PRO FOOTBALL REGISTER

2003 EDITION

Editors/Pro Football Register
TONY NISTLER
DAVID WALTON
STEVE MEYERHOFF

Withdrawn

CONTENTS

EXPLANATION OF ABBREVIATIONS AND TERMS

LEAGUES: AFL: American Football League. **Ar.FL., Arena Football:** Arena Football League. **CFL:** Canadian Football League. **CoFL:** Continental Football League. **NFL:** National Football League. **NFLE:** NFL Europe League. **USFL:** United States Football League. **WFL:** World Football League. **W.L.:** World League. **WLAF:** World League of American Football.

TEAMS: Birm.: Birmingham. **Jack., Jax.:** Jacksonville. **L.A. Raiders:** Los Angeles Raiders. **L.A. Rams:** Los Angeles Rams. **New Eng.:** New England. **N.Y. Giants:** New York Giants. **N.Y. Jets:** New York Jets. **N.Y./N.J.:** New York/New Jersey. **San Ant.:** San Antonio. **San Fran.:** San Francisco. **Sask.:** Saskatchewan. **StL.:** St. Louis.

STATISTICS: Ast.: Assists. **Att.:** Attempts. **Avg.:** Average. **Blk.:** Blocked punts. **Cmp.:** Completions. **FGA:** Field goals attempted. **FGM:** Field goals made. **50+:** Field goals of 50 yards or longer. **F., Fum.:** Fumbles. **G:** Games. **In. 20:** Punts inside 20-yard line. **Int.:** Interceptions. **Lg.:** Longest made field goal. **L:** Lost. **Net avg.:** Net punting average. **No.:** Number. **Rat.:** Passer rating. **Pct.:** Percentage. **Pts.:** Points scored. **Skd.:** Times sacked. **Sks.:** Sacks. **T:** Tied. **TD:** Touchdowns. **Tk.:** Tackles. **2-pt.:** Two-point conversions. **W:** Won. **XPA:** Extra points attempted. **XPM:** Extra points made. **Yds.:** Yards.

POSITIONS: C: Center. **CB:** Cornerback. **DB:** Defensive back. **DE:** Defensive end. **DL:** Defensive lineman. **DT:** Defensive tackle. **FB:** Fullback. **G:** Guard. **K:** Kicker. **LB:** Linebacker. **OL:** Offensive lineman. **OT:** Offensive tackle. **P:** Punter. **QB:** Quarterback. **RB:** Running back. **S:** Safety. **TE:** Tight end. **WR:** Wide receiver.

SINGLE GAME HIGHS (regular season): If a player reached a single game high on numerous occasions—had one rushing touchdown in a game, for example—the most recent occurrence is listed.

EXPLANATION OF AWARDS

AWARDS: Butkus Award: Nation's top college linebacker. **Chuck Bednarik Award:** Nation's top defensive player. **Davey O'Brien Award:** Nation's top college quarterback. **Doak Walker Award:** Nation's top college junior or senior running back. **Fred Biletnikoff Award:** Nation's top college wide receiver. **Harlon Hill Trophy:** Nation's top college Division II player. **Heisman Trophy:** Nation's top college player. **Jim Thorpe Award:** Nation's top college defensive back. **Lombardi Award:** Nation's top college lineman. **Lou Groza Award:** Nation's top college kicker. **Maxwell Award:** Nation's top college player. **Outland Trophy:** Nation's top college interior lineman. **Walter Payton Award:** Nation's top college Division I-AA player.

A Note on Tackles:

Nearly all of the numbers in the career section are official NFL statistics. However, tackle data is not official. For the sake of consistency, we use NFL game summaries to collect this information, assuming that the standards used in crediting tackles and assists are relatively uniform among the various stat crews at NFL game sites. However, for seasons before 1994 we list the team-supplied totals because no other data is available. For this reason, you may notice that many regular defenders' assist totals have dropped off substantially since 1994. One final note: a few teams never listed assists; instead, they threw them in with overall tackle numbers. This results in zeroes in the assists column for some players prior to 1995, which suggested that those players never assisted on tackles. In all likelihood they probably did pick up some assists, but it's impossible to find out how many.

ON THE COVER: Large photo of Clinton Portis by Albert Dickson/THE SPORTING NEWS. Bottom left to right: Rich Gannon by Tom Hauck for THE SPORTING NEWS; Warren Sapp by Bob Leverone/THE SPORTING NEWS; Priest Holmes by Albert Dickson/THE SPORTING NEWS. Spine photo of Warren sapp by Bob Leverone/THE SPORTING NEWS.

NFL statistics compiled by STATS, Inc., a News Corporation company; 8130 Lehigh Avenue, Morton Grove, IL 60053. STATS is a trademark of Sports Team Analysis and Tracking Systems, Inc.

ISBN: 0-89204-708-9   10 9 8 7 6 5 4 3 2 1

VETERAN PLAYERS

Please note for statistical comparisons: In 1982, only nine of 16 games were played due to the cancellation of games because of a player's strike. In 1987, only 15 of 16 games were played due to the cancellation of games in the third week because of a player's strike. Most NFL players also missed games scheduled in the fourth, fifth and sixth weeks.

Sacks became an official NFL statistic in 1982.

Two-point conversions became an official NFL statistic in 1994.

* Indicates league leader.   † Indicates tied for league lead.   ... Statistics unavailable, unofficial, or mathematically
‡ Indicates NFC leader.   § Indicates AFC leader.   impossible to calculate.
∞ Indicates tied for NFC lead.   ▲ Indicates tied for AFC lead.

ABDULLAH, RABIH   RB   BEARS

PERSONAL: Born April 27, 1975, in Martinsville, Va. ... 6-0/220. ... Full name: Rabih Fard Abdullah. ... Name pronounced RAH-bee ab-DUE-lah.
HIGH SCHOOL: Barham Clark (Roselle, N.J.).
COLLEGE: Lehigh.
TRANSACTIONS/CAREER NOTES: Signed as non-drafted free agent by Tampa Bay Buccaneers (April 20, 1998). ... Inactive for all 16 games (1998). ... On injured reserve with thumb injury (December 28, 1999-remainder of season). ... Granted free agency (March 2, 2001). ... Re-signed by Buccaneers (March 2, 2001). ... Granted unconditional free agency (March 1, 2002). ... Signed by Chicago Bears (March 6, 2002).
SINGLE GAME HIGHS (regular season): Attempts—10 (December 3, 2000, vs. Dallas); yards—38 (December 3, 2000, vs. Dallas); and rushing touchdowns—0.

			RUSHING				RECEIVING				KICKOFF RETURNS				TOTALS			
Year—Team	G	GS	Att.	Yds.	Avg.	TD	No.	Yds.	Avg.	TD	No.	Yds.	Avg.	TD	TD	2pt.	Pts.	Fum.
1999—Tampa Bay NFL	15	1	5	12	2.4	0	2	11	5.5	0	0	0	0.0	0	0	0	0	0
2000—Tampa Bay NFL	12	0	16	70	4.4	0	2	14	7.0	0	1	16	16.0	0	0	0	0	0
2001—Tampa Bay NFL	16	0	11	40	3.6	0	2	26	13.0	0	5	92	18.4	0	0	0	0	0
2002—Chicago NFL	16	0	0	0	0.0	0	0	0	0.0	0	9	182	20.2	0	0	0	0	1
Pro totals (4 years)	59	1	32	122	3.8	0	6	51	8.5	0	15	290	19.3	0	0	0	0	1

ABRAHAM, DONNIE   CB   JETS

PERSONAL: Born October 8, 1973, in Orangeburg, S.C. ... 5-10/192. ... Full name: Nathaniel Donnell Abraham.
HIGH SCHOOL: Orangeburg-Wilkinson (Orangeburg, S.C.).
COLLEGE: East Tennessee State (degree in business management, 1995).
TRANSACTIONS/CAREER NOTES: Selected by Tampa Bay Buccaneers in third round (71st pick overall) of 1996 NFL draft. ... Signed by Buccaneers (July 13, 1996). ... Released by Buccaneers (March 14, 2002). ... Signed by New York Jets (April 24, 2002).
CHAMPIONSHIP GAME EXPERIENCE: Played in NFC championship game (1999 season).
HONORS: Played in Pro Bowl (2000 season).
MISCELLANEOUS: Holds Tampa Bay Buccaneers all-time record for most interceptions (31).

			TOTALS			INTERCEPTIONS			
Year—Team	G	GS	Tk.	Ast.	Sks.	No.	Yds.	Avg.	TD
1996—Tampa Bay NFL	16	12	50	8	0.0	5	27	5.4	0
1997—Tampa Bay NFL	16	16	44	10	0.0	5	16	3.2	0
1998—Tampa Bay NFL	13	13	32	6	0.0	1	3	3.0	0
1999—Tampa Bay NFL	16	16	65	14	2.0	†7	115	16.4	†2
2000—Tampa Bay NFL	16	16	46	11	0.0	7	82	11.7	0
2001—Tampa Bay NFL	15	5	29	10	0.0	6	98	16.3	0
2002—New York Jets NFL	16	16	47	6	0.0	4	49	12.3	0
Pro totals (7 years)	108	94	313	65	2.0	35	390	11.1	2

ABRAHAM, JOHN   LB   JETS

PERSONAL: Born May 6, 1978, in Timmonsville, S.C. ... 6-4/256.
HIGH SCHOOL: Lamar (Timmonsville, S.C.).
COLLEGE: South Carolina.
TRANSACTIONS/CAREER NOTES: Selected by New York Jets in first round (13th pick overall) of 2000 NFL draft. ... Signed by Jets (July 10, 2000). ... On injured reserve with hernia (November 17, 2000-remainder of season).
HONORS: Named defensive end on THE SPORTING NEWS NFL All-Pro team (2001). ... Played in Pro Bowl (2001 and 2002 seasons).

			TOTALS			INTERCEPTIONS			
Year—Team	G	GS	Tk.	Ast.	Sks.	No.	Yds.	Avg.	TD
2000—New York Jets NFL	6	0	8	4	4.5	0	0	0.0	0
2001—New York Jets NFL	16	15	57	10	13.0	0	0	0.0	0
2002—New York Jets NFL	16	16	48	13	10.0	0	0	0.0	0
Pro totals (3 years)	38	31	113	27	27.5	0	0	0.0	0

ACKERMAN, TOM   G   TITANS

PERSONAL: Born September 6, 1972, in Bellingham, Wash. ... 6-4/300. ... Full name: Thomas Michael Ackerman.
HIGH SCHOOL: Nooksack (Wash.) Valley.
COLLEGE: Eastern Washington.
TRANSACTIONS/CAREER NOTES: Selected by New Orleans Saints in fifth round (145th pick overall) of 1996 NFL draft. ... Signed by Saints (July 14, 1996). ... Granted free agency (February 12, 1999). ... Re-signed by Saints (April 14, 1999). ... Granted unconditional free agency

(February 11, 2000). ... Re-signed by Saints (February 15, 2000). ... Released by Saints (March 12, 2002). ... Signed by Oakland Raiders (May 22, 2002). ... Released by Raiders (September 1, 2002). ... Signed by Tennessee Titans (September 3, 2002). ... Granted unconditional free agency (February 28, 2003). ... Re-signed by Titans (April 2, 2003).

PLAYING EXPERIENCE: New Orleans NFL, 1996-2001; Tennessee NFL, 2002. ... Games/Games started: 1996 (2/0), 1997 (14/0), 1998 (15/10), 1999 (16/8), 2000 (15/0), 2001 (16/0), 2002 (11/3). Total: 89/21.

CHAMPIONSHIP GAME EXPERIENCE: Played in AFC championship game (2002 season).

ADAMS, FLOZELL — OT — COWBOYS

PERSONAL: Born May 18, 1975, in Chicago. ... 6-7/357. ... Full name: Flozell Jootin Adams. ... Cousin of Hersey Hawkins, guard, with five NBA teams (1988-89 through 2000-01).
HIGH SCHOOL: Proviso West (Hillside, Ill.).
COLLEGE: Michigan State.
TRANSACTIONS/CAREER NOTES: Selected by Dallas Cowboys in second round (38th pick overall) of 1998 NFL draft. ... Signed by Cowboys (July 17, 1998). ... Designated by Cowboys as franchise player (February 21, 2002). ... Granted unconditional free agency (February 28, 2003). ... Re-signed by Cowboys (February 28, 2003).
PLAYING EXPERIENCE: Dallas NFL, 1998-2002. ... Games/Games started: 1998 (16/12), 1999 (16/16), 2000 (16/16), 2001 (16/16), 2002 (16/16). Total: 80/76.
HONORS: Named offensive tackle on THE SPORTING NEWS college All-America third team (1997).

ADAMS, KEITH — LB — EAGLES

PERSONAL: Born November 22, 1979, in College Park, Ga. ... 5-11/223.
HIGH SCHOOL: Westlake (Atlanta).
COLLEGE: Clemson.
TRANSACTIONS/CAREER NOTES: Selected after junior season by Tennessee Titans in seventh round (232nd pick overall) of 2001 NFL draft. ... Signed by Titans (July 13, 2001). ... Released by Titans (August 31, 2001). ... Signed by Dallas Cowboys to practice squad (November 8, 2001). ... Activated (November 21, 2001). ... Claimed on waivers by Philadelphia Eagles (October 21, 2002). ... Re-signed by Eagles (March 3, 2003).
CHAMPIONSHIP GAME EXPERIENCE: Played in NFC championship game (2002 season).
HONORS: Named linebacker on THE SPORTING NEWS college All-America third team (1999). ... Named linebacker on THE SPORTING NEWS college All-America first team (2000).

| | | | TOTALS | | | INTERCEPTIONS | | | |
Year Team	G	GS	Tk.	Ast.	Sks.	No.	Yds.	Avg.	TD
2001—Dallas NFL	4	0	0	0	0.0	0	0	0.0	0
2002—Dallas NFL	6	5	15	3	0.0	0	0	0.0	0
—Philadelphia NFL	10	0	0	0	0.0	0	0	0.0	0
Pro totals (2 years)	20	5	15	3	0.0	0	0	0.0	0

ADAMS, SAM — DT — BILLS

PERSONAL: Born June 13, 1973, in Houston. ... 6-3/330. ... Full name: Sam Aaron Adams. ... Son of Sam Adams Sr., guard with New England Patriots (1972-80) and New Orleans Saints (1981).
HIGH SCHOOL: Cypress Creek (Houston).
COLLEGE: Texas A&M.
TRANSACTIONS/CAREER NOTES: Selected after junior season by Seattle Seahawks in first round (eighth pick overall) of 1994 NFL draft. ... Signed by Seahawks (July 30, 1994). ... Granted unconditional free agency (February 11, 2000). ... Signed by Baltimore Ravens (April 17, 2000). ... Released by Ravens (March 1, 2002). ... Signed by Oakland Raiders (August 19, 2002). ... Released by Raiders (February 27, 2003). ... Signed by Buffalo Bills (March 23, 2003).
CHAMPIONSHIP GAME EXPERIENCE: Played in AFC championship game (2000 and 2002 seasons). ... Member of Super Bowl championship team (2000 season). ... Played in Super Bowl XXXVII (2002 season).
HONORS: Named defensive lineman on THE SPORTING NEWS college All-America first team (1993). ... Played in Pro Bowl (2000 and 2001 seasons).

| | | | TOTALS | | | INTERCEPTIONS | | | |
Year Team	G	GS	Tk.	Ast.	Sks.	No.	Yds.	Avg.	TD
1994—Seattle NFL	12	7	20	7	4.0	0	0	0.0	0
1995—Seattle NFL	16	5	16	10	3.5	0	0	0.0	0
1996—Seattle NFL	16	15	35	5	5.5	0	0	0.0	0
1997—Seattle NFL	16	15	37	15	7.0	0	0	0.0	0
1998—Seattle NFL	16	11	28	3	2.0	1	25	25.0	1
1999—Seattle NFL	13	13	31	7	1.0	0	0	0.0	0
2000—Baltimore NFL	16	16	23	4	2.0	0	0	0.0	0
2001—Baltimore NFL	14	14	18	5	2.0	0	0	0.0	0
2002—Oakland NFL	15	14	18	4	2.0	0	0	0.0	0
Pro totals (9 years)	134	110	226	60	29.0	1	25	25.0	1

AHANOTU, CHIDI — DE

PERSONAL: Born October 11, 1970, in Modesto, Calif. ... 6-2/285. ... Full name: Chidi Obioma Ahanotu. ... Name pronounced CHEE-dee a-HA-noe-too.
HIGH SCHOOL: Berkeley (Calif.).
COLLEGE: California (degree in physical education).

TRANSACTIONS/CAREER NOTES: Selected by Tampa Bay Buccaneers in sixth round (145th pick overall) of 1993 NFL draft. ... Signed by Buccaneers (July 9, 1993). ... Granted free agency (February 16, 1996). ... Re-signed by Buccaneers (February 20, 1996). ... On injured reserve with shoulder injury (October 27, 1998-remainder of season). ... Designated by Buccaneers as franchise player (February 12, 1999). ... Re-signed by Buccaneers (July 30, 1999). ... Released by Buccaneers (April 20, 2001). ... Signed by St. Louis Rams (August 20, 2001). ... Granted unconditional free agency (March 1, 2002). ... Signed by Buffalo Bills (August 19, 2002). ... Granted unconditional free agency (February 28, 2003).

CHAMPIONSHIP GAME EXPERIENCE: Played in NFC championship game (1999 and 2001 seasons). ... Played in Super Bowl XXXVI (2001 season).

| | | | TOTALS | | |
Year Team	G	GS	Tk.	Ast.	Sks.
1993—Tampa Bay NFL	16	10	15	16	1.5
1994—Tampa Bay NFL	16	16	31	15	1.0
1995—Tampa Bay NFL	16	15	36	12	3.0
1996—Tampa Bay NFL	13	13	37	10	5.5
1997—Tampa Bay NFL	16	15	38	10	10.0
1998—Tampa Bay NFL	4	4	9	8	0.0
1999—Tampa Bay NFL	16	15	24	9	6.5
2000—Tampa Bay NFL	16	16	28	19	3.5
2001—St. Louis NFL	16	16	21	8	2.0
2002—Buffalo NFL	16	14	30	14	5.0
Pro totals (10 years)	145	134	269	121	38.0

AKBAR, HAKIM — S — RAMS

PERSONAL: Born August 11, 1980, in Riverside, Calif. ... 6-0/212.
HIGH SCHOOL: Polytechnic (Riverside, Calif.).
COLLEGE: Washington.
TRANSACTIONS/CAREER NOTES: Selected after junior season by New England Patriots in fifth round (163rd pick overall) of 2001 NFL draft. ... Signed by Patriots (June 15, 2001). ... On non-football injury list with multiple injuries (November 16, 2001-remainder of season). ... Claimed on waivers by Houston Texans (March 26, 2002). ... Released by Texans (September 1, 2002). ... Signed by St. Louis Rams (November 5, 2002).

| | | | TOTALS | | | INTERCEPTIONS | | | |
Year Team	G	GS	Tk.	Ast.	Sks.	No.	Yds.	Avg.	TD
2001—New England NFL	6	0	0	0	0.0	0	0	0.0	0
2002—St. Louis NFL	4	0	0	0	0.0	0	0	0.0	0
Pro totals (2 years)	10	0	0	0	0.0	0	0	0.0	0

AKERS, DAVID — K — EAGLES

PERSONAL: Born December 9, 1974, in Lexington, Ky. ... 5-10/200. ... Full name: David Roy Akers. ... Name pronounced A-kers.
HIGH SCHOOL: Tates Creek (Lexington, Ky.).
COLLEGE: Louisville.
TRANSACTIONS/CAREER NOTES: Signed as non-drafted free agent by Carolina Panthers (April 19, 1997). ... Released by Panthers (August 17, 1997). ... Signed by Atlanta Falcons (April 28, 1998). ... Released by Falcons (July 7, 1998). ... Re-signed by Falcons (July 21, 1998). ... Released by Falcons (August 24, 1998). ... Signed by Washington Redskins to practice squad (September 1, 1998). ... Activated (September 15, 1998). ... Released by Redskins (September 22, 1998). ... Signed by Philadelphia Eagles (January 11, 1999). ... Assigned by Eagles to Berlin Thunder in 1999 NFL Europe enhancement allocation program (February 22, 1999).

CHAMPIONSHIP GAME EXPERIENCE: Played in NFC championship game (2001 and 2002 seasons).

HONORS: Named kicker on THE SPORTING NEWS NFL All-Pro team (2001 and 2002). ... Played in Pro Bowl (2001 and 2002 seasons).

| | | FIELD GOALS | | | | | | | TOTALS | | |
Year Team	G	1-29	30-39	40-49	50+	Tot.	Pct.	Lg.	XPM	XPA	Pts.
1998—Washington NFL	1	0-0	0-0	0-2	0-0	0-2	0.0	0	2	2	2
1999—Berlin NFLE	...	...	...	...	2-5	10-15	66.7	...	3	3	33
—Philadelphia NFL	16	0-0	0-0	2-3	1-3	3-6	50.0	∞53	2	2	11
2000—Philadelphia NFL	16	7-7	14-15	7-10	1-1	29-33	87.9	51	34	36	121
2001—Philadelphia NFL	16	10-10	7-8	7-10	2-3	26-31	83.9	50	37	38	115
2002—Philadelphia NFL	16	9-9	14-16	6-7	1-2	30-34	88.2	51	43	43	133
NFL Europe totals (1 year)	...	...	...	...	2-5	10-15	66.7	...	3	3	33
NFL totals (5 years)	65	26-26	35-39	22-32	5-9	88-106	83.0	53	118	121	382
Pro totals (6 years)	...	...	...	...	7-14	98-121	81.0	...	121	124	415

AKINS, CHRIS — DB — PATRIOTS

PERSONAL: Born November 29, 1976, in Little Rock, Ark. ... 5-11/195. ... Full name: Christopher Drew Akins. ... Second cousin of Jackie Harris, tight end, with four NFL teams (1990-2001). ... Name pronounced A-kenz.
HIGH SCHOOL: Little Rock (Ark.) Hall.
COLLEGE: Arkansas, then Arkansas-Pine Bluff.
TRANSACTIONS/CAREER NOTES: Selected by Green Bay Packers in seventh round (212th pick overall) of 1999 NFL draft. ... Signed by Packers (June 1, 1999). ... Released by Packers (September 5, 1999). ... Re-signed by Packers to practice squad (September 14, 1999). ... Signed by Dallas Cowboys off Packers practice squad (October 27, 1999). ... Assigned by Cowboys to Rhein Fire in 2000 NFL Europe enhancement allocation program (February 18, 2000). ... Claimed on waivers by Packers (November 2, 2000). ... Claimed on waivers by Cleveland Browns (December 11, 2001). ... Granted free agency (March 1, 2002). ... Re-signed by Browns (May 5, 2002). ... Granted unconditional free agency (February 28, 2003). ... Signed by New England Patriots (March 12, 2003).

Year Team	G	GS	TOTALS			INTERCEPTIONS			
			Tk.	Ast.	Sks.	No.	Yds.	Avg.	TD
1999—Dallas NFL	9	0	0	0	0.0	0	0	0.0	0
2000—Rhein NFLE	...	...	...	...	0.0	1	13	13.0	0
—Dallas NFL	8	0	0	0	0.0	0	0	0.0	0
—Green Bay NFL	2	0	0	0	0.0	0	0	0.0	0
2001—Green Bay NFL	11	0	9	5	0.0	0	0	0.0	0
—Cleveland NFL	4	0	3	0	0.0	0	0	0.0	0
2002—Cleveland NFL	15	0	0	0	0.0	0	0	0.0	0
NFL Europe totals (1 year)	...	...	...	...	0.0	1	13	13.0	0
NFL totals (4 years)	49	0	12	5	0.0	0	0	0.0	0
Pro totals (5 years)	...	...	...	...	0.0	1	13	13.0	0

ALBRIGHT, ETHAN — OL — REDSKINS

PERSONAL: Born May 1, 1971, in Greensboro, N.C. ... 5-7/273. ... Full name: Lawrence Ethan Albright.
HIGH SCHOOL: Grimsley (Greensboro, N.C.).
COLLEGE: North Carolina.
TRANSACTIONS/CAREER NOTES: Signed as non-drafted free agent by Miami Dolphins (April 28, 1994). ... Released by Dolphins (August 22, 1994). ... Re-signed by Dolphins to practice squad (August 29, 1994). ... Released by Dolphins (September 14, 1994). ... Re-signed by Dolphins to practice squad (September 28, 1994). ... Released by Dolphins (November 2, 1994). ... Re-signed by Dolphins (February 16, 1995). ... On injured reserve with knee injury (November 15, 1995-remainder of season). ... Released by Dolphins (August 20, 1996). ... Signed by Buffalo Bills (August 26, 1996). ... Granted free agency (February 13, 1998). ... Re-signed by Bills (April 15, 1998). ... Granted unconditional free agency (February 12, 1999). ... Re-signed by Bills (April 1, 1999). ... Released by Bills (March 1, 2001). ... Signed by Washington Redskins (March 9, 2001). ... Re-signed by Redskins (March 23, 2003)
PLAYING EXPERIENCE: Miami NFL, 1995; Buffalo NFL, 1996-2000; Washington NFL, 2001-2002. ... Games/Games started: 1995 (10/0), 1996 (16/0), 1997 (16/0), 1998 (16/0), 1999 (16/0), 2000 (16/0), 2001 (16/0), 2002 (16/0). Total: 122/0.

ALDRIDGE, KEVIN — DE — TITANS

PERSONAL: Born March 30, 1980, in Palestine, Texas. ... 6-1/271. ... Full name: Kevin Lamar Aldridge. ... Nephew of Jerry Aldridge, running back with San Francisco 49ers (1980).
HIGH SCHOOL: Jacksonville (Texas).
COLLEGE: Southern Methodist.
TRANSACTIONS/CAREER NOTES: Signed as non-drafted free agent by Tennessee Titans (April 22, 2002). ... Released by Titans (September 1, 2002). ... Re-signed by Titans to practice squad (September 3, 2002). ... Released by Titans (September 10, 2002). ... Re-signed by Titans (September 11, 2002). ... Released by Titans (November 1, 2002). ... Re-signed by Titans to practice squad (November 5, 2002). ... Released by Titans (November 15, 2002). ... Re-signed by Titans to practice squad (November 22, 2002). ... Assigned by Titans to Barcelona Dragons in 2003 NFL Europe enhancement allocation program (February 4, 2003).

Year Team	G	GS	TOTALS		
			Tk.	Ast.	Sks.
2002—Tennessee NFL	6	0	5	3	0.0

ALEXANDER, BRENT — S — STEELERS

PERSONAL: Born July 10, 1971, in Detroit. ... 5-11/200. ... Full name: Ronald Brent Alexander.
HIGH SCHOOL: Gallatin (Tenn.).
COLLEGE: Tennessee State.
TRANSACTIONS/CAREER NOTES: Signed as non-drafted free agent by Arizona Cardinals (April 28, 1994). ... Granted unconditional free agency (February 13, 1998). ... Signed by Carolina Panthers (March 20, 1998). ... Released by Panthers (April 18, 2000). ... Signed by Pittsburgh Steelers (May 30, 2000).
CHAMPIONSHIP GAME EXPERIENCE: Played in AFC championship game (2001 season).

Year Team	G	GS	TOTALS			INTERCEPTIONS			
			Tk.	Ast.	Sks.	No.	Yds.	Avg.	TD
1994—Arizona NFL	16	7	26	10	0.0	0	0	0.0	0
1995—Arizona NFL	16	13	51	17	0.5	2	14	7.0	0
1996—Arizona NFL	16	15	52	29	0.0	2	3	1.5	0
1997—Arizona NFL	16	15	54	22	0.0	0	0	0.0	0
1998—Carolina NFL	16	16	68	29	0.0	0	0	0.0	0
1999—Carolina NFL	16	16	65	12	0.0	2	18	9.0	0
2000—Pittsburgh NFL	16	16	61	15	1.5	3	31	10.3	0
2001—Pittsburgh NFL	16	16	52	17	2.0	4	39	9.8	0
2002—Pittsburgh NFL	16	16	50	25	1.0	4	37	9.3	0
Pro totals (9 years)	144	130	479	176	5.0	17	142	8.4	0

ALEXANDER, DAN — RB/FB — JAGUARS

PERSONAL: Born March 17, 1978, in Wentzville, Mo. ... 6-0/250.
HIGH SCHOOL: Wentzville (Mo.).
COLLEGE: Nebraska.
TRANSACTIONS/CAREER NOTES: Selected by Tennessee Titans in sixth round (192nd pick overall) of 2001 NFL draft. ... Signed by Titans (July 10, 2001). ... Released by Titans (September 6, 2001). ... Re-signed by Titans to practice squad (September 8, 2001). ... Activated (November 21, 2001). ... Claimed on waivers by Jacksonville Jaguars (August 29, 2002). ... Re-signed by Jaguars (March 23, 2003).

Year Team	G	GS	RUSHING				TOTALS			
			Att.	Yds.	Avg.	TD	TD	2pt.	Pts.	Fum.
2001—Tennessee NFL	7	0	0	0	0.0	0	0	0	0	0
2002—Jacksonville NFL	3	0	0	0	0.0	0	0	0	0	0
Pro totals (2 years)	10	0	0	0	0.0	0	0	0	0	0

ALEXANDER, DERRICK — WR — VIKINGS

PERSONAL: Born November 6, 1971, in Detroit. ... 6-2/206. ... Full name: Derrick Scott Alexander.
HIGH SCHOOL: Benedictine (Detroit).
COLLEGE: Michigan (degree in sports management).
TRANSACTIONS/CAREER NOTES: Selected by Cleveland Browns in first round (29th pick overall) of 1994 NFL draft. ... Signed by Browns (August 3, 1994). ... Browns franchise moved to Baltimore and renamed Ravens for 1996 season (March 11, 1996). ... Granted unconditional free agency (February 13, 1998). ... Signed by Kansas City Chiefs (March 2, 1998). ... Released by Chiefs (June 3, 2002). ... Signed by Minnesota Vikings (June 7, 2002). ... On injured reserve with knee injury (November 6, 2002-remainder of season).
SINGLE GAME HIGHS (regular season): Receptions—9 (November 5, 2000, vs. Oakland); yards—198 (December 1, 1996, vs. Pittsburgh); and touchdown receptions—2 (November 5, 2000, vs. Oakland).
STATISTICAL PLATEAUS: 100-yard receiving games: 1994 (3), 1996 (3), 1997 (3), 1998 (2), 1999 (4), 2000 (6). Total: 21.
MISCELLANEOUS: Shares Baltimore Ravens all-time record for most touchdown receptions (18).

Year Team	G	GS	RUSHING				RECEIVING				PUNT RETURNS				KICKOFF RETURNS				TOTALS		
			Att.	Yds.	Avg.	TD	No.	Yds.	Avg.	TD	No.	Yds.	Avg.	TD	No.	Yds.	Avg.	TD	TD	2pt.	Pts.
1994—Cleveland NFL	14	12	4	38	9.5	0	48	828	17.3	2	0	0	0.0	0	0	0	0.0	0	2	1	14
1995—Cleveland NFL	14	2	1	29	29.0	0	15	216	14.4	0	9	122	13.6	†1	21	419	20.0	0	1	0	6
1996—Baltimore NFL	15	14	3	0	0.0	0	62	1099	17.7	9	1	15	15.0	0	1	13	13.0	0	9	1	56
1997—Baltimore NFL	15	13	1	0	0.0	0	65	1009	15.5	9	1	34	34.0	0	0	0	0.0	0	9	0	54
1998—Kansas City NFL	15	14	0	0	0.0	0	54	992	18.4	4	0	0	0.0	0	0	0	0.0	0	4	0	24
1999—Kansas City NFL	16	15	2	82	41.0	1	54	832	15.4	2	0	0	0.0	0	0	0	0.0	0	3	0	18
2000—Kansas City NFL	16	16	3	45	15.0	0	78	1391	§17.8	10	0	0	0.0	0	0	0	0.0	0	10	0	60
2001—Kansas City NFL	13	11	2	16	8.0	0	27	470	17.4	3	0	0	0.0	0	0	0	0.0	0	3	0	18
2002—Minnesota NFL	8	5	0	0	0.0	0	14	134	9.6	1	0	0	0.0	0	0	0	0.0	0	1	0	6
Pro totals (9 years)	126	102	16	210	13.1	1	417	6971	16.7	40	11	171	15.5	1	22	432	19.6	0	42	2	256

ALEXANDER, SHAUN — RB — SEAHAWKS

PERSONAL: Born August 30, 1977, in Florence, Ky. ... 5-11/229.
HIGH SCHOOL: Boone County (Ky.).
COLLEGE: Alabama (degree in marketing, 1999).
TRANSACTIONS/CAREER NOTES: Selected by Seattle Seahawks in first round (19th pick overall) of 2000 NFL draft. ... Signed by Seahawks (July 20, 2000).
HONORS: Named running back on THE SPORTING NEWS college All-America second team (1999).
SINGLE GAME HIGHS (regular season): Attempts—35 (November 11, 2001, vs. Oakland); yards—266 (November 11, 2001, vs. Oakland); and rushing touchdowns—4 (September 29, 2002, vs. Minnesota).
STATISTICAL PLATEAUS: 100-yard rushing games: 2001 (4), 2002 (4). Total: 8.

Year Team	G	GS	RUSHING				RECEIVING				TOTALS			
			Att.	Yds.	Avg.	TD	No.	Yds.	Avg.	TD	TD	2pt.	Pts.	Fum.
2000—Seattle NFL	16	1	64	313	4.9	2	5	41	8.2	0	2	0	12	2
2001—Seattle NFL	16	12	309	1318	4.3	*14	44	343	7.8	2	§16	0	96	4
2002—Seattle NFL	16	16	295	1175	4.0	‡16	59	460	7.8	2	‡18	0	108	3
Pro totals (3 years)	48	29	668	2806	4.2	32	108	844	7.8	4	36	0	216	9

ALEXANDER, STEPHEN — TE — CHARGERS

PERSONAL: Born November 7, 1975, in Chickasha, Okla. ... 6-4/250.
HIGH SCHOOL: Chickasha (Okla.).
COLLEGE: Oklahoma.
TRANSACTIONS/CAREER NOTES: Selected by Washington Redskins in second round (48th pick overall) of 1998 NFL draft. ... Signed by Redskins (July 13, 1998). ... On injured reserve with ankle injury (December 26, 2001-remainder of season). ... Granted unconditional free agency (March 1, 2002). ... Signed by San Diego Chargers (March 21, 2002).
HONORS: Played in Pro Bowl (2000 season).
SINGLE GAME HIGHS (regular season): Receptions—8 (December 29, 2002, vs. Seattle); yards—129 (December 29, 2002, vs. Seattle); and touchdown receptions—2 (September 19, 1999, vs. New York Giants).
STATISTICAL PLATEAUS: 100-yard receiving games: 2002 (1).

Year Team	G	GS	RECEIVING				TOTALS			
			No.	Yds.	Avg.	TD	TD	2pt.	Pts.	Fum.
1998—Washington NFL	15	5	37	383	10.4	4	4	0	24	2
1999—Washington NFL	15	15	29	324	11.2	3	3	0	18	0
2000—Washington NFL	16	16	47	510	10.9	2	2	0	12	2
2001—Washington NFL	7	5	9	85	9.4	0	0	0	0	0
2002—San Diego NFL	14	14	45	510	11.3	1	1	0	6	1
Pro totals (5 years)	67	55	167	1812	10.9	10	10	0	60	5

ALFORD, DARNELL — OT

PERSONAL: Born June 11, 1977, in Fredricksburg, Va. ... 6-4/328. ... Full name: Darnell LaShawn Alford.
HIGH SCHOOL: Chancellor (Fredricksburg, Va.).
COLLEGE: Boston College.

TRANSACTIONS/CAREER NOTES: Selected by Kansas City Chiefs in sixth round (188th pick overall) of 2000 NFL draft. ... Signed by Chiefs (July 20, 2000). ... Assigned by Chiefs to Barcelona Dragons in 2002 NFL Europe enhancement allocation program (February 12, 2002). ... Released by Chiefs (September 1, 2002). ... Signed by Green Bay Packers to practice squad (September 4, 2002). ... Signed by New York Jets off Packers practice squad (September 9, 2002). ... Claimed on waivers by Dallas Cowboys (November 20, 2002). ... Released by Cowboys (December 11, 2002). ... Signed by Chiefs (December 12, 2002). ... Granted free agency (February 28, 2003).
PLAYING EXPERIENCE: Kansas City NFL, 2000-2002; New York Jets NFL, 2002. ... Games/Games started: 2000 (1/0), 2001 (2/0), 2002 (3/0). Total: 6/0.

ALLEN, BRIAN — LB — PANTHERS

PERSONAL: Born April 1, 1978, in Lake City, Fla. ... 6-0/232. ... Cousin of Reinard Wilson, defensive end, Cincinnati Bengals.
HIGH SCHOOL: Columbia (Lake City, Fla.).
COLLEGE: Florida State.
TRANSACTIONS/CAREER NOTES: Selected by St. Louis Rams in third round (83rd pick overall) of 2001 NFL draft. ... Signed by Rams (June 5, 2001). ... Selected by Houston Texans from Rams in NFL expansion draft (February 18, 2002). ... Claimed on waivers by Carolina Panthers (May 30, 2003).
CHAMPIONSHIP GAME EXPERIENCE: Member of Rams for NFC championship game (2001 season); inactive. ... Member of Rams for Super Bowl XXXVI (2001 season); inactive.

Year Team	G	GS	TOTALS Tk.	Ast.	Sks.	INTERCEPTIONS No.	Yds.	Avg.	TD
2001—St. Louis NFL	3	0	0	0	0.0	0	0	0.0	0
2002—Carolina NFL	16	5	27	6	0.0	0	0	0.0	0
Pro totals (2 years)	19	5	27	6	0.0	0	0	0.0	0

ALLEN, IAN — OT — GIANTS

PERSONAL: Born July 22, 1978, in Newark, N.J. ... 6-4/320. ... Full name: Ian Ramon Allen.
HIGH SCHOOL: Westlake (Atlanta).
COLLEGE: Purdue.
TRANSACTIONS/CAREER NOTES: Signed as non-drafted free agent by Kansas City Chiefs (April 30, 2001). ... Released by Chiefs (August 28, 2001). ... Signed by Atlanta Falcons to practice squad (January 2, 2002). ... Granted free agency following 2001 season. ... Allocated by Chiefs to Scottish Claymores in 2002 NFL Europe enhancement allocation program (February 12, 2002). ... Signed by Kansas City Chiefs (January 14, 2002). ... Released by Chiefs (September 1, 2002). ... Signed by New York Giants to practice squad (September 10, 2002). ... Activated (October 3, 2002).
PLAYING EXPERIENCE: New York Giants NFL, 2002. ... Games/Games started: 2002 (3/0).

ALLEN, JAMES — LB — SAINTS

PERSONAL: Born November 11, 1979, in Portland, Ore. ... 6-2/240.
HIGH SCHOOL: Thomas Jefferson (Portland, Ore.).
COLLEGE: Oregon State.
TRANSACTIONS/CAREER NOTES: Selected by New Orleans Saints in third round (82nd pick overall) of 2002 NFL draft. ... Signed by Saints (July 22, 2002).

Year Team	G	GS	TOTALS Tk.	Ast.	Sks.	INTERCEPTIONS No.	Yds.	Avg.	TD
2002—New Orleans NFL	14	1	6	2	0.0	1	0	0.0	1

ALLEN, JAMES — RB — TEXANS

PERSONAL: Born March 28, 1975, in Wynnewood, Okla. ... 5-10/215.
HIGH SCHOOL: Wynnewood (Okla.).
COLLEGE: Oklahoma.
TRANSACTIONS/CAREER NOTES: Signed as non-drafted free agent by Tennessee Oilers (May 14, 1997). ... Released by Oilers (August 20, 1997). ... Signed by Philadelphia Eagles to practice squad (August 27, 1997). ... Released by Eagles (September 2, 1997). ... Re-signed by Eagles to practice squad (September 10, 1997). ... Signed by Chicago Bears off Eagles practice squad (December 9, 1997). ... Inactive for two games (1997). ... Released by Bears (August 25, 1998). ... Re-signed by Bears to practice squad (August 31, 1998). ... Activated (October 13, 1998). ... Granted free agency (March 2, 2001). ... Re-signed by Bears (April 24, 2001). ... Granted unconditional free agency (March 1, 2002). ... Signed by Houston Texans (March 15, 2002). ... Granted unconditional free agency (February 28, 2003). ... Re-signed by Texans (May 11, 2003).
SINGLE GAME HIGHS (regular season): Attempts—37 (December 10, 2000, vs. New England); yards—163 (December 20, 1998, vs. Baltimore); and rushing touchdowns—1 (October 14, 2001, vs. Arizona).
STATISTICAL PLATEAUS: 100-yard rushing games: 1998 (1), 2000 (1), 2001 (1). Total: 3.

Year Team	G	GS	RUSHING Att.	Yds.	Avg.	TD	RECEIVING No.	Yds.	Avg.	TD	TOTALS TD	2pt.	Pts.	Fum.
1997—Chicago NFL			Did not play.											
1998—Chicago NFL	6	2	58	270	4.7	1	8	77	9.6	1	2	0	12	1
1999—Chicago NFL	12	3	32	119	3.7	0	9	91	10.1	0	0	0	0	0
2000—Chicago NFL	16	15	290	1120	3.9	2	39	291	7.5	1	3	0	18	5
2001—Chicago NFL	16	7	135	469	3.5	1	30	203	6.8	1	2	0	12	1
2002—Houston NFL	16	5	155	519	3.3	0	47	302	6.4	0	0	1	2	1
Pro totals (5 years)	66	32	670	2497	3.7	4	133	964	7.2	3	7	1	44	8

ALLEN, LARRY   G   COWBOYS

PERSONAL: Born November 27, 1971, in Los Angeles. ... 6-3/335. ... Full name: Larry Christopher Allen.
HIGH SCHOOL: Centennial (Compton, Calif.), then Vintage (Napa, Calif.).
JUNIOR COLLEGE: Butte College (Calif.).
COLLEGE: Sonoma State (Calif.).
TRANSACTIONS/CAREER NOTES: Selected by Dallas Cowboys in second round (46th pick overall) of 1994 NFL draft. ... Signed by Cowboys (July 16, 1994). ... On injured reserve with ankle injury (November 21, 2002-remainder of season).
PLAYING EXPERIENCE: Dallas NFL, 1994-2002. ... Games/Games started: 1994 (16/10), 1995 (16/16), 1996 (16/16), 1997 (16/16), 1998 (16/16), 1999 (11/11), 2000 (16/16), 2001 (16/16), 2002 (5/5). Total: 128/122.
CHAMPIONSHIP GAME EXPERIENCE: Played in NFC championship game (1994 and 1995 seasons). ... Member of Super Bowl championship team (1995 season).
HONORS: Named guard on THE SPORTING NEWS NFL All-Pro team (1995-97 and 1999). ... Played in Pro Bowl (1995-1998 and 2000 seasons). ... Named to play in Pro Bowl (1999 season); replaced by Adam Timmerman due to injury. ... Named offensive tackle on THE SPORTING NEWS NFL All-Pro team (1998). ... Named guard on THE SPORTING NEWS NFL All-Pro team (2000 and 2001). ... Named to play in Pro Bowl (2001 season); replaced by Adam Timmerman due to injury.

ALLEN, MATT   P

PERSONAL: Born October 23, 1977, in Montgomery, Ala. ... 6-4/230.
HIGH SCHOOL: Calvary (Montgomery, Ala.).
COLLEGE: Troy State.
TRANSACTIONS/CAREER NOTES: Signed as non-drafted free agent by Atlanta Falcons (May 4, 2001). ... Released by Falcons (August 20, 2001). ... Signed by Seattle Seahawks (January 17, 2002). ... Claimed on waivers by Falcons (April 17, 2002). ... Released by Falcons (August 22, 2002). ... Signed by New York Giants (August 30, 2002). ... Released by Giants (February 22, 2003).

		PUNTING					
Year Team	G	No.	Yds.	Avg.	Net avg.	In. 20	Blk.
2002—New York Giants NFL	14	63	2326	36.9	32.5	20	0

ALLEN, TAJE   CB

PERSONAL: Born November 6, 1973, in Fairburn, Ga. ... 5-11/184. ... Full name: Taje LaQuane Allen.
HIGH SCHOOL: Estacado (Lubbock, Texas).
COLLEGE: Texas.
TRANSACTIONS/CAREER NOTES: Selected by St. Louis Rams in fifth round (158th pick overall) of 1997 NFL draft. ... Signed by Rams (July 3, 1997). ... Granted free agency (February 11, 2000). ... Re-signed by Rams (June 2, 2000). ... Granted unconditional free agency (March 2, 2001). ... Signed by Kansas City Chiefs (April 17, 2001). ... Granted unconditional free agency (February 28, 2003).
CHAMPIONSHIP GAME EXPERIENCE: Played in NFC championship game (1999 season). ... Member of Super Bowl championship team (1999 season); did not play.

			TOTALS			INTERCEPTIONS			
Year Team	G	GS	Tk.	Ast.	Sks.	No.	Yds.	Avg.	TD
1997—St. Louis NFL	14	1	18	1	0.0	0	0	0.0	0
1998—St. Louis NFL	16	0	1	0	0.0	0	0	0.0	0
1999—St. Louis NFL	16	2	31	2	0.5	2	76	38.0	0
2000—St. Louis NFL	11	1	1	0	0.0	0	0	0.0	0
2001—Kansas City NFL	16	0	10	0	0.0	0	0	0.0	0
2002—Kansas City NFL	6	0	0	0	0.0	0	0	0.0	0
Pro totals (6 years)	79	4	61	3	0.5	2	76	38.0	0

ALLEN, WILL   CB   GIANTS

PERSONAL: Born August 5, 1978, in Syracuse, N.Y. ... 5-10/195. ... Full name: Will D. Allen.
HIGH SCHOOL: Corcoran (Syracuse, N.Y.).
COLLEGE: Syracuse.
TRANSACTIONS/CAREER NOTES: Selected by New York Giants in first round (22nd pick overall) of 2001 NFL draft. ... Signed by Giants (July 26, 2001).
HONORS: Named cornerback to THE SPORTING NEWS college All-America third team (2000).

			TOTALS			INTERCEPTIONS			
Year Team	G	GS	Tk.	Ast.	Sks.	No.	Yds.	Avg.	TD
2001—New York Giants NFL	13	12	38	4	0.0	4	27	6.8	0
2002—New York Giants NFL	15	15	50	5	0.0	1	0	0.0	0
Pro totals (2 years)	28	27	88	9	0.0	5	27	5.4	0

ALLRED, JOHN   TE

PERSONAL: Born September 9, 1974, in Del Mar, Calif. ... 6-4/246.
HIGH SCHOOL: Torrey Pines (Encinitas, Calif.).
COLLEGE: Southern California.
TRANSACTIONS/CAREER NOTES: Selected by Chicago Bears in second round (38th pick overall) of 1997 NFL draft. ... Signed by Bears (July 14, 1997). ... Granted free agency (February 11, 2000). ... Re-signed by Bears (April 20, 2000). ... On injured reserve with knee injury (October 10, 2000-remainder of season). ... Granted unconditional free agency (March 2, 2001). ... Signed by St. Louis Rams (June 15, 2001). ... Released by Rams (July 19, 2001). ... Signed by Pittsburgh Steelers (April 26, 2002). ... Granted unconditional free agency (February 28, 2003).

SINGLE GAME HIGHS (regular season): Receptions—4 (October 1, 2000, vs. Green Bay); yards—36 (September 3, 2000, vs. Minnesota); and touchdown receptions—1 (September 3, 2000, vs. Minnesota).

Year Team	G	GS	RECEIVING				TOTALS			
			No.	Yds.	Avg.	TD	TD	2pt.	Pts.	Fum.
1997—Chicago NFL	15	4	8	70	8.8	0	0	0	0	0
1998—Chicago NFL	4	0	0	0	0.0	0	0	0	0	0
1999—Chicago NFL	16	5	13	102	7.8	1	1	0	6	0
2000—Chicago NFL	5	3	9	109	12.1	1	1	0	6	0
2002—Pittsburgh NFL	13	0	0	0	0.0	0	0	0	0	0
Pro totals (5 years)	53	12	30	281	9.4	2	2	0	12	0

ALSTOTT, MIKE — FB — BUCCANEERS

PERSONAL: Born December 21, 1973, in Joliet, Ill. ... 6-1/248. ... Full name: Michael Joseph Alstott.
HIGH SCHOOL: Joliet (Ill.) Catholic.
COLLEGE: Purdue (degree in business, 1995).
TRANSACTIONS/CAREER NOTES: Selected by Tampa Bay Buccaneers in second round (35th pick overall) of 1996 NFL draft. ... Signed by Buccaneers (July 21, 1996).
CHAMPIONSHIP GAME EXPERIENCE: Played in NFC championship game (1999 and 2002 seasons). ... Member of Super Bowl championship team (2002 season).
HONORS: Played in Pro Bowl (1997-2002 seasons).
SINGLE GAME HIGHS (regular season): Attempts—28 (October 28, 2001, vs. Minnesota); yards—131 (September 26, 1999, vs. Denver); and rushing touchdowns—3 (October 28, 2001, vs. Minnesota).
STATISTICAL PLATEAUS: 100-yard rushing games: 1998 (2), 1999 (2), 2001 (2), 2002 (1). Total: 7.
MISCELLANEOUS: Holds Tampa Bay Buccaneers all-time records for most rushing touchdowns (45) and most touchdowns (57).

Year Team	G	GS	RUSHING				RECEIVING				TOTALS			
			Att.	Yds.	Avg.	TD	No.	Yds.	Avg.	TD	TD	2pt.	Pts.	Fum.
1996—Tampa Bay NFL	16	16	96	377	3.9	3	65	557	8.6	3	6	0	36	4
1997—Tampa Bay NFL	15	15	176	665	3.8	7	23	178	7.7	3	10	0	60	5
1998—Tampa Bay NFL	16	16	215	846	3.9	8	22	152	6.9	1	9	0	54	5
1999—Tampa Bay NFL	16	16	242	949	3.9	7	27	239	8.9	2	9	0	54	6
2000—Tampa Bay NFL	13	13	131	465	3.5	5	13	93	7.2	0	5	0	30	3
2001—Tampa Bay NFL	16	16	165	680	4.1	10	35	231	6.6	1	11	2	70	2
2002—Tampa Bay NFL	16	9	146	548	3.8	5	35	242	6.9	2	7	0	42	4
Pro totals (7 years)	108	101	1171	4530	3.9	45	220	1692	7.7	12	57	2	346	29

AMBROSE, ASHLEY — CB — SAINTS

PERSONAL: Born September 17, 1970, in New Orleans. ... 5-10/187. ... Full name: Ashley Avery Ambrose.
HIGH SCHOOL: Alcee Fortier (New Orleans).
COLLEGE: Mississippi Valley State (degree in industrial technology).
TRANSACTIONS/CAREER NOTES: Selected by Indianapolis Colts in second round (29th pick overall) of 1992 NFL draft. ... Signed by Colts (August 11, 1992). ... On injured reserve with leg injury (September 14-October 29, 1992); on practice squad (October 21-29, 1992). ... Granted free agency (February 17, 1995). ... Re-signed by Colts (April 29, 1995). ... Granted unconditional free agency (February 16, 1996). ... Signed by Cincinnati Bengals (February 25, 1996). ... Granted unconditional free agency (February 12, 1999). ... Signed by New Orleans Saints (July 13, 1999). ... Granted unconditional free agency (February 11, 2000). ... Signed by Atlanta Falcons (February 12, 2000). ... Released by Falcons (February 21, 2003). ... Signed by Saints (March 3, 2003).
CHAMPIONSHIP GAME EXPERIENCE: Played in AFC championship game (1995 season).
HONORS: Played in Pro Bowl (1996 season).

Year Team	G	GS	TOTALS			INTERCEPTIONS			
			Tk.	Ast.	Sks.	No.	Yds.	Avg.	TD
1992—Indianapolis NFL	10	2	6	2	0.0	0	0	0.0	0
1993—Indianapolis NFL	14	6	36	8	0.0	0	0	0.0	0
1994—Indianapolis NFL	16	4	31	4	0.0	2	50	25.0	0
1995—Indianapolis NFL	16	0	11	3	0.0	3	12	4.0	0
1996—Cincinnati NFL	16	16	44	6	0.0	8	63	7.9	1
1997—Cincinnati NFL	16	16	57	2	1.0	3	56	18.7	0
1998—Cincinnati NFL	15	15	36	4	0.0	2	0	0.0	0
1999—New Orleans NFL	16	16	51	6	0.0	6	27	4.5	0
2000—Atlanta NFL	16	16	37	1	0.0	4 ‡139	34.8	1
2001—Atlanta NFL	16	16	49	3	0.0	5	43	8.6	0
2002—Atlanta NFL	16	16	42	2	0.0	3	25	8.3	0
Pro totals (11 years)	167	123	400	41	1.0	36	415	11.5	2

ANDERSEN, JASON — C — CHIEFS

PERSONAL: Born September 3, 1975, in Hayward, Calif. ... 6-6/319. ... Full name: Jason Allen Andersen.
HIGH SCHOOL: Piedmont (Calif.).
COLLEGE: Brigham Young.
TRANSACTIONS/CAREER NOTES: Selected by New England Patriots in seventh round (211th pick overall) of 1998 NFL draft. ... Signed by Patriots (June 18, 1998). ... Active for seven games (1998); did not play. ... Released by Patriots (October 21, 2000). ... Signed by Miami Dolphins (November 14, 2000). ... Inactive for six games (2000). ... Released by Dolphins (August 26, 2001). ... Released by Chiefs (September 1, 2002). ... Re-signed by Chiefs (December 11, 2002).
PLAYING EXPERIENCE: New England NFL, 1999-2002. Kansas City NFL, 2002. ... Games/Games started: 1999 (9/0), 2000 (7/0), 2002 (3/0). Total: 19/0.

ANDERSEN, MORTEN   K   CHIEFS

PERSONAL: Born August 19, 1960, in Copenhagen, Denmark. ... 6-2/217.
HIGH SCHOOL: Ben Davis (Indianapolis).
COLLEGE: Michigan State (degrees in communications and German).
TRANSACTIONS/CAREER NOTES: Selected by New Orleans Saints in fourth round (86th pick overall) of 1982 NFL draft. ... On injured reserve with sprained ankle (September 15-November 20, 1982). ... Designated by Saints as transition player (February 25, 1993). ... Released by Saints (July 19, 1995). ... Signed by Atlanta Falcons (July 21, 1995). ... Granted unconditional free agency (March 2, 2001). ... Signed by New York Giants (August 29, 2001). ... Granted unconditional free agency (March 1, 2002). ... Signed by Kansas City Chiefs (March 25, 2002). ... On injured reserve with knee injury (December 17, 2002-remainder of season). ... Granted unconditional free agency (February 28, 2003). ... Re-signed by Chiefs (March 18, 2003).
CHAMPIONSHIP GAME EXPERIENCE: Played in NFC championship game (1998 season). ... Played in Super Bowl XXXIII (1998 season).
HONORS: Named kicker on THE SPORTING NEWS college All-America first team (1981). ... Named kicker on THE SPORTING NEWS NFL All-Pro team (1985-1987 and 1995). ... Played in Pro Bowl (1985-1988, 1990, 1992 and 1995 seasons).
RECORDS: Holds NFL career records for most consecutive games scoring—300 (December 11, 1983-present); and for most made field goals of 50 or more yards—40. ... Holds NFL single-season record for most made field goals of 50 or more yards—8 (1995). ... Holds NFL single-game record for most made field goals of 50 or more yards—3 (December 10, 1995, vs. New Orleans). ... Shares NFL record for most seasons with 100 or more points—13 (1985-89, 1991-95, 1997, 1998 and 2002).

| | | FIELD GOALS | | | | | | | TOTALS | | |
Year Team	G	1-29	30-39	40-49	50+	Tot.	Pct.	Lg.	XPM	XPA	Pts.
1982—New Orleans NFL	8	0-0	1-1	1-3	0-1	2-5	40.0	45	6	6	12
1983—New Orleans NFL	16	10-10	3-4	2-6	3-4	18-24	75.0	52	37	38	91
1984—New Orleans NFL	16	9-9	4-5	5-10	2-3	20-27	74.1	53	34	34	94
1985—New Orleans NFL	16	4-5	13-14	11-12	3-4	31-35	88.6	§55	27	29	120
1986—New Orleans NFL	16	12-12	6-7	6-6	2-5	26-30	86.7	53	30	30	108
1987—New Orleans NFL	12	9-9	9-9	8-12	2-6	*28-*36	77.8	52	37	37	121
1988—New Orleans NFL	16	12-13	8-11	5-8	1-4	26-36	72.2	51	32	33	110
1989—New Orleans NFL	16	7-8	10-11	3-6	0-4	20-29	69.0	49	44	45	104
1990—New Orleans NFL	16	5-5	5-6	8-12	3-4	21-27	77.8	52	29	29	92
1991—New Orleans NFL	16	6-6	11-13	6-9	2-4	25-32	78.1	*60	38	38	113
1992—New Orleans NFL	16	10-10	8-10	8-11	3-3	29-34	85.3	52	33	34	∞120
1993—New Orleans NFL	16	9-9	7-7	11-14	1-5	28-35	80.0	56	33	33	117
1994—New Orleans NFL	16	9-9	11-14	8-10	0-6	28-†39	71.8	48	32	32	116
1995—Atlanta NFL	16	9-9	11-11	3-8	8-9	‡31-37	83.8	*59	29	30	122
1996—Atlanta NFL	16	5-5	9-11	7-8	1-5	22-29	75.9	∞54	31	31	97
1997—Atlanta NFL	16	11-11	7-7	3-6	2-3	23-27	85.2	∞55	35	35	104
1998—Atlanta NFL	16	8-10	7-7	6-9	2-2	23-28	82.1	53	51	52	120
1999—Atlanta NFL	16	6-6	5-8	4-6	0-1	15-21	71.4	49	34	34	79
2000—Atlanta NFL	16	6-6	6-7	11-15	2-3	25-31	80.6	51	23	23	98
2001—New York Giants NFL	16	8-8	7-8	6-7	2-5	23-28	82.1	51	29	30	98
2002—Kansas City NFL	14	6-6	10-10	5-9	1-1	22-26	84.6	50	*51	*51	117
Pro totals (21 years)	322	161-166	158-181	127-187	40-82	486-616	78.9	60	695	704	2153

ANDERSON, BENNIE   G   RAVENS

PERSONAL: Born February 17, 1977, in St. Louis. ... 6-5/335. ... Full name: Tyrone Lamar Anderson.
HIGH SCHOOL: Cleveland Junior Naval Academy (St. Louis).
COLLEGE: Tennessee State.
TRANSACTIONS/CAREER NOTES: Signed as non-drafted free agent by St. Louis Rams (May 3, 2000). ... Released by Rams (July 19, 2000). ... Signed by Baltimore Ravens (June 14, 2001).
PLAYING EXPERIENCE: Baltimore NFL, 2001-2002. ... Games/Games started: 2001 (16/13), 2002 (16/16), Totals (32/29).

ANDERSON, DAMIEN   RB   CARDINALS

PERSONAL: Born July 17, 1979, in Wilmington, Ill. ... 5-11/217. ... Full name: Damien Ramone Anderson.
HIGH SCHOOL: Wilmington (Ill.).
COLLEGE: Northwestern.
TRANSACTIONS/CAREER NOTES: Signed as non-drafted free agent by Arizona Cardinals (April 23, 2002). ... Released by Cardinals (September 1, 2002). ... Re-signed by Cardinals to practice squad (September 2, 2002). ... Activated (October 5, 2002).
SINGLE GAME HIGHS (regular season): Attempts—23 (October 6, 2002, vs. Carolina); yards—61 (October 6, 2002, vs. Carolina); and rushing touchdowns—0.

| | | | RUSHING | | | | RECEIVING | | | | KICKOFF RETURNS | | | | TOTALS | | |
Year Team	G	GS	Att.	Yds.	Avg.	TD	No.	Yds.	Avg.	TD	No.	Yds.	Avg.	TD	TD	2pt.	Pts.	Fum.
2002—Arizona NFL	10	1	24	65	2.7	0	3	36	12.0	0	12	227	18.9	0	0	0	0	0

ANDERSON, GARY   K

PERSONAL: Born July 16, 1959, in Parys, Orange Free State, South Africa. ... 5-11/193. ... Full name: Gary Allan Anderson. ... Son of Rev. Douglas Anderson, former professional soccer player in England.
HIGH SCHOOL: Brettonwood (Durban, South Africa).
COLLEGE: Syracuse (degree in management and accounting, 1982).
TRANSACTIONS/CAREER NOTES: Selected by Buffalo Bills in seventh round (171st pick overall) of 1982 NFL draft. ... Signed by Bills for 1982 season. ... Claimed on waivers by Pittsburgh Steelers (September 7, 1982). ... Designated by Steelers as transition player (February 15, 1994). ... On reserve/did not report list (August 23-25, 1994). ... Free agency status changed by Steelers from transition to unconditional (February 17, 1995). ... Signed by Philadelphia Eagles (July 23, 1995). ... Released by Eagles (April 22, 1997). ... Signed by San Francisco 49ers (June 11, 1997). ... Granted unconditional free agency (February 13, 1998). ... Signed by Minnesota Vikings (February 20, 1998). ... Granted unconditional free agency (March 1, 2002). ... Re-signed by Vikings (September 17, 2002). ... Granted unconditional free agency (February 28, 2003).

A

CHAMPIONSHIP GAME EXPERIENCE: Played in AFC championship game (1984 and 1994 seasons). ... Played in NFC championship game (1997 and 1998 seasons). ... Member of Vikings for NFC Championship game (2000 season); did not play.
HONORS: Played in Pro Bowl (1983, 1985, 1993 and 1998 seasons). ... Named kicker on The Sporting News NFL All-Pro team (1998).
RECORDS: Holds NFL career record for most points—2,223; most field goals made—494; and most consecutive field goals made—40. ... Holds NFL single-season record for most points scored without a touchdown—164 (1998). ... Shares NFL record for most seasons with 100 or more points—13 (1983-2000). ... Shares NFL single-season record for highest field-goal percentage—100.0 (1998).
POST SEASON RECORDS: Holds NFL postseason career record for most made field goals—30. ... Holds NFL postseason record for most consecutive made field goals—16 (1989-95).

		FIELD GOALS							TOTALS		
Year Team	**G**	**1-29**	**30-39**	**40-49**	**50+**	**Tot.**	**Pct.**	**Lg.**	**XPM**	**XPA**	**Pts.**
1982—Pittsburgh NFL	9	4-4	1-2	5-5	0-1	10-12	83.3	48	22	22	52
1983—Pittsburgh NFL	16	10-11	9-10	8-10	0-0	27-31	87.1	49	38	39	§119
1984—Pittsburgh NFL	16	8-9	6-9	8-11	2-3	▲24-32	75.0	55	45	45	§117
1985—Pittsburgh NFL	16	13-14	14-15	5-9	1-4	*33-*42	78.6	52	40	40	§139
1986—Pittsburgh NFL	16	6-8	6-7	9-14	0-3	21-32	65.6	45	32	32	95
1987—Pittsburgh NFL	12	8-9	5-5	7-11	2-2	22-27	81.5	52	21	21	87
1988—Pittsburgh NFL	16	12-12	9-10	6-12	1-2	28-36	77.8	52	34	35	118
1989—Pittsburgh NFL	16	7-7	5-8	9-15	0-0	21-30	70.0	49	28	28	91
1990—Pittsburgh NFL	16	4-4	8-8	8-11	0-2	20-25	80.0	48	32	32	92
1991—Pittsburgh NFL	16	8-10	9-11	5-6	1-6	23-33	69.7	54	31	31	100
1992—Pittsburgh NFL	16	12-13	12-15	4-6	0-2	28-36	77.8	49	29	31	113
1993—Pittsburgh NFL	16	9-10	14-14	5-6	0-0	28-30	93.3	46	32	32	*116
1994—Pittsburgh NFL	16	8-9	8-9	7-9	1-2	24-29	82.8	50	32	32	104
1995—Philadelphia NFL	16	5-5	9-10	8-12	0-3	22-30	73.3	43	32	33	98
1996—Philadelphia NFL	16	10-11	8-9	7-9	0-0	25-29	86.2	46	40	40	115
1997—San Francisco NFL	16	11-11	9-12	8-10	1-3	29-36	80.6	51	38	38	125
1998—Minnesota NFL	16	12-12	9-9	12-12	2-2	‡35-∞35	100.0	53	*59	*59	*164
1999—Minnesota NFL	16	6-8	9-11	4-9	0-2	19-30	63.3	44	46	46	103
2000—Minnesota NFL	16	6-6	9-9	7-7	0-1	22-23	95.7	49	‡45	∞45	111
2001—Minnesota NFL	16	7-7	2-4	6-7	0-0	15-18	83.3	44	29	30	74
2002—Minnesota NFL	14	9-9	5-5	3-8	1-1	18-23	78.3	∞53	36	37	90
Pro totals (21 years)	323	175-189	166-192	141-199	12-39	494-619	79.8	55	741	748	2223

ANDERSON, MARQUES — S — PACKERS

PERSONAL: Born May 26, 1979, in Harbor City, Calif. ... 5-11/213. ... Full name: Marques Deon Anderson.
HIGH SCHOOL: Polytechnic (Pasadena, Calif.).
COLLEGE: UCLA.
TRANSACTIONS/CAREER NOTES: Selected by Green Bay Packers in third round (92nd pick overall) of 2002 NFL draft. ... Signed by Packers (July 9, 2002).

			TOTALS			INTERCEPTIONS			
Year Team	**G**	**GS**	**Tk.**	**Ast.**	**Sks.**	**No.**	**Yds.**	**Avg.**	**TD**
2002—Green Bay NFL	14	11	41	20	0.0	4	114	28.5	2

ANDERSON, MIKE — RB — BRONCOS

PERSONAL: Born September 21, 1973, in Winnsboro, S.C. ... 6-0/230. ... Full name: Michael Moschello Anderson.
HIGH SCHOOL: Fairfield (S.C.).
JUNIOR COLLEGE: Mount San Jacinto Community College (Calif.).
COLLEGE: Utah.
TRANSACTIONS/CAREER NOTES: Selected by Denver Broncos in sixth round (189th pick overall) of 2000 NFL draft. ... Signed by Broncos (July 14, 2000).
SINGLE GAME HIGHS (regular season): Attempts—37 (December 3, 2000, vs. New Orleans); yards—251 (December 3, 2000, vs. New Orleans); and rushing touchdowns—4 (December 3, 2000, vs. New Orleans).
STATISTICAL PLATEAUS: 100-yard rushing games: 2000 (6), 2001 (2). Total: 8.

			RUSHING				RECEIVING				TOTALS			
Year Team	**G**	**GS**	**Att.**	**Yds.**	**Avg.**	**TD**	**No.**	**Yds.**	**Avg.**	**TD**	**TD**	**2pt.**	**Pts.**	**Fum.**
2000—Denver NFL	16	12	297	1487	§5.0	§15	23	169	7.3	0	15	1	92	4
2001—Denver NFL	16	7	175	678	3.9	4	8	46	5.8	0	4	1	26	1
2002—Denver NFL	15	12	84	386	4.6	2	18	167	9.3	2	4	0	24	2
Pro totals (3 years)	47	31	556	2551	4.6	21	49	382	7.8	2	23	2	142	7

ANDERSON, RASHARD — CB — PANTHERS

PERSONAL: Born June 14, 1977, in Forest, Miss. ... 6-2/204.
HIGH SCHOOL: Forest (Miss.).
COLLEGE: Jackson State.
TRANSACTIONS/CAREER NOTES: Selected by Carolina Panthers in first round (23rd pick overall) of 2000 NFL draft. ... Signed by Panthers (July 17, 2000). ... On suspended list for violating league substance abuse policy (May 23, 2002-present).

			TOTALS			INTERCEPTIONS			
Year Team	**G**	**GS**	**Tk.**	**Ast.**	**Sks.**	**No.**	**Yds.**	**Avg.**	**TD**
2000—Carolina NFL	12	0	13	1	0.0	0	0	0.0	0
2001—Carolina NFL	15	9	41	4	0.0	1	0	0.0	0
2002—Carolina NFL	Did not play.								
Pro totals (2 years)	27	9	54	5	0.0	1	0	0.0	0

ANDERSON, RICHIE   FB   COWBOYS

PERSONAL: Born September 13, 1971, in Sandy Spring, Md. ... 6-2/230. ... Full name: Richard Darnoll Anderson II.
HIGH SCHOOL: Sherwood (Sandy Spring, Md.).
COLLEGE: Penn State.
TRANSACTIONS/CAREER NOTES: Selected after junior season by New York Jets in sixth round (144th pick overall) of 1993 NFL draft. ... Signed by Jets (June 10, 1993). ... On injured reserve with ankle injury (December 31, 1993-remainder of season). ... On injured reserve with ankle injury (November 30, 1995-remainder of season). ... Granted unconditional free agency (February 28, 2003). ... Signed by Dallas Cowboys (March 4, 2003).
CHAMPIONSHIP GAME EXPERIENCE: Member of Jets for AFC championship game (1998 season); did not play.
HONORS: Played in Pro Bowl (2000 season).
SINGLE GAME HIGHS (regular season): Attempts—9 (November 13, 1994, vs. Green Bay); yards—74 (November 13, 1994, vs. Green Bay); and rushing touchdowns—1 (October 27, 1996, vs. Arizona).
STATISTICAL PLATEAUS: 100-yard receiving games: 2000 (3).

			RUSHING				RECEIVING				KICKOFF RETURNS				TOTALS			
Year Team	G	GS	Att.	Yds.	Avg.	TD	No.	Yds.	Avg.	TD	No.	Yds.	Avg.	TD	TD	2pt.	Pts.	Fum.
1993—New York Jets NFL	7	0	0	0	0.0	0	0	0	0.0	0	4	66	16.5	0	0	0	0	1
1994—New York Jets NFL	13	5	43	207	4.8	1	25	212	8.5	1	3	43	14.3	0	2	0	12	1
1995—New York Jets NFL	10	0	5	17	3.4	0	5	26	5.2	0	0	0	0.0	0	0	0	0	2
1996—New York Jets NFL	16	13	47	150	3.2	1	44	385	8.8	0	0	0	0.0	0	1	0	6	0
1997—New York Jets NFL	16	3	21	70	3.3	0	26	150	5.8	1	0	0	0.0	0	1	0	6	2
1998—New York Jets NFL	8	1	1	2	2.0	0	3	12	4.0	0	0	0	0.0	0	0	0	0	0
1999—New York Jets NFL	16	9	16	84	5.3	0	29	302	10.4	3	0	0	0.0	0	3	0	18	0
2000—New York Jets NFL	16	15	27	63	2.3	0	88	853	9.7	2	0	0	0.0	0	2	0	12	2
2001—New York Jets NFL	16	16	26	102	3.9	0	40	252	6.3	2	0	0	0.0	0	2	0	12	1
2002—New York Jets NFL	16	14	5	27	5.4	0	45	257	5.7	1	0	0	0.0	0	1	0	6	0
Pro totals (10 years)	134	76	191	722	3.8	2	305	2449	8.0	10	7	109	15.6	0	12	0	72	9

ANDERSON, SCOTTY   WR   LIONS

PERSONAL: Born November 24, 1979, in Jonesboro, La. ... 6-2/191. ... Brother of Stevie Anderson, wide receiver with New York Jets (1994) and Arizona Cardinals (1995 and 1996); and brother of Anthony Anderson, defensive back with San Diego Chargers (1987).
HIGH SCHOOL: Jonesboro-Hodge (Jonesboro, La.).
COLLEGE: Grambling State.
TRANSACTIONS/CAREER NOTES: Selected by Detroit Lions in fifth round (148th pick overall) of 2001 NFL draft. ... Signed by Lions (July 16, 2001).
SINGLE GAME HIGHS (regular season): Receptions—5 (November 24, 2002, vs. Chicago); yards—70 (November 24, 2002, vs. Chicago); and touchdown receptions—1 (December 29, 2002, vs. Minnesota).

			RECEIVING			
Year Team	G	GS	No.	Yds.	Avg.	TD
2001—Detroit NFL	9	4	12	211	17.6	1
2002—Detroit NFL	16	4	25	322	12.9	1
Pro totals (2 years)	25	8	37	533	14.4	2

ANDERSON, WILLIE   OT   BENGALS

PERSONAL: Born July 11, 1975, in Mobile, Ala. ... 6-5/340. ... Full name: Willie Aaron Anderson.
HIGH SCHOOL: Vigor (Prichard, Ala.).
COLLEGE: Auburn.
TRANSACTIONS/CAREER NOTES: Selected after junior season by Cincinnati Bengals in first round (10th pick overall) of 1996 NFL draft. ... Signed by Bengals (August 5, 1996).
PLAYING EXPERIENCE: Cincinnati NFL, 1996-2002.. ... Games/Games started: 1996 (16/10), 1997 (16/16), 1998 (16/16), 1999 (14/14), 2000 (16/16), 2001 (16/16), 2002 (16/16). Total: 110/104.

ANDRUZZI, JOE   G   PATRIOTS

PERSONAL: Born August 23, 1975, in Staten Island, N.Y. ... 6-3/312. ... Full name: Joseph Dominick Andruzzi. ... Name pronounced ann-DROOZ-ee.
HIGH SCHOOL: Tottenville (Staten Island, N.Y.).
COLLEGE: Southern Connecticut State.
TRANSACTIONS/CAREER NOTES: Signed as non-drafted free agent by Green Bay Packers (April 25, 1997). ... Inactive for all 16 games (1997). ... Assigned by Packers to Scottish Claymores in 1998 NFL Europe enhancement allocations program (February 18, 1998). ... On injured reserve with knee injury (November 23, 1999-remainder of season). ... Released by Packers (August 27, 2000). ... Signed by New England Patriots (September 9, 2000). ... On injured reserve with knee injury (December 7, 2000-remainder of season).
PLAYING EXPERIENCE: Scottish NFLE, 1998; Green Bay NFL, 1998 and 1999; New England NFL, 2000-2002. ... Games/Games started: NFLE 1998 (10/10), NFL 1998 (15/1), 1999 (8/3), 2000 (11/11), 2001 (16/16), 2002 (13/13). Total NFLE: 10/10. Total NFL: 63/44. Total Pro: 73/54.
CHAMPIONSHIP GAME EXPERIENCE: Member of Packers for NFC championship game (1997 season); inactive. ... Member of Packers for Super Bowl XXXII (1997 season); inactive. ... Played in AFC championship game (2001 season). ... Member of Super Bowl championship team (2001 season).

ANELLI, MARK   TE   49ERS

PERSONAL: Born June 5, 1979, in Addison, Ill. ... 6-3/265.
HIGH SCHOOL: Addison Trail (Addison, Ill.).
COLLEGE: Wisconsin.
TRANSACTIONS/CAREER NOTES: Selected by San Francisco 49ers in sixth round (201st pick overall) of 2002 NFL draft. ... Signed by 49ers (July 21, 2002). ... Released by 49ers (September 24, 2002). ... Re-signed by 49ers to practice squad (September 30, 2002). ... Activated (October 26, 2002). ... Released by 49ers (November 25, 2002). ... Re-signed by 49ers to practice squad (November 26, 2002).

Year Team	G	GS	RECEIVING No.	Yds.	Avg.	TD
2002—San Francisco NFL	2	0	0	0	0.0	0

ANTHONY, CORNELIUS   LB   49ERS

PERSONAL: Born July 7, 1978, in Missouri City, Texas. ... 6-0/235. ... Full name: Cornelius Armand Anthony.
HIGH SCHOOL: Elkins (Missouri City, Texas).
COLLEGE: Texas A&M.
TRANSACTIONS/CAREER NOTES: Signed as non-drafted free agent by Washington Redskins (April 24, 2001). ... Released by Redskins (August 27, 2001). ... Signed by San Francisco 49ers (February 5, 2002). ... Assigned by 49ers to Frankfurt Galaxy in 2002 NFL Europe enhancement allocation program (February 12, 2002). ... Released by 49ers (August 31, 2002). ... Re-signed by 49ers (October 23, 2002).

Year Team	G	GS	TOTALS Tk.	Ast.	Sks.	INTERCEPTIONS No.	Yds.	Avg.	TD
2002—Frankfurt NFLE	...	...	...	...	2.0	1	8	8.0	0
—San Francisco NFL	10	0	0	0	0.0	0	0	0.0	0
NFL Europe totals (1 year)	...	...	...	...	2.0	1	8	8.0	0
NFL totals (1 year)	10	0	0	0	0.0	0	0	0.0	0
Pro totals (2 years)	...	...	...	...	2.0	1	8	8.0	0

ARCHULETA, ADAM   S   RAMS

PERSONAL: Born November 27, 1977, in Chandler, Ariz. ... 6-0/215. ... Full name: Adam J. Archuleta.
HIGH SCHOOL: Chandler (Ariz.).
COLLEGE: Arizona State.
TRANSACTIONS/CAREER NOTES: Selected by St. Louis Rams in first round (20th pick overall) of 2001 NFL draft. ... Signed by Rams (July 29, 2001).
CHAMPIONSHIP GAME EXPERIENCE: Played in NFC championship game (2001 season). ... Played in Super Bowl XXXVI (2001 season).

Year Team	G	GS	TOTALS Tk.	Ast.	Sks.	INTERCEPTIONS No.	Yds.	Avg.	TD
2001—St. Louis NFL	13	12	47	9	2.0	0	0	0.0	0
2002—St. Louis NFL	16	16	94	14	2.5	1	2	2.0	0
Pro totals (2 years)	29	28	141	23	4.5	1	2	2.0	0

ARMOUR, JO JUAN   S   BENGALS

PERSONAL: Born July 10, 1976, in Toledo, Ohio. ... 5-11/220. ... Full name: JoJuan Armour. ... Name pronounced JOE-wan.
HIGH SCHOOL: Central Catholic (Cleveland).
COLLEGE: Miami of Ohio.
TRANSACTIONS/CAREER NOTES: Selected by Oakland Raiders in seventh round (224th pick overall) of 1999 NFL draft. ... Signed by Raiders (July 24, 1999). ... Claimed on waivers by Jacksonville Jaguars (September 7, 1999). ... Inactive for two games with Jaguars (1999). ... Claimed on waivers by Cincinnati Bengals (September 21, 1999). ... Released by Bengals (October 15, 1999). ... Re-signed by Bengals to practice squad (October 16, 1999). ... Activated (December 16, 1999). ... Released by Bengals (August 27, 2000). ... Re-signed by Bengals to practice squad (August 28, 2000). ... Activated (October 2, 2000). ... Assigned by Bengals to Barcelona Dragons in 2001 NFL Europe enhancement allocation program (February 19, 2001). ... Granted free agency (March 1, 2002). ... Re-signed by Bengals (April 23, 2002).
HONORS: Named outside linebacker on The Sporting News college All-America second team (1997).

Year Team	G	GS	TOTALS Tk.	Ast.	Sks.	INTERCEPTIONS No.	Yds.	Avg.	TD
1999—Cincinnati NFL	2	0	0	0	0.0	0	0	0.0	0
2000—Cincinnati NFL	4	0	0	0	0.0	0	0	0.0	0
2001—Cincinnati NFL	16	11	36	11	0.0	0	0	0.0	0
2002—Cincinnati NFL	16	8	32	20	0.0	0	0	0.0	0
Pro totals (4 years)	38	19	68	31	0.0	0	0	0.0	0

ARMSTEAD, JESSIE   LB   REDSKINS

PERSONAL: Born October 26, 1970, in Dallas. ... 6-1/232. ... Full name: Jessie W. Armstead.
HIGH SCHOOL: David W. Carter (Dallas).
COLLEGE: Miami (Fla.) (degree in criminal justice, 1992).
TRANSACTIONS/CAREER NOTES: Selected by New York Giants in eighth round (207th pick overall) of 1993 NFL draft. ... Signed by Giants (July 19, 1993). ... Released by Giants (February 28, 2002). ... Signed by Washington Redskins (March 1, 2002).
CHAMPIONSHIP GAME EXPERIENCE: Played in NFC championship game (2000 season). ... Played in Super Bowl XXXV (2000 season).
HONORS: Named outside linebacker on The Sporting News NFL All-Pro team (1997). ... Played in Pro Bowl (1997-2001 seasons).

Year Team	G	GS	TOTALS Tk.	Ast.	Sks.	INTERCEPTIONS No.	Yds.	Avg.	TD
1993—New York Giants NFL	16	0	28	3	0.0	1	0	0.0	0
1994—New York Giants NFL	16	0	33	8	3.0	1	0	0.0	0
1995—New York Giants NFL	16	2	36	10	0.5	1	58	58.0	1
1996—New York Giants NFL	16	16	83	31	3.0	2	23	11.5	0
1997—New York Giants NFL	16	16	101	31	3.5	2	57	28.5	1
1998—New York Giants NFL	16	16	75	26	5.0	2	4	2.0	0
1999—New York Giants NFL	16	16	97	27	9.0	2	35	17.5	0
2000—New York Giants NFL	16	16	76	26	5.0	1	-2	-2.0	0
2001—New York Giants NFL	16	16	64	24	1.5	0	0	0.0	0
2002—Washington NFL	16	14	79	21	3.0	0	0	0.0	0
Pro totals (10 years)	160	112	672	207	33.5	12	175	14.6	2

ARMSTRONG, TRACE   DE   RAIDERS

PERSONAL: Born October 5, 1965, in Bethesda, Md. ... 6-4/275. ... Full name: Raymond Lester Armstrong.
HIGH SCHOOL: John Carroll (Birmingham, Ala.).
COLLEGE: Arizona State, then Florida (degree in psychology, 1989).
TRANSACTIONS/CAREER NOTES: Selected by Chicago Bears in first round (12th pick overall) of 1989 NFL draft. ... Signed by Bears (August 18, 1989). ... On injured reserve with knee injury (September 24-November 3, 1991). ... Granted free agency (March 1, 1993). ... Re-signed by Bears (March 14, 1993). ... Traded by Bears to Miami Dolphins for second- (P Todd Sauerbrun) and third-round (G Evan Pilgrim) picks in 1995 draft (April 4, 1995). ... Granted unconditional free agency (March 2, 2001). ... Signed by Oakland Raiders (March 5, 2001). ... On injured reserve with Achilles' tendon injury (October 2, 2001-remainder of season). ... On injured reserve with groin injury (January 15, 2003-remainder of season).
HONORS: Named defensive lineman on THE SPORTING NEWS college All-America first team (1988). ... Played in Pro Bowl (2000 season).

Year Team	G	GS	TOTALS Tk.	Ast.	Sks.	INTERCEPTIONS No.	Yds.	Avg.	TD
1989—Chicago NFL	15	14	37	43	5.0	0	0	0.0	0
1990—Chicago NFL	16	16	33	49	10.0	0	0	0.0	0
1991—Chicago NFL	12	12	26	30	1.5	0	0	0.0	0
1992—Chicago NFL	14	14	40	35	6.5	0	0	0.0	0
1993—Chicago NFL	16	16	34	24	11.5	0	0	0.0	0
1994—Chicago NFL	15	15	31	10	7.5	0	0	0.0	0
1995—Miami NFL	15	0	21	5	4.5	0	0	0.0	0
1996—Miami NFL	16	9	22	11	12.0	0	0	0.0	0
1997—Miami NFL	16	16	25	22	5.5	0	0	0.0	0
1998—Miami NFL	16	0	20	2	10.5	0	0	0.0	0
1999—Miami NFL	16	2	16	9	7.5	0	0	0.0	0
2000—Miami NFL	16	0	24	10	§16.5	0	0	0.0	0
2001—Oakland NFL	3	0	1	3	0.5	0	0	0.0	0
2002—Oakland NFL	15	8	15	5	4.0	1	0	0.0	0
Pro totals (14 years)	201	122	345	258	103.0	1	0	0.0	0

ARRINGTON, LAVAR   LB   REDSKINS

PERSONAL: Born June 20, 1978, in Pittsburgh. ... 6-3/247. ... Full name: LaVar RaShad Arrington.
HIGH SCHOOL: North Hills (Pittsburgh).
COLLEGE: Penn State.
TRANSACTIONS/CAREER NOTES: Selected after junior season by Washington Redskins in first round (second pick overall) of 2000 NFL draft. ... Signed by Redskins (July 22, 2000).
HONORS: Named linebacker on THE SPORTING NEWS college All-America first team (1998 and 1999). ... Butkus Award winner (1999). ... Played in Pro Bowl (2001 and 2002 seasons).

Year Team	G	GS	TOTALS Tk.	Ast.	Sks.	INTERCEPTIONS No.	Yds.	Avg.	TD
2000—Washington NFL	16	11	43	9	4.0	0	0	0.0	0
2001—Washington NFL	14	14	82	17	0.5	3	120	40.0	1
2002—Washington NFL	16	16	70	25	11.0	0	0	0.0	0
Pro totals (3 years)	46	41	195	51	15.5	3	120	40.0	1

ASHMORE, DARRYL   G/OT

PERSONAL: Born November 1, 1969, in Peoria, Ill. ... 6-7/310. ... Full name: Darryl Allan Ashmore.
HIGH SCHOOL: Peoria (Ill.) Central.
COLLEGE: Northwestern (degree in business).
TRANSACTIONS/CAREER NOTES: Selected by Los Angeles Rams in seventh round (171st pick overall) of 1992 NFL draft. ... Signed by Rams (July 13, 1992). ... On injured reserve with knee injury (September 3-October 7, 1992). ... On practice squad (October 7, 1992-remainder of season). ... Granted free agency (February 17, 1995). ... Rams franchise moved to St. Louis (April 12, 1995). ... Re-signed by Rams (July 20, 1995). ... Released by Rams (October 14, 1996). ... Signed by Washington Redskins (October 26, 1996). ... Granted unconditional free agency (February 14, 1997). ... Re-signed by Redskins (May 9, 1997). ... Granted unconditional free agency (February 13, 1998). ... Signed by Oakland Raiders (April 25, 1998). ... Granted unconditional free agency (February 11, 2000). ... Re-signed by Raiders (February 22, 2000). ... Granted unconditional free agency (March 1, 2002). ... Re-signed by Raiders (March 22, 2002). ... On injured reserve with arm injury (August 15, 2002-entire season). ... Granted unconditional free agency (February 28, 2003).
PLAYING EXPERIENCE: Los Angeles Rams NFL, 1993 and 1994; St. Louis NFL, 1995; St. Louis (6)-Washington (5) NFL, 1996; Washington NFL, 1997; Oakland NFL, 1998-2002. ... Games/Games started: 1993 (9/7), 1994 (11/3), 1995 (16/15), 1996 (St.L-6/0; Wash.-5/0; Total: 11/0), 1997 (11/2), 1998 (15/4), 1999 (16/2), 2000 (16/2), 2001 (14/1), 2002 (0/0). Total: 119/36.
CHAMPIONSHIP GAME EXPERIENCE: Played in AFC championship game (2000 season).

ASHWORTH, THOMAS OT PATRIOTS

PERSONAL: Born October 10, 1977, in Denver. ... 6-6/305. ... Full name: Thomas F. Ashworth.
HIGH SCHOOL: Cherry Creek (Englewood, Colo.).
COLLEGE: Colorado.
TRANSACTIONS/CAREER NOTES: Signed as non-drafted free agent by San Francisco 49ers (April 27, 2001). ... Released by 49ers (August 27, 2001). ... Signed by New England Patriots to practice squad (September 4, 2001). ... Released by Patriots (October 9, 2001). ... Re-signed by Patriots to practice squad (October 31, 2001). ... Re-signed by Patriots (April 8, 2003).
PLAYING EXPERIENCE: New England NFL, 2002. ... Games/Games started: 2002 (1/0).

ATKINS, LARRY LB CHIEFS

PERSONAL: Born July 21, 1975, in Santa Monica, Calif. ... 6-3/250. ... Full name: Larry Tabay Atkins III.
HIGH SCHOOL: Venice (Los Angeles).
COLLEGE: UCLA.
TRANSACTIONS/CAREER NOTES: Selected by Kansas City Chiefs in third round (84th pick overall) of 1999 NFL draft. ... Signed by Chiefs (July 15, 1999). ... Granted free agency (March 1, 2002). ... Re-signed by Chiefs (March 18, 2002). ... On injured reserve with knee injury (December 4, 2002-remainder of season). ... Granted unconditional free agency (February 28, 2003). ... Re-signed by Chiefs (March 21, 2003).
HONORS: Named free safety on THE SPORTING NEWS college All-America second team (1998).

			TOTALS			INTERCEPTIONS			
Year Team	G	GS	Tk.	Ast.	Sks.	No.	Yds.	Avg.	TD
1999—Kansas City NFL	9	0	0	0	0.0	0	0	0.0	0
2000—Kansas City NFL	15	0	0	0	0.0	0	0	0.0	0
2001—Kansas City NFL	12	0	1	0	0.0	0	0	0.0	0
2002—Kansas City NFL	10	0	7	0	0.0	0	0	0.0	0
Pro totals (4 years)	46	0	8	0	0.0	0	0	0.0	0

AUSTIN, REGGIE CB

PERSONAL: Born January 21, 1977, in Atlanta. ... 5-9/185. ... Full name: Reggie Antonio Austin.
HIGH SCHOOL: Harper (Atlanta).
COLLEGE: Wake Forest.
TRANSACTIONS/CAREER NOTES: Selected by Chicago Bears in fourth round (125th pick overall) of 2000 NFL draft. ... Signed by Bears (June 8, 2000). ... On injured reserve with heel injury (August 23, 2000-entire season). ... On injured reserve with knee injury (November 11, 2002-remainder of season). ... Granted free agency (February 28, 2003).

			TOTALS			INTERCEPTIONS			
Year Team	G	GS	Tk.	Ast.	Sks.	No.	Yds.	Avg.	TD
2000—Chicago NFL			Did not play.						
2001—Chicago NFL	9	0	0	0	0.0	0	0	0.0	0
2002—Chicago NFL	9	4	16	5	0.0	2	0	0.0	0
Pro totals (2 years)	18	4	16	5	0.0	2	0	0.0	0

AYI, KOLE LB RAMS

PERSONAL: Born September 27, 1978, in Ann Arbor, Mich. ... 6-1/231. ... Full name: Bamikole Richard Ayi.
HIGH SCHOOL: Nashua (N.H.).
COLLEGE: Massachusetts.
TRANSACTIONS/CAREER NOTES: Signed as non-drafted free agent by St. Louis Rams (May 3, 2001). ... Released by Rams (October 23, 2001). ... Re-signed by Rams to practice squad (October 24, 2001). ... Signed by New York Giants off Rams practice squad (October 25, 2001); did not play. ... Claimed on waivers by New England Patriots (November 15, 2001). ... On injured reserve with leg injury (November 28, 2001-remainder of season). ... Traded by Patriots to Rams for undisclosed draft pick (June 26, 2002). ... On injured reserve with shoulder injury (October 16, 2002-remainder of season).

			TOTALS			INTERCEPTIONS			
Year Team	G	GS	Tk.	Ast.	Sks.	No.	Yds.	Avg.	TD
2001—St. Louis NFL	6	0	0	2	0.0	0	0	0.0	0
—New England NFL	1	0	0	0	0.0	0	0	0.0	0
2002—St. Louis NFL	6	0	0	0	0.0	0	0	0.0	0
Pro totals (2 years)	13	0	0	2	0.0	0	0	0.0	0

AYODELE, AKIN LB JAGUARS

PERSONAL: Born September 17, 1979, in Grand Prairie, Texas. ... 6-2/252. ... Full name: Akinola James Ayodele.
HIGH SCHOOL: MacArthur (Irving, Texas).
COLLEGE: Purdue.
TRANSACTIONS/CAREER NOTES: Selected by Jacksonville Jaguars in third round (89th pick overall) of 2002 NFL draft. ... Signed by Jaguars (July 11, 2002).

			TOTALS			INTERCEPTIONS			
Year Team	G	GS	Tk.	Ast.	Sks.	No.	Yds.	Avg.	TD
2002—Jacksonville NFL	16	3	49	7	3.0	1	22	22.0	0

AZUMAH, JERRY — CB — BEARS

PERSONAL: Born September 1, 1977, in Worcester, Mass. ... 5-10/189. ... Name pronounced ah-ZOO-muh.
HIGH SCHOOL: St. Peter-Marian (Worcester, Mass.).
COLLEGE: New Hampshire.
TRANSACTIONS/CAREER NOTES: Selected by Chicago Bears in fifth round (147th pick overall) of 1999 NFL draft. ... Signed by Bears (June 8, 1999).
HONORS: Walter Payton Award winner (1998).

			TOTALS			INTERCEPTIONS			
Year Team	G	GS	Tk.	Ast.	Sks.	No.	Yds.	Avg.	TD
1999—Chicago NFL	16	2	17	2	0.0	0	0	0.0	0
2000—Chicago NFL	14	4	21	5	0.0	1	2	2.0	0
2001—Chicago NFL	16	5	42	7	2.0	1	14	14.0	0
2002—Chicago NFL	16	16	69	13	1.0	0	18	0.0	0
Pro totals (4 years)	62	27	149	27	3.0	2	34	17.0	0

BABER, BILLY — TE — CHIEFS

PERSONAL: Born January 17, 1979, in Charlottesville, Va. ... 6-3/252. ... Full name: William Franklin Baber.
HIGH SCHOOL: Western Albermarle (Va.).
COLLEGE: Virginia.
TRANSACTIONS/CAREER NOTES: Selected by Kansas City Chiefs in fifth round (141st pick overall) of 2001 NFL draft. ... Signed by Chiefs (May 24, 2001). ... Released by Chiefs (September 2, 2001). ... Re-signed by Chiefs to practice squad (September 3, 2001). ... Activated (December 3, 2001).
SINGLE GAME HIGHS (regular season): Receptions—1 (September 29, 2002, vs. Miami); yards—7 (September 29, 2002, vs. New England); and touchdown receptions—1 (September 29, 2002, vs. Miami).

			RECEIVING			
Year Team	G	GS	No.	Yds.	Avg.	TD
2001—Kansas City NFL	1	0	0	0	0.0	0
2002—Kansas City NFL	12	2	2	10	5.0	1
Pro totals (2 years)	13	2	2	10	5.0	1

BACKUS, JEFF — OT — LIONS

PERSONAL: Born September 21, 1977, in Midland, Mich. ... 6-5/309. ... Full name: Jeffrey Carl Backus.
HIGH SCHOOL: Norcross (Ga.).
COLLEGE: Michigan.
TRANSACTIONS/CAREER NOTES: Selected by Detriot Lions in first round (18th pick overall) of 2001 NFL draft. ... Signed by Lions (July 23, 2001).
PLAYING EXPERIENCE: Detroit NFL, 2001-2002 ... Games/Games started: 2001 (16/16), 2002 (16/16). Total: 32/32.

BADGER, BRAD — OT — RAIDERS

PERSONAL: Born January 11, 1975, in Corvallis, Ore. ... 6-4/320.
HIGH SCHOOL: Corvallis (Ore.).
COLLEGE: Stanford.
TRANSACTIONS/CAREER NOTES: Selected by Washington Redskins in fifth round (162nd pick overall) of 1997 NFL draft. ... Signed by Redskins (May 5, 1997). ... Granted free agency (February 11, 2000). ... Tendered offer sheet by Minnesota Vikings (April 10, 2000). ... Redskins declined to match offer (April 11, 2000). ... Released by Vikings (March 12, 2002). ... Signed by Oakland Raiders (April 12, 2002). ... Granted unconditional free agency (February 28, 2003). ... Re-signed by Raiders (March 4, 2003).
PLAYING EXPERIENCE: Washington NFL, 1997-1999; Minnesota NFL, 2000-2001. Oakland NFL, 2002. ... Games/Games started: 1997 (12/1), 1998 (16/16), 1999 (14/4), 2000 (16/0), 2001 (13/12), 2002 (7/0). Total: 78/33.
CHAMPIONSHIP GAME EXPERIENCE: Member of Vikings for NFC Championship game (2000 season); did not play. ... Member of Raiders for AFC championship game (2002 season); inactive. ... Played in Super Bowl XXXVII (2002 season).

BAILEY, CHAMP — CB — REDSKINS

PERSONAL: Born June 22, 1978 ... 6-0/192. ... Full name: Roland Champ Bailey. ... Brother of Boss Bailey, linebacker, Detroit Lions.
HIGH SCHOOL: Charlton County (Folkson, Ga.).
COLLEGE: Georgia.
TRANSACTIONS/CAREER NOTES: Selected after junior season by Washington Redskins in first round (seventh pick overall) of 1999 NFL draft. ... Signed by Redskins (July 24, 1999).
HONORS: Named cornerback on THE SPORTING NEWS college All-America second team (1998). ... Bronko Nagurski Award winner (1998). ... Played in Pro Bowl (2000-2002 seasons).

			TOTALS			INTERCEPTIONS				PUNT RETURNS				KICKOFF RETURNS				TOTALS			
Year Team	G	GS	Tk.	Ast.	Sks.	No.	Yds.	Avg.	TD	No.	Yds.	Avg.	TD	No.	Yds.	Avg.	TD	TD	2pt.	Pts.	Fum.
1999—Washington NFL	16	16	61	5	1.0	5	55	11.0	1	0	0	0.0	0	0	0	0.0	0	1	0	6	0
2000—Washington NFL	16	16	52	5	0.0	5	48	9.6	0	1	65	65.0	0	0	0	0.0	0	1	0	6	0
2001—Washington NFL	16	16	49	2	0.0	3	17	5.7	0	0	0	0.0	0	0	0	0.0	0	0	0	0	0
2002—Washington NFL	16	16	62	6	0.0	3	2	0.7	0	24	238	9.9	0	1	17	17.0	0	0	0	0	4
Pro totals (4 years)	64	64	224	18	1.0	16	122	7.6	1	25	303	12.1	0	1	17	17.0	0	2	0	12	4

BAILEY, KARSTEN — WR — PACKERS

PERSONAL: Born April 26, 1977, in Newnan, Ga. ... 6-0/205. ... Full name: Karsten Mario Bailey.
HIGH SCHOOL: East Coweta (Sharpsburg, Ga.).
COLLEGE: Auburn.
TRANSACTIONS/CAREER NOTES: Selected by Seattle Seahawks in third round (82nd pick overall) of 1999 NFL draft. ... Signed by Seahawks (July 29, 1999). ... Released by Seahawks (September 2, 2001). ... Signed by Green Bay Packers (January 24, 2002). ... Granted free agency (February 28, 2003). ... Re-signed by Packers (March 3, 2003).
SINGLE GAME HIGHS (regular season): Receptions—2 (September 29, 2002, vs. Carolina); yards—34 (December 23, 2000, vs. Buffalo); and touchdown receptions—1 (October 15, 2000, vs. Indianapolis).

			RECEIVING			
Year Team	G	GS	No.	Yds.	Avg.	TD
1999—Seattle NFL	2	0	0	0	0.0	0
2000—Seattle NFL	9	0	6	62	10.3	1
2002—Green Bay NFL	7	0	3	26	8.7	0
Pro totals (3 years)	18	0	9	88	9.8	1

BAILEY, RODNEY — DE — STEELERS

PERSONAL: Born October 7, 1979, in Cleveland. ... 6-3/300. ... Full name: Rodney Dwayne Bailey.
HIGH SCHOOL: St. Edwards (Cleveland).
COLLEGE: Ohio State.
TRANSACTIONS/CAREER NOTES: Selected by Pittsburgh Steelers in sixth round (181st pick overall) of 2001 NFL draft. ... Signed by Steelers (June 6, 2001).
CHAMPIONSHIP GAME EXPERIENCE: Played in AFC championship game (2001 season).

			TOTALS		
Year Team	G	GS	Tk.	Ast.	Sks.
2001—Pittsburgh NFL	16	1	8	4	2.0
2002—Pittsburgh NFL	16	0	17	7	5.5
Pro totals (2 years)	32	1	25	11	7.5

BAKER, CHRIS — TE — JETS

PERSONAL: Born November 18, 1979, in Saline, Mich. ... 6-3/258.
HIGH SCHOOL: Saline (Mich.).
COLLEGE: Michigan State.
TRANSACTIONS/CAREER NOTES: Selected by New York Jets in third round (88th pick overall) of 2002 NFL draft. ... Signed by Jets (July 16, 2002).
SINGLE GAME HIGHS (regular season): Receptions—1 (December 22, 2002, vs. New England); yards—10 (November 3, 2002, vs. San Diego); and touchdown receptions—0.

			RECEIVING				KICKOFF RETURNS				TOTALS			
Year Team	G	GS	No.	Yds.	Avg.	TD	No.	Yds.	Avg.	TD	TD	2pt.	Pts.	Fum.
2002—New York Jets NFL	11	1	2	14	7.0	0	3	23	7.7	0	0	0	0	0

BAKER, JASON — P — CHIEFS

PERSONAL: Born May 17, 1978, in Fort Wayne, Ind. ... 6-1/201.
HIGH SCHOOL: Wayne (Fort Wayne, Ind.).
COLLEGE: Iowa.
TRANSACTIONS/CAREER NOTES: Signed as non-drafted free agent by Philadelphia Eagles (April 23, 2001). ... Released by Eagles (August 28, 2001). ... Signed by San Francisco 49ers (August 29, 2001). ... Released by 49ers (November 26, 2002). ... Signed by Philadelphia Eagles (December 3, 2002). ... Released by Eagles (December 16, 2002). ... Signed by Kansas City Chiefs (May 14, 2003).

		PUNTING					
Year Team	G	No.	Yds.	Avg.	Net avg.	In. 20	Blk.
2001—San Francisco NFL	16	69	2813	40.8	35.4	21	0
2002—Philadelphia NFL	2	13	445	34.2	29.8	2	0
—San Francisco NFL	11	42	1688	40.2	32.0	12	0
Pro totals (2 years)	29	124	4946	39.9	33.7	35	0

BAKER, ROBERT — WR — DOLPHINS

PERSONAL: Born May 14, 1976, in Gainesville, Fla. ... 5-11/200. ... Full name: Robert Cedrick Baker III.
HIGH SCHOOL: P.K. Yonge (Gainesville, Fla.).
COLLEGE: Auburn.
TRANSACTIONS/CAREER NOTES: Signed as non-drafted free agent by Miami Dolphins (July 13, 1999). ... On injured reserve with knee injury (August 31, 1999-entire season). ... Released by Dolphins (August 27, 2000). ... Re-signed by Dolphins to practice squad (August 30, 2000). ... Released by Dolphins (September 12, 2000). ... Re-signed by Dolphins (April 11, 2001). ... Released by Dolphins (September 2, 2001). ... Re-signed by Dolphins to practice squad (September 3, 2001). ... Activated (January 12, 2002); did not play. ... Released by Dolphins (August 30, 2002). ... Re-signed by Dolphins (October 1, 2002). ... Assigned by Dolphins to Frankfurt Galaxy in 2003 NFL Europe enhancement allocation program (February 4, 2003).
SINGLE GAME HIGHS (regular season): Receptions—1 (November 24, 2002, vs. San Diego); yards—17 (November 24, 2002, vs. San Diego); and touchdown receptions—0.

			RECEIVING				PUNT RETURNS				TOTALS			
Year Team	G	GS	No.	Yds.	Avg.	TD	No.	Yds.	Avg.	TD	TD	2pt.	Pts.	Fum.
2002—Miami NFL	10	0	1	17	17.0	0	7	55	7.9	0	0	0	0	0

BALL, JASON   C   CHARGERS

PERSONAL: Born March 21, 1979, in Fayetteville, N.C. ... 6-2/301.
HIGH SCHOOL: Londerry (N.H.).
COLLEGE: New Hampshire.
TRANSACTIONS/CAREER NOTES: Signed as non-drafted free agent by San Diego Chargers (April 26, 2002).
PLAYING EXPERIENCE: San Diego NFL, 2002. ... Games/games started: 2002 (16/13).

BANKS, MIKE   TE   CARDINALS

PERSONAL: Born November 5, 1979, in Mason City, Iowa. ... 6-4/263.
HIGH SCHOOL: Ogden (Iowa).
COLLEGE: Iowa State.
TRANSACTIONS/CAREER NOTES: Selected by Arizona Cardinals in seventh round (223rd pick overall) of 2002 NFL draft. ... Signed by Cardinals (May 28, 2002).

| | | | | RECEIVING | | |
Year Team	G	GS	No.	Yds.	Avg.	TD
2002—Arizona NFL	12	0	0	0	0.0	0

BANKS, TONY   QB   TEXANS

PERSONAL: Born April 5, 1973, in San Diego. ... 6-4/230. ... Full name: Anthony Lamar Banks. ... Cousin of Chip Banks, linebacker with Cleveland Browns (1982-86), San Diego Chargers (1987) and Indianapolis Colts (1989-92).
HIGH SCHOOL: Herbert Hoover (San Diego).
JUNIOR COLLEGE: San Diego Mesa College.
COLLEGE: Michigan State.
TRANSACTIONS/CAREER NOTES: Selected by St. Louis Rams in second round (42nd pick overall) of 1996 NFL draft. ... Signed by Rams (July 15, 1996). ... On injured reserve list with knee injury (December 14, 1998-remainder of season). ... Granted free agency (February 12, 1999). ... Re-signed by Rams (April 17, 1999). ... Traded by Rams to Baltimore Ravens for fifth-round pick (G Cameron Spikes) in 1999 draft and seventh-round pick (traded to Chicago) in 2000 draft (April 17, 1999). ... Granted unconditional free agency (February 11, 2000). ... Re-signed by Ravens (February 17, 2000). ... Released by Ravens (March 1, 2001). ... Signed by Dallas Cowboys (March 28, 2001). ... Released by Cowboys (August 14, 2001). ... Signed by Washington Redskins (August 16, 2001). ... Granted unconditional free agency (March 1, 2002). ... Signed by Houston Texans (August 19, 2002). ... Granted unconditional free agency (February 28, 2003). ... Re-signed by Texans (April 3, 2003).
CHAMPIONSHIP GAME EXPERIENCE: Member of Ravens for AFC championship game (2000 season); did not play. ... Member of Super Bowl championship team (2000 season).
SINGLE GAME HIGHS (regular season): Attempts—49 (September 28, 1997, vs. Oakland); completions—29 (September 6, 1998, vs. New Orleans); yards—401 (November 2, 1997, vs. Atlanta); and touchdown passes—5 (September 10, 2000, vs. Jacksonville).
STATISTICAL PLATEAUS: 300-yard passing games: 1996 (2), 1997 (1), 1999 (1), 2001 (1). Total: 5.
MISCELLANEOUS: Regular-season record as starting NFL quarterback: 33-42 (.440).

| | | | PASSING | | | | | | | | RUSHING | | | | TOTALS | | |
Year Team	G	GS	Att.	Cmp.	Pct.	Yds.	TD	Int.	Avg.	Skd.	Rat.	Att.	Yds.	Avg.	TD	TD	2pt.	Pts.
1996—St. Louis NFL	14	13	368	192	52.2	2544	15	15	6.91	48	71.0	61	212	3.5	0	0	1	2
1997—St. Louis NFL	16	16	487	252	51.7	3254	14	13	6.68	43	71.5	47	186	4.0	1	1	0	6
1998—St. Louis NFL	14	14	408	241	59.1	2535	7	14	6.21	41	68.6	40	156	3.9	3	3	1	20
1999—Baltimore NFL	12	10	320	169	52.8	2136	17	8	6.68	33	81.2	24	93	3.9	0	0	0	0
2000—Baltimore NFL	11	8	274	150	54.7	1578	8	8	5.76	20	69.3	19	57	3.0	0	0	0	0
2001—Washington NFL	15	14	370	198	53.5	2386	10	10	6.45	29	71.3	47	152	3.2	2	2	0	12
2002—Houston NFL								Did not play.										
Pro totals (6 years)	82	75	2227	1202	54.0	14433	71	68	6.48	214	72.0	238	856	3.6	6	6	2	40

BANNAN, JUSTIN   DT   BILLS

PERSONAL: Born April 18, 1979, in Sacramento, Calif. ... 6-3/300.
HIGH SCHOOL: Bella Vista (Fair Oaks, Calif.).
COLLEGE: Colorado.
TRANSACTIONS/CAREER NOTES: Selected by Buffalo Bills in fifth round (139th pick overall) of 2002 NFL draft. ... Signed by Bills (June 21, 2002).

| | | | TOTALS | | |
Year Team	G	GS	Tk.	Ast.	Sks.
2002—Buffalo NFL	15	0	15	6	1.0

BANNISTER, ALEX   WR   SEAHAWKS

PERSONAL: Born April 23, 1979, in Cincinnati. ... 6-5/207.
HIGH SCHOOL: Hughes Center (Cincinnati).
COLLEGE: Eastern Kentucky.
TRANSACTIONS/CAREER NOTES: Selected by Seattle Seahawks in fifth round (140th pick overall) of 2001 NFL draft. ... Signed by Seahawks (July 9, 2001).
SINGLE GAME HIGHS (regular season): Receptions—1 (December 23, 2001, vs. New York Giants); yards—17 (December 2, 2001, vs. San Diego); and touchdown receptions—0.

| | | | RECEIVING | | | |
Year Team	G	GS	No.	Yds.	Avg.	TD
2001—Seattle NFL	16	0	4	50	12.5	0
2002—Seattle NFL	16	1	0	0	0.0	0
Pro totals (2 years)	32	1	4	50	12.5	0

BANTA, BRADFORD — TE — LIONS

PERSONAL: Born December 14, 1970, in Baton Rouge, La. ... 6-6/253. ... Full name: Dennis Bradford Banta.
HIGH SCHOOL: University (Baton Rouge, La.).
COLLEGE: Southern California.
TRANSACTIONS/CAREER NOTES: Selected by Indianapolis Colts in fourth round (106th pick overall) of 1994 NFL draft. ... Signed by Colts (July 22, 1994). ... Granted free agency (February 14, 1997). ... Re-signed by Colts (May 14, 1997). ... Granted unconditional free agency (February 11, 2000). ... Re-signed by Colts (March 9, 2000). ... Released by Colts (August 27, 2000). ... Signed by New York Jets (August 29, 2000). ... Granted unconditional free agency (March 2, 2001). ... Signed by Detroit Lions (April 19, 2001).
CHAMPIONSHIP GAME EXPERIENCE: Played in AFC championship game (1995 season).
SINGLE GAME HIGHS (regular season): Receptions—1 (November 1, 1998, vs. New England); yards—7 (November 1, 1998, vs. New England); and touchdown receptions—0.

| | | | RECEIVING | | | |
Year Team	G	GS	No.	Yds.	Avg.	TD
1994—Indianapolis NFL	16	0	0	0	0.0	0
1995—Indianapolis NFL	16	2	1	6	6.0	0
1996—Indianapolis NFL	13	0	0	0	0.0	0
1997—Indianapolis NFL	15	0	0	0	0.0	0
1998—Indianapolis NFL	16	0	1	7	7.0	0
1999—Indianapolis NFL	16	0	0	0	0.0	0
2000—New York Jets NFL	16	0	0	0	0.0	0
2001—Detroit NFL	16	0	0	0	0.0	0
2002—Detroit NFL	16	0	0	0	0.0	0
Pro totals (9 years)	140	2	2	13	6.5	0

BARBER, RONDE — CB — BUCCANEERS

PERSONAL: Born April 7, 1975, in Montgomery County, Va. ... 5-10/184. ... Full name: Jamael Oronde Barber. ... Twin brother of Tiki Barber, running back, New York Giants. ... Name pronounced RON-day.
HIGH SCHOOL: Cave Spring (Roanoke, Va.).
COLLEGE: Virginia (degree in commerce, 1996).
TRANSACTIONS/CAREER NOTES: Selected after junior season by Tampa Bay Buccaneers in third round (66th pick overall) of 1997 NFL draft. ... Signed by Buccaneers (July 18, 1997). ... Granted free agency (February 11, 2000). ... Re-signed by Buccaneers (June 13, 2000). ... Granted unconditional free agency (March 2, 2001). ... Re-signed by Buccaneers (April 10, 2001).
CHAMPIONSHIP GAME EXPERIENCE: Played in NFC championship game (1999 and 2002 seasons). ... Member of Super Bowl championship team (2002 season).
HONORS: Played in Pro Bowl (2001 season).

| | | | TOTALS | | | INTERCEPTIONS | | | |
Year Team	G	GS	Tk.	Ast.	Sks.	No.	Yds.	Avg.	TD
1997—Tampa Bay NFL	1	0	4	0	0.0	0	0	0.0	0
1998—Tampa Bay NFL	16	9	59	11	3.0	2	67	33.5	0
1999—Tampa Bay NFL	16	15	54	16	1.0	2	60	30.0	0
2000—Tampa Bay NFL	16	16	67	15	5.5	2	46	23.0	1
2001—Tampa Bay NFL	16	16	56	13	1.0	†10	86	8.6	1
2002—Tampa Bay NFL	16	16	63	12	3.0	2	9	4.5	0
Pro totals (6 years)	81	72	303	67	13.5	18	268	14.9	2

BARBER, SHAWN — LB — CHIEFS

PERSONAL: Born January 14, 1975, in Richmond, Va. ... 6-2/237.
HIGH SCHOOL: Hermitage (Richmond, Va.).
COLLEGE: Richmond.
TRANSACTIONS/CAREER NOTES: Selected by Washington Redskins in fourth round (113th pick overall) of 1998 NFL draft. ... Signed by Redskins (May 13, 1998). ... Granted free agency (March 2, 2001). ... Re-signed by Redskins (June 1, 2001). ... On injured reserve with knee injury (October 2, 2001-remainder of season). ... Granted unconditional free agency (March 1, 2002). ... Signed by Philadelphia Eagles (March 15, 2002). ... Granted unconditional free agency (February 28, 2003). ... Signed by Kansas City Chiefs (March 3, 2003).
CHAMPIONSHIP GAME EXPERIENCE: Played in NFC championship game (2002 season).

| | | | TOTALS | | | INTERCEPTIONS | | | |
Year Team	G	GS	Tk.	Ast.	Sks.	No.	Yds.	Avg.	TD
1998—Washington NFL	16	1	21	6	0.0	1	0	0.0	0
1999—Washington NFL	16	16	82	19	1.0	2	70	35.0	1
2000—Washington NFL	14	14	56	7	2.0	0	0	0.0	0
2001—Washington NFL	3	3	14	3	0.0	0	0	0.0	0
2002—Philadelphia NFL	16	16	69	22	1.0	2	81	40.5	1
Pro totals (5 years)	65	50	242	57	4.0	5	151	30.2	2

BARBER, TIKI — RB — GIANTS

PERSONAL: Born April 7, 1975, in Roanoke, Va. ... 5-10/200. ... Full name: Atiim Kiambu Barber. ... Twin brother of Ronde Barber, cornerback, Tampa Bay Buccaneers. ... Name pronounced TEE-kee.
HIGH SCHOOL: Cave Spring (Roanoke, Va.).
COLLEGE: Virginia.
TRANSACTIONS/CAREER NOTES: Selected by New York Giants in second round (36th pick overall) of 1997 NFL draft. ... Signed by Giants for 1997 season. ... Granted free agency (February 11, 2000). ... Re-signed by Giants (June 8, 2000). ... Granted unconditional free agency (March 2, 2001). ... Re-signed by Giants (March 8, 2001).

CHAMPIONSHIP GAME EXPERIENCE: Played in NFC championship game (2000 season). ... Played in Super Bowl XXXV (2000 season).
SINGLE GAME HIGHS (regular season): Attempts—32 (December 28, 2002, vs. Philadelphia); yards—203 (December 28, 2002, vs. Philadelphia); and rushing touchdowns—2 (December 22, 2002, vs. Indianapolis).
STATISTICAL PLATEAUS: 100-yard rushing games: 1997 (1), 2000 (1), 2001 (3), 2002 (4). Total: 9. ... 100-yard receiving games: 1999 (1).

Year	Team	G	GS	RUSHING				RECEIVING				PUNT RETURNS				KICKOFF RETURNS				TOTALS			
				Att.	Yds.	Avg.	TD	No.	Yds.	Avg.	TD	No.	Yds.	Avg.	TD	No.	Yds.	Avg.	TD	TD	2pt.	Pts.	Fum.
1997—NYG NFL		12	6	136	511	3.8	3	34	299	8.8	1	0	0	0.0	0	0	0	0.0	0	4	1	26	3
1998—NYG NFL		16	4	52	166	3.2	0	42	348	8.3	3	0	0	0.0	0	14	250	17.9	0	3	0	18	1
1999—NYG NFL		16	1	62	258	4.2	0	66	609	9.2	2	∞44	‡506	11.5	∞1	12	266	22.2	0	3	0	18	5
2000—NYG NFL		16	12	213	1006	4.7	8	70	719	10.3	1	‡39	332	8.5	0	1	28	28.0	0	9	0	54	9
2001—NYG NFL		14	9	166	865	5.2	4	72	577	8.0	0	38	338	8.9	0	0	0	0.0	0	4	1	26	8
2002—NYG NFL		16	15	304	1387	4.6	11	69	597	8.7	0	1	5	5.0	0	0	0	0.0	0	11	0	66	9
Pro totals (6 yrs)		90	47	933	4193	4.5	26	353	3149	8.9	7	122	1181	9.7	1	27	544	20.1	0	34	2	208	35

BARKER, BRYAN   P   REDSKINS

PERSONAL: Born June 28, 1964, in Jacksonville Beach, Fla. ... 6-1/203. ... Full name: Bryan Christopher Barker.
HIGH SCHOOL: Miramonte (Orinda, Calif.).
COLLEGE: Santa Clara (degree in economics).
TRANSACTIONS/CAREER NOTES: Signed as non-drafted free agent by Denver Broncos (May 1988). ... Released by Broncos (July 19, 1988). ... Signed by Seattle Seahawks (1989). ... Released by Seahawks (August 30, 1989). ... Signed by Kansas City Chiefs (May 1, 1990). ... Released by Chiefs (August 28, 1990). ... Re-signed by Chiefs (September 26, 1990). ... Granted unconditional free agency (February 1-April 1, 1991). ... Re-signed by Chiefs for 1991 season. ... Granted unconditional free agency (February 1-April 1, 1992). ... Re-signed by Chiefs for 1992 season. ... Released by Chiefs (1994). ... Signed by Minnesota Vikings (May 18, 1994). ... Released by Vikings (August 30, 1994). ... Signed by Philadelphia Eagles (October 11, 1994). ... Granted unconditional free agency (February 17, 1995). ... Signed by Jacksonville Jaguars (March 7, 1995). ... Granted unconditional free agency (March 2, 2001). ... Signed by Washington Redskins (April 12, 2001). ... On injured reserve with head injury (December 4, 2002-remainder of season).
CHAMPIONSHIP GAME EXPERIENCE: Played in AFC championship game (1993, 1996 and 1999 seasons).
HONORS: Played in Pro Bowl (1997 season).

Year	Team	G	PUNTING					
			No.	Yds.	Avg.	Net avg.	In. 20	Blk.
1990—Kansas City NFL		13	64	2479	38.7	33.3	16	0
1991—Kansas City NFL		16	57	2303	40.4	35.0	11	0
1992—Kansas City NFL		15	75	3245	43.3	35.2	16	1
1993—Kansas City NFL		16	76	3240	42.6	35.3	19	1
1994—Philadelphia NFL		11	66	2696	40.8	‡36.2	20	0
1995—Jacksonville NFL		16	82	3591	43.8	*38.6	19	0
1996—Jacksonville NFL		16	69	3016	43.7	35.6	16	0
1997—Jacksonville NFL		16	66	2964	44.9	38.8	27	0
1998—Jacksonville NFL		16	85	3824	45.0	38.5	28	0
1999—Jacksonville NFL		16	78	3260	41.8	36.9	32	0
2000—Jacksonville NFL		16	76	3194	42.0	34.4	29	0
2001—Washington NFL		16	90	3747	41.6	34.8	27	0
2002—Washington NFL		12	48	1924	40.1	30.0	13	0
Pro totals (13 years)		195	932	39483	42.4	35.8	273	2

BARLOW, KEVAN   RB   49ERS

PERSONAL: Born January 7, 1979, in Pittsburgh. ... 6-1/238. ... Full name: Kevan C. Barlow.
HIGH SCHOOL: Peabody (Pittsburgh).
COLLEGE: Pittsburgh.
TRANSACTIONS/CAREER NOTES: Selected by San Francisco 49ers in third round (80th pick overall) of 2001 NFL draft. ... Signed by 49ers (July 25, 2001).
SINGLE GAME HIGHS (regular season): Attempts—18 (October 27, 2002, vs. Arizona); yards—94 (September 22, 2002, vs. Washington); and rushing touchdowns—2 (December 16, 2001, vs. Miami).

Year	Team	G	GS	RUSHING				RECEIVING				TOTALS			
				Att.	Yds.	Avg.	TD	No.	Yds.	Avg.	TD	TD	2pt.	Pts.	Fum.
2001—San Francisco NFL		15	0	125	512	4.1	4	22	247	11.2	1	5	0	30	1
2002—San Francisco NFL		14	0	145	675	4.7	4	14	136	9.7	1	5	0	30	2
Pro totals (2 years)		29	0	270	1187	4.4	8	36	383	10.6	2	10	0	60	3

BARLOW, REGGIE   WR/PR/KR

PERSONAL: Born January 22, 1973, in Montgomery, Ala. ... 6-0/190. ... Full name: Reggie Devon Barlow.
HIGH SCHOOL: Lanier (Montgomery, Ala.).
COLLEGE: Alabama State.
TRANSACTIONS/CAREER NOTES: Selected by Jacksonville Jaguars in fourth round (110th pick overall) of 1996 NFL draft. ... Signed by Jaguars (May 28, 1996). ... Granted free agency (February 12, 1999). ... Re-signed by Jaguars (March 23, 1999). ... Released by Jaguars (February 27. 2001). ... Signed by Oakland Raiders (March 21, 2001). ... On injured reserve with foot injury (August 28, 2001-entire season). ... Released by Raiders (September 1, 2002). ... Signed by Tampa Bay Buccaneers (September 4, 2002). ... Granted unconditional free agency (February 28, 2003).
CHAMPIONSHIP GAME EXPERIENCE: Played in AFC championship game (1996 and 1999 seasons). ... Member of Buccaneers for NFC championship game (2002 season); inactive. ... Member of Super Bowl championship team (2002 season); inactive.
SINGLE GAME HIGHS (regular season): Receptions—4 (December 2, 1999, vs. Pittsburgh); yards—50 (October 12, 1998, vs. Miami); and touchdown receptions—0.

Year Team	G	GS	RECEIVING				PUNT RETURNS				KICKOFF RETURNS				TOTALS			
			No.	Yds.	Avg.	TD	No.	Yds.	Avg.	TD	No.	Yds.	Avg.	TD	TD	2pt.	Pts.	Fum.
1996—Jacksonville NFL........	7	0	0	0	0.0	0	0	0	0.0	0	0	0	0.0	0	0	0	0	0
1997—Jacksonville NFL........	16	0	5	74	14.8	0	36	412	11.4	0	10	267	26.7	▲1	1	0	6	2
1998—Jacksonville NFL........	16	2	11	168	15.3	0 .	43	*555	§12.9	1	30	747	24.9	0	1	0	6	1
1999—Jacksonville NFL........	14	2	16	202	12.6	0	38	414	10.9	1	19	396	20.8	0	1	0	6	4
2000—Jacksonville NFL........	16	0	1	28	28.0	0	29	200	6.9	0	11	224	20.4	0	0	0	0	0
2001—Oakland NFL..............									Did not play.									
2002—Tampa Bay NFL..........	2	1	3	23	7.7	0	0	0	0.0	0	0	0	0.0	0	0	0	0	0
Pro totals (6 years)...............	71	5	36	495	13.8	0	146	1581	10.8	2	70	1634	23.3	1	3	0	18	7

BARNES, DARIAN — FB — BUCCANEERS

PERSONAL: Born February 29, 1980, in Neptune, N.J. ... 6-2/250. ... Full name: Darian Durrell Barnes.
HIGH SCHOOL: North (Toms River, N.J.).
COLLEGE: Rutgers, then Hampton.
TRANSACTIONS/CAREER NOTES: Signed as non-drafted free agent by New York Giants (July 24, 2002). ... Claimed on waivers by Tampa Bay Buccaneers (September 2, 2002).
CHAMPIONSHIP GAME EXPERIENCE: Played in NFC championship game (2002 season). ... Member of Super Bowl championship team (2002 season).

Year Team	G	GS	RUSHING				TOTALS			
			Att.	Yds.	Avg.	TD	TD	2pt.	Pts.	Fum.
2002—Tampa Bay NFL..	6	0	0	0	0.0	0	0	0	0	0

BARRETT, DAVID — CB — CARDINALS

PERSONAL: Born December 22, 1977, in Osceola, Ark. ... 5-10/198.
HIGH SCHOOL: Osceola (Ark.).
COLLEGE: Arkansas.
TRANSACTIONS/CAREER NOTES: Selected by Arizona Cardinals in fourth round (102nd pick overall) of 2000 NFL draft. ... Signed by Cardinals (June 15, 2000). ... Granted free agency (February 28, 2003). ... Re-signed by Cardinals (May 8, 2003).

Year Team	G	GS	TOTALS			INTERCEPTIONS			
			Tk.	Ast.	Sks.	No.	Yds.	Avg.	TD
2000—Arizona NFL	16	0	6	2	0.0	0	0	0.0	0
2001—Arizona NFL	16	9	49	9	0.0	2	30	15.0	0
2002—Arizona NFL	14	14	57	17	0.0	3	40	13.3	0
Pro totals (3 years)	46	23	112	28	0.0	5	70	14.0	0

BARROW, MIKE — LB — GIANTS

PERSONAL: Born April 19, 1970, in Homestead, Fla. ... 6-2/245. ... Full name: Micheal Colvin Barrow.
HIGH SCHOOL: Homestead (Fla.) Senior.
COLLEGE: Miami (Fla.) (degree in accounting, 1992).
TRANSACTIONS/CAREER NOTES: Selected by Houston Oilers in second round (47th pick overall) of 1993 NFL draft. ... Signed by Oilers (July 30, 1993). ... Granted free agency (February 16, 1996). ... Re-signed by Oilers (August 9, 1996). ... Granted unconditional free agency (February 14, 1997). ... Signed by Carolina Panthers (February 20, 1997). ... Released by Panthers (February 22, 2000). ... Signed by New York Giants (March 2, 2000).
CHAMPIONSHIP GAME EXPERIENCE: Played in NFC championship game (2000 season). ... Played in Super Bowl XXXV (2000 season).
HONORS: Named linebacker on THE SPORTING NEWS college All-America first team (1992).

Year Team	G	GS	TOTALS			INTERCEPTIONS			
			Tk.	Ast.	Sks.	No.	Yds.	Avg.	TD
1993—Houston NFL..	16	0	21	5	1.0	0	0	0.0	0
1994—Houston NFL..	16	16	57	37	2.5	0	0	0.0	0
1995—Houston NFL..	13	12	54	32	3.0	0	0	0.0	0
1996—Houston NFL..	16	16	67	39	6.0	0	0	0.0	0
1997—Carolina NFL..	16	16	68	21	8.5	0	0	0.0	0
1998—Carolina NFL..	16	16	97	32	4.0	1	10	10.0	0
1999—Carolina NFL..	16	16	81	25	4.0	0	0	0.0	0
2000—New York Giants NFL...	15	15	72	22	3.5	1	7	7.0	0
2001—New York Giants NFL...	16	16	91	44	6.0	0	0	0.0	0
2002—New York Giants NFL...	15	14	73	37	2.5	0	0	0.0	0
Pro totals (10 years)	155	137	681	294	41.0	2	17	8.5	0

BARRY, KEVIN — OT — PACKERS

PERSONAL: Born July 20, 1979, in Racine, Wis. ... 6-4/325.
HIGH SCHOOL: Washington Park (Racine, Wis.).
COLLEGE: Arizona.
TRANSACTIONS/CAREER NOTES: Signed as non-drafted free agent by Green Bay Packers (April 21, 2002).
PLAYING EXPERIENCE: Green Bay NFL, 2002. ... Games/games started: 2002 (14/3).

BARTEE, WILLIAM   CB   CHIEFS

PERSONAL: Born June 25, 1977, in Daytona Beach, Fla. ... 6-1/200.
HIGH SCHOOL: Atlantic (Daytona Beach, Fla.).
JUNIOR COLLEGE: Butler County Community College (Kan.).
COLLEGE: Oklahoma.
TRANSACTIONS/CAREER NOTES: Selected by Kansas City Chiefs in second round (54th pick overall) of 2000 NFL draft. ... Signed by Chiefs (July 21, 2000).

				TOTALS			INTERCEPTIONS		
Year Team	G	GS	Tk.	Ast.	Sks.	No.	Yds.	Avg.	TD
2000—Kansas City NFL	16	3	23	4	1.0	0	0	0.0	0
2001—Kansas City NFL	16	5	30	2	1.0	0	0	0.0	0
2002—Kansas City NFL	14	13	71	6	0.0	0	0	0.0	0
Pro totals (3 years)	46	21	124	12	2.0	0	0	0.0	0

BARTON, ERIC   LB   RAIDERS

PERSONAL: Born September 29, 1977, in Alexandria, Va. ... 6-2/245.
HIGH SCHOOL: Thomas A. Edison (Alexandria, Va.).
COLLEGE: Maryland.
TRANSACTIONS/CAREER NOTES: Selected by Oakland Raiders in fifth round (146th pick overall) of 1999 NFL draft. ... Signed by Raiders for 1999 season.
CHAMPIONSHIP GAME EXPERIENCE: Member of Raiders for AFC Championship game (2000 season); inactive. ... Played in AFC championship game (2002 season). ... Played in Super Bowl XXXVII (2002 season).

				TOTALS			INTERCEPTIONS		
Year Team	G	GS	Tk.	Ast.	Sks.	No.	Yds.	Avg.	TD
1999—Oakland NFL	16	3	20	2	3.0	0	0	0.0	0
2000—Oakland NFL	4	0	4	2	0.0	0	0	0.0	0
2001—Oakland NFL	16	1	19	5	0.0	0	0	0.0	0
2002—Oakland NFL	16	16	95	29	6.0	2	5	2.5	0
Pro totals (4 years)	52	20	138	38	9.0	2	5	2.5	0

BARTRUM, MIKE   TE

PERSONAL: Born June 23, 1970, in Galliapolis, Ohio. ... 6-4/245. ... Full name: Michael Weldon Bartrum.
HIGH SCHOOL: Meigs (Pomeroy, Ohio).
COLLEGE: Marshall (degree in education).
TRANSACTIONS/CAREER NOTES: Signed as non-drafted free agent by Kansas City Chiefs (May 5, 1993). ... Released by Chiefs (August 30, 1993). ... Re-signed by Chiefs to practice squad (August 31, 1993). ... Activated (October 27, 1993). ... Released by Chiefs (August 23, 1994). ... Signed by Green Bay Packers (January 20, 1995). ... On injured reserve with broken arm (October 11, 1995-remainder of season). ... Traded by Packers with DE Walter Scott to New England Patriots for past considerations (August 25, 1996). ... On injured reserve with forearm injury (November 12, 1997-remainder of season). ... Granted unconditional free agency (February 13, 1998). ... Re-signed by Patriots (April 7, 1998). ... Released by Patriots (April 10, 2000). ... Signed by Philadelphia Eagles (April 17, 2000). ... Granted unconditional free agency (March 1, 2002). ... Re-signed by Eagles (March 6, 2002). ... Granted unconditional free agency (February 28, 2003).
CHAMPIONSHIP GAME EXPERIENCE: Member of Chiefs for AFC championship game (1993 season); inactive. ... Played in AFC championship game (1996 season). ... Played in Super Bowl XXXI (1996 season). ... Played in NFC championship game (2001 and 2002 seasons).
SINGLE GAME HIGHS (regular season): Receptions—1 (September 22, 2002, vs. Dallas); yards—8 (September 22, 2002, vs. Dallas); and touchdown receptions—1 (November 11, 2001, vs. Minnesota).

			RECEIVING		
Year Team	G	GS	No.	Yds.	Avg.	TD
1993—Kansas City NFL	3	0	0	0	0.0	0
1995—Green Bay NFL	4	0	0	0	0.0	0
1996—New England NFL	16	0	1	1	1.0	1
1997—New England NFL	9	0	0	0	0.0	0
1998—New England NFL	16	0	0	0	0.0	0
1999—New England NFL	16	0	1	1	1.0	1
2000—Philadelphia NFL	16	0	0	0	0.0	0
2001—Philadelphia NFL	16	0	1	4	4.0	1
2002—Philadelphia NFL	●16	0	1	8	8.0	0
Pro totals (9 years)	112	0	4	14	3.5	3

BASHIR, IDREES   DB   COLTS

PERSONAL: Born December 7, 1978, in Decatur, Ga. ... 6-2/198.
HIGH SCHOOL: Dunwoody (Decatur, Ga.).
COLLEGE: Memphis.
TRANSACTIONS/CAREER NOTES: Selected by Indianapolis Colts in second round (37th pick overall) of 2001 NFL draft. ... Signed by Colts (July 25, 2001).

				TOTALS			INTERCEPTIONS		
Year Team	G	GS	Tk.	Ast.	Sks.	No.	Yds.	Avg.	TD
2001—Indianapolis NFL	15	15	53	24	0.0	1	0	0.0	0
2002—Indianapolis NFL	14	14	36	14	0.0	2	4	2.0	0
Pro totals (2 years)	29	29	89	38	0.0	3	4	1.3	0

BATCH, CHARLIE   QB   STEELERS

PERSONAL: Born December 5, 1974, in Homestead, Pa. ... 6-2/220. ... Full name: Charles D'Donte Batch.
HIGH SCHOOL: Steel Valley (Munhall, Pa.).
COLLEGE: Eastern Michigan (degree in business, 1997).
TRANSACTIONS/CAREER NOTES: Selected by Detroit Lions in second round (60th pick overall) of 1998 NFL draft. ... Signed by Lions (July 19, 1998). ... On injured reserve with back injury (December 24, 1998-remainder of season). ... On injured reserve with shoulder injury (December 5, 2001-remainder of season). ... Released by Lions (June 3, 2002). ... Signed by Pittsburgh Steelers (June 17, 2002). ... On physically unable to perform list with knee injury (July 25-26, 2002). ... Granted unconditional free agency (February 28, 2003). ... Re-signed by Steelers (March 14, 2003).
RECORDS: Holds NFL rookie-season record for lowest interception percentage—1.98.
SINGLE GAME HIGHS (regular season): Attempts—62 (November 18, 2001, vs. Arizona); completions—36 (November 18, 2001, vs. Arizona); yards—436 (November 18, 2001, vs. Arizona); and touchdown passes—3 (November 18, 2001, vs. Arizona).
STATISTICAL PLATEAUS: 300-yard passing games: 2001 (3).
MISCELLANEOUS: Regular-season record as starting NFL quarterback: 19-27 (.413).

					PASSING							RUSHING				TOTALS		
Year Team	G	GS	Att.	Cmp.	Pct.	Yds.	TD	Int.	Avg.	Skd.	Rat.	Att.	Yds.	Avg.	TD	TD	2pt.	Pts.
1998—Detroit NFL	12	12	303	173	57.1	2178	11	6	7.19	37	83.5	41	229	5.6	1	1	0	6
1999—Detroit NFL	11	10	270	151	55.9	1957	13	7	7.25	36	84.1	28	87	3.1	2	2	0	12
2000—Detroit NFL	15	15	412	221	53.6	2489	13	15	6.04	41	67.3	44	199	4.5	2	2	0	12
2001—Detroit NFL	10	9	341	198	58.1	2392	12	12	7.01	33	76.8	12	45	3.8	0	0	0	0
2002—Pittsburgh NFL									Did not play.									
Pro totals (4 years)	48	46	1326	743	56.0	9016	49	40	6.80	147	76.9	125	560	4.5	5	5	0	30

BATES, D'WAYNE   WR   VIKINGS

PERSONAL: Born December 4, 1975, in Aiken, S.C. ... 6-2/215. ... Full name: D'Wayne Lavoris Bates.
HIGH SCHOOL: Silver Bluff (Aiken, S.C.).
COLLEGE: Northwestern.
TRANSACTIONS/CAREER NOTES: Selected by Chicago Bears in third round (71st pick overall) of 1999 NFL draft. ... Signed by Bears (July 22, 1999). ... Granted free agency (March 1, 2002). ... Tendered offer sheet by Minnesota Vikings (March 27, 2002). ... Offer matched by Bears (April 3, 2002). ... Claimed on waivers by Vikings (April 9, 2002).
SINGLE GAME HIGHS (regular season): Receptions—7 (December 21, 2002, vs. Miami); yards—107 (December 30, 2001, vs. Detroit); and touchdown receptions—1 (December 21, 2002, vs. Miami).
STATISTICAL PLATEAUS: 100-yard receiving games: 2001 (1).
MISCELLANEOUS: Selected by Toronto Blue Jays organization in 53rd round of free-agent draft (June 2, 1994); did not sign.

			RECEIVING				PUNT RETURNS				TOTALS			
Year Team	G	GS	No.	Yds.	Avg.	TD	No.	Yds.	Avg.	TD	TD	2pt.	Pts.	Fum.
1999—Chicago NFL	7	1	2	19	9.5	0	0	0	0.0	0	0	0	0	0
2000—Chicago NFL	5	0	4	42	10.5	0	0	0	0.0	0	0	0	0	0
2001—Chicago NFL	11	1	9	160	17.8	1	0	0	0.0	0	1	0	6	0
2002—Minnesota NFL	14	11	50	689	13.8	4	4	93	23.3	0	4	0	24	2
Pro totals (4 years)	37	13	65	910	14.0	5	4	93	23.3	0	5	0	30	2

BATTAGLIA, MARCO   TE   DOLPHINS

PERSONAL: Born January 25, 1973, in Howard Beach, N.Y. ... 6-3/249. ... Name pronounced buh-TAG-lee-uh.
HIGH SCHOOL: St. Francis (Fresh Meadows, N.Y.).
COLLEGE: Rutgers.
TRANSACTIONS/CAREER NOTES: Selected by Cincinnati Bengals in second round (39th pick overall) of 1996 NFL draft. ... Signed by Bengals (July 15, 1996). ... Granted free agency (February 12, 1999). ... Re-signed by Bengals (May 25, 1999). ... On non-football illness list with appendectomy (November 17-December 10, 2001). ... Claimed on waivers by Washington Redskins (December 11, 2001). ... Granted unconditional free agency (March 1, 2002). ... Signed by Tampa Bay Buccaneers (March 19, 2002). ... Released by Buccaneers (September 24, 2002). ... Signed by Pittsburgh Steelers (December 10, 2002). ... Granted unconditional free agency (February 28, 2003). ... Signed by Miami Dolphins (March 25, 2003).
HONORS: Named tight end on THE SPORTING NEWS college All-America first team (1995).
SINGLE GAME HIGHS (regular season): Receptions—4 (November 11, 2001, vs. Jacksonville); yards—57 (October 21, 2001, vs. Chicago); and touchdown receptions—1 (November 1, 1998, vs. Denver).

			RECEIVING				TOTALS			
Year Team	G	GS	No.	Yds.	Avg.	TD	TD	2pt.	Pts.	Fum.
1996—Cincinnati NFL	16	0	8	79	9.9	0	0	0	0	0
1997—Cincinnati NFL	16	0	12	149	12.4	1	1	0	6	2
1998—Cincinnati NFL	16	0	10	47	4.7	1	1	0	6	1
1999—Cincinnati NFL	16	0	14	153	10.9	0	0	0	0	0
2000—Cincinnati NFL	16	10	13	105	8.1	0	0	0	0	0
2001—Cincinnati NFL	8	1	13	118	9.1	0	0	0	0	1
—Washington NFL	3	0	1	9	9.0	0	0	0	0	0
2002—Pittsburgh NFL	1	0	0	0	0.0	0	0	0	0	0
—Tampa Bay NFL	2	0	0	0	0.0	0	0	0	0	0
Pro totals (7 years)	94	11	71	660	9.3	2	2	0	12	4

BATTLES, AINSLEY   S   JAGUARS

PERSONAL: Born November 6, 1978, in Lilburn, Ga. ... 5-11/195.
HIGH SCHOOL: Parkview (Lilburn, Ga.).
COLLEGE: Vanderbilt.

TRANSACTIONS/CAREER NOTES: Signed as non-drafted free agent by Pittsburgh Steelers (April 21, 2000). ... Claimed on waivers by Jacksonville Jaguars (September 3, 2001). ... Granted free agency (February 28, 2003). ... Re-signed by Jaguars (April 23, 2003).

Year Team	G	GS	TOTALS Tk.	Ast.	Sks.	INTERCEPTIONS No.	Yds.	Avg.	TD
2000—Pittsburgh NFL	16	2	13	4	1.0	0	0	0.0	0
2001—Jacksonville NFL	13	11	46	4	1.0	2	26	13.0	0
2002—Jacksonville NFL	16	4	16	2	0.0	1	6	6.0	0
Pro totals (3 years)	45	17	75	10	2.0	3	32	10.7	0

BAUMAN, RASHAD   CB   REDSKINS

PERSONAL: Born May 7, 1979, in Tempe, Ariz. ... 5-8/181. ... Full name: Leddure Rashad Bauman.
HIGH SCHOOL: South Mountain (Phoenix).
COLLEGE: Oregon.
TRANSACTIONS/CAREER NOTES: Selected by Washington Redskins in third round (79th pick overall) of 2002 NFL draft. ... Signed by Redskins (July 22, 2002).

Year Team	G	GS	TOTALS Tk.	Ast.	Sks.	INTERCEPTIONS No.	Yds.	Avg.	TD
2002—Washington NFL	16	0	9	0	0.0	0	0	0.0	0

BAXTER, FRED   TE   PATRIOTS

PERSONAL: Born June 14, 1971, in Brundidge, Ala. ... 6-3/260. ... Full name: Frederick Denard Baxter.
HIGH SCHOOL: Pike County (Brundidge, Ala.).
COLLEGE: Auburn.
TRANSACTIONS/CAREER NOTES: Selected by New York Jets in fifth round (115th pick overall) of 1993 NFL draft. ... Signed by Jets (July 13, 1993). ... On injured reserve with broken hand (November 21, 2000-remainder of season). ... Released by Jets (December 23, 2000). ... Signed by Chicago Bears (February 27, 2001). ... Released by Bears (November 12, 2002). ... Signed by New England Patriots (December 24, 2002). ... Granted unconditional free agency (February 28, 2003). ... Re-signed by Patriots (March 6, 2003).
CHAMPIONSHIP GAME EXPERIENCE: Played in AFC championship game (1998 season).
SINGLE GAME HIGHS (regular season): Receptions—6 (September 17, 1995, vs. Jacksonville); yards—99 (September 17, 1995, vs. Jacksonville); and touchdown receptions—1 (December 16, 2001, vs. Tampa Bay).

Year Team	G	GS	RECEIVING No.	Yds.	Avg.	TD	TOTALS TD	2pt.	Pts.	Fum.
1993—New York Jets NFL	7	0	3	48	16.0	1	1	0	6	0
1994—New York Jets NFL	11	1	3	11	3.7	1	1	0	6	0
1995—New York Jets NFL	15	3	18	222	12.3	1	1	0	6	1
1996—New York Jets NFL	16	4	7	114	16.3	0	0	0	0	1
1997—New York Jets NFL	16	9	27	276	10.2	3	3	0	18	1
1998—New York Jets NFL	14	2	3	50	16.7	0	0	0	0	0
1999—New York Jets NFL	14	8	8	66	8.3	2	2	0	12	0
2000—New York Jets NFL	9	6	4	22	5.5	2	2	0	12	0
2001—Chicago NFL	14	14	22	148	6.7	2	2	0	12	0
2002—Chicago NFL	5	3	5	51	10.2	0	0	0	0	0
—New England NFL	1	0	0	0	0.0	0	0	0	0	0
Pro totals (10 years)	122	50	100	1008	10.1	12	12	0	72	3

BAXTER, GARY   CB   RAVENS

PERSONAL: Born November 24, 1978, in Tyler, Texas. ... 6-2/204. ... Full name: Gary Wayne Baxter.
HIGH SCHOOL: John Tyler (Tyler, Texas).
COLLEGE: Baylor.
TRANSACTIONS/CAREER NOTES: Selected by Baltimore Ravens in second round (62nd pick overall) of 2001 NFL draft. ... Signed by Ravens (July 20, 2001).

Year Team	G	GS	TOTALS Tk.	Ast.	Sks.	INTERCEPTIONS No.	Yds.	Avg.	TD
2001—Baltimore NFL	6	0	0	0	0.0	0	0	0.0	0
2002—Baltimore NFL	16	14	69	9	0.0	1	0	0.0	0
Pro totals (2 years)	22	14	69	9	0.0	1	0	0.0	0

BAXTER, JARROD   FB   TEXANS

PERSONAL: Born March 9, 1979, in Dayton, Ohio. ... 6-1/245. ... Full name: Jarrod Anthony Baxter.
HIGH SCHOOL: Highland (Albuquerque, N.M.).
COLLEGE: New Mexico.
TRANSACTIONS/CAREER NOTES: Selected by Houston Texans in fifth round (136th pick overall) of 2002 NFL draft. ... Signed by Texans (July 19, 2002).
SINGLE GAME HIGHS (regular season): Attempts—2 (September 15, 2002, vs. San Diego); yards—7 (September 15, 2002, vs. San Diego); and rushing touchdowns—0.

Year Team	G	GS	RUSHING Att.	Yds.	Avg.	TD	RECEIVING No.	Yds.	Avg.	TD	TOTALS TD	2pt.	Pts.	Fum.
2002—Houston NFL	16	10	7	14	2.0	0	5	33	6.6	1	1	0	6	0

BEAN, ROBERT — CB

PERSONAL: Born January 6, 1978, in Atlanta. ... 5-11/178. ... Full name: Robert D. Bean Jr.
HIGH SCHOOL: Lakeside (Atlanta).
JUNIOR COLLEGE: Georgia Military College.
COLLEGE: Mississippi State.
TRANSACTIONS/CAREER NOTES: Selected by Cincinnati Bengals in fifth round (133rd pick overall) of 2000 NFL draft. ... Signed by Bengals (June 16, 2000). ... Claimed on waivers by Jacksonville Jaguars (September 3, 2002). ... On injured reserve with hamstring injury (December 3, 2002-remainder of season). ... Granted free agency (February 28, 2003).

			TOTALS			INTERCEPTIONS			
Year Team	G	GS	Tk.	Ast.	Sks.	No.	Yds.	Avg.	TD
2000—Cincinnati NFL	12	4	17	2	0.0	1	0	0.0	0
2001—Cincinnati NFL	15	4	39	3	0.0	0	0	0.0	0
2002—Jacksonville NFL	5	0	1	0	0.0	0	0	0.0	0
Pro totals (3 years)	32	8	57	5	0.0	1	0	0.0	0

BEASLEY, AARON — CB — JETS

PERSONAL: Born July 7, 1973, in Pottstown, Pa. ... 6-0/205. ... Full name: Aaron Bruce Beasley.
HIGH SCHOOL: Pottstown (Pa.), then Valley Forge Military Academy (Wayne, Pa.).
COLLEGE: West Virginia.
TRANSACTIONS/CAREER NOTES: Selected by Jacksonville Jaguars in third round (63rd pick overall) of 1996 NFL draft. ... Signed by Jaguars (May 24, 1996). ... Granted free agency (February 12, 1999). ... Re-signed by Jaguars (March 3, 1999). ... Granted unconditional free agency (February 11, 2000). ... Re-signed by Jaguars (February 11, 2000). ... On injured reserve with shoulder injury (December 21, 2001-remainder of season). ... Released by Jaguars (February 28, 2002). ... Signed by New York Jets (March 8, 2002).
CHAMPIONSHIP GAME EXPERIENCE: Played in AFC championship game (1996 and 1999 seasons).
MISCELLANEOUS: Holds Jacksonville Jaguars all-time record for most interceptions (15).

			TOTALS			INTERCEPTIONS			
Year Team	G	GS	Tk.	Ast.	Sks.	No.	Yds.	Avg.	TD
1996—Jacksonville NFL	9	7	20	9	1.0	1	0	0.0	0
1997—Jacksonville NFL	9	7	25	0	0.0	1	5	5.0	0
1998—Jacksonville NFL	16	15	58	9	0.0	3	35	11.7	0
1999—Jacksonville NFL	16	16	57	9	1.5	6	*200	§33.3	†2
2000—Jacksonville NFL	14	14	45	7	5.0	1	39	39.0	0
2001—Jacksonville NFL	12	12	36	3	0.0	3	0	0.0	0
2002—New York Jets NFL	15	15	59	7	0.0	2	29	14.5	0
Pro totals (7 years)	91	86	300	44	7.5	17	308	18.1	2

BEASLEY, FRED — FB — 49ERS

PERSONAL: Born September 18, 1974, in Montgomery, Ala. ... 6-0/246. ... Full name: Frederick Jerome Beasley.
HIGH SCHOOL: Robert E. Lee (Montgomery, Ala.).
COLLEGE: Auburn.
TRANSACTIONS/CAREER NOTES: Selected by San Francisco 49ers in sixth round (180th pick overall) of 1998 NFL draft. ... Signed by 49ers (July 18, 1998). ... Granted free agency (March 2, 2001). ... Re-signed by 49ers (March 2, 2001). ... Granted unconditional free agency (March 1, 2002). ... Re-signed by 49ers (March 12, 2002).
SINGLE GAME HIGHS (regular season): Attempts—12 (December 26, 1999, vs. Washington); yards—65 (December 26, 1999, vs. Washington); and rushing touchdowns—2 (December 12, 1999, vs. Atlanta).

			RUSHING				RECEIVING				TOTALS			
Year Team	G	GS	Att.	Yds.	Avg.	TD	No.	Yds.	Avg.	TD	TD	2pt.	Pts.	Fum.
1998—San Francisco NFL	16	0	0	0	0.0	0	1	11	11.0	0	0	0	0	0
1999—San Francisco NFL	13	11	58	276	4.8	4	32	282	8.8	0	4	0	24	2
2000—San Francisco NFL	15	15	50	147	2.9	3	31	233	7.5	3	6	0	36	0
2001—San Francisco NFL	15	12	23	73	3.2	1	16	99	6.2	0	1	0	6	1
2002—San Francisco NFL	16	14	26	75	2.9	0	22	152	6.9	1	1	0	6	0
Pro totals (5 years)	75	52	157	571	3.6	8	102	777	7.6	4	12	0	72	3

BECHT, ANTHONY — TE — JETS

PERSONAL: Born August 8, 1977, in Media, Pa. ... 6-5/272.
HIGH SCHOOL: Monsignor Bonner (Drexel Hill, Pa.).
COLLEGE: West Virginia (degree in business, 1999).
TRANSACTIONS/CAREER NOTES: Selected by New York Jets in first round (27th pick overall) of 2000 NFL draft. ... Signed by Jets (May 26, 2000).
SINGLE GAME HIGHS (regular season): Receptions—5 (October 21, 2001, vs. St. Louis); yards—58 (September 9, 2001, vs. Indianapolis); and touchdown receptions—2 (October 21, 2001, vs. St. Louis).

			RECEIVING			
Year Team	G	GS	No.	Yds.	Avg.	TD
2000—New York Jets NFL	14	10	16	144	9.0	2
2001—New York Jets NFL	16	16	36	321	8.9	5
2002—New York Jets NFL	16	15	28	243	8.7	5
Pro totals (3 years)	46	41	80	708	8.9	12

BECKETT, ROGERS   S   CHARGERS

PERSONAL: Born January 31, 1977, in Apopka, Fla. ... 6-3/205.
HIGH SCHOOL: Apopka (Fla.).
COLLEGE: Marshall (degree in political science).
TRANSACTIONS/CAREER NOTES: Selected by San Diego Chargers in second round (43rd pick overall) of 2000 NFL draft. ... Signed by Chargers (July 24, 2000).
HONORS: Named free safety on THE SPORTING NEWS college All-America third team (1999).

			TOTALS			INTERCEPTIONS			
Year Team	G	GS	Tk.	Ast.	Sks.	No.	Yds.	Avg.	TD
2000—San Diego NFL	16	3	28	11	1.0	1	7	7.0	0
2001—San Diego NFL	16	16	73	21	0.0	1	8	8.0	0
2002—San Diego NFL	16	10	32	2	0.0	0	0	0.0	0
Pro totals (3 years)	48	29	133	34	1.0	2	15	7.5	0

BECKHAM, TONY   CB   TITANS

PERSONAL: Born October 1, 1978, in Ocala, Fla. ... 6-1/189.
HIGH SCHOOL: Forest (Ocala, Fla.).
COLLEGE: Wisconsin-Stout.
TRANSACTIONS/CAREER NOTES: Selected by Tennesse Titans in fourth round (115th pick overall) of 2002 NFL draft. ... Signed by Titans (July 18, 2002).
CHAMPIONSHIP GAME EXPERIENCE: Played in AFC championship game (2002 season).

			TOTALS			INTERCEPTIONS				KICKOFF RETURNS				TOTALS			
Year Team	G	GS	Tk.	Ast.	Sks.	No.	Yds.	Avg.	TD	No.	Yds.	Avg.	TD	TD	2pt.	Pts.	Fum.
2002—Tennessee NFL	14	0	1	1	0.0	0	0	0.0	0	0	0	0.0	0	0	0	0	0

BEISEL, MONTY   LB   CHIEFS

PERSONAL: Born August 20, 1978, in Douglass, Kan. ... 6-3/254.
HIGH SCHOOL: Douglass (Kan.).
COLLEGE: Kansas State.
TRANSACTIONS/CAREER NOTES: Selected by Kansas City Chiefs in fourth round (107th pick overall) of 2001 NFL draft. ... Signed by Chiefs (July 23, 2001).

			TOTALS			INTERCEPTIONS			
Year Team	G	GS	Tk.	Ast.	Sks.	No.	Yds.	Avg.	TD
2001—Kansas City NFL	16	0	3	3	0.0	0	0	0.0	0
2002—Kansas City NFL	16	0	0	0	0.0	0	0	0.0	0
Pro totals (2 years)	32	0	3	3	0.0	0	0	0.0	0

BELL, JASON   CB   TEXANS

PERSONAL: Born April 1, 1978, in Long Beach, Calif. ... 6-0/182. ... Full name: Jason Dewande Bell.
HIGH SCHOOL: Millikan (Long Beach, Calif.).
COLLEGE: UCLA.
TRANSACTIONS/CAREER NOTES: Signed as non-drafted free agent by Dallas Cowboys (April 27, 2001). ... Claimed on waivers by Houston Texans (September 2, 2002). ... Re-signed by Texans (March 18, 2003).

			TOTALS			INTERCEPTIONS			
Year Team	G	GS	Tk.	Ast.	Sks.	No.	Yds.	Avg.	TD
2001—Dallas NFL	16	0	0	0	0.0	0	0	0.0	0
2002—Houston NFL	13	0	2	0	0.0	0	0	0.0	0
Pro totals (2 years)	29	0	2	0	0.0	0	0	0.0	0

BELL, KENDRELL   LB   STEELERS

PERSONAL: Born July 17, 1980, in Augusta, Ga. ... 6-1/254.
HIGH SCHOOL: Laney (August, Ga.).
JUNIOR COLLEGE: Middle Georgia College.
COLLEGE: Georgia.
TRANSACTIONS/CAREER NOTES: Selected by Pittsburgh Steelers in second round (39th pick overall) of 2001 NFL draft. ... Signed by Steelers (June 11, 2001).
CHAMPIONSHIP GAME EXPERIENCE: Played in AFC championship game (2001 season).
HONORS: Named NFL Rookie of the Year by THE SPORTING NEWS (2001). ... Played in Pro Bowl (2001 season). ... Named to play in Pro Bowl (2002 season); replaced by Donnie Edwards due to injury.

			TOTALS			INTERCEPTIONS			
Year Team	G	GS	Tk.	Ast.	Sks.	No.	Yds.	Avg.	TD
2001—Pittsburgh NFL	16	16	69	13	9.0	0	0	0.0	0
2002—Pittsburgh NFL	12	12	37	13	4.0	0	0	0.0	0
Pro totals (2 years)	28	28	106	26	13.0	0	0	0.0	0

BELL, MARCUS — DT — CARDINALS

PERSONAL: Born June 1, 1979, in Memphis, Tenn. ... 6-2/330.
HIGH SCHOOL: Kingsbury (Memphis, Tenn.).
COLLEGE: Memphis.
TRANSACTIONS/CAREER NOTES: Selected by Arizona Cardinals in fourth round (123rd pick overall) of 2001 NFL draft. ... Signed by Cardinals (June 4, 2001).

Year Team	G	GS	TOTALS Tk.	Ast.	Sks.
2001—Arizona NFL	13	0	16	7	0.5
2002—Arizona NFL	16	4	25	9	2.0
Pro totals (2 years)	29	4	41	16	2.5

BELL, MARCUS — LB — SEAHAWKS

PERSONAL: Born July 19, 1977, in St. John's, Ariz. ... 6-1/245. ... Full name: Marcus Udall Bell.
HIGH SCHOOL: St. John's (Ariz.).
COLLEGE: Arizona.
TRANSACTIONS/CAREER NOTES: Selected by Seattle Seahawks in fourth round (116th pick overall) of 2000 NFL draft. ... Signed by Seahawks (June 13, 2000). ... Granted free agency (February 28, 2003). ... Re-signed by Seahawks (March 18, 2003).

Year Team	G	GS	TOTALS Tk.	Ast.	Sks.	INTERCEPTIONS No.	Yds.	Avg.	TD
2000—Seattle NFL	16	0	2	0	0.0	1	30	30.0	0
2001—Seattle NFL	13	0	21	2	1.0	0	0	0.0	0
2002—Seattle NFL	16	9	63	11	1.0	0	0	0.0	0
Pro totals (3 years)	45	9	86	13	2.0	1	30	30.0	0

BELLAMY, JAY — S — SAINTS

PERSONAL: Born July 8, 1972, in Perth Amboy, N.J. ... 5-11/200. ... Full name: John Jay Bellamy. ... Name pronounced BELL-a-me.
HIGH SCHOOL: Matawan Regional (Aberdeen, N.J.).
COLLEGE: Rutgers.
TRANSACTIONS/CAREER NOTES: Signed as non-drafted free agent by Seattle Seahawks (April 27, 1994). ... On injured reserve with shoulder injury (November 11, 1994-remainder of season). ... Granted unconditional free agency (March 2, 2001). ... Signed by New Orleans Saints (April 4, 2001).

Year Team	G	GS	TOTALS Tk.	Ast.	Sks.	INTERCEPTIONS No.	Yds.	Avg.	TD
1994—Seattle NFL	3	0	0	0	0.0	0	0	0.0	0
1995—Seattle NFL	15	0	2	1	0.0	0	0	0.0	0
1996—Seattle NFL	16	0	16	2	0.0	3	18	6.0	0
1997—Seattle NFL	16	7	42	10	2.0	1	13	13.0	0
1998—Seattle NFL	16	16	80	18	1.0	3	40	13.3	0
1999—Seattle NFL	16	16	85	11	0.0	4	4	1.0	0
2000—Seattle NFL	16	16	69	18	2.0	4	132	33.0	1
2001—New Orleans NFL	16	16	69	22	2.0	3	21	7.0	0
2002—New Orleans NFL	16	16	67	19	1.5	3	39	13.0	0
Pro totals (9 years)	130	87	430	101	8.5	21	267	12.7	1

BELSER, JASON — DB

PERSONAL: Born May 28, 1970, in Kansas City, Mo. ... 5-10/197. ... Full name: Jason Daks Belser. ... Son of Caeser Belser, defensive back with Kansas City Chiefs (1968-71) and linebacker with San Francisco 49ers (1974). ... Name pronounced BELL-sir.
HIGH SCHOOL: Raytown (Mo.) South.
COLLEGE: Oklahoma.
TRANSACTIONS/CAREER NOTES: Selected by Indianapolis Colts in eighth round (197th pick overall) of 1992 NFL draft. ... Signed by Colts (July 22, 1992). ... Granted free agency (February 17, 1995). ... Tendered offer sheet by Carolina Panthers (April 17, 1995). ... Offer matched by Colts (April 19, 1995). ... Granted unconditional free agency (March 2, 2001). ... Signed by Kansas City Chiefs (June 12, 2001). ... Granted unconditional free agency (February 28, 2003).
CHAMPIONSHIP GAME EXPERIENCE: Played in AFC championship game (1995 season).

Year Team	G	GS	TOTALS Tk.	Ast.	Sks.	INTERCEPTIONS No.	Yds.	Avg.	TD	KICKOFF RETURNS No.	Yds.	Avg.	TD	TOTALS TD	2pt.	Pts.	Fum.
1992—Indianapolis NFL	16	2	55	0	0.0	3	27	9.0	0	0	0	0.0	0	0	0	0	1
1993—Indianapolis NFL	16	16	94	33	0.0	1	14	14.0	0	0	0	0.0	0	0	0	0	0
1994—Indianapolis NFL	13	12	43	25	0.0	1	31	31.0	0	0	0	0.0	0	0	0	0	0
1995—Indianapolis NFL	16	16	63	13	0.0	1	0	0.0	0	1	15	15.0	0	0	0	0	0
1996—Indianapolis NFL	16	16	74	22	1.0	4	81	20.3	†2	0	0	0.0	0	2	0	12	0
1997—Indianapolis NFL	16	16	67	27	1.0	2	121	60.5	1	0	0	0.0	0	1	0	6	0
1998—Indianapolis NFL	16	16	76	20	1.0	1	19	19.0	0	0	0	0.0	0	0	0	0	0
1999—Indianapolis NFL	16	16	63	14	1.0	0	0	0.0	0	0	0	0.0	0	0	0	0	0
2000—Indianapolis NFL	16	16	80	16	5.0	0	0	0.0	0	0	0	0.0	0	0	0	0	0
2001—Kansas City NFL	16	0	1	0	0.0	0	0	0.0	0	3	58	19.3	0	0	0	0	0
2002—Kansas City NFL	16	8	40	14	0.0	1	45	45.0	0	2	39	19.5	0	0	0	0	0
Pro totals (11 years)	173	134	656	184	9.0	14	338	24.1	3	6	112	18.7	0	3	0	18	1

BENJAMIN, RYAN — C — BUCCANEERS

PERSONAL: Born November 11, 1977, in Greenfield, Mass. ... 6-1/242. ... Full name: Ryan Arthur Benjamin.
HIGH SCHOOL: River Ridge (New Port Richey, Fla.).
COLLEGE: South Florida.
TRANSACTIONS/CAREER NOTES: Signed as non-drafted free agent by Tampa Bay Buccaneers (April 23, 2001). ... Released by Buccaneers (June 7, 2001). ... Signed by New England Patriots (August 13, 2001). ... Released by Patriots (August 26, 2001). ... Signed by Chicago Bears (October 13, 2001). ... Released by Bears (October 16, 2001). ... Signed by Patriots (February 11, 2002). ... Released by Patriots (August 27, 2002). ... Signed by Buccaneers (October 14, 2002). ... Re-signed by Buccaneers (April 4, 2003).
PLAYING EXPERIENCE: Chicago NFL, 2001; Tampa Bay NFL, 2002. ... Games/Games started: 2001 (1/0), 2002 (10/0). Total: 11/0.
CHAMPIONSHIP GAME EXPERIENCE: Played in NFC championship game (2002 season). ... Member of Super Bowl championship team (2002 season).

BENNETT, BRANDON — RB — BENGALS

B

PERSONAL: Born February 3, 1973, in Taylors, S.C. ... 5-11/220.
HIGH SCHOOL: Riverside (Greer, S.C.).
COLLEGE: South Carolina.
TRANSACTIONS/CAREER NOTES: Signed as non-drafted free agent by Cleveland Browns (July 25, 1995). ... Released by Browns (August 18, 1995). ... Signed by Chicago Bears to practice squad (December 6, 1995). ... Released by Bears (August 19, 1996). ... Re-signed by Bears to practice squad (September 24, 1996). ... Released by Bears (November 1, 1996). ... Signed by Miami Dolphins to practice squad (November 5, 1996). ... Activated (December 17, 1996); did not play. ... Released by Dolphins (August 12, 1997). ... Signed by Cincinnati Bengals (April 20, 1998). ... Released by Bengals (August 30, 1998). ... Re-signed by Bengals (September 7, 1998). ... Released by Bengals (June 3, 1999). ... Re-signed by Bengals (March 2, 2001).
SINGLE GAME HIGHS (regular season): Attempts—25 (December 20, 1998, vs. Pittsburgh); yards—87 (December 13, 1998, vs. Indianapolis); and rushing touchdowns—1 (December 3, 2000, vs. Arizona).
STATISTICAL PLATEAUS: 100-yard receiving games: 1998 (1).

			RUSHING				RECEIVING				KICKOFF RETURNS				TOTALS			
Year Team	G	GS	Att.	Yds.	Avg.	TD	No.	Yds.	Avg.	TD	No.	Yds.	Avg.	TD	TD	2pt.	Pts.	Fum.
1995—Chicago NFL									Did not play.									
1996—Miami NFL									Did not play.									
1997—									Did not play.									
1998—Cincinnati NFL	14	1	77	243	3.2	2	8	153	19.1	0	3	61	20.3	0	2	0	12	1
1999—									Did not play.									
2000—Cincinnati NFL	16	0	90	324	3.6	3	19	168	8.8	0	0	0	0.0	0	3	0	18	2
2001—Cincinnati NFL	16	1	50	232	4.6	0	20	150	7.5	0	4	60	15.0	0	0	0	0	1
2002—Cincinnati NFL	12	0	33	155	4.7	0	18	109	6.1	0	49	1231	25.1	1	1	0	6	2
Pro totals (4 years)	58	2	250	954	3.8	5	65	580	8.9	0	56	1352	24.1	1	6	0	36	6

BENNETT, DARREN — P — CHARGERS

PERSONAL: Born January 9, 1965, in Sydney, Australia. ... 6-5/235. ... Full name: Darren Leslie Bennett.
HIGH SCHOOL: Applecross (Perth, Western Australia).
COLLEGE: None.
TRANSACTIONS/CAREER NOTES: Played Australian Rules Football (1987-1993). ... Signed as non-drafted free agent by San Diego Chargers (April 14, 1994). ... Released by Chargers (August 28, 1994). ... Re-signed by Chargers to practice squad (August 29, 1994). ... Assigned by Chargers to Amsterdam Admirals in 1995 World League enhancement allocation program (February 20, 1995). ... Granted unconditional free agency (February 11, 2000). ... Re-signed by Chargers (March 7, 2000).
HONORS: Named punter on THE SPORTING NEWS NFL All-Pro team (1995). ... Played in Pro Bowl (1995 and 2000 seasons).

				PUNTING			
Year Team	G	No.	Yds.	Avg.	Net avg.	In. 20	Blk.
1994—San Diego NFL				Did not play.			
1995—Amsterdam W.L.	10	60	2296	38.3	35.1	24	1
—San Diego NFL	16	72	3221	44.7	36.6	28	0
1996—San Diego NFL	16	87	3967	45.6	37.2	23	0
1997—San Diego NFL	16	89	3972	44.6	37.7	26	1
1998—San Diego NFL	16	95	4174	43.9	36.8	27	0
1999—San Diego NFL	16	89	3910	43.9	*38.7	32	0
2000—San Diego NFL	16	92	4248	*46.2	36.2	23	0
2001—San Diego NFL	16	78	3308	42.4	36.9	25	0
2002—San Diego NFL	16	87	3540	40.7	34.3	31	2
W.L. totals (1 year)	10	60	2296	38.3	35.1	24	1
NFL totals (8 years)	128	689	30340	44.0	36.8	215	3
Pro totals (9 years)	138	749	32636	43.6	36.7	239	4

BENNETT, DREW — WR — TITANS

PERSONAL: Born August 26, 1978, in Berkeley, Calif. ... 6-5/203. ... Full name: Andrew Russell Bennett.
HIGH SCHOOL: Miramonte (Calif.).
COLLEGE: UCLA.
TRANSACTIONS/CAREER NOTES: Singed as non-drafted free agent by Tennessee Titans (April 22, 2001).
CHAMPIONSHIP GAME EXPERIENCE: Played in AFC championship game (2002 season).
SINGLE GAME HIGHS (regular season): Receptions—6 (October 13, 2002, vs. Jacksonville); yards—87 (December 9, 2001, vs. Minnesota); and touchdown receptions—1 (December 1, 2002, vs. New York Giants).

			RECEIVING				TOTALS			
Year Team	G	GS	No.	Yds.	Avg.	TD	TD	2pt.	Pts.	Fum.
2001—Tennessee NFL	14	1	24	329	13.7	1	1	1	8	0
2002—Tennessee NFL	16	7	33	478	14.5	2	2	0	12	0
Pro totals (2 years)	30	8	57	807	14.2	3	3	1	20	0

BENNETT, MICHAEL　　　　RB　　　　VIKINGS

PERSONAL: Born August 13, 1978, in Milwaukee. ... 5-9/211.
HIGH SCHOOL: Milwaukee Tech.
COLLEGE: Wisconsin.
TRANSACTIONS/CAREER NOTES: Selected after junior season by Minnesota Vikings in first round (27th pick overall) of 2001 NFL draft. ... Signed by Vikings (July 30, 2001).
HONORS: Played in Pro Bowl (2002 season).
SINGLE GAME HIGHS (regular season): Attempts—29 (October 27, 2002, vs. Chicago); yards—167 (November 10, 2002, vs. New York Giants); and rushing touchdowns—2 (December 9, 2001, vs. Tennessee).
STATISTICAL PLATEAUS: 100-yard rushing games: 2001 (2), 2002 (5). Total: 7.

			RUSHING				RECEIVING				TOTALS			
Year　Team	G	GS	Att.	Yds.	Avg.	TD	No.	Yds.	Avg.	TD	TD	2pt.	Pts.	Fum.
2001—Minnesota NFL	13	13	172	682	4.0	2	29	226	7.8	1	3	0	18	0
2002—Minnesota NFL	16	16	255	1296	5.1	5	37	351	9.5	1	6	0	36	4
Pro totals (2 years)	29	29	427	1978	4.6	7	66	577	8.7	2	9	0	54	4

BENNETT, SEAN　　　　RB　　　　JETS

PERSONAL: Born November 9, 1975, in Evansville, Ind. ... 6-1/230. ... Full name: William Sean Bennett.
HIGH SCHOOL: Harrison (Evansville, Ind.).
COLLEGE: Illinois (did not play football), then Evansville, then Northwestern.
TRANSACTIONS/CAREER NOTES: Selected by New York Giants in fourth round (112th pick overall) of 1999 NFL draft. ... Signed by Giants (July 27, 1999). ... On injured reserve with knee injury (August 25, 2000-entire season). ... On physically unable to perform list with hamstring injury (August 28-September 2, 2001). ... Released by Giants (September 2, 2001). ... Re-signed by Giants (January 15, 2002). ... Released by Giants (December 4, 2002). ... Signed by New York Jets (April 1, 2003).
SINGLE GAME HIGHS (regular season): Attempts—13 (September 12, 1999, vs. Tampa Bay); yards—45 (September 19, 1999, vs. Washington); and rushing touchdowns—1 (November 28, 1999, vs. Arizona).

			RUSHING				RECEIVING				TOTALS			
Year　Team	G	GS	Att.	Yds.	Avg.	TD	No.	Yds.	Avg.	TD	TD	2pt.	Pts.	Fum.
1999—New York Giants NFL	9	2	29	126	4.3	1	4	27	6.8	0	1	0	6	0
2000—New York Giants NFL					Did not play.									
2002—New York Giants NFL	7	0	0	0	0.0	0	5	37	7.4	0	0	0	0	0
Pro totals (2 years)	16	2	29	126	4.3	1	9	64	7.1	0	1	0	6	0

BENTLEY, KEVIN　　　　LB　　　　BROWNS

PERSONAL: Born December 29, 1979, in Northridge, Calif. ... 6-0/243. ... Full name: Kevin Kinte Bentley.
HIGH SCHOOL: Montclair (Calif.).
COLLEGE: Northwestern.
TRANSACTIONS/CAREER NOTES: Selected by Cleveland Browns in fourth round (101st pick overall) of 2002 NFL draft. ... Signed by Browns (July 16, 2002).

			TOTALS			INTERCEPTIONS			
Year　Team	G	GS	Tk.	Ast.	Sks.	No.	Yds.	Avg.	TD
2002—Cleveland NFL	12	0	20	14	0.0	0	0	0.0	0

BENTLEY, LECHARLES　　　　C　　　　SAINTS

PERSONAL: Born November 7, 1979, in Cleveland. ... 6-2/299.
HIGH SCHOOL: St. Ignatius (Cleveland).
COLLEGE: Ohio State.
TRANSACTIONS/CAREER NOTES: Selected by New Orleans Saints in second round (44th pick overall) of 2002 NFL draft. ... Signed by Saints (July 28, 2002).
PLAYING EXPERIENCE: New Orleans NFL, 2002. ... Games/games started: 2002 (14/14).
HONORS: Named center on THE SPORTING NEWS college All-America first team (2001).

BERGER, MITCH　　　　P　　　　SAINTS

PERSONAL: Born June 24, 1972, in Kamloops, B.C. ... 6-4/220.
HIGH SCHOOL: North Delta (Vancouver).
JUNIOR COLLEGE: Tyler (Texas) Junior College.
COLLEGE: Colorado.
TRANSACTIONS/CAREER NOTES: Selected by Philadelphia Eagles in sixth round (193rd pick overall) of 1994 NFL draft. ... Signed by Eagles (July 11, 1994). ... Released by Eagles (October 10, 1994). ... Signed by Cincinnati Bengals to practice squad (October 13, 1994). ... Released by Bengals (November 30, 1994). ... Signed by Chicago Bears (March 7, 1995). ... Released by Bears (May 4, 1995). ... Signed by Indianapolis Colts (May 16, 1995). ... Claimed on waivers by Green Bay Packers (August 24, 1995). ... Released by Packers (August 27, 1995). ... Signed by Bears (November 7, 1995). ... Released by Bears (November 13, 1995). ... Signed by Minnesota Vikings (April 19, 1996). ... Granted unconditional free agency (February 11, 2000). ... Re-signed by Vikings (February 21, 2000). ... On injured reserve with knee injury (December 18, 2001-remainder of season). ... Released by Vikings (February 22, 2002). ... Signed by St. Louis Rams (April 22, 2002). ... Granted unconditional free agency (February 28, 2003). ... Signed by New Orleans Saints (March 7, 2003).
CHAMPIONSHIP GAME EXPERIENCE: Played in NFC championship game (1998 and 2000 seasons).
HONORS: Named punter on THE SPORTING NEWS NFL All-Pro team (1999). ... Played in Pro Bowl (1999 season).

		PUNTING						
Year Team	G	No.	Yds.	Avg.	Net avg.	In. 20	Blk.
1994—Philadelphia NFL	5	25	951	38.0	31.3	8	0
1995—				Did not play.			
1996—Minnesota NFL	16	88	3616	41.1	32.4	26	2
1997—Minnesota NFL	14	73	3133	42.9	34.1	22	0
1998—Minnesota NFL	16	55	2458	44.7	37.0	17	0
1999—Minnesota NFL	16	61	2769	‡45.4	‡38.4	18	0
2000—Minnesota NFL	16	62	2773	‡44.7	36.2	16	0
2001—Minnesota NFL	12	47	2046	43.5	32.9	10	0
2002—St. Louis NFL	16	72	3020	41.9	32.7	26	0
Pro totals (8 years)	111	483	20766	43.0	34.5	143	2

BERLIN, EDDIE　　　　WR　　　　TITANS

B

PERSONAL: Born January 14, 1978, in Urbandale, Iowa. ... 5-11/194.
HIGH SCHOOL: Urbandale (Iowa).
COLLEGE: Northern Iowa.
TRANSACTIONS/CAREER NOTES: Selected by Tennessee Titans in fifth round (159th pick overall) of 2001 NFL draft. ... Signed by Titans (July 9, 2001).
CHAMPIONSHIP GAME EXPERIENCE: Played in AFC championship game (2002 season).
SINGLE GAME HIGHS (regular season): Receptions—2 (September 23, 2001, vs. Jacksonville); yards—28 (September 23, 2001, vs. Jacksonville); and touchdown receptions—0.

			RECEIVING				KICKOFF RETURNS				TOTALS		
Year Team	G	GS	No.	Yds.	Avg.	TD	No.	Yds.	Avg.	TD	TD	2pt.	Pts.	Fum.
2001—Tennessee NFL	11	0	2	28	14.0	0	13	253	19.5	0	0	0	0	0
2002—Tennessee NFL	16	0	1	14	14.0	0	13	260	20.0	0	0	0	0	0
Pro totals (2 years)	27	0	3	42	14.0	0	26	513	19.7	0	0	0	0	0

BERNARD, ROCKY　　　　DT　　　　SEAHAWKS

PERSONAL: Born April 19, 1979, in Baytown, Texas. ... 6-3/293. ... Full name: Robert Bernard.
HIGH SCHOOL: Sterling (Baytown, Texas).
COLLEGE: Texas A&M.
TRANSACTIONS/CAREER NOTES: Selected by Seattle Seahawks in fifth round (146th pick overall) of 2002 NFL draft. ... Signed by Seahawks (July 11, 2002).

			TOTALS		
Year Team	G	GS	Tk.	Ast.	Sks.
2002—Seattle NFL	16	2	34	15	4.0

BERNARD, WALTER　　　　CB　　　　SEAHAWKS

PERSONAL: Born May 3, 1978, in San Diego. ... 6-2/200. ... Full name: Walter Anton Bernard. ... Nephew of Popeye Jones, forward, Dallas Mavericks.
HIGH SCHOOL: Rancho Buena Vista (Vista, Calif.).
COLLEGE: New Mexico.
TRANSACTIONS/CAREER NOTES: Signed as non-drafted free agent by San Diego Chargers (April 24, 2001). ... Released by Chargers (August 27, 2001). ... Signed by Indianapolis Colts (February 12, 2002). ... Assigned by Colts to Frankfurt Galaxy in 2002 NFL Europe enhancement allocation program (February 12, 2002). ... Released by Colts (September 1, 2002). ... Signed by Seattle Seahawks to practice squad (December 11, 2002). ... Activated (December 13, 2002).

			TOTALS			INTERCEPTIONS			
Year Team	G	GS	Tk.	Ast.	Sks.	No.	Yds.	Avg.	TD
2002—Frankfurt NFLE	...	...	...	...	0.0	1	0	0.0	0
—Seattle NFL	1	0	0	0	0.0	0	0	0.0	0
NFL Europe totals (1 year)	...	...	...	...	0.0	1	0	0.0	0
NFL totals (1 year)	1	0	0	0	0.0	0	0	0.0	0
Pro totals (2 years)	...	...	...	...	0.0	1	0	0.0	0

BERRY, BERTRAND　　　　DE　　　　BRONCOS

PERSONAL: Born August 15, 1975, in Houston. ... 6-3/250. ... Full name: Bertrand Demond Berry.
HIGH SCHOOL: Humble (Texas).
COLLEGE: Notre Dame.
TRANSACTIONS/CAREER NOTES: Selected by Indianapolis Colts in third round (86th pick overall) of 1997 NFL draft. ... Signed by Colts (July 9, 1997). ... Granted free agency (February 11, 2000). ... Signed by St. Louis Rams (July 20, 2000). ... Released by Rams (August 20, 2000). ... Signed by Denver Broncos (January 3, 2001).

			TOTALS		
Year Team	G	GS	Tk.	Ast.	Sks.
1997—Indianapolis NFL	10	1	4	7	0.0
1998—Indianapolis NFL	16	12	38	11	4.0
1999—Indianapolis NFL	16	0	5	2	1.0
2000—			Did not play.		
2001—Denver NFL	14	0	14	2	2.0
2002—Denver NFL	16	1	10	2	6.5
Pro totals (5 years)	72	14	71	24	13.5

BETTIS, JEROME   RB   STEELERS

PERSONAL: Born February 16, 1972, in Detroit. ... 5-11/256. ... Full name: Jerome Abram Bettis. ... Nickname: The Bus.
HIGH SCHOOL: Mackenzie (Detroit).
COLLEGE: Notre Dame.
TRANSACTIONS/CAREER NOTES: Selected after junior season by Los Angeles Rams in first round (10th pick overall) of 1993 NFL draft. ... Signed by Rams (July 22, 1993). ... Rams franchise moved to St. Louis (April 12, 1995). ... Traded by Rams with third-round pick (LB Steven Conley) in 1996 draft to Pittsburgh Steelers for second-round pick (TE Ernie Conwell) in 1996 draft and fourth-round pick (traded to Miami) in 1997 draft (April 20, 1996). ... Granted unconditional free agency (February 14, 1997). ... Re-signed by Steelers (February 17, 1997). ... Granted unconditional free agency (March 2, 2001). ... Re-signed by Steelers (March 2, 2001).
CHAMPIONSHIP GAME EXPERIENCE: Played in AFC championship game (1997 and 2001 seasons).
HONORS: Named NFL Rookie of the Year by THE SPORTING NEWS (1993). ... Played in Pro Bowl (1993, 1994, 1996 and 1997 seasons). ... Named to play in Pro Bowl (2001 season); replaced by Corey Dillon due to injury.
SINGLE GAME HIGHS (regular season): Attempts—39 (January 2, 1994, vs. Chicago); yards—212 (December 12, 1993, vs. New Orleans); and rushing touchdowns—3 (November 30, 1997, vs. Arizona).
STATISTICAL PLATEAUS: 100-yard rushing games: 1993 (7), 1994 (4), 1996 (10), 1997 (10), 1998 (6), 1999 (2), 2000 (7), 2001 (5), 2002 (1). Total: 52.

			RUSHING				RECEIVING				TOTALS			
Year Team	G	GS	Att.	Yds.	Avg.	TD	No.	Yds.	Avg.	TD	TD	2pt.	Pts.	Fum.
1993—Los Angeles Rams NFL	16	12	‡294	1429	4.9	7	26	244	9.4	0	7	0	42	4
1994—Los Angeles Rams NFL	16	16	319	1025	3.2	3	31	293	9.5	1	4	∞2	28	5
1995—St. Louis NFL	15	13	183	637	3.5	3	18	106	5.9	0	3	0	18	4
1996—Pittsburgh NFL	16	12	320	1431	4.5	11	22	122	5.5	0	11	0	66	7
1997—Pittsburgh NFL	15	15	*375	1665	4.4	7	15	110	7.3	2	9	0	54	6
1998—Pittsburgh NFL	15	15	316	1185	3.8	3	16	90	5.6	0	3	0	18	2
1999—Pittsburgh NFL	16	16	299	1091	3.6	7	21	110	5.2	0	7	0	42	2
2000—Pittsburgh NFL	16	16	355	1341	3.8	8	13	97	7.5	0	8	0	48	1
2001—Pittsburgh NFL	11	11	225	1072	§4.8	4	8	48	6.0	0	4	0	24	3
2002—Pittsburgh NFL	13	11	187	666	3.6	9	7	57	8.1	0	9	0	54	1
Pro totals (10 years)	149	137	2873	11542	4.0	62	177	1277	7.2	3	65	2	394	35

BETTS, LADELL   RB   REDSKINS

PERSONAL: Born August 27, 1979, in Blue Springs, Mo. ... 5-10/221. ... Full name: Matthew Betts.
HIGH SCHOOL: Blue Springs (Mo.).
COLLEGE: Iowa.
TRANSACTIONS/CAREER NOTES: Selected by Washington Redskins in second round (56th pick overall) of 2002 NFL draft. ... Signed by Redskins (July 23, 2002).
SINGLE GAME HIGHS (regular season): Attempts—20 (December 22, 2002, vs. Houston); yards—116 (December 22, 2002, vs. Houston); and rushing touchdowns—1 (December 22, 2002, vs. Houston).
STATISTICAL PLATEAUS: 100-yard rushing games: 2002 (1).

			RUSHING				RECEIVING				KICKOFF RETURNS				TOTALS			
Year Team	G	GS	Att.	Yds.	Avg.	TD	No.	Yds.	Avg.	TD	No.	Yds.	Avg.	TD	TD	2pt.	Pts.	Fum.
2002—Washington NFL	11	0	65	307	4.7	1	12	154	12.8	0	28	690	24.6	0	1	0	6	2

BEUERLEIN, STEVE   QB   BRONCOS

PERSONAL: Born March 7, 1965, in Hollywood, Calif. ... 6-3/220. ... Full name: Stephen Taylor Beuerlein. ... Name pronounced BURR-line.
HIGH SCHOOL: Servite (Anaheim, Calif.).
COLLEGE: Notre Dame (degree in American studies, 1987).
TRANSACTIONS/CAREER NOTES: Selected by Los Angeles Raiders in fourth round (110th pick overall) of 1987 NFL draft. ... Signed by Raiders (July 24, 1987). ... On injured reserve with elbow and shoulder injuries (September 7, 1987-entire season). ... Granted free agency (February 1, 1990). ... Re-signed by Raiders (September 3, 1990). ... Granted roster exemption (September 3-16, 1990). ... Inactive for all 16 games (1990). ... Granted free agency (February 1, 1991). ... Re-signed by Raiders (July 8, 1991). ... Traded by Raiders to Dallas Cowboys for fourth-round pick (traded to Indianapolis) in 1992 draft (August 25, 1991). ... Granted unconditional free agency (March 1, 1993). ... Signed by Phoenix Cardinals (April 21, 1993). ... Cardinals franchise renamed Arizona Cardinals for 1994 season. ... Selected by Jacksonville Jaguars from Cardinals in NFL expansion draft (February 15, 1995). ... Granted free agency (February 16, 1996). ... Signed by Carolina Panthers (April 10, 1996). ... Released by Panthers (March 19, 2001). ... Signed by Denver Broncos (May 30, 2001). ... On injured reserve with elbow injury (October 5, 2001-remainder of season).
CHAMPIONSHIP GAME EXPERIENCE: Member of Raiders for AFC championship game (1990 season); inactive. ... Played in NFC championship game (1992 season). ... Member of Super Bowl championship team (1992 season). ... Member of Panthers for NFC championship game (1996 season); did not play.
HONORS: Played in Pro Bowl (1999 season).
SINGLE GAME HIGHS (regular season): Attempts—53 (December 19, 1993, vs. Seattle); completions—34 (December 19, 1993, vs. Seattle); yards—431 (December 19, 1993, vs. Seattle); and touchdown passes—5 (January 2, 2000, vs. New Orleans).
STATISTICAL PLATEAUS: 300-yard passing games: 1988 (1), 1993 (2), 1999 (5), 2000 (3). Total: 11.
MISCELLANEOUS: Regular-season record as starting NFL quarterback: 46-54 (.460). ... Postseason record as starting NFL quarterback: 1-1 (.500). ... Holds Carolina Panthers all-time records for most passing yards (12,690) and touchdown passes (86).

			PASSING									RUSHING				TOTALS		
Year Team	G	GS	Att.	Cmp.	Pct.	Yds.	TD	Int.	Avg.	Skd.	Rat.	Att.	Yds.	Avg.	TD	TD	2pt.	Pts.
1987—L.A. Raiders NFL							Did not play.											
1988—L.A. Raiders NFL	10	8	238	105	44.1	1643	8	7	6.90	26	66.6	30	35	1.2	0	0	0	0
1989—L.A. Raiders NFL	10	7	217	108	49.8	1677	13	9	7.73	22	78.4	16	39	2.4	0	0	0	0
1990—L.A. Raiders NFL							Did not play.											
1991—Dallas NFL	8	4	137	68	49.6	909	5	2	6.64	6	77.2	7	-14	-2.0	0	0	0	0
1992—Dallas NFL	16	0	18	12	66.7	152	0	1	8.44	0	69.7	4	-7	-1.8	0	0	0	0

Year Team	G	GS	PASSING Att.	Cmp.	Pct.	Yds.	TD	Int.	Avg.	Skd.	Rat.	RUSHING Att.	Yds.	Avg.	TD	TOTALS TD	2pt.	Pts.
1993—Phoenix NFL...............	16	14	418	258	61.7	3164	18	17	7.57	29	82.5	22	45	2.0	0	0	0	0
1994—Arizona NFL	9	7	255	130	51.0	1545	5	9	6.06	20	61.6	22	39	1.8	1	1	0	6
1995—Jacksonville NFL........	7	6	142	71	50.0	952	4	7	6.70	17	60.5	5	32	6.4	0	0	0	0
1996—Carolina NFL	8	4	123	69	56.1	879	8	2	7.15	18	93.5	12	17	1.4	0	0	0	0
1997—Carolina NFL	7	3	153	89	58.2	1032	6	3	6.75	17	83.6	4	32	8.0	0	0	0	0
1998—Carolina NFL	12	12	343	216	63.0	2613	17	12	7.62	44	88.2	22	26	1.2	0	0	0	0
1999—Carolina NFL	16	16	571	*343	60.1	*4436	36	15	7.77	‡50	94.6	27	124	4.6	2	2	0	12
2000—Carolina NFL	16	16	533	324	60.8	3730	19	18	7.00	*62	79.7	44	106	2.4	1	1	1	8
2001—Denver NFL								Did not play.										
2002—Denver NFL	8	3	117	68	58.1	925	6	5	7.91	12	82.7	5	9	1.8	1	1	0	6
Pro totals (13 years)	143	100	3265	1861	57.0	23657	145	107	7.25	323	80.9	220	483	2.2	5	5	1	32

BEVERLY, ERIC   C   LIONS   B

PERSONAL: Born March 28, 1974, in Cleveland. ... 6-3/300. ... Full name: Eric Raymonde Beverly.
HIGH SCHOOL: Bedford Heights (Ohio).
COLLEGE: Miami of Ohio.
TRANSACTIONS/CAREER NOTES: Signed as non-drafted free agent by Detroit Lions (April 24, 1997). ... Released by Lions (August 24, 1997). ... Re-signed by Lions to practice squad (August 26, 1997). ... Activated (December 20, 1997). ... Active for one game (1997); did not play. ... Granted free agency (March 2, 2001). ... Tendered offer sheet by Miami Dolphins (March 8, 2001). ... Offer matched by Lions (March 15, 2001).
PLAYING EXPERIENCE: Detroit NFL, 1998-2002. ... Games/Games started: 1998 (16/0), 1999 (16/2), 2000 (16/7), 2001 (16/16), 2002 (15/3). Total: 79/28.

BIBLA, MARTIN   G   FALCONS

PERSONAL: Born October 4, 1979, in Mountaintop, Pa. ... 6-3/306. ... Full name: Martin John Bibla.
HIGH SCHOOL: Crestwood (Mountaintop, Pa.).
COLLEGE: Miami (Fla.).
TRANSACTIONS/CAREER NOTES: Selected by Atlanta Falcons in fourth round (116th pick overall) of 2002 NFL draft. ... Signed by Falcons (June 19, 2002).
PLAYING EXPERIENCE: Atlanta NFL, 2002. ... Games/games started: 2002 (10/0).

BIDWELL, JOSH   P   PACKERS

PERSONAL: Born March 13, 1976, in Roseburg, Ore. ... 6-3/220. ... Full name: Joshua John Bidwell.
HIGH SCHOOL: Douglas (Winston, Ore.).
COLLEGE: Oregon (degree in English).
TRANSACTIONS/CAREER NOTES: Selected by Green Bay Packers in fourth round (133rd pick overall) of 1999 NFL draft. ... Signed by Packers (July 27, 1999). ... On non-football illness list with cancer (September 5, 1999-entire season). ... Granted free agency (February 28, 2003). ... Re-signed by Packers (April 30, 2003).
HONORS: Named punter on THE SPORTING NEWS college All-America second team (1998).

Year Team	G	PUNTING No.	Yds.	Avg.	Net avg.	In. 20	Blk.
1999—Green Bay NFL..				Did not play.			
2000—Green Bay NFL..	16	78	3003	38.5	34.6	22	0
2001—Green Bay NFL..	16	82	3485	42.5	36.5	21	0
2002—Green Bay NFL..	16	79	3296	41.7	35.7	26	0
Pro totals (3 years)	48	239	9784	40.9	35.6	69	0

BIEKERT, GREG   LB   VIKINGS

PERSONAL: Born March 14, 1969, in Iowa City, Iowa. ... 6-2/255. ... Name pronounced BEEK-ert.
HIGH SCHOOL: Longmont (Colo.).
COLLEGE: Colorado (degree in marketing, 1992).
TRANSACTIONS/CAREER NOTES: Selected by Los Angeles Raiders in seventh round (181st pick overall) of 1993 NFL draft. ... Signed by Raiders (July 13, 1993). ... Raiders franchise moved to Oakland (July 21, 1995). ... Released by Raiders (September 1, 2002). ... Signed by Minnesota Vikings (September 2, 2002).
CHAMPIONSHIP GAME EXPERIENCE: Played in AFC championship game (2000 season).

Year Team	G	GS	TOTALS Tk.	Ast.	Sks.	INTERCEPTIONS No.	Yds.	Avg.	TD
1993—Los Angeles Raiders NFL.......................................	16	0	8	2	0.0	0	0	0.0	0
1994—Los Angeles Raiders NFL.......................................	16	14	75	25	1.5	1	11	11.0	0
1995—Oakland NFL..	16	14	69	16	1.0	0	0	0.0	0
1996—Oakland NFL..	16	15	75	23	0.0	0	0	0.0	0
1997—Oakland NFL..	16	16	73	26	2.5	0	0	0.0	0
1998—Oakland NFL..	16	16	115	31	3.0	0	0	0.0	0
1999—Oakland NFL..	16	16	104	32	2.0	2	57	28.5	0
2000—Oakland NFL..	16	16	100	34	2.0	0	0	0.0	0
2001—Oakland NFL..	16	16	81	27	3.0	0	0	0.0	0
2002—Minnesota NFL..	16	16	70	31	0.0	4	26	6.5	0
Pro totals (10 years)	160	139	770	247	15.0	7	94	13.4	0

BIERRIA, TERREAL　　　　S　　　　SEAHAWKS

PERSONAL: Born October 10, 1980, in Slidell, La. ... 6-3/211.
HIGH SCHOOL: Salmen (Slidell, La.).
COLLEGE: Georgia.
TRANSACTIONS/CAREER NOTES: Selected after junior season by Seattle Seahawks in fourth round (120th pick overall) of 2002 NFL draft. ... Signed by Seahawks (July 25, 2002).

Year Team	G	GS	TOTALS Tk.	Ast.	Sks.	INTERCEPTIONS No.	Yds.	Avg.	TD
2002—Seattle NFL	14	0	0	0	0.0	0	0	0.0	0

BINN, DAVID　　　　C　　　　CHARGERS

PERSONAL: Born February 6, 1972, in San Mateo, Calif. ... 6-3/245. ... Full name: David Aaron Binn.
HIGH SCHOOL: San Mateo (Calif.).
COLLEGE: California (degree in ecology and the social system, 1993).
TRANSACTIONS/CAREER NOTES: Signed as non-drafted free agent by San Diego Chargers (April 28, 1994). ... Granted unconditional free agency (February 13, 1998). ... Re-signed by Chargers (February 25, 1998). ... Granted unconditional free agency (February 11, 2000). ... Re-signed by Chargers (February 11, 2000). ... Granted unconditional free agency (March 1, 2002). ... Re-signed by Chargers (March 5, 2002). ... Granted unconditional free agency (February 28, 2003). ... Re-signed by Chargers (March 3, 2003).
PLAYING EXPERIENCE: San Diego NFL, 1994-2002. ... Games/Games started: 1994 (16/0), 1995 (16/0), 1996 (16/0), 1997 (16/0), 1998 (15/0), 1999 (16/0), 2000 (16/0), 2001 (16/0), 2002 (16/0). Total: 143/0.
CHAMPIONSHIP GAME EXPERIENCE: Played in AFC championship game (1994 season). ... Played in Super Bowl XXIX (1994 season).

BIRD, CORY　　　　DB　　　　COLTS

PERSONAL: Born August 10, 1978, in Atlantic City, N.J. ... 5-10/213. ... Full name: Cory James Bird.
HIGH SCHOOL: Oakcrest (Mays Landing, N.J.).
COLLEGE: Virginia Tech.
TRANSACTIONS/CAREER NOTES: Selected by Indianapolis Colts in third round (91st pick overall) of 2001 NFL draft. ... Signed by Colts (July 25, 2001). ... On injured reserve with hip injury (November 20, 2002-remainder of season).

Year Team	G	GS	TOTALS Tk.	Ast.	Sks.	INTERCEPTIONS No.	Yds.	Avg.	TD
2001—Indianapolis NFL	14	0	20	5	0.5	0	0	0.0	0
2002—Indianapolis NFL	6	4	10	5	0.0	0	0	0.0	0
Pro totals (2 years)	20	4	30	10	0.5	0	0	0.0	0

BIRK, MATT　　　　C　　　　VIKINGS

PERSONAL: Born July 23, 1976, in St. Paul, Minn. ... 6-4/308. ... Full name: Matthew Robert Birk.
HIGH SCHOOL: Cretin-Derham Hall (St. Paul, Minn.).
COLLEGE: Harvard (degree in economics, 1998).
TRANSACTIONS/CAREER NOTES: Selected by Minnesota Vikings in sixth round (173rd pick overall) of 1998 NFL draft. ... Signed by Vikings (June 24, 1998). ... Granted free agency (March 2, 2001). ... Re-signed by Vikings (March 6, 2001).
PLAYING EXPERIENCE: Minnesota NFL, 1998-2002. ... Games/Games started: 1998 (7/0), 1999 (15/0), 2000 (16/16), 2001 (16/16), 2002 (16/16). Total: 70/48.
CHAMPIONSHIP GAME EXPERIENCE: Member of Vikings for NFC championship game (1998 season); did not play. ... Played in NFC championship game (2000 season).
HONORS: Played in Pro Bowl (2000 seasons). ... Named to play in Pro Bowl (2001 season); replaced by Jeremy Newberry due to injury.

BISHOP, BLAINE　　　　S

PERSONAL: Born July 24, 1970, in Indianapolis. ... 5-9/203. ... Full name: Blaine Elwood Bishop.
HIGH SCHOOL: Cathedral (Indianapolis).
COLLEGE: Saint Joseph's College (Ind.), then Ball State (degree in insurance, 1993).
TRANSACTIONS/CAREER NOTES: Selected by Houston Oilers in eighth round (214th pick overall) of 1993 NFL draft. ... Signed by Oilers (July 16, 1993). ... Granted free agency (February 16, 1996). ... Re-signed by Oilers (June 17, 1996). ... Designated by Oilers as franchise player (February 14, 1997). ... Oilers franchise moved to Tennessee for 1997 season. ... Re-signed by Oilers (August 27, 1997). ... Oilers franchise renamed Tennessee Titans for 1999 season (December 26, 1998). ... On injured reserve with foot injury (December 22, 2001-remainder of season). ... Released by Titans (February 28, 2002). ... Signed by Philadelphia Eagles (March 14, 2002). ... Released by Eagles (March 6, 2003).
CHAMPIONSHIP GAME EXPERIENCE: Played in AFC championship game (1999 season). ... Played in Super Bowl XXXIV (1999 season). ... Played in NFC championship game (2002 season).
HONORS: Played in Pro Bowl (1995, 1997 and 2000 seasons). ... Named to play in Pro Bowl (1996 season); replaced by Tyrone Braxton due to injury.

Year Team	G	GS	TOTALS Tk.	Ast.	Sks.	INTERCEPTIONS No.	Yds.	Avg.	TD
1993—Houston NFL	16	2	24	3	1.0	1	1	1.0	0
1994—Houston NFL	16	13	76	36	1.5	1	21	21.0	0
1995—Houston NFL	16	16	75	22	1.5	1	62	62.0	▲1
1996—Houston NFL	15	15	73	36	0.0	1	6	6.0	0
1997—Tennessee NFL	14	14	67	14	1.5	0	0	0.0	0
1998—Tennessee NFL	13	13	63	22	3.0	1	13	13.0	0
1999—Tennessee NFL	15	15	58	17	2.5	0	0	0.0	0
2000—Tennessee NFL	16	16	57	27	2.5	0	0	0.0	0
2001—Tennessee NFL	5	4	21	5	0.0	0	0	0.0	0
2002—Philadelphia NFL	12	12	29	12	2.0	0	0	0.0	0
Pro totals (10 years)	138	120	543	194	15.5	5	103	20.6	1

BLACK, AVION   WR   TEXANS

PERSONAL: Born April 24, 1977, in Nashville. ... 5-11/185. ... Full name: Avion Carlos Black.
HIGH SCHOOL: Maplewood (Nashville).
COLLEGE: Tennessee State.
TRANSACTIONS/CAREER NOTES: Selected by Buffalo Bills in fourth round (121st pick overall) of 2000 NFL draft. ... Signed by Bills (July 10, 2000). ... Selected by Houston Texans from Bills in NFL expansion draft (February 18, 2002). ... Granted free agency (February 28, 2003). ... Re-signed by Texans (May 29, 2003).
SINGLE GAME HIGHS (regular season): Receptions—4 (October 20, 2002, vs. Cleveland); yards—31 (October 20, 2002, vs. Cleveland); and touchdown receptions—0.

			RECEIVING				PUNT RETURNS				KICKOFF RETURNS				TOTALS			
Year Team	G	GS	No.	Yds.	Avg.	TD	No.	Yds.	Avg.	TD	No.	Yds.	Avg.	TD	TD	2pt.	Pts.	Fum.
2000—Buffalo NFL	2	0	0	0	0.0	0	0	0	0.0	0	9	165	18.3	0	0	0	0	0
2001—Buffalo NFL	14	0	8	90	11.3	0	1	34	34.0	0	25	498	19.9	0	0	0	0	0
2002—Houston NFL	11	0	6	52	8.7	0	14	188	13.4	1	24	529	22.0	0	1	0	6	2
Pro totals (3 years)	27	0	14	142	10.1	0	15	222	14.8	1	58	1192	20.6	0	1	0	6	2

BLACK, NATHAN   WR   PANTHERS

PERSONAL: Born June 20, 1978, in Baton Rouge, La. ... 6-0/190. ... Full name: Nathan Austin Black.
HIGH SCHOOL: East Ascension (Baton Rouge, La.).
COLLEGE: Northwestern State (La.).
TRANSACTIONS/CAREER NOTES: Signed as non-drafted free agent by Carolina Panthers (April 29, 2002). ... Released by Panthers (September 1, 2002). ... Re-signed by Panthers to practice squad (September 3, 2002). ... Activated (October 11, 2002).

			RECEIVING				KICKOFF RETURNS				TOTALS			
Year Team	G	GS	No.	Yds.	Avg.	TD	No.	Yds.	Avg.	TD	TD	2pt.	Pts.	Fum.
2002—Carolina NFL	5	0	0	0	0.0	0	3	44	14.7	0	0	0	0	0

BLACKMON, HAROLD   CB   SEAHAWKS

PERSONAL: Born May 20, 1978, in Chicago. ... 5-11/216. ... Full name: Harold Gene Blackmon.
HIGH SCHOOL: Leo (Chicago).
COLLEGE: Northwestern.
TRANSACTIONS/CAREER NOTES: Selected by Seattle Seahawks in seventh round (210th pick overall) of 2001 NFL draft. ... Signed by Seahawks (July 12, 2001). ... Released by Seahawks (October 2, 2001). ... Re-signed by Seahawks to practice squad (October 3, 2001). ... Activated (January 4, 2001).

			TOTALS			INTERCEPTIONS			
Year Team	G	GS	Tk.	Ast.	Sks.	No.	Yds.	Avg.	TD
2001—Seattle NFL	2	0	0	0	0.0	0	0	0.0	0
2002—Seattle NFL	7	0	1	1	0.0	0	0	0.0	0
Pro totals (2 years)	9	0	1	1	0.0	0	0	0.0	0

BLACKSHEAR, JEFF   G

PERSONAL: Born March 29, 1969, in Fort Pierce, Fla. ... 6-6/323. ... Full name: Jeffrey Leon Blackshear.
HIGH SCHOOL: Westwood Christian (Miami).
JUNIOR COLLEGE: Northwest Mississippi Junior College.
COLLEGE: Northeast Louisiana.
TRANSACTIONS/CAREER NOTES: Selected by Seattle Seahawks in eighth round (197th pick overall) of 1993 NFL draft. ... Signed by Seahawks (July 15, 1993). ... Traded by Seahawks to Cleveland Browns for fourth-round pick (traded to Atlanta) in 1997 draft (March 12, 1996). ... Browns franchise moved to Baltimore and renamed Ravens for 1996 season (March 11, 1996). ... Granted unconditional free agency (February 14, 1997). ... Re-signed by Ravens (March 13, 1997). ... Released by Ravens (February 23, 2000). ... Signed by Kansas City Chiefs (May 4, 2000). ... Released by Chiefs (June 8, 2001). ... Signed by Green Bay Packers (July 31, 2002). ... Released by Packers (September 1, 2002). ... Re-signed by Packers (December 24, 2002). ... Granted unconditional free agency (February 28, 2003).
PLAYING EXPERIENCE: Seattle NFL, 1993 and 1994; Cleveland NFL, 1995; Baltimore NFL, 1996-1999; Kansas City NFL, 2000; Green Bay NFL, 2002. ... Games/Games started: 1993 (15/2), 1994 (16/16), 1995 (16/3), 1996 (16/12), 1997 (16/16), 1998 (16/16), 1999 (16/16), 2000 (16/15), 2002 (1/0). Total: 128/96.

BLAISE, KERLIN   G

PERSONAL: Born December 25, 1974, in Orlando, Fla. ... 6-5/315.
HIGH SCHOOL: Maynard Evans (Orlando, Fla.).
COLLEGE: Miami (Fla.).
TRANSACTIONS/CAREER NOTES: Signed as non-drafted free agent by Detroit Lions (April 24, 1998). ... Released by Lions (August 30, 1998). ... Re-signed by Lions to practice squad (September 1, 1998). ... Activated (October 27, 1998); did not play. ... On injured reserve with knee injury (December 1, 1998-remainder of season). ... Granted free agency (March 2, 2001). ... Re-signed by Lions (April 26, 2001). ... Granted unconditional free agency (March 1, 2002). ... Re-signed by Lions (April 2, 2002). ... On injured reserve with knee injury (September 17, 2002-remainder of season). ... Granted unconditional free agency (February 28, 2003).
PLAYING EXPERIENCE: Detroit NFL, 1999-2002. ... Games/Games started: 1999 (16/4), 2000 (12/0), 2001 (6/0), 2002 (2/2). Total: 36/6.

PERSONAL: Born December 4, 1970, in Daytona Beach, Fla. ... 6-0/210. ... Son of Emory Blake, running back with Toronto Argonauts of CFL (1974).

HIGH SCHOOL: Seminole (Sanford, Fla.).

COLLEGE: East Carolina.

TRANSACTIONS/CAREER NOTES: Selected by New York Jets in sixth round (166th pick overall) of 1992 NFL draft. ... Signed by Jets (July 14, 1992). ... Inactive for all 16 games (1993). ... Claimed on waivers by Cincinnati Bengals (August 29, 1994). ... Granted free agency (February 17, 1995). ... Re-signed by Bengals (May 8, 1995). ... On injured reserve with wrist injury (December 24, 1998-remainder of season). ... Granted unconditional free agency (February 11, 2000). ... Signed by New Orleans Saints (February 11, 2000). ... On injured reserve with broken foot (November 20, 2000-remainder of season). ... Released by Saints (March 1, 2002). ... Signed by Baltimore Ravens (April 24, 2002). ... Granted unconditional free agency (February 28, 2003). ... Signed by Arizona Cardinals (March 12, 2003).

HONORS: Played in Pro Bowl (1995 season).

SINGLE GAME HIGHS (regular season): Attempts—50 (October 27, 2002, vs. Pittsburgh); completions—33 (September 10, 2000, vs. San Diego); yards—387 (November 6, 1994, vs. Seattle); and touchdown passes—4 (December 5, 1999, vs. San Francisco).

STATISTICAL PLATEAUS: 300-yard passing games: 1994 (2), 1995 (1), 1996 (2), 1997 (1), 1998 (1), 1999 (1), 2002 (2). Total: 10.

MISCELLANEOUS: Regular-season record as starting NFL quarterback: 36-51 (.414).

				PASSING							RUSHING				TOTALS		
Year Team	G	GS	Att.	Cmp.	Pct.	Yds.	TD	Int.	Avg.	Skd.	Rat.	Att.	Yds.	Avg.	TD	TD	2pt.	Pts.
1992—New York Jets NFL......	3	0	9	4	44.4	40	0	1	4.44	2	18.1	2	-2	-1.0	0	0	0	0
1993—New York Jets NFL......								Did not play.										
1994—Cincinnati NFL............	10	9	306	156	51.0	2154	14	9	7.04	19	76.9	37	204	5.5	1	1	1	8
1995—Cincinnati NFL............	16	16	567	§326	57.5	3822	§28	17	6.74	24	82.1	53	309	5.8	2	2	1	14
1996—Cincinnati NFL............	16	16	549	308	56.1	3624	24	14	6.60	44	80.3	72	317	4.4	2	2	0	12
1997—Cincinnati NFL............	11	11	317	184	58.0	2125	8	7	6.70	39	77.6	45	234	5.2	3	3	0	18
1998—Cincinnati NFL............	8	2	93	51	54.8	739	3	3	7.95	15	78.2	15	103	6.9	0	0	0	0
1999—Cincinnati NFL............	14	12	389	215	55.3	2670	16	12	6.86	30	77.6	63	332	5.3	2	2	0	12
2000—New Orleans NFL	11	11	302	184	60.9	2025	13	9	6.71	24	82.7	57	243	4.3	1	1	0	6
2001—New Orleans NFL	1	0	1	0	0.0	0	0	0	0.0	0	39.6	1	-1	-1.0	0	0	0	0
2002—Baltimore NFL............	11	10	295	165	55.9	2084	13	11	7.06	30	77.3	39	106	2.7	1	1	0	6
Pro totals (10 years)............	101	87	2828	1593	56.3	19283	119	83	6.82	227	79.2	384	1845	4.8	12	12	2	76

PERSONAL: Born August 23, 1979, in Atlanta, Texas. ... 5-9/195.

HIGH SCHOOL: Atlanta (Texas).

COLLEGE: Stephen F. Austin.

TRANSACTIONS/CAREER NOTES: Selected by Kansas City Chiefs in fifth round (150th pick overall) of 2001 NFL draft. ... Signed by Chiefs (June 8, 2001).

SINGLE GAME HIGHS (regular season): Attempts—7 (December 1, 2002, vs. Arizona); yards—23 (December 1, 2002, vs. Arizona); and rushing touchdowns—0.

			RUSHING				RECEIVING				KICKOFF RETURNS				TOTALS			
Year Team	G	GS	Att.	Yds.	Avg.	TD	No.	Yds.	Avg.	TD	No.	Yds.	Avg.	TD	TD	2pt.	Pts.	Fum.
2002—Kansas City NFL.........	12	0	16	72	4.5	0	5	47	9.4	0	3	49	16.3	0	0	0	0	0

PERSONAL: Born February 14, 1972, in Ellensburg, Wash. ... 6-5/240.

HIGH SCHOOL: Walla Walla (Wash.).

COLLEGE: Washington State.

TRANSACTIONS/CAREER NOTES: Selected after junior season by New England Patriots in first round (first pick overall) of 1993 NFL draft. ... Signed by Patriots (July 6, 1993). ... Traded by Patriots to Buffalo Bills for first-round pick (traded to Chicago) in 2003 draft (April 21, 2002).

CHAMPIONSHIP GAME EXPERIENCE: Played in AFC championship game (1996 and 2001 seasons). ... Played in Super Bowl XXXI (1996 season). ... Member of Super Bowl championship team (2001 season); did not play.

HONORS: Played in Pro Bowl (1994, 1996, 1997 and 2002 seasons).

RECORDS: Holds NFL single-season record for most passes attempted—691 (1994). ... Holds NFL single-game records for most passes completed—45; most passes attempted—70; and most passes attempted without an interception—70 (November 13, 1994, vs. Minnesota). ... Tied for most consecutive years leading league in passing attempts—3 (1994-1996).

SINGLE GAME HIGHS (regular season): Attempts—70 (November 13, 1994, vs. Minnesota); completions—45 (November 13, 1994, vs. Minnesota); yards—463 (September 15, 2002, vs. Minnesota); and touchdown passes—4 (September 29, 2002, vs. Chicago).

STATISTICAL PLATEAUS: 300-yard passing games: 1993 (1), 1994 (6), 1995 (2), 1996 (4), 1997 (3), 1998 (4), 1999 (5), 2000 (1), 2002 (7). Total: 33.

MISCELLANEOUS: Regular-season record as starting NFL quarterback: 71-68 (.511). ... Postseason record as starting NFL quarterback: 3-3 (.500). ... Holds New England Patriots all-time record for most yards passing (29,657).

				PASSING							RUSHING				TOTALS		
Year Team	G	GS	Att.	Cmp.	Pct.	Yds.	TD	Int.	Avg.	Skd.	Rat.	Att.	Yds.	Avg.	TD	TD	2pt.	Pts.
1993—New England NFL........	13	12	429	214	49.9	2494	15	15	5.81	16	65.0	32	82	2.6	0	0	0	0
1994—New England NFL........	16	16	*691	*400	57.9	*4555	25	*27	6.59	22	73.6	44	40	0.9	0	0	0	0
1995—New England NFL........	15	15	*636	323	50.8	3507	13	16	5.51	23	63.7	20	28	1.4	0	0	0	0
1996—New England NFL........	16	16	*623	*373	59.9	4086	27	15	6.56	30	83.7	24	27	1.1	0	0	0	0
1997—New England NFL........	16	16	522	314	60.2	3706	28	15	7.10	30	87.7	28	55	2.0	0	0	0	0
1998—New England NFL........	14	14	481	263	54.7	3633	20	14	7.55	§36	80.9	28	44	1.6	0	0	0	0
1999—New England NFL........	16	16	§539	305	56.6	3985	19	§21	7.39	55	75.6	42	101	2.4	0	0	0	0
2000—New England NFL........	16	16	531	312	58.8	3291	17	13	6.20	45	77.3	47	158	3.4	2	2	0	12
2001—New England NFL........	2	2	66	40	60.6	400	2	2	6.06	5	75.3	5	18	3.6	0	0	0	0
2002—Buffalo NFL.................	16	16	610	375	61.5	4359	24	15	7.15	54	86.0	27	67	2.5	2	2	0	12
Pro totals (10 years)............	140	139	5128	2919	56.9	34016	190	153	6.63	316	77.1	297	620	2.1	4	4	0	24

BLY, DRE' CB LIONS

PERSONAL: Born May 22, 1977, in Chesapeake, Va. ... 5-9/190. ... Full name: Donald Andre Bly.
HIGH SCHOOL: Western Branch (Chesapeake, Va.).
COLLEGE: North Carolina (degree in exercise and sports science).
TRANSACTIONS/CAREER NOTES: Selected after junior season by St. Louis Rams in second round (41st pick overall) of 1999 NFL draft. ... Signed by Rams (July 16, 1999). ... Granted unconditional free agency (February 28, 2003). ... Signed by Detroit Lions (March 1, 2003).
CHAMPIONSHIP GAME EXPERIENCE: Played in NFC championship game (1999 and 2001 seasons). ... Member of Super Bowl championship team (1999 season). ... Played in Super Bowl XXXVI (2001 season).
HONORS: Named cornerback on THE SPORTING NEWS college All-America first team (1996). ... Named cornerback on THE SPORTING NEWS college All-America third team (1997).

			TOTALS			INTERCEPTIONS				PUNT RETURNS				KICKOFF RETURNS				TOTALS			
Year Team	G	GS	Tk.	Ast.	Sks.	No.	Yds.	Avg.	TD	No.	Yds.	Avg.	TD	No.	Yds.	Avg.	TD	TD	2pt.	Pts.	Fum.
1999—St. Louis NFL	16	2	16	1	0.0	3	53	17.7	1	0	0	0.0	0	1	1	1.0	0	1	0	6	0
2000—St. Louis NFL	16	3	39	4	1.0	3	44	14.7	0	0	0	0.0	0	9	163	18.1	0	0	0	0	1
2001—St. Louis NFL	16	4	28	2	0.0	6	150	25.0	†2	7	71	10.1	0	6	128	21.3	0	2	0	12	1
2002—St. Louis NFL	16	16	58	6	1.0	2	0	0.0	0	8	138	17.3	1	1	5	5.0	0	2	0	12	0
Pro totals (4 years)	64	25	141	13	2.0	14	247	17.6	3	15	209	13.9	1	17	297	17.5	0	5	0	30	2

BOBER, CHRIS OT GIANTS

PERSONAL: Born December 24, 1976, in Omaha, Neb. ... 6-5/310.
HIGH SCHOOL: South (Omaha, Neb.).
COLLEGE: Nebraska-Omaha.
TRANSACTIONS/CAREER NOTES: Signed as non-drafted free agent by New York Giants (April 20, 2000). ... Released by Giants (August 27, 2000). ... Re-signed by Giants to practice squad (August 29, 2000). ... Activated (November 6, 2000); did not play. ... Granted free agency (February 28, 2003). ... Re-signed by Giants (April 21, 2003).
PLAYING EXPERIENCE: New York Giants NFL, 2001-2002. ... Games/Games started: 2001 (16/0), 2002 (15/15). Total: 31/15.

BOERIGTER, MARC WR CHIEFS

PERSONAL: Born May 4, 1978, in Hastings, Neb. ... 6-3/223. ... Full name: Marc Robert Boerigter.
HIGH SCHOOL: Hastings (Neb.).
COLLEGE: Hastings (Neb.) College.
TRANSACTIONS/CAREER NOTES: Signed by Calgary Stampeders of CFL (May 12, 2000). ... Signed as non-drafted free agent by Kansas City Chiefs (February 7, 2002).
CHAMPIONSHIP GAME EXPERIENCE: Member of CFL championship team (2001).
RECORDS: Shares NFL record for longest pass reception (from Trent Green)—99 yards, touchdown (December 22, 2002, vs. San Diego).
SINGLE GAME HIGHS (regular season): Receptions—5 (December 22, 2002, vs. San Diego); yards—144 (December 22, 2002, vs. San Diego); and touchdown receptions—2 (December 22, 2002, vs. San Diego).
STATISTICAL PLATEAUS: 100-yard receiving games: 2002 (1).

			RECEIVING			
Year Team	G	GS	No.	Yds.	Avg.	TD
2000—Calgary CFL	18	0	63	1092	17.3	8
2001—Calgary CFL	18	0	48	931	19.4	11
2002—Kansas City NFL	16	2	20	420	21.0	8
CFL totals (2 years)	36	0	111	2023	18.2	19
NFL totals (1 year)	16	2	20	420	21.0	8
Pro totals (3 years)	52	2	131	2443	18.6	27

BOIMAN, ROCKY LB TITANS

PERSONAL: Born January 24, 1980, in Cincinnati. ... 6-4/233. ... Full name: Rocky Michael Boiman.
HIGH SCHOOL: St. Xavier (Cincinnati).
COLLEGE: Notre Dame.
TRANSACTIONS/CAREER NOTES: Selected by Tennessee Titans in fourth round (133rd pick overall) of 2002 NFL draft. ... Signed by Titans (July 24, 2002).
CHAMPIONSHIP GAME EXPERIENCE: Played in AFC championship game (2002 season).

			TOTALS			INTERCEPTIONS			
Year Team	G	GS	Tk.	Ast.	Sks.	No.	Yds.	Avg.	TD
2002—Tennessee NFL	16	0	1	0	0.0	0	0	0.0	0

BOLDEN, JURAN CB FALCONS

PERSONAL: Born June 27, 1974, in Tampa. ... 6-2/207. ... Cousin of K.D. Williams, linebacker, New Orleans Saints.
HIGH SCHOOL: Hillsborough (Tampa).
JUNIOR COLLEGE: Mississippi Delta Community College.
TRANSACTIONS/CAREER NOTES: Signed by Winnipeg Blue Bombers of CFL (April 1995). ... Selected by Atlanta Falcons in fourth round (127th pick overall) of 1996 NFL draft. ... Signed by Falcons (July 20, 1996). ... On injured reserve with knee injury (December 9, 1996-remainder of season). ... Claimed on waivers by Green Bay Packers (September 30, 1998). ... Claimed on waivers by Carolina Panthers (October 27, 1998). ... Released by Panthers (February 12, 1999). ... Signed by Kansas City Chiefs (April 19, 1999). ... Released by Chiefs (September 5, 1999). ... Re-signed by Chiefs (September 21, 1999). ... Released by Chiefs (December 21, 1999). ... Signed by Blue Bombers of CFL (June 8, 2000). ... Signed by Atlanta Falcons (January 10, 2002). ... Granted unconditional free agency (February 28, 2003). ... Re-signed by Falcons (April 28, 2003),

Year	Team	G	GS	TOTALS			INTERCEPTIONS			
				Tk.	Ast.	Sks.	No.	Yds.	Avg.	TD
1995—Winnipeg CFL		9	9	17	...	0.0	6	28	4.7	0
1996—Atlanta NFL		9	0	0	0	0.0	0	0	0.0	0
1997—Atlanta NFL		14	1	7	0	0.0	0	0	0.0	0
1998—Atlanta NFL		3	0	3	0	0.0	0	0	0.0	0
—Green Bay NFL		3	0	0	0	0.0	0	0	0.0	0
—Carolina NFL		6	0	0	0	0.0	0	0	0.0	0
1999—Kansas City NFL		7	0	0	0	0.0	0	0	0.0	0
2002—Atlanta NFL		14	6	23	6	0.0	4	25	6.3	0
CFL totals (1 year)		9	9	17	...	0.0	6	28	4.7	0
NFL totals (5 years)		56	7	33	6	0.0	4	25	6.3	0
Pro totals (6 years)		65	16	50	...	0.0	10	53	5.3	0

B

BOOKER, MARTY   WR   BEARS

PERSONAL: Born July 31, 1976, in Marrero, La. ... 6-0/210. ... Full name: Marty Montez Booker.
HIGH SCHOOL: Jonesboro-Hodge (Jonesboro, La.).
COLLEGE: Northeastern Louisiana.
TRANSACTIONS/CAREER NOTES: Selected by Chicago Bears in third round (78th pick overall) of 1999 NFL draft. ... Signed by Bears (July 22, 1999). ... Granted free agency (March 1, 2002). ... Re-signed by Bears (June 21, 2002).
HONORS: Played in Pro Bowl (2002 season).
SINGLE GAME HIGHS (regular season): Receptions—12 (October 7, 2002, vs. Green Bay); yards—198 (September 8, 2002, vs. Minnesota); and touchdown receptions—3 (November 18, 2001, vs. Tampa Bay).
STATISTICAL PLATEAUS: 100-yard receiving games: 1999 (1), 2001 (2), 2002 (3). Total: 6.

Year	Team	G	GS	RECEIVING				TOTALS			
				No.	Yds.	Avg.	TD	TD	2pt.	Pts.	Fum.
1999—Chicago NFL		9	4	19	219	11.5	3	3	0	18	0
2000—Chicago NFL		15	7	47	490	10.4	2	2	0	12	2
2001—Chicago NFL		16	16	100	1071	10.7	8	8	0	48	2
2002—Chicago NFL		16	16	97	1189	12.3	6	6	0	36	0
Pro totals (4 years)		56	43	263	2969	11.3	19	19	0	114	4

BOOKER, VAUGHN   DE

PERSONAL: Born February 24, 1968, in Cincinnati. ... 6-5/300. ... Full name: Vaughn Jamel Booker.
HIGH SCHOOL: Taft (Cincinnati).
COLLEGE: Cincinnati.
TRANSACTIONS/CAREER NOTES: Signed by Winnipeg Blue Bombers of CFL (June 1992). ... Granted free agency after 1993 season. ... Signed as non-drafted free agent by Kansas City Chiefs (May 2, 1994). ... Traded by Chiefs to Green Bay Packers for DT Darius Holland (May 13, 1998). ... Granted unconditional free agency (February 11, 2000). ... Signed by Cincinnati Bengals (February 16, 2000). ... On injured reserve with knee injury (December 7, 2000-remainder of season). ... Released by Bengals (April 1, 2003).
MISCELLANEOUS: Served in U.S. Army (1988-90).

Year	Team	G	GS	TOTALS		
				Tk.	Ast.	Sks.
1992—Winnipeg CFL		15	...	29	...	2.0
1993—Winnipeg CFL		9	...	18	...	4.0
1994—Kansas City NFL		13	0	13	2	0.0
1995—Kansas City NFL		16	10	27	5	1.5
1996—Kansas City NFL		14	12	31	4	1.0
1997—Kansas City NFL		13	13	25	5	4.0
1998—Green Bay NFL		16	4	14	6	3.0
1999—Green Bay NFL		14	14	32	14	3.5
2000—Cincinnati NFL		9	9	13	4	0.0
2001—Cincinnati NFL		14	13	34	6	1.5
2002—Cincinnati NFL		6	5	5	2	0.0
CFL totals (2 years)		24	...	47	...	6.0
NFL totals (9 years)		115	80	194	48	14.5
Pro totals (11 years)		139	...	241	...	20.5

BOONE, ALFONSO   DT   BEARS

PERSONAL: Born January 11, 1976, in Saginaw, Mich. ... 6-4/325.
HIGH SCHOOL: Arthur Hill (Saginaw, Mich.).
JUNIOR COLLEGE: Mount San Antonio College (Calif.).
COLLEGE: Central State (did not play football).
TRANSACTIONS/CAREER NOTES: Selected after sophomore season by Detroit Lions in seventh round (253rd pick overall) of 2000 NFL draft. ... Signed by Lions (July 16, 2000). ... Released by Lions (August 27, 2000). ... Re-signed by Lions to practice squad (August 29, 2000). ... Signed by Chicago Bears off Lions practice squad (November 21, 2000). ... Inactive for five games (2000).

Year	Team	G	GS	TOTALS		
				Tk.	Ast.	Sks.
2001—Chicago NFL		11	0	7	2	2.0
2002—Chicago NFL		16	5	19	2	1.5
Pro totals (2 years)		27	5	26	4	3.5

BOSELLI, TONY — OT — TEXANS

PERSONAL: Born April 17, 1972, in Boulder, Colo. ... 6-7/322. ... Full name: Don Anthony Boselli Jr.
HIGH SCHOOL: Fairview (Boulder, Colo.).
COLLEGE: Southern California (degree in business administration, 1995).
TRANSACTIONS/CAREER NOTES: Selected by Jacksonville Jaguars in first round (second pick overall) of 1995 NFL draft. ... Signed by Jaguars (June 1, 1995). ... On injured reserve with knee injury (January 4, 2000-remainder of playoffs). ... On injured reserve with shoulder injury (October 22, 2001-remainder of season). ... Selected by Houston Texans from Jaguars in NFL expansion draft (February 18, 2002). ... On injured reserve with shoulder injury (October 15, 2002-remainder of season).
PLAYING EXPERIENCE: Jacksonville NFL, 1995-2001; Houston NFL, 2002. ... Games/Games started: 1995 (13/12), 1996 (16/16), 1997 (12/12), 1998 (15/15), 1999 (16/16), 2000 (16/16), 2001 (3/3), 2002 (0/0). Total: 91/90.
CHAMPIONSHIP GAME EXPERIENCE: Played in AFC championship game (1996 season).
HONORS: Named offensive lineman on The Sporting News college All-America first team (1994). ... Played in Pro Bowl (1996-1998 seasons). ... Named offensive tackle on The Sporting News NFL All-Pro team (1997-99). ... Named to play in Pro Bowl (1999 season); replaced by Walter Jones due to injury. ... Named to play in Pro Bowl (2000 season); replaced by Lincoln Kennedy due to injury.

BOSTIC, JASON — S — BILLS

PERSONAL: Born June 30, 1976, in Lauderhill, Fla. ... 5-9/190. ... Full name: Jason Devon Bostic.
HIGH SCHOOL: Cardinal Gibbons (Lauderhill, Fla.).
COLLEGE: Georgia Tech.
TRANSACTIONS/CAREER NOTES: Signed as non-drafted free agent by Philadelphia Eagles (April 19, 1999). ... Released by Eagles (September 5, 1999). ... Re-signed by Eagles to practice squad (September 8, 1999). ... Activated (December 27, 1999). ... Released by Eagles (September 2, 2001). ... Signed by Buffalo Bills (February 6, 2002). ... On injured reserve with knee injury (December 18, 2002-remainder of season).

			TOTALS			INTERCEPTIONS			
Year Team	G	GS	Tk.	Ast.	Sks.	No.	Yds.	Avg.	TD
1999—Philadelphia NFL	1	0	0	0	0.0	0	0	0.0	0
2000—Philadelphia NFL	16	0	1	0	0.0	0	0	0.0	0
2002—Buffalo NFL	14	0	8	2	0.0	0	0	0.0	0
Pro totals (3 years)	31	0	9	2	0.0	0	0	0.0	0

BOSTON, DAVID — WR — CHARGERS

PERSONAL: Born August 19, 1978, in Humble, Texas. ... 6-2/236.
HIGH SCHOOL: Humble (Texas).
COLLEGE: Ohio State.
TRANSACTIONS/CAREER NOTES: Selected after junior season by Arizona Cardinals in first round (eighth pick overall) of 1999 NFL draft. ... Signed by Cardinals (August 2, 1999). ... Granted unconditional free agency (February 28, 2003). ... Signed by San Diego Chargers (March 5, 2003).
HONORS: Named wide receiver on The Sporting News college All-America second team (1998). ... Named wide receiver on The Sporting News NFL All-Pro team (2001). ... Played in Pro Bowl (2001 season).
SINGLE GAME HIGHS (regular season): Receptions—9 (November 11, 2001, vs. New York Giants); yards—184 (December 3, 2000, vs. Cincinnati); and touchdown receptions—2 (December 30, 2001, vs. Carolina).
STATISTICAL PLATEAUS: 100-yard receiving games: 1999 (1), 2000 (4), 2001 (9), 2002 (2). Total: 16.

			RUSHING				RECEIVING				PUNT RETURNS				TOTALS			
Year Team	G	GS	Att.	Yds.	Avg.	TD	No.	Yds.	Avg.	TD	No.	Yds.	Avg.	TD	TD	2pt.	Pts.	Fum.
1999—Arizona NFL	16	8	5	0	0.0	0	40	473	11.8	2	7	62	8.9	0	2	0	12	2
2000—Arizona NFL	16	16	3	9	3.0	0	71	1156	16.3	7	0	0	0.0	0	7	0	42	2
2001—Arizona NFL	16	16	5	35	7.0	0	98	*1598	16.3	8	0	0	0.0	0	8	0	48	1
2002—Arizona NFL	8	8	2	29	14.5	0	32	512	16.0	1	0	0	0.0	0	1	0	6	0
Pro totals (4 years)	56	48	15	73	4.9	0	241	3739	15.5	18	7	62	8.9	0	18	0	108	5

BOULWARE, PETER — LB — RAVENS

PERSONAL: Born December 18, 1974, in Columbia, S.C. ... 6-4/255. ... Full name: Peter Nicholas Boulware. ... Name pronounced BOWL-ware.
HIGH SCHOOL: Spring Valley (Columbia, S.C.).
COLLEGE: Florida State (degree in management information systems, 1997).
TRANSACTIONS/CAREER NOTES: Selected after junior season by Baltimore Ravens in first round (fourth pick overall) of 1997 NFL draft. ... Signed by Ravens (August 16, 1997). ... On physically unable to perform list with ankle injury (July 26-August 16, 2002).
CHAMPIONSHIP GAME EXPERIENCE: Played in AFC championship game (2000 season). ... Member of Super Bowl championship team (2000 season).
HONORS: Named defensive end on The Sporting News college All-America first team (1996). ... Played in Pro Bowl (1998, 1999 and 2002 seasons).
MISCELLANEOUS: Holds Baltimore Ravens all-time record for most sacks (59).

			TOTALS			INTERCEPTIONS			
Year Team	G	GS	Tk.	Ast.	Sks.	No.	Yds.	Avg.	TD
1997—Baltimore NFL	16	16	43	15	11.5	0	0	0.0	0
1998—Baltimore NFL	16	16	38	23	8.5	0	0	0.0	0
1999—Baltimore NFL	16	11	31	8	10.0	0	0	0.0	0
2000—Baltimore NFL	16	15	33	6	7.0	0	0	0.0	0
2001—Baltimore NFL	16	14	45	22	§15.0	0	0	0.0	0
2002—Baltimore NFL	16	16	57	16	7.0	1	6	6.0	0
Pro totals (6 years)	96	88	247	90	59.0	1	6	6.0	0

BOUMAN, TODD   QB   SAINTS

PERSONAL: Born August 1, 1972, in Ruthton, Minn. ... 6-2/229. ... Name pronounced Bow-man.
HIGH SCHOOL: Ruthton (Minn.).
COLLEGE: South Dakota State, then St. Cloud State.
TRANSACTIONS/CAREER NOTES: Signed as non-drafted free agent by Minnesota Vikings (April 25, 1997). ... Released by Vikings (August 23, 1997). ... Re-signed by Vikings to practice squad (August 25, 1997). ... Activated (December 5, 1997). ... Inactive for all 16 games (1999). ... Assigned by Vikings to Barcelona Dragons in 1999 NFL Europe enhancement allocation program (February 22, 1999). ... Inactive for all 16 games (2000). ... Traded by Vikings to New Orleans Saints for sixth-round pick in 2003 draft (LB Mike Nattiel) (March 13, 2003).
CHAMPIONSHIP GAME EXPERIENCE: Member of Vikings for NFC championship game (1998 and 2000 seasons); inactive.
SINGLE GAME HIGHS (regular season): Attempts—38 (December 16, 2001, vs. Detroit); completions—21 (December 9, 2001, vs. Tennessee); yards—348 (December 9, 2001, vs. Tennessee); and touchdown passes—4 (December 9, 2001, vs. Tennessee).
STATISTICAL PLATEAUS: 300-yard passing games: 2001 (1).
MISCELLANEOUS: Regular-season record as starting NFL quarterback: 1-2 (.333).

			PASSING									RUSHING				TOTALS		
Year Team	G	GS	Att.	Cmp.	Pct.	Yds.	TD	Int.	Avg.	Skd.	Rat.	Att.	Yds.	Avg.	TD	TD	2pt.	Pts.
1999—Barcelona W.L.	...	...	324	170	52.5	2296	16	11	7.09	0	77.6	47	213	4.5	2	2	0	12
2000—Minnesota NFL						Did not play.												
2001—Minnesota NFL	5	3	89	51	57.3	795	8	4	8.93	4	98.3	9	61	6.8	0	0	0	0
2002—Minnesota NFL	1	0	6	3	50.0	85	0	0	14.17	2	95.8	1	9	9.0	0	0	0	0
W.L. totals (1 year)	...	...	324	170	52.5	2296	16	11	7.09	0	77.6	47	213	4.5	2	2	0	12
NFL totals (2 years)	6	3	95	54	56.8	880	8	4	9.26	6	98.6	10	70	7.0	0	0	0	0
Pro totals (3 years)	...	...	419	224	53.5	3176	24	15	7.58	6	82.4	57	283	5.0	2	2	0	12

BOWEN, MATT   S   REDSKINS

PERSONAL: Born November 12, 1976, in Glen Ellyn, Ill. ... 6-1/210.
HIGH SCHOOL: Glenbard West (Glen Ellyn, Ill.).
COLLEGE: Iowa.
TRANSACTIONS/CAREER NOTES: Selected by St. Louis Rams in sixth round (198th pick overall) of 2000 NFL draft. ... Signed by Rams (July 7, 2000). ... On injured reserve with broken foot (October 3-November 6, 2001). ... Released by Rams (November 6, 2001). ... Signed by Green Bay Packers (November 30, 2001). ... Granted free agency (February 28, 2003). ... Tendered offer sheet by Washington Redskins (March 8, 2003). ... Packers declined to match offer (March 11, 2003).

			TOTALS			INTERCEPTIONS			
Year Team	G	GS	Tk.	Ast.	Sks.	No.	Yds.	Avg.	TD
2000—St. Louis NFL	16	2	14	2	0.0	0	0	0.0	0
2001—St. Louis NFL	1	0	0	0	0.0	0	0	0.0	0
—Green Bay NFL	5	0	0	0	0.0	0	0	0.0	0
2002—Green Bay NFL	16	6	29	16	0.0	1	0	0.0	0
Pro totals (3 years)	38	8	43	18	0.0	1	0	0.0	0

BOWENS, DAVID   DE   DOLPHINS

PERSONAL: Born July 3, 1977, in Denver. ... 6-3/260. ... Full name: David Walter Bowens.
HIGH SCHOOL: St. Mary's (Orchard Lake, Mich.).
COLLEGE: Michigan, then Western Illinois.
TRANSACTIONS/CAREER NOTES: Selected after junior season by Denver Broncos in fifth round (158th pick overall) of 1999 NFL draft. ... Signed by Broncos (July 22, 1999). ... Traded by Broncos to Green Bay Packers for fourth-round pick (C Ben Hamilton) in 2001 draft (February 24, 2000). ... Traded by Packers to Buffalo Bills for TE Bobby Collins (August 7, 2001). ... Claimed on waivers by Washington Redskins (September 3, 2001). ... Released by Redskins (September 26, 2001). ... Signed by Miami Dolphins (October 22, 2001). ... Granted unconditional free agency (February 28, 2003). ... Re-signed by Dolphins (March 6, 2003).

			TOTALS		
Year Team	G	GS	Tk.	Ast.	Sks.
1999—Denver NFL	16	0	7	0	1.0
2000—Green Bay NFL	14	0	19	7	3.5
2001—Miami NFL	8	0	5	1	1.0
2002—Miami NFL	14	0	9	7	1.5
Pro totals (4 years)	52	0	40	15	7.0

BOWENS, TIM   DT   DOLPHINS

PERSONAL: Born February 7, 1973, in Okolona, Miss. ... 6-4/320. ... Full name: Timothy L. Bowens.
HIGH SCHOOL: Okolona (Miss.).
JUNIOR COLLEGE: Itawamba Community College (Miss.).
COLLEGE: Mississippi.
TRANSACTIONS/CAREER NOTES: Selected after junior season by Miami Dolphins in first round (20th pick overall) of 1994 NFL draft. ... Signed by Dolphins (June 2, 1994). ... Designated by Dolphins as franchise player (February 13, 1998). ... Re-signed by Dolphins (August 21, 1998). ... On injured reserve with torn biceps muscle (January 3, 1999-remainder of playoffs). ... Released by Dolphins (February 28, 2002). ... Re-signed by Dolphins (February 28, 2002).
HONORS: Named to play in Pro Bowl (1998 season); replaced by Cortez Kennedy due to injury. ... Played in Pro Bowl (2002 season).

Year	Team	G	GS	TOTALS			INTERCEPTIONS			
				Tk.	Ast.	Sks.	No.	Yds.	Avg.	TD
1994—Miami NFL		16	15	44	8	3.0	0	0	0.0	0
1995—Miami NFL		16	16	34	7	2.0	0	0	0.0	0
1996—Miami NFL		16	16	41	7	3.0	0	0	0.0	0
1997—Miami NFL		16	16	34	14	5.0	0	0	0.0	0
1998—Miami NFL		16	16	21	9	0.0	0	0	0.0	0
1999—Miami NFL		16	15	18	16	1.5	0	0	0.0	0
2000—Miami NFL		15	15	29	11	2.5	1	0	0.0	0
2001—Miami NFL		15	15	30	18	3.0	0	0	0.0	0
2002—Miami NFL		16	16	24	12	0.0	0	0	0.0	0
Pro totals (9 years)		142	140	275	102	20.0	1	0	0.0	0

BOWERS, R.J.   FB   BROWNS

PERSONAL: Born February 10, 1974, in Honolulu, Hawaii. ... 6-0/245. ... Full name: Raymond Keith Bowers Jr.
HIGH SCHOOL: West Middlesex (Pa.).
COLLEGE: Grove City (Pa.).
TRANSACTIONS/CAREER NOTES: Signed as non-drafted free agent by Carolina Panthers (April 23, 2001). ... Released by Panthers (August 28, 2001). ... Signed by Pittsburgh Steelers to practice squad (September 3, 2001). ... Activated (December 21, 2001). ... Claimed on waivers by Cleveland Browns (August 28, 2002). ... Released by Browns (October 2, 2002). ... Re-signed by Browns to practice squad (October 2, 2002). ... Activated (November 19, 2002). ... Released by Browns (November 26, 2002). ... Re-signed by Browns (November 29, 2002).
CHAMPIONSHIP GAME EXPERIENCE: Member of Steelers for AFC championship game (2001 season); inactive.
SINGLE GAME HIGHS (regular season): Attempts—11 (January 6, 2002, vs. Cleveland); yards—67 (January 6, 2002, vs. Cleveland); and rushing touchdowns—1 (January 6, 2002, vs. Cleveland).

Year	Team	G	GS	RUSHING				RECEIVING				TOTALS			
				Att.	Yds.	Avg.	TD	No.	Yds.	Avg.	TD	TD	2pt.	Pts.	Fum.
2001—Pittsburgh NFL		3	0	18	84	4.7	1	1	0	0.0	0	1	0	6	0
2002—Cleveland NFL		4	0	0	0	0.0	0	0	0	0.0	0	0	0	0	0
Pro totals (2 years)		7	0	18	84	4.7	1	1	0	0.0	0	1	0	6	0

BOYD, DANNY   K   JAGUARS

PERSONAL: Born June 1, 1978, in Bradenton, Fla. ... 6-0/213. ... Full name: Daniel Edward Boyd.
HIGH SCHOOL: Southeast (Bradenton, Fla.).
COLLEGE: Louisana State (degree in music education).
TRANSACTIONS/CAREER NOTES: Signed as non-drafted free agent by New York Jets (January 15, 2002). ... Allocated by Jets to Berlin Thunder in NFL Europe enhance allocation program (February 12, 2002). ... Released by Jets (September 2, 2002). ... Signed by New York Giants to practice squad (September 3, 2002). ... Released by Giants (September 26, 2002). ... Signed by Jacksonville Jaguars (December 3, 2002). ... Re-signed by Jaguars (March 24, 2003).

Year	Team	G	1-29	30-39	40-49	50+	FIELD GOALS			TOTALS		
							Tot.	Pct.	Lg.	XPM	XPA	Pts.
2002—Berlin NFLE		...	...	...	...	0-0	10-19	52.6	...	9	9	39
—Jacksonville NFL		4	3-3	2-2	0-0	0-0	5-5	100.0	33	7	7	22
NFL Europe totals (1 year)		...	...	...	...	0-0	10-19	52.6	...	9	9	39
NFL totals (1 year)		4	3-3	2-2	0-0	0-0	5-5	100.0	33	7	7	22
Pro totals (2 years)		...	...	...	...	0-0	15-24	62.5	...	16	16	61

BOYD, JAMES   S

PERSONAL: Born October 17, 1977, in Norfolk, Va. ... 5-11/207. ... Full name: James Aaron Boyd.
HIGH SCHOOL: Indian River (Chesapeake, Va.).
COLLEGE: Penn State.
TRANSACTIONS/CAREER NOTES: Selected by Jacksonville Jaguars in third round (94th pick overall) of 2001 NFL draft. ... Signed by Jaguars (June 14, 2001). ... Released by Jaguars (May 19, 2003).
HONORS: Named strong safety on THE SPORTING NEWS college All-America third team (2000).

Year	Team	G	GS	TOTALS			INTERCEPTIONS			
				Tk.	Ast.	Sks.	No.	Yds.	Avg.	TD
2001—Jacksonville NFL		16	0	2	1	0.0	0	0	0.0	0
2002—Jacksonville NFL		10	0	3	0	0.0	0	0	0.0	0
Pro totals (2 years)		26	0	5	1	0.0	0	0	0.0	0

BOYER, BRANT   LB   BROWNS

PERSONAL: Born June 27, 1971, in Ogden, Utah. ... 6-1/230. ... Full name: Brant T. Boyer.
HIGH SCHOOL: North Summit (Coalville, Utah).
JUNIOR COLLEGE: Snow College (Utah).
COLLEGE: Arizona.
TRANSACTIONS/CAREER NOTES: Selected by Miami Dolphins in sixth round (177th pick overall) of 1994 NFL draft. ... Signed by Dolphins (July 11, 1994). ... Released by Dolphins (September 21, 1994). ... Re-signed by Dolphins to practice squad (September 22, 1994). ... Activated (October 5, 1994). ... Selected by Jacksonville Jaguars from Dolphins in NFL expansion draft (February 15, 1995). ... Released by Jaguars (August 27, 1995). ... Re-signed by Jaguars (December 13, 1995). ... Released by Jaguars (August 25, 1996). ... Re-signed by Jaguars (September 24, 1996). ... Released by Jaguars (September 25, 1996). ... Re-signed by Jaguars (September 27, 1996). ... Granted free agency (February 13, 1998). ... Re-signed by Jaguars (March 18, 1998). ... On injured reserve with neck injury (December 2, 1998-remainder of season). ... Granted unconditional free agency (February 12, 1999). ... Re-signed by Jaguars (March 15, 1999). ... Released by Jaguars (March 1, 2001). ... Signed by Cleveland Browns (March 12, 2001).
CHAMPIONSHIP GAME EXPERIENCE: Played in AFC championship game (1996 and 1999 seasons).

Year Team	G	GS	TOTALS Tk.	Ast.	Sks.	INTERCEPTIONS No.	Yds.	Avg.	TD
1994—Miami NFL	14	0	1	1	0.0	0	0	0.0	0
1995—Jacksonville NFL	2	0	0	0	0.0	0	0	0.0	0
1996—Jacksonville NFL	12	0	4	1	0.0	0	0	0.0	0
1997—Jacksonville NFL	16	2	18	6	1.5	0	0	0.0	0
1998—Jacksonville NFL	11	0	10	2	1.0	0	0	0.0	0
1999—Jacksonville NFL	15	0	18	5	4.0	1	5	5.0	0
2000—Jacksonville NFL	12	5	19	4	3.5	1	12	12.0	0
2001—Cleveland NFL	16	1	50	15	0.0	2	12	6.0	0
2002—Cleveland NFL	16	1	34	7	3.0	1	1	1.0	0
Pro totals (9 years)	114	9	154	41	13.0	5	30	6.0	0

B

BRACKENS, TONY   DE   JAGUARS

PERSONAL: Born December 26, 1974, in Fairfield, Texas. ... 6-4/265. ... Full name: Tony Lynn Brackens Jr.
HIGH SCHOOL: Fairfield (Texas).
COLLEGE: Texas.
TRANSACTIONS/CAREER NOTES: Selected after junior season by Jacksonville Jaguars in second round (33rd pick overall) of 1996 NFL draft. ... Signed by Jaguars (May 28, 1996). ... Designated by Jaguars as franchise player (February 11, 2000). ... On injured reserve with knee injury (October 15, 2002-remainder of season).
CHAMPIONSHIP GAME EXPERIENCE: Played in AFC championship game (1996 and 1999 seasons).
HONORS: Named defensive lineman on THE SPORTING NEWS college All-America first team (1995). ... Played in Pro Bowl (1999 season).
MISCELLANEOUS: Holds Jacksonville Jaguars all-time record for most sacks (49).

Year Team	G	GS	TOTALS Tk.	Ast.	Sks.	INTERCEPTIONS No.	Yds.	Avg.	TD
1996—Jacksonville NFL	16	1	45	10	7.0	1	27	27.0	0
1997—Jacksonville NFL	15	3	41	3	7.0	0	0	0.0	0
1998—Jacksonville NFL	12	8	27	12	3.5	0	0	0.0	0
1999—Jacksonville NFL	16	15	55	13	12.0	2	16	8.0	1
2000—Jacksonville NFL	16	16	54	9	7.5	1	7	7.0	0
2001—Jacksonville NFL	12	12	39	3	11.0	0	0	0.0	0
2002—Jacksonville NFL	5	5	9	2	1.0	0	0	0.0	0
Pro totals (7 years)	92	60	270	52	49.0	4	50	12.5	1

BRADFORD, COREY   WR   TEXANS

PERSONAL: Born December 8, 1975, in Baton Rouge, La. ... 6-1/197. ... Full name: Corey Lamon Bradford.
HIGH SCHOOL: Clinton (La.).
JUNIOR COLLEGE: Hinds Community College (Miss.).
COLLEGE: Jackson State.
TRANSACTIONS/CAREER NOTES: Selected by Green Bay Packers in fifth round (150th pick overall) of 1998 NFL draft. ... Signed by Packers (July 17, 1998). ... Granted free agency (March 2, 2001). ... Re-signed by Packers (March 20, 2001). ... Granted unconditional free agency (March 1, 2002). ... Signed by Houston Texans (March 11, 2002).
SINGLE GAME HIGHS (regular season): Receptions—7 (September 29, 2002, vs. Philadelphia); yards—126 (October 13, 2002, vs. Buffalo); and touchdown receptions—2 (October 20, 2002, vs. Cleveland).
STATISTICAL PLATEAUS: 100-yard receiving games: 1999 (1), 2001 (2), 2002 (1). Total: 4.
MISCELLANEOUS: Holds Houston Texans all-time records for most touchdown receptions (6) and receiving yards (697).

Year Team	G	GS	RECEIVING No.	Yds.	Avg.	TD	TOTALS TD	2pt.	Pts.	Fum.
1998—Green Bay NFL	8	0	3	27	9.0	0	0	0	0	1
1999—Green Bay NFL	16	2	37	637	17.2	5	5	1	32	1
2000—Green Bay NFL	2	2	0	0	0.0	0	0	0	0	0
2001—Green Bay NFL	16	6	31	526	17.0	2	2	0	12	1
2002—Houston NFL	16	16	45	697	15.5	6	6	0	36	0
Pro totals (5 years)	58	26	116	1887	16.3	13	13	1	80	3

BRADFORD, RONNIE   CB

PERSONAL: Born October 1, 1970, in Minot, N.D. ... 5-10/198. ... Full name: Ronald L. Bradford.
HIGH SCHOOL: Adams City (Commerce City, Colo.).
COLLEGE: Colorado.
TRANSACTIONS/CAREER NOTES: Selected by Miami Dolphins in fourth round (105th pick overall) of 1993 NFL draft. ... Signed by Dolphins (July 14, 1993). ... Released by Dolphins (August 24, 1993). ... Signed by Denver Broncos to practice squad (September 1, 1993). ... Activated (October 12, 1993). ... On injured reserve with knee injury (September 28, 1995-remainder of season). ... Released by Broncos (August 25, 1996). ... Signed by Arizona Cardinals (August 27, 1996). ... Granted unconditional free agency (February 14, 1997). ... Signed by Atlanta Falcons (April 11, 1997). ... Granted unconditional free agency (February 12, 1999). ... Re-signed by Falcons (March 11, 1999). ... Released by Falcons (February 25, 2002). ... Signed by Minnesota Vikings (May 21, 2002). ... Granted unconditional free agency (February 28, 2003).
CHAMPIONSHIP GAME EXPERIENCE: Played in NFC championship game (1998 season). ... Played in Super Bowl XXXIII (1998 season).

Year Team	G	GS	TOTALS Tk.	Ast.	Sks.	INTERCEPTIONS No.	Yds.	Avg.	TD
1993—Denver NFL	10	3	10	3	0.0	1	0	0.0	0
1994—Denver NFL	12	0	20	2	1.0	0	0	0.0	0
1995—Denver NFL	4	0	2	0	0.0	0	0	0.0	0
1996—Arizona NFL	15	11	49	15	0.0	1	0	0.0	0
1997—Atlanta NFL	16	14	43	8	0.0	4	9	2.3	0

			TOTALS			INTERCEPTIONS			
Year Team	G	GS	Tk.	Ast.	Sks.	No.	Yds.	Avg.	TD
1998—Atlanta NFL	14	11	31	1	0.0	3	11	3.7	1
1999—Atlanta NFL	16	16	36	4	0.0	0	0	0.0	0
2000—Atlanta NFL	16	15	57	12	0.0	3	25	8.3	0
2001—Atlanta NFL	14	14	49	10	1.0	0	0	0.0	0
2002—Minnesota NFL	16	15	50	17	0.0	1	20	20.0	0
Pro totals (10 years)	133	99	347	72	2.0	13	65	5.0	1

BRADY, KYLE — TE — JAGUARS

PERSONAL: Born January 14, 1972, in New Cumberland, Pa. ... 6-6/278. ... Full name: Kyle James Brady.
HIGH SCHOOL: Cedar Cliff (Camp Hill, Pa.).
COLLEGE: Penn State.
TRANSACTIONS/CAREER NOTES: Selected by New York Jets in first round (ninth pick overall) of 1995 NFL draft. ... Signed by Jets (July 17, 1995). ... Designated by Jets as transition player (February 12, 1999). ... Tendered offer sheet by Jacksonville Jaguars (February 16, 1999). ... Jets declined to match offer (February 18, 1999).
CHAMPIONSHIP GAME EXPERIENCE: Played in AFC championship game (1998 and 1999 seasons).
HONORS: Named tight end on THE SPORTING NEWS college All-America second team (1994).
SINGLE GAME HIGHS (regular season): Receptions—10 (October 29, 2000, vs. Dallas); yards—138 (October 29, 2000, vs. Dallas); and touchdown receptions—2 (October 19, 1998, vs. New England).
STATISTICAL PLATEAUS: 100-yard receiving games: 2000 (2).

			RECEIVING				TOTALS			
Year Team	G	GS	No.	Yds.	Avg.	TD	TD	2pt.	Pts.	Fum.
1995—New York Jets NFL	15	11	26	252	9.7	2	2	0	12	0
1996—New York Jets NFL	16	16	15	144	9.6	1	1	1	8	1
1997—New York Jets NFL	16	14	22	238	10.8	2	2	0	12	1
1998—New York Jets NFL	16	16	30	315	10.5	5	5	0	30	1
1999—Jacksonville NFL	13	12	32	346	10.8	1	1	1	8	0
2000—Jacksonville NFL	16	15	64	729	11.4	3	3	1	20	0
2001—Jacksonville NFL	16	16	36	386	10.7	2	2	0	12	0
2002—Jacksonville NFL	16	16	43	461	10.7	4	4	0	24	0
Pro totals (8 years)	124	116	268	2871	10.7	20	20	3	126	3

BRADY, TOM — QB — PATRIOTS

PERSONAL: Born August 3, 1977, in San Mateo, Calif. ... 6-4/225. ... Full name: Thomas Brady.
HIGH SCHOOL: Serra (San Mateo, Calif.).
COLLEGE: Michigan.
TRANSACTIONS/CAREER NOTES: Selected by New England Patriots in sixth round (199th pick overall) of 2000 NFL draft. ... Signed by Patriots (July 14, 2000).
CHAMPIONSHIP GAME EXPERIENCE: Played in AFC championship game (2001 season). ... Member of Super Bowl championship team (2001 season).
HONORS: Named Most Valuable Player of Super Bowl XXXVI (2001 season). ... Played in Pro Bowl (2001 season).
SINGLE GAME HIGHS (regular season): Attempts—55 (November 10, 2002, vs. Chicago); completions—39 (September 22, 2002, vs. Kansas City); yards—410 (September 22, 2002, vs. Kansas City); and touchdown passes—4 (September 22, 2002, vs. Kansas City).
STATISTICAL PLATEAUS: 300-yard passing games: 2001 (1), 2002 (3). Total: 4.
MISCELLANEOUS: Selected by Montreal Expos organization in 18th round of free-agent draft (June 1, 1995); did not sign. ... Regular-season record as starting NFL quarterback: 20-10 (.667). ... Postseason record as starting NFL quarterback: 3-0.

			PASSING								RUSHING				TOTALS		
Year Team	G	GS	Att.	Cmp.	Pct.	Yds.	TD	Int.	Avg.	Skd.	Rat.	Att.	Yds.	Avg.	TD	TD	2pt.	Pts.
2000—New England NFL	1	0	3	1	33.3	6	0	0	2.00	0	42.4	0	0	0.0	0	0	0	0
2001—New England NFL	15	14	413	264	63.9	2843	18	12	6.88	41	86.5	36	43	1.2	0	0	0	0
2002—New England NFL	16	16	601	373	62.1	3764	*28	14	6.26	31	85.7	42	110	2.6	1	1	0	6
Pro totals (3 years)	32	30	1017	638	62.7	6613	46	26	6.50	72	85.9	78	153	2.0	1	1	0	6

BRAHAM, RICH — C — BENGALS

PERSONAL: Born November 6, 1970, in Morgantown, W.Va. ... 6-4/305. ... Name pronounced BRAY-um.
HIGH SCHOOL: University (Morgantown, W.Va.).
COLLEGE: West Virginia (degree in finance).
TRANSACTIONS/CAREER NOTES: Selected by Arizona Cardinals in third round (76th pick overall) of 1994 NFL draft. ... Signed by Cardinals (July 30, 1994). ... Claimed on waivers by Cincinnati Bengals (November 18, 1994). ... On injured reserve with ankle injury (August 29, 1995-entire season). ... Granted free agency (February 14, 1997). ... Tendered offer sheet by New England Patriots (April 8, 1997). ... Offer matched by Bengals (April 15, 1997). ... On injured reserve with knee injury (December 3, 1998-remainder of season). ... Granted unconditional free agency (March 2, 2001). ... Re-signed by Bengals (March 12, 2001). ... Granted free agency (February 28, 2003). ... Re-signed by Bengals (April 30, 2003).
PLAYING EXPERIENCE: Cincinnati NFL, 1994 and 1996-2002. ... Games/Games started: 1994 (3/0), 1996 (16/16), 1997 (16/16), 1998 (12/12), 1999 (16/16), 2000 (9/9), 2001 (16/16), 2002 (15/15). Total: 103/100.
HONORS: Named offensive lineman on THE SPORTING NEWS college All-America second team (1993).

BRANCH, BRUCE — CB — REDSKINS

PERSONAL: Born September 14, 1978, in Queens, N.Y. ... 5-11/189. ... Full name: Bruce Lamont Branch.
HIGH SCHOOL: Huguenot (Richmond, Va.).
COLLEGE: Penn State.

TRANSACTIONS/CAREER NOTES: Signed as non-drafted free agent by Jacksonville Jaguars (April 21, 2002). ... Released by Jaguars (September 1, 2002). ... Signed by Green Bay Packers to practice squad (October 15, 2002). ... Released by Packers (October 31, 2002). ... Signed by Tennessee Titans to practice squad (November 15, 2002). ... Released by Titans (November 22, 2002). ... Signed by Washington Redskins to practice squad (November 26, 2002). ... Activated (December 17, 2002). ... Assigned by Redskins to Barcelona Dragons in 2003 NFL Europe enhancement allocation program (February 4, 2003).

			TOTALS			INTERCEPTIONS				PUNT RETURNS				KICKOFF RETURNS				TOTALS			
Year Team	G	GS	Tk.	Ast.	Sks.	No.	Yds.	Avg.	TD	No.	Yds.	Avg.	TD	No.	Yds.	Avg.	TD	TD	2pt.	Pts.	Fum.
2002—Washington NFL........	1	0	0	0	0.0	0	0	0.0	0	2	3	1.5	0	2	29	14.5	0	0	0	0	0

BRANCH, DEION — WR — PATRIOTS

PERSONAL: Born July 18, 1979, in Albany, Ga. ... 5-9/193. ... Full name: Anthony Branch.
HIGH SCHOOL: Monroe (Ga.).
JUNIOR COLLEGE: Jones County Junior College (Miss.).
COLLEGE: Louisville.
TRANSACTIONS/CAREER NOTES: Selected by New England Patrios in second round (65th pick overall) of 2002 NFL draft.
HONORS: Named wide receiver on THE SPORTING NEWS college All-America third team (2001).
SINGLE GAME HIGHS (regular season): Receptions—13 (September 29, 2002, vs. San Diego); yards—128 (September 29, 2002, vs. San Diego); and touchdown receptions—1 (September 15, 2002, vs. New York Jets).
STATISTICAL PLATEAUS: 100-yard receiving games: 2002 (1).

			RECEIVING				PUNT RETURNS				KICKOFF RETURNS				TOTALS			
Year Team	G	GS	No.	Yds.	Avg.	TD	No.	Yds.	Avg.	TD	No.	Yds.	Avg.	TD	TD	2pt.	Pts.	Fum.
2002—New England NFL........	13	7	43	489	11.4	2	2	58	29.0	0	36	863	24.0	0	2	0	12	1

BRANDON, SAM — S — BRONCOS

PERSONAL: Born July 5, 1979, in Toledo, Ohio. ... 6-2/200.
HIGH SCHOOL: Riverside (Calif.).
COLLEGE: UNLV.
TRANSACTIONS/CAREER NOTES: Selected by Denver Broncos in fourth round (131st pick overall) of 2002 NFL draft. ... Signed by Broncos (July 19, 2002).

			TOTALS			INTERCEPTIONS			
Year Team	G	GS	Tk.	Ast.	Sks.	No.	Yds.	Avg.	TD
2002—Denver NFL	16	2	14	3	0.0	0	0	0.0	0

BRATZKE, CHAD — DE — COLTS

PERSONAL: Born September 15, 1971, in Waukegan, Ill. ... 6-5/270. ... Full name: Chad Allen Bratzke. ... Name pronounced BRAT-ski.
HIGH SCHOOL: Bloomingdale (Valrico, Fla.).
COLLEGE: Eastern Kentucky.
TRANSACTIONS/CAREER NOTES: Selected by New York Giants in fifth round (155th pick overall) of 1994 NFL draft. ... Signed by Giants (July 17, 1994). ... On injured reserve with knee injury (November 12, 1997-remainder of season). ... Granted unconditional free agency (February 12, 1999). ... Signed by Indianapolis Colts (March 1, 1999).

			TOTALS		
Year Team	G	GS	Tk.	Ast.	Sks.
1994—New York Giants NFL..........................	2	0	0	0	0.0
1995—New York Giants NFL..........................	6	0	2	3	0.0
1996—New York Giants NFL..........................	16	16	43	9	5.0
1997—New York Giants NFL..........................	10	10	23	12	3.5
1998—New York Giants NFL..........................	16	16	57	22	11.0
1999—Indianapolis NFL.................................	16	16	34	14	12.0
2000—Indianapolis NFL.................................	16	16	45	19	7.5
2001—Indianapolis NFL.................................	15	15	45	15	8.5
2002—Indianapolis NFL.................................	16	16	34	11	6.0
Pro totals (9 years).................................	113	105	283	105	53.5

BREES, DREW — QB — CHARGERS

PERSONAL: Born January 15, 1979, in Austin, Texas. ... 6-0/221. ... Full name: Drew Christopher Brees.
HIGH SCHOOL: Westlake (Austin, Texas).
COLLEGE: Purdue.
TRANSACTIONS/CAREER NOTES: Selected by San Diego Chargers in second round (32nd pick overall) of 2001 NFL draft. ... Signed by Chargers (August 7, 2001).
HONORS: Named quarterback to THE SPORTING NEWS college All-America third team (2000). ... Maxwell Award winner (2000).
SINGLE GAME HIGHS (regular season): Attempts—50 (November 17, 2002, vs. San Francisco); completions—29 (November 17, 2002, vs. San Francisco); yards—336 (November 17, 2002, vs. San Francisco); and touchdown passes—3 (December 29, 2002, vs. Seattle).
STATISTICAL PLATEAUS: 300-yard passing games: 2002 (3).
MISCELLANEOUS: Regular-season record as starting NFL quarterback: 8-8 (.500).

			PASSING									RUSHING				TOTALS		
Year Team	G	GS	Att.	Cmp.	Pct.	Yds.	TD	Int.	Avg.	Skd.	Rat.	Att.	Yds.	Avg.	TD	TD	2pt.	Pts.
2001—San Diego NFL	1	0	27	15	55.6	221	1	0	8.19	2	94.8	2	18	9.0	0	0	0	0
2002—San Diego NFL	16	16	526	320	60.8	3284	17	16	6.24	24	76.9	38	130	3.4	1	1	0	6
Pro totals (2 years)	17	16	553	335	60.6	3505	18	16	6.34	26	77.8	40	148	3.7	1	1	0	6

BREWER, JACK　　　　　S　　　　　VIKINGS

PERSONAL: Born January 8, 1979, in Grapevine, Texas. ... 6-0/194.
HIGH SCHOOL: Grapevine (Texas).
COLLEGE: Minnesota (degree in sports studies).
TRANSACTIONS/CAREER NOTES: Signed as non-drafted free agent by Minnesota Vikings (April 24, 2002).

			TOTALS			INTERCEPTIONS			
Year Team	G	GS	Tk.	Ast.	Sks.	No.	Yds.	Avg.	TD
2002—Minnesota NFL	15	1	8	2	0.0	2	24	12.0	0

BREWER, SEAN　　　　　TE　　　　　BENGALS

PERSONAL: Born October 5, 1977, in Riverside, Calif. ... 6-4/255.
HIGH SCHOOL: Polytechnic (Riverside, Calif.).
JUNIOR COLLEGE: Riverside.
COLLEGE: San Jose State.
TRANSACTIONS/CAREER NOTES: Selected by Cincinnati Bengals in third round (66th pick overall) of 2001 NFL draft. ... Signed by Bengals (July 18, 2001). ... On injured reserve with leg injury (September 1, 2001-entire season). ... On injured reserve with knee injury (November 5, 2002-remainder of season).

			RECEIVING			
Year Team	G	GS	No.	Yds.	Avg.	TD
2001—Cincinnati NFL				Did not play.		
2002—Cincinnati NFL	3	2	0	0	0.0	0
Pro totals (1 years)	3	2	0	0	0.0	0

BRIEN, DOUG　　　　　K　　　　　JETS

PERSONAL: Born November 24, 1970, in Bloomfield, N.J. ... 6-0/180. ... Full name: Douglas Robert Zachariah Brien.
HIGH SCHOOL: De La Salle Catholic (Concord, Calif.).
COLLEGE: California (degree in political economies).
TRANSACTIONS/CAREER NOTES: Selected by San Francisco 49ers in third round (85th pick overall) of 1994 NFL draft. ... Signed by 49ers (July 27, 1994). ... Released by 49ers (October 16, 1995). ... Signed by New Orleans Saints (October 31, 1995). ... Granted free agency (February 14, 1997). ... Re-signed by Saints (July 17, 1997). ... Released by Saints (March 1, 2001). ... Signed by Indianapolis Colts (December 5, 2001). ... Released by Colts (December 15, 2001). ... Signed by Tampa Bay Buccaneers (December 27, 2001). ... Granted unconditional free agency (March 1, 2002). ... Signed by Minnesota Vikings (April 29, 2002). ... On physically unable to perform list with knee injury (July 27-August 2, 2002). ... Released by Vikings (October 23, 2002). ... Signed by New York Jets (March 21, 2003).
CHAMPIONSHIP GAME EXPERIENCE: Played in NFC championship game (1994 season). ... Member of Super Bowl championship team (1994 season).
POST SEASON RECORDS: Shares Super Bowl single-game record for most extra points—7 (January 29, 1995, vs. San Diego).

		FIELD GOALS								TOTALS		
Year Team	G	1-29	30-39	40-49	50+	Tot.	Pct.	Lg.		XPM	XPA	Pts.
1994—San Francisco NFL	16	5-5	5-6	5-8	0-1	15-20	75.0	48		*60	*62	105
1995—San Francisco NFL	6	4-4	0-1	2-6	1-1	7-12	58.3	51		19	19	40
—New Orleans NFL	8	4-4	4-6	4-6	0-1	12-17	70.6	47		16	16	52
1996—New Orleans NFL	16	4-4	9-10	5-7	3-4	21-25	84.0	‡54		18	18	81
1997—New Orleans NFL	16	3-3	10-10	6-9	4-5	23-27	85.2	53		22	22	91
1998—New Orleans NFL	16	7-7	3-3	6-6	4-6	20-22	90.9	56		31	31	91
1999—New Orleans NFL	16	9-11	6-7	7-9	2-2	24-29	82.8	52		20	21	92
2000—New Orleans NFL	16	7-7	4-5	12-15	0-2	23-29	79.3	48		37	37	106
2001—Indianapolis NFL	1	0-0	0-0	0-0	0-0	0-0	0.0	0		0	0	0
—Tampa Bay NFL	2	2-2	1-1	2-3	0-0	5-6	83.3	42		2	2	17
2002—Minnesota NFL	6	3-3	1-1	1-2	0-0	5-6	83.3	42		5	7	20
Pro totals (9 years)	119	48-50	43-50	50-71	14-22	155-193	80.3	56		230	235	695

BRIGANCE, O.J.　　　　　LB

PERSONAL: Born September 29, 1969, in Houston. ... 6-0/236. ... Full name: Orenthial James Brigance.
HIGH SCHOOL: Willowridge (Sugar Land, Texas).
COLLEGE: Rice (degree in managerial studies).
TRANSACTIONS/CAREER NOTES: Signed by B.C. Lions of CFL (May 1991). ... Granted free agency (February 1994). ... Signed by Baltimore Stallions of CFL (April 1994). ... Granted free agency (February 16, 1996). ... Signed as non-drafted free agent by Miami Dolphins (May 17, 1996). ... Granted free agency (February 12, 1999). ... Re-signed by Dolphins (May 20, 1999). ... On physically unable to perform list with back injury (July 30-August 25, 1999). ... Granted unconditional free agency (February 11, 2000). ... Signed by Baltimore Ravens (June 15, 2000). ... Granted unconditional free agency (March 2, 2001). ... Signed by St. Louis Rams (June 1, 2001). ... Released by Rams (August 20, 2001). ... Re-signed by St. Louis Rams (November 12, 2001). ... Granted unconditional free agency (March 1, 2002). ... Signed by New England Patriots (August 12, 2002). ... Released by Patriots (August 27, 2002). ... Re-signed by Patriots (September 11, 2002). ... Released by Patriots (September 17, 2002). ... Signed by Rams (September 25, 2002). ... Granted unconditional free agency (February 28, 2003).
CHAMPIONSHIP GAME EXPERIENCE: Played in AFC championship game (2000 season). ... Member of Super Bowl championship team (2000 season). ... Played in NFC championship game (2001 season). ... Played in Super Bowl XXXVI (2001 season).

Year—Team	G	GS	TOTALS Tk.	Ast.	Sks.	INTERCEPTIONS No.	Yds.	Avg.	TD
1991—British Columbia CFL	18	...	92	...	2.0	1	7	7.0	0
1992—British Columbia CFL	18	...	87	...	0.0	0	0	0.0	0
1993—British Columbia CFL	18	...	46	...	20.0	0	0	0.0	0
1994—Baltimore CFL	18	...	38	...	6.0	0	0	0.0	0
1995—Baltimore CFL	18	...	59	...	7.0	1	13	13.0	0
1996—Miami NFL	12	0	1	0	0.0	0	0	0.0	0
1997—Miami NFL	16	0	0	0	0.0	0	0	0.0	0
1998—Miami NFL	16	0	0	0	0.0	0	0	0.0	0
1999—Miami NFL	16	0	0	0	0.0	0	0	0.0	0
2000—Baltimore NFL	16	0	0	1	0.0	0	0	0.0	0
2001—St. Louis NFL	8	0	1	2	0.0	0	0	0.0	0
2002—St. Louis NFL	13	0	1	0	0.0	0	0	0.0	0
—New England NFL	1	0	0	0	0.0	0	0	0.0	0
CFL totals (5 years)	90	...	322	...	35.0	2	20	10.0	0
NFL totals (7 years)	98	0	3	3	0.0	0	0	0.0	0
Pro totals (12 years)	188	...	325	...	35.0	2	20	10.0	0

BRIGHAM, JEREMY TE

PERSONAL: Born March 22, 1975, in Boston. ... 6-6/250.
HIGH SCHOOL: Saguaro (Scottsdale, Ariz.).
COLLEGE: Washington.
TRANSACTIONS/CAREER NOTES: Selected by Oakland Raiders in fifth round (127th pick overall) of 1998 NFL draft. ... Signed by Raiders (July 18, 1998). ... On injured reserve with knee injury (September 1-27, 2002). ... Released by Raiders (September 27, 2002). ... Re-signed by Raiders (January 21, 2003). ... Granted unconditional free agency (February 28, 2003).
CHAMPIONSHIP GAME EXPERIENCE: Played in AFC championship game (2000). ... Played in Super Bowl XXXVII (2002 season).
SINGLE GAME HIGHS (regular season): Receptions—3 (December 30, 2001, vs. Denver); yards—39 (September 19, 1999, vs. Minnesota); and touchdown receptions—2 (December 24, 2000, vs. Carolina).

Year—Team	G	GS	RECEIVING No.	Yds.	Avg.	TD
1998—Oakland NFL	2	0	0	0	0.0	0
1999—Oakland NFL	16	2	8	108	13.5	0
2000—Oakland NFL	15	3	13	107	8.2	2
2001—Oakland NFL	14	3	12	85	7.1	1
2002—Oakland NFL			Did not play.			
Pro totals (3 years)	47	8	33	300	9.1	3

BRIGHT, ANTHONY WR PANTHERS

PERSONAL: Born March 28, 1977, in Starke, Fla. ... 6-1/170.
HIGH SCHOOL: Bradford (Starke, Fla.).
JUNIOR COLLEGE: Valencia Community College (Fla.).
TRANSACTIONS/CAREER NOTES: Signed as non-drafted free agent by Carolina Panthers (July 31, 2001). ... Released by Panthers (August 15, 2001). ... Re-signed by Panthers to practice squad (November 20, 2001). ... Released by Panthers (October 11, 2002). ... Re-signed by Panthers to practice squad (October 16, 2002).

Year—Team	G	GS	RECEIVING No.	Yds.	Avg.	TD
2002—Carolina NFL	1	0	0	0	0.0	0

BRIGHTFUL, LAMONT DB RAVENS

PERSONAL: Born January 29, 1979, in Oak Harbor, Wash. ... 5-10/170. ... Full name: Lamont Eugene Brightful.
HIGH SCHOOL: Mariner (Everett, Wash.).
COLLEGE: Eastern Washington.
TRANSACTIONS/CAREER NOTES: Selected by Baltimore Ravens in sixth round (195th pick overall) of 2002 NFL draft. ... Signed by Ravens (July 25, 2002).

Year—Team	G	GS	TOTALS Tk.	Ast.	Sks.	INTERCEPTIONS No.	Yds.	Avg.	TD	PUNT RETURNS No.	Yds.	Avg.	TD	KICKOFF RETURNS No.	Yds.	Avg.	TD	TOTALS TD	2pt.	Pts.	Fum.
2002—Baltimore NFL	12	0	0	0	0.0	0	0	0.0	0	15	241	16.1	1	34	701	20.6	0	1	0	6	3

BROCK, RAHEEM DE

PERSONAL: Born June 10, 1978, in Philadelphia. ... 6-4/257.
HIGH SCHOOL: Dobbins (Germantown, Md.).
COLLEGE: Temple.
TRANSACTIONS/CAREER NOTES: Selected by Philadelphia Eagles in seventh round (238th pick overall) of 2002 NFL draft. ... Signed by Eagles (July 25, 2002). ... Released by Eagles (July 25, 2002).

Year—Team	G	GS	TOTALS Tk.	Ast.	Sks.	INTERCEPTIONS No.	Yds.	Avg.	TD
2002—Indianapolis NFL	13	6	12	7	1.0	0	0	0.0	0

BROCKERMEYER, BLAKE   OT

PERSONAL: Born April 11, 1973, in Fort Worth, Texas. ... 6-4/295. ... Full name: Blake Weeks Brockermeyer.
HIGH SCHOOL: Arlington Heights (Texas).
COLLEGE: Texas.
TRANSACTIONS/CAREER NOTES: Selected after junior season by Carolina Panthers in first round (29th pick overall) of 1995 NFL draft. ... Signed by Panthers (July 14, 1995). ... Granted unconditional free agency (February 12, 1999). ... Signed by Chicago Bears (February 27, 1999). ... Released by Bears (April 5, 2002). ... Signed by Denver Broncos (June 24, 2002). ... Released by Broncos (February 25, 2003).
PLAYING EXPERIENCE: Carolina NFL, 1995-1998; Chicago NFL, 1999-2001; Denver NFL, 2002. ... Games/Games started: 1995 (16/16), 1996 (12/12), 1997 (16/13), 1998 (14/14), 1999 (15/15), 2000 (15/14), 2001 (16/16), 2002 (16/1). Total: 120/101.
CHAMPIONSHIP GAME EXPERIENCE: Played in NFC championship game (1996 season).
HONORS: Named offensive lineman on THE SPORTING NEWS college All-America first team (1994).

BROMELL, LORENZO   DE   VIKINGS

B

PERSONAL: Born September 23, 1975, in Georgetown, S.C. ... 6-6/268. ... Full name: Lorenzo Alexis Bromell.
HIGH SCHOOL: Choppee (Georgetown, S.C.).
JUNIOR COLLEGE: Georgia Military College.
COLLEGE: Clemson.
TRANSACTIONS/CAREER NOTES: Selected by Miami Dolphins in fourth round (102nd pick overall) of 1998 draft. ... Signed by Dolphins (July 10, 1998). ... Granted free agency (March 2, 2001). ... Re-signed by Dolphins (April 19, 2001). ... Granted unconditional free agency (March 1, 2002). ... Signed by Minnesota Vikings (April 12, 2002).

			TOTALS		
Year Team	G	GS	Tk.	Ast.	Sks.
1998—Miami NFL	14	0	16	7	8.0
1999—Miami NFL	15	1	10	7	5.0
2000—Miami NFL	8	0	11	1	2.0
2001—Miami NFL	16	1	20	12	6.5
2002—Minnesota NFL	16	2	22	7	4.0
Pro totals (5 years)	69	4	79	34	25.5

BRONSON, ZACK   S   49ERS

PERSONAL: Born January 28, 1974, in Jasper, Texas. ... 6-1/204. ... Full name: Robert Zack Bronson.
HIGH SCHOOL: Jasper (Texas).
COLLEGE: McNeese State.
TRANSACTIONS/CAREER NOTES: Signed as non-drafted free agent by San Francisco 49ers (May 2, 1997). ... On injured reserve with foot injury (December 29, 1999-remainder of season). ... Granted free agency (February 11, 2000). ... Re-signed by 49ers (June 15, 2000). ... Granted unconditional free agency (March 2, 2001). ... Re-signed by 49ers (May 15, 2001).
CHAMPIONSHIP GAME EXPERIENCE: Played in NFC championship game (1997 season).

			TOTALS			INTERCEPTIONS			
Year Team	G	GS	Tk.	Ast.	Sks.	No.	Yds.	Avg.	TD
1997—San Francisco NFL	16	0	18	6	0.0	1	22	22.0	0
1998—San Francisco NFL	11	0	17	0	0.0	4	34	8.5	0
1999—San Francisco NFL	15	2	17	6	0.0	0	0	0.0	0
2000—San Francisco NFL	9	7	31	7	0.0	3	75	25.0	0
2001—San Francisco NFL	16	16	57	6	0.0	7	‡165	23.6	†2
2002—San Francisco NFL	5	5	16	5	0.0	3	28	9.3	0
Pro totals (6 years)	72	30	156	30	0.0	18	324	18.0	2

BROOKING, KEITH   LB   FALCONS

PERSONAL: Born October 30, 1975, in Senoia, Ga. ... 6-2/245. ... Full name: Keith Howard Brooking.
HIGH SCHOOL: East Coweta (Sharpsburg, Ga.).
COLLEGE: Georgia Tech.
TRANSACTIONS/CAREER NOTES: Selected by Atlanta Falcons in first round (12th pick overall) of 1998 NFL draft. ... Signed by Falcons (June 29, 1998). ... On injured reserve with foot injury (November 1, 2000-remainder of season).
CHAMPIONSHIP GAME EXPERIENCE: Played in NFC championship game (1998 season). ... Played in Super Bowl XXXIII (1998 season).
HONORS: Played in Pro Bowl (2001). ... Named to play in Pro Bowl (2002 season); replaced by Shelton Quarles due to injury.

			TOTALS			INTERCEPTIONS			
Year Team	G	GS	Tk.	Ast.	Sks.	No.	Yds.	Avg.	TD
1998—Atlanta NFL	15	0	21	5	0.0	1	12	12.0	0
1999—Atlanta NFL	13	13	73	21	2.0	0	0	0.0	0
2000—Atlanta NFL	5	5	28	8	1.0	0	0	0.0	0
2001—Atlanta NFL	16	16	102	25	3.5	2	17	8.5	0
2002—Atlanta NFL	16	16	111	29	0.0	2	24	12.0	0
Pro totals (5 years)	65	50	335	88	6.5	5	53	10.6	0

BROOKS, AARON   QB   SAINTS

PERSONAL: Born March 24, 1976, in Newport News, Va. ... 6-4/205. ... Full name: Aaron Lafette Brooks.
HIGH SCHOOL: Homer L. Ferguson (Newport News, Va.).
COLLEGE: Virginia (degree in anthropology).

TRANSACTIONS/CAREER NOTES: Selected by Green Bay Packers in fourth round (131st pick overall) of 1999 NFL draft. ... Signed by Packers (July 27, 1999). ... Traded by Packers with TE Lamont Hall to New Orleans Saints for LB K.D. Williams and third-round pick (traded to San Francisco) in 2001 draft (July 31, 2000).
SINGLE GAME HIGHS (regular season): Attempts—54 (September 30, 2001, vs. New York Giants); completions—30 (December 3, 2000, vs. Denver); yards—441 (December 3, 2000, vs. Denver); and touchdown passes—3 (October 20, 2002, vs. San Francisco).
STATISTICAL PLATEAUS: 300-yard passing games: 2000 (1), 2001 (3), 2002 (1). Total: 5. ... 100-yard rushing games: 2000 (1).
MISCELLANEOUS: Regular-season record as starting NFL quarterback: 19-18 (.514). ... Postseason record as starting NFL quarterback: 1-1 (.500).

Year Team	G	GS	PASSING Att.	Cmp.	Pct.	Yds.	TD	Int.	Avg.	Skd.	Rat.	RUSHING Att.	Yds.	Avg.	TD	TOTALS TD	2pt.	Pts.
1999—Green Bay NFL								Did not play.										
2000—New Orleans NFL	8	5	194	113	58.2	1514	9	6	7.80	15	85.7	41	170	4.1	2	2	0	12
2001—New Orleans NFL	16	16	558	312	55.9	3832	26	∞22	6.87	‡50	76.4	80	358	4.5	1	1	0	6
2002—New Orleans NFL	16	16	528	283	53.6	3572	∞27	15	6.77	36	80.1	62	253	4.1	2	2	∞2	16
Pro totals (3 years)	40	37	1280	708	55.3	8918	62	43	6.97	101	79.4	183	781	4.3	5	5	2	34

BROOKS, AHMAD　　　CB　　　BILLS

PERSONAL: Born March 13, 1980, in Abilene, Texas. ... 5-8/180. ... Full name: Ahmad Drushane Brooks.
HIGH SCHOOL: Abilene (Texas).
COLLEGE: Texas.
TRANSACTIONS/CAREER NOTES: Signed as non-drafted free agent by Buffalo Bills (April 23, 2002). ... Released by Bills (September 1, 2002). ... Re-signed by Bills to practice squad (September 2, 2002). ... Activated (October 18, 2002).

Year Team	G	GS	TOTALS Tk.	Ast.	Sks.	INTERCEPTIONS No.	Yds.	Avg.	TD
2002—Buffalo NFL	6	2	7	2	0.0	1	13	13.0	0

BROOKS, BARRETT　　　OT　　　GIANTS

PERSONAL: Born May 5, 1972, in St. Louis. ... 6-5/314.
HIGH SCHOOL: McCluer North (Florissant, Mo.).
COLLEGE: Kansas State.
TRANSACTIONS/CAREER NOTES: Selected by Philadelphia Eagles in second round (58th pick overall) of 1995 NFL draft. ... Signed by Eagles (July 19, 1995). ... Granted free agency (February 13, 1998). ... Re-signed by Eagles (April 21, 1998). ... Granted unconditional free agency (February 12, 1999). ... Signed by Detroit Lions (April 12, 1999). ... Granted unconditional free agency (March 2, 2001). ... Signed by Cleveland Browns (July 29, 2001). ... Released by Browns (September 1, 2001). ... Signed by Denver Broncos (September 1, 2002). ... Released by Broncos (September 1, 2002). ... Signed by Green Bay Packers (September 26, 2002). ... Released by Packers (October 12, 2002). ... Re-signed by Packers (October 15, 2002). ... Released by Packers (December 9, 2002). ... Signed by Giants (December 17, 2002). ... Granted unconditional free agency (February 28, 2003). ... Re-signed by Giants (March 4, 2003).
PLAYING EXPERIENCE: Philadelphia NFL, 1995-1998; Detroit NFL, 1999-2000; Green Bay NFL, 2002. ... Games/Games started: 1995 (16/16), 1996 (16/15), 1997 (16/14), 1998 (16/1), 1999 (16/12), 2000 (15/4), 2002 (2/0). Total: 97/62.

BROOKS, BOBBY　　　LB　　　JAGUARS

PERSONAL: Born March 3, 1976, in Vallejo, Calif. ... 6-2/240.
HIGH SCHOOL: Hogan (Vallejo, Calif.).
COLLEGE: Fresno State.
TRANSACTIONS/CAREER NOTES: Signed as non-drafted free agent by Oakland Raiders (April 1999). ... Released by Raiders (September 5, 1999). ... Re-signed by Raiders to practice squad (October 20, 1999). ... Activated (December 1999). ... Released by Raiders (September 1, 2002). ... Signed by Jacksonville Jaguars (September 10, 2002). ... Granted free agency (February 28, 2003). ... Re-signed by Jaguars (March 25, 2003).
CHAMPIONSHIP GAME EXPERIENCE: Played in AFC championship game (2000 season).

Year Team	G	GS	TOTALS Tk.	Ast.	Sks.	INTERCEPTIONS No.	Yds.	Avg.	TD
1999—Oakland NFL	1	0	0	0	0.0	0	0	0.0	0
2000—Oakland NFL	16	0	6	1	0.0	0	0	0.0	0
2001—Oakland NFL	16	0	0	0	0.0	0	0	0.0	0
2002—Jacksonville NFL	3	0	0	0	0.0	0	0	0.0	0
Pro totals (4 years)	36	0	6	1	0.0	0	0	0.0	0

BROOKS, DERRICK　　　LB　　　BUCCANEERS

PERSONAL: Born April 18, 1973, in Pensacola, Fla. ... 6-0/235. ... Full name: Derrick Dewan Brooks.
HIGH SCHOOL: Booker T. Washington (Pensacola, Fla.).
COLLEGE: Florida State (degree in communications, 1994).
TRANSACTIONS/CAREER NOTES: Selected by Tampa Bay Buccaneers in first round (28th pick overall) of 1995 NFL draft. ... Signed by Buccaneers (May 3, 1995).
CHAMPIONSHIP GAME EXPERIENCE: Played in NFC championship game (1999 and 2002 seasons). ... Member of Super Bowl championship team (2002 season).
HONORS: Named linebacker on THE SPORTING NEWS college All-America first team (1993 and 1994). ... Played in Pro Bowl (1997-2000 and 2002 seasons). ... Named linebacker on THE SPORTING NEWS NFL All-Pro team (1999, 2000 and 2002). ... Named to play in Pro Bowl (2001 season); replaced by Dexter Coakley due to injury.

Year Team	G	GS	TOTALS Tk.	Ast.	Sks.	INTERCEPTIONS No.	Yds.	Avg.	TD
1995—Tampa Bay NFL	16	13	60	19	1.0	0	0	0.0	0
1996—Tampa Bay NFL	16	16	92	41	0.0	1	6	6.0	0
1997—Tampa Bay NFL	16	16	102	43	1.5	2	13	6.5	0
1998—Tampa Bay NFL	16	16	123	35	0.0	1	25	25.0	0
1999—Tampa Bay NFL	16	16	118	36	2.0	4	61	15.3	0
2000—Tampa Bay NFL	16	16	123	23	1.0	1	34	34.0	1
2001—Tampa Bay NFL	16	16	80	33	0.0	3	65	21.7	0
2002—Tampa Bay NFL	16	16	88	30	1.0	5	218	43.6	*3
Pro totals (8 years)	128	125	786	260	6.5	17	422	24.8	4

BROOKS, ETHAN　　OT　　RAVENS

PERSONAL: Born April 27, 1972, in Hartford, Conn. ... 6-6/297.
HIGH SCHOOL: Westminster (Simsbury, Conn.).
COLLEGE: Williams, Conn. (degree in psychology, 1995).
TRANSACTIONS/CAREER NOTES: Selected by Atlanta Falcons in seventh round (229th pick overall) of 1996 NFL draft. ... Signed by Falcons (June 7, 1996). ... Assigned by Falcons to Frankfurt Galaxy in 1997 World League enhancement allocation program (February 19, 1997). ... Released by Falcons (August 27, 1997). ... Signed by St. Louis Rams (November 20, 1997). ... Inactive for five games (1997). ... Released by Rams (July 19, 1999). ... Signed by Arizona Cardinals (February 3, 2000). ... Granted unconditional free agency (March 2, 2001). ... Signed by Denver Broncos (March 15, 2001). ... Released by Broncos (August 28, 2001). ... Signed by Baltimore Ravens (August 2, 2002). ... Granted unconditional free agency (February 28, 2003). ... Re-signed by Ravens (March 13, 2003).
PLAYING EXPERIENCE: Atlanta NFL, 1996; Frankfurt W.L., 1997; St. Louis NFL, 1998; Arizona NFL, 2000. Baltimore 2002. ... Games/Games started: 1996 (2/0), 1997 (games played unavailable), 1998 (15/0), 2000 (14/3), 2002 (15/13). Total NFL: 46/16.

BROOKS, JAMAL　　LB　　COWBOYS

PERSONAL: Born November 9, 1976, in Los Angeles. ... 6-2/240.
HIGH SCHOOL: Grenada Hills (Calif.).
JUNIOR COLLEGE: Pasadena City College.
COLLEGE: Hampton.
TRANSACTIONS/CAREER NOTES: Signed as non-drafted free agent by New Orleans Saints (April 27, 2000). ... Released by Saints (August 22, 2000). ... Selected by Scottish Claymores in 2001 NFL Europe draft (February 18, 2001). ... Signed by Dallas Cowboys (July 10, 2001). ... On injured reserve with ankle injury (September 1, 2002-entire season).

Year Team	G	GS	TOTALS Tk.	Ast.	Sks.	INTERCEPTIONS No.	Yds.	Avg.	TD
2001—Scottish NFLE	...	...	...	...	1.5	1	0	0.0	0
—Dallas NFL	16	1	11	4	0.0	0	0	0.0	0
2002—Dallas NFL				Did not play.					
NFL Europe totals (1 year)	...	...	...	...	1.5	1	0	0.0	0
NFL totals (1 year)	16	1	11	4	0.0	0	0	0.0	0
Pro totals (2 years)	...	...	...	...	1.5	1	0	0.0	0

BROWN, ALEX　　DE　　BEARS

PERSONAL: Born June 4, 1979, in Jasper, Fla. ... 6-3/268. ... Full name: Alex James Brown.
HIGH SCHOOL: Hamilton County (White Springs, Fla.).
COLLEGE: Florida.
TRANSACTIONS/CAREER NOTES: Selected by Chicago Bears in fourth round (104th pick overall) of 2002 NFL draft. ... Signed by Bears (July 24, 2002).
HONORS: Named defensive end on THE SPORTING NEWS college All-America first team (1999). ... Named defensive end on THE SPORTING NEWS college All-America second team (2001).

Year Team	G	GS	TOTALS Tk.	Ast.	Sks.	INTERCEPTIONS No.	Yds.	Avg.	TD
2002—Chicago NFL	15	9	31	9	2.5	0	0	0.0	0

BROWN, CHAD　　LB　　SEAHAWKS

PERSONAL: Born July 12, 1970, in Altadena, Calif. ... 6-2/245. ... Full name: Chadwick Everett Brown.
HIGH SCHOOL: John Muir (Pasadena, Calif.).
COLLEGE: Colorado (degree in marketing, 1992).
TRANSACTIONS/CAREER NOTES: Selected by Pittsburgh Steelers in second round (44th pick overall) of 1993 NFL draft. ... Signed by Steelers (July 26, 1993). ... Granted unconditional free agency (February 14, 1997). ... Signed by Seattle Seahawks (February 15, 1997). ... On injured reserve with broken foot (November 12, 2002-remainder of season).
CHAMPIONSHIP GAME EXPERIENCE: Played in AFC championship game (1994 and 1995 seasons). ... Played in Super Bowl XXX (1995 season).
HONORS: Named linebacker on THE SPORTING NEWS NFL All-Pro team (1996 and 1998). ... Played in Pro Bowl (1996, 1998 and 1999 seasons).

Year Team	G	GS	TOTALS Tk.	Ast.	Sks.	INTERCEPTIONS No.	Yds.	Avg.	TD
1993—Pittsburgh NFL	16	9	43	26	3.0	0	0	0.0	0
1994—Pittsburgh NFL	16	16	90	29	8.5	1	9	9.0	0
1995—Pittsburgh NFL	10	10	20	10	5.5	0	0	0.0	0
1996—Pittsburgh NFL	14	14	50	31	13.0	2	20	10.0	0
1997—Seattle NFL	15	15	75	29	6.5	0	0	0.0	0
1998—Seattle NFL	16	16	117	32	7.5	1	11	11.0	0
1999—Seattle NFL	15	15	87	30	5.5	0	0	0.0	0
2000—Seattle NFL	16	16	71	23	6.0	1	0	0.0	0
2001—Seattle NFL	16	16	80	26	8.5	0	0	0.0	0
2002—Seattle NFL	8	8	42	8	6.0	0	0	0.0	0
Pro totals (10 years)	142	135	675	244	70.0	5	40	8.0	0

BROWN, CORNELL   LB   RAVENS

PERSONAL: Born March 15, 1975, in Englewood, N.J. ... 6-0/245. ... Full name: Cornell Desmond Brown. ... Brother of Ruben Brown, guard, Buffalo Bills.

HIGH SCHOOL: E.C. Glass (Lynchburg, Va.).

COLLEGE: Virginia Tech.

TRANSACTIONS/CAREER NOTES: Selected by Baltimore Ravens in sixth round (194th pick overall) of 1997 NFL draft. ... Signed by Ravens (July 10, 1997). ... Granted free agency (February 11, 2000). ... Re-signed by Ravens (April 25, 2000) ... Signed by Ravens (March 2, 2001). ... Re-signed by Ravens (May 23, 2001). ... Released by Ravens (September 5, 2001). ... Re-signed by Ravens (August 20, 2002). ... Granted unconditional free agency (February 28, 2003). ... Re-signed by Ravens (March 18, 2003).

CHAMPIONSHIP GAME EXPERIENCE: Member of Ravens for AFC Championship game (2000 season); inactive. ... Member of Super Bowl championship team (2000 season).

HONORS: Named defensive lineman on The Sporting News college All-America first team (1995).

Year Team	G	GS	TOTALS Tk.	Ast.	Sks.	INTERCEPTIONS No.	Yds.	Avg.	TD
1997—Baltimore NFL	16	1	11	0	0.5	1	21	21.0	0
1998—Baltimore NFL	16	1	3	2	0.0	0	0	0.0	0
1999—Baltimore NFL	16	5	21	7	1.0	0	0	0.0	0
2000—Baltimore NFL	16	1	13	6	3.0	0	0	0.0	0
2002—Baltimore NFL	16	14	36	23	1.5	0	0	0.0	0
Pro totals (5 years)	80	22	84	38	6.0	1	21	21.0	0

BROWN, COURTNEY   DE   BROWNS

PERSONAL: Born February 14, 1978, in Charleston, S.C. ... 6-4/280. ... Full name: Courtney Lanair Brown.

HIGH SCHOOL: Macedonia (Alvin, S.C.).

COLLEGE: Penn State (degree in integrative arts, 1999).

TRANSACTIONS/CAREER NOTES: Selected by Cleveland Browns in first round (first pick overall) of 2000 NFL draft. ... Signed by Browns (May 10, 2000). ... On injured reserve with ankle injury (January 2, 2002-remainder of season). ... On injured reserve with knee injury (December 18, 2002-remainder of season).

HONORS: Named defensive end on The Sporting News college All-America first team (1999).

Year Team	G	GS	TOTALS Tk.	Ast.	Sks.
2000—Cleveland NFL	16	16	61	8	4.5
2001—Cleveland NFL	5	5	14	7	4.5
2002—Cleveland NFL	11	11	30	12	2.0
Pro totals (3 years)	32	32	105	27	11.0

BROWN, DEE   RB   PANTHERS

PERSONAL: Born May 12, 1978, in Clearwater, Fla. ... 5-10/209. ... Full name: Dadrian L. Brown.

HIGH SCHOOL: Lake Brantley (Fla.).

COLLEGE: Syracuse (degree in psychology).

TRANSACTIONS/CAREER NOTES: Selected by Carolina Panthers in sixth round (175th pick overall) of 2001 NFL draft. ... Signed by Carolina (July 18, 2001). ... On injured reserve with ankle injury (September 1, 2001-entire season).

SINGLE GAME HIGHS (regular season): Attempts—27 (December 1, 2002, vs. Cleveland); yards—122 (December 1, 2002, vs. Cleveland); and rushing touchdowns—2 (December 22, 2002, vs. Chicago).

STATISTICAL PLATEAUS: 100-yard rushing games: 2002 (1).

Year Team	G	GS	RUSHING Att.	Yds.	Avg.	TD	RECEIVING No.	Yds.	Avg.	TD	KICKOFF RETURNS No.	Yds.	Avg.	TD	TOTALS TD	2pt.	Pts.	Fum.
2002—Carolina NFL	14	3	102	360	3.5	4	17	86	5.1	1	13	253	19.5	0	5	0	30	4

BROWN, ERIC   S   TEXANS

PERSONAL: Born March 20, 1975, in San Antonio. ... 6-1/210. ... Full name: Eric Jon Brown.

HIGH SCHOOL: Judson (Converse, Texas).

JUNIOR COLLEGE: Blinn College (Texas).

COLLEGE: Mississippi State.

TRANSACTIONS/CAREER NOTES: Selected by Denver Broncos in second round (61st pick overall) of 1998 NFL draft. ... Signed by Broncos (July 16, 1998). ... On injured reserve with knee injury (November 18, 1999-remainder of season). ... Granted unconditional free agency (March 1, 2002). ... Signed by Houston Texans (August 5, 2002). ... Granted unconditional free agency (February 28, 2003). ... Re-signed by Texans (March 17, 2003).

CHAMPIONSHIP GAME EXPERIENCE: Member of Broncos for AFC championship game (1998 season); inactive. ... Member of Super Bowl championship team (1998 season); inactive.

Year Team	G	GS	TOTALS Tk.	Ast.	Sks.	INTERCEPTIONS No.	Yds.	Avg.	TD
1998—Denver NFL	11	10	24	7	0.0	0	0	0.0	0
1999—Denver NFL	10	10	59	15	1.5	1	13	13.0	0
2000—Denver NFL	16	16	77	14	1.0	3	9	3.0	0
2001—Denver NFL	16	16	64	13	3.0	2	0	0.0	0
2002—Houston NFL	15	15	58	9	0.5	2	7	3.5	0
Pro totals (5 years)	68	67	282	58	6.0	8	29	3.6	0

BROWN, FAKHIR — CB — SAINTS

PERSONAL: Born September 21, 1977, in Detroit. ... 5-11/192. ... Full name: Fakhir Hamin Brown. ... Name pronounced fah-KEAR.
HIGH SCHOOL: Mansfield (La.).
COLLEGE: Grambling State.
TRANSACTIONS/CAREER NOTES: Signed by Toronto Argonauts of CFL (April 6, 1998). ... Signed as non-drafted free agent by San Diego Chargers (April 20, 1999). ... Released by Chargers (September 4, 1999). ... Re-signed by Chargers to practice squad (September 7, 1999). ... Activated (October 9, 1999). ... Released by Chargers (October 15, 1999). ... Re-signed by Chargers to practice squad (October 16, 1999). ... Activated (October 22, 1999). ... Released by Chargers (September 3, 2001). ... Signed by Oakland Raiders (January 24, 2002). ... Released by Raiders (April 26, 2002). ... Signed by New Orleans Saints (July 17, 2002).

| | | | TOTALS | | | INTERCEPTIONS | | | |
Year Team	G	GS	Tk.	Ast.	Sks.	No.	Yds.	Avg.	TD
1998—Toronto CFL	6	...	...	...	0.0	1	0	0.0	0
1999—San Diego NFL	9	3	29	2	0.0	0	0	0.0	0
2000—San Diego NFL	9	8	28	7	0.0	1	0	0.0	0
2002—New Orleans NFL	12	0	15	0	0.0	0	0	0.0	0
CFL totals (1 year)	6	...	...	...	0.0	1	0	0.0	0
NFL totals (3 years)	30	11	72	9	0.0	1	0	0.0	0
Pro totals (4 years)	36	...	...	...	0.0	2	0	0.0	0

BROWN, GILBERT — DT

PERSONAL: Born February 22, 1971, in Detroit. ... 6-2/339. ... Full name: Gilbert Jesse Brown.
HIGH SCHOOL: Mackenzie (Detroit).
COLLEGE: Kansas.
TRANSACTIONS/CAREER NOTES: Selected by Minnesota Vikings in third round (79th pick overall) of 1993 NFL draft. ... Signed by Vikings (July 16, 1993). ... Claimed on waivers by Green Bay Packers (August 31, 1993). ... On injured reserve with knee injury (December 6, 1994-remainder of season). ... Granted unconditional free agency (February 14, 1997). ... Re-signed by Packers (February 18, 1997). ... Granted unconditional free agency (February 11, 2000). ... Re-signed by Packers (March 23, 2001). ... Granted unconditional free agency (March 1, 2002). ... Re-signed by Packers (April 23, 2002). ... Granted unconditional free agency (February 28, 2003).
CHAMPIONSHIP GAME EXPERIENCE: Played in NFC championship game (1995-97 seasons). ... Member of Super Bowl championship team (1996 season). ... Played in Super Bowl XXXII (1997 season).

| | | | TOTALS | | |
Year Team	G	GS	Tk.	Ast.	Sks.
1993—Green Bay NFL	2	0	1	0	0.0
1994—Green Bay NFL	13	1	25	6	3.0
1995—Green Bay NFL	13	7	17	6	0.0
1996—Green Bay NFL	16	16	38	13	1.0
1997—Green Bay NFL	12	12	15	12	3.0
1998—Green Bay NFL	16	16	9	17	0.0
1999—Green Bay NFL	16	15	22	18	0.0
2000—Green Bay NFL			Did not play.		
2001—Green Bay NFL	11	11	15	8	0.0
2002—Green Bay NFL	12	11	17	10	0.0
Pro totals (9 years)	111	89	159	90	7.0

BROWN, KRIS — K — TEXANS

PERSONAL: Born December 23, 1976, in Southlake, Texas. ... 5-11/206.
HIGH SCHOOL: Carroll (Southlake, Texas).
COLLEGE: Nebraska.
TRANSACTIONS/CAREER NOTES: Selected by Pittsburgh Steelers in seventh round (228th pick overall) of 1999 NFL draft. ... Signed by Steelers (June 29, 1999). ... Granted free agency (March 1, 2002). ... Signed by Houston Texans (March 25, 2002).
CHAMPIONSHIP GAME EXPERIENCE: Played in AFC championship game (2001 season).

| | | FIELD GOALS | | | | | | | TOTALS | | |
Year Team	G	1-29	30-39	40-49	50+	Tot.	Pct.	Lg.	XPM	XPA	Pts.
1999—Pittsburgh NFL	16	7-7	9-10	8-11	1-1	25-29	86.2	51	30	31	105
2000—Pittsburgh NFL	16	9-9	9-10	6-9	1-2	25-30	83.3	52	32	33	107
2001—Pittsburgh NFL	16	7-7	15-20	6-15	2-2	30-*44	68.2	†55	34	37	124
2002—Houston NFL	16	3-4	1-1	11-14	2-5	17-24	70.8	51	20	20	71
Pro totals (4 years)	64	26-27	34-41	31-49	6-10	97-127	76.4	55	116	121	407

BROWN, LOMAS — OT

PERSONAL: Born March 30, 1963, in Miami. ... 6-4/280. ... Full name: Lomas Brown Jr. ... Cousin of Joe Taylor, defensive back with Chicago Bears (1967-74); cousin of Guy McIntyre, guard with San Francisco 49ers (1984-93), Green Bay Packers (1994) and Philadelphia Eagles (1995 and 1996); and cousin of Eric Curry, defensive end, with Tampa Bay Buccaneers (1993-97) and Jacksonville Jaguars (1998-99).
HIGH SCHOOL: Miami Springs Senior.
COLLEGE: Florida (degree in public recreation, 1996).
TRANSACTIONS/CAREER NOTES: Selected by Orlando Renegades in second round (18th pick overall) of 1985 USFL draft. ... Selected by Detroit Lions in first round (sixth pick overall) of 1985 NFL draft. ... Signed by Lions (August 9, 1985). ... Designated by Lions as franchise player (February 25, 1993). ... Granted roster exemption (September 1-3, 1993). ... Designated by Lions as franchise player (February 15, 1995). ... Re-signed by Lions (September 7, 1995). ... Granted unconditional free agency (February 16, 1996). ... Signed by Arizona Cardinals (February 28, 1996). ... Granted unconditional free agency (February 12, 1999). ... Signed by Cleveland Browns (March 9, 1999). ... On injured reserve with knee injury (December 14, 1999-remainder of season). ... Released by Browns (February 8, 2000). ... Signed by New York Giants

(February 2, 2000). ... Released by Giants (February 28, 2002). ... Signed by Tampa Bay Buccaneers (July 25, 2002). ... Granted unconditional free agency (February 28, 2003).

PLAYING EXPERIENCE: Detroit NFL, 1985-1995; Arizona NFL, 1996-1998; Cleveland NFL, 1999; New York Giants NFL, 2000 and 2001; Tampa Bay NFL, 2002. ... Games/Games started: 1985 (16/16), 1986 (16/16), 1987 (11/11), 1988 (16/16), 1989 (16/16), 1990 (16/16), 1991 (15/15), 1992 (16/16), 1993 (11/11), 1994 (16/16), 1995 (15/14), 1996 (16/16), 1997 (14/14), 1998 (16/16), 1999 (10/10), 2000 (16/16), 2001 (16/16), 2002 (11/0). Total: 263/251.

CHAMPIONSHIP GAME EXPERIENCE: Played in NFC championship game (1991, 2000 and 2002 seasons). ... Played in Super Bowl XXXV (2000 season). ... Member of Super Bowl championship team (2002 season).

HONORS: Named tackle on The Sporting News college All-America first team (1984). ... Played in Pro Bowl (1990-1996 seasons). ... Named offensive tackle on The Sporting News NFL All-Pro team (1992).

BROWN, MIKE   S   BEARS

PERSONAL: Born February 13, 1978, in Scottsdale, Ariz. ... 5-10/207.
HIGH SCHOOL: Saguaro (Scottsdale, Ariz.).
COLLEGE: Nebraska.
TRANSACTIONS/CAREER NOTES: Selected by Chicago Bears in second round (39th pick overall) of 2000 NFL draft. ... Signed by Bears (July 23, 2000).

			TOTALS			INTERCEPTIONS			
Year Team	G	GS	Tk.	Ast.	Sks.	No.	Yds.	Avg.	TD
2000—Chicago NFL	16	16	79	17	0.0	1	35	35.0	1
2001—Chicago NFL	16	16	51	11	3.0	5	81	16.2	†2
2002—Chicago NFL	16	15	72	12	0.0	3	16	5.3	0
Pro totals (3 years)	48	47	202	40	3.0	9	132	14.7	3

BROWN, RALPH   CB   GIANTS

PERSONAL: Born September 16, 1978, in Hacienda Heights, Calif. ... 5-10/185. ... Full name: Ralph Brown II.
HIGH SCHOOL: Bishop Amat (La Puente, Calif.).
COLLEGE: Nebraska.
TRANSACTIONS/CAREER NOTES: Selected by New York Giants in fifth round (140th pick overall) of 2000 NFL draft. ... Signed by Giants (July 18, 2000). ... On injured reserve with kidney injury (October 3, 2000-remainder of season). ... Granted free agency (February 28, 2003). ... Re-signed by Giants (April 19, 2003).
HONORS: Named cornerback on The Sporting News college All-America first team (1999).

			TOTALS			INTERCEPTIONS			
Year Team	G	GS	Tk.	Ast.	Sks.	No.	Yds.	Avg.	TD
2000—New York Giants NFL	2	0	0	0	0.0	0	0	0.0	0
2001—New York Giants NFL	8	0	0	2	0.0	0	0	0.0	0
2002—New York Giants NFL	16	2	18	4	0.0	1	19	19.0	0
Pro totals (3 years)	26	2	18	6	0.0	1	19	19.0	0

BROWN, RAY   G   LIONS

PERSONAL: Born December 12, 1962, in Marion, Ark. ... 6-5/318. ... Full name: Leonard Ray Brown Jr.
HIGH SCHOOL: Marion (Ark.).
COLLEGE: Memphis State, then Arizona State, then Arkansas State.
TRANSACTIONS/CAREER NOTES: Selected by St. Louis Cardinals in eighth round (201st pick overall) of 1986 NFL draft. ... Signed by Cardinals (July 14, 1986). ... On injured reserve with knee injury (October 17-November 21, 1986). ... Released by Cardinals (September 7, 1987). ... Re-signed by Cardinals as replacement player (September 25, 1987). ... On injured reserve with finger injury (November 12-December 12, 1987). ... Cardinals franchise moved to Phoenix (March 15, 1988). ... Granted unconditional free agency (February 1, 1989). ... Signed by Washington Redskins (March 10, 1989). ... On injured reserve with knee injury (September 5-November 4, 1989). ... On injured reserve with knee injury (September 4, 1990-January 4, 1991). ... Granted unconditional free agency (February 1-April 1, 1991). ... Re-signed by Redskins for 1991 season. ... On injured reserve with elbow injury (August 27, 1991-entire season). ... Granted unconditional free agency (February 16, 1996). ... Signed by San Francisco 49ers (March 1, 1996). ... Released by 49ers (June 3, 2002). ... Signed by Detroit Lions (August 20, 2002). ... Granted unconditional free agency (February 28, 2003). ... Re-signed by Lions (March 13, 2003).
PLAYING EXPERIENCE: St. Louis NFL, 1986 and 1987; Phoenix NFL, 1988; Washington NFL, 1989, 1992-1995; San Francisco NFL, 1996-2001; Detroit NFL, 2002. ... Games/Games started: 1986 (11/4), 1987 (7/3), 1988 (15/1), 1989 (7/0), 1992 (16/8), 1993 (16/14), 1994 (16/16), 1995 (16/16), 1996 (16/16), 1997 (15/15), 1998 (16/16), 1999 (16/16), 2000 (16/16), 2001 (16/16), 2002 (16/16). Total: 215/173.
CHAMPIONSHIP GAME EXPERIENCE: Played in NFC championship game (1997 season).
HONORS: Played in Pro Bowl (2001 season).

BROWN, RUBEN   G   BILLS

PERSONAL: Born February 13, 1972, in Englewood, N.J. ... 6-3/304. ... Full name: Ruben Pernell Brown. ... Brother of Cornell Brown, linebacker, with Baltimore Ravens (1997-2000).
HIGH SCHOOL: E.C. Glass (Lynchburg, Va.).
COLLEGE: Pittsburgh.
TRANSACTIONS/CAREER NOTES: Selected by Buffalo Bills in first round (14th pick overall) of 1995 NFL draft. ... Signed by Bills (June 20, 1995). ... Granted unconditional free agency (February 11, 2000). ... Re-signed by Bills (March 31, 2000).
PLAYING EXPERIENCE: Buffalo NFL, 1995-2001; Buffalo NFL, 2002. ... Games/Games started: 1995 (16/16), 1996 (14/14), 1997 (16/16), 1998 (13/13), 1999 (14/14), 2000 (16/16), 2001 (16/16), 2002 (16/16). Total: 121/121.
HONORS: Named offensive lineman on The Sporting News college All-America second team (1994). ... Played in Pro Bowl (1996-2002 seasons).

BROWN, SHELDON   CB   EAGLES

PERSONAL: Born March 19, 1979, in Fort Lawn, S.C. ... 5-10/196.
HIGH SCHOOL: Lewisville (Richburg, S.C.).
COLLEGE: South Carolina.
TRANSACTIONS/CAREER NOTES: Selected by Philadelphia Eagles in second round (59th pick overall) of 2002 NFL draft. ... Signed by Eagles (July 25, 2002).
CHAMPIONSHIP GAME EXPERIENCE: Played in NFC championship game (2002 season).

Year Team	G	GS	TOTALS			INTERCEPTIONS			
			Tk.	Ast.	Sks.	No.	Yds.	Avg.	TD
2002—Philadelphia NFL	16	0	8	4	1.0	2	41	20.5	0

BROWN, TIM   WR   RAIDERS

PERSONAL: Born July 22, 1966, in Dallas. ... 6-0/195. ... Full name: Timothy Donell Brown.
HIGH SCHOOL: Woodrow Wilson (Dallas).
COLLEGE: Notre Dame (degree in sociology).
TRANSACTIONS/CAREER NOTES: Selected by Los Angeles Raiders in first round (sixth pick overall) of 1988 NFL draft. ... Signed by Raiders (July 14, 1988). ... On injured reserve with knee injury (September 12, 1989-remainder of season). ... Granted free agency (February 1, 1992). ... Re-signed by Raiders (August 13, 1992). ... Designated by Raiders as transition player (February 25, 1993). ... Tendered offer sheet by Denver Broncos (March 11, 1994). ... Offer matched by Raiders (March 16, 1994). ... Raiders franchise moved to Oakland (July 21, 1995).
CHAMPIONSHIP GAME EXPERIENCE: Played in AFC championship game (1990, 2000 and 2002 seasons). ... Played in Super Bowl XXXVII (2002 season).
HONORS: Named wide receiver on THE SPORTING NEWS college All-America first team (1986 and 1987). ... Heisman Trophy winner (1987). ... Named College Football Player of the Year by THE SPORTING NEWS (1987). ... Named kick returner on THE SPORTING NEWS NFL All-Pro team (1988). ... Played in Pro Bowl (1988, 1991, 1993-1997 and 2001 seasons). ... Named wide receiver on THE SPORTING NEWS NFL All-Pro team (1997). ... Named to play in Pro Bowl (1999 season); replaced by Terry Glenn due to injury.
RECORDS: Holds NFL rookie-season record for most combined yards gained—2,317 (1988).
SINGLE GAME HIGHS (regular season): Receptions—14 (December 21, 1997, vs. Jacksonville); yards—190 (October 24, 1999, vs. New York Jets); and touchdown receptions—2 (August 31, 1997, vs. Tennessee).
STATISTICAL PLATEAUS: 100-yard receiving games: 1988 (1), 1991 (1), 1992 (1), 1993 (4), 1994 (4), 1995 (6), 1996 (2), 1997 (7), 1998 (3), 1999 (6), 2000 (2), 2001 (4), 2002 (1). Total: 42.
MISCELLANEOUS: Holds Raiders franchise all-time record for most receptions (1,018), most yards receiving (14,167), most touchdowns (102) and most receiving touchdowns (97).

Year Team	G	GS	RUSHING				RECEIVING				PUNT RETURNS				KICKOFF RETURNS				TOTALS		
			Att.	Yds.	Avg.	TD	No.	Yds.	Avg.	TD	No.	Yds.	Avg.	TD	No.	Yds.	Avg.	TD	TD	2pt.	Pts.
1988—LA Raiders NFL	16	9	14	50	3.6	1	43	725	16.9	5	§49	§444	9.1	0	†41	*1098	*26.8	†1	7	0	42
1989—LA Raiders NFL	1	1	0	0	0.0	0	1	8	8.0	0	4	43	10.8	0	3	63	21.0	0	0	0	0
1990—LA Raiders NFL	16	0	0	0	0.0	0	18	265	14.7	3	34	295	8.7	0	0	0	0.0	0	3	0	18
1991—LA Raiders NFL	16	1	5	16	3.2	0	36	554	15.4	5	29	§330	11.4	▲1	1	29	29.0	0	6	0	36
1992—LA Raiders NFL	15	12	3	-4	-1.3	0	49	693	14.1	7	37	383	10.4	0	2	14	7.0	0	7	0	42
1993—LA Raiders NFL	16	16	2	7	3.5	0	80	§1180	14.8	7	40	§465	11.6	1	0	0	0.0	0	8	0	48
1994—LA Raiders NFL	16	16	0	0	0.0	0	89	§1309	14.7	9	40	*487	12.2	0	0	0	0.0	0	9	0	54
1995—Oakland NFL	16	16	0	0	0.0	0	89	§1342	15.1	10	36	364	10.1	0	0	0	0.0	0	10	0	60
1996—Oakland NFL	16	16	6	35	5.8	0	90	1104	12.3	9	32	272	8.5	0	1	24	24.0	0	9	0	54
1997—Oakland NFL	16	16	5	19	3.8	0	†104	§1408	13.5	5	0	0	0.0	0	1	7	7.0	0	5	1	32
1998—Oakland NFL	16	16	1	-7	-7.0	0	81	1012	12.5	9	3	23	7.7	0	0	0	0.0	0	9	0	54
1999—Oakland NFL	16	16	1	4	4.0	0	90	1344	14.9	6	0	0	0.0	0	0	0	0.0	0	6	0	36
2000—Oakland NFL	16	16	3	12	4.0	0	76	1128	14.8	11	0	0	0.0	0	0	0	0.0	0	11	0	66
2001—Oakland NFL	16	16	4	39	9.8	0	91	1165	12.8	9	6	111	18.5	1	0	0	0.0	0	10	0	60
2002—Oakland NFL	16	16	6	19	3.2	0	81	930	11.5	2	10	55	5.5	0	0	0	0.0	0	2	0	12
Pro totals (15 years)	224	183	50	190	3.8	1	1018	14167	13.9	97	320	3272	10.2	3	49	1235	25.2	1	102	1	614

BROWN, TROY   WR   PATRIOTS

PERSONAL: Born July 2, 1971, in Barnwell, S.C. ... 5-10/193. ... Full name: Troy Fitzgerald Brown.
HIGH SCHOOL: Blackville (S.C.)-Hilda.
JUNIOR COLLEGE: Lees-McRae College (N.C.).
COLLEGE: Marshall.
TRANSACTIONS/CAREER NOTES: Selected by New England Patriots in eighth round (198th pick overall) of 1993 NFL draft. ... Signed by Patriots (July 16, 1993). ... On injured reserve with quadriceps injury (December 31, 1993-remainder of season). ... Released by Patriots (August 28, 1994). ... Re-signed by Patriots (October 19, 1994). ... Granted unconditional free agency (February 14, 1997). ... Re-signed by Patriots (March 10, 1997). ... Granted unconditional free agency (February 1, 2000). ... Re-signed by Patriots (February 26, 2000).
CHAMPIONSHIP GAME EXPERIENCE: Played in AFC championship game (1996 and 2001 seasons). ... Member of Patriots for Super Bowl XXXI (1996 season); inactive. ... Member of Super Bowl championship team (2001 season).
HONORS: Played in Pro Bowl (2001 season).
SINGLE GAME HIGHS (regular season): Receptions—16 (September 22, 2002, vs. Kansas City); yards—176 (September 22, 2002, vs. Kansas City); and touchdown receptions—2 (October 1, 2000, vs. Denver).
STATISTICAL PLATEAUS: 100-yard receiving games: 1997 (2), 1999 (1), 2000 (4), 2001 (3), 2002 (2). Total: 12.

Year Team	G	GS	RUSHING				RECEIVING				PUNT RETURNS				KICKOFF RETURNS				TOTALS		
			Att.	Yds.	Avg.	TD	No.	Yds.	Avg.	TD	No.	Yds.	Avg.	TD	No.	Yds.	Avg.	TD	TD	2pt.	Pts.
1993—New England NFL	12	0	0	0	0.0	0	2	22	11.0	0	25	224	9.0	0	15	243	16.2	0	0	0	0
1994—New England NFL	9	0	0	0	0.0	0	0	0	0.0	0	24	202	8.4	0	1	14	14.0	0	0	0	0
1995—New England NFL	16	0	0	0	0.0	0	14	159	11.4	0	0	0	0.0	0	31	672	21.7	0	1	0	6
1996—New England NFL	16	0	0	0	0.0	0	21	222	10.6	0	0	0	0.0	0	29	634	21.9	0	0	0	0
1997—New England NFL	16	6	1	-18	-18.0	0	41	607	14.8	6	0	0	0.0	0	0	0	0.0	0	6	0	36

Year Team	G	GS	RUSHING				RECEIVING				PUNT RETURNS				KICKOFF RETURNS				TOTALS		
			Att.	Yds.	Avg.	TD	No.	Yds.	Avg.	TD	No.	Yds.	Avg.	TD	No.	Yds.	Avg.	TD	TD	2pt.	Pts.
1998—New England NFL	10	0	0	0	0.0	0	23	346	15.0	1	17	225	13.2	0	0	0	0.0	0	1	0	6
1999—New England NFL	13	1	0	0	0.0	0	36	471	13.1	1	38	405	10.7	0	8	271	33.9	0	1	0	6
2000—New England NFL	16	15	6	46	7.7	0	83	944	11.4	4	39	504	12.9	1	2	15	7.5	0	5	0	30
2001—New England NFL	16	13	11	91	8.3	0	101	1199	11.9	5	29	413*14.2		*2	1	13	13.0	0	7	0	42
2002—New England NFL	14	13	3	14	4.7	0	97	890	9.2	3	24	175	7.3	0	0	0	0.0	0	3	1	20
Pro totals (10 years)	138	48	21	133	6.3	0	418	4860	11.6	20	196	2148	11.0	3	87	1862	21.4	0	24	1	146

BROWN, WILBERT — G — REDSKINS

PERSONAL: Born May 9, 1977, in Texarkana, Texas. ... 6-2/315. ... Full name: Wilbert Lemon Brown. ... Cousin of Curtis Enis, running back, Chicago Bears.

HIGH SCHOOL: Hooks (Texas).

COLLEGE: Houston.

TRANSACTIONS/CAREER NOTES: Signed as non-drafted free agent by San Diego Chargers (April 20, 1999). ... Released by Chargers (September 4, 1999). ... Re-signed by Chargers to practice squad (September 6, 1999). ... Released by Chargers (September 14, 1999). ... Re-signed by Chargers to practice squad (September 21, 1999). ... Activated (December 4, 1999). ... Released by Chargers (August 27, 2000). ... Re-signed by Chargers to practice squad (August 29, 2000). ... Released by Chargers (November 25, 2000). ... Re-signed by Chargers to practice squad (November 27, 2000). ... Granted free agency following 2000 season. ... Signed by Tampa Bay Buccaneers (January 5, 2001). ... Assigned by Buccaneers to Frankfurt Galaxy in 2001 NFL Europe enhancement allocation program (February 19, 2001). ... Released by Buccaneers (September 2, 2001). ... Signed by Washington Redskins (July 16, 2002). ... Re-signed by Redskins (March 31, 2003).

PLAYING EXPERIENCE: San Diego NFL, 1999. Washington NFL, 2002. ... Games/Games started: 1999 (5/0), 2002 (14/9). Total: 19/9.

BROWNING, JOHN — DT — CHIEFS

PERSONAL: Born September 30, 1973, in Miami. ... 6-4/297.

HIGH SCHOOL: North Miami (Fla.).

COLLEGE: West Virginia.

TRANSACTIONS/CAREER NOTES: Selected by Kansas City Chiefs in third round (68th pick overall) of 1996 NFL draft. ... Signed by Chiefs (July 24, 1996). ... On injured reserve with Achilles' tendon injury (September 1, 1999-entire season). ... Granted unconditional free agency (February 11, 2000). ... Re-signed by Chiefs (February 11, 2000). ... On injured reserve with shoulder injury (October 25, 2001-remainder of season).

Year Team	G	GS	TOTALS			INTERCEPTIONS			
			Tk.	Ast.	Sks.	No.	Yds.	Avg.	TD
1996—Kansas City NFL	13	2	17	4	2.0	0	0	0.0	0
1997—Kansas City NFL	14	13	29	4	4.0	0	0	0.0	0
1998—Kansas City NFL	8	8	20	10	0.0	0	0	0.0	0
1999—Kansas City NFL			Did not play.						
2000—Kansas City NFL	16	16	38	10	6.0	1	0	0.0	0
2001—Kansas City NFL	6	6	15	5	1.5	0	0	0.0	0
2002—Kansas City NFL	16	16	33	6	7.0	0	0	0.0	0
Pro totals (6 years)	73	61	152	39	20.5	1	0	0.0	0

BROYLES, JAMES — G — RAMS

PERSONAL: Born May 18, 1978, in Hammond, Ind. ... 6-4/312. ... Full name: James Franklin Broyles.

HIGH SCHOOL: Kankakee Valley (Rensselaer, Ind.).

COLLEGE: Indiana, then Southwest Missouri State.

TRANSACTIONS/CAREER NOTES: Signed as non-drafted free agent by St. Louis Rams (May 30, 2002). ... Released by Rams (September 1, 2002). ... Re-signed by Rams to practice squad (September 3, 2002). ... Activated (December 6, 2002). ... Assigned by Rams to Scottish Claymores in 2003 NFL Europe enhancement allocation program (February 4, 2003).

PLAYING EXPERIENCE: St. Louis NFL, 2002. ... Games/Games started: 2002 (1/0).

BRUCE, ISAAC — WR — RAMS

PERSONAL: Born November 10, 1972, in Fort Lauderdale, Fla. ... 6-0/188. ... Full name: Isaac Isidore Bruce. ... Cousin of Derrick Moore, running back with Detroit Lions (1993 and 1994) and Carolina Panthers (1995).

HIGH SCHOOL: Dillard (Fort Lauderdale, Fla.).

JUNIOR COLLEGE: West Los Angeles Junior College, then Santa Monica (Calif.) Junior College.

COLLEGE: Memphis State.

TRANSACTIONS/CAREER NOTES: Selected by Los Angeles Rams in second round (33rd pick overall) of 1994 NFL draft. ... Signed by Rams (July 13, 1994). ... On injured reserve with sprained right knee (December 9, 1994-remainder of season). ... Rams franchise moved to St. Louis (April 12, 1995). ... On injured reserve with hamstring injury (December 9, 1998-remainder of season).

CHAMPIONSHIP GAME EXPERIENCE: Played in NFC championship game (1999 and 2001 seasons). ... Member of Super Bowl championship team (1999 season). ... Played in Super Bowl XXXVI (2001 season).

HONORS: Named wide receiver on THE SPORTING NEWS NFL All-Pro team (1999). ... Played in Pro Bowl (1996 and 1999 season). ... Named to play in Pro Bowl (2000 season); replaced by Torry Holt due to injury. ... Named to play in Pro Bowl (2001 season); replaced by Joe Horn due to injury.

SINGLE GAME HIGHS (regular season): Receptions—15 (December 24, 1995, vs. Miami); yards—233 (November 2, 1997, vs. Atlanta); touchdown receptions—4 (October 10, 1999, vs. San Francisco).

STATISTICAL PLATEAUS: 100-yard receiving games: 1995 (9), 1996 (4), 1997 (2), 1998 (2), 1999 (4), 2000 (4), 2001 (3), 2002 (2). Total: 30.

MISCELLANEOUS: Holds St. Louis Rams all-time records for most receptions (619) and most receiving touchdowns (63).

Year Team	G	GS	RUSHING Att.	Yds.	Avg.	TD	RECEIVING No.	Yds.	Avg.	TD	TD	TOTALS 2pt.	Pts.	Fum.
1994—Los Angeles Rams NFL	12	0	1	2	2.0	0	21	272	13.0	3	3	0	18	0
1995—St. Louis NFL	16	16	3	17	5.7	0	119	1781	15.0	13	13	1	80	2
1996—St. Louis NFL	16	16	1	4	4.0	0	84	*1338	15.9	7	7	0	42	1
1997—St. Louis NFL	12	12	0	0	0.0	0	56	815	14.6	5	5	0	30	1
1998—St. Louis NFL	5	5	1	30	30.0	0	32	457	14.3	1	1	0	6	0
1999—St. Louis NFL	16	16	5	32	6.4	0	77	1165	15.1	12	12	1	74	0
2000—St. Louis NFL	16	16	1	11	11.0	0	87	1471	16.9	9	9	0	54	1
2001—St. Louis NFL	16	16	4	23	5.8	0	64	1106	17.3	6	6	0	36	4
2002—St. Louis NFL	16	16	3	18	6.0	0	79	1075	13.6	7	7	0	42	2
Pro totals (9 years)	125	113	19	137	7.2	0	619	9480	15.3	63	63	2	382	11

BRUENER, MARK   TE   STEELERS

B

PERSONAL: Born September 16, 1972, in Olympia, Wash. ... 6-4/260. ... Full name: Mark Frederick Bruener. ... Name pronounced BREW-ner.
HIGH SCHOOL: Aberdeen (Wash.).
COLLEGE: Washington (degree in economics).
TRANSACTIONS/CAREER NOTES: Selected by Pittsburgh Steelers in first round (27th pick overall) of 1995 NFL draft. ... Signed by Steelers (July 25, 1995). ... On injured reserve with knee injury (November 29, 1996-remainder of season). ... On injured reserve with shoulder injury (November 21, 2001-remainder of season). ... On physically unable to perform list with foot injury (July 25-30, 2002). ... On injured reserve with knee injury (December 3, 2002-remainder of season).
CHAMPIONSHIP GAME EXPERIENCE: Played in AFC championship game (1995 and 1997 seasons). ... Played in Super Bowl XXX (1995 season).
SINGLE GAME HIGHS (regular season): Receptions—5 (December 13, 1997, vs. New England); yards—51 (November 28, 1999, vs. Cincinnati); and touchdown receptions—1 (November 3, 2002, vs. Cleveland).

Year Team	G	GS	RECEIVING No.	Yds.	Avg.	TD	TD	TOTALS 2pt.	Pts.	Fum.
1995—Pittsburgh NFL	16	13	26	238	9.2	3	3	0	18	0
1996—Pittsburgh NFL	12	12	12	141	11.8	0	0	1	2	0
1997—Pittsburgh NFL	16	16	18	117	6.5	6	6	0	36	1
1998—Pittsburgh NFL	16	16	19	157	8.3	2	2	0	12	0
1999—Pittsburgh NFL	14	14	18	176	9.8	0	0	0	0	0
2000—Pittsburgh NFL	16	16	17	192	11.3	3	3	0	18	0
2001—Pittsburgh NFL	9	9	12	98	8.2	0	0	0	0	0
2002—Pittsburgh NFL	12	12	13	66	5.1	1	1	0	6	0
Pro totals (8 years)	111	108	135	1185	8.8	15	15	1	92	1

BRUNELL, MARK   QB   JAGUARS

PERSONAL: Born September 17, 1970, in Los Angeles. ... 6-1/217. ... Full name: Mark Allen Brunell.
HIGH SCHOOL: St. Joseph (Santa Maria, Calif.).
COLLEGE: Washington (degree in history).
TRANSACTIONS/CAREER NOTES: Selected by Green Bay Packers in fifth round (118th pick overall) of 1993 NFL draft. ... Signed by Packers (July 1, 1993). ... Traded by Packers to Jacksonville Jaguars for third- (FB William Henderson) and fifth-round (RB Travis Jervey) picks in 1995 draft (April 21, 1995).
CHAMPIONSHIP GAME EXPERIENCE: Played in AFC championship game (1996 and 1999 seasons).
HONORS: Played in Pro Bowl (1996, 1997 and 1999 seasons). ... Named Outstanding Player of Pro Bowl (1996 season).
SINGLE GAME HIGHS (regular season): Attempts—52 (October 20, 1996, vs. St. Louis); completions—37 (October 20, 1996, vs. St. Louis); yards—432 (September 22, 1996, vs. New England); and touchdown passes—4 (November 29, 1998, vs. Cincinnati).
STATISTICAL PLATEAUS: 300-yard passing games: 1995 (1), 1996 (6), 1997 (3), 1998 (2), 1999 (2), 2000 (3), 2001 (2), 2002 (1). Total: 22.
MISCELLANEOUS: Regular-season record as starting NFL quarterback: 63-51 (.553). ... Postseason record as starting NFL quarterback: 4-4 (.500). ... Holds Jacksonville Jaguars all-time record for most yards passing (25,214) and most touchdown passes (142).

Year Team	G	GS	PASSING Att.	Cmp.	Pct.	Yds.	TD	Int.	Avg.	Skd.	Rat.	RUSHING Att.	Yds.	Avg.	TD	TOTALS TD	2pt.	Pts.
1993—Green Bay NFL									Did not play.									
1994—Green Bay NFL	2	0	27	12	44.4	95	0	0	3.52	2	53.8	6	7	1.2	1	1	0	6
1995—Jacksonville NFL	13	10	346	201	58.1	2168	15	7	6.27	39	82.6	67	480	7.2	4	4	0	24
1996—Jacksonville NFL	16	16	557	353	§63.4	*4367	19	§20	*7.84	*50	84.0	80	396	5.0	3	3	2	22
1997—Jacksonville NFL	14	14	435	264	60.7	3281	18	7	§7.54	33	§91.2	48	257	5.4	2	2	0	12
1998—Jacksonville NFL	13	13	354	208	58.8	2601	20	9	7.35	28	89.9	49	192	3.9	0	0	0	0
1999—Jacksonville NFL	15	15	441	259	58.7	3060	14	9	6.94	29	82.0	47	208	4.4	1	1	†1	8
2000—Jacksonville NFL	16	16	512	311	60.7	3640	20	14	7.11	§54	84.0	48	236	4.9	2	2	0	12
2001—Jacksonville NFL	15	15	473	289	61.1	3309	19	13	7.00	*57	84.1	39	224	5.7	1	1	0	6
2002—Jacksonville NFL	15	15	416	245	58.9	2788	17	7	6.70	34	85.7	43	207	4.8	0	0	0	0
Pro totals (9 years)	119	114	3561	2142	60.2	25309	142	86	7.11	326	85.1	427	2207	5.2	14	14	3	90

BRUSCHI, TEDY   LB   PATRIOTS

PERSONAL: Born June 9, 1973, in San Francisco. ... 6-1/245. ... Full name: Tedy Lacap Bruschi. ... Stepson of Ronald Sandys, former professional tennis player. ... Name pronounced BREW-ski.
HIGH SCHOOL: Roseville (Calif.).
COLLEGE: Arizona (degree in communications).
TRANSACTIONS/CAREER NOTES: Selected by New England Patriots in third round (86th pick overall) of 1996 NFL draft. ... Signed by Patriots (July 17, 1996). ... Granted free agency (February 12, 1999). ... Re-signed by Patriots (June 1, 1999). ... Granted unconditional free agency (February 11, 2000). ... Re-signed by Patriots (March 22, 2000).

CHAMPIONSHIP GAME EXPERIENCE: Played in AFC championship game (1996 and 2001 seasons). ... Played in Super Bowl XXXI (1996 season). ... Member of Super Bowl championship team (2001 season).
HONORS: Named defensive lineman on THE SPORTING NEWS college All-America first team (1994 and 1995).

				TOTALS			INTERCEPTIONS			
Year Team	G	GS	Tk.	Ast.	Sks.	No.	Yds.	Avg.	TD
1996—New England NFL	16	0	10	1	4.0	0	0	0.0	0
1997—New England NFL	16	1	25	5	4.0	0	0	0.0	0
1998—New England NFL	16	7	48	26	2.0	0	0	0.0	0
1999—New England NFL	14	14	71	36	2.0	1	1	1.0	0
2000—New England NFL	16	16	68	38	1.0	0	0	0.0	0
2001—New England NFL	15	9	54	19	2.0	2	7	3.5	0
2002—New England NFL	11	9	45	20	4.5	2	75	37.5	▲2
Pro totals (7 years)	104	56	321	145	19.5	5	83	16.6	2

B

BRYANT, ANTONIO   WR   COWBOYS

PERSONAL: Born March 9, 1981, in Miami. ... 6-1/192.
HIGH SCHOOL: Miami Northwestern.
COLLEGE: Pittsburgh.
TRANSACTIONS/CAREER NOTES: Selected after junior season by Dallas Cowboys in second round (63rd pick overall) of 2002 NFL draft. ... Signed by Cowboys (July 26, 2002).
HONORS: Named wide receiver on THE SPORTING NEWS college All-America second team (2000).
SINGLE GAME HIGHS (regular season): Receptions—7 (December 29, 2002, vs. Washington); yards—170 (December 29, 2002, vs. Washington); and touchdown receptions—1 (December 29, 2002, vs. Washington).
STATISTICAL PLATEAUS: 100-yard receiving games: 2002 (1).

			RECEIVING				PUNT RETURNS				TOTALS			
Year Team	G	GS	No.	Yds.	Avg.	TD	No.	Yds.	Avg.	TD	TD	2pt.	Pts.	Fum.
2002—Dallas NFL	16	15	44	733	‡16.7	6	0	0	0.0	0	6	0	36	3

BRYANT, FERNANDO   CB   JAGUARS

PERSONAL: Born March 26, 1977, in Albany, Ga. ... 5-10/180. ... Full name: Fernando Antoneiyo Bryant. ... Nephew of Don Griffin, cornerback with San Francisco 49ers (1986-93), Cleveland Browns (1994 and 1995) and Philadelphia Eagles (1996); and nephew of James Griffin, defensive back with Cincinnati Bengals (1983-85) and Detroit Lions (1986-89).
HIGH SCHOOL: Riverdale (Murfreesboro, Tenn.).
COLLEGE: Alabama.
TRANSACTIONS/CAREER NOTES: Selected by Jacksonville Jaguars in first round (26th pick overall) of 1999 NFL draft. ... Signed by Jaguars (August 9, 1999). ... On injured reserve with foot injury (January 1, 2002-remainder of season).
CHAMPIONSHIP GAME EXPERIENCE: Played in AFC championship game (1999 season).

				TOTALS			INTERCEPTIONS			
Year Team	G	GS	Tk.	Ast.	Sks.	No.	Yds.	Avg.	TD
1999—Jacksonville NFL	16	16	61	9	0.0	2	0	0.0	0
2000—Jacksonville NFL	14	14	37	6	0.0	1	0	0.0	0
2001—Jacksonville NFL	10	9	49	5	0.0	0	0	0.0	0
2002—Jacksonville NFL	16	16	57	2	0.0	1	26	26.0	0
Pro totals (4 years)	56	55	204	22	0.0	4	26	6.5	0

BRYANT, MATT   K   GIANTS

PERSONAL: Born May 21, 1975, in Orange, Texas. ... 5-9/191.
HIGH SCHOOL: Bridge City (Orange, Texas).
JUNIOR COLLEGE: Panola Junior College, then Trinity Valley Community College (Texas).
COLLEGE: Oregon State, then Baylor.
TRANSACTIONS/CAREER NOTES: Signed as non-drafted free agent by New York Giants (January 15, 2002). ... Assigned by Giants to Frankfurt Galaxy in 2002 NFL Europe enhancement allocation program (February 12, 2002). ... Released by Giants (August 30, 2002). ... Re-signed by Giants to practice squad (September 2, 2002). ... Activated (September 3, 2002).

		FIELD GOALS							TOTALS		
Year Team	G	1-29	30-39	40-49	50+	Tot.	Pct.	Lg.	XPM	XPA	Pts.
2002—Frankfurt NFLE	...	...	...	...	0-0	0-1	0.0	...	0	0	0
—New York Giants NFL	16	9-9	14-19	3-4	0-0	26-32	81.3	47	30	32	108
NFL Europe totals (1 year)	...	...	...	...	0-0	0-1	0.0	...	0	0	0
NFL totals (1 year)	16	9-9	14-19	3-4	0-0	26-32	81.3	47	30	32	108
Pro totals (2 years)	...	...	...	...	0-0	26-33	78.8	...	30	32	108

BRYANT, TONY   DE   RAIDERS

PERSONAL: Born September 3, 1976, in Marathon, Fla. ... 6-6/275.
HIGH SCHOOL: Marathon (Fla.).
JUNIOR COLLEGE: Copiah-Lincoln Junior College (Miss.).
COLLEGE: Florida State.
TRANSACTIONS/CAREER NOTES: Selected by Oakland Raiders in second round (40th pick overall) of 1999 NFL draft. ... Signed by Raiders (July 22, 1999).
CHAMPIONSHIP GAME EXPERIENCE: Played in AFC championship game (2000 season).

		TOTALS		
Year Team	G	GS	Tk.	Ast.	Sks.

Year Team	G	GS	Tk.	Ast.	Sks.
1999—Oakland NFL	10	0	13	3	4.5
2000—Oakland NFL	16	16	25	13	5.5
2001—Oakland NFL	16	16	28	12	5.0
2002—Oakland NFL	8	8	26	7	2.5
Pro totals (4 years)	50	40	92	35	17.5

BRYANT, WENDELL   DT   CARDINALS

PERSONAL: Born September 12, 1980, in St. Louis. ... 6-4/314.
HIGH SCHOOL: Ritenour (St. Louis).
COLLEGE: Wisconsin.
TRANSACTIONS/CAREER NOTES: Selected by Arizona Cardinals in first round (12th pick overall) of 2002 NFL draft. ... Signed by Cardinals (September 12, 2002).
HONORS: Named defensive tackle on THE SPORTING NEWS college All-America second team (2001).

Year Team	G	GS	Tk.	Ast.	Sks.
2002—Arizona NFL	14	4	12	8	1.5

BRYSON, SHAWN   RB   LIONS

PERSONAL: Born August 26, 1976, in Franklin, N.C. ... 6-1/228. ... Full name: Adrian Shawn Bryson.
HIGH SCHOOL: Franklin (N.C.).
COLLEGE: Tennessee.
TRANSACTIONS/CAREER NOTES: Selected by Buffalo Bills in third round (86th pick overall) of 1999 NFL draft. ... Signed by Bills (July 27, 1999). ... On injured reserve with knee injury (August 30, 1999-entire season). ... Granted free agency (March 1, 2002). ... Re-signed by Bills (May 6, 2002). ... On injured reserve with knee injury (October 18, 2002-remainder of season). ... Granted unconditional free agency (February 28, 2003). ... Signed by Detroit Lions (March 24, 2003).
SINGLE GAME HIGHS (regular season): Attempts—28 (December 30, 2001, vs. New York Jets); yards—130 (December 23, 2001, vs. Atlanta); and rushing touchdowns—2 (December 23, 2001, vs. Atlanta).
STATISTICAL PLATEAUS: 100-yard rushing games: 2001 (2).

Year Team	G	GS	RUSHING Att.	Yds.	Avg.	TD	RECEIVING No.	Yds.	Avg.	TD	KICKOFF RETURNS No.	Yds.	Avg.	TD	TOTALS TD	2pt.	Pts.	Fum.
1999—Buffalo NFL									Did not play.									
2000—Buffalo NFL	16	7	161	591	3.7	0	32	271	8.5	2	8	122	15.3	0	2	1	14	1
2001—Buffalo NFL	15	3	80	341	4.3	2	9	59	6.6	0	16	299	18.7	0	2	0	12	0
2002—Buffalo NFL	6	0	13	35	2.7	0	1	9	9.0	0	1	18	18.0	0	0	0	0	1
Pro totals (3 years)	37	10	254	967	3.8	2	42	339	8.1	2	25	439	17.6	0	4	1	26	2

BRZEZINSKI, DOUG   G   PANTHERS

PERSONAL: Born March 11, 1976, in Livonia, Mich. ... 6-4/305. ... Full name: Douglas Gregory Brzezinski. ... Name pronounced bruh-ZHIN-skee.
HIGH SCHOOL: Detroit Catholic Central.
COLLEGE: Boston College.
TRANSACTIONS/CAREER NOTES: Selected by Philadelphia Eagles in third round (64th pick overall) of 1999 NFL draft. ... Signed by Eagles (July 28, 1999). ... Granted free agency (March 1, 2002). ... Re-signed by Eagles (March 28, 2002). ... Granted unconditional free agency (February 28, 2003). ... Signed by Carolina Panthers (March 12, 2003).
PLAYING EXPERIENCE: Philadelphia NFL, 1999-2002. ... Games/Games started: 1999 (16/16), 2000 (16/0), 2001 (16/1), 2002 (16/5). Total: 64/22.
CHAMPIONSHIP GAME EXPERIENCE: Played in NFC championship game (2001 and 2002 seasons).
HONORS: Named offensive guard on THE SPORTING NEWS college All-America first team (1998).

BUCHANAN, RAY   CB   FALCONS

PERSONAL: Born September 29, 1971, in Chicago. ... 5-9/186. ... Full name: Raymond Louis Buchanan.
HIGH SCHOOL: Proviso East (Maywood, Ill.).
COLLEGE: Louisville.
TRANSACTIONS/CAREER NOTES: Selected by Indianapolis Colts in third round (65th pick overall) of 1993 NFL draft. ... Signed by Colts (July 26, 1993). ... Designated by Colts as transition player (February 13, 1997). ... Tendered offer sheet by Atlanta Falcons (February 25, 1997). ... Colts declined to match offer (March 3, 1997). ... Granted unconditional free agency (February 21, 2001). ... Re-signed by Falcons (February 21, 2001). ... On suspended list for violating league substance abuse policy (September 11-October 14, 2002).
CHAMPIONSHIP GAME EXPERIENCE: Played in AFC championship game (1995 season). ... Played in NFC championship game (1998 season). ... Played in Super Bowl XXXIII (1998 season).
HONORS: Played in Pro Bowl (1998 season).

Year Team	G	GS	TOTALS Tk.	Ast.	Sks.	INTERCEPTIONS No.	Yds.	Avg.	TD	PUNT RETURNS No.	Yds.	Avg.	TD	TOTALS TD	2pt.	Pts.	Fum.
1993—Indianapolis NFL	16	5	44	21	0.0	4	45	11.3	0	0	0	0.0	0	0	0	0	0
1994—Indianapolis NFL	16	16	76	24	1.0	8	221	27.6	†3	0	0	0.0	0	3	0	18	0
1995—Indianapolis NFL	16	16	68	15	1.0	2	60	30.0	0	16	113	7.1	0	0	0	0	1
1996—Indianapolis NFL	13	13	53	9	0.5	2	32	16.0	0	12	201	16.8	0	0	0	0	0
1997—Atlanta NFL	16	16	48	4	0.0	5	49	9.8	0	0	37	0.0	0	0	0	0	0
1998—Atlanta NFL	16	16	54	7	0.0	7	102	14.6	0	1	4	4.0	0	0	0	0	0
1999—Atlanta NFL	16	16	59	5	1.0	4	81	20.3	1	0	0	0.0	0	1	0	6	0
2000—Atlanta NFL	16	16	69	11	0.0	6	114	19.0	0	0	0	0.0	0	0	0	0	0
2001—Atlanta NFL	16	16	63	8	0.0	5	85	17.0	0	0	0	0.0	0	0	0	0	0
2002—Atlanta NFL	12	11	42	5	0.0	2	9	4.5	0	0	0	0.0	0	0	0	0	0
Pro totals (10 years)	153	141	576	109	3.5	45	798	17.7	4	29	355	12.2	0	4	0	24	1

B

BUCHANON, PHILLIP   CB   RAIDERS

PERSONAL: Born September 19, 1980, in Lehigh, Fla. ... 5-10/185. ... Full name: Phillip Darren Buchanon.
HIGH SCHOOL: Lehigh (Fla.).
COLLEGE: Miami (Fla.).
TRANSACTIONS/CAREER NOTES: Selected after junior season by Oakland Raiders in first round (17th pick overall) of 2002 NFL draft. ... Signed by Raiders (July 25, 2002).

Year Team	G	GS	TOTALS Tk.	Ast.	Sks.	INTERCEPTIONS No.	Yds.	Avg.	TD	PUNT RETURNS No.	Yds.	Avg.	TD	KICKOFF RETURNS No.	Yds.	Avg.	TD	TOTALS TD	2pt.	Pts.	Fum.
2002—Oakland NFL.............	6	2	21	0	0.0	2	81	40.5	1	15	178	11.9	1	0	0	0.0	0	2	0	12	2

BUCKHALTER, CORRELL   RB   EAGLES

PERSONAL: Born October 6, 1978, in Collins, Miss. ... 6-0/222.
HIGH SCHOOL: Collins (Miss.).
COLLEGE: Nebraska.
TRANSACTIONS/CAREER NOTES: Selected by Philadelphia Eagles in fourth round (121st pick overall) of 2001 NFL draft. ... Signed by Eagles (May 24, 2001). ... On physically unable to perform list with knee injury (July 27, 2002-entire season).
CHAMPIONSHIP GAME EXPERIENCE: Played in NFC championship game (2001 season).
SINGLE GAME HIGHS (regular season): Attempts—21 (October 7, 2001, vs. Arizona); yards—134 (October 7, 2001, vs. Arizona; and rushing touchdowns—1 (November 11, 2001, vs. Minnesota).
STATISTICAL PLATEAUS: 100-yard rushing games: 2001 (1).

Year Team	G	GS	RUSHING Att.	Yds.	Avg.	TD	RECEIVING No.	Yds.	Avg.	TD	TOTALS TD	2pt.	Pts.	Fum.
2001—Philadelphia NFL.....................	15	6	129	586	4.5	2	13	130	10.0	0	2	0	12	2
2002—Philadelphia NFL.....................							Did not play.							
Pro totals (1 years).....................	**15**	**6**	**129**	**586**	**4.5**	**2**	**13**	**130**	**10.0**	**0**	**2**	**0**	**12**	**2**

BUCKLEY, TERRELL   CB   DOLPHINS

PERSONAL: Born June 7, 1971, in Pascagoula, Miss. ... 5-9/176. ... Full name: Douglas Terrell Buckley.
HIGH SCHOOL: Pascagoula (Miss.).
COLLEGE: Florida State.
TRANSACTIONS/CAREER NOTES: Selected after junior season by Green Bay Packers in first round (fifth pick overall) of 1992 NFL draft. ... Signed by Packers (September 11, 1992). ... Granted roster exemption for one game (September 1992). ... Traded by Packers to Miami Dolphins for past considerations (April 3, 1995). ... Granted unconditional free agency (February 11, 2000). ... Signed by Denver Broncos (July 20, 2000). ... Granted unconditional free agency (March 2, 2001). ... Signed by New England Patriots (July 13, 2001). ... Granted unconditional free agency (March 1, 2002). ... Signed by Tampa Bay Buccaneers (July 8, 2002). ... Released by Buccaneers (September 1, 2002). ... Signed by New England Patriots (September 5, 2002). ... Granted unconditional free agency (February 28, 2003). ... Signed by Dolphins (March 13, 2003).
CHAMPIONSHIP GAME EXPERIENCE: Played in AFC championship game (2001 season). ... Member of Super Bowl championship team (2001 season).
HONORS: Named defensive back on THE SPORTING NEWS college All-America second team (1990). ... Jim Thorpe Award winner (1991). ... Named defensive back on THE SPORTING NEWS college All-America first team (1991).

Year Team	G	GS	TOTALS Tk.	Ast.	Sks.	INTERCEPTIONS No.	Yds.	Avg.	TD	PUNT RETURNS No.	Yds.	Avg.	TD	TOTALS TD	2pt.	Pts.	Fum.
1992—Green Bay NFL	14	12	30	2	0.0	3	33	11.0	1	21	211	10.0	1	2	0	12	7
1993—Green Bay NFL	16	16	47	1	0.0	2	31	15.5	0	11	76	6.9	0	0	0	0	1
1994—Green Bay NFL	16	16	48	11	0.0	5	38	7.6	0	0	0	0.0	0	0	0	0	0
1995—Miami NFL	16	4	23	3	0.0	1	0	0.0	0	0	0	0.0	0	0	0	0	0
1996—Miami NFL	16	16	46	7	0.0	6	*164	27.3	1	3	24	8.0	0	1	0	6	1
1997—Miami NFL	16	16	67	18	0.0	4	26	6.5	0	4	58	14.5	0	1	0	6	0
1998—Miami NFL	16	16	44	7	0.0	8	157	19.6	1	29	354	12.2	0	1	0	6	1
1999—Miami NFL	16	11	30	5	1.0	3	3	1.0	0	8	13	1.6	0	0	0	0	1
2000—Denver NFL	16	16	35	3	0.0	6	110	18.3	0	2	10	5.0	0	1	0	6	0
2001—New England NFL	15	1	24	2	1.0	3	76	25.3	1	0	0	0.0	0	1	0	6	0
2002—New England NFL	16	2	21	0	0.0	4	50	12.5	0	0	0	0.0	0	0	0	0	1
Pro totals (11 years)	**173**	**126**	**415**	**59**	**2.0**	**45**	**688**	**15.3**	**5**	**78**	**746**	**9.6**	**1**	**7**	**0**	**42**	**12**

BUCKNER, BRENTSON   DT   PANTHERS

PERSONAL: Born September 30, 1971, in Columbus, Ga. ... 6-2/305. ... Full name: Brentson Andre Buckner. ... Name pronounced BRENT-son.
HIGH SCHOOL: Carver (Columbus, Ga.).
COLLEGE: Clemson (degree in English, 1993).
TRANSACTIONS/CAREER NOTES: Selected by Pittsburgh Steelers in second round (50th pick overall) of 1994 NFL Draft. ... Signed by Steelers (July 23, 1994). ... Traded by Steelers to Kansas City Chiefs for seventh-round pick (traded to San Diego) in 1997 draft (April 4, 1997). ... Claimed on waivers by Cincinnati Bengals (August 25, 1997). ... Granted unconditional free agency (February 13, 1998). ... Signed by San Francisco 49ers (May 26, 1998). ... On physically unable to perform list with pulled quadricep muscle (July 17-August 15, 1998). ... Granted unconditional free agency (February 12, 1999). ... Re-signed by 49ers (April 7, 1999). ... Granted unconditional free agency (February 11, 2000). ... Re-signed by 49ers (August 8, 2000). ... Granted unconditional free agency (March 2, 2001). ... Signed by Carolina Panthers (April 21, 2001). ... On suspended list for violating league substance abuse policy (November 4-December 2, 2002).
CHAMPIONSHIP GAME EXPERIENCE: Played in AFC championship game (1994 and 1995 seasons). ... Played in Super Bowl XXX (1995 season).

Year	Team	G	GS	TOTALS Tk.	Ast.	Sks.	INTERCEPTIONS No.	Yds.	Avg.	TD
1994—Pittsburgh NFL		13	5	13	5	2.0	0	0	0.0	0
1995—Pittsburgh NFL		16	16	29	19	3.0	0	0	0.0	0
1996—Pittsburgh NFL		15	14	24	12	3.0	0	0	0.0	0
1997—Cincinnati NFL		14	5	32	7	0.0	0	0	0.0	0
1998—San Francisco NFL		13	0	10	6	0.5	0	0	0.0	0
1999—San Francisco NFL		16	5	29	15	1.0	0	0	0.0	0
2000—San Francisco NFL		16	16	41	14	7.0	0	0	0.0	0
2001—Carolina NFL		16	10	28	10	4.5	1	29	29.0	0
2002—Carolina NFL		12	12	24	8	5.0	0	0	0.0	0
Pro totals (9 years)		131	83	230	96	26.0	1	29	29.0	0

BULGER, MARC — QB — RAMS

PERSONAL: Born April 5, 1977, in Pittsburgh, Pa. ... 6-3/215. ... Full name: Marc Robert Bulger.
HIGH SCHOOL: Central Catholic (Pittsburgh).
COLLEGE: West Virginia.
TRANSACTIONS/CAREER NOTES: Selected by New Orleans Saints in sixth round (168th pick overall) of 2000 NFL draft. ... Signed by Saints (July 13, 2000). ... Released by Saints (August 22, 2000). ... Signed by St. Louis Rams to practice squad (October 24, 2000). ... Released by Rams (October 31, 2000). ... Signed by Atlanta Falcons to practice squad (December 1, 2000). ... Released by Falcons (December 13, 2000). ... Re-signed by Rams (January 12, 2001).
CHAMPIONSHIP GAME EXPERIENCE: Member of Rams for NFC championship game (2001 season); inactive. ... Member of Rams for Super Bowl XXXVI (2001 season); inactive.
SINGLE GAME HIGHS (regular season): Attempts—48 (November 10, 2002, vs. San Diego); completions—36 (November 10, 2002, vs. San Diego); yards—453 (November 10, 2002, vs. San Diego); and touchdown passes—4 (November 10, 2002, vs. San Diego).
STATISTICAL PLATEAUS: 300-yard passing games: 2002 (3).
MISCELLANEOUS: Regular-season record as starting NFL quarterback: 6-1 (.857).

				PASSING								RUSHING				TOTALS		
Year	Team	G	GS	Att.	Cmp.	Pct.	Yds.	TD	Int.	Avg.	Skd.	Rat.	Att.	Yds.	Avg.	TD	TD	2pt.	Pts.
2002—St. Louis NFL		7	7	214	138	64.5	1826	14	6	8.53	12	101.5	12	-13	-1.1	1	1	0	6

BULLARD, COURTLAND — LB — RAMS

PERSONAL: Born August 2, 1978, in Miami. ... 6-3/234.
HIGH SCHOOL: Southridge (Miami).
COLLEGE: Ohio State.
TRANSACTIONS/CAREER NOTES: Selected by St. Louis Rams in fifth round (167th pick overall) of 2002 NFL draft. ... Signed by Rams (July 10, 2002).

Year	Team	G	GS	TOTALS Tk.	Ast.	Sks.	INTERCEPTIONS No.	Yds.	Avg.	TD
2002—St. Louis NFL		11	1	1	0	0.0	0	0	0.0	0

BULLUCK, KEITH — LB — TITANS

PERSONAL: Born April 4, 1977, in Suffern, N.Y. ... 6-3/232. ... Full name: Keith J. Bulluck.
HIGH SCHOOL: Clarkstown (New City, N.Y.).
COLLEGE: Syracuse.
TRANSACTIONS/CAREER NOTES: Selected by Tennessee Titans in first round (30th pick overall) of 2000 NFL draft. ... Signed by Titans (July 19, 2000).
CHAMPIONSHIP GAME EXPERIENCE: Played in AFC championship game (2002 season).

Year	Team	G	GS	TOTALS Tk.	Ast.	Sks.	INTERCEPTIONS No.	Yds.	Avg.	TD
2000—Tennessee NFL		16	1	10	7	0.0	1	8	8.0	1
2001—Tennessee NFL		15	3	26	19	1.0	2	21	10.5	0
2002—Tennessee NFL		16	16	101	26	1.0	1	5	5.0	0
Pro totals (3 years)		47	20	137	52	2.0	4	34	8.5	1

BURGESS, DERRICK — LB/DE — EAGLES

PERSONAL: Born August 12, 1978, in Riverdale, Md. ... 6-2/266.
HIGH SCHOOL: Eleanor Roosevelt (Greenbelt, Md.).
COLLEGE: Mississippi.
TRANSACTIONS/CAREER NOTES: Selected by Philadelphia Eagles in third round (63rd pick overall) of 2001 NFL draft. ... Signed by Eagles (July 26, 2001).
CHAMPIONSHIP GAME EXPERIENCE: Played in NFC championship game (2001 season). ... Member of Eagles for NFC championship game (2002 season); inactive.

Year	Team	G	GS	TOTALS Tk.	Ast.	Sks.	INTERCEPTIONS No.	Yds.	Avg.	TD
2001—Philadelphia NFL		16	4	24	6	6.0	0	0	0.0	0
2002—Philadelphia NFL		1	0	1	0	0.0	0	0	0.0	0
Pro totals (2 years)		17	4	25	6	6.0	0	0	0.0	0

BURKE, THOMAS — DE

PERSONAL: Born October 12, 1976, in Poplar, Wis. ... 6-3/275.
HIGH SCHOOL: Northwestern (Poplar, Wis.).
COLLEGE: Wisconsin.
TRANSACTIONS/CAREER NOTES: Selected by Arizona Cardinals in third round (83rd pick overall) of 1999 NFL draft. ... Signed by Cardinals (June 18, 1999). ... On injured reserve with abdominal injury (December 15, 2000-remainder of season). ... Granted free agency (March 1, 2002). ... Re-signed by Cardinals (May 2, 2002). ... On injured reserve with thigh injury (December 4, 2002-remainder of season). ... Granted unconditional free agency (February 28, 2003).
HONORS: Named defensive end on THE SPORTING NEWS college All-America first team (1998).

			TOTALS		
Year Team	G	GS	Tk.	Ast.	Sks.
1999—Arizona NFL	16	3	24	11	2.5
2000—Arizona NFL	3	0	2	1	0.0
2001—Arizona NFL	12	9	16	7	2.0
2002—Arizona NFL	6	0	7	2	0.0
Pro totals (4 years)	37	12	49	21	4.5

BURNETT, ROB — DE — DOLPHINS

PERSONAL: Born August 27, 1967, in East Orange, N.J. ... 6-4/267. ... Full name: Robert Barry Burnett.
HIGH SCHOOL: Newfield (Selden, N.Y.).
COLLEGE: Syracuse (degree in economics).
TRANSACTIONS/CAREER NOTES: Selected by Cleveland Browns in fifth round (129th pick overall) of 1990 NFL draft. ... Signed by Browns (July 22, 1990). ... Granted free agency (March 1, 1993). ... Re-signed by Browns (June 11, 1993). ... Browns franchise moved to Baltimore and renamed Ravens for 1996 season (March 11, 1996). ... Granted unconditional free agency (February 11, 2000). ... Re-signed by Ravens (February 17, 2000). ... Released by Ravens (February 27, 2002). ... Signed by Miami Dolphins (June 12, 2002).
CHAMPIONSHIP GAME EXPERIENCE: Played in AFC championship game (2000 season). ... Member of Super Bowl championship team (2000 season).
HONORS: Played in Pro Bowl (1994 season).

			TOTALS			INTERCEPTIONS			
Year Team	G	GS	Tk.	Ast.	Sks.	No.	Yds.	Avg.	TD
1990—Cleveland NFL	16	6	38	19	2.0	0	0	0.0	0
1991—Cleveland NFL	13	8	17	14	3.0	0	0	0.0	0
1992—Cleveland NFL	16	16	37	23	9.0	0	0	0.0	0
1993—Cleveland NFL	16	16	39	37	9.0	0	0	0.0	0
1994—Cleveland NFL	16	16	41	13	10.0	0	0	0.0	0
1995—Cleveland NFL	16	16	40	15	7.5	0	0	0.0	0
1996—Baltimore NFL	6	6	21	2	3.0	0	0	0.0	0
1997—Baltimore NFL	15	15	33	7	4.0	0	0	0.0	0
1998—Baltimore NFL	16	16	37	12	2.5	0	0	0.0	0
1999—Baltimore NFL	16	16	39	17	6.5	0	0	0.0	0
2000—Baltimore NFL	16	16	40	9	10.5	1	3	3.0	0
2001—Baltimore NFL	13	13	16	10	0.0	0	0	0.0	0
2002—Miami NFL	15	0	10	5	4.0	0	0	0.0	0
Pro totals (13 years)	190	160	408	183	71.0	1	3	3.0	0

BURNS, JOE — RB — BILLS

PERSONAL: Born September 15, 1979, in Thomasville, Ga. ... 5-9/215. ... Full name: Joe Frank Burns.
HIGH SCHOOL: Thomas County (Ga.).
COLLEGE: Georgia Tech.
TRANSACTIONS/CAREER NOTES: Signed as non-drafted free agent by Buffalo Bills (April 26, 2002).
SINGLE GAME HIGHS (regular season): Attempts—4 (December 29, 2002, vs. Cincinnati); yards—7 (December 29, 2002, vs. Cincinnati); and rushing touchdowns—0.

			RUSHING				TOTALS			
Year Team	G	GS	Att.	Yds.	Avg.	TD	TD	2pt.	Pts.	Fum.
2002—Buffalo NFL	10	0	5	7	1.4	0	0	0	0	0

BURNS, KEITH — LB

PERSONAL: Born May 16, 1972, in Greelyville, S.C. ... 6-2/235. ... Full name: Keith Bernard Burns.
HIGH SCHOOL: T. C. Williams (Alexandria, Va.).
JUNIOR COLLEGE: Navarro College (Texas).
COLLEGE: Oklahoma State.
TRANSACTIONS/CAREER NOTES: Selected by Denver Broncos in seventh round (210th pick overall) of 1994 NFL draft. ... Signed by Broncos (July 12, 1994). ... Granted free agency (February 14, 1997). ... Re-signed by Broncos (June 30, 1997). ... Granted unconditional free agency (February 12, 1999). ... Signed by Chicago Bears (April 6, 1999). ... Released by Bears (August 27, 2000). ... Signed by Broncos (September 19, 2000). ... Granted unconditional free agency (March 2, 2001). ... Re-signed by Broncos (April 6, 2001). ... Released by Broncos (February 26, 2003).
CHAMPIONSHIP GAME EXPERIENCE: Played in AFC championship game (1997 and 1998 seasons). ... Member of Super Bowl championship team (1997 and 1998 seasons).

B

Year	Team	G	GS	TOTALS			INTERCEPTIONS			
				Tk.	Ast.	Sks.	No.	Yds.	Avg.	TD
1994	Denver NFL	11	1	15	3	0.0	0	0	0.0	0
1995	Denver NFL	16	0	10	3	1.5	0	0	0.0	0
1996	Denver NFL	16	0	1	0	0.0	0	0	0.0	0
1997	Denver NFL	16	0	1	0	0.0	0	0	0.0	0
1998	Denver NFL	16	0	7	2	0.0	0	0	0.0	0
1999	Chicago NFL	15	0	5	0	0.0	1	15	15.0	0
2000	Denver NFL	13	0	0	0	0.0	0	0	0.0	0
2001	Denver NFL	16	0	0	0	0.0	0	0	0.0	0
2002	Denver NFL	16	1	0	0	0.0	0	0	0.0	0
Pro totals (9 years)		135	2	39	8	1.5	1	15	15.0	0

BURRESS, PLAXICO — WR — STEELERS

PERSONAL: Born August 12, 1977, in Norfolk, Va. ... 6-5/226.
HIGH SCHOOL: Green Run (Virginia Beach, Va.).
COLLEGE: Michigan State.
TRANSACTIONS/CAREER NOTES: Selected after junior season by Pittsburgh Steelers in first round (eighth pick overall) of 2000 NFL draft. ... Signed by Steelers (July 20, 2000). ... On injured reserve with wrist injury (December 1, 2000-remainder of season).
CHAMPIONSHIP GAME EXPERIENCE: Played in AFC championship game (2001 season).
SINGLE GAME HIGHS (regular season): Receptions—9 (November 10, 2002, vs. Atlanta); yards—253 (November 10, 2002, vs. Atlanta); and touchdown receptions—2 (November 10, 2002, vs. Atlanta).
STATISTICAL PLATEAUS: 100-yard receiving games: 2001 (4), 2002 (4). Total: 8.

Year	Team	G	GS	RECEIVING			
				No.	Yds.	Avg.	TD
2000	Pittsburgh NFL	12	8	22	273	12.4	0
2001	Pittsburgh NFL	16	16	66	1008	15.3	6
2002	Pittsburgh NFL	16	15	78	1325	17.0	7
Pro totals (3 years)		44	39	166	2606	15.7	13

BURRIS, HENRY — QB — BEARS

PERSONAL: Born June 4, 1975, in Fort Smith, Ark. ... 6-0/195. ... Full name: Henry Armand Burris. ... Cousin of Priest Holmes, running back, Kansas City Chiefs.
HIGH SCHOOL: Spiro (Okla.).
COLLEGE: Temple (degree in broadcasting/communications).
TRANSACTIONS/CAREER NOTES: Signed by Calgary Stampeders of CFL (May 1997). ... Signed by Saskatchewan Roughriders of CFL (March 7, 2000). ... Signed as non-drafted free agent by Green Bay Packers (February 27, 2001). ... Released by Packers (November 30, 2001). ... Re-signed by Packers to practice squad (December 2, 2001). ... Granted free agency following 2001 season. ... Signed by Chicago Bears (February 8, 2002). ... Assigned by Bears to Berlin Thunder in 2003 NFL Europe enhancement allocation program (February 4, 2003).
CHAMPIONSHIP GAME EXPERIENCE: Member of CFL championship team (1998).
SINGLE GAME HIGHS (regular season): Attempts—22 (December 22, 2002, vs. Carolina); completions—8 (December 22, 2002, vs. Carolina); yards—78 (December 29, 2002, vs. Tampa Bay); and touchdown passes—1 (December 22, 2002, vs. Carolina).
MISCELLANEOUS: Regular-season record as starting NFL quarterback: 0-1.

Year	Team	G	GS	PASSING								RUSHING				TOTALS		
				Att.	Cmp.	Pct.	Yds.	TD	Int.	Avg.	Skd.	Rat.	Att.	Yds.	Avg.	TD	TD	2pt.	Pts.
1997	Calgary CFL									Did not play.									
1998	Calgary CFL	3	0	11	5	45.5	83	0	1	7.55	0	33.5	2	4	2.0	0	0	0	0
1999	Calgary CFL	3	2	60	36	60.0	529	4	4	8.82	0	83.3	13	81	6.2	0	0	0	0
2000	Saskatchewan CFL	16	16	576	308	53.5	4647	30	25	8.07	0	79.5	68	188	2.8	8	8	0	48
2002	Berlin NFLE	...	...	0	0	0.0	0	0	0	0.0	0	...	0	0	0.0	0	0	0	0
—	Chicago NFL	6	1	51	18	35.3	207	3	5	4.06	4	28.4	15	104	6.9	0	0	0	0
NFL Europe totals (1 year)		...	...	0	0	0.0	0	0	0	0.0	0	...	0	0	0.0	0	0	0	0
CFL totals (3 years)		22	18	647	349	53.9	5259	34	30	8.13	0	79.1	83	273	3.3	8	8	0	48
NFL totals (1 year)		6	1	51	18	35.3	207	3	5	4.06	4	28.4	15	104	6.9	0	0	0	0
Pro totals (5 years)		...	...	698	367	52.6	5466	37	35	7.83	4	75.3	98	377	3.8	8	8	0	48

BURRIS, JEFF — CB — BENGALS

PERSONAL: Born June 7, 1972, in Rock Hill, S.C. ... 6-0/190. ... Full name: Jeffrey Lamar Burris.
HIGH SCHOOL: Northwestern (Rock Hill, S.C.).
COLLEGE: Notre Dame.
TRANSACTIONS/CAREER NOTES: Selected by Buffalo Bills in first round (27th pick overall) of 1994 NFL draft. ... Signed by Bills (July 18, 1994). ... On injured reserve with knee injury (November 20, 1995-remainder of season). ... Granted unconditional free agency (February 13, 1998). ... Signed by Indianapolis Colts (February 18, 1998). ... Released by Colts (February 21, 2002). ... Signed by Cincinnati Bengals (March 26, 2002).
HONORS: Named defensive back on THE SPORTING NEWS college All-America second team (1993).

Year	Team	G	GS	TOTALS			INTERCEPTIONS				PUNT RETURNS				TOTALS			
				Tk.	Ast.	Sks.	No.	Yds.	Avg.	TD	No.	Yds.	Avg.	TD	TD	2pt.	Pts.	Fum.
1994	Buffalo NFL	16	0	13	3	0.0	2	24	12.0	0	32	332	10.4	0	0	0	0	2
1995	Buffalo NFL	9	9	28	6	0.0	1	19	19.0	0	20	229	11.5	0	0	0	0	0
1996	Buffalo NFL	15	15	41	9	0.0	1	28	28.0	0	27	286	10.6	0	0	0	0	1
1997	Buffalo NFL	14	14	39	6	0.0	2	19	9.5	0	21	198	9.4	0	0	0	0	3
1998	Indianapolis NFL	14	14	57	11	0.0	1	0	0.0	0	0	0	0.0	0	0	0	0	0
1999	Indianapolis NFL	16	16	67	16	2.0	2	83	41.5	0	0	0	0.0	0	0	0	0	0
2000	Indianapolis NFL	16	16	69	8	3.0	4	38	9.5	1	0	0	0.0	0	1	0	6	0
2001	Indianapolis NFL	15	15	54	4	0.0	3	69	23.0	1	0	0	0.0	0	1	0	6	0
2002	Cincinnati NFL	16	12	50	12	0.0	1	5	5.0	0	0	0	0.0	0	0	0	0	0
Pro totals (9 years)		131	111	418	75	5.0	17	285	16.8	2	100	1045	10.5	0	2	0	12	6

BURROUGH, JOHN   DE

PERSONAL: Born May 17, 1972, in Laramie, Wyo. ... 6-4/276.
HIGH SCHOOL: Pinedale (Wyo.).
COLLEGE: Wyoming.
TRANSACTIONS/CAREER NOTES: Selected by Atlanta Falcons in seventh round (245th pick overall) of 1995 NFL draft. ... Signed by Falcons (June 30, 1995). ... Granted free agency (February 13, 1998). ... Re-signed by Falcons (April 1, 1998). ... Granted unconditional free agency (February 12, 1999). ... Signed by Minnesota Vikings (February 17, 1999). ... Released by Vikings (March 1, 2001). ... Signed by St. Louis Rams (April 23, 2002). ... Released by Rams (September 25, 2002).
CHAMPIONSHIP GAME EXPERIENCE: Played in NFC championship game (1998 and 2000 seasons). ... Played in Super Bowl XXXIII (1998 season).

Year Team	G	GS	TOTALS Tk.	Ast.	Sks.
1995—Atlanta NFL	16	0	4	1	0.0
1996—Atlanta NFL	16	1	8	4	0.0
1997—Atlanta NFL	16	1	10	3	1.0
1998—Atlanta NFL	16	3	11	10	0.5
1999—Minnesota NFL	10	3	10	4	1.0
2000—Minnesota NFL	14	6	19	10	2.0
2002—St. Louis NFL	1	0	0	0	0.0
Pro totals (7 years)	**89**	**14**	**62**	**32**	**4.5**

BURTON, SHANE   DT   PANTHERS

PERSONAL: Born January 18, 1974, in Logan, W.Va. ... 6-6/305. ... Full name: Franklin Shane Burton.
HIGH SCHOOL: Bandys (Catawba, N.C.).
COLLEGE: Tennessee.
TRANSACTIONS/CAREER NOTES: Selected by Miami Dolphins in fifth round (150th pick overall) of 1996 NFL draft. ... Signed by Dolphins (June 18, 1996). ... Granted free agency (February 12, 1999). ... Re-signed by Dolphins (April 13, 1999). ... Claimed on waivers by Chicago Bears (August 24, 1999). ... Granted unconditional free agency (February 11, 2000). ... Signed by New York Jets (March 20, 2000). ... Released by Jets (February 26, 2002). ... Signed by Carolina Panthers (March 27, 2002).

Year Team	G	GS	TOTALS Tk.	Ast.	Sks.	INTERCEPTIONS No.	Yds.	Avg.	TD
1996—Miami NFL	16	8	26	3	3.0	0	0	0.0	0
1997—Miami NFL	16	4	18	9	4.0	0	0	0.0	0
1998—Miami NFL	15	0	12	5	2.0	0	0	0.0	0
1999—Chicago NFL	15	0	7	4	3.0	1	37	37.0	0
2000—New York Jets NFL	16	16	31	18	1.0	0	0	0.0	0
2001—New York Jets NFL	15	13	24	16	2.0	1	0	0.0	0
2002—Carolina NFL	16	4	16	6	1.0	0	0	0.0	0
Pro totals (7 years)	**109**	**45**	**134**	**61**	**16.0**	**2**	**37**	**18.5**	**0**

BUSH, DEVIN   S

PERSONAL: Born July 3, 1973, in Miami. ... 6-0/210. ... Full name: Devin Marquese Bush.
HIGH SCHOOL: Hialeah (Fla.) Miami Lakes.
COLLEGE: Florida State.
TRANSACTIONS/CAREER NOTES: Selected after junior season by Atlanta Falcons in first round (26th pick overall) of 1995 NFL draft. ... Signed by Falcons (August 8, 1995). ... Granted unconditional free agency (February 12, 1999). ... Signed by St. Louis Rams (February 18, 1999). ... Released by Rams (September 2, 2001). ... Signed by Cleveland Browns (September 3, 2001). ... Granted unconditional free agency (February 28, 2003).
CHAMPIONSHIP GAME EXPERIENCE: Member of Falcons for NFC championship game (1998 season); inactive. ... Played in Super Bowl XXXI-II (1998 season). ... Played in NFC championship game (1999 season). ... Member of Super Bowl championship team (1999 season).

Year Team	G	GS	TOTALS Tk.	Ast.	Sks.	INTERCEPTIONS No.	Yds.	Avg.	TD
1995—Atlanta NFL	11	5	21	14	0.0	1	0	0.0	0
1996—Atlanta NFL	16	15	51	8	0.0	1	2	2.0	0
1997—Atlanta NFL	16	16	70	15	0.0	1	4	4.0	0
1998—Atlanta NFL	13	0	15	4	0.0	0	0	0.0	0
1999—St. Louis NFL	16	7	35	7	0.0	2	45	22.5	1
2000—St. Louis NFL	13	12	50	17	1.0	0	0	0.0	0
2001—Cleveland NFL	16	7	39	19	0.0	2	62	31.0	1
2002—Cleveland NFL	15	9	34	6	0.0	0	0	0.0	0
Pro totals (8 years)	**116**	**71**	**315**	**90**	**1.0**	**7**	**113**	**16.1**	**2**

BUSH, LEW   LB   CHIEFS

PERSONAL: Born December 2, 1969, in Atlanta. ... 6-2/250. ... Full name: Lewis Fitzgerald Bush.
HIGH SCHOOL: Washington (Tacoma, Wash.).
COLLEGE: Washington State.
TRANSACTIONS/CAREER NOTES: Selected by San Diego Chargers in fourth round (99th pick overall) of 1993 NFL draft. ... Signed by Chargers (July 9, 1993). ... Granted free agency (February 16, 1996). ... Re-signed by Chargers (June 14, 1996). ... Granted unconditional free agency (February 14, 1997). ... Re-signed by Chargers (May 13, 1997). ... On injured reserve with knee injury (December 26, 1998-remainder of season). ... Released by Chargers (March 1, 2000). ... Signed by Kansas City Chiefs (March 4, 2000). ... On suspended list for violating league substance abuse policy (November 6-December 2, 2002).
CHAMPIONSHIP GAME EXPERIENCE: Played in AFC championship game (1994 season). ... Played in Super Bowl XXIX (1994 season).

Year	Team	G	GS	TOTALS			INTERCEPTIONS			
				Tk.	Ast.	Sks.	No.	Yds.	Avg.	TD
1993—San Diego NFL		16	0	1	1	0.0	0	0	0.0	0
1994—San Diego NFL		16	0	3	0	0.0	0	0	0.0	0
1995—San Diego NFL		16	15	45	11	0.0	1	0	0.0	0
1996—San Diego NFL		16	16	48	16	1.0	0	0	0.0	0
1997—San Diego NFL		14	13	51	5	0.0	0	0	0.0	0
1998—San Diego NFL		10	10	12	6	1.0	0	0	0.0	0
1999—San Diego NFL		16	14	40	4	1.0	0	0	0.0	0
2000—Kansas City NFL		16	8	26	3	1.0	1	33	33.0	0
2001—Kansas City NFL		12	11	26	6	0.0	0	0	0.0	0
2002—Kansas City NFL		9	5	19	2	0.0	0	0	0.0	0
Pro totals (10 years)		141	92	271	54	4.0	2	33	16.5	0

BUSH, STEVE — TE/FB — CARDINALS

PERSONAL: Born July 4, 1974, in Phoenix. ... 6-3/274. ... Full name: Steven Jack Bush.

HIGH SCHOOL: Paradise Valley (Phoenix).

COLLEGE: Arizona State.

TRANSACTIONS/CAREER NOTES: Signed as non-drafted free agent by Cincinnati Bengals (April 25, 1997). ... Granted free agency (February 11, 2000). ... Re-signed by Bengals (April 25, 2000). ... Granted unconditional free agency (March 2, 2001). ... Signed by St. Louis Rams (July 20, 2001). ... Released by Rams (August 27, 2001). ... Signed by Arizona Cardinals (November 6, 2001).

SINGLE GAME HIGHS (regular season): Receptions—4 (December 21, 2002, vs. San Francisco); yards—31 (December 24, 2000, vs. Philadelphia); and touchdown receptions—1 (December 15, 2002, vs. St. Louis).

Year	Team	G	GS	RECEIVING			
				No.	Yds.	Avg.	TD
1997—Cincinnati NFL		16	0	0	0	0.0	0
1998—Cincinnati NFL		12	2	4	39	9.8	0
1999—Cincinnati NFL		13	0	1	4	4.0	0
2000—Cincinnati NFL		16	0	3	39	13.0	0
2001—Arizona NFL		9	7	8	80	10.0	0
2002—Arizona NFL		16	12	19	121	6.4	1
Pro totals (6 years)		82	21	35	283	8.1	1

BUTLER, JERAMETRIUS — CB — RAMS

PERSONAL: Born November 28, 1978, in Dallas. ... 5-10/181.

HIGH SCHOOL: Carter (Dallas).

COLLEGE: Kansas State.

TRANSACTIONS/CAREER NOTES: Selected after junior season by St. Louis Rams in fifth round (145th pick overall) of 2001 NFL draft. ... Signed by Rams (June 27, 2001).

CHAMPIONSHIP GAME EXPERIENCE: Played in NFC championship game (2001 season). ... Played in Super Bowl XXXVI (2001 season).

Year	Team	G	GS	TOTALS			INTERCEPTIONS			
				Tk.	Ast.	Sks.	No.	Yds.	Avg.	TD
2001—St. Louis NFL		16	0	8	2	0.0	0	0	0.0	0
2002—St. Louis NFL		9	0	2	0	0.0	0	0	0.0	0
Pro totals (2 years)		25	0	10	2	0.0	0	0	0.0	0

BYRD, ISAAC — WR

PERSONAL: Born November 16, 1974, in St. Louis. ... 6-1/188. ... Full name: Isaac Byrd III. ... Brother of Israel Byrd, defensive back with New Orleans Saints (1994-95).

HIGH SCHOOL: Parkway Central (Chesterfield, Mo.).

COLLEGE: Kansas.

TRANSACTIONS/CAREER NOTES: Selected by Kansas City Chiefs in sixth round (195th pick overall) of 1997 NFL draft. ... Signed by Chiefs (May 6, 1997). ... Released by Chiefs (August 23, 1997). ... Re-signed by Chiefs to practice squad (August 25, 1997). ... Signed by Tennessee Oilers off Chiefs practice squad (November 7, 1997). ... Oilers franchise renamed Tennessee Titans for 1999 season (December 26, 1998). ... Granted free agency (February 11, 2000). ... Re-signed by Titans (June 6, 2000). ... Claimed on waivers by Carolina Panthers (August 29, 2000). ... Granted unconditional free agency (February 28, 2003).

CHAMPIONSHIP GAME EXPERIENCE: Played in AFC championship game (1999 season). ... Played in Super Bowl XXXIV (1999 season).

SINGLE GAME HIGHS (regular season): Receptions—7 (December 30, 2001, vs. Arizona); yards—84 (December 19, 1999, vs. Atlanta); and touchdown receptions—1 (October 6, 2002, vs. Arizona).

Year	Team	G	GS	RECEIVING				PUNT RETURNS				KICKOFF RETURNS				TOTALS			
				No.	Yds.	Avg.	TD	No.	Yds.	Avg.	TD	No.	Yds.	Avg.	TD	TD	2pt.	Pts.	Fum.
1997—Tennessee NFL		2	0	0	0	0.0	0	0	0	0.0	0	0	0	0.0	0	0	0	0	0
1998—Tennessee NFL		4	3	6	71	11.8	0	0	0	0.0	0	0	0	0.0	0	0	0	0	0
1999—Tennessee NFL		12	6	14	261	18.6	2	2	8	4.0	0	2	16	8.0	0	2	0	12	1
2000—Carolina NFL		15	4	22	241	11.0	2	1	10	10.0	0	9	172	19.1	0	2	0	12	0
2001—Carolina NFL		15	5	37	492	13.3	1	5	56	11.2	0	10	225	22.5	0	1	0	6	0
2002—Carolina NFL		13	3	14	164	11.7	1	2	17	8.5	0	14	294	21.0	0	1	0	6	1
Pro totals (6 years)		61	21	93	1229	13.2	6	10	91	9.1	0	35	707	20.2	0	6	0	36	2

BYRDSONG, SHAWN   S   SAINTS

PERSONAL: Born October 2, 1979, in Longview, Texas. ... 5-10/188. ... Full name: Rodrick Shawn Byrdsong.
HIGH SCHOOL: Longview (Texas).
COLLEGE: Mississippi State.
TRANSACTIONS/CAREER NOTES: Signed as non-drafted free agent by Baltimore Ravens (April 26, 2002). ... Released by Ravens (September 24, 2002). ... Signed by New Orleans Saints (February 4, 2003). ... Assigned by Saints to Berlin Thunder in 2003 NFL Europe enhancement allocation program (February 4, 2003).

			TOTALS			INTERCEPTIONS			
Year Team	G	GS	Tk.	Ast.	Sks.	No.	Yds.	Avg.	TD
2002—Baltimore NFL	1	0	0	0	0.0	0	0	0.0	0

CADREZ, GLENN   LB

PERSONAL: Born January 2, 1970, in El Centro, Calif. ... 6-2/247. ... Full name: Glenn E. Cadrez. ... Name pronounced ku-DREZ.
HIGH SCHOOL: El Centro Central Union (El Centro, Calif.).
JUNIOR COLLEGE: Chaffey College (Calif.).
COLLEGE: Houston.
TRANSACTIONS/CAREER NOTES: Selected by New York Jets in sixth round (154th pick overall) of 1992 NFL draft. ... Signed by Jets (July 13, 1992). ... Released by Jets (September 19, 1995). ... Signed by Denver Broncos (September 27, 1995). ... Released by Broncos (May 2, 2001). ... Signed by Kansas City Chiefs (June 6, 2001). ... Granted unconditional free agency (March 1, 2002). ... Re-signed by Chiefs (March 13, 2002). ... On injured reserve with neck injury (December 7, 2002-remainder of season). ... Granted unconditional free agency (February 28, 2003).
CHAMPIONSHIP GAME EXPERIENCE: Played in AFC championship game (1997 and 1998 seasons). ... Member of Super Bowl championship team (1997 and 1998 seasons).

			TOTALS			INTERCEPTIONS			
Year Team	G	GS	Tk.	Ast.	Sks.	No.	Yds.	Avg.	TD
1992—New York Jets NFL	16	0	1	0	0.0	0	0	0.0	0
1993—New York Jets NFL	16	0	5	1	0.0	0	0	0.0	0
1994—New York Jets NFL	16	0	0	0	0.0	0	0	0.0	0
1995—New York Jets NFL	1	0	0	0	0.0	0	0	0.0	0
—Denver NFL	10	7	20	4	2.0	0	0	0.0	0
1996—Denver NFL	16	0	7	1	0.0	0	0	0.0	0
1997—Denver NFL	16	0	4	1	0.0	0	0	0.0	0
1998—Denver NFL	16	15	56	20	4.0	2	11	5.5	0
1999—Denver NFL	16	15	60	22	7.0	0	0	0.0	0
2000—Denver NFL	16	3	7	0	0.0	0	0	0.0	0
2001—Kansas City NFL	16	5	23	9	1.5	1	0	0.0	0
2002—Kansas City NFL	12	1	11	1	0.0	0	0	0.0	0
Pro totals (11 years)	167	46	194	59	14.5	3	11	3.7	0

CALDWELL, MIKE   LB   BEARS

PERSONAL: Born August 31, 1971, in Oak Ridge, Tenn. ... 6-2/235. ... Full name: Mike Isiah Caldwell. ... Nickname: Zeke.
HIGH SCHOOL: Oak Ridge (Tenn.).
COLLEGE: Middle Tennessee State (degree in business administration, 1996).
TRANSACTIONS/CAREER NOTES: Selected by Cleveland Browns in third round (83rd pick overall) of 1993 NFL draft. ... Signed by Browns (July 14, 1993). ... Granted free agency (February 16, 1996). ... Browns franchise moved to Baltimore and renamed Ravens for 1996 season (March 11, 1996). ... Re-signed by Ravens for 1996 season. ... Granted unconditional free agency (February 14, 1997). ... Signed by Arizona Cardinals (July 16, 1997). ... Granted unconditional free agency (February 13, 1998). ... Signed by Philadelphia Eagles (April 9, 1998). ... Granted unconditional free agency (March 1, 2002). ... Signed by Chicago Bears (March 15, 2002).
CHAMPIONSHIP GAME EXPERIENCE: Played in NFC championship game (2001 season).

			TOTALS			INTERCEPTIONS			
Year Team	G	GS	Tk.	Ast.	Sks.	No.	Yds.	Avg.	TD
1993—Cleveland NFL	15	1	13	29	0.0	0	0	0.0	0
1994—Cleveland NFL	16	1	30	10	0.0	1	0	0.0	0
1995—Cleveland NFL	16	6	58	12	0.0	2	24	12.0	▲1
1996—Baltimore NFL	9	9	43	11	4.5	1	45	45.0	1
1997—Arizona NFL	16	0	24	5	2.0	1	5	5.0	0
1998—Philadelphia NFL	16	8	33	14	1.0	1	33	33.0	0
1999—Philadelphia NFL	14	2	19	9	1.0	1	12	12.0	0
2000—Philadelphia NFL	16	3	42	5	0.0	1	26	26.0	1
2001—Philadelphia NFL	16	16	72	23	3.0	0	0	0.0	0
2002—Chicago NFL	16	3	43	15	3.0	0	0	0.0	0
Pro totals (10 years)	150	49	377	133	14.5	8	145	18.1	3

CALDWELL, RECHE   WR   CHARGERS

PERSONAL: Born March 28, 1979, in Tampa, Fla. ... 5-11/194. ... Full name: Donald Reche Caldwell Jr..
HIGH SCHOOL: Jefferson (Tampa, Fla.).
COLLEGE: Florida.
TRANSACTIONS/CAREER NOTES: Selected after junior season by San Diego Chargers in second round (48th pick overall) of 2002 NFL draft. ... Signed by Chargers (July 22, 2002).
SINGLE GAME HIGHS (regular season): Receptions—4 (December 29, 2002, vs. Seattle); yards—53 (December 22, 2002, vs. Kansas City); and touchdown receptions—1 (November 17, 2002, vs. San Francisco).

			RUSHING				RECEIVING				PUNT RETURNS				KICKOFF RETURNS				TOTALS		
Year Team	G	GS	Att.	Yds.	Avg.	TD	No.	Yds.	Avg.	TD	No.	Yds.	Avg.	TD	No.	Yds.	Avg.	TD	TD	2pt.	Pts.
2002—San Diego NFL....	16	2	2	9	4.5	0	22	208	9.5	3	2	-2	-1.0	0	9	220	24.4	0	3	1	20

CALMUS, ROCKY　　　　　LB　　　　　TITANS

PERSONAL: Born August 1, 1979, in Tulsa, Okla. ... 6-3/235.
HIGH SCHOOL: Jenks (Okla.).
COLLEGE: Oklahoma.
TRANSACTIONS/CAREER NOTES: Selected by Tennessee Titans in third round (77th pick overall) of 2002 NFL draft. ... Signed by Titans (July 24, 2002).
CHAMPIONSHIP GAME EXPERIENCE: Member of Titans for AFC championship game (2002 season); inactive.
HONORS: Named linebacker on THE SPORTING NEWS college All-America first team (2001). ... Butkus Award winner (2001).

			TOTALS			INTERCEPTIONS			
Year	Team	G	GS	Tk.	Ast.	Sks.	No.	Yds.	Avg.	TD
2002—Tennessee NFL		13	1	7	4	0.0	0	0	0.0	0

CAMPBELL, DANIEL　　　　　TE　　　　　COWBOYS

PERSONAL: Born April 13, 1976, in Glen Rose, Texas. ... 6-5/263. ... Full name: Daniel Allen Campbell.
HIGH SCHOOL: Glen Rose (Texas).
COLLEGE: Texas A&M.
TRANSACTIONS/CAREER NOTES: Selected by New York Giants in third round (79th pick overall) of 1999 NFL draft. ... Signed by Giants (July 29, 1999). ... Granted free agency (March 1, 2002). ... Re-signed by Giants (March 27, 2002). ... Granted unconditional free agency (February 28, 2003). ... Signed by Dallas Cowboys (March 11, 2003).
CHAMPIONSHIP GAME EXPERIENCE: Played in NFC championship game (2000 season). ... Played in Super Bowl XXXV (2000 season).
SINGLE GAME HIGHS (regular season): Receptions—4 (November 10, 2002, vs. Minnesota); yards—35 (November 10, 2002, vs. Minnesota); and touchdown receptions—1 (December 1, 2002, vs. Tennessee).

				RECEIVING			
Year	Team	G	GS	No.	Yds.	Avg.	TD
1999—New York Giants NFL		12	1	0	0	0.0	0
2000—New York Giants NFL		16	4	8	46	5.8	3
2001—New York Giants NFL		16	13	13	148	11.4	1
2002—New York Giants NFL		16	16	22	175	8.0	1
Pro totals (4 years)		60	34	43	369	8.6	5

CAMPBELL, KELLY　　　　　WR　　　　　VIKINGS

PERSONAL: Born July 23, 1980, in Atlanta. ... 5-10/171.
HIGH SCHOOL: Mays (Atlanta).
COLLEGE: Georgia Tech.
TRANSACTIONS/CAREER NOTES: Signed non-drafted free agent by Minnesota Vikings (April 26, 2002). ... Released by Vikings (September 24, 2002). ... Re-signed by Vikings to practice squad (September 26, 2002). ... Activated (November 6, 2002).
SINGLE GAME HIGHS (regular season): Receptions—6 (November 24, 2002, vs. New England); yards—63 (November 24, 2002, vs. New England); and touchdown receptions—2 (December 29, 2002, vs. Detroit).

				RECEIVING			
Year	Team	G	GS	No.	Yds.	Avg.	TD
2002—Minnesota NFL		6	2	13	176	13.5	3

CAMPBELL, KHARY　　　　　LB　　　　　JETS

PERSONAL: Born April 4, 1979, in Toledo, Ohio. ... 6-1/230.
HIGH SCHOOL: Sylvania Southview (Toledo, Ohio).
COLLEGE: Bowling Green.
TRANSACTIONS/CAREER NOTES: Signed as non-drafted free agent by Dallas Cowboys (April 26, 2002). ... Released by Cowboys (August 27, 2002). ... Re-signed by Cowboys to practice squad (September 3, 2002). ... Signed by New York Jets off Cowboys practice squad (September 25, 2002). ... Re-signed by Jets (April 2, 2003).

				TOTALS			INTERCEPTIONS			
Year	Team	G	GS	Tk.	Ast.	Sks.	No.	Yds.	Avg.	TD
2002—New York Jets NFL		9	0	0	0	0.0	0	0	0.0	0

CAMPBELL, LAMAR　　　　　S　　　　　LIONS

PERSONAL: Born August 29, 1976, in Chester, Pa. ... 5-11/198.
HIGH SCHOOL: Strath Haven (Wallingford, Pa.).
COLLEGE: Wisconsin.
TRANSACTIONS/CAREER NOTES: Signed as non-drafted free agent by Detroit Lions (April 24, 1998). ... Granted free agency (March 2, 2001). ... Re-signed by Lions (April 19, 2001). ... Granted unconditional free agency (March 1, 2002). ... Re-signed by Lions (March 14, 2002).

				TOTALS			INTERCEPTIONS			
Year	Team	G	GS	Tk.	Ast.	Sks.	No.	Yds.	Avg.	TD
1998—Detroit NFL		12	0	1	0	0.0	0	0	0.0	0
1999—Detroit NFL		15	2	15	4	0.0	0	0	0.0	0
2000—Detroit NFL		16	2	23	15	0.0	1	42	42.0	1
2001—Detroit NFL		12	12	35	15	1.0	0	0	0.0	0
2002—Detroit NFL		9	2	6	3	0.0	0	0	0.0	0
Pro totals (5 years)		64	18	80	37	1.0	1	42	42.0	1

CAMPBELL, MARK — TE — BILLS

PERSONAL: Born December 6, 1975, in Clawson, Mich. ... 6-6/260.
HIGH SCHOOL: Bishop Foley (Madison Heights, Mich.).
COLLEGE: Michigan.
TRANSACTIONS/CAREER NOTES: Signed as non-drafted free agent by Cleveland Browns (April 23, 1999). ... On injured reserve with ankle injury (December 14, 1999-remainder of season). ... On injured reserve with leg injury (September 1, 2001-entire season). ... Traded by Browns to Buffalo Bills for undisclosed pick in 2004 draft (February 28, 2003).
SINGLE GAME HIGHS (regular season): Receptions—7 (October 27, 2002, vs. New York Jets); yards—34 (October 27, 2002, vs. New York Jets); and touchdown receptions—1 (December 22, 2002, vs. Baltimore).

			RECEIVING				KICKOFF RETURNS				TOTALS			
Year Team	G	GS	No.	Yds.	Avg.	TD	No.	Yds.	Avg.	TD	TD	2pt.	Pts.	Fum.
1999—Cleveland NFL	14	4	9	131	14.6	0	3	28	9.3	0	0	0	0	0
2000—Cleveland NFL	16	10	12	80	6.7	1	3	30	10.0	0	1	0	6	0
2002—Cleveland NFL	16	16	25	179	7.2	3	2	21	10.5	0	3	0	18	0
Pro totals (3 years)	46	30	46	390	8.5	4	8	79	9.9	0	4	0	24	0

CANIDATE, TRUNG — RB — REDSKINS

PERSONAL: Born March 3, 1977, in Phoenix. ... 5-11/205. ... Full name: Trung Jered Canidate.
HIGH SCHOOL: Central (Phoenix).
COLLEGE: Arizona.
TRANSACTIONS/CAREER NOTES: Selected by St. Louis Rams in first round (31st pick overall) of 2000 NFL draft. ... Signed by Rams (July 20, 2000). ... On injured reserve with wrist injury (November 13, 2000-remainder of season). ... Traded by Rams to Washington Redskins for G David Loverne and fourth-round pick (DB DeJuan Groce) in 2003 draft (February 28, 2003).
CHAMPIONSHIP GAME EXPERIENCE: Played in NFC championship game (2001 season). ... Played in Super Bowl XXXVI (2001 season).
SINGLE GAME HIGHS (regular season): Attempts—23 (October 21, 2001, vs. New York Jets); yards—195 (October 21, 2001, vs. New York Jets); and rushing touchdowns—2 (October 21, 2001, vs. New York Jets).
STATISTICAL PLATEAUS: 100-yard rushing games: 2001 (2). ... 100-yard receiving games: 2001 (1).

			RUSHING				RECEIVING				KICKOFF RETURNS				TOTALS			
Year Team	G	GS	Att.	Yds.	Avg.	TD	No.	Yds.	Avg.	TD	No.	Yds.	Avg.	TD	TD	2pt.	Pts.	Fum.
2000—St. Louis NFL	3	0	3	6	2.0	0	1	4	4.0	0	0	0	0.0	0	0	0	0	0
2001—St. Louis NFL	16	2	78	441	5.7	6	17	154	9.1	0	36	748	20.8	0	6	0	36	3
2002—St. Louis NFL	16	1	17	48	2.8	0	4	31	7.8	0	7	197	28.1	0	0	0	0	1
Pro totals (3 years)	35	3	98	495	5.1	6	22	189	8.6	0	43	945	22.0	0	6	0	36	4

CANNIDA, JAMES — DT

PERSONAL: Born January 3, 1975, in Savannah, Ga. ... 6-2/305. ... Full name: James Thomas Cannida II.
HIGH SCHOOL: American (Fremont, Calif.).
COLLEGE: Nevada-Reno.
TRANSACTIONS/CAREER NOTES: Selected by Tampa Bay Buccaneers in sixth round (175th pick overall) of 1998 NFL draft. ... Signed by Buccaneers (June 4, 1998). ... Granted free agency (March 2, 2001). ... Re-signed by Buccaneers (March 2, 2001). ... Granted unconditional free agency (March 1, 2002). ... Signed by Indianapolis Colts (April 20, 2002). ... Released by Colts (February 27, 2003).
CHAMPIONSHIP GAME EXPERIENCE: Member of Buccaneers for NFC championship game (1999 season); inactive.

			TOTALS		
Year Team	G	GS	Tk.	Ast.	Sks.
1998—Tampa Bay NFL	10	0	0	0	0.0
1999—Tampa Bay NFL	2	1	0	2	0.0
2000—Tampa Bay NFL	16	0	5	3	2.0
2001—Tampa Bay NFL	12	2	9	10	0.0
2002—Indianapolis NFL	10	7	18	6	1.0
Pro totals (5 years)	50	10	32	21	3.0

CARLISLE, COOPER — OT — BRONCOS

PERSONAL: Born August 11, 1977, in Greenville, Miss. ... 6-5/295. ... Full name: Cooper Morrison Carlisle.
HIGH SCHOOL: McComb (Miss.).
COLLEGE: Florida.
TRANSACTIONS/CAREER NOTES: Selected by Denver Broncos in fourth round (112th pick overall) of 2000 NFL draft. ... Signed by Broncos (July 19, 2000).
PLAYING EXPERIENCE: Denver NFL, 2000-2002. ... Games/Games started: 2000 (13/0), 2001 (16/0), 2002 (1/0). Total: 30/0.

CARNEY, JOHN — K — SAINTS

PERSONAL: Born April 20, 1964, in Hartford, Conn. ... 5-11/180. ... Full name: John Michael Carney.
HIGH SCHOOL: Cardinal Newman (West Palm Beach, Fla.).
COLLEGE: Notre Dame (degree in marketing, 1987).
TRANSACTIONS/CAREER NOTES: Signed as non-drafted free agent by Cincinnati Bengals (May 1, 1987). ... Released by Bengals (August 10, 1987). ... Signed as replacement player by Tampa Bay Buccaneers (September 24, 1987). ... Released by Buccaneers (October 14, 1987). ... Re-signed by Buccaneers (April 5, 1988). ... Released by Buccaneers (August 23, 1988). ... Re-signed by Buccaneers (November 22, 1988).

... Granted unconditional free agency (February 1-April 1, 1989). ... Re-signed by Buccaneers (April 13, 1989). ... Released by Buccaneers (September 5, 1989). ... Re-signed by Buccaneers (December 13, 1989). ... Granted unconditional free agency (February 1, 1990). ... Signed by San Diego Chargers (April 1, 1990). ... Released by Chargers (August 28, 1990). ... Signed by Los Angeles Rams (September 21, 1990). ... Released by Rams (September 26, 1990). ... Signed by Chargers (October 3, 1990). ... Granted free agency (February 1, 1992). ... Re-signed by Chargers (July 27, 1992). ... Granted free agency (March 1, 1993). ... Re-signed by Chargers (June 9, 1993). ... Granted unconditional free agency (February 17, 1994). ... Re-signed by Chargers (April 6, 1994). ... On injured reserve with knee injury (November 15, 1997-remainder of season). ... Granted unconditional free agency (March 2, 2001). ... Signed by New Orleans Saints (August 5, 2001). ... Granted unconditional free agency (March 1, 2002). ... Re-signed by Saints (March 12, 2002). ... Granted unconditional free agency (February 28, 2003). ... Re-signed by Saints (March 7, 2003).

CHAMPIONSHIP GAME EXPERIENCE: Played in AFC championship game (1994 season). ... Played in Super Bowl XXIX (1994 season).

HONORS: Named kicker on THE SPORTING NEWS NFL All-Pro team (1994). ... Played in Pro Bowl (1994 season).

Year Team	G	FIELD GOALS							TOTALS		
		1-29	30-39	40-49	50+	Tot.	Pct.	Lg.	XPM	XPA	Pts.
1988—Tampa Bay NFL	4	2-3	0-1	0-1	0-0	2-5	40.0	29	6	6	12
1989—Tampa Bay NFL	1	0-0	0-0	0-0	0-0	0-0	0.0	0	0	0	0
1990—Los Angeles Rams NFL	1	0-0	0-0	0-0	0-0	0-0	0.0	0	0	0	0
—San Diego NFL	12	10-10	6-7	3-3	0-1	19-21	90.5	43	27	28	84
1991—San Diego NFL	16	7-7	6-8	4-10	2-4	19-29	65.5	54	31	31	88
1992—San Diego NFL	16	13-14	5-7	7-8	1-3	26-32	81.3	50	35	35	113
1993—San Diego NFL	16	8-8	14-17	7-12	2-3	31-40	77.5	51	31	33	124
1994—San Diego NFL	16	12-12	15-15	5-9	2-2	†34-§38	89.5	50	33	33	*135
1995—San Diego NFL	16	8-8	10-11	3-5	0-2	21-26	80.8	45	32	33	95
1996—San Diego NFL	16	11-13	8-8	7-12	3-3	29-36	80.6	53	31	31	118
1997—San Diego NFL	4	3-3	2-2	2-2	0-0	7-7	100.0	41	5	5	26
1998—San Diego NFL	16	11-12	5-5	8-10	2-3	26-30	86.7	54	19	19	97
1999—San Diego NFL	16	15-15	6-8	9-12	1-1	31-36	86.1	50	22	23	115
2000—San Diego NFL	16	4-4	5-7	7-10	2-4	18-25	72.0	▲54	27	27	81
2001—New Orleans NFL	15	7-7	11-11	8-12	1-1	27-31	87.1	50	32	32	113
2002—New Orleans NFL	16	9-9	11-13	11-12	0-1	31-35	88.6	48	37	37	130
Pro totals (15 years)	197	120-125	104-120	81-118	16-28	321-391	82.1	54	368	373	1331

CARPENTER, KEION   S   FALCONS

PERSONAL: Born October 31, 1977, in Baltimore. ... 5-11/205. ... Full name: Keion Eric Carpenter.
HIGH SCHOOL: Woodlawn (Baltimore).
COLLEGE: Virginia Tech.
TRANSACTIONS/CAREER NOTES: Signed as non-drafted free agent by Buffalo Bills (April 19, 1999). ... Granted free agency (March 1, 2002). ... Signed by Atlanta Falcons (March 6, 2002). ... Granted unconditional free agency (February 28, 2003). ... Re-signed by Falcons (April 10, 2003).

Year Team	G	GS	TOTALS			INTERCEPTIONS			
			Tk.	Ast.	Sks.	No.	Yds.	Avg.	TD
1999—Buffalo NFL	10	0	0	0	0.0	0	0	0.0	0
2000—Buffalo NFL	12	12	30	3	0.0	5	63	12.6	0
2001—Buffalo NFL	15	10	24	10	0.0	0	0	0.0	0
2002—Atlanta NFL	16	16	43	6	0.0	4	82	20.5	1
Pro totals (4 years)	53	38	97	19	0.0	9	145	16.1	1

CARR, DAVID   QB   TEXANS

PERSONAL: Born July 21, 1979, in Bakersfield, Calif. ... 6-3/223.
HIGH SCHOOL: Stockdale (Bakersfield, Calf.).
COLLEGE: Fresno State.
TRANSACTIONS/CAREER NOTES: Selected by Houston Texans in first round (first pick overall) of 2002 NFL draft. ... Signed by Texans (April 20, 2002).
RECORDS: Holds NFL single-season record for most times sacked—76 (2002).
SINGLE GAME HIGHS (regular season): Attempts—40 (December 29, 2002, vs. Tennessee); completions—22 (November 17, 2002, vs. Jacksonville); yards—267 (October 20, 2002, vs. Cleveland); and touchdown passes—2 (September 29, 2002, vs. Philadelphia).
MISCELLANEOUS: Regular-season record as starting NFL quarterback: 4-12 (.250). ... Holds Houston Texans all-time records for most yards passing (2,592) and passing touchdowns (9). ... Shares Houston Texans all-time record for most rushing touchdowns (3).

Year Team	G	GS	PASSING								RUSHING				TOTALS		
			Att.	Cmp.	Pct.	Yds.	TD	Int.	Avg.	Skd.	Rat.	Att.	Yds.	Avg.	TD	TD	2pt.	Pts.
2002—Houston NFL	16	16	444	233	52.5	2592	9	15	5.84	*76	62.8	59	282	4.8	3	3	0	18

CARROLL, TRAVIS   LB   SAINTS

PERSONAL: Born October 26, 1978, in Jacksonville, Fla. ... 6-4/240. ... Full name: Travis C. Carroll.
HIGH SCHOOL: The Bolles School (Jacksonville, Fla.).
COLLEGE: Alabama, then Florida.
TRANSACTIONS/CAREER NOTES: Signed as non-drafted free agent by New Orleans Saints (April 23, 2002).

Year Team	G	GS	TOTALS			INTERCEPTIONS			
			Tk.	Ast.	Sks.	No.	Yds.	Avg.	TD
2002—New Orleans NFL	6	0	0	0	0.0	0	0	0.0	0

CARSON, LEONARDO DT CHARGERS

PERSONAL: Born February 11, 1977, in Mobile, Ala. ... 6-2/305. ... Full name: Leonardo Tremayne Carson.
HIGH SCHOOL: Shaw (Mobile, Ala.).
COLLEGE: Auburn.
TRANSACTIONS/CAREER NOTES: Selected by San Diego Chargers in fourth round (113th pick overall) of 2000 NFL draft. ... Signed by Chargers (July 20, 2000). ... On injured reserve with shoulder injury (November 17, 2000-remainder of season). ... Granted free agency (February 28, 2003). ... Re-signed by Chargers (April 15, 2003).

			TOTALS		
Year Team	G	GS	Tk.	Ast.	Sks.
2000—San Diego NFL	4	0	2	0	0.0
2001—San Diego NFL	16	13	24	9	3.0
2002—San Diego NFL	16	6	22	9	3.5
Pro totals (3 years)	36	19	48	18	6.5

CARSWELL, DWAYNE TE BRONCOS

PERSONAL: Born January 18, 1972, in Jacksonville. ... 6-3/260.
HIGH SCHOOL: University Christian (Jacksonville).
COLLEGE: Liberty (Va.).
TRANSACTIONS/CAREER NOTES: Signed as non-drafted free agent by Denver Broncos (May 2, 1994). ... Released by Broncos (August 26, 1994). ... Re-signed by Broncos to practice squad (August 30, 1994). ... Activated (November 25, 1994).
CHAMPIONSHIP GAME EXPERIENCE: Played in AFC championship game (1997 and 1998 seasons). ... Member of Super Bowl championship team (1997 and 1998 seasons).
HONORS: Played in Pro Bowl (2001 season).
SINGLE GAME HIGHS (regular season): Receptions—6 (December 16, 2001, vs. Kansas City); yards—68 (October 22, 2000, vs. Cincinnati); and touchdown receptions—1 (September 22, 2002, vs. Buffalo).

			RECEIVING				TOTALS			
Year Team	G	GS	No.	Yds.	Avg.	TD	TD	2pt.	Pts.	Fum.
1994—Denver NFL	4	0	0	0	0.0	0	0	0	0	0
1995—Denver NFL	9	2	3	37	12.3	0	0	0	0	0
1996—Denver NFL	16	2	15	85	5.7	0	0	0	0	0
1997—Denver NFL	16	3	12	96	8.0	1	1	0	6	0
1998—Denver NFL	16	1	4	51	12.8	0	0	0	0	0
1999—Denver NFL	16	11	24	201	8.4	2	2	0	12	0
2000—Denver NFL	16	16	49	495	10.1	3	3	0	18	0
2001—Denver NFL	16	16	34	299	8.8	4	4	1	26	0
2002—Denver NFL	16	7	21	189	9.0	1	1	0	6	0
Pro totals (9 years)	125	58	162	1453	9.0	11	11	1	68	0

CARSWELL, ROBERT S

PERSONAL: Born October 26, 1978, in Gary, Ind. ... 5-11/215. ... Full name: Robert Lee Carswell.
HIGH SCHOOL: Stone Mountain (Ga.).
COLLEGE: Clemson.
TRANSACTIONS/CAREER NOTES: Selected by San Diego Chargers in seventh round (244th pick overall) of 2001 NFL draft. ... Signed by Chargers (June 20, 2001). ... Released by Chargers (October 15, 2002).
HONORS: Named free safety on THE SPORTING NEWS college All-America third team (2000).

			TOTALS			INTERCEPTIONS			
Year Team	G	GS	Tk.	Ast.	Sks.	No.	Yds.	Avg.	TD
2001—San Diego NFL	16	0	4	3	0.0	0	0	0.0	0
2002—San Diego NFL	2	0	0	0	0.0	0	0	0.0	0
Pro totals (2 years)	18	0	4	3	0.0	0	0	0.0	0

CARTER, ANDRE DE 49ERS

PERSONAL: Born May 12, 1979, in Denver, Colo. ... 6-4/265.
HIGH SCHOOL: Oak Grove (San Jose, Calif.).
COLLEGE: California.
TRANSACTIONS/CAREER NOTES: Selected by San Francisco 49ers in first round (seventh pick overall) of 2001 NFL draft. ... Signed by 49ers (July 26, 2001).
HONORS: Named defensive end on THE SPORTING NEWS college All-America first team (2000).

			TOTALS		
Year Team	G	GS	Tk.	Ast.	Sks.
2001—San Francisco NFL	15	15	40	7	6.5
2002—San Francisco NFL	16	16	44	10	12.5
Pro totals (2 years)	31	31	84	17	19.0

CARTER, CHRIS   S

PERSONAL: Born September 27, 1974, in Tyler, Texas. ... 6-2/212. ... Full name: Christopher Cary Carter. ... Cousin of Joe Carter, first baseman/outfielder with five major league baseball teams (1984-98).

HIGH SCHOOL: John Tyler (Tyler, Texas).

COLLEGE: Texas.

TRANSACTIONS/CAREER NOTES: Selected by New England Patriots in third round (89th pick overall) of 1997 NFL draft. ... Signed by Patriots (July 15, 1997). ... Granted free agency (February 11, 2000). ... Re-signed by Patriots (July 14, 2000). ... Claimed on waivers by Cincinnati Bengals (August 28, 2000). ... Granted unconditional free agency (March 1, 2002). ... Signed by Houston Texans (April 5, 2002). ... Released by Texans (December 18, 2002).

			TOTALS			INTERCEPTIONS			
Year Team	G	GS	Tk.	Ast.	Sks.	No.	Yds.	Avg.	TD
1997—New England NFL	16	0	1	0	0.0	0	0	0.0	0
1998—New England NFL	16	0	9	4	1.0	0	0	0.0	0
1999—New England NFL	15	15	44	24	1.0	3	13	4.3	0
2000—Cincinnati NFL	16	10	49	11	1.0	1	6	6.0	0
2001—Cincinnati NFL	16	4	34	15	0.0	1	10	10.0	0
2002—Houston NFL	13	0	3	0	1.0	0	0	0.0	0
Pro totals (6 years)	92	29	140	54	4.0	5	29	5.8	0

CARTER, CRIS   WR   C

PERSONAL: Born November 25, 1965, in Troy, Ohio. ... 6-3/208. ... Full name: Christopher D. Carter. ... Brother of Butch Carter, head coach with Toronto Raptors (February 13, 1998-99).

HIGH SCHOOL: Middletown (Ohio).

COLLEGE: Ohio State.

TRANSACTIONS/CAREER NOTES: Selected by Philadelphia Eagles in fourth round of 1987 NFL supplemental draft (September 4, 1987). ... Signed by Eagles (September 17, 1987). ... Granted roster exemption (September 17-October 26, 1987). ... Claimed on waivers by Minnesota Vikings (September 4, 1990). ... Granted free agency (February 1, 1991). ... Re-signed by Vikings (July 9, 1991). ... Granted free agency (February 1, 1992). ... Re-signed by Vikings (July 26, 1992). ... On injured reserve with broken collarbone (December 4-30, 1992). ... Granted unconditional free agency (March 1, 2002). ... Announced retirement (May 21, 2002). ... Signed by Miami Dolphins (October 21, 2002). ... Granted unconditional free agency (February 28, 2003).

CHAMPIONSHIP GAME EXPERIENCE: Played in NFC championship game (1998 and 2000 seasons).

HONORS: Played in Pro Bowl (1993-2000 seasons). ... Named wide receiver on The Sporting News NFL All-Pro team (1994).

SINGLE GAME HIGHS (regular season): Receptions—14 (October 2, 1994, vs. Arizona); yards—168 (September 10, 2000, vs. Miami); and touchdown receptions—3 (November 14, 1999, vs. Chicago).

STATISTICAL PLATEAUS: 100-yard receiving games: 1988 (1), 1989 (1), 1990 (2), 1991 (4), 1992 (1), 1993 (3), 1994 (5), 1995 (5), 1996 (1), 1997 (4), 1998 (3), 1999 (5), 2000 (6), 2001 (1). Total: 42.

MISCELLANEOUS: Holds Minnesota Vikings all-time records for most receptions (1,004), most yards receiving (12,383), most touchdowns (110) and most touchdown receptions (110).

			RUSHING				RECEIVING				TOTALS			
Year Team	G	GS	Att.	Yds.	Avg.	TD	No.	Yds.	Avg.	TD	TD	2pt.	Pts.	Fum.
1987—Philadelphia NFL	9	0	0	0	0.0	0	5	84	16.8	2	2	0	12	0
1988—Philadelphia NFL	16	16	1	1	1.0	0	39	761	19.5	6	7	0	42	0
1989—Philadelphia NFL	16	15	2	16	8.0	0	45	605	13.4	11	11	0	66	1
1990—Minnesota NFL	16	5	2	6	3.0	0	27	413	15.3	3	3	0	18	0
1991—Minnesota NFL	16	16	0	0	0.0	0	72	962	13.4	5	5	0	30	1
1992—Minnesota NFL	12	12	5	15	3.0	0	53	681	12.8	6	6	0	36	1
1993—Minnesota NFL	16	16	0	0	0.0	0	86	1071	12.5	9	9	0	54	0
1994—Minnesota NFL	16	16	0	0	0.0	0	*122	1256	10.3	7	7	2	46	4
1995—Minnesota NFL	16	16	1	0	0.0	0	122	1371	11.2	†17	17	0	102	0
1996—Minnesota NFL	16	16	0	0	0.0	0	96	1163	12.1	10	10	0	60	1
1997—Minnesota NFL	16	16	0	0	0.0	0	89	1069	12.0	*13	13	3	84	3
1998—Minnesota NFL	16	16	1	-1	-1.0	0	78	1011	13.0	12	12	0	72	0
1999—Minnesota NFL	16	16	0	0	0.0	0	90	1241	13.8	*13	13	0	78	0
2000—Minnesota NFL	16	16	0	0	0.0	0	96	1274	13.3	9	9	0	54	3
2001—Minnesota NFL	16	16	1	4	4.0	0	73	871	11.9	6	6	0	36	2
2002—Miami NFL	5	1	0	0	0.0	0	8	66	8.3	1	1	0	6	1
Pro totals (16 years)	234	209	13	41	3.2	0	1101	13899	12.6	130	131	5	796	17

CARTER, DALE   CB   SAINTS

PERSONAL: Born November 28, 1969, in Covington, Ga. ... 6-1/188. ... Full name: Dale Lavelle Carter. ... Brother of Jake Reed, wide receiver, New Orleans Saints.

HIGH SCHOOL: Newton County (Covington, Ga.).

JUNIOR COLLEGE: Ellsworth (Iowa) Community College.

COLLEGE: Tennessee.

TRANSACTIONS/CAREER NOTES: Selected by Kansas City Chiefs in first round (20th pick overall) of 1992 NFL draft. ... Signed by Chiefs (June 2, 1992). ... Designated by Chiefs as transition player (February 25, 1993). ... On injured reserve with broken arm (January 7, 1994-remainder of 1993 playoffs). ... Tendered offer sheet by Minnesota Vikings (July 12, 1996). ... Offer matched by Chiefs (July 19, 1996). ... Granted unconditional free agency (February 12, 1999). ... Signed by Denver Broncos (February 19, 1999). ... Suspended by NFL for violating league substance abuse policy (April 25, 2000-November 6, 2001). ... Released by Broncos (November 6, 2001). ... Signed by Minnesota Vikings (November 8, 2001). ... Granted unconditional free agency (March 1, 2002). ... Signed by New Orleans Saints (March 12, 2002). ... On suspended list for violating league substance abuse policy (July 19-November 4, 2002).

HONORS: Named kick returner on The Sporting News college All-America first team (1990). ... Named defensive back on The Sporting News college All-America first team (1991). ... Played in Pro Bowl (1994, 1995 and 1997 seasons). ... Named cornerback on The Sporting News NFL All-Pro team (1996). ... Named to play in Pro Bowl (1996 season); replaced by Terry McDaniel due to injury.

Year Team	G	GS	TOTALS			INTERCEPTIONS				PUNT RETURNS				KICKOFF RETURNS				TOTALS			
			Tk.	Ast.	Sks.	No.	Yds.	Avg.	TD	No.	Yds.	Avg.	TD	No.	Yds.	Avg.	TD	TD	2pt.	Pts.	Fum.
1992—Kansas City NFL	16	9	39	16	0.0	7	65	9.3	1	38	398	10.5	†2	11	190	17.3	0	3	0	18	7
1993—Kansas City NFL	15	11	43	15	0.0	1	0	0.0	0	27	247	9.1	0	0	0	0.0	0	0	0	0	4
1994—Kansas City NFL	16	16	78	3	0.0	2	24	12.0	0	16	124	7.8	0	0	0	0.0	0	0	0	0	1
1995—Kansas City NFL	16	14	48	5	0.0	4	45	11.3	0	0	0	0.0	0	0	0	0.0	0	0	0	0	0
1996—Kansas City NFL	14	14	41	10	0.0	3	17	5.7	0	2	18	9.0	0	0	0	0.0	0	1	0	6	1
1997—Kansas City NFL	16	15	49	6	0.0	2	9	4.5	0	0	0	0.0	0	0	0	0.0	0	0	0	0	0
1998—Kansas City NFL	11	9	31	8	0.0	2	23	11.5	0	0	0	0.0	0	0	0	0.0	0	0	0	0	0
1999—Denver NFL	14	14	54	18	0.0	2	48	24.0	0	0	0	0.0	0	0	0	0.0	0	0	0	0	0
2000—Denver NFL										Did not play.											
2001—Minnesota NFL	8	8	24	9	0.0	0	0	0.0	0	0	0	0.0	0	0	0	0.0	0	0	0	0	0
2002—New Orleans NFL	7	7	26	4	0.0	1	25	25.0	0	0	0	0.0	0	0	0	0.0	0	0	0	0	0
Pro totals (10 years)	133	117	433	94	0.0	24	256	10.7	1	83	787	9.5	2	11	190	17.3	0	4	0	24	13

CARTER, JONATHAN — WR — JETS

PERSONAL: Born March 20, 1979, in Anniston, Ala. ... 6-0/180.
HIGH SCHOOL: Lineville (Ala.).
COLLEGE: Troy State.
TRANSACTIONS/CAREER NOTES: Selected by New York Giants in fifth round (162nd pick overall) of 2001 NFL draft. ... Signed by Giants (July 26, 2001). ... Released by Giants (September 2, 2001). ... Re-signed by Giants to practice squad (September 3, 2001). ... Activated (December 29, 2001). ... Claimed on waivers by New York Jets (October 8, 2002). ... Re-signed by Jets (April 2, 2003)

Year Team	G	GS	RECEIVING			
			No.	Yds.	Avg.	TD
2001—New York Giants NFL	2	0	0	0	0.0	0
2002—New York Giants NFL	1	0	0	0	0.0	0
Pro totals (2 years)	3	0	0	0	0.0	0

CARTER, KEVIN — DE — TITANS

PERSONAL: Born September 21, 1973, in Miami. ... 6-5/290. ... Full name: Kevin Louis Carter. ... Brother of Bernard Carter, linebacker with Jacksonville Jaguars (1995).
HIGH SCHOOL: Lincoln (Tallahassee, Fla.).
COLLEGE: Florida.
TRANSACTIONS/CAREER NOTES: Selected by St. Louis Rams in first round (sixth pick overall) of 1995 NFL draft. ... Signed by Rams (July 17, 1995). ... Designated by Rams as franchise player (February 22, 2001). ... Traded by Rams to Tennessee Titans for first-round pick (DT Ryan Pickett) in 2001 draft (March 28, 2001).
CHAMPIONSHIP GAME EXPERIENCE: Played in NFC championship game (1999 season). ... Member of Super Bowl championship team (1999 season). ... Played in AFC championship game (2002 season).
HONORS: Named defensive lineman on THE SPORTING NEWS college All-America first team (1994). ... Named defensive end on THE SPORTING NEWS NFL All-Pro team (1999). ... Played in Pro Bowl (1999 and 2002 seasons).

Year Team	G	GS	TOTALS		
			Tk.	Ast.	Sks.
1995—St. Louis NFL	16	16	33	4	6.0
1996—St. Louis NFL	16	16	39	16	9.5
1997—St. Louis NFL	16	16	32	10	7.5
1998—St. Louis NFL	16	16	49	11	12.0
1999—St. Louis NFL	16	16	30	4	*17.0
2000—St. Louis NFL	16	13	31	4	10.5
2001—Tennessee NFL	16	16	28	8	2.0
2002—Tennessee NFL	16	16	27	15	10.0
Pro totals (8 years)	128	125	269	72	74.5

CARTER, QUINCY — QB — COWBOYS

PERSONAL: Born October 13, 1977, in Decatur, Ga. ... 6-2/213.
HIGH SCHOOL: Southwest DeKalb (Decatur, Ga.).
COLLEGE: Georgia.
TRANSACTIONS/CAREER NOTES: Selected after junior season by Dallas Cowboys in second round (53rd pick overall) of 2001 NFL draft. ... Signed by Cowboys (July 19, 2001).
HONORS: Named College Football Freshman of the Year by THE SPORTING NEWS (1998).
SINGLE GAME HIGHS (regular season): Attempts—42 (October 6, 2002, vs. New York Giants); completions—26 (September 29, 2002, vs. St. Louis); yards—262 (October 6, 2002, vs. New York Giants); and touchdown passes—2 (October 13, 2002, vs. Carolina).
MISCELLANEOUS: Regular-season record as starting NFL quarterback: 6-9 (.400).

Year Team	G	GS	PASSING									RUSHING				TOTALS		
			Att.	Cmp.	Pct.	Yds.	TD	Int.	Avg.	Skd.	Rat.	Att.	Yds.	Avg.	TD	TD	2pt.	Pts.
2001—Dallas NFL	8	8	176	90	51.1	1072	5	7	6.09	12	63.0	45	150	3.3	1	1	0	6
2002—Dallas NFL	7	7	221	125	56.6	1465	7	8	6.63	19	72.3	27	91	3.4	0	0	0	0
Pro totals (2 years)	15	15	397	215	54.2	2537	12	15	6.39	31	68.2	72	241	3.3	1	1	0	6

CARTER, TIM — WR — GIANTS

PERSONAL: Born September 21, 1979, in Atlanta. ... 5-11/190. ... Full name: Timothy M. Carter.
HIGH SCHOOL: Lakewood (St. Petersburg, Fla.).
COLLEGE: Auburn.

TRANSACTIONS/CAREER NOTES: Selected by New York Giants in second round (46th pick overall) of 2002 NFL draft. ... Signed by Giants (July 25, 2002). ... On injured reserve with Achilles' tendon injury (November 12, 2002-remainder of season).

SINGLE GAME HIGHS (regular season): Receptions—1 (November 3, 2002, vs. Jacksonville); yards—27 (November 3, 2002, vs. Jacksonville); and touchdown receptions—0.

			RUSHING				RECEIVING				PUNT RETURNS				KICKOFF RETURNS				TOTALS		
Year Team	G	GS	Att.	Yds.	Avg.	TD	No.	Yds.	Avg.	TD	No.	Yds.	Avg.	TD	No.	Yds.	Avg.	TD	TD	2pt.	Pts.
2002—NY Giants NFL	5	0	3	28	9.3	0	2	37	18.5	0	0	0	0.0	0	5	78	15.6	0	0	0	0

CARTER, TONY — FB

PERSONAL: Born August 23, 1972, in Columbus, Ohio. ... 6-0/235. ... Full name: Antonio Marcus Carter.
HIGH SCHOOL: South (Columbus, Ohio).
COLLEGE: Minnesota.
TRANSACTIONS/CAREER NOTES: Signed as non-drafted free agent by Chicago Bears (April 28, 1994). ... Granted unconditional free agency (February 13, 1998). ... Signed by New England Patriots (February 25, 1998). ... Granted unconditional free agency (March 2, 2001). ... Signed by Denver Broncos (May 4, 2001). ... Released by Broncos (September 1, 2002). ... Signed by Green Bay Packers (September 25, 2002). ... Granted unconditional free agency (February 28, 2003).
SINGLE GAME HIGHS (regular season): Attempts—9 (December 17, 2000, vs. Buffalo); yards—37 (October 13, 1996, vs. New Orleans); and rushing touchdowns—1 (December 24, 2000, vs. Miami).

			RUSHING				RECEIVING				KICKOFF RETURNS				TOTALS			
Year Team	G	GS	Att.	Yds.	Avg.	TD	No.	Yds.	Avg.	TD	No.	Yds.	Avg.	TD	TD	2pt.	Pts.	Fum.
1994—Chicago NFL..............	14	0	0	0	0.0	0	1	24	24.0	0	6	99	16.5	0	0	0	0	0
1995—Chicago NFL..............	16	11	10	34	3.4	0	40	329	8.2	1	3	24	8.0	0	1	0	6	1
1996—Chicago NFL..............	16	11	11	43	3.9	0	41	233	5.7	0	0	0	0.0	0	0	0	0	1
1997—Chicago NFL..............	16	10	9	56	6.2	0	24	152	6.3	0	2	34	17.0	0	0	0	0	0
1998—New England NFL.......	11	7	2	3	1.5	0	18	166	9.2	0	0	0	0.0	0	0	0	0	0
1999—New England NFL.......	16	14	6	26	4.3	0	20	108	5.4	0	0	0	0.0	0	0	0	0	0
2000—New England NFL.......	16	6	37	90	2.4	2	9	73	8.1	0	1	16	16.0	0	2	0	12	0
2001—Denver NFL..............	16	6	1	4	4.0	0	11	83	7.5	0	2	44	22.0	0	0	0	0	1
2002—Green Bay NFL..........	12	0	0	0	0.0	0	0	0	0.0	0	2	42	21.0	0	0	0	0	0
Pro totals (9 years)..............	133	65	76	256	3.4	2	164	1168	7.1	1	16	259	16.2	0	3	0	18	3

CARTER, TYRONE — S — JETS

PERSONAL: Born March 31, 1976, in Pompano Beach, Fla. ... 5-8/190.
HIGH SCHOOL: Ely (Pompano Beach, Fla.).
COLLEGE: Minnesota.
TRANSACTIONS/CAREER NOTES: Selected by Minnesota Vikings in fourth round (118th pick overall) of 2000 NFL draft. ... Signed by Vikings (July 5, 2000). ... Granted free agency (February 28, 2003). ... Signed by New York Jets (April 14, 2003).
CHAMPIONSHIP GAME EXPERIENCE: Played in NFC championship game (2000 season).
HONORS: Jim Thorpe Award winner (1999). ... Named strong safety on THE SPORTING NEWS college All-America first team (1999).

			TOTALS			INTERCEPTIONS				KICKOFF RETURNS				TOTALS			
Year Team	G	GS	Tk.	Ast.	Sks.	No.	Yds.	Avg.	TD	No.	Yds.	Avg.	TD	TD	2pt.	Pts.	Fum.
2000—Minnesota NFL................................	15	7	29	9	0.0	0	0	0.0	0	17	389	22.9	0	0	0	0	0
2001—Minnesota NFL................................	15	7	45	5	1.0	0	0	0.0	0	0	0	0.0	0	1	0	6	0
2002—Minnesota NFL................................	16	8	42	6	0.0	1	13	13.0	0	17	350	20.6	0	0	0	0	0
Pro totals (3 years).................................	46	22	116	20	1.0	1	13	13.0	0	34	739	21.7	0	1	0	6	0

CARTWRIGHT, ROCK — FB — REDSKINS

PERSONAL: Born December 3, 1979, in Conroe, Texas. ... 5-7/239.
HIGH SCHOOL: Conroe (Texas).
JUNIOR COLLEGE: Trinity Valley Community College (Texas).
COLLEGE: Kansas State.
TRANSACTIONS/CAREER NOTES: Selected by Washington Redskins in seventh round (257th pick overall) of 2002 NFL draft.. ... Signed by Redskins (July 19, 2002).
SINGLE GAME HIGHS (regular season): Attempts—2 (December 22, 2002, vs. Houston); yards—21 (December 22, 2002, vs. Houston); and rushing touchdowns—0.

			RUSHING				RECEIVING				KICKOFF RETURNS				TOTALS			
Year Team	G	GS	Att.	Yds.	Avg.	TD	No.	Yds.	Avg.	TD	No.	Yds.	Avg.	TD	TD	2pt.	Pts.	Fum.
2002—Washington NFL	16	0	3	22	7.3	0	11	121	11.0	1	10	169	16.9	0	1	0	6	1

CARTY, JOHNDALE — S — JAGUARS

PERSONAL: Born August 27, 1977, in Miami. ... 6-0/196.
HIGH SCHOOL: Hialeah (Fla.) Miami Lakes.
COLLEGE: Utah State.
TRANSACTIONS/CAREER NOTES: Selected by Atlanta Falcons in fourth round (126th pick overall) of 1999 NFL draft. ... Signed by Falcons (July 8, 1999). ... Released by Falcons (May 15, 2003). ... Signed by Jacksonville Jaguars (May 27, 2003).

			TOTALS			INTERCEPTIONS			
Year Team	G	GS	Tk.	Ast.	Sks.	No.	Yds.	Avg.	TD
1999—Atlanta NFL	14	0	1	0	0.0	0	0	0.0	0
2000—Atlanta NFL	16	0	2	0	0.0	0	0	0.0	0
2001—Atlanta NFL	16	2	4	3	0.0	1	0	0.0	0
2002—Atlanta NFL	16	1	7	1	1.0	1	37	37.0	0
Pro totals (4 years)..	62	3	14	4	1.0	2	37	18.5	0

CASH, CHRISTOPHER   CB   LIONS

PERSONAL: Born July 13, 1980, in Stockton, Calif. ... 5-11/170. ... Full name: Chris Cash.
HIGH SCHOOL: Franklin (Stockton, Calif.).
JUNIOR COLLEGE: Palomar College (Calif.).
COLLEGE: Southern California.
TRANSACTIONS/CAREER NOTES: Selected by Detroit Lions in sixth round (175th pick overall) of 2002 NFL draft. ... Signed by Lions (July 23, 2002).

			TOTALS			INTERCEPTIONS			
Year Team	G	GS	Tk.	Ast.	Sks.	No.	Yds.	Avg.	TD
2002—Detroit NFL	16	12	79	12	0.0	1	11	11.0	0

CASON, AVEION   RB   COWBOYS

PERSONAL: Born July 12, 1977, in St. Petersburg, Fla. ... 5-10/204. ... Full name: Aveion Marquel Cason.
HIGH SCHOOL: Lakewood (St. Petersburg, Fla.).
COLLEGE: Illinois State.
TRANSACTIONS/CAREER NOTES: Signed as non-drafted free agent by St. Louis Rams (April 23, 2001). ... Released by Rams (September 25, 2001). ... Re-signed by Rams to practice squad (September 26, 2001). ... Released by Rams (September 28, 2001). ... Signed by Detroit Lions (November 19, 2001). ... Traded by Lions to Dallas Cowboys for seventh-round pick (RB Brandon Drumm) in 2003 draft (April 27, 2003).
SINGLE GAME HIGHS (regular season): Attempts—10 (December 15, 2002, vs. Tampa Bay); yards—62 (December 15, 2002, vs. Tampa Bay); and rushing touchdowns—0.

			RUSHING				RECEIVING				KICKOFF RETURNS				TOTALS			
Year Team	G	GS	Att.	Yds.	Avg.	TD	No.	Yds.	Avg.	TD	No.	Yds.	Avg.	TD	TD	2pt.	Pts.	Fum.
2001—St. Louis NFL	1	0	0	0	0.0	0	0	0	0.0	0	4	73	18.3	0	0	0	0	1
—Detroit NFL	5	0	11	31	2.8	0	4	32	8.0	0	0	0	0.0	0	0	0	0	1
2002—Detroit NFL	10	3	26	107	4.1	0	19	288	15.2	2	2	48	24.0	0	2	0	12	0
Pro totals (2 years)	16	3	37	138	3.7	0	23	320	13.9	2	6	121	20.2	0	2	0	12	2

CAVER, QUINTON   LB   CHIEFS

PERSONAL: Born August 22, 1978, in Anniston, Ala. ... 6-4/230.
HIGH SCHOOL: Anniston (Ala.).
COLLEGE: Arkansas.
TRANSACTIONS/CAREER NOTES: Selected by Philadelphia Eagles in second round (55th pick overall) of 2001 NFL draft. ... Signed by Eagles (July 27, 2001). ... Released by Eagles (October 21, 2002). ... Signed by Kansas City Chiefs (October 28, 2002). ... On injured reserve with shoulder injury (December 14, 2002-remainder of season).
CHAMPIONSHIP GAME EXPERIENCE: Played in NFC championship game (2001 season).

			TOTALS			INTERCEPTIONS			
Year Team	G	GS	Tk.	Ast.	Sks.	No.	Yds.	Avg.	TD
2001—Philadelphia NFL	11	0	7	2	0.0	0	0	0.0	0
2002—Kansas City NFL	1	0	0	0	0.0	0	0	0.0	0
—Philadelphia NFL	5	0	0	0	0.0	0	0	0.0	0
Pro totals (2 years)	17	0	7	2	0.0	0	0	0.0	0

CENTERS, LARRY   FB

PERSONAL: Born June 1, 1968, in Tatum, Texas. ... 6-0/225. ... Full name: Larry E. Centers.
HIGH SCHOOL: Tatum (Texas).
COLLEGE: Stephen F. Austin State.
TRANSACTIONS/CAREER NOTES: Selected by Phoenix Cardinals in fifth round (115th pick overall) of 1990 NFL draft. ... Signed by Cardinals (July 23, 1990). ... On injured reserve with broken foot (September 11-October 30, 1991). ... Granted free agency (February 1, 1992). ... Re-signed by Cardinals (July 23, 1992). ... Granted unconditional free agency (February 17, 1994). ... Re-signed by Cardinals (March 15, 1994). ... Cardinals franchise renamed Arizona Cardinals for 1994 season. ... Granted unconditional free agency (February 14, 1997). ... Re-signed by Cardinals (March 14, 1997). ... Released by Cardinals (June 18, 1999). ... Signed by Washington Redskins (July 6, 1999). ... Released by Redskins (April 20, 2001). ... Signed by Buffalo Bills (May 8, 2001). ... Released by Bills (March 20, 2003).
HONORS: Played in Pro Bowl (1995, 1996 and 2001 seasons).
SINGLE GAME HIGHS (regular season): Attempts—15 (September 4, 1994, vs. Los Angeles Rams); yards—62 (November 26, 1995, vs. Atlanta); and rushing touchdowns—2 (December 4, 1994, vs. Houston).
STATISTICAL PLATEAUS: 100-yard receiving games: 1995 (2), 1996 (1). Total: 3.
MISCELLANEOUS: Holds Cardinals franchise all-time record for most receptions (535).

			RUSHING				RECEIVING				KICKOFF RETURNS				TOTALS			
Year Team	G	GS	Att.	Yds.	Avg.	TD	No.	Yds.	Avg.	TD	No.	Yds.	Avg.	TD	TD	2pt.	Pts.	Fum.
1990—Phoenix NFL	6	0	0	0	0.0	0	0	0	0.0	0	16	272	17.0	0	0	0	0	1
1991—Phoenix NFL	9	2	14	44	3.1	0	19	176	9.3	0	16	330	20.6	0	0	0	0	4
1992—Phoenix NFL	16	1	37	139	3.8	0	50	417	8.3	2	0	0	0.0	0	2	0	12	1
1993—Phoenix NFL	16	9	25	152	6.1	0	66	603	9.1	3	0	0	0.0	0	3	0	18	1
1994—Arizona NFL	16	5	115	336	2.9	5	77	647	8.4	2	0	0	0.0	0	7	0	42	2
1995—Arizona NFL	16	10	78	254	3.3	2	101	962	9.5	2	1	15	15.0	0	4	0	24	2
1996—Arizona NFL	16	14	116	425	3.7	7	99	766	7.7	7	0	0	0.0	0	9	0	54	1
1997—Arizona NFL	15	14	101	276	2.7	1	54	409	7.6	1	0	0	0.0	0	2	0	12	1
1998—Arizona NFL	16	12	31	110	3.5	0	69	559	8.1	2	0	0	0.0	0	2	0	12	1
1999—Washington NFL	16	12	13	51	3.9	0	69	544	7.9	3	0	0	0.0	0	3	0	18	2
2000—Washington NFL	15	5	19	103	5.4	0	81	600	7.4	3	0	0	0.0	0	3	0	18	0
2001—Buffalo NFL	16	13	34	160	4.7	2	80	620	7.8	2	0	0	0.0	0	4	0	24	2
2002—Buffalo NFL	16	7	11	56	5.1	2	43	388	9.0	0	0	0	0.0	0	2	0	12	1
Pro totals (13 years)	189	104	594	2106	3.5	14	808	6691	8.3	27	33	617	18.7	0	41	0	246	19

CERCONE, MATT — TE — JAGUARS

PERSONAL: Born November 30, 1975, in Bakersfield, Calif. ... 6-5/252. ... Full name: Matthew Anthony Cercone.
HIGH SCHOOL: South High (Calif.).
COLLEGE: Arizona State.
TRANSACTIONS/CAREER NOTES: Signed as non-drafted free agent by Minnesota Vikings (April 30, 1999). ... Released by Vikings (August 27, 1999). ... Re-signed by Vikings (February 1, 2000). ... Released by Vikings (August 27, 2000). ... Re-signed by Vikings to practice squad (August 28, 2000). ... Released by Vikings (September 5, 2000). ... Re-signed by Vikings to practice squad (September 25, 2000). ... Activated (November 15, 2000). ... Released by Vikings (December 5, 2000). ... Re-signed by Vikings to practice squad (December 5, 2000). ... Released by Vikings (September 2, 2001). ... Re-signed by Vikings to practice squad (September 4, 2001). ... Activated (September 11, 2001). ... Released by Vikings (September 25, 2001). ... Re-signed by Vikings to practice squad (September 27, 2001). ... Released by Vikings (October 1, 2002). ... Signed by Jacksonville Jaguars (January 30, 2003). ... Assigned by Jaguars to Barcelona Dragons in 2003 NFL Europe enhancement allocation program (February 4, 2003).

			RECEIVING			
Year Team	G	GS	No.	Yds.	Avg.	TD
2000—Minnesota NFL	2	0	0	0	0.0	0
2002—Minnesota NFL	3	0	0	0	0.0	0
Pro totals (2 years)	5	0	0	0	0.0	0

CERQUA, MARQ — LB — BEARS

PERSONAL: Born April 3, 1977, in Miami. ... 6-2/223. ... Full name: Marq Vincent Cerqua.
HIGH SCHOOL: Daniel (Central, S.C.).
COLLEGE: Furman, then Carson-Newman.
TRANSACTIONS/CAREER NOTES: Signed as non-drafted free agent by Tampa Bay Buccaneers (April 23, 2001). ... Claimed on waivers by Dallas Cowboys (December 24, 2001; did not play. ... Released by Cowboys (April 29, 2002). ... Signed by Chicago Bears to practice squad (November 5, 2002). ... Activated (December 20, 2002).

			TOTALS			INTERCEPTIONS			
Year Team	G	GS	Tk.	Ast.	Sks.	No.	Yds.	Avg.	TD
2001—Tampa Bay NFL	3	0	0	0	0.0	0	0	0.0	0
2002—Chicago NFL	2	0	0	0	0.0	0	0	0.0	0
Pro totals (2 years)	5	0	0	0	0.0	0	0	0.0	0

CHAMBERLAIN, BYRON — TE — VIKINGS

PERSONAL: Born October 17, 1971, in Honolulu. ... 6-1/242.
HIGH SCHOOL: Eastern Hills (Fort Worth, Texas).
COLLEGE: Missouri, then Wayne State (Neb.).
TRANSACTIONS/CAREER NOTES: Selected by Denver Broncos in seventh round (222nd pick overall) of 1995 NFL draft. ... Signed by Broncos (August 27, 1995). ... Released by Broncos to practice squad (August 28, 1995). ... Activated (November 24, 1995). ... Assigned by Broncos to Rhein Fire in 1996 World League enhancement allocation program (February 19, 1996). ... Granted unconditional free agency (March 2, 2001). ... Signed by Minnesota Vikings (March 16, 2001). ... Granted unconditional free agency (March 1, 2002). ... Re-signed by Vikings (March 27, 2002).
CHAMPIONSHIP GAME EXPERIENCE: Played in AFC championship game (1997 and 1998 seasons). ... Member of Super Bowl championship team (1997 season); did not play. ... Member of Super Bowl championship team (1998 season).
HONORS: Played in Pro Bowl (2001 season).
SINGLE GAME HIGHS (regular season): Receptions—7 (December 23, 2001, vs. Jacksonville); yards—123 (October 17, 1999, vs. Green Bay); and touchdown receptions—1 (December 30, 2001, vs. Green Bay).
STATISTICAL PLATEAUS: 100-yard receiving games: 1999 (1).

			RECEIVING				TOTALS			
Year Team	G	GS	No.	Yds.	Avg.	TD	TD	2pt.	Pts.	Fum.
1995—Denver NFL	5	0	1	11	11.0	0	0	0	0	0
1996—Rhein W.L.	10	10	58	685	11.8	8	8	0	48	0
—Denver NFL	11	0	12	129	10.8	0	0	0	0	1
1997—Denver NFL	10	0	2	18	9.0	0	0	0	0	1
1998—Denver NFL	16	0	3	35	11.7	0	0	0	0	0
1999—Denver NFL	16	0	32	488	15.3	2	2	0	12	0
2000—Denver NFL	15	0	22	283	12.9	1	1	0	6	0
2001—Minnesota NFL	16	15	57	666	11.7	3	3	0	18	1
2002—Minnesota NFL	13	9	34	389	11.4	0	0	0	0	0
W.L. totals (1 year)	10	10	58	685	11.8	8	8	0	48	0
NFL totals (8 years)	102	24	163	2019	12.4	6	6	0	36	3
Pro totals (9 years)	112	34	221	2704	12.2	14	14	0	84	3

CHAMBERLIN, FRANK — LB — TITANS

PERSONAL: Born January 2, 1978, in Paramus, N.J. ... 6-1/238. ... Full name: Frank Jacob Chamberlin.
HIGH SCHOOL: Mahwah (N.J.).
COLLEGE: Boston College.
TRANSACTIONS/CAREER NOTES: Selected by Tennessee Titans in fifth round (160th pick overall) of 2000 NFL draft. ... Signed by Titans (July 7, 2000). ... Granted free agency (February 28, 2003). ... Re-signed by Titans (March 9, 2003).
CHAMPIONSHIP GAME EXPERIENCE: Played in AFC championship game (2002 season).

			TOTALS			INTERCEPTIONS			
Year Team	G	GS	Tk.	Ast.	Sks.	No.	Yds.	Avg.	TD
2000—Tennessee NFL	12	0	0	1	0.0	0	0	0.0	0
2001—Tennessee NFL	16	0	8	3	1.0	0	0	0.0	0
2002—Tennessee NFL	15	3	11	5	0.0	0	0	0.0	0
Pro totals (3 years)	43	3	19	9	1.0	0	0	0.0	0

C

CHAMBERS, CHRIS   WR   DOLPHINS

PERSONAL: Born August 12, 1978, in Cleveland. ... 5-11/210.
HIGH SCHOOL: Bedford (Ohio).
COLLEGE: Wisconsin.
TRANSACTIONS/CAREER NOTES: Selected by Miami Dolphins in second round (52nd pick overall) of 2001 NFL draft. ... Signed by Dolphins (July 23, 2001).
SINGLE GAME HIGHS (regular season): Receptions—7 (December 15, 2002, vs. Oakland); yards—138 (December 15, 2002, vs. Oakland); and touchdown receptions—2 (December 10, 2001, vs. Indianapolis).
STATISTICAL PLATEAUS: 100-yard receiving games: 2001 (3), 2002 (2). Total: 5.

Year Team	G	GS	RUSHING Att.	Yds.	Avg.	TD	RECEIVING No.	Yds.	Avg.	TD	TOTALS TD	2pt.	Pts.	Fum.
2001—Miami NFL	16	7	1	-11	-11.0	0	48	883	*18.4	7	7	0	42	2
2002—Miami NFL	15	15	6	78	13.0	0	52	734	14.1	3	3	0	18	1
Pro totals (2 years)	31	22	7	67	9.6	0	100	1617	16.2	10	10	0	60	3

CHANDLER, CHRIS   QB   BEARS

PERSONAL: Born October 12, 1965, in Everett, Wash. ... 6-4/228. ... Full name: Christopher Mark Chandler. ... Brother of Greg Chandler, catcher with San Francisco Giants organization (1978); and son-in-law of John Brodie, quarterback with San Francisco 49ers (1957-73).
HIGH SCHOOL: Everett (Wash.).
COLLEGE: Washington (degree in economics, 1988).
TRANSACTIONS/CAREER NOTES: Selected by Indianapolis Colts in third round (76th pick overall) of 1988 NFL draft. ... Signed by Colts (July 23, 1988). ... On injured reserve with knee injury (October 3, 1989-remainder of season). ... Traded by Colts to Tampa Bay Buccaneers for first round pick (LB Quentin Coryatt) in 1992 draft (August 7, 1990). ... Claimed on waivers by Phoenix Cardinals (November 6, 1991). ... Granted unconditional free agency (February 17, 1994). ... Signed by Los Angeles Rams (May 4, 1994). ... Granted unconditional free agency (February 17, 1995). ... Signed by Houston Oilers (March 10, 1995). ... Traded by Oilers to Atlanta Falcons for fourth- (WR Derrick Mason) and sixth-round (traded to New Orleans) picks in 1997 draft (February 24, 1997). ... Released by Falcons (February 25, 2002). ... Signed by Chicago Bears (April 12, 2002).
CHAMPIONSHIP GAME EXPERIENCE: Played in NFC championship game (1998 season). ... Played in Super Bowl XXXIII (1998 season).
HONORS: Played in Pro Bowl (1997 and 1998 seasons).
SINGLE GAME HIGHS (regular season): Attempts—50 (November 18, 2001, vs. Green Bay); completions—29 (November 18, 2001, vs. Green Bay); yards—431 (December 23, 2001, vs. Buffalo); and touchdown passes—4 (November 28, 1999, vs. Carolina).
STATISTICAL PLATEAUS: 300-yard passing games: 1992 (1), 1995 (1), 1998 (1), 1999 (2), 2001 (2). Total: 7.
MISCELLANEOUS: Regular-season record as starting NFL quarterback: 64-80 (.444). ... Postseason record as starting NFL quarterback: 2-1 (.667).

Year Team	G	GS	PASSING Att.	Cmp.	Pct.	Yds.	TD	Int.	Avg.	Skd.	Rat.	RUSHING Att.	Yds.	Avg.	TD	TOTALS TD	2pt.	Pts.
1988—Indianapolis NFL	15	13	233	129	55.4	1619	8	12	6.95	18	67.2	46	139	3.0	3	3	0	18
1989—Indianapolis NFL	3	3	80	39	48.8	537	2	3	6.71	3	63.4	7	57	8.1	1	1	0	6
1990—Tampa Bay NFL	7	3	83	42	50.6	464	1	6	5.59	15	41.4	13	71	5.5	1	1	0	6
1991—Tampa Bay NFL	6	3	104	53	51.0	557	4	8	5.36	10	47.6	18	79	4.4	0	0	0	0
—Phoenix NFL	3	2	50	25	50.0	289	1	2	5.78	7	57.8	8	32	4.0	0	0	0	0
1992—Phoenix NFL	15	13	413	245	59.3	2832	15	15	6.86	29	77.1	36	149	4.1	1	1	0	6
1993—Phoenix NFL	4	2	103	52	50.5	471	3	2	4.57	4	64.8	3	2	0.7	0	0	0	0
1994—L.A. Rams NFL	12	6	176	108	61.4	1352	7	2	7.68	7	93.8	18	61	3.4	1	1	0	6
1995—Houston NFL	13	13	356	225	63.2	2460	17	10	6.91	21	87.8	28	58	2.1	2	2	1	14
1996—Houston NFL	12	12	320	184	57.5	2099	16	11	6.56	25	79.7	28	113	4.0	0	0	0	0
1997—Atlanta NFL	14	14	342	202	59.1	2692	20	7	7.87	39	95.1	43	158	3.7	0	0	0	0
1998—Atlanta NFL	14	14	327	190	58.1	3154	25	12	*9.65	45	100.9	36	121	3.4	2	2	0	12
1999—Atlanta NFL	12	12	307	174	56.7	2339	16	11	7.62	32	83.5	16	57	3.6	1	1	0	6
2000—Atlanta NFL	14	13	331	192	58.0	2236	10	12	6.76	40	73.5	21	60	2.9	0	0	0	0
2001—Atlanta NFL	14	14	365	223	61.1	2847	16	14	7.80	41	84.1	25	84	3.4	0	0	0	0
2002—Chicago NFL	9	7	161	103	64.0	1023	4	4	6.35	23	79.8	10	32	3.2	0	0	0	0
Pro totals (15 years)	167	144	3751	2186	58.3	26971	165	131	7.19	359	80.7	356	1273	3.6	12	12	1	74

CHANDLER, JEFF   K   49ERS

PERSONAL: Born June 18, 1979, in Jacksonville, Fla. ... 6-2/218. ... Full name: Jeffrey Robin Chandler.
HIGH SCHOOL: Mandarin (Jacksonville, Fla.).
COLLEGE: Florida.
TRANSACTIONS/CAREER NOTES: Selected by San Francisco 49ers in fourth round (102nd pick overall) of 2002 NFL draft. ... Signed by 49ers (July 21, 2002).

Year Team	G	FIELD GOALS 1-29	30-39	40-49	50+	Tot.	Pct.	Lg.	TOTALS XPM	XPA	Pts.
2002—San Francisco NFL	6	3-3	1-1	4-7	0-1	8-12	66.7	47	14	14	38

CHANOINE, ROGER   OT

PERSONAL: Born September 11, 1976, in Linden, N.J. ... 6-4/305. ... Full name: Roger Chanoine Jr. ... Name pronounced SHAN-wah.
HIGH SCHOOL: Linden (N.J.).
COLLEGE: Temple.
TRANSACTIONS/CAREER NOTES: Signed as non-drafted free agent by St. Louis Rams (April 20, 1998). ... On injured reserve with ankle injury (August 25, 1998-entire season). ... Released by Rams (August 30, 1999). ... Signed by Cleveland Browns to practice squad (September 7, 1999). ... Activated (December 8, 1999). ... Granted free agency (March 1, 2002). ... Re-signed by Browns (April 20, 2002). ... Released by Browns (November 5, 2002). ... Signed by Jacksonville Jaguars (November 6, 2002). ... Released by Jaguars (December 24, 2002).
PLAYING EXPERIENCE: Cleveland NFL, 1999-2002. ... Games/Games started: 1999 (1/0), 2000 (7/0), 2001 (16/16), 2002 (9/2). Total: 34/18.

CHAPMAN, DOUG — RB — VIKINGS

PERSONAL: Born August 22, 1977, in Chesterfield, Va. ... 5-10/213.
HIGH SCHOOL: Lloyd C. Bird (Chesterfield, Va.).
COLLEGE: Marshall.
TRANSACTIONS/CAREER NOTES: Selected by Minnesota Vikings in third round (88th pick overall) of 2000 NFL draft. ... Signed by Vikings (July 23, 2000). ... Inactive for 16 games (2000). ... On injured reserve with internal injury (October 23, 2002-remainder of season). ... Granted free agency (February 28, 2003). ... Re-signed by Vikings (April 1, 2003).
CHAMPIONSHIP GAME EXPERIENCE: Member of Vikings for NFC championship game (2000 season); inactive.
SINGLE GAME HIGHS (regular season): Attempts—22 (October 21, 2001, vs. Green Bay); yards—90 (October 21, 2001, vs. Green Bay); and rushing touchdowns—0.

			RUSHING				RECEIVING				KICKOFF RETURNS				TOTALS		
Year Team	G	GS	Att.	Yds.	Avg.	TD	No.	Yds.	Avg.	TD	No.	Yds.	Avg.	TD	TD 2pt.	Pts.	Fum.
2000—Minnesota NFL							Did not play.										
2001—Minnesota NFL	16	3	63	195	3.1	0	16	135	8.4	1	0	0	0.0	0	1 0	6	1
2002—Minnesota NFL	6	0	12	89	7.4	0	0	0	0.0	0	11	225	20.5	0	0 0	0	1
Pro totals (2 years)	22	3	75	284	3.8	0	16	135	8.4	1	11	225	20.5	0	1 0	6	2

CHARLTON, IKE — CB — JAGUARS

PERSONAL: Born October 6, 1977, in Orlando, Fla. ... 5-11/204. ... Full name: Isaac C. Charlton IV.
HIGH SCHOOL: Dr. Phillips (Orlando, Fla.).
COLLEGE: Virginia Tech.
TRANSACTIONS/CAREER NOTES: Selected after junior season by Seattle Seahawks in second round (52nd pick overall) of 2000 NFL draft. ... Signed by Seahawks (July 20, 2000). ... Traded by Seahawks to Jacksonville Jaguars for conditional seventh-round draft pick (K Josh Brown) in 2003 draft (June 21, 2002).

			TOTALS			INTERCEPTIONS				KICKOFF RETURNS				TOTALS		
Year Team	G	GS	Tk.	Ast.	Sks.	No.	Yds.	Avg.	TD	No.	Yds.	Avg.	TD	TD 2pt.	Pts.	Fum.
2000—Seattle NFL	16	0	11	2	0.0	0	0	0.0	0	0	0	0.0	0	0 0	0	0
2001—Seattle NFL	15	1	25	2	1.0	2	43	21.5	1	0	0	0.0	0	1 0	6	0
2002—Jacksonville NFL	15	0	22	0	1.0	0	0	0.0	0	10	236	23.6	0	0 0	0	1
Pro totals (3 years)	46	1	58	4	2.0	2	43	21.5	1	10	236	23.6	0	1 0	6	1

CHASE, MARTIN — DT — SAINTS

PERSONAL: Born December 19, 1974, in Lawton, Okla. ... 6-2/310. ... Full name: Cecil Martin Chase.
HIGH SCHOOL: Eisenhower (Lawton, Okla.).
COLLEGE: Oklahoma.
TRANSACTIONS/CAREER NOTES: Selected by Baltimore Ravens in fifth round (124th pick overall) of 1998 NFL draft. ... Signed by Ravens (July 17, 1998). ... On injured reserve with ankle injury (August 25, 1998-entire season). ... Assigned by Ravens to Frankfurt Galaxy in 2000 NFL Europe enhancement allocation program (February 18, 2000). ... Claimed on waivers by New Orleans Saints (August 28, 2000). ... Granted free agency (March 2, 2001). ... Re-signed by Saints (April 16, 2001).

			TOTALS		
Year Team	G	GS	Tk.	Ast.	Sks.
1998—Baltimore NFL			Did not play.		
1999—Baltimore NFL	3	0	0	1	0.0
2000—New Orleans NFL	9	0	3	0	0.0
2001—New Orleans NFL	16	3	16	6	1.0
2002—New Orleans NFL	13	2	15	4	0.0
Pro totals (4 years)	41	5	34	11	1.0

CHATHAM, MATT — LB — PATRIOTS

PERSONAL: Born June 28, 1977, in Sioux City, Iowa. ... 6-4/248.
HIGH SCHOOL: Sioux City (Iowa).
COLLEGE: South Dakota.
TRANSACTIONS/CAREER NOTES: Signed as non-drafted free agent by St. Louis Rams (April 26, 1999). ... Released by Rams (June 26, 1999). ... Signed by Rams (February 11, 2000). ... Claimed on waivers by New England Patriots (August 28, 2000). ... Released by Patriots (September 2, 2001). ... Re-signed by Patriots to practice squad (September 4, 2001). ... Activated (September 22, 2001). ... Released by Patriots (September 25, 2001). ... Re-signed by Patriots to practice squad (September 26, 2001). ... Activated (October 3, 2001). ... On injured reserve with hand injury (December 11, 2002-remainder of season). ... Granted free agency (February 28, 2003). ... Re-signed by Patriots (April 11, 2003).
CHAMPIONSHIP GAME EXPERIENCE: Played in AFC championship game (2001 season). ... Member of Super Bowl championship team (2001 season).

			TOTALS			INTERCEPTIONS			
Year Team	G	GS	Tk.	Ast.	Sks.	No.	Yds.	Avg.	TD
2000—New England NFL	6	0	0	0	0.0	0	0	0.0	0
2001—New England NFL	11	0	2	0	0.0	0	0	0.0	0
2002—New England NFL	13	0	2	0	0.0	0	0	0.0	0
Pro totals (3 years)	30	0	4	0	0.0	0	0	0.0	0

C

CHATMAN, JESSE — RB — CHARGERS

PERSONAL: Born September 22, 1979, in Houston. ... 5-8/215.
HIGH SCHOOL: Franklin (Seattle).
COLLEGE: Eastern Washington.
TRANSACTIONS/CAREER NOTES: Signed as non-drafted free agent by San Diego Chargers (April 26, 2002).
SINGLE GAME HIGHS (regular season): Attempts—4 (November 24, 2002, vs. Miami); yards—18 (November 24, 2002, vs. Miami); and rushing touchdowns—0.

			RUSHING				RECEIVING				TOTALS			
Year Team	G	GS	Att.	Yds.	Avg.	TD	No.	Yds.	Avg.	TD	TD	2pt.	Pts.	Fum.
2002—San Diego NFL	10	0	6	19	3.2	0	3	44	14.7	0	0	0	0	0

CHAVOUS, COREY — CB — VIKINGS

PERSONAL: Born January 15, 1976, in Petticoat Junction, S.C. ... 6-1/206. ... Cousin of Fred Vinson, cornerback, Carolina Panthers. ... Name pronounced CHAY-vus.
HIGH SCHOOL: Silver Bluff (Aiken, S.C.).
COLLEGE: Vanderbilt.
TRANSACTIONS/CAREER NOTES: Selected by Arizona Cardinals in second round (33rd pick overall) of 1998 NFL draft. ... Signed by Cardinals (July 23, 1998). ... Granted free agency (March 2, 2001). ... Re-signed by Cardinals (July 13, 2001). ... Granted unconditional free agency (March 1, 2002). ... Signed by Minnesota Vikings (March 25, 2002).

			TOTALS			INTERCEPTIONS			
Year Team	G	GS	Tk.	Ast.	Sks.	No.	Yds.	Avg.	TD
1998—Arizona NFL	16	5	20	5	0.0	2	0	0.0	0
1999—Arizona NFL	15	4	28	8	0.0	1	1	1.0	0
2000—Arizona NFL	16	1	39	3	0.0	1	0	0.0	0
2001—Arizona NFL	14	14	59	12	0.0	1	0	0.0	0
2002—Minnesota NFL	16	16	66	17	1.0	3	76	25.3	1
Pro totals (5 years)	77	40	212	45	1.0	8	77	9.6	1

CHERRY, JE'ROD — S — PATRIOTS

PERSONAL: Born May 30, 1973, in Charlotte. ... 6-1/210. ... Full name: Je'Rod L. Cherry. ... Name pronounced juh-ROD.
HIGH SCHOOL: Berkeley (Calif.).
COLLEGE: California (degree in political science, 1995).
TRANSACTIONS/CAREER NOTES: Selected by New Orleans Saints in second round (40th pick overall) of 1996 NFL draft. ... Signed by Saints (July 3, 1996). ... Granted free agency (February 12, 1999). ... Re-signed by Saints (July 21, 1999). ... Granted unconditional free agency (February 11, 2000). ... Signed by Oakland Raiders (February 19, 2000). ... Released by Raiders (August 27, 2000). ... Signed by Philadelphia Eagles (September 20, 2000). ... Granted unconditional free agency (March 2, 2001). ... Signed by New England Patriots (July 25, 2001). ... Granted unconditional free agency (February 28, 2003). ... Re-signed by Patriots (March 5, 2003).
CHAMPIONSHIP GAME EXPERIENCE: Played in AFC championship game (2001 season). ... Member of Super Bowl championship team (2001 season).

			TOTALS			INTERCEPTIONS			
Year Team	G	GS	Tk.	Ast.	Sks.	No.	Yds.	Avg.	TD
1996—New Orleans NFL	13	0	6	2	0.0	0	0	0.0	0
1997—New Orleans NFL	16	0	6	0	0.0	0	0	0.0	0
1998—New Orleans NFL	14	0	23	4	2.0	0	0	0.0	0
1999—New Orleans NFL	16	0	13	1	0.0	0	0	0.0	0
2000—Philadelphia NFL	13	0	0	0	0.0	0	0	0.0	0
2001—New England NFL	16	0	2	1	0.0	0	0	0.0	0
2002—New England NFL	16	0	1	0	0.0	0	0	0.0	0
Pro totals (7 years)	104	0	51	8	2.0	0	0	0.0	0

CHESTER, LARRY — DT — DOLPHINS

PERSONAL: Born October 17, 1975, in Hammond, La. ... 6-2/325.
HIGH SCHOOL: Hammond (La.).
JUNIOR COLLEGE: Southwest Mississippi Junior College.
COLLEGE: Temple.
TRANSACTIONS/CAREER NOTES: Signed as non-drafted free agent by Indianapolis Colts (April 24, 1998). ... Released by Colts (August 31, 1998). ... Re-signed by Colts to practice squad (September 2, 1998). ... Activated (September 11, 1998). ... Granted free agency (March 2, 2001). ... Signed by Carolina Panthers (May 15, 2001). ... Granted unconditional free agency (March 1, 2002). ... Signed by Miami Dolphins (March 5, 2002).

			TOTALS		
Year Team	G	GS	Tk.	Ast.	Sks.
1998—Indianapolis NFL	14	2	20	3	3.0
1999—Indianapolis NFL	16	8	31	10	1.0
2000—Indianapolis NFL	16	0	10	6	2.5
2001—Carolina NFL	11	5	26	10	0.5
2002—Miami NFL	16	16	26	11	1.5
Pro totals (5 years)	73	31	113	40	8.5

CHIAVERINI, DARRIN — WR

PERSONAL: Born October 12, 1977, in Orange County, Calif. ... 6-2/210. ... Name pronounced SHEVV-er-re-nee.
HIGH SCHOOL: Corona (Calif.).
COLLEGE: Colorado.
TRANSACTIONS/CAREER NOTES: Selected by Cleveland Browns in fifth round (148th pick overall) of 1999 NFL draft. ... Signed by Browns (July 22, 1999). ... Traded by Browns to Dallas Cowboys for conditional seventh-round pick (August 28, 2001). ... Granted free agency (March 1, 2002). ... Re-signed by Cowboys (April 26, 2002). ... Released by Cowboys (June 13, 2002). ... Signed by Atlanta Falcons (July 2, 2002). ... Granted unconditional free agency (February 28, 2003).
SINGLE GAME HIGHS (regular season): Receptions—10 (December 19, 1999, vs. Jacksonville); yards—108 (December 19, 1999, vs. Jacksonville); and touchdown receptions—1 (December 30, 2001, vs. San Francisco).
STATISTICAL PLATEAUS: 100-yard receiving games: 1999 (1).

Year Team	G	GS	RECEIVING No.	Yds.	Avg.	TD	TOTALS TD	2pt.	Pts.	Fum.
1999—Cleveland NFL	16	8	44	487	11.1	4	4	0	24	0
2000—Cleveland NFL	10	2	8	68	8.5	1	1	0	6	1
2001—Dallas NFL	16	0	10	107	10.7	2	2	0	12	0
2002—Atlanta NFL	7	0	0	0	0.0	0	0	0	0	0
Pro totals (4 years)	49	10	62	662	10.7	7	7	0	42	1

CHREBET, WAYNE — WR — JETS

C

PERSONAL: Born August 14, 1973, in Garfield, N.J. ... 5-10/188. ... Name pronounced kra-BET.
HIGH SCHOOL: Garfield (N.J.).
COLLEGE: Hofstra.
TRANSACTIONS/CAREER NOTES: Signed as non-drafted free agent by New York Jets (April 25, 1995).
CHAMPIONSHIP GAME EXPERIENCE: Played in AFC championship game (1998 season).
SINGLE GAME HIGHS (regular season): Receptions—12 (October 13, 1996, vs. Jacksonville); yards—162 (October 13, 1996, vs. Jacksonville); and touchdown receptions—2 (December 29, 2002, vs. Green Bay).
STATISTICAL PLATEAUS: 100-yard receiving games: 1996 (1); 1991 (1); 1995 (5); 1999 (1); 2000 (2); 2001 (1). Total: 11

Year Team	G	GS	RECEIVING No.	Yds.	Avg.	TD	PUNT RETURNS No.	Yds.	Avg.	TD	TOTALS TD	2pt.	Pts.	Fum.
1995—New York Jets NFL	16	16	66	726	11.0	4	0	0	0.0	0	4	0	24	1
1996—New York Jets NFL	16	9	84	909	10.8	3	28	139	5.0	0	3	0	18	5
1997—New York Jets NFL	16	1	58	799	13.8	3	0	0	0.0	0	3	0	18	0
1998—New York Jets NFL	16	15	75	1083	14.4	8	0	0	0.0	0	8	0	48	0
1999—New York Jets NFL	11	11	48	631	13.1	3	0	0	0.0	0	3	0	18	0
2000—New York Jets NFL	16	16	69	937	13.6	8	0	0	0.0	0	8	0	48	0
2001—New York Jets NFL	15	15	56	750	13.4	1	0	0	0.0	0	1	0	6	0
2002—New York Jets NFL	15	15	51	691	13.5	9	0	0	0.0	0	9	0	54	2
Pro totals (8 years)	121	98	507	6526	12.9	39	28	139	5.0	0	39	0	234	8

CHRISTIAN, BOB — FB

PERSONAL: Born November 14, 1968, in St. Louis. ... 5-11/232. ... Full name: Robert Douglas Christian.
HIGH SCHOOL: McCluer North (Florissant, Mo.).
COLLEGE: Northwestern.
TRANSACTIONS/CAREER NOTES: Selected by Atlanta Falcons in 12th round (310th pick overall) of 1991 NFL draft. ... Signed by Falcons (July 18, 1991). ... Released by Falcons (August 20, 1991). ... Selected by London Monarchs in 16th round (175th pick overall) of 1992 World League draft. ... Signed by San Diego Chargers (July 10, 1992). ... Released by Chargers (August 25, 1992). ... Signed by Chicago Bears to practice squad (September 8, 1992). ... Activated (December 18, 1992). ... On injured reserve with knee injury (December 2, 1994-remainder of season). ... Selected by Carolina Panthers from Bears in NFL expansion draft (February 15, 1995). ... Granted free agency (February 16, 1996). ... Re-signed by Panthers (July 19, 1996). ... On injured reserve with shoulder injury (August 25, 1996-entire season). ... Granted unconditional free agency (February 14, 1997). ... Signed by Falcons (March 6, 1997). ... On injured reserve with knee injury (December 11, 1998-remainder of season). ... On injured reserve with concussion (January 1, 2003-remainder of season). ... Announced retirement (March 11, 2003).
SINGLE GAME HIGHS (regular season): Attempts—10 (December 30, 2001, vs. Miami); yards—78 (November 25, 2001, vs. Carolina); and rushing touchdowns—2 (December 26, 1999, vs. Arizona).

Year Team	G	GS	RUSHING Att.	Yds.	Avg.	TD	RECEIVING No.	Yds.	Avg.	TD	TOTALS TD	2pt.	Pts.	Fum.
1992—Chicago NFL	2	0	0	0	0.0	0	0	0	0.0	0	0	0	0	0
1993—Chicago NFL	14	1	8	19	2.4	0	16	160	10.0	0	0	0	0	0
1994—Chicago NFL	12	0	7	29	4.1	0	2	30	15.0	0	0	0	0	0
1995—Carolina NFL	14	12	41	158	3.9	0	29	255	8.8	1	1	1	8	1
1996—Carolina NFL						Did not play.								
1997—Atlanta NFL	16	12	7	8	1.1	0	22	154	7.0	1	1	0	6	3
1998—Atlanta NFL	14	10	8	21	2.6	2	19	214	11.3	1	3	0	18	1
1999—Atlanta NFL	16	14	38	174	4.6	5	40	354	8.9	2	7	0	42	1
2000—Atlanta NFL	16	14	9	19	2.1	0	44	315	7.2	0	0	0	0	0
2001—Atlanta NFL	16	8	44	284	6.5	2	45	392	8.7	2	4	0	24	0
2002—Atlanta NFL	15	10	31	119	3.8	3	13	174	13.4	0	3	0	18	1
Pro totals (10 years)	135	81	193	831	4.3	12	230	2048	8.9	7	19	1	116	7

CHRISTIE, STEVE — K

PERSONAL: Born November 13, 1967, in Oakville, Ont. ... 6-0/195. ... Full name: Geoffrey Stephen Christie.
HIGH SCHOOL: Trafalgar (Oakville, Ont.).
COLLEGE: William & Mary.
TRANSACTIONS/CAREER NOTES: Signed as non-drafted free agent by Tampa Bay Buccaneers (May 8, 1990). ... Granted unconditional free agency (February 1, 1992). ... Signed by Buffalo Bills (February 5, 1992). ... Granted unconditional free agency (March 2, 2001). ... Re-signed by Bills (April 22, 2001). ... On injured reserve with groin injury (September 8-October 3, 2001). ... Released by Bills (October 3, 2001). ... Signed by San Diego Chargers (November 29, 2001). ... Granted unconditional free agency (March 1, 2002). ... Re-signed by Chargers (March 29, 2002). ... Granted unconditional free agency (February 28, 2003).
CHAMPIONSHIP GAME EXPERIENCE: Played in AFC championship game (1992 and 1993 seasons). ... Played in Super Bowl XXVII (1992 season) and Super Bowl XXVIII (1993 season).
POST SEASON RECORDS: Holds Super Bowl single-game record for longest field goal—54 yards (January 30, 1994, vs. Dallas). ... Shares NFL postseason single-game record for most field goals made—5; and most field goals attempted—6 (January 17, 1993, at Miami).

Year Team	G	1-29	30-39	40-49	50+	Tot.	Pct.	Lg.	XPM	XPA	Pts.
1990—Tampa Bay NFL	16	7-7	10-13	4-5	2-2	23-27	85.2	54	27	27	96
1991—Tampa Bay NFL	16	5-5	7-11	3-4	0-0	15-20	75.0	49	22	22	67
1992—Buffalo NFL	16	11-11	3-6	7-8	3-5	24-30	80.0	†54	§43	§44	115
1993—Buffalo NFL	16	4-5	12-12	6-9	1-6	23-32	71.9	*59	36	37	105
1994—Buffalo NFL	16	11-12	6-7	5-7	2-2	24-28	85.7	52	§38	§38	110
1995—Buffalo NFL	16	13-14	13-15	3-6	2-5	31-40	77.5	51	33	35	126
1996—Buffalo NFL	16	5-6	12-14	7-8	0-1	24-29	82.8	48	33	33	105
1997—Buffalo NFL	16	6-6	9-12	8-10	1-2	24-30	80.0	†55	21	21	93
1998—Buffalo NFL	16	11-13	12-14	9-11	1-3	33-*41	80.5	52	41	41	§140
1999—Buffalo NFL	16	12-12	7-10	3-9	3-3	25-34	73.5	52	33	33	108
2000—Buffalo NFL	16	13-15	4-6	9-13	0-1	26-35	74.3	48	31	31	109
2001—San Diego NFL	5	4-4	3-5	2-2	0-0	9-11	81.8	41	6	6	33
2002—San Diego NFL	16	8-8	5-6	4-9	1-3	18-26	69.2	53	35	36	89
Pro totals (13 years)	197	110-118	103-131	70-101	16-33	299-383	78.1	59	399	404	1296

CHRISTY, JEFF — C — BUCCANEERS

PERSONAL: Born February 3, 1969, in Natrona Heights, Pa. ... 6-2/285. ... Full name: Jeffrey Allen Christy. ... Brother of Greg Christy, offensive tackle with Buffalo Bills (1985).
HIGH SCHOOL: Freeport (Pa.) Area.
COLLEGE: Pittsburgh.
TRANSACTIONS/CAREER NOTES: Selected by Phoenix Cardinals in fourth round (91st pick overall) of 1992 NFL draft. ... Signed by Cardinals (July 21, 1992). ... Released by Cardinals (August 31, 1992). ... Signed by Minnesota Vikings (March 16, 1993). ... On injured reserve with ankle injury (November 26, 1997-remainder of season). ... Granted unconditional free agency (February 11, 2000). ... Signed by Tampa Bay Buccaneers (February 15, 2000).
PLAYING EXPERIENCE: Minnesota NFL, 1993-1999; Tampa Bay NFL, 2000-2002. ... Games/Games started: 1993 (9/0), 1994 (16/16), 1995 (16/16), 1996 (16/16), 1997 (12/12), 1998 (16/16), 1999 (16/16), 2000 (16/16), 2001 (15/15), 2002 (16/16). Total: 148/139.
CHAMPIONSHIP GAME EXPERIENCE: Played in NFC championship game (1998 and 2002 seasons). ... Member of Super Bowl championship team (2002 season).
HONORS: Played in Pro Bowl (1998-2000 seasons).

CHUKWURAH, PATRICK — LB — SAINTS

PERSONAL: Born March 1, 1979, in Nigeria. ... 6-1/250.
HIGH SCHOOL: MacArthur (Texas).
COLLEGE: Wyoming.
TRANSACTIONS/CAREER NOTES: Selected by Minnesota Vikings in fifth round (157th pick overall) of 2001 NFL draft. ... Signed by Vikings (July 24, 2001). ... Claimed on waivers by New Orleans Saints (March 2, 2003).

Year Team	G	GS	Tk.	Ast.	Sks.	No.	Yds.	Avg.	TD
2001—Minnesota NFL	16	3	5	3	2.5	0	0	0.0	0
2002—Minnesota NFL	11	2	7	2	0.0	0	0	0.0	0
Pro totals (2 years)	27	5	12	5	2.5	0	0	0.0	0

CLAIBORNE, CHRIS — LB — VIKINGS

PERSONAL: Born July 26, 1978, in Riverdale, Calif. ... 6-3/258.
HIGH SCHOOL: John W. North (Riverside, Calif.).
COLLEGE: Southern California.
TRANSACTIONS/CAREER NOTES: Selected after junior season by Detroit Lions in first round (ninth pick overall) of 1999 NFL draft. ... Signed by Lions (July 24, 1999). ... Granted unconditional free agency (February 28, 2003). ... Signed by Minnesota Vikings (March 24, 2003).
HONORS: Butkus Award winner (1998). ... Named inside linebacker on THE SPORTING NEWS college All-America first team (1998).

Year Team	G	GS	Tk.	Ast.	Sks.	No.	Yds.	Avg.	TD
1999—Detroit NFL	15	13	50	16	1.5	0	0	0.0	0
2000—Detroit NFL	16	14	65	39	0.5	1	1	1.0	0
2001—Detroit NFL	16	16	77	43	4.0	2	11	5.5	0
2002—Detroit NFL	16	15	72	29	4.5	3	63	21.0	1
Pro totals (4 years)	63	58	264	127	10.5	6	75	12.5	1

CLANCY, KENDRICK   NT   STEELERS

PERSONAL: Born September 17, 1978, in Tuscaloosa, Ala. ... 6-1/289.
HIGH SCHOOL: Holt (Tuscaloosa, Ala.).
JUNIOR COLLEGE: East Central Community College (Miss.).
COLLEGE: Mississippi.
TRANSACTIONS/CAREER NOTES: Selected by Pittsburgh Steelers in third round (72nd pick overall) of 2000 NFL draft. ... Signed by Steelers (July 16, 2000). ... Granted free agency (February 28, 2003). ... Re-signed by Steelers (April 16, 2003).
CHAMPIONSHIP GAME EXPERIENCE: Played in AFC championship game (2001 season).
HONORS: Named defensive tackle on THE SPORTING NEWS college All-America third team (1999).

			TOTALS			INTERCEPTIONS			
Year Team	G	GS	Tk.	Ast.	Sks.	No.	Yds.	Avg.	TD
2000—Pittsburgh NFL	9	0	5	3	0.0	0	0	0.0	0
2001—Pittsburgh NFL	16	4	6	4	0.0	1	3	3.0	0
2002—Pittsburgh NFL	7	0	1	0	0.0	0	0	0.0	0
Pro totals (3 years)	32	4	12	7	0.0	1	3	3.0	0

CLARIDGE, TRAVIS   OT/OG   FALCONS

PERSONAL: Born March 23, 1978, in Detroit. ... 6-5/300.
HIGH SCHOOL: Fort Vancouver (Vancouver, Wash.).
COLLEGE: Southern California.
TRANSACTIONS/CAREER NOTES: Selected by Atlanta Falcons in second round (37th pick overall) of 2000 NFL draft. ... Signed by Falcons (May 16, 2000).
PLAYING EXPERIENCE: Atlanta NFL, 2000-2002. ... Games/Games started: 2000 (16/16), 2001 (14/11), 2002 (16/16). Total: 46/43.
HONORS: Named guard on THE SPORTING NEWS college All-America third team (1999).

CLARK, DANNY   LB   JAGUARS

PERSONAL: Born May 9, 1977, in Blue Island, Ill. ... 6-2/243. ... Full name: Daniel Clark IV.
HIGH SCHOOL: Hillcrest (Ill.).
COLLEGE: Illinois (degree in speech communications).
TRANSACTIONS/CAREER NOTES: Selected by Jacksonville Jaguars in seventh round (245th pick overall) of 2000 NFL draft. ... Signed by Jaguars (June 6, 2000). ... Granted free agency (February 28, 2003). ... Re-signed by Jaguars (May 5, 2003).

			TOTALS			INTERCEPTIONS			
Year Team	G	GS	Tk.	Ast.	Sks.	No.	Yds.	Avg.	TD
2000—Jacksonville NFL	16	0	4	0	0.0	0	0	0.0	0
2001—Jacksonville NFL	13	3	18	3	0.0	0	0	0.0	0
2002—Jacksonville NFL	16	16	69	22	2.0	1	7	7.0	0
Pro totals (3 years)	45	19	91	25	2.0	1	7	7.0	0

CLARK, DESMOND   TE   BEARS

PERSONAL: Born April 20, 1977, in Bartow, Fla. ... 6-3/255. ... Full name: Desmond Darice Clark.
HIGH SCHOOL: Kathleen (Lakeland, Fla.).
COLLEGE: Wake Forest.
TRANSACTIONS/CAREER NOTES: Selected by Denver Broncos in sixth round (179th pick overall) of 1999 NFL draft. ... Signed by Broncos (June 14, 1999). ... Granted free agency (March 1, 2002). ... Re-signed by Broncos (April 16, 2002). ... Claimed on waivers by Miami Dolphins (September 2, 2002). ... Granted unconditional free agency (February 28, 2003). ... Signed by Chicago Bears (March 1, 2003).
SINGLE GAME HIGHS (regular season): Receptions—7 (November 5, 2001, vs. Oakland); yards—94 (October 28, 2001, vs. New England); and touchdown receptions—1 (January 6, 2002, vs. Indianapolis).

			RECEIVING				TOTALS			
Year Team	G	GS	No.	Yds.	Avg.	TD	TD	2pt.	Pts.	Fum.
1999—Denver NFL	9	0	1	5	5.0	0	0	0	0	0
2000—Denver NFL	16	2	27	339	12.6	3	3	0	18	0
2001—Denver NFL	16	4	51	566	11.1	6	6	0	36	3
2002—Miami NFL	11	0	2	42	21.0	0	0	0	0	0
Pro totals (4 years)	52	6	81	952	11.8	9	9	0	54	3

CLARK, RYAN   S

PERSONAL: Born October 12, 1979, in New Orleans. ... 5-11/192. ... Full name: Ryan Terry Clark.
HIGH SCHOOL: Shaw (New Orleans).
COLLEGE: Louisiana State.
TRANSACTIONS/CAREER NOTES: Signed as non-drafted free agent by New York Giants (April 26, 2002). ... Released by Giants (October 21, 2002).

			TOTALS			INTERCEPTIONS			
Year Team	G	GS	Tk.	Ast.	Sks.	No.	Yds.	Avg.	TD
2002—New York Giants NFL	6	0	0	1	0.0	0	0	0.0	0

CLAYBROOKS, DEVONE — DT — BUCCANEERS

PERSONAL: Born September 15, 1977, in Martinsville, Va. ... 6-3/292. ... Full name: Natravis DeVone Claybrooks. ... Cousin of Shawn Moore, quarterback with Denver Broncos (1991-93).
HIGH SCHOOL: Bassett (Va.).
COLLEGE: East Carolina.
TRANSACTIONS/CAREER NOTES: Signed as non-drafted free agent by Green Bay Packers (May 18, 2001). ... Released by Packers (September 2, 2001). ... Signed by Tampa Bay Buccaneers to practice squad (September 4, 2001). ... Released by Buccaneers (October 16, 2001). ... Signed by Cleveland Browns to practice squad (October 30, 2001). ... Activated (November 7, 2001); did not play. ... Assigned by Browns to Rhein Fire in 2002 NFL Europe enhancement allocation program (February 12, 2002). ... Released by Browns (July 26, 2002). ... Signed by Buccaneers to practice squad (November 6, 2002). ... Activated (November 15, 2002). ... Released by Buccaneers (November 18, 2002). ... Re-signed by Buccaneers to practice squad (November 20, 2002). ... Activated (November 23, 2002).
CHAMPIONSHIP GAME EXPERIENCE: Played in NFC championship game (2002 season). ... Member of Super Bowl championship team (2002 season).

Year Team	G	GS	TOTALS Tk.	Ast.	Sks.	INTERCEPTIONS No.	Yds.	Avg.	TD
2002—Rhein NFLE	...	...	...	...	2.0	1	0	0.0	0
—Tampa Bay NFL	2	0	2	3	0.0	0	0	0.0	0
NFL Europe totals (1 year)	...	...	...	...	2.0	1	0	0.0	0
NFL totals (1 year)	2	0	2	3	0.0	0	0	0.0	0
Pro totals (2 years)	...	...	...	...	2.0	1	0	0.0	0

CLEELAND, CAM — TE — RAMS

PERSONAL: Born August 15, 1975, in Sedro Woolley, Wash. ... 6-4/272. ... Full name: Cameron Ross Cleeland. ... Nephew of Phil Misley, pitcher in Milwaukee Braves organization (1956-58).
HIGH SCHOOL: Sedro Woolley (Wash.).
COLLEGE: Washington.
TRANSACTIONS/CAREER NOTES: Selected by New Orleans Saints in second round (40th pick overall) of 1998 NFL draft. ... Signed by Saints (June 9, 1998). ... On injured reserve with Achilles' tendon injury (August 22, 2000-entire season). ... Granted free agency (March 2, 2001). ... Re-signed by Saints (March 19, 2001). ... On injured reserve with Achilles' tendon injury (December 26, 2001-remainder of season). ... Granted unconditional free agency (March 1, 2002). ... Signed by New England Patriots (March 28, 2002). ... Granted unconditional free agency (February 28, 2003). ... Signed by St. Louis Rams (April 4, 2003).
SINGLE GAME HIGHS (regular season): Receptions—10 (December 27, 1998, vs. Buffalo); yards—112 (December 27, 1998, vs. Buffalo); and touchdown receptions—2 (October 14, 2001, vs. Carolina).
STATISTICAL PLATEAUS: 100-yard receiving games: 1998 (1).

Year Team	G	GS	RECEIVING No.	Yds.	Avg.	TD	TOTALS TD	2pt.	Pts.	Fum.
1998—New Orleans NFL	16	16	54	684	12.7	6	6	0	36	1
1999—New Orleans NFL	11	8	26	325	12.5	1	1	†1	8	1
2000—New Orleans NFL					Did not play.					
2001—New Orleans NFL	9	7	13	138	10.6	4	4	0	24	1
2002—New England NFL	12	1	16	112	7.0	1	1	0	6	0
Pro totals (4 years)	48	32	109	1259	11.6	12	12	1	74	3

CLEMENT, ANTHONY — OT — CARDINALS

PERSONAL: Born April 10, 1976, in Lafayette, La. ... 6-8/328.
HIGH SCHOOL: Cecilia (La.).
COLLEGE: Southwestern Louisiana.
TRANSACTIONS/CAREER NOTES: Selected by Arizona Cardinals in second round (36th pick overall) of 1998 NFL draft. ... Signed by Cardinals (June 16, 1998). ... On injured reserve with back injury (November 17, 1998-remainder of season). ... Granted free agency (March 2, 2001). ... Re-signed by Cardinals (May 7, 2001). ... Granted unconditional free agency (March 1, 2002). ... Re-signed by Cardinals (March 3, 2002). ... On injured reserve with triceps injury (November 23, 2002-remainder of season).
PLAYING EXPERIENCE: Arizona NFL, 1998-2002. ... Games/Games started: 1998 (1/0), 1999 (16/14), 2000 (16/16), 2001 (16/16), 2002 (1/0). Total: 50/46.

CLEMENTS, NATE — CB — BILLS

PERSONAL: Born December 12, 1979, in Shaker Heights, Ohio. ... 5-11/204.
HIGH SCHOOL: Shaker Heights (Ohio).
COLLEGE: Ohio State.
TRANSACTIONS/CAREER NOTES: Selected after junior season by Buffalo Bills in first round (21st pick overall) of 2001 NFL draft. ... Signed by Bills (July 28, 2001).

Year Team	G	GS	TOTALS Tk.	Ast.	Sks.	INTERCEPTIONS No.	Yds.	Avg.	TD	PUNT RETURNS No.	Yds.	Avg.	TD	KICKOFF RETURNS No.	Yds.	Avg.	TD	TOTALS TD	2pt.	Pts.	Fum.
2001—Buffalo NFL	16	11	55	10	1.0	3	48	16.0	1	4	81	20.3	1	30	628	20.9	0	2	0	12	1
2002—Buffalo NFL	16	16	51	13	0.0	6	82	13.7	1	4	20	5.0	0	0	0	0.0	0	1	0	6	1
Pro totals (2 years)	32	27	106	23	1.0	9	130	14.4	2	8	101	12.6	1	30	628	20.9	0	3	0	18	2

CLEMONS, CHARLIE — LB — TEXANS

PERSONAL: Born July 4, 1972, in Griffin, Ga. ... 6-2/250. ... Full name: Charlie Fitzgerald Clemons.
HIGH SCHOOL: Griffin (Ga.).

JUNIOR COLLEGE: Northeast Oklahoma Junior College.
COLLEGE: Georgia (degree in recreation and leisure studies, 1993).
TRANSACTIONS/CAREER NOTES: Signed by Winnipeg Blue Bombers of CFL (May 1994). ... Transferred to Ottawa Rough Riders of CFL (August 1995). ... Transferred back to Blue Bombers (January 1996). ... Signed as non-drafted free agent by St. Louis Rams (February 19, 1997). ... On injured reserve with hamstring injury (November 24, 1997-remainder of season). ... Granted free agency (February 11, 2000). ... Tendered offer sheet by New Orleans Saints (February 16, 2000). ... Rams declined to match offer (February 22, 2000). ... On injured reserve with Achilles' tendon injury (October 2, 2000-remainder of season). ... Granted unconditional free agency (February 28, 2003). ... Signed by Houston Texans (April 2, 2003).
CHAMPIONSHIP GAME EXPERIENCE: Played in NFC championship game (1999 season). ... Member of Super Bowl championship team (1999 season).

			TOTALS			INTERCEPTIONS			
Year Team	G	GS	Tk.	Ast.	Sks.	No.	Yds.	Avg.	TD
1994—Winnipeg CFL	7	...	28	...	0.0	0	0	0.0	0
1995—Winnipeg CFL	6	...	16	...	3.0	0	0	0.0	0
—Ottawa CFL	7	...	26	...	3.0	0	0	0.0	0
1996—Winnipeg CFL	14	...	37	...	6.0	0	0	0.0	0
1997—St. Louis NFL	5	0	1	0	0.0	0	0	0.0	0
1998—St. Louis NFL	16	0	13	2	2.0	0	0	0.0	0
1999—St. Louis NFL	16	0	30	4	3.0	1	0	0.0	0
2000—New Orleans NFL			Did not play.						
2001—New Orleans NFL	16	15	75	18	13.5	1	3	3.0	0
2002—New Orleans NFL	16	15	60	24	0.5	0	0	0.0	0
CFL totals (3 years)	34	...	107	...	12.0	0	0	0.0	0
NFL totals (5 years)	69	30	179	48	19.0	2	3	1.5	0
Pro totals (8 years)	103	...	286	...	31.0	2	3	1.5	0

CLEMONS, DUANE   DE   BENGALS

PERSONAL: Born May 23, 1974, in Riverside, Calif. ... 6-5/270.
HIGH SCHOOL: John W. North (Riverside, Calif.).
COLLEGE: California (degree in ethnic studies, 1993).
TRANSACTIONS/CAREER NOTES: Selected after junior season by Minnesota Vikings in first round (16th pick overall) of 1996 NFL draft. ... Signed by Vikings (July 25, 1996). ... Granted unconditional free agency (February 11, 2000). ... Signed by Kansas City Chiefs (March 24, 2000). ... Released by Chiefs (February 26, 2003). ... Signed by Cincinnati Bengals (May 13, 2003).
CHAMPIONSHIP GAME EXPERIENCE: Played in NFC championship game (1998 season).

			TOTALS		
Year Team	G	GS	Tk.	Ast.	Sks.
1996—Minnesota NFL	13	0	2	5	0.0
1997—Minnesota NFL	13	3	23	1	7.0
1998—Minnesota NFL	16	3	17	8	2.5
1999—Minnesota NFL	16	9	29	7	9.0
2000—Kansas City NFL	12	12	47	9	7.5
2001—Kansas City NFL	16	15	37	12	7.0
2002—Kansas City NFL	16	16	28	8	2.0
Pro totals (7 years)	102	58	183	50	35.0

CLIFTON, CHAD   OT   PACKERS

PERSONAL: Born June 26, 1976, in Martin, Tenn. ... 6-5/327. ... Full name: Jeffrey Chad Clifton.
HIGH SCHOOL: Westview (Martin, Tenn.).
COLLEGE: Tennessee.
TRANSACTIONS/CAREER NOTES: Selected by Green Bay Packers in second round (44th pick overall) of 2000 NFL draft. ... Signed by Packers (July 24, 2000). ... On injured reserve with hip injury (December 4, 2002-remainder of season).
PLAYING EXPERIENCE: Green Bay NFL, 2000-2002. ... Games/Games started: 2000 (13/10), 2001 (14/13), 2002 (10/9). Total: 37/32.
HONORS: Named offensive tackle on THE SPORTING NEWS college All-America second team (1999).

CLOUD, MIKE   RB

PERSONAL: Born July 1, 1975, in Charleston, S.C. ... 5-10/205. ... Full name: Michael Alexander Cloud.
HIGH SCHOOL: Portsmouth (R.I.).
COLLEGE: Boston College.
TRANSACTIONS/CAREER NOTES: Selected by Kansas City Chiefs in second round (54th pick overall) of 1999 NFL draft. ... Signed by Chiefs (July 30, 1999). ... Granted unconditional free agency (February 28, 2003).
SINGLE GAME HIGHS (regular season): Attempts—16 (December 22, 2002, vs. San Diego); yards—58 (November 28, 1999, vs. Oakland); and rushing touchdowns—1 (December 15, 2002, vs. Denver).

			RUSHING				RECEIVING				KICKOFF RETURNS				TOTALS			
Year Team	G	GS	Att.	Yds.	Avg.	TD	No.	Yds.	Avg.	TD	No.	Yds.	Avg.	TD	TD	2pt.	Pts.	Fum.
1999—Kansas City NFL	11	0	35	128	3.7	0	3	25	8.3	0	2	28	14.0	0	0	0	0	0
2000—Kansas City NFL	16	4	30	84	2.8	1	2	16	8.0	0	36	779	21.6	0	2	0	12	0
2001—Kansas City NFL	15	0	7	54	7.7	1	0	0	0.0	0	8	174	21.8	0	1	0	6	0
2002—Kansas City NFL	14	2	49	115	2.3	2	6	48	8.0	0	0	0	0.0	0	2	0	12	0
Pro totals (4 years)	56	6	121	381	3.1	4	11	89	8.1	0	46	981	21.3	0	5	0	30	0

COADY, RICH   S   COLTS

PERSONAL: Born January 26, 1976, in Dallas. ... 6-1/215. ... Full name: Richard Joseph Coady IV. ... Son of Rich Coady, tight end/center with Chicago Bears (1970-74).
HIGH SCHOOL: J.J. Pearce (Richardson, Texas).
COLLEGE: Texas A&M.
TRANSACTIONS/CAREER NOTES: Selected by St. Louis Rams in third round (68th pick overall) of 1999 NFL draft. ... Signed by Rams (July 16, 1999). ... On injured reserve with neck injury (December 13, 2000-remainder of season). ... Claimed on waivers by Tennessee Titans (August 29, 2002). ... Granted unconditional free agency (February 28, 2003). ... Signed by Indianapolis Colts (March 6, 2003).
CHAMPIONSHIP GAME EXPERIENCE: Played in NFC championship game (1999 season). ... Member of Super Bowl championship team (1999 season). ... Member of Rams for NFC championship game (2001 season); inactive. ... Member of Rams for Super Bowl XXXVI (2001 season); inactive. ... Played in AFC championship game (2002 season).

Year Team	G	GS	TOTALS Tk.	Ast.	Sks.	INTERCEPTIONS No.	Yds.	Avg.	TD
1999—St. Louis NFL	16	0	3	0	0.0	1	11	11.0	0
2000—St. Louis NFL	12	2	17	1	0.0	0	0	0.0	0
2001—St. Louis NFL	12	2	18	3	1.0	0	0	0.0	0
2002—Tennessee NFL	14	2	10	3	0.0	1	24	24.0	1
Pro totals (4 years)	54	6	48	7	1.0	2	35	17.5	1

COAKLEY, DEXTER   LB   COWBOYS

C

PERSONAL: Born October 20, 1972, in Charleston, S.C. ... 5-10/236. ... Full name: William Dexter Coakley.
HIGH SCHOOL: Wando (Mt. Pleasant, S.C.), then Fork Union (Va.) Military Academy.
COLLEGE: Appalachian State (degree in communications and advertising.).
TRANSACTIONS/CAREER NOTES: Selected by Dallas Cowboys in third round (65th pick overall) of 1997 NFL draft. ... Signed by Cowboys (July 14, 1997). ... Granted free agency (February 11, 2000). ... Re-signed by Cowboys (April 28, 2000). ... Granted unconditional free agency (March 2, 2001). ... Re-signed by Cowboys (March 8, 2001).
HONORS: Played in Pro Bowl (1999 and 2001 seasons).

Year Team	G	GS	TOTALS Tk.	Ast.	Sks.	INTERCEPTIONS No.	Yds.	Avg.	TD
1997—Dallas NFL	16	16	69	20	2.5	1	6	6.0	0
1998—Dallas NFL	16	16	55	17	2.0	1	18	18.0	0
1999—Dallas NFL	16	16	62	14	1.0	4	119	29.8	1
2000—Dallas NFL	16	16	75	12	0.0	0	0	0.0	0
2001—Dallas NFL	15	15	72	23	0.0	2	39	19.5	†2
2002—Dallas NFL	16	16	81	23	1.0	1	52	52.0	1
Pro totals (6 years)	95	95	414	109	6.5	9	234	26.0	4

COCHRAN, ANTONIO   DT   SEAHAWKS

PERSONAL: Born June 21, 1976, in Montezuma, Ga. ... 6-4/292. ... Full name: Antonio Desez Cochran.
HIGH SCHOOL: Macon County (Montezuma, Ga.).
JUNIOR COLLEGE: Middle Georgia College.
COLLEGE: Georgia.
TRANSACTIONS/CAREER NOTES: Selected by Seattle Seahawks in fourth round (115th pick overall) of 1999 NFL draft. ... Signed by Seahawks (July 27, 1999). ... Granted free agency (March 1, 2002). ... Re-signed by Seahawks (May 2, 2002). ... Granted unconditional free agency (February 28, 2003). ... Re-signed by Seahawks (February 28, 2003).

Year Team	G	GS	TOTALS Tk.	Ast.	Sks.	INTERCEPTIONS No.	Yds.	Avg.	TD
1999—Seattle NFL	4	0	2	0	0.0	0	0	0.0	0
2000—Seattle NFL	15	0	19	3	0.5	0	0	0.0	0
2001—Seattle NFL	16	2	26	5	4.5	0	0	0.0	0
2002—Seattle NFL	16	16	37	15	3.0	1	9	9.0	0
Pro totals (4 years)	51	18	84	23	8.0	1	9	9.0	0

CODY, TAY   CB   CHARGERS

PERSONAL: Born October 6, 1977, in Blakely, Ga. ... 5-9/180.
HIGH SCHOOL: Earl County (Blakely, Ga.).
COLLEGE: Florida State.
TRANSACTIONS/CAREER NOTES: Selected by San Diego Chargers in third round (67th pick overall) of 2001 NFL draft. ... Signed by Chargers (July 24, 2001). ... On injured reserve with toe injury (October 3, 2002-remainder of season).
HONORS: Named cornerback on THE SPORTING NEWS college All-America first team (2000).

Year Team	G	GS	TOTALS Tk.	Ast.	Sks.	INTERCEPTIONS No.	Yds.	Avg.	TD
2001—San Diego NFL	14	11	53	6	0.0	2	3	1.5	0
2002—San Diego NFL	4	0	3	1	0.0	0	0	0.0	0
Pro totals (2 years)	18	11	56	7	0.0	2	3	1.5	0

COLEMAN, COSEY   G   BUCCANEERS

PERSONAL: Born October 27, 1978, in Clarkston, Ga. ... 6-4/322. ... Full name: Cosey Clinton Coleman.
HIGH SCHOOL: DeKalb (Clarkston, Ga.).
COLLEGE: Tennessee.

TRANSACTIONS/CAREER NOTES: Selected after junior season by Tampa Bay Buccaneers in second round (51st pick overall) of 2000 NFL draft. ... Signed by Buccaneers (July 23, 2000).
PLAYING EXPERIENCE: Tampa Bay NFL, 2000-2002. ... Games/Games started: 2000 (8/0), 2001 (16/16), 2002 (15/15). Total: 39/31.
CHAMPIONSHIP GAME EXPERIENCE: Played in NFC championship game (2002 season). ... Member of Super Bowl championship team (2002 season).

COLEMAN, FRED — WR

PERSONAL: Born January 31, 1975, in Tyler, Texas. ... 6-0/190. ... Full name: Fred Dewayne Coleman.
HIGH SCHOOL: Robert E. Lee (Tyler, Texas).
COLLEGE: Washington.
TRANSACTIONS/CAREER NOTES: Selected by Buffalo Bills in sixth round (160th pick overall) of 1998 NFL draft. ... Signed by Bills (June 19, 1998). ... Released by Bills (August 30, 1998). ... Re-signed by Bills to practice squad (August 31, 1998). ... Granted free agency after 1998 season. ... Signed by Philadelphia Eagles (January 11, 1999). ... Released by Eagles (August 31, 1999). ... Signed by New York Jets to practice squad (October 18, 1999). ... Released by Jets (August 20, 2000). ... Signed by Chicago Bears (April 24, 2001). ... Released by Bears (August 31, 2001). ... Signed by New England Patriots (November 8, 2001). ... Released by Patriots (September 1, 2002). ... Re-signed by Patriots (December 24, 2002). ... Granted free agency (February 28, 2003).
CHAMPIONSHIP GAME EXPERIENCE: Played in AFC championship game (2001 season). ... Member of Super Bowl championship team (2001 season).
SINGLE GAME HIGHS (regular season): Receptions—1 (January 6, 2002, vs. Carolina); yards—46 (December 2, 2001, vs. New York Jets); and touchdown receptions—0.

| | | | RECEIVING | | | |
Year Team	G	GS	No.	Yds.	Avg.	TD
2001—New England NFL	8	0	2	50	25.0	0
2002—New England NFL	1	0	0	0	0.0	0
Pro totals (2 years)	9	0	2	50	25.0	0

COLEMAN, KARON — RB — BRONCOS

PERSONAL: Born May 22, 1978, in Missouri City, Texas. ... 5-7/198.
HIGH SCHOOL: Elkins (Missouri City, Texas).
COLLEGE: Stephen F. Austin State.
TRANSACTIONS/CAREER NOTES: Signed as non-drafted free agent by Denver Broncos (April 17, 2000). ... Released by Broncos (August 27, 2000). ... Re-signed by Broncos to practice squad (August 28, 2000). ... Activated (September 9, 2000). ... Released by Broncos (September 12, 2000). ... Re-signed by Broncos to practice squad (September 9, 2000). ... Activated (October 4, 2000). ... Released by Broncos (September 2, 2001). ... Re-signed by Broncos (November 26, 2001).
SINGLE GAME HIGHS (regular season): Attempts—14 (October 8, 2000, vs. San Diego); yards—52 (December 23, 2000, vs. San Francisco); and rushing touchdowns—1 (December 23, 2000, vs. San Francisco).

| | | | RUSHING | | | | RECEIVING | | | | TOTALS | | | |
Year Team	G	GS	Att.	Yds.	Avg.	TD	No.	Yds.	Avg.	TD	TD	2pt.	Pts.	Fum.
2000—Denver NFL	9	0	54	183	3.4	1	1	5	5.0	0	1	0	6	2
2001—Denver NFL	4	0	4	17	4.3	0	6	45	7.5	0	0	0	0	0
2002—Denver NFL	2	0	0	0	0.0	0	0	0	0.0	0	0	0	0	0
Pro totals (3 years)	15	0	58	200	3.4	1	7	50	7.1	0	1	0	6	2

COLEMAN, KENYON — DE — RAIDERS

PERSONAL: Born April 10, 1979, in Fontana, Calif. ... 6-5/285. ... Full name: Kenyon Octavia Coleman.
HIGH SCHOOL: Alta Loma (Calif.).
COLLEGE: UCLA.
TRANSACTIONS/CAREER NOTES: Selected by Oakland Raiders in fifth round (147th pick overall) of 2002 NFL draft. ... Signed by Raiders (July 24, 2002).
CHAMPIONSHIP GAME EXPERIENCE: Member of Raiders for AFC championship game (2002 season); inactive. ... Member of Raiders for Super Bowl XXXVII (2002 season); inactive.
HONORS: Named defensive end on THE SPORTING NEWS college All-America third team (2001).

| | | | TOTALS | | |
Year Team	G	GS	Tk.	Ast.	Sks.
2002—Oakland NFL	1	0	1	0	0.0

COLEMAN, MARCO — DE — JAGUARS

PERSONAL: Born December 18, 1969, in Dayton, Ohio. ... 6-3/270. ... Full name: Marco Darnell Coleman.
HIGH SCHOOL: Patterson Co-op (Dayton, Ohio).
COLLEGE: Georgia Tech.
TRANSACTIONS/CAREER NOTES: Selected after junior season by Miami Dolphins in first round (12th pick overall) of 1992 NFL draft. ... Signed by Dolphins (August 1, 1992). ... Designated by Dolphins as transition player (February 25, 1993). ... Tendered offer sheet by San Diego Chargers (February 28, 1996). ... Dolphins declined to match offer (March 7, 1996). ... Granted unconditional free agency (February 12, 1999). ... Signed by Washington Redskins (June 3, 1999). ... Granted unconditional free agency (February 11, 2000). ... Re-signed by Redskins (February 29, 2000). ... Released by Redskins (June 3, 2002). ... Signed by Jacksonville Jaguars (June 20, 2002).
CHAMPIONSHIP GAME EXPERIENCE: Played in AFC championship game (1992 season).
HONORS: Named linebacker on THE SPORTING NEWS college All-America second team (1991). ... Played in Pro Bowl (2000 season).

Year Team	G	GS	TOTALS			INTERCEPTIONS			
			Tk.	Ast.	Sks.	No.	Yds.	Avg.	TD
1992—Miami NFL	16	15	61	23	6.0	0	0	0.0	0
1993—Miami NFL	15	15	35	19	5.5	0	0	0.0	0
1994—Miami NFL	16	16	34	9	6.0	0	0	0.0	0
1995—Miami NFL	16	16	33	12	6.5	0	0	0.0	0
1996—San Diego NFL	16	15	34	8	4.0	0	0	0.0	0
1997—San Diego NFL	16	16	39	9	2.0	1	2	2.0	0
1998—San Diego NFL	16	16	46	5	3.5	0	0	0.0	0
1999—Washington NFL	16	16	54	13	6.5	0	0	0.0	0
2000—Washington NFL	16	16	41	11	12.0	0	0	0.0	0
2001—Washington NFL	12	12	33	6	4.5	0	0	0.0	0
2002—Jacksonville NFL	16	16	29	7	5.0	0	0	0.0	0
Pro totals (11 years)	171	169	439	122	61.5	1	2	2.0	0

COLEMAN, MARCUS — CB — TEXANS

PERSONAL: Born May 24, 1974, in Dallas. ... 6-2/210.
HIGH SCHOOL: Lake Highlands (Dallas).
COLLEGE: Texas Tech.
TRANSACTIONS/CAREER NOTES: Selected by New York Jets in fifth round (133rd pick overall) of 1996 NFL draft. ... Signed by Jets (July 11, 1996). ... Granted unconditional free agency (February 11, 2000). ... Re-signed by Jets (February 14, 2000). ... Selected by Houston Texans from Jets in NFL expansion draft (February 18, 2002).
CHAMPIONSHIP GAME EXPERIENCE: Played in AFC championship game (1998 season).

Year Team	G	GS	TOTALS			INTERCEPTIONS			
			Tk.	Ast.	Sks.	No.	Yds.	Avg.	TD
1996—New York Jets NFL	13	4	25	6	0.0	1	23	23.0	0
1997—New York Jets NFL	16	2	8	2	0.0	1	24	24.0	0
1998—New York Jets NFL	14	0	5	1	0.0	0	0	0.0	0
1999—New York Jets NFL	16	10	51	11	0.0	6	165	27.5	1
2000—New York Jets NFL	16	16	50	6	0.0	4	6	1.5	0
2001—New York Jets NFL	16	16	58	11	0.0	2	41	20.5	0
2002—Houston NFL	16	16	60	12	0.0	1	0	0.0	0
Pro totals (7 years)	107	64	257	49	0.0	15	259	17.3	1

COLEMAN, ROD — DE — RAIDERS

PERSONAL: Born August 16, 1976, in Philadelphia. ... 6-2/285. ... Full name: Roderick Coleman.
HIGH SCHOOL: Simon Gratz (Philadelphia).
COLLEGE: East Carolina.
TRANSACTIONS/CAREER NOTES: Selected by Oakland Raiders in fifth round (153rd pick overall) of 1999 NFL draft. ... Signed by Raiders (July 24, 1999).
CHAMPIONSHIP GAME EXPERIENCE: Played in AFC championship game (2000 and 2002 seasons). ... Played in Super Bowl XXXVII (2002 season).

Year Team	G	GS	TOTALS		
			Tk.	Ast.	Sks.
1999—Oakland NFL	3	0	1	0	0.0
2000—Oakland NFL	13	1	16	4	6.0
2001—Oakland NFL	14	6	35	11	6.0
2002—Oakland NFL	14	2	33	5	11.0
Pro totals (4 years)	44	9	85	20	23.0

COLEMAN, TRAVIS — DB — BEARS

PERSONAL: Born January 4, 1980, in Goldsboro, N.C. ... 5-11/180. ... Full name: Travis Lee Coleman.
HIGH SCHOOL: Goldsboro (N.C.).
COLLEGE: Hampton.
TRANSACTIONS/CAREER NOTES: Signed as non-drafted free agent by Chicago Bears (April 29, 2002). ... Released by Bears (September 1, 2002). ... Re-signed by Bears to practice squad (September 3, 2002). ... Activated (November 12, 2002). ... Assigned by Bears to Berlin Thunder in 2003 NFL Europe enhancement allocation program (February 4, 2003).

Year Team	G	GS	TOTALS			INTERCEPTIONS			
			Tk.	Ast.	Sks.	No.	Yds.	Avg.	TD
2002—Chicago NFL	7	0	2	0	0.0	0	0	0.0	0

COLES, LAVERANUES — WR/KR — REDSKINS

PERSONAL: Born December 29, 1977, in Jacksonville. ... 5-11/196.
HIGH SCHOOL: Jean Ribault (Jacksonville).
COLLEGE: Florida State.
TRANSACTIONS/CAREER NOTES: Selected by New York Jets in third round (78th pick overall) of 2000 NFL draft. ... Signed by Jets (May 1, 2000). ... Granted free agency (February 28, 2003). ... Tendered offer sheet by Washington Redskins (March 13, 2003). ... Jets declined to match offer (March 19, 2003).
SINGLE GAME HIGHS (regular season): Receptions—10 (December 2, 2002, vs. Oakland); yards—158 (December 2, 2002, vs. Oakland); and touchdown receptions—2 (October 14, 2001, vs. Miami).
STATISTICAL PLATEAUS: 100-yard receiving games: 2000 (1), 2001 (1), 2002 (4). Total: 6.

Year Team	G	GS	RUSHING				RECEIVING				KICKOFF RETURNS				TOTALS			
			Att.	Yds.	Avg.	TD	No.	Yds.	Avg.	TD	No.	Yds.	Avg.	TD	TD	2pt.	Pts.	Fum.
2000—New York Jets NFL......	13	3	2	15	7.5	0	22	370	16.8	1	11	207	18.8	0	1	1	8	0
2001—New York Jets NFL......	16	16	10	108	10.8	0	59	868	14.7	7	9	211	23.4	0	7	0	42	1
2002—New York Jets NFL......	16	16	6	39	6.5	0	89	1264	14.2	5	0	0	0.0	0	5	1	32	1
Pro totals (3 years)..............	45	35	18	162	9.0	0	170	2502	14.7	13	20	418	20.9	0	13	2	82	2

COLINET, STALIN   DT

PERSONAL: Born July 17, 1974, in Bronx, N.Y. ... 6-6/288.
HIGH SCHOOL: Cardinal Hayes (Bronx, N.Y.).
COLLEGE: Boston College (degree in sociology, 1996).
TRANSACTIONS/CAREER NOTES: Selected by Minnesota Vikings in third round (78th pick overall) of 1997 NFL draft. ... Signed by Vikings (June 30, 1997). ... Traded by Vikings to Cleveland Browns for DT Jerry Ball (September 28, 1999). ... Granted free agency (February 11, 2000). ... Re-signed by Browns (April 18, 2000). ... Granted unconditional free agency (March 2, 2001). ... Re-signed by Browns (March 2, 2001). ... Traded by Browns to Vikings for future pick in draft (October 16, 2001). ... Released by Vikings (February 21, 2002). ... Signed by Jacksonville Jaguars (March 11, 2002). ... Released by Jaguars (October 26, 2002).
CHAMPIONSHIP GAME EXPERIENCE: Played in NFC championship game (1998 season).

Year Team	G	GS	TOTALS		
			Tk.	Ast.	Sks.
1997—Minnesota NFL	10	2	14	4	0.0
1998—Minnesota NFL	11	3	5	6	1.0
1999—Minnesota NFL	3	1	2	0	0.0
—Cleveland NFL..	11	9	10	2	0.0
2000—Cleveland NFL	16	16	24	9	3.5
2001—Cleveland NFL	5	0	1	0	0.0
—Minnesota NFL...	11	11	11	2	1.0
2002—Jacksonville NFL	1	0	0	0	0.0
Pro totals (6 years)..	68	42	67	23	5.5

COLLINS, JAVIAR   OT   COWBOYS

PERSONAL: Born April 13, 1978, in St. Paul, Minn. ... 6-6/322.
HIGH SCHOOL: St. Thomas Academy (St. Paul, Minn.).
COLLEGE: Northwestern.
TRANSACTIONS/CAREER NOTES: Signed as non-drafted free agent by Dallas Cowboys (April 26, 2001). ... Inactive for all 16 games (2001). ... Assigned by Cowboys to Frankfurt Galaxy in 2002 NFL Europe enhancement allocation program (February 12, 2002).
PLAYING EXPERIENCE: Dallas NFL, 2002. ... Games/games started: 2002 (9/4).

COLLINS, KERRY   QB   GIANTS

PERSONAL: Born December 30, 1972, in Lebanon, Pa. ... 6-5/248. ... Full name: Kerry Michael Collins.
HIGH SCHOOL: Wilson (West Lawn, Pa.).
COLLEGE: Penn State.
TRANSACTIONS/CAREER NOTES: Selected by Carolina Panthers in first round (fifth pick overall) of 1995 NFL draft. ... Signed by Panthers (July 17, 1995). ... Granted free agency (February 13, 1998). ... Re-signed by Panthers (July 24, 1998). ... Claimed on waivers by New Orleans Saints (October 14, 1998). ... Granted unconditional free agency (February 12, 1999). ... Signed by New York Giants (February 19, 1999).
CHAMPIONSHIP GAME EXPERIENCE: Played in NFC championship game (1996 and 2000 season). ... Played in Super Bowl XXXV (2000 season).
HONORS: Maxwell Award winner (1994). ... Davey O'Brien Award winner (1994). ... Named quarterback on THE SPORTING NEWS college All-America first team (1994). ... Played in Pro Bowl (1996 season).
RECORDS: Shares NFL single-season record for most fumbles—23 (2001).
SINGLE GAME HIGHS (regular season): Attempts—59 (January 6, 2002, vs. Green Bay); completions—36 (January 6, 2002, vs. Green Bay); passing yards—386 (January 6, 2002, vs. Green Bay); and touchdown passes—4 (December 22, 2002, vs. Indianapolis).
STATISTICAL PLATEAUS: 300-yard passing games: 1995 (2), 1996 (1), 1997 (1), 1998 (2), 1999 (2), 2000 (3), 2001 (5), 2002 (4). Total: 20.
MISCELLANEOUS: Selected by Detroit Tigers organization in 26th round of free-agent draft (June 4, 1990); did not sign. ... Selected by Toronto Blue Jays organization in 58th round of free-agent draft (June 4, 1994); did not sign. ... Regular-season record as starting NFL quarterback: 55-49 (.529). ... Postseason record as starting NFL quarterback: 3-3 (.500).

Year Team	G	GS	PASSING									RUSHING				TOTALS		
			Att.	Cmp.	Pct.	Yds.	TD	Int.	Avg.	Skd.	Rat.	Att.	Yds.	Avg.	TD	TD	2pt.	Pts.
1995—Carolina NFL	15	13	433	214	49.4	2717	14	19	6.27	24	61.9	42	74	1.8	3	3	0	18
1996—Carolina NFL	13	12	364	204	56.0	2454	14	9	6.74	18	79.4	32	38	1.2	0	0	1	2
1997—Carolina NFL	13	13	381	200	52.5	2124	11	*21	5.57	27	55.7	26	65	2.5	1	1	0	6
1998—Carolina NFL	4	4	162	76	46.9	1011	8	5	6.24	10	70.8	7	40	5.7	0	0	1	2
—New Orleans NFL........	7	7	191	94	49.2	1202	4	10	6.29	21	54.5	23	113	4.9	1	1	0	6
1999—N.Y. Giants NFL..........	10	7	331	190	57.4	2318	8	11	7.00	16	73.3	19	36	1.9	2	2	†1	14
2000—N.Y. Giants NFL..........	16	16	529	311	58.8	3610	22	13	6.82	28	83.1	41	65	1.6	1	1	0	6
2001—N.Y. Giants NFL..........	16	16	‡568	327	57.6	3764	19	16	6.63	36	77.1	39	73	1.9	0	0	0	0
2002—N.Y. Giants NFL..........	16	16	545	335	61.5	‡4073	19	14	‡7.47	24	85.4	44	-3	-0.1	0	0	0	0
Pro totals (8 years)..............	110	104	3504	1951	55.7	23273	119	118	6.64	204	73.4	273	501	1.8	8	8	3	54

COLLINS, MO — OT — RAIDERS

PERSONAL: Born September 22, 1976, in Charlotte. ... 6-4/325. ... Full name: Damon Jamal Collins.
HIGH SCHOOL: West Charlotte.
COLLEGE: Florida.
TRANSACTIONS/CAREER NOTES: Selected after junior season by Oakland Raiders in first round (23rd pick overall) of 1998 NFL draft. ... Signed by Raiders (July 15, 1998). ... Granted unconditional free agency (February 28, 2003). ... Re-signed by Raiders (May 8, 2003).
PLAYING EXPERIENCE: Oakland NFL, 1998-2002. ... Games/Games started: 1998 (16/11), 1999 (13/12), 2000 (16/16), 2001 (6/5), 2002 (10/10). Total: 61/54.
CHAMPIONSHIP GAME EXPERIENCE: Played in AFC championship game (2000 and 2002 seasons). ... Played in Super Bowl XXXVII (2002 season).

COLLINS, TODD — QB — CHIEFS

PERSONAL: Born November 5, 1971, in Walpole, Mass. ... 6-4/225.
HIGH SCHOOL: Walpole (Mass.).
COLLEGE: Michigan.
TRANSACTIONS/CAREER NOTES: Selected by Buffalo Bills in second round (45th pick overall) of 1995 NFL draft. ... Signed by Bills (July 10, 1995). ... Claimed on waivers by Kansas City Chiefs (August 25, 1998). ... Active for three games (1998); did not play. ... Active for all 16 games (1999); did not play. ... Active for all 16 games (2000); did not play. ... Granted unconditional free agency (February 28, 2003). ... Re-signed by Chiefs (March 24, 2003).
SINGLE GAME HIGHS (regular season): Attempts—44 (October 6, 1996, vs. Indianapolis); completions—25 (November 23, 1997, vs. Tennessee); yards—309 (October 6, 1996, vs. Indianapolis); and touchdown passes—3 (September 7, 1997, vs. New York Jets).
STATISTICAL PLATEAUS: 300-yard passing games: 1996 (1).
MISCELLANEOUS: Regular-season record as starting NFL quarterback: 7-10 (.412).

Year Team	G	GS	Att.	Cmp.	Pct.	Yds.	TD	Int.	Avg.	Skd.	Rat.	Att.	Yds.	Avg.	TD	TD	2pt.	Pts.
						PASSING						RUSHING				TOTALS		
1995—Buffalo NFL	7	1	29	14	48.3	112	0	1	3.86	6	44.0	9	23	2.6	0	0	0	0
1996—Buffalo NFL	7	3	99	55	55.6	739	4	5	7.46	11	71.9	21	43	2.0	0	0	0	0
1997—Buffalo NFL	14	13	391	215	55.0	2367	12	13	6.05	39	69.5	30	77	2.6	0	0	0	0
1998—Kansas City NFL									Did not play.									
1999—Kansas City NFL									Did not play.									
2000—Kansas City NFL									Did not play.									
2001—Kansas City NFL	1	0	4	3	75.0	40	0	0	10.00	0	106.3	2	6	3.0	0	0	0	0
2002—Kansas City NFL	3	0	6	5	83.3	73	1	0	12.17	0	156.9	1	7	7.0	0	0	0	0
Pro totals (5 years)	32	17	529	292	55.2	3331	17	19	6.30	56	70.1	63	156	2.5	0	0	0	0

COLOMBO, MARC — OT — BEARS

PERSONAL: Born October 8, 1978, in Bridgewater, Mass. ... 6-7/320. ... Full name: Marc Edward Colombo.
HIGH SCHOOL: Bridgewater-Raynham (Bridgewater, Mass.).
COLLEGE: Boston College.
TRANSACTIONS/CAREER NOTES: Selected by Chicago Bears in first round (29th pick overall) of 2002 NFL draft. ... Signed by Bears (July 25, 2002). ... On injured reserve with knee injury (November 26, 2002-remainder of season).
PLAYING EXPERIENCE: Chicago NFL, 2002. ... Games/games started: 2002 (10/5).

COLVIN, ROSEVELT — LB — PATRIOTS

PERSONAL: Born September 5, 1977, in Indianapolis. ... 6-3/245.
HIGH SCHOOL: Broad Ripple (Indianapolis).
COLLEGE: Purdue.
TRANSACTIONS/CAREER NOTES: Selected by Chicago Bears in fourth round (111th pick overall) of 1999 NFL draft. ... Signed by Bears (July 21, 1999). ... Granted free agency (March 1, 2002). ... Re-signed by Bears (April 19, 2002). ... Granted unconditional free agency (February 28, 2003). ... Signed by New England Patriots (March 11, 2003).

Year Team	G	GS	Tk.	Ast.	Sks.	No.	Yds.	Avg.	TD
			TOTALS			INTERCEPTIONS			
1999—Chicago NFL	11	0	10	2	2.0	0	0	0.0	0
2000—Chicago NFL	13	8	25	9	3.0	0	0	0.0	0
2001—Chicago NFL	16	13	60	10	10.5	2	22	11.0	0
2002—Chicago NFL	16	15	55	9	10.5	0	0	0.0	0
Pro totals (4 years)	56	36	150	30	26.0	2	22	11.0	0

COMBS, CHRIS — DE — JAGUARS

PERSONAL: Born December 15, 1976, in Roanoke, Va. ... 6-5/291. ... Full name: Christopher Brandon Combs. ... Son of Glen Combs, guard with five American Basketball Association teams (1968-69 through 1974-75).
HIGH SCHOOL: Patrick Henry (Roanoke, Va.).
COLLEGE: Duke (degree in sociology).
TRANSACTIONS/CAREER NOTES: Selected by Pittsburgh Steelers in sixth round (173rd pick overall) of 2000 NFL draft. ... Signed by Steelers (July 16, 2000). ... Released by Steelers (September 1, 2002). ... Signed by Jacksonville Jaguars to practice squad (September 17, 2002). ... Activated (December 17, 2002). ... Re-signed by Jaguars (March 12, 2003).
CHAMPIONSHIP GAME EXPERIENCE: Member of Steelers for AFC championship game (2001 season); inactive.

Year Team	G	GS	Tk.	Ast.	Sks.
			TOTALS		
2000—Pittsburgh NFL	6	0	3	0	0.0
2001—Pittsburgh NFL	2	0	1	0	0.0
2002—Jacksonville NFL	2	0	0	0	0.0
Pro totals (3 years)	10	0	4	0	0.0

COMBS, DEREK · CB · PACKERS

PERSONAL: Born February 28, 1979, in Urbancrest, Ohio. ... 6-0/195.
HIGH SCHOOL: Grove City (Urbancrest, Ohio).
COLLEGE: Ohio State.
TRANSACTIONS/CAREER NOTES: Selected by Oakland Raiders in seventh round (228th pick overall) of 2001 NFL draft. ... Signed by Raiders (July 21, 2001). ... Released by Raiders (September 2, 2001). ... Signed by Tennessee Titans to practice squad (September 4, 2001). ... Released by Titans (September 5, 2001). ... Signed by Miami Dolphins to practice squad (September 11, 2001). ... Released by Dolphins (September 18, 2001). ... Re-signed by Dolphins to practice squad (September 26, 2001). ... Released by Dolphins (October 2, 2001). ... Signed by Raiders to practice squad (October 18, 2001). ... Released by Raiders (November 1, 2001). ... Re-signed by Raiders to practice squad (November 7, 2001). ... Released by Raiders (October 9, 2002). ... Signed by Kansas City Chiefs (February 1, 2003). ... Traded by Chiefs to Green Bay Packers for conditional pick in draft (April 24, 2003).

			RUSHING				RECEIVING				KICKOFF RETURNS				TOTALS			
Year Team	G	GS	Att.	Yds.	Avg.	TD	No.	Yds.	Avg.	TD	No.	Yds.	Avg.	TD	TD	2pt.	Pts.	Fum.
2002—Amsterdam NFLE........	...	...	9	15	1.7	0	1	8	8.0	0	12	282	23.5	0	0	0	0	0
—Oakland NFL..............	4	0	0	0	0.0	0	0	0	0.0	0	5	71	14.2	0	0	0	0	0
NFL Europe totals (1 year)	...	...	9	15	1.7	0	1	8	8.0	0	12	282	23.5	0	0	0	0	0
NFL totals (1 year)................	4	0	0	0	0.0	0	0	0	0.0	0	5	71	14.2	0	0	0	0	0
Pro totals (2 years)...............	...	...	9	15	1.7	0	1	8	8.0	0	17	353	20.8	0	0	0	0	0

COMELLA, GREG · FB · TITANS

PERSONAL: Born July 29, 1975, in Wellesley, Mass. ... 6-1/248. ... Name pronounced Ka-MELL-uh.
HIGH SCHOOL: Xaverian Brothers (Westwood, Mass.).
COLLEGE: Stanford.
TRANSACTIONS/CAREER NOTES: Signed as non-drafted free agent by New York Giants (April 24, 1998). ... Granted free agency (March 2, 2001). ... Re-signed by Giants (April 18, 2001). ... Granted unconditional free agency (March 1, 2002). ... Signed by Tennessee Titans (April 19, 2002).
CHAMPIONSHIP GAME EXPERIENCE: Played in NFC championship game (2000 season). ... Played in Super Bowl XXXV (2000 season). ... Member of Titans for AFC championship game (2002 season); inactive.
SINGLE GAME HIGHS (regular season): Attempts—3 (November 5, 2000, vs. Cleveland); yards—19 (September 10, 2000, vs. Philadelphia); and rushing touchdowns—0.

			RUSHING				RECEIVING				TOTALS			
Year Team	G	GS	Att.	Yds.	Avg.	TD	No.	Yds.	Avg.	TD	TD	2pt.	Pts.	Fum.
1998—New York Giants NFL............................	16	0	1	6	6.0	0	1	3	3.0	0	0	0	0	0
1999—New York Giants NFL............................	16	3	1	0	0.0	0	8	39	4.9	0	0	0	0	0
2000—New York Giants NFL............................	16	12	10	45	4.5	0	36	274	7.6	0	0	0	0	2
2001—New York Giants NFL............................	16	13	4	15	3.8	0	39	253	6.5	1	1	0	6	2
2002—Tennessee NFL....................................	12	7	1	0	0.0	0	10	70	7.0	0	0	0	0	1
Pro totals (5 years)...................................	76	35	17	66	3.9	0	94	639	6.8	1	1	0	6	5

COMPTON, MIKE · OL · PATRIOTS

PERSONAL: Born September 18, 1970, in Richlands, Va. ... 6-6/310. ... Full name: Michael Eugene Compton.
HIGH SCHOOL: Richlands (Va.).
COLLEGE: West Virginia.
TRANSACTIONS/CAREER NOTES: Selected by Detroit Lions in third round (68th pick overall) of 1993 NFL draft. ... Signed by Lions (June 4, 1993). ... Granted unconditional free agency (March 2, 2001). ... Signed by New England Patriots (April 2, 2001).
PLAYING EXPERIENCE: Detroit NFL, 1993-2000; New England NFL, 2001-2002. ... Games/Games started: 1993 (8/0), 1994 (2/0), 1995 (16/7), 1996 (15/15), 1997 (16/16), 1998 (16/16), 1999 (15/15), 2000 (16/16), 2001 (16/16), 2002 (16/16). Total: 136/117.
CHAMPIONSHIP GAME EXPERIENCE: Played in AFC championship game (2001 season). ... Member of Super Bowl championship team (2001 season).
HONORS: Named center on THE SPORTING NEWS college All-America first team (1992).

CONATY, BILL · C

PERSONAL: Born March 8, 1973, in Baltimore. ... 6-2/300. ... Full name: William B. Conaty. ... Name pronounced CON-uh-tee.
HIGH SCHOOL: Milford (Conn.) Academy, then Camden Catholic (Cherry Hill, N.J.).
COLLEGE: Virginia Tech.
TRANSACTIONS/CAREER NOTES: Signed as non-drafted free agent by Buffalo Bills (April 25, 1997). ... Released by Bills (August 24, 1997). ... Re-signed by Bills to practice squad (August 26, 1997). ... Activated (September 6, 1997). ... Released by Bills (September 22, 1997). ... Re-signed by Bills to practice squad (September 24, 1997). ... Granted free agency (March 2, 2001). ... Re-signed by Bills (June 12, 2001). ... Granted unconditional free agency (March 1, 2002). ... Re-signed by Bills (March 8, 2002). ... Granted unconditional free agency (February 28, 2003).
PLAYING EXPERIENCE: Buffalo NFL, 1997-2002. ... Games/Games started: 1997 (1/0), 1998 (15/1), 1999 (7/1), 2000 (16/0), 2001 (16/16), 2002 (11/0). Totals: 66/18.
HONORS: Named center on THE SPORTING NEWS college All-America first team (1996).

CONWAY, BRETT · K · COLTS

PERSONAL: Born March 8, 1975, in Atlanta. ... 6-2/208. ... Full name: Brett Alan Conway.
HIGH SCHOOL: Parkview (Lilburn, Ga.).
COLLEGE: Penn State.

TRANSACTIONS/CAREER NOTES: Selected by Green Bay Packers in third round (90th pick overall) of 1997 NFL draft. ... Signed by Packers (July 8, 1997). ... On injured reserve with thigh injury (September 3, 1997-entire season). ... Traded by Packers to New York Jets for an undisclosed draft pick (August 21, 1998). ... Released by Jets (August 30, 1998). ... Re-signed by Jets to practice squad (September 1, 1998). ... Released by Jets (September 23, 1998). ... Signed by Washington Redskins (November 12, 1998). ... Granted free agency (February 11, 2000). ... Re-signed by Redskins (May 31, 2000). ... Released by Redskins (September 20, 2000). ... Signed by Oakland Raiders (November 11, 2000). ... Released by Raiders (November 21, 2000). ... Signed by Jets (December 18, 2000). ... Granted unconditional free agency (March 2, 2001). ... Signed by Redskins (March 15, 2001). ... On injured reserve with leg injury (September 10-December 5, 2002). ... Released by Redskins (December 5, 2002). ... Signed by Indianapolis Colts (January 23, 2003).

Year Team	G	FIELD GOALS							TOTALS		
		1-29	30-39	40-49	50+	Tot.	Pct.	Lg.	XPM	XPA	Pts.
1997—Green Bay NFL					Did not play.						
1998—Washington NFL	6	0-0	0-0	0-0	0-0	0-0	0	0	0	0	0
1999—Washington NFL	16	7-9	6-7	6-7	3-9	22-∞32	68.8	51	49	50	115
2000—Washington NFL	2	3-3	0-0	0-0	0-0	3-3	100.0	26	3	3	12
—Oakland NFL	1	1-1	0-0	0-0	0-0	1-1	100.0	19	3	3	6
—New York Jets NFL	1	1-1	0-0	1-1	0-0	2-2	100.0	40	2	2	8
2001—Washington NFL	16	8-8	8-11	8-12	2-2	26-33	78.8	†55	22	22	100
2002—Washington NFL	1	0-0	1-1	0-0	0-0	1-1	100.0	35	4	4	7
Pro totals (5 years)	43	20-22	15-19	15-20	5-11	55-72	76.4	55	83	84	248

CONWAY, CURTIS — WR — JETS

PERSONAL: Born January 13, 1971, in Los Angeles. ... 6-1/196. ... Full name: Curtis LaMont Conway.
HIGH SCHOOL: Hawthorne (Calif.).
JUNIOR COLLEGE: El Camino College (Calif.).
COLLEGE: Southern California.
TRANSACTIONS/CAREER NOTES: Selected after junior season by Chicago Bears in first round (seventh pick overall) of 1993 NFL draft. ... Signed by Bears (May 24, 1993). ... Granted free agency (February 16, 1996). ... Re-signed by Bears (March 4, 1996). ... On injured reserve with (shoulder) injury (December 22, 1999-remainder of season). ... Granted unconditional free agency (February 11, 2000). ... Signed by San Diego Chargers (February 22, 2000). ... Released by Chargers (February 27, 2003). ... Signed by New York Jets (March 20, 2003).
HONORS: Named kick returner on The Sporting News college All-America second team (1992).
SINGLE GAME HIGHS (regular season): Receptions—11 (December 30, 2001, vs. Seattle); yards—156 (December 30, 2001, vs. Seattle); and touchdown receptions—3 (October 15, 1995, vs. Jacksonville).
STATISTICAL PLATEAUS: 100-yard receiving games: 1994 (1), 1995 (3), 1996 (4), 1997 (3), 1999 (1), 2000 (2), 2001 (4), 2002 (3). Total: 21.

Year Team	G	GS	RUSHING				RECEIVING				KICKOFF RETURNS				TOTALS			
			Att.	Yds.	Avg.	TD	No.	Yds.	Avg.	TD	No.	Yds.	Avg.	TD	TD	2pt.	Pts.	Fum.
1993—Chicago NFL	16	7	5	44	8.8	0	19	231	12.2	2	21	450	21.4	0	2	0	12	1
1994—Chicago NFL	13	12	6	31	5.2	0	39	546	14.0	2	10	228	22.8	0	2	1	14	2
1995—Chicago NFL	16	16	5	77	15.4	0	62	1037	16.7	12	0	0	0.0	0	12	0	72	0
1996—Chicago NFL	16	16	8	50	6.3	0	81	1049	13.0	7	0	0	0.0	0	7	0	42	1
1997—Chicago NFL	7	7	3	17	5.7	0	30	476	15.9	1	0	0	0.0	0	1	0	6	0
1998—Chicago NFL	15	15	5	48	9.6	0	54	733	13.6	3	0	0	0.0	0	3	0	18	1
1999—Chicago NFL	9	8	1	-2	-2.0	0	44	426	9.7	4	0	0	0.0	0	4	0	24	2
2000—San Diego NFL	14	14	3	31	10.3	0	53	712	13.4	5	0	0	0.0	0	5	0	30	0
2001—San Diego NFL	16	16	7	116	16.6	0	71	1125	15.8	6	0	0	0.0	0	7	0	42	1
2002—San Diego NFL	13	13	7	53	7.6	2	57	852	14.9	5	0	0	0.0	0	7	0	42	2
Pro totals (10 years)	135	124	50	465	9.3	3	510	7187	14.1	47	31	678	21.9	0	50	1	302	10

CONWELL, ERNIE — TE — SAINTS

PERSONAL: Born August 17, 1972, in Renton, Wash. ... 6-2/265. ... Full name: Ernest Harold Conwell.
HIGH SCHOOL: Kentwood (Kent, Wash.).
COLLEGE: Washington (degree in sociology, 1995).
TRANSACTIONS/CAREER NOTES: Selected by St. Louis Rams in second round (59th pick overall) of 1996 NFL draft. ... Signed by Rams (June 25, 1996). ... On injured reserve with knee injury (October 28, 1998-remainder of season). ... On physically unable to perform list with knee injury (August 30-November 9, 1999). ... Granted unconditional free agency (February 11, 2000). ... Re-signed by Rams (February 11, 2000). ... Granted unconditional free agency (February 28, 2003). ... Signed by New Orleans Saints (April 14, 2003).
CHAMPIONSHIP GAME EXPERIENCE: Played in NFC championship game (1999 and 2001 seasons). ... Member of Super Bowl championship team (1999 season). ... Played in Super Bowl XXXVI (2001 season).
SINGLE GAME HIGHS (regular season): Receptions—6 (October 28, 2001, vs. New Orleans); yards—75 (January 6, 2002, vs. Atlanta); and touchdown receptions—1 (December 30, 2002, vs. San Francisco).

Year Team	G	GS	RUSHING				RECEIVING				TOTALS			
			Att.	Yds.	Avg.	TD	No.	Yds.	Avg.	TD	TD	2pt.	Pts.	Fum.
1996—St. Louis NFL	10	8	0	0	0.0	0	15	164	10.9	0	0	0	0	0
1997—St. Louis NFL	16	16	0	0	0.0	0	38	404	10.6	4	4	0	24	0
1998—St. Louis NFL	7	7	0	0	0.0	0	15	105	7.0	0	0	0	0	0
1999—St. Louis NFL	3	0	0	0	0.0	0	1	11	11.0	0	0	0	0	0
2000—St. Louis NFL	16	1	2	23	11.5	0	5	40	8.0	0	0	0	0	0
2001—St. Louis NFL	16	13	7	28	4.0	1	38	431	11.3	4	5	0	30	2
2002—St. Louis NFL	16	10	6	30	5.0	1	34	419	12.3	2	3	0	18	0
Pro totals (7 years)	84	55	15	81	5.4	2	146	1574	10.8	10	12	0	72	2

COOK, DAMION — OT — RAVENS

PERSONAL: Born April 16, 1979, in Fort Lauderdale, Fla. ... 6-6/343. ... Full name: Damion Lamar Cook.
HIGH SCHOOL: American Heritage (Fort Lauderdale, Fla.).
COLLEGE: Bethune-Cookman.

TRANSACTIONS/CAREER NOTES: Signed as non-drafted free agent by Baltimore Ravens (April 27, 2001). ... Released by Ravens (September 1, 2001). ... Signed by Chicago Bears (September 28, 2001). ... Inactive for 15 games (2001). ... Assigned by Bears to Barcelona Dragons in 2002 NFL Europe enhancement allocation program (February 12, 2002). ... Released by Bears (September 1, 2002). ... Signed by Miami Dolphins to practice squad (September 10, 2002). ... Signed by Ravens off Dolphins practice squad (September 23, 2002).
PLAYING EXPERIENCE: Baltimore NFL, 2002. ... Games/games started: 2002 (3/0).

COOK, JAMEEL — FB — BUCCANEERS

PERSONAL: Born February 8, 1979, in Miami. ... 5-10/237. ... Full name: Jameel A. Cook.
HIGH SCHOOL: Southridge (Miami).
COLLEGE: Illinois.
TRANSACTIONS/CAREER NOTES: Selected after junior season by Tampa Bay Buccaneers in sixth round (174th pick overall) of 2001 NFL draft. ... Signed by Buccaneers (July 16, 2001).
CHAMPIONSHIP GAME EXPERIENCE: Played in NFC championship game (2002 season). ... Member of Super Bowl championship team (2002 season).
SINGLE GAME HIGHS (regular season): Attempts—2 (October 28, 2001, vs. Minnesota); yards—2 (October 28, 2001, vs. Minnesota); and rushing touchdowns—0.

			RUSHING				RECEIVING				TOTALS		
Year Team	G	GS	Att.	Yds.	Avg.	TD	No.	Yds.	Avg.	TD	TD	2pt.	Pts.	Fum.
2001—Tampa Bay NFL	16	3	2	2	1.0	0	17	89	5.2	0	0	0	0	0
2002—Tampa Bay NFL	14	1	0	0	0.0	0	4	43	10.8	0	0	0	0	0
Pro totals (2 years)	30	4	2	2	1.0	0	21	132	6.3	0	0	0	0	0

COOK, RASHARD — S

PERSONAL: Born April 18, 1977, in San Diego. ... 5-11/205. ... Cousin of Kareem Kelly, wide receiver, New Orleans Saints.
HIGH SCHOOL: Samuel F.B. Morse (San Diego).
COLLEGE: Southern California.
TRANSACTIONS/CAREER NOTES: Selected by Chicago Bears in sixth round (184th pick overall) of 1999 NFL draft. ... Signed by Bears (June 25, 1999). ... Claimed on waivers by Philadelphia Eagles (September 7, 1999). ... Granted free agency (March 1, 2002). ... Re-signed by Eagles (April 26, 2002). ... On injured reserve with knee injury (November 1, 2002-remainder of season). ... Granted unconditional free agency (February 28, 2003).
CHAMPIONSHIP GAME EXPERIENCE: Played in NFC championship game (2001 season).

			TOTALS			INTERCEPTIONS			
Year Team	G	GS	Tk.	Ast.	Sks.	No.	Yds.	Avg.	TD
1999—Philadelphia NFL	13	0	3	1	1.0	1	29	29.0	0
2000—Philadelphia NFL	14	0	0	1	0.0	0	0	0.0	0
2001—Philadelphia NFL	16	3	8	3	1.0	1	11	11.0	0
2002—Philadelphia NFL	4	0	2	0	1.0	0	0	0.0	0
Pro totals (4 years)	47	3	13	5	3.0	2	40	20.0	0

COOPER, CHRIS — DT — RAIDERS

PERSONAL: Born December 27, 1977, in Lincoln, Neb. ... 6-5/275.
HIGH SCHOOL: Lincoln Southeast (Neb.).
COLLEGE: Nebraska-Omaha.
TRANSACTIONS/CAREER NOTES: Selected by Oakland Raiders in sixth round (184th pick overall) of 2001 NFL draft. ... Signed by Raiders (July 21, 2001).
CHAMPIONSHIP GAME EXPERIENCE: Played in AFC championship game (2002 season). ... Played in Super Bowl XXXVII (2002 season).

			TOTALS			INTERCEPTIONS			
Year Team	G	GS	Tk.	Ast.	Sks.	No.	Yds.	Avg.	TD
2001—Oakland NFL	11	1	14	8	2.0	1	0	0.0	0
2002—Oakland NFL	16	1	14	5	1.0	0	0	0.0	0
Pro totals (2 years)	27	2	28	13	3.0	1	0	0.0	0

COOPER, DEKE — S — PANTHERS

PERSONAL: Born October 18, 1977, in Swainsboro, Ga. ... 6-3/215.
HIGH SCHOOL: Evansville (Ind.).
COLLEGE: Notre Dame.
TRANSACTIONS/CAREER NOTES: Signed as non-drafted free agent by Arizona Cardinals (April 18, 2000). ... Released by Cardinals (August 22, 2000). ... Re-signed by Cardinals (February 15, 2001). ... Assigned by Cardinals to Rhein Fire in 2001 NFL Europe enhancement allocation program (February 18, 2001). ... Released by Cardinals (September 1, 2001). ... Signed by Cleveland Browns to practice squad (September 20, 2001). ... Released by Browns (October 9, 2001). ... Signed by Carolina Panthers (January 16, 2002). ... Assigned by Panthers to Rhein Fire in 2002 NFL Europe enhancement allocation program (February 12, 2002). ... Released by Panthers (September 1, 2002). ... Re-signed by Panthers to practice squad (September 3, 2002). ... Activated (October 10, 2002).

			TOTALS			INTERCEPTIONS			
Year Team	G	GS	Tk.	Ast.	Sks.	No.	Yds.	Avg.	TD
2001—Rhein NFLE	...	...	...	...	0.0	6	30	5.0	0
2002—Rhein NFLE	...	...	...	...	0.0	5	27	5.4	0
—Carolina NFL	10	0	0	0	0.0	0	0	0.0	0
NFL Europe totals (2 years)	...	...	...	...	0.0	11	57	5.2	0
NFL totals (1 year)	10	0	0	0	0.0	0	0	0.0	0
Pro totals (3 years)	...	...	...	...	0.0	11	57	5.2	0

C

COOPER, JARROD   S   PANTHERS

PERSONAL: Born March 31, 1978, in Pearland, Texas. ... 6-0/210.
HIGH SCHOOL: Pearland (Texas).
COLLEGE: Kansas State.
TRANSACTIONS/CAREER NOTES: Selected by Carolina Panthers in fifth round (143rd pick overall) of 2001 NFL draft. ... Signed by Panthers (July 19, 2001). ... On injured reserve with knee injury (October 16, 2002-remainder of season).

			TOTALS			INTERCEPTIONS			
Year Team	G	GS	Tk.	Ast.	Sks.	No.	Yds.	Avg.	TD
2001—Carolina NFL	16	0	9	1	0.0	0	0	0.0	0
2002—Carolina NFL	6	0	2	0	0.0	0	0	0.0	0
Pro totals (2 years)	22	0	11	1	0.0	0	0	0.0	0

COOPER, RAFAEL   RB   LIONS

PERSONAL: Born January 8, 1975, in Detroit. ... 5-11/205.
HIGH SCHOOL: Chadsey (Detroit).
COLLEGE: Minnesota, then Louisville.
TRANSACTIONS/CAREER NOTES: Signed as non-drafted free agent by Green Bay Packers (August 8, 2000). ... Released by Packers (August 7, 2000). ... Re-signed by Packers (June 6, 2001). ... Released by Packers (July 20, 2001). ... Signed by Tennessee Titans (July 31, 2001). ... Released by Titans (August 25, 2001). ... Re-signed by Titans (February 5, 2002). ... Assigned by Titans to Amsterdam Admirals in 2002 NFL Europe enhancement allocation program (February 12, 2002). ... Released by Titans (August 22, 2002). ... Signed by Detroit Lions to practice squad (September 2, 2002). ... Released by Lions (September 17, 2002). ... Re-signed by Lions to practice squad (September 24, 2002). ... Activated (November 5, 2002). ... Re-signed by Lions (March 23, 2003).
SINGLE GAME HIGHS (regular season): Attempts—8 (December 15, 2002, vs. Tampa Bay); yards—50 (December 15, 2002, vs. Tampa Bay); and rushing touchdowns—0.

			RUSHING				RECEIVING				KICKOFF RETURNS				TOTALS			
Year Team	G	GS	Att.	Yds.	Avg.	TD	No.	Yds.	Avg.	TD	No.	Yds.	Avg.	TD	TD	2pt.	Pts.	Fum.
2002—Amsterdam NFLE	10	8	155	751	4.8	8	29	238	8.2	1	11	370	33.6	1	10	0	60	0
—Detroit NFL	5	0	12	57	4.8	0	1	4	4.0	0	1	55	55.0	0	0	0	0	0
NFL Europe totals (1 year)	10	8	155	751	4.8	8	29	238	8.2	1	11	370	33.6	1	10	0	60	0
NFL totals (1 year)	5	0	12	57	4.8	0	1	4	4.0	0	1	55	55.0	0	0	0	0	0
Pro totals (2 years)	15	8	167	808	4.8	8	30	242	8.1	1	12	425	35.4	1	10	0	60	0

CORTEZ, JOSE   K   REDSKINS

PERSONAL: Born May 27, 1975, in San Vicente, El Salvador. ... 5-11/200. ... Full name: Jose Antonio Cortez.
HIGH SCHOOL: Van Nuys (Calif.).
JUNIOR COLLEGE: Los Angeles Valley College.
COLLEGE: Oregon State.
TRANSACTIONS/CAREER NOTES: Signed as non-drafted free agent by Cleveland Browns (April 23, 1999). ... Released by Browns (June 3, 1999). ... Signed by San Diego Chargers (June 14, 1999). ... Released by Chargers (August 30, 1999). ... Signed by New York Giants to practice squad (December 14, 1999). ... Activated (December 17, 1999). ... Released by Giants (December 21, 1999). ... Signed by San Diego Chargers (January 18, 2000). ... Released by Chargers (August 27, 2000). ... Signed by San Francisco 49ers (May 9, 2001). ... Released by 49ers (November 26, 2002). ... Signed by Washington Redskins (December 2, 2002).

		FIELD GOALS								TOTALS		
Year Team	G	1-29	30-39	40-49	50+	Tot.	Pct.	Lg.		XPM	XPA	Pts.
1999—New York Giants NFL	1	0-0	0-0	0-0	0-0	0-0	0.0	0		0	0	0
2000—Amsterdam NFLE	...	...	...	...	...	9-13	69.2	...		0	0	27
2001—San Francisco NFL	16	7-9	6-7	4-8	1-1	18-25	72.0	52		47	47	101
2002—San Francisco NFL	10	8-10	7-8	3-6	0-0	18-24	75.0	45		25	25	79
—Washington NFL	4	3-3	1-1	1-4	0-0	5-8	62.5	44		9	9	24
NFL Europe totals (1 year)	...	...	...	...	...	9-13	69.2	...		0	0	27
NFL totals (3 years)	31	18-22	14-16	8-18	1-1	41-57	71.9	52		81	81	204
Pro totals (4 years)	...	...	...	...	...	50-70	71.4	...		81	81	231

COTA, CHAD   DB

PERSONAL: Born August 8, 1971, in Ashland, Ore. ... 6-0/196. ... Full name: Chad Garrett Cota.
HIGH SCHOOL: Ashland (Ore.).
COLLEGE: Oregon (degree in sociology).
TRANSACTIONS/CAREER NOTES: Selected by Carolina Panthers in seventh round (209th pick overall) of 1995 NFL draft. ... Signed by Panthers (July 14, 1995). ... Granted free agency (February 13, 1998). ... Tendered offer sheet by New Orleans Saints (March 11, 1998). ... Panthers declined to match offer (March 19, 1998). ... Granted unconditional free agency (February 12, 1999). ... Signed by Indianapolis Colts (February 23, 1999). ... Released by Colts (February 21, 2002). ... Signed by San Francisco 49ers (August 14, 2002). ... Released by 49ers (August 31, 2002). ... Signed by St. Louis Rams (September 3, 2002). ... Granted unconditional free agency (February 28, 2003).
CHAMPIONSHIP GAME EXPERIENCE: Played in NFC championship game (1996 season).

			TOTALS			INTERCEPTIONS			
Year Team	G	GS	Tk.	Ast.	Sks.	No.	Yds.	Avg.	TD
1995—Carolina NFL	16	0	4	0	0.0	0	0	0.0	0
1996—Carolina NFL	16	2	31	11	1.0	5	63	12.6	0
1997—Carolina NFL	16	16	86	31	1.0	2	28	14.0	0
1998—New Orleans NFL	16	16	71	25	2.0	4	16	4.0	0
1999—Indianapolis NFL	15	15	65	23	0.0	0	0	0.0	0
2000—Indianapolis NFL	16	16	67	20	0.0	2	3	1.5	0
2001—Indianapolis NFL	16	16	73	21	0.0	2	21	10.5	0
2002—St. Louis NFL	14	1	4	0	0.0	0	0	0.0	0
Pro totals (8 years)	125	82	401	131	4.0	15	131	8.7	0

COUCH, TIM — QB — BROWNS

PERSONAL: Born July 31, 1977, in Hyden, Ky. ... 6-4/227. ... Full name: Timothy Scott Couch.
HIGH SCHOOL: Leslie County (Hyden, Ky.).
COLLEGE: Kentucky.
TRANSACTIONS/CAREER NOTES: Selected after junior season by Cleveland Browns in first round (first pick overall) of 1999 NFL draft. ... Signed by Browns (April 17, 1999). ... On injured reserve with broken thumb (October 20, 2000-remainder of season).
HONORS: Named quarterback on THE SPORTING NEWS college All-America third team (1998).
SINGLE GAME HIGHS (regular season): Attempts—50 (September 22, 2002, vs. Tennessee); completions—36 (September 22, 2002, vs. Tennessee); passing yards—336 (December 30, 2001, vs. Tennessee); and touchdown passes—3 (November 17, 2002, vs. Cincinnati).
STATISTICAL PLATEAUS: 300-yard passing games: 2000 (1), 2001 (1), 2002 (1). Total: 3.
MISCELLANEOUS: Regular-season record as starting NFL quarterback: 19-32 (.373).

				PASSING								RUSHING				TOTALS		
Year Team	G	GS	Att.	Cmp.	Pct.	Yds.	TD	Int.	Avg.	Skd.	Rat.	Att.	Yds.	Avg.	TD	TD	2pt.	Pts.
1999—Cleveland NFL	15	14	399	223	55.9	2447	15	13	6.13	*56	73.2	40	267	6.7	1	1	†1	8
2000—Cleveland NFL	7	7	215	137	63.7	1483	7	9	6.90	10	77.3	12	45	3.8	0	0	0	0
2001—Cleveland NFL	16	16	454	272	59.9	3040	17	21	6.70	51	73.1	38	128	3.4	0	0	0	0
2002—Cleveland NFL	14	14	443	273	61.6	2842	18	18	6.42	30	76.8	23	77	3.3	0	0	0	0
Pro totals (4 years)	52	51	1511	905	59.9	9812	57	61	6.49	147	74.8	113	517	4.6	1	1	1	8

COUSIN, TERRY — CB — PANTHERS

PERSONAL: Born March 11, 1975, in Miami. ... 5-9/181.
HIGH SCHOOL: Miami Beach Senior.
COLLEGE: South Carolina.
TRANSACTIONS/CAREER NOTES: Signed as non-drafted free agent by Chicago Bears (April 25, 1997). ... Released by Bears (August 24, 1997). ... Re-signed by Bears to practice squad (August 26, 1997). ... Activated (October 25, 1997). ... Released by Bears (October 28, 1997). ... Re-signed by Bears to practice squad (October 30, 1997). ... Activated (November 15, 1997). ... Granted free agency (February 11, 2000). ... Re-signed by Bears (April 18, 2000). ... Claimed on waivers by Atlanta Falcons (August 28, 2000). ... Granted unconditional free agency (March 2, 2001). ... Signed by Miami Dolphins (March 15, 2001). ... Granted unconditional free agency (March 1, 2002). ... Signed by Carolina Panthers (March 19, 2002).

			TOTALS			INTERCEPTIONS			
Year Team	G	GS	Tk.	Ast.	Sks.	No.	Yds.	Avg.	TD
1997—Chicago NFL	6	0	2	2	0.0	0	0	0.0	0
1998—Chicago NFL	16	12	50	12	0.0	1	0	0.0	0
1999—Chicago NFL	16	9	43	12	0.0	2	1	0.5	0
2000—Atlanta NFL	15	0	4	0	0.0	0	0	0.0	0
2001—Miami NFL	16	3	37	13	2.0	0	0	0.0	0
2002—Carolina NFL	16	16	44	15	1.0	2	4	2.0	0
Pro totals (6 years)	85	40	180	54	3.0	5	5	1.0	0

COVINGTON, SCOTT — QB — RAMS

PERSONAL: Born January 17, 1976, in Laguna Niguel, Calif. ... 6-2/217.
HIGH SCHOOL: Dana Hills (Dana Point, Calif.).
COLLEGE: Miami (Fla.).
TRANSACTIONS/CAREER NOTES: Selected by Cincinnati Bengals in seventh round (245th pick overall) of 1999 NFL draft. ... Signed by Bengals (June 14, 1999). ... Released by Bengals (August 27, 2001). ... Re-signed by Bengals (September 2, 2001). ... Released by Bengals (September 10, 2001). ... Re-signed by Bengals (December 20, 2001). ... Released by Bengals (August 26, 2002). ... Signed by St. Louis Rams (October 1, 2002). ... Released by Rams (November 27, 2002). ... Re-signed by Rams (December 3, 2002). ... Granted free agency (February 28, 2003). ... Re-signed by Rams (March 23, 2003).
SINGLE GAME HIGHS (regular season): Attempts—5 (December 30, 2002, vs. San Francisco); completions—2 (December 30, 2002, vs. San Francisco); passing yards—15 (November 7, 1999, vs. Seattle); and touchdown passes—0.
MISCELLANEOUS: Regular-season record as starting NFL quarterback: 1-0 (1.000).

				PASSING								RUSHING				TOTALS		
Year Team	G	GS	Att.	Cmp.	Pct.	Yds.	TD	Int.	Avg.	Skd.	Rat.	Att.	Yds.	Avg.	TD	TD	2pt.	Pts.
1999—Cincinnati NFL	3	0	5	4	80.0	23	0	0	4.60	0	85.8	2	-4	-2.0	0	0	0	0
2002—St. Louis NFL	1	1	5	2	40.0	7	0	0	1.40	2	47.9	0	0	0.0	0	0	0	0
Pro totals (2 years)	4	1	10	6	60.0	30	0	0	3.00	2	64.6	2	-4	-2.0	0	0	0	0

COWART, SAM — LB — JETS

PERSONAL: Born February 26, 1975, in Jacksonville. ... 6-2/245.
HIGH SCHOOL: Mandarin (Jacksonville).
COLLEGE: Florida State.
TRANSACTIONS/CAREER NOTES: Selected by Buffalo Bills in second round (39th pick overall) of 1998 NFL draft. ... Signed by Bills (July 20, 1998). ... On injured reserve with Achilles' tendon injury (September 26, 2001-remainder of season). ... Granted unconditional free agency (March 1, 2002). ... Signed by New York Jets (March 6, 2002).
HONORS: Named outside linebacker on THE SPORTING NEWS college All-America first team (1997). ... Played in Pro Bowl (2000 season).

			TOTALS			INTERCEPTIONS			
Year Team	G	GS	Tk.	Ast.	Sks.	No.	Yds.	Avg.	TD
1998—Buffalo NFL	16	11	54	18	0.0	2	23	11.5	0
1999—Buffalo NFL	16	16	79	46	1.0	0	0	0.0	0
2000—Buffalo NFL	12	12	88	41	5.5	2	4	2.0	0
2001—Buffalo NFL	1	1	0	2	0.0	0	0	0.0	0
2002—New York Jets NFL	16	16	91	36	2.0	0	0	0.0	0
Pro totals (5 years)	61	56	312	143	8.5	4	27	6.8	0

COWSETTE, DELBERT   DT   REDSKINS

PERSONAL: Born September 3, 1977, in Cleveland. ... 6-1/287. ... Full name: Delbert Ray Cowsette.
HIGH SCHOOL: Central Catholic (Cleveland).
COLLEGE: Maryland.
TRANSACTIONS/CAREER NOTES: Selected by Washington Redskins in seventh round (216th pick overall) of 2000 NFL draft. ... Signed by Redskins (May 18, 2000). ... Released by Redskins (August 27, 2000). ... Re-signed by Redskins to practice squad (August 28, 2000). ... Released by Redskins (November 13, 2000). ... Signed by Indianapolis Colts to practice squad (December 7, 2000). ... Signed by Redskins off Colts practice squad (December 19, 2000).

			TOTALS		
Year Team	G	GS	Tk.	Ast.	Sks.
2001—Washington NFL	16	0	8	2	0.0
2002—Washington NFL	16	0	10	4	2.0
Pro totals (2 years)	32	0	18	6	2.0

COX, BRYAN   LB

PERSONAL: Born February 17, 1968, in St. Louis. ... 6-4/250. ... Full name: Bryan Keith Cox.
HIGH SCHOOL: East St. Louis (Ill.) Senior.
COLLEGE: Western Illinois (bachelor of science degree in mass communications).
TRANSACTIONS/CAREER NOTES: Selected by Miami Dolphins in fifth round (113th pick overall) of 1991 NFL draft. ... Signed by Dolphins (July 11, 1991). ... On injured reserve with sprained ankle (October 5-November 2, 1991). ... Granted unconditional free agency (February 16, 1996). ... Signed by Chicago Bears (February 20, 1996). ... On injured reserve with thumb injury (November 5, 1996-remainder of season). ... Released by Bears (June 2, 1998). ... Signed by New York Jets (August 1, 1998). ... On injured reserve with abdominal injury (December 10, 1999-remainder of season). ... On injured reserve with broken leg (December 18, 2000-remainder of season). ... Released by Jets (February 23, 2001). ... Signed by New England Patriots (July 31, 2001). ... Granted unconditional free agency (March 1, 2002). ... Signed by New Orleans Saints (March 28, 2002). ... Granted unconditional free agency (February 28, 2003).
CHAMPIONSHIP GAME EXPERIENCE: Played in AFC championship game (1992, 1998 and 2001 seasons). ... Member of Super Bowl championship team (2001 season).
HONORS: Played in Pro Bowl (1992, 1994 and 1995 seasons).

			TOTALS			INTERCEPTIONS			
Year Team	G	GS	Tk.	Ast.	Sks.	No.	Yds.	Avg.	TD
1991—Miami NFL	13	13	51	10	2.0	0	0	0.0	0
1992—Miami NFL	16	16	84	43	14.0	1	0	0.0	0
1993—Miami NFL	16	16	87	35	5.0	1	26	26.0	0
1994—Miami NFL	16	16	75	25	3.0	0	0	0.0	0
1995—Miami NFL	16	16	95	24	7.5	1	12	12.0	0
1996—Chicago NFL	9	9	45	14	3.0	0	0	0.0	0
1997—Chicago NFL	16	15	68	33	5.0	0	0	0.0	0
1998—New York Jets NFL	16	10	48	22	6.0	0	0	0.0	0
1999—New York Jets NFL	12	11	32	13	0.0	1	27	27.0	1
2000—New York Jets NFL	15	15	54	27	6.0	0	0	0.0	0
2001—New England NFL	11	7	34	15	0.0	0	0	0.0	0
2002—New Orleans NFL	9	1	3	1	0.0	0	0	0.0	0
Pro totals (12 years)	165	145	676	262	51.5	4	65	16.3	1

CRAFT, JASON   CB   JAGUARS

PERSONAL: Born February 13, 1976, in Denver. ... 5-10/179. ... Full name: Jason Donell Andre Craft.
HIGH SCHOOL: Denver East.
JUNIOR COLLEGE: Denver Community College.
COLLEGE: Colorado State.
TRANSACTIONS/CAREER NOTES: Selected by Jacksonville Jaguars in fifth round (160th pick overall) of 1999 NFL draft. ... Signed by Jaguars (May 18, 1999). ... Granted free agency (March 1, 2002). ... Tendered offer sheet by New Orleans Saints (March 5, 2002). ... Offer sheet matched by Jaguars (March 12, 2002).
CHAMPIONSHIP GAME EXPERIENCE: Played in AFC championship game (1999 season).

			TOTALS			INTERCEPTIONS			
Year Team	G	GS	Tk.	Ast.	Sks.	No.	Yds.	Avg.	TD
1999—Jacksonville NFL	16	0	2	0	0.0	0	0	0.0	0
2000—Jacksonville NFL	16	3	22	5	0.0	0	0	0.0	0
2001—Jacksonville NFL	16	8	45	6	0.0	2	4	2.0	0
2002—Jacksonville NFL	16	16	49	9	0.0	3	0	0.0	0
Pro totals (4 years)	64	27	118	20	0.0	5	4	0.8	0

CRAVER, KEYUO   CB   SAINTS

PERSONAL: Born August 22, 1980, in Harleton, Texas. ... 5-10/195.
HIGH SCHOOL: Harleton (Texas).
COLLEGE: Nebraska.
TRANSACTIONS/CAREER NOTES: Selected by New Orleans Saints in fourth round (125th pick overall) of 2002 NFL draft. ... Signed by Saints (July 24, 2002).
HONORS: Named cornerback on THE SPORTING NEWS college All-America first team (2001).

			TOTALS			INTERCEPTIONS				PUNT RETURNS				TOTALS			
Year Team	G	GS	Tk.	Ast.	Sks.	No.	Yds.	Avg.	TD	No.	Yds.	Avg.	TD	TD	2pt.	Pts.	Fum.
2002—New Orleans NFL	10	1	9	3	0.0	0	0	0.0	0	1	0	0.0	0	1	0	6	1

CRAWFORD, CASEY   TE   BUCCANEERS

PERSONAL: Born August 1, 1977, in Washington, D.C. ... 6-6/255. ... Full name: Casey Stuart Crawford.
HIGH SCHOOL: Bishop O'Connell (Falls Church, Va.).
COLLEGE: Virginia.
TRANSACTIONS/CAREER NOTES: Signed as non-drafted free agent by Carolina Panthers (April 25, 2000). ... Released by Panthers (September 1, 2002). ... Signed by Tampa Bay Buccaneers to practice squad (September 10, 2002). ... Activated (October 29, 2002).
CHAMPIONSHIP GAME EXPERIENCE: Member of Buccaneers for NFC championship game (2002 season); inactive. ... Member of Super Bowl championship team (2002 season); inactive.
SINGLE GAME HIGHS (regular season): Receptions—1 (December 23, 2001, vs. St. Louis); yards—16 (November 5, 2000, vs. St. Louis); and touchdown receptions—1 (November 5, 2000, vs. St. Louis).

			RECEIVING			
Year Team	G	GS	No.	Yds.	Avg.	TD
2000—Carolina NFL	8	0	4	47	11.8	1
2001—Carolina NFL	3	1	1	10	10.0	0
2002—Tampa Bay NFL	4	0	0	0	0.0	0
Pro totals (3 years)	15	1	5	57	11.4	1

CROCKETT, HENRI   LB   VIKINGS

PERSONAL: Born October 28, 1974, in Pompano Beach, Fla. ... 6-2/238. ... Full name: Henri W. Crockett. ... Brother of Zack Crockett, fullback, Oakland Raiders.
HIGH SCHOOL: Ely (Pompano Beach, Fla.).
COLLEGE: Florida State (degree in criminology, 1996).
TRANSACTIONS/CAREER NOTES: Selected by Atlanta Falcons in fourth round (100th pick overall) of 1997 NFL draft. ... Signed by Falcons (July 14, 1997). ... Granted free agency (February 11, 2000). ... Re-signed by Falcons (June 1, 2000). ... Granted unconditional free agency (March 2, 2001). ... Signed by Denver Broncos (May 4, 2001). ... Traded by Broncos to Falcons for conditional pick in 2002 draft (August 2, 2001). ... Granted unconditional free agency (March 1, 2002). ... Signed by Minnesota Vikings (March 19, 2002).
CHAMPIONSHIP GAME EXPERIENCE: Played in NFC championship game (1998 season). ... Played in Super Bowl XXXIII (1998 season).

			TOTALS			INTERCEPTIONS			
Year Team	G	GS	Tk.	Ast.	Sks.	No.	Yds.	Avg.	TD
1997—Atlanta NFL	16	10	26	4	2.0	0	0	0.0	0
1998—Atlanta NFL	10	10	22	7	1.0	0	0	0.0	0
1999—Atlanta NFL	16	14	30	12	1.5	0	0	0.0	0
2000—Atlanta NFL	15	12	34	6	2.0	0	0	0.0	0
2001—Atlanta NFL	16	15	46	8	0.0	1	7	7.0	0
2002—Minnesota NFL	14	10	47	14	1.0	0	0	0.0	0
Pro totals (6 years)	87	71	205	51	7.5	1	7	7.0	0

CROCKETT, RAY   CB

PERSONAL: Born January 5, 1967, in Dallas. ... 5-10/185. ... Full name: Donald Ray Crockett.
HIGH SCHOOL: Duncanville (Texas).
COLLEGE: Baylor.
TRANSACTIONS/CAREER NOTES: Selected by Detroit Lions in fourth round (86th pick overall) of 1989 NFL draft. ... Signed by Lions (July 18, 1989). ... Granted unconditional free agency (February 17, 1994). ... Signed by Denver Broncos (March 9, 1994). ... Granted unconditional free agency (March 2, 2001). ... Signed by Kansas City Chiefs (April 5, 2001). ... Released by Chiefs (June 3, 2003).
CHAMPIONSHIP GAME EXPERIENCE: Played in NFC championship game (1991 season). ... Played in AFC championship game (1997 and 1998 seasons). ... Member of Super Bowl championship team (1997 and 1998 seasons).

			TOTALS			INTERCEPTIONS			
Year Team	G	GS	Tk.	Ast.	Sks.	No.	Yds.	Avg.	TD
1989—Detroit NFL	16	0	34	12	0.0	1	5	5.0	0
1990—Detroit NFL	16	6	62	29	1.0	3	17	5.7	0
1991—Detroit NFL	16	16	74	12	1.0	∞6	141	23.5	∞1
1992—Detroit NFL	15	15	41	11	1.0	4	50	12.5	0
1993—Detroit NFL	16	16	57	11	1.0	2	31	15.5	0
1994—Denver NFL	14	14	58	6	0.0	2	6	3.0	0
1995—Denver NFL	16	16	60	12	3.0	0	0	0.0	0
1996—Denver NFL	15	15	52	6	4.0	2	34	17.0	0
1997—Denver NFL	16	16	68	14	0.0	4	18	4.5	0
1998—Denver NFL	16	16	46	5	0.5	3	105	35.0	1
1999—Denver NFL	16	16	61	3	2.0	2	14	7.0	0
2000—Denver NFL	13	11	35	3	1.0	4	31	7.8	1
2001—Kansas City NFL	14	12	41	4	0.0	1	8	8.0	0
2002—Kansas City NFL	15	5	38	6	1.0	2	0	0.0	0
Pro totals (14 years)	214	174	727	134	15.5	36	460	12.8	3

CROCKETT, ZACK   RB   RAIDERS

PERSONAL: Born December 2, 1972, in Pompano Beach, Fla. ... 6-2/240. ... Brother of Henri Crockett, linebacker, Minnesota Vikings.
HIGH SCHOOL: Ely (Pompano Beach, Fla.).
JUNIOR COLLEGE: Hinds Community College (Miss.).
COLLEGE: Florida State.
TRANSACTIONS/CAREER NOTES: Selected by Indianapolis Colts in third round (79th pick overall) of 1995 NFL draft. ... Signed by Colts (July 21, 1995). ... On injured reserve with knee injury (October 22, 1996-remainder of season). ... Granted free agency (February 13, 1998). ... Re-

signed by Colts (July 23, 1998). ... Claimed on waivers by Jacksonville Jaguars (October 21, 1998). ... Granted unconditional free agency (February 12, 1999). ... Signed by Oakland Raiders (March 16, 1999). ... Granted unconditional free agency (February 28, 2003). ... Re-signed by Raiders (March 4, 2003).

CHAMPIONSHIP GAME EXPERIENCE: Played in AFC championship game (1995, 2000 and 2002 seasons). ... Played in Super Bowl XXXVII (2002 season).

SINGLE GAME HIGHS (regular season): Attempts—17 (October 28, 2001, vs. Philadelphia); yards—81 (November 2, 1997, vs. Tampa Bay); and rushing touchdowns—2 (December 22, 2002, vs. Denver).

Year Team	G	GS	RUSHING				RECEIVING				TOTALS			
			Att.	Yds.	Avg.	TD	No.	Yds.	Avg.	TD	TD	2pt.	Pts.	Fum.
1995—Indianapolis NFL	16	0	1	0	0.0	0	2	35	17.5	0	0	0	0	0
1996—Indianapolis NFL	5	5	31	164	5.3	0	11	96	8.7	1	1	0	6	2
1997—Indianapolis NFL	16	11	95	300	3.2	1	15	112	7.5	0	1	0	6	3
1998—Indianapolis NFL	2	1	2	5	2.5	0	1	1	1.0	0	0	0	0	1
—Jacksonville NFL	10	1	0	0	0.0	0	1	4	4.0	0	0	0	0	0
1999—Oakland NFL	13	1	45	91	2.0	4	8	56	7.0	1	5	0	30	0
2000—Oakland NFL	16	3	43	130	3.0	7	10	62	6.2	0	7	0	42	0
2001—Oakland NFL	16	1	57	145	2.5	6	2	10	5.0	0	6	0	36	1
2002—Oakland NFL	16	0	40	118	3.0	8	0	0	0.0	0	8	0	48	0
Pro totals (8 years)	110	23	314	953	3.0	26	50	376	7.5	2	28	0	168	7

CROSBY, CLIFTON　　　CB　　　COLTS

PERSONAL: Born September 17, 1974, in Erie, Pa. ... 5-10/179.
HIGH SCHOOL: East (Erie, Pa.).
COLLEGE: Maryland.
TRANSACTIONS/CAREER NOTES: Signed as non-drafted free agent by St. Louis Rams (April 20, 1999). ... Released by Rams (September 5, 1999). ... Re-signed by Rams (September 6, 1999). ... Released by Rams (September 13, 1999). ... Re-signed by Rams to practice squad (September 30, 1999). ... Released by Rams (August 27, 2000). ... Re-signed by Rams to practice squad (August 29, 2000). ... Released by Rams (October 24, 2000). ... Signed by Indianapolis Colts (November 1, 2000). ... Granted free agency (February 28, 2003). ... Re-signed by Colts (April 22, 2003).

Year Team	G	GS	TOTALS			INTERCEPTIONS			
			Tk.	Ast.	Sks.	No.	Yds.	Avg.	TD
1999—St. Louis NFL	1	0	0	0	0.0	0	0	0.0	0
2001—Indianapolis NFL	14	0	2	0	0.0	0	0	0.0	0
2002—Indianapolis NFL	16	0	15	3	0.0	0	0	0.0	0
Pro totals (3 years)	31	0	17	3	0.0	0	0	0.0	0

CROSBY, PHILLIP　　　FB　　　BILLS

PERSONAL: Born November 5, 1976, in Bessemer City, N.C. ... 6-0/242. ... Full name: Phillip Jermaine Crosby.
HIGH SCHOOL: Bessemer City (N.C.).
JUNIOR COLLEGE: Coffeyville Community College.
COLLEGE: Tennessee.
TRANSACTIONS/CAREER NOTES: Signed as non-drafted free agent by Buffalo Bills (April 22, 2000). ... Released by Bills (August 21, 2000). ... Re-signed by Bills (April 24, 2001).

Year Team	G	GS	RUSHING				RECEIVING				KICKOFF RETURNS				TOTALS			
			Att.	Yds.	Avg.	TD	No.	Yds.	Avg.	TD	No.	Yds.	Avg.	TD	TD	2pt.	Pts.	Fum.
2001—Buffalo NFL	16	2	0	0	0.0	0	2	16	8.0	0	0	0	0.0	0	0	0	0	0
2002—Buffalo NFL	16	4	0	0	0.0	0	4	33	8.3	0	3	45	15.0	0	0	0	0	0
Pro totals (2 years)	32	6	0	0	0.0	0	6	49	8.2	0	3	45	15.0	0	0	0	0	0

CROWELL, GERMANE　　　WR

PERSONAL: Born September 13, 1976, in Winston-Salem, N.C. ... 6-3/216. ... Full name: Germane L. Crowell. ... Brother of Angelo Crowell, linebacker, Buffalo Bills.
HIGH SCHOOL: North Forsyth (Winston-Salem, N.C.).
COLLEGE: Virginia.
TRANSACTIONS/CAREER NOTES: Selected by Detroit Lions in second round (50th pick overall) of 1998 NFL draft. ... Signed by Lions (July 20, 1998). ... On injured reserve with knee injury (October 24, 2001-remainder of season). ... Granted unconditional free agency (March 1, 2002). ... Re-signed by Lions (March 26, 2002). ... On physically unable to perform list with knee injury (August 26-October 19, 2002). ... Released by Lions (February 25, 2003).
SINGLE GAME HIGHS (regular season): Receptions—9 (October 14, 2001, vs. Minnesota); yards—163 (November 7, 1999, vs. St. Louis); and touchdown receptions—2 (September 12, 1999, vs. Seattle).
STATISTICAL PLATEAUS: 100-yard receiving games: 1999 (6), 2001 (1). Total: 7.

Year Team	G	GS	RUSHING				RECEIVING				TOTALS			
			Att.	Yds.	Avg.	TD	No.	Yds.	Avg.	TD	TD	2pt.	Pts.	Fum.
1998—Detroit NFL	14	2	1	35	35.0	0	25	464	18.6	3	3	0	18	1
1999—Detroit NFL	16	15	5	38	7.6	0	81	1338	16.5	7	7	†1	44	1
2000—Detroit NFL	9	7	1	12	12.0	0	34	430	12.6	3	3	0	18	0
2001—Detroit NFL	5	4	1	6	6.0	0	22	289	13.1	2	2	0	12	1
2002—Detroit NFL	10	5	0	0	0.0	0	22	201	9.1	1	1	0	6	0
Pro totals (5 years)	54	33	8	91	11.4	0	184	2722	14.8	16	16	1	98	3

CRUMPLER, ALGE — TE — FALCONS

PERSONAL: Born December 23, 1977, in Wilmington, N.C. ... 6-2/262. ... Full name: Algernon Darius Crumpler.
HIGH SCHOOL: New Hanover (Wilmington, N.C.).
COLLEGE: North Carolina.
TRANSACTIONS/CAREER NOTES: Selected by Atlanta Falcons in second round (35th pick overall) of 2001 NFL draft. ... Signed by Falcons (May 29, 2001).
SINGLE GAME HIGHS (regular season): Receptions—5 (December 15, 2002, vs. Seattle); yards—78 (October 21, 2001, vs. New Orleans); and touchdown receptions—1 (December 15, 2002, vs. Seattle).

			RECEIVING			
Year Team	G	GS	No.	Yds.	Avg.	TD
2001—Atlanta NFL	16	12	25	330	13.2	3
2002—Atlanta NFL	16	9	36	455	12.6	5
Pro totals (2 years)	32	21	61	785	12.9	8

CULPEPPER, DAUNTE — QB — VIKINGS

PERSONAL: Born January 28, 1977, in Ocala, Fla. ... 6-4/260.
HIGH SCHOOL: Vanguard (Ocala, Fla.).
COLLEGE: Central Florida.
TRANSACTIONS/CAREER NOTES: Selected by Minnesota Vikings in first round (11th pick overall) of 1999 NFL draft. ... Signed by Vikings (July 30, 1999).
CHAMPIONSHIP GAME EXPERIENCE: Played in NFC championship game (2000 season).
HONORS: Played in Pro Bowl (2000 season).
RECORDS: Shares NFL single-season record for most fumbles—23 (2002).
SINGLE GAME HIGHS (regular season): Attempts—53 (September 29, 2002, vs. Seattle); completions—30 (September 30, 2001, vs. Tampa Bay); yards—357 (November 19, 2000, vs. Carolina); and touchdown passes—4 (November 19, 2001, vs. New York Giants).
STATISTICAL PLATEAUS: 300-yard passing games: 2000 (5), 2001 (2), 2002 (2). Total: 9.
MISCELLANEOUS: Selected by New York Yankees organization in 26th round of free-agent baseball draft (June 1, 1995); did not sign. ... Regular-season record as starting NFL quarterback: 21-22 (.488). ... Postseason record as starting NFL quarterback: 1-1 (.500).

			PASSING								RUSHING				TOTALS		
Year Team	G	GS	Att.	Cmp.	Pct.	Yds.	TD	Int.	Avg.	Skd.	Rat.	Att.	Yds.	Avg.	TD	TD	2pt.	Pts.
1999—Minnesota NFL	1	0	0	0	0.0	0	0	0	0.0	0	...	3	6	2.0	0	0	0	0
2000—Minnesota NFL	16	16	474	297	62.7	3937	†33	16	8.31	34	98.0	89	470	5.3	7	7	0	42
2001—Minnesota NFL	11	11	366	235	64.2	2612	14	13	7.14	33	83.3	71	416	5.9	5	5	2	34
2002—Minnesota NFL	16	16	549	333	60.7	3853	18	*23	7.02	‡47	75.3	106	609	5.7	10	10	1	62
Pro totals (4 years)	44	43	1389	865	62.3	10402	65	52	7.49	114	85.2	269	1501	5.6	22	22	3	138

CUNDIFF, BILL — K — COWBOYS

PERSONAL: Born March 30, 1980, in Harlan, Iowa. ... 6-1/201.
HIGH SCHOOL: Harlan (Iowa).
COLLEGE: Drake.
TRANSACTIONS/CAREER NOTES: Signed as non-drafted free agent by Dallas Cowboys (April 26, 2002).

		FIELD GOALS							TOTALS		
Year Team	G	1-29	30-39	40-49	50+	Tot.	Pct.	Lg.	XPM	XPA	Pts.
2002—Dallas NFL	16	3-3	5-7	4-8	0-1	12-19	63.2	48	25	25	61

CUNNINGHAM, RICHIE — K

PERSONAL: Born August 18, 1970, in Terrebonne, La. ... 5-10/167. ... Full name: Richard Anthony Cunningham.
HIGH SCHOOL: Terrebonne (La.).
COLLEGE: Southwestern Louisiana (degree in marketing).
TRANSACTIONS/CAREER NOTES: Signed as non-drafted free agent by Dallas Cowboys (May 2, 1994). ... Released by Cowboys (August 17, 1994). ... Signed by Green Bay Packers (April 22, 1996). ... Released by Packers (August 19, 1996). ... Signed by Cowboys (April 15, 1997). ... Released by Cowboys (December 7, 1999). ... Signed by Carolina Panthers (December 14, 1999). ... Released by Panthers (February 10, 2000). ... Re-signed by Panthers (August 18, 2000). ... Released by Panthers (October 3, 2000). ... Signed by Cincinnati Bengals (March 16, 2001). ... Released by Bengals (August 27, 2001). ... Signed by Jacksonville Jaguars (November 27, 2002). ... Released by Jaguars (December 3, 2002).
HONORS: Named kicker on THE SPORTING NEWS NFL All-Pro team (1997).

		FIELD GOALS							TOTALS		
Year Team	G	1-29	30-39	40-49	50+	Tot.	Pct.	Lg.	XPM	XPA	Pts.
1997—Dallas NFL	16	17-17	9-9	7-10	1-1	*34-∞37	91.9	53	24	24	‡126
1998—Dallas NFL	16	10-10	8-11	10-11	1-3	29-35	82.9	54	40	40	127
1999—Dallas NFL	12	4-6	5-6	3-9	0-1	12-22	54.5	47	31	31	67
—Carolina NFL	3	2-2	0-0	1-1	0-0	3-3	100.0	43	13	14	22
2000—Carolina NFL	4	3-5	2-2	0-0	0-0	5-7	71.4	39	9	9	24
2002—Jacksonville NFL	1	1-1	0-0	0-0	0-0	1-1	100.0	23	2	2	5
Pro totals (5 years)	52	37-41	24-28	21-31	2-5	84-105	80.0	54	119	120	371

CURRY, DONTE' — LB — LIONS

PERSONAL: Born July 22, 1978, in Savannah, Ga. ... 6-1/233. ... Full name: Donte Curry.
HIGH SCHOOL: Savannah (Ga.).
JUNIOR COLLEGE: Middle Georgia Junior College.
COLLEGE: Morris Brown.

C

Year Team	G	GS	TOTALS			INTERCEPTIONS			
			Tk.	Ast.	Sks.	No.	Yds.	Avg.	TD
2001—Washington NFL	8	0	0	0	0.0	0	0	0.0	0
2002—Detroit NFL	16	10	39	16	3.0	0	0	0.0	0
Pro totals (2 years)	24	10	39	16	3.0	0	0	0.0	0

CURRY, RONALD — QB — RAIDERS

PERSONAL: Born May 28, 1979, in Hampton, Va. ... 6-3/220. ... Full name: Ronald Antonio Curry.
HIGH SCHOOL: Hampton (Va.).
COLLEGE: North Carolina.
TRANSACTIONS/CAREER NOTES: Selected by Oakland Raiders in seventh round (235th pick overall) of 2002 NFL draft. ... Signed by Raiders (July 26, 2002). ... Released by Raiders (September 1, 2002). ... Re-signed by Raiders to practice squad (September 3, 2002). ... Released by Raiders (November 2, 2002). ... Re-signed by Raiders to practice squad (January 22, 2003).
CHAMPIONSHIP GAME EXPERIENCE: Member of Raiders for Super Bowl XXXVII (2002 season); inactive.

Year Team	G	GS	PASSING								PUNT RETURNS			KICKOFF RETURNS			TOTALS		
			Att.	Cmp.	Pct.	Yds.	TD	Int.	Avg.	Rat.	Att.	Yds.	Avg.	TD	No.	Yds.	Avg.	TD	TD	2pt.	Pts.
2002—Oakland NFL	1	0	0	0	0.0	0	0	0	0.0		0	0	0.0	0	3	68	22.7	0	0	0	0

CURTIS, CANUTE — LB

PERSONAL: Born August 4, 1974, in Amityville, N.Y. ... 6-2/257. ... Name pronounced kuh-NOOT.
HIGH SCHOOL: Farmingdale (N.Y.).
COLLEGE: West Virginia.
TRANSACTIONS/CAREER NOTES: Selected by Cincinnati Bengals in sixth round (176th pick overall) of 1997 NFL draft. ... Signed by Bengals (July 11, 1997). ... Released by Bengals (August 24, 1997). ... Re-signed by Bengals to practice squad (August 26, 1997). ... Activated (October 21, 1997). ... Released by Bengals (August 30, 1998). ... Re-signed by Bengals to practice squad (August 31, 1998). ... Activated (November 10, 1998). ... Granted free agency (February 11, 2000). ... Re-signed by Bengals (March 1, 2000). ... Released by Bengals (May 27, 2003).
HONORS: Named outside linebacker on THE SPORTING NEWS college All-America first team (1996).

Year Team	G	GS	TOTALS			INTERCEPTIONS			
			Tk.	Ast.	Sks.	No.	Yds.	Avg.	TD
1997—Cincinnati NFL	3	0	2	0	0.0	0	0	0.0	0
1998—Cincinnati NFL	5	0	1	1	0.0	0	0	0.0	0
1999—Cincinnati NFL	15	0	6	1	1.0	0	0	0.0	0
2000—Cincinnati NFL	15	0	8	2	2.0	0	0	0.0	0
2001—Cincinnati NFL	16	4	11	8	0.0	0	0	0.0	0
2002—Cincinnati NFL	16	11	38	8	0.0	0	0	0.0	0
Pro totals (6 years)	70	15	66	20	3.0	0	0	0.0	0

CUSHING, MATT — TE — STEELERS

PERSONAL: Born July 2, 1975, in Chicago. ... 6-4/260. ... Full name: Matt Jay Cushing.
HIGH SCHOOL: Mount Carmel (Chicago).
COLLEGE: Illinois.
TRANSACTIONS/CAREER NOTES: Signed as non-drafted free agent by Pittsburgh Steelers (April 24, 1998). ... Released by Steelers (August 24, 1998). ... Re-signed by Steelers (February 22, 1999). ... Assigned by Steelers to Amsterdam Admirals in 1999 NFL Europe enhancement allocation program (February 22, 1999). ... Released by Steelers (September 5, 1999). ... Re-signed by Steelers (October 28, 1999). ... Released by Steelers (August 27, 2000). ... Re-signed by Steelers (November 7, 2000). ... Granted free agency (March 1, 2002). ... Re-signed by Steelers (April 12, 2002). ... Released by Steelers (September 24, 2002). ... Re-signed by Steelers (October 22, 2002). ... Released by Steelers (November 5, 2002). ... Re-signed by Steelers (December 3, 2002). ... Granted unconditional free agency (February 28, 2003). ... Re-signed by Steelers (March 17, 2003).
CHAMPIONSHIP GAME EXPERIENCE: Played in AFC championship game (2001 season).
SINGLE GAME HIGHS (regular season): Receptions—2 (December 23, 2001, vs. Detroit); yards—29 (January 2, 2000, vs. Tennessee); and touchdown receptions—1 (December 23, 2001, vs. Detroit).

Year Team	G	GS	RECEIVING				TOTALS			
			No.	Yds.	Avg.	TD	TD	2pt.	Pts.	Fum.
1999—Amsterdam NFLE	...	...	6	62	10.3	0	0	0	0	0
—Pittsburgh NFL	7	1	2	29	14.5	0	0	0	0	0
2000—Pittsburgh NFL	7	1	4	17	4.3	0	0	0	0	0
2001—Pittsburgh NFL	13	3	5	24	4.8	1	1	0	6	0
2002—Pittsburgh NFL	6	0	1	4	4.0	0	0	0	0	0
NFL Europe totals (1 year)	...		6	62	10.3	0	0	0	0	0
NFL totals (4 years)	33	5	12	74	6.2	1	1	0	6	0
Pro totals (5 years)	...	...	18	136	7.6	1	1	0	6	0

DALTON, LIONAL — DT — BRONCOS

PERSONAL: Born February 21, 1975, in Detroit. ... 6-1/309.
HIGH SCHOOL: Cooley (Detroit).
COLLEGE: Eastern Michigan.

TRANSACTIONS/CAREER NOTES: Signed as non-drafted free agent by Baltimore Ravens (April 23, 1998). ... Granted free agency (March 2, 2001). ... Re-signed by Ravens (March 29, 2001). ... Granted unconditional free agency (March 1, 2002). ... Signed by Denver Broncos (March 20, 2002).
CHAMPIONSHIP GAME EXPERIENCE: Played in AFC championship game (2000 season). ... Member of Super Bowl championship team (2000 season).

				TOTALS	
Year Team	G	GS	Tk.	Ast.	Sks.
1998—Baltimore NFL	2	1	3	1	0.0
1999—Baltimore NFL	16	2	12	5	1.0
2000—Baltimore NFL	16	1	9	1	0.0
2001—Baltimore NFL	16	3	12	4	0.0
2002—Denver NFL	16	13	24	5	1.0
Pro totals (5 years)	66	20	60	16	2.0

DANIELS, PHILLIP   DE   BEARS

PERSONAL: Born March 4, 1973, in Donaldsonville, Ga. ... 6-5/288. ... Full name: Phillip Bernard Daniels.
HIGH SCHOOL: Seminole County (Donaldsonville, Ga.).
COLLEGE: Georgia.
TRANSACTIONS/CAREER NOTES: Selected by Seattle Seahawks in fourth round (99th pick overall) of 1996 NFL draft. ... Signed by Seahawks (July 17, 1996). ... Granted free agency (February 12, 1999). ... Re-signed by Seahawks (April 6, 1999). ... Granted unconditional free agency (February 11, 2000). ... Signed by Chicago Bears (February 12, 2000). ... On injured reserve with ankle injury (December 13, 2000-remainder of season).

				TOTALS	
Year Team	G	GS	Tk.	Ast.	Sks.
1996—Seattle NFL	15	0	9	2	2.0
1997—Seattle NFL	13	10	24	10	4.0
1998—Seattle NFL	16	15	34	14	6.5
1999—Seattle NFL	16	16	40	8	9.0
2000—Chicago NFL	14	14	37	5	6.0
2001—Chicago NFL	16	16	43	7	9.0
2002—Chicago NFL	13	13	34	9	5.5
Pro totals (7 years)	103	84	221	55	42.0

DANTZLER, WOODROW   RB   COWBOYS

PERSONAL: Born October 4, 1979, in Orangeburg, S.C. ... 5-10/209.
HIGH SCHOOL: Wilkinsburg (Orangeburg, S.C.).
COLLEGE: Clemson (degree in marketing).
TRANSACTIONS/CAREER NOTES: Signed as non-drafted free agent by Dallas Cowboys (April 26, 2002). ... Released by Cowboys (September 1, 2002). ... Re-signed by Cowboys to practice squad (September 3, 2002). ... Activated (November 27, 2002).

			RUSHING				KICKOFF RETURNS				TOTALS		
Year Team	G	GS	Att.	Yds.	Avg.	TD	No.	Yds.	Avg.	TD	TD	2pt.	Pts.	Fum.
2002—Dallas NFL	5	0	0	0	0.0	0	27	602	22.3	1	1	0	6	2

DARBY, CHARTRIC   DT   BUCCANEERS

PERSONAL: Born October 22, 1975, in North, S.C. ... 6-0/270. ... Full name: Chartric Terrell Darby.
HIGH SCHOOL: North (S.C.).
COLLEGE: South Carolina State.
TRANSACTIONS/CAREER NOTES: Signed as non-drafted free agent by Baltimore Ravens (April 23, 1998). ... Released by Ravens (August 30, 1998). ... Re-signed by Ravens to practice squad (September 1, 1998). ... Granted free agency after 1998 season. ... Signed by Indianapolis Colts (January 19, 1999). ... Claimed on waivers by Carolina Panthers (April 28, 1999). ... Released by Panthers (August 30, 1999). ... Selected by Rhein Fire in 2000 NFL Europe draft (February 22, 2000). ... Signed by Buccaneers (July 10, 2000). ... Released by Buccaneers (August 27, 2000). ... Re-signed by Buccaneers to practice squad (August 28, 2000).
CHAMPIONSHIP GAME EXPERIENCE: Played in NFC championship game (2002 season). ... Member of Super Bowl championship team (2002 season).

				TOTALS	
Year Team	G	GS	Tk.	Ast.	Sks.
2000—Barcelona NFLE	...	...	...	...	8.5
2001—Tampa Bay NFL	13	0	6	0	2.0
2002—Tampa Bay NFL	16	6	22	6	1.5
NFL Europe totals (1 year)	...	...	...	...	8.5
NFL totals (2 years)	29	6	28	6	3.5
Pro totals (3 years)	...	...	...	...	12.0

DARCHE, JEAN-PHILIPPE   TE   SEAHAWKS

PERSONAL: Born February 28, 1975, in Montreal. ... 6-0/246. ... Full name: Jean-Philipe Darche. ... Brother of Mathieu Darche, left winger, Columbus Blue Jackets.
HIGH SCHOOL: Andre Grassett Junior College (Montreal).
COLLEGE: McGill (Montreal).
TRANSACTIONS/CAREER NOTES: Signed as non-drafted free agent by Seattle Seahawks (May 11, 2000). ... Granted free agency (February 28, 2003). ... Re-signed by Seahawks (March 26, 2003).

Year Team	G	GS	No.	RECEIVING Yds.	Avg.	TD
2000—Seattle NFL	16	0	0	0	0.0	0
2001—Seattle NFL	16	0	0	0	0.0	0
2002—Seattle NFL	16	0	0	0	0.0	0
Pro totals (3 years)	48	0	0	0	0.0	0

DARIUS, DONOVIN — S — JAGUARS

PERSONAL: Born August 12, 1975, in Camden, N.J. ... 6-1/214. ... Full name: Donovin Lee Darius.
HIGH SCHOOL: Woodrow Wilson (Camden, N.J.).
COLLEGE: Syracuse (degree in exercise science, 1997).
TRANSACTIONS/CAREER NOTES: Selected by Jacksonville Jaguars in first round (25th pick overall) of 1998 NFL draft. ... Signed by Jaguars (July 23, 1998). ... Designated by Jaguars as franchise player (February 20, 2003). ... Re-signed by Jaguars (March 25, 2003).
CHAMPIONSHIP GAME EXPERIENCE: Played in AFC championship game (1999 season).
HONORS: Named free safety on THE SPORTING NEWS college All-America first team (1997).

Year Team	G	GS	TOTALS Tk.	Ast.	Sks.	INTERCEPTIONS No.	Yds.	Avg.	TD
1998—Jacksonville NFL	14	14	58	16	0.0	0	0	0.0	0
1999—Jacksonville NFL	16	16	56	19	0.0	4	37	9.3	0
2000—Jacksonville NFL	16	16	65	20	1.0	2	26	13.0	0
2001—Jacksonville NFL	11	11	64	12	0.0	1	39	39.0	0
2002—Jacksonville NFL	14	14	70	8	1.0	1	3	3.0	0
Pro totals (5 years)	71	71	313	75	2.0	8	105	13.1	0

DARLING, JAMES — LB — CARDINALS

PERSONAL: Born December 29, 1974, in Denver. ... 6-0/250. ... Full name: James Jackson Darling.
HIGH SCHOOL: Kettle Falls (Wash.).
COLLEGE: Washington State.
TRANSACTIONS/CAREER NOTES: Selected by Philadelphia Eagles in second round (57th pick overall) of 1997 NFL draft. ... Signed by Eagles (July 16, 1997). ... Granted free agency (February 11, 2000). ... Re-signed by Eagles (April 10, 2000). ... Granted unconditional free agency (March 2, 2001). ... Signed by New York Jets (March 21, 2001). ... Granted unconditional free agency (February 28, 2003). ... Signed by Arizona Cardinals (March 12, 2003).
HONORS: Named inside linebacker on THE SPORTING NEWS college All-America second team (1996).

Year Team	G	GS	TOTALS Tk.	Ast.	Sks.	INTERCEPTIONS No.	Yds.	Avg.	TD
1997—Philadelphia NFL	16	6	20	8	0.0	0	0	0.0	0
1998—Philadelphia NFL	12	8	20	6	2.0	0	0	0.0	0
1999—Philadelphia NFL	15	10	40	18	0.0	1	33	33.0	0
2000—Philadelphia NFL	16	0	1	3	0.5	0	0	0.0	0
2001—New York Jets NFL	16	0	7	4	0.0	0	0	0.0	0
2002—New York Jets NFL	16	0	28	9	1.0	2	38	19.0	0
Pro totals (6 years)	91	24	116	48	3.5	3	71	23.7	0

DAVENPORT, JOE DEAN — TE — COLTS

PERSONAL: Born October 29, 1976, in Springdale, Ark. ... 6-6/268. ... Full name: Joe Dean Davenport.
HIGH SCHOOL: Springdale (Ark.).
COLLEGE: Arkansas.
TRANSACTIONS/CAREER NOTES: Signed as non-drafted free agent by Indianapolis Colts (May 9, 2001).
SINGLE GAME HIGHS (regular season): Receptions—3 (November 24, 2002, vs. Denver); yards—22 (December 15, 2002, vs. Cleveland); and touchdown receptions—0.

Year Team	G	GS	No.	RECEIVING Yds.	Avg.	TD
2001—Indianapolis NFL	3	0	0	0	0.0	0
2002—Indianapolis NFL	10	7	8	70	8.8	0
Pro totals (2 years)	13	7	8	70	8.8	0

DAVENPORT, NAJEH — FB — PACKERS

PERSONAL: Born February 8, 1979, in Miami. ... 6-1/247. ... Full name: Najeh Trenadious Monte Davenport.
HIGH SCHOOL: Miami Central (Fla.).
COLLEGE: Miami (Fla.).
TRANSACTIONS/CAREER NOTES: Selected by Green Bay Packers in fourth round (135th pick overall) of 2002 NFL draft. ... Signed by Packers (July 26, 2002). ... On injured reserve with eye injury (November 20, 2002-remainder of season).
SINGLE GAME HIGHS (regular season): Attempts—22 (September 22, 2002, vs. Detroit); yards—84 (September 22, 2002, vs. Detroit); and rushing touchdowns—1 (November 10, 2002, vs. Detroit).

Year Team	G	GS	RUSHING Att.	Yds.	Avg.	TD	RECEIVING No.	Yds.	Avg.	TD	KICKOFF RETURNS No.	Yds.	Avg.	TD	TOTALS TD	2pt.	Pts.	Fum.
2002—Green Bay NFL	8	0	39	184	4.7	1	5	33	6.6	0	6	130	21.7	0	1	0	6	1

DAVEY, ROHAN   QB   PATRIOTS

PERSONAL: Born April 14, 1978, in Claredon, Jamaica. ... 6-2/245. ... Full name: Rohan St. Patrick Davey.
HIGH SCHOOL: Miami Lakes (Fla.).
COLLEGE: Louisiana State.
TRANSACTIONS/CAREER NOTES: Selected by New England Patriots in fourth round (117th pick overall) of 2002 NFL draft. ... Signed by Patriots (July 21, 2002).
SINGLE GAME HIGHS (regular season): Attempts—2 (December 16, 2002, vs. Tennessee); completions—1 (December 16, 2002, vs. Tennessee); yards—3 (December 16, 2002, vs. Tennessee); and touchdown passes—0.

| | | | PASSING | | | | | | | | RUSHING | | | | TOTALS | | |
Year Team	G	GS	Att.	Cmp.	Pct.	Yds.	TD	Int.	Avg.	Skd.	Rat.	Att.	Yds.	Avg.	TD	TD	2pt.	Pts.
2002—New England NFL	2	0	2	1	50.0	3	0	0	1.50	0	56.3	2	-4	-2.0	0	0	0	0

DAVIS, ANDRA   LB   BROWNS

PERSONAL: Born December 23, 1978, in Live Oak, Fla. ... 6-1/244. ... Full name: Andra Raynard Davis.
HIGH SCHOOL: Suwanee (Live Oak, Fla.).
COLLEGE: Florida.
TRANSACTIONS/CAREER NOTES: Selected by Cleveland Browns in fifth round (141st pick overall) of 2002 NFL draft. ... Signed by Browns (July 18, 2002).
HONORS: Named linebacker on THE SPORTING NEWS college All-America second team (2001).

| | | | TOTALS | | | INTERCEPTIONS | | | |
Year Team	G	GS	Tk.	Ast.	Sks.	No.	Yds.	Avg.	TD
2002—Cleveland NFL	16	0	1	4	0.0	1	0	0.0	0

DAVIS, ANDRE'   WR   BROWNS

PERSONAL: Born June 12, 1979, in Niskayuna, N.Y. ... 6-1/194. ... Full name: Andre' N. Davis.
HIGH SCHOOL: Niskayuna (N.Y.).
COLLEGE: Virginia Tech.
TRANSACTIONS/CAREER NOTES: Selected by Cleveland Browns in second round (47th pick overall) of 2002 NFL draft. ... Signed by Browns (July 22, 2002).
SINGLE GAME HIGHS (regular season): Receptions—5 (October 6, 2002, vs. Baltimore); yards—99 (September 22, 2002, vs. Tennessee); and touchdown receptions—2 (September 22, 2002, vs. Tennessee).

| | | | RUSHING | | | | RECEIVING | | | | PUNT RETURNS | | | | KICKOFF RETURNS | | | | TOTALS | | |
Year Team	G	GS	Att.	Yds.	Avg.	TD	No.	Yds.	Avg.	TD	No.	Yds.	Avg.	TD	No.	Yds.	Avg.	TD	TD	2pt.	Pts.
2002—Cleveland NFL	16	4	3	7	2.3	0	37	420	11.4	6	7	33	4.7	0	50	1068	21.4	1	7	0	42

DAVIS, DON   LB   PATRIOTS

PERSONAL: Born December 17, 1972, in Olathe, Kan. ... 6-1/234.
HIGH SCHOOL: Olathe (Kan.) South.
COLLEGE: Kansas.
TRANSACTIONS/CAREER NOTES: Signed as non-drafted free agent by New York Jets (April 28, 1995). ... Released by Jets (August 27, 1995). ... Signed by Kansas City Chiefs (January 9, 1996). ... Released by Chiefs (August 20, 1996). ... Signed by New Orleans Saints to practice squad (August 27, 1996). ... Activated (October 4, 1996). ... On injured reserve with wrist injury (November 19, 1997-remainder of season). ... Claimed on waivers by Tampa Bay Buccaneers (November 25, 1998). ... Granted free agency (February 12, 1999). ... Re-signed by Buccaneers (May 21, 1999). ... Released by Buccaneers (October 9, 1999). ... Re-signed by Buccaneers (October 19, 1999). ... Granted unconditional free agency (February 11, 2000). ... Re-signed by Buccaneers (July 1, 2000). ... Granted unconditional free agency (March 2, 2001). ... Signed by St. Louis Rams (March 3, 2001). ... Granted unconditional free agency (February 28, 2003). ... Signed by New England Patriots (May 16, 2003).
CHAMPIONSHIP GAME EXPERIENCE: Played in NFC championship game (1999 and 2001 seasons). ... Played in Super Bowl XXXVI (2001 season).

| | | | TOTALS | | | INTERCEPTIONS | | | |
Year Team	G	GS	Tk.	Ast.	Sks.	No.	Yds.	Avg.	TD
1996—New Orleans NFL	11	0	0	0	0.0	0	0	0.0	0
1997—New Orleans NFL	11	0	0	0	0.0	0	0	0.0	0
1998—New Orleans NFL	4	0	2	2	0.0	0	0	0.0	0
—Tampa Bay NFL	5	0	0	0	0.0	0	0	0.0	0
1999—Tampa Bay NFL	14	0	0	1	0.0	0	0	0.0	0
2000—Tampa Bay NFL	16	0	2	5	0.0	0	0	0.0	0
2001—St. Louis NFL	12	8	16	9	0.0	0	0	0.0	0
2002—St. Louis NFL	16	7	33	6	0.0	1	29	29.0	0
Pro totals (7 years)	89	15	53	23	0.0	1	29	29.0	0

DAVIS, ERIC   CB

PERSONAL: Born January 26, 1968, in Anniston, Ala. ... 5-11/185. ... Full name: Eric Wayne Davis.
HIGH SCHOOL: Anniston (Ala.).
COLLEGE: Jacksonville (Ala.) State.
TRANSACTIONS/CAREER NOTES: Selected by San Francisco 49ers in second round (53rd pick overall) of 1990 NFL draft. ... Signed by 49ers (July 28, 1990). ... On injured reserve with shoulder injury (September 11, 1991-remainder of season). ... Granted free agency (March 1, 1993). ... Re-signed by 49ers (July 20, 1993). ... Granted unconditional free agency (February 16, 1996). ... Signed by Carolina Panthers

(February 21, 1996). ... Released by Panthers (February 28, 2001). ... Signed by Denver Broncos (August 2, 2001). ... Granted unconditional free agency (March 1, 2002). ... Signed by Detroit Lions (June 30, 2002). ... Granted unconditional free agency (February 28, 2003).

CHAMPIONSHIP GAME EXPERIENCE: Played in NFC championship game (1990, 1992-1994 and 1996 seasons). ... Member of Super Bowl championship team (1994 season).

HONORS: Played in Pro Bowl (1995 and 1996 seasons).

MISCELLANEOUS: Holds Carolina Panthers all-time record for most interceptions (25).

				TOTALS			INTERCEPTIONS		
Year Team	G	GS	Tk.	Ast.	Sks.	No.	Yds.	Avg.	TD
1990—San Francisco NFL	16	0	20	1	0.0	1	13	13.0	0
1991—San Francisco NFL	2	2	9	1	0.0	0	0	0.0	0
1992—San Francisco NFL	16	16	58	3	0.0	3	52	17.3	0
1993—San Francisco NFL	16	16	63	6	0.0	4	45	11.3	1
1994—San Francisco NFL	16	16	68	6	0.0	1	8	8.0	0
1995—San Francisco NFL	15	15	43	8	1.0	3	84	28.0	1
1996—Carolina NFL	16	16	56	4	0.0	5	57	11.4	0
1997—Carolina NFL	14	14	35	6	0.0	5	25	5.0	0
1998—Carolina NFL	16	16	64	7	1.0	5	81	16.2	2
1999—Carolina NFL	16	16	59	17	0.0	5	49	9.8	0
2000—Carolina NFL	16	16	61	12	0.0	5	14	2.8	0
2001—Denver NFL	16	0	13	0	0.0	0	0	0.0	0
2002—Detroit NFL	13	8	31	6	0.0	1	14	14.0	0
Pro totals (13 years)	188	151	580	77	2.0	38	442	11.6	4

DAVIS, JEROME   DE   49ERS

PERSONAL: Born April 4, 1974, in Detroit. ... 6-5/290.

HIGH SCHOOL: Chadsey (Detroit).

COLLEGE: Minnesota.

TRANSACTIONS/CAREER NOTES: Signed as non-drafted free agent by Detroit Lions (April 24, 1997). ... Released by Lions (August 19, 1997). ... Re-signed by Lions to practice squad (December 23, 1997). ... Assigned by Lions to Frankfurt Galaxy in 1998 NFL Europe enhancement allocation program (February 18, 1998). ... On injured reserve list with leg injury (August 17, 1998-entire season). ... Released by Lions (February 12, 1999). ... Signed by Carolina Panthers (August 2, 1999). ... Released by Panthers (August 30, 1999). ... Signed by Denver Broncos (February 16, 2000). ... Released by Broncos (August 21, 2000). ... Signed by Calgary Stampeders of CFL (October 2000). ... Released by Stampeders (June 27, 2001). ... Signed by San Francisco 49ers (August 7, 2001). ... Released by 49ers (September 3, 2001). ... Re-signed by 49ers (January 23, 2002). ... Assigned by 49ers to Frankfurt Galaxy in 2002 NFL Europe enhancement allocation program (February 12, 2002). ... Released by 49ers (September 7, 2002). ... Re-signed by 49ers to practice squad (September 9, 2002). ... Activated (December 30, 2002).

			TOTALS		
Year Team	G	GS	Tk.	Ast.	Sks.
1998—Frankfurt NFLE	10	10	...	...	2.0
—Detroit NFL			Did not play.		
2000—Calgary CFL	2	0	...	...	0.0
2002—Frankfurt NFLE	...	...	...	...	5.5
—San Francisco NFL	2	0	0	0	0.0
NFL Europe totals (2 years)	...	...	...	...	7.5
CFL totals (1 year)	2	0	...	...	0.0
NFL totals (1 year)	2	0	0	0	0.0
Pro totals (4 years)	...	...	...	...	7.5

DAVIS, JOHN   TE   BEARS

PERSONAL: Born May 14, 1973, in Jasper, Texas. ... 6-4/264.

HIGH SCHOOL: Jasper (Texas).

JUNIOR COLLEGE: Cisco (Texas) Junior College.

COLLEGE: Emporia (Kan.) State.

TRANSACTIONS/CAREER NOTES: Selected by Dallas Cowboys in fifth round of 1994 supplemental draft. ... Signed by Cowboys for 1994 season. ... Released by Cowboys (August 28, 1994). ... Re-signed by Cowboys to practice squad (August 30, 1994). ... On injured reserve with ankle injury (prior to 1995 season-October 31, 1995). ... Released by Cowboys (October 31, 1995). ... Signed by New Orleans Saints (June 3, 1996). ... Released by Saints (August 12, 1996). ... Signed by Tampa Bay Buccaneers (January 20, 1997). ... Granted free agency (February 12, 1999). ... Re-signed by Buccaneers (April 18, 1999). ... Granted unconditional free agency (February 11, 2000). ... Signed by Minnesota Vikings (May 31, 2000). ... Released by Vikings (August 8, 2001). ... Signed by Chicago Bears (August 14, 2001). ... Granted unconditional free agency (February 28, 2003). ... Re-signed by Bears (March 1, 2003).

CHAMPIONSHIP GAME EXPERIENCE: Played in NFC championship game (1999 and 2000 seasons).

SINGLE GAME HIGHS (regular season): Receptions—4 (November 18, 2002, vs. St. Louis); yards—42 (September 10, 2000, vs. Miami); and touchdown receptions—2 (October 7, 2002, vs. Green Bay).

			RECEIVING				TOTALS			
Year Team	G	GS	No.	Yds.	Avg.	TD	TD	2pt.	Pts.	Fum.
1997—Tampa Bay NFL	8	2	3	35	11.7	0	0	0	0	0
1998—Tampa Bay NFL	16	0	2	12	6.0	1	1	0	6	0
1999—Tampa Bay NFL	16	0	2	7	3.5	1	1	0	6	0
2000—Minnesota NFL	15	9	17	202	11.9	1	1	0	6	0
2001—Chicago NFL	16	6	11	68	6.2	0	0	0	0	0
2002—Chicago NFL	10	8	20	193	9.7	3	3	0	18	0
Pro totals (6 years)	81	25	55	517	9.4	6	6	0	36	0

DAVIS, KEITH   S   COWBOYS

PERSONAL: Born December 30, 1978, in Italy, Texas. ... 5-10/193.
HIGH SCHOOL: Italy (Texas).
COLLEGE: Sam Houston State.
TRANSACTIONS/CAREER NOTES: Signed as non-drafted free agent by Dallas Cowboys (April 26, 2002). ... Released by Cowboys (August 31, 2002). ... Re-signed by Cowboys to practice squad (September 3, 2002). ... Released by Cowboys (September 10, 2002). ... Re-signed by Cowboys to practice squad (September 16, 2002). ... Activated (October 12, 2002). ... Released by Cowboys (October 21, 2002). ... Re-signed by Cowboys to practice squad (October 23, 2002). ... Activated (November 21, 2002). ... Re-signed by Cowboys (March 7, 2003).

			TOTALS			INTERCEPTIONS			
Year Team	G	GS	Tk.	Ast.	Sks.	No.	Yds.	Avg.	TD
2002—Dallas NFL	8	0	2	0	0.0	0	0	0.0	0

DAVIS, LEONARD   OT   CARDINALS

PERSONAL: Born September 5, 1978, in Wortham, Texas. ... 6-6/372. ... Full name: Leonard Barnett Davis.
HIGH SCHOOL: Wortham (Texas).
COLLEGE: Texas.
TRANSACTIONS/CAREER NOTES: Selected by Arizona Cardinals in first round (second pick overall) of 2001 NFL draft. ... Signed by Cardinals (August 8, 2001). ... On injured reserve with knee injury (December 24, 2002-remainder of season).
PLAYING EXPERIENCE: Arizona NFL, 2001-2002. ... Games/Games started: 2001 (16/16), 2002 (15/15). Total: 31/31.
HONORS: Named offensive tackle on THE SPORTING NEWS college All-America first team (2000).

DAVIS, NICK   WR   VIKINGS

PERSONAL: Born October 6, 1979, in Manchester, Mich. ... 6-0/180.
HIGH SCHOOL: Manchester (Mich.).
COLLEGE: Wisconsin.
TRANSACTIONS/CAREER NOTES: Signed as non-drafted free agent by Minnesota Vikings (April 25, 2002).

			PUNT RETURNS				KICKOFF RETURNS				TOTALS			
Year Team	G	GS	No.	Yds.	Avg.	TD	No.	Yds.	Avg.	TD	TD	2pt.	Pts.	Fum.
2002—Minnesota NFL	15	0	24	190	7.9	0	18	368	20.4	0	0	0	0	4

D

DAVIS, ROB   C   PACKERS

PERSONAL: Born December 10, 1968, in Washington, D.C. ... 6-3/284. ... Full name: Robert Emmett Davis.
HIGH SCHOOL: Eleanor Roosevelt (Greenbelt, Md.).
COLLEGE: Shippensburg, Pa. (degree in criminal justice/law enforcement).
TRANSACTIONS/CAREER NOTES: Signed as non-drafted free agent by New York Jets (April 27, 1993). ... Released by Jets (August 24, 1993). ... Re-signed by Jets (April 29, 1994). ... Released by Jets (August 22, 1994). ... Signed by Baltimore Stallions of CFL (April 1995). ... Signed by Kansas City Chiefs (April 22, 1996). ... Released by Chiefs (August 20, 1996). ... Signed by Chicago Bears (August 28, 1996). ... Released by Bears (August 27, 1997). ... Signed by Green Bay Packers (November 4, 1997). ... On physically unable to perform list with back injury (July 18-August 10, 1998). ... Granted unconditional free agency (March 2, 2001). ... Re-signed by Packers (March 20, 2001).
PLAYING EXPERIENCE: Baltimore CFL, 1995; Chicago NFL, 1996; Green Bay NFL, 1997-2002. ... Games/Games started: 1995 (18/games started unavailable), 1996 (16/0), 1997 (7/0), 1998 (16/0), 1999 (16/0), 2000 (16/0), 2001 (16/0), 2002 (16/0). Total CFL: 18/-. Total NFL:103/0. Total Pro: 121/-.
CHAMPIONSHIP GAME EXPERIENCE: Played in NFC championship game (1997 season). ... Played in Super Bowl XXXII (1997 season).

DAVIS, RUSSELL   DT   CARDINALS

PERSONAL: Born March 28, 1975, in Fayetteville, N.C. ... 6-4/316. ... Full name: Russell Morgan Davis.
HIGH SCHOOL: E.E. Smith (Fayetteville, N.C.).
COLLEGE: North Carolina.
TRANSACTIONS/CAREER NOTES: Selected by Chicago Bears in second round (48th pick overall) of 1999 NFL draft. ... Signed by Bears (July 22, 1999). ... Claimed on waivers by Arizona Cardinals (August 28, 2000). ... Granted unconditional free agency (February 28, 2003). ... Re-signed by Cardinals (March 16, 2003).

			TOTALS		
Year Team	G	GS	Tk.	Ast.	Sks.
1999—Chicago NFL	11	8	13	4	2.0
2000—Arizona NFL	13	9	29	9	0.5
2001—Arizona NFL	16	16	37	17	2.0
2002—Arizona NFL	16	16	35	9	2.0
Pro totals (4 years)	56	49	114	39	6.5

DAVIS, STEPHEN   RB   PANTHERS

PERSONAL: Born March 1, 1974, in Spartanburg, S.C. ... 6-0/230.
HIGH SCHOOL: Spartanburg (S.C.).
COLLEGE: Auburn (degree in vocational education, 1995).

TRANSACTIONS/CAREER NOTES: Selected by Washington Redskins in fourth round (102nd pick overall) of 1996 NFL draft. ... Signed by Redskins (July 16, 1996). ... Granted free agency (February 12, 1999). ... Re-signed by Redskins (May 12, 1999). ... Designated by Redskins as franchise player (February 11, 2000). ... Released by Redskins (February 26, 2003). ... Signed by Carolina Panthers (March 14, 2003).
HONORS: Played in Pro Bowl (1999 and 2000 seasons).
SINGLE GAME HIGHS (regular season): Attempts—38 (January 6, 2002, vs. Arizona); yards—189 (December 12, 1999, vs. Arizona); and rushing touchdowns—3 (November 24, 2002, vs. St. Louis).
STATISTICAL PLATEAUS: 100-yard rushing games: 1999 (6), 2000 (5), 2001 (6), 2002 (1). Total: 18. ... 100-yard receiving games: 1998 (1).

Year Team	G	GS	RUSHING Att.	Yds.	Avg.	TD	RECEIVING No.	Yds.	Avg.	TD	TOTALS TD	2pt.	Pts.	Fum.
1996—Washington NFL	12	0	23	139	6.0	2	0	0	0.0	0	2	0	12	0
1997—Washington NFL	14	6	141	567	4.0	3	18	134	7.4	0	3	0	18	1
1998—Washington NFL	16	12	34	109	3.2	0	21	263	12.5	2	2	0	12	0
1999—Washington NFL	14	14	290	‡1405	4.8	*17	23	111	4.8	0	†17	†1	104	4
2000—Washington NFL	15	15	332	1318	4.0	11	33	313	9.5	0	11	0	66	4
2001—Washington NFL	16	16	*356	‡1432	4.0	5	28	205	7.3	0	5	1	32	6
2002—Washington NFL	12	12	207	820	4.0	7	23	142	6.2	1	8	0	48	4
Pro totals (7 years)	99	75	1383	5790	4.2	45	146	1168	8.0	3	48	2	292	19

DAVIS, TYRONE   TE   PACKERS

PERSONAL: Born June 30, 1972, in Halifax, Va. ... 6-4/260.
HIGH SCHOOL: Halifax County (South Boston, Va.), then Fork Union (Va.) Military Academy.
COLLEGE: Virginia.
TRANSACTIONS/CAREER NOTES: Selected by New York Jets in fourth round (107th pick overall) of 1995 NFL draft. ... Signed by Jets (June 14, 1995). ... Released by Jets (September 13, 1995). ... Re-signed by Jets to practice squad (September 15, 1995). ... Activated (December 11, 1995). ... Granted free agency (February 14, 1997). ... Re-signed by Jets for 1997 season. ... Traded by Jets to Green Bay Packers for past considerations (August 25, 1997). ... Released by Packers (September 24, 1997). ... Re-signed by Packers (September 29, 1997). ... Granted unconditional free agency (March 2, 2001). ... Re-signed by Packers (March 21, 2001). ... On physically unable to perform list with hamstring injury (August 28-November 27, 2001). ... Granted unconditional free agency (March 1, 2002). ... Re-signed by Packers (April 23, 2002). ... Granted unconditional free agency (February 28, 2003). ... Re-signed by Packers (April 30, 2003).
CHAMPIONSHIP GAME EXPERIENCE: Played in NFC championship game (1997 season). ... Played in Super Bowl XXXII (1997 season).
SINGLE GAME HIGHS (regular season): Receptions—5 (September 17, 2000, vs. Philadelphia); yards—83 (November 15, 1998, vs. New York Giants); and touchdown receptions—2 (November 22, 1998, vs. Minnesota).

Year Team	G	GS	RECEIVING No.	Yds.	Avg.	TD	TOTALS TD	2pt.	Pts.	Fum.
1995—New York Jets NFL	4	0	1	9	9.0	0	0	0	0	0
1996—New York Jets NFL	2	0	1	6	6.0	0	0	0	0	0
1997—Green Bay NFL	13	0	2	28	14.0	1	2	0	12	0
1998—Green Bay NFL	13	1	18	250	13.9	7	7	0	42	1
1999—Green Bay NFL	16	13	20	204	10.2	2	2	0	12	0
2000—Green Bay NFL	14	9	19	177	9.3	2	2	1	14	2
2001—Green Bay NFL	4	2	3	14	4.7	0	0	0	0	0
2002—Green Bay NFL	9	2	9	107	11.9	1	1	0	6	0
Pro totals (8 years)	75	27	73	795	10.9	13	14	1	86	3

DAVISON, ANDREW   CB   JETS

PERSONAL: Born December 9, 1979, in Detroit. ... 5-11/185.
HIGH SCHOOL: Chadsey (Detroit).
COLLEGE: Kansas.
TRANSACTIONS/CAREER NOTES: Signed as non-drafted free agent by New York Jets (April 26, 2002).

Year Team	G	GS	TOTALS Tk.	Ast.	Sks.	INTERCEPTIONS No.	Yds.	Avg.	TD
2002—New York Jets NFL	6	0	1	0	0.0	0	0	0.0	0

DAWKINS, BRIAN   S   EAGLES

PERSONAL: Born October 13, 1973, in Jacksonville. ... 5-11/200.
HIGH SCHOOL: Raines (Jacksonville).
COLLEGE: Clemson (degree in education, 1995).
TRANSACTIONS/CAREER NOTES: Selected by Philadelphia Eagles in second round (61st pick overall) of 1996 NFL draft. ... Signed by Eagles (July 17, 1996).
CHAMPIONSHIP GAME EXPERIENCE: Played in NFC championship game (2001 and 2002 seasons).
HONORS: Named defensive back on The Sporting News college All-America second team (1995). ... Played in Pro Bowl (1999, 2001 and 2002 seasons). ... Named safety on The Sporting News NFL All-Pro team (2001 and 2002).

Year Team	G	GS	TOTALS Tk.	Ast.	Sks.	INTERCEPTIONS No.	Yds.	Avg.	TD
1996—Philadelphia NFL	14	13	53	21	1.0	3	41	13.7	0
1997—Philadelphia NFL	15	15	61	13	0.0	3	76	25.3	1
1998—Philadelphia NFL	14	14	45	11	1.0	2	39	19.5	0
1999—Philadelphia NFL	16	16	58	20	1.5	4	127	31.8	1
2000—Philadelphia NFL	13	13	54	17	2.0	4	62	15.5	0
2001—Philadelphia NFL	15	15	58	12	1.5	2	15	7.5	0
2002—Philadelphia NFL	16	16	66	29	3.0	2	27	13.5	0
Pro totals (7 years)	103	102	395	123	10.0	20	387	19.4	2

DAWSON, JAJUAN   WR   TEXANS

PERSONAL: Born November 5, 1977, in Houston. ... 6-1/197. ... Full name: JaJuan LaTroy Dawson.
HIGH SCHOOL: H.L. Bourgeois (Gibson, La.).
COLLEGE: Tulane.
TRANSACTIONS/CAREER NOTES: Selected by Cleveland Browns in third round (79th pick overall) of 2000 NFL draft. ... Signed by Browns (June 3, 2000). ... On injured reserve with clavicle injury (September 20, 2000-remainder of season). ... Released by Browns (September 1, 2002). ... Signed by Houston Texans (September 10, 2002). ... Granted free agency (February 28, 2003). ... Re-signed by Texans (March 25, 2003).
SINGLE GAME HIGHS (regular season): Receptions—6 (September 3, 2000, vs. Jacksonville); yards—83 (September 3, 2000, vs. Jacksonville); and touchdown receptions—1 (December 30, 2001, vs. Tennessee).

				RECEIVING		
Year Team	G	GS	No.	Yds.	Avg.	TD
2000—Cleveland NFL	2	2	9	97	10.8	1
2001—Cleveland NFL	14	0	22	281	12.8	1
2002—Houston NFL	14	2	21	286	13.6	0
Pro totals (3 years)	30	4	52	664	12.8	2

DAWSON, PHIL   K   BROWNS

PERSONAL: Born January 23, 1975, in West Palm Beach, Fla. ... 5-11/190.
HIGH SCHOOL: Lake Highlands (Dallas).
COLLEGE: Texas.
TRANSACTIONS/CAREER NOTES: Signed as non-drafted free agent by Oakland Raiders (April 24, 1998). ... Claimed on waivers by New England Patriots (August 21, 1998). ... Released by Patriots (August 30, 1998). ... Re-signed by Patriots to practice squad (August 31, 1998). ... Granted free agency after 1998 season. ... Signed by Cleveland Browns (March 25, 1999). ... Granted free agency (March 1, 2002). ... Re-signed by Browns (April 26, 2002).

		FIELD GOALS							TOTALS		
Year Team	G	1-29	30-39	40-49	50+	Tot.	Pct.	Lg.	XPM	XPA	Pts.
1999—Cleveland NFL	15	2-2	3-5	3-5	0-0	8-12	66.7	49	23	24	53
2000—Cleveland NFL	16	7-7	5-5	2-5	0-0	14-17	82.4	45	17	17	59
2001—Cleveland NFL	16	10-10	8-9	4-6	0-0	22-25	88.0	48	29	30	95
2002—Cleveland NFL	16	9-10	6-8	5-7	2-3	22-28	78.6	52	34	35	100
Pro totals (4 years)	63	28-29	22-27	14-23	2-3	66-82	80.5	52	103	106	307

DAYNE, RON   RB   GIANTS

PERSONAL: Born March 14, 1978, in Berlin, N.J. ... 5-10/250.
HIGH SCHOOL: Overbrook (Berlin, N.J.).
COLLEGE: Wisconsin.
TRANSACTIONS/CAREER NOTES: Selected by New York Giants in first round (11th pick overall) of 2000 NFL draft. ... Signed by Giants (July 21, 2000).
CHAMPIONSHIP GAME EXPERIENCE: Played in NFC championship game (2000 season). ... Played in Super Bowl XXXV (2000 season).
HONORS: Heisman Trophy winner (1999). ... Doak Walker Award winner (1999). ... Maxwell Award winner (1999). ... Named running back on THE SPORTING NEWS college All-America first team (1999). ... Named College Football Player of the Year by THE SPORTING NEWS (1999).
SINGLE GAME HIGHS (regular season): Attempts—25 (October 29, 2000, vs. Philadelphia); yards—111 (September 30, 2001, vs. New Orleans); and rushing touchdowns—2 (December 15, 2002, vs. Dallas).
STATISTICAL PLATEAUS: 100-yard rushing games: 2000 (1), 2001 (1). Total: 2.

			RUSHING				RECEIVING				TOTALS			
Year Team	G	GS	Att.	Yds.	Avg.	TD	No.	Yds.	Avg.	TD	TD	2pt.	Pts.	Fum.
2000—New York Giants NFL	16	4	228	770	3.4	5	3	11	3.7	0	5	0	30	1
2001—New York Giants NFL	16	7	180	690	3.8	7	8	67	8.4	0	7	1	44	2
2002—New York Giants NFL	16	1	125	428	3.4	3	11	49	4.5	0	3	0	18	1
Pro totals (3 years)	48	12	533	1888	3.5	15	22	127	5.8	0	15	1	92	4

DEARTH, JAMES   TE   JETS

PERSONAL: Born January 22, 1976, in Scurry, Texas. ... 6-4/270.
HIGH SCHOOL: Scurry (Texas)-Rosser.
COLLEGE: Tulsa, then Tarleton State (Texas).
TRANSACTIONS/CAREER NOTES: Selected by Cleveland Browns in sixth round (191st pick overall) of 1999 NFL draft. ... Signed by Browns (July 22, 1999). ... Released by Browns (September 3, 1999). ... Re-signed by Browns to practice squad (November 23, 1999). ... Activated (December 14, 1999). ... Assigned by Browns to Scottish Claymores in 2000 NFL Europe enhancement allocation program (February 11, 2000). ... Released by Browns (April 18, 2000). ... Signed by Titans (July 14, 2000). ... Released by Titans (August 22, 2000). ... Re-signed by Titans to practice squad (November 8, 2000). ... Granted free agency following 2000 season. ... Signed by New York Jets (January 24, 2001).
SINGLE GAME HIGHS (regular season): Receptions—1 (December 16, 2001, vs. Cincinnati); yards—9 (November 11, 2001, vs. Kansas City); and touchdown receptions—1 (December 16, 2001, vs. Cincinnati).

				RECEIVING		
Year Team	G	GS	No.	Yds.	Avg.	TD
1999—Cleveland NFL	2	0	0	0	0.0	0
2001—New York Jets NFL	16	0	3	10	3.3	1
2002—New York Jets NFL	16	0	0	0	0.0	0
Pro totals (3 years)	34	0	3	10	3.3	1

DEESE, DERRICK OT 49ERS

PERSONAL: Born May 17, 1970, in Culver City, Calif. ... 6-3/289.
HIGH SCHOOL: Culver City (Calif.).
JUNIOR COLLEGE: El Camino Junior College (Calif.).
COLLEGE: Southern California.
TRANSACTIONS/CAREER NOTES: Signed as non-drafted free agent by San Francisco 49ers (May 8, 1992). ... On injured reserve with elbow injury (August 4, 1992-entire season). ... Inactive for six games (1993). ... On injured reserve with broken wrist (October 23, 1993-remainder of season). ... Granted free agency (February 17, 1995). ... Tendered offer sheet by St. Louis Rams (April 20, 1995). ... Offer matched by 49ers (April 21, 1995). ... Granted unconditional free agency (February 16, 1996). ... Re-signed by 49ers (June 4, 1996). ... Granted unconditional free agency (February 14, 1997). ... Re-signed by 49ers (April 22, 1997).
PLAYING EXPERIENCE: San Francisco NFL, 1994-2002. ... Games/Games started: 1994 (16/15), 1995 (2/2), 1996 (16/0), 1997 (16/13), 1998 (16/16), 1999 (16/16), 2000 (13/13), 2001 (16/16), 2002 (14/14). Total: 125/105.
CHAMPIONSHIP GAME EXPERIENCE: Played in NFC championship game (1994 and 1997 seasons). ... Member of Super Bowl championship team (1994 season).

DELHOMME, JAKE QB PANTHERS

PERSONAL: Born January 10, 1975, in Lafayette, La. ... 6-2/205.
HIGH SCHOOL: Teurlings (La.).
COLLEGE: Southwestern Louisiana.
TRANSACTIONS/CAREER NOTES: Signed as non-drafted free agent by New Orleans Saints (June 10, 1997). ... Released by Saints (August 18, 1997). ... Re-signed by Saints to practice sqaud (November 19, 1997). ... Assigned by Saints to Amsterdam Admirals in 1998 NFL Europe enhancement allocation program (February 18, 1998). ... Inactive for five games (1998). ... Released by Saints (October 14, 1998). ... Re-signed by Saints to practice squad (October 15, 1998). ... Assigned by Saints to Frankfurt Galaxy in 1999 NFL Europe enhancement allocation program (February 22, 1999). ... Released by Saints (September 5, 1999). ... Re-signed by Saints (November 23, 1999). ... Granted free agency (March 1, 2002). ... Re-signed by Saints (April 19, 2002). ... Granted unconditional free agency (February 28, 2003). ... Signed by Carolina Panthers (March 5, 2003).
SINGLE GAME HIGHS (regular season): Attempts—49 (January 2, 2000, vs. Carolina); completions—26 (January 2, 2000, vs. Carolina); passing yards—278 (December 24, 1999, vs. Dallas); and touchdown passes—2 (December 24, 1999, vs. Dallas).
MISCELLANEOUS: Regular-season record as starting NFL quarterback: 1-1 (.500).

Year Team	G	GS	PASSING Att.	Cmp.	Pct.	Yds.	TD	Int.	Avg.	Skd.	Rat.	RUSHING Att.	Yds.	Avg.	TD	TOTALS TD	2pt.	Pts.
1998—Amsterdam NFLE	...	...	47	15	31.9	247	0	4	5.26	0	15.1	2	20	10.0	0	0	0	0
1999—Frankfurt NFLE	...	...	202	136	67.3	1410	12	5	6.98	0	96.8	21	126	6.0	0	0	0	0
—New Orleans NFL	2	2	76	42	55.3	521	3	5	6.86	6	62.4	11	72	6.5	2	2	0	12
2000—New Orleans NFL	...	...							Did not play.									
2002—New Orleans NFL	4	0	10	8	80.0	113	0	0	11.30	0	113.8	4	-2	-0.5	0	0	0	0
NFL Europe totals (2 years)	...	...	249	151	60.6	1657	12	9	6.65	0	81.4	23	146	6.3	0	0	0	0
NFL totals (2 years)	6	2	86	50	58.1	634	3	5	7.37	6	68.7	15	70	4.7	2	2	0	12
Pro totals (4 years)	...	...	335	201	60.0	2291	15	14	6.84	6	78.1	38	216	5.7	2	2	0	12

DELOACH, JERRY DT TEXANS

PERSONAL: Born July 17, 1977, in Sacramento, Calif. ... 6-2/315.
HIGH SCHOOL: Valley (Calif.).
COLLEGE: California.
TRANSACTIONS/CAREER NOTES: Singed as non-drafted free agent by Washington Redskins (April 28, 2000). ... Traded by Redskins to Houston Texans for QB Danny Wuerffel (March 4, 2002). ... Re-signed by Texans (March 21, 2003).

Year Team	G	GS	TOTALS Tk.	Ast.	Sks.
2001—Washington NFL	15	4	9	2	1.0
2002—Houston NFL	16	16	24	8	1.0
Pro totals (2 years)	31	20	33	10	2.0

DEMAREE, CHRIS DE BEARS

PERSONAL: Born March 12, 1980, in Louisville, Ky. ... 6-3/260.
HIGH SCHOOL: Male (Louisville, Ky.).
COLLEGE: Kentucky.
TRANSACTIONS/CAREER NOTES: Signed as non-drafted free agent by San Diego Chargers (April 26, 2002). ... Released by Chargers (November 20, 2002). ... Signed by Chicago Bears to practice squad (November 26, 2002).

Year Team	G	GS	TOTALS Tk.	Ast.	Sks.
2002—San Diego NFL	2	0	0	0	0.0

DEMPS, WILL S RAVENS

PERSONAL: Born November 7, 1979, in Charleston, S.C. ... 5-11/205. ... Full name: Will Henry Demps.
HIGH SCHOOL: Highlands (Palmdale, Calif.).
COLLEGE: San Diego State.
TRANSACTIONS/CAREER NOTES: Signed as non-drafted free agent by Baltimore Ravens (April 26, 2002).

Year Team	G	GS	TOTALS Tk.	Ast.	Sks.	INTERCEPTIONS No.	Yds.	Avg.	TD
2002—Baltimore NFL	14	10	43	6	1.0	1	18	18.0	0

DEMULLING, RICK   G   COLTS

PERSONAL: Born July 21, 1977, in Cheney, Wash. ... 6-4/304. ... Full name: Rick Elwood DeMulling.
HIGH SCHOOL: Cheney (Wash.).
COLLEGE: Idaho.
TRANSACTIONS/CAREER NOTES: Selected by Indianapolis Colts in seventh round (220th pick overall) of 2001 NFL draft. ... Signed by Colts (June 19, 2001).
PLAYING EXPERIENCE: Indianapolis NFL, 2001-2002. ... Games/Games started: 2001 (7/0), 2002 (14/14). Total: 21/14.

DENMAN, ANTHONY   LB   BILLS

PERSONAL: Born October 30, 1979, in Lufkin, Texas. ... 5-11/235. ... Full name: Anthony Ray Denman.
HIGH SCHOOL: Rusk (Texas).
COLLEGE: Notre Dame.
TRANSACTIONS/CAREER NOTES: Selected by Jacksonville Jaguars in seventh round (213th pick overall) of 2001 NFL draft. ... Signed by Jaguars (June 26, 2001). ... Claimed on waivers by Cleveland Browns (August 28, 2001). ... Released by Browns (September 1, 2001). ... Re-signed by Browns to practice squad (September 3, 2001). ... Activated (September 18, 2001). ... Claimed on waivers by Buffalo Bills (September 3, 2002).
HONORS: Named linebacker on THE SPORTING NEWS college All-America second team (2000).

			TOTALS			INTERCEPTIONS			
Year Team	G	GS	Tk.	Ast.	Sks.	No.	Yds.	Avg.	TD
2001—Cleveland NFL	11	0	3	1	0.0	0	0	0.0	0
2002—Buffalo NFL	16	0	0	0	0.0	0	0	0.0	0
Pro totals (2 years)	27	0	3	1	0.0	0	0	0.0	0

DENNEY, RYAN   DE   BILLS

PERSONAL: Born June 15, 1977, in Denver. ... 6-7/276.
HIGH SCHOOL: Horizon (Thornton, Colo.).
COLLEGE: Brigham Young.
TRANSACTIONS/CAREER NOTES: Selected by Buffalo Bills in second round (61st pick overall) of 2002 NFL draft. ... Signed by Bills (July 26, 2002).

			TOTALS			INTERCEPTIONS			
Year Team	G	GS	Tk.	Ast.	Sks.	No.	Yds.	Avg.	TD
2002—Buffalo NFL	8	0	6	3	0.0	0	0	0.0	0

DENNIS, PAT   CB   TEXANS

PERSONAL: Born June 30, 1978, in Shreveport, La. ... 6-0/203. ... Full name: Patrick Dennis.
HIGH SCHOOL: Southwood (Shreveport, La.).
COLLEGE: Louisiana-Monroe.
TRANSACTIONS/CAREER NOTES: Selected after junior season by Kansas City Chiefs in fifth round (162nd pick overall) of 2000 NFL draft. ... Signed by Chiefs (July 20, 2000). ... On injured reserve with knee injury (September 1-October 3, 2001). ... Claimed on waivers by Dallas Cowboys (October 3, 2001). ... Claimed on waivers by Houston Texans (September 2, 2002). ... On injured reserve with knee injury (October 22, 2002-remainder of season). ... Granted free agency (February 28, 2003). ... Re-signed by Texans (March 18, 2003).

			TOTALS			INTERCEPTIONS			
Year Team	G	GS	Tk.	Ast.	Sks.	No.	Yds.	Avg.	TD
2000—Kansas City NFL	16	13	60	7	0.0	1	0	0.0	0
2001—Dallas NFL	11	0	14	1	0.0	0	0	0.0	0
2002—Houston NFL	3	0	0	0	0.0	0	0	0.0	0
Pro totals (3 years)	30	13	74	8	0.0	1	0	0.0	0

DENSON, AUTRY   RB   LIONS

PERSONAL: Born December 8, 1976, in Lauderhill, Fla. ... 5-10/203. ... Full name: Autry Lamont Denson.
HIGH SCHOOL: Nova (Fort Lauderdale, Fla.).
COLLEGE: Notre Dame.
TRANSACTIONS/CAREER NOTES: Selected by Tampa Bay Buccaneers in seventh round (233rd pick overall) of 1999 NFL draft. ... Signed by Buccaneers (July 29, 1999). ... Released by Buccaneers (September 5, 1999). ... Re-signed by Buccaneers to practice squad (September 6, 1999). ... Signed by Miami Dolphins off Buccaneers practice squad (October 20, 1999). ... Claimed on waivers by Chicago Bears (September 5, 2001). ... Granted free agency (March 1, 2002). ... Signed by Cleveland Browns (July 26, 2002). ... Released by Browns (September 1, 2002). ... Signed by Indianapolis Colts (November 5, 2002). ... Released by Colts (November 15, 2002). ... Signed by Detroit Lions (December 11, 2002). ... Assigned by Lions to Rhein Fire in 2003 NFL Europe enhancement allocation program (February 4, 2003).
SINGLE GAME HIGHS (regular season): Attempts—21 (January 2, 2000, vs. Washington); yards—80 (January 2, 2000, vs. Washington); and rushing touchdowns—0.

			RUSHING				RECEIVING				TOTALS			
Year Team	G	GS	Att.	Yds.	Avg.	TD	No.	Yds.	Avg.	TD	TD	2pt.	Pts.	Fum.
1999—Miami NFL	6	1	28	98	3.5	0	4	28	7.0	0	0	0	0	0
2000—Miami NFL	11	0	31	108	3.5	0	14	105	7.5	0	0	0	0	1
2001—Chicago NFL	16	0	1	4	4.0	0	0	0	0.0	0	0	0	0	1
2002—Indianapolis NFL	1	0	2	2	1.0	0	0	0	0.0	0	0	0	0	0
Pro totals (4 years)	34	1	62	212	3.4	0	18	133	7.4	0	0	0	0	2

D

DETMER, KOY   QB

PERSONAL: Born July 5, 1973, in San Antonio. ... 6-1/195. ... Full name: Koy Dennis Detmer. ... Brother of Ty Detmer, quarterback, Detroit Lions.
HIGH SCHOOL: Mission (Texas).
COLLEGE: Colorado (degree in communications, 1996).
TRANSACTIONS/CAREER NOTES: Selected by Philadelphia Eagles in seventh round (207th pick overall) of 1997 NFL draft. ... Signed by Eagles (June 4, 1997). ... On injured reserve with knee injury (August 22, 1997-entire season). ... Granted free agency (February 11, 2000). ... Re-signed by Eagles (April 17, 2000). ... Granted unconditional free agency (February 28, 2003).
CHAMPIONSHIP GAME EXPERIENCE: Played in NFC championship game (2001 and 2002 seasons).
SINGLE GAME HIGHS (regular season): Attempts—43 (December 20, 1998, vs. Dallas); completions—24 (December 20, 1998, vs. Dallas); yards—231 (December 20, 1998, vs. Dallas); and touchdown passes—3 (December 19, 1999, vs. New England).
MISCELLANEOUS: Regular-season record as starting NFL quarterback: 3-4 (.429).

Year Team	G	GS	Att.	Cmp.	Pct.	Yds.	TD	Int.	Avg.	Skd.	Rat.	Att.	Yds.	Avg.	TD	TD	2pt.	Pts.
										PASSING				RUSHING				TOTALS
1997—Philadelphia NFL										Did not play.								
1998—Philadelphia NFL	8	5	181	97	53.6	1011	5	5	5.59	5	67.7	7	20	2.9	0	0	0	0
1999—Philadelphia NFL	1	1	29	10	34.5	181	3	2	6.24	0	62.6	2	-2	-1.0	0	0	0	0
2000—Philadelphia NFL	16	0	1	0	0.0	0	0	1	0.0	0	0.0	1	8	8.0	0	0	0	0
2001—Philadelphia NFL	16	0	14	5	35.7	51	0	1	3.64	1	17.3	8	6	0.8	0	0	0	0
2002—Philadelphia NFL	14	1	28	19	67.9	224	2	0	8.00	1	115.8	2	4	2.0	1	1	0	6
Pro totals (5 years)	55	7	253	131	51.8	1467	10	9	5.80	7	67.7	20	36	1.8	1	1	0	6

DEVRIES, JARED   DE   LIONS

PERSONAL: Born June 11, 1976, in Aplington, Iowa. ... 6-4/269.
HIGH SCHOOL: Aplington-Parkersburg (Aplington, Iowa).
COLLEGE: Iowa.
TRANSACTIONS/CAREER NOTES: Selected by Detroit Lions in third round (70th pick overall) of 1999 NFL draft. ... Signed by Lions (July 28, 1999). ... On physically unable to perform list with blood clot (July 24-October 27, 2001). ... Granted free agency (March 1, 2002). ... Re-signed by Lions (April 16, 2002). ... On injured reserve with foot injury (December 11, 2002-remainder of season). ... Granted unconditional free agency (February 28, 2003). ... Re-signed by Lions (March 5, 2003).
HONORS: Named defensive tackle on THE SPORTING NEWS college All-America third team (1997). ... Named defensive tackle on THE SPORTING NEWS college All-America first team (1998).

Year Team	G	GS	Tk.	Ast.	Sks.
					TOTALS
1999—Detroit NFL	2	0	0	0	0.0
2000—Detroit NFL	15	1	14	8	0.0
2001—Detroit NFL	11	0	9	4	0.0
2002—Detroit NFL	10	0	5	5	1.0
Pro totals (4 years)	38	1	28	17	1.0

DIEM, RYAN   G   COLTS

PERSONAL: Born July 1, 1979, in Carol Stream, Ill. ... 6-6/331.
HIGH SCHOOL: Glenbard North (Carol Stream, Ill.).
COLLEGE: Northern Illinois.
TRANSACTIONS/CAREER NOTES: Selected by Indianapolis Colts in fourth round (118th pick overall) of 2001 NFL draft. ... Signed by Colts (July 19, 2001).
PLAYING EXPERIENCE: Indianapolis NFL, 2001-2002. ... Games/Games started: 2001 (15/8), 2002 (16/16). Totals: 31/24.

DIGGS, NA'IL   LB   PACKERS

PERSONAL: Born July 8, 1978, in Phoenix. ... 6-4/238. ... Full name: Na'il Ronald Diggs.
HIGH SCHOOL: Dorsey (Los Angeles).
COLLEGE: Ohio State.
TRANSACTIONS/CAREER NOTES: Selected after junior season by Green Bay Packers in fourth round (98th pick overall) of 2000 NFL draft. ... Signed by Packers (June 19, 2000). ... Granted free agency (February 28, 2003). ... Tendered offer sheet by Detroit Lions (March 21, 2003). ... Offer matched by Packers (March 28, 2003).

Year Team	G	GS	Tk.	Ast.	Sks.	No.	Yds.	Avg.	TD
				TOTALS			INTERCEPTIONS		
2000—Green Bay NFL	13	12	24	9	0.0	0	0	0.0	0
2001—Green Bay NFL	16	16	51	16	2.0	0	0	0.0	0
2002—Green Bay NFL	16	16	65	19	3.0	2	62	31.0	0
Pro totals (3 years)	45	44	140	44	5.0	2	62	31.0	0

DILFER, TRENT   QB   SEAHAWKS

PERSONAL: Born March 13, 1972, in Santa Cruz, Calif. ... 6-4/225. ... Full name: Trent Farris Dilfer.
HIGH SCHOOL: Aptos (Calif.).
COLLEGE: Fresno State.
TRANSACTIONS/CAREER NOTES: Selected after junior season by Tampa Bay Buccaneers in first round (sixth pick overall) of 1994 NFL draft. ... Signed by Buccaneers (August 3, 1994). ... Granted unconditional free agency (January 25, 2000). ... Signed by Baltimore Ravens (March

8, 2000). ... Granted unconditional free agency (March 2, 2001). ... Signed by Seattle Seahawks (August 3, 2001). ... Granted unconditional free agency (March 1, 2002). ... Re-signed by Seahawks (March 5, 2002). ... On injured reserve with knee and Achilles' injuries (October 29, 2002-remainder of season).
CHAMPIONSHIP GAME EXPERIENCE: Member of Buccaneers for NFC championship game (1999 season); inactive. ... Played in AFC championship game (2000 season). ... Member of Super Bowl championship team (2000 season).
HONORS: Played in Pro Bowl (1997 season).
SINGLE GAME HIGHS (regular season): Attempts—48 (November 26, 1995, vs. Green Bay); completions—30 (November 17, 1996, vs. San Diego); yards—352 (September 15, 2002, vs. Arizona); and touchdown passes—4 (September 21, 1997, vs. Miami).
STATISTICAL PLATEAUS: 300-yard passing games: 1995 (1), 1996 (1), 1999 (1), 2002 (1). Total: 4.
MISCELLANEOUS: Regular-season record as starting NFL quarterback: 51-43 (.543). ... Postseason record as starting NFL quarterback: 5-1 (.833).

			PASSING									RUSHING				TOTALS		
Year Team	G	GS	Att.	Cmp.	Pct.	Yds.	TD	Int.	Avg.	Skd.	Rat.	Att.	Yds.	Avg.	TD	TD	2pt.	Pts.
1994—Tampa Bay NFL..........	5	2	82	38	46.3	433	1	6	5.28	8	36.3	2	27	13.5	0	0	0	0
1995—Tampa Bay NFL..........	16	16	415	224	54.0	2774	4	18	6.68	‡47	60.1	23	115	5.0	2	2	0	12
1996—Tampa Bay NFL..........	16	16	482	267	55.4	2859	12	19	5.93	28	64.8	32	124	3.9	0	0	0	0
1997—Tampa Bay NFL..........	16	16	386	217	56.2	2555	21	11	6.62	32	82.8	33	99	3.0	1	1	0	6
1998—Tampa Bay NFL..........	16	16	429	225	52.4	2729	21	15	6.36	27	74.0	40	141	3.5	2	2	0	12
1999—Tampa Bay NFL..........	10	10	244	146	59.8	1619	11	11	6.64	26	75.8	35	144	4.1	0	0	0	0
2000—Baltimore NFL..........	11	8	226	134	59.3	1502	12	11	6.65	23	76.6	20	75	3.8	0	0	0	0
2001—Seattle NFL................	7	4	122	73	59.8	1014	7	4	8.31	10	92.0	11	17	1.5	0	0	0	0
2002—Seattle NFL................	6	6	168	94	56.0	1182	4	6	7.04	7	71.1	10	27	2.7	0	0	0	0
Pro totals (9 years)................	103	94	2554	1418	55.5	16667	93	101	6.53	208	71.2	206	769	3.7	5	5	0	30

DILGER, KEN   TE   BUCCANEERS

PERSONAL: Born February 2, 1971, in Mariah Hill, Ind. ... 6-5/250. ... Full name: Kenneth Ray Dilger. ... Name pronounced DIL-gur.
HIGH SCHOOL: Heritage Hills (Lincoln City, Ind.).
COLLEGE: Illinois (degree in marketing).
TRANSACTIONS/CAREER NOTES: Selected by Indianapolis Colts in second round (48th pick overall) of 1995 NFL draft. ... Signed by Colts (July 15, 1995). ... Released by Colts (February 21, 2002). ... Signed by Tampa Bay Buccaneers (April 17, 2002).
CHAMPIONSHIP GAME EXPERIENCE: Played in AFC championship game (1995 season). ... Played in NFC championship game (2002 season). ... Member of Super Bowl championship team (2002 season).
HONORS: Played in Pro Bowl (2001 season).
SINGLE GAME HIGHS (regular season): Receptions—8 (September 10, 2000, vs. Oakland); yards—156 (September 8, 1996, vs. New York Jets); and touchdown receptions—3 (December 14, 1997, vs. Miami).
STATISTICAL PLATEAUS: 100-yard receiving games: 1995 (1), 1996 (1), 1997 (1). Total: 3.

			RECEIVING				TOTALS			
Year Team	G	GS	No.	Yds.	Avg.	TD	TD	2pt.	Pts.	Fum.
1995—Indianapolis NFL	16	13	42	635	15.1	4	4	0	24	0
1996—Indianapolis NFL	16	16	42	503	12.0	4	4	0	24	1
1997—Indianapolis NFL	14	14	27	380	14.1	3	3	0	18	0
1998—Indianapolis NFL	16	16	31	303	9.8	1	1	1	8	0
1999—Indianapolis NFL	15	15	40	479	12.0	2	2	0	12	1
2000—Indianapolis NFL	16	16	47	538	11.4	3	3	0	18	1
2001—Indianapolis NFL	16	16	32	343	10.7	1	1	1	8	2
2002—Tampa Bay NFL	16	15	34	329	9.7	2	2	0	12	1
Pro totals (8 years)	125	121	295	3510	11.9	20	20	2	124	6

DILLON, COREY   RB   BENGALS

PERSONAL: Born October 24, 1974, in Seattle. ... 6-1/225.
HIGH SCHOOL: Franklin (Seattle).
JUNIOR COLLEGE: Garden City (Kan.) Community College, then Dixie College (Utah).
COLLEGE: Washington.
TRANSACTIONS/CAREER NOTES: Selected after junior season by Cincinnati Bengals in second round (43rd pick overall) of 1997 NFL draft. ... Signed by Bengals (July 21, 1997). ... Granted free agency (February 11, 2000). ... Re-signed by Bengals (August 9, 2000). ... Designated by Bengals as transition player (February 12, 2001). ... Re-signed by Bengals (May 11, 2001).
HONORS: Named running back on THE SPORTING NEWS college All-America second team (1996). ... Played in Pro Bowl (1999-2001 seasons).
RECORDS: Holds NFL record for most yards rushing in a game—278 (October 22, 2000, vs. Denver).
SINGLE GAME HIGHS (regular season): Attempts—39 (December 4, 1997, vs. Tennessee); yards—278 (October 22, 2000, vs. Denver); and rushing touchdowns—4 (December 4, 1997, vs. Tennessee).
STATISTICAL PLATEAUS: 100-yard rushing games: 1997 (4), 1998 (4), 1999 (5), 2000 (5), 2001 (4), 2002 (5). Total: 27.
MISCELLANEOUS: Selected by San Diego Padres organization in 34th round of free agent draft (June 3, 1993); did not sign. ... Holds Cincinnati Bengals all-time record for most yards rushing (7,520).

			RUSHING				RECEIVING				KICKOFF RETURNS				TOTALS			
Year Team	G	GS	Att.	Yds.	Avg.	TD	No.	Yds.	Avg.	TD	No.	Yds.	Avg.	TD	TD	2pt.	Pts.	Fum.
1997—Cincinnati NFL............	16	6	233	1129	4.8	10	27	259	9.6	0	6	182	30.3	0	10	0	60	1
1998—Cincinnati NFL............	15	15	262	1130	4.3	4	28	178	6.4	1	0	0	0.0	0	5	0	30	2
1999—Cincinnati NFL............	15	15	263	1200	4.6	5	31	290	9.4	1	1	4	4.0	0	6	0	36	3
2000—Cincinnati NFL............	16	16	315	1435	4.6	7	18	158	8.8	0	0	0	0.0	0	7	0	42	4
2001—Cincinnati NFL............	16	16	§340	1315	3.9	10	34	228	6.7	3	0	0	0.0	0	13	0	78	5
2002—Cincinnati NFL............	16	16	314	1311	4.2	7	43	298	6.9	0	0	0	0.0	0	7	0	42	5
Pro totals (6 years)................	94	84	1727	7520	4.4	43	181	1411	7.8	5	7	186	26.6	0	48	0	288	20

DINAPOLI, GENNARO   C/OG   TITANS

PERSONAL: Born May 25, 1975, in Manhasset, N.Y. ... 6-3/287. ... Full name: Gennaro L. DiNapoli. ... Name pronounced den-ah-POLE-e.
HIGH SCHOOL: Cazenovia (N.Y.), then Milford (Conn.) Academy.
COLLEGE: Virginia Tech.
TRANSACTIONS/CAREER NOTES: Selected by Oakland Raiders in fourth round (109th pick overall) of 1998 NFL draft. ... Signed by Raiders (July 24, 1998). ... Active for four games (1998); did not play. ... Traded by Raiders to Tennessee Titans for undisclosed pick (August 27, 2000). ... Granted unconditional free agency (March 1, 2002). ... Re-signed by Titans (April 19, 2002).
PLAYING EXPERIENCE: Oakland NFL, 1999; Tennessee NFL, 2001-2002. ... Games/Games started: 1999 (11/9), 2001 (5/2), 2002 (16/16). Total: 32/27.
CHAMPIONSHIP GAME EXPERIENCE: Played in AFC championship game (2002 season).

DINGLE, ADRIAN   DE   CHARGERS

PERSONAL: Born June 25, 1977, in Holly Hill, S.C. ... 6-3/272. ... Full name: Adrian Kennell Dingle.
HIGH SCHOOL: Holly Hill (S.C.)-Roberts.
COLLEGE: Clemson.
TRANSACTIONS/CAREER NOTES: Selected by San Diego Chargers in fifth round (139th pick overall) of 1999 NFL draft. ... Signed by Chargers (July 23, 1999). ... On physically unable to perform list with knee injury (August 31-November 17, 1999). ... Active for two games (1999); did not play. ... Granted free agency (March 1, 2002). ... Re-signed by Chargers (March 29, 2002). ... Granted unconditional free agency (February 28, 2003). ... Re-signed by Chargers (March 11, 2003).

Year Team	G	GS	TOTALS Tk.	Ast.	Sks.
1999—San Diego NFL			Did not play.		
2000—San Diego NFL	14	1	15	1	2.5
2001—San Diego NFL	14	0	10	1	1.0
2002—San Diego NFL	16	3	24	1	4.0
Pro totals (3 years)	44	4	49	3	7.5

DINKINS, DARNELL   DB   GIANTS

PERSONAL: Born January 20, 1977, in Pittsburgh. ... 6-3/234. ... Full name: Darnell Joseph Dinkins.
HIGH SCHOOL: Schenley (Pittsburgh).
COLLEGE: Pittsburgh.
TRANSACTIONS/CAREER NOTES: Signed as non-drafted free agent by New York Giants (January 31, 2002). ... Assigned by Giants to Rhein Fire in 2002 NFL Europe enhancement allocation program (February 12, 2002). ... On injured reserve with foot injury (November 1, 2002-remainder of season).

Year Team	G	GS	TOTALS Tk.	Ast.	Sks.	INTERCEPTIONS No.	Yds.	Avg.	TD
2002—Rhein NFLE	...	...	...	...	0.0	0	0	0.0	0
—New York Giants NFL	2	0	0	0	0.0	0	0	0.0	0
NFL Europe totals (1 year)	...	...	...	...	0.0	0	0	0.0	0
NFL totals (1 year)	2	0	0	0	0.0	0	0	0.0	0
Pro totals (2 years)	...	...	...	...	0.0	0	0	0.0	0

DISHMAN, CHRIS   G   CARDINALS

PERSONAL: Born February 27, 1974, in Cozad, Neb. ... 6-3/340.
HIGH SCHOOL: Cozad (Neb.).
COLLEGE: Nebraska.
TRANSACTIONS/CAREER NOTES: Selected by Arizona Cardinals in fourth round (106th pick overall) of 1997 NFL draft. ... Signed by Cardinals (July 9, 1997). ... Granted free agency (February 11, 2000). ... Re-signed by Cardinals (April 28, 2000) ... Granted unconditional free agency (March 2, 2001). ... Re-signed by Cardinals (March 5, 2001).
PLAYING EXPERIENCE: Arizona NFL, 1997-2002. ... Games/Games started: 1997 (8/0), 1998 (12/11), 1999 (13/10), 2000 (14/12), 2001 (16/5), 2002 (14/14). Total: 77/52.

DIXON, DAVID   G   VIKINGS

PERSONAL: Born January 5, 1969, in Papakura, New Zealand. ... 6-5/359. ... Full name: David Tukatahi Dixon.
HIGH SCHOOL: Pukekohe (New Zealand).
JUNIOR COLLEGE: Ricks College (Idaho).
COLLEGE: Arizona State.
TRANSACTIONS/CAREER NOTES: Selected by New England Patriots in ninth-round (232nd pick overall) of 1992 draft. ... Signed by Patriots for 1992 season. ... Released by Patriots (August 1992). ... Signed by Minnesota Vikings to practice squad (October 20, 1992). ... Released by Vikings (August 23, 1993). ... Signed by Dallas Cowboys to practice squad (September 8, 1993). ... Granted free agency after 1993 season. ... Signed by Vikings (July 12, 1994). ... Granted free agency (February 14, 1997). ... Re-signed by Vikings (May 1, 1997). ... Granted unconditional free agency (February 13, 1998). ... Re-signed by Vikings (February 17, 1998). ... On physically unable to perform list with knee injury (August 1-10, 1999).
PLAYING EXPERIENCE: Minnesota NFL, 1994-2002. ... Games/Games started: 1994 (1/0), 1995 (15/6), 1996 (13/6), 1997 (13/13), 1998 (16/16), 1999 (16/16), 2000 (16/16), 2001 (15/14), 2002 (15/15). Total: 120/102.
CHAMPIONSHIP GAME EXPERIENCE: Played in NFC championship game (1998 and 2000 seasons).

DIXON, MARK   G   DOLPHINS

PERSONAL: Born November 26, 1970, in Charlottesville, N.C. ... 6-4/295. ... Full name: Mark Keller Dixon.
HIGH SCHOOL: Ragsdale (Jamestown, N.C.).
COLLEGE: Virginia.
TRANSACTIONS/CAREER NOTES: Signed as non-drafted free agent by Philadelphia Eagles (April 1994). ... Released by Eagles (August 1994). ... Played with Frankfurt Galaxy of World League (1995). ... Signed by Atlanta Falcons (July 18, 1995). ... Released by Falcons (August 21, 1995). ... Signed by Baltimore Stallions of CFL (August 30, 1995). ... Signed by Miami Dolphins (January 22, 1998). ... On injured reserve with neck injury (November 24, 1998-remainder of season). ... On injured reserve with broken leg (December 4, 2001-remainder of season).
PLAYING EXPERIENCE: Frankfurt W.L., 1995; Baltimore Stallions CFL, 1995; Montreal Alouettes CFL, 1996 and 1997; Miami NFL, 1998-2002. ... Games/Games started: W.L. 1995 (games played unavailable), CFL 1995 (9/5), 1996 (18/18), 1997 (7/7), 1998 (11/10), 1999 (13/13), 2000 (15/15), 2001 (10/10), 2002 (13/12). Total CFL: 34/30. Total NFL 62/60. Total Pro: 96/90.
CHAMPIONSHIP GAME EXPERIENCE: Member of CFL championship team (1995).

DIXON, RON   WR/KR   GIANTS

PERSONAL: Born May 28, 1976, in Wildwood, Fla. ... 6-0/190. ... Full name: Ronald Dixon.
HIGH SCHOOL: Wildwood (Fla.).
JUNIOR COLLEGE: Itawamba Community College (Miss.).
COLLEGE: West Georgia, then Lambuth University.
TRANSACTIONS/CAREER NOTES: Selected by New York Giants in third round (73rd pick overall) of 2000 NFL draft. ... Signed by Giants (July 16, 2000). ... Granted free agency (February 28, 2003). ... Re-signed by Giants (March 25, 2003).
CHAMPIONSHIP GAME EXPERIENCE: Played in NFC championship game (2000 season). ... Played in Super Bowl XXXV (2000 season).
POST SEASON RECORDS: Holds NFL career record for kickoff returns for touchdowns—2.
SINGLE GAME HIGHS (regular season): Receptions—5 (December 1, 2002, vs. Tennessee); yards—107 (November 10, 2002, vs. Minnesota); and touchdown receptions—1 (December 1, 2002, vs. Tennessee).
STATISTICAL PLATEAUS: 100-yard receiving games: 2002 (1).

			RECEIVING				KICKOFF RETURNS				TOTALS			
Year Team	G	GS	No.	Yds.	Avg.	TD	No.	Yds.	Avg.	TD	TD	2pt.	Pts.	Fum.
2000—New York Giants NFL	12	0	6	92	15.3	1	31	658	21.2	0	1	0	6	0
2001—New York Giants NFL	15	0	8	227	28.4	1	34	645	19.0	0	1	0	6	2
2002—New York Giants NFL	10	3	22	377	17.1	2	2	61	30.5	0	2	0	12	1
Pro totals (3 years)	37	3	36	696	19.3	4	67	1364	20.4	0	4	0	24	3

DIXON, TONY   S   COWBOYS

PERSONAL: Born June 18, 1979, in Reform, Ala. ... 6-1/213.
HIGH SCHOOL: Pickens County (Reform, Ala.).
COLLEGE: Alabama (degree in management).
TRANSACTIONS/CAREER NOTES: Selected by Dallas Cowboys in second round (56th pick overall) of 2001 NFL draft. ... Signed by Cowboys (July 21, 2001).

			TOTALS			INTERCEPTIONS			
Year Team	G	GS	Tk.	Ast.	Sks.	No.	Yds.	Avg.	TD
2001—Dallas NFL	8	0	5	2	1.0	0	0	0.0	0
2002—Dallas NFL	16	8	31	9	2.0	1	0	0.0	0
Pro totals (2 years)	24	8	36	11	3.0	1	0	0.0	0

DOERING, CHRIS   WR   STEELERS

PERSONAL: Born May 19, 1973, in Gainesville, Fla. ... 6-4/199. ... Full name: Christopher Paul Doering. ... Name pronounced DOOR-ing.
HIGH SCHOOL: P.K. Yonge (Gainesville, Fla.).
COLLEGE: Florida.
TRANSACTIONS/CAREER NOTES: Selected by Jacksonville Jaguars in sixth round (185th pick overall) of 1996 NFL draft. ... Signed by Jaguars (June 5, 1996). ... Claimed on waivers by New York Jets (August 20, 1996). ... Released by Jets (August 25, 1996). ... Signed by Indianapolis Colts to practice squad (August 27, 1996). ... Activated (December 20, 1996). ... Released by Colts (August 24, 1997). ... Re-signed by Colts to practice squad (August 25, 1997). ... Activated (December 5, 1997). ... Claimed on waivers by Cincinnati Bengals (February 25, 1998). ... Released by Bengals (September 2, 1998). ... Signed by Denver Broncos (February 3, 1999). ... Released by Broncos (August 7, 2000). ... Re-signed by Broncos (August 6, 2001). ... Released by Broncos (August 28, 2001). ... Signed by Washington Redskins (February 21, 2002). ... Granted free agency (February 28, 2003). ... Signed by Pittsburgh Steelers (May 20, 2003).
SINGLE GAME HIGHS (regular season): Receptions—4 (October 6, 2002, vs. Tennessee); yards—34 (October 6, 2002, vs. Tennessee); and touchdown receptions—1 (December 15, 2002, vs. Philadelphia).

			RECEIVING			
Year Team	G	GS	No.	Yds.	Avg.	TD
1996—Indianapolis NFL	1	0	1	10	10.0	0
1997—Indianapolis NFL	2	0	2	12	6.0	0
1999—Denver NFL	3	0	3	22	7.3	0
2002—Washington NFL	15	3	18	192	10.7	2
Pro totals (4 years)	21	3	24	236	9.8	2

DOERING, JASON — DB — COLTS

PERSONAL: Born April 22, 1978, in Rhinelander, Wis. ... 6-0/201. ... Full name: Jason James Doering.
HIGH SCHOOL: Rhinelander (Wis.).
COLLEGE: Wisconsin.
TRANSACTIONS/CAREER NOTES: Selected by Indianapolis Colts in sixth round (193rd pick overall) of 2001 NFL draft. ... Signed by Colts (June 7, 2001).

Year Team	G	GS	TOTALS			INTERCEPTIONS			
			Tk.	Ast.	Sks.	No.	Yds.	Avg.	TD
2001—Indianapolis NFL	16	1	10	1	0.0	0	0	0.0	0
2002—Indianapolis NFL	15	6	24	12	0.0	0	0	0.0	0
Pro totals (2 years)	31	7	34	13	0.0	0	0	0.0	0

DOGINS, KEVIN — C — FALCONS

PERSONAL: Born December 7, 1972, in Eagle Lake, Texas. ... 6-1/310. ... Full name: Kevin Ray Dogins.
HIGH SCHOOL: Rice (Texas).
COLLEGE: Texas A&M-Kingsville.
TRANSACTIONS/CAREER NOTES: Signed as non-drafted free agent by Dallas Cowboys (April 25, 1996). ... Released by Cowboys (August 19, 1996). ... Signed by Tampa Bay Buccaneers to practice squad (August 27, 1996). ... Activated (December 17, 1996). ... Inactive for all 16 games (1997). ... Granted free agency (February 11, 2000). ... Re-signed by Buccaneers (May 26, 2000). ... Granted unconditional free agency (March 2, 2001). ... Signed by Chicago Bears (June 22, 2001). ... Granted unconditional free agency (February 28, 2003). ... Signed by Atlanta Falcons (April 10, 2003).
PLAYING EXPERIENCE: Tampa Bay NFL, 1996, 1998 and 1999; Chicago NFL, 2001-2002. ... Games/Games started: 1996 (1/0), 1998 (6/4), 1999 (11/5), 2001 (16/0), 2002 (15/8). Total: 49/17.
CHAMPIONSHIP GAME EXPERIENCE: Played in NFC championship game (1999 season).

DONNALLEY, KEVIN — G — PANTHERS

PERSONAL: Born June 10, 1968, in St. Louis. ... 6-5/310. ... Full name: Kevin Thomas Donnalley. ... Brother of Rick Donnalley, center with Pittsburgh Steelers (1982 and 1983), Washington Redskins (1984 and 1985) and Kansas City Chiefs (1986 and 1987).
HIGH SCHOOL: Athens Drive Senior (Raleigh, N.C.).
COLLEGE: Davidson, then North Carolina (degree in economics).
TRANSACTIONS/CAREER NOTES: Selected by Houston Oilers in third round (79th pick overall) of 1991 NFL draft. ... Signed by Oilers (July 10, 1991). ... Granted free agency (February 17, 1994). ... Tendered offer sheet by Los Angeles Rams (March 17, 1994). ... Offer matched by Oilers (March 23, 1994). ... Oilers franchise moved to Tennessee for 1997 season. ... Granted unconditional free agency (February 13, 1998). ... Signed by Miami Dolphins (February 17, 1998). ... Released by Dolphins (June 2, 2000). ... Re-signed by Dolphins (June 13, 2000). ... Granted unconditional free agency (March 2, 2001). ... Signed by Carolina Panthers (March 16, 2001). ... On injured reserve with knee injury (October 23, 2001-remainder of season).
PLAYING EXPERIENCE: Houston NFL, 1991-1996; Tennessee NFL, 1997; Miami NFL, 1998-2000; Carolina NFL, 2001-2002. ... Games/Games started: 1991 (16/0), 1992 (16/2), 1993 (16/6), 1994 (13/11), 1995 (16/16), 1996 (16/16), 1997 (16/16), 1998 (14/14), 1999 (16/9), 2000 (16/16), 2001 (6/6), 2002 (16/16). Total: 177/128.

DORRIS, DEREK — WR — GIANTS

PERSONAL: Born December 1, 1978 ... 6-2/206.
COLLEGE: Texas Tech.
TRANSACTIONS/CAREER NOTES: Signed as non-drafted free agent by New Orleans Saints (April 24, 2001). ... Claimed on waivers by Washington Redskins (August 24, 2001). ... Released by Redskins (August 28, 2001). ... Signed by New York Giants (April 20, 2002). ... Claimed on waivers by New York Jets (September 1, 2002). ... Released by Jets (September 6, 2002). ... Signed by Giants to practice squad (November 13, 2002). ... Activated (November 16, 2002).

Year Team	G	GS	RECEIVING			
			No.	Yds.	Avg.	TD
2002—New York Giants NFL	6	0	0	0	0.0	0

DORSCH, TRAVIS — P/K — BENGALS

PERSONAL: Born September 4, 1979, in Bozeman, Mont. ... 6-6/227. ... Full name: Travis Edward Dorsch.
HIGH SCHOOL: Bozeman (Mont.).
COLLEGE: Purdue.
TRANSACTIONS/CAREER NOTES: Selected by Cincinnati Bengals in fourth round (109th pick overall) of 2002 NFL draft. ... Signed by Bengals (July 24, 2002).
HONORS: Named kicker on THE SPORTING NEWS college All-America first team (2001). ... Named punter on THE SPORTING NEWS college All-America second team (2001).

Year Team	G	PUNTING					
		No.	Yds.	Avg.	Net avg.	In. 20	Blk.
2002—Cincinnati NFL	1	5	162	32.4	1.8	0	0

DORSETT, ANTHONY — S

PERSONAL: Born September 14, 1973, in Aliquippa, Pa. ... 5-11/205. ... Full name: Anthony Drew Dorsett Jr. ... Son of Tony Dorsett, Hall of Fame running back with Dallas Cowboys (1977-87) and Denver Broncos (1988).

HIGH SCHOOL: Richland (Dallas), then J.J. Pearce (Dallas).
COLLEGE: Pittsburgh.
TRANSACTIONS/CAREER NOTES: Selected by Houston Oilers in sixth round (177th pick overall) of 1996 NFL draft. ... Signed by Oilers (June 21, 1996). ... Assigned by Oilers to Barcelona Dragons in 1997 World League enhancement allocation program (February 19, 1997). ... Oilers franchise moved to Tennessee for 1997 season. ... Oilers franchise renamed Tennessee Titans for 1999 season (December 26, 1998). ... Granted free agency (February 12, 1999). ... Re-signed by Titans (June 15, 1999). ... Granted unconditional free agency (February 11, 2000). ... Signed by Oakland Raiders (March 21, 2000). ... Released by Raiders (February 27, 2003).
CHAMPIONSHIP GAME EXPERIENCE: Played in AFC championship game (1999, 2000 and 2002 seasons). ... Played in Super Bowl XXXIV (1999 season). ... Played in Super Bowl XXXVII (2002 season).

			TOTALS			INTERCEPTIONS			
Year Team	G	GS	Tk.	Ast.	Sks.	No.	Yds.	Avg.	TD
1996—Houston NFL	8	0	0	0	0.0	0	0	0.0	0
1997—Tennessee NFL	16	0	5	3	0.0	0	0	0.0	0
1998—Tennessee NFL	16	0	3	1	0.0	0	0	0.0	0
1999—Tennessee NFL	16	1	8	2	0.0	1	43	43.0	0
2000—Oakland NFL	16	16	52	20	1.0	0	0	0.0	0
2001—Oakland NFL	16	16	62	9	1.0	2	65	32.5	†2
2002—Oakland NFL	16	7	26	10	0.0	0	0	0.0	0
Pro totals (7 years)	104	40	156	45	2.0	3	108	36.0	2

DORSEY, CHAR-RON   OT   GIANTS

PERSONAL: Born November 5, 1978, in Jacksonville. ... 6-6/388.
HIGH SCHOOL: The Bolles School (Jacksonville).
COLLEGE: Florida State.
TRANSACTIONS/CAREER NOTES: Selected by Dallas Cowboys in seventh round (242nd pick overall) of 2001 NFL draft. ... Signed by Cowboys (July 17, 2001). ... Released by Cowboys (September 9, 2002). ... Signed by Houston Texans (September 14, 2002). ... Released by Texans (November 29, 2002). ... Signed by New York Giants (January 7, 2003).
PLAYING EXPERIENCE: Dallas NFL, 2001; Dallas (1)-Houston (2) NFL, 2002. ... Games/Games started: 2001 (8/2), 2002 (Dal.-1/0; Hou.-2/1; Total: 3/1). Total: 11/3.

DOTSON, EARL   OT

PERSONAL: Born December 17, 1970, in Beaumont, Texas. ... 6-4/317. ... Full name: Earl Christopher Dotson.
HIGH SCHOOL: Westbrook (Texas).
JUNIOR COLLEGE: Tyler (Texas) Junior College.
COLLEGE: Texas A&I.
TRANSACTIONS/CAREER NOTES: Selected by Green Bay Packers in third round (81st pick overall) of 1993 NFL draft. ... Signed by Packers (June 14, 1993). ... Released by Packers (February 27, 2001). ... Re-signed by Packers (March 8, 2001). ... Granted unconditional free agency (March 1, 2002). ... Re-signed by Packers (April 10, 2002). ... On physically unable to perform list with knee injury (July 25-August 28, 2002). ... Granted unconditional free agency (February 28, 2003).
PLAYING EXPERIENCE: Green Bay NFL, 1993-2002. ... Games/Games started: 1993 (13/0), 1994 (4/0), 1995 (16/16), 1996 (15/15), 1997 (13/13), 1998 (16/16), 1999 (15/15), 2000 (2/2), 2001 (12/0), 2002 (14/11). Total: 102/88.
CHAMPIONSHIP GAME EXPERIENCE: Played in NFC championship game (1995-97 seasons). ... Member of Super Bowl championship team (1996 season). ... Played in Super Bowl XXXII (1997 season).

DOTSON, SANTANA   DT

PERSONAL: Born December 19, 1969, in New Orleans. ... 6-5/285. ... Full name: Santana N. Dotson. ... Son of Alphonse Dotson, defensive tackle with Kansas City Chiefs (1965), Miami Dolphins (1966) and Oakland Raiders (1968-70).
HIGH SCHOOL: Jack Yates (Houston).
COLLEGE: Baylor.
TRANSACTIONS/CAREER NOTES: Selected by Tampa Bay Buccaneers in fifth round (132nd pick overall) of 1992 NFL draft. ... Signed by Buccaneers (July 7, 1992). ... Granted free agency (February 17, 1995). ... Re-signed by Buccaneers (June 14, 1995). ... Granted unconditional free agency (February 16, 1996). ... Signed by Green Bay Packers (March 7, 1996). ... Granted unconditional free agency (February 12, 1999). ... Re-signed by Packers (February 19, 1999). ... On injured reserve with knee injury (November 29, 2000-remainder of season). ... Released by Packers (February 27, 2002). ... Signed by Washington Redskins (June 4, 2002). ... On injured reserve with Achilles' injury (August 7, 2002-entire season). ... Granted unconditional free agency (February 28, 2003).
CHAMPIONSHIP GAME EXPERIENCE: Played in NFC championship game (1996 and 1997 seasons). ... Member of Super Bowl championship team (1996 season). ... Played in Super Bowl XXXII (1997 season).
HONORS: Named defensive lineman on The Sporting News college All-America first team (1991). ... Named NFL Rookie of the Year by The Sporting News (1992).

			TOTALS		
Year Team	G	GS	Tk.	Ast.	Sks.
1992—Tampa Bay NFL	16	16	57	14	10.0
1993—Tampa Bay NFL	16	13	41	22	5.0
1994—Tampa Bay NFL	16	9	18	5	3.0
1995—Tampa Bay NFL	16	8	24	14	5.0
1996—Green Bay NFL	16	15	25	12	5.5
1997—Green Bay NFL	16	16	38	33	5.5
1998—Green Bay NFL	16	16	33	17	3.0
1999—Green Bay NFL	12	12	17	18	2.5
2000—Green Bay NFL	12	12	23	15	6.0
2001—Green Bay NFL	16	13	22	12	3.5
2002—Washington NFL			Did not play.		
Pro totals (10 years)	152	130	298	162	49.0

DOUGLAS, DAMEANE — WR — CHIEFS

PERSONAL: Born March 15, 1976, in Hanford, Calif. ... 6-0/195.
HIGH SCHOOL: Hanford (Calif.).
COLLEGE: California.
TRANSACTIONS/CAREER NOTES: Selected by Oakland Raiders in fourth round (102nd pick overall) of 1999 NFL draft. ... Signed by Raiders for 1999 season. ... Claimed on waivers by Philadelphia Eagles (September 7, 1999). ... Granted unconditional free agency (February 28, 2003). ... Signed by Kansas City Chiefs (April 29, 2003).
CHAMPIONSHIP GAME EXPERIENCE: Played in NFC championship game (2001 and 2002 seasons).
SINGLE GAME HIGHS (regular season): Receptions—5 (January 6, 2002, vs. Tampa Bay); yards—77 (January 6, 2002, vs. Tampa Bay); and touchdown receptions—2 (January 6, 2002, vs. Tampa Bay).

Year Team	G	GS	RECEIVING				KICKOFF RETURNS				TOTALS			
			No.	Yds.	Avg.	TD	No.	Yds.	Avg.	TD	TD	2pt.	Pts.	Fum.
1999—Philadelphia NFL	14	0	8	79	9.9	1	0	0	0.0	0	1	0	6	0
2000—Philadelphia NFL	6	0	1	9	9.0	0	2	50	25.0	0	0	0	0	0
2001—Philadelphia NFL	16	0	5	77	15.4	2	2	32	16.0	0	2	0	12	0
2002—Philadelphia NFL	16	0	0	0	0.0	0	4	77	19.3	0	0	0	0	0
Pro totals (4 years)	52	0	14	165	11.8	3	8	159	19.9	0	3	0	18	0

DOUGLAS, HUGH — LB/DE — JAGUARS

PERSONAL: Born August 23, 1971, in Mansfield, Ohio. ... 6-2/280.
HIGH SCHOOL: Mansfield (Ohio).
COLLEGE: Central State (Ohio).
TRANSACTIONS/CAREER NOTES: Selected after junior season by New York Jets in first round (16th pick overall) of 1995 NFL draft. ... Signed by Jets (June 8, 1995). ... Traded by Jets to Philadelphia Eagles for second- (traded to Pittsburgh) and fifth-round (LB Casey Dailey) picks in 1998 draft (March 13, 1998). ... On injured reserve with bicep injury (October 20, 1999-remainder of season). ... Granted unconditional free agency (February 28, 2003). ... Signed by Jacksonville Jaguars (March 16, 2003).
CHAMPIONSHIP GAME EXPERIENCE: Played in NFC championship game (2001 and 2002 seasons).
HONORS: Named defensive end on THE SPORTING NEWS NFL All-Pro team (2000). ... Played in Pro Bowl (2000-2002 seasons).

Year Team	G	GS	TOTALS			INTERCEPTIONS			
			Tk.	Ast.	Sks.	No.	Yds.	Avg.	TD
1995—New York Jets NFL	15	3	25	8	10.0	0	0	0.0	0
1996—New York Jets NFL	10	10	28	8	8.0	0	0	0.0	0
1997—New York Jets NFL	15	15	31	8	4.0	0	0	0.0	0
1998—Philadelphia NFL	15	13	37	9	12.5	0	0	0.0	0
1999—Philadelphia NFL	4	2	5	3	2.0	0	0	0.0	0
2000—Philadelphia NFL	16	15	44	12	15.0	1	9	9.0	0
2001—Philadelphia NFL	15	15	39	8	9.5	0	0	0.0	0
2002—Philadelphia NFL	16	16	45	8	12.5	0	0	0.0	0
Pro totals (8 years)	106	89	254	64	73.5	1	9	9.0	0

DOUGLAS, MARQUES — DE — RAVENS

PERSONAL: Born March 5, 1977, in Greensboro, N.C. ... 6-2/280. ... Full name: Marques Lamont Douglas.
HIGH SCHOOL: Dudley (Greensboro, N.C.).
COLLEGE: Howard.
TRANSACTIONS/CAREER NOTES: Signed by Baltimore Ravens as non-drafted free agent (April 23, 1999). ... Released by Ravens (September 4, 1999). ... Re-signed by Ravens (December 22, 1999). ... Claimed on waivers by New Orleans Saints (August 28, 2000). ... Released by Saints (September 14, 2000). ... Re-signed by Saints (September 20, 2000). ... On injured reserve with knee injury (October 12, 2000-remainder of season). ... Released by Saints (September 2, 2001). ... Re-signed by Saints to practice squad (September 3, 2001). ... Signed by Baltimore Ravens off Saints practice squad (November 28, 2001). ... Re-signed by Ravens (March 13, 2003).

Year Team	G	GS	TOTALS		
			Tk.	Ast.	Sks.
2000—New Orleans NFL	1	0	1	0	0.0
2001—Baltimore NFL	2	0	1	1	1.0
2002—Baltimore NFL	5	1	6	4	1.0
Pro totals (3 years)	8	1	8	5	2.0

DOWNING, ERIC — DT — CHIEFS

PERSONAL: Born September 16, 1978, in Ahoskie, N.C. ... 6-3/315. ... Full name: Eric Lamont Downing.
HIGH SCHOOL: John F. Kennedy (Paterson, N.J.).
JUNIOR COLLEGE: Coffeyville (Kan.) Community College.
COLLEGE: Syracuse.
TRANSACTIONS/CAREER NOTES: Selected by Kansas City Chiefs in third round (75th pick overall) of 2001 NFL draft. ... Signed by Chiefs (May 23, 2001).

Year Team	G	GS	TOTALS		
			Tk.	Ast.	Sks.
2001—Kansas City NFL	15	9	13	6	1.5
2002—Kansas City NFL	13	4	10	4	0.5
Pro totals (2 years)	28	13	23	10	2.0

DRAFT, CHRIS   LB   FALCONS

PERSONAL: Born February 26, 1976, in Anaheim. ... 5-11/232.
HIGH SCHOOL: Valencia (Placentia, Calif.).
COLLEGE: Stanford.
TRANSACTIONS/CAREER NOTES: Selected by Chicago Bears in sixth round (157th pick overall) of 1998 NFL draft. ... Signed by Bears (June 16, 1998). ... Released by Bears (August 30, 1998). ... Re-signed by Bears to practice squad (August 31, 1998). ... Activated (December 2, 1998). ... Released by Bears (August 30, 1999). ... Signed by San Francisco 49ers to practice squad (September 29, 1999). ... Activated (November 19, 1999). ... Released by 49ers (February 10, 2000). ... Signed by Atlanta Falcons (February 14, 2000). ... Granted free agency (March 1, 2002).

			TOTALS			INTERCEPTIONS			
Year Team	G	GS	Tk.	Ast.	Sks.	No.	Yds.	Avg.	TD
1998—Chicago NFL	1	0	0	0	0.0	0	0	0.0	0
1999—San Francisco NFL	7	0	0	0	0.0	0	0	0.0	0
2000—Atlanta NFL	13	8	41	15	1.0	0	0	0.0	0
2001—Atlanta NFL	13	10	53	19	0.0	0	0	0.0	0
2002—Atlanta NFL	15	5	49	15	3.5	2	12	6.0	0
Pro totals (5 years)	49	23	143	49	4.5	2	12	6.0	0

DRIVER, DONALD   WR   PACKERS

PERSONAL: Born February 2, 1975, in Houston. ... 6-0/188. ... Full name: Donald Jerome Driver.
HIGH SCHOOL: Milby (Houston).
COLLEGE: Alcorn State (degree in accounting).
TRANSACTIONS/CAREER NOTES: Selected by Green Bay Packers in seventh round (213th pick overall) of 1999 NFL draft. ... Signed by Packers (June 2, 1999). ... Granted free agency (March 1, 2002). ... Re-signed by Packers (April 16, 2002).
HONORS: Played in Pro Bowl (2002 season).
SINGLE GAME HIGHS (regular season): Receptions—11 (November 10, 2002, vs. Detroit); yards—130 (November 10, 2002, vs. Detroit); and touchdown receptions—2 (September 29, 2002, vs. Carolina).
STATISTICAL PLATEAUS: 100-yard receiving games: 2002 (3).

			RUSHING				RECEIVING				TOTALS			
Year Team	G	GS	Att.	Yds.	Avg.	TD	No.	Yds.	Avg.	TD	TD	2pt.	Pts.	Fum.
1999—Green Bay NFL	6	0	0	0	0.0	0	3	31	10.3	1	1	0	6	0
2000—Green Bay NFL	16	2	1	4	4.0	0	21	322	15.3	1	1	1	8	0
2001—Green Bay NFL	13	2	3	38	12.7	1	13	167	12.8	1	2	0	12	0
2002—Green Bay NFL	16	16	8	70	8.8	0	70	1064	15.2	9	9	0	54	1
Pro totals (4 years)	51	20	12	112	9.3	1	107	1584	14.8	12	13	1	80	1

D

DRIVER, TONY   S   BILLS

PERSONAL: Born August 4, 1977, in Louisville, Ky. ... 6-1/207.
HIGH SCHOOL: Male (Louisville, Ky.).
COLLEGE: Notre Dame.
TRANSACTIONS/CAREER NOTES: Selected by Buffalo Bills in sixth round (178th pick overall) of 2001 NFL draft. ... Signed by Bills (June 18, 2001). ... On injured reserve with shoulder and knee injuries (November 7, 2001-remainder of season).

			TOTALS			INTERCEPTIONS				KICKOFF RETURNS				TOTALS			
Year Team	G	GS	Tk.	Ast.	Sks.	No.	Yds.	Avg.	TD	No.	Yds.	Avg.	TD	TD	2pt.	Pts.	Fum.
2001—Buffalo NFL	5	0	0	0	0.0	0	0	0.0	0	7	130	18.6	0	0	0	0	0
2002—Buffalo NFL	6	0	0	0	0.0	0	0	0.0	0	1	27	27.0	0	0	0	0	0
Pro totals (2 years)	11	0	0	0	0.0	0	0	0.0	0	8	157	19.6	0	0	0	0	0

DROUGHNS, REUBEN   RB   BRONCOS

PERSONAL: Born August 21, 1978, in Chicago. ... 5-11/207.
HIGH SCHOOL: Anaheim (Calif.).
JUNIOR COLLEGE: Merced (Calif.) College.
COLLEGE: Oregon.
TRANSACTIONS/CAREER NOTES: Selected by Detroit Lions in third round (81st pick overall) of 2000 NFL draft. ... Signed by Lions (July 15, 2000). ... On injured reserve with shoulder injury (August 22, 2000-entire season). ... Released by Lions (September 12, 2001). ... Signed by Miami Dolphins to practice squad (September 18, 2001). ... Signed by Lions off Dolphins practice squad (October 9, 2001). ... Granted free agency (March 1, 2002). ... Signed by Denver Broncos (April 1, 2002). ... Granted free agency (February 28, 2003). ... Re-signed by Broncos (April 24, 2003).
SINGLE GAME HIGHS (regular season): Attempts—13 (November 11, 2001, vs. Tampa Bay); yards—36 (November 4, 2001, vs. San Francisco); and rushing touchdowns—1 (September 30, 2002, vs. Baltimore).

			RUSHING				RECEIVING				KICKOFF RETURNS				TOTALS			
Year Team	G	GS	Att.	Yds.	Avg.	TD	No.	Yds.	Avg.	TD	No.	Yds.	Avg.	TD	TD	2pt.	Pts.	Fum.
2000—Detroit NFL							Did not play.											
2001—Detroit NFL	9	3	30	72	2.4	0	4	21	5.3	1	0	0	0.0	0	1	0	6	0
2002—Denver NFL	16	0	4	11	2.8	1	5	53	10.6	1	20	516	25.8	0	2	0	12	0
Pro totals (2 years)	25	3	34	83	2.4	1	9	74	8.2	2	20	516	25.8	0	3	0	18	0

DRUMMOND, EDDIE   WR   LIONS

PERSONAL: Born April 12, 1980, in Pittsburgh ... 5-9/185.
HIGH SCHOOL: Linsley (Pittsburgh).
COLLEGE: Penn State.
TRANSACTIONS/CAREER NOTES: Signed as non-drafted free agent by Detroit Lions (April 26, 2002).
SINGLE GAME HIGHS (regular season): Receptions—1 (December 8, 2002, vs. Arizona); yards—1 (December 8, 2002, vs. Arizona); and touchdown receptions—0.

				RUSHING				RECEIVING				PUNT RETURNS				KICKOFF RETURNS				TOTALS	
Year	Team	G	GS	Att.	Yds.	Avg.	TD	No.	Yds.	Avg.	TD	No.	Yds.	Avg.	TD	No.	Yds.	Avg.	TD	TD	2pt. Pts.
2002—Detroit NFL		9	0	4	38	9.5	0	2	-3	-1.5	0	18	138	7.7	1	40	1039	26.0	0	1	0 6

DUCKETT, T.J.   RB   FALCONS

PERSONAL: Born February 17, 1981, in Kalamazoo, Mich. ... 6-0/254.
HIGH SCHOOL: Loy Norrix (Kalamazoo, Mich.).
COLLEGE: Michigan State.
TRANSACTIONS/CAREER NOTES: Selected after junior season by Atlanta Falcons in first round (18th pick overall) of 2002 NFL draft. ... Signed by Falcons (August 3, 2002).
SINGLE GAME HIGHS (regular season): Attempts—22 (November 24, 2002, vs. Carolina); yards—75 (November 3, 2002, vs. Baltimore); and rushing touchdowns—2 (October 20, 2002, vs. Carolina).

				RUSHING				RECEIVING				TOTALS			
Year	Team	G	GS	Att.	Yds.	Avg.	TD	No.	Yds.	Avg.	TD	TD	2pt.	Pts.	Fum.
2002—Atlanta NFL		12	3	130	507	3.9	4	9	61	6.8	0	4	0	24	0

DUDLEY, RICKEY   TE   BUCCANEERS

D

PERSONAL: Born July 15, 1972, in Henderson, Texas. ... 6-6/255.
HIGH SCHOOL: Henderson (Texas).
COLLEGE: Ohio State.
TRANSACTIONS/CAREER NOTES: Selected by Oakland Raiders in first round (ninth pick overall) of 1996 NFL draft. ... Signed by Raiders (July 12, 1996). ... Granted unconditional free agency (March 2, 2001). ... Signed by Cleveland Browns (March 30, 2001). ... On injured reserve with foot injury (October 9, 2001-remainder of season). ... Released by Browns (September 1, 2002). ... Signed by Tampa Bay Buccaneers (September 17, 2002). ... Granted unconditional free agency (February 28, 2003). ... Re-signed by Buccaneers (April 25, 2003).
CHAMPIONSHIP GAME EXPERIENCE: Played in AFC championship game (2000 season). ... Played in NFC championship game (2002 season). ... Member of Super Bowl championship team (2002 season).
SINGLE GAME HIGHS (regular season): Receptions—6 (November 8, 1998, vs. Baltimore); yards—116 (November 9, 1997, vs. New Orleans); and touchdown receptions—2 (December 24, 2000, vs. Carolina).
STATISTICAL PLATEAUS: 100-yard receiving games: 1997 (2), 1998 (1). Total: 3.
MISCELLANEOUS: Member of Ohio State basketball team (1991-92 through 1993-94).

				RECEIVING				TOTALS			
Year	Team	G	GS	No.	Yds.	Avg.	TD	TD	2pt.	Pts.	Fum.
1996—Oakland NFL		16	15	34	386	11.4	4	4	0	24	1
1997—Oakland NFL		16	16	48	787	16.4	7	7	0	42	0
1998—Oakland NFL		16	15	36	549	15.3	5	5	1	32	1
1999—Oakland NFL		16	16	39	555	14.2	9	9	0	54	0
2000—Oakland NFL		16	16	29	350	12.1	4	4	0	24	1
2001—Cleveland NFL		4	4	9	115	12.8	0	0	0	0	0
2002—Tampa Bay NFL		14	3	16	192	12.0	3	3	0	18	0
Pro totals (7 years)		98	85	211	2934	13.9	32	32	1	194	3

DUGANS, RON   WR   BENGALS

PERSONAL: Born April 27, 1977, in Tallahassee, Fla. ... 6-2/205.
HIGH SCHOOL: Florida A&M University Develop Research (Tallahassee, Fla.).
COLLEGE: Florida State (degree in political science, 1999).
TRANSACTIONS/CAREER NOTES: Selected by Cincinnati Bengals in third round (66th pick overall) of 2000 NFL draft. ... Signed by Bengals (July 25, 2000). ... Granted free agency (February 28, 2003). ... Re-signed by Bengals (April 25, 2003).
SINGLE GAME HIGHS (regular season): Receptions—7 (December 1, 2002, vs. Baltimore); yards—81 (December 1, 2002, vs. Baltimore); and touchdown receptions—1 (December 30, 2001, vs. Pittsburgh).

				RECEIVING				TOTALS			
Year	Team	G	GS	No.	Yds.	Avg.	TD	TD	2pt.	Pts.	Fum.
2000—Cincinnati NFL		14	5	14	125	8.9	1	1	0	6	0
2001—Cincinnati NFL		16	3	28	251	9.0	2	2	1	14	0
2002—Cincinnati NFL		16	5	47	421	9.0	0	0	0	0	0
Pro totals (3 years)		46	13	89	797	9.0	3	3	1	20	0

DUNCAN, JAMIE   LB   RAMS

PERSONAL: Born July 20, 1975, in Wilmington, Del. ... 6-1/238. ... Full name: Jamie Robert Duncan.
HIGH SCHOOL: Christiana (Newark, Del.).
COLLEGE: Vanderbilt (degree in human and organizational development, 1998).

TRANSACTIONS/CAREER NOTES: Selected by Tampa Bay Buccaneers in third round (84th pick overall) of 1998 NFL draft. ... Signed by Buccaneers (July 10, 1998). ... Granted unconditional free agency (March 1, 2002). ... Signed by St. Louis Rams (March 7, 2002).
CHAMPIONSHIP GAME EXPERIENCE: Played in NFC championship game (1999 season).
HONORS: Named inside linebacker on THE SPORTING NEWS college All-America second team (1997).

			TOTALS			INTERCEPTIONS			
Year Team	G	GS	Tk.	Ast.	Sks.	No.	Yds.	Avg.	TD
1998—Tampa Bay NFL	14	6	30	6	0.0	0	0	0.0	0
1999—Tampa Bay NFL	16	0	0	0	0.0	0	0	0.0	0
2000—Tampa Bay NFL	15	15	48	17	0.0	4	55	13.8	1
2001—Tampa Bay NFL	15	15	66	21	2.0	1	9	9.0	0
2002—St. Louis NFL	16	12	47	16	0.0	0	0	0.0	0
Pro totals (5 years)	76	48	191	60	2.0	5	64	12.8	1

DUNN, JASON   TE   CHIEFS

PERSONAL: Born November 15, 1973, in Harrodsburg, Ky. ... 6-6/276. ... Full name: Jason Adam Dunn.
HIGH SCHOOL: Harrodsburg (Ky.).
COLLEGE: Eastern Kentucky.
TRANSACTIONS/CAREER NOTES: Selected by Philadelphia Eagles in second round (54th pick overall) of 1996 NFL draft. ... Signed by Eagles (July 17, 1996). ... On injured reserve with knee injury (December 1, 1998-remainder of season). ... Granted free agency (February 12, 1999). ... Re-signed by Eagles for 1999 season. ... Released by Eagles (June 17, 1999). ... Signed by Kansas City Chiefs (July 11, 2000). ... Granted unconditional free agency (March 2, 2001). ... Re-signed by Chiefs (March 26, 2001). ... On injured reserve with elbow injury (January 4, 2001-remainder of season).
SINGLE GAME HIGHS (regular season): Receptions—4 (November 15, 1998, vs. Washington); yards—58 (September 22, 1996, vs. Atlanta); and touchdown receptions—1 (December 23, 2001, vs. San Diego).

			RECEIVING				TOTALS			
Year Team	G	GS	No.	Yds.	Avg.	TD	TD	2pt.	Pts.	Fum.
1996—Philadelphia NFL	16	12	15	332	22.1	2	2	0	12	0
1997—Philadelphia NFL	15	4	7	93	13.3	2	2	0	12	0
1998—Philadelphia NFL	10	10	18	132	7.3	0	0	0	0	1
2000—Kansas City NFL	14	2	2	26	13.0	0	0	0	0	0
2001—Kansas City NFL	15	5	4	54	13.5	1	1	0	6	0
2002—Kansas City NFL	11	4	2	16	8.0	0	0	0	0	0
Pro totals (6 years)	81	37	48	653	13.6	5	5	0	30	1

DUNN, WARRICK   RB   FALCONS

PERSONAL: Born January 5, 1975, in Baton Rouge, La. ... 5-9/180. ... Full name: Warrick De'Mon Dunn.
HIGH SCHOOL: Catholic (Baton Rouge, La.).
COLLEGE: Florida State (degree in information studies, 1997).
TRANSACTIONS/CAREER NOTES: Selected by Tampa Bay Buccaneers in first round (12th pick overall) of 1997 NFL draft. ... Signed by Buccaneers (July 24, 1997). ... Granted unconditional free agency (March 1, 2002). ... Signed by Atlanta Falcons (March 15, 2002).
CHAMPIONSHIP GAME EXPERIENCE: Played in NFC championship game (1999 season).
HONORS: Named NFL Rookie of the Year by THE SPORTING NEWS (1997). ... Played in Pro Bowl (1997 and 2000 seasons).
SINGLE GAME HIGHS (regular season): Attempts—30 (December 22, 2002, vs. Detroit); yards—210 (December 3, 2000, vs. Dallas); and rushing touchdowns—3 (December 18, 2000, vs. St. Louis).
STATISTICAL PLATEAUS: 100-yard rushing games: 1997 (5), 1998 (2), 2000 (3), 2002 (4). Total: 14. ... 100-yard receiving games: 1997 (1), 1999 (1), 2001 (1). Total: 3.

			RUSHING				RECEIVING				KICKOFF RETURNS				TOTALS			
Year Team	G	GS	Att.	Yds.	Avg.	TD	No.	Yds.	Avg.	TD	No.	Yds.	Avg.	TD	TD	2pt.	Pts.	Fum.
1997—Tampa Bay NFL	16	10	224	978	4.4	4	39	462	11.8	3	6	129	21.5	0	7	0	42	4
1998—Tampa Bay NFL	16	14	245	1026	4.2	2	44	344	7.8	0	1	25	25.0	0	2	0	12	1
1999—Tampa Bay NFL	15	15	195	616	3.2	0	64	589	9.2	2	8	156	19.5	0	2	0	12	3
2000—Tampa Bay NFL	16	14	248	1133	4.6	8	44	422	9.6	1	0	0	0.0	0	9	0	54	1
2001—Tampa Bay NFL	13	12	158	447	2.8	3	68	557	8.2	3	0	0	0.0	0	6	0	36	2
2002—Atlanta NFL	15	14	230	927	4.0	7	50	377	7.5	2	0	0	0.0	0	9	0	54	4
Pro totals (6 years)	91	79	1300	5127	3.9	24	309	2751	8.9	11	15	310	20.7	0	35	0	210	15

DWIGHT, TIM   WR/PR   CHARGERS

PERSONAL: Born July 13, 1975, in Iowa City, Iowa. ... 5-9/180. ... Full name: Timothy John Dwight Jr.
HIGH SCHOOL: Iowa City (Iowa) High.
COLLEGE: Iowa.
TRANSACTIONS/CAREER NOTES: Selected by Atlanta Falcons in fourth round (114th pick overall) of 1998 NFL draft. ... Signed by Falcons (June 25, 1998). ... Granted free agency (March 2, 2001). ... Re-signed by Falcons (April 21, 2001). ... Traded by Falcons with first-(RB LaDainian Tomlinson) and third-round (DB Tay Cody) picks in 2001 draft and second-round pick in 2002 draft to San Diego Chargers for first-round pick (QB Michael Vick) in 2001 draft (April 20, 2001).
CHAMPIONSHIP GAME EXPERIENCE: Played in NFC championship game (1998 season). ... Played in Super Bowl XXXIII (1998 season).
HONORS: Named kick returner on THE SPORTING NEWS college All-America second team (1996). ... Named kick returner on THE SPORTING NEWS college All-America first team (1997).
POST SEASON RECORDS: Holds Super Bowl career record for highest kickoff return average (minimum four returns)—42.0. ... Shares Super Bowl single-game record for most touchdowns by kickoff return—1 (January 31, 1999, vs. Denver).
SINGLE GAME HIGHS (regular season): Receptions—7 (January 3, 2000, vs. San Francisco); yards—162 (January 3, 2000, vs. San Francisco); and touchdown receptions—2 (January 3, 2000, vs. San Francisco).
STATISTICAL PLATEAUS: 100-yard receiving games: 1999 (2).

Year	Team	G	GS	RUSHING Att	Yds	Avg	TD	RECEIVING No	Yds	Avg	TD	PUNT RETURNS No	Yds	Avg	TD	KICKOFF RETURNS No	Yds	Avg	TD	TOTALS TD	2pt	Pts.
1998—Atlanta NFL		12	0	8	19	2.4	0	4	94	23.5	1	31	263	8.5	0	36	973	27.0	1	2	0	12
1999—Atlanta NFL		12	8	5	28	5.6	1	32	669	*20.9	7	20	220	11.0	∞1	44	944	21.5	0	9	0	54
2000—Atlanta NFL		14	1	5	8	1.6	0	26	406	16.6	3	33	309	9.4	1	32	680	21.3	0	4	0	24
2001—San Diego NFL		10	2	2	24	12.0	1	25	406	16.2	0	24	271	11.3	1	0	0	0.0	0	2	0	12
2002—San Diego NFL		16	14	12	108	9.0	1	50	623	12.5	2	19	231	12.2	0	8	166	20.8	0	3	0	18
Pro totals (5 years)		64	25	32	187	5.8	3	137	2198	16.0	13	127	1294	10.2	3	120	2763	23.0	1	20	0	120

DYER, DEON — FB — DOLPHINS

PERSONAL: Born October 2, 1977, in Chesapeake, Va. ... 5-11/255. ... Full name: Deon Joseph Dyer.
HIGH SCHOOL: Deep Creek (Chesapeake, Va.).
COLLEGE: North Carolina.
TRANSACTIONS/CAREER NOTES: Selected by Miami Dolphins in fourth round (117th pick overall) of 2000 NFL draft. ... Signed by Dolphins (June 2, 2000).

Year	Team	G	GS	RUSHING Att	Yds	Avg	TD	RECEIVING No	Yds	Avg	TD	TOTALS TD	2pt	Pts.	Fum.
2000—Miami NFL		16	0	0	0	0.0	0	2	14	7.0	0	0	0	0	0
2001—Miami NFL		16	0	0	0	0.0	0	0	0	0.0	0	0	0	0	0
2002—Miami NFL		13	0	0	0	0.0	0	0	0	0.0	0	0	0	0	0
Pro totals (3 years)		45	0	0	0	0.0	0	2	14	7.0	0	0	0	0	0

DYSON, ANDRE — CB — TITANS

PERSONAL: Born May 25, 1979, in Layton, Utah. ... 5-10/187. ... Brother of Kevin Dyson, wide receiver, Carolina Panthers.
HIGH SCHOOL: Clearfield (Utah).
COLLEGE: Utah.
TRANSACTIONS/CAREER NOTES: Selected by Tennessee Titans in second round (60th pick overall) of 2001 NFL draft. ... Signed by Titans (July 24, 2001).
CHAMPIONSHIP GAME EXPERIENCE: Played in AFC championship game (2002 season).

Year	Team	G	GS	TOTALS Tk.	Ast.	Sks.	INTERCEPTIONS No.	Yds.	Avg.	TD
2001—Tennessee NFL		14	12	54	4	0.0	3	36	12.0	0
2002—Tennessee NFL		16	16	56	5	1.0	3	27	9.0	1
Pro totals (2 years)		30	28	110	9	1.0	6	63	10.5	1

DYSON, KEVIN — WR — PANTHERS

PERSONAL: Born June 23, 1975, in Logan, Utah ... 6-1/208. ... Full name: Kevin Tyree Dyson. ... Brother of Andre Dyson, cornerback, Tennessee Titans.
HIGH SCHOOL: Clearfield (Utah).
COLLEGE: Utah.
TRANSACTIONS/CAREER NOTES: Selected by Tennessee Oilers in first round (16th pick overall) of 1998 NFL draft. ... Signed by Oilers (July 24, 1998). ... Oilers franchise renamed Tennessee Titans for 1999 season (December 26, 1998). ... On injured reserve with knee injury (September 29, 2000-remainder of season). ... On injured reserve with hamstring injury (December 20, 2002-remainder of season). ... Granted unconditional free agency (February 28, 2003). ... Signed by Carolina Panthers (March 19, 2003).
CHAMPIONSHIP GAME EXPERIENCE: Played in AFC championship game (1999 season). ... Played in Super Bowl XXXIV (1999 season).
SINGLE GAME HIGHS (regular season): Receptions—9 (September 12, 1999, vs. Cincinnati); yards—162 (September 12, 1999, vs. Cincinnati); and touchdown receptions—2 (November 17, 2002, vs. Pittsburgh).
STATISTICAL PLATEAUS: 100-yard receiving games: 1999 (1), 2000 (1), 2001 (2). Total: 4.

Year	Team	G	GS	RECEIVING No.	Yds.	Avg.	TD	TOTALS TD	2pt.	Pts.	Fum.
1998—Tennessee NFL		13	9	21	263	12.5	2	2	0	12	0
1999—Tennessee NFL		16	16	54	658	12.2	4	4	0	24	0
2000—Tennessee NFL		2	2	6	104	17.3	1	1	0	6	0
2001—Tennessee NFL		16	16	54	825	15.3	7	7	1	44	0
2002—Tennessee NFL		11	11	41	460	11.2	4	4	0	24	1
Pro totals (5 years)		58	54	176	2310	13.1	18	18	1	110	1

EASON, NIJRELL — S — CARDINALS

PERSONAL: Born May 20, 1979, in Long Beach, Calif. ... 6-1/205.
HIGH SCHOOL: Woodrow Wilson (Long Beach, Calif.).
JUNIOR COLLEGE: Long Beach (Calif.) City College.
COLLEGE: Arizona State.
TRANSACTIONS/CAREER NOTES: Signed as non-drafted free agent by Arizona Cardinals (April 23, 2001). ... Released by Cardinals (August 8, 2001). ... Signed by Pittsburgh Steelers (February 5, 2002). ... Assigned by Steelers to Frankfurt Galaxy in 2002 NFL Europe enhancement allocation program (February 12, 2002). ... Released by Steelers (September 1, 2002). ... Signed by Arizona Cardinals (December 27, 2002). ... Re-signed by Cardinals (March 23, 2003).

Year	Team	G	GS	TOTALS Tk.	Ast.	Sks.	INTERCEPTIONS No.	Yds.	Avg.	TD
2002—Arizona NFL		1	0	0	0	0.0	0	0	0.0	0

EASY, OMAR   RB   CHIEFS

PERSONAL: Born October 29, 1977, in Jamaica. ... 6-1/245. ... Full name: Omar Xavier Easy.
HIGH SCHOOL: Everett (Mass.).
COLLEGE: Penn State.
TRANSACTIONS/CAREER NOTES: Selected by Kansas City Chiefs in fourth round (107th pick overall) of 2002 NFL draft. ... Signed by Chiefs (June 11, 2002).

			RUSHING				RECEIVING				TOTALS		
Year Team	G	GS	Att.	Yds.	Avg.	TD	No.	Yds.	Avg.	TD	TD	2pt.	Pts.	Fum.
2002—Kansas City NFL	7	0	0	0	0.0	0	3	23	7.7	1	1	0	6	0

EATON, CHAD   DT   SEAHAWKS

PERSONAL: Born April 6, 1972, in Exeter, N.H. ... 6-5/303. ... Full name: Chad Everett Eaton.
HIGH SCHOOL: Rogers (Puyallup, Wash.).
COLLEGE: Washington State.
TRANSACTIONS/CAREER NOTES: Selected by Arizona Cardinals in seventh round (241st pick overall) of 1995 NFL draft. ... Signed by Cardinals (July 24, 1995). ... Released by Cardinals (August 14, 1995). ... Signed by New York Jets (August 15, 1995). ... Released by Jets (August 27, 1995). ... Signed by Cleveland Browns to practice squad (September 28, 1995). ... Activated (December 15, 1995); did not play. ... Browns franchise moved to Baltimore and renamed Ravens for 1996 season (March 11, 1996). ... Released by Ravens (August 19, 1996). ... Signed by New England Patriots to practice squad (August 27, 1996). ... Activated (November 28, 1996). ... Granted unconditional free agency (March 2, 2001). ... Signed by Seattle Seahawks (March 9, 2001).
CHAMPIONSHIP GAME EXPERIENCE: Played in AFC championship game (1996 season). ... Played in Super Bowl XXXI (1996 season).
HONORS: Named defensive lineman on THE SPORTING NEWS college All-America second team (1994).

			TOTALS		
Year Team	G	GS	Tk.	Ast.	Sks.
1995—Cleveland NFL			Did not play.		
1996—New England NFL	4	0	3	1	1.0
1997—New England NFL	16	1	13	8	1.0
1998—New England NFL	15	14	49	31	6.0
1999—New England NFL	16	16	38	18	3.0
2000—New England NFL	14	13	59	19	2.5
2001—Seattle NFL	16	16	44	13	1.0
2002—Seattle NFL	16	16	48	25	1.0
Pro totals (7 years)	97	76	254	115	15.5

ECHOLS, MIKE   CB   TITANS

PERSONAL: Born October 13, 1978, in Youngstown, Ohio. ... 5-10/190.
HIGH SCHOOL: Ursuline (Youngstown, Ohio).
COLLEGE: Wisconsin.
TRANSACTIONS/CAREER NOTES: Selected by Tennessee Titans in fourth round (110th pick overall) of 2002 NFL draft. ... Signed by Titans (July 26, 2002). ... On injured reserve with leg injury (November 27, 2002-remainder of season).

			TOTALS			INTERCEPTIONS			
Year Team	G	GS	Tk.	Ast.	Sks.	No.	Yds.	Avg.	TD
2002—Tennessee NFL	4	0	13	7	0.0	0	0	0.0	0

EDINGER, PAUL   K   BEARS

PERSONAL: Born January 17, 1978, in Frankfort, Mich. ... 5-8/168. ... Full name: Paul E. Edinger.
HIGH SCHOOL: Kathleen (Lakeland, Fla.).
COLLEGE: Michigan State.
TRANSACTIONS/CAREER NOTES: Selected by Chicago Bears in sixth round (174th pick overall) of 2000 NFL draft. ... Signed by Bears (June 8, 2000). ... Granted free agency (February 28, 2003). ... Tendered offer sheet by Minnesota Vikings (March 9, 2003). ... Offer matched by Bears (March 12, 2003).

		FIELD GOALS							TOTALS		
Year Team	G	1-29	30-39	40-49	50+	Tot.	Pct.	Lg.	XPM	XPA	Pts.
2000—Chicago NFL	16	6-6	7-9	6-10	2-2	21-27	77.8	54	21	21	84
2001—Chicago NFL	16	6-7	7-8	13-16	0-0	26-31	83.9	48	34	34	112
2002—Chicago NFL	16	4-4	5-6	8-10	5-8	22-28	78.6	∞53	29	29	95
Pro totals (3 years)	48	16-17	19-23	27-36	7-10	69-86	80.2	54	84	84	291

EDMONDS, CHRIS   FB   BENGALS

PERSONAL: Born January 1, 1978, in Newark, N.J. ... 6-3/250.
HIGH SCHOOL: Woodland Hills (Pittsburgh).
COLLEGE: West Virginia.
TRANSACTIONS/CAREER NOTES: Signed as non-drafted free agent by Cincinnati Bengals (April 24, 2001). ... Released by Bengals (September 2, 2001). ... Re-signed by Bengals to practice squad (September 3, 2001). ... Activated (December 18, 2001); did not play. ... Released by Bengals (September 1, 2002). ... Re-signed by Bengals to practice squad (September 2, 2002). ... Activated (November 5, 2002).

			RECEIVING			
Year Team	G	GS	No.	Yds.	Avg.	TD
2002—Cincinnati NFL	8	0	0	0	0.0	0

E

EDWARDS, ANTUAN   CB/SS   PACKERS

PERSONAL: Born May 26, 1977, in Starkville, Miss. ... 6-1/210. ... Full name: Antuan Minye' Edwards. ... Name pronounced AN-twan.
HIGH SCHOOL: Starkville (Miss.).
COLLEGE: Clemson.
TRANSACTIONS/CAREER NOTES: Selected by Green Bay Packers in first round (25th pick overall) of 1999 NFL draft. ... Signed by Packers (June 7, 1999). ... On injured reserve with knee injury (October 3, 2001-remainder of season).

Year Team	G	GS	TOTALS Tk.	Ast.	Sks.	INTERCEPTIONS No.	Yds.	Avg.	TD	PUNT RETURNS No.	Yds.	Avg.	TD	TOTALS TD	2pt.	Pts.	Fum.
1999—Green Bay NFL	16	1	26	4	0.0	4	26	6.5	1	10	90	9.0	0	1	0	6	1
2000—Green Bay NFL	12	3	21	4	0.0	2	4	2.0	0	0	0	0.0	0	0	0	0	0
2001—Green Bay NFL	3	0	2	0	0.0	0	0	0.0	0	0	0	0.0	0	0	0	0	0
2002—Green Bay NFL	12	4	25	14	1.0	0	0	0.0	0	1	0	0.0	0	0	0	0	0
Pro totals (4 years)	43	8	74	22	1.0	6	30	5.0	1	11	90	8.2	0	1	0	6	1

EDWARDS, DONNIE   LB   CHARGERS

PERSONAL: Born April 6, 1973, in San Diego. ... 6-2/227. ... Full name: Donnie Lewis Edwards Jr.
HIGH SCHOOL: Chula Vista (San Diego).
COLLEGE: UCLA (degree in political science).
TRANSACTIONS/CAREER NOTES: Selected by Kansas City Chiefs in fourth round (98th pick overall) of 1996 NFL draft. ... Signed by Chiefs (July 24, 1996). ... Released by Chiefs (March 1, 2002). ... Signed by San Diego Chargers (April 25, 2002).
HONORS: Played in Pro Bowl (2002).

Year Team	G	GS	TOTALS Tk.	Ast.	Sks.	INTERCEPTIONS No.	Yds.	Avg.	TD
1996—Kansas City NFL	15	1	8	3	0.0	1	22	22.0	0
1997—Kansas City NFL	16	16	80	20	2.5	2	15	7.5	0
1998—Kansas City NFL	15	15	80	44	6.0	0	0	0.0	0
1999—Kansas City NFL	16	16	98	25	3.0	5	50	10.0	1
2000—Kansas City NFL	16	16	114	18	1.0	2	45	22.5	1
2001—Kansas City NFL	16	16	98	32	2.0	0	0	0.0	0
2002—San Diego NFL	16	16	100	29	0.0	5	95	19.0	1
Pro totals (7 years)	110	96	578	171	14.5	15	227	15.1	3

EDWARDS, KALIMBA   DE   LIONS

E

PERSONAL: Born December 26, 1979, in East Point, Ga. ... 6-5/264.
HIGH SCHOOL: Tri-Cities (Atlanta).
COLLEGE: South Carolina.
TRANSACTIONS/CAREER NOTES: Selected by Detroit Lions in second round (35th pick overall) of 2002 NFL draft. ... Signed by Lions (July 23, 2002).
HONORS: Named linebacker on THE SPORTING NEWS college All-America first team (2001).

Year Team	G	GS	TOTALS Tk.	Ast.	Sks.	INTERCEPTIONS No.	Yds.	Avg.	TD
2002—Detroit NFL	16	4	23	8	6.5	0	0	0.0	0

EDWARDS, MARC   FB   JAGUARS

PERSONAL: Born November 17, 1974, in Cincinnati. ... 6-0/245. ... Full name: Marc Alexander Edwards.
HIGH SCHOOL: Norwood (Cincinnati).
COLLEGE: Notre Dame (degree in business management, 1996).
TRANSACTIONS/CAREER NOTES: Selected by San Francisco 49ers in second round (55th pick overall) of 1997 NFL draft. ... Signed by 49ers (July 23, 1997). ... On physically unable to perform list with back injury (July 17-August 10, 1998). ... Traded by 49ers to Cleveland Browns for fourth-round pick (DB Pierson Prioleau) in 1999 draft (April 18, 1999). ... Granted unconditional free agency (March 2, 2001). ... Signed by New England Patriots (March 19, 2001). ... Granted unconditional free agency (February 28, 2003). ... Signed by Jacksonville Jaguars (March 16, 2003).
CHAMPIONSHIP GAME EXPERIENCE: Played in NFC championship game (1997 season). ... Played in AFC championship game (2001 season). ... Member of Super Bowl championship team (2001 season).
SINGLE GAME HIGHS (regular season): Attempts—7 (September 15, 2002, vs. New York Jets); yards—41 (September 27, 1998, vs. Atlanta); and rushing touchdowns—1 (December 2, 2001, vs. New York Jets).

Year Team	G	GS	RUSHING Att.	Yds.	Avg.	TD	RECEIVING No.	Yds.	Avg.	TD	TOTALS TD	2pt.	Pts.	Fum.
1997—San Francisco NFL	15	1	5	17	3.4	0	6	48	8.0	0	0	0	0	0
1998—San Francisco NFL	16	10	22	94	4.3	1	22	218	9.9	2	3	0	18	0
1999—Cleveland NFL	16	14	6	35	5.8	0	27	212	7.9	2	2	0	12	1
2000—Cleveland NFL	16	8	2	9	4.5	0	16	128	8.0	2	2	0	12	2
2001—New England NFL	16	13	51	141	2.8	1	25	166	6.6	2	3	0	18	3
2002—New England NFL	16	10	31	96	3.1	0	23	196	8.5	0	0	0	0	1
Pro totals (6 years)	95	56	117	392	3.4	2	119	968	8.1	8	10	0	60	7

EDWARDS, MARIO   CB   COWBOYS

PERSONAL: Born December 1, 1975, in Gautier, Miss. ... 6-0/199. ... Full name: Mario L. Edwards.
HIGH SCHOOL: Pascagoula (Miss.).
COLLEGE: Florida State.
TRANSACTIONS/CAREER NOTES: Selected by Dallas Cowboys in sixth round (180th pick overall) of 2000 NFL draft. ... Signed by Cowboys (July 14, 2000). ... Granted free agency (February 28, 2003). ... Re-signed by Cowboys (April 15, 2003).

			TOTALS			INTERCEPTIONS			
Year Team	G	GS	Tk.	Ast.	Sks.	No.	Yds.	Avg.	TD
2000—Dallas NFL	11	1	5	0	0.0	0	0	0.0	0
2001—Dallas NFL	16	15	42	7	0.0	1	71	71.0	1
2002—Dallas NFL	15	15	53	4	0.0	2	29	14.5	0
Pro totals (3 years)	42	31	100	11	0.0	3	100	33.3	1

EDWARDS, ROBERT   RB   DOLPHINS

PERSONAL: Born October 2, 1974, in Tennille, Ga. ... 5-11/220. ... Full name: Robert Lee Edwards III.
HIGH SCHOOL: Washington County (Sandersville, Ga.).
COLLEGE: Georgia.
TRANSACTIONS/CAREER NOTES: Selected by New England Patriots in first round (18th pick overall) of 1998 NFL draft. ... Signed by Patriots (July 17, 1998). ... On non-football injury list with knee injury (August 31, 1999-entire season). ... On non-football injury list with knee injury (August 22, 2000-entire season). ... On physically unable to perform list with knee injury (July 23-August 24, 2001). ... Released by Patriots (August 24, 2001). ... Signed by Miami Dolphins (March 6, 2002).
SINGLE GAME HIGHS (regular season): Attempts—28 (December 6, 1998, vs. Pittsburgh); yards—196 (December 13, 1998, vs. St. Louis); and rushing touchdowns—1 (September 8, 2002, vs. Detroit).
STATISTICAL PLATEAUS: 100-yard rushing games: 1998 (4).

			RUSHING				RECEIVING				TOTALS			
Year Team	G	GS	Att.	Yds.	Avg.	TD	No.	Yds.	Avg.	TD	TD	2pt.	Pts.	Fum.
1998—New England NFL	16	15	291	1115	3.8	9	35	331	9.5	3	12	0	72	5
1999—New England NFL							Did not play.							
2000—New England NFL							Did not play.							
2001—							Did not play.							
2002—Miami NFL	12	0	20	107	5.4	1	18	126	7.0	1	2	0	12	0
Pro totals (2 years)	28	15	311	1222	3.9	10	53	457	8.6	4	14	0	84	5

EDWARDS, RON   DT   BILLS

PERSONAL: Born July 12, 1979, in Houston. ... 6-3/305.
HIGH SCHOOL: Klein Forest (Houston).
COLLEGE: Texas A&M.
TRANSACTIONS/CAREER NOTES: Selected by Buffalo Bills in third round (76th pick overall) of 2001 NFL draft. ... Signed by Bills (June 1, 2001).

			TOTALS		
Year Team	G	GS	Tk.	Ast.	Sks.
2001—Buffalo NFL	7	3	7	3	0.0
2002—Buffalo NFL	16	16	25	15	2.5
Pro totals (2 years)	23	19	32	18	2.5

EDWARDS, STEVE   OT   BEARS

PERSONAL: Born February 20, 1979, in Chicago. ... 6-5/350.
HIGH SCHOOL: Mount Carmel (Chicago).
JUNIOR COLLEGE: West Hills Community College (Calif.).
COLLEGE: Tennessee State, then Central Florida.
TRANSACTIONS/CAREER NOTES: Signed as non-drafted free agent by Philadelphia Eagles (April 23, 2002). ... Released by Eagles (September 1, 2002). ... Re-signed by Eagles to practice squad (September 3, 2002). ... Signed by Chicago Bears off Eagles practice squad (October 9, 2002).
PLAYING EXPERIENCE: Chicago NFL, 2002. ... Games/Games started: (1-0).

EDWARDS, TROY   WR   RAMS

PERSONAL: Born April 7, 1977, in Shreveport, La. ... 5-10/191.
HIGH SCHOOL: Huntington (Shreveport, La.).
COLLEGE: Louisiana Tech.
TRANSACTIONS/CAREER NOTES: Selected by Pittsburgh Steelers in first round (13th pick overall) of 1999 NFL draft. ... Signed by Steelers (July 28, 1999). ... Traded by Steelers to St. Louis Rams for sixth-round pick in 2004 draft (September 1, 2002).
CHAMPIONSHIP GAME EXPERIENCE: Played in AFC championship game (2001 season).
HONORS: Fred Biletnikoff Award winner (1998). ... Named wide receiver on THE SPORTING NEWS college All-America second team (1998).
SINGLE GAME HIGHS (regular season): Receptions—7 (November 28, 1999, vs. Cincinnati); yards—86 (November 28, 1999, vs. Cincinnati); and touchdown receptions—1 (December 15, 2002, vs. Arizona).

			RUSHING				RECEIVING				PUNT RETURNS				KICKOFF RETURNS				TOTALS		
Year Team	G	GS	Att.	Yds.	Avg.	TD	No.	Yds.	Avg.	TD	No.	Yds.	Avg.	TD	No.	Yds.	Avg.	TD	TD	2pt.	Pts.
1999—Pittsburgh NFL	16	6	0	0	0.0	0	61	714	11.7	5	25	234	9.4	0	13	234	18.0	0	5	0	30
2000—Pittsburgh NFL	14	1	3	4	1.3	0	18	215	11.9	0	0	0	0.0	0	15	298	19.9	0	0	0	0
2001—Pittsburgh NFL	16	0	5	28	5.6	1	19	283	14.9	0	10	83	8.3	0	20	462	23.1	0	2	0	12
2002—St. Louis NFL	14	0	3	21	7.0	0	18	157	8.7	2	0	0	0.0	0	10	211	21.1	0	2	0	12
Pro totals (4 years)	60	7	11	53	4.8	1	116	1369	11.8	7	35	317	9.1	0	58	1205	20.8	0	9	0	54

EKUBAN, EBENEZER · DE · COWBOYS

PERSONAL: Born May 29, 1976, in Ghana, Africa. ... 6-3/265. ... Full name: Ebenezer Ekuban Jr. ... Name pronounced ECK-you-bon.
HIGH SCHOOL: Bladensburg (Md.).
COLLEGE: North Carolina.
TRANSACTIONS/CAREER NOTES: Selected by Dallas Cowboys in first round (20th pick overall) of 1999 NFL draft. ... Signed by Cowboys (July 27, 1999). ... On injured reserve with back injury (December 21, 2001-remainder of season).

Year Team	G	GS	TOTALS Tk.	Ast.	Sks.
1999—Dallas NFL	16	2	20	3	2.5
2000—Dallas NFL	12	2	22	7	6.5
2001—Dallas NFL	1	1	1	1	0.0
2002—Dallas NFL	16	15	26	5	1.0
Pro totals (4 years)	45	20	69	16	10.0

ELAM, JASON · K · BRONCOS

PERSONAL: Born March 8, 1970, in Fort Walton Beach, Fla. ... 5-11/200. ... Name pronounced EE-lum.
HIGH SCHOOL: Brookwood (Snellville, Ga.).
COLLEGE: Hawaii.
TRANSACTIONS/CAREER NOTES: Selected by Denver Broncos in third round (70th pick overall) of 1993 NFL draft. ... Signed by Broncos (July 12, 1993). ... Designated by Broncos as franchise player (February 21, 2002). ... Granted free agency (March 1, 2002). ... Re-signed by Broncos (July 25, 2002).
CHAMPIONSHIP GAME EXPERIENCE: Played in AFC championship game (1997 and 1998 seasons). ... Member of Super Bowl championship team (1997 and 1998 seasons).
HONORS: Named kicker on THE SPORTING NEWS college All-America second team (1989 and 1991). ... Played in Pro Bowl (1995, 1998 and 2001 seasons).
RECORDS: Holds NFL career record for most consecutive PATs made—371 (1993-2002). ... Holds NFL career record for highest PAT percentage—99.51. ... Shares NFL career record for longest field goal—63 (October 25, 1998, vs. Jacksonville).

Year Team	G	FIELD GOALS 1-29	30-39	40-49	50+	Tot.	Pct.	Lg.	TOTALS XPM	XPA	Pts.
1993—Denver NFL	16	11-12	7-7	4-10	4-6	26-35	74.3	54	§41	§42	119
1994—Denver NFL	16	11-11	11-11	7-12	1-3	30-37	81.1	†54	29	29	119
1995—Denver NFL	16	7-9	14-15	5-7	5-7	31-38	81.6	§56	39	39	132
1996—Denver NFL	16	10-10	4-5	6-10	1-3	21-28	75.0	51	§46	§46	109
1997—Denver NFL	15	10-11	10-12	3-8	3-5	26-36	72.2	53	§46	§46	124
1998—Denver NFL	16	3-3	13-14	4-6	3-4	23-27	85.2	*63	§58	§58	§127
1999—Denver NFL	16	9-9	7-8	8-11	5-8	29-36	80.6	*55	29	29	116
2000—Denver NFL	13	7-7	6-7	4-9	1-1	18-24	75.0	51	*49	*49	103
2001—Denver NFL	16	11-11	8-8	10-13	2-4	*31-36	86.1	50	31	31	124
2002—Denver NFL	16	10-10	7-9	5-11	4-6	26-§36	72.2	55	42	43	120
Pro totals (10 years)	156	89-93	87-96	56-97	29-47	261-333	78.4	63	410	412	1193

ELLIOTT, JAMIN · WR · BEARS

PERSONAL: Born October 5, 1979, in Portsmouth, Va. ... 6-0/187.
HIGH SCHOOL: Churchland (Portsmouth, Va.).
COLLEGE: Delaware.
TRANSACTIONS/CAREER NOTES: Selected by Chicago Bears in sixth round (203rd pick overall) of 2002 NFL draft. ... Signed by Bears (July 25, 2002). ... Released by Bears (October 3, 2002). ... Re-signed by Bears to practice squad (October 5, 2002). ... Activated (November 20, 2002).

Year Team	G	GS	RECEIVING No.	Yds.	Avg.	TD	TOTALS TD	2pt.	Pts.	Fum.
2002—Chicago NFL	1	0	0	0	0.0	0	0	0	0	0

ELLIOTT, JUMBO · OT

PERSONAL: Born April 1, 1965, in Lake Ronkonkoma, N.Y. ... 6-7/305. ... Full name: John Elliott.
HIGH SCHOOL: Sachem (Lake Ronkonkoma, N.Y.).
COLLEGE: Michigan.
TRANSACTIONS/CAREER NOTES: Selected by New York Giants in second round (36th pick overall) of 1988 NFL draft. ... Signed by Giants (July 18, 1988). ... Granted free agency (February 1, 1991). ... Re-signed by Giants (August 22, 1991). ... Designated by Giants as franchise player (February 25, 1993). ... On injured reserve with back injury (January 7, 1994-remainder of playoffs). ... Granted unconditional free agency (February 16, 1996). ... Signed by New York Jets (February 24, 1996). ... On injured reserve with ankle injury (December 1, 1997-remainder of season). ... Announced retirement (March 6, 2000). ... Re-signed by Jets (August 14, 2000). ... On suspended list (August 29-September 4, 2000). ... Released by Jets (July 19, 2001). ... Re-signed by Jets (April 5, 2002). ... Granted unconditional free agency (February 28, 2003).
PLAYING EXPERIENCE: New York Giants NFL, 1988-1995; New York Jets NFL, 1996-2002. ... Games/Games started: 1988 (16/5), 1989 (13/11), 1990 (8/8), 1991 (16/16), 1992 (16/16), 1993 (11/11), 1994 (16/15), 1995 (16/16), 1996 (14/14), 1997 (13/13), 1998 (16/16), 1999 (16/15), 2000 (9/0), 2002 (16/0). Total: 196/156.
CHAMPIONSHIP GAME EXPERIENCE: Played in NFC championship game (1990 season). ... Member of Super Bowl championship team (1990 season). ... Played in AFC championship game (1998 season).
HONORS: Played in Pro Bowl (1993 season).

ELLIS, ED   OT   BRONCOS

PERSONAL: Born October 13, 1975, in Hamden, Conn. ... 6-7/325. ... Full name: Edward Key Ellis.
HIGH SCHOOL: Hamden (Conn.).
COLLEGE: Buffalo.
TRANSACTIONS/CAREER NOTES: Selected by New England Patriots in fourth round (125th pick overall) of 1997 NFL draft. ... Signed by Patriots (June 19, 1997). ... Granted free agency (February 11, 2000). ... Assigned by Patriots to Barcelona Dragons in 2000 NFL Europe enhancement allocation program (February 18, 2000). ... Re-signed by Patriots (March 13, 2000). ... Released by Patriots (July 17, 2000). ... Signed by Washington Redskins (July 20, 2000). ... Granted unconditional free agency (March 2, 2001). ... Signed by San Diego Chargers (April 2, 2001). ... Released by Chargers (February 27, 2003). ... Signed by Denver Broncos (April 24, 2003).
PLAYING EXPERIENCE: New England NFL, 1997-1999; Barcelona NFLE 2000; Washington NFL, 2000; San Diego NFL, 2001-2002. ... Games/Games started: 1997 (1/0), 1998 (7/0), 1999 (1/1), NFLE 2000 (games played unavailable), NFL 2000 (12/0), 2001 (16/2), 2002 (15/3). Total: 50/6.

ELLIS, GREG   DE   COWBOYS

PERSONAL: Born August 14, 1975, in Wendell. N.C. ... 6-6/275. ... Full name: Gregory Lemont Ellis.
HIGH SCHOOL: East Wake (Wendell, N.C.).
COLLEGE: North Carolina.
TRANSACTIONS/CAREER NOTES: Selected by Dallas Cowboys in first round (eighth pick overall) of 1998 NFL draft. ... Signed by Cowboys (July 13, 1998). ... On injured reserve with leg injury (December 16, 1999-remainder of season).
HONORS: Named defensive end on THE SPORTING NEWS college All-America second team (1996 and 1997).

			TOTALS			INTERCEPTIONS			
Year Team	G	GS	Tk.	Ast.	Sks.	No.	Yds.	Avg.	TD
1998—Dallas NFL	16	16	27	12	3.0	0	0	0.0	0
1999—Dallas NFL	13	13	37	7	7.5	1	87	87.0	1
2000—Dallas NFL	16	16	39	13	3.0	0	0	0.0	0
2001—Dallas NFL	16	16	45	16	6.0	0	0	0.0	0
2002—Dallas NFL	15	15	50	17	7.5	1	0	0.0	0
Pro totals (5 years)	76	76	198	65	27.0	2	87	43.5	1

ELLIS, SHAUN   DT/DE   JETS

PERSONAL: Born June 24, 1977, in Anderson, S.C. ... 6-5/294. ... Full name: MeShaunda Pizarrur Ellis.
HIGH SCHOOL: Westside (Anderson, S.C.).
COLLEGE: Tennessee.
TRANSACTIONS/CAREER NOTES: Selected by New York Jets in first round (12th pick overall) of 2000 NFL draft. ... Signed by Jets (July 10, 2000).

			TOTALS			INTERCEPTIONS			
Year Team	G	GS	Tk.	Ast.	Sks.	No.	Yds.	Avg.	TD
2000—New York Jets NFL	16	3	38	15	8.5	1	1	1.0	0
2001—New York Jets NFL	16	16	28	12	5.0	0	0	0.0	0
2002—New York Jets NFL	16	16	31	10	4.0	0	0	0.0	0
Pro totals (3 years)	48	35	97	37	17.5	1	1	1.0	0

E

ELLISS, LUTHER   DT   LIONS

PERSONAL: Born March 22, 1973, in Mancos, Colo. ... 6-5/318.
HIGH SCHOOL: Mancos (Colo.).
COLLEGE: Utah.
TRANSACTIONS/CAREER NOTES: Selected by Detroit Lions in first round (20th pick overall) of 1995 NFL draft. ... Signed by Lions (July 19, 1995). ... On injured reserve with ankle injury (December 19, 2002-remainder of season).
HONORS: Named defensive lineman on THE SPORTING NEWS college All-America first team (1994). ... Played in Pro Bowl (1999 and 2000 seasons).

			TOTALS		
Year Team	G	GS	Tk.	Ast.	Sks.
1995—Detroit NFL	16	16	9	10	0.0
1996—Detroit NFL	14	14	26	23	6.5
1997—Detroit NFL	16	16	35	28	8.5
1998—Detroit NFL	16	16	38	12	3.0
1999—Detroit NFL	15	14	31	16	3.5
2000—Detroit NFL	16	16	23	16	3.0
2001—Detroit NFL	14	13	26	5	0.0
2002—Detroit NFL	14	14	19	7	2.5
Pro totals (8 years)	121	119	207	117	27.0

EMMONS, CARLOS   LB   EAGLES

PERSONAL: Born September 3, 1973, in Greenwood, Miss. ... 6-5/250. ... Name pronounced EM-mins.
HIGH SCHOOL: Greenwood (Miss.).
COLLEGE: Arkansas State (degree in business management, 1995).

TRANSACTIONS/CAREER NOTES: Selected by Pittsburgh Steelers in seventh round (242nd pick overall) of 1996 NFL draft. ... Signed by Steelers (July 16, 1996). ... Granted free agency (February 12, 1999). ... Re-signed by Steelers (April 23, 1999). ... Granted unconditional free agency (February 11, 2000). ... Signed by Philadelphia Eagles (March 23, 2000).
CHAMPIONSHIP GAME EXPERIENCE: Played in AFC championship game (1997 season). ... Played in NFC championship game (2001 and 2002 seasons).

			TOTALS			INTERCEPTIONS			
Year Team	G	GS	Tk.	Ast.	Sks.	No.	Yds.	Avg.	TD
1996—Pittsburgh NFL	15	0	5	2	2.5	0	0	0.0	0
1997—Pittsburgh NFL	5	0	1	0	0.0	0	0	0.0	0
1998—Pittsburgh NFL	15	14	46	17	3.5	1	2	2.0	0
1999—Pittsburgh NFL	16	16	51	16	6.0	1	22	22.0	0
2000—Philadelphia NFL	16	13	55	23	0.5	2	8	4.0	0
2001—Philadelphia NFL	16	15	61	18	1.0	0	0	0.0	0
2002—Philadelphia NFL	13	13	51	9	3.5	0	0	0.0	0
Pro totals (7 years)	96	71	270	85	17.0	4	32	8.0	0

ENA, JUSTIN   LB   EAGLES

PERSONAL: Born November 20, 1977, in Provo, Utah. ... 6-3/247.
HIGH SCHOOL: Shelton (Calif.).
COLLEGE: Brigham Young (degree in history).
TRANSACTIONS/CAREER NOTES: Signed as non-drafted free agent by Philadelphia Eagles (April 23, 2002).
CHAMPIONSHIP GAME EXPERIENCE: Played in NFC championship game (2002).

			TOTALS			INTERCEPTIONS			
Year Team	G	GS	Tk.	Ast.	Sks.	No.	Yds.	Avg.	TD
2002—Philadelphia NFL	9	0	1	0	0.0	0	0	0.0	0

ENGELBERGER, JOHN   DE   49ERS

PERSONAL: Born October 18, 1976, in Heidelburg, Germany. ... 6-4/268. ... Full name: John Albert Engelberger.
HIGH SCHOOL: Robert E. Lee (Springfield, Va.).
COLLEGE: Virginia Tech.
TRANSACTIONS/CAREER NOTES: Selected by San Francisco 49ers in second round (35th pick overall) of 2000 NFL draft. ... Signed by 49ers (July 18, 2000).

			TOTALS		
Year Team	G	GS	Tk.	Ast.	Sks.
2000—San Francisco NFL	16	13	21	9	3.0
2001—San Francisco NFL	15	14	30	1	4.0
2002—San Francisco NFL	15	0	9	1	0.0
Pro totals (3 years)	46	27	60	11	7.0

ENGRAM, BOBBY   WR   SEAHAWKS

PERSONAL: Born January 7, 1973, in Camden, S.C. ... 5-10/188. ... Full name: Simon Engram III.
HIGH SCHOOL: Camden (S.C.).
COLLEGE: Penn State.
TRANSACTIONS/CAREER NOTES: Selected by Chicago Bears in second round (52nd pick overall) of 1996 NFL draft. ... Signed by Bears (July 17, 1996). ... Granted free agency (February 12, 1999). ... Re-signed by Bears (April 16, 1999). ... Granted unconditional free agency (February 11, 2000). ... Re-signed by Bears (April 26, 2000). ... On injured reserve with knee injury (September 19, 2000-remainder of season). ... Released by Bears (August 28, 2001). ... Signed by Seattle Seahawks (August 30, 2001). ... Granted unconditional free agency (February 28, 2003). ... Re-signed by Seahawks (March 5, 2003).
HONORS: Named wide receiver on THE SPORTING NEWS college All-America second team (1994 and 1995).
SINGLE GAME HIGHS (regular season): Receptions—13 (December 26, 1999, vs. St. Louis); yards—143 (December 26, 1999, vs. St. Louis); and touchdown receptions—2 (December 26, 1999, vs. St. Louis).
STATISTICAL PLATEAUS: 100-yard receiving games: 1998 (3), 1999 (2). Total: 5.

			RECEIVING				PUNT RETURNS				KICKOFF RETURNS				TOTALS			
Year Team	G	GS	No.	Yds.	Avg.	TD	No.	Yds.	Avg.	TD	No.	Yds.	Avg.	TD	TD	2pt.	Pts.	Fum.
1996—Chicago NFL	16	2	33	389	11.8	6	31	282	9.1	0	25	580	23.2	0	6	0	36	2
1997—Chicago NFL	11	11	45	399	8.9	2	1	4	4.0	0	2	27	13.5	0	2	1	14	1
1998—Chicago NFL	16	16	64	987	15.4	5	0	0	0.0	0	0	0	0.0	0	5	0	30	1
1999—Chicago NFL	16	14	88	947	10.8	4	0	0	0.0	0	0	0	0.0	0	4	0	24	2
2000—Chicago NFL	3	3	16	109	6.8	0	0	0	0.0	0	0	0	0.0	0	0	0	0	1
2001—Seattle NFL	16	4	29	400	13.8	0	6	96	16.0	0	1	6	6.0	0	0	0	0	0
2002—Seattle NFL	15	6	50	619	12.4	0	21	224	10.7	1	0	0	0.0	0	1	0	6	2
Pro totals (7 years)	93	56	325	3850	11.8	17	59	606	10.3	1	28	613	21.9	0	18	1	110	9

EPSTEIN, HAYDEN   K/P   VIKINGS

PERSONAL: Born November 16, 1980, in San Diego. ... 6-2/214.
HIGH SCHOOL: Torrey Pines (Cardiff, Calif.).
COLLEGE: Michigan.
TRANSACTIONS/CAREER NOTES: Selected by Jacksonville Jaguars in seventh round (247th pick overall) of 2002 NFL draft. ... Signed by Jaguars (July 19, 2002). ... Claimed on waivers by Minnesota Vikings (October 23, 2002).

Year Team	G	FIELD GOALS							TOTALS		
		1-29	30-39	40-49	50+	Tot.	Pct.	Lg.	XPM	XPA	Pts.
1990—Tampa Bay NFL	16	7-7	10-13	4-5	2-2	23-27	85.2	54	27	27	96
2002—Minnesota NFL	9	0-0	0-0	0-0	0-0	0-0	0.0	0	0	0	0
—Jacksonville NFL	6	3-3	2-3	0-2	0-1	5-9	55.6	34	13	13	28
Pro totals (1 years)	15	3-3	2-3	0-2	0-1	5-9	55.6	34	13	13	28

EVANS, DEMETRIC — DE — COWBOYS

PERSONAL: Born September 3, 1979, in Haynesville, La. ... 6-3/293. ... Full name: Demetric Untrell Evans.
HIGH SCHOOL: Haynesville (La.).
COLLEGE: Georgia.
TRANSACTIONS/CAREER NOTES: Signed as non-drafted free agent by Dallas Cowboys (April 27, 2001).

Year Team	G	GS	TOTALS		
			Tk.	Ast.	Sks.
2001—Dallas NFL	16	0	16	3	1.0
2002—Dallas NFL	4	0	3	1	0.0
Pro totals (2 years)	20	0	19	4	1.0

EVANS, DOUG — CB — SEAHAWKS

PERSONAL: Born May 13, 1970, in Shreveport, La. ... 6-1/188. ... Full name: Douglas Edwards Evans. ... Brother of Bobby Evans, safety with Winnipeg Blue Bombers of the CFL (1990-94).
HIGH SCHOOL: Haynesville (La.).
COLLEGE: Louisiana Tech (degree in finance).
TRANSACTIONS/CAREER NOTES: Selected by Green Bay Packers in sixth round (141st pick overall) of 1993 NFL draft. ... Signed by Packers (July 9, 1993). ... Granted unconditional free agency (February 13, 1998). ... Signed by Carolina Panthers (February 18, 1998). ... On injured reserve with broken collarbone (November 10, 1998-remainder of season). ... Released by Panthers (February 22, 2002). ... Signed by Seattle Seahawks (April 10, 2002).
CHAMPIONSHIP GAME EXPERIENCE: Played in NFC championship game (1995-1997 seasons). ... Member of Super Bowl championship team (1996 season). ... Played in Super Bowl XXXII (1997 season).

Year Team	G	GS	TOTALS			INTERCEPTIONS			
			Tk.	Ast.	Sks.	No.	Yds.	Avg.	TD
1993—Green Bay NFL	16	0	9	5	0.0	1	0	0.0	0
1994—Green Bay NFL	16	15	46	12	1.0	1	0	0.0	0
1995—Green Bay NFL	16	16	74	15	1.0	2	24	12.0	0
1996—Green Bay NFL	16	16	62	16	3.0	5	102	20.4	1
1997—Green Bay NFL	15	15	66	10	1.0	3	33	11.0	0
1998—Carolina NFL	9	7	32	5	0.0	2	18	9.0	0
1999—Carolina NFL	16	16	60	10	0.0	2	1	0.5	0
2000—Carolina NFL	16	16	66	13	0.0	2	17	8.5	0
2001—Carolina NFL	16	16	60	7	0.0	8	126	15.8	1
2002—Seattle NFL	15	0	26	3	0.0	1	0	0.0	0
Pro totals (10 years)	151	117	501	96	6.0	27	321	11.9	2

EVANS, HEATH — FB — SEAHAWKS

PERSONAL: Born December 30, 1978, in West Palm Beach, Fla. ... 6-0/252. ... Full name: Bryan Heath Evans.
HIGH SCHOOL: Kings Academy (Miami).
COLLEGE: Auburn.
TRANSACTIONS/CAREER NOTES: Selected by Seattle Seahawks in third round (82nd pick overall) of 2001 NFL draft. ... Signed by Seahawks (July 26, 2001).
SINGLE GAME HIGHS (regular season): Attempts—5 (December 29, 2002, vs. San Diego); yards—22 (December 29, 2002, vs. San Diego); and rushing touchdowns—0.

Year Team	G	GS	RUSHING				RECEIVING				KICKOFF RETURNS				TOTALS			
			Att.	Yds.	Avg.	TD	No.	Yds.	Avg.	TD	No.	Yds.	Avg.	TD	TD	2pt.	Pts.	Fum.
2001—Seattle NFL	16	0	2	11	5.5	0	0	0	0.0	0	3	40	13.3	0	0	0	0	0
2002—Seattle NFL	16	1	17	53	3.1	0	8	41	5.1	0	6	84	14.0	0	0	0	0	1
Pro totals (2 years)	32	1	19	64	3.4	0	8	41	5.1	0	9	124	13.8	0	0	0	0	1

EVANS, JOSH — DT/DE — JETS

PERSONAL: Born September 6, 1972, in Langdale, Ala. ... 6-3/280. ... Full name: Mijoshki Antwon Evans.
HIGH SCHOOL: Lanett (Ala.).
COLLEGE: Alabama-Birmingham.
TRANSACTIONS/CAREER NOTES: Signed as non-drafted free agent by Dallas Cowboys (April 27, 1995). ... Released by Cowboys (August 22, 1995). ... Signed by Houston Oilers to practice squad (September 1, 1995). ... Activated (November 10, 1995). ... On injured reserve with knee injury (November 29, 1996-remainder of season). ... Oilers franchise moved to Tennessee for 1997 season. ... Granted free agency (February 13, 1998). ... Re-signed by Oilers (July 25, 1998). ... Oilers franchise renamed Tennessee Titans for 1999 season (December 26, 1998). ... On suspended list for violating league substance abuse policy (September 6-October 4, 1999). ... On suspended list for violating league substance abuse policy (March 1, 2000-April 13, 2001). ... Granted unconditional free agency (March 1, 2002). ... Signed by New York Jets (July 17, 2002).
CHAMPIONSHIP GAME EXPERIENCE: Played in AFC championship game (1999 season). ... Played in Super Bowl XXXIV (1999 season).

E

Year Team	G	GS	TOTALS Tk.	TOTALS Ast.	TOTALS Sks.
1995—Houston NFL	7	0	2	1	0.0
1996—Houston NFL	8	0	4	7	0.0
1997—Tennessee NFL	15	0	23	3	2.0
1998—Tennessee NFL	14	11	30	13	3.5
1999—Tennessee NFL	11	10	21	5	3.5
2000—Tennessee NFL			Did not play.		
2001—Tennessee NFL	16	16	41	12	5.5
2002—New York Jets NFL	16	16	40	7	6.0
Pro totals (7 years)	87	53	161	48	20.5

EVANS, TROY   LB   TEXANS

PERSONAL: Born December 3, 1977, in Bay City, Mich. ... 6-3/243. ... Full name: Troy Lyn Evans.
HIGH SCHOOL: Lakota (Cincinnati).
COLLEGE: Cincinnati.
TRANSACTIONS/CAREER NOTES: Signed as non-drafted free agent by St. Louis Rams (April 25, 2001). ... Released by Rams (August 27, 2001). ... Re-signed by Rams to practice squad (November 21, 2001). ... Granted free agency following 2001 season. ... Signed by Houston Texans (February 12, 2002). ... Released by Texans (September 23, 2002). ... Re-signed by Texans (October 30, 2002). ... Re-signed by Texans (April 1, 2003).

Year Team	G	GS	TOTALS Tk.	TOTALS Ast.	TOTALS Sks.	INTERCEPTIONS No.	INTERCEPTIONS Yds.	INTERCEPTIONS Avg.	INTERCEPTIONS TD
2002—Houston NFL	12	0	0	0	0.0	0	0	0.0	0

FABINI, JASON   OT   JETS

PERSONAL: Born August 25, 1974, in Fort Wayne, Ind. ... 6-7/304.
HIGH SCHOOL: Bishop Dwenger (Fort Wayne, Ind.).
COLLEGE: Cincinnati.
TRANSACTIONS/CAREER NOTES: Selected by New York Jets in fourth round (111th pick overall) of 1998 NFL draft. ... Signed by Jets (July 13, 1998). ... On injured reserve with knee injury (November 16, 1999-remainder of season). ... Granted free agency (March 2, 2001). ... Re-signed by Jets (May 30, 2001).
PLAYING EXPERIENCE: New York Jets NFL, 1998-2002. ... Games/Games started: 1998 (16/16), 1999 (9/9), 2000 (16/16), 2001 (16/16), 2002 (16/16). Total: 73/73.
CHAMPIONSHIP GAME EXPERIENCE: Played in AFC championship game (1998 season).

FAGGINS, DEMARCUS   CB   TEXANS

PERSONAL: Born June 13, 1979, in Irving, Texas. ... 5-10/178. ... Full name: Demarcus Faggins.
HIGH SCHOOL: Irving (Texas).
JUNIOR COLLEGE: Navarro College (Texas).
COLLEGE: Kansas State.
TRANSACTIONS/CAREER NOTES: Selected by Houston Texans in sixth round (173rd pick overall) of 2002 NFL draft. ... Signed by Texans (July 13, 2002).

Year Team	G	GS	TOTALS Tk.	TOTALS Ast.	TOTALS Sks.	INTERCEPTIONS No.	INTERCEPTIONS Yds.	INTERCEPTIONS Avg.	INTERCEPTIONS TD
2002—Houston NFL	2	0	0	0	0.0	0	0	0.0	0

FAIR, TERRY   CB

PERSONAL: Born July 20, 1976, in Phoenix. ... 5-9/184. ... Full name: Terrance Delon Fair.
HIGH SCHOOL: South Mountain (Phoenix).
COLLEGE: Tennessee.
TRANSACTIONS/CAREER NOTES: Selected by Detroit Lions in first round (20th pick overall) of 1998 NFL draft. ... Signed by Lions (July 20, 1998). ... On non-football injury list with hand injury (December 14, 1999-remainder of season). ... On physically unable to perform list with foot injury (July 23-August 19, 2002). ... Released by Lions (September 1, 2002). ... Signed by Carolina Panthers (September 5, 2002). ... On injured reserve with broken ankle (September 24, 2002-remainder of season). ... Granted unconditional free agency (February 28, 2003).
HONORS: Named kick returner on THE SPORTING NEWS NFL All-Pro team (1998).

Year Team	G	GS	TOTALS Tk.	TOTALS Ast.	TOTALS Sks.	INTERCEPTIONS No.	INTERCEPTIONS Yds.	INTERCEPTIONS Avg.	INTERCEPTIONS TD	PUNT RETURNS No.	PUNT RETURNS Yds.	PUNT RETURNS Avg.	PUNT RETURNS TD	KICKOFF RETURNS No.	KICKOFF RETURNS Yds.	KICKOFF RETURNS Avg.	KICKOFF RETURNS TD	TOTALS TD	TOTALS 2pt.	TOTALS Pts.	TOTALS Fum.
1998—Detroit NFL	14	10	39	18	1.0	0	0	0.0	0	30	189	6.3	0	51	1428	*28.0	†2	2	0	12	5
1999—Detroit NFL	11	11	46	6	0.0	3	49	16.3	1	11	97	8.8	0	34	752	22.1	0	2	0	12	2
2000—Detroit NFL	15	15	46	11	0.0	2	0	0.0	0	2	15	7.5	0	6	149	24.8	0	0	0	0	1
2001—Detroit NFL	12	12	37	6	0.0	2	29	14.5	1	4	37	9.3	0	10	187	18.7	0	1	0	6	0
2002—Carolina NFL	3	0	0	0	0.0	0	0	0.0	0	0	0	0.0	0	0	0	0.0	0	0	0	0	0
Pro totals (5 years)	55	48	168	41	1.0	7	78	11.1	2	47	338	7.2	0	101	2516	24.9	2	5	0	30	8

FANECA, ALAN   G   STEELERS

PERSONAL: Born December 7, 1976, in New Orleans. ... 6-5/305. ... Full name: Alan Joseph Faneca Jr.
HIGH SCHOOL: John Curtis Christian (New Orleans), then Lamar (Houston).
COLLEGE: Louisiana State.
TRANSACTIONS/CAREER NOTES: Selected after junior season by Pittsburgh Steelers in first round (26th pick overall) of 1998 NFL draft. ... Signed by Steelers (July 29, 1998).

PLAYING EXPERIENCE: Pittsburgh NFL, 1998-2002. ... Games/Games started: 1998 (16/12), 1999 (15/14), 2000 (16/16), 2001 (15/15), 2002 (16/16). Total: 78/73.
CHAMPIONSHIP GAME EXPERIENCE: Played in AFC championship game (2001 season).
HONORS: Named guard on THE SPORTING NEWS college All-America first team (1997). ... Named guard on THE SPORTING NEWS NFL All-Pro team (2001 and 2002). ... Played in Pro Bowl (2001and 2002 seasons).

FARMER, DANNY — WR — BENGALS

PERSONAL: Born May 21, 1977, in Los Angeles. ... 6-3/215. ... Full name: Daniel Steven Farmer. ... Son of George Farmer, wide receiver with Chicago Bears (1970-75) and Detroit Lions (1975); nephew of Dave Farmer, running back with Tampa Bay Buccaneers (1978).
HIGH SCHOOL: Loyola (Los Angeles).
COLLEGE: UCLA.
TRANSACTIONS/CAREER NOTES: Selected by Pittsburgh Steelers in fourth round (103rd pick overall) of 2000 NFL draft. ... Signed by Steelers (July 7, 2000). ... Claimed on waivers by Cincinnati Bengals (August 28, 2000). ... Granted free agency (February 28, 2003). ... Re-signed by Bengals (April 22, 2003).
SINGLE GAME HIGHS (regular season): Receptions—5 (December 24, 2000, vs. Philadelphia); yards—102 (December 17, 2000, vs. Jacksonville); and touchdown receptions—1 (December 30, 2001, vs. Pittsburgh).
STATISTICAL PLATEAUS: 100-yard receiving games: 2000 (1).

			RECEIVING			
Year Team	G	GS	No.	Yds.	Avg.	TD
2000—Cincinnati NFL	13	2	19	268	14.1	0
2001—Cincinnati NFL	12	1	15	228	15.2	1
2002—Cincinnati NFL	8	1	9	115	12.8	0
Pro totals (3 years)	33	4	43	611	14.2	1

FARRIOR, JAMES — LB — STEELERS

PERSONAL: Born January 6, 1975, in Ettrick, Va. ... 6-2/242. ... Full name: James Alfred Farrior.
HIGH SCHOOL: Matoaca (Ettrick, Va.).
COLLEGE: Virginia.
TRANSACTIONS/CAREER NOTES: Selected by New York Jets in first round (eighth pick overall) of 1997 NFL draft. ... Signed by Jets (July 20, 1997). ... Granted unconditional free agency (March 1, 2002). ... Signed by Pittsburgh Steelers (April 12, 2002).
CHAMPIONSHIP GAME EXPERIENCE: Played in AFC championship game (1998 season).

			TOTALS			INTERCEPTIONS			
Year Team	G	GS	Tk.	Ast.	Sks.	No.	Yds.	Avg.	TD
1997—New York Jets NFL	16	15	53	18	1.5	0	0	0.0	0
1998—New York Jets NFL	12	2	17	10	0.0	0	0	0.0	0
1999—New York Jets NFL	16	4	30	8	2.0	0	0	0.0	0
2000—New York Jets NFL	16	6	46	10	1.0	1	0	0.0	0
2001—New York Jets NFL	16	16	107	36	1.0	2	84	42.0	0
2002—Pittsburgh NFL	14	14	55	22	0.0	0	0	0.0	0
Pro totals (6 years)	90	57	308	104	5.5	3	84	28.0	0

FASANI, RANDY — QB — PANTHERS

PERSONAL: Born September 18, 1978, in Granite City, Calif. ... 6-3/234.
HIGH SCHOOL: Del Oro (Loomis, Calif.).
COLLEGE: Stanford.
TRANSACTIONS/CAREER NOTES: Selected by Carolina Panthers in fifth round (137th pick overall) of 2002 NFL draft. ... Signed by Panthers (July 23, 2002).
SINGLE GAME HIGHS (regular season): Attempts—18 (October 27, 2002, vs. Tampa Bay); completions—6 (October 20, 2002, vs. Atlanta); yards—100 (October 20, 2002, vs. Atlanta); and touchdown passes—0.
MISCELLANEOUS: Regular-season record as starting NFL quarterback: 0-1.

			PASSING								RUSHING				TOTALS		
Year Team	G	GS	Att.	Cmp.	Pct.	Yds.	TD	Int.	Avg.	Skd.	Rat.	Att.	Yds.	Avg.	TD	TD	2pt.	Pts.
2002—Carolina NFL	4	1	44	15	34.1	171	0	4	3.89	7	8.8	18	95	5.3	0	0	0	0

F

FATAFEHI, MARIO — DT — PANTHERS

PERSONAL: Born January 27, 1979, in Chicago. ... 6-2/300.
HIGH SCHOOL: Ferrington (Honolulu, Hawaii).
JUNIOR COLLEGE: Snow College (Utah).
COLLEGE: Kansas State.
TRANSACTIONS/CAREER NOTES: Selected by Arizona Cardinals in fifth round (133rd pick overall) of 2001 NFL draft. ... Signed by Cardinals (June 5, 2001). ... On injured reserve with hand injury (November 30, 2001-remainder of season). ... Released by Cardinals (October 5, 2002). ... Signed by Carolina Panthers (November 1, 2002).

			TOTALS		
Year Team	G	GS	Tk.	Ast.	Sks.
2001—Arizona NFL	7	1	4	4	0.0
2002—Carolina NFL	6	0	0	0	0.0
Pro totals (2 years)	13	1	4	4	0.0

FAULK, KEVIN   RB   PATRIOTS

PERSONAL: Born June 5, 1976, in Lafayette, La. ... 5-8/202. ... Full name: Kevin Tony Faulk.
HIGH SCHOOL: Carencro (Lafayette, La.).
COLLEGE: Louisiana State (degree in kinesiology).
TRANSACTIONS/CAREER NOTES: Selected by New England Patriots in second round (46th pick overall) of 1999 NFL draft. ... Signed by Patriots (July 28, 1999). ... On injured reserve with broken ankle (December 15, 1999-remainder of season).
CHAMPIONSHIP GAME EXPERIENCE: Played in AFC championship game (2001 season). ... Member of Super Bowl championship team (2001 season).
HONORS: Named kick returner on THE SPORTING NEWS college All-America second team (1998).
SINGLE GAME HIGHS (regular season): Attempts—22 (December 4, 2000, vs. Kansas City); yards—82 (September 11, 2000, vs. New York Jets); and rushing touchdowns—1 (November 3, 2002, vs. Buffalo).
STATISTICAL PLATEAUS: 100-yard receiving games: 2002 (1).

			RUSHING				RECEIVING				PUNT RETURNS				KICKOFF RETURNS				TOTALS		
Year Team	G	GS	Att.	Yds.	Avg.	TD	No.	Yds.	Avg.	TD	No.	Yds.	Avg.	TD	No.	Yds.	Avg.	TD	TD	2pt.Pts.Fum.
1999—NE NFL	11	2	67	227	3.4	1	12	98	8.2	1	10	90	9.0	0	39	943	24.2	0	2	0 12 3
2000—NE NFL	16	9	164	570	3.5	4	51	465	9.1	1	6	58	9.7	0	38	816	21.5	0	5	1 32 6
2001—NE NFL	15	1	41	169	4.1	1	30	189	6.3	2	4	27	6.8	0	33	662	20.1	0	3	0 18 2
2002—NE NFL	15	0	52	271	5.2	2	37	379	10.2	3	8	65	8.1	0	26	725	§27.9	†2	7	0 42 1
Pro totals (4 yrs)	57	12	324	1237	3.8	8	130	1131	8.7	7	28	240	8.6	0	136	3146	23.1	2	17	1 104 12

FAULK, MARSHALL   RB   RAMS

PERSONAL: Born February 26, 1973, in New Orleans. ... 5-10/211. ... Full name: Marshall William Faulk.
HIGH SCHOOL: G. W. Carver (New Orleans).
COLLEGE: San Diego State.
TRANSACTIONS/CAREER NOTES: Selected after junior season by Indianapolis Colts in first round (second pick overall) of 1994 NFL draft. ... Signed by Colts (July 24, 1994). ... Traded by Colts to St. Louis Rams for second- (LB Mike Peterson) and fifth-round (DE Brad Scioli) picks in 1999 draft (April 15, 1999).
CHAMPIONSHIP GAME EXPERIENCE: Member of Colts for AFC championship game (1995 season); inactive due to injury. ... Played in NFC championship game (1999 and 2001 seasons). ... Member of Super Bowl championship team (1999 season). ... Played in Super Bowl XXXVI (2001 season).
HONORS: Named running back on THE SPORTING NEWS college All-America first team (1991-1993). ... Named NFL Rookie of the Year by THE SPORTING NEWS (1994). ... Played in Pro Bowl (1994, 1995, 1998, 1999, 2001 and 2002 seasons). ... Named Outstanding Player of Pro Bowl (1994 season). ... Named running back on THE SPORTING NEWS NFL All-Pro team (1999-2001). ... Named NFL Player of the Year by THE SPORTING NEWS (2000 and 2001). ... Named to play in Pro Bowl (2000 season); replaced by Stephen Davis due to injury.
RECORDS: Holds NFL single-season record for most touchdowns—26 (2000). ... Shares NFL single-game record for most two-point conversions—2 (October 15, 2000).
SINGLE GAME HIGHS (regular season): Attempts—32 (October 20, 2002, vs. Seattle); yards—220 (December 24, 2000, vs. New Orleans); and rushing touchdowns—4 (December 10, 2000, vs. Minnesota).
STATISTICAL PLATEAUS: 100-yard rushing games: 1994 (4), 1995 (1), 1996 (1), 1997 (4), 1998 (4), 1999 (7), 2000 (4), 2001 (5), 2002 (3). Total: 33. ... 100-yard receiving games: 1994 (1), 1998 (3), 1999 (1), 2000 (2), 2001 (1). Total: 8.
MISCELLANEOUS: Holds St. Louis Rams all-time record for most touchdowns (69).

			RUSHING				RECEIVING				TOTALS			
Year Team	G	GS	Att.	Yds.	Avg.	TD	No.	Yds.	Avg.	TD	TD	2pt.	Pts.	Fum.
1994—Indianapolis NFL	16	16	314	1282	4.1	11	52	522	10.0	1	▲12	0	72	5
1995—Indianapolis NFL	16	16	289	1078	3.7	11	56	475	8.5	3	14	0	84	8
1996—Indianapolis NFL	13	13	198	587	3.0	7	56	428	7.6	0	7	0	42	2
1997—Indianapolis NFL	16	16	264	1054	4.0	7	47	471	10.0	1	8	0	48	5
1998—Indianapolis NFL	16	15	324	1319	4.1	6	86	908	10.6	4	10	0	60	3
1999—St. Louis NFL	16	16	253	1381	*5.5	7	87	1048	12.0	5	12	†1	74	2
2000—St. Louis NFL	14	14	253	1359	*5.4	*18	81	830	10.2	8	*26	2	*160	0
2001—St. Louis NFL	14	14	260	1382	*5.3	‡12	83	765	9.2	9	*21	1	*128	3
2002—St. Louis NFL	14	10	212	953	4.5	8	80	537	6.7	2	10	0	60	4
Pro totals (9 years)	135	130	2367	10395	4.4	87	628	5984	9.5	33	120	4	728	32

FAURIA, CHRISTIAN   TE   PATRIOTS

PERSONAL: Born September 22, 1971, in Harbor City, Calif. ... 6-4/250. ... Name pronounced FOUR-ee-ah.
HIGH SCHOOL: Crespi Carmelite (Encino, Calif.).
COLLEGE: Colorado (degree in communications, 1995).
TRANSACTIONS/CAREER NOTES: Selected by Seattle Seahawks in second round (39th pick overall) of 1995 NFL draft. ... Signed by Seahawks (July 17, 1995). ... Granted free agency (February 13, 1998). ... Re-signed by Seahawks (April 20, 1998). ... Granted unconditional free agency (February 12, 1999). ... Re-signed by Seahawks (March 5, 1999). ... Granted unconditional free agency (March 1, 2002). ... Signed by New England Patriots (March 22, 2002).
SINGLE GAME HIGHS (regular season): Receptions—6 (December 26, 1999, vs. Kansas City); yards—84 (December 26, 1999, vs. Kansas City); and touchdown receptions—2 (November 24, 2002, vs. Minnesota).

			RECEIVING				TOTALS			
Year Team	G	GS	No.	Yds.	Avg.	TD	TD	2pt.	Pts.	Fum.
1995—Seattle NFL	14	9	17	181	10.6	1	1	0	6	0
1996—Seattle NFL	10	9	18	214	11.9	1	1	0	6	0
1997—Seattle NFL	16	3	10	110	11.0	0	0	0	0	0
1998—Seattle NFL	16	15	37	377	10.2	2	2	0	12	1
1999—Seattle NFL	16	16	35	376	10.7	0	0	0	0	1
2000—Seattle NFL	15	10	28	237	8.5	2	2	0	12	1
2001—Seattle NFL	16	11	21	188	9.0	1	1	1	8	2
2002—New England NFL	16	13	27	253	9.4	7	7	1	44	0
Pro totals (8 years)	119	86	193	1936	10.0	14	14	2	88	5

FAVORS, GREG — LB — PANTHERS

PERSONAL: Born September 30, 1974, in Atlanta. ... 6-1/242. ... Full name: Gregory Bernard Favors.
HIGH SCHOOL: Southside (Atlanta).
COLLEGE: Mississippi State (degree in correction, 1997).
TRANSACTIONS/CAREER NOTES: Selected by Kansas City Chiefs in fourth round (120th pick overall) of 1998 NFL draft. ... Signed by Chiefs (July 17, 1998). ... Claimed on waivers by Tennessee Titans (September 8, 1999). ... Granted free agency (March 2, 2001). ... Re-signed by Titans (May 9, 2001). ... Granted unconditional free agency (March 1, 2002). ... Signed by Indianapolis Colts (April 9, 2002). ... Released by Colts (November 4, 2002). ... Signed by Buffalo Bills (November 19, 2002). ... Granted unconditional free agency (February 28, 2003). ... Signed by Carolina Panthers (March 25, 2003).
CHAMPIONSHIP GAME EXPERIENCE: Played in AFC championship game (1999 season). ... Played in Super Bowl XXXIV (1999 season).

				TOTALS			INTERCEPTIONS			
Year Team	G	GS	Tk.	Ast.	Sks.	No.	Yds.	Avg.	TD
1998—Kansas City NFL	16	4	17	2	2.0	0	0	0.0	0
1999—Tennessee NFL	15	0	0	0	0.0	0	0	0.0	0
2000—Tennessee NFL	16	16	28	9	5.5	0	0	0.0	0
2001—Tennessee NFL	16	12	30	17	1.5	1	0	0.0	0
2002—Buffalo NFL	6	0	0	0	0.0	0	0	0.0	0
Pro totals (5 years)	69	32	75	28	9.0	1	0	0.0	0

FAVRE, BRETT — QB — PACKERS

PERSONAL: Born October 10, 1969, in Gulfport, Miss. ... 6-2/225. ... Full name: Brett Lorenzo Favre. ... Name pronounced FARVE.
HIGH SCHOOL: Hancock North Central (Kiln, Miss.).
COLLEGE: Southern Mississippi.
TRANSACTIONS/CAREER NOTES: Selected by Atlanta Falcons in second round (33rd pick overall) of 1991 NFL draft. ... Signed by Falcons (July 18, 1991). ... Traded by Falcons to Green Bay Packers for first-round pick (OT Bob Whitfield) in 1992 draft (February 11, 1992). ... Granted free agency (February 17, 1994). ... Re-signed by Packers (July 14, 1994).
CHAMPIONSHIP GAME EXPERIENCE: Played in NFC championship game (1995-1997 seasons). ... Member of Super Bowl championship team (1996 season). ... Played in Super Bowl XXXII (1997 season).
HONORS: Played in Pro Bowl (1992, 1993, 1995 and 1996 seasons). ... Named NFL Player of the Year by THE SPORTING NEWS (1995 and 1996). ... Named quarterback on THE SPORTING NEWS NFL All-Pro team (1995-97). ... Named to play in Pro Bowl (1997 season); replaced by Chris Chandler due to injury. ... Named to play in Pro Bowl (2001 season); replaced by Donovan McNabb due to injury. ... Named to play in Pro Bowl (2002 season); replaced by Donovan McNabb due to injury.
RECORDS: Shares NFL record for longest pass completion (to Robert Brooks)—99 yards, touchdown (September 11, 1995, at Chicago).
POST SEASON RECORDS: Holds Super Bowl record for longest pass completion (to Antonio Freeman)—81 yards (January 26, 1997, vs. New England).
SINGLE GAME HIGHS (regular season): Attempts—61 (October 14, 1996, vs. San Francisco); completions—36 (December 5, 1993, vs. Chicago); yards—402 (December 5, 1993, vs. Chicago); and touchdown passes—5 (September 27, 1998, vs. Carolina).
STATISTICAL PLATEAUS: 300-yard passing games: 1993 (1), 1994 (4), 1995 (7), 1996 (2), 1997 (2), 1998 (4), 1999 (6), 2000 (2), 2001 (4), 2002 (3). Total: 35.
MISCELLANEOUS: Regular-season record as starting NFL quarterback: 115-58 (.665). ... Postseason record as starting NFL quarterback: 10-7 (.588). ... Active NFL leader in touchdown passes (314). ... Holds Green Bay Packers all-time records for most yards passing (42,285) and most touchdown passes (314).

			PASSING									RUSHING				TOTALS		
Year Team	G	GS	Att.	Cmp.	Pct.	Yds.	TD	Int.	Avg.	Skd.	Rat.	Att.	Yds.	Avg.	TD	TD	2pt.	Pts.
1991—Atlanta NFL	2	0	5	0	0.0	0	0	2	0.0	1	0.0	0	0	0.0	0	0	0	0
1992—Green Bay NFL	15	13	471	∞302	64.1	3227	18	13	6.85	34	85.3	47	198	4.2	1	1	0	6
1993—Green Bay NFL	16	16	‡522	‡318	60.9	3303	19	*24	6.33	30	72.2	58	216	3.7	1	1	0	6
1994—Green Bay NFL	16	16	582	363	62.4	3882	33	14	6.67	31	90.7	42	202	4.8	2	2	0	12
1995—Green Bay NFL	16	16	570	359	63.0	*4413	*38	13	‡7.74	33	‡99.5	39	181	4.6	3	3	0	18
1996—Green Bay NFL	16	16	‡543	‡325	59.9	‡3899	*39	13	7.18	40	95.8	49	136	2.8	2	2	0	12
1997—Green Bay NFL	16	16	513	‡304	59.3	‡3867	*35	16	7.54	25	92.6	58	187	3.2	1	1	0	6
1998—Green Bay NFL	16	16	‡551	*347	*63.0	*4212	31	‡23	7.64	38	87.8	40	133	3.3	1	1	0	6
1999—Green Bay NFL	16	16	*595	341	57.3	4091	22	23	6.88	35	74.7	28	142	5.1	0	0	0	0
2000—Green Bay NFL	16	16	‡580	338	58.3	3812	20	16	6.57	33	78.0	27	108	4.0	0	0	0	0
2001—Green Bay NFL	16	16	510	314	61.6	3921	32	15	7.69	22	94.1	38	56	1.5	1	1	0	6
2002—Green Bay NFL	16	16	‡551	‡341	61.9	3658	∞27	16	6.64	26	85.6	25	73	2.9	0	0	0	0
Pro totals (12 years)	177	173	5993	3652	60.9	42285	314	188	7.06	348	86.7	451	1632	3.6	12	12	0	72

FEAGLES, JEFF — P — GIANTS

PERSONAL: Born March 7, 1966, in Anaheim. ... 6-1/211. ... Full name: Jeffrey Allan Feagles.
HIGH SCHOOL: Gerard Catholic (Phoenix).
JUNIOR COLLEGE: Scottsdale (Ariz.) Community College.
COLLEGE: Miami (Fla.) (degree in business administration, 1988).
TRANSACTIONS/CAREER NOTES: Signed as non-drafted free agent by New England Patriots (May 1, 1988). ... Claimed on waivers by Philadelphia Eagles (June 5, 1990). ... Granted unconditional free agency (February 1-April 1, 1992). ... Re-signed by Eagles for 1992 season. ... Granted unconditional free agency (February 17, 1994). ... Signed by Phoenix Cardinals (March 2, 1994). ... Cardinals franchise renamed Arizona Cardinals for 1994 season. ... Granted unconditional free agency (February 13, 1998). ... Signed by Seattle Seahawks (March 4, 1998). ... Granted unconditional free agency (February 28, 2003). ... Signed by New York Giants (March 7, 2003).
HONORS: Played in Pro Bowl (1995 season).

Year	Team	G	No.	Yds.	Avg.	Net avg.	In. 20	Blk.
			PUNTING					
1988—New England NFL		16	▲91	3482	38.3	34.1	24	0
1989—New England NFL		16	63	2392	38.0	31.3	13	1
1990—Philadelphia NFL		16	72	3026	42.0	35.5	20	2
1991—Philadelphia NFL		16	*87	3640	41.8	34.0	*29	1
1992—Philadelphia NFL		16	‡82	‡3459	42.2	36.9	‡26	1
1993—Philadelphia NFL		16	83	3323	40.0	35.3	*31	0
1994—Arizona NFL		16	*98	‡3997	40.8	36.0	‡33	0
1995—Arizona NFL		16	72	3150	43.8	‡38.2	20	0
1996—Arizona NFL		16	76	3328	43.8	36.4	23	1
1997—Arizona NFL		16	91	4028	44.3	36.8	24	1
1998—Seattle NFL		16	81	3568	44.0	36.5	27	0
1999—Seattle NFL		16	84	3425	40.8	35.2	34	0
2000—Seattle NFL		16	74	2960	40.0	36.9	24	▲1
2001—Seattle NFL		16	85	3730	43.9	36.4	26	1
2002—Seattle NFL		16	61	2542	41.7	37.0	22	0
Pro totals (15 years)		240	1200	50050	41.7	35.8	376	8

FEELEY, A.J.　　　QB　　　EAGLES

PERSONAL: Born May 16, 1977, in Caldwell, Idaho. ... 6-3/217. ... Full name: Adam Joshua Feeley.
HIGH SCHOOL: Ontario (Ore.).
COLLEGE: Oregon.
TRANSACTIONS/CAREER NOTES: Selected by Philadelphia Eagles in fifth round (155th pick overall) of 2001 NFL draft. ... Signed by Eagles (June 6, 2001). ... Released by Eagles (September 26, 2002). ... Re-signed by Eagles to practice squad (September 28, 2002). ... Activated (October 8, 2002).
CHAMPIONSHIP GAME EXPERIENCE: Member of Eagles for NFC championship game (2001 and 2002 seasons); inactive.
SINGLE GAME HIGHS (regular season): Attempts—35 (December 8, 2002, vs. Seattle); completions—21 (December 8, 2002, vs. Seattle); passing yards—253 (December 21, 2002, vs. Dallas); and touchdown passes—2 (December 15, 2002, vs. Washington).
MISCELLANEOUS: Regular-season record as starting NFL quarterback: 4-1 (.800).

Year	Team	G	GS	PASSING									RUSHING				TOTALS		
				Att.	Cmp.	Pct.	Yds.	TD	Int.	Avg.	Skd.	Rat.	Att.	Yds.	Avg.	TD	TD	2pt.	Pts.
2001—Philadelphia NFL		1	0	14	10	71.4	143	2	1	10.21	0	114.0	0	0	0.0	0	0	0	0
2002—Philadelphia NFL		6	5	154	86	55.8	1011	6	5	6.56	7	75.4	12	6	0.5	0	0	0	0
Pro totals (2 years)		7	5	168	96	57.1	1154	8	6	6.87	7	79.3	12	6	0.5	0	0	0	0

FEELY, JAY　　　K　　　FALCONS

PERSONAL: Born May 23, 1976, in Odessa, Fla. ... 5-10/206.
HIGH SCHOOL: Tampa Jesuit (Fla.).
COLLEGE: Michigan.
TRANSACTIONS/CAREER NOTES: Signed as non-drafted free agent by Atlanta Falcons (April 12, 2001). ... Re-signed by Falcons (May 18, 2003).

Year	Team	G	FIELD GOALS							TOTALS		
			1-29	30-39	40-49	50+	Tot.	Pct.	Lg.	XPM	XPA	Pts.
2001—Atlanta NFL		16	9-9	14-15	4-9	2-4	‡29-‡37	78.4	†55	28	28	115
2002—Atlanta NFL		16	8-10	12-14	11-13	1-3	†32-*40	80.0	52	42	43	‡138
Pro totals (2 years)		32	17-19	26-29	15-22	3-7	61-77	79.2	55	70	71	253

FENDERSON, JAMES　　　FB　　　SAINTS

F

PERSONAL: Born October 24, 1976, in Long Beach, Calif. ... 5-9/200. ... Full name: James E. Fenderson.
HIGH SCHOOL: Mililani (Oahu, Hawaii).
COLLEGE: Hawaii.
TRANSACTIONS/CAREER NOTES: Signed as non-drafted free agent by New Orleans Saints (April 26, 2001). ... Released by Saints (September 7, 2001). ... Re-signed by Saints (December 14, 2001).
SINGLE GAME HIGHS (regular season): Attempts—7 (November 24, 2002, vs. Cleveland); yards—35 (November 24, 2002, vs. Cleveland); and rushing touchdowns—1 (November 24, 2002, vs. Cleveland).

Year	Team	G	GS	RUSHING				RECEIVING				KICKOFF RETURNS				TOTALS			
				Att.	Yds.	Avg.	TD	No.	Yds.	Avg.	TD	No.	Yds.	Avg.	TD	TD	2pt.	Pts.	Fum.
2001—New Orleans NFL		4	0	0	0	0.0	0	0	0	0.0	0	0	0	0.0	0	0	0	0	0
2002—New Orleans NFL		16	1	13	65	5.0	1	6	38	6.3	0	2	43	21.5	0	1	0	6	1
Pro totals (2 years)		20	1	13	65	5.0	1	6	38	6.3	0	2	43	21.5	0	1	0	6	1

FERGUSON, JASON　　　DT　　　JETS

PERSONAL: Born November 28, 1974, in Nettleton, Miss. ... 6-3/305. ... Full name: Jason O. Ferguson. ... Cousin of Terance Mathis, wide receiver, with New York Jets (1990-93) and Atlanta Falcons (1994-2001).
HIGH SCHOOL: Nettleton (Miss.).
JUNIOR COLLEGE: Itawamba Community College (Miss.).
COLLEGE: Georgia.
TRANSACTIONS/CAREER NOTES: Selected by New York Jets in seventh round (229th pick overall) of 1997 NFL draft. ... Signed by Jets (April 30, 1997). ... On suspended list for violating league substance abuse policy (November 24-December 22, 1999). ... Granted free agency (February 11, 2000). ... Re-signed by Jets (May 24, 2000). ... Granted unconditional free agency (March 2, 2001). ... Re-signed by Jets (March 11, 2001). ... On injured reserve with shoulder injury (September 3, 2001-entire season).
CHAMPIONSHIP GAME EXPERIENCE: Played in AFC championship game (1998 season).

Year	Team	G	GS	TOTALS Tk.	Ast.	Sks.
1997—New York Jets NFL		13	1	23	8	3.5
1998—New York Jets NFL		16	16	42	21	4.0
1999—New York Jets NFL		9	9	23	10	1.0
2000—New York Jets NFL		15	11	34	11	1.0
2001—New York Jets NFL				Did not play.		
2002—New York Jets NFL		16	16	42	21	3.0
Pro totals (5 years)		69	53	164	71	12.5

FERGUSON, NICK — S — BRONCOS

PERSONAL: Born November 27, 1974, in Miami. ... 5-11/201.
HIGH SCHOOL: Jackson (Miami).
COLLEGE: Morris Brown College, then Georgia Tech.
TRANSACTIONS/CAREER NOTES: Signed as non-drafted free agent by Cincinnati Bengals (April 23, 1996). ... Released by Bengals (August 5, 1996). ... Signed by Sasketchewan Roughriders of CFL (September 27, 1996). ... Traded by Roughriders to Winnipeg Blue Bombers (May 9, 1997). ... Signed by Chicago Bears (February 12, 1999). ... Assigned by Bears to Rhein Fire in 1999 NFL Europe enhancement allocation program (February 22, 1999). ... Released by Bears (August 30, 1999). ... Signed by Buffalo Bills (July 6, 2000). ... Released by Bills (August 27, 2000). ... Re-signed by Bills to practice squad (August 28, 2000). ... Signed by New York Jets off Bills practice squad (November 7, 2000). ... Granted free agency (February 28, 2003). ... Signed by Denver Broncos (April 2, 2003).

Year	Team	G	GS	TOTALS Tk.	Ast.	Sks.	INTERCEPTIONS No.	Yds.	Avg.	TD
1996—Saskatchewan CFL		5	...	...	...	0.0	0	0	0.0	0
1997—Winnipeg CFL		15	...	...	...	0.0	2	35	17.5	0
1998—Winnipeg CFL		16	...	...	...	0.0	1	0	0.0	0
1999—Rhein NFLE		...	...	...	...	0.0	0	0	0.0	0
—Winnipeg CFL		3	...	...	...	0.0	0	0	0.0	0
2000—Rhein NFLE		...	...	...	...	0.0	2	0	0.0	0
—New York Jets NFL		7	0	5	4	0.0	1	20	20.0	0
2001—New York Jets NFL		16	1	10	3	0.0	0	0	0.0	0
2002—New York Jets NFL		16	0	7	2	0.0	0	0	0.0	0
NFL Europe totals (2 years)		...	...	...	...	0.0	2	0	0.0	0
CFL totals (4 years)		39	...	...	...	0.0	3	35	11.7	0
NFL totals (3 years)		39	1	22	9	0.0	1	20	20.0	0
Pro totals (9 years)		...	...	...	...	0.0	6	55	9.2	0

FERGUSON, ROBERT — WR — PACKERS

PERSONAL: Born December 17, 1979, in Houston. ... 6-1/209.
HIGH SCHOOL: Spring Woods (Houston).
JUNIOR COLLEGE: Tyler (Texas) Junor College.
COLLEGE: Texas A&M.
TRANSACTIONS/CAREER NOTES: Selected after junior season by Green Bay Packers in second round (41st pick overall) of 2001 NFL draft. ... Signed by Packers (July 23, 2001).
SINGLE GAME HIGHS (regular season): Receptions—6 (December 8, 2002, vs. Minnesota); yards—105 (December 8, 2002, vs. Minnesota); and touchdown receptions—2 (December 8, 2002, vs. Minnesota).
STATISTICAL PLATEAUS: 100-yard receiving games: 2002 (1).

Year	Team	G	GS	RECEIVING No.	Yds.	Avg.	TD	KICKOFF RETURNS No.	Yds.	Avg.	TD	TOTALS TD	2pt.	Pts.	Fum.
2001—Green Bay NFL		1	0	0	0	0.0	0	2	32	16.0	0	0	0	0	0
2002—Green Bay NFL		16	1	22	293	13.3	3	6	113	18.8	0	3	0	18	0
Pro totals (2 years)		17	1	22	293	13.3	3	8	145	18.1	0	3	0	18	0

FERRARA, FRANK — DE — GIANTS

PERSONAL: Born December 7, 1975, in Staten Island, N.Y. ... 6-3/280.
HIGH SCHOOL: New Dorp (N.Y.).
COLLEGE: Rhode Island.
TRANSACTIONS/CAREER NOTES: Signed as non-drafted free agent by New York Giants (April 19, 2000). ... Released by Giants (August 27, 2000). ... Re-signed by Giants to practice squad (August 29, 2000). ... Released by Giants (November 20, 2000). ... Re-signed by Giants to practice squad (December 13, 2000). ... Assigned by Giants to Amsterdam Admirals in 2000 NFL Europe enhancement allocation program (February 17, 2000).

Year	Team	G	GS	TOTALS Tk.	Ast.	Sks.
2001—New York Giants NFL		9	0	4	3	1.0
2002—New York Giants NFL		16	1	20	6	2.5
Pro totals (2 years)		25	1	24	9	3.5

F

FERRARIO, BILL — G — PACKERS

PERSONAL: Born September 22, 1978, in Scranton, Pa. ... 6-2/315. ... Full name: William Ferrario.
HIGH SCHOOL: West (Scranton, Pa.).
COLLEGE: Wisconsin (degree in history.).
TRANSACTIONS/CAREER NOTES: Selected by Green Bay Packers in fourth round (105th pick overall) of 2001 NFL draft. ... Signed by Packers (June 28, 2001). ... Assigned by Packers to Berlin Thunder in 2003 NFL Europe enhancement allocation program (February 4, 2003).
PLAYING EXPERIENCE: Green Bay NFL, 2002. ... Games/games started: 2002 (16/0).
HONORS: Named guard on THE SPORTING NEWS college All-America third team (2000).

FIALA, JOHN — LB — STEELERS

PERSONAL: Born November 25, 1973, in Fullerton, Calif. ... 6-3/237. ... Full name: John Charles Fiala. ... Name pronounced FEE-ah-lah.
HIGH SCHOOL: Lake Washington (Kirkland, Wash.).
COLLEGE: Washington.
TRANSACTIONS/CAREER NOTES: Selected by Miami Dolphins in sixth round (166th pick overall) of 1997 NFL draft. ... Signed by Dolphins (June 17, 1997). ... Released by Dolphins (July 31, 1997). ... Signed by Pittsburgh Steelers to practice squad (August 26, 1997). ... Granted free agency (March 2, 2001). ... Re-signed by Steelers (May 13, 2001). ... On injured reserve with knee injury (November 26, 2002-remainder of season).
CHAMPIONSHIP GAME EXPERIENCE: Played in AFC championship game (2001 season).

			TOTALS			INTERCEPTIONS			
Year Team	G	GS	Tk.	Ast.	Sks.	No.	Yds.	Avg.	TD
1998—Pittsburgh NFL	16	0	0	2	0.0	0	0	0.0	0
1999—Pittsburgh NFL	16	0	0	0	0.0	0	0	0.0	0
2000—Pittsburgh NFL	16	0	4	2	0.0	0	0	0.0	0
2001—Pittsburgh NFL	16	0	1	2	0.0	0	0	0.0	0
2002—Pittsburgh NFL	11	1	4	1	0.0	0	0	0.0	0
Pro totals (5 years)	75	1	9	7	0.0	0	0	0.0	0

FIEDLER, JAY — QB — DOLPHINS

PERSONAL: Born December 29, 1971, in Oceanside, N.Y. ... 6-2/225. ... Full name: Jay Brian Fiedler.
HIGH SCHOOL: Oceanside (N.Y.).
COLLEGE: Dartmouth (degree in engineering sciences).
TRANSACTIONS/CAREER NOTES: Signed as non-drafted free agent by Philadelphia Eagles (April 29, 1994). ... Inactive for all 16 games (1994). ... Claimed on waivers by Cincinnati Bengals (July 31, 1996). ... Released by Bengals (August 25, 1996). ... Played for Amsterdam Admirals of World League (1997). ... Signed by Minnesota Vikings (April 3, 1998). ... Released by Vikings (August 30, 1998). ... Re-signed by Vikings (September 15, 1998). ... Granted free agency (February 12, 1999). ... Signed by Jacksonville Jaguars (April 16, 1999). ... Granted unconditional free agency (February 11, 2000). ... Signed by Miami Dolphins (February 17, 2000). ... On physically unable to perform list with hip injury (July 26-31, 2002).
CHAMPIONSHIP GAME EXPERIENCE: Member of Vikings for NFC championship game (1998 season); inactive. ... Member of Jaguars for AFC championship game (1999 season); did not play.
SINGLE GAME HIGHS (regular season): Attempts—45 (September 29, 2002, vs. Kansas City); completions—30 (December 24, 2000, vs.New England); yards—320 (December 22, 2001, vs. New England); and touchdown passes—3 (September 8, 2002, vs. Detroit).
STATISTICAL PLATEAUS: 300-yard passing games: 1999 (1), 2001 (1), 2002 (1). Total: 3.
MISCELLANEOUS: Regular-season record as starting NFL quarterback: 29-13 (.690). ... Postseason record as starting NFL quarterback: 1-2 (.333).

			PASSING								RUSHING				TOTALS		
Year Team	G	GS	Att.	Cmp.	Pct.	Yds.	TD	Int.	Avg.	Skd.	Rat.	Att.	Yds.	Avg.	TD	TD	2pt.	Pts.
1994—Philadelphia NFL										Did not play.								
1995—Philadelphia NFL										Did not play.								
1996—										Did not play.								
1997—Amsterdam W.L.	...	...	109	46	42.2	678	2	8	6.22	0	38.7	16	93	5.8	0	0	0	0
1998—Minnesota NFL	5	0	7	3	42.9	41	0	1	5.86	0	22.6	4	-6	-1.5	0	0	0	0
1999—Jacksonville NFL	7	1	94	61	64.9	656	2	2	6.98	7	83.5	13	26	2.0	0	0	0	0
2000—Miami NFL	15	15	357	204	57.1	2402	14	14	6.73	23	74.5	54	267	4.9	1	1	0	6
2001—Miami NFL	16	16	450	273	60.7	3290	20	19	7.31	27	80.3	73	321	4.4	4	4	0	24
2002—Miami NFL	11	10	292	179	61.3	2024	14	9	6.93	13	85.2	28	99	3.5	3	3	0	18
W.L. totals (1 year)	...	...	109	46	42.2	678	2	8	6.22	0	38.7	16	93	5.8	0	0	0	0
NFL totals (5 years)	54	42	1200	720	60.0	8413	50	45	7.01	70	79.6	172	707	4.1	8	8	0	48
Pro totals (6 years)	...	...	1309	766	58.5	9091	52	53	6.94	70	76.2	188	800	4.3	8	8	0	48

FIELDS, MARK — LB — PANTHERS

PERSONAL: Born November 9, 1972, in Los Angeles. ... 6-2/244. ... Full name: Mark Lee Fields.
HIGH SCHOOL: Washington (Cerritos, Calif.).
JUNIOR COLLEGE: Los Angeles Southwest Community College.
COLLEGE: Washington State.
TRANSACTIONS/CAREER NOTES: Selected by New Orleans Saints in first round (13th pick overall) of 1995 NFL draft. ... Signed by Saints (July 20, 1995). ... Released by Saints (March 30, 2001). ... Signed by St. Louis Rams (April 10, 2001). ... Released by Rams (March 7, 2002). ... Signed by Carolina Panthers (March 21, 2002).
CHAMPIONSHIP GAME EXPERIENCE: Played in NFC championship game (2001 season). ... Played in Super Bowl XXXVI (2001 season).
HONORS: Played in Pro Bowl (2000 season).

Year	Team	G	GS	TOTALS			INTERCEPTIONS			
				Tk.	Ast.	Sks.	No.	Yds.	Avg.	TD
1995—New Orleans NFL		16	3	31	9	1.0	0	0	0.0	0
1996—New Orleans NFL		16	15	85	22	2.0	0	0	0.0	0
1997—New Orleans NFL		16	15	88	20	8.0	0	0	0.0	0
1998—New Orleans NFL		15	15	82	27	6.0	0	0	0.0	0
1999—New Orleans NFL		14	14	63	18	4.0	2	0	0.0	0
2000—New Orleans NFL		16	14	63	21	2.0	0	0	0.0	0
2001—St. Louis NFL		14	12	48	15	0.0	1	30	30.0	0
2002—Carolina NFL		15	15	76	27	7.5	1	37	37.0	0
Pro totals (8 years)		122	103	536	159	30.5	4	67	16.8	0

FILIPOVIC, FILIP   P   COWBOYS

PERSONAL: Born November 5, 1977, in Belgrade, Yugoslavia. ... 6-2/216.
COLLEGE: South Dakota.
TRANSACTIONS/CAREER NOTES: Signed as non-drafted free agent by Dallas Cowboys (April 26, 2002). ... Released by Cowboys (September 1, 2002). ... Re-signed by Cowboys (October 23, 2002).

Year	Team	G	PUNTING					
			No.	Yds.	Avg.	Net avg.	In. 20	Blk.
2002—Dallas NFL		9	65	2640	40.6	31.5	14	1

FINA, JOHN   OT

PERSONAL: Born March 11, 1969, in Rochester, Minn. ... 6-5/300. ... Full name: John Joseph Fina. ... Name pronounced FEE-nuh.
HIGH SCHOOL: Salpointe Catholic (Tucson, Ariz.).
COLLEGE: Arizona.
TRANSACTIONS/CAREER NOTES: Selected by Buffalo Bills in first round (27th pick overall) of 1992 NFL draft. ... Signed by Bills (July 21, 1992). ... Designated by Bills as franchise player (February 16, 1996). ... Released by Bills (June 3, 2002). ... Signed by Arizona Cardinals (September 9, 2002). ... On injured reserve with ankle injury (December 24, 2002-remainder of season). ... Granted unconditional free agency (February 28, 2003).
PLAYING EXPERIENCE: Buffalo NFL, 1992-2001; Buffalo NFL, 2002. ... Games/Games started: 1992 (16/0), 1993 (16/16), 1994 (12/12), 1995 (16/16), 1996 (15/15), 1997 (16/16), 1998 (14/14), 1999 (16/16), 2000 (14/14), 2001 (13/12), 2002 (7/0). Total: 156/131.
CHAMPIONSHIP GAME EXPERIENCE: Played in AFC championship game (1992 and 1993 seasons). ... Played in Super Bowl XXVII (1992 season) and Super Bowl XXVIII (1993 season).

FINLEY, CLINT   S   CHIEFS

PERSONAL: Born March 27, 1977, in Andrews, Texas. ... 6-0/210. ... Full name: Clint Cade Finley.
HIGH SCHOOL: Cuero (Texas).
COLLEGE: Nebraska.
TRANSACTIONS/CAREER NOTES: Signed as non-drafted free agent by Kansas City Chiefs (February 20, 2002). ... Released by Chiefs (September 1, 2002). ... Re-signed by Chiefs to practice squad (September 3, 2002). ... Activated (December 26, 2002). ... Assigned by Chiefs to Berlin Thunder in 2003 NFL Europe enhancement allocation program (February 4, 2003).

Year	Team	G	GS	TOTALS			INTERCEPTIONS			
				Tk.	Ast.	Sks.	No.	Yds.	Avg.	TD
2002—Kansas City NFL		1	0	0	1	0.0	0	0	0.0	0

FINN, JIM   RB   GIANTS

PERSONAL: Born December 9, 1976, in Teaneck, N.J. ... 6-0/242.
HIGH SCHOOL: Bergen Catholic (Oradell, N.J.).
COLLEGE: Pennsylvania.
TRANSACTIONS/CAREER NOTES: Selected by Chicago Bears in seventh round (253rd pick overall) of 1999 NFL draft. ... Signed by Bears (June 3, 1999). ... Released by Bears (August 30, 1999). ... Re-signed by Bears to practice squad (September 21, 1999). ... Released by Bears (October 11, 1999). ... Signed by Indianapolis Colts (January 25, 2000). ... Granted free agency (February 28, 2003). ... Signed by New York Giants (March 11, 2003).
SINGLE GAME HIGHS (regular season): Attempts—3 (November 10, 2002, vs. Philadelphia); yards—8 (November 3, 2002, vs. Tennessee); and rushing touchdowns—0.

Year	Team	G	GS	RUSHING				TOTALS			
				Att.	Yds.	Avg.	TD	TD	2pt.	Pts.	Fum.
2000—Indianapolis NFL		16	1	1	1	1.0	0	1	0	6	1
2001—Indianapolis NFL		15	0	0	0	0.0	0	0	0	0	0
2002—Indianapolis NFL		12	2	5	8	1.6	0	0	0	0	2
Pro totals (3 years)		43	3	6	9	1.5	0	1	0	6	3

FINNERAN, BRIAN   WR   FALCONS

PERSONAL: Born January 31, 1976, in Mission Viejo, Calif. ... 6-5/210.
HIGH SCHOOL: Santa Margarita (Mission Viejo, Calif.).
COLLEGE: Villanova.
TRANSACTIONS/CAREER NOTES: Signed as non-drafted free agent by Seattle Seahawks (April 21, 1998). ... Released by Seahawks (August 24, 1998). ... Selected by Barcelona Dragons in 1999 NFL Europe draft (February 18, 1999). ... Signed by Philadelphia Eagles (July 6, 1999). ... Released by Eagles (October 12, 1999). ... Signed by Atlanta Falcons to practice squad (December 13, 1999). ... Granted free agency (February 28, 2003). ... Re-signed by Falcons (March 23, 2003).

F

HONORS: Won Walter Payton Award (1997).

SINGLE GAME HIGHS (regular season): Receptions—6 (November 10, 2002, vs. Pittsburgh); yards—114 (December 1, 2002, vs. Minnesota); and touchdown receptions—2 (September 22, 2002, vs. Cincinnati).

STATISTICAL PLATEAUS: 100-yard receiving games: 2002 (2).

Year Team	G	GS	RECEIVING				TOTALS			
			No.	Yds.	Avg.	TD	TD	2pt.	Pts.	Fum.
1999—Barcelona NFLE	...	...	54	844	15.6	8	8	1	50	0
—Philadelphia NFL	3	0	2	21	10.5	0	0	0	0	0
2000—Atlanta NFL	12	0	7	60	8.6	0	0	0	0	0
2001—Atlanta NFL	16	1	23	491	21.3	3	3	0	18	0
2002—Atlanta NFL	16	16	56	838	15.0	6	6	0	36	2
NFL Europe totals (1 year)	...	...	54	844	15.6	8	8	1	50	0
NFL totals (4 years)	47	17	88	1410	16.0	9	9	0	54	2
Pro totals (5 years)	...	...	142	2254	15.9	17	17	1	104	2

FIORE, DAVE — OT

PERSONAL: Born August 10, 1974, in Hackensack, N.J. ... 6-4/290. ... Full name: David Allan Fiore. ... Name pronounced fee-OR-ee.
HIGH SCHOOL: Waldwick (N.J.).
COLLEGE: Hofstra.
TRANSACTIONS/CAREER NOTES: Signed as non-drafted free agent by San Francisco 49ers (April 23, 1996). ... Claimed on waivers by New York Jets (October 14, 1996). ... Active for nine games (1996); did not play. ... Released by Jets (July 31, 1997). ... Signed by 49ers (August 1, 1997). ... On injured reserve with knee injury (August 19, 1997-entire season). ... On injured reserve with knee injury (September 25, 2002-remainder of season). ... Released by 49ers (February 26, 2003).
PLAYING EXPERIENCE: San Francisco NFL, 1998-2002. ... Games/Games started: 1998 (9/3), 1999 (16/16), 2000 (15/15), 2001 (16/16), 2002 (3/3). Total: 59/53.

FISHER, BRYCE — DE — RAMS

PERSONAL: Born May 12, 1977, in Renton, Wash. ... 6-3/268.
HIGH SCHOOL: Seattle Prep.
COLLEGE: Air Force.
TRANSACTIONS/CAREER NOTES: Selected by Buffalo Bills in seventh round (248th pick overall) of 1999 NFL draft. ... Signed by Bills (July 27, 1999). ... On military reserve list (August 30, 1999-entire season). ... On military reserve list (August 27, 2000-entire season). ... Claimed on waivers by St. Louis Rams (September 3, 2002).

Year Team	G	GS	TOTALS		
			Tk.	Ast.	Sks.
1999—Buffalo NFL			Did not play.		
2001—Buffalo NFL	13	2	19	13	3.0
2002—St. Louis NFL	4	0	2	1	0.0
Pro totals (2 years)	17	2	21	14	3.0

FISHER, LEVAR — LB — CARDINALS

PERSONAL: Born July 2, 1979, in Beaufort, N.C. ... 6-1/233.
HIGH SCHOOL: East Carteret (Beaufort, N.C.).
COLLEGE: North Carolina State.
TRANSACTIONS/CAREER NOTES: Selected by Arizona Cardinals in second round (49th pick overall) of 2002 NFL draft. ... Signed by Cardinals (July 22, 2002). ... On injured reserve with knee injury (December 18, 2002-remainder of season).
HONORS: Named linebacker on THE SPORTING NEWS college All-America third team (2001). ... Named linebacker on THE SPORTING NEWS college All-America second team (2000).

Year Team	G	GS	TOTALS			INTERCEPTIONS			
			Tk.	Ast.	Sks.	No.	Yds.	Avg.	TD
2002—Arizona NFL	7	0	18	2	0.0	0	0	0.0	0

FISHER, TONY — RB — PACKERS

PERSONAL: Born October 12, 1979, in Euclid, Ohio. ... 6-1/222. ... Full name: Antoine Maurice Fisher.
HIGH SCHOOL: Euclid (Ohio).
COLLEGE: Notre Dame.
TRANSACTIONS/CAREER NOTES: Signed as non-drafted free agent by Green Bay Packers (April 25, 2002).
SINGLE GAME HIGHS (regular season): Attempts—25 (December 8, 2002, vs. Minnesota); yards—96 (December 8, 2002, vs. Minnesota); and rushing touchdowns—1 (December 8, 2002, vs. Minnesota).

Year Team	G	GS	RUSHING				RECEIVING				KICKOFF RETURNS				TOTALS			
			Att.	Yds.	Avg.	TD	No.	Yds.	Avg.	TD	No.	Yds.	Avg.	TD	TD	2pt.	Pts.	Fum.
2002—Green Bay NFL	15	1	70	283	4.0	2	18	70	3.9	0	2	42	21.0	0	2	0	12	2

FISHER, TRAVIS — CB — RAMS

PERSONAL: Born September 12, 1979, in Tallahassee, Fla. ... 5-10/189.
HIGH SCHOOL: Godby (Tallahassee, Fla.).
JUNIOR COLLEGE: Coffeyville (Kan.) Community College.

F

COLLEGE: Central Florida.
TRANSACTIONS/CAREER NOTES: Selected by St. Louis Rams in second round (64th pick overall) of 2002 NFL draft. ... Signed by Rams (June 21, 2002).

			TOTALS			INTERCEPTIONS			
Year	Team	G	GS	Tk.	Ast.	Sks.	No.	Yds.	Avg.	TD
2002—St. Louis NFL		14	11	54	7	0.0	2	0	0.0	0

FISK, JASON   DT   CHARGERS

PERSONAL: Born September 4, 1972, in Davis, Calif. ... 6-3/295.
HIGH SCHOOL: Davis (Calif.).
COLLEGE: Stanford.
TRANSACTIONS/CAREER NOTES: Selected by Minnesota Vikings in seventh round (243rd pick overall) of 1995 NFL draft. ... Signed by Vikings (July 24, 1995). ... Granted unconditional free agency (February 12, 1999). ... Signed by Tennessee Titans (March 3, 1999). ... Granted unconditional free agency (March 1, 2002). ... Signed by San Diego Chargers (March 8, 2002).
CHAMPIONSHIP GAME EXPERIENCE: Played in NFC championship game (1998 season). ... Played in AFC championship game (1999 season). ... Played in Super Bowl XXXIV (1999 season).

			TOTALS			INTERCEPTIONS			
Year	Team	G	GS	Tk.	Ast.	Sks.	No.	Yds.	Avg.	TD
1995—Minnesota NFL		8	0	0	0	0.0	0	0	0.0	0
1996—Minnesota NFL		16	6	22	9	1.0	1	0	0.0	0
1997—Minnesota NFL		16	10	20	8	3.0	1	1	1.0	0
1998—Minnesota NFL		16	0	12	5	1.5	0	0	0.0	0
1999—Tennessee NFL		16	16	35	13	4.0	1	17	17.0	0
2000—Tennessee NFL		15	15	30	10	2.0	0	0	0.0	0
2001—Tennessee NFL		16	16	26	16	2.5	0	0	0.0	0
2002—San Diego NFL		16	14	28	10	3.0	0	0	0.0	0
Pro totals (8 years)		119	77	173	71	17.0	3	18	6.0	0

FLANAGAN, MIKE   C   PACKERS

PERSONAL: Born November 10, 1973, in Washington, D.C. ... 6-5/297. ... Full name: Michael Christopher Flanagan.
HIGH SCHOOL: Rio Americano (Sacramento).
COLLEGE: UCLA.
TRANSACTIONS/CAREER NOTES: Selected by Green Bay Packers in third round (90th pick overall) of 1996 NFL draft. ... Signed by Packers (July 17, 1996). ... On injured reserve with leg injury (August 19, 1996-entire season). ... On physically unable to perform list with ankle injury (August 19, 1997-entire season). ... Traded by Packers to Carolina Panthers for an undisclosed draft pick (August 31, 1998); trade later voided because Flanagan failed physical (September 1, 1998). ... Granted free agency (February 12, 1999). ... Re-signed by Packers (March 25, 1999).
PLAYING EXPERIENCE: Green Bay NFL, 1998-2002. ... Games/Games started: 1998 (2/0), 1999 (15/0), 2000 (16/2), 2001 (16/16), 2002 (16/13). Total: 55/31.

FLANIGAN, JIM   DT   49ERS

PERSONAL: Born August 27, 1971, in Green Bay. ... 6-2/290. ... Full name: James Michael Flanigan. ... Son of Jim Flanigan, linebacker with Green Bay Packers (1967-70) and New Orleans Saints (1971).
HIGH SCHOOL: Southern Door (Brussels, Wis.).
COLLEGE: Notre Dame.
TRANSACTIONS/CAREER NOTES: Selected by Chicago Bears in third round (74th pick overall) of 1994 NFL draft. ... Signed by Bears (July 14, 1994). ... Granted free agency (February 14, 1997). ... Re-signed by Bears (June 1, 1997). ... Granted unconditional free agency (February 13, 1998). ... Re-signed by Bears (February 13, 1998). ... Released by Bears (April 26, 2001). ... Signed by Green Bay Packers (May 29, 2001). ... Granted unconditional free agency (March 1, 2002). ... Signed by San Francisco 49ers (June 13, 2002).

			TOTALS			INTERCEPTIONS			
Year	Team	G	GS	Tk.	Ast.	Sks.	No.	Yds.	Avg.	TD
1994—Chicago NFL		14	0	10	1	0.0	0	0	0.0	0
1995—Chicago NFL		16	12	39	10	11.0	0	0	0.0	0
1996—Chicago NFL		14	14	36	5	5.0	0	0	0.0	0
1997—Chicago NFL		16	16	38	12	6.0	0	0	0.0	0
1998—Chicago NFL		16	16	32	14	8.5	0	0	0.0	0
1999—Chicago NFL		16	16	35	8	6.0	1	6	6.0	0
2000—Chicago NFL		16	14	33	13	4.0	0	0	0.0	0
2001—Green Bay NFL		16	8	26	14	4.5	0	0	0.0	0
2002—San Francisco NFL		15	1	7	5	1.0	0	0	0.0	0
Pro totals (9 years)		139	97	256	82	46.0	1	6	6.0	0

FLEMISTER, ZERON   TE   REDSKINS

PERSONAL: Born September 8, 1976, in Sioux City, Iowa. ... 6-4/245.
HIGH SCHOOL: West (Iowa).
COLLEGE: Iowa.
TRANSACTIONS/CAREER NOTES: Signed as non-drafted free agent by Washington Redskins (April 18, 2000).
SINGLE GAME HIGHS (regular season): Receptions—3 (September 22, 2002, vs. San Francisco); yards—57 (September 22, 2002, vs. San Francisco); and touchdown receptions—1 (November 28, 2002, vs. Dallas).

F

Year Team	G	GS	RECEIVING				TOTALS			
			No.	Yds.	Avg.	TD	TD	2pt.	Pts.	Fum.
2000—Washington NFL	5	0	1	8	8.0	0	0	0	0	0
2001—Washington NFL	16	1	18	196	10.9	2	2	0	12	0
2002—Washington NFL	15	7	10	146	14.6	2	2	0	12	1
Pro totals (3 years)	36	8	29	350	12.1	4	4	0	24	1

FLEMONS, RONALD   DE   FALCONS

PERSONAL: Born October 20, 1979, in San Antonio. ... 6-5/265.
HIGH SCHOOL: Marshall (San Antonio).
COLLEGE: Texas A&M.
TRANSACTIONS/CAREER NOTES: Selected by Atlanta Falcons in seventh round (226th pick overall) of 2001 NFL draft. ... Signed by Falcons (May 21, 2001). ... Released by Falcons (September 17, 2002). ... Re-signed by Falcons to practice squad (September 19, 2002). ... Released by Falcons (October 22, 2002). ... Signed by New Orleans Saints to practice squad (November 5, 2002). ... Signed off Saints practice squad by Falcons (November 21, 2002).

Year Team	G	GS	TOTALS		
			Tk.	Ast.	Sks.
2001—Atlanta NFL	1	0	0	0	0.0
2002—Atlanta NFL	4	0	0	1	0.5
Pro totals (2 years)	5	0	0	1	0.5

FLETCHER, DERRICK   G   PANTHERS

PERSONAL: Born September 9, 1975, in Houston. ... 6-6/350. ... Full name: Derrick W. Fletcher.
HIGH SCHOOL: Aldine (Houston).
COLLEGE: Baylor.
TRANSACTIONS/CAREER NOTES: Selected by New England Patriots in fifth round (154th pick overall) of 1999 NFL draft. ... Signed by Patriots (July 28, 1999). ... Active for one game (1999); did not play. ... Released by Patriots (September 19, 2000). ... Signed by Washington Redskins (October 3, 2000). ... Released by Redskins (November 9, 2000). ... Re-signed by Redskins to practice squad (November 13, 2000). ... Activated (November 14, 2000). ... Released by Redskins (September 2, 2001). ... Signed by Carolina Panthers (March 6, 2002).
PLAYING EXPERIENCE: New England (2)-Washington (1) NFL, 2000; Carolina NFL, 2002. ... Games/Games started: 2000 (N.E.-2/2; Wash.-1/0; Total: 3/2), 2002 (5/0). Total: 8/2.

FLETCHER, JAMAR   CB   DOLPHINS

PERSONAL: Born August 28, 1979, in St. Louis. ... 5-9/187. ... Full name: Jamar Mondell Fletcher.
HIGH SCHOOL: Hazelwood East (St. Louis).
COLLEGE: Wisconsin.
TRANSACTIONS/CAREER NOTES: Selected after junior season by Miami Dolphins in first round (26th pick overall) of 2001 NFL draft. ... Signed by Dolphins (July 25, 2001).
HONORS: Named cornerback on THE SPORTING NEWS college All-America first team (1999). ... Named cornerback on THE SPORTING NEWS college All-America second team (2000). ... Jim Thorpe Award winner (2000).

Year Team	G	GS	TOTALS			INTERCEPTIONS			
			Tk.	Ast.	Sks.	No.	Yds.	Avg.	TD
2001—Miami NFL	14	2	8	2	0.0	0	0	0.0	0
2002—Miami NFL	16	4	35	2	0.0	2	30	15.0	0
Pro totals (2 years)	30	6	43	4	0.0	2	30	15.0	0

FLETCHER, LONDON   LB   BILLS

PERSONAL: Born May 19, 1975, in Cleveland. ... 5-9/245. ... Full name: London Levi Fletcher.
HIGH SCHOOL: Villa Angela-St. Joseph (Cleveland).
COLLEGE: John Carroll (degree in sociology).
TRANSACTIONS/CAREER NOTES: Signed as non-drafted free agent by St. Louis Rams (April 28, 1998). ... Granted free agency (March 2, 2001). ... Re-signed by Rams (May 9, 2001). ... Granted unconditional free agency (March 1, 2002). ... Signed by Buffalo Bills (March 7, 2002).
CHAMPIONSHIP GAME EXPERIENCE: Played in NFC championship game (1999 and 2001 seasons). ... Member of Super Bowl championship team (1999 season). ... Played in Super Bowl XXXVI (2001 season).

Year Team	G	GS	TOTALS			INTERCEPTIONS			
			Tk.	Ast.	Sks.	No.	Yds.	Avg.	TD
1998—St. Louis NFL	16	1	11	1	0.0	0	0	0.0	0
1999—St. Louis NFL	16	16	66	24	3.0	0	0	0.0	0
2000—St. Louis NFL	16	15	106	27	5.5	4	33	8.3	0
2001—St. Louis NFL	16	16	90	29	4.5	2	18	9.0	0
2002—Buffalo NFL	16	16	98	51	3.0	0	0	0.0	0
Pro totals (5 years)	80	64	371	132	16.0	6	51	8.5	0

FLETCHER, TERRELL   RB

PERSONAL: Born September 14, 1973, in St. Louis. ... 5-8/196. ... Full name: Terrell Antoine Fletcher.
HIGH SCHOOL: Hazelwood East (St. Louis).

COLLEGE: Wisconsin (degree in English, 1994).
TRANSACTIONS/CAREER NOTES: Selected by San Diego Chargers in second round (51st pick overall) of 1995 NFL draft. ... Signed by Chargers (July 12, 1995). ... On injured reserve with knee injury (December 17, 1997-remainder of season). ... Granted free agency (February 13, 1998). ... Re-signed by Chargers (June 1998). ... Released by Chargers (April 20, 2001). ... Re-signed by Chargers (April 25, 2001). ... Released by Chargers (February 27, 2003).
SINGLE GAME HIGHS (regular season): Attempts—34 (December 6, 1998, vs. Washington); yards—127 (December 27, 1998, vs. Arizona); and rushing touchdowns—2 (November 22, 1998, vs. Kansas City).
STATISTICAL PLATEAUS: 100-yard rushing games: 1998 (2).

			RUSHING				RECEIVING				KICKOFF RETURNS				TOTALS			
Year Team	G	GS	Att.	Yds.	Avg.	TD	No.	Yds.	Avg.	TD	No.	Yds.	Avg.	TD	TD	2pt.	Pts.	Fum.
1995—San Diego NFL	16	0	26	140	5.4	1	3	26	8.7	0	4	65	16.3	0	1	0	6	2
1996—San Diego NFL	16	0	77	282	3.7	0	61	476	7.8	2	0	0	0.0	0	2	0	12	1
1997—San Diego NFL	13	1	51	161	3.2	0	39	292	7.5	0	0	0	0.0	0	0	0	0	4
1998—San Diego NFL	12	5	153	543	3.5	5	30	188	6.3	0	3	71	23.7	0	5	0	30	1
1999—San Diego NFL	15	2	48	126	2.6	0	45	360	8.0	0	7	112	16.0	0	0	0	0	1
2000—San Diego NFL	16	6	116	384	3.3	3	48	355	7.4	1	0	0	0.0	0	4	0	24	2
2001—San Diego NFL	13	0	29	107	3.7	0	23	184	8.0	0	1	11	11.0	0	0	0	0	1
2002—San Diego NFL	10	0	26	128	4.9	1	10	62	6.2	0	1	22	22.0	0	1	0	6	0
Pro totals (8 years)	111	14	526	1871	3.6	10	259	1943	7.5	3	16	281	17.6	0	13	0	78	12

FLOWERS, ERIK   DE   TEXANS

PERSONAL: Born March 1, 1978, in San Antonio, Texas. ... 6-4/273. ... Full name: Erik Mathews Flowers.
HIGH SCHOOL: Theodore Roosevelt (San Antonio, Texas).
JUNIOR COLLEGE: Trinity Valley Community College (Texas).
COLLEGE: Arizona State.
TRANSACTIONS/CAREER NOTES: Selected by Buffalo Bills in first round (26th pick overall) of 2000 NFL draft. ... Signed by Bills (July 23, 2000). ... Claimed on waivers by Houston Texans (August 21, 2002).

			TOTALS			INTERCEPTIONS			
Year Team	G	GS	Tk.	Ast.	Sks.	No.	Yds.	Avg.	TD
2000—Buffalo NFL	16	0	11	9	2.0	1	0	0.0	0
2001—Buffalo NFL	15	5	15	6	2.0	0	0	0.0	0
2002—Houston NFL	14	0	0	1	0.0	0	0	0.0	0
Pro totals (3 years)	45	5	26	16	4.0	1	0	0.0	0

FLOWERS, LEE   S   BRONCOS

PERSONAL: Born January 14, 1973, in Columbia, S.C. ... 5-11/214. ... Full name: Lethon Flowers III.
HIGH SCHOOL: Spring Valley (Columbia, S.C.).
COLLEGE: Georgia Tech.
TRANSACTIONS/CAREER NOTES: Selected by Pittsburgh Steelers in fifth round (151st pick overall) of 1995 NFL draft. ... Signed by Steelers (July 18, 1995). ... Granted free agency (February 13, 1998). ... Re-signed by Steelers (June 9, 1998). ... Granted unconditional free agency (February 12, 1999). ... Re-signed by Steelers (February 16, 1999). ... Granted unconditional free agency (February 28, 2003). ... Signed by Denver Broncos (June 3, 2003).
CHAMPIONSHIP GAME EXPERIENCE: Played in AFC championship game (1995, 1997 and 2001 seasons). ... Played in Super Bowl XXX (1995 season).

			TOTALS			INTERCEPTIONS			
Year Team	G	GS	Tk.	Ast.	Sks.	No.	Yds.	Avg.	TD
1995—Pittsburgh NFL	10	0	0	0	0.0	0	0	0.0	0
1996—Pittsburgh NFL	16	0	3	0	0.0	0	0	0.0	0
1997—Pittsburgh NFL	10	0	1	0	0.0	0	0	0.0	0
1998—Pittsburgh NFL	16	16	78	23	1.0	1	2	2.0	0
1999—Pittsburgh NFL	15	15	64	15	5.0	0	0	0.0	0
2000—Pittsburgh NFL	14	14	61	24	1.0	1	0	0.0	0
2001—Pittsburgh NFL	15	15	48	13	1.0	0	0	0.0	0
2002—Pittsburgh NFL	16	15	52	21	4.0	2	31	15.5	0
Pro totals (8 years)	112	75	307	96	12.0	4	33	8.3	0

F

FLOYD, MARCUS   CB   BILLS

PERSONAL: Born October 12, 1978, in Bartow, Fla. ... 5-9/180.
HIGH SCHOOL: Bartow (Fla.).
COLLEGE: Indiana (degree in sports communication).
TRANSACTIONS/CAREER NOTES: Signed as non-drafted free agent by New York Jets (April 27, 2002). ... Released by Jets (September 24, 2002). ... Signed by Buffalo Bills to practice squad (October 21, 2002). ... Activated (December 18, 2002).

			TOTALS			INTERCEPTIONS			
Year Team	G	GS	Tk.	Ast.	Sks.	No.	Yds.	Avg.	TD
2002—Buffalo NFL	2	0	0	0	0.0	0	0	0.0	0
—New York Jets NFL	2	0	0	0	0.0	0	0	0.0	0
Pro totals (1 year)	4	0	0	0	0.0	0	0	0.0	0

PERSONAL: Born October 23, 1962, in Manchester, Md. ... 5-10/180. ... Full name: Douglas Richard Flutie. ... Brother of Darren Flutie, wide receiver with San Diego Chargers (1998), B.C. Lions of CFL (1991-95), Edmonton Eskimos of CFL (1996 and 1997) and Hamilton Tiger-Cats of CFL (1998).

HIGH SCHOOL: Natick (Mass.).

COLLEGE: Boston College (degrees in computer science and speech communications, 1984).

TRANSACTIONS/CAREER NOTES: Selected by New Jersey Generals in 1985 USFL territorial draft. ... Signed by Generals (February 4, 1985). ... Granted roster exemption (February 4-14, 1985). ... Activated (February 15, 1985). ... On developmental squad for three games with Generals (1985). ... Selected by Los Angeles Rams in 11th round (285th pick overall) of 1985 NFL draft. ... On developmental squad (June 10, 1995-remainder of season). ... Rights traded by Rams with fourth-round pick in 1987 draft to Chicago Bears for third- and sixth-round picks in 1987 draft (October 14, 1986). ... Signed by Bears (October 21, 1986). ... Granted roster exemption (October 21-November 3, 1986). ... Activated (November 4, 1986). ... Crossed picket line during players strike (October 13, 1907). ... Traded by Bears to New England Patriots for eighth-round pick in 1988 draft (October 13, 1987). ... Released by Patriots after 1989 season. ... Signed by B.C. Lions of CFL (June 1990). ... Granted free agency (February 1992). ... Signed by Calgary Stampeders of CFL (March 1992). ... Rights assigned to Toronto Argonauts of CFL (March 15, 1996). ... Signed by Buffalo Bills (January 16, 1998). ... Released by Bills (March 1, 2001). ... Signed by San Diego Chargers (March 9, 2001).

CHAMPIONSHIP GAME EXPERIENCE: Member of CFL championship team (1992, 1996 and 1997). ... Named Most Valuable Player of Grey Cup, CFL championship game (1992, 1996 and 1997). ... Played in Grey Cup (1993 and 1995).

HONORS: Heisman Trophy winner (1984). ... Named College Football Player of the Year by THE SPORTING NEWS (1984). ... Named quarterback on THE SPORTING NEWS college All-America first team (1984). ... Most Outstanding Player of CFL (1991-1994, 1996 and 1997). ... Played in Pro Bowl (1998 season).

SINGLE GAME HIGHS (regular season): Attempts—53 (December 30, 2001, vs. Seattle); completions—34 (December 30, 2001, vs. Seattle); yards—377 (December 30, 2001, vs. Seattle); and touchdown passes—4 (October 30, 1988, vs. Chicago).

STATISTICAL PLATEAUS: 300-yard passing games: 1998 (2), 1999 (1), 2000 (1), 2001 (4). Total: 8.

MISCELLANEOUS: Regular-season record as starting NFL quarterback: 35-25 (.583). ... Postseason record as starting NFL quarterback: 0-2.

Year	Team	G	GS	PASSING									RUSHING				TOTALS		
				Att.	Cmp.	Pct.	Yds.	TD	Int.	Avg.	Skd.	Rat.	Att.	Yds.	Avg.	TD	TD	2pt.	Pts.
1985—New Jersey USFL		15	...	281	134	47.7	2109	13	14	7.51	0	67.8	65	465	7.2	6	6	0	36
1986—Chicago NFL		4	1	46	23	50.0	361	3	2	7.85	6	80.1	9	36	4.0	1	1	0	6
1987—Chicago NFL		1	0	0	0	0.0	0	0	0	0.0	0	...	0	0	0.0	0	0	0	0
—New England NFL		1	1	25	15	60.0	199	1	0	7.96	1	98.6	6	43	7.2	0	0	0	0
1988—New England NFL		11	9	179	92	51.4	1150	8	10	6.42	11	63.3	38	179	4.7	1	1	0	6
1989—New England NFL		5	3	91	36	39.6	493	2	4	5.42	6	46.6	16	87	5.4	0	0	0	0
1990—British Columbia CFL		16	...	392	207	52.8	2960	16	19	7.55	0	71.0	79	662	8.4	3	3	0	18
1991—British Columbia CFL		18	...	730	466	63.8	6619	38	24	9.07	0	96.7	120	610	5.1	14	14	1	86
1992—Calgary CFL		18	...	688	396	57.6	5945	32	30	8.64	0	83.4	96	669	7.0	11	11	0	66
1993—Calgary CFL		18	...	703	416	59.2	6092	44	17	8.67	0	98.3	74	373	5.0	11	11	0	66
1994—Calgary CFL		18	...	659	403	61.2	5726	48	19	8.69	0	101.5	96	760	7.9	8	8	0	48
1995—Calgary CFL		12	...	332	223	67.2	2788	16	5	8.40	0	102.8	46	288	6.3	5	5	0	30
1996—Toronto CFL		18	...	677	434	64.1	5720	29	17	8.45	0	94.5	101	756	7.5	9	9	0	54
1997—Toronto CFL		18	18	673	430	63.9	5505	47	24	8.18	0	97.8	92	542	5.9	9	9	0	54
1998—Buffalo NFL		13	10	354	202	57.1	2711	20	11	7.66	12	87.4	48	248	5.2	1	1	0	6
1999—Buffalo NFL		15	15	478	264	55.2	3171	19	16	6.63	26	75.1	88	476	5.4	1	1	0	6
2000—Buffalo NFL		11	5	231	132	57.1	1700	8	3	7.36	10	86.5	36	161	4.5	1	1	0	6
2001—San Diego NFL		16	16	521	294	56.4	3464	15	18	6.65	25	72.0	53	192	3.6	1	1	0	6
2002—San Diego NFL		1	0	11	3	27.3	64	0	0	5.82	0	51.3	1	6	6.0	0	0	0	0
USFL totals (1 year)		15	...	281	134	47.7	2109	13	14	7.51	0	67.8	65	465	7.2	6	6	0	36
CFL totals (8 years)		136	...	4854	2975	61.3	41355	270	155	8.52	0	93.9	704	4660	6.6	70	70	1	422
NFL totals (9 years)		78	60	1936	1061	54.8	13313	76	64	6.88	97	75.7	295	1428	4.8	6	6	0	36
Pro totals (18 years)		229	...	7071	4170	59.0	56777	359	233	8.03	97	87.9	1064	6553	6.2	82	82	1	494

PERSONAL: Born June 15, 1974, in Doylestown, Pa. ... 6-3/305. ... Full name: Michael Patrick Flynn.

HIGH SCHOOL: Cathedral (Springfield, Mass.).

COLLEGE: Maine.

TRANSACTIONS/CAREER NOTES: Signed as non-drafted free agent by Baltimore Ravens (April 25, 1997). ... Released by Ravens (August 24, 1997). ... Signed by Tampa Bay Buccaneers to practice squad (August 27, 1997). ... Released by Buccaneers (September 2, 1997). ... Signed by Jacksonville Jaguars to practice squad (November 4, 1997). ... Signed by Ravens off Jaguars practice squad (December 3, 1997). ... Inactive for three games (1997). ... Granted free agency (March 2, 2001). ... Re-signed by Ravens (March 13, 2001).

PLAYING EXPERIENCE: Baltimore NFL, 1998-2002. ... Games/Games started: 1998 (2/0), 1999 (12/0), 2000 (16/16), 2001 (16/16), 2002 (15/15). Total: 61/47.

CHAMPIONSHIP GAME EXPERIENCE: Played in AFC championship game (2000 season). ... Member of Super Bowl championship team (2000 season).

PERSONAL: Born April 5, 1973, in Nuk 'Alofa, Tonga, Samoan Islands. ... 6-5/315. ... Full name: Spencer Sione Folau. ... Name pronounced fah-LOWE.

HIGH SCHOOL: Sequoia (Redwood City, Calif.).

COLLEGE: Idaho.

TRANSACTIONS/CAREER NOTES: Signed as non-drafted free agent by Baltimore Ravens (April 26, 1996). ... Released by Ravens (August 25, 1996). ... Re-signed by Ravens to practice squad (October 29, 1996). ... Assigned by Ravens to Rhein Fire in 1997 World League enhancement allocation program (February 1997). ... Released by Ravens (October 28, 1998). ... Re-signed by Ravens (November 3, 1998). ... Granted free agency (February 11, 2000). ... Tendered offer sheet by New England Patriots (April 10, 2000). ... Offer matched by Ravens (April 12, 2000). ... Released by Ravens (March 1, 2001). ... Signed by Miami Dolphins (July 28, 2001). ... Granted unconditional free agency (March 1, 2002). ... Signed by New Orleans Saints (April 1, 2002).

PLAYING EXPERIENCE: Rhein W.L., 1997; Baltimore NFL, 1997-2000; Miami NFL, 2001; New Orleans NFL, 2002. ... Games/Games started: W.L. 1997 (games played unavailable), NFL 1997 (10/0), 1998 (3/3), 1999 (5/1), 2000 (11/4), 2001 (16/15), 2002 (16/16). Total NFL: 61/39.

CHAMPIONSHIP GAME EXPERIENCE: Played in AFC championship game (2000 season). ... Member of Super Bowl championship team (2000 season).

FOLEY, STEVE   LB   BENGALS

PERSONAL: Born September 9, 1975, in Little Rock, Ark. ... 6-3/260.
HIGH SCHOOL: Hall (Little Rock, Ark.).
COLLEGE: Northeast Louisiana.
TRANSACTIONS/CAREER NOTES: Selected by Cincinnati Bengals in third round (75th pick overall) of 1998 NFL draft. ... Signed by Bengals (July 19, 1998). ... On injured reserve with shoulder injury (September 1, 2002-entire season).

			TOTALS			INTERCEPTIONS			
Year Team	G	GS	Tk.	Ast.	Sks.	No.	Yds.	Avg.	TD
1998—Cincinnati NFL	10	1	11	1	2.0	0	0	0.0	0
1999—Cincinnati NFL	16	16	34	3	3.5	0	0	0.0	0
2000—Cincinnati NFL	16	16	34	9	4.0	1	1	1.0	0
2001—Cincinnati NFL	12	12	25	14	0.0	0	0	0.0	0
2002—Cincinnati NFL			Did not play.						
Pro totals (4 years)	54	45	104	27	9.5	1	1	1.0	0

FONOTI, TONIU   G   CHARGERS

PERSONAL: Born November 26, 1981, in American Samoa. ... 6-4/349. ... Full name: Toniuolevaiavea Satele Fonoti.
HIGH SCHOOL: Kahuku (Hauula, Hawaii).
COLLEGE: Nebraska.
TRANSACTIONS/CAREER NOTES: Selected after junior season by San Diego Chargers in second round (39th pick overall) of 2002 NFL draft. ... Signed by Chargers (July 30, 2002).
PLAYING EXPERIENCE: San Diego NFL, 2002. ... Games/games started: 2002 (15/14).

FONTENOT, JERRY   C

PERSONAL: Born November 21, 1966, in Lafayette, La. ... 6-3/300. ... Full name: Jerry Paul Fontenot.
HIGH SCHOOL: Lafayette (La.).
COLLEGE: Texas A&M.
TRANSACTIONS/CAREER NOTES: Selected by Chicago Bears in third round (65th pick overall) of 1989 NFL draft. ... Signed by Bears (July 27, 1989). ... Granted free agency (March 1, 1993). ... Re-signed by Bears (June 16, 1993). ... Granted free agency (February 16, 1996). ... Re-signed by Bears (July 10, 1996). ... Granted unconditional free agency (February 14, 1997). ... Signed by New Orleans Saints (May 28, 1997). ... On injured reserve with knee injury (October 14, 1998-remainder of season). ... Granted unconditional free agency (February 12, 1999). ... Re-signed by Saints (February 15, 1999). ... Granted unconditional free agency (February 28, 2003).
PLAYING EXPERIENCE: Chicago NFL, 1989-1996; New Orleans NFL, 1997-2002. ... Games/Games started: 1989 (16/0), 1990 (16/2), 1991 (16/7), 1992 (16/16), 1993 (16/16), 1994 (16/16), 1995 (16/16), 1996 (16/16), 1997 (16/16), 1998 (4/4), 1999 (16/16), 2000 (16/16), 2001 (16/16), 2002 (16/16). Total: 212/173.

FOOTE, LARRY   LB   STEELERS

PERSONAL: Born June 12, 1980, in Detroit. ... 6-0/234. ... Full name: Lawrence Edward Foote Jr..
HIGH SCHOOL: Pershing (Detroit).
COLLEGE: Michigan.
TRANSACTIONS/CAREER NOTES: Selected by Pittsburgh Steelers in fourth round (128th pick overall) of 2002 NFL draft. ... Signed by Steelers (July 18, 2002).
HONORS: Named linebacker on THE SPORTING NEWS college All-America second team (2001).

			TOTALS			INTERCEPTIONS			
Year Team	G	GS	Tk.	Ast.	Sks.	No.	Yds.	Avg.	TD
2002—Pittsburgh NFL	14	4	11	7	0.0	0	0	0.0	0

FORD, HENRY   DT   TITANS

F

PERSONAL: Born October 30, 1971, in Fort Worth, Texas. ... 6-3/295.
HIGH SCHOOL: Trimble Technical (Fort Worth, Texas).
COLLEGE: Arkansas.
TRANSACTIONS/CAREER NOTES: Selected by Houston Oilers in first round (26th pick overall) of 1994 NFL draft. ... Signed by Oilers (June 16, 1994). ... Oilers franchise moved to Tennessee for 1997 season. ... Granted unconditional free agency (February 13, 1998). ... Re-signed by Oilers (March 2, 1998). ... Oilers franchise renamed Tennessee Titans for 1999 season (December 26, 1998).
CHAMPIONSHIP GAME EXPERIENCE: Played in AFC championship game (1999 and 2002 seasons). ... Played in Super Bowl XXXIV (1999 season).

			TOTALS		
Year Team	G	GS	Tk.	Ast.	Sks.
1994—Houston NFL	11	0	10	1	0.0
1995—Houston NFL	16	16	27	16	4.5
1996—Houston NFL	15	14	24	15	1.0
1997—Tennessee NFL	16	16	38	12	5.0
1998—Tennessee NFL	13	5	14	8	1.5
1999—Tennessee NFL	12	9	14	13	5.5
2000—Tennessee NFL	14	3	20	12	2.0
2001—Tennessee NFL	16	0	16	11	1.0
2002—Tennessee NFL	16	13	15	7	3.5
Pro totals (9 years)	129	76	178	95	24.0

FORDHAM, TODD   OT   STEELERS

PERSONAL: Born October 9, 1973, in Atlanta. ... 6-5/315. ... Full name: Lindsey Todd Fordham.
HIGH SCHOOL: Tift County (Tifton, Ga.).
COLLEGE: Florida State (degree in business, 1996).

TRANSACTIONS/CAREER NOTES: Signed as non-drafted free agent by Jacksonville Jaguars (April 21, 1997). ... Released by Jaguars (August 24, 1997). ... Re-signed by Jaguars to practice squad (August 25, 1997). ... Activated (September 23, 1997). ... On injured reserve with knee injury (August 31, 1999-entire season). ... Granted free agency (February 11, 2000). ... Re-signed by Jaguars (February 24, 2000). ... Granted unconditional free agency (March 2, 2001). ... Signed by Denver Broncos (April 13, 2001). ... Released by Broncos (September 2, 2001). ... Signed by Jaguars (October 2, 2001). ... Granted unconditional free agency (March 1, 2002). ... Re-signed by Jaguars (April 16, 2002). ... Granted unconditional free agency (February 28, 2003). ... Signed by Pittsburgh Steelers (March 18, 2003).
PLAYING EXPERIENCE: Jacksonville NFL, 1997-2002. ... Games/Games started: 1997 (1/0), 1998 (11/1), 2000 (16/8), 2001 (12/12), 2002 (16/9). Total: 56/30.

FOREMAN, JAY — LB — TEXANS

PERSONAL: Born February 18, 1976, in Eden Prairie, Minn. ... 6-1/240. ... Full name: Jamal A. Foreman. ... Son of Chuck Foreman, running back with Minnesota Vikings (1973-79) and New England Patriots (1980).
HIGH SCHOOL: Eden Prairie (Minn.).
COLLEGE: Nebraska (degree in business administration).
TRANSACTIONS/CAREER NOTES: Selected by Buffalo Bills in fifth round (156th pick overall) of 1999 NFL draft. ... Signed by Bills (July 27, 1999). ... Granted free agency (March 1, 2002). ... Re-signed by Bills (April 17, 2002). ... Traded by Bills to Houston Texans for KR/PR Charlie Rogers (April 17, 2002). ... Granted unconditional free agency (February 28, 2003). ... Re-signed by Texans (March 4, 2003).

			TOTALS			INTERCEPTIONS			
Year Team	G	GS	Tk.	Ast.	Sks.	No.	Yds.	Avg.	TD
1999—Buffalo NFL	7	0	0	0	0.0	0	0	0.0	0
2000—Buffalo NFL	15	4	32	18	0.0	0	0	0.0	0
2001—Buffalo NFL	16	16	69	28	2.5	0	0	0.0	0
2002—Houston NFL	16	16	101	36	0.0	0	0	0.0	0
Pro totals (4 years)	54	36	202	82	2.5	0	0	0.0	0

FORNEY, KYNAN — G — FALCONS

PERSONAL: Born September 8, 1978, in Nacogdoches, Texas. ... 6-2/305.
HIGH SCHOOL: Nacogdoches (Texas).
JUNIOR COLLEGE: Trinity Valley Community College (Texas).
COLLEGE: Hawaii.
TRANSACTIONS/CAREER NOTES: Selected by Atlanta Falcons in seventh round (219th pick overall) of 2001 NFL draft. ... Signed by Falcons (May 21, 2001).
PLAYING EXPERIENCE: Atlanta NFL, 2001-2002. ... Games/Games started: 2001 (12/8), 2002 (14/12). Total: 26/20.

FOSTER, DESHAUN — RB — PANTHERS

PERSONAL: Born January 10, 1980, in Charlotte, N.C. ... 6-0/222. ... Full name: DeShaun Xavier Foster.
HIGH SCHOOL: Tustin (Calif.).
COLLEGE: UCLA.
TRANSACTIONS/CAREER NOTES: Selected by Carolina Panthers in second round (34th pick overall) of 2002 NFL draft. ... Signed by Panthers (July 30, 2002). ... On injured reserve with knee injury (October 25, 2002-remainder of season).
HONORS: Named running back on THE SPORTING NEWS college All-America second team (2001).

			RUSHING				RECEIVING				KICKOFF RETURNS				TOTALS		
Year Team	G	GS	Att.	Yds.	Avg.	TD	No.	Yds.	Avg.	TD	No.	Yds.	Avg.	TD	TD	2pt.	Pts. Fum.
2002—Carolina NFL																	

Did not play.

FOSTER, LARRY — WR — CARDINALS

PERSONAL: Born November 7, 1976, in Shreveport, La. ... 5-10/188.
HIGH SCHOOL: West Jefferson (La.).
COLLEGE: Louisiana State.
TRANSACTIONS/CAREER NOTES: Signed as non-drafted free agent by Detroit Lions (April 28, 2000). ... Released by Lions (August 27, 2000). ... Re-signed by Lions to practice squad (August 29, 2000). ... Activated (October 16, 2000). ... Granted free agency (February 28, 2003). ... Re-signed by Lions (April 27, 2003). ... Traded by Lions to Arizona Cardinals for seventh-round pick (DB Blue Adams) in 2003 draft (April 27, 2003).
SINGLE GAME HIGHS (regular season): Receptions—8 (November 30, 2000, vs. Minnesota); yards—106 (November 30, 2000, vs. Minnesota); and touchdown receptions—1 (November 30, 2000, vs. Minnesota).
STATISTICAL PLATEAUS: 100-yard receiving games: 2000 (1).

			RUSHING				RECEIVING				PUNT RETURNS				KICKOFF RETURNS				TOTALS		
Year Team	G	GS	Att.	Yds.	Avg.	TD	No.	Yds.	Avg.	TD	No.	Yds.	Avg.	TD	No.	Yds.	Avg.	TD	TD	2pt.	Pts.
2000—Detroit NFL	10	0	2	31	15.5	0	17	175	10.3	1	0	0	0.0	0	0	0	0.0	0	1	0	6
2001—Detroit NFL	13	5	2	6	3.0	0	22	283	12.9	0	3	17	5.7	0	9	182	20.2	0	0	0	0
2002—Detroit NFL	13	0	0	0	0.0	0	14	152	10.9	0	4	29	7.3	0	12	286	23.8	0	0	0	0
Pro totals (3 years)	36	5	4	37	9.3	0	53	610	11.5	1	7	46	6.6	0	21	468	22.3	0	1	0	6

FOWLER, MELVIN — C — BROWNS

PERSONAL: Born March 31, 1979, in Wheatley Heights, N.Y. ... 6-3/300. ... Full name: Melvin Thaddeus Fowler Jr..
HIGH SCHOOL: Half Hollow Hills (Long Island, N.Y.).
COLLEGE: Maryland.
TRANSACTIONS/CAREER NOTES: Selected by Cleveland Browns in third round (76th pick overall) of 2002 NFL draft. ... Signed by Browns (July 22, 2002).
PLAYING EXPERIENCE: Cleveland NFL, 2002. ... Games/games started: 2002 (1/1).

FOX, VERNON   S   CHARGERS

PERSONAL: Born October 9, 1979, in Las Vegas, Nev. ... 5-9/200. ... Full name: Vernon Lee Fox III.
HIGH SCHOOL: Caimarron-Memorial (Las Vegas).
COLLEGE: Fresno State.
TRANSACTIONS/CAREER NOTES: Signed as non-drafted free agent by San Diego Chargers (April 26, 2002).

Year Team	G	GS	TOTALS			INTERCEPTIONS			
			Tk.	Ast.	Sks.	No.	Yds.	Avg.	TD
2002—San Diego NFL	16	3	17	6	0.0	1	25	25.0	0

FRALEY, HANK   C/OG   EAGLES

PERSONAL: Born September 21, 1977, in Gaithersburg, Md. ... 6-2/300.
HIGH SCHOOL: Gaithersburg (Md.).
COLLEGE: Robert Morris.
TRANSACTIONS/CAREER NOTES: Signed as non-drafted free agent by Pittsburgh Steelers (April 21, 2000). ... Claimed on waivers by Philadelphia Eagles (August 28, 2000). ... Inactive for all 16 games (2000).
PLAYING EXPERIENCE: Philadelphia NFL, 2001-2002. ... Games/Games started: 2001 (16/15), 2002 (16/16). Total: 32/31.
CHAMPIONSHIP GAME EXPERIENCE: Played in NFC championship game (2001 and 2002 seasons).

FRANKS, BUBBA   TE   PACKERS

PERSONAL: Born January 6, 1978, in Riverside, Calif. ... 6-6/263. ... Full name: Daniel Lamont Franks.
HIGH SCHOOL: Big Springs (Texas).
COLLEGE: Miami (Fla.).
TRANSACTIONS/CAREER NOTES: Selected after junior season by Green Bay Packers in first round (14th pick overall) of 2000 NFL draft. ... Signed by Packers (July 19, 2000).
HONORS: Named tight end on THE SPORTING NEWS college All-America first team (1999). ... Played in Pro Bowl (2001 and 2002 seasons).
SINGLE GAME HIGHS (regular season): Receptions—9 (September 22, 2002, vs. Detroit); yards—62 (September 22, 2002, vs. Detroit); and touchdown receptions—2 (December 23, 2001, vs. Cleveland).

Year Team	G	GS	RECEIVING			
			No.	Yds.	Avg.	TD
2000—Green Bay NFL	16	13	34	363	10.7	1
2001—Green Bay NFL	16	14	36	322	8.9	9
2002—Green Bay NFL	16	15	54	442	8.2	7
Pro totals (3 years)	48	42	124	1127	9.1	17

FRANZ, TODD   CB   REDSKINS

PERSONAL: Born April 12, 1976, in Enid, Okla. ... 6-0/194. ... Full name: Stephen Todd Franz.
HIGH SCHOOL: Weatherford (Okla.).
COLLEGE: Tulsa.
TRANSACTIONS/CAREER NOTES: Selected by Detroit Lions in fifth round (145th pick overall) of 2000 NFL draft. ... Signed by Lions (July 15, 2000). ... Claimed on waivers by New Orleans Saints (August 28, 2000). ... Released by Saints (October 10, 2000). ... Signed by Cleveland Browns (November 14, 2000). ... Released by Browns (August 4, 2001). ... Signed by New York Jets (January 15, 2002). ... Claimed on waivers by Green Bay Packers (July 22, 2002). ... Released by Packers (September 1, 2002). ... Re-signed by Packers to practice squad (September 4, 2002). ... Released by Packers (September 9, 2002). ... Re-signed by Packers to practice squad (October 9, 2002). ... Activated (October 12, 2002). ... Released by Packers (October 23, 2002). ... Re-signed by Packers to practice squad (October 24, 2002). ... Released by Packers (November 13, 2002). ... Signed by Washington Redskins to practice squad (November 19, 2002). ... Activated (December 17, 2002).

Year Team	G	GS	TOTALS			INTERCEPTIONS			
			Tk.	Ast.	Sks.	No.	Yds.	Avg.	TD
2000—New Orleans NFL	5	0	0	0	0.0	0	0	0.0	0
—Cleveland NFL	2	0	2	0	0.0	0	0	0.0	0
2002—Scottish NFLE	...	...	...	...	0.0	1	33	33.0	1
—Green Bay NFL	2	0	2	1	0.0	0	0	0.0	0
NFL Europe totals (1 year)	...	...	...	...	0.0	1	33	33.0	1
NFL totals (2 years)	9	0	4	1	0.0	0	0	0.0	0
Pro totals (3 years)	...	...	...	...	0.0	1	33	33.0	1

F

FREDRICKSON, ROB   LB

PERSONAL: Born May 13, 1971, in Saint Joseph, Mich. ... 6-4/239. ... Full name: Robert J. Fredrickson.
HIGH SCHOOL: Saint Joseph (Mich.) Senior.
COLLEGE: Michigan State.
TRANSACTIONS/CAREER NOTES: Selected by Los Angeles Raiders in first round (22nd pick overall) of 1994 NFL draft. ... Signed by Raiders (July 19, 1994). ... Raiders franchise moved to Oakland (July 21, 1995). ... On injured reserve with shoulder injury (November 20, 1996-remainder of season). ... Traded by Raiders to Detroit Lions for fourth-round pick (traded to Washington) in 1998 draft (March 25, 1998). ... Granted unconditional free agency (February 12, 1999). ... Signed by Arizona Cardinals (March 26, 1999). ... On injured reserve with neck injury (December 11, 2002-remainder of season). ... Granted unconditional free agency (February 28, 2003).

Year Team	G	GS	TOTALS			INTERCEPTIONS			
			Tk.	Ast.	Sks.	No.	Yds.	Avg.	TD
1994—Los Angeles Raiders NFL	16	12	58	23	3.0	0	0	0.0	0
1995—Oakland NFL	16	15	71	14	0.0	1	14	14.0	0
1996—Oakland NFL	10	10	36	11	0.0	0	0	0.0	0
1997—Oakland NFL	16	14	60	15	2.0	0	0	0.0	0
1998—Detroit NFL	16	16	56	30	2.5	1	0	0.0	0
1999—Arizona NFL	16	16	91	34	2.0	2	57	28.5	1
2000—Arizona NFL	13	12	61	38	1.0	1	8	8.0	0
2001—Arizona NFL	15	15	72	21	4.0	0	0	0.0	0
2002—Arizona NFL	10	10	35	12	1.0	0	0	0.0	0
Pro totals (9 years)	128	120	540	198	15.5	5	79	15.8	1

FREEMAN, ANTONIO   WR

PERSONAL: Born May 27, 1972, in Baltimore. ... 6-1/198. ... Full name: Antonio Michael Freeman.
HIGH SCHOOL: Polytechnic (Baltimore).
COLLEGE: Virginia Tech.
TRANSACTIONS/CAREER NOTES: Selected by Green Bay Packers in third round (90th pick overall) of 1995 NFL draft. ... Signed by Packers (June 22, 1995). ... Granted free agency (February 13, 1998). ... Re-signed by Packers (June 16, 1998). ... Designated by Packers as franchise player (February 12, 1999). ... Released by Packers (June 3, 2002). ... Signed by Philadelphia Eagles (August 24, 2002). ... Granted unconditional free agency (February 28, 2003).
CHAMPIONSHIP GAME EXPERIENCE: Played in NFC championship game (1995-1997 and 2002 seasons). ... Member of Super Bowl championship team (1996 season). ... Played in Super Bowl XXXII (1997 season).
HONORS: Named wide receiver on THE SPORTING NEWS NFL All-Pro team (1998). ... Played in Pro Bowl (1998 season).
POST SEASON RECORDS: Holds Super Bowl record for longest pass reception (from Brett Favre)—81 yards (January 26, 1997, vs. New England). ... Shares NFL postseason record for most touchdowns by punt return—1(December 31, 1995, vs. Atlanta).
SINGLE GAME HIGHS (regular season): Receptions—10 (December 14, 1997, vs. Carolina); yards—193 (November 1, 1998, vs. San Francisco); and touchdown receptions—3 (December 20, 1998, vs. Tennessee).
STATISTICAL PLATEAUS: 100-yard receiving games: 1996 (4), 1997 (3), 1998 (6), 1999 (3), 2000 (2), 2001 (2), 2002 (1). Total: 21.

Year Team	G	GS	RECEIVING				PUNT RETURNS				KICKOFF RETURNS				TOTALS			
			No.	Yds.	Avg.	TD	No.	Yds.	Avg.	TD	No.	Yds.	Avg.	TD	TD	2pt.	Pts.	Fum.
1995—Green Bay NFL	11	0	8	106	13.3	1	37	292	7.9	0	24	556	23.2	0	1	0	6	7
1996—Green Bay NFL	12	12	56	933	16.7	9	0	0	0.0	0	1	16	16.0	0	9	0	54	3
1997—Green Bay NFL	16	16	81	1243	15.3	12	0	0	0.0	0	0	0	0.0	0	12	0	72	1
1998—Green Bay NFL	15	15	84	*1424	17.0	14	0	0	0.0	0	0	0	0.0	0	14	1	86	0
1999—Green Bay NFL	16	16	74	1074	14.5	6	0	0	0.0	0	0	0	0.0	0	6	0	36	1
2000—Green Bay NFL	15	15	62	912	14.7	9	0	0	0.0	0	0	0	0.0	0	9	0	54	1
2001—Green Bay NFL	16	16	52	818	15.7	6	17	114	6.7	0	2	28	14.0	0	6	1	38	1
2002—Philadelphia NFL	16	1	46	600	13.0	4	0	0	0.0	0	0	0	0.0	0	4	0	24	0
Pro totals (8 years)	117	91	463	7110	15.4	61	54	406	7.5	0	27	600	22.2	0	61	2	370	14

FREEMAN, ARTURO   S   DOLPHINS

PERSONAL: Born October 27, 1976, in Orangeburg, S.C. ... 6-0/198. ... Full name: Arturo C. Freeman.
HIGH SCHOOL: Orangeburg-Wilkinson (Orangeburg, S.C.).
COLLEGE: South Carolina.
TRANSACTIONS/CAREER NOTES: Selected by Miami Dolphins in fifth round (152nd pick overall) of 2000 NFL draft. ... Signed by Dolphins (July 11, 2000). ... Granted free agency (February 28, 2003).

Year Team	G	GS	TOTALS			INTERCEPTIONS			
			Tk.	Ast.	Sks.	No.	Yds.	Avg.	TD
2000—Miami NFL	8	0	0	0	0.0	0	0	0.0	0
2001—Miami NFL	16	4	25	7	1.0	1	0	0.0	0
2002—Miami NFL	16	16	56	16	1.5	0	0	0.0	0
Pro totals (3 years)	40	20	81	23	2.5	1	0	0.0	0

F

FREEMAN, EDDIE   DT   CHIEFS

PERSONAL: Born January 4, 1978, in Mobile, Ala. ... 6-5/307.
HIGH SCHOOL: B.C. Rain (Mobile, Ala.).
COLLEGE: Alabama-Birmingham.
TRANSACTIONS/CAREER NOTES: Selected by Kansas City Chiefs in second round (43rd pick overall) of 2002 NFL draft. ... Signed by Chiefs (June 4, 2002).

Year Team	G	GS	TOTALS		
			Tk.	Ast.	Sks.
2002—Kansas City NFL	15	0	13	4	4.0

FREENEY, DWIGHT   DE   COLTS

PERSONAL: Born January 4, 1978, in Hartford, Conn. ... 6-1/268. ... Full name: Dwight Jason Freeney.
HIGH SCHOOL: Bloomfield (Conn.).
COLLEGE: Syracuse.
TRANSACTIONS/CAREER NOTES: Selected by Indianapolis Colts in first round (11th pick overall) of 2002 NFL draft. ... Signed by Colts (July 28, 2002).
HONORS: Named defensive end on THE SPORTING NEWS college All-America first team (2001).

Year Team	G	GS	TOTALS		
			Tk.	Ast.	Sks.
2002—Indianapolis NFL	16	8	45	1	13.0

FREROTTE, GUS　　　　QB　　　　VIKINGS

PERSONAL: Born July 31, 1971, in Kittanning, Pa. ... 6-3/225. ... Full name: Gustave Joseph Frerotte. ... Cousin of Mitch Frerotte, guard with Buffalo Bills (1987 and 1990-92).
HIGH SCHOOL: Ford City (Pa.) Junior-Senior.
COLLEGE: Tulsa.
TRANSACTIONS/CAREER NOTES: Selected by Washington Redskins in seventh round (197th pick overall) of 1994 NFL draft. ... Signed by Redskins (July 19, 1994). ... Granted free agency (February 14, 1997). ... Re-signed by Redskins (July 18, 1997). ... On injured reserve with hip injury (December 2, 1997-remainder of season). ... Released by Redskins (February 11, 1999). ... Signed by Detroit Lions (March 3, 1999). ... Granted unconditional free agency (February 11, 2000). ... Signed by Denver Broncos (March 7, 2000). ... Granted unconditional free agency (March 2, 2001). ... Re-signed by Broncos (March 13, 2001). ... On injured reserve with shoulder injury (December 19, 2001-remainder of season). ... Granted unconditional free agency (March 1, 2002). ... Signed by Cincinnati Bengals (May 1, 2002). ... Granted unconditional free agency (February 28, 2003). ... Signed by Minnesota Vikings (March 19, 2003).
HONORS: Played in Pro Bowl (1996 season).
SINGLE GAME HIGHS (regular season): Attempts—58 (November 19, 2000, vs. San Diego); completions—36 (November 19, 2000, vs. San Diego); yards—462 (November 19, 2000, vs. San Diego); and touchdown passes—5 (November 19, 2000, vs. San Diego).
STATISTICAL PLATEAUS: 300-yard passing games: 1995 (1), 1996 (1), 1999 (2), 2000 (1). Total: 5.
MISCELLANEOUS: Regular-season record as starting NFL quarterback: 25-36-1 (.411). ... Postseason record as starting NFL quarterback: 0-2.

				PASSING								RUSHING				TOTALS		
Year Team	G	GS	Att.	Cmp.	Pct.	Yds.	TD	Int.	Avg.	Skd.	Rat.	Att.	Yds.	Avg.	TD	TD	2pt.	Pts.
1994—Washington NFL	4	4	100	46	46.0	600	5	5	6.00	3	61.3	4	1	0.3	0	0	0	0
1995—Washington NFL	16	11	396	199	50.3	2751	13	13	6.95	23	70.2	22	16	0.7	1	1	0	6
1996—Washington NFL	16	16	470	270	57.4	3453	12	11	7.35	22	79.3	28	16	0.6	0	0	0	0
1997—Washington NFL	13	13	402	204	50.7	2682	17	12	6.67	23	73.8	24	65	2.7	2	2	0	12
1998—Washington NFL	3	2	54	25	46.3	283	1	3	5.24	12	45.5	3	20	6.7	0	0	0	0
1999—Detroit NFL	9	6	288	175	60.8	2117	9	7	7.35	28	83.6	15	33	2.2	0	0	0	0
2000—Denver NFL	10	6	232	138	59.5	1776	9	8	7.66	12	82.1	22	64	2.9	1	1	0	6
2001—Denver NFL	4	1	48	30	62.5	308	3	0	6.42	3	101.7	10	9	0.9	1	1	0	6
2002—Cincinnati NFL	4	3	85	44	51.8	437	1	5	5.14	10	46.1	4	22	5.5	0	0	0	0
Pro totals (9 years)	79	62	2075	1131	54.5	14407	70	64	6.94	136	74.8	132	246	1.9	5	5	0	30

FRIEDMAN, LENNIE　　　　G　　　　REDSKINS

PERSONAL: Born October 13, 1976, in Livingston, N.J. ... 6-3/285. ... Full name: Leonard Lebrecht Friedman.
HIGH SCHOOL: West Milford (N.J.).
COLLEGE: Duke.
TRANSACTIONS/CAREER NOTES: Selected by Denver Broncos in second round (61st pick overall) of 1999 NFL draft. ... Signed by Broncos (June 14, 1999). ... On injured reserve with knee injury (August 31, 1999-entire season). ... Assigned by Broncos to Barcelona Dragons in 2000 NFL Europe enhancement allocation program (February 18, 2000). ... Released by Broncos (February 25, 2003). ... Signed by Washington Redskins (March 3, 2003).
PLAYING EXPERIENCE: Barcelona NFLE, 2000; Denver NFL, 2000-2002. ... Games/Games started: NFLE 2000 (games played unavailable), NFL 2000 (16/8), 2001 (15/14), 2002 (2/0). Total: 33/22.

FRISCH, BYRON　　　　DE

PERSONAL: Born December 17, 1976, in Roseville, Calif. ... 6-5/267.
HIGH SCHOOL: Bonita Vista (Bonita, Calif.).
COLLEGE: Brigham Young.
TRANSACTIONS/CAREER NOTES: Selected by Tennessee Titans in third round (93rd pick overall) of 2000 NFL draft. ... Signed by Titans (July 19, 2000). ... Released by Titans (September 2, 2001). ... Signed by Dallas Cowboys (September 24, 2001). ... Released by Cowboys (August 27, 2002). ... Signed by New York Giants (October 15, 2002). ... Granted free agency (February 28, 2003).

			TOTALS		
Year Team	G	GS	Tk.	Ast.	Sks.
2001—Dallas NFL	13	0	7	2	3.0
2002—New York Giants NFL	10	0	6	1	2.0
Pro totals (2 years)	23	0	13	3	5.0

F

FUAMATU-MA'AFALA, CHRIS　　　　RB　　　　STEELERS

PERSONAL: Born March 4, 1977, in Honolulu. ... 5-11/254. ... Name pronounced fu-ah-MAH-tu ma-ah-FAH-la.
HIGH SCHOOL: St. Louis (Honolulu).
COLLEGE: Utah.
TRANSACTIONS/CAREER NOTES: Selected after junior season by Pittsburgh Steelers in sixth round (178th pick overall) of 1998 NFL draft. ... Signed by Steelers (July 10, 1998). ... On injured reserve with broken foot (December 20, 2000-remainder of season). ... Granted free agency (March 2, 2001). ... Tendered offer sheet by New England Patriots (April 14, 2001). ... Offer matched by Steelers (April 19, 2001).
CHAMPIONSHIP GAME EXPERIENCE: Played in AFC championship game (2001 season).
SINGLE GAME HIGHS (regular season): Attempts—26 (December 23, 2001, vs. Detroit); yards—126 (December 23, 2001, vs. Detroit); and rushing touchdowns—1 (January 6, 2002, vs. Cleveland).
STATISTICAL PLATEAUS: 100-yard rushing games: 2001 (1).

			RUSHING				RECEIVING				TOTALS		
Year Team	G	GS	Att.	Yds.	Avg.	TD	No.	Yds.	Avg.	TD	TD	2pt.	Pts.	Fum.
1998—Pittsburgh NFL	12	0	7	30	4.3	2	9	84	9.3	1	3	0	18	0
1999—Pittsburgh NFL	9	0	1	4	4.0	0	0	0	0.0	0	0	0	0	0
2000—Pittsburgh NFL	7	1	21	149	7.1	0	11	109	9.7	0	1	0	6	0
2001—Pittsburgh NFL	16	5	120	453	3.8	3	16	127	7.9	1	4	0	24	0
2002—Pittsburgh NFL	8	0	23	115	5.0	0	2	12	6.0	0	0	0	0	0
Pro totals (5 years)	52	6	172	751	4.4	6	38	330	8.7	2	8	0	48	0

FUJITA, SCOTT   LB   CHIEFS

PERSONAL: Born April 28, 1979, in Ventura, Calif. ... 6-5/247.
HIGH SCHOOL: Rio Mesa (Calif.).
COLLEGE: California.
TRANSACTIONS/CAREER NOTES: Selected by Kansas City Chiefs in fifth round (143rd pick overall) of 2002 NFL draft. ... Signed by Chiefs (June 21, 2002).

Year Team	G	GS	TOTALS Tk.	Ast.	Sks.	INTERCEPTIONS No.	Yds.	Avg.	TD
2002—Kansas City NFL	16	9	50	5	1.0	0	0	0.0	0

FULCHER, MONDRIEL   TE   RAIDERS

PERSONAL: Born October 15, 1976, in Coffeyville, Kan. ... 6-3/250. ... Full name: Mondriel DeCarlos A. Fulcher.
HIGH SCHOOL: Field Kindley (Coffeyville, Kan.).
COLLEGE: Miami (Fla.).
TRANSACTIONS/CAREER NOTES: Selected by Oakland Raiders in seventh round (227th pick overall) of 2000 NFL draft. ... Signed by Raiders (July 11, 2000).
CHAMPIONSHIP GAME EXPERIENCE: Member of Raiders for AFC Championship game (2000 season); inactive.

Year Team	G	GS	RECEIVING No.	Yds.	Avg.	TD
2000—Oakland NFL	10	0	0	0	0.0	0
2001—Oakland NFL	13	1	0	0	0.0	0
2002—Oakland NFL	2	0	0	0	0.0	0
Pro totals (3 years)	25	1	0	0	0.0	0

FULLER, COREY   DB   RAVENS

PERSONAL: Born May 1, 1971, in Tallahassee, Fla. ... 5-10/210.
HIGH SCHOOL: James S. Rickards (Tallahassee, Fla.).
COLLEGE: Florida State (degree in criminology and child development, 1994).
TRANSACTIONS/CAREER NOTES: Selected by Minnesota Vikings in second round (55th pick overall) of 1995 NFL draft. ... Signed by Vikings (July 24, 1995). ... Granted unconditional free agency (February 12, 1999). ... Signed by Cleveland Browns (February 18, 1999). ... Released by Browns (February 26, 2003). ... Signed by Baltimore Ravens (March 4, 2003).
CHAMPIONSHIP GAME EXPERIENCE: Played in NFC championship game (1998 season).

Year Team	G	GS	TOTALS Tk.	Ast.	Sks.	INTERCEPTIONS No.	Yds.	Avg.	TD
1995—Minnesota NFL	16	10	57	9	0.5	1	0	0.0	0
1996—Minnesota NFL	16	14	53	11	0.0	3	3	1.0	0
1997—Minnesota NFL	16	16	82	9	0.0	2	24	12.0	0
1998—Minnesota NFL	16	16	70	9	1.0	4	36	9.0	0
1999—Cleveland NFL	16	16	64	13	0.0	0	0	0.0	0
2000—Cleveland NFL	15	15	37	5	0.0	3	0	0.0	0
2001—Cleveland NFL	16	16	72	15	0.0	3	82	27.3	1
2002—Cleveland NFL	13	12	27	5	0.0	1	0	0.0	0
Pro totals (8 years)	124	115	462	76	1.5	17	145	8.5	1

FULLER, CURTIS   S   SEAHAWKS

PERSONAL: Born July 25, 1978, in North Richland Hill, Texas. ... 5-10/191.
HIGH SCHOOL: Christian (Fort Worth, Texas).
JUNIOR COLLEGE: Trinity Valley Community College (Texas).
COLLEGE: Texas Christian (degree in psychology).
TRANSACTIONS/CAREER NOTES: Selected by Seattle Seahawks in fourth round (127th pick overall) of 2001 NFL draft. ... Signed by Seahawks (June 8, 2001).

Year Team	G	GS	TOTALS Tk.	Ast.	Sks.	INTERCEPTIONS No.	Yds.	Avg.	TD
2001—Seattle NFL	10	1	12	2	0.0	0	0	0.0	0
2002—Seattle NFL	16	1	22	11	0.0	1	3	3.0	0
Pro totals (2 years)	26	2	34	13	0.0	1	3	3.0	0

GADSDEN, ORONDE   WR

PERSONAL: Born August 20, 1971, in Charleston, S.C. ... 6-2/215. ... Full name: Oronde Benjamin Gadsden. ... Name pronounced o-RON-day.
HIGH SCHOOL: Burke (Charleston, S.C.).
COLLEGE: Winston-Salem (degree in marketing).
TRANSACTIONS/CAREER NOTES: Signed as non-drafted free agent by Dallas Cowboys (August 1995). ... Released by Cowboys (August 22, 1995). ... Re-signed by Cowboys to practice squad (August 30, 1995). ... Activated (January 8, 1996). ... On injured reserve with left ankle sprain (January 11, 1996-remainder of playoffs). ... Released by Cowboys (August 27, 1996). ... Signed by Pittsburgh Steelers (February 4, 1997). ... Released by Steelers (August 19, 1997). ... Signed by Cowboys (August 21, 1997). ... Released by Cowboys (August 27, 1997). ... Played with Portland Forest Dragons of Arena League (1998). ... Signed by Miami Dolphins (August 3, 1998). ... On injured reserve with wrist injury (October 21, 2002-remainder of season). ... Granted unconditional free agency (February 28, 2003).

F
G

SINGLE GAME HIGHS (regular season): Receptions—9 (January 2, 2000, vs. Washington); yards—153 (December 27, 1998, vs. Atlanta); and touchdown receptions—2 (October 1, 2000, vs. Cincinnati).
STATISTICAL PLATEAUS: 100-yard receiving games: 1998 (1), 1999 (3), 2000 (1), 2001 (2). Total: 7.

Year Team	G	GS	RECEIVING No.	Yds.	Avg.	TD	TD	TOTALS 2pt.	Pts.	Fum.
1995—Dallas NFL						Did not play.				
1996—						Did not play.				
1997—						Did not play.				
1998—Miami NFL	16	12	48	713	14.9	7	7	0	42	2
1999—Miami NFL	16	7	48	803	16.7	6	6	0	36	0
2000—Miami NFL	16	16	56	786	14.0	6	6	0	36	0
2001—Miami NFL	14	14	55	674	12.3	3	3	0	18	1
2002—Miami NFL	6	6	16	228	14.3	0	0	0	0	0
Pro totals (5 years)	68	55	223	3204	14.4	22	22	0	132	3

GAFFNEY, JABAR   WR   TEXANS

PERSONAL: Born December 1, 1980, in San Antonio. ... 6-1/193. ... Full name: Derrick Jabar Gaffney.
HIGH SCHOOL: Raines (Jacksonville, Fla.).
COLLEGE: Florida.
TRANSACTIONS/CAREER NOTES: Selected after sophomore season by Houston Texans in second round (33rd pick overall) of 2002 NFL draft. ... Signed by Texans (July 19, 2002).
HONORS: Named College Football Freshman of the Year by THE SPORTING NEWS (2000). ... Named wide receiver on THE SPORTING NEWS college All-America first team (2001).
SINGLE GAME HIGHS (regular season): Receptions—6 (December 29, 2002, vs. Tennessee); yards—73 (December 29, 2002, vs. Tennessee); and touchdown receptions—1 (October 13, 2002, vs. Buffalo).

Year Team	G	GS	RECEIVING No.	Yds.	Avg.	TD
2002—Houston NFL	16	14	41	483	11.8	1

GALLOWAY, JOEY   WR   COWBOYS

PERSONAL: Born November 20, 1971, in Bellaire, Ohio. ... 5-11/197.
HIGH SCHOOL: Bellaire (Ohio).
COLLEGE: Ohio State (degree in business/marketing, 1994).
TRANSACTIONS/CAREER NOTES: Selected by Seattle Seahawks in first round (eighth pick overall) of 1995 NFL draft. ... Signed by Seahawks (July 20, 1995). ... On did not report list (September 4-November 9, 1999). ... Designated by Seahawks as franchise player (February 11, 2000). ... Traded by Seahawks to Dallas Cowboys for first-round pick (RB Shaun Alexander) in 2000 draft and first round pick (traded to San Francisco) in 2001 draft (February 12, 2000). ... On injured reserve with knee injury (September 8, 2000-remainder of season).
SINGLE GAME HIGHS (regular season): Receptions—8 (October 6, 2002, vs. New York Giants); yards—146 (December 30, 2001, vs. San Francisco); and touchdown receptions—3 (October 26, 1997, vs. Oakland).
STATISTICAL PLATEAUS: 100-yard receiving games: 1995 (3), 1996 (2), 1997 (3), 1998 (4), 2001 (1), 2002 (3). Total: 16.

Year Team	G	GS	RUSHING Att.	Yds.	Avg.	TD	RECEIVING No.	Yds.	Avg.	TD	PUNT RETURNS No.	Yds.	Avg.	TD	TOTALS TD	2pt.	Pts.	Fum.
1995—Seattle NFL	16	16	11	154	14.0	1	67	1039	15.5	7	36	360	10.0	†1	9	0	54	1
1996—Seattle NFL	16	16	15	127	8.5	0	57	987	17.3	7	15	158	10.5	▲1	8	0	48	2
1997—Seattle NFL	15	15	9	72	8.0	0	72	1049	14.6 ▲12		0	0	0.0	0	12	0	72	1
1998—Seattle NFL	16	16	9	26	2.9	0	65	1047	16.1 ▲10		25	251	10.0	†2	12	0	72	1
1999—Seattle NFL	8	4	1	-1	-1.0	0	22	335	15.2	1	3	54	18.0	0	1	0	6	0
2000—Dallas NFL	1	1	0	0	0.0	0	4	62	15.5	1	1	2	2.0	0	1	0	6	0
2001—Dallas NFL	16	16	3	32	10.7	0	52	699	13.4	3	1	6	6.0	0	3	0	18	1
2002—Dallas NFL	16	16	4	31	7.8	0	61	908	14.9	6	15	181	12.1	0	6	0	36	2
Pro totals (8 years)	104	100	52	441	8.5	1	400	6126	15.3	47	96	1012	10.5	4	52	0	312	8

GALYON, SCOTT   LB

PERSONAL: Born March 23, 1974, in Seymour, Tenn. ... 6-2/235. ... Name pronounced GAL-yun.
HIGH SCHOOL: Seymour (Tenn.).
COLLEGE: Tennessee.
TRANSACTIONS/CAREER NOTES: Selected by New York Giants in sixth round (182nd pick overall) of 1996 NFL draft. ... Signed by Giants (July 17, 1996). ... On injured reserve with knee injury (December 8, 1998-remainder of season). ... Granted free agency (February 12, 1999). ... Re-signed by Giants (May 3, 1999). ... Granted unconditional free agency (February 11, 2000). ... Signed by Miami Dolphins (February 25, 2000). ... On injured reserve with knee injury (October 11, 2000-remainder of season). ... On physically unable to perform list with knee injury (July 24-31, 2001). ... Released by Dolphins (September 2, 2002). ... Re-signed by Dolphins (September 9, 2002). ... Granted unconditional free agency (February 28, 2003).

Year Team	G	GS	TOTALS Tk.	Ast.	Sks.	INTERCEPTIONS No.	Yds.	Avg.	TD
1996—New York Giants NFL	16	0	2	0	0.0	0	0	0.0	0
1997—New York Giants NFL	16	0	31	6	3.0	0	0	0.0	0
1998—New York Giants NFL	10	1	19	5	1.0	0	0	0.0	0
1999—New York Giants NFL	16	0	14	5	1.0	0	0	0.0	0
2000—Miami NFL	6	1	8	1	0.0	0	0	0.0	0
2001—Miami NFL	16	2	6	6	1.0	1	0	0.0	0
2002—Miami NFL	15	0	1	0	0.0	0	0	0.0	0
Pro totals (7 years)	95	4	81	23	6.0	1	0	0.0	0

G

GAMBLE, TRENT   S   DOLPHINS

PERSONAL: Born July 24, 1977, in Denver. ... 5-9/195. ... Full name: Trent Ashford Gamble.
HIGH SCHOOL: Ponderosa (Parker, Colo.).
COLLEGE: Wyoming (degree in finance).
TRANSACTIONS/CAREER NOTES: Signed as non-drafted free agent by Miami Dolphins (April 25, 2000). ... On injured reserve with knee injury (October 23, 2001-remainder of season). ... Granted free agency (February 28, 2003).

Year Team	G	GS	TOTALS			INTERCEPTIONS			
			Tk.	Ast.	Sks.	No.	Yds.	Avg.	TD
2000—Miami NFL	16	0	2	1	0.0	0	0	0.0	0
2001—Miami NFL	1	0	0	0	0.0	0	0	0.0	0
2002—Miami NFL	13	0	6	2	0.0	0	0	0.0	0
Pro totals (3 years)	30	0	8	3	0.0	0	0	0.0	0

GAMMON, KENDALL   TE   CHIEFS

PERSONAL: Born October 23, 1968, in Wichita, Kan. ... 6-4/255. ... Full name: Kendall Robert Gammon.
HIGH SCHOOL: Rose Hill (Kan.).
COLLEGE: Pittsburg (Kan.) State (degree in physical education).
TRANSACTIONS/CAREER NOTES: Selected by Pittsburgh Steelers in 11th round (291st pick overall) of 1992 NFL draft. ... Signed by Steelers (July 14, 1992). ... Released by Steelers (August 30, 1993). ... Re-signed by Steelers (August 31, 1993). ... Granted unconditional free agency (February 17, 1995). ... Re-signed by Steelers (May 8, 1995). ... Released by Steelers (August 26, 1996). ... Signed by New Orleans Saints (August 28, 1996). ... Granted unconditional free agency (February 11, 2000). ... Signed by Kansas City Chiefs (February 23, 2000). ... Granted unconditional free agency (February 28, 2003). ... Re-signed by Chiefs (March 23, 2003).
CHAMPIONSHIP GAME EXPERIENCE: Played in AFC championship game (1994 and 1995 seasons). ... Played in Super Bowl XXX (1995 season).

Year Team	G	GS	RECEIVING			
			No.	Yds.	Avg.	TD
1992—Pittsburgh NFL	16	0	0	0	0.0	0
1993—Pittsburgh NFL	16	0	0	0	0.0	0
1994—Pittsburgh NFL	16	0	0	0	0.0	0
1995—Pittsburgh NFL	16	0	0	0	0.0	0
1996—New Orleans NFL	16	0	0	0	0.0	0
1997—New Orleans NFL	16	0	0	0	0.0	0
1998—New Orleans NFL	16	0	0	0	0.0	0
1999—New Orleans NFL	16	0	0	0	0.0	0
2000—Kansas City NFL	16	0	0	0	0.0	0
2001—Kansas City NFL	16	0	0	0	0.0	0
2002—Kansas City NFL	16	0	0	0	0.0	0
Pro totals (11 years)	176	0	0	0	0.0	0

GANDY, MIKE   G   BEARS

PERSONAL: Born January 3, 1979, in Rockford, Ill. ... 6-4/302. ... Full name: Michael Joseph Gandy.
HIGH SCHOOL: Garland (Texas).
COLLEGE: Notre Dame (degree in sociology and computer applications).
TRANSACTIONS/CAREER NOTES: Selected by Chicago Bears in third round (68th pick overall) of 2001 NFL draft. ... Signed by Bears (July 20, 2001). ... Inactive for all 16 games (2001).
PLAYING EXPERIENCE: Chicago NFL, 2002. ... Games/games started: 2002 (13/11).
HONORS: Named guard on THE SPORTING NEWS college All-America first team (2000).

GANDY, WAYNE   OT   SAINTS

PERSONAL: Born February 10, 1971, in Haines City, Fla. ... 6-4/308. ... Full name: Wayne Lamar Gandy.
HIGH SCHOOL: Haines City (Fla.).
COLLEGE: Auburn.
TRANSACTIONS/CAREER NOTES: Selected by Los Angeles Rams in first round (15th pick overall) of 1994 NFL draft. ... Signed by Rams (July 23, 1994). ... Rams franchise moved to St. Louis (April 12, 1995). ... Granted unconditional free agency (February 12, 1999). ... Signed by Pittsburgh Steelers (April 6, 1999). ... Granted unconditional free agency (February 28, 2003). ... Signed by New Orleans Saints (March 2, 2003).
PLAYING EXPERIENCE: Los Angeles Rams NFL, 1994; St. Louis NFL, 1995-1998; Pittsburgh NFL, 1999-2002. ... Games/Games started: 1994 (16/9), 1995 (16/16), 1996 (16/16), 1997 (16/16), 1998 (16/16), 1999 (16/16), 2000 (16/16), 2001 (15/15), 2002 (16/16). Total: 143/136.
CHAMPIONSHIP GAME EXPERIENCE: Played in AFC championship game (2001 season).
HONORS: Named offensive lineman on THE SPORTING NEWS college All-America first team (1993).

GANNON, RICH   QB   RAIDERS

PERSONAL: Born December 20, 1965, in Philadelphia. ... 6-3/210. ... Full name: Richard Joseph Gannon.
HIGH SCHOOL: St. Joseph's Prep (Philadelphia).
COLLEGE: Delaware (degree in criminal justice, 1987).
TRANSACTIONS/CAREER NOTES: Selected by New England Patriots in fourth round (98th pick overall) of 1987 NFL draft. ... Rights traded by Patriots to Minnesota Vikings for fourth- (WR Sammy Martin) and 11th-round (traded) picks in 1988 draft (May 6, 1987). ... Signed by Vikings (July 30, 1987). ... Active for 13 games (1989); did not play. ... Granted free agency (February 1, 1990). ... Re-signed by Vikings (July 30, 1990). ... Granted free agency (February 1, 1991). ... Re-signed by Vikings (July 25, 1991). ... Granted free agency (February 1, 1992). ... Re-signed by Vikings (August 8, 1992). ... Traded by Vikings to Washington Redskins for conditional draft pick (August 20, 1993). ... Granted unconditional free agency (February 17, 1994). ... Signed by Kansas City Chiefs (March 29, 1995). ... Released by Chiefs (February 15, 1996).

... Re-signed by Chiefs (April 3, 1996). ... Granted unconditional free agency (February 12, 1999). ... Signed by Oakland Raiders (February 16, 1999).
CHAMPIONSHIP GAME EXPERIENCE: Member of Vikings for NFC championship game (1987 season); did not play. ... Played in AFC championship game (2000 and 2002 seasons). ... Played in Super Bowl XXXVII (2002 season).
HONORS: Played in Pro Bowl (1999-2003 seasons). ... Named quarterback on THE SPORTING NEWS NFL All-Pro team (2000 and 2002). ... Named Outstanding Player of Pro Bowl (2000 and 2001). ... Named NFL Player of the Year by THE SPORTING NEWS (2002).
RECORDS: Holds NFL single-season record for most completions—418 (2002); and most games with 300 or more yards passing—10 (2002). ... Shares NFL record for most consecutive games with 300 or more yards passing—6 (September 15-October 27, 2002). ... Holds NFL single-game record for most consecutive completions—21 (November 11, 2002, vs. Denver).
POST SEASON RECORDS: Holds Super Bowl single-game record for most passes intercepted—5 (January 26, 2003, vs. Tampa Bay).
SINGLE GAME HIGHS (regular season): Attempts—64 (September 15, 2002, vs. Pittsburgh); completions—43 (September 15, 2002, vs. Pittsburgh); yards—403 (September 15, 2002, vs. Pittsburgh); and touchdown passes—5 (December 24, 2000, vs. Carolina).
STATISTICAL PLATEAUS: 300-yard passing games: 1991 (1), 1992 (1), 1997 (1), 1998 (1), 1999 (2), 2000 (2), 2001 (4), 2002 (10). Total: 22.
MISCELLANEOUS: Regular-season record as starting NFL quarterback: 72-50 (.590). ... Postseason record as starting NFL quarterback: 4-3 (.571).

			PASSING								RUSHING				TOTALS		
Year Team	G	GS	Att.	Cmp.	Pct.	Yds.	TD	Int.	Avg.	Skd.	Rat.	Att.	Yds.	Avg.	TD	TD	2pt.	Pts.
1987—Minnesota NFL	4	0	6	2	33.3	18	0	1	3.00	0	2.8	0	0	0.0	0	0	0	0
1988—Minnesota NFL	3	0	15	7	46.7	90	0	0	6.00	3	66.0	4	29	7.3	0	0	0	0
1989—Minnesota NFL									Did not play.									
1990—Minnesota NFL	14	12	349	182	52.1	2278	16	16	6.53	34	68.9	52	268	5.2	1	1	0	6
1991—Minnesota NFL	15	11	354	211	59.6	2166	12	6	6.12	19	81.5	43	236	5.5	2	2	0	12
1992—Minnesota NFL	12	12	279	159	57.0	1905	12	13	6.83	25	72.9	45	187	4.2	0	0	0	0
1993—Washington NFL	8	4	125	74	59.2	704	3	7	5.63	16	59.6	21	88	4.2	1	1	0	6
1994—									Did not play.									
1995—Kansas City NFL	2	0	11	7	63.6	57	0	0	5.18	0	76.7	8	25	3.1	1	1	0	6
1996—Kansas City NFL	4	3	90	54	60.0	491	6	1	5.46	5	92.4	12	81	6.8	0	0	0	0
1997—Kansas City NFL	9	6	175	98	56.0	1144	7	4	6.54	13	79.8	33	109	3.3	2	2	0	12
1998—Kansas City NFL	12	10	354	206	58.2	2305	10	6	6.51	25	80.1	44	168	3.8	3	3	0	18
1999—Oakland NFL	16	16	515	304	59.0	3840	24	14	7.46	49	86.5	46	298	6.5	2	2	0	12
2000—Oakland NFL	16	16	473	284	60.0	3430	28	11	7.25	28	92.4	89	529	5.9	4	4	1	26
2001—Oakland NFL	16	16	549	§361	§65.8	3828	§27	9	6.97	27	§95.5	63	231	3.7	2	2	0	14
2002—Oakland NFL	16	16	*618	*418	67.6	*4689	26	10	7.59	36	97.3	50	156	3.1	3	3	0	18
Pro totals (14 years)	147	122	3913	2367	60.5	26945	171	98	6.89	280	85.3	510	2405	4.7	21	21	2	130

GARCIA, FRANK — C — CARDINALS

PERSONAL: Born January 28, 1972, in Phoenix. ... 6-2/302. ... Full name: Frank Christopher Garcia.
HIGH SCHOOL: Maryvale (Phoenix).
COLLEGE: Washington.
TRANSACTIONS/CAREER NOTES: Selected by Carolina Panthers in fourth round (132nd pick overall) of 1995 NFL draft. ... Signed by Panthers (July 14, 1995). ... Granted free agency (February 13, 1998). ... Re-signed by Panthers (March 16, 1998). ... Granted unconditional free agency (March 2, 2001). ... Signed by St. Louis Rams (April 26, 2001). ... Granted unconditional free agency (February 28, 2003). ... Signed by Arizona Cardinals (March 14, 2003).
PLAYING EXPERIENCE: Carolina NFL, 1995-2000; St. Louis NFL, 2001-2002. ... Games/Games started: 1995 (15/14), 1996 (14/8), 1997 (16/16), 1998 (14/14), 1999 (16/16), 2000 (16/16), 2001 (13/2), 2002 (14/3). Total: 118/89.
CHAMPIONSHIP GAME EXPERIENCE: Played in NFC championship game (1996 and 2001 seasons). ... Played in Super Bowl XXXVI (2001 season).

GARCIA, JEFF — QB — 49ERS

PERSONAL: Born February 24, 1970, in Gilroy, Calif. ... 6-1/195.
HIGH SCHOOL: Gilroy (Calif.).
JUNIOR COLLEGE: Gavilan College (Calif.).
COLLEGE: San Jose State.
TRANSACTIONS/CAREER NOTES: Signed by Calgary Stampeders of CFL (1994). ... Granted free agency (February 16, 1997). ... Re-signed by Stampeders (April 30, 1997). ... Signed as non-drafted free agent by San Francisco 49ers (February 16, 1999).
CHAMPIONSHIP GAME EXPERIENCE: Played in Grey Cup (1995). ... Member of CFL Championship team (1998). ... Named Most Valuable Player of Grey Cup, CFL championship game (1998).
HONORS: Played in Pro Bowl (2000-2002 seasons).
SINGLE GAME HIGHS (regular season): Attempts—55 (December 8, 2002, vs. Dallas); completions—36 (December 8, 2002, vs. Dallas); passing yards—437 (December 5, 1999, vs. Cincinnati); and touchdown passes—4 (October 27, 2002, vs. Arizona).
STATISTICAL PLATEAUS: 300-yard passing games: 1999 (3), 2000 (6), 2001 (3), 2002 (1). Total: 13.
MISCELLANEOUS: Regular-season record as starting NFL quarterback: 30-28 (.517). ... Postseason record as starting NFL quarterback: 1-2 (.333).

			PASSING								RUSHING				TOTALS		
Year Team	G	GS	Att.	Cmp.	Pct.	Yds.	TD	Int.	Avg.	Skd.	Rat.	Att.	Yds.	Avg.	TD	TD	2pt.	Pts.
1994—Calgary CFL	7	...	3	2	66.7	10	0	0	3.33	...	71.5	2	3	1.5	0	0	0	0
1995—Calgary CFL	18	...	364	230	63.2	3358	25	7	9.23	...	108.1	61	396	6.5	5	5	0	30
1996—Calgary CFL	18	...	537	315	58.7	4225	25	16	7.87	...	86.9	92	657	7.1	6	6	0	36
1997—Calgary CFL	17	...	566	354	62.5	4573	33	14	8.08	...	97.0	135	727	5.4	7	7	1	44
1998—Calgary CFL	18	...	554	348	62.8	4276	28	15	7.72	...	92.2	94	575	6.1	6	6	0	36
1999—San Francisco NFL	13	10	375	225	60.0	2544	11	11	6.78	15	77.9	45	231	5.1	2	2	0	12
2000—San Francisco NFL	16	16	561	‡355	63.3	‡4278	‡31	10	7.63	24	97.6	72	414	5.8	4	4	0	24
2001—San Francisco NFL	16	16	504	316	62.7	3538	32	12	7.02	26	94.8	72	254	3.5	5	5	0	30
2002—San Francisco NFL	16	16	528	328	62.1	3344	21	10	6.33	17	85.6	73	353	4.8	3	3	1	20
CFL totals (5 years)	78	...	2024	1249	61.7	16442	111	52	8.12	...	94.9	384	2358	6.1	24	24	1	146
NFL totals (4 years)	61	58	1968	1224	62.2	13704	95	43	6.96	82	89.9	262	1252	4.8	14	14	1	86
Pro totals (9 years)	139	...	3992	2473	61.9	30146	206	95	7.55	...	92.5	646	3610	5.6	38	38	2	232

G

GARDENER, DARYL   DT   BRONCOS

PERSONAL: Born February 25, 1973, in Baltimore. ... 6-6/295. ... Full name: Daryl Ronald Gardener.
HIGH SCHOOL: Lawton (Okla.).
COLLEGE: Baylor.
TRANSACTIONS/CAREER NOTES: Selected by Miami Dolphins in first round (20th pick overall) of 1996 NFL draft. ... Signed by Dolphins (June 6, 1996). ... On injured reserve with back injury (December 4, 2001-remainder of season). ... Released by Dolphins (July 19, 2002). ... Signed by Washington Redskins (July 30, 2002). ... Granted unconditional free agency (February 28, 2003). ... Signed by Denver Broncos (March 7, 2003).

			TOTALS			INTERCEPTIONS			
Year Team	G	GS	Tk.	Ast.	Sks.	No.	Yds.	Avg.	TD
1996—Miami NFL	16	12	24	9	1.0	0	0	0.0	0
1997—Miami NFL	16	16	32	20	1.5	0	0	0.0	0
1998—Miami NFL	16	16	27	12	1.0	1	-1	-1.0	0
1999—Miami NFL	16	15	28	24	5.0	0	0	0.0	0
2000—Miami NFL	10	10	35	14	2.5	0	0	0.0	0
2001—Miami NFL	8	8	17	11	4.0	0	0	0.0	0
2002—Washington NFL	15	15	45	7	4.0	0	0	0.0	0
Pro totals (7 years)	97	92	200	97	19.0	1	-1	-1.0	0

GARDNER, BARRY   LB   BROWNS

PERSONAL: Born December 13, 1976, in Harvey, Ill. ... 6-0/248. ... Full name: Barry Allan Gardner.
HIGH SCHOOL: Thornton (Harvey, Ill.).
COLLEGE: Northwestern.
TRANSACTIONS/CAREER NOTES: Selected by Philadelphia Eagles in second round (35th pick overall) of 1999 NFL draft. ... Signed by Eagles (July 25, 1999). ... Granted unconditional free agency (February 28, 2003). ... Signed by Cleveland Browns (March 14, 2003).
CHAMPIONSHIP GAME EXPERIENCE: Played in NFC championship game (2001 and 2002 seasons).

			TOTALS			INTERCEPTIONS			
Year Team	G	GS	Tk.	Ast.	Sks.	No.	Yds.	Avg.	TD
1999—Philadelphia NFL	16	5	27	10	0.0	0	0	0.0	0
2000—Philadelphia NFL	16	13	42	15	1.0	0	0	0.0	0
2001—Philadelphia NFL	16	0	10	5	0.0	0	0	0.0	0
2002—Philadelphia NFL	16	0	19	9	1.0	0	0	0.0	0
Pro totals (4 years)	64	18	98	39	2.0	0	0	0.0	0

GARDNER, ROD   WR   REDSKINS

PERSONAL: Born October 26, 1977, in Jacksonville, Fla. ... 6-2/217. ... Full name: Roderick F. Gardner.
HIGH SCHOOL: Raines (Jacksonville, Fla.).
COLLEGE: Clemson.
TRANSACTIONS/CAREER NOTES: Selected by Washington Redskins in first round (15th pick overall) of 2001 NFL draft. ... Signed by Redskins (August 2, 2001).
SINGLE GAME HIGHS (regular season): Receptions—7 (November 10, 2002, vs. Jacksonville); yards—208 (October 21, 2001, vs. Carolina); and touchdown receptions—1 (December 15, 2002, vs. Philadelphia).
STATISTICAL PLATEAUS: 100-yard receiving games: 2001 (1), 2002 (2). Total: 3.

			RECEIVING			
Year Team	G	GS	No.	Yds.	Avg.	TD
2001—Washington NFL	16	16	46	741	16.1	4
2002—Washington NFL	16	15	71	1006	14.2	8
Pro totals (2 years)	32	31	117	1747	14.9	12

GARDOCKI, CHRIS   P   BROWNS

PERSONAL: Born February 7, 1970, in Stone Mountain, Ga. ... 6-1/200. ... Full name: Christopher Allen Gardocki.
HIGH SCHOOL: Redan (Stone Mountain, Ga.).
COLLEGE: Clemson.
TRANSACTIONS/CAREER NOTES: Selected after junior season by Chicago Bears in third round (78th pick overall) of 1991 NFL draft. ... Signed by Bears (June 24, 1991). ... On injured reserve with groin injury (August 27-November 27, 1991). ... Granted unconditional free agency (February 17, 1995). ... Signed by Indianapolis Colts (February 24, 1995). ... Granted unconditional free agency (February 12, 1999). ... Signed by Cleveland Browns (February 16, 1999).
CHAMPIONSHIP GAME EXPERIENCE: Played in AFC championship game (1995 season).
HONORS: Named kicker on THE SPORTING NEWS college All-America second team (1990). ... Named punter on THE SPORTING NEWS NFL All-Pro team (1996). ... Played in Pro Bowl (1996 season).
RECORDS: Holds NFL career record for most consecutive punts without a block—906.

		PUNTING					
Year Team	G	No.	Yds.	Avg.	Net avg.	In. 20	Blk.
1991—Chicago NFL	4	0	0	0.0	.0	0	0
1992—Chicago NFL	16	79	3393	42.9	36.2	19	0
1993—Chicago NFL	16	80	3080	38.5	36.6	28	0
1994—Chicago NFL	16	76	2871	37.8	32.3	23	0
1995—Indianapolis NFL	16	63	2681	42.6	33.3	16	0
1996—Indianapolis NFL	16	68	3105	45.7	§39.0	23	0
1997—Indianapolis NFL	16	67	3034	45.3	36.2	18	0
1998—Indianapolis NFL	16	79	3583	45.4	37.1	23	0
1999—Cleveland NFL	16	§106	*4645	43.8	34.6	20	0
2000—Cleveland NFL	16	*108	*4919	45.5	37.3	25	0
2001—Cleveland NFL	16	*99	§4249	42.9	34.6	25	0
2002—Cleveland NFL	16	81	3388	41.8	35.3	27	0
Pro totals (12 years)	180	906	38948	43.0	35.7	247	0

G

GARMON, KELVIN   G   CHARGERS

PERSONAL: Born October 26, 1976, in Fort Worth, Texas ... 6-2/350.
HIGH SCHOOL: Haltom (Fort Worth, Texas).
COLLEGE: Baylor.
TRANSACTIONS/CAREER NOTES: Selected by Dallas Cowboys in seventh round (243rd pick overall) of 1999 NFL draft. ... Signed by Cowboys (August 8, 1999). ... On non-football injury list with leg injury (August 31, 1999-entire season). ... Active for one game (2000); did not play. ... Traded by Cowboys to San Diego Chargers for conditional seventh-round pick (traded to Detroit) in 2003 draft (October 13, 2002).
PLAYING EXPERIENCE: Dallas NFL, 2001. Dallas (5)-San Diego (7) NFL, 2002. ... Games/Games started: 2001 (16/16), 2002 (Dal.-5/5; SD-7/5; Total: 12/10). Total: 28/26.

GARNER, CHARLIE   RB   RAIDERS

PERSONAL: Born February 13, 1972, in Falls Church, Va. ... 5-10/190.
HIGH SCHOOL: Jeb Stuart (Falls Church, Va.).
JUNIOR COLLEGE: Scottsdale (Ariz.) Community College.
COLLEGE: Tennessee.
TRANSACTIONS/CAREER NOTES: Selected by Philadelphia Eagles in second round (42nd pick overall) of 1994 NFL draft. ... Signed by Eagles (July 18, 1994). ... Granted free agency (February 14, 1997). ... Re-signed by Eagles (June 16, 1997). ... Granted unconditional free agency (February 13, 1998). ... Re-signed by Eagles (February 23, 1998). ... On injured reserve with rib injury (December 10, 1998-remainder of season). ... Released by Eagles (April 20, 1999). ... Signed by San Francisco 49ers (July 19, 1999). ... Granted unconditional free agency (March 2, 2001). ... Signed by Oakland Raiders (April 13, 2001).
CHAMPIONSHIP GAME EXPERIENCE: Played in AFC championship game (2002 season). ... Played in Super Bowl XXXVII (2002 season).
HONORS: Played in Pro Bowl (2000 season).
SINGLE GAME HIGHS (regular season): Attempts—36 (September 24, 2000, vs. Dallas); yards—201 (September 24, 2000, vs. Dallas); and rushing touchdowns—3 (October 8, 1995, vs. Washington).
STATISTICAL PLATEAUS: 100-yard rushing games: 1994 (2), 1995 (1), 1997 (1), 1998 (1), 1999 (3), 2000 (3), 2002 (3). Total: 14. ... 100-yard receiving games: 2000 (1).

			RUSHING				RECEIVING				KICKOFF RETURNS				TOTALS			
Year Team	G	GS	Att.	Yds.	Avg.	TD	No.	Yds.	Avg.	TD	No.	Yds.	Avg.	TD	TD	2pt.	Pts.	Fum.
1994—Philadelphia NFL	10	8	109	399	3.7	3	8	74	9.3	0	0	0	0.0	0	3	0	18	3
1995—Philadelphia NFL	15	3	108	588	*5.4	6	10	61	6.1	0	29	590	20.3	0	6	0	36	2
1996—Philadelphia NFL	15	1	66	346	5.2	1	14	92	6.6	0	6	117	19.5	0	1	0	6	1
1997—Philadelphia NFL	16	2	116	547	4.7	3	24	225	9.4	0	0	0	0.0	0	3	0	18	1
1998—Philadelphia NFL	10	3	96	381	4.0	4	19	110	5.8	0	0	0	0.0	0	4	0	24	1
1999—San Francisco NFL	16	15	241	1229	5.1	4	56	535	9.6	2	0	0	0.0	0	6	0	36	4
2000—San Francisco NFL	16	15	258	1142	4.4	7	68	647	9.5	3	0	0	0.0	0	10	0	60	4
2001—Oakland NFL	16	16	211	839	4.0	1	72	578	8.0	2	0	0	0.0	0	3	0	18	2
2002—Oakland NFL	16	15	182	962	5.3	7	91	941	10.3	4	0	0	0.0	0	11	0	66	0
Pro totals (9 years)	130	78	1387	6433	4.6	36	362	3263	9.0	11	35	707	20.2	0	47	0	282	18

GARNES, SAM   S   JETS

PERSONAL: Born July 12, 1974, in Bronx, N.Y. ... 6-3/225. ... Full name: Sam Aaron Garnes.
HIGH SCHOOL: DeWitt Clinton (Bronx, N.Y.).
COLLEGE: Cincinnati.
TRANSACTIONS/CAREER NOTES: Selected by New York Giants in fifth round (136th pick overall) of 1997 NFL draft. ... Signed by Giants for 1997 season. ... Granted free agency (February 11, 2000). ... Re-signed by Giants (February 12, 2000). ... Released by Giants (February 28, 2002). ... Signed by New York Jets (March 5, 2002).

			TOTALS			INTERCEPTIONS			
Year Team	G	GS	Tk.	Ast.	Sks.	No.	Yds.	Avg.	TD
1997—New York Giants NFL	16	15	40	19	0.0	1	95	95.0	1
1998—New York Giants NFL	11	11	37	12	0.0	1	13	13.0	0
1999—New York Giants NFL	16	16	73	18	1.0	2	7	3.5	0
2000—New York Giants NFL	15	15	51	12	1.0	1	4	4.0	0
2001—New York Giants NFL	16	16	58	15	0.0	1	5	5.0	0
2002—New York Jets NFL	16	16	55	12	0.5	2	65	32.5	0
Pro totals (6 years)	90	89	314	88	2.5	8	189	23.6	1

GARRARD, DAVID   QB   JAGUARS   G

PERSONAL: Born February 14, 1978, in East Orange, N.J. ... 6-1/237. ... Full name: David Douglas Garrard.
HIGH SCHOOL: Southern Durham (N.C.).
COLLEGE: East Carolina.
TRANSACTIONS/CAREER NOTES: Selected by Jacksonville Jaguars in fourth round (108th pick overall) of 2002 NFL draft. ... Signed by Jaguars (July 22, 2002).
SINGLE GAME HIGHS (regular season): Attempts—26 (December 29, 2002, vs. Indianapolis); completions—13 (December 29, 2002, vs. Indianapolis); yards—135 (December 29, 2002, vs. Indianapolis); and touchdown passes—1 (December 22, 2002, vs. Tennessee).
MISCELLANEOUS: Regular-season record as starting NFL quarterback: 0-1.

			PASSING									RUSHING				TOTALS		
Year Team	G	GS	Att.	Cmp.	Pct.	Yds.	TD	Int.	Avg.	Skd.	Rat.	Att.	Yds.	Avg.	TD	TD	2pt.	Pts.
2002—Jacksonville NFL	4	1	46	23	50.0	231	1	2	5.02	7	53.8	25	139	5.6	2	2	0	12

GARRETT, JASON QB GIANTS

PERSONAL: Born March 28, 1966, in Abington, Pa. ... 6-2/200. ... Full name: Jason Calvin Garrett. ... Son of Jim Garrett, scout, Dallas Cowboys; brother of John Garrett, wide receiver with Cincinnati Bengals (1989) and San Antonio Riders of World League (1991); and brother of Judd Garrett, running back with London of World League (1991-92).
HIGH SCHOOL: University (Chargin Falls, Ohio).
COLLEGE: Princeton (degree in history).
TRANSACTIONS/CAREER NOTES: Signed as non-drafted free agent by New Orleans Saints (1989). ... Released by Saints (August 30, 1989). ... Re-signed by Saints to developmental squad (September 6, 1989). ... Released by Saints (December 29, 1989). ... Re-signed by Saints for 1990 season. ... Released by Saints (September 3, 1990). ... Signed by WLAF (January 3, 1991). ... Selected by San Antonio Riders in first round (seventh quarterback) of 1991 WLAF positional draft. ... Signed by Ottawa Rough Riders of CFL (1991). ... Released by San Antonio Riders (March 3, 1992). ... Signed by Dallas Cowboys (March 23, 1992). ... Released by Cowboys (August 31, 1992). ... Re-signed by Cowboys to practice squad (September 1, 1992). ... Granted unconditional free agency (February 16, 1996). ... Re-signed by Cowboys (April 3, 1996). ... Granted unconditional free agency (February 14, 1997). ... Re-signed by Cowboys (April 8, 1997). ... Granted unconditional free agency (February 11, 2000). ... Signed by New York Giants (February 22, 2000). ... Released by Giants (February 28, 2002). ... Re-signed by Giants (July 24, 2002). ... Granted unconditional free agency (February 28, 2003). ... Re-signed by Giants (March 4, 2003).
CHAMPIONSHIP GAME EXPERIENCE: Member of Cowboys for NFC championship game (1993-1995 seasons); inactive. ... Member of Super Bowl championship team (1993 and 1995 seasons). ... Played in NFC championship game (2000 season). ... Member of Giants for Super Bowl XXXV (2000 season); did not play.
SINGLE GAME HIGHS (regular season): Attempts—33 (September 27, 1998, vs. Oakland); completions—18 (September 27, 1998, vs. Oakland); yards—311 (November 24, 1994, vs. Green Bay); and touchdown passes—2 (November 14, 1999, vs. Green Bay).
STATISTICAL PLATEAUS: 300-yard passing games: 1994 (1).
MISCELLANEOUS: Regular-season record as starting NFL quarterback: 6-3 (.667).

			PASSING									RUSHING				TOTALS		
Year Team	G	GS	Att.	Cmp.	Pct.	Yds.	TD	Int.	Avg.	Skd.	Rat.	Att.	Yds.	Avg.	TD	TD	2pt.	Pts.
1991—San Antonio W.L.	5	3	113	66	58.4	609	3	3	5.39	0	71.0	7	7	1.0	0	0	0	0
—Ottawa CFL	13	0	3	2	66.7	28	0	0	9.33	0	96.5	0	0	0.0	0	0	0	0
1992—Dallas NFL									Did not play.									
1993—Dallas NFL	5	1	19	9	47.4	61	0	0	3.21	1	54.9	8	-8	-1.0	0	0	0	0
1994—Dallas NFL	2	1	31	16	51.6	315	2	1	10.16	2	95.5	3	-2	-0.7	0	0	0	0
1995—Dallas NFL	1	0	5	4	80.0	46	1	0	9.20	0	144.6	1	-1	-1.0	0	0	0	0
1996—Dallas NFL	1	0	3	3	100.0	44	0	0	14.67	0	118.8	0	0	0.0	0	0	0	0
1997—Dallas NFL	1	0	14	10	71.4	56	0	0	4.00	2	78.3	0	0	0.0	0	0	0	0
1998—Dallas NFL	8	5	158	91	57.6	1206	5	3	7.63	10	84.5	11	14	1.3	0	0	0	0
1999—Dallas NFL	5	2	64	32	50.0	314	3	1	4.91	5	73.3	6	12	2.0	0	0	0	0
2000—N.Y. Giants NFL	2	0	0	0	0.0	0	0	0	0.0	0	...	4	-4	-1.0	0	0	0	0
2001—N.Y. Giants NFL	15	0	0	0	0.0	0	0	0	0.0	0	...	0	0	0	0	0	0	0
2002—N.Y. Giants NFL									Did not play.									
W.L. totals (1 year)	5	3	113	66	58.4	609	3	3	5.39	0	71.0	7	7	1.0	0	0	0	0
CFL totals (1 year)	13	0	3	2	66.7	28	0	0	9.33	0	96.5	0	0	0.0	0	0	0	0
NFL totals (9 years)	40	9	294	165	56.1	2042	11	5	6.95	20	83.2	33	11	0.3	0	0	0	0
Pro totals (11 years)	58	12	410	233	56.8	2679	14	8	6.53	20	79.9	40	18	0.5	0	0	0	0

GARY, OLANDIS RB BILLS

PERSONAL: Born May 18, 1975, in Washington, D.C. ... 5-11/218. ... Full name: Olandis C. Gary.
HIGH SCHOOL: Riverdale Baptist (Upper Marlboro, Md.).
COLLEGE: Marshall, then Georgia.
TRANSACTIONS/CAREER NOTES: Selected by Denver Broncos in fourth round (127th pick overall) of 1999 NFL draft. ... Signed by Broncos (July 20, 1999). ... On injured reserve with knee injury (September 8, 2000-remainder of season). ... On injured reserve with broken leg (November 26, 2001-remainder of season). ... Granted free agency (March 1, 2002). ... Re-signed by Broncos (April 19, 2002). ... Granted unconditional free agency (February 28, 2003). ... Signed by Buffalo Bills (April 21, 2003).
SINGLE GAME HIGHS (regular season): Attempts—37 (October 17, 1999, vs. Green Bay); yards—185 (December 25, 1999, vs. Detroit); and rushing touchdowns—2 (November 7, 1999, vs. San Diego).
STATISTICAL PLATEAUS: 100-yard rushing games: 1999 (4).

			RUSHING				RECEIVING				TOTALS			
Year Team	G	GS	Att.	Yds.	Avg.	TD	No.	Yds.	Avg.	TD	TD	2pt.	Pts.	Fum.
1999—Denver NFL	12	12	276	1159	4.2	7	21	159	7.6	0	7	†1	44	2
2000—Denver NFL	1	0	13	80	6.2	0	3	10	3.3	0	0	0	0	0
2001—Denver NFL	9	1	57	228	4.0	1	4	29	7.3	0	1	0	6	0
2002—Denver NFL	13	2	37	147	4.0	1	18	148	8.2	0	1	0	6	0
Pro totals (4 years)	35	15	383	1614	4.2	9	46	346	7.5	0	9	1	56	2

GARZA, ROBERTO C FALCONS

PERSONAL: Born March 2, 1979, in Rio Hondo, Texas. ... 6-2/296. ... Full name: Robert Garza.
HIGH SCHOOL: Rio Hondo (Texas).
COLLEGE: Texas A&M-Kingsville.
TRANSACTIONS/CAREER NOTES: Selected by Atlanta Falcons in fourth round (99th pick overall) of 2001 NFL draft. ... Signed by Falcons (May 21, 2001).
PLAYING EXPERIENCE: Atlanta NFL, 2001-2002. ... Games/Games started: 2001 (16/4), 2002 (6/4). Total: 22/8.

GASH, SAM FB BILLS

PERSONAL: Born March 7, 1969, in Hendersonville, N.C. ... 6-0/240. ... Full name: Samuel Lee Gash Jr. ... Cousin of Thane Gash, safety with Cleveland Browns (1988-90) and San Francisco 49ers (1992).
HIGH SCHOOL: Hendersonville (N.C.).
COLLEGE: Penn State (degree in liberal arts).

G

TRANSACTIONS/CAREER NOTES: Selected by New England Patriots in eighth round (205th pick overall) of 1992 NFL draft. ... Signed by Patriots (June 10, 1992). ... Granted free agency (February 17, 1995). ... Re-signed by Patriots (May 5, 1995). ... On injured reserve with knee injury (December 10, 1996-remainder of season). ... Granted unconditional free agency (February 13, 1998). ... Signed by Buffalo Bills (March 5, 1998). ... Released by Bills (April 14, 2000). ... Signed by Baltimore Ravens (August 7, 2000). ... Granted unconditional free agency (March 2, 2001). ... Re-signed by Ravens (June 11, 2001). ... Released by Ravens (February 27, 2002). ... Re-signed by Ravens (September 2, 2002). ... Granted unconditional free agency (February 28, 2003). ... Signed by Bills (March 31, 2003).
CHAMPIONSHIP GAME EXPERIENCE: Played in AFC championship game (2000 season). ... Member of Super Bowl championship team (2000 season).
HONORS: Played in Pro Bowl (1998 and 1999 seasons).
SINGLE GAME HIGHS (regular season): Attempts—15 (December 18, 1994, vs. Buffalo); yards—56 (December 18, 1994, vs. Buffalo); and rushing touchdowns—1 (September 19, 1993, vs. Seattle).

			RUSHING				RECEIVING				TOTALS			
Year Team	G	GS	Att.	Yds.	Avg.	TD	No.	Yds.	Avg.	TD	TD	2pt.	Pts.	Fum.
1992—New England NFL	15	0	5	7	1.4	1	0	0	0.0	0	1	0	6	1
1993—New England NFL	15	4	48	149	3.1	1	14	93	6.6	0	1	0	6	1
1994—New England NFL	13	6	30	86	2.9	0	9	61	6.8	0	0	0	0	1
1995—New England NFL	15	12	8	24	3.0	0	26	242	9.3	1	1	0	6	0
1996—New England NFL	14	9	8	15	1.9	0	33	276	8.4	2	2	1	14	0
1997—New England NFL	16	5	6	10	1.7	0	22	154	7.0	3	3	0	18	0
1998—Buffalo NFL	16	12	11	32	2.9	0	19	165	8.7	3	3	0	18	0
1999—Buffalo NFL	15	11	0	0	0.0	0	20	163	8.2	2	2	0	12	0
2000—Baltimore NFL	15	4	2	2	1.0	0	6	30	5.0	1	1	0	6	0
2001—Baltimore NFL	16	4	2	-1	-0.5	0	9	80	8.9	1	1	0	6	0
2002—Baltimore NFL	11	0	0	0	0.0	0	0	0	0.0	0	0	0	0	0
Pro totals (11 years)	161	67	120	324	2.7	2	158	1264	8.0	13	15	1	92	3

GAYLOR, TREVOR   WR   FALCONS

PERSONAL: Born November 3, 1977, in St. Louis. ... 6-3/195. ... Full name: Trevor Alexander Gaylor.
HIGH SCHOOL: Hazelwood (Mo.) West.
COLLEGE: Miami of Ohio.
TRANSACTIONS/CAREER NOTES: Selected by San Diego Chargers in fourth round (111th pick overall) of 2000 NFL draft. ... Signed by Chargers (July 20, 2000). ... Traded by Chargers to Atlanta Falcons for undisclosed pick in 2004 draft (September 1, 2002). ... Granted free agency (February 28, 2003). ... Re-signed by Falcons (March 19, 2003).
SINGLE GAME HIGHS (regular season): Receptions—5 (December 30, 2001, vs. Seattle); yards—100 (November 17, 2002, vs. New Orleans); and touchdown receptions—1 (December 15, 2002, vs. Seattle).
STATISTICAL PLATEAUS: 100-yard receiving games: 2002 (1).

			RECEIVING			
Year Team	G	GS	No.	Yds.	Avg.	TD
2000—San Diego NFL	14	2	13	182	14.0	1
2001—San Diego NFL	7	3	14	217	15.5	0
2002—Atlanta NFL	13	2	25	385	15.4	3
Pro totals (3 years)	34	7	52	784	15.1	4

GBAJA-BIAMILA, KABEER   DE   PACKERS

PERSONAL: Born September 24, 1977, in Los Angeles. ... 6-4/255. ... Full name: Muhammed-Kabeer Olarewaja Gbaja-Biamila.
HIGH SCHOOL: Crenshaw (Los Angeles).
COLLEGE: San Diego State.
TRANSACTIONS/CAREER NOTES: Selected by Green Bay Packers in fifth round (149th pick overall) of 2000 NFL draft. ... Signed by Packers (July 17, 2000). ... Released by Packers (August 27, 2000). ... Re-signed by Packers to practice squad (August 28, 2000). ... Activated (October 10, 2000). ... Granted free agency (February 28, 2003). ... Re-signed by Packers (April 2, 2003).

			TOTALS			INTERCEPTIONS			
Year Team	G	GS	Tk.	Ast.	Sks.	No.	Yds.	Avg.	TD
2000—Green Bay NFL	7	0	3	1	1.5	0	0	0.0	0
2001—Green Bay NFL	16	0	19	5	13.5	0	0	0.0	0
2002—Green Bay NFL	15	11	35	11	12.0	1	72	72.0	1
Pro totals (3 years)	38	11	57	17	27.0	1	72	72.0	1

GEASON, CORY   TE

G

PERSONAL: Born August 12, 1975, in St. James, La. ... 6-3/255. ... Full name: Corey Geason.
HIGH SCHOOL: St. James (La.).
COLLEGE: Tulane.
TRANSACTIONS/CAREER NOTES: Signed as non-drafted free agent by Dallas Cowboys (April 21, 1998). ... Released by Cowboys (August 24, 1998). ... Signed by Tampa Bay Buccaneers (July 14, 1999). ... Released by Buccaneers (September 5, 1999). ... Signed by Pittsburgh Steelers to practice squad (December 21, 1999). ... On injured reserve with knee injury (November 7, 2000-remainder of season). ... Released by Steelers (September 2, 2001). ... Re-signed by Steelers (November 21, 2001). ... Claimed on waivers by Buffalo Bills (September 3, 2002). ... Released by Bills (November 18, 2002).
CHAMPIONSHIP GAME EXPERIENCE: Member of Steelers for AFC championship game (2001 season); inactive.
SINGLE GAME HIGHS (regular season): Receptions—1 (November 5, 2000, vs. Tennessee); yards—36 (September 24, 2000, vs. Tennessee); and touchdown receptions—0.

			RECEIVING			
Year Team	G	GS	No.	Yds.	Avg.	TD
2000—Pittsburgh NFL	9	3	3	66	22.0	0
2001—Pittsburgh NFL	7	0	0	0	0.0	0
2002—Buffalo NFL	10	0	0	0	0.0	0
Pro totals (3 years)	26	3	3	66	22.0	0

GEORGE, EDDIE   RB   TITANS

PERSONAL: Born September 24, 1973, in Philadelphia. ... 6-3/236. ... Full name: Edward Nathan George.
HIGH SCHOOL: Abington (Philadelphia), then Fork Union (Va.) Military Academy.
COLLEGE: Ohio State.
TRANSACTIONS/CAREER NOTES: Selected by Houston Oilers in first round (14th pick overall) of 1996 NFL draft. ... Signed by Oilers (July 20, 1996). ... Oilers franchise moved to Tennessee for 1997 season. ... Oilers franchise renamed Tennessee Titans for 1999 season (December 26, 1998). ... On physically unable to perform list with toe injury (July 28-31, 2001).
CHAMPIONSHIP GAME EXPERIENCE: Played in AFC championship game (1999 and 2002 seasons). ... Played in Super Bowl XXXIV (1999 season).
HONORS: Heisman Trophy winner (1995). ... Maxwell Award winner (1995). ... Doak Walker Award winner (1995). ... Named running back on THE SPORTING NEWS college All-America first team (1995). ... Named NFL Rookie of the Year by THE SPORTING NEWS (1996). ... Played in Pro Bowl (1997-2000 seasons).
SINGLE GAME HIGHS (regular season): Attempts—36 (November 19, 2000, vs. Cleveland); yards—216 (August 31, 1997, vs. Oakland); and rushing touchdowns—3 (December 17, 2000, vs. Cleveland).
STATISTICAL PLATEAUS: 100-yard rushing games: 1996 (4), 1997 (8), 1998 (6), 1999 (5), 2000 (6), 2001 (1), 2002 (4). Total: 34. ... 100-yard receiving games: 2000 (1).
MISCELLANEOUS: Holds Tennessee Titans franchise all-time record for most yards rushing (8,978).

			RUSHING				RECEIVING				TOTALS		
Year Team	G	GS	Att.	Yds.	Avg.	TD	No.	Yds.	Avg.	TD	TD	2pt.	Pts.	Fum.
1996—Houston NFL	16	16	335	1368	4.1	8	23	182	7.9	0	8	0	48	3
1997—Tennessee NFL	16	16	357	1399	3.9	6	7	44	6.3	1	7	1	44	4
1998—Tennessee NFL	16	16	348	1294	3.7	5	37	310	8.4	1	6	1	38	7
1999—Tennessee NFL	16	16	320	1304	4.1	9	47	458	9.7	4	13	0	78	5
2000—Tennessee NFL	16	16	*403	1509	3.7	14	50	453	9.1	2	16	0	96	5
2001—Tennessee NFL	16	16	315	939	3.0	5	37	279	7.5	0	5	0	30	8
2002—Tennessee NFL	16	16	343	1165	3.4	12	36	255	7.1	2	14	1	86	1
Pro totals (7 years)	112	112	2421	8978	3.7	59	237	1981	8.4	10	69	3	420	33

GIBSON, AARON   OT   BEARS

PERSONAL: Born September 27, 1977, in Indianapolis. ... 6-6/410.
HIGH SCHOOL: Decatur Central (Indianapolis).
COLLEGE: Wisconsin.
TRANSACTIONS/CAREER NOTES: Selected by Detroit Lions in first round (27th pick overall) of 1999 NFL draft. ... Signed by Lions (July 24, 1999). ... On injured reserve with shoulder injury (August 31, 1999-entire season). ... On injured reserve with shoulder injury (December 4, 2000-remainder of season). ... Claimed on waivers by Dallas Cowboys (October 31, 2001). ... Released by Cowboys (September 18, 2002). ... Signed by Chicago Bears (November 26, 2002).
PLAYING EXPERIENCE: Detroit NFL, 2000; Detroit (6)-Dallas (1) NFL, 2001; Dallas 2002. ... Games/Games started: 2000 (10/10), 2001 (Det-6/5; Dal.-1/0; Total: 7/5), 2002 (1/0). Total: 18/15.
HONORS: Named offensive tackle on THE SPORTING NEWS college All-America second team (1998).

GIBSON, DAMON   WR/KR

PERSONAL: Born February 25, 1975, in Houston. ... 5-9/183.
HIGH SCHOOL: Forest Brook (Houston).
COLLEGE: Iowa.
TRANSACTIONS/CAREER NOTES: Signed as non-drafted free agent by Cincinnati Bengals (April 20, 1998). ... Selected by Cleveland Browns from Bengals in 1999 NFL expansion draft (February 9, 1999). ... Released by Browns (September 28, 1999). ... Selected by Scottish Claymores in 2000 NFL Europe draft (February 22, 2000). ... Signed by Jacksonville Jaguars (June 29, 2000). ... Released by Jaguars (August 22, 2000). ... Re-signed by Jaguars (June 29, 2001). ... Released by Jaguars (September 10, 2002). ... Signed by Atlanta Falcons (September 17, 2002). ... Released by Falcons (October 18, 2002).
SINGLE GAME HIGHS (regular season): Receptions—3 (November 1, 1998, vs. Denver); yards—76 (October 18, 1998, vs. Tennessee); and touchdown receptions—1 (November 8, 1998, vs. Jacksonville).

			RECEIVING				PUNT RETURNS				KICKOFF RETURNS				TOTALS		
Year Team	G	GS	No.	Yds.	Avg.	TD	No.	Yds.	Avg.	TD	No.	Yds.	Avg.	TD	TD	2pt.	Pts.	Fum.
1998—Cincinnati NFL	16	0	19	258	13.6	3	27	218	8.1	1	17	372	21.9	0	4	0	24	3
1999—Cleveland NFL	2	0	0	0	0.0	0	2	9	4.5	0	0	0	0.0	0	0	0	0	0
2000—Scottish NFLE	...	...	23	378	16.4	3	22	328	14.9	0	13	260	20.0	0	0	0	0	0
2001—Jacksonville NFL	16	0	2	13	6.5	0	38	333	8.8	0	26	511	19.7	0	0	0	0	3
2002—Atlanta NFL	1	0	0	0	0.0	0	2	25	12.5	0	0	0	0.0	0	0	0	0	0
—Jacksonville NFL	1	0	0	0	0.0	0	1	0	0.0	0	0	0	0.0	0	0	0	0	1
NFL Europe totals (1 year)	...	...	23	378	16.4	3	22	328	14.9	0	13	260	20.0	0	0	0	0	0
NFL totals (4 years)	36	0	21	271	12.9	3	70	585	8.4	1	43	883	20.5	0	4	0	24	7
Pro totals (5 years)	...	...	44	649	14.8	6	92	913	9.9	1	56	1143	20.4	0	4	0	24	7

GIBSON, DAVID   S   COLTS

PERSONAL: Born November 5, 1977, in Santa Ana, Calif. ... 6-1/210.
HIGH SCHOOL: Mater Dei (Santa, Ana, Calif.).
COLLEGE: Southern California.
TRANSACTIONS/CAREER NOTES: Selected by Tampa Bay Buccaneers in sixth round (193rd pick overall) of 2000 NFL draft. ... Signed by Buccaneers (July 10, 2000). ... Traded by Buccaneers to Indianapolis Colts for undisclosed draft pick (September 24, 2002). ... Granted free agency (February 28, 2003). ... Re-signed by Colts (May 6, 2003).

G

Year Team	G	GS	TOTALS Tk.	Ast.	Sks.	INTERCEPTIONS No.	Yds.	Avg.	TD
2000—Tampa Bay NFL	9	0	2	0	0.0	0	0	0.0	0
2001—Tampa Bay NFL	13	0	4	2	0.0	0	0	0.0	0
2002—Indianapolis NFL	13	9	43	18	1.0	1	0	0.0	0
—Tampa Bay NFL	3	0	0	0	0.0	0	0	0.0	0
Pro totals (3 years)	38	9	49	20	1.0	1	0	0.0	0

GIBSON, DERRICK   S   RAIDERS

PERSONAL: Born March 22, 1979, in Miami. ... 6-2/215.
HIGH SCHOOL: Killian (Miami).
COLLEGE: Florida State.
TRANSACTIONS/CAREER NOTES: Selected by Oakland Raiders in first round (28th pick overall) of 2001 NFL draft. ... Signed by Raiders (July 21, 2001).
CHAMPIONSHIP GAME EXPERIENCE: Played in AFC championship game (2002 season). ... Played in Super Bowl XXXVII (2002 season).

Year Team	G	GS	TOTALS Tk.	Ast.	Sks.	INTERCEPTIONS No.	Yds.	Avg.	TD
2001—Oakland NFL	16	0	10	0	0.0	1	9	9.0	0
2002—Oakland NFL	16	11	50	14	0.0	0	0	0.0	0
Pro totals (2 years)	32	11	60	14	0.0	1	9	9.0	0

GIBSON, OLIVER   DT   BENGALS

PERSONAL: Born March 15, 1972, in Chicago. ... 6-2/310. ... Full name: Oliver Donnovan Gibson. ... Cousin of Godfrey Myles, linebacker with Dallas Cowboys (1991-96).
HIGH SCHOOL: Romeoville (Ill.).
COLLEGE: Notre Dame (degree in economics, 1994).
TRANSACTIONS/CAREER NOTES: Selected by Pittsburgh Steelers in fourth round (120th pick overall) of 1995 NFL draft. ... Signed by Steelers (July 18, 1995). ... Granted free agency (February 13, 1998). ... Re-signed by Steelers (June 9, 1998). ... Granted unconditional free agency (February 12, 1999). ... Signed by Cincinnati Bengals (March 9, 1999). ... On injured reserve with Achilles' injury (November 11, 2002-remainder of season).
CHAMPIONSHIP GAME EXPERIENCE: Member of Steelers for AFC championship game (1995 season); inactive. ... Played in AFC championship game (1997 season).
HONORS: Earned first-team All-Independent honors from THE SPORTING NEWS (1994).

Year Team	G	GS	TOTALS Tk.	Ast.	Sks.	INTERCEPTIONS No.	Yds.	Avg.	TD
1995—Pittsburgh NFL	12	0	1	1	0.0	0	0	0.0	0
1996—Pittsburgh NFL	16	0	7	8	2.5	0	0	0.0	0
1997—Pittsburgh NFL	16	0	9	1	1.0	0	0	0.0	0
1998—Pittsburgh NFL	16	0	10	5	2.0	0	0	0.0	0
1999—Cincinnati NFL	16	16	31	10	4.5	0	0	0.0	0
2000—Cincinnati NFL	16	16	43	9	4.0	0	0	0.0	0
2001—Cincinnati NFL	16	16	45	10	3.0	0	0	0.0	0
2002—Cincinnati NFL	9	9	19	10	0.0	1	6	6.0	0
Pro totals (8 years)	117	57	165	54	17.0	1	6	6.0	0

GILBERT, SEAN   DT

PERSONAL: Born April 10, 1970, in Aliquippa, Pa. ... 6-5/318.
HIGH SCHOOL: Aliquippa (Pa.).
COLLEGE: Pittsburgh.
TRANSACTIONS/CAREER NOTES: Selected after junior season by Los Angeles Rams in first round (third pick overall) of 1992 NFL draft. ... Signed by Rams (July 28, 1992). ... Designated by Rams as transition player (February 25, 1993). ... Rams franchise moved to St. Louis (April 12, 1995). ... Traded by Rams to Washington Redskins for first-round pick (RB Lawrence Phillips) in 1996 draft (April 8, 1996). ... Designated by Redskins as franchise player (February 12, 1997). ... Sat out 1997 season due to contract dispute. ... Designated by Redskins as franchise player (February 11, 1998). ... Tendered offer sheet by Carolina Panthers (March 24, 1998). ... Redskins declined to match offer (April 21, 1998). ... On injured reserve with hip injury (November 21, 2002-remainder of season). ... Released by Panthers (March 10, 2003).
HONORS: Played in Pro Bowl (1993 season).

Year Team	G	GS	TOTALS Tk.	Ast.	Sks.	INTERCEPTIONS No.	Yds.	Avg.	TD
1992—Los Angeles Rams NFL	16	16	46	8	5.0	0	0	0.0	0
1993—Los Angeles Rams NFL	16	16	54	27	10.5	0	0	0.0	0
1994—Los Angeles Rams NFL	14	14	36	11	3.0	0	0	0.0	0
1995—St. Louis NFL	14	14	24	9	5.5	0	0	0.0	0
1996—Washington NFL	16	16	55	13	3.0	0	0	0.0	0
1997—Washington NFL			Did not play.						
1998—Carolina NFL	16	16	39	14	6.0	0	0	0.0	0
1999—Carolina NFL	16	16	36	11	2.5	1	4	4.0	0
2000—Carolina NFL	15	15	38	15	4.0	1	0	0.0	0
2001—Carolina NFL	9	9	23	2	2.0	0	0	0.0	0
2002—Carolina NFL	8	0	5	0	1.0	0	0	0.0	0
Pro totals (10 years)	140	132	356	110	42.5	2	4	2.0	0

G

GILDON, JASON   LB   STEELERS

PERSONAL: Born July 31, 1972, in Altus, Okla. ... 6-4/250. ... Full name: Jason Larue Gildon. ... Related to Wendall Gaines, guard with Arizona Cardinals (1995).
HIGH SCHOOL: Altus (Okla.).
COLLEGE: Oklahoma State.
TRANSACTIONS/CAREER NOTES: Selected by Pittsburgh Steelers in third round (88th pick overall) of 1994 NFL draft. ... Signed by Steelers (July 15, 1994). ... Granted free agency (February 14, 1997). ... Re-signed by Steelers (July 21, 1997). ... Granted unconditional free agency (February 13, 1998). ... Re-signed by Steelers (April 7, 1998). ... Designated by Steelers as franchise player (February 21, 2002). ... Re-signed by Steelers (February 25, 2002).
CHAMPIONSHIP GAME EXPERIENCE: Played in AFC championship game (1994, 1995, 1997 and 2001 seasons). ... Played in Super Bowl XXX (1995 season).
HONORS: Played in Pro Bowl (2000-2002 seasons).

Year Team	G	GS	TOTALS Tk.	Ast.	Sks.	INTERCEPTIONS No.	Yds.	Avg.	TD
1994—Pittsburgh NFL	16	1	4	0	2.0	0	0	0.0	0
1995—Pittsburgh NFL	16	0	8	4	3.0	0	0	0.0	0
1996—Pittsburgh NFL	14	13	47	12	7.0	0	0	0.0	0
1997—Pittsburgh NFL	16	16	41	12	5.0	0	0	0.0	0
1998—Pittsburgh NFL	16	16	42	12	11.0	0	0	0.0	0
1999—Pittsburgh NFL	16	16	42	15	8.5	0	0	0.0	0
2000—Pittsburgh NFL	16	16	58	19	13.5	0	0	0.0	0
2001—Pittsburgh NFL	16	16	43	13	12.0	1	0	0.0	0
2002—Pittsburgh NFL	16	16	45	22	9.0	0	0	0.0	0
Pro totals (9 years)	142	110	330	109	71.0	1	0	0.0	0

GILLIAM, DONDRE   WR   CHARGERS

PERSONAL: Born February 9, 1977, in Baltimore. ... 6-0/185.
HIGH SCHOOL: Aberdeen (Md.).
COLLEGE: Cheyney (Pa.), then Millersville (Pa.).
TRANSACTIONS/CAREER NOTES: Signed as non-drafted free agent by San Diego Chargers (April 24, 2001). ... On injured reserve with hip injury (August 28-September 8, 2001). ... Assigned by Chargers to Scottish Claymores in 2002 NFL Europe enhancement allocation program (February 12, 2002). ... Released by Chargers (September 1, 2002). ... Re-signed by Chargers to practice squad (September 3, 2002). ... Activated (November 14, 2002). ... Released by Chargers (November 19, 2002). ... Re-signed by Chargers to practice squad (November 21, 2002). ... Activated (December 21, 2002). ... Re-signed by Chargers (April 4, 2003).

Year Team	G	GS	RECEIVING No.	Yds.	Avg.	TD	KICKOFF RETURNS No.	Yds.	Avg.	TD	TOTALS TD	2pt.	Pts.	Fum.
2002—Scottish NFLE	...	...	20	400	20.0	4	6	64	10.7	0	4	0	24	0
—San Diego NFL	2	0	0	0	0.0	0	0	0	0.0	0	0	0	0	0
NFL Europe totals (1 year)	...	...	20	400	20.0	4	6	64	10.7	0	4	0	24	0
NFL totals (1 year)	2	0	0	0	0.0	0	0	0	0.0	0	0	0	0	0
Pro totals (2 years)	...	...	20	400	20.0	4	6	64	10.7	0	4	0	24	0

GILMORE, BRYAN   WR   CARDINALS

PERSONAL: Born July 21, 1978, in Lufkin, Texas. ... 6-0/193.
HIGH SCHOOL: Lufkin (Texas).
COLLEGE: Midwestern State (Texas).
TRANSACTIONS/CAREER NOTES: Signed as non-drafted free agent by Arizona Cardinals (April 17, 2000). ... Released by Cardinals (August 27, 2000). ... Re-signed by Cardinals to practice squad (August 28, 2000). ... Activated (December 15, 2000). ... Assigned by Cardinals to Barcelona Dragons in 2001 NFL Europe enhancement allocation program (February 19, 2001). ... Released by Cardinals (September 2, 2001). ... Re-signed by Cardinals to practice squad (September 3, 2001). ... Activated (November 29, 2001). ... On injured reserve with ankle injury (October 30, 2002-remainder of season).
SINGLE GAME HIGHS (regular season): Receptions—1 (September 29, 2002, vs. New York Giants); yards—14 (September 29, 2002, vs. Arizona); and touchdown receptions—0.

Year Team	G	GS	RECEIVING No.	Yds.	Avg.	TD
2000—Arizona NFL	1	0	0	0	0.0	0
2001—Barcelona NFLE	...	...	30	403	13.4	5
—Arizona NFL	2	0	0	0	0.0	0
2002—Arizona NFL	7	0	1	14	14.0	0
NFL Europe totals (1 year)	...	...	30	403	13.4	5
NFL totals (3 years)	10	0	1	14	14.0	0
Pro totals (4 years)	...	...	31	417	13.5	5

GILMORE, JOHN   TE   BEARS

PERSONAL: Born September 21, 1979, in Marquette, Mich. ... 6-3/265. ... Full name: John Henry Gilmore.
HIGH SCHOOL: Wilson (West Lawn, Pa.).
COLLEGE: Penn State.
TRANSACTIONS/CAREER NOTES: Selected by New Orleans Saints in sixth round (196th pick overall) of 2002 NFL draft. ... Signed by Saints (July 22, 2002). ... Released by Saints (September 1, 2002). ... Signed by Chicago Bears to practice squad (September 3, 2002). ... Activated (October 25, 2002).
SINGLE GAME HIGHS (regular season): Receptions—3 (December 15, 2002, vs. New York Jets); yards—32 (December 22, 2002, vs. Carolina); and touchdown receptions—0.

Year Team	G	GS	RECEIVING No.	Yds.	Avg.	TD
2002—Chicago NFL	8	4	10	130	13.0	0

G

GIVENS, DAVID — WR — PATRIOTS

PERSONAL: Born August 16, 1980, in Youngstown, Ohio. ... 6-0/212. ... Full name: David Lamar Givens.
HIGH SCHOOL: Humble (Texas).
COLLEGE: Notre Dame.
TRANSACTIONS/CAREER NOTES: Selected by New England Patriots in seventh round (253rd pick overall) of 2002 NFL draft. ... Signed by Patriots (July 21, 2002).
SINGLE GAME HIGHS (regular season): Receptions—3 (October 13, 2002, vs. Green Bay); yards—30 (December 8, 2002, vs. Buffalo); and touchdown receptions—1 (October 13, 2002, vs. Green Bay).

			RUSHING				RECEIVING				KICKOFF RETURNS				TOTALS		
Year Team	G	GS	Att.	Yds.	Avg.	TD	No.	Yds.	Avg.	TD	No.	Yds.	Avg.	TD	TD 2pt.	Pts.	Fum.
2002—New England NFL........	12	0	0	0	0.0	0	9	92	10.2	1	0	0	0.0	0	1 0	6	1

GLEASON, STEVE — DB — SAINTS

PERSONAL: Born March 19, 1977, in Spokane, Wash. ... 5-11/215. ... Full name: Stephen Gleason.
HIGH SCHOOL: Gonzaga (Wash.) Prep.
COLLEGE: Washington State.
TRANSACTIONS/CAREER NOTES: Signed as non-drafted free agent by Indianapolis Colts (April 16, 2000). ... Released by Colts (August 27, 2000). ... Signed by New Orleans Saints to practice squad (November 21, 2000). ... Activated (December 3, 2000). ... Released by Saints (September 2, 2001). ... Re-signed by Saints (November 23, 2001).

			TOTALS			INTERCEPTIONS			
Year Team	G	GS	Tk.	Ast.	Sks.	No.	Yds.	Avg.	TD
2000—New Orleans NFL	3	0	0	0	0.0	0	0	0.0	0
2001—New Orleans NFL	7	0	0	0	0.0	0	0	0.0	0
2002—New Orleans NFL	14	0	1	1	0.0	0	0	0.0	0
Pro totals (3 years)	24	0	1	1	0.0	0	0	0.0	0

GLENN, AARON — CB/KR — TEXANS

PERSONAL: Born July 16, 1972, in Humble, Texas. ... 5-9/185. ... Full name: Aaron DeVon Glenn.
HIGH SCHOOL: Nimitz (Irving, Texas).
JUNIOR COLLEGE: Navarro College (Texas).
COLLEGE: Texas A&M.
TRANSACTIONS/CAREER NOTES: Selected by New York Jets in first round (12th pick overall) of 1994 NFL draft. ... Signed by Jets (July 21, 1994). ... Selected by Houston Texans from Jets in NFL expansion draft (February 18, 2002).
CHAMPIONSHIP GAME EXPERIENCE: Played in AFC championship game (1998 season).
HONORS: Named defensive back on The Sporting News college All-America first team (1993). ... Played in Pro Bowl (1997 and 2002 seasons). ... Named to play in Pro Bowl (1998 season); replaced by Charles Woodson due to injury. ... Named cornerback on The Sporting News NFL All-Pro team (2002).
MISCELLANEOUS: Holds Houston Texans all-time record for most interceptions (5).

			TOTALS			INTERCEPTIONS				KICKOFF RETURNS				TOTALS		
Year Team	G	GS	Tk.	Ast.	Sks.	No.	Yds.	Avg.	TD	No.	Yds.	Avg.	TD	TD 2pt.	Pts.	Fum.
1994—New York Jets NFL............................	15	15	58	9	0.0	0	0	0.0	0	27	582	21.6	0	0 0	0	2
1995—New York Jets NFL............................	16	16	42	10	0.0	1	17	17.0	0	1	12	12.0	0	0 0	0	0
1996—New York Jets NFL............................	16	16	38	6	0.0	4	113	28.3	†2	1	6	6.0	0	2 0	12	0
1997—New York Jets NFL............................	16	16	54	11	0.0	1	5	5.0	0	28	741§26.5	▲1	1 0	6	1
1998—New York Jets NFL............................	13	13	47	1	0.0	6	23	3.8	0	24	585	24.4	0	1 0	6	1
1999—New York Jets NFL............................	16	16	46	5	0.0	3	20	6.7	0	27	601	22.3	0	0 0	0	0
2000—New York Jets NFL............................	16	16	28	9	0.0	4	34	8.5	0	3	51	17.0	0	0 0	0	0
2001—New York Jets NFL............................	13	12	28	5	0.0	5	82	16.4	1	0	0	0.0	0	1 0	6	1
2002—Houston NFL	16	16	56	11	1.0	5	181	36.2	▲2	0	0	0.0	0	2 0	12	0
Pro totals (9 years)	137	136	397	67	1.0	29	475	16.4	5	111	2578	23.2	1	7 0	42	5

GLENN, JASON — LB — JETS

PERSONAL: Born August 20, 1979, in Aldine, Texas. ... 6-0/231.
HIGH SCHOOL: Nimitz (Aldine, Texas).
COLLEGE: Texas A&M.
TRANSACTIONS/CAREER NOTES: Selected by Detroit Lions in sixth round (173rd pick overall) of 2001 NFL draft. ... Signed by Lions (July 20, 2001). ... Claimed on waivers by New York Jets (September 3, 2001).

			TOTALS			INTERCEPTIONS			
Year Team	G	GS	Tk.	Ast.	Sks.	No.	Yds.	Avg.	TD
2001—New York Jets NFL	15	0	0	0	0.0	0	0	0.0	0
2002—New York Jets NFL	16	0	0	0	0.0	0	0	0.0	0
Pro totals (2 years)	31	0	0	0	0.0	0	0	0.0	0

G

GLENN, TARIK — OT — COLTS

PERSONAL: Born May 25, 1976, in Cleveland. ... 6-5/332.
HIGH SCHOOL: Bishop O'Dowd (Oakland).
COLLEGE: California.
TRANSACTIONS/CAREER NOTES: Selected by Indianapolis Colts in first round (19th pick overall) of 1997 NFL draft. ... Signed by Colts (August 11, 1997). ... Granted free agency (March 1, 2002). ... Re-signed by Colts (March 15, 2002).
PLAYING EXPERIENCE: Indianapolis NFL, 1997-2002. ... Games/Games started: 1997 (16/16), 1998 (16/16), 1999 (16/16), 2000 (16/16), 2001 (16/16), 2002 (16/16). Total: 96/96.
HONORS: Named offensive tackle on The Sporting News college All-America second team (1996).

PERSONAL: Born July 23, 1974, in Columbus, Ohio. ... 5-11/195.
HIGH SCHOOL: Brookhaven (Columbus, Ohio).
COLLEGE: Ohio State.
TRANSACTIONS/CAREER NOTES: Selected after junior season by New England Patriots in first round (seventh pick overall) of 1996 NFL draft. ... Signed by Patriots (July 12, 1996). ... On injured reserve with fractured ankle (December 18, 1998-remainder of season). ... On suspended list for violating league substance abuse policy (Sepetmber 9-October 7, 2001). ... On reserve/left squad list (August 15-September 13, 2001). ... Traded by Patriots to Green Bay Packers for fourth-round pick (DE Jarvis Green) in 2002 draft and conditional pick in 2003 draft (March 8, 2002). ... Traded by Packers to Dallas Cowboys for undisclosed draft pick (February 28, 2003).
CHAMPIONSHIP GAME EXPERIENCE: Played in AFC championship game (1996 season). ... Played in Super Bowl XXXI (1996 season).
HONORS: Fred Biletnikoff Award winner (1995). ... Named wide receiver on THE SPORTING NEWS college All-America first team (1995).
RECORDS: Holds NFL single-season record for most receptions by a rookie—90 (1996).
SINGLE GAME HIGHS (regular season): Receptions—13 (October 3, 1999, vs. Cleveland); yards—214 (October 3, 1999, vs. Cleveland); and touchdown receptions—1 (December 29, 2002, vs. New York Jets).
STATISTICAL PLATEAUS: 100-yard receiving games: 1996 (2), 1997 (1), 1998 (4), 1999 (4), 2000 (1), 2001 (1), 2002 (1). Total: 14.

Year Team	G	GS	RUSHING Att.	Yds.	Avg.	TD	RECEIVING No.	Yds.	Avg.	TD	TOTALS TD	2pt.	Pts.	Fum.
1996—New England NFL	15	15	5	42	8.4	0	90	1132	12.6	6	6	0	36	1
1997—New England NFL	9	9	0	0	0.0	0	27	431	16.0	2	2	0	12	1
1998—New England NFL	10	9	2	-1	-0.5	0	50	792	15.8	3	3	0	18	0
1999—New England NFL	14	13	0	0	0.0	0	69	1147	16.6	4	4	0	24	2
2000—New England NFL	16	15	4	39	9.8	0	79	963	12.2	6	6	0	36	0
2001—New England NFL	4	1	0	0	0.0	0	14	204	14.6	1	1	0	6	0
2002—Green Bay NFL	15	14	0	0	0.0	0	56	817	14.6	2	2	0	12	1
Pro totals (7 years)	83	76	11	80	7.3	0	385	5486	14.2	24	24	0	144	5

PERSONAL: Born July 4, 1974, in San Diego. ... 6-2/285. ... Full name: La'Roi Damon Glover. ... Name pronounced la-ROY.
HIGH SCHOOL: Point Loma (San Diego).
COLLEGE: San Diego State.
TRANSACTIONS/CAREER NOTES: Selected by Oakland Raiders in fifth round (166th pick overall) of 1996 NFL draft. ... Signed by Raiders (July 12, 1996). ... Assigned by Raiders to Barcelona Dragons in 1997 World League enhancement allocation program (February 19, 1997). ... Claimed on waivers by New Orleans Saints (August 25, 1997). ... Granted unconditional free agency (March 1, 2002). ... Signed by Dallas Cowboys (March 12, 2002).
HONORS: Named defensive tackle on THE SPORTING NEWS NFL All-Pro team (2000 and 2002). ... Played in Pro Bowl (2000-2002 seasons).

Year Team	G	GS	TOTALS Tk.	Ast.	Sks.	INTERCEPTIONS No.	Yds.	Avg.	TD
1996—Oakland NFL	2	0	2	0	0.0	0	0	0.0	0
1997—Barcelona W.L.	10	10	...	...	6.5	0	0	0.0	0
—New Orleans NFL	15	2	24	9	6.5	0	0	0.0	0
1998—New Orleans NFL	16	15	59	8	10.0	1	0	0.0	0
1999—New Orleans NFL	16	16	46	16	8.5	0	0	0.0	0
2000—New Orleans NFL	16	16	53	14	*17.0	0	0	0.0	0
2001—New Orleans NFL	16	16	36	11	8.0	0	0	0.0	0
2002—Dallas NFL	16	16	39	11	6.5	1	7	7.0	0
W.L. totals (1 year)	10	10	...	...	6.5	0	0	0.0	0
NFL totals (7 years)	97	81	259	69	56.5	2	7	3.5	0
Pro totals (8 years)	107	91	...	...	63.0	2	7	3.5	0

PERSONAL: Born December 17, 1978, in Dayton, Ohio. ... 5-9/177. ... Full name: Lavar Glover.
HIGH SCHOOL: Jefferson (Dayton, Ohio).
COLLEGE: Cincinnati.
TRANSACTIONS/CAREER NOTES: Selected by Pittsburgh Steelers in seventh round (212th pick overall) of 2002 NFL draft. ... Signed by Steelers (July 12, 2002). ... Claimed on waivers by Cincinnati Bengals (August 28, 2002). ... Released by Bengals (September 1, 2002). ... Re-signed by Bengals to practice squad (September 2, 2002). ... Released by Bengals (October 16, 2002). ... Signed by Detroit Lions to practice squad (November 5, 2002). ... Signed by Bengals off Lions practice squad (November 12, 2002).

Year Team	G	GS	TOTALS Tk.	Ast.	Sks.	INTERCEPTIONS No.	Yds.	Avg.	TD
2002—Cincinnati NFL	2	0	0	0	0.0	0	0	0.0	0

PERSONAL: Born April 6, 1973, in Valdosta, Ga. ... 6-2/245. ... Full name: Randall Euralentris Godfrey.
HIGH SCHOOL: Lowndes County (Valdosta, Ga.).
COLLEGE: Georgia.
TRANSACTIONS/CAREER NOTES: Selected by Dallas Cowboys in second round (49th pick overall) of 1996 NFL draft. ... Signed by Cowboys (July 17, 1996). ... Granted free agency (February 12, 1999). ... Re-signed by Cowboys (June 25, 1999). ... Granted unconditional free agency (February 11, 2000). ... Signed by Tennessee Titans (February 16, 2000).
CHAMPIONSHIP GAME EXPERIENCE: Played in AFC championship game (2002 season).

G

Year Team	G	GS	TOTALS			INTERCEPTIONS			
			Tk.	Ast.	Sks.	No.	Yds.	Avg.	TD
1996—Dallas NFL	16	6	25	3	0.0	0	0	0.0	0
1997—Dallas NFL	16	16	66	31	1.0	0	0	0.0	0
1998—Dallas NFL	16	16	70	16	3.0	1	0	0.0	0
1999—Dallas NFL	16	16	81	15	1.0	1	10	10.0	0
2000—Tennessee NFL	16	16	98	23	3.0	2	25	12.5	1
2001—Tennessee NFL	14	14	62	16	1.0	1	5	5.0	0
2002—Tennessee NFL	8	5	25	7	1.0	0	0	0.0	0
Pro totals (7 years)	102	89	427	111	10.0	5	40	8.0	1

GOFF, MIKE　　　　G　　　　BENGALS

PERSONAL: Born January 6, 1976, in Spring Valley, Ill. ... 6-5/311. ... Full name: Michael J. Goff.
HIGH SCHOOL: Lasalle-Peru (Peru, Ill.).
COLLEGE: Iowa.
TRANSACTIONS/CAREER NOTES: Selected by Cincinnati Bengals in third round (78th pick overall) of 1998 NFL draft. ... Signed by Bengals (July 20, 1998).
PLAYING EXPERIENCE: Cincinnati NFL, 1998-2002. ... Games/Games started: 1998 (10/5), 1999 (12/1), 2000 (16/16), 2001 (16/16), 2002 (13/13). Total: 67/51.

GOINGS, NICK　　　　RB　　　　PANTHERS

PERSONAL: Born January 26, 1978, in Dublin, Ohio. ... 6-0/225. ... Full name: Nick Aaron Goings.
HIGH SCHOOL: Dublin Scioto (Ohio).
COLLEGE: Ohio State, then Pittsburgh.
TRANSACTIONS/CAREER NOTES: Signed as non-drafted free agent by Carolina Panthers (April 23, 2001).
SINGLE GAME HIGHS (regular season): Attempts—25 (September 9, 2001, vs. Minnesota); yards—86 (September 9, 2001, vs. Minnesota); and rushing touchdowns—0.

Year Team	G	GS	RUSHING				RECEIVING				TOTALS			
			Att.	Yds.	Avg.	TD	No.	Yds.	Avg.	TD	TD	2pt.	Pts.	Fum.
2001—Carolina NFL	13	2	66	197	3.0	0	8	39	4.9	0	0	0	0	1
2002—Carolina NFL	14	2	50	188	3.8	0	18	91	5.1	0	0	1	2	2
Pro totals (2 years)	27	4	116	385	3.3	0	26	130	5.0	0	0	1	2	3

GOLD, IAN　　　　LB　　　　BRONCOS

PERSONAL: Born August 23, 1978, in Ann Arbor, Mich. ... 6-0/223. ... Full name: Ian Maurice Gold.
HIGH SCHOOL: Belleville (Mich.).
COLLEGE: Michigan.
TRANSACTIONS/CAREER NOTES: Selected by Denver Broncos in second round (40th pick overall) of 2000 NFL draft. ... Signed by Broncos (July 23, 2000).
HONORS: Played in Pro Bowl (2001 season).

Year Team	G	GS	TOTALS			INTERCEPTIONS			
			Tk.	Ast.	Sks.	No.	Yds.	Avg.	TD
2000—Denver NFL	16	0	16	3	2.0	0	0	0.0	0
2001—Denver NFL	16	0	21	3	3.0	0	0	0.0	0
2002—Denver NFL	16	16	85	14	6.5	0	0	0.0	0
Pro totals (3 years)	48	16	122	20	11.5	0	0	0.0	0

GOLDEN, JACK　　　　LB　　　　BUCCANEERS

PERSONAL: Born January 28, 1977, in Harvey, Ill. ... 6-1/240.
HIGH SCHOOL: Thornton (Harvey, Ill.).
COLLEGE: Oklahoma State.
TRANSACTIONS/CAREER NOTES: Signed as non-drafted free agent by New York Giants (April 20, 2000). ... Claimed on waivers by Tampa Bay Buccaneers (April 4, 2002). ... Released by Buccaneers (September 4, 2002). ... Re-signed by Buccaneers (September 25, 2002). ... Granted free agency (February 28, 2003). ... Re-signed by Buccaneers (May 12, 2003).
CHAMPIONSHIP GAME EXPERIENCE: Played in NFC championship game (2000 and 2002 seasons). ... Played in Super Bowl XXXV (2000 season). ... Member of Super Bowl championship team (2002 season).

Year Team	G	GS	TOTALS			INTERCEPTIONS			
			Tk.	Ast.	Sks.	No.	Yds.	Avg.	TD
2000—New York Giants NFL	16	0	0	0	0.0	0	0	0.0	0
2001—New York Giants NFL	16	0	0	0	0.0	0	0	0.0	0
2002—Tampa Bay NFL	13	0	0	0	0.0	0	0	0.0	0
Pro totals (3 years)	45	0	0	0	0.0	0	0	0.0	0

GONZALEZ, JOAQUIN　　　　OT　　　　BROWNS

PERSONAL: Born September 7, 1979, in Miami. ... 6-3/302. ... Full name: Joaquin Antonio Gonzalez.
HIGH SCHOOL: Columbus (Miami).
COLLEGE: Miami (Fla.).
TRANSACTIONS/CAREER NOTES: Selected by Cleveland Browns in seventh round (227th pick overall) of 2002 NFL draft. ... Signed by Browns (July 16, 2002).
PLAYING EXPERIENCE: Cleveland NFL, 2002. ... Games/games started: 2002 (9/0).
HONORS: Named offensive tackle on THE SPORTING NEWS college All-America second team (2001).

G

GONZALEZ, TONY   TE   CHIEFS

PERSONAL: Born February 27, 1976, in Torrance, Calif. ... 6-4/248. ... Full name: Anthony Gonzalez.
HIGH SCHOOL: Huntington Beach (Calif.).
COLLEGE: California.
TRANSACTIONS/CAREER NOTES: Selected by Kansas City Chiefs in first round (13th pick overall) of 1997 NFL draft. ... Signed by Chiefs (July 29, 1997). ... Designated by Chiefs as franchise player (February 21, 2002). ... Re-signed by Chiefs (August 30, 2002).
HONORS: Named tight end on THE SPORTING NEWS college All-America first team (1996). ... Named tight end on THE SPORTING NEWS NFL All-Pro team (1999-2002). ... Played in Pro Bowl (1999, 2000 and 2002 seasons). ... Named to play in Pro Bowl (2001 season); replaced by Ken Dilger due to injury.
SINGLE GAME HIGHS (regular season): Receptions—11 (December 4, 2000, vs. New England); yards—147 (December 4, 2000, vs. New England); and touchdown receptions—3 (September 29, 2002, vs. Miami).
STATISTICAL PLATEAUS: 100-yard receiving games: 2000 (6), 2001 (1), 2002 (1). Total: 8.

			RECEIVING				TOTALS			
Year Team	G	GS	No.	Yds.	Avg.	TD	TD	2pt.	Pts.	Fum.
1997—Kansas City NFL	16	0	33	368	11.2	2	2	1	14	0
1998—Kansas City NFL	16	16	59	621	10.5	2	2	0	12	3
1999—Kansas City NFL	15	15	76	849	11.2	11	11	0	66	2
2000—Kansas City NFL	16	16	93	1203	12.9	9	9	0	54	0
2001—Kansas City NFL	16	16	73	917	12.6	6	6	1	38	0
2002—Kansas City NFL	16	16	63	773	12.3	7	7	0	42	0
Pro totals (6 years)	95	79	397	4731	11.9	37	37	2	226	5

GOOCH, JEFF   LB   LIONS

PERSONAL: Born October 31, 1974, in Nashville. ... 5-11/226. ... Full name: Jeffery Lance Gooch.
HIGH SCHOOL: Overton (Nashville).
COLLEGE: Austin Peay State.
TRANSACTIONS/CAREER NOTES: Signed as non-drafted free agent by Tampa Bay Buccaneers (April 23, 1996). ... On injured reserve with knee injury (December 17, 1996-remainder of season). ... Granted free agency (February 12, 1999). ... Re-signed by Buccaneers (April 13, 1999). ... Traded by Buccaneers to St. Louis Rams for fifth-round pick in 2001 draft (March 19, 2001); traded voided because Gooch failed physical (March 23, 2001). ... Released by Buccaneers (February 26, 2002). ... Signed by Detroit Lions (April 16, 2002).
CHAMPIONSHIP GAME EXPERIENCE: Played in NFC championship game (1999 season).

			TOTALS			INTERCEPTIONS			
Year Team	G	GS	Tk.	Ast.	Sks.	No.	Yds.	Avg.	TD
1996—Tampa Bay NFL	15	0	4	2	0.0	0	0	0.0	0
1997—Tampa Bay NFL	14	5	18	8	0.0	0	0	0.0	0
1998—Tampa Bay NFL	16	16	35	18	1.0	0	0	0.0	0
1999—Tampa Bay NFL	15	0	3	1	0.0	0	0	0.0	0
2000—Tampa Bay NFL	16	0	6	1	0.0	0	0	0.0	0
2001—Tampa Bay NFL	13	0	6	5	0.5	0	0	0.0	0
2002—Detroit NFL	16	2	24	9	0.0	1	3	3.0	0
Pro totals (7 years)	105	23	96	44	1.5	1	3	3.0	0

GOODMAN, ANDRE'   CB   LIONS

PERSONAL: Born August 8, 1978, in Greenville, S.C. ... 5-10/182.
HIGH SCHOOL: Eastwood (Greenville, S.C.).
COLLEGE: South Carolina.
TRANSACTIONS/CAREER NOTES: Selected by Detroit Lions in third round (68th pick overall) of 2002 NFL draft. ... Signed by Lions (July 16, 2002).

			TOTALS			INTERCEPTIONS			
Year Team	G	GS	Tk.	Ast.	Sks.	No.	Yds.	Avg.	TD
2002—Detroit NFL	14	6	34	8	0.0	1	2	2.0	0

GOODRICH, DWAYNE   CB

PERSONAL: Born May 29, 1978, in Oak Lawn, Ill. ... 5-11/207. ... Full name: Dwayne Lewis Goodrich.
HIGH SCHOOL: H.L. Richards (Oak Lawn, Ill.).
COLLEGE: Tennessee.
TRANSACTIONS/CAREER NOTES: Selected by Dallas Cowboys in second round (49th pick overall) of 2000 NFL draft. ... Signed by Cowboys (July 17, 2000). ... On injured reserve with Achilles' tendon injury (August 28, 2001-entire season). ... Released by Cowboys (February 20, 2003).

			TOTALS			INTERCEPTIONS			
Year Team	G	GS	Tk.	Ast.	Sks.	No.	Yds.	Avg.	TD
2000—Dallas NFL	5	0	0	0	0.0	0	0	0.0	0
2002—Dallas NFL	11	1	8	0	0.0	0	0	0.0	0
Pro totals (2 years)	16	1	8	0	0.0	0	0	0.0	0

GOODSPEED, JOEY   FB   CHARGERS

PERSONAL: Born February 22, 1978, in Berwyn, Ill. ... 6-1/247. ... Full name: Joey Allen Goodspeed.
HIGH SCHOOL: Oswego (Ill.).

G

COLLEGE: Notre Dame (degree in management).
TRANSACTIONS/CAREER NOTES: Signed as non-drafted free agent by Pittsburgh Steelers (April 18, 2000). ... Released by Steelers (August 21, 2000). ... Re-signed by Steelers to practice squad (October 18, 2000). ... Granted free agency following 2000 season. ... Signed by New Orleans Saints (February 10, 2001). ... Released by Saints (September 1, 2001). ... Signed by San Diego Chargers (February 14, 2002). ... Re-signed by Chargers (April 4, 2003).

			RUSHING					TOTALS		
Year Team	G	GS	Att.	Yds.	Avg.	TD	TD	2pt.	Pts.	Fum.
2002—San Diego NFL	12	0	0	0	0.0	0	0	0	0	0

GOODWIN, HUNTER   TE   VIKINGS

PERSONAL: Born October 10, 1972, in Bellville, Texas. ... 6-5/270. ... Full name: Robert Hunter Goodwin.
HIGH SCHOOL: Bellville (Texas).
COLLEGE: Texas A&M-Kingsville, then Texas A&M.
TRANSACTIONS/CAREER NOTES: Selected by Minnesota Vikings in fourth round (97th pick overall) of 1996 NFL draft. ... Signed by Vikings (July 20, 1996). ... Granted free agency (February 12, 1999). ... Tendered offer sheet by Miami Dolphins (April 8, 1999). ... Vikings declined to match offer (April 9, 1999). ... Released by Dolphins (March 14, 2001). ... Re-signed by Dolphins (March 16, 2001). ... Released by Dolphins (February 21, 2002). ... Signed by Vikings (April 23, 2002). ... Granted unconditional free agency (February 28, 2003). ... Re-signed by Vikings (April 2, 2003).
CHAMPIONSHIP GAME EXPERIENCE: Played in NFC championship game (1998 season).
SINGLE GAME HIGHS (regular season): Receptions—3 (December 27, 1999, vs. New York Jets); yards—24 (December 1, 1996, vs. Arizona); and touchdown receptions—1 (December 1, 2002, vs. Atlanta).

			RECEIVING					TOTALS		
Year Team	G	GS	No.	Yds.	Avg.	TD	TD	2pt.	Pts.	Fum.
1996—Minnesota NFL	9	6	1	24	24.0	0	0	0	0	0
1997—Minnesota NFL	16	5	7	61	8.7	0	0	0	0	0
1998—Minnesota NFL	15	0	3	16	5.3	0	0	0	0	0
1999—Miami NFL	15	5	8	55	6.9	0	0	0	0	1
2000—Miami NFL	16	16	6	36	6.0	1	1	0	6	0
2001—Miami NFL	16	11	4	27	6.8	0	0	0	0	0
2002—Minnesota NFL	16	6	4	20	5.0	1	1	0	6	0
Pro totals (7 years)	103	49	33	239	7.2	2	2	0	12	1

GOODWIN, JONATHAN   OL   JETS

PERSONAL: Born December 2, 1978, in Columbia, S.C. ... 6-3/318. ... Full name: Jonathan Scott Goodwin.
HIGH SCHOOL: Lower Richland (S.C.).
COLLEGE: Ohio, then Michigan.
TRANSACTIONS/CAREER NOTES: Selected by New York Jets in fifth round (154th pick overall) of 2002 NFL draft. ... Signed by Jets (July 24, 2002).
PLAYING EXPERIENCE: New York Jets NFL, 2002. ... Games/games started: 2002 (12/0).
HONORS: Named guard on THE SPORTING NEWS college All-America third team (2001).

GORDON, DARRIEN   CB/PR

PERSONAL: Born November 14, 1970, in Shawnee, Okla. ... 5-11/190. ... Full name: Darrien Jamal Gordon.
HIGH SCHOOL: Shawnee (Okla.).
COLLEGE: Stanford.
TRANSACTIONS/CAREER NOTES: Selected by San Diego Chargers in first round (22nd pick overall) of 1993 NFL draft. ... Signed by Chargers (July 16, 1993). ... Inactive for all 16 games due to shoulder injury (1995 season). ... Granted unconditional free agency (February 14, 1997). ... Signed by Denver Broncos (April 30, 1997). ... Granted unconditional free agency (February 12, 1999). ... Signed by Oakland Raiders (June 9, 1999). ... Released by Raiders (February 10, 2000). ... Re-signed by Raiders (February 28, 2000). ... Released by Raiders (March 1, 2001). ... Signed by Atlanta Falcons (August 15, 2001). ... Granted unconditional free agency (March 1, 2002). ... Signed by Green Bay Packers (July 17, 2002). ... Released by Packers (December 11, 2002). ... Signed by Raiders (December 13, 2002). ... Granted unconditional free agency (February 28, 2003).
CHAMPIONSHIP GAME EXPERIENCE: Played in AFC championship game (1994, 1997, 1998 and 2000 seasons). ... Played in Super Bowl XXIX (1994 season). ... Member of Super Bowl championship team (1997 and 1998 seasons). ... Member of Raiders for AFC championship game (2002 season); inactive. ... Played in Super Bowl XXXVII (2002 season).
HONORS: Named punt returner on THE SPORTING NEWS NFL All-Pro team (1997).
RECORDS: Shares NFL single-game records for most touchdowns by punt return—2; and most touchdowns by combined kick return—2 (November 9, 1997, vs. Carolina).
POST SEASON RECORDS: Holds Super Bowl career and single-game records for most interception return yards—108 (January 31, 1999, vs. Atlanta).

			TOTALS			INTERCEPTIONS				PUNT RETURNS				TOTALS		
Year Team	G	GS	Tk.	Ast.	Sks.	No.	Yds.	Avg.	TD	No.	Yds.	Avg.	TD	TD	2pt.	Pts.	Fum.
1993—San Diego NFL	16	7	40	1	0.0	1	3	3.0	0	31	395	12.7	0	0	0	0	4
1994—San Diego NFL	16	16	75	14	0.0	4	32	8.0	0	36	475§13.2		†2	2	0	12	2
1995—San Diego NFL								Did not play.									
1996—San Diego NFL	16	6	44	6	2.0	2	55	27.5	0	36	537§14.9	▲1	1	0	6	3
1997—Denver NFL	16	16	51	11	2.0	4	64	16.0	1	40	543	13.6	†3	4	0	24	3
1998—Denver NFL	16	16	58	6	0.0	4	125	31.3	1	34	379	11.1	0	1	0	6	1
1999—Oakland NFL	16	2	28	4	1.0	3	44	14.7	0	42	397	9.5	0	0	0	0	3
2000—Oakland NFL	13	0	12	1	0.0	0	0	0.0	0	29	258	8.9	0	1	0	6	2
2001—Atlanta NFL	16	2	9	4	0.0	1	7	7.0	0	31	437‡14.1		0	0	0	0	4
2002—Green Bay NFL	13	0	4	1	0.0	0	0	0.0	0	35	180	5.1	0	0	0	0	5
Pro totals (9 years)	138	65	321	48	5.0	19	330	17.4	2	314	3601	11.5	6	9	0	54	27

G

GORDON, LAMAR   RB   RAMS

PERSONAL: Born January 7, 1980, in Milwaukee. ... 6-1/214.
HIGH SCHOOL: Cudahy (Milwaukee).
COLLEGE: North Dakota State.
TRANSACTIONS/CAREER NOTES: Selected by St. Louis Rams in third round (84th pick overall) of 2002 NFL draft. ... Signed by Rams (July 2, 2002).
SINGLE GAME HIGHS (regular season): Attempts—16 (November 18, 2002, vs. Chicago); yards—45 (November 18, 2002, vs. Chicago); and rushing touchdowns—1 (September 23, 2002, vs. Tampa Bay).

			RUSHING				RECEIVING				KICKOFF RETURNS				TOTALS		
Year Team	G	GS	Att.	Yds.	Avg.	TD	No.	Yds.	Avg.	TD	No.	Yds.	Avg.	TD	TD	2pt.	Pts. Fum.
2002—St. Louis NFL	13	5	65	228	3.5	1	30	278	9.3	2	6	104	17.3	0	3	0	18	4

GOWIN, TOBY   P   COWBOYS

PERSONAL: Born March 30, 1975, in Jacksonville, Texas. ... 5-10/167. ... Name pronounced GO-in.
HIGH SCHOOL: Jacksonville (Texas).
COLLEGE: North Texas (degree in kinesiology).
TRANSACTIONS/CAREER NOTES: Signed as non-drafted free agent by Dallas Cowboys (April 24, 1997). ... Granted free agency (February 11, 2000). ... Tendered offer sheet by New Orleans Saints (April 6, 2000). ... Cowboys declined to match offer (April 6, 2000). ... Granted unconditional free agency (February 28, 2003). ... Signed by Cowboys (March 3, 2003).

				PUNTING			
Year Team	G	No.	Yds.	Avg.	Net avg.	In. 20	Blk.
1997—Dallas NFL	16	86	3592	41.8	35.4	26	0
1998—Dallas NFL	16	77	3342	43.4	36.6	31	∞1
1999—Dallas NFL	16	81	3500	43.2	35.1	24	0
2000—New Orleans NFL	16	74	3043	41.1	32.3	22	0
2001—New Orleans NFL	16	76	3180	41.8	35.8	24	0
2002—New Orleans NFL	15	61	2553	41.9	36.9	15	0
Pro totals (6 years)	95	455	19210	42.2	35.3	142	1

GRACE, STEVE   C   CARDINALS

PERSONAL: Born February 13, 1979, in Honolulu, Hawaii. ... 6-3/296. ... Full name: Steven Kanoeau Grace.
HIGH SCHOOL: Kamehameha (Honolulu, Hawaii).
COLLEGE: Arizona.
TRANSACTIONS/CAREER NOTES: Signed as non-drafted free agent by Arizona Cardinals (April 22, 2002). ... Released by Cardinals (September 9, 2002). ... Re-signed by Cardinals to practice squad (September 11, 2002). ... Activated (December 4, 2002). ... Re-signed by Cardinals (March 5, 2003).
PLAYING EXPERIENCE: Arizona NFL, 2002. ... Games/games started: 2002 (1/0).

GRAGG, SCOTT   OT   49ERS

PERSONAL: Born February 28, 1972, in Silverton, Ore. ... 6-8/315.
HIGH SCHOOL: Silverton (Ore.) Union.
COLLEGE: Montana.
TRANSACTIONS/CAREER NOTES: Selected by New York Giants in second round (54th pick overall) of 1995 NFL draft. ... Signed by Giants (July 23, 1995). ... Granted free agency (February 13, 1998). ... Re-signed by Giants (September 4, 1998). ... Released by Giants (March 28, 2000). ... Signed by San Francisco 49ers (July 19, 2000). ... Granted unconditional free agency (March 2, 2001). ... Re-signed by 49ers (April 5, 2001).
PLAYING EXPERIENCE: New York Giants NFL, 1995-1999; San Francisco NFL, 2000-2002. ... Games/Games started: 1995 (13/0), 1996 (16/16), 1997 (16/16), 1998 (16/16), 1999 (16/16), 2000 (16/16), 2001 (16/16), 2002 (16/16). Total: 125/112.

GRAHAM, AARON   C/OG

PERSONAL: Born May 22, 1973, in Las Vegas, N.M. ... 6-4/301.
HIGH SCHOOL: Denton (Texas).
COLLEGE: Nebraska.
TRANSACTIONS/CAREER NOTES: Selected by Arizona Cardinals in fourth round (112th pick overall) of 1996 NFL draft. ... Signed by Cardinals for 1996 season. ... Granted free agency (February 12, 1999). ... Re-signed by Cardinals (May 21, 1999). ... Granted unconditional free agency (February 11, 2000). ... Signed by Kansas City Chiefs (April 13, 2000) ... Released by Chiefs (August 22, 2000). ... Signed by Oakland Raiders (August 7, 2001). ... Released by Raiders (September 2, 2001). ... Re-signed by Raiders (September 26, 2001). ... Granted unconditional free agency (March 1, 2002). ... Signed by Tennessee Titans (June 3, 2002). ... Granted unconditional free agency (February 28, 2003).
PLAYING EXPERIENCE: Arizona NFL, 1996-1999; Oakland NFL, 2001; Tennessee NFL, 2002. ... Games/Games started: 1996 (16/7), 1997 (16/4), 1998 (14/13), 1999 (16/16), 2001 (14/0), 2002 (16/0). Total: 92/40.
CHAMPIONSHIP GAME EXPERIENCE: Played in AFC championship game (2002 season).

GRAHAM, DANIEL   TE   PATRIOTS

PERSONAL: Born November 16, 1978, in Torrance, Calif. ... 6-3/253.
HIGH SCHOOL: Thomas Jefferson (Denver).
COLLEGE: Colorado.

G

TRANSACTIONS/CAREER NOTES: Selected by New England Patriots in first round (21st pick overall) of 2002 NFL draft. ... Signed by Patriots (July 21, 2002). ... On injured reserve with rib injury (December 24, 2002-remainder of season).
HONORS: Named tight end on THE SPORTING NEWS college All-America first team (2001).
SINGLE GAME HIGHS (regular season): Receptions—3 (November 3, 2002, vs. Buffalo); yards—68 (November 3, 2002, vs. Buffalo); and touchdown receptions—1 (September 22, 2002, vs. Kansas City).

			RECEIVING		
Year Team	G	GS	No.	Yds.	Avg.	TD
2002—New England NFL	12	6	15	150	10.0	1

GRAHAM, DEMINGO   G   49ERS

PERSONAL: Born September 10, 1973, in Newark, N.J. ... 6-3/310.
HIGH SCHOOL: Newark (N.J.) Central.
COLLEGE: Hofstra.
TRANSACTIONS/CAREER NOTES: Signed as non-drafted free agent by San Diego Chargers (April 20, 1998). ... Inactive for all 16 games (1998). ... Granted free agency (March 2, 2001). ... Re-signed by Chargers (April 19, 2001). ... Granted unconditional free agency (March 1, 2002). ... Signed by Houston Texans (April 9, 2002). ... On suspended list for violating league substance abusy policy (December 18, 2002-remainder of season). ... Granted unconditional free agency (February 28, 2003). ... Signed by San Francisco 49ers (June 1, 2003).
PLAYING EXPERIENCE: San Diego NFL, 1999-2001; Houston NFL, 2002. ... Games/Games started: 1999 (16/10), 2000 (13/1), 2001 (16/16), 2002 (14/11). Total: 59/38.

GRAHAM, JAY   RB

PERSONAL: Born July 14, 1975, in Concord, N.C. ... 6-0/225. ... Full name: Herman Jason Graham.
HIGH SCHOOL: Concord (N.C.).
COLLEGE: Tennessee.
TRANSACTIONS/CAREER NOTES: Selected by Baltimore Ravens in third round (64th pick overall) of 1997 NFL draft. ... Signed by Ravens (June 19, 1997). ... On injured reserve with knee injury (December 10, 1998-remainder of season). ... Granted free agency (February 11, 2000). ... Re-signed by Ravens (August 22, 2000). ... Released by Ravens (August 27, 2000). ... Signed by Seattle Seahawks (April 27, 2001). ... Released by Seahawks (September 2, 2001). ... Re-signed by Seahawks (October 2, 2001). ... Released by Seahawks (September 1, 2002). ... Signed by Green Bay Packers (November 21, 2002). ... Released by Packers (December 10, 2002).
SINGLE GAME HIGHS (regular season): Attempts—35 (November 16, 1997, vs. Philadelphia); yards—154 (November 16, 1997, vs. Philadelphia); and rushing touchdowns—1 (September 14, 1997, vs. New York Giants).
STATISTICAL PLATEAUS: 100-yard rushing games: 1997 (1).

			RUSHING				RECEIVING				TOTALS			
Year Team	G	GS	Att.	Yds.	Avg.	TD	No.	Yds.	Avg.	TD	TD	2pt.	Pts.	Fum.
1997—Baltimore NFL	13	3	81	299	3.7	2	12	51	4.3	0	2	0	12	2
1998—Baltimore NFL	5	1	35	109	3.1	0	5	41	8.2	0	0	0	0	0
1999—Baltimore NFL	4	0	0	0	0.0	0	0	0	0.0	0	0	0	0	0
2000—							Did not play.							
2001—Seattle NFL	11	0	12	43	3.6	0	1	6	6.0	0	0	0	0	0
2002—Green Bay NFL	3	0	1	3	3.0	0	2	6	3.0	0	0	0	0	0
Pro totals (5 years)	36	4	129	454	3.5	2	20	104	5.2	0	2	0	12	2

GRAHAM, SHAYNE   K   PANTHERS

PERSONAL: Born December 9, 1977, in Radford, Va. ... 6-0/192. ... Full name: Michael Shayne Graham.
HIGH SCHOOL: Pulaski County (Va.).
COLLEGE: Virginia Tech.
TRANSACTIONS/CAREER NOTES: Signed as non-drafted free agent by New Orleans Saints (June 30, 2000). ... Released by Saints (August 22, 2000). ... Signed by Seattle Seahawks (April 27, 2001). ... Released by Seahawks (September 2, 2001). ... Signed by Buffalo Bills (November 27, 2001). ... Released by Bills (April 24, 2002). ... Signed by Seattle Seahawks (May 13, 2002). ... Released by Seahawks (August 13, 2002). ... Signed by Carolina Panthers (September 28, 2002).

		FIELD GOALS							TOTALS		
Year Team	G	1-29	30-39	40-49	50+	Tot.	Pct.	Lg.	XPM	XPA	Pts.
2001—Buffalo NFL	6	4-4	0-0	2-4	0-0	6-8	75.0	41	7	7	25
2002—Carolina NFL	11	3-5	2-3	6-8	2-2	13-18	72.2	50	21	21	60
Pro totals (2 years)	17	7-9	2-3	8-12	2-2	19-26	73.1	50	28	28	85

GRAMATICA, BILL   K   CARDINALS

PERSONAL: Born July 10, 1978, in Buenos Aires, Argentina. ... 5-10/187. ... Full name: Guillermo Gramatica. ... Brother of Martin Gramatica, kicker, Tampa Bay Buccaneers.
HIGH SCHOOL: LaBelle (Fla.).
COLLEGE: Florida State, then South Florida.
TRANSACTIONS/CAREER NOTES: Selected by Arizona Cardinals in fourth round (98th pick overall) of 2001 NFL draft. ... Signed by Cardinals (June 4, 2001). ... On injured reserve with knee injury (December 18, 2001-remainder of season).

		FIELD GOALS							TOTALS		
Year Team	G	1-29	30-39	40-49	50+	Tot.	Pct.	Lg.	XPM	XPA	Pts.
2001—Arizona NFL	13	8-8	3-4	4-7	1-1	16-20	80.0	50	25	25	73
2002—Arizona NFL	16	6-7	2-2	6-8	1-4	15-21	71.4	50	29	29	74
Pro totals (2 years)	29	14-15	5-6	10-15	2-5	31-41	75.6	50	54	54	147

G

GRAMATICA, MARTIN   K   BUCCANEERS

PERSONAL: Born November 27, 1975, in Buenos Aires, Argentina. ... 5-8/170. ... Brother of Bill Gramatica, kicker, Arizona Cardinals. ... Name pronounced mar-TEEN gruh-MAT-ee-ka.
HIGH SCHOOL: La Belle (Fla.).
COLLEGE: Kansas State.
TRANSACTIONS/CAREER NOTES: Selected by Tampa Bay Buccaneers in third round (80th pick overall) of 1999 NFL draft. ... Signed by Buccaneers (July 29, 1999).
CHAMPIONSHIP GAME EXPERIENCE: Played in NFC championship game (1999 and 2002 seasons). ... Member of Super Bowl championship team (2002 season).
HONORS: Named kicker on THE SPORTING NEWS college All-America first team (1997). ... Named kicker on THE SPORTING NEWS college All-America second team (1998). ... Won Lou Groza Award (1997). ... Played in Pro Bowl (2000 season).

		FIELD GOALS							TOTALS		
Year Team	G	1-29	30-39	40-49	50+	Tot.	Pct.	Lg.	XPM	XPA	Pts.
1999—Tampa Bay NFL	16	8-8	10-12	6-8	3-4	‡27-∞32	84.4	∞53	25	25	106
2000—Tampa Bay NFL	16	8-8	8-10	7-9	5-7	28-34	82.4	*55	42	42	126
2001—Tampa Bay NFL	14	9-10	9-9	5-7	0-3	23-29	79.3	49	28	28	97
2002—Tampa Bay NFL	16	7-8	14-15	6-10	5-6	†32-39	82.1	∞53	32	32	128
Pro totals (4 years)	62	32-34	41-46	24-34	13-20	110-134	82.1	55	127	127	457

GRANT, CHARLES   DE   SAINTS

PERSONAL: Born September 3, 1978, in Colquitt, Ga. ... 6-3/282.
HIGH SCHOOL: Miller County (Colquitt, Ga.).
COLLEGE: Georgia.
TRANSACTIONS/CAREER NOTES: Selected by New Orleans Saints in first round (25th pick overall) of 2002 NFL draft. ... Signed by Saints (July 27, 2002).

			TOTALS		
Year Team	G	GS	Tk.	Ast.	Sks.
2002—New Orleans NFL	16	6	30	7	7.0

GRANT, DELAWRENCE   DE   RAIDERS

PERSONAL: Born November 18, 1979, in Compton, Calif. ... 6-3/280. ... Full name: DeLawrence Grant Jr..
HIGH SCHOOL: Centennial (Compton, Calif.).
JUNIOR COLLEGE: El Camino College (Calif.).
COLLEGE: Oregon State.
TRANSACTIONS/CAREER NOTES: Selected by Oakland Raiders in third round (89th pick overall) of 2001 NFL draft. ... Signed by Raiders (July 22, 2001).
CHAMPIONSHIP GAME EXPERIENCE: Played in AFC championship game (2002 season). ... Played in Super Bowl XXXVII (2002 season).
HONORS: Named defensive end on THE SPORTING NEWS college All-America second team (2000).

			TOTALS		
Year Team	G	GS	Tk.	Ast.	Sks.
2001—Oakland NFL	2	0	0	0	0.0
2002—Oakland NFL	16	14	21	5	3.0
Pro totals (2 years)	18	14	21	5	3.0

GRANT, DEON   S   PANTHERS

PERSONAL: Born March 14, 1979, in Augusta, Ga. ... 6-2/207.
HIGH SCHOOL: Josey (Augusta, Ga.).
COLLEGE: Tennessee.
TRANSACTIONS/CAREER NOTES: Selected after junior season by Carolina Panthers in second round (57th pick overall) of 2000 NFL draft. ... Signed by Panthers (July 13, 2000). ... On injured reserve with hip injury (August 20, 2000-entire season).
HONORS: Named free safety on THE SPORTING NEWS college All-America first team (1999).

			TOTALS			INTERCEPTIONS			
Year Team	G	GS	Tk.	Ast.	Sks.	No.	Yds.	Avg.	TD
2000—Carolina NFL			Did not play.						
2001—Carolina NFL	16	16	59	12	1.0	5	96	19.2	0
2002—Carolina NFL	16	16	54	14	0.0	3	16	5.3	0
Pro totals (2 years)	32	32	113	26	1.0	8	112	14.0	0

GRANT, ERNEST   DT   BEARS

PERSONAL: Born May 17, 1976, in Atlanta. ... 6-5/312. ... Full name: Ernest Jouoa Grant.
HIGH SCHOOL: Forest (Atlanta).
COLLEGE: Arkansas-Pine Bluff.
TRANSACTIONS/CAREER NOTES: Selected by Miami Dolphins in sixth round (167th pick overall) of 2000 NFL draft. ... Signed by Dolphins (July 17, 2000). ... Released by Dolphins (September 1, 2002). ... Signed by Chicago Bears (September 24, 2002). ... Released by Bears (September 27, 2002). ... Re-signed by Bears (October 1, 2002).

Year	Team	G	GS	TOTALS Tk.	Ast.	Sks.
2000—Miami NFL		2	0	1	0	0.0
2001—Miami NFL		11	3	13	7	0.5
2002—Chicago NFL		11	0	5	4	0.0
Pro totals (3 years)		24	3	19	11	0.5

GRANT, ORANTES — LB — REDSKINS

PERSONAL: Born March 18, 1978, in Atlanta. ... 6-0/236. ... Full name: Orantes Laquay Grant.
HIGH SCHOOL: Dunwoody (Atlanta).
COLLEGE: Georgia.
TRANSACTIONS/CAREER NOTES: Selected by Dallas Cowboys in seventh round (219th pick overall) of 2000 NFL draft. ... Signed by Cowboys (July 17, 2000). ... Released by Cowboys (September 1, 2002). ... Signed by Washington Redskins (December 4, 2002).

Year	Team	G	GS	TOTALS Tk.	Ast.	Sks.	INTERCEPTIONS No.	Yds.	Avg.	TD
2000—Dallas NFL		13	0	3	0	0.0	0	0	0.0	0
2001—Dallas NFL		10	1	8	3	0.0	0	0	0.0	0
2002—Washington NFL		1	0	0	0	0.0	0	0	0.0	0
Pro totals (3 years)		24	1	11	3	0.0	0	0	0.0	0

GRASMANIS, PAUL — DT — EAGLES

PERSONAL: Born August 2, 1974, in Grand Rapids, Mich. ... 6-3/298. ... Full name: Paul Ryan Grasmanis.
HIGH SCHOOL: Jenison (Mich.).
COLLEGE: Notre Dame.
TRANSACTIONS/CAREER NOTES: Selected by Chicago Bears in fourth round (116th pick overall) of 1996 NFL draft. ... Signed by Bears (June 13, 1996). ... Granted free agency (February 12, 1999). ... Re-signed by Bears (April 13, 1999). ... Released by Bears (September 5, 1999). ... Signed by St. Louis Rams (September 7, 1999). ... Inactive for one game with Rams (1999). ... Released by Rams (September 13, 1999). ... Signed by Denver Broncos (November 1, 1999). ... Granted unconditional free agency (February 11, 2000). ... Signed by Philadelphia Eagles (March 3, 2000). ... Granted unconditional free agency (March 2, 2001). ... Re-signed by Eagles (April 24, 2001).
CHAMPIONSHIP GAME EXPERIENCE: Played in NFC championship game (2001 and 2002 seasons).

Year	Team	G	GS	TOTALS Tk.	Ast.	Sks.
1996—Chicago NFL		14	3	8	3	0.0
1997—Chicago NFL		16	0	9	5	0.5
1998—Chicago NFL		15	0	15	2	1.0
1999—Denver NFL		5	0	5	2	0.0
2000—Philadelphia NFL		16	0	30	5	3.5
2001—Philadelphia NFL		14	2	14	5	2.0
2002—Philadelphia NFL		16	3	20	11	4.0
Pro totals (7 years)		96	8	101	33	11.0

GRAU, JEFF — TE — COWBOYS

PERSONAL: Born December 16, 1979, in Inglewood, Calif. ... 6-3/257. ... Full name: Jeffrey Alan Grau.
HIGH SCHOOL: Loyola (Torrance, Calif.).
COLLEGE: UCLA.
TRANSACTIONS/CAREER NOTES: Selected by Washington Redskins in seventh round (230th pick overall) of 2002 NFL draft. ... Signed by Redskins (July 22, 2002). ... Claimed on waivers by Dallas Cowboys (August 28, 2002).

Year	Team	G	GS	RECEIVING No.	Yds.	Avg.	TD
2002—Dallas NFL		16	0	0	0	0.0	0

GRAY, BOBBY — S — BEARS

PERSONAL: Born April 30, 1978, in Houston. ... 6-0/205. ... Full name: Bobby Wayne Gray.
HIGH SCHOOL: Aldine (Texas).
COLLEGE: Louisiana Tech.
TRANSACTIONS/CAREER NOTES: Selected by Chicago Bears in fifth round (140th pick overall) of 2002 NFL draft. ... Signed by Bears (July 19, 2002). ... On injured reserve with wrist injury (September 23, 2002-remainder of season).

Year	Team	G	GS	TOTALS Tk.	Ast.	Sks.	INTERCEPTIONS No.	Yds.	Avg.	TD
2002—Chicago NFL		3	0	4	1	0.0	0	0	0.0	0

GRAY, CHRIS — G/OC — SEAHAWKS

PERSONAL: Born June 19, 1970, in Birmingham, Ala. ... 6-4/308. ... Full name: Christopher William Gray.
HIGH SCHOOL: Homewood (Ala.).
COLLEGE: Auburn (degree in marketing, 1992).
TRANSACTIONS/CAREER NOTES: Selected by Miami Dolphins in fifth round (132nd pick overall) of 1993 NFL draft. ... Signed by Dolphins (July 12, 1993). ... On injured reserve with ankle injury (November 15, 1995-remainder of season). ... On injured reserve with broken leg (November 19, 1996-remainder of season). ... Released by Dolphins (August 12, 1997). ... Signed by Chicago Bears (September 9, 1997). ... Granted unconditional free agency (February 13, 1998). ... Signed by Seattle Seahawks (February 20, 1998).
PLAYING EXPERIENCE: Miami NFL, 1993-1996; Chicago NFL, 1997; Seattle NFL, 1998-2002. ... Games/Games started: 1993 (5/0), 1994 (16/2), 1995 (10/10), 1996 (11/11), 1997 (8/2), 1998 (15/8), 1999 (16/10), 2000 (16/16), 2001 (16/16), 2002 (16/16). Total: 129/91.

G

GREEN, AHMAN   RB   PACKERS

PERSONAL: Born February 16, 1977, in Omaha, Neb. ... 6-0/217.

HIGH SCHOOL: North (Omaha, Neb.), then Central Christian (Omaha, Neb.).

COLLEGE: Nebraska.

TRANSACTIONS/CAREER NOTES: Selected after junior season by Seattle Seahawks in third round (76th pick overall) of 1998 NFL draft. ... Signed by Seahawks (July 18, 1998). ... Traded by Seahawks with fifth-round pick (WR/KR Joey Jamison) in 2000 draft to Green Bay Packers for CB Fred Vinson and sixth-round pick (DT Tim Watson) in 2000 draft (April 14, 2000). ... Granted free agency (March 2, 2001). ... Re-signed by Packers (July 24, 2001).

HONORS: Named running back on THE SPORTING NEWS college All-America second team (1997). ... Played in Pro Bowl (2001 season). ... Named to play in Pro Bowl (2002 season); replaced by Michael Bennett due to injury.

SINGLE GAME HIGHS (regular season): Attempts—31 (October 13, 2002, vs. New England); yards—169 (November 4, 2001, vs. Tampa Bay); and rushing touchdowns—3 (October 20, 2002, vs. Washington).

STATISTICAL PLATEAUS: 100-yard rushing games: 1998 (1), 2000 (3), 2001 (7), 2002 (4). Total: 15.

			RUSHING				RECEIVING				KICKOFF RETURNS				TOTALS			
Year Team	G	GS	Att.	Yds.	Avg.	TD	No.	Yds.	Avg.	TD	No.	Yds.	Avg.	TD	TD	2pt.	Pts.	Fum.
1998—Seattle NFL	16	0	35	209	6.0	1	3	2	0.7	0	27	620	23.0	0	1	0	6	1
1999—Seattle NFL	14	0	26	120	4.6	0	0	0	0.0	0	36	818	22.7	0	0	0	0	2
2000—Green Bay NFL	16	11	263	1175	4.5	10	73	559	7.7	3	0	0	0.0	0	13	0	78	6
2001—Green Bay NFL	16	16	304	1387	4.6	9	62	594	9.6	2	0	0	0.0	0	11	0	66	5
2002—Green Bay NFL	14	14	286	1240	4.3	7	57	393	6.9	2	0	0	0.0	0	9	0	54	4
Pro totals (5 years)	76	41	914	4131	4.5	27	195	1548	7.9	7	63	1438	22.8	0	34	0	204	18

GREEN, BARRETT   LB   LIONS

PERSONAL: Born October 29, 1977, in West Palm Beach, Fla. ... 6-0/225. ... Son of Joe Green, defensive back with New York Giants (1970 and 1971).

HIGH SCHOOL: Suncoast (West Palm Beach, Fla.).

COLLEGE: West Virginia.

TRANSACTIONS/CAREER NOTES: Selected by Detroit Lions in second round (50th pick overall) of 2000 NFL draft. ... Signed by Lions (July 15, 2000).

			TOTALS			INTERCEPTIONS			
Year Team	G	GS	Tk.	Ast.	Sks.	No.	Yds.	Avg.	TD
2000—Detroit NFL	9	0	0	0	0.0	0	0	0.0	0
2001—Detroit NFL	14	10	51	24	1.0	0	0	0.0	0
2002—Detroit NFL	15	14	50	23	1.0	0	0	0.0	0
Pro totals (3 years)	38	24	101	47	2.0	0	0	0.0	0

GREEN, CORNELL   OT   BUCCANEERS

PERSONAL: Born August 25, 1976, in St. Petersburg, Fla. ... 6-6/315.

HIGH SCHOOL: Lakewood (St. Petersburg, Fla.).

COLLEGE: Central Florida.

TRANSACTIONS/CAREER NOTES: Signed as non-drafted free agent by Atlanta Falcons (May 18, 1999). ... Released by Falcons (August 30, 1999). ... Signed by Washington Redskins (July 14, 2000). ... Claimed on waivers by New York Jets (August 29, 2000). ... Released by Jets (September 6, 2000). ... Re-signed by Jets to practice squad (September 7, 2000). ... Activated (November 17, 2000); did not play. ... Released by Jets (December 3, 2001). ... Signed by Miami Dolphins to practice squad (December 11, 2001). ... Traded by Dolphins to Tampa Bay Buccaneers for seventh-round pick (traded to Carolina) in 2003 draft (August 20, 2002).

PLAYING EXPERIENCE: Tampa Bay NFL, 2002. ... Games/games started: 2002 (16/3).

CHAMPIONSHIP GAME EXPERIENCE: Played in NFC championship game (2002 season). ... Member of Super Bowl championship team (2002 season).

GREEN, DARRELL   CB   REDSKINS

PERSONAL: Born February 15, 1960, in Houston. ... 5-9/184.

HIGH SCHOOL: Jesse H. Jones Senior (Houston).

COLLEGE: Texas A&I.

TRANSACTIONS/CAREER NOTES: Selected by Denver Gold in 10th round (112th pick overall) of 1983 USFL draft. ... Selected by Washington Redskins in first round (28th pick overall) of 1983 NFL draft. ... Signed by Redskins (June 10, 1983). ... On injured reserve with broken hand (December 13, 1988-remainder of season). ... On injured reserve with broken bone in wrist (October 24, 1989-remainder of season). ... Granted free agency (February 1, 1992). ... Re-signed by Redskins (August 25, 1992). ... On injured reserve with broken forearm (September 16-November 23, 1992). ... Granted unconditional free agency (February 17, 1995). ... Re-signed by Redskins (March 10, 1995). ... Granted unconditional free agency (February 14, 1997). ... Re-signed by Redskins (April 25, 1997).

CHAMPIONSHIP GAME EXPERIENCE: Played in NFC championship game (1983, 1986, 1987 and 1991 seasons). ... Played in Super Bowl XVIII (1983 season). ... Member of Super Bowl championship team (1987 and 1991 seasons).

HONORS: Played in Pro Bowl (1984, 1986, 1987, 1990, 1991, 1996 and 1997 seasons). ... Named cornerback on THE SPORTING NEWS NFL All-Pro team (1991).

RECORDS: Shares NFL career record for most seasons with one club—20 (Washington Redskins, 1983-2002).

POST SEASON RECORDS: Shares NFL postseason career record for most touchdowns by punt return—1 (January 10, 1988, at Chicago).

MISCELLANEOUS: Holds Washington Redskins all-time record for most interceptions (54).

G

Year Team	G	GS	TOTALS Tk.	Ast.	Sks.	INTERCEPTIONS No.	Yds.	Avg.	TD	PUNT RETURNS No.	Yds.	Avg.	TD	TOTALS TD	2pt.	Pts.	Fum.
1983—Washington NFL	16	16	79	30	0.0	2	7	3.5	0	4	29	7.3	0	0	0	0	1
1984—Washington NFL	16	16	69	19	0.0	5	91	18.2	1	2	13	6.5	0	1	0	6	0
1985—Washington NFL	16	16	60	24	0.0	2	0	0.0	0	16	214	13.4	0	0	0	0	2
1986—Washington NFL	16	15	58	12	0.0	5	9	1.8	0	12	120	10.0	0	0	0	0	1
1987—Washington NFL	12	12	38	10	0.0	3	65	21.7	0	5	53	10.6	0	1	0	6	0
1988—Washington NFL	15	15	50	13	1.0	1	12	12.0	0	9	103	11.4	0	0	0	0	1
1989—Washington NFL	7	7	21	8	0.0	2	0	0.0	0	1	11	11.0	0	0	0	0	1
1990—Washington NFL	16	16	56	22	0.0	4	20	5.0	1	1	6	6.0	0	1	0	6	0
1991—Washington NFL	16	16	64	15	0.0	5	47	9.4	0	0	0	0.0	0	0	0	0	0
1992—Washington NFL	8	7	25	10	0.0	1	15	15.0	0	0	0	0.0	0	0	0	0	0
1993—Washington NFL	16	16	71	18	0.0	4	10	2.5	0	1	27	27.0	0	1	0	6	0
1994—Washington NFL	16	16	52	3	0.0	3	32	10.7	1	0	0	0.0	0	1	0	6	0
1995—Washington NFL	16	16	48	5	0.0	3	42	14.0	0	0	0	0.0	0	1	0	6	0
1996—Washington NFL	16	16	57	5	0.0	3	84	28.0	1	0	0	0.0	0	1	0	6	0
1997—Washington NFL	16	16	41	13	0.0	1	83	83.0	1	0	0	0.0	0	1	0	6	0
1998—Washington NFL	16	16	64	1	0.0	3	36	12.0	0	0	0	0.0	0	0	0	0	0
1999—Washington NFL	16	16	52	4	0.0	3	33	11.0	0	0	0	0.0	0	0	0	0	0
2000—Washington NFL	13	2	22	1	0.0	3	35	11.7	0	0	0	0.0	0	0	0	0	0
2001—Washington NFL	16	4	32	4	0.0	1	0	0.0	0	0	0	0.0	0	0	0	0	0
2002—Washington NFL	16	4	19	2	0.0	0	0	0.0	0	1	35	0.0	0	0	0	0	0
Pro totals (20 years)	295	258	978	219	1.0	54	621	11.5	6	51	611	12.0	0	8	0	48	6

GREEN, HOWARD — DT — TEXANS

PERSONAL: Born January 12, 1979, in Donaldsonville, La. ... 6-2/320. ... Full name: Howard Green Jr..
HIGH SCHOOL: Donaldsonville (La.).
JUNIOR COLLEGE: Southwest Mississippi College.
COLLEGE: Louisiana State.
TRANSACTIONS/CAREER NOTES: Selected by Houston Texans in sixth round (190th pick overall) of 2002 NFL draft. ... Signed by Texans (June 19, 2002). ... Claimed on waivers by Baltimore Ravens (September 3, 2002). ... Released by Ravens (October 29, 2002). ... Signed by Texans to practice squad (October 31, 2002). ... Activated (December 18, 2002). ... Re-signed by Texans (March 24, 2003).

Year Team	G	GS	TOTALS Tk.	Ast.	Sks.
2002—Baltimore NFL	1	0	0	0	0.0

GREEN, JACQUEZ — WR — BUCCANEERS

PERSONAL: Born January 15, 1976, in Fort Valley, Ga. ... 5-10/170. ... Full name: D'Tanyian Jacquez Green.
HIGH SCHOOL: Peach County (Fort Valley, Ga.).
COLLEGE: Florida.
TRANSACTIONS/CAREER NOTES: Selected after junior season by Tampa Bay Buccaneers in second round (34th pick overall) of 1998 NFL draft. ... Signed by Buccaneers (July 19, 1998). ... Granted unconditional free agency (March 1, 2002). ... Signed by Washington Redskins (March 8, 2002). ... Claimed on waivers by Detroit Lions (November 13, 2002). ... Released by Lions (April 2, 2003). ... Signed by Buccaneers (April 24, 2003).
CHAMPIONSHIP GAME EXPERIENCE: Played in NFC championship game (1999 season).
HONORS: Named wide receiver on THE SPORTING NEWS college All-America second team (1997).
SINGLE GAME HIGHS (regular season): Receptions—11 (October 9, 2000, vs. Minnesota); yards—164 (November 14, 1999, vs. Kansas City); and touchdown receptions—1 (October 14, 2001, vs. Tennessee).
STATISTICAL PLATEAUS: 100-yard receiving games: 1999 (2), 2000 (2). Total: 4.

Year Team	G	GS	RUSHING Att.	Yds.	Avg.	TD	RECEIVING No.	Yds.	Avg.	TD	PUNT RETURNS No.	Yds.	Avg.	TD	KICKOFF RETURNS No.	Yds.	Avg.	TD	TOTALS TD	2pt.	Pts.
1998—Tampa Bay NFL	12	1	3	12	4.0	0	14	251	17.9	2	30	453	15.1	1	10	229	22.9	0	3	0	18
1999—Tampa Bay NFL	16	10	3	8	2.7	0	56	791	14.1	3	23	204	8.9	0	10	185	18.5	0	3	0	18
2000—Tampa Bay NFL	16	16	5	13	2.6	0	51	773	15.2	1	2	1	0.5	0	1	11	11.0	0	1	0	6
2001—Tampa Bay NFL	12	10	0	0	0.0	0	36	402	11.2	1	0	0	0.0	0	0	0	0.0	0	1	0	6
2002—Detroit NFL	1	0	0	0	0.0	0	0	0	0.0	0	0	0	0.0	0	0	0	0.0	0	0	0	0
—Washington NFL	9	0	2	9	4.5	0	5	94	18.8	0	17	174	10.2	1	3	58	19.3	0	1	0	6
Pro totals (5 years)	66	37	13	42	3.2	0	162	2311	14.3	7	72	832	11.6	2	24	483	20.1	0	9	0	54

GREEN, JARVIS — DE — PATRIOTS

G

PERSONAL: Born January 12, 1979, in Thibodaux, La. ... 6-3/285. ... Full name: Jarvis Pernell Green.
HIGH SCHOOL: Donaldsville (La.).
COLLEGE: Louisiana State.
TRANSACTIONS/CAREER NOTES: Selected by New England Patriots in fourth round (126th pick overall) of 2002 NFL draft. ... Signed by Patriots (July 18, 2002).

Year Team	G	GS	TOTALS Tk.	Ast.	Sks.
2002—New England NFL	15	4	14	7	2.5

GREEN, MIKE — RB

PERSONAL: Born September 2, 1976, in Houston. ... 6-0/250. ... Full name: Mike Lewayne Green.
HIGH SCHOOL: Klein (Houston).
JUNIOR COLLEGE: Blinn College (Texas).
COLLEGE: Houston.

TRANSACTIONS/CAREER NOTES: Selected by Tennessee Titans in seventh round (213th pick overall) of 2000 NFL draft. ... Signed by Titans (July 10, 2000). ... Assigned by Titans to Barcelona Dragons in 2001 NFL Europe enhancement allocation program (February 19, 2001). ... Released by Titans (April 10, 2001). ... Re-signed by Titans (April 25, 2001). ... Granted free agency (February 28, 2003). ... Signed by Cincinnati Bengals (April 3, 2003). ... Released by Bengals (May 27, 2003).
CHAMPIONSHIP GAME EXPERIENCE: Played in AFC championship game (2002 season).
SINGLE GAME HIGHS (regular season): Attempts—5 (December 22, 2002, vs. Jacksonville); yards—27 (October 29, 2001, vs. Pittsburgh); and rushing touchdowns—1 (December 30, 2001, vs. Cleveland).

			RUSHING				RECEIVING				TOTALS			
Year Team	G	GS	Att.	Yds.	Avg.	TD	No.	Yds.	Avg.	TD	TD	2pt.	Pts.	Fum.
2000—Tennessee NFL............................	1	0	0	0	0.0	0	0	0	0.0	0	0	0	0	0
2001—Barcelona NFLE	...	...	183	1057	5.8	8	12	67	5.6	0	8	0	48	0
—Tennessee NFL	16	1	15	71	4.7	1	12	64	5.3	1	2	0	12	1
2002—Tennessee NFL............................	15	2	21	71	3.4	0	7	57	8.1	1	1	0	6	0
NFL Europe totals (1 year)	...	...	183	1057	5.8	8	12	67	5.6	0	8	0	48	0
NFL totals (3 years)	32	3	36	142	3.9	1	19	121	6.4	2	3	0	18	1
Pro totals (4 years)	...	...	219	1199	5.5	9	31	188	6.1	2	11	0	66	1

GREEN, MIKE   S   BEARS

PERSONAL: Born December 6, 1976, in Ruston, La. ... 6-0/195.
HIGH SCHOOL: Ruston (La.).
COLLEGE: Louisiana-Lafayette.
TRANSACTIONS/CAREER NOTES: Selected by Chicago Bears in seventh round (254th pick overall) of 2000 NFL draft. ... Signed by Bears (May 30, 2000).

			TOTALS			INTERCEPTIONS			
Year Team	G	GS	Tk.	Ast.	Sks.	No.	Yds.	Avg.	TD
2000—Chicago NFL............................	7	0	0	0	0.0	0	0	0.0	0
2001—Chicago NFL............................	16	2	53	4	3.0	0	0	0.0	0
2002—Chicago NFL............................	16	16	91	27	1.0	0	0	0.0	0
NFL totals (3 years)	39	18	144	31	4.0	0	0	0.0	0

GREEN, RAY   CB   GIANTS

PERSONAL: Born March 22, 1977, in Queens, New York. ... 6-3/190.
HIGH SCHOOL: Burke (Charleston, S.C.).
COLLEGE: South Carolina.
TRANSACTIONS/CAREER NOTES: Signed as non-drafted free agent by Carolina Panthers (April 17, 2000). ... Released by Panthers (September 1, 2001). ... Signed by Miami Dolphins (October 23, 2001). ... On injured reserve with elbow injury (November 5, 2002-remainder of season). ... Granted free agency (February 28, 2003). ... Signed by New York Giants (March 12, 2003).

			TOTALS			INTERCEPTIONS			
Year Team	G	GS	Tk.	Ast.	Sks.	No.	Yds.	Avg.	TD
2000—Carolina NFL	16	0	0	0	0.0	0	0	0.0	0
2001—Miami NFL	4	0	0	0	0.0	0	0	0.0	0
2002—Miami NFL	8	0	3	0	0.0	0	0	0.0	0
Pro totals (3 years)	28	0	3	0	0.0	0	0	0.0	0

GREEN, TRENT   QB   CHIEFS

PERSONAL: Born July 9, 1970, in Cedar Rapids, Iowa. ... 6-3/217. ... Full name: Trent Jason Green.
HIGH SCHOOL: Vianney (St. Louis).
COLLEGE: Indiana.
TRANSACTIONS/CAREER NOTES: Selected by San Diego Chargers in eighth round (222nd pick overall) of 1993 NFL draft. ... Signed by Chargers (July 15, 1993). ... Inactive for all 16 games (1993). ... Released by Chargers (August 22, 1994). ... Signed by Washington Redskins (April 5, 1995). ... Inactive for all 16 games (1995). ... Inactive for all 16 games (1996). ... Granted free agency (February 14, 1997). ... Re-signed by Redskins (June 6, 1997). ... Granted unconditional free agency (February 12, 1999). ... Signed by St. Louis Rams (February 16, 1999). ... On injured reserve with knee injury (August 30, 1999-entire season). ... Traded by Rams with fifth-round pick (RB Derrick Blaylock) in 2001 draft to Kansas City Chiefs for first-round pick (DT Damione Lewis) in 2001 draft (April 20, 2001).
RECORDS: Shares NFL record for longest pass completion (to Marc Boerigter)—99 yards, touchdown (December 22, 2002, vs. San Diego).
SINGLE GAME HIGHS (regular season): Attempts—54 (September 20, 1998, vs. Seattle); completions—30 (November 22, 1998, vs. Arizona); yards—431 (November 5, 2000, vs. Carolina); and touchdown passes—5 (September 29, 2002, vs. Miami).
STATISTICAL PLATEAUS: 300-yard passing games: 1998 (2), 2000 (3), 2001 (3), 2002 (4). Total: 12.
MISCELLANEOUS: Regular-season record as starting NFL quarterback: 22-29 (.431).

			PASSING									RUSHING				TOTALS		
Year Team	G	GS	Att.	Cmp.	Pct.	Yds.	TD	Int.	Avg.	Skd.	Rat.	Att.	Yds.	Avg.	TD	TD	2pt.	Pts.
1993—San Diego NFL............						Did not play.												
1994—						Did not play.												
1995—Washington NFL						Did not play.												
1996—Washington NFL						Did not play.												
1997—Washington NFL	1	0	1	0	0.0	0	0	0	0.0	0	39.6	0	0	0.0	0	0	0	0
1998—Washington NFL	15	14	509	278	54.6	3441	23	11	6.76	49	81.8	42	117	2.8	2	2	0	12
1999—St. Louis NFL..............						Did not play.												
2000—St. Louis NFL..............	8	5	240	145	60.4	2063	16	5	8.60	24	‡101.8	20	69	3.5	1	1	0	6
2001—Kansas City NFL..........	16	16	523	296	56.6	3783	17	*24	7.23	39	71.1	35	158	4.5	0	0	1	2
2002—Kansas City NFL..........	16	16	470	287	61.1	3690	26	13	*7.85	26	92.6	31	225	7.3	1	1	0	8
Pro totals (5 years)	56	51	1743	1006	57.7	12977	82	53	7.45	138	84.2	128	569	4.4	4	4	2	28

G

GREEN, VICTOR — S — PATRIOTS

PERSONAL: Born December 8, 1969, in Americus, Ga. ... 5-11/210. ... Full name: Victor Bernard Green. ... Cousin of Tommy Sims, defensive back with Indianapolis Colts (1986).
HIGH SCHOOL: Americus (Ga.).
JUNIOR COLLEGE: Copiah-Lincoln Junior College (Miss.).
COLLEGE: Akron (degree in criminal justice, 1993).
TRANSACTIONS/CAREER NOTES: Signed as non-drafted free agent by New York Jets (April 29, 1993). ... Released by Jets (August 30, 1993). ... Re-signed by Jets to practice squad (September 1, 1993). ... Activated (September 28, 1993). ... Released by Jets (February 28, 2002). ... Signed by New England Patriots (July 16, 2002). ... Granted free agency (February 28, 2003).
CHAMPIONSHIP GAME EXPERIENCE: Played in AFC championship game (1998 season).

				TOTALS			INTERCEPTIONS			
Year Team	G	GS	Tk.	Ast.	Sks.	No.	Yds.	Avg.	TD	
1993—New York Jets NFL	11	0	0	0	0.0	0	0	0.0	0	
1994—New York Jets NFL	16	0	16	1	1.0	0	0	0.0	0	
1995—New York Jets NFL	16	12	103	34	2.0	1	2	2.0	0	
1996—New York Jets NFL	16	16	123	42	2.0	2	27	13.5	0	
1997—New York Jets NFL	16	16	89	34	1.0	3	89	29.7	0	
1998—New York Jets NFL	16	16	69	24	1.0	4	99	24.8	0	
1999—New York Jets NFL	16	16	90	32	0.0	5	92	18.4	0	
2000—New York Jets NFL	16	16	64	41	0.0	6	144	24.0	1	
2001—New York Jets NFL	16	16	55	29	0.0	3	76	25.3	1	
2002—New England NFL	16	6	62	22	0.0	1	90	90.0	1	
Pro totals (10 years)	155	114	671	259	7.0	25	619	24.8	3	

GREEN, WILLIAM — RB — BROWNS

PERSONAL: Born December 17, 1979, in Atlantic City, N.J. ... 6-0/221.
HIGH SCHOOL: Holy Spirit (Atlantic City, N.J.).
COLLEGE: Boston College.
TRANSACTIONS/CAREER NOTES: Selected after junior season by Cleveland Browns in first round (16th pick overall) of 2002 NFL draft. ... Signed by Browns (July 27, 2002).
HONORS: Named running back on THE SPORTING NEWS college All-America first team (2001).
SINGLE GAME HIGHS (regular season): Attempts—28 (November 24, 2002, vs. New Orleans); yards—178 (December 29, 2002, vs. Atlanta); and rushing touchdowns—2 (December 29, 2002, vs. Atlanta).
STATISTICAL PLATEAUS: 100-yard rushing games: 2002 (3).

			RUSHING				RECEIVING				TOTALS			
Year Team	G	GS	Att.	Yds.	Avg.	TD	No.	Yds.	Avg.	TD	TD	2pt.	Pts.	Fum.
2002—Cleveland NFL	16	10	243	887	3.7	6	16	113	7.1	0	6	0	36	4

GREENWOOD, MORLON — LB — DOLPHINS

PERSONAL: Born July 17, 1978, in Jamaica, West Indies. ... 6-0/238. ... Full name: Morlon O'Neil Greenwood.
HIGH SCHOOL: Freeport (N.Y.).
COLLEGE: Syracuse.
TRANSACTIONS/CAREER NOTES: Selected by Miami Dolphins in third round (88th pick overall) of 2001 NFL draft. ... Signed by Dolphins (July 23, 2001).

			TOTALS			INTERCEPTIONS			
Year Team	G	GS	Tk.	Ast.	Sks.	No.	Yds.	Avg.	TD
2001—Miami NFL	14	12	30	28	1.5	0	0	0.0	0
2002—Miami NFL	16	14	33	18	1.0	0	0	0.0	0
Pro totals (2 years)	30	26	63	46	2.5	0	0	0.0	0

GREER, DONOVAN — DB

PERSONAL: Born September 11, 1974, in Houston. ... 5-9/178.
HIGH SCHOOL: Elsik (Alief, Texas).
COLLEGE: Texas A&M.
TRANSACTIONS/CAREER NOTES: Signed as non-drafted free agent by New Orleans Saints (April 25, 1997). ... Released by Saints (August 24, 1997). ... Signed by Atlanta Falcons (August 26, 1997). ... Released by Falcons (September 3, 1997). ... Signed by Saints to practice squad (September 4, 1997). ... Activated (November 15, 1997). ... Released by Saints (August 24, 1998). ... Signed by Buffalo Bills to practice squad (September 9, 1998). ... Activated (September 30, 1998). ... Granted free agency (February 11, 2000). ... Re-signed by Bills (April 14, 2000). ... Granted unconditional free agency (March 2, 2001). ... Signed by Washington Redskins (April 20, 2001). ... On injured reserve with knee injury (September 26, 2001-remainder of season). ... Released by Redskins (June 21, 2002). ... Signed by Detroit Lions (November 26, 2002). ... Granted unconditional free agency (February 28, 2003).

			TOTALS			INTERCEPTIONS			
Year Team	G	GS	Tk.	Ast.	Sks.	No.	Yds.	Avg.	TD
1997—Atlanta NFL	1	0	0	0	0.0	0	0	0.0	0
—New Orleans NFL	6	1	1	0	0.0	0	0	0.0	0
1998—Buffalo NFL	11	2	14	4	0.0	0	0	0.0	0
1999—Buffalo NFL	16	0	3	3	0.0	1	0	0.0	0
2000—Buffalo NFL	13	1	11	6	0.0	0	0	0.0	0
2001—Washington NFL	2	0	0	1	0.0	0	0	0.0	0
2002—Detroit NFL	1	0	0	0	0.0	0	0	0.0	0
Pro totals (6 years)	50	4	29	14	0.0	1	0	0.0	0

G

GREGG, KELLY   DT   RAVENS

PERSONAL: Born November 1, 1976, in Edmond, Okla. ... 6-0/310.
HIGH SCHOOL: Edmond (Okla.).
COLLEGE: Oklahoma.
TRANSACTIONS/CAREER NOTES: Selected by Cincinnati Bengals in sixth round (173rd pick overall) of 1999 NFL draft. ... Signed by Bengals (June 23, 1999). ... Released by Bengals (September 6, 1999). ... Re-signed by Bengals to practice squad (September 7, 1999). ... Signed by Philadelphia Eagles off Bengals practice squad (December 7, 1999). ... Released by Eagles (September 12, 2000). ... Signed by Baltimore Ravens to practice squad (September 13, 2000). ... Assigned by Ravens to Rhein Fire in 2001 NFL Europe enhancement allocation program (February 19, 2001).

Year Team	G	GS	TOTALS Tk.	Ast.	Sks.
1999—Philadelphia NFL	3	0	2	0	0.0
2000—Baltimore NFL			Did not play.		
2001—Rhein NFLE	...	...	...	...	6.0
—Baltimore NFL	8	1	7	3	1.0
2002—Baltimore NFL	16	16	45	11	2.0
NFL Europe totals (1 year)	...	...	...	...	6.0
NFL totals (3 years)	27	17	54	14	3.0
Pro totals (4 years)	...	...	...	...	9.0

GREGORY, DAMIAN   DT   RAIDERS

PERSONAL: Born January 21, 1977, in Ann Arbor, Mich. ... 6-2/305. ... Full name: Damian K. Gregory.
HIGH SCHOOL: Sexton (Lansing, Mich.).
COLLEGE: Illinois State.
TRANSACTIONS/CAREER NOTES: Signed as non-drafted free agent by Miami Dolphins (April 27, 2000). ... On injured reserve with knee injury (August 22, 2000-remainder of season). ... On non-football injury list with spleen surgery (October 16, 2001-remainder of season). ... Claimed on waivers by Cleveland Browns (March 4, 2002). ... Released by Browns (September 1, 2002). ... Re-signed by Browns to practice squad (September 4, 2002). ... Activated (November 14, 2002). ... Released by Browns (November 27, 2002). ... Re-signed by Browns to practice squad (November 29, 2002). ... Signed by Oakland Raiders (March 23, 2003).

Year Team	G	GS	TOTALS Tk.	Ast.	Sks.
2001—Miami NFL	2	0	1	1	0.0
2002—Cleveland NFL	1	0	1	0	0.0
Pro totals (2 years)	3	0	2	1	0.0

GREISEN, NICK   LB   GIANTS

PERSONAL: Born August 10, 1979, in Sturgeon Bay, Wis. ... 6-1/242.
HIGH SCHOOL: Sturgeon Bay (Wis.).
COLLEGE: Wisconsin.
TRANSACTIONS/CAREER NOTES: Selected by New York Giants in fifth round (152nd pick overall) of 2002 NFL draft.

Year Team	G	GS	TOTALS Tk.	Ast.	Sks.	INTERCEPTIONS No.	Yds.	Avg.	TD
2002—New York Giants NFL	8	1	3	0	1.0	0	0	0.0	0

GRIESE, BRIAN   QB   DOLPHINS

PERSONAL: Born March 18, 1975, in Miami. ... 6-3/215. ... Full name: Brian David Griese. ... Son of Bob Griese, Hall of Fame quarterback with Miami Dolphins (1967-80). ... Name pronounced GREE-see.
HIGH SCHOOL: Columbus (Miami).
COLLEGE: Michigan.
TRANSACTIONS/CAREER NOTES: Selected by Denver Broncos in third round (91st pick overall) of 1998 NFL draft. ... Signed by Broncos (July 22, 1998). ... Granted free agency (March 2, 2001). ... Re-signed by Broncos (April 11, 2001). ... Released by Broncos (June 1, 2003). ... Signed by Miami Dolphins (June 9, 2003).
CHAMPIONSHIP GAME EXPERIENCE: Member of Broncos for AFC championship game (1998 season); inactive. ... Member of Super Bowl championship team (1998 season); inactive.
HONORS: Played in Pro Bowl (2000 season).
SINGLE GAME HIGHS (regular season): Attempts—53 (September 30, 2002, vs. Baltimore); completions—35 (September 30, 2002, vs. Baltimore); yards—376 (October 20, 2002, vs. Kansas City); and touchdown passes—3 (September 23, 2001, vs. Arizona).
STATISTICAL PLATEAUS: 300-yard passing games: 1999 (2), 2000 (5), 2001 (1), 2002 (4). Total: 12.
MISCELLANEOUS: Regular-season record as starting NFL quarterback: 27-24 (.529).

Year Team	G	GS	PASSING Att.	Cmp.	Pct.	Yds.	TD	Int.	Avg.	Skd.	Rat.	RUSHING Att.	Yds.	Avg.	TD	TOTALS TD	2pt.	Pts.
1998—Denver NFL	1	0	3	1	33.3	2	0	1	0.67	0	2.8	4	-4	-1.0	0	0	0	0
1999—Denver NFL	14	13	452	261	57.7	3032	14	14	6.71	27	75.6	46	138	3.0	2	2	0	12
2000—Denver NFL	10	10	336	216	§64.3	2688	19	4	§8.00	17	*102.9	29	102	3.5	1	1	0	6
2001—Denver NFL	15	15	451	275	61.0	2827	23	19	6.27	38	78.5	50	173	3.5	1	1	0	6
2002—Denver NFL	13	13	436	291	66.7	3214	15	15	7.37	34	85.6	37	107	2.9	1	1	0	6
Pro totals (5 years)	53	51	1678	1044	62.2	11763	71	53	7.01	116	84.1	166	516	3.1	5	5	0	30

G

GRIFFIN, CORNELIUS　　　　　DT　　　　　GIANTS

PERSONAL: Born December 3, 1976, in Brundidge, Ala. ... 6-3/300.
HIGH SCHOOL: Pike County (Brundidge, Ala.).
JUNIOR COLLEGE: Pearl River Community College (Miss.).
COLLEGE: Alabama.
TRANSACTIONS/CAREER NOTES: Selected by New York Giants in second round (42nd pick overall) of 2000 NFL draft. ... Signed by Giants (July 25, 2000).
CHAMPIONSHIP GAME EXPERIENCE: Played in NFC championship game (2000 season). ... Played in Super Bowl XXXV (2000 season).

			TOTALS		
Year　Team	G	GS	Tk.	Ast.	Sks.
2000—New York Giants NFL	15	0	20	4	5.0
2001—New York Giants NFL	16	16	47	16	2.5
2002—New York Giants NFL	14	14	32	17	4.0
Pro totals (3 years)	45	30	99	37	11.5

GRIFFITH, ROBERT　　　　　S　　　　　BROWNS

PERSONAL: Born November 30, 1970, in Landham, Md. ... 5-11/197. ... Full name: Robert Otis Griffith.
HIGH SCHOOL: Mount Miguel (Spring Valley, Calif.).
COLLEGE: San Diego State.
TRANSACTIONS/CAREER NOTES: Signed by Sacramento Gold Miners of CFL to practice squad (August 8, 1993). ... Granted free agency after 1993 season. ... Signed as non-drafted free agent by Minnesota Vikings (April 21, 1994). ... Granted free agency (February 14, 1997). ... Re-signed by Vikings (May 7, 1997). ... Granted unconditional free agency (March 1, 2002). ... Signed by Cleveland Browns (March 6, 2002).
CHAMPIONSHIP GAME EXPERIENCE: Played in NFC championship game (1998 and 2000 seasons).
HONORS: Named safety on THE SPORTING NEWS NFL All-Pro team (1998). ... Played in Pro Bowl (2000 season).

			TOTALS			INTERCEPTIONS			
Year　Team	G	GS	Tk.	Ast.	Sks.	No.	Yds.	Avg.	TD
1994—Minnesota NFL	15	0	8	3	0.0	0	0	0.0	0
1995—Minnesota NFL	16	1	30	8	0.5	0	0	0.0	0
1996—Minnesota NFL	14	14	78	17	2.0	4	67	16.8	0
1997—Minnesota NFL	16	16	90	25	0.0	2	26	13.0	0
1998—Minnesota NFL	16	16	74	15	0.0	5	25	5.0	0
1999—Minnesota NFL	16	16	94	26	4.0	3	0	0.0	0
2000—Minnesota NFL	16	16	75	29	1.0	1	25	25.0	0
2001—Minnesota NFL	10	9	47	16	0.0	2	25	12.5	0
2002—Cleveland NFL	12	12	62	11	0.0	3	0	0.0	0
Pro totals (9 years)	131	100	558	150	7.5	20	168	8.4	0

GRUTTADAURIA, MIKE　　　　　C

PERSONAL: Born December 6, 1972, in Fort Lauderdale, Fla. ... 6-3/280. ... Full name: Michael Jason Gruttadauria. ... Name pronounced GRU-da-DOOR-ri-ah.
HIGH SCHOOL: Tarpon Springs (Fla.).
COLLEGE: Central Florida.
TRANSACTIONS/CAREER NOTES: Signed as non-drafted free agent by Dallas Cowboys (April 26, 1995). ... Released by Cowboys (August 22, 1995). ... Signed by St. Louis Rams (February 9, 1996). ... Granted free agency (February 12, 1999). ... Re-signed by Rams (June 8, 1999). ... Granted unconditional free agency (February 11, 2000). ... Signed by Arizona Cardinals (February 19, 2000). ... On injured reserve with neck injury (November 24, 2000-remainder of season). ... On injured reserve with knee injury (December 11, 2002-remainder of season). ... Released by Cardinals (April 2, 2003).
PLAYING EXPERIENCE: St. Louis NFL, 1996-1999; Arizona NFL, 2000-2002. ... Games/Games started: 1996 (9/4), 1997 (14/14), 1998 (11/2), 1999 (16/16), 2000 (8/8), 2001 (15/15), 2002 (8/8). Total: 82/67.
CHAMPIONSHIP GAME EXPERIENCE: Played in NFC championship game (1999 season). ... Member of Super Bowl championship team (1999 season).

GURLEY, BUCK　　　　　DT　　　　　BUCCANEERS

PERSONAL: Born April 7, 1978, in Quincy, Fla. ... 6-2/295. ... Full name: Sheddrick Gurley.
HIGH SCHOOL: Godby (Tallahassee, Fla.).
COLLEGE: Florida.
TRANSACTIONS/CAREER NOTES: Signed as non-drafted free agent by Miami Dolphins (April 26, 2001). ... Released by Dolphins (August 26, 2001). ... Signed by Chicago Bears (August 31, 2001). ... Released by Bears (September 2, 2001). ... Signed by Tampa Bay Buccaneers (March 7, 2002).
CHAMPIONSHIP GAME EXPERIENCE: Member of Buccaneers for NFC championship game (2002 season); inactive. ... Member of Super Bowl championship team (2002 season); inactive.

			TOTALS		
Year　Team	G	GS	Tk.	Ast.	Sks.
2002—Tampa Bay NFL	7	0	2	0	0.0

G

GURODE, ANDRE　　　　　G/OC　　　　　COWBOYS

PERSONAL: Born March 6, 1978, in Houston. ... 6-4/326.
HIGH SCHOOL: North Shore (Houston).

COLLEGE: Colorado.
TRANSACTIONS/CAREER NOTES: Selected by Dallas Cowboys in second round (37th pick overall) of 2002 NFL draft. ... Signed by Cowboys (July 26, 2002).
PLAYING EXPERIENCE: Dallas NFL, 2002. ... Games/games started: 2002 (14/14).
HONORS: Named guard on THE SPORTING NEWS college All-America first team (2001).

GUTIERREZ, BROCK — C

PERSONAL: Born September 25, 1973, in Charlotte, Mich. ... 6-3/304.
HIGH SCHOOL: Charlotte (Mich.).
COLLEGE: Central Michigan.
TRANSACTIONS/CAREER NOTES: Signed as non-drafted free agent by Cincinnati Bengals (April 23, 1996). ... Active for two games (1996). ... Released by Bengals (August 30, 1998). ... Re-signed by Bengals (November 4, 1998). ... Released by Bengals (November 17, 1998). ... Signed by Jacksonville Jaguars to practice squad (November 30, 1998). ... Signed by Bengals off Jaguars practice squad (December 15, 1998). ... Granted free agency (February 11, 2000). ... Re-signed by Bengals (March 17, 2000). ... Released by Bengals (May 27, 2003).
PLAYING EXPERIENCE: Cincinnati NFL, 1997-2002. ... Games/Games started: 1997 (5/0), 1998 (1/0), 1999 (16/0), 2000 (16/7), 2001 (14/0), 2002 (16/1). Total: 68/8.

HAAYER, ADAM — OT — VIKINGS

PERSONAL: Born February 22, 1977, in Wyoming, Minn. ... 6-6/298.
HIGH SCHOOL: Forest Lake (Minn.).
COLLEGE: Minnesota.
TRANSACTIONS/CAREER NOTES: Selected by Tennessee Titans in sixth round (199th pick overall) of 2001 NFL draft. ... Signed by Titans (July 6, 2001). ... On injured reserve with knee injury (August 25, 2001-entire season). ... Claimed on waivers by Minnesota Vikings (August 27, 2002).
PLAYING EXPERIENCE: Minnesota NFL, 2002. ... Games/games started: 2002 (4/0).

HADDAD, DREW — WR — COLTS

PERSONAL: Born August 15, 1978, in Westlake, Ohio. ... 5-11/187.
HIGH SCHOOL: St. Ignatius (Westlake, Ohio).
COLLEGE: Buffalo.
TRANSACTIONS/CAREER NOTES: Selected by Buffalo Bills in seventh round (233rd pick overall) of 2000 NFL draft. ... Signed by Bills (July 17, 2000). ... Released by Bills (August 27, 2000). ... Re-signed by Bills to practice squad (August 28, 2000). ... Released by Bills (November 22, 2000). ... Signed by Indianapolis Colts to practice squad (December 7, 2000). ... On injured reserve with hamstring injury (October 8, 2001-remainder of season).
SINGLE GAME HIGHS (regular season): Receptions—1 (November 3, 2002, vs. Tennessee); yards—11 (November 3, 2002, vs. Tennessee); and touchdown receptions—0.

			RECEIVING				PUNT RETURNS				KICKOFF RETURNS				TOTALS			
Year Team	G	GS	No.	Yds.	Avg.	TD	No.	Yds.	Avg.	TD	No.	Yds.	Avg.	TD	TD	2pt.	Pts.	Fum.
2002—Indianapolis NFL	1	0	1	11	11.0	0	0	0	0.0	0	2	19	9.5	0	0	0	0	0

HAGGANS, CLARK — DE — STEELERS

PERSONAL: Born January 10, 1977, in Torrance, Calif. ... 6-3/251. ... Full name: Clark Cromwell Haggans.
HIGH SCHOOL: Peninsula (Torrance, Calif.).
COLLEGE: Colorado State.
TRANSACTIONS/CAREER NOTES: Selected by Pittsburgh Steelers in fifth round (137th pick overall) of 2000 NFL draft. ... Signed by Steelers (July 7, 2000). ... Granted free agency (February 28, 2003). ... Re-signed by Steelers (April 21, 2003).
CHAMPIONSHIP GAME EXPERIENCE: Played in AFC championship game (2001 season).

			TOTALS		
Year Team	G	GS	Tk.	Ast.	Sks.
2000—Pittsburgh NFL	2	0	0	0	0.0
2001—Pittsburgh NFL	16	1	3	2	0.0
2002—Pittsburgh NFL	16	0	17	9	6.5
Pro totals (3 years)	34	1	20	11	6.5

HAKIM, AZ-ZAHIR — WR — LIONS

PERSONAL: Born June 3, 1977, in Los Angeles. ... 5-10/189. ... Full name: Az-Zahir Ali Hakim. ... Name pronounced oz-za-HERE ha-KEEM.
HIGH SCHOOL: Fairfax (Los Angeles).
COLLEGE: San Diego State.
TRANSACTIONS/CAREER NOTES: Selected by St. Louis Rams in fourth round (96th pick overall) of 1998 NFL draft. ... Signed by Rams (July 13, 1998). ... Granted free agency (March 2, 2001). ... Re-signed by Rams (May 23, 2001). ... Granted unconditional free agency (March 1, 2002). ... Signed by Detroit Lions (March 7, 2002). ... On injured reserve with hip injury (November 20, 2002-remainder of season).
CHAMPIONSHIP GAME EXPERIENCE: Played in NFC championship game (1999 and 2001 seasons). ... Member of Super Bowl championship team (1999 season). ... Played in Super Bowl XXXVI (2001 season).
HONORS: Named punt returner on THE SPORTING NEWS NFL All-Pro team (2000).
SINGLE GAME HIGHS (regular season): Receptions—9 (September 8, 2002, vs. Miami); yards—147 (November 5, 2000, vs. Carolina); and touchdown receptions—3 (October 3, 1999, vs. Cincinnati).
STATISTICAL PLATEAUS: 100-yard receiving games: 1999 (1), 2000 (3), 2002 (1). Total: 5.

G
H

Year Team	G	GS	RUSHING				RECEIVING				PUNT RETURNS				KICKOFF RETURNS				TOTALS		
			Att.	Yds.	Avg.	TD	No.	Yds.	Avg.	TD	No.	Yds.	Avg.	TD	No.	Yds.	Avg.	TD	TD	2pt.	Pts.
1998—St. Louis NFL	9	4	2	30	15.0	1	20	247	12.4	1	0	0	0.0	0	0	0	0.0	0	2	0	12
1999—St. Louis NFL	15	0	4	44	11.0	0	36	677	18.8	8	∞44	461	10.5	∞1	2	35	17.5	0	9	0	54
2000—St. Louis NFL	16	4	5	19	3.8	0	53	734	13.8	4	32	‡489‡	15.3	1	1	2	2.0	0	5	0	30
2001—St. Louis NFL	16	2	11	50	4.5	0	39	374	9.6	3	36	330	9.2	0	0	0	0.0	0	3	0	18
2002—Detroit NFL	10	10	4	3	0.8	0	37	541	14.6	3	10	148	14.8	1	0	0	0.0	0	4	0	24
Pro totals (5 years)	66	20	26	146	5.6	1	185	2573	13.9	19	122	1428	11.7	3	3	37	12.3	0	23	0	138

HALEY, JERMAINE — DT — REDSKINS

PERSONAL: Born February 23, 1973, in Fresno, Calif. ... 6-4/305.
HIGH SCHOOL: Hanford (Calif.).
JUNIOR COLLEGE: Butte Junior College (Calif.).
TRANSACTIONS/CAREER NOTES: Signed by Toronto Argonauts of CFL (May 1998). ... Selected by Miami Dolphins in seventh round (232nd pick overall) of 1999 NFL draft. ... Signed by Dolphins (March 2, 2000). ... Granted free agency (February 28, 2003). ... Tendered offer sheet by Washington Redskins (April 18, 2003). ... Dolphins declined to match offer (April 25, 2003).

Year Team	G	GS	TOTALS			INTERCEPTIONS			
			Tk.	Ast.	Sks.	No.	Yds.	Avg.	TD
1998—Toronto CFL	16	...	...	...	7.0	0	0	0.0	0
1999—Toronto CFL	15	...	...	...	3.0	1	0	0.0	0
2000—Miami NFL	15	4	15	7	1.5	0	0	0.0	0
2001—Miami NFL	12	5	10	8	0.5	0	0	0.0	0
2002—Miami NFL	16	0	13	14	0.5	1	0	0.0	0
CFL totals (2 years)	31	...	...	...	10.0	1	0	0.0	0
NFL totals (3 years)	43	9	38	29	2.5	1	0	0.0	0
Pro totals (5 years)	74	...	...	...	12.5	2	0	0.0	0

HALL, CARLOS — DE — TITANS

PERSONAL: Born January 16, 1979, in Moro, Ark. ... 6-4/251.
HIGH SCHOOL: Lee (Mariana, Ark.).
COLLEGE: Arkansas.
TRANSACTIONS/CAREER NOTES: Selected by Tennessee Titans in seventh round (240th pick overall) of 2002 NFL draft. ... Signed by Titans (July 9, 2002).
CHAMPIONSHIP GAME EXPERIENCE: Played in AFC championship game (2002 season).

Year Team	G	GS	TOTALS		
			Tk.	Ast.	Sks.
2002—Tennessee NFL	15	13	27	15	8.0

HALL, CORY — S — FALCONS

PERSONAL: Born December 5, 1976, in Bakersfield, Calif. ... 6-0/213.
HIGH SCHOOL: South (Bakersfield, Calif.).
COLLEGE: Fresno State.
TRANSACTIONS/CAREER NOTES: Selected by Cincinnati Bengals in third round (65th pick overall) of 1999 NFL draft. ... Signed by Bengals (May 7, 1999). ... Granted free agency (March 1, 2002). ... Re-signed by Bengals (April 23, 2002). ... On injured reserve with shoulder injury (December 17, 2002-remainder of season). ... Granted unconditional free agency (February 28, 2003). ... Signed by Atlanta Falcons (March 3, 2003).

Year Team	G	GS	TOTALS			INTERCEPTIONS			
			Tk.	Ast.	Sks.	No.	Yds.	Avg.	TD
1999—Cincinnati NFL	16	12	36	13	0.0	1	0	0.0	0
2000—Cincinnati NFL	16	6	36	5	4.0	1	12	12.0	0
2001—Cincinnati NFL	16	15	31	16	0.0	0	0	0.0	0
2002—Cincinnati NFL	14	14	43	15	2.0	1	2	2.0	0
Pro totals (4 years)	62	47	146	49	6.0	3	14	4.7	0

HALL, DANTE — WR/KR — CHIEFS

PERSONAL: Born September 1, 1978, in Lufkin, Texas. ... 5-8/187. ... Full name: Damieon Dante Hall.
HIGH SCHOOL: Nimitz (Irving, Texas).
COLLEGE: Texas A&M.
TRANSACTIONS/CAREER NOTES: Selected by Kansas City Chiefs in fifth round (153rd pick overall) of 2000 NFL draft. ... Signed by Chiefs (July 6, 2000). ... Assigned by Chiefs to Scottish Claymores in 2001 NFL Europe enhancement allocation program (February 19, 2001).
HONORS: Played in Pro Bowl (2002 season).
SINGLE GAME HIGHS (regular season): Receptions—5 (December 15, 2002, vs. Denver); yards—143 (December 15, 2002, vs. Denver); and touchdown receptions—2 (December 15, 2002, vs. Denver).
STATISTICAL PLATEAUS: 100-yard receiving games: 2002 (1).

Year Team	G	GS	RUSHING				RECEIVING				PUNT RETURNS				KICKOFF RETURNS				TOTALS		
			Att.	Yds.	Avg.	TD	No.	Yds.	Avg.	TD	No.	Yds.	Avg.	TD	No.	Yds.	Avg.	TD	TD	2pt.	Pts.
2000—Kansas City NFL	5	0	0	0	0.0	0	0	0	0.0	0	6	37	6.2	0	17	358	21.1	0	0	0	0
2001—Scottish NFLE	...	...	4	12	3.0	0	34	462	13.6	5	15	177	11.8	0	26	635	24.4	0	5	0	30
—Kansas City NFL	13	0	2	10	5.0	0	0	0	0.0	0	32	235	7.3	0	43	969	22.5	0	0	0	0
2002—Kansas City NFL	16	0	11	54	4.9	0	20	322	16.1	3	29	390	13.4	†2	57	1354	23.8	1	6	0	36
NFLEurope totals (1 year)	...	...	4	12	3.0	0	34	462	13.6	5	15	177	11.8	0	26	635	24.4	0	5	0	30
NFL totals (3 years)	34	0	13	64	4.9	0	20	322	16.1	3	67	662	9.9	2	117	2681	22.9	1	6	0	36
Pro totals (4 years)	...	...	17	76	4.5	0	54	784	14.5	8	82	839	10.2	2	143	3316	23.2	1	11	0	66

H

HALL, JAMES   DE   LIONS

PERSONAL: Born February 4, 1977, in New Orleans. ... 6-2/274.
HIGH SCHOOL: St. Augustine (La.).
COLLEGE: Michigan.
TRANSACTIONS/CAREER NOTES: Signed as non-drafted free agent by Detroit Lions (April 28, 2000). ... Granted free agency (February 28, 2003). ... Re-signed by Lions (May 28, 2003).
HONORS: Named linebacker on THE SPORTING NEWS college All-America third team (1999).

			TOTALS		
Year Team	G	GS	Tk.	Ast.	Sks.
2000—Detroit NFL	5	0	1	0	1.0
2001—Detroit NFL	15	0	25	8	4.0
2002—Detroit NFL	16	14	34	15	2.0
Pro totals (3 years)	36	14	60	23	7.0

HALL, JOHN   K   REDSKINS

PERSONAL: Born March 17, 1974, in Port Charlotte, Fla. ... 6-3/228.
HIGH SCHOOL: Port Charlotte (Fla.).
COLLEGE: Wisconsin.
TRANSACTIONS/CAREER NOTES: Signed as non-drafted free agent by New York Jets (April 25, 1997). ... Granted free agency (February 11, 2000). ... Re-signed by Jets (April 13, 2000). ... Granted unconditional free agency (February 28, 2003). ... Signed by Washington Redskins (March 2, 2003).
CHAMPIONSHIP GAME EXPERIENCE: Played in AFC championship game (1998 season).

		FIELD GOALS							TOTALS		
Year Team	G	1-29	30-39	40-49	50+	Tot.	Pct.	Lg.	XPM	XPA	Pts.
1997—New York Jets NFL	16	11-12	11-17	2-6	4-6	28-†41	68.3	†55	36	36	120
1998—New York Jets NFL	16	9-9	9-13	6-10	1-3	25-35	71.4	54	45	46	120
1999—New York Jets NFL	16	3-4	17-17	7-12	0-0	27-33	81.8	48	27	29	108
2000—New York Jets NFL	15	8-9	6-8	6-12	1-3	21-32	65.6	51	30	30	93
2001—New York Jets NFL	16	9-9	5-7	7-9	3-6	24-31	77.4	53	32	32	104
2002—New York Jets NFL	16	9-9	9-11	6-10	0-1	24-31	77.4	46	35	37	107
Pro totals (6 years)	95	49-52	57-73	34-59	9-19	149-203	73.4	55	205	210	652

HALL, LAMONT   TE   FALCONS

PERSONAL: Born November 16, 1974, in Clover, S.C. ... 6-4/260. ... Full name: James Lamont Hall.
HIGH SCHOOL: Clover (S.C.).
COLLEGE: Clemson (degree in history).
TRANSACTIONS/CAREER NOTES: Signed as non-drafted free agent by Tampa Bay Buccaneers (April 24, 1998). ... Released by Buccaneers (August 25, 1998). ... Re-signed by Buccaneers to practice squad (October 21, 1998). ... Granted free agency following 1998 season. ... Selected by Rhein Fire in 1999 NFL Europe draft (February 18, 1999). ... Signed by Green Bay Packers (July 7, 1999). ... Traded by Packers with QB Aaron Brooks to New Orleans Saints for LB K.D. Williams and third-round pick (traded to San Francisco) in 2001 draft (July 31, 2000). ... Granted free agency (March 1, 2002). ... Re-signed by Saints (May 31, 2002). ... Granted unconditional free agency (February 28, 2003). ... Signed by Atlanta Falcons (April 1, 2003).
SINGLE GAME HIGHS (regular season): Receptions—2 (October 22, 2000, vs. Atlanta); yards—20 (October 22, 2000, vs. Atlanta); and touchdown receptions—1 (October 29, 2000, vs. Arizona).

			RECEIVING					TOTALS		
Year Team	G	GS	No.	Yds.	Avg.	TD	TD	2pt.	Pts.	Fum.
1998—Tampa Bay NFL						Did not play.				
1999—Rhein NFLE	...	...	5	60	12.0	0	0	0	0	0
—Green Bay NFL	14	0	3	33	11.0	0	0	0	0	0
2000—New Orleans NFL	16	5	5	33	6.6	1	1	0	6	0
2001—New Orleans NFL	16	6	2	15	7.5	0	0	0	0	1
2002—New Orleans NFL	16	1	2	6	3.0	0	0	0	0	0
NFL Europe totals (1 year)	...	...	5	60	12.0	0	0	0	0	0
NFL totals (3 years)	62	12	12	87	7.3	1	1	0	6	1
Pro totals (4 years)	...	...	17	147	8.6	1	1	0	6	1

HALL, LEMANSKI   LB

PERSONAL: Born November 24, 1970, in Valley, Ala. ... 6-0/234. ... Full name: Lemanski S. Hall.
HIGH SCHOOL: Valley (Ala.).
COLLEGE: Alabama.
TRANSACTIONS/CAREER NOTES: Selected by Houston Oilers in seventh round (220th pick overall) of 1994 NFL draft. ... Signed by Oilers (June 20, 1994). ... Released by Oilers (August 28, 1994). ... Re-signed by Oilers to practice squad (August 30, 1994). ... Activated (December 23, 1994); did not play. ... Assigned by Oilers to Frankfurt Galaxy in 1995 World League enhancement allocation program (February 20, 1995). ... Assigned by Oilers to Amsterdam Admirals in 1996 World League enhancement allocation program (February 19, 1996). ... Oilers franchise moved to Tennessee for 1997 season. ... Granted free agency (February 13, 1998). ... Re-signed by Oilers (May 28, 1998). ... Traded by Oilers to Chicago Bears for seventh-round pick (RB Mike Green) in 2000 draft (September 1, 1998). ... Released by Bears (September 5, 1999). ... Signed by Dallas Cowboys (October 27, 1999). ... Granted unconditional free agency (February 11, 2000). ... Signed by Minnesota Vikings (February 24, 2000). ... Released by Vikings (September 1, 2002). ... Re-signed by Vikings (September 11, 2002). ... Granted unconditional free agency (February 28, 2003).
CHAMPIONSHIP GAME EXPERIENCE: Played in NFC championship game (2000 season).

H

Year Team	G	GS	TOTALS			INTERCEPTIONS			
			Tk.	Ast.	Sks.	No.	Yds.	Avg.	TD
1995—Houston NFL	12	0	1	1	0.0	0	0	0.0	0
1996—Houston NFL	3	0	0	0	0.0	0	0	0.0	0
1997—Tennessee NFL	16	2	6	2	2.0	0	0	0.0	0
1998—Chicago NFL	15	0	5	2	0.0	0	0	0.0	0
1999—Dallas NFL	10	0	0	0	0.0	0	0	0.0	0
2000—Minnesota NFL	15	1	8	1	0.0	0	0	0.0	0
2001—Minnesota NFL	16	13	46	12	1.0	0	0	0.0	0
2002—Minnesota NFL	14	4	20	9	1.0	0	0	0.0	0
Pro totals (8 years)	101	20	86	27	4.0	0	0	0.0	0

HALL, TRAVIS　　　　DT　　　　FALCONS

PERSONAL: Born August 3, 1972, in Kenai, Alaska. ... 6-5/295.
HIGH SCHOOL: West Jordan (Utah).
COLLEGE: Brigham Young.
TRANSACTIONS/CAREER NOTES: Selected by Atlanta Falcons in sixth round (181st pick overall) of 1995 NFL draft. ... Signed by Falcons (June 30, 1995).
CHAMPIONSHIP GAME EXPERIENCE: Played in NFC championship game (1998 season). ... Played in Super Bowl XXXIII (1998 season).

Year Team	G	GS	TOTALS		
			Tk.	Ast.	Sks.
1995—Atlanta NFL	1	0	0	0	0.0
1996—Atlanta NFL	14	13	44	7	6.0
1997—Atlanta NFL	16	16	61	17	10.5
1998—Atlanta NFL	14	13	39	10	4.5
1999—Atlanta NFL	16	15	36	9	4.5
2000—Atlanta NFL	16	16	45	18	4.5
2001—Atlanta NFL	16	16	39	12	2.5
2002—Atlanta NFL	11	1	14	11	1.0
Pro totals (8 years)	104	90	278	84	33.5

HALLEN, BOB　　　　G　　　　CHARGERS

PERSONAL: Born March 9, 1975, in Mentor, Ohio. ... 6-3/295. ... Full name: Robert Joseph Hallen.
HIGH SCHOOL: Mentor (Ohio).
COLLEGE: Kent.
TRANSACTIONS/CAREER NOTES: Selected by Atlanta Falcons in second round (53rd pick overall) of 1998 NFL draft. ... Signed by Falcons (June 3, 1998). ... Granted unconditional free agency (March 1, 2002). ... Signed by San Diego Chargers (May 2, 2002).
PLAYING EXPERIENCE: Atlanta NFL, 1998-2001; San Diego NFL, 2002. ... Games/Games started: 1998 (12/0), 1999 (16/14), 2000 (16/5), 2001 (15/12), 2002 (13/11). Total: 72/42.
CHAMPIONSHIP GAME EXPERIENCE: Played in NFC championship game (1998 season). ... Played in Super Bowl XXXIII (1998 season).

HAMBRICK, DARREN　　　　LB

PERSONAL: Born August 30, 1975, in Lacoochee, Fla. ... 6-2/227. ... Nephew of Mudcat Grant, pitcher for seven major league teams (1958-71).
HIGH SCHOOL: Pasco (Dade City, Fla.).
COLLEGE: Florida, then South Carolina.
TRANSACTIONS/CAREER NOTES: Selected by Dallas Cowboys in fifth round (130th pick overall) of 1998 NFL draft. ... Signed by Cowboys (July 14, 1998). ... Granted free agency (March 2, 2001). ... Re-signed by Cowboys (May 18, 2001). ... Claimed on waivers by Carolina Panthers (October 24, 2001). ... Granted unconditional free agency (March 1, 2002). ... Signed by Cleveland Browns (August 11, 2002). ... Granted unconditional free agency (February 28, 2003).

Year Team	G	GS	TOTALS			INTERCEPTIONS			
			Tk.	Ast.	Sks.	No.	Yds.	Avg.	TD
1998—Dallas NFL	14	0	0	0	0.0	0	0	0.0	0
1999—Dallas NFL	16	12	43	11	2.5	2	44	22.0	0
2000—Dallas NFL	16	16	61	16	1.0	0	0	0.0	0
2001—Dallas NFL	5	5	14	6	0.0	0	0	0.0	0
—Carolina NFL	9	8	42	11	0.0	0	0	0.0	0
2002—Cleveland NFL	16	15	41	16	0.0	1	6	6.0	0
Pro totals (5 years)	76	56	201	60	3.5	3	50	16.7	0

HAMBRICK, TROY　　　　RB　　　　COWBOYS

PERSONAL: Born November 6, 1976, in Pasco, Fla. ... 6-1/233.
HIGH SCHOOL: Pasco (Fla.).
COLLEGE: Savannah (Ga.) State.
TRANSACTIONS/CAREER NOTES: Signed as non-drafted free agent by Dallas Cowboys (June 1, 2000). ... Released by Cowboys (August 27, 2000). ... Re-signed by Cowboys to practice squad (August 29, 2000). ... Activated (December 8, 2000).
SINGLE GAME HIGHS (regular season): Attempts—30 (November 4, 2001, vs. New York Giants); yards—127 (November 11, 2001, vs. Atlanta); and rushing touchdowns—2 (November 22, 2001, vs. Denver).
STATISTICAL PLATEAUS: 100-yard rushing games: 2001 (2).

Year Team	G	GS	RUSHING				RECEIVING				TOTALS			
			Att.	Yds.	Avg.	TD	No.	Yds.	Avg.	TD	TD	2pt.	Pts.	Fum.
2000—Dallas NFL	3	0	6	28	4.7	0	0	0	0.0	0	0	0	0	0
2001—Dallas NFL	16	11	113	579	5.1	2	4	62	15.5	0	2	0	12	1
2002—Dallas NFL	16	0	79	317	4.0	1	21	99	4.7	0	1	0	6	2
Pro totals (3 years)	35	11	198	924	4.7	3	25	161	6.4	0	3	0	18	3

H

HAMILTON, BEN   C   BRONCOS

PERSONAL: Born August 18, 1977, in Minneapolis, Minn. ... 6-4/283. ... Son of Wes Hamilton, guard with Minnesota Vikings (1976-84).
HIGH SCHOOL: Wayzata (Minn.).
COLLEGE: Minnesota.
TRANSACTIONS/CAREER NOTES: Selected by Denver Broncos in fourth round (113th pick overall) of 2001 NFL draft. ... Signed by Broncos (July 10, 2001).
PLAYING EXPERIENCE: Denver NFL, 2002. ... Games/games started: 2002 (16/16).
HONORS: Named center on THE SPORTING NEWS college All-America first team (1999 and 2000).

HAMILTON, BOBBY   DE   PATRIOTS

PERSONAL: Born July 1, 1971, in Columbia, Miss. ... 6-5/280.
HIGH SCHOOL: East Marion (Columbia, Miss.).
COLLEGE: Southern Mississippi.
TRANSACTIONS/CAREER NOTES: Signed as non-drafted free agent by Seattle Seahawks (April 19, 1994). ... On injured reserve with knee injury (August 17, 1994-entire season). ... Assigned by Seahawks to Amsterdam Admirals in 1995 World League enhancement allocation draft. ... Released by Seahawks (August 15, 1995). ... Signed by New York Jets (June, 1996). ... Released by Jets (August 24, 1996). ... Re-signed by Jets to practice squad (August 26, 1996). ... Activated (September 4, 1996). ... Granted unconditional free agency (February 11, 2000). ... Signed by New England Patriots (July 16, 2000).
CHAMPIONSHIP GAME EXPERIENCE: Played in AFC championship game (1998 and 2001 season). ... Member of Super Bowl championship team (2001 season).

Year Team	G	GS	Tk.	Ast.	Sks.	No.	Yds.	Avg.	TD
			TOTALS			**INTERCEPTIONS**			
1994—Seattle NFL			Did not play.						
1995—Amsterdam W.L.	10	9	...	...	5.0	0	0	0.0	0
1996—Amsterdam W.L.	11	9	...	...	5.0	0	0	0.0	0
—New York Jets NFL	15	11	32	17	4.5	0	0	0.0	0
1997—New York Jets NFL	16	0	13	11	1.0	0	0	0.0	0
1998—New York Jets NFL	16	1	13	8	0.0	0	0	0.0	0
1999—New York Jets NFL	7	0	4	2	0.0	0	0	0.0	0
2000—New England NFL	16	16	41	38	1.5	0	0	0.0	0
2001—New England NFL	16	15	31	21	7.0	0	0	0.0	0
2002—New England NFL	16	15	34	21	2.0	1	0	0.0	0
W.L. totals (2 years)	21	18	...	...	10.0	0	0	0.0	0
NFL totals (6 years)	102	58	168	118	16.0	1	0	0.0	0
Pro totals (8 years)	123	76	...	...	26.0	1	0	0.0	0

HAMILTON, KEITH   DT   GIANTS

PERSONAL: Born May 25, 1971, in Paterson, N.J. ... 6-6/295. ... Full name: Keith Lamarr Hamilton.
HIGH SCHOOL: Heritage (Lynchburg, Va.).
COLLEGE: Pittsburgh.
TRANSACTIONS/CAREER NOTES: Selected after junior season by New York Giants in fourth round (99th pick overall) of 1992 NFL draft. ... Signed by Giants (July 21, 1992). ... On injured reserve with Achilles' tendon injury (October 15, 2002-remainder of season).
CHAMPIONSHIP GAME EXPERIENCE: Played in NFC championship game (2000 season). ... Played in Super Bowl XXXV (2000 season).

Year Team	G	GS	Tk.	Ast.	Sks.
			TOTALS		
1992—New York Giants NFL	16	0	15	6	3.5
1993—New York Giants NFL	16	16	40	11	11.5
1994—New York Giants NFL	15	15	27	14	6.5
1995—New York Giants NFL	14	14	29	13	2.0
1996—New York Giants NFL	14	14	31	6	3.0
1997—New York Giants NFL	16	16	40	17	8.0
1998—New York Giants NFL	16	16	35	12	7.0
1999—New York Giants NFL	16	16	36	18	4.0
2000—New York Giants NFL	16	16	43	14	10.0
2001—New York Giants NFL	13	13	19	16	6.0
2002—New York Giants NFL	6	6	11	3	0.0
Pro totals (11 years)	158	142	326	130	61.5

HAMPTON, CASEY   DT   STEELERS

PERSONAL: Born September 3, 1977, in Galveston, Texas. ... 6-1/320.
HIGH SCHOOL: Ball (Galveston, Texas).
COLLEGE: Texas.
TRANSACTIONS/CAREER NOTES: Selected by Pittsburgh Steelers in first round (19th pick overall) of 2001 NFL draft. ... Signed by Steelers (July 21, 2001).
CHAMPIONSHIP GAME EXPERIENCE: Played in AFC championship game (2001 season).
HONORS: Named defensive tackle on THE SPORTING NEWS college All-America second team (1999). ... Named defensive tackle on THE SPORTING NEWS college All-America first team (2000).

Year Team	G	GS	Tk.	Ast.	Sks.
			TOTALS		
2001—Pittsburgh NFL	16	11	10	13	1.0
2002—Pittsburgh NFL	16	15	24	17	2.0
Pro totals (2 years)	32	26	34	30	3.0

H

HAND, NORMAN — DT — SEAHAWKS

PERSONAL: Born September 4, 1972, in Queens, N.Y. ... 6-3/310. ... Full name: Norman L. Hand.
HIGH SCHOOL: Walterboro (S.C.).
JUNIOR COLLEGE: Itawamba Community College (Miss.).
COLLEGE: Mississippi.
TRANSACTIONS/CAREER NOTES: Selected by Miami Dolphins in fifth round (158th pick overall) of 1995 NFL draft. ... Signed by Dolphins (May 17, 1995). ... Inactive for all 16 games (1995). ... Claimed on waivers by San Diego Chargers (August 25, 1997). ... Granted free agency (February 13, 1998). ... Re-signed by Chargers (July 14, 1998). ... Designated by Chargers as franchise player (February 11, 2000). ... Free agency status changed from franchise to unconditional (February 16, 2000). ... Signed by New Orleans Saints (February 23, 2000). ... On injured reserve with foot injury (January 4, 2002-remainder of season). ... Traded by Saints to Seattle Seahawks for sixth-round pick (WR Kareem Kelly) in 2003 draft (April 27, 2003).

			TOTALS			INTERCEPTIONS			
Year Team	G	GS	Tk.	Ast.	Sks.	No.	Yds.	Avg.	TD
1995—Miami NFL			Did not play.						
1996—Miami NFL	9	0	2	3	0.5	0	0	0.0	0
1997—San Diego NFL	15	1	16	3	1.0	0	0	0.0	0
1998—San Diego NFL	16	16	42	7	6.0	2	47	23.5	0
1999—San Diego NFL	14	14	41	14	4.0	0	0	0.0	0
2000—New Orleans NFL	15	15	44	10	3.0	0	0	0.0	0
2001—New Orleans NFL	13	13	25	11	3.5	0	0	0.0	0
2002—New Orleans NFL	16	13	30	9	2.5	0	0	0.0	0
Pro totals (7 years)	98	72	200	57	20.5	2	47	23.5	0

HANKTON, KARL — WR — PANTHERS

PERSONAL: Born July 24, 1970, in New Orleans. ... 6-2/202.
HIGH SCHOOL: De La Salle (New Orleans), then Valley Forge Military Academy (Wayne, Penn.).
COLLEGE: Louisiana State, then Trinity (III.).
TRANSACTIONS/CAREER NOTES: Signed as non-drafted free agent by Washington Redskins (April 1, 1997). ... Released by Redskins (February 25, 1998). ... Signed by Philadelphia Eagles (April 9, 1998). ... Released by Eagles (August 31, 1998). ... Re-signed by Eagles to practice squad (September 2, 1998). ... Released by Eagles (August 31, 1998). ... Re-signed by Eagles to practice squad (September 25, 1998). ... Activated (September 25, 1998). ... Released by Eagles (September 7, 1999). ... Signed by Carolina Panthers (February 29, 2000). ... Granted free agency (March 2, 2001).
SINGLE GAME HIGHS (regular season): Receptions—2 (November 24, 2002, vs. Atlanta); yards—38 (October 13, 2002, vs. Dallas); and touchdown receptions—0.

			RECEIVING			
Year Team	G	GS	No.	Yds.	Avg.	TD
1998—Philadelphia NFL	10	0	0	0	0.0	0
2000—Carolina NFL	16	0	4	38	9.5	0
2001—Carolina NFL	11	0	0	0	0.0	0
2002—Carolina NFL	16	1	9	146	16.2	0
Pro totals (4 years)	53	1	13	184	14.2	0

HANNAM, RYAN — TE — SEAHAWKS

PERSONAL: Born February 24, 1980, in St. Ansgar, Iowa. ... 6-2/248.
HIGH SCHOOL: St. Ansgar (Iowa).
COLLEGE: Northern Iowa.
TRANSACTIONS/CAREER NOTES: Selected by Seattle Seahawks in fifth round (169th pick overall) of 2002 NFL draft. ... Signed by Seahawks (July 25, 2002).
SINGLE GAME HIGHS (regular season): Receptions—1 (November 10, 2002, vs. Arizona); yards—16 (November 10, 2002, vs. Arizona); and touchdown receptions—1 (November 10, 2002, vs. Arizona).

			RECEIVING			
Year Team	G	GS	No.	Yds.	Avg.	TD
2002—Seattle NFL	14	0	1	16	16.0	1

HANSON, CHRIS — P — JAGUARS

PERSONAL: Born October 25, 1976, in Riverdale, Ga. ... 6-2/215.
HIGH SCHOOL: East Coweta (Ga.).
COLLEGE: Marshall.
TRANSACTIONS/CAREER NOTES: Signed as non-drafted free agent by Cleveland Browns (April 23, 1999). ... Claimed on waivers by Green Bay Packers (September 1, 1999). ... Released by Packers (September 14, 1999). ... Re-signed by Packers to practice squad (September 16, 1999). ... Released by Packers (October 12, 1999). ... Signed by Miami Dolphins (February 8, 2000). ... Assigned by Dolphins to Barcelona Dragons in 2000 NFL Europe enhancement allocation program (February 18, 2000). ... On injured reserve with knee injury (July 21, 2000-entire season). ... Released by Dolphins (August 15, 2001). ... Signed by Jacksonville Jaguars (August 18, 2001).
HONORS: Played in Pro Bowl (2002 season).

				PUNTING			
Year Team	G	No.	Yds.	Avg.	Net avg.	In. 20	Blk.
1999—Green Bay NFL	1	4	157	39.3	38.5	0	0
2000—Barcelona NFLE	...	50	2141	42.8	36.9	16	0
—Miami NFL			Did not play.				
2001—Jacksonville NFL	16	82	3577	43.6	37.1	24	0
2002—Jacksonville NFL	16	81	3583	§44.2	§37.6	27	0
NFL Europe totals (1 year)	...	50	2141	42.8	36.9	16	0
NFL totals (3 years)	33	167	7317	43.8	37.4	51	0
Pro totals (4 years)	...	217	9458	43.6	37.3	67	0

H

HANSON, JASON — K — LIONS

PERSONAL: Born June 17, 1970, in Spokane, Wash. ... 5-11/182. ... Full name: Jason Douglas Hanson.
HIGH SCHOOL: Mead (Spokane, Wash.).
COLLEGE: Washington State (degree in pre-med).
TRANSACTIONS/CAREER NOTES: Selected by Detroit Lions in second round (56th pick overall) of 1992 NFL draft. ... Signed by Lions (July 23, 1992). ... Designated by Lions as transition player (February 15, 1994).
HONORS: Named kicker on THE SPORTING NEWS college All-America first team (1989). ... Named kicker on THE SPORTING NEWS NFL All-Pro team (1993). ... Played in Pro Bowl (1997 and 1999 season).

Year Team	G	FIELD GOALS							TOTALS		
		1-29	30-39	40-49	50+	Tot.	Pct.	Lg.	XPM	XPA	Pts.
1992—Detroit NFL	16	5-5	10-10	4-6	2-5	21-26	80.8	52	30	30	93
1993—Detroit NFL	16	9-9	15-15	7-12	3-7	‡34-‡43	79.1	53	28	28	‡130
1994—Detroit NFL	16	6-7	7-7	5-8	0-5	18-27	66.7	49	39	40	93
1995—Detroit NFL	16	6-6	16-17	5-10	1-1	28-34	82.4	56	*48	†48	132
1996—Detroit NFL	16	4-4	4-5	3-5	1-3	12-17	70.6	51	36	36	72
1997—Detroit NFL	16	10-10	8-9	5-5	3-5	26-29	89.7	†55	39	40	117
1998—Detroit NFL	16	8-8	7-7	13-15	1-3	29-33	87.9	51	27	29	114
1999—Detroit NFL	16	8-8	4-4	10-12	4-8	26-∞32	81.3	52	28	29	106
2000—Detroit NFL	16	8-9	10-12	4-7	2-2	24-30	80.0	54	29	29	101
2001—Detroit NFL	16	3-3	8-8	6-12	4-7	21-30	70.0	54	23	23	86
2002—Detroit NFL	16	8-8	8-9	7-8	0-3	23-28	82.1	49	31	31	100
Pro totals (11 years)	176	75-77	97-103	69-100	21-49	262-329	79.6	56	358	363	1144

HAPE, PATRICK — FB/TE — BRONCOS

PERSONAL: Born June 6, 1974, in Killen, Ala. ... 6-4/262. ... Full name: Patrick Stephen Hape.
HIGH SCHOOL: Brooks (Killen, Ala.).
COLLEGE: Alabama.
TRANSACTIONS/CAREER NOTES: Selected by Tampa Bay Buccaneers in fifth round (137th pick overall) of 1997 NFL draft. ... Signed by Buccaneers (July 20, 1997). ... Granted free agency (February 11, 2000). ... Re-signed by Buccaneers (July 23, 2000). ... Granted unconditional free agency (March 2, 2001). ... Signed by Denver Broncos (March 14, 2001).
CHAMPIONSHIP GAME EXPERIENCE: Played in NFC championship game (1999 season).
SINGLE GAME HIGHS (regular season): Receptions—2 (December 16, 2001, vs. Kansas City); yards—35 (December 16, 2001, vs. Kansas City); and touchdown receptions—1 (November 17, 2002, vs. Seattle). ... Attempts—2 (September 10, 2001, vs. New York Giants); yards—1 (August 31, 1997, vs. San Francisco); and rushing touchdowns—0.

Year Team	G	GS	RECEIVING				TOTALS			
			No.	Yds.	Avg.	TD	TD	2pt.	Pts.	Fum.
1997—Tampa Bay NFL	14	3	4	22	5.5	1	1	0	6	1
1998—Tampa Bay NFL	16	2	4	27	6.8	0	0	1	2	1
1999—Tampa Bay NFL	15	1	5	12	2.4	1	1	0	6	0
2000—Tampa Bay NFL	16	2	6	39	6.5	0	0	0	0	0
2001—Denver NFL	15	8	15	96	6.4	3	3	0	18	0
2002—Denver NFL	16	0	6	26	4.3	2	2	0	12	0
Pro totals (6 years)	92	16	40	222	5.6	7	7	1	44	2

HARDY, KEVIN — LB — BENGALS

PERSONAL: Born July 24, 1973, in Evansville, Ind. ... 6-4/259. ... Full name: Kevin Lamont Hardy.
HIGH SCHOOL: Harrison (Evansville, Ind.).
COLLEGE: Illinois (degree in marketing, 1995).
TRANSACTIONS/CAREER NOTES: Selected by Jacksonville Jaguars in first round (second pick overall) of 1996 NFL draft. ... Signed by Jaguars (July 17, 1996). ... On injured reserve with knee injury (December 11, 2001-remainder of season). ... Granted unconditional free agency (March 1, 2002). ... Signed by Dallas Cowboys (April 14, 2002). ... Granted unconditional free agency (February 28, 2003). ... Signed by Cincinnati Bengals (March 7, 2003).
CHAMPIONSHIP GAME EXPERIENCE: Played in AFC championship game (1996 and 1999 seasons).
HONORS: Butkus Award winner (1995). ... Named linebacker on THE SPORTING NEWS college All-America first team (1995). ... Named linebacker on THE SPORTING NEWS NFL All-Pro team (1999). ... Played in Pro Bowl (1999 season).

Year Team	G	GS	TOTALS			INTERCEPTIONS			
			Tk.	Ast.	Sks.	No.	Yds.	Avg.	TD
1996—Jacksonville NFL	16	15	64	22	5.5	2	19	9.5	0
1997—Jacksonville NFL	13	11	48	7	2.5	0	0	0.0	0
1998—Jacksonville NFL	16	16	87	25	1.5	2	40	20.0	0
1999—Jacksonville NFL	16	16	74	24	10.5	0	0	0.0	0
2000—Jacksonville NFL	16	16	72	14	3.0	1	0	0.0	0
2001—Jacksonville NFL	9	9	57	12	5.5	0	0	0.0	0
2002—Dallas NFL	16	15	60	15	2.0	0	0	0.0	0
Pro totals (7 years)	102	98	462	119	30.5	5	59	11.8	0

HARPER, NICK — DB — COLTS

PERSONAL: Born September 10, 1974, in Baldwin, Ga. ... 5-10/182. ... Full name: Nicholas Necosi Harper.
HIGH SCHOOL: Baldwin (Milledgeville, Ga.).
COLLEGE: Fort Valley State.
TRANSACTIONS/CAREER NOTES: Signed as non-drafted free agent by Indianapolis Colts (January 16, 2001).

Year Team	G	GS	Tk.	Ast.	Sks.	No.	Yds.	Avg.	TD
			TOTALS			**INTERCEPTIONS**			
2001—Indianapolis NFL	13	2	19	4	0.0	2	17	8.5	0
2002—Indianapolis NFL	16	1	35	5	0.0	0	0	0.0	0
Pro totals (2 years)	29	3	54	9	0.0	2	17	8.5	0

HARRINGTON, JOEY   QB   LIONS

PERSONAL: Born October 21, 1978, in Portland, Ore. ... 6-4/220. ... Full name: John Joseph Harrington.
HIGH SCHOOL: Central Catholic (Portland, Ore.).
COLLEGE: Oregon.
TRANSACTIONS/CAREER NOTES: Selected by Detroit Lions in first round (third pick overall) of 2002 NFL draft. ... Signed by Lions (July 23, 2002).
HONORS: Named quarterback on THE SPORTING NEWS college All-America second team (2001).
SINGLE GAME HIGHS (regular season): Attempts—44 (November 28, 2002, vs. New England); completions—25 (October 13, 2002, vs. Minnesota); yards—309 (October 13, 2002, vs. Minnesota); and touchdown passes—2 (November 17, 2002, vs. New York Jets).
STATISTICAL PLATEAUS: 300-yard passing games: 2002 (1).
MISCELLANEOUS: Regular-season record as starting NFL quarterback: 3-9 (.250).

Year Team	G	GS	Att.	Cmp.	Pct.	Yds.	TD	Int.	Avg.	Skd.	Rat.	Att.	Yds.	Avg.	TD	TD	2pt.	Pts.
			PASSING									**RUSHING**				**TOTALS**		
2002—Detroit NFL	14	12	429	215	50.1	2294	12	16	5.35	8	59.9	7	4	0.6	0	0	0	0

HARRIS, AL   CB   PACKERS

PERSONAL: Born December 7, 1974, in Pompano Beach, Fla. ... 6-1/185. ... Full name: Alshinard Harris.
HIGH SCHOOL: Ely (Pompano Beach, Fla.).
JUNIOR COLLEGE: Trinity Valley Community College (Texas).
COLLEGE: Texas A&M-Kingsville.
TRANSACTIONS/CAREER NOTES: Selected by Tampa Bay Buccaneers in sixth round (169th pick overall) of 1997 NFL draft. ... Signed by Buccaneers (July 1, 1997). ... Released by Buccaneers (August 24, 1997). ... Re-signed by Buccaneers to practice squad (August 26, 1997). ... Claimed on waivers by Philadelphia Eagles (August 31, 1998). ... Traded by Eagles to Green Bay Packers for second-round pick (traded to San Diego) in 2003 draft (March 1, 2003).
CHAMPIONSHIP GAME EXPERIENCE: Played in NFC championship game (2001 and 2002 seasons).

Year Team	G	GS	Tk.	Ast.	Sks.	No.	Yds.	Avg.	TD
			TOTALS			**INTERCEPTIONS**			
1998—Philadelphia NFL	16	7	40	1	0.0	0	0	0.0	0
1999—Philadelphia NFL	16	6	32	6	0.0	4	‡151	37.8	1
2000—Philadelphia NFL	16	4	25	2	0.0	0	1	0.0	0
2001—Philadelphia NFL	16	2	20	2	0.0	2	22	11.0	0
2002—Philadelphia NFL	16	2	22	2	0.0	1	0	0.0	0
Pro totals (5 years)	80	21	139	13	0.0	7	174	24.9	1

HARRIS, ANTWAN   CB   PATRIOTS

PERSONAL: Born May 29, 1977, in Raleigh, N.C. ... 5-9/194. ... Full name: Melvin Antwan Harris.
HIGH SCHOOL: Ravenscroft (Raleigh, N.C.).
COLLEGE: Virginia.
TRANSACTIONS/CAREER NOTES: Selected by New England Patriots in sixth round (187th pick overall) of 2000 NFL draft. ... Signed by Patriots (July 14, 2000).

Year Team	G	GS	Tk.	Ast.	Sks.	No.	Yds.	Avg.	TD
			TOTALS			**INTERCEPTIONS**			
2000—New England NFL	14	0	6	1	1.0	1	11	11.0	0
2001—New England NFL	11	1	2	2	0.0	0	0	0.0	0
2002—New England NFL	14	0	9	1	0.0	0	0	0.0	0
Pro totals (3 years)	39	1	17	4	1.0	1	11	11.0	0

HARRIS, ATNAF   WR   TEXANS

PERSONAL: Born February 27, 1979, in Fresno, Calif. ... 6-1/182.
HIGH SCHOOL: Edison (Huntington Beach, Calif.).
COLLEGE: Cal State Northridge.
TRANSACTIONS/CAREER NOTES: Signed as non-drafted free agent by Houston Texans (May 22, 2002). ... Released by Texans (September 1, 2002). ... Re-signed by Texans to practice squad (September 2, 2002). ... Released by Texans (September 10, 2002). ... Re-signed by Texans to practice squad (September 14, 2002). ... Activated (November 26, 2002).
SINGLE GAME HIGHS (regular season): Receptions—1 (December 29, 2002, vs. Tennessee); yards—8 (December 29, 2002, vs. Tennessee); and touchdown receptions—0.

Year Team	G	GS	No.	Yds.	Avg.	TD
			RECEIVING			
2002—Houston NFL	1	1	1	8	8.0	0

H

HARRIS, BERNARDO   LB   RAVENS

PERSONAL: Born October 15, 1971, in Chapel Hill, N.C. ... 6-2/250. ... Full name: Bernardo Jamaine Harris.
HIGH SCHOOL: Chapel Hill (N.C.).
COLLEGE: North Carolina.
TRANSACTIONS/CAREER NOTES: Signed as non-drafted free agent by Kansas City Chiefs (June 2, 1994). ... Released by Chiefs (August 2, 1994). ... Signed by Green Bay Packers (January 20, 1995). ... Released by Packers (February 27, 2002). ... Signed by Baltimore Ravens (August 6, 2002). ... Granted unconditional free agency (February 28, 2003). ... Re-signed by Ravens (April 1, 2003).
CHAMPIONSHIP GAME EXPERIENCE: Played in NFC championship game (1995-1997 seasons). ... Member of Super Bowl championship team (1996 season). ... Played in Super Bowl XXXII (1997 season).

Year Team	G	GS	TOTALS Tk.	Ast.	Sks.	INTERCEPTIONS No.	Yds.	Avg.	TD
1995—Green Bay NFL	11	0	4	1	0.0	0	0	0.0	0
1996—Green Bay NFL	16	0	7	1	0.0	0	0	0.0	0
1997—Green Bay NFL	16	16	65	48	1.0	1	0	0.0	0
1998—Green Bay NFL	16	16	67	38	2.0	0	0	0.0	0
1999—Green Bay NFL	16	15	69	40	0.0	0	0	0.0	0
2000—Green Bay NFL	16	16	76	21	2.0	0	0	0.0	0
2001—Green Bay NFL	16	16	69	29	2.5	2	12	6.0	0
2002—Baltimore NFL	13	11	50	12	2.0	2	11	5.5	0
Pro totals (8 years)	120	90	407	190	9.5	5	23	4.6	0

HARRIS, COREY   CB   CHIEFS

PERSONAL: Born November 28, 1976, in Warner Robins, Ga. ... 5-10/187.
HIGH SCHOOL: Northside (Warner Robins, Ga.).
COLLEGE: The Citadel, then North Alabama.
TRANSACTIONS/CAREER NOTES: Signed as non-drafted free agent by New Orleans Saints (May 20, 1999). ... Released by Saints (September 5, 1999). ... Re-signed by Saints to practice squad (September 6, 1999). ... Released by Saints (September 28, 1999). ... Re-signed by Saints to practice squad (October 27, 1999). ... Activated (December 17, 1999). ... Released by Saints (September 20, 2000). ... Assigned by Saints to Rhein Fire in 2001 NFL Europe enhancement allocation program (February 19, 2001). ... Released by Saints (May 8, 2001). ... Signed by Kansas City Chiefs (September 18, 2001).

Year Team	G	GS	TOTALS Tk.	Ast.	Sks.	INTERCEPTIONS No.	Yds.	Avg.	TD
1999—New Orleans NFL	3	0	0	0	0.0	0	0	0.0	0
2000—New Orleans NFL	3	1	0	0	0.0	0	0	0.0	0
2001—Rhein NFLE	...	...	...	...	0.0	2	57	28.5	1
—Kansas City NFL	4	0	0	0	0.0	0	0	0.0	0
2002—Kansas City NFL	14	0	15	2	1.0	0	0	0.0	0
NFL Europe totals (1 year)	...	...	...	...	0.0	2	57	28.5	1
NFL totals (4 years)	24	1	15	2	1.0	0	0	0.0	0
Pro totals (5 years)	...	...	...	...	1.0	2	57	28.5	1

HARRIS, COREY   S   LIONS

PERSONAL: Born October 25, 1969, in Indianapolis. ... 5-11/213. ... Full name: Corey Lamont Harris.
HIGH SCHOOL: Ben Davis (Indianapolis).
COLLEGE: Vanderbilt (degree in human resources).
TRANSACTIONS/CAREER NOTES: Selected by Houston Oilers in third round (77th pick overall) of 1992 NFL draft. ... Signed by Oilers (August 5, 1992). ... Claimed on waivers by Green Bay Packers (October 14, 1992). ... Granted free agency (February 17, 1995). ... Tendered offer sheet by Seattle Seahawks (March 3, 1995). ... Packers declined to match offer (March 10, 1995). ... Granted unconditional free agency (February 14, 1997). ... Signed by Miami Dolphins (March 17, 1997). ... Released by Dolphins (August 3, 1998). ... Signed by Baltimore Ravens (August 17, 1998). ... Granted unconditional free agency (February 12, 1999). ... Re-signed by Ravens (May 17, 1999). ... Granted unconditional free agency (February 11, 2000). ... Re-signed by Ravens (March 21, 2000). ... Granted unconditional free agency (March 1, 2002). ... Signed by Detroit Lions (April 2, 2002).
CHAMPIONSHIP GAME EXPERIENCE: Played in AFC championship game (2000 season). ... Member of Super Bowl championship team (2000 season).
MISCELLANEOUS: Played wide receiver (1992 and 1993).

Year Team	G	GS	TOTALS Tk.	Ast.	Sks.	INTERCEPTIONS No.	Yds.	Avg.	TD	KICKOFF RETURNS No.	Yds.	Avg.	TD	TOTALS TD	2pt.	Pts.	Fum.
1992—Houston NFL	5	0	0	0	0.0	0	0	0.0	0	0	0	0.0	0	0	0	0	0
—Green Bay NFL	10	0	0	0	0.0	0	0	0.0	0	33	691	20.9	0	0	0	0	0
1993—Green Bay NFL	11	0	4	0	0.0	0	0	0.0	0	16	482	30.1	0	0	0	0	1
1994—Green Bay NFL	16	2	32	6	0.0	0	0	0.0	0	29	618	21.3	0	0	0	0	0
1995—Seattle NFL	16	16	76	9	0.0	3	-5	-1.7	0	19	397	20.9	0	1	0	6	0
1996—Seattle NFL	16	16	69	6	1.0	1	25	25.0	0	7	166	23.7	0	0	0	0	0
1997—Miami NFL	16	7	29	14	0.0	0	0	0.0	0	11	224	20.4	0	0	0	0	0
1998—Baltimore NFL	16	6	45	12	1.0	0	0	0.0	0	35	965§27.6 ▲1			1	0	6	2
1999—Baltimore NFL	16	0	31	6	1.0	1	24	24.0	1	38	843	22.2	0	1	0	6	0
2000—Baltimore NFL	16	0	31	3	0.0	2	44	22.0	0	39	907	23.3	0	0	0	0	1
2001—Baltimore NFL	16	16	74	10	0.0	2	1	0.5	0	11	235	21.4	0	0	0	0	0
2002—Detroit NFL	16	16	58	21	2.5	1	49	49.0	0	0	0	0.0	0	0	0	0	0
Pro totals (11 years)	170	79	449	87	5.5	10	138	13.8	1	238	5528	23.2	1	3	0	18	4

H

PERSONAL: Born August 21, 1972, in Chicago. ... 6-2/210.
HIGH SCHOOL: Martin Luther King (Chicago).
JUNIOR COLLEGE: San Bernardino (Calif.) Valley.
COLLEGE: Mississippi State.
TRANSACTIONS/CAREER NOTES: Signed by San Antonio Texans of CFL (October 17, 1995). ... Selected by Edmonton Eskimos in 1996 U.S. Team Dispersal draft. ... Released by Eskimos (June 5, 1996). ... Played with Tampa Bay Storm of Arena League (1996-98). ... Signed by Toronto Argonauts of CFL (October 12, 1996). ... Released by Argonauts (May 15, 1997). ... Re-signed by Argonauts (June 2, 1997). ... Signed as non-drafted free agent by Oakland Raiders (February 28, 1999). ... Released by Raiders (September 5, 1999). ... Re-signed by Raiders to practice squad (September 7, 1999). ... Activated (December 1999). ... Released by Raiders (September 1, 2002). ... Signed by New York Giants (October 21, 2002).
CHAMPIONSHIP GAME EXPERIENCE: Member of CFL championship team (1996). ... Played in AFC championship game (2000 season).

Year Team	G	GS	TOTALS			INTERCEPTIONS			
			Tk.	Ast.	Sks.	No.	Yds.	Avg.	TD
1996—Toronto CFL	4	...	...	...	0.0	0	0	0.0	0
1997—Toronto CFL	18	...	...	...	0.0	5	72	14.4	0
1998—			Did not play.						
1999—Oakland NFL	4	0	0	0	0.0	0	0	0.0	0
2000—Oakland NFL	15	2	27	6	0.0	0	0	0.0	0
2001—Oakland NFL	16	5	31	7	0.5	0	0	0.0	0
2002—New York Giants NFL	9	0	9	0	0.0	1	11	11.0	0
CFL totals (2 years)	22	...	...	...	0.0	5	72	14.4	0
NFL totals (4 years)	44	7	67	13	0.5	1	11	11.0	0
Pro totals (6 years)	66	...	...	...	0.5	6	83	13.8	0

PERSONAL: Born February 25, 1979, in Dixmoor, Ill. ... 6-2/255. ... Full name: Napoleon Bill Harris.
HIGH SCHOOL: Thornton (Harvey, Ill.).
COLLEGE: Northwestern.
TRANSACTIONS/CAREER NOTES: Selected by Oakland Raiders in first round (23rd pick overall) of 2002 NFL draft. ... Signed by Raiders (July 19, 2002).
CHAMPIONSHIP GAME EXPERIENCE: Played in AFC championship game (2002 season). ... Played in Super Bowl XXXVII (2002 season).

Year Team	G	GS	TOTALS			INTERCEPTIONS			
			Tk.	Ast.	Sks.	No.	Yds.	Avg.	TD
2002—Oakland NFL	15	13	59	22	0.5	0	0	0.0	0

PERSONAL: Born July 23, 1978, in Phoenix. ... 6-2/218.
HIGH SCHOOL: Westview (Phoenix).
COLLEGE: California (degree in business administration).
TRANSACTIONS/CAREER NOTES: Selected by Denver Broncos in fourth round (120th pick overall) of 2001 NFL draft. ... Signed by Broncos (May 22, 2001). ... Claimed on waivers by Cincinnati Bengals (August 29, 2001).

Year Team	G	PUNTING					
		No.	Yds.	Avg.	Net avg.	In. 20	Blk.
2001—Cincinnati NFL	16	84	3372	40.1	33.9	21	1
2002—Cincinnati NFL	15	65	2608	40.1	31.4	11	1
Pro totals (2 years)	31	149	5980	40.1	32.8	32	2

PERSONAL: Born January 26, 1977, in Wilkes-Barre, Pa. ... 6-1/214. ... Full name: Quentin Hugh Harris.
HIGH SCHOOL: Wilkes-Barre (Pa.).
COLLEGE: Syracuse.
TRANSACTIONS/CAREER NOTES: Signed as non-drafted free agent by Arizona Cardinals (April 22, 2002). ... Released by Cardinals (September 1, 2002). ... Re-signed by Cardinals to practice squad (September 3, 2002). ... Activated (November 14, 2002).

Year Team	G	GS	TOTALS			INTERCEPTIONS			
			Tk.	Ast.	Sks.	No.	Yds.	Avg.	TD
2002—Arizona NFL	6	0	0	0	0.0	0	0	0.0	0

PERSONAL: Born August 10, 1974, in La Grange, Ga. ... 5-11/192. ... Full name: Walter Lee Harris.
HIGH SCHOOL: La Grange (Ga.).
COLLEGE: Mississippi State.
TRANSACTIONS/CAREER NOTES: Selected by Chicago Bears in first round (13th pick overall) of 1996 NFL draft. ... Signed by Bears (July 11, 1996). ... On injured reserve with knee injury (December 22, 1998-remainder of season). ... On injured reserve with knee injury (December 22, 2000-remainder of season). ... Granted unconditional free agency (March 2, 2001). ... Re-signed by Bears (April 25, 2001). ... Granted unconditional free agency (March 1, 2002). ... Signed by Indianapolis Colts (March 15, 2002).

H

Year Team	G	GS	TOTALS Tk.	Ast.	Sks.	INTERCEPTIONS No.	Yds.	Avg.	TD
1996—Chicago NFL	15	13	84	14	0.0	2	0	0.0	0
1997—Chicago NFL	16	16	76	7	0.0	5	30	6.0	0
1998—Chicago NFL	14	14	64	5	0.0	4	41	10.3	1
1999—Chicago NFL	15	15	60	10	1.0	1	-1	-1.0	0
2000—Chicago NFL	12	12	33	9	0.0	2	35	17.5	1
2001—Chicago NFL	15	13	49	2	0.0	1	45	45.0	1
2002—Indianapolis NFL	15	15	35	9	0.0	2	0	0.0	0
Pro totals (7 years)	102	98	401	56	1.0	17	150	8.8	3

HARRISON, JAMES — LB — STEELERS

PERSONAL: Born May 4, 1978, in Akron, Ohio. ... 6-0/242. ... Full name: James Harrison Jr.
HIGH SCHOOL: Coventry (Akron, Ohio).
COLLEGE: Kent State.
TRANSACTIONS/CAREER NOTES: Signed as non-drafted free agent by Pittsburgh Steelers (April 22, 2002). ... Released by Steelers (September 1, 2002). ... Re-signed by Steelers to practice squad (September 3, 2002). ... Activated (December 17, 2002).

HARRISON, LLOYD — CB

PERSONAL: Born June 21, 1977, in Jamaica. ... 5-10/190.
HIGH SCHOOL: Sewanhaka (Floral Park, N.Y.).
COLLEGE: North Carolina State.
TRANSACTIONS/CAREER NOTES: Selected by Washington Redskins in third round (64th pick overall) of 2000 NFL draft. ... Signed by Redskins (July 7, 2000). ... Claimed on waivers by San Diego Chargers (September 3, 2001). ... Claimed on waivers by Miami Dolphins (September 2, 2002). ... Released by Dolphins (September 23, 2002).

Year Team	G	GS	TOTALS Tk.	Ast.	Sks.	INTERCEPTIONS No.	Yds.	Avg.	TD
2000—Washington NFL	2	0	0	0	0.0	0	0	0.0	0
2001—San Diego NFL	12	1	15	2	1.0	0	0	0.0	0
2002—Miami NFL	2	0	0	0	0.0	0	0	0.0	0
Pro totals (3 years)	16	1	15	2	1.0	0	0	0.0	0

HARRISON, MARVIN — WR — COLTS

PERSONAL: Born August 25, 1972, in Philadelphia. ... 6-0/175. ... Full name: Marvin Daniel Harrison.
HIGH SCHOOL: Roman Catholic (Philadelphia).
COLLEGE: Syracuse.
TRANSACTIONS/CAREER NOTES: Selected by Indianapolis Colts in first round (19th pick overall) of 1996 NFL draft. ... Signed by Colts (July 8, 1996). ... On injured reserve with shoulder injury (December 2, 1998-remainder of season).
HONORS: Named kick returner on THE SPORTING NEWS All-America first team (1995). ... Named wide receiver on THE SPORTING NEWS NFL All-Pro team (1999, 2000 and 2002). ... Played in Pro Bowl (1999-2002 seasons).
RECORDS: Holds NFL single-season record for most pass receptions—143 (2002).
SINGLE GAME HIGHS (regular season): Receptions—14 (November 17, 2002, vs. Dallas); yards—196 (September 26, 1999, vs. San Diego); and touchdown receptions—3 (November 11, 2001, vs. Miami).
STATISTICAL PLATEAUS: 100-yard receiving games: 1996 (2), 1998 (2), 1999 (9), 2000 (8), 2001 (6), 2002 (10). Total: 37.
MISCELLANEOUS: Holds Indianapolis Colts all-time records for most receptions (665) and most touchdown receptions (73).

Year Team	G	GS	RECEIVING No.	Yds.	Avg.	TD	PUNT RETURNS No.	Yds.	Avg.	TD	TOTALS TD	2pt.	Pts.	Fum.
1996—Indianapolis NFL	16	15	64	836	13.1	8	18	177	9.8	0	8	0	48	1
1997—Indianapolis NFL	16	15	73	866	11.9	6	0	0	0.0	0	6	2	40	2
1998—Indianapolis NFL	12	12	59	776	13.2	7	0	0	0.0	0	7	1	44	0
1999—Indianapolis NFL	16	16	115	*1663	14.5	§12	0	0	0.0	0	12	†1	74	2
2000—Indianapolis NFL	16	16	†102	1413	13.9	§14	0	0	0.0	0	14	0	84	2
2001—Indianapolis NFL	16	16	109	§1524	14.0	§15	0	0	0.0	0	15	0	90	0
2002—Indianapolis NFL	16	16	*143	*1722	12.0	11	0	0	0.0	0	11	1	68	0
Pro totals (7 years)	108	106	665	8800	13.2	73	18	177	9.8	0	73	5	448	7

HARRISON, RODNEY — S — PATRIOTS

PERSONAL: Born December 15, 1972, in Markham, Ill. ... 6-1/220. ... Full name: Rodney Scott Harrison.
HIGH SCHOOL: Marian Catholic (Chicago Heights, Ill.).
COLLEGE: Western Illinois.
TRANSACTIONS/CAREER NOTES: Selected after junior season by San Diego Chargers in fifth round (145th pick overall) of 1994 NFL draft. ... Signed by Chargers (June 29, 1994). ... Released by Chargers (February 27, 2003). ... Signed by New England Patriots (March 12, 2003).
CHAMPIONSHIP GAME EXPERIENCE: Played in AFC championship game (1994 season). ... Played in Super Bowl XXIX (1994 season).
HONORS: Named safety on THE SPORTING NEWS NFL All-Pro team (1998 and 2001). ... Played in Pro Bowl (1998 and 2001 seasons).

Year Team	G	GS	TOTALS			INTERCEPTIONS			
			Tk.	Ast.	Sks.	No.	Yds.	Avg.	TD
1994—San Diego NFL	15	0	0	0	0.0	0	0	0.0	0
1995—San Diego NFL	11	0	21	3	0.0	5	22	4.4	0
1996—San Diego NFL	16	16	105	20	1.0	5	56	11.2	0
1997—San Diego NFL	16	16	96	36	4.0	2	75	37.5	1
1998—San Diego NFL	16	16	89	25	4.0	3	42	14.0	0
1999—San Diego NFL	6	6	30	11	1.0	1	0	0.0	0
2000—San Diego NFL	16	16	101	26	6.0	6	97	16.2	1
2001—San Diego NFL	14	14	91	17	3.5	2	51	25.5	0
2002—San Diego NFL	13	13	69	19	2.0	2	2	1.0	0
Pro totals (9 years)	123	97	602	157	21.5	26	345	13.3	2

HARRISON, TYREO   LB

PERSONAL: Born May 15, 1980, in Sulphur Springs, Texas. ... 6-2/238. ... Full name: Tyreo Tremayne Harrison.
HIGH SCHOOL: Sulphur Springs (Texas).
COLLEGE: Notre Dame.
TRANSACTIONS/CAREER NOTES: Selected by Philadelphia Eagles in sixth round (198th pick overall) of 2002 NFL draft. ... Signed by Eagles (May 13, 2002). ... Released by Eagles (September 26, 2002). ... Re-signed by Eagles to practice squad (September 28, 2002). ... Activated (October 22, 2002).
CHAMPIONSHIP GAME EXPERIENCE: Member of Eagles for NFC championship game (2002 season); inactive.

Year Team	G	GS	TOTALS			INTERCEPTIONS			
			Tk.	Ast.	Sks.	No.	Yds.	Avg.	TD
2002—Philadelphia NFL	2	0	0	0	0.0	0	0	0.0	0

HARTINGS, JEFF   C   STEELERS

PERSONAL: Born September 7, 1972, in St. Henry, Ohio. ... 6-3/295. ... Full name: Jeffrey Allen Hartings.
HIGH SCHOOL: St. Henry (Ohio).
COLLEGE: Penn State.
TRANSACTIONS/CAREER NOTES: Selected by Detroit Lions in first round (23rd pick overall) of 1996 NFL draft. ... Signed by Lions (September 27, 1996). ... Granted unconditional free agency (March 2, 2001). ... Signed by Pittsburgh Steelers (March 8, 2001).
PLAYING EXPERIENCE: Detroit NFL, 1996-2000; Pittsburgh NFL, 2001-2002. ... Games/Games started: 1996 (11/10), 1997 (16/16), 1998 (13/13), 1999 (16/16), 2000 (16/16), 2001 (16/16), 2002 (13/11). Total: 101/98.
CHAMPIONSHIP GAME EXPERIENCE: Played in AFC championship game (2001 season).
HONORS: Named offensive lineman on THE SPORTING NEWS college All-America second team (1994). ... Named offensive lineman on THE SPORTING NEWS college All-America first team (1995).

HARTS, SHAUNARD   DB   CHIEFS

PERSONAL: Born August 4, 1978, in Pittsburg, Calif. ... 5-11/207.
HIGH SCHOOL: Pittsburg (Calif.).
COLLEGE: Boise State.
TRANSACTIONS/CAREER NOTES: Selected by Kansas City Chiefs in seventh round (212th pick overall) of 2001 NFL draft. ... Signed by Chiefs (July 3, 2001). ... Released by Chiefs (September 2, 2001). ... Re-signed by Chiefs to practice squad (September 3, 2001). ... Activated (December 22, 2001).

Year Team	G	GS	TOTALS			INTERCEPTIONS			
			Tk.	Ast.	Sks.	No.	Yds.	Avg.	TD
2001—Kansas City NFL	3	0	0	0	0.0	0	0	0.0	0
2002—Kansas City NFL	16	11	71	9	2.0	0	0	0.0	0
Pro totals (2 years)	19	11	71	9	2.0	0	0	0.0	0

HARTWELL, EDGERTON   LB   RAVENS

PERSONAL: Born May 27, 1978, in Las Vegas, Nev. ... 6-1/250.
HIGH SCHOOL: Cheyenne (Las Vegas, Nev.).
COLLEGE: Wisconsin, then Western Illinois.
TRANSACTIONS/CAREER NOTES: Selected by Baltimore Ravens in fourth round (126th pick overall) of 2001 NFL draft. ... Signed by Ravens (June 8, 2001).

Year Team	G	GS	TOTALS			INTERCEPTIONS			
			Tk.	Ast.	Sks.	No.	Yds.	Avg.	TD
2001—Baltimore NFL	16	0	0	0	0.0	0	0	0.0	0
2002—Baltimore NFL	16	15	105	39	3.0	0	0	0.0	0
Pro totals (2 years)	32	15	105	39	3.0	0	0	0.0	0

HARTWIG, JUSTIN   G   TITANS

PERSONAL: Born November 21, 1978, in Mankato, Minn. ... 6-4/300.
HIGH SCHOOL: Valley (West Des Moines, Iowa).
COLLEGE: Kansas.
TRANSACTIONS/CAREER NOTES: Selected by Tennessee Titans in sixth round (187th pick overall) of 2002 NFL draft. ... Signed by Titans (July 11, 2002).
PLAYING EXPERIENCE: Tennessee NFL, 2002. ... Games/games started: 2002 (3/0).
CHAMPIONSHIP GAME EXPERIENCE: Member of Titans for AFC championship game (2002 season); inactive.

H

PERSONAL: Born September 25, 1975, in Boulder, Colo. ... 6-4/223. ... Full name: Matthew Michael Hasselbeck. ... Son of Don Hasselbeck, tight end with New England Patriots (1977-85); and brother of Tim Hasselbeck, quarterback, Philadelphia Eagles.
HIGH SCHOOL: Xaverian Brothers (Westwood, Mass.).
COLLEGE: Boston College (degree in marketing and finance, 1997).
TRANSACTIONS/CAREER NOTES: Selected by Green Bay Packers in sixth round (187th pick overall) of 1998 NFL draft. ... Signed by Packers (July 17, 1998). ... Released by Packers (September 3, 1998). ... Re-signed by Packers to practice squad (September 5, 1998). ... Traded by Packers with first-round pick (G Steve Hutchinson) in 2001 draft to Seattle Seahawks for first-round pick (DE Jamal Reynolds) in 2001 draft (March 2, 2001).
SINGLE GAME HIGHS (regular season): Attempts—55 (December 1, 2002, vs. San Francisco); completions—36 (December 29, 2002, vs. San Diego); passing yards—449 (December 29, 2002, vs. San Diego); and touchdown passes—3 (December 1, 2002, vs. San Francisco).
STATISTICAL PLATEAUS: 300-yard passing games: 2002 (4).
MISCELLANEOUS: Regular-season record as starting NFL quarterback: 10-12 (.455).

Year Team	G	GS	Att.	Cmp.	Pct.	Yds.	TD	Int.	Avg.	Skd.	Rat.	Att.	Yds.	Avg.	TD	TD	2pt.	Pts.
					PASSING								**RUSHING**				**TOTALS**	
1999—Green Bay NFL	16	0	10	3	30.0	41	1	0	4.10	1	77.5	6	15	2.5	0	0	0	0
2000—Green Bay NFL	16	0	19	10	52.6	104	1	0	5.47	1	86.3	4	-5	-1.3	0	0	0	0
2001—Seattle NFL	13	12	321	176	54.8	2023	7	8	6.30	38	70.9	40	141	3.5	0	0	0	0
2002—Seattle NFL	16	10	419	267	‡63.7	3075	15	10	7.34	26	87.8	40	202	5.1	1	1	1	8
Pro totals (4 years)	61	22	769	456	59.3	5243	24	18	6.82	66	80.6	90	353	3.9	1	1	1	8

PERSONAL: Born April 6, 1978, in Norfolk, Mass. ... 6-1/211. ... Son of Don Hasselbeck, tight end with New England Patriots (1977-85); and brother of Matt Hasselbeck, quarterback, Seattle Seahawks.
HIGH SCHOOL: Xaverian Brothers (Westwood, Mass.).
COLLEGE: Boston College.
TRANSACTIONS/CAREER NOTES: Signed as non-drafted free agent by Buffalo Bills (April 24, 2001). ... Released by Bills (July 23, 2001). ... Signed by Baltimore Ravens (August 1, 2001). ... Released by Ravens (August 24, 2001). ... Signed by Philadelphia Eagles (February 6, 2002). ... Assigned by Eagles to Berlin Thunder in 2002 NFL Europe enhancement allocation program (February 12, 2002). ... Released by Eagles (September 1, 2002). ... Signed by Carolina Panthers to practice squad (October 22, 2002). ... Activated (October 25, 2002). ... Released by Panthers (October 29, 2002). ... Re-signed by Eagles to practice squad (November 19, 2002). ... Activated (November 27, 2002).
CHAMPIONSHIP GAME EXPERIENCE: Member of Eagles for NFC championship game (2002 season); inactive.

Year Team	G	GS	Att.	Cmp.	Pct.	Yds.	TD	Int.	Avg.	Skd.	Rat.	Att.	Yds.	Avg.	TD	TD	2pt.	Pts.
					PASSING								**RUSHING**				**TOTALS**	
2002—Berlin NFLE	...	...	47	30	63.8	342	1	0	7.28	0	92.7	6	6	1.0	0	0	0	0
—Philadelphia NFL	2	0	0	0	0.0	0	0	0	0.0	0	...	0	0	0.0	0	0	0	0
NFL Europe totals (1 year)	...	...	47	30	63.8	342	1	0	7.28	0	92.7	6	6	1.0	0	0	0	0
NFL totals (1 year)	2	0	0	0	0.0	0	0	0	0.0	0	...	0	0	0.0	0	0	0	0
Pro totals (2 years)	...	...	47	30	63.8	342	1	0	7.28	0	92.7	6	6	1.0	0	0	0	0

PERSONAL: Born December 20, 1966, in Butte, Mont. ... 5-10/187. ... Full name: Timothy Christian Hauck. ... Name pronounced HOWK.
HIGH SCHOOL: Sweet Grass County (Big Timber, Mont.).
COLLEGE: Pacific (Ore.), then Montana.
TRANSACTIONS/CAREER NOTES: Signed as non-drafted free agent by New England Patriots (May 1, 1990). ... Released by Patriots (August 26, 1990). ... Re-signed by Patriots to practice squad (October 1, 1990). ... Activated (October 27, 1990). ... Granted unconditional free agency (February 1, 1991). ... Signed by Green Bay Packers (April 1, 1991). ... Granted unconditional free agency (February 1-April 1, 1992). ... Re-signed by Packers for 1992 season. ... Granted free agency (March 1, 1993). ... Re-signed by Packers (July 13, 1993). ... Granted unconditional free agency (February 17, 1994). ... Re-signed by Packers (July 20, 1994). ... Granted unconditional free agency (February 17, 1995). ... Signed by Denver Broncos (March 6, 1995). ... Granted unconditional free agency (February 14, 1997). ... Signed by Seattle Seahawks (June 2, 1997). ... Granted unconditional free agency (February 13, 1998). ... Signed by Indianapolis Colts (July 26, 1998). ... Granted unconditional free agency (February 12, 1999). ... Signed by Philadelphia Eagles (April 20, 1999). ... Granted unconditional free agency (February 11, 2000). ... Re-signed by Eagles (August 24, 2000). ... Granted unconditional free agency (March 2, 2001). ... Re-signed by Eagles (August 18, 2001). ... Granted unconditional free agency (March 1, 2002). ... Re-signed by Eagles (November 6, 2002). ... Released by Eagles (November 26, 2002). ... Signed by San Francisco 49ers (December 3, 2002). ... Granted unconditional free agency (February 28, 2003).
CHAMPIONSHIP GAME EXPERIENCE: Played in NFC championship game (2001 season).

Year Team	G	GS	Tk.	Ast.	Sks.	No.	Yds.	Avg.	TD
				TOTALS			**INTERCEPTIONS**		
1990—New England NFL	10	0	3	1	0.0	0	0	0.0	0
1991—Green Bay NFL	16	0	6	1	0.0	0	0	0.0	0
1992—Green Bay NFL	16	0	15	0	0.0	0	0	0.0	0
1993—Green Bay NFL	13	0	0	2	0.0	0	0	0.0	0
1994—Green Bay NFL	13	3	28	12	0.0	0	0	0.0	0
1995—Denver NFL	16	0	12	2	0.0	0	0	0.0	0
1996—Denver NFL	16	0	7	3	0.0	0	0	0.0	0
1997—Seattle NFL	16	0	13	1	0.0	0	0	0.0	0
1998—Indianapolis NFL	16	7	53	10	0.0	0	0	0.0	0
1999—Philadelphia NFL	16	15	60	25	0.0	1	2	2.0	0
2000—Philadelphia NFL	16	3	15	10	0.0	0	0	0.0	0
2001—Philadelphia NFL	16	0	3	4	0.0	0	0	0.0	0
2002—San Francisco NFL	3	0	2	0	0.0	0	0	0.0	0
Pro totals (13 years)	183	28	217	71	0.0	1	2	2.0	0

H

HAWKINS, ARTRELL CB BENGALS

PERSONAL: Born November 24, 1976, in Johnstown, Pa. ... 5-10/190. ... Cousin of Carlton Haselrig, guard with Pittsburgh Steelers (1990-93) and New York Jets (1995).
HIGH SCHOOL: Bishop McCort (Johnstown, Pa.).
COLLEGE: Cincinnati.
TRANSACTIONS/CAREER NOTES: Selected by Cincinnati Bengals in second round (43rd pick overall) of 1998 NFL draft. ... Signed by Bengals (May 14, 1998). ... Granted free agency (March 2, 2001). ... Re-signed by Bengals (April 4, 2001). ... Granted unconditional free agency (March 1, 2002). ... Re-signed by Bengals (March 18, 2002).

			TOTALS			INTERCEPTIONS			
Year Team	G	GS	Tk.	Ast.	Sks.	No.	Yds.	Avg.	TD
1998—Cincinnati NFL	16	16	65	5	1.0	3	21	7.0	0
1999—Cincinnati NFL	14	13	61	7	0.0	0	0	0.0	0
2000—Cincinnati NFL	16	6	43	4	0.0	0	0	0.0	0
2001—Cincinnati NFL	14	13	49	10	0.0	3	26	8.7	0
2002—Cincinnati NFL	15	15	69	7	2.0	2	102	51.0	1
Pro totals (5 years)	75	63	287	33	3.0	8	149	18.6	1

HAWTHORNE, DUANE CB

PERSONAL: Born August 26, 1976, in St. Louis. ... 5-10/175. ... Name pronounced DUH-wann.
HIGH SCHOOL: Ladue (Mo.).
COLLEGE: Northern Illinois.
TRANSACTIONS/CAREER NOTES: Signed as non-drafted free agent by Dallas Cowboys (April 23, 1999). ... Assigned by Cowboys to Scottish Claymores in 2000 NFL Europe enhancement allocation program (February 18, 2000). ... Granted free agency (March 1, 2002). ... Re-signed by Cowboys (April 25, 2002). ... Released by Cowboys (December 7, 2002). ... Signed by San Francisco 49ers (December 11, 2002). ... Granted unconditional free agency (February 28, 2003).

			TOTALS			INTERCEPTIONS			
Year Team	G	GS	Tk.	Ast.	Sks.	No.	Yds.	Avg.	TD
1999—Dallas NFL	13	0	17	3	0.0	3	-2	-0.7	0
2000—Scottish NFLE	...	...	...	...	0.0	4	51	12.8	0
—Dallas NFL	14	0	1	0	0.0	0	0	0.0	0
2001—Dallas NFL	16	11	51	12	0.0	2	28	14.0	0
2002—Dallas NFL	10	5	17	4	0.0	1	15	15.0	0
—San Francisco NFL	3	0	0	0	0.0	0	0	0.0	0
NFL Europe totals (1 year)	...	...	...	...	0.0	4	51	12.8	0
NFL totals (4 years)	56	16	86	19	0.0	6	41	6.8	0
Pro totals (5 years)	...	...	...	...	0.0	10	92	9.2	0

HAWTHORNE, MICHAEL CB SAINTS

PERSONAL: Born January 26, 1977, in Sarasota, Fla. ... 6-3/200. ... Full name: Michael Seneca Hawthorne.
HIGH SCHOOL: Booker (Sarasota, Fla.).
COLLEGE: Purdue.
TRANSACTIONS/CAREER NOTES: Selected by New Orleans Saints in sixth round (195th pick overall) of 2000 NFL draft. ... Signed by Saints (June 23, 2000). ... On injured reserve with knee injury (December 22, 2002-remainder of season). ... Granted free agency (February 28, 2003). ... Re-signed by Saints (May 7, 2003).

			TOTALS			INTERCEPTIONS			
Year Team	G	GS	Tk.	Ast.	Sks.	No.	Yds.	Avg.	TD
2000—New Orleans NFL	11	0	6	1	0.0	0	0	0.0	0
2001—New Orleans NFL	11	2	15	3	0.0	0	0	0.0	0
2002—New Orleans NFL	6	4	25	9	0.0	1	0	0.0	0
Pro totals (3 years)	28	6	46	13	0.0	1	0	0.0	0

HAYES, CHRIS S

PERSONAL: Born May 7, 1972, in San Bernardino, Calif. ... 6-0/205.
HIGH SCHOOL: San Gorgonio (San Bernardino, Calif.).
COLLEGE: Washington State.
TRANSACTIONS/CAREER NOTES: Selected by New York Jets in seventh round (210th pick overall) of 1996 NFL draft. ... Signed by Jets (June 26, 1996). ... Released by Jets (August 19, 1996). ... Signed by Washington Redskins to practice squad (September 11, 1996). ... Released by Redskins (October 2, 1996). ... Signed by Green Bay Packers to practice squad (October 4, 1996). ... Activated (December 9, 1996). ... Traded by Packers to Jets for CB Carl Greenwood (June 5, 1997). ... Granted free agency (February 11, 2000). ... Re-signed by Jets (May 8, 2000). ... Granted unconditional free agency (March 2, 2001). ... Re-signed by Jets (March 13, 2001). ... Released by Jets (February 25, 2002). ... Signed by New England Patriots (March 12, 2002). ... Released by Patriots (August 30, 2002). ... Re-signed by Patriots (December 2, 2002). ... Granted unconditional free agency (February 28, 2003).
CHAMPIONSHIP GAME EXPERIENCE: Played in NFC championship game (1996 season). ... Member of Super Bowl championship team (1996 season). ... Played in AFC championship game (1998 season).

			TOTALS			INTERCEPTIONS			
Year Team	G	GS	Tk.	Ast.	Sks.	No.	Yds.	Avg.	TD
1996—Green Bay NFL	2	0	0	0	0.0	0	0	0.0	0
1997—New York Jets NFL	16	0	0	0	0.0	0	0	0.0	0
1998—New York Jets NFL	15	0	4	1	0.0	0	0	0.0	0
1999—New York Jets NFL	15	0	0	0	0.0	0	0	0.0	0
2000—New York Jets NFL	16	8	23	6	0.0	1	0	0.0	0
2001—New York Jets NFL	16	1	5	2	0.0	0	0	0.0	0
2002—New England NFL	4	0	0	0	0.0	0	0	0.0	0
Pro totals (7 years)	84	9	32	9	0.0	1	0	0.0	0

H

HAYES, DONALD   WR   JAGUARS

PERSONAL: Born July 13, 1975, in Madison, Wis. ... 6-4/220. ... Full name: Donald Ross Hayes Jr.
HIGH SCHOOL: Madison East (Wis.).
COLLEGE: Wisconsin.
TRANSACTIONS/CAREER NOTES: Selected by Carolina Panthers in fourth round (106th pick overall) of 1998 NFL draft. ... Signed by Panthers (July 8, 1998). ... Granted free agency (March 2, 2001). ... Re-signed by Panthers (March 2, 2001). ... Granted unconditional free agency (March 1, 2002). ... Signed by New England Patriots (March 12, 2002). ... Released by Patriots (February 21, 2003). ... Signed by Jacksonville Jaguars (March 11, 2003).
SINGLE GAME HIGHS (regular season): Receptions—7 (October 14, 2001, vs. New Orleans); yards—133 (November 28, 1999, vs. Atlanta); and touchdown receptions—1 (December 8, 2002, vs. Buffalo).
STATISTICAL PLATEAUS: 100-yard receiving games: 1999 (1), 2000 (1). Total: 2.

				RECEIVING		
Year Team	G	GS	No.	Yds.	Avg.	TD
1998—Carolina NFL	7	0	3	62	20.7	0
1999—Carolina NFL	13	1	11	270	24.5	2
2000—Carolina NFL	15	15	66	926	14.0	3
2001—Carolina NFL	16	15	52	597	11.5	2
2002—New England NFL	12	1	12	133	11.1	2
Pro totals (5 years)	63	32	144	1988	13.8	9

HAYGOOD, HERB   WR   BRONCOS

PERSONAL: Born December 30, 1977, in Sarasota, Fla. ... 5-11/193.
HIGH SCHOOL: Sarasota (Fla.).
COLLEGE: Michigan State.
TRANSACTIONS/CAREER NOTES: Selected by Denver Broncos in fifth round (144th pick overall) of 2002 NFL draft. ... Signed by Broncos (June 18, 2002). ... Released by Broncos (September 1, 2002). ... Re-signed by Broncos to practice squad (September 3, 2002). ... Activated (November 4, 2002).
HONORS: Named kick returner on THE SPORTING NEWS college All-America second team (2001).

			RUSHING				RECEIVING				KICKOFF RETURNS				TOTALS			
Year Team	G	GS	Att.	Yds.	Avg.	TD	No.	Yds.	Avg.	TD	No.	Yds.	Avg.	TD	TD	2pt.	Pts.	Fum.
2002—Denver NFL	4	0	0	0	0.0	0	0	0	0.0	0	0	0	0.0	0	0	0	0	0

HAYNES, VERRON   FB   STEELERS

PERSONAL: Born February 17, 1979, in Bronx, N.Y. ... 5-10/223.
HIGH SCHOOL: North Springs (Atlanta).
COLLEGE: Western Kentucky, then Georgia.
TRANSACTIONS/CAREER NOTES: Selected by Pittsburgh Steelers in fifth round (166th pick overall) of 2002 NFL draft. ... Signed by Steelers (July 24, 2002). ... On injured reserve with broken leg (December 17, 2002-remainder of season).
SINGLE GAME HIGHS (regular season): Attempts—4 (November 3, 2002, vs. Cleveland); yards—23 (October 27, 2002, vs. Baltimore); and rushing touchdowns—0.

			RUSHING				RECEIVING				TOTALS			
Year Team	G	GS	Att.	Yds.	Avg.	TD	No.	Yds.	Avg.	TD	TD	2pt.	Pts.	Fum.
2002—Pittsburgh NFL	14	0	10	51	5.1	0	3	10	3.3	0	0	0	0	0

HAYNESWORTH, ALBERT   DT   TITANS

PERSONAL: Born June 17, 1981, in Hartsville, S.C. ... 6-6/320. ... Full name: Albert Haynesworth III.
HIGH SCHOOL: Hartsville (S.C.).
COLLEGE: Tennessee.
TRANSACTIONS/CAREER NOTES: Selected after junior season by Tennessee Titans in first round (15th pick overall) of 2002 NFL draft. ... Signed by Titans (July 29, 2002).
CHAMPIONSHIP GAME EXPERIENCE: Played in AFC championship game (2002 season).

			TOTALS		
Year Team	G	GS	Tk.	Ast.	Sks.
2002—Tennessee NFL	16	3	21	9	1.0

HAYWARD, REGGIE   DE   BRONCOS

PERSONAL: Born March 14, 1979, in Chicago. ... 6-5/270.
HIGH SCHOOL: Thornridge (Dolton, Ill.).
COLLEGE: Iowa State.
TRANSACTIONS/CAREER NOTES: Selected by Denver Broncos in third round (87th pick overall) of 2001 NFL draft. ... Signed by Broncos (July 26, 2001). ... On injured reserve with hand injury (December 4, 2002-remainder of season).

			TOTALS		
Year Team	G	GS	Tk.	Ast.	Sks.
2001—Denver NFL	6	2	15	3	3.0
2002—Denver NFL	9	0	6	3	0.0
Pro totals (2 years)	15	2	21	6	3.0

H

HEAP, TODD   TE   RAVENS

PERSONAL: Born March 16, 1980, in Mesa, Ariz. ... 6-5/252. ... Full name: Todd Benjamin Heap.
HIGH SCHOOL: Mountain View (Mesa, Ariz.).
COLLEGE: Arizona State.
TRANSACTIONS/CAREER NOTES: Selected after junior season by Baltimore Ravens in first round (31st pick overall) of 2001 NFL draft. ... Signed by Ravens (July 28, 2001).
HONORS: Named tight end on THE SPORTING NEWS college All-America first team (2000). ... Played in Pro Bowl (2002 season).
SINGLE GAME HIGHS (regular season): Receptions—7 (December 29, 2002, vs. Pittsburgh); yards—146 (December 29, 2002, vs. Pittsburgh); and touchdown receptions—2 (October 20, 2002, vs. Jacksonville).
STATISTICAL PLATEAUS: 100-yard receiving games: 2002 (1).

			RECEIVING			
Year Team	G	GS	No.	Yds.	Avg.	TD
2001—Baltimore NFL	12	7	16	206	12.9	1
2002—Baltimore NFL	16	16	68	836	12.3	6
Pro totals (2 years)	28	23	84	1042	12.4	7

HEARD, RONNIE   S   49ERS

PERSONAL: Born October 5, 1976, in Bay City, Texas. ... 6-3/215.
HIGH SCHOOL: Brazoswood (Clute, Texas).
COLLEGE: Mississippi.
TRANSACTIONS/CAREER NOTES: Signed as non-drafted free agent by San Francisco 49ers (April 20, 2000). ... Released by 49ers (August 27, 2000). ... Re-signed by 49ers to practice squad (August 29, 2000). ... Activated (October 16, 2000). ... Granted free agency (February 28, 2003). ... Released by 49ers (March 23, 2003). ... Re-signed by 49ers (May 16, 2003).

			TOTALS			INTERCEPTIONS			
Year Team	G	GS	Tk.	Ast.	Sks.	No.	Yds.	Avg.	TD
2000—San Francisco NFL	13	3	13	3	2.0	0	0	0.0	0
2001—San Francisco NFL	16	0	24	6	1.0	0	0	0.0	0
2002—San Francisco NFL	12	6	34	8	0.0	4	60	15.0	0
Pro totals (3 years)	41	9	71	17	3.0	4	60	15.0	0

HEARST, GARRISON   RB   49ERS

PERSONAL: Born January 4, 1971, in Lincolnton, Ga. ... 5-11/215. ... Full name: Gerald Garrison Hearst.
HIGH SCHOOL: Lincoln County (Lincolnton, Ga.).
COLLEGE: Georgia.
TRANSACTIONS/CAREER NOTES: Selected after junior season by Phoenix Cardinals in first round (third pick overall) of 1993 NFL draft. ... Signed by Cardinals (August 28, 1993). ... On injured reserve with knee injury (November 4, 1993-remainder of season). ... Cardinals franchise renamed Arizona Cardinals for 1994 season. ... On physically unable to perform list with knee injury (August 23-October 13, 1994). ... Granted free agency (February 16, 1996). ... Re-signed by Cardinals (May 23, 1996). ... Claimed on waivers by Cincinnati Bengals (August 21, 1996). ... Granted unconditional free agency (February 14, 1997). ... Signed by San Francisco 49ers (March 7, 1997). ... On physically unable to perform list with leg injury (July 30, 1999-entire season). ... On physically unable to perform list with leg injury (August 22-November 21, 2000). ... Granted unconditional free agency (March 1, 2002). ... Re-signed by 49ers (March 19, 2002).
CHAMPIONSHIP GAME EXPERIENCE: Played in NFC championship game (1997 season).
HONORS: Doak Walker Award winner (1992). ... Named running back on THE SPORTING NEWS college All-America first team (1992). ... Named to play in Pro Bowl (1998 season); replaced by Emmitt Smith due to injury. ... Played in Pro Bowl (2001 season).
SINGLE GAME HIGHS (regular season): Attempts—31 (December 1, 2002, vs. Seattle); yards—198 (December 14, 1998, vs. Detroit); and rushing touchdowns—3 (December 1, 2002, vs. Seattle).
STATISTICAL PLATEAUS: 100-yard rushing games: 1995 (3), 1997 (3), 1998 (6), 2001 (4), 2002 (2). Total: 18. ... 100-yard receiving games: 1998 (2), 2001 (1). Total: 3.

			RUSHING				RECEIVING				TOTALS			
Year Team	G	GS	Att.	Yds.	Avg.	TD	No.	Yds.	Avg.	TD	TD	2pt.	Pts.	Fum.
1993—Phoenix NFL	6	5	76	264	3.5	1	6	18	3.0	0	1	0	6	2
1994—Arizona NFL	8	0	37	169	4.6	1	6	49	8.2	0	1	0	6	0
1995—Arizona NFL	16	15	284	1070	3.8	1	29	243	8.4	1	2	0	12	12
1996—Cincinnati NFL	16	12	225	847	3.8	0	12	131	10.9	1	1	1	8	1
1997—San Francisco NFL	13	13	234	1019	4.4	4	21	194	9.2	2	6	0	36	2
1998—San Francisco NFL	16	16	310	1570	‡5.1	7	39	535	13.7	2	9	1	56	4
1999—San Francisco NFL			Did not play.											
2000—San Francisco NFL			Did not play.											
2001—San Francisco NFL	16	16	252	1206	4.8	4	41	347	8.5	1	5	0	30	1
2002—San Francisco NFL	16	16	215	972	4.5	8	48	317	6.6	1	9	1	56	4
Pro totals (8 years)	107	93	1633	7117	4.4	26	202	1834	9.1	8	34	3	210	26

HEATH, RODNEY   CB

PERSONAL: Born October 29, 1974, in Cincinnati. ... 5-10/177. ... Full name: Rodney Larece Heath.
HIGH SCHOOL: Western Hills (Cincinnati).
COLLEGE: Minnesota (degree in sports studies).
TRANSACTIONS/CAREER NOTES: Signed as non-drafted free agent by Cincinnati Bengals (January 27, 1999). ... On injured reserve with shoulder injury (December 4, 2000-remainder of season). ... On injured reserve with hamstring injury (October 16, 2001-remainder of season). ... Claimed on waivers by Carolina Panthers (September 2, 2002). ... Released by Panthers (September 5, 2002). ... Signed by Atlanta Falcons (September 11, 2002). ... Released by Falcons (September 17, 2002).

H

Year Team	G	GS	TOTALS Tk.	Ast.	Sks.	INTERCEPTIONS No.	Yds.	Avg.	TD
1999—Cincinnati NFL	16	9	43	3	0.0	3	72	24.0	1
2000—Cincinnati NFL	13	9	40	4	0.0	0	0	0.0	0
2001—Cincinnati NFL	5	5	16	3	0.0	0	0	0.0	0
2002—Atlanta NFL	1	0	0	0	0.0	0	0	0.0	0
Pro totals (4 years)	35	23	99	10	0.0	3	72	24.0	1

HEFFNER-LIDDIARD, BRODY   TE

PERSONAL: Born June 12, 1977, in Salt Lake City. ... 6-4/250. ... Full name: Jon Brody Heffner-Liddiard.
HIGH SCHOOL: Torrey Pines (San Diego).
COLLEGE: Colorado.
TRANSACTIONS/CAREER NOTES: Signed as non-drafted free agent by Minnesota Vikings (April 25, 2000). ... Released by Vikings (August 14, 2000). ... Signed by New York Giants (August 20, 2000). ... Released by Giants (September 4, 2000). ... Re-signed by Giants to practice squad (September 5, 2000). ... Activated (September 9, 2000). ... Released by Giants (September 12, 2000). ... Signed by Miami Dolphins (November 23, 2000). ... Released by Dolphins (July 11, 2001). ... Signed by Minnesota Vikings (July 23, 2001). ... Granted free agency (February 28, 2003).

Year Team	G	GS	RECEIVING No.	Yds.	Avg.	TD
2000—Miami NFL	5	0	0	0	0.0	0
2001—Minnesota NFL	16	0	0	0	0.0	0
2002—Minnesota NFL	16	0	0	0	0.0	0
Pro totals (3 years)	37	0	0	0	0.0	0

HEIDEN, STEVE   TE   BROWNS

PERSONAL: Born September 21, 1976, in Rushford, Minn. ... 6-5/270. ... Full name: Steve Allen Heiden. ... Name pronounced HIGH-den.
HIGH SCHOOL: Rushford-Peterson (Rushford, Minn.).
COLLEGE: South Dakota State.
TRANSACTIONS/CAREER NOTES: Selected by San Diego Chargers in third round (69th pick overall) of 1999 NFL draft. ... Signed by Chargers (July 22, 1999). ... Granted free agency (March 1, 2002). ... Re-signed by Chargers (April 3, 2002). ... Traded by Chargers to Cleveland Browns for seventh-round pick (traded to Dallas) in 2003 draft (September 1, 2002).
SINGLE GAME HIGHS (regular season): Receptions—5 (December 8, 2002, vs. Jacksonville); yards—24 (November 24, 2001, vs. Arizona); and touchdown receptions—1 (November 3, 2002, vs. Pittsburgh).

Year Team	G	GS	RECEIVING No.	Yds.	Avg.	TD
1999—San Diego NFL	11	0	0	0	0.0	0
2000—San Diego NFL	15	2	6	32	5.3	1
2001—San Diego NFL	16	9	8	55	6.9	1
2002—Cleveland NFL	16	6	17	105	6.2	1
Pro totals (4 years)	58	17	31	192	6.2	3

HEINRICH, KEITH   TE   PANTHERS

PERSONAL: Born March 19, 1979, in Tomball, Texas. ... 6-5/255.
HIGH SCHOOL: Tomball (Texas).
COLLEGE: Sam Houston State.
TRANSACTIONS/CAREER NOTES: Selected by Carolina Panthers in sixth round (174th pick overall) of 2002 NFL draft. ... Signed by Panthers (July 12, 2002). ... On injured reserve with foot injury (October 17, 2002-remainder of season).

Year Team	G	GS	RECEIVING No.	Yds.	Avg.	TD
2002—Carolina NFL	4	0	0	0	0.0	0

HEINRICH-TAVES, JOSH   DE   PANTHERS

PERSONAL: Born May 13, 1972, in Watsonville, Calif. ... 6-7/285. ... Name pronounced TAAVS.
HIGH SCHOOL: Dennis-Yarmouth Regional (South Yarmouth, Mass.), then New Hampton Prep.
COLLEGE: Northeastern.
TRANSACTIONS/CAREER NOTES: Signed as non-drafted free agent by Detroit Lions (May 3, 1995). ... Released by Lions (August 28, 1995). ... Re-signed by Lions (August 30, 1995). ... Activated (December 21, 1995); did not play. ... Assigned by Lions to Barcelona Dragons in 1996 World League enhancement allocation program (February 1996). ... Released by Lions (August 21, 1996). ... Signed by Jacksonville Jaguars (November 13, 1996); did not play. ... Released by Jaguars (December 4, 1996). ... Signed by New England Patriots to practice squad (December 31, 1996). ... On injured reserve with ankle injury (August 21-September 22, 1997). ... Released by Patriots (September 22, 1997). ... Signed by Miami Dolphins (June 22, 1998). ... Claimed on waivers by New Orleans Saints (August 18, 1998). ... Released by Saints (September 5, 1998). ... Signed by Oakland Raiders (March 10, 1999). ... Released by Raiders (September 4, 1999). ... Re-signed by Raiders (February 17, 2000). ... Released by Raiders (September 1, 2002). ... Signed by Carolina Panthers (November 26, 2002).
CHAMPIONSHIP GAME EXPERIENCE: Played in AFC championship game (2000 season).

Year Team	G	GS	TOTALS Tk.	Ast.	Sks.	INTERCEPTIONS No.	Yds.	Avg.	TD
1995—Detroit NFL			Did not play.						
1996—Barcelona W.L.	...	...	...	...	6.0	0	0	0.0	0
—Jacksonville NFL			Did not play.						
1997—New England NFL			Did not play.						

– 184 –

Year	Team	G	GS	TOTALS			INTERCEPTIONS			
				Tk.	Ast.	Sks.	No.	Yds.	Avg.	TD
1998—Barcelona NFLE		10	10	...	...	9.0	0	0	0.0	0
—New Orleans NFL				Did not play.						
2000—Oakland NFL		16	0	21	3	3.0	1	24	24.0	0
2001—Oakland NFL		8	3	7	5	1.0	0	0	0.0	0
2002—Carolina NFL		5	0	3	2	0.0	0	0	0.0	0
NFL Europe totals (1 year)		10	10	...	...	9.0	0	0	0.0	0
W.L. totals (1 year)		...	...	...	...	6.0	0	0	0.0	0
NFL totals (3 years)		29	3	31	10	4.0	1	24	24.0	0
Pro totals (5 years)		...	...	...	...	19.0	1	24	24.0	0

HEITMANN, ERIC   G   49ERS

PERSONAL: Born February 24, 1980, in Brookshire, Texas. ... 6-3/305.
HIGH SCHOOL: Katy (Texas).
COLLEGE: Stanford.
TRANSACTIONS/CAREER NOTES: Selected by San Francisco 49ers in seventh round (239th pick overall) of 2002 NFL draft. ... Signed by 49ers (July 21, 2002).
PLAYING EXPERIENCE: San Francisco NFL, 2002. ... Games/games started: 2002 (16/12).
HONORS: Named guard on THE SPORTING NEWS college All-America second team (2001).

HENDERSON, JAMIE   CB   JETS

PERSONAL: Born January 1, 1979, in Carrolton, Ga. ... 6-2/202. ... Full name: Jamie Concepcion Henderson.
HIGH SCHOOL: Carrolton (Ga.).
JUNIOR COLLEGE: Mississippi Gulf Coast Junior College.
COLLEGE: Georgia.
TRANSACTIONS/CAREER NOTES: Selected by New York Jets in fourth round (101st pick overall) of 2001 NFL draft. ... Signed by Jets (June 28, 2001). ... On injured reserve with shoulder injury (October 8, 2002-remainder of season).

Year	Team	G	GS	TOTALS			INTERCEPTIONS			
				Tk.	Ast.	Sks.	No.	Yds.	Avg.	TD
2001—New York Jets NFL		16	0	8	4	0.0	1	5	5.0	0
2002—New York Jets NFL		2	0	3	0	0.0	0	0	0.0	0
Pro totals (2 years)		18	0	11	4	0.0	1	5	5.0	0

HENDERSON, JOHN   DT   JAGUARS

PERSONAL: Born January 9, 1979, in Nashville, Tenn. ... 6-7/316. ... Full name: John Nathan Henderson.
HIGH SCHOOL: Pearl-Cohn (Nashville, Tenn.).
COLLEGE: Tennessee.
TRANSACTIONS/CAREER NOTES: Selected by Jacksonville Jaguars in first round (ninth pick overall) of 2002 NFL draft. ... Signed by Jaguars (July 25, 2002).
HONORS: Named defensive tackle on THE SPORTING NEWS college All-America first team (2000 and 2001). ... Outland Trophy winner (2000).

Year	Team	G	GS	TOTALS		
				Tk.	Ast.	Sks.
2002—Jacksonville NFL		16	13	45	9	6.5

HENDERSON, WILLIAM   FB   PACKERS

PERSONAL: Born February 19, 1971, in Richmond, Va. ... 6-1/249. ... Full name: William Terrelle Henderson.
HIGH SCHOOL: Thomas Dale (Chester, Va.).
COLLEGE: North Carolina.
TRANSACTIONS/CAREER NOTES: Selected by Green Bay Packers in third round (66th pick overall) of 1995 NFL draft. ... Signed by Packers (July 17, 1995). ... Granted free agency (February 13, 1998). ... Re-signed by Packers (June 15, 1998). ... Granted unconditional free agency (February 12, 1999). ... Re-signed by Packers (April 6, 1999). ... Granted unconditional free agency (March 1, 2002). ... Re-signed by Packers (March 1, 2002).
CHAMPIONSHIP GAME EXPERIENCE: Played in NFC championship game (1995-1997 seasons). ... Member of Super Bowl championship team (1996 season). ... Played in Super Bowl XXXII (1997 season).
SINGLE GAME HIGHS (regular season): Attempts—6 (December 29, 2002, vs. New York Jets); yards—40 (September 9, 1996, vs. Philadelphia); and rushing touchdowns—1 (September 8, 2002, vs. Atlanta).

Year	Team	G	GS	RUSHING				RECEIVING				TOTALS			
				Att.	Yds.	Avg.	TD	No.	Yds.	Avg.	TD	TD	2pt.	Pts.	Fum.
1995—Green Bay NFL		15	1	7	35	5.0	0	3	21	7.0	0	0	0	0	0
1996—Green Bay NFL		16	11	39	130	3.3	0	27	203	7.5	1	1	0	6	1
1997—Green Bay NFL		16	14	31	113	3.6	0	41	367	9.0	1	1	0	6	1
1998—Green Bay NFL		16	10	23	70	3.0	2	37	241	6.5	1	3	0	18	1
1999—Green Bay NFL		16	13	7	29	4.1	2	30	203	6.8	1	3	0	18	1
2000—Green Bay NFL		16	6	2	16	8.0	0	35	234	6.7	1	1	0	6	1
2001—Green Bay NFL		16	8	6	11	1.8	0	21	193	9.2	0	0	0	0	0
2002—Green Bay NFL		15	12	7	27	3.9	1	26	168	6.5	3	4	0	24	0
Pro totals (8 years)		126	75	122	431	3.5	5	220	1630	7.4	8	13	0	78	5

HENDRICKS, TOMMY — LB — DOLPHINS

PERSONAL: Born October 23, 1978, in Houston. ... 6-2/235. ... Full name: Thomas Emmett Hendricks III.
HIGH SCHOOL: Scarborough (Texas), then Eiserhower (Houston).
COLLEGE: Michigan.
TRANSACTIONS/CAREER NOTES: Signed as non-drafted free agent by Miami Dolphins (April 25, 2000). ... Released by Dolphins (August 27, 2000). ... Re-signed by Dophins (September 26, 2000). ... Released by Dolphins (October 2, 2000). ... Re-signed by Dolphins to practice squad (October 4, 2000). ... Activated (November 10, 2000).

Year Team	G	GS	TOTALS Tk.	Ast.	Sks.	INTERCEPTIONS No.	Yds.	Avg.	TD
2000—Miami NFL	8	0	0	1	0.0	0	0	0.0	0
2001—Miami NFL	16	1	2	2	0.0	0	0	0.0	0
2002—Miami NFL	16	0	2	0	0.0	0	0	0.0	0
Pro totals (3 years)	40	1	4	3	0.0	0	0	0.0	0

HENRY, ANTHONY — CB — BROWNS

PERSONAL: Born November 3, 1976, in Fort Myers, Fla. ... 6-1/204. ... Full name: Anthony Daniel Henry.
HIGH SCHOOL: Estero (Fla.).
COLLEGE: South Florida.
TRANSACTIONS/CAREER NOTES: Selected by Cleveland Browns in fourth round (97th pick overall) of 2001 NFL draft. ... Signed by Browns (June 15, 2001).

Year Team	G	GS	TOTALS Tk.	Ast.	Sks.	INTERCEPTIONS No.	Yds.	Avg.	TD
2001—Cleveland NFL	16	2	37	9	0.0	†10	177	17.7	1
2002—Cleveland NFL	16	10	57	5	0.0	2	4	2.0	0
Pro totals (2 years)	32	12	94	14	0.0	12	181	15.1	1

HENRY, TRAVIS — RB — BILLS

PERSONAL: Born October 29, 1978, in Frostproof, Fla. ... 5-9/220. ... Full name: Travis Deion Henry.
HIGH SCHOOL: Frostproof (Fla.).
COLLEGE: Tennessee.
TRANSACTIONS/CAREER NOTES: Selected by Buffalo Bills in second round (58th pick overall) of 2001 NFL draft. ... Signed by Bills (July 26, 2001).
HONORS: Played in Pro Bowl (2002 season).
SINGLE GAME HIGHS (regular season): Attempts—35 (December 1, 2002, vs. Miami); yards—159 (October 13, 2002, vs. Houston); and rushing touchdowns—3 (September 8, 2002, vs. New York Jets).
STATISTICAL PLATEAUS: 100-yard rushing games: 2001 (2), 2002 (6). Total: 8.

Year Team	G	GS	RUSHING Att.	Yds.	Avg.	TD	RECEIVING No.	Yds.	Avg.	TD	TOTALS TD	2pt.	Pts.	Fum.
2001—Buffalo NFL	13	12	213	729	3.4	4	22	179	8.1	0	4	0	24	5
2002—Buffalo NFL	16	16	325	1438	4.4	13	43	309	7.2	1	14	0	84	11
Pro totals (2 years)	29	28	538	2167	4.0	17	65	488	7.5	1	18	0	108	16

HENTRICH, CRAIG — P — TITANS

PERSONAL: Born May 18, 1971, in Alton, Ill. ... 6-3/202. ... Full name: Craig Anthony Hentrich. ... Name pronounced HEN-trick.
HIGH SCHOOL: Alton-Marquette (Ill.).
COLLEGE: Notre Dame.
TRANSACTIONS/CAREER NOTES: Selected by New York Jets in eighth round (200th pick overall) of 1993 NFL draft. ... Signed by Jets (July 14, 1993). ... Released by Jets (August 24, 1993). ... Signed by Green Bay Packers to practice squad (September 7, 1993). ... Activated (January 14, 1994); did not play. ... Granted unconditional free agency (February 13, 1998). ... Signed by Tennessee Oilers (February 19, 1998). ... Oilers franchise renamed Tennessee Titans for 1999 season (December 26, 1998). ... Designated by Titans as transition player (February 20, 2003).
CHAMPIONSHIP GAME EXPERIENCE: Played in NFC championship game (1995-1997 seasons). ... Member of Super Bowl championship team (1996 season). ... Played in Super Bowl XXXII (1997 season) and Super Bowl XXXIV (1999 season). ... Played in AFC championship game (1999 and 2002 seasons).
HONORS: Named punter on THE SPORTING NEWS NFL All-Pro team (1998). ... Played in Pro Bowl (1998 season).

Year Team	G	PUNTING No.	Yds.	Avg.	Net avg.	In. 20	Blk.	KICKING 50+	Tot.	Pct.	Lg.	TOTALS XPM	XPA	Pts.
1993—Green Bay NFL					Did not play.									
1994—Green Bay NFL	16	81	3351	41.4	35.5	24	0	0-0	0-0	0.0	0	0	0	0
1995—Green Bay NFL	16	65	2740	42.2	34.6	26	2	0-0	3-5	60.0	49	5	5	14
1996—Green Bay NFL	16	68	2886	42.4	36.2	28	0	0-0	0-0	0.0	0	0	0	0
1997—Green Bay NFL	16	75	3378	45.0	36.0	26	0	0-0	0-0	0.0	0	0	0	0
1998—Tennessee NFL	16	69	3258	*47.2	*39.2	18	0	0-0	0-1	0.0	0	0	0	0
1999—Tennessee NFL	16	90	3824	42.5	38.1	35	0	0-0	0-0	0.0	0	0	0	0
2000—Tennessee NFL	16	76	3101	40.8	36.3	33	0	0-1	0-1	0.0	0	0	0	0
2001—Tennessee NFL	16	85	3567	42.0	37.0	28	0	0-0	0-0	0.0	0	0	0	0
2002—Tennessee NFL	16	65	2725	41.9	33.9	28	1	0-0	0-0	0.0	0	0	0	0
Pro totals (9 years)	144	674	28830	42.8	36.4	246	3	0-1	3-7	42.9	49	5	5	14

H

HERNDON, JIMMY   OT   TEXANS

PERSONAL: Born August 30, 1973, in Baytown, Texas. ... 6-8/318.
HIGH SCHOOL: Lee (Baytown, Texas).
COLLEGE: Houston (degree in sociology, 1996).
TRANSACTIONS/CAREER NOTES: Selected by Jacksonville Jaguars in fifth round (146th pick overall) of 1996 NFL draft. ... Signed by Jaguars (May 24, 1996). ... Active for eight games (1996); did not play. ... Traded by Jaguars to Chicago Bears for seventh-round pick (WR Alvis Whitted) in 1998 draft (August 24, 1997). ... On injured reserve with knee injury (August 31, 1999-entire season). ... Granted unconditional free agency (March 1, 2002). ... Signed by Houston Texans (April 3, 2002). ... Granted unconditional free agency (February 28, 2003). ... Re-signed by Texans (March 27, 2003).
PLAYING EXPERIENCE: Chicago NFL, 1997, 1998, 2000 and 2001; Houston NFL, 2002. ... Games/Games started: 1997 (7/0), 1998 (9/2), 2000 (9/2), 2001 (16/0), 2002 (12/7). Total: 53/11.
CHAMPIONSHIP GAME EXPERIENCE: Member of Jaguars for AFC championship game (1996 season); inactive.

HERNDON, KELLY   CB   BRONCOS

PERSONAL: Born November 3, 1976, in Chamberlain, Ohio. ... 5-10/180.
HIGH SCHOOL: Chamberlain (Ohio).
COLLEGE: Toledo.
TRANSACTIONS/CAREER NOTES: Signed as non-drafted free agent by San Francisco 49ers (April 23, 1999). ... Released by 49ers (Seotember 6, 1999). ... Re-signed by 49ers (July 7, 2000). ... Released by 49ers (August 28, 2000). ... Signed by New York Giants (May 15, 2001). ... Released by Giants (September 2, 2001). ... Re-signed by Giants to practice squad (September 4, 2001). ... Released by Giants (September 18, 2001). ... Signed by Denver Broncos to practice squad (October 24, 2001).

| | | | TOTALS | | | INTERCEPTIONS | | | |
Year Team	G	GS	Tk.	Ast.	Sks.	No.	Yds.	Avg.	TD
2002—Denver NFL	14	0	0	0	0.0	1	0	0.0	0

HERNDON, STEVE   G   BRONCOS

PERSONAL: Born May 25, 1977, in LaGrange, Ga. ... 6-4/305. ... Full name: Steven Marshall Herndon.
HIGH SCHOOL: Troup County (LaGrange, Ga.).
COLLEGE: Georgia.
TRANSACTIONS/CAREER NOTES: Signed as non-drafted free agent by Miami Dolphins (April 25, 2000). ... Released by Dolphins (August 22, 2000). ... Signed by Denver Broncos to practice squad (August 29, 2000). ... Assigned by Broncos to Barcelona Dragons in 2001 NFL Europe enhancement allocation program (February 17, 2001).
PLAYING EXPERIENCE: Barcelona NFLE, 2000; Denver NFL, 2001-2002. ... Games/Games started: 2000 (games played unavailable), 2001 (5/3), 2002 (15/9). Total: 20/12.

HERRING, KIM   S   RAMS

PERSONAL: Born September 10, 1975, in Detroit. ... 6-0/200. ... Full name: Kimani Masai Herring.
HIGH SCHOOL: Solon (Ohio).
COLLEGE: Penn State.
TRANSACTIONS/CAREER NOTES: Selected by Baltimore Ravens in second round (58th pick overall) of 1997 NFL draft. ... Signed by Ravens (July 18, 1997). ... On injured reserve with shoulder injury (December 2, 1998-remainder of season). ... Granted free agency (February 11, 2000). ... Re-signed by Ravens (April 18, 2000) ... Granted unconditional free agency (March 2, 2001). ... Signed by St. Louis Rams (March 22, 2001).
CHAMPIONSHIP GAME EXPERIENCE: Member of Ravens for AFC Championship game (2000 season); inactive. ... Member of Super Bowl championship team (2000 season). ... Played in NFC championship game (2001 season). ... Played in Super Bowl XXXVI (2001 season).
HONORS: Named free safety on The Sporting News college All-America first team (1996).

| | | | TOTALS | | | INTERCEPTIONS | | | |
Year Team	G	GS	Tk.	Ast.	Sks.	No.	Yds.	Avg.	TD
1997—Baltimore NFL	15	4	44	8	1.0	0	0	0.0	0
1998—Baltimore NFL	7	7	20	7	0.0	0	0	0.0	0
1999—Baltimore NFL	16	16	48	10	0.0	0	0	0.0	0
2000—Baltimore NFL	16	16	47	7	1.0	3	74	24.7	0
2001—St. Louis NFL	16	15	49	6	0.0	1	15	15.0	0
2002—St. Louis NFL	16	16	66	9	0.0	3	38	12.7	0
Pro totals (6 years)	86	74	274	47	2.0	7	127	18.1	0

HERRON, ANTHONY   DE   LIONS

PERSONAL: Born September 24, 1979, in Bolingbrook, Ill. ... 6-3/280.
HIGH SCHOOL: Bolingbrook (Ill.).
COLLEGE: Iowa.
TRANSACTIONS/CAREER NOTES: Signed as non-drafted free agent by Detriot Lions (April 27, 2001). ... Released by Lions (September 2, 2001). ... Re-signed by Lions (November 27, 2001). ... On physically unable to perform list with foot injury (July 23, 2002-entire season).

| | | | TOTALS | | |
Year Team	G	GS	Tk.	Ast.	Sks.
2001—Detroit NFL	1	0	0	0	0.0
2002—Detroit NFL			Did not play.		
Pro totals (1 year)	1	0	0	0	0.0

H

HETHERINGTON, CHRIS   FB   RAIDERS

PERSONAL: Born November 27, 1972, in North Branford, Conn. ... 6-3/250. ... Full name: Christopher Raymond Hetherington.
HIGH SCHOOL: Avon (Conn.) Old Farms.
COLLEGE: Yale (degree in psychology).
TRANSACTIONS/CAREER NOTES: Signed as non-drafted free agent by Cincinnati Bengals (April 23, 1996). ... Released by Bengals (August 21, 1996). ... Re-signed by Bengals to practice squad (August 26, 1996). ... Signed by Indianapolis Colts off Bengals practice squad (October 22, 1996). ... Released by Colts (August 24, 1998). ... Re-signed by Colts (August 31, 1998). ... Released by Colts (February 12, 1999). ... Signed by Carolina Panthers (March 5, 1999). ... Granted unconditional free agency (February 11, 2000). ... Re-signed by Panthers (February 23, 2000). ... Granted unconditional free agency (March 1, 2002). ... Signed by St. Louis Rams (April 30, 2002). ... Granted unconditional free agency (February 28, 2003). ... Signed by Oakland Raiders (March 19, 2003).
SINGLE GAME HIGHS (regular season): Attempts—5 (December 10, 2000, vs. Kansas City); yards—29 (December 24, 2000, vs. Oakland); and rushing touchdowns—1 (December 10, 2000, vs. Kansas City).

Year Team	G	GS	RUSHING Att.	Yds.	Avg.	TD	RECEIVING No.	Yds.	Avg.	TD	KICKOFF RETURNS No.	Yds.	Avg.	TD	TOTALS TD	2pt.	Pts.	Fum.
1996—Indianapolis NFL	6	0	0	0	0.0	0	0	0	0.0	0	1	16	16.0	0	0	0	0	0
1997—Indianapolis NFL	16	0	0	0	0.0	0	0	0	0.0	0	2	23	11.5	0	0	0	0	0
1998—Indianapolis NFL	14	1	0	0	0.0	0	0	0	0.0	0	5	71	14.2	0	0	0	0	1
1999—Carolina NFL	14	0	2	7	3.5	0	0	0	0.0	0	1	16	16.0	0	0	0	0	0
2000—Carolina NFL	16	5	23	65	2.8	2	14	116	8.3	1	2	21	10.5	0	3	0	18	0
2001—Carolina NFL	16	1	5	12	2.4	0	23	124	5.4	0	4	31	7.8	0	0	0	0	0
2002—St. Louis NFL	6	4	1	0	0.0	0	1	2	2.0	0	0	0	0.0	0	0	0	0	0
Pro totals (7 years)	88	11	31	84	2.7	2	38	242	6.4	1	15	178	11.9	0	3	0	18	1

HICKS, ERIC   DE   CHIEFS

PERSONAL: Born June 17, 1976, in Erie, Pa. ... 6-6/280. ... Full name: Eric David Hicks.
HIGH SCHOOL: Mercyhurst (Erie, Pa.).
COLLEGE: Maryland.
TRANSACTIONS/CAREER NOTES: Signed as non-drafted free agent by Kansas City Chiefs (April 25, 1998).

Year Team	G	GS	TOTALS Tk.	Ast.	Sks.
1998—Kansas City NFL	3	0	0	0	0.0
1999—Kansas City NFL	16	16	28	9	4.0
2000—Kansas City NFL	13	11	37	9	14.0
2001—Kansas City NFL	16	16	44	9	3.5
2002—Kansas City NFL	16	15	40	14	9.0
Pro totals (5 years)	64	58	149	41	30.5

HILBERT, JON   K

PERSONAL: Born July 15, 1975, in West Palm Beach, Fla. ... 6-2/228. ... Full name: Jonathan Samuel Hilbert.
HIGH SCHOOL: Boonville (Ind.).
COLLEGE: Louisville.
TRANSACTIONS/CAREER NOTES: Signed as non-drafted free agent by Dallas Cowboys (April 15, 2000). ... Released by Cowboys (July 16, 2000). ... Signed by Buffalo Bills (July 20, 2000). ... Released by Bills (August 22, 2000). ... Signed by New Orleans Saints (March 26, 2001). ... Released by Saints (August 28, 2001). ... Signed by Cowboys (November 14, 2001). ... Granted free agency (March 1, 2002). ... Signed by Chicago Bears (March 15, 2002). ... Released by Bears (August 25, 2002). ... Signed by Carolina Panthers to practice squad (September 19, 2002). ... Activated (September 21, 2002). ... Released by Panthers (September 28, 2002).

Year Team	G	FIELD GOALS 1-29	30-39	40-49	50+	Tot.	Pct.	Lg.	TOTALS XPM	XPA	Pts.
2001—Dallas NFL	8	3-3	6-6	2-7	0-0	11-16	68.8	43	12	12	45
2002—Carolina NFL	1	0-0	0-1	0-1	0-0	0-2	0.0	0	3	3	3
Pro totals (2 years)	9	3-3	6-7	2-8	0-0	11-18	61.1	43	15	15	48

HILL, CHARLES   DT   TEXANS

PERSONAL: Born November 1, 1980, in Palmer Park, Md. ... 6-2/293. ... Full name: Charles LeDawnta Hill.
HIGH SCHOOL: Eleanor Roosevelt (Palmer Park, Md.).
COLLEGE: Maryland.
TRANSACTIONS/CAREER NOTES: Selected by Houston Texans in third round (83rd pick overall) of 2002 NFL draft. ... Signed by Texans (July 15, 2002).

Year Team	G	GS	TOTALS Tk.	Ast.	Sks.
2002—Houston NFL	16	0	1	1	0.0

HILL, DARRELL   WR   TITANS

PERSONAL: Born June 19, 1979, in Chicago. ... 6-3/197.
HIGH SCHOOL: Mount Carmel (Chicago).
COLLEGE: Northern Illinois.
TRANSACTIONS/CAREER NOTES: Selected by Tennessee Titans in seventh round (225th pick overall) of 2002 NFL draft. ... Signed by Titans (July 22, 2002).
CHAMPIONSHIP GAME EXPERIENCE: Member of Titans for AFC championship game (2002 season); inactive.

H

Year Team	G	GS	RECEIVING No.	Yds.	Avg.	TD
2002—Tennessee NFL	7	0	0	0	0.0	0

HILL, KAHLIL   WR   LIONS

PERSONAL: Born March 18, 1979, in Iowa City, Iowa. ... 6-2/200.
HIGH SCHOOL: Iowa City (Iowa).
COLLEGE: Iowa.
TRANSACTIONS/CAREER NOTES: Selected by Atlanta Falcons in sixth round (184th pick overall) of 2002 NFL draft. ... Signed by Falcons (June 14, 2002). ... Released by Falcons (August 31, 2002). ... Re-signed by Falcons to practice squad (September 3, 2002). ... Activated (September 14, 2002). ... Released by Falcons (September 17, 2002). ... Signed by New Orleans Saints to practice squad (October 3, 2002). ... Signed by Detroit Lions to practice squad (December 12, 2002).

			RUSHING				RECEIVING				PUNT RETURNS				KICKOFF RETURNS				TOTALS		
Year Team	G	GS	Att.	Yds.	Avg.	TD	No.	Yds.	Avg.	TD	No.	Yds.	Avg.	TD	No.	Yds.	Avg.	TD	TD	2pt.	Pts.
2002—Atlanta NFL	1	0	0	0	0.0	0	0	0	0.0	0	4	12	3.0	0	0	0	0.0	0	0	0	0

HILL, MADRE   RB   RAIDERS

PERSONAL: Born January 2, 1976, in Malvern, Ark. ... 5-11/199.
HIGH SCHOOL: Malvern (Ark.).
COLLEGE: Arkansas.
TRANSACTIONS/CAREER NOTES: Selected by Cleveland Browns in seventh round (207th pick overall) of 1999 NFL draft. ... Signed by Browns (July 22, 1999). ... Released by Browns (September 5, 1999). ... Re-signed by Browns to practice squad (September 6, 1999). ... Activated (November 23, 1999). ... On injured reserve with neck injury (August 27, 2000-entire season). ... Assigned by Browns to Berlin Thunder in 2001 NFL Europe enhancement allocation program (February 19, 2001). ... Released by Browns (February 22, 2001). ... Signed by San Diego Chargers (July 27, 2001). ... Released by Chargers (August 27, 2001). ... Signed by Oakland Raiders (February 8, 2002). ... Released by Raiders (September 1, 2002). ... Re-signed by Raiders to practice squad (September 3, 2002). ... Activated (October 22, 2002). ... Released by Raiders (November 15, 2002). ... Re-signed by Raiders to practice squad (November 26, 2002). ... Activated (January 18, 2003).
CHAMPIONSHIP GAME EXPERIENCE: Member of Raiders for AFC championship game (2002 season); inactive. ... Member of Raiders for Super Bowl XXXVII (2002 season); inactive.

			KICKOFF RETURNS				TOTALS			
Year Team	G	GS	No.	Yds.	Avg.	TD	TD	2pt.	Pts.	Fum.
1999—Cleveland NFL	5	0	8	137	17.1	0	0	0	0	0
2001—Berlin NFLE	...	...	7	98	14.0	0	4	0	24	0
2002—Oakland NFL	2	0	0	0	0.0	0	0	0	0	0
NFL Europe totals (1 year)	...	...	7	98	14.0	0	4	0	24	0
NFL totals (2 years)	7	0	8	137	17.1	0	0	0	0	0
Pro totals (3 years)	...	...	15	235	15.7	0	4	0	24	0

HILL, MATT   OT   SEAHAWKS

PERSONAL: Born November 10, 1978, in Grangeville, Idaho. ... 6-6/304.
HIGH SCHOOL: Grangeville (Idaho).
COLLEGE: Boise State.
TRANSACTIONS/CAREER NOTES: Selected by Seattle Seahawks in fifth round (171st pick overall) of 2002 NFL draft. ... Signed by Seahawks (July 25, 2002).
PLAYING EXPERIENCE: Seattle NFL, 2002. ... Games/games started: 2002 (14/0).

HILL, RENALDO   DB   CARDINALS

PERSONAL: Born November 12, 1978, in Detroit. ... 5-11/183.
HIGH SCHOOL: Chadsey (Mich.).
COLLEGE: Michigan State.
TRANSACTIONS/CAREER NOTES: Selected by Arizona Cardinals in seventh round (202nd pick overall) of 2001 NFL draft. ... Signed by Cardinals (May 29, 2001).

			TOTALS			INTERCEPTIONS			
Year Team	G	GS	Tk.	Ast.	Sks.	No.	Yds.	Avg.	TD
2001—Arizona NFL	14	1	16	6	0.5	0	0	0.0	0
2002—Arizona NFL	14	7	52	4	1.0	2	4	2.0	0
Pro totals (2 years)	28	8	68	10	1.5	2	4	2.0	0

HILLIARD, IKE   WR   GIANTS

PERSONAL: Born April 5, 1976, in Patterson, La. ... 5-11/205. ... Full name: Isaac Jason Hilliard. ... Nephew of Dalton Hilliard, running back with New Orleans Saints (1986-93).
HIGH SCHOOL: Patterson (La.).
COLLEGE: Florida.
TRANSACTIONS/CAREER NOTES: Selected by New York Giants in first round (seventh pick overall) of 1997 NFL draft. ... Signed by Giants (July 19, 1997). ... On injured reserve with neck injury (September 30, 1997-remainder of season). ... On injured reserve with shoulder injury (November 1, 2002-remainder of season). ... Granted unconditional free agency (February 28, 2003). ... Re-signed by Giants (March 6, 2003).
CHAMPIONSHIP GAME EXPERIENCE: Played in NFC championship game (2000 season).
SINGLE GAME HIGHS (regular season): Receptions—8 (September 10, 2000, vs. Philadelphia); yards—141 (November 30, 1998, vs. San Francisco); and touchdown receptions—2 (November 12, 2000, vs. St. Louis).
STATISTICAL PLATEAUS: 100-yard receiving games: 1998 (1), 1999 (3), 2000 (1), 2001 (2). Total: 7.

H

			RECEIVING				TOTALS			
Year Team	G	GS	No.	Yds.	Avg.	TD	TD	2pt.	Pts.	Fum.
1997—New York Giants NFL	2	2	2	42	21.0	0	0	0	0	0
1998—New York Giants NFL	16	16	51	715	14.0	2	2	0	12	2
1999—New York Giants NFL	16	16	72	996	13.8	3	3	0	18	0
2000—New York Giants NFL	14	14	55	787	14.3	8	8	0	48	0
2001—New York Giants NFL	14	9	52	659	12.7	6	6	0	36	0
2002—New York Giants NFL	7	7	27	386	14.3	2	2	0	12	0
Pro totals (6 years)	69	64	259	3585	13.8	21	21	0	126	2

HILLIARD, JOHN — DE — SEAHAWKS

PERSONAL: Born April 16, 1976, in Coushatta, La. ... 6-2/296. ... Full name: John Edward Hilliard.
HIGH SCHOOL: Sterling (Houston).
COLLEGE: Mississippi State.
TRANSACTIONS/CAREER NOTES: Selected by Seattle Seahawks in sixth round (190th pick overall) of 2000 NFL draft. ... Signed by Seahawks (July 13, 2000). ... Granted free agency (February 28, 2003). ... Re-signed by Seahawks (April 25, 2003).

			TOTALS		
Year Team	G	GS	Tk.	Ast.	Sks.
2000—Seattle NFL	5	0	3	0	0.0
2001—Seattle NFL	16	8	9	8	0.0
2002—Seattle NFL	6	3	12	2	0.0
Pro totals (3 years)	27	11	24	10	0.0

HITCHCOCK, JIMMY — CB

PERSONAL: Born September 11, 1970, in Concord, N.C. ... 5-10/187. ... Full name: Jimmy Davis Hitchcock Jr.
HIGH SCHOOL: Concord (N.C.).
COLLEGE: North Carolina.
TRANSACTIONS/CAREER NOTES: Selected by New England Patriots in third round (88th pick overall) of 1995 NFL draft. ... Signed by Patriots (July 19, 1995). ... Granted free agency (February 13, 1998). ... Re-signed by Patriots (April 18, 1998). ... Traded by Patriots to Minnesota Vikings for third-round pick (S Tony George) in 1999 draft (April 18, 1998). ... Granted unconditional free agency (February 11, 2000). ... Signed by Carolina Panthers (February 24, 2000). ... Released by Panthers (February 22, 2002). ... Signed by Patriots (August 14, 2002). ... Released by Patriots (September 6, 2002). ... Re-signed by Patriots (September 17, 2002). ... Claimed on waivers by Detroit Lions (November 20, 2002). ... Released by Lions (November 23, 2002).
CHAMPIONSHIP GAME EXPERIENCE: Member of Patriots for AFC championship game (1996 season); inactive. ... Member of Patriots for Super Bowl XXXI (1996 season); inactive. ... Played in NFC championship game (1998 season).

			TOTALS			INTERCEPTIONS			
Year Team	G	GS	Tk.	Ast.	Sks.	No.	Yds.	Avg.	TD
1995—New England NFL	8	0	4	0	0.0	0	0	0.0	0
1996—New England NFL	13	5	27	5	0.0	2	14	7.0	0
1997—New England NFL	15	15	65	18	0.0	2	104	52.0	1
1998—Minnesota NFL	16	16	58	9	0.0	7	*242	‡34.6	*3
1999—Minnesota NFL	16	16	73	9	2.0	2	0	0.0	0
2000—Carolina NFL	16	2	29	1	0.0	3	116	38.7	1
2001—Carolina NFL	16	7	45	8	0.0	3	65	21.7	0
2002—New England NFL	1	0	0	0	0.0	0	0	0.0	0
Pro totals (8 years)	101	61	301	50	2.0	19	541	28.5	5

HOBGOOD-CHITTICK, NATE — DT

PERSONAL: Born November 30, 1974, in New Haven, Conn. ... 6-3/296. ... Full name: Nate Broe Hobgood-Chittick.
HIGH SCHOOL: William Allen (Allentown, Pa.).
COLLEGE: North Carolina.
TRANSACTIONS/CAREER NOTES: Signed as non drafted free agent by New York Giants (April 24, 1998). ... Inactive for four games with Giants (1998). ... Released by Giants (September 30, 1998). ... Re-signed by Giants to practice squad (October 2, 1998). ... Signed by Indianapolis Colts off Giants practice squad (November 25, 1998). ... Inactive for five games with Colts (1998). ... Released by Colts (September 7, 1999). ... Signed by St. Louis Rams (September 13, 1999). ... Released by Rams (October 10, 2000). ... Signed by San Francisco 49ers (October 11, 2000). ... Granted free agency (March 2, 2001). ... Signed by Kansas City Chiefs (June 27, 2001). ... Released by Chiefs (September 18, 2001). ... Re-signed by Chiefs (October 3, 2001). ... Released by Chiefs (September 1, 2002). ... Signed by Rams (September 2, 2002). ... Released by Rams (September 3, 2002). ... Signed by Chiefs (October 16, 2002). ... Granted unconditional free agency (February 28, 2003).
CHAMPIONSHIP GAME EXPERIENCE: Played in NFC championship game (1999 season). ... Member of Super Bowl championship team (1999 season).

			TOTALS		
Year Team	G	GS	Tk.	Ast.	Sks.
1998—Indianapolis NFL			Did not play.		
1999—St. Louis NFL	10	0	9	4	0.5
2000—St. Louis NFL	5	0	2	3	1.0
—San Francisco NFL	5	0	3	3	0.0
2001—Kansas City NFL	10	1	7	0	0.0
2002—Kansas City NFL	3	0	2	1	0.0
Pro totals (4 years)	33	1	23	11	1.5

H

HOCHSTEIN, RUSS   G   PATRIOTS

PERSONAL: Born October 7, 1977, in Hartington, Neb. ... 6-4/300.
HIGH SCHOOL: Cedar Catholic (Hartington, Neb.).
COLLEGE: Nebraska.
TRANSACTIONS/CAREER NOTES: Selected by Tampa Bay Buccaneers in fifth round (151st pick overall) of 2001 NFL draft. ... Signed by Buccaneers (July 16, 2001). ... Inactive for 16 games (2001). ... Released by Buccaneers (September 17, 2002). ... Re-signed by Buccaneers (September 24, 2002). ... Released by Buccaneers (October 1, 2002). ... Re-signed by Buccaneers to practice squad (October 1, 2002). ... Released by Buccaneers (October 16, 2002). ... Signed by New England Patriots to practice squad (October 21, 2002). ... Activated (November 17, 2002).
PLAYING EXPERIENCE: New England (1)-Tampa Bay (1) NFL, 2002. ... Games/games started: 2002 (N.E.-1/0; T.B.-1/0; Total: 2/0).
HONORS: Named guard on THE SPORTING NEWS college All-America first team (2000).

HODEL, NATHAN   TE   CARDINALS

PERSONAL: Born November 12, 1977, in Maryville, Ill. ... 6-2/245.
HIGH SCHOOL: East (Belleville, Ill.).
COLLEGE: Illinois (degree in business administration).
TRANSACTIONS/CAREER NOTES: Signed as non-drafted free agent by Carolina Panthers (April 23, 2001). ... Released by Panthers (September 1, 2001). ... Re-signed by Panthers to practice squad (September 4, 2001). ... Released by Panthers (October 24, 2001). ... Signed by Arizona Cardinals to practice squad (October 26, 2001). ... Activated (December 27, 2001); did not play.

| | | | RECEIVING | | |
Year Team	G	GS	No.	Yds.	Avg.	TD
2002—Arizona NFL	16	0	0	0	0.0	0

HODGE, SEDRICK   LB   SAINTS

PERSONAL: Born September 13, 1978, in Fayettesville, Ga. ... 6-4/244. ... Full name: Sedrick Jamaine Hodge.
HIGH SCHOOL: Westminster (Atlanta).
COLLEGE: North Carolina.
TRANSACTIONS/CAREER NOTES: Selected by New Orleans Saints in third round (70th pick overall) of 2001 NFL draft. ... Signed by Saints (June 6, 2001).

| | | | TOTALS | | | INTERCEPTIONS | | | |
Year Team	G	GS	Tk.	Ast.	Sks.	No.	Yds.	Avg.	TD
2001—New Orleans NFL	16	0	6	2	0.0	0	0	0.0	0
2002—New Orleans NFL	16	15	58	17	0.0	0	0	0.0	0
Pro totals (2 years)	32	15	64	19	0.0	0	0	0.0	0

HODGINS, JAMES   FB   CARDINALS

PERSONAL: Born April 30, 1977, in San Jose, Calif. ... 6-1/270.
HIGH SCHOOL: Oak Grove (San Jose, Calif.).
COLLEGE: San Jose State.
TRANSACTIONS/CAREER NOTES: Signed as non-drafted free agent by St. Louis Rams (April 20, 1999). ... Granted free agency (March 1, 2002). ... Tendered offer sheet by Denver Broncos (April 13, 2002). ... Offer matched by Rams (April 19, 2002). ... Released by Rams (February 27, 2003). ... Signed by Arizona Cardinals (March 12, 2003).
CHAMPIONSHIP GAME EXPERIENCE: Played in NFC championship game (1999 and 2001 seasons). ... Member of Super Bowl championship team (1999 season). ... Played in Super Bowl XXXVI (2001 season).
SINGLE GAME HIGHS (regular season): Attempts—3 (November 28, 1999, vs. New Orleans); yards—5 (December 15, 2002, vs. Arizona); and rushing touchdowns—1 (November 28, 1999, vs. New Orleans).

| | | | RUSHING | | | | RECEIVING | | | | TOTALS | | | |
Year Team	G	GS	Att.	Yds.	Avg.	TD	No.	Yds.	Avg.	TD	TD	2pt.	Pts.	Fum.
1999—St. Louis NFL	15	0	7	10	1.4	1	6	35	5.8	0	1	0	6	0
2000—St. Louis NFL	15	2	1	3	3.0	0	2	5	2.5	0	0	0	0	0
2001—St. Louis NFL	16	10	2	5	2.5	0	4	24	6.0	1	1	0	6	0
2002—St. Louis NFL	9	8	3	7	2.3	0	9	47	5.2	0	0	0	0	0
Pro totals (4 years)	55	20	13	25	1.9	1	21	111	5.3	1	2	0	12	0

HOLCOMB, KELLY   QB   BROWNS

PERSONAL: Born July 9, 1973, in Fayetteville, Tenn. ... 6-2/212. ... Full name: Bryan Kelly Holcomb.
HIGH SCHOOL: Lincoln County (Fayetteville, Tenn.).
COLLEGE: Middle Tennessee State.
TRANSACTIONS/CAREER NOTES: Signed as non-drafted free agent by Tampa Bay Buccaneers (May 1, 1995). ... Released by Buccaneers (August 22, 1995). ... Re-signed by Buccaneers to practice squad (August 29, 1995). ... Released by Buccaneers (September 19, 1995). ... Re-signed by Buccaneers to practice squad (October 4, 1995). ... Released by Buccaneers (October 17, 1995). ... Re-signed by Buccaneers to practice squad (December 19, 1995). ... Played for Barcelona Dragons of World League (1996). ... Released by Buccaneers (August 19, 1996). ... Signed by Indianapolis Colts to practice squad (November 27, 1996). ... Active for all 16 games (1998); did not play. ... Granted free agency (February 11, 2000). ... Re-signed by Colts (February 26, 2000). ... Released by Colts (February 28, 2001) ... Signed by Cleveland Browns (March 2, 2001).
SINGLE GAME HIGHS (regular season): Attempts—39 (September 8, 2002, vs. Kansas City); completions—27 (September 8, 2002, vs. Kansas City); yards—326 (September 8, 2002, vs. Kansas City); touchdown passes—3 (September 8, 2002, vs. Kansas City).
STATISTICAL PLATEAUS: 300-yard passing games: 2002 (1).
MISCELLANEOUS: Regular-season record as starting NFL quarterback: 1-2 (.333). ... Postseason record as starting NFL quarterback: 0-1.

H

Year Team	G	GS	Att.	Cmp.	Pct.	Yds.	TD	Int.	Avg.	Skd.	Rat.	Att.	Yds.	Avg.	TD	TD	2pt.	Pts.
						PASSING							RUSHING				TOTALS	
1995—Tampa Bay NFL									Did not play.									
1996—Barcelona W.L.	10	10	319	191	59.9	2382	14	16	7.47	0	76.8	38	111	2.9	2	2	0	12
—Indianapolis NFL									Did not play.									
1997—Indianapolis NFL	5	1	73	45	61.6	454	1	8	6.22	11	44.3	5	5	1.0	0	0	0	0
1998—Indianapolis NFL									Did not play.									
1999—Indianapolis NFL									Did not play.									
2000—Indianapolis NFL									Did not play.									
2001—Cleveland NFL	4	0	12	7	58.3	114	1	0	9.50	0	118.1	1	0	0.0	0	0	0	0
2002—Cleveland NFL	5	2	106	64	60.4	790	8	4	7.45	5	92.9	8	9	1.1	0	0	0	0
W.L. totals (1 year)	10	10	319	191	59.9	2382	14	16	7.47	0	76.8	38	111	2.9	2	2	0	12
NFL totals (3 years)	14	3	191	116	60.7	1358	10	12	7.11	16	73.6	14	14	1.0	0	0	0	0
Pro totals (4 years)	24	13	510	307	60.2	3740	24	28	7.33	16	75.6	52	125	2.4	2	2	0	12

HOLCOMBE, ROBERT   RB   TITANS

PERSONAL: Born December 11, 1975, in Houston. ... 5-11/215. ... Full name: Robert Wayne Holcombe.

HIGH SCHOOL: Jeff Davis Senior (Houston), then Mesa (Ariz.).

COLLEGE: Illinois.

TRANSACTIONS/CAREER NOTES: Selected by St. Louis Rams in second round (37th pick overall) of 1998 NFL draft. ... Signed by Rams (July 2, 1998). ... Granted unconditional free agency (March 1, 2002). ... Signed by Tennessee Titans (May 28, 2002).

CHAMPIONSHIP GAME EXPERIENCE: Played in NFC championship game (1999 and 2001 seasons). ... Member of Super Bowl championship team (1999 season). ... Played in Super Bowl XXXVI (2001 season). ... Played in AFC championship game (2002 season).

SINGLE GAME HIGHS (regular season): Attempts—21 (September 27, 1998, vs. Arizona); yards—86 (January 2, 2000, vs. Philadelphia); and rushing touchdowns—2 (September 27, 1998, vs. Arizona).

Year Team	G	GS	Att.	Yds.	Avg.	TD	No.	Yds.	Avg.	TD	TD	2pt.	Pts.	Fum.
			RUSHING				RECEIVING				TOTALS			
1998—St. Louis NFL	13	6	98	230	2.3	2	6	34	5.7	0	2	0	12	0
1999—St. Louis NFL	15	7	78	294	3.8	4	14	163	11.6	1	5	0	30	4
2000—St. Louis NFL	14	9	21	70	3.3	3	8	90	11.3	1	4	0	24	0
2001—St. Louis NFL	16	0	13	42	3.2	1	1	14	14.0	0	1	0	6	1
2002—Tennessee NFL	8	0	47	242	5.1	0	10	91	9.1	0	0	0	0	1
Pro totals (5 years)	66	22	257	878	3.4	10	39	392	10.1	2	12	0	72	6

HOLDMAN, WARRICK   LB   BEARS

PERSONAL: Born November 22, 1975, in Alief, Texas. ... 6-1/234. ... Full name: Warrick Donte Holdman.

HIGH SCHOOL: Elsik (Alief, Texas).

COLLEGE: Texas A&M.

TRANSACTIONS/CAREER NOTES: Selected by Chicago Bears in fourth round (106th pick overall) of 1999 NFL draft. ... Signed by Bears (July 25, 1999). ... On injured reserve with knee injury (November 21, 2000-remainder of season). ... Granted free agency (March 1, 2002). ... Tendered offer sheet by Kansas City Chiefs (April 16, 2002). ... Offer matched by Bears (April 19, 2002). ... On injured reserve with knee injury (October 1, 2002-remainder of season).

Year Team	G	GS	Tk.	Ast.	Sks.	No.	Yds.	Avg.	TD
			TOTALS			INTERCEPTIONS			
1999—Chicago NFL	16	5	47	13	2.0	0	0	0.0	0
2000—Chicago NFL	10	10	57	16	0.0	0	0	0.0	0
2001—Chicago NFL	16	15	95	14	1.5	1	0	0.0	0
2002—Chicago NFL	4	4	16	4	0.0	0	0	0.0	0
Pro totals (4 years)	46	34	215	47	3.5	1	0	0.0	0

HOLECEK, JOHN   LB

PERSONAL: Born May 7, 1972, in Steger, Ill. ... 6-2/242. ... Full name: John Francis Holecek. ... Name pronounced HOLL-uh-sek.

HIGH SCHOOL: Marian Catholic (Chicago Heights, Ill.).

COLLEGE: Illinois.

TRANSACTIONS/CAREER NOTES: Selected by Buffalo Bills in fifth round (144th pick overall) of 1995 NFL draft. ... Signed by Bills (June 12, 1995). ... On physically unable to perform list with hamstring injury (August 22-November 21, 1995). ... On injured reserve with knee injury (August 16, 1996-entire season). ... Granted free agency (February 13, 1998). ... Re-signed by Bills (April 27, 1998). ... Released by Bills (July 12, 2001). ... Signed by San Diego Chargers (July 31, 2001). ... On injured reserve with knee injury (November 28, 2001-remainder of season). ... Granted unconditional free agency (March 1, 2002). ... Signed by Atlanta Falcons (April 1, 2002). ... On injured reserve with knee injury (January 7, 2003-remainder of playoffs). ... Granted unconditional free agency (February 28, 2003).

Year Team	G	GS	Tk.	Ast.	Sks.	No.	Yds.	Avg.	TD
			TOTALS			INTERCEPTIONS			
1995—Buffalo NFL	1	0	3	2	0.0	0	0	0.0	0
1997—Buffalo NFL	14	8	38	20	1.5	0	0	0.0	0
1998—Buffalo NFL	13	13	57	21	0.0	0	0	0.0	0
1999—Buffalo NFL	14	14	44	19	1.0	1	35	35.0	0
2000—Buffalo NFL	16	16	69	41	0.0	1	0	0.0	0
2001—San Diego NFL	11	0	8	1	0.0	0	0	0.0	0
2002—Atlanta NFL	12	11	43	10	1.0	0	0	0.0	0
Pro totals (7 years)	81	62	262	114	3.5	2	35	17.5	0

HOLLAND, DARIUS — DT

PERSONAL: Born November 10, 1973, in Petersburg, Va. ... 6-5/330. ... Full name: Darius Jerome Holland.
HIGH SCHOOL: Mayfield (Las Cruces, N.M.).
COLLEGE: Colorado.
TRANSACTIONS/CAREER NOTES: Selected by Green Bay Packers in third round (65th pick overall) of 1995 NFL draft. ... Signed by Packers (July 18, 1995). ... Granted free agency (February 13, 1998). ... Re-signed by Packers (April 10, 1998). ... Traded by Packers to Kansas City Chiefs for DE Vaughn Booker (May 13, 1998). ... Released by Chiefs (October 13, 1998). ... Signed by Detroit Lions (October 19, 1998). ... Granted unconditional free agency (February 12, 1999). ... Signed by Cleveland Browns (April 23, 1999). ... Granted unconditional free agency (February 11, 2000). ... Re-signed by Browns (February 15, 2000). ... Released by Browns (September 1, 2001). ... Signed by Minnesota Vikings (March 12, 2002). ... Granted unconditional free agency (February 28, 2003).
CHAMPIONSHIP GAME EXPERIENCE: Played in NFC championship game (1995-1997 seasons). ... Member of Super Bowl championship team (1996 season). ... Played in Super Bowl XXXII (1997 season).

			TOTALS			INTERCEPTIONS			
Year Team	G	GS	Tk.	Ast.	Sks.	No.	Yds.	Avg.	TD
1995—Green Bay NFL	14	4	9	8	1.5	0	0	0.0	0
1996—Green Bay NFL	16	0	9	1	0.0	0	0	0.0	0
1997—Green Bay NFL	12	1	5	7	0.0	0	0	0.0	0
1998—Kansas City NFL	6	0	0	0	0.0	0	0	0.0	0
—Detroit NFL	10	4	11	0	0.0	0	0	0.0	0
1999—Cleveland NFL	15	11	30	6	2.0	0	0	0.0	0
2000—Cleveland NFL	16	1	28	4	1.0	1	0	0.0	0
2002—Minnesota NFL	4	0	0	2	0.0	0	0	0.0	0
Pro totals (7 years)	93	21	92	28	4.5	1	0	0.0	0

HOLLIDAY, VONNIE — DE — CHIEFS

PERSONAL: Born December 11, 1975, in Camden, S.C. ... 6-5/290. ... Full name: Dimetry Giovonni Holliday. ... Cousin of Corey Holliday, wide receiver with Pittsburgh Steelers (1995-97).
HIGH SCHOOL: Camden (S.C.).
COLLEGE: North Carolina.
TRANSACTIONS/CAREER NOTES: Selected by Green Bay Packers in first round (19th pick overall) of 1998 NFL draft. ... Signed by Packers (June 15, 1998). ... Granted unconditional free agency (February 28, 2003). ... Signed by Kansas City Chiefs (April 7, 2003).

			TOTALS			INTERCEPTIONS			
Year Team	G	GS	Tk.	Ast.	Sks.	No.	Yds.	Avg.	TD
1998—Green Bay NFL	12	12	34	18	8.0	0	0	0.0	0
1999—Green Bay NFL	16	16	47	20	6.0	0	0	0.0	0
2000—Green Bay NFL	12	9	22	13	5.0	1	3	3.0	0
2001—Green Bay NFL	16	16	47	25	7.0	0	0	0.0	0
2002—Green Bay NFL	10	10	18	8	6.0	1	3	3.0	0
Pro totals (5 years)	66	63	168	84	32.0	2	6	3.0	0

HOLLIS, MIKE — K — GIANTS

PERSONAL: Born May 22, 1972, in Kellogg, Idaho. ... 5-7/178. ... Full name: Michael Shane Hollis.
HIGH SCHOOL: Central Valley (Veradale, Wash.).
COLLEGE: Idaho (degree in sports science, 1996).
TRANSACTIONS/CAREER NOTES: Signed as non-drafted free agent by San Diego Chargers (May 6, 1994). ... Released by Chargers (August 22, 1994). ... Signed by Jacksonville Jaguars (June 5, 1995). ... Granted unconditional free agency (March 1, 2002). ... Signed by Buffalo Bills (April 18, 2002). ... Granted unconditional free agency (February 28, 2003). ... Signed by New York Giants (April 10, 2003).
CHAMPIONSHIP GAME EXPERIENCE: Played in AFC championship game (1996 and 1999 seasons).
HONORS: Played in Pro Bowl (1997 season).

		FIELD GOALS							TOTALS		
Year Team	G	1-29	30-39	40-49	50+	Tot.	Pct.	Lg.	XPM	XPA	Pts.
1995—Jacksonville NFL	16	7-9	7-8	4-7	2-3	20-27	74.1	53	27	28	87
1996—Jacksonville NFL	16	11-11	12-14	5-8	2-3	30-36	83.3	53	27	27	117
1997—Jacksonville NFL	16	14-16	8-9	7-9	2-2	31-36	86.1	52	41	41	*134
1998—Jacksonville NFL	16	9-11	8-9	4-5	0-1	21-26	80.8	47	45	45	108
1999—Jacksonville NFL	16	12-13	8-9	10-15	1-1	31-38	81.6	50	37	37	130
2000—Jacksonville NFL	12	6-7	8-8	7-8	3-3	24-26	92.3	51	33	33	105
2001—Jacksonville NFL	16	4-5	8-11	6-11	0-1	18-28	64.3	48	29	31	83
2002—Buffalo NFL	16	7-8	8-10	7-10	3-5	25-33	75.8	54	40	40	115
Pro totals (8 years)	124	70-80	67-78	50-73	13-19	200-250	80.0	54	279	282	879

HOLLOWAY, JABARI — TE — TEXANS

PERSONAL: Born December 18, 1978, in Atlanta. ... 6-2/260. ... Full name: Jabari Jelani Holloway.
HIGH SCHOOL: Sandy Creek (Tyrone, Ga.).
COLLEGE: Notre Dame.
TRANSACTIONS/CAREER NOTES: Selected by New England Patriots in fourth round (119th pick overall) of 2001 NFL draft. ... Signed by Patriots (July 13, 2001). ... On physically unable to perform list with hamstring injury (July 23-August 28, 2001). ... On injured reserve with hamstring injury (August 28, 2001-entire season). ... Claimed on waivers by Houston Texans (August 26, 2002). ... Released by Texans (September 6, 2002). ... Re-signed by Texans to practice squad (September 10, 2002). ... Activated (October 18, 2002). ... Re-signed by Texans (March 21, 2003).
SINGLE GAME HIGHS (regular season): Receptions—2 (October 27, 2002, vs. Jacksonville); yards—24 (December 15, 2002, vs. Baltimore); and touchdown receptions—0.

H

			RECEIVING			
Year Team	G	GS	No.	Yds.	Avg.	TD
2002—Houston NFL	11	7	7	73	10.4	0

HOLMAN, RASHAD   CB   49ERS

PERSONAL: Born January 17, 1978, in Louisville, Ky. ... 5-11/191.
HIGH SCHOOL: Male (Louisville, Ky.).
COLLEGE: Louisville.
TRANSACTIONS/CAREER NOTES: Selected by San Francisco 49ers in sixth round (179th pick overall) of 2001 NFL draft. ... Signed by 49ers (July 24, 2001).

				TOTALS			INTERCEPTIONS			
Year Team	G	GS	Tk.	Ast.	Sks.	No.	Yds.	Avg.	TD
2001—San Francisco NFL	16	1	42	4	0.0	1	19	19.0	0
2002—San Francisco NFL	16	0	19	0	0.0	1	1	1.0	0
Pro totals (2 years)	32	1	61	4	0.0	2	20	10.0	0

HOLMES, EARL   LB   LIONS

PERSONAL: Born April 28, 1973, in Tallahassee, Fla. ... 6-2/250. ... Full name: Earl L. Holmes.
HIGH SCHOOL: Florida A&M University (Tallahassee, Fla.).
COLLEGE: Florida A&M.
TRANSACTIONS/CAREER NOTES: Selected by Pittsburgh Steelers in fourth round (126th pick overall) of 1996 NFL draft. ... Signed by Steelers (July 16, 1996). ... Granted unconditional free agency (March 1, 2002). ... Signed by Cleveland Browns (April 5, 2002). ... Released by Browns (February 27, 2003). ... Signed by Detroit Lions (April 9, 2003).
CHAMPIONSHIP GAME EXPERIENCE: Played in AFC championship game (1997 and 2001 seasons).

				TOTALS			INTERCEPTIONS			
Year Team	G	GS	Tk.	Ast.	Sks.	No.	Yds.	Avg.	TD
1996—Pittsburgh NFL	3	1	9	1	1.0	0	0	0.0	0
1997—Pittsburgh NFL	16	16	67	29	4.0	0	0	0.0	0
1998—Pittsburgh NFL	14	14	55	25	1.5	1	36	36.0	0
1999—Pittsburgh NFL	16	16	89	26	0.0	0	0	0.0	0
2000—Pittsburgh NFL	16	16	87	41	1.0	0	0	0.0	0
2001—Pittsburgh NFL	16	16	85	33	2.0	0	0	0.0	0
2002—Cleveland NFL	16	15	96	32	0.0	0	0	0.0	0
Pro totals (7 years)	97	94	488	187	9.5	1	36	36.0	0

HOLMES, KENNY   DE   GIANTS

PERSONAL: Born October 24, 1973, in Vero Beach, Fla. ... 6-4/265. ... Full name: Kenneth Holmes.
HIGH SCHOOL: Vero Beach (Fla.).
COLLEGE: Miami, Fla. (degree in criminal justice).
TRANSACTIONS/CAREER NOTES: Selected by Houston Oilers in first round (18th pick overall) of 1997 NFL draft. ... Oilers franchise moved to Tennessee for 1997 season. ... Signed by Oilers (July 18, 1997). ... Oilers franchise renamed Tennessee Titans for 1999 season (December 26, 1998). ... Granted unconditional free agency (March 2, 2001). ... Signed by New York Giants (March 14, 2001).
CHAMPIONSHIP GAME EXPERIENCE: Played in AFC championship game (1999 season). ... Played in Super Bowl XXXIV (1999 season).

				TOTALS			INTERCEPTIONS			
Year Team	G	GS	Tk.	Ast.	Sks.	No.	Yds.	Avg.	TD
1997—Tennessee NFL	16	5	28	5	7.0	0	0	0.0	0
1998—Tennessee NFL	14	11	22	11	2.5	0	0	0.0	0
1999—Tennessee NFL	14	7	13	6	4.0	2	17	8.5	0
2000—Tennessee NFL	14	13	32	5	8.0	0	0	0.0	0
2001—New York Giants NFL	16	16	38	18	3.5	0	0	0.0	0
2002—New York Giants NFL	15	15	32	15	8.0	0	0	0.0	0
Pro totals (6 years)	89	67	165	60	33.0	2	17	8.5	0

HOLMES, PRIEST   RB   CHIEFS

PERSONAL: Born October 7, 1973, in Fort Smith, Ark. ... 5-9/213. ... Full name: Priest Anthony Holmes. ... Cousin of Henry Burris, quarterback, Chicago Bears.
HIGH SCHOOL: Marshall (Texas).
COLLEGE: Texas.
TRANSACTIONS/CAREER NOTES: Signed as non-drafted free agent by Baltimore Ravens (April 25, 1997). ... Granted free agency (February 11, 2000). ... Re-signed by Ravens (June 9, 2000). ... Granted unconditional free agency (March 2, 2001). ... Signed by Kansas City Chiefs (April 1, 2001).
CHAMPIONSHIP GAME EXPERIENCE: Played in AFC championship game (2000 season). ... Member of Super Bowl championship team (2000 season).
HONORS: Played in Pro Bowl (2001 season). ... Named to play in Pro Bowl (2002 season); replaced by Travis Henry due to injury. ... Named running back on THE SPORTING NEWS NFL All-Pro team (2002).
SINGLE GAME HIGHS (regular season): Attempts—36 (November 22, 1998, vs. Cincinnati); yards—227 (November 22, 1998, vs. Cincinnati); and rushing touchdowns—4 (September 8, 2002, vs. Cleveland).
STATISTICAL PLATEAUS: 100-yard rushing games: 1998 (4), 1999 (2), 2000 (1), 2001 (7), 2002 (9). Total: 23. ... 100-yard receiving games: 2001 (2), 2002 (1). Total: 3.

			RUSHING				RECEIVING				TOTALS			
Year Team	G	GS	Att.	Yds.	Avg.	TD	No.	Yds.	Avg.	TD	TD	2pt.	Pts.	Fum.
1997—Baltimore NFL	7	0	0	0	0.0	0	0	0	0.0	0	0	0	0	0
1998—Baltimore NFL	16	13	233	1008	4.3	7	43	260	6.0	0	7	0	42	3
1999—Baltimore NFL	9	4	89	506	5.7	1	13	104	8.0	1	2	0	12	0
2000—Baltimore NFL	16	2	137	588	4.3	2	32	221	6.9	0	2	0	12	2
2001—Kansas City NFL	16	16	327	*1555	4.8	8	62	614	9.9	2	10	0	60	4
2002—Kansas City NFL	14	14	313	1615	5.2	*21	70	672	9.6	3	*24	0	*144	1
Pro totals (6 years)	78	49	1099	5272	4.8	39	220	1871	8.5	6	45	0	270	10

H

HOLSEY, BERNARD — DL

PERSONAL: Born December 10, 1973, in Rome, Ga. ... 6-2/286.
HIGH SCHOOL: Coosa (Rome, Ga.).
COLLEGE: Duke.
TRANSACTIONS/CAREER NOTES: Signed as non-drafted free agent by New York Giants (April 26, 1996). ... Granted free agency (February 12, 1999). ... Re-signed by Giants (June 2, 1999). ... Granted unconditional free agency (February 11, 2000). ... Signed by Indianapolis Colts (March 15, 2000). ... Released by Colts (August 20, 2001). ... Signed by New England Patriots (July 25, 2002). ... Granted unconditional free agency (February 28, 2003).

				TOTALS	
Year Team	G	GS	Tk.	Ast.	Sks.
1996—New York Giants NFL	16	0	10	2	0.0
1997—New York Giants NFL	16	4	10	7	3.5
1998—New York Giants NFL	16	0	4	4	0.0
1999—New York Giants NFL	16	0	15	5	0.0
2000—Indianapolis NFL	16	13	28	14	2.0
2002—New England NFL	8	0	3	2	1.0
Pro totals (6 years)	88	17	70	34	6.5

HOLT, TORRY — WR — RAMS

PERSONAL: Born June 5, 1976, in Greensboro, N.C. ... 6-0/190. ... Full name: Torry Jabar Holt. ... Brother of Terrence Holt, safety, Detroit Lions.
HIGH SCHOOL: Eastern Guilford (Gibsonville, N.C.).
COLLEGE: North Carolina State.
TRANSACTIONS/CAREER NOTES: Selected by St. Louis Rams in first round (sixth pick overall) of 1999 NFL draft. ... Signed by Rams (June 5, 1999).
CHAMPIONSHIP GAME EXPERIENCE: Played in NFC championship game (1999 and 2001 seasons). ... Member of Super Bowl championship team (1999 season). ... Played in Super Bowl XXXVI (2001 season).
HONORS: Named wide receiver on THE SPORTING NEWS college All-America first team (1998). ... Played in Pro Bowl (2000 and 2001 seasons).
SINGLE GAME HIGHS (regular season): Receptions—12 (September 23, 2002, vs. Tampa Bay); yards—203 (December 30, 2001, vs. Indianapolis); and touchdown receptions—2 (December 30, 2001, vs. Indianapolis).
STATISTICAL PLATEAUS: 100-yard receiving games: 1999 (2), 2000 (8), 2001 (3), 2002 (4). Total: 17.

			RUSHING				RECEIVING				TOTALS			
Year Team	G	GS	Att.	Yds.	Avg.	TD	No.	Yds.	Avg.	TD	TD	2pt.	Pts.	Fum.
1999—St. Louis NFL	16	15	3	25	8.3	0	52	788	15.2	6	6	0	36	4
2000—St. Louis NFL	16	15	2	7	3.5	0	82	*1635	*19.9	6	6	0	36	2
2001—St. Louis NFL	16	14	2	0	0.0	0	81	1363	16.8	7	7	0	42	2
2002—St. Louis NFL	16	12	2	18	9.0	0	91	1302	14.3	4	4	0	24	1
Pro totals (4 years)	64	56	9	50	5.6	0	306	5088	16.6	23	23	0	138	9

HOOVER, BRAD — FB — PANTHERS

PERSONAL: Born November 11, 1976, in High Point, N.C. ... 6-0/242. ... Full name: Bradley R. Hoover.
HIGH SCHOOL: Ledford (Thomasville, N.C.).
COLLEGE: Western Carolina.
TRANSACTIONS/CAREER NOTES: Signed as non-drafted free agent by Carolina Panthers (April 17, 2000).
SINGLE GAME HIGHS (regular season): Attempts—24 (November 27, 2000, vs. Green Bay); yards—117 (November 27, 2000, vs. Green Bay); and rushing touchdowns—1 (November 27, 2000, vs. Green Bay).
STATISTICAL PLATEAUS: 100-yard rushing games: 2000 (1).

			RUSHING				RECEIVING				TOTALS			
Year Team	G	GS	Att.	Yds.	Avg.	TD	No.	Yds.	Avg.	TD	TD	2pt.	Pts.	Fum.
2000—Carolina NFL	16	4	89	290	3.3	1	15	112	7.5	0	1	0	6	1
2001—Carolina NFL	16	7	17	71	4.2	0	26	185	7.1	0	0	0	0	1
2002—Carolina NFL	16	10	31	129	4.2	0	17	187	11.0	2	2	0	12	1
Pro totals (3 years)	48	21	137	490	3.6	1	58	484	8.3	2	3	0	18	3

HOPE, CHRIS — S — STEELERS

PERSONAL: Born September 29, 1980, in Rock Hill, S.C. ... 6-0/204.
HIGH SCHOOL: Rock Hill (S.C.).
COLLEGE: Florida State.
TRANSACTIONS/CAREER NOTES: Selected by Pittsburgh Steelers in third round (94th pick overall) of 2002 NFL draft. ... Signed by Steelers (July 12, 2002).
HONORS: Named free safety on THE SPORTING NEWS college All-America second team (2000).

			TOTALS			INTERCEPTIONS			
Year Team	G	GS	Tk.	Ast.	Sks.	No.	Yds.	Avg.	TD
2002—Pittsburgh NFL	14	0	12	0	0.0	0	0	0.0	0

HOPKINS, BRAD — OT — TITANS

PERSONAL: Born September 5, 1970, in Columbia, S.C. ... 6-3/305. ... Full name: Bradley D. Hopkins.
HIGH SCHOOL: Moline (Ill.).
COLLEGE: Illinois (degree in speech communications, 1993).

TRANSACTIONS/CAREER NOTES: Selected by Houston Oilers in first round (13th pick overall) of 1993 NFL draft. ... Signed by Oilers (August 10, 1993). ... Granted unconditional free agency (February 14, 1997). ... Re-signed by Oilers (March 10, 1997). ... Oilers franchise moved to Tennessee for 1997 season. ... Oilers franchise renamed Tennessee Titans for 1999 season (December 26, 1998).
PLAYING EXPERIENCE: Houston NFL, 1993-1996; Tennessee NFL, 1997-2002. ... Games/Games started: 1993 (16/11), 1994 (16/15), 1995 (16/16), 1996 (16/16), 1997 (16/16), 1998 (13/13), 1999 (16/16), 2000 (15/15), 2001 (14/14), 2002 (14/14). Total: 152/146.
CHAMPIONSHIP GAME EXPERIENCE: Played in AFC championship game (1999 and 2002 seasons). ... Played in Super Bowl XXXIV (1999 season).
HONORS: Played in Pro Bowl (2000 season).

HOPKINS, TAM — G — GIANTS

PERSONAL: Born March 22, 1978, in Winter Park, Fla. ... 6-4/315.
HIGH SCHOOL: Lake Howell (Casselberry, Fla.).
COLLEGE: Ohio State.
TRANSACTIONS/CAREER NOTES: Signed as non-drafted free agent by Washington Redskins (April 23, 2001). ... Released by Redskins (August 27, 2001). ... Signed by New York Giants (January 24, 2002).
PLAYING EXPERIENCE: New York Giants NFL, 2002. ... Games/Games started: 2002 (16/1).

HOPSON, TYRONE — G — LIONS

PERSONAL: Born May 28, 1976, in Hopkinsville, Ky. ... 6-2/305. ... Full name: Tyrone Hopson Jr.
HIGH SCHOOL: Davies County (Owensboro, Ky.).
COLLEGE: Eastern Kentucky.
TRANSACTIONS/CAREER NOTES: Selected by San Francisco 49ers in fifth round (161st pick overall) of 1999 NFL draft. ... Signed by 49ers (July 26, 1999). ... On injured reserve with shoulder injury (October 20, 1999-remainder of season). ... Released by 49ers (August 27, 2000). ... Re-signed by 49ers to practice squad (August 29, 2000). ... Activated (November 14, 2000). ... Released by 49ers (September 2, 2001). ... Signed by Jacksonville Jaguars to practice squad (October 14, 2001). ... Released by Jaguars (October 22, 2001). ... Signed by Detroit Lions to practice squad (October 31, 2001). ... Activated (December 18, 2001).
PLAYING EXPERIENCE: San Francisco NFL, 1999 and 2000; Detroit NFL, 2002. ... Games/Games started: 1999 (1/0), 2000 (2/1), 2002 (8/0). Total: 11/1.

HORN, JOE — WR — SAINTS

PERSONAL: Born January 16, 1972, in New Haven, Conn. ... 6-1/206. ... Full name: Joseph Horn.
HIGH SCHOOL: Douglas Bird (Fayetteville, N.C.).
JUNIOR COLLEGE: Itawamba Community College (Miss.).
COLLEGE: None.
TRANSACTIONS/CAREER NOTES: Signed by Memphis Mad Dogs of CFL (March 25, 1995). ... Selected by Kansas City Chiefs in fifth round (135th pick overall) of 1996 NFL draft. ... Signed by Chiefs (June 25, 1996). ... Granted free agency (February 12, 1999). ... Re-signed by Chiefs (June 16, 1999). ... Granted unconditional free agency (February 11, 2000). ... Signed by New Orleans Saints (February 13, 2000).
HONORS: Played in Pro Bowl (2000 and 2002 seasons). ... Named to play in Pro Bowl (2001 season); replaced by Torry Holt due to injury.
SINGLE GAME HIGHS (regular season): Receptions—13 (December 2, 2001, vs. Carolina); yards—180 (November 5, 2000, vs. San Francisco); and touchdown receptions—2 (October 20, 2002, vs. San Francisco).
STATISTICAL PLATEAUS: 100-yard receiving games: 2000 (5), 2001 (4), 2002 (6). Total: 15.

				RECEIVING				KICKOFF RETURNS				TOTALS			
Year Team	G	GS	No.	Yds.	Avg.	TD	No.	Yds.	Avg.	TD	TD	2pt.	Pts.	Fum.
1995—Memphis CFL	17	17	71	1415	19.9	5	2	17	8.5	0	5	0	30	0
1996—Kansas City NFL	9	0	2	30	15.0	0	0	0	0.0	0	0	0	0	0
1997—Kansas City NFL	8	0	2	65	32.5	0	0	0	0.0	0	0	0	0	0
1998—Kansas City NFL	16	1	14	198	14.1	1	11	233	21.2	0	1	0	6	2
1999—Kansas City NFL	16	1	35	586	16.7	6	9	165	18.3	0	6	0	36	0
2000—New Orleans NFL	16	16	94	1340	14.3	8	0	0	0.0	0	8	0	48	1
2001—New Orleans NFL	16	16	83	1265	15.2	9	0	0	0.0	0	9	0	54	1
2002—New Orleans NFL	16	16	88	1312	14.9	7	0	0	0.0	0	7	1	44	1
CFL totals (1 year)	17	17	71	1415	19.9	5	2	17	8.5	0	5	0	30	0
NFL totals (7 years)	97	50	318	4796	15.1	31	20	398	19.9	0	31	1	188	5
Pro totals (8 years)	114	67	389	6211	16.0	36	22	415	18.9	0	36	1	218	5

HOUGHTON, MIKE — G/OT — BILLS

PERSONAL: Born December 1, 1979, in Northridge, Calif. ... 6-3/315. ... Full name: Michael Christopher Houghton.
HIGH SCHOOL: Mission Bay (San Diego).
COLLEGE: San Diego State.
TRANSACTIONS/CAREER NOTES: Selected by Green Bay Packers in sixth round (200th pick overall) of 2002 NFL draft. ... Signed by Packers (July 23, 2002). ... Claimed on waivers by Buffalo Bills (September 3, 2002).
PLAYING EXPERIENCE: Buffalo NFL, 2002. ... Games/games started: 2002 (1/0).

H — HOUSE, KEVIN — CB — CHARGERS

PERSONAL: Born January 9, 1979, in St. Louis. ... 5-11/175. ... Full name: Kevin N. House. ... Son of Kevin House, wide receiver with Los Angeles Rams and Tampa Bay Buccaneers (Tampa Bay: 1980-1986, Los Angeles Rams: 1986-1987).
HIGH SCHOOL: Chamberlain (Tampa).
COLLEGE: South Carolina.

				TOTALS			INTERCEPTIONS			
Year	Team	G	GS	Tk.	Ast.	Sks.	No.	Yds.	Avg.	TD
2002—San Diego NFL		1	0	0	0	0.0	0	0	0.0	0

HOUSER, KEVIN   CB   CHARGERS

PERSONAL: Born August 23, 1977, in Westlake, Ohio. ... 6-2/250. ... Full name: Kevin J. Houser.
HIGH SCHOOL: Westlake (Ohio).
COLLEGE: Ohio State.
TRANSACTIONS/CAREER NOTES: Selected by New Orleans Saints in seventh round (228th pick overall) of 2000 NFL draft. ... Signed by Saints (June 20, 2000).

				TOTALS			INTERCEPTIONS			
Year	Team	G	GS	Tk.	Ast.	Sks.	No.	Yds.	Avg.	TD
2000—New Orleans NFL		16	0	0	0	0.0	0	0	0.0	0
2001—New Orleans NFL		16	0	0	0	0.0	0	0	0.0	0
2002—New Orleans NFL		16	0	0	0	0.0	0	0	0.0	0
Pro totals (3 years)		48	0	0	0	0.0	0	0	0.0	0

HOUSHMANDZADEH, T.J.   WR   BENGALS

PERSONAL: Born September 26, 1977, in Victor Valley, Calif. ... 6-1/197. ... Full name: Touraj Houshmandzadeh.
HIGH SCHOOL: Barstow (Calif.).
JUNIOR COLLEGE: Cerritos (Calif.).
COLLEGE: Oregon State.
TRANSACTIONS/CAREER NOTES: Selected by Cincinnati Bengals in seventh round (204th pick overall) of 2001 NFL draft. ... Signed by Bengals (July 18, 2001).
SINGLE GAME HIGHS (regular season): Receptions—9 (December 30, 2001, vs. Pittsburgh); yards—98 (December 30, 2001, vs. Pittsburgh); and touchdown receptions—1 (December 1, 2002, vs. Baltimore).

				RECEIVING				PUNT RETURNS				KICKOFF RETURNS				TOTALS			
Year	Team	G	GS	No.	Yds.	Avg.	TD	No.	Yds.	Avg.	TD	No.	Yds.	Avg.	TD	TD	2pt.	Pts.	Fum.
2001—Cincinnati NFL		12	1	21	228	10.9	0	12	163	13.6	0	10	185	18.5	0	0	0	0	3
2002—Cincinnati NFL		16	5	41	492	12.0	1	24	117	4.9	0	13	288	22.2	0	1	0	6	3
Pro totals (2 years)		28	6	62	720	11.6	1	36	280	7.8	0	23	473	20.6	0	1	0	6	6

HOVAN, CHRIS   DT   VIKINGS

PERSONAL: Born May 12, 1978, in Rocky River, Ohio. ... 6-2/294. ... Full name: Christopher James Hovan.
HIGH SCHOOL: St. Ignatius (Cleveland).
COLLEGE: Boston College.
TRANSACTIONS/CAREER NOTES: Selected by Minnesota Vikings in first round (25th pick overall) of 2000 NFL draft. ... Signed by Vikings (July 24, 2000).
CHAMPIONSHIP GAME EXPERIENCE: Played in NFC championship game (2000 season).
HONORS: Named defensive end on THE SPORTING NEWS college All-America third team (1999).

				TOTALS		
Year	Team	G	GS	Tk.	Ast.	Sks.
2000—Minnesota NFL		16	13	43	5	2.0
2001—Minnesota NFL		16	16	30	15	6.0
2002—Minnesota NFL		16	16	38	14	5.5
Pro totals (3 years)		48	45	111	34	13.5

HOWARD, BOBBIE   LB   BEARS

PERSONAL: Born June 14, 1977, in Charleston, W.Va. ... 5-10/232. ... Full name: Bobbie Allen Howard.
HIGH SCHOOL: DuPont (Belle, W.Va.).
COLLEGE: Notre Dame.
TRANSACTIONS/CAREER NOTES: Signed as non-drafted free agent by Tampa Bay Buccaneers (April 19, 1999). ... Released by Buccaneers (September 5, 1999). ... Re-signed by Buccaneers (January 25, 2000). ... Assigned by Buccaneers to Frankfurt Galaxy in 2000 NFL Europe enhancement allocation program (February 18, 2000). ... Released by Buccaneers (August 27, 2000). ... Signed by Chicago Bears to practice squad (December 6, 2000). ... Activated (December 22, 2000); did not play.

				TOTALS			INTERCEPTIONS			
Year	Team	G	GS	Tk.	Ast.	Sks.	No.	Yds.	Avg.	TD
2000—Frankfurt NFLE		...	...	...	...	4.0	0	0	0.0	0
2001—Chicago NFL		16	0	0	0	0.0	0	0	0.0	0
2002—Chicago NFL		16	9	38	11	0.5	1	9	9.0	0
NFL Europe totals (1 year)		...	...	...	...	4.0	0	0	0.0	0
NFL totals (2 years)		32	9	38	11	0.5	1	9	9.0	0
Pro totals (3 years)		...	...	...	...	4.5	1	9	9.0	0

H

HOWARD, DARREN   DE   SAINTS

PERSONAL: Born November 19, 1976, in St. Petersburg, Fla. ... 6-3/281.
HIGH SCHOOL: Boca Ciega (Fla.).
COLLEGE: Kansas State.
TRANSACTIONS/CAREER NOTES: Selected by New Orleans Saints in second round (33rd pick overall) of 2000 NFL draft. ... Signed by Saints (July 17, 2000).

Year Team	G	GS	TOTALS Tk.	Ast.	Sks.	INTERCEPTIONS No.	Yds.	Avg.	TD
2000—New Orleans NFL	16	16	37	15	11.0	1	46	46.0	0
2001—New Orleans NFL	16	16	36	18	6.0	1	37	37.0	0
2002—New Orleans NFL	16	16	35	13	8.0	0	0	0.0	0
Pro totals (3 years)	48	48	108	46	25.0	2	83	41.5	0

HOWARD, DESMOND   WR

PERSONAL: Born May 15, 1970, in Cleveland. ... 5-10/188. ... Full name: Desmond Kevin Howard.
HIGH SCHOOL: St. Joseph (Cleveland) Academy.
COLLEGE: Michigan (degree in communication studies).
TRANSACTIONS/CAREER NOTES: Selected by Washington Redskins in first round (fourth pick overall) of 1992 NFL draft. ... Signed by Redskins (August 25, 1992). ... On injured reserve with separated shoulder (December 29, 1992-remainder of 1992 playoffs). ... Selected by Jacksonville Jaguars from Redskins in NFL expansion draft (February 15, 1995). ... Granted unconditional free agency (February 16, 1996). ... Signed by Green Bay Packers (July 11, 1996). ... Granted unconditional free agency (February 14, 1997). ... Signed by Oakland Raiders (March 4, 1997). ... Released by Raiders (June 9, 1999). ... Signed by Packers (June 29, 1999). ... Released by Packers (November 30, 1999). ... Signed by Detroit Lions (December 4, 1999). ... Granted unconditional free agency (February 11, 2000). ... Re-signed by Lions (July 19, 2000). ... Granted unconditional free agency (March 2, 2001). ... Re-signed by Lions (March 2, 2001). ... On injured reserve with neck injury (November 13, 2002-remainder of season). ... Released by Lions (February 25, 2003).
CHAMPIONSHIP GAME EXPERIENCE: Played in NFC championship game (1996 season). ... Member of Super Bowl championship team (1996 season).
HONORS: Heisman Trophy winner (1991). ... Named College Football Player of the Year by The Sporting News (1991). ... Maxwell Award winner (1991). ... Named wide receiver on The Sporting News college All-America first team (1991). ... Named punt returner on The Sporting News NFL All-Pro team (1996). ... Named Most Valuable Player of Super Bowl XXXI (1996 season). ... Played in Pro Bowl (2000 season).
RECORDS: Holds NFL single-season record for most yards by punt return—875 (1996). ... Holds NFL single-game record for most kickoff returns—10 (October 26, 1997, Oakland at Seattle).
POST SEASON RECORDS: Holds Super Bowl record for longest kickoff return—99 yards (January 26, 1997, vs. New England). ... Holds Super Bowl single-game record for most yards by punt return—90 (January 26, 1997, vs. New England). ... Shares Super Bowl career and single-game records for most punt returns—6. ... Shares Super Bowl single-game records for most combined yards—244; most combined yards by kick returns—244; most touchdowns by kickoff return—1 (January 26, 1997, vs. New England). ... Shares NFL postseason single-game record for most combined yards —244; most combined kick return yards—244; and most touchdowns by kickoff return—1 (January 26, 1997, vs. New England).
SINGLE GAME HIGHS (regular season): Receptions—7 (November 20, 1994, vs. Dallas); yards—130 (December 4, 1994, vs. Tampa Bay); and touchdown receptions—1 (October 21, 2001, vs. Tennessee).
STATISTICAL PLATEAUS: 100-yard receiving games: 1994 (2).

Year Team	G	GS	RUSHING Att.	Yds.	Avg.	TD	RECEIVING No.	Yds.	Avg.	TD	PUNT RETURNS No.	Yds.	Avg.	TD	KICKOFF RETURNS No.	Yds.	Avg.	TD	TOTALS TD	2pt.	Pts.
1992—Washington NFL	16	1	3	14	4.7	0	3	20	6.7	0	6	84	14.0	1	22	462	21.0	0	1	0	6
1993—Washington NFL	16	5	2	17	8.5	0	23	286	12.4	0	4	25	6.3	0	21	405	19.3	0	0	0	0
1994—Washington NFL	16	15	1	4	4.0	0	40	727	18.2	5	0	0	0.0	0	0	0	0.0	0	5	1	32
1995—Jacksonville NFL	13	7	1	8	8.0	0	26	276	10.6	1	24	246	10.3	0	10	178	17.8	0	1	0	6
1996—Green Bay NFL	16	0	0	0	0.0	0	13	95	7.3	0	*58	*875	*15.1	*3	22	460	20.9	0	3	0	18
1997—Oakland NFL	15	0	0	0	0.0	0	4	30	7.5	0	27	210	7.8	0	*61	§1318	21.6	0	0	0	0
1998—Oakland NFL	15	1	0	0	0.0	0	2	16	8.0	0	§45	541	12.0	†2	§49	1040	21.2	0	2	0	12
1999—Green Bay NFL	8	0	0	0	0.0	0	0	0	0.0	0	12	93	7.8	0	19	364	19.2	0	0	0	0
—Detroit NFL	5	0	0	0	0.0	0	0	0	0.0	0	6	115	19.2	∞1	15	298	19.9	0	1	0	6
2000—Detroit NFL	15	0	0	0	0.0	0	2	14	7.0	0	31	457	14.7	1	57	1401	24.6	0	1	0	6
2001—Detroit NFL	14	1	5	25	5.0	0	10	133	13.3	1	22	201	9.1	0	57	1446	25.4	0	1	0	6
2002—Detroit NFL	7	0	0	0	0.0	0	0	0	0.0	0	9	48	5.3	0	26	587	22.6	0	0	0	0
Pro totals (11 years)	156	30	12	68	5.7	0	123	1597	13.0	7	244	2895	11.9	8	359	7959	22.2	0	15	1	92

HOWARD, REGGIE   CB   PANTHERS

PERSONAL: Born May 17, 1977, in Memphis, Tenn. ... 6-0/190. ... Full name: Reginald Clement Howard.
HIGH SCHOOL: Kirby (Memphis,Tenn.).
COLLEGE: Memphis.
TRANSACTIONS/CAREER NOTES: Signed as non-drafted free agent by Carolina Panthers (April 17, 2000). ... Released by Panthers (August 29, 2000). ... Signed by New Orleans Saints to practice squad (September 1, 2000). ... Activated (October 22, 2000). ... Claimed on waivers by Panthers (October 25, 2000). ... Granted free agency (February 28, 2003). ... Re-signed by Panthers (May 2, 2003).

Year Team	G	GS	TOTALS Tk.	Ast.	Sks.	INTERCEPTIONS No.	Yds.	Avg.	TD
2000—New Orleans NFL	1	0	0	0	0.0	0	0	0.0	0
—Carolina NFL	1	0	0	0	0.0	0	0	0.0	0
2001—Carolina NFL	11	0	15	0	1.0	1	16	16.0	0
2002—Carolina NFL	14	14	75	9	1.0	2	19	9.5	0
Pro totals (3 years)	27	14	90	9	2.0	3	35	11.7	0

H

HOWELL, JOHN   S   BUCCANEERS

PERSONAL: Born April 28, 1978, in North Platte, Neb. ... 5-11/204. ... Full name: John Thomas Howell.
HIGH SCHOOL: Mullen (Neb.).
COLLEGE: Colorado State.
TRANSACTIONS/CAREER NOTES: Selected by Tampa Bay Buccaneers in fourth round (117th pick overall) of 2001 NFL draft. ... Signed by Buccaneers (July 25, 2001).
CHAMPIONSHIP GAME EXPERIENCE: Played in NFC championship game (2002 season). ... Member of Super Bowl championship team (2002 season).

			TOTALS			INTERCEPTIONS			
Year Team	G	GS	Tk.	Ast.	Sks.	No.	Yds.	Avg.	TD
2001—Tampa Bay NFL	14	1	16	8	0.0	0	0	0.0	0
2002—Tampa Bay NFL	16	1	14	1	0.0	0	0	0.0	0
Pro totals (2 years)	30	2	30	9	0.0	0	0	0.0	0

HUARD, BROCK   QB   COLTS

PERSONAL: Born April 15, 1976, in Seattle. ... 6-4/232. ... Brother of Damon Huard, quarterback, New England Patriots.
HIGH SCHOOL: Puyallup (Wash.).
COLLEGE: Washington.
TRANSACTIONS/CAREER NOTES: Selected after junior season by Seattle Seahawks in third round (77th pick overall) of 1999 NFL draft. ... Signed by Seahawks (July 29, 1999). ... Inactive for all 16 games (1999). ... Granted free agency (March 1, 2002). ... Re-signed by Seahawks (April 19, 2002). ... Traded by Seahawks to Indianapolis Colts for fifth-round pick (DL Rocky Bernard) in 2002 draft (April 19, 2002).
SINGLE GAME HIGHS (regular season): Attempts—34 (October 8, 2000, vs. Carolina); completions—19 (October 15, 2000, vs. Indianapolis); yards—226 (October 15, 2000, vs. Indianapolis); and touchdown passes—3 (October 15, 2000, vs. Indianapolis).
MISCELLANEOUS: Regular-season record as starting NFL quarterback: 0-4.

			PASSING								RUSHING				TOTALS		
Year Team	G	GS	Att.	Cmp.	Pct.	Yds.	TD	Int.	Avg.	Skd.	Rat.	Att.	Yds.	Avg.	TD	TD	2pt.	Pts.
1999—Seattle NFL						Did not play.												
2000—Seattle NFL	5	4	87	49	56.3	540	3	2	6.21	13	76.8	5	29	5.8	0	0	0	0
2001—Seattle NFL	1	0	17	9	52.9	127	1	0	7.47	1	96.9	1	11	11.0	0	0	0	0
2002—Indianapolis NFL						Did not play.												
Pro totals (2 years)	6	4	104	58	55.8	667	4	2	6.41	14	80.1	6	40	6.7	0	0	0	0

HUARD, DAMON   QB   PATRIOTS

PERSONAL: Born July 9, 1973, in Yakima, Wash. ... 6-3/215. ... Brother of Brock Huard, quarterback, Seattle Seahawks.
HIGH SCHOOL: Puyallup (Wash.).
COLLEGE: Washington.
TRANSACTIONS/CAREER NOTES: Signed as non-drafted free agent by Cincinnati Bengals (April 23, 1996). ... Released by Bengals (August 19, 1996). ... Signed by Miami Dolphins (April 24, 1997). ... Released by Dolphins (August 24, 1997). ... Re-signed by Dolphins to practice squad (August 26, 1997). ... Activated (September 6, 1997); did not play. ... Assigned by Dolphins to Frankfurt Galaxy in 1998 NFL Europe enhancement allocation program (February 18, 1998). ... Released by Dolphins (March 19, 2001). ... Signed by New England Patriots (April 2, 2001).
CHAMPIONSHIP GAME EXPERIENCE: Played in AFC championship game (2001 season). ... Member of Super Bowl championship team (2001 season); inactive.
SINGLE GAME HIGHS (regular season): Attempts—42 (October 17, 1999, vs. New England); completions—24 (October 17, 1999, vs. New England); yards—240 (October 17, 1999, vs. New England); and touchdown passes—2 (November 21, 1999, vs. New England).
MISCELLANEOUS: Regular-season record as starting NFL quarterback: 5-1 (.833).

			PASSING								RUSHING				TOTALS		
Year Team	G	GS	Att.	Cmp.	Pct.	Yds.	TD	Int.	Avg.	Skd.	Rat.	Att.	Yds.	Avg.	TD	TD	2pt.	Pts.
1997—Miami NFL						Did not play.												
1998—Frankfurt NFLE	10	10	290	159	54.8	1857	12	7	6.40	0	78.2	28	65	2.3	1	1	0	6
—Miami NFL	2	0	9	6	66.7	85	0	1	9.44	1	57.4	0	0	0.0	0	0	0	0
1999—Miami NFL	16	5	216	125	57.9	1288	8	4	5.96	28	79.8	28	124	4.4	0	0	0	0
2000—Miami NFL	16	1	63	39	61.9	318	1	3	5.05	4	60.2	0	0	0.0	0	0	0	0
2002—New England NFL	2	0	0	0	0.0	0	0	0	0.0	0	...	1	4	4.0	0	0	0	0
NFL Europe totals (1 year)	10	10	290	159	54.8	1857	12	7	6.40	0	78.2	28	65	2.3	1	1	0	6
NFL totals (3 years)	36	6	288	170	59.0	1691	9	8	5.87	33	74.6	29	128	4.4	0	0	0	0
Pro totals (4 years)	46	16	578	329	56.9	3548	21	15	6.14	33	76.4	57	193	3.4	1	1	0	6

HUFF, ORLANDO   LB   SEAHAWKS

PERSONAL: Born August 14, 1978, in Mobile, Alabama. ... 6-2/250.
HIGH SCHOOL: Upland (Calif.).
JUNIOR COLLEGE: Eastern Arizona Junior College.
COLLEGE: Fresno State.
TRANSACTIONS/CAREER NOTES: Selected by Seattle Seahawks in fourth round (104th pick overall) of 2001 NFL draft. ... Signed by Seahawks (July 9, 2001).

			TOTALS			INTERCEPTIONS			
Year Team	G	GS	Tk.	Ast.	Sks.	No.	Yds.	Avg.	TD
2001—Seattle NFL	12	0	0	0	0.0	0	0	0.0	0
2002—Seattle NFL	16	7	38	13	0.0	1	0	0.0	0
Pro totals (2 years)	28	7	38	13	0.0	1	0	0.0	0

H

HUNT, CLETIDUS — DT/DE — PACKERS

PERSONAL: Born January 2, 1976, in Memphis, Tenn. ... 6-4/303. ... Full name: Cletidus Marquell Hunt.
HIGH SCHOOL: Whitehaven (Memphis, Tenn.).
JUNIOR COLLEGE: Northwest Mississippi Community College.
COLLEGE: Kentucky State.
TRANSACTIONS/CAREER NOTES: Selected by Green Bay Packers in third round (94th pick overall) of NFL draft. ... Signed by Packers (July 26, 1999). ... On suspended list for violating league substance abuse policy (July 20-October 14, 2001). ... Granted free agency (March 1, 2002). ... Re-signed by Packers (April 24, 2002). ... Designated by Packers as franchise player (February 20, 2003). ... Re-signed by Packers (March 5, 2003).

				TOTALS		
Year Team	G	GS	Tk.	Ast.	Sks.	
1999—Green Bay NFL	11	1	10	10	0.5	
2000—Green Bay NFL	16	11	18	10	5.0	
2001—Green Bay NFL	12	4	15	10	0.0	
2002—Green Bay NFL	14	14	31	5	5.5	
Pro totals (4 years)	53	30	74	35	11.0	

HUNTER, DAMEON — RB — RAVENS

PERSONAL: Born February 18, 1979, in San Bernardino, Calif. ... 5-11/221. ... Full name: Dameon DeShawn Hunter.
HIGH SCHOOL: Rialto (Calif.).
JUNIOR COLLEGE: Chaffey College (Calif.).
COLLEGE: Utah.
TRANSACTIONS/CAREER NOTES: Signed as non-drafted free agent by Baltimore Ravens (April 26, 2002). ... Assigned by Ravens to Barcelona Dragons in 2003 NFL Europe enhancement allocation program (February 4, 2003).

			RUSHING				TOTALS			
Year Team	G	GS	Att.	Yds.	Avg.	TD	TD	2pt.	Pts.	Fum.
2002—Baltimore NFL	1	0	0	0	0.0	0	0	0	0	0

HUNTER, JAVIN — WR — RAVENS

PERSONAL: Born May 9, 1980, in Detroit. ... 5-11/190. ... Full name: Javin Edward Hunter.
HIGH SCHOOL: Detroit Country Day (Beverly Hills, Mich.).
COLLEGE: Notre Dame.
TRANSACTIONS/CAREER NOTES: Selected by Baltimore Ravens in sixth round (206th pick overall) of 2002 NFL draft. ... Signed by Ravens (July 26, 2002).
SINGLE GAME HIGHS (regular season): Receptions—2 (November 17, 2002, vs. Miami); yards—15 (November 17, 2002, vs. Miami); and touchdown receptions—0.

			RUSHING				RECEIVING				KICKOFF RETURNS				TOTALS			
Year Team	G	GS	Att.	Yds.	Avg.	TD	No.	Yds.	Avg.	TD	No.	Yds.	Avg.	TD	TD	2pt.	Pts.	Fum.
2002—Baltimore NFL	12	3	1	9	9.0	0	5	35	7.0	0	4	105	26.3	0	0	0	0	2

HUNTER, PETE — CB — COWBOYS

PERSONAL: Born May 25, 1980, in Atlantic City, N.J. ... 6-2/212. ... Full name: Ralph Hunter.
HIGH SCHOOL: Atlantic City (N.J.).
COLLEGE: Virgina Union.
TRANSACTIONS/CAREER NOTES: Selected by Dallas Cowboys in fifth round (168th pick overall) of 2002 NFL draft. ... Signed by Cowboys (July 25, 2002).

			TOTALS			INTERCEPTIONS			
Year Team	G	GS	Tk.	Ast.	Sks.	No.	Yds.	Avg.	TD
2002—Dallas NFL	11	2	18	2	0.0	1	16	16.0	0

HUNTLEY, RICHARD — RB

PERSONAL: Born September 18, 1972, in Monroe, N.C. ... 5-11/225. ... Full name: Richard Earl Huntley.
HIGH SCHOOL: Monroe (N.C.).
COLLEGE: Winston-Salem (N.C.) State.
TRANSACTIONS/CAREER NOTES: Selected by Atlanta Falcons in fourth round (117th pick overall) of 1996 NFL draft. ... Signed by Falcons for 1996 season. ... Released by Falcons (August 18, 1997). ... Signed by Pittsburgh Steelers (February 13, 1998). ... Granted free agency (February 11, 2000). ... Re-signed by Steelers (March 14, 2000). ... Released by Steelers (June 4, 2001). ... Signed by Carolina Panthers (June 6, 2001). ... Released by Panthers (March 22, 2002). ... Signed by Buffalo Bills (June 4, 2002). ... Released by Bills (September 1, 2002). ... Signed by Detroit Lions (September 18, 2002). ... Released by Detroit Lions (November 4, 2002).
SINGLE GAME HIGHS (regular season): Attempts—22 (December 9, 2001, vs. Buffalo); yards—168 (January 6, 2002, vs. New England); and rushing touchdowns—2 (December 16, 2000, vs. Washington).
STATISTICAL PLATEAUS: 100-yard rushing games: 2001 (1).

			RUSHING				RECEIVING				KICKOFF RETURNS				TOTALS			
Year Team	G	GS	Att.	Yds.	Avg.	TD	No.	Yds.	Avg.	TD	No.	Yds.	Avg.	TD	TD	2pt.	Pts.	Fum.
1996—Atlanta NFL	1	0	2	8	4.0	0	1	14	14.0	0	0	0	0.0	0	0	0	0	0
1997—									Did not play.									
1998—Pittsburgh NFL	16	1	55	242	4.4	1	3	18	6.0	0	6	119	19.8	0	1	0	6	5
1999—Pittsburgh NFL	16	2	93	567	6.1	5	27	253	9.4	3	15	336	22.4	0	8	0	48	3
2000—Pittsburgh NFL	13	0	46	215	4.7	3	10	91	9.1	0	0	0	0.0	0	3	1	20	1
2001—Carolina NFL	14	9	165	665	4.0	2	21	101	4.8	1	1	20	20.0	0	3	0	18	3
2002—Detroit NFL	3	1	3	4	1.3	0	0	0	0.0	0	0	0	0.0	0	0	0	0	0
Pro totals (6 years)	63	13	364	1701	4.7	11	62	477	7.7	4	22	475	21.6	0	15	1	92	12

H

HUSTED, MICHAEL　　　　K

PERSONAL: Born June 16, 1970, in El Paso, Texas. ... 6-0/195. ... Full name: Michael James Husted.
HIGH SCHOOL: Hampton (Va.).
COLLEGE: Virginia (degree in sociology, 1992).
TRANSACTIONS/CAREER NOTES: Signed as non-drafted free agent by Tampa Bay Buccaneers (May 3, 1993). ... Granted free agency (February 16, 1996). ... Tendered offer sheet by San Francisco 49ers (February 21, 1996). ... Offer matched by Buccaneers (February 28, 1996). ... Released by Buccaneers (February 11, 1999). ... Signed by Oakland Raiders (February 24, 1999). ... Released by Raiders (July 21, 2000). ... Signed by Chicago Bears (July 27, 2000). ... Released by Bears (August 7, 2000). ... Signed by Washington Redskins (September 18, 2000). ... Released by Redskins (October 10, 2000). ... Released by Colts (August 26, 2002). ... Signed by Kansas City Chiefs (October 12, 2002). ... Released by Chiefs (October 28, 2002). ... Re-signed by Chiefs (December 14, 2002). ... Granted unconditional free agency (February 28, 2003).

		FIELD GOALS							TOTALS		
Year　Team	G	1-29	30-39	40-49	50+	Tot.	Pct.	Lg.	XPM	XPA	Pts.
1993—Tampa Bay NFL	16	5-5	5-6	3-6	3-5	16-22	72.7	‡57	27	27	75
1994—Tampa Bay NFL	16	8-8	10-12	4-10	1-5	23-35	65.7	53	20	20	89
1995—Tampa Bay NFL	16	6-7	5-7	5-9	3-3	19-26	73.1	53	25	25	82
1996—Tampa Bay NFL	16	9-10	8-11	7-8	1-3	25-32	78.1	50	18	19	93
1997—Tampa Bay NFL	16	5-5	2-3	5-6	1-3	13-17	76.5	54	32	35	71
1998—Tampa Bay NFL	16	7-8	8-12	5-7	1-1	21-28	75.0	52	29	30	92
1999—Oakland NFL	13	5-5	7-11	8-12	0-3	20-31	64.5	49	30	30	90
2000—Washington NFL	4	4-4	0-3	0-1	0-0	4-8	50.0	28	8	9	20
2002—Kansas City NFL	6	0-0	1-1	0-0	0-0	1-1	100.0	38	3	3	6
Pro totals (9 years)	119	49-52	46-66	37-59	10-23	142-200	71.0	57	192	198	618

HUTCHINSON, CHAD　　　QB　　　COWBOYS

PERSONAL: Born February 21, 1977, in Encinitas, Calif. ... 6-5/237. ... Full name: Chad Martin Hutchinson.
HIGH SCHOOL: Torrey Pines (Encinitas, Calif.).
COLLEGE: Stanford.
TRANSACTIONS/CAREER NOTES: Signed as non-drafted free agent by Dallas Cowboys (January 26, 2002).
SINGLE GAME HIGHS (regular season): Attempts—40 (December 15, 2002, vs. New York Giants); completions—22 (November 3, 2002, vs. Detroit); yards—301 (November 24, 2002, vs. Jacksonville); and touchdown passes—2 (November 28, 2002, vs. Washington).
STATISTICAL PLATEAUS: 300-yard passing games: 2002 (1).
MISCELLANEOUS: Regular-season record as starting NFL quarterback: 2-7 (.222).

			PASSING							RUSHING				TOTALS		
Year　Team	G	GS	Att.	Cmp.	Pct.	Yds.	TD	Int.	Avg.	Skd.	Rat.	Att.	Yds.	Avg.	TD	TD	2pt.	Pts.
2002—Dallas NFL	9	9	250	127	50.8	1555	7	8	6.22	34	66.3	18	74	4.1	0	0	0	0

HUTCHINSON, STEVE　　　G　　　SEAHAWKS

PERSONAL: Born November 1, 1977, in Coral Springs, Fla. ... 6-5/313.
HIGH SCHOOL: Coral Springs (Fla.).
COLLEGE: Michigan.
TRANSACTIONS/CAREER NOTES: Selected by Seattle Seahawks in first round (17th pick overall) of 2001 NFL draft. ... Signed by Seahawks (July 25, 2001). ... On injured reserve with broken leg (November 12, 2002-remainder of season).
PLAYING EXPERIENCE: Seattle NFL, 2001-2002. ... Games/Games started: 2001 (16/16), 2002 (4/4). Total: 20/20.
HONORS: Named guard on THE SPORTING NEWS college All-America first team (2000).

HYMES, RANDY　　　WR　　　RAVENS

PERSONAL: Born August 7, 1979, in Galveston, Texas. ... 6-3/211.
HIGH SCHOOL: Hitchcock (Texas).
COLLEGE: Grambling State.
TRANSACTIONS/CAREER NOTES: Signed as non-drafted free agent by Baltimore Ravens (April 26, 2002). ... Released by Ravens (August 30, 2002). ... Re-signed by Ravens to practice squad (September 3, 2002). ... Activated (November 14, 2002).
SINGLE GAME HIGHS (regular season): Receptions—3 (December 22, 2002, vs. Cleveland); yards—76 (December 29, 2002, vs. Pittsburgh); and touchdown receptions—0.

			RECEIVING			
Year　Team	G	GS	No.	Yds.	Avg.	TD
2002—Baltimore NFL	7	2	6	123	20.5	0

IOANE, JUNIOR　　　DT　　　RAIDERS

PERSONAL: Born July 21, 1977, in American Samoa. ... 6-4/320. ... Full name: Junior Burton Ioane.
HIGH SCHOOL: North Sanpete (Mount Pleasant, Utah).
JUNIOR COLLEGE: Snow College (Utah).
COLLEGE: Arizona State.
TRANSACTIONS/CAREER NOTES: Selected by Oakland Raiders in fourth round (107th pick overall) of 2000 NFL draft. ... Signed by Raiders (June 1, 2000). ... Inactive for all 16 games (2000).
CHAMPIONSHIP GAME EXPERIENCE: Played in AFC championship game (2002 season). ... Played in Super Bowl XXXVII (2002 season).

			TOTALS		
Year　Team	G	GS	Tk.	Ast.	Sks.
2001—Oakland NFL	3	0	0	0	0.0
2002—Oakland NFL	6	0	2	1	1.0
Pro totals (2 years)	9	0	2	1	1.0

IRONS, GRANT   DE   BILLS

PERSONAL: Born July 7, 1979, in The Woodlands, Texas. ... 6-5/270. ... Full name: Grant Michael Irons. ... Son of Gerald Irons, linebacker with Oakland Raiders (1970-1975) and Cleveland Browns (1976-1979).
HIGH SCHOOL: Woodlands (Texas).
COLLEGE: Notre Dame.
TRANSACTIONS/CAREER NOTES: Signed as non-drafted free agent by Buffalo Bills (April 26, 2002).

Year Team	G	GS	TOTALS		
			Tk.	Ast.	Sks.
2002—Buffalo NFL	15	0	5	3	2.5

IRVIN, KEN   CB   VIKINGS

PERSONAL: Born July 11, 1972, in Rome, Ga. ... 5-11/186. ... Full name: Kenneth Irvin.
HIGH SCHOOL: Pepperell (Lindale, Ga.).
COLLEGE: Memphis (degree in criminal justice, 1998).
TRANSACTIONS/CAREER NOTES: Selected by Buffalo Bills in fourth round (109th pick overall) of 1995 NFL draft. ... Signed by Bills (July 10, 1995). ... Granted free agency (February 13, 1998). ... Re-signed by Bills (April 17, 1998). ... Granted unconditional free agency (February 12, 1999). ... Re-signed by Bills (March 17, 1999). ... On injured reserve with foot injury (December 23, 1999-remainder of season). ... Released by Bills (February 28, 2002). ... Signed by New Orleans Saints (April 24, 2002). ... Granted unconditional free agency (February 28, 2003). ... Signed by Minnesota Vikings (March 20, 2003).

Year Team	G	GS	TOTALS			INTERCEPTIONS			
			Tk.	Ast.	Sks.	No.	Yds.	Avg.	TD
1995—Buffalo NFL	16	3	18	2	0.0	0	0	0.0	0
1996—Buffalo NFL	16	1	17	4	2.0	0	0	0.0	0
1997—Buffalo NFL	16	0	5	0	0.0	2	28	14.0	0
1998—Buffalo NFL	16	16	46	5	0.0	1	43	43.0	0
1999—Buffalo NFL	14	14	40	5	0.0	1	1	1.0	0
2000—Buffalo NFL	16	16	29	2	0.0	2	1	0.5	0
2001—Buffalo NFL	14	4	33	3	0.0	1	0	0.0	0
2002—New Orleans NFL	16	9	58	4	0.0	2	10	5.0	0
Pro totals (8 years)	124	63	246	25	2.0	9	83	9.2	0

IRWIN, HEATH   G   BRONCOS

PERSONAL: Born June 27, 1973, in Boulder, Colo. ... 6-4/300. ... Nephew of Hale Irwin, professional golfer.
HIGH SCHOOL: Boulder (Colo.).
COLLEGE: Colorado.
TRANSACTIONS/CAREER NOTES: Selected by New England Patriots in fourth round (101st pick overall) of 1996 NFL draft. ... Signed by Patriots (July 17, 1996). ... Inactive for all 16 games (1996). ... Granted free agency (February 12, 1999). ... Re-signed by Patriots (June 24, 1999). ... Granted unconditional free agency (February 11, 2000). ... Signed by Miami Dolphins (February 25, 2000). ... Released by Dolphins (February 21, 2002). ... Signed by St. Louis Rams (June 5, 2002). ... Granted unconditional free agency (February 28, 2003). ... Signed by Denver Broncos (March 27, 2003).
PLAYING EXPERIENCE: New England NFL, 1997-1999; Miami NFL, 2000 and 2001; St. Louis NFL, 2002. ... Games/Games started: 1997 (16/1), 1998 (13/3), 1999 (15/13), 2000 (13/0), 2001 (16/7), 2002 (14/5). Total: 87/29.
CHAMPIONSHIP GAME EXPERIENCE: Member of Patriots for AFC championship game (1996 season); inactive. ... Member of Patriots for Super Bowl XXXI (1996 season); inactive.

ISMAIL, QADRY   WR

PERSONAL: Born November 8, 1970, in Newark, N.J. ... 6-0/196. ... Full name: Qadry Rahmadan Ismail. ... Brother of Rocket Ismail, wide receiver, Dallas Cowboys. ... Name pronounced KAH-dree ISS-my-el.
HIGH SCHOOL: Elmer L. Meyers (Wilkes-Barre, Pa.).
COLLEGE: Syracuse (degree in communications).
TRANSACTIONS/CAREER NOTES: Selected by Minnesota Vikings in second round (52nd pick overall) of 1993 NFL draft. ... Signed by Vikings (July 20, 1993). ... Granted unconditional free agency (February 14, 1997). ... Signed by Green Bay Packers (June 2, 1997). ... Traded by Packers to Miami Dolphins for first-round pick in (DT Vonnie Holliday) in 1998 draft (August 24, 1997). ... Granted unconditional free agency (February 13, 1998). ... Signed by New Orleans Saints (February 27, 1998). ... Released by Saints (February 10, 1999). ... Signed by Baltimore Ravens (April 27, 1999). ... Granted unconditional free agency (February 11, 2000). ... Re-signed by Ravens (April 28, 2000). ... Released by Ravens (February 27, 2002). ... Signed by Indianapolis Colts (March 18, 2002). ... On injured reserve with head injury (December 28, 2002-remainder of season). ... Released by Colts (February 27, 2003).
CHAMPIONSHIP GAME EXPERIENCE: Played in AFC championship game (2000 season). ... Member of Super Bowl championship team (2000 season).
HONORS: Named kick returner on THE SPORTING NEWS college All-America second team (1991).
SINGLE GAME HIGHS (regular season): Receptions—9 (October 8, 2000, vs. Jacksonville); yards—258 (December 12, 1999, vs. Pittsburgh); and touchdown receptions—3 (December 12, 1999, vs. Pittsburgh).
STATISTICAL PLATEAUS: 100-yard receiving games: 1994 (2), 1995 (1), 1999 (3), 2000 (1), 2001 (1). Total: 8.
MISCELLANEOUS: Holds Baltimore Ravens all-time records for most receiving yards (2,819) and receptions (191). ... Shares Baltimore Ravens all-time record for most touchdown receptions (18).

Year Team	G	GS	RECEIVING				KICKOFF RETURNS				TOTALS			
			No.	Yds.	Avg.	TD	No.	Yds.	Avg.	TD	TD	2pt.	Pts.	Fum.
1993—Minnesota NFL	15	3	19	212	11.2	1	‡42	902	21.5	0	1	0	6	1
1994—Minnesota NFL	16	3	45	696	15.5	5	35	807	23.1	0	5	0	30	2
1995—Minnesota NFL	16	1	32	597	18.7	3	42	1037	24.7	0	3	0	18	3
1996—Minnesota NFL	16	2	22	351	16.0	3	28	527	18.8	0	3	0	18	2
1997—Miami NFL	3	0	0	0	0.0	0	8	166	20.8	0	0	0	0	0
1998—New Orleans NFL	10	1	0	0	0.0	0	28	590	21.1	0	0	0	0	2
1999—Baltimore NFL	16	16	68	1105	16.3	6	4	55	13.8	0	6	0	36	2
2000—Baltimore NFL	15	13	49	655	13.4	5	2	51	25.5	0	5	0	30	0
2001—Baltimore NFL	16	15	74	1059	14.3	7	0	0	0.0	0	7	1	44	1
2002—Indianapolis NFL	14	14	44	462	10.5	3	0	0	0.0	0	3	0	18	0
Pro totals (10 years)	137	68	353	5137	14.6	33	189	4135	21.9	0	33	1	200	13

ISMAIL, ROCKET — WR

PERSONAL: Born November 18, 1969, in Elizabeth, N.J. ... 5-11/183. ... Full name: Raghib Ramadian Ismail. ... Brother of Qadry Ismail, wide receiver, Indianapolis Colts. ... Name pronounced rah-GIBB ISS-my-ell.

HIGH SCHOOL: Elmer L. Meyers (Wilkes-Barre, Pa.).

COLLEGE: Notre Dame (degree in sociology, 1994).

TRANSACTIONS/CAREER NOTES: Signed after junior season by Toronto Argonauts of CFL (April 21, 1991). ... Selected by Los Angeles Raiders in fourth round (100th pick overall) of 1991 NFL draft. ... Granted free agency from Argonauts (February 15, 1993). ... Signed by Raiders (August 30, 1993). ... Raiders franchise moved to Oakland (July 21, 1995). ... Granted free agency (February 16, 1996). ... Re-signed by Raiders (August 25, 1996). ... Traded by Raiders to Carolina Panthers for fifth-round pick (traded to Miami) in 1997 draft (August 25, 1996). ... Granted unconditional free agency (February 14, 1997). ... Re-signed by Panthers (February 26, 1997). ... Granted unconditional free agency (February 13, 1998). ... Re-signed by Panthers (June 2, 1998). ... Granted unconditional free agency (February 12, 1999). ... Signed by Dallas Cowboys (April 15, 1999). ... On injured reserve with knee injury (November 8, 2000-remainder of season). ... On injured reserve with neck injury (September 1, 2002-entire season). ... Released by Cowboys (February 26, 2003).

CHAMPIONSHIP GAME EXPERIENCE: Played in Grey Cup, CFL championship game (1991). ... Played in NFC championship game (1996 season).

HONORS: Named kick returner on THE SPORTING NEWS college All-America first team (1989). ... Named College Football Player of the Year by THE SPORTING NEWS (1990). ... Named wide receiver on THE SPORTING NEWS college All-America first team (1990).

SINGLE GAME HIGHS (regular season): Receptions—10 (December 9, 2001, vs. New York Giants); yards—149 (September 12, 1999, vs. Washington); and touchdown receptions—2 (October 11, 1998, vs. Dallas).

STATISTICAL PLATEAUS: 100-yard receiving games: 1995 (1), 1996 (1), 1997 (1), 1998 (3), 1999 (3), 2001 (2). Total: 11.

Year Team	G	GS	RUSHING				RECEIVING				PUNT RETURNS				KICKOFF RETURNS				TOTALS		
			Att.	Yds.	Avg.	TD	No.	Yds.	Avg.	TD	No.	Yds.	Avg.	TD	No.	Yds.	Avg.	TD	TD	2pt.	Pts.
1991—Toronto CFL	17	17	36	271	7.5	3	64	1300	20.3	9	48	602	12.5	1	31	786	25.4	0	13	0	78
1992—Toronto CFL	16	16	34	154	4.5	3	36	651	18.1	4	59	614	10.4	1	43	*1139	26.5	0	8	0	48
1993—LA Raiders NFL	13	0	4	-5	-1.3	0	26	353	13.6	1	0	0	0.0	0	25	605	§24.2	0	1	0	6
1994—LA Raiders NFL	16	0	4	31	7.8	0	34	513	15.1	5	0	0	0.0	0	43	923	21.5	0	5	0	30
1995—Oakland NFL	16	15	6	29	4.8	0	28	491	17.5	3	0	0	0.0	0	36	706	19.6	0	3	0	18
1996—Carolina NFL	13	5	8	80	10.0	1	12	214	17.8	0	0	0	0.0	0	5	100	20.0	0	1	0	6
1997—Carolina NFL	13	2	4	32	8.0	0	36	419	11.6	2	0	0	0.0	0	0	0	0.0	0	2	0	12
1998—Carolina NFL	16	15	3	42	14.0	0	69	1024	14.8	8	0	0	0.0	0	0	0	0.0	0	8	0	48
1999—Dallas NFL	16	14	13	110	8.5	1	80	1097	13.7	6	0	0	0.0	0	0	0	0.0	0	7	0	42
2000—Dallas NFL	9	9	8	73	9.1	0	25	350	14.0	1	0	0	0.0	0	0	0	0.0	0	1	1	8
2001—Dallas NFL	14	13	8	31	3.9	0	53	834	15.7	2	1	20	20.0	0	0	0	0.0	0	2	0	12
2002—Dallas NFL									Did not play.												
CFL totals (2 years)	33	33	70	425	6.1	6	100	1951	19.5	13	107	1216	11.4	2	74	1925	26.0	0	21	0	126
NFL totals (9 years)	126	73	58	423	7.3	2	363	5295	14.6	28	1	20	20.0	0	109	2334	21.4	0	30	1	182
Pro totals (11 years)	159	106	128	848	6.6	8	463	7246	15.7	41	108	1236	11.4	2	183	4259	23.3	0	51	1	308

IVY, COREY — CB — BUCCANEERS

PERSONAL: Born March 29, 1977, in St. Louis. ... 5-8/183. ... Full name: Corey Terrell Ivy.

HIGH SCHOOL: Moore (Oklahoma).

JUNIOR COLLEGE: Northeastern Oklahoma.

COLLEGE: Oklahoma.

TRANSACTIONS/CAREER NOTES: Signed as non-drafted free agent by New England Patriots (May 13, 1999). :.. Released by Patriots (September 5, 1999). ... Re-signed by Patriots to practice squad (December 29, 1999). ... Signed by Cleveland Browns (July 12, 2000). ... Released by Browns (August 27, 2000). ... Signed by Tampa Bay Buccaneers (June 4, 2001). ... Released by Buccaneers (September 2, 2001). ... Re-signed by Buccaneers to practice squad (September 3, 2001). ... Activated (November 10, 2001). ... Released by Buccaneers (December 4, 2001). ... Re-signed by Buccaneers to practice squad (December 5, 2001). ... Assigned by Buccaneers to Rhein Fire in 2002 NFL Europe enhancement allocation program (February 12, 2002).

CHAMPIONSHIP GAME EXPERIENCE: Played in NFC championship game (2002 season). ... Member of Super Bowl championship team (2002 season).

Year Team	G	GS	TOTALS			INTERCEPTIONS			
			Tk.	Ast.	Sks.	No.	Yds.	Avg.	TD
2001—Tampa Bay NFL	1	0	3	2	0.0	0	0	0.0	0
2002—Frankfurt NFLE	...	...	...	...	0.0	0	0	0.0	0
—Tampa Bay NFL	16	0	0	0	0.0	0	0	0.0	0
NFL Europe totals (1 year)	...	...	...	...	0.0	0	0	0.0	0
NFL totals (2 years)	17	0	3	2	0.0	0	0	0.0	0
Pro totals (3 years)	...	...	...	...	0.0	0	0	0.0	0

IWUOMA, CHIDI   CB   STEELERS

PERSONAL: Born February 19, 1978, in Pasadena, Calif. ... 5-8/180.
HIGH SCHOOL: Pasadena (Calif.).
COLLEGE: California.
TRANSACTIONS/CAREER NOTES: Signed as non-drafted free agent by Detroit Lions (April 27, 2000). ... Released by Lions (September 2, 2001). ... Re-signed by Lions to practice squad (September 4, 2001). ... Activated (September 8, 2001). ... Released by Lions (September 1, 2002). ... Signed by Pittsburgh Steelers (September 11, 2002).

			TOTALS			INTERCEPTIONS			
Year Team	G	GS	Tk.	Ast.	Sks.	No.	Yds.	Avg.	TD
2001—Detroit NFL	13	1	5	0	0.0	0	0	0.0	0
2002—Pittsburgh NFL	13	0	0	1	0.0	0	0	0.0	0
Pro totals (2 years)	26	1	5	1	0.0	0	0	0.0	0

IZZO, LARRY   LB   PATRIOTS

PERSONAL: Born September 26, 1974, in Fort Belvoir, Va. ... 5-10/228. ... Full name: Lawrence Alexander Izzo.
HIGH SCHOOL: McCullough (Houston).
COLLEGE: Rice.
TRANSACTIONS/CAREER NOTES: Signed as non-drafted free agent by Miami Dolphins (April 25, 1996). ... On injured reserve with foot injury (August 18, 1997-entire season). ... Granted free agency (February 12, 1999). ... Re-signed by Dolphins (March 31, 1999). ... Granted unconditional free agency (March 2, 2001). ... Signed by New England Patriots (March 6, 2001).
CHAMPIONSHIP GAME EXPERIENCE: Played in AFC championship game (2001 season). ... Member of Super Bowl championship team (2001 season).
HONORS: Played in Pro Bowl (2000 and 2002 seasons).

			TOTALS			INTERCEPTIONS			
Year Team	G	GS	Tk.	Ast.	Sks.	No.	Yds.	Avg.	TD
1996—Miami NFL	16	0	1	0	0.0	0	0	0.0	0
1997—Miami NFL			Did not play.						
1998—Miami NFL	13	0	0	0	0.0	0	0	0.0	0
1999—Miami NFL	16	0	0	0	0.0	0	0	0.0	0
2000—Miami NFL	16	0	4	0	0.0	0	0	0.0	0
2001—New England NFL	16	0	1	1	0.0	0	0	0.0	0
2002—New England NFL	15	0	1	0	0.0	0	0	0.0	0
Pro totals (6 years)	92	0	7	1	0.0	0	0	0.0	0

JACKSON, ALCENDER   G

PERSONAL: Born May 18, 1977, in Moss Point, Miss. ... 6-3/311. ... Full name: Alcender O'Neal Jackson.
HIGH SCHOOL: Moss Point (Miss.).
COLLEGE: Louisiana State.
TRANSACTIONS/CAREER NOTES: Signed as non-drafted free agent by Dallas Cowboys (April 17, 2000). ... Released by Cowboys (September 1, 2002). ... Signed by Green Bay Packers to practice squad (October 2, 2002). ... Released by Packers (October 9, 2002). ... Re-signed by Packers (December 4, 2002). ... Released by Packers (December 23, 2002).
PLAYING EXPERIENCE: Dallas NFL, 2000; Green Bay NFL, 2002. ... Games/Games started: 2000 (3/0), 2002 (2/0). Total: 5/0.

JACKSON, ARNOLD   WR/PR

PERSONAL: Born April 9, 1977, in Jacksonville. ... 5-8/173.
HIGH SCHOOL: Andrew Jackson (Fla.).
COLLEGE: Louisville.
TRANSACTIONS/CAREER NOTES: Signed as non-drafted free agent by Arizona Cardinals (April 23, 2001). ... Granted free agency (February 28, 2003). ... Released by Cardinals (March 23, 2003).
SINGLE GAME HIGHS (regular season): Receptions—4 (December 23, 2001, vs. Dallas); yards—25 (November 24, 2002, vs. Oakland); and touchdown receptions—1 (November 24, 2002, vs. Oakland).

			RECEIVING				PUNT RETURNS				KICKOFF RETURNS				TOTALS			
Year Team	G	GS	No.	Yds.	Avg.	TD	No.	Yds.	Avg.	TD	No.	Yds.	Avg.	TD	TD	2pt.	Pts.	Fum.
2001—Arizona NFL	16	1	9	44	4.9	0	‡40	461	11.5	0	2	46	23.0	0	0	0	0	0
2002—Arizona NFL	16	0	5	42	8.4	1	31	182	5.9	0	0	0	0.0	0	1	0	6	2
Pro totals (2 years)	32	1	14	86	6.1	1	71	643	9.1	0	2	46	23.0	0	1	0	6	2

JACKSON, BERNARD   DL   REDSKINS

PERSONAL: Born May 10, 1980, in Louisville, Ky. ... 6-4/281.
HIGH SCHOOL: St. Xavier (Louisville, Ky.).
COLLEGE: Tennessee.
TRANSACTIONS/CAREER NOTES: Signed as non-drafted free agent by Washington Redskins (April 25, 2002). ... Released by Redskins (September 1, 2002). ... Re-signed by Redskins to practice squad (September 3, 2002). ... Activated (November 18, 2002).

			TOTALS		
Year Team	G	GS	Tk.	Ast.	Sks.
2002—Washington NFL	4	0	1	1	0.0

JACKSON, BRAD — LB

PERSONAL: Born January 11, 1975, in Canton, Ohio. ... 6-0/230. ... Full name: Bradley Michael Jackson.
HIGH SCHOOL: Firestone (Akron, Ohio).
COLLEGE: Cincinnati.
TRANSACTIONS/CAREER NOTES: Selected by Miami Dolphins in third round (79th pick overall) of 1998 NFL draft. ... Signed by Dolphins (July 21, 1998). ... Released by Dolphins (August 25, 1998). ... Signed by Tennessee Oilers to practice squad (September 1, 1998). ... Released by Oilers (September 29, 1998). ... Signed by Baltimore Ravens to practice squad (September 30, 1998). ... Activated (December 17, 1998); did not play. ... Granted free agency (March 1, 2002). ... Signed by Carolina Panthers (March 13, 2002). ... Released by Panthers (September 2, 2002). ... Re-signed by Panthers (September 24, 2002). ... Released by Panthers (October 8, 2002). ... Re-signed by Panthers (October 17, 2002). ... Granted unconditional free agency (February 28, 2003).
CHAMPIONSHIP GAME EXPERIENCE: Played in AFC championship game (2000 season). ... Member of Super Bowl championship team (2000 season).
HONORS: Named outside linebacker on THE SPORTING NEWS college All-America third team (1997).

			TOTALS			INTERCEPTIONS			
Year Team	G	GS	Tk.	Ast.	Sks.	No.	Yds.	Avg.	TD
1998—Baltimore NFL			Did not play.						
1999—Baltimore NFL	13	0	0	0	0.0	0	0	0.0	0
2000—Baltimore NFL	10	0	2	0	0.0	0	0	0.0	0
2001—Baltimore NFL	16	5	10	8	0.0	0	0	0.0	0
2002—Carolina NFL	11	0	5	1	0.0	0	0	0.0	0
Pro totals (4 years)	50	5	17	9	0.0	0	0	0.0	0

JACKSON, CHRIS — WR

PERSONAL: Born February 26, 1975, in Bristol, Pa. ... 6-2/204.
HIGH SCHOOL: Mater Dei (Santa Ana, Calif.).
COLLEGE: Washington State.
TRANSACTIONS/CAREER NOTES: Signed as non-drafted free agent by Seattle Seahawks (April 21, 1998). ... Released by Seahawks (August 24, 1998). ... Signed by Tampa Bay Buccaneers to practice squad (September 1, 1998). ... Released by Buccaneers (October 21, 1998). ... Signed by Seahawks (March 23, 1999). ... Released by Seahawks (September 6, 1999). ... Signed by Tennessee Titans to practice squad (October 8, 2000). ... Activated (November 4, 2000). ... On injured reserve with back injury (December 1, 2000-remainder of season). ... Released by Titans (February 28, 2001). ... Signed by Green Bay Packers (August 1, 2002). ... Released by Packers (September 1, 2002). ... Re-signed by Packers (September 29, 2002). ... Released by Packers (October 1, 2002).

			RECEIVING			
Year Team	G	GS	No.	Yds.	Avg.	TD
2000—Tennessee NFL	1	0	0	0	0.0	0
2002—Green Bay NFL	1	0	0	0	0.0	0
Pro totals (2 years)	2	0	0	0	0.0	0

JACKSON, DARRELL — WR — SEAHAWKS

PERSONAL: Born December 6, 1978, in Dayton, Ohio. ... 6-0/201. ... Full name: Darrell Lamont Jackson.
HIGH SCHOOL: Tampa Catholic.
COLLEGE: Florida.
TRANSACTIONS/CAREER NOTES: Selected after junior season by Seattle Seahawks in third round (80th pick overall) of 2000 NFL draft. ... Signed by Seahawks (July 19, 2000). ... Granted free agency (February 28, 2003). ... Re-signed by Seahawks (April 25, 2003).
SINGLE GAME HIGHS (regular season): Receptions—10 (September 15, 2002, vs. Arizona); yards—174 (September 15, 2002, vs. Arizona); and touchdown receptions—2 (December 1, 2002, vs. San Francisco).
STATISTICAL PLATEAUS: 100-yard receiving games: 2001 (5), 2002 (2). Total: 7.

			RUSHING				RECEIVING				PUNT RETURNS				TOTALS			
Year Team	G	GS	Att.	Yds.	Avg.	TD	No.	Yds.	Avg.	TD	No.	Yds.	Avg.	TD	TD	2pt.	Pts.	Fum.
2000—Seattle NFL	16	10	1	-1	-1.0	0	53	713	13.5	6	0	0	0.0	0	6	0	36	2
2001—Seattle NFL	16	16	1	9	9.0	0	70	1081	15.4	8	0	0	0.0	0	8	0	48	0
2002—Seattle NFL	13	13	3	3	1.0	0	62	877	14.1	4	4	32	8.0	0	4	0	24	3
Pro totals (3 years)	45	39	5	11	2.2	0	185	2671	14.4	18	4	32	8.0	0	18	0	108	5

JACKSON, DEXTER — S — CARDINALS

PERSONAL: Born July 28, 1977, in Quincy, Fla. ... 6-1/203. ... Full name: Dexter Lamar Jackson.
HIGH SCHOOL: James A. Shanks (Quincy, Fla.).
COLLEGE: Florida State.
TRANSACTIONS/CAREER NOTES: Selected by Tampa Bay Buccaneers in fourth round (113th pick overall) of 1999 NFL draft. ... Signed by Buccaneers (July 29, 1999). ... Granted free agency (March 1, 2002). ... Re-signed by Buccaneers (April 26, 2002). ... Granted unconditional free agency (February 28, 2003). ... Signed by Arizona Cardinals (March 12, 2003).
CHAMPIONSHIP GAME EXPERIENCE: Played in NFC championship game (1999 and 2002 seasons). ... Member of Super Bowl championship team (2002 season).
HONORS: Named Most Valuable Player of Super Bowl XXXVII (2002 season).

			TOTALS			INTERCEPTIONS			
Year Team	G	GS	Tk.	Ast.	Sks.	No.	Yds.	Avg.	TD
1999—Tampa Bay NFL	12	0	0	0	0.0	0	0	0.0	0
2000—Tampa Bay NFL	13	0	18	2	0.0	0	0	0.0	0
2001—Tampa Bay NFL	15	15	54	11	2.5	4	42	10.5	0
2002—Tampa Bay NFL	16	16	56	15	0.0	3	101	33.7	0
Pro totals (4 years)	56	31	128	28	2.5	7	143	20.4	0

JACKSON, FRISMAN   WR   BROWNS

PERSONAL: Born June 12, 1979, in Chicago. ... 6-3/205.
HIGH SCHOOL: Morgan Park (Chicago).
COLLEGE: Northern Illinois, then Western Illinois.
TRANSACTIONS/CAREER NOTES: Signed as non-drafted free agent by Cleveland Browns (April 26, 2002).
SINGLE GAME HIGHS (regular season): Receptions—1 (November 17, 2002, vs. Cincinnati); yards—6 (November 17, 2002, vs. Cincinnati); and touchdown receptions—0.

			RECEIVING				KICKOFF RETURNS				TOTALS			
Year Team	G	GS	No.	Yds.	Avg.	TD	No.	Yds.	Avg.	TD	TD	2pt.	Pts.	Fum.
2002—Cleveland NFL	7	0	1	6	6.0	0	3	58	19.3	0	0	0	0	0

JACKSON, GRADY   DT   SAINTS

PERSONAL: Born January 21, 1973, in Greensboro, Ala. ... 6-2/330.
HIGH SCHOOL: Greensboro (Ala.) East.
JUNIOR COLLEGE: Hinds Community College (Miss.).
COLLEGE: Knoxville (Tenn.) College.
TRANSACTIONS/CAREER NOTES: Selected by Oakland Raiders in sixth round (193rd pick overall) of 1997 NFL draft. ... Signed by Raiders (July 18, 1997). ... Granted unconditional free agency (March 1, 2002). ... Signed by New Orleans Saints (April 11, 2002).
CHAMPIONSHIP GAME EXPERIENCE: Played in AFC championship game (2000 season).

			TOTALS		
Year Team	G	GS	Tk.	Ast.	Sks.
1997—Oakland NFL	5	0	4	2	0.0
1998—Oakland NFL	15	1	29	10	3.0
1999—Oakland NFL	15	0	25	9	4.0
2000—Oakland NFL	16	15	51	17	8.0
2001—Oakland NFL	16	16	52	17	4.0
2002—New Orleans NFL	15	14	31	12	5.5
Pro totals (6 years)	82	46	192	67	24.5

JACKSON, JAMES   RB   BROWNS

PERSONAL: Born August 4, 1976, in Belle Glade, Fla. ... 5-10/215. ... Full name: James Shurrate Jackson.
HIGH SCHOOL: Glades Central (Belle Glade, Fla.).
COLLEGE: Miami.
TRANSACTIONS/CAREER NOTES: Selected by Cleveland Browns in third round (65th pick overall) of 2001 NFL draft. ... Signed by Browns (July 23, 2001). ... On injured reserve with ankle injury (December 20, 2001-remainder of season).
SINGLE GAME HIGHS (regular season): Attempts—31 (September 23, 2001, vs. Detroit); yards—124 (September 23, 2001, vs. Detroit); and rushing touchdowns—1 (October 21, 2001, vs. Baltimore).
STATISTICAL PLATEAUS: 100-yard rushing games: 2001 (1).

			RUSHING				RECEIVING				TOTALS			
Year Team	G	GS	Att.	Yds.	Avg.	TD	No.	Yds.	Avg.	TD	TD	2pt.	Pts.	Fum.
2001—Cleveland NFL	11	10	195	554	2.8	2	7	56	8.0	0	2	0	12	1
2002—Cleveland NFL	15	0	12	54	4.5	0	3	9	3.0	0	0	0	0	0
Pro totals (2 years)	26	10	207	608	2.9	2	10	65	6.5	0	2	0	12	1

JACKSON, JARIOUS   QB   BRONCOS

PERSONAL: Born May 3, 1977, in Tupelo, Miss. ... 6-0/228. ... Full name: Jarious K. Jackson.
HIGH SCHOOL: Tupelo (Miss.).
COLLEGE: Notre Dame.
TRANSACTIONS/CAREER NOTES: Selected by Denver Broncos in seventh round (214th pick overall) of 2000 NFL draft. ... Signed by Broncos (July 20, 2000). ... Assigned by Broncos to Bracelona Dragons in 2001 NFL Europe enhancement allocation program (February 19, 2001). ... Granted free agency (February 28, 2003). ... Re-signed by Broncos (April 18, 2003).
SINGLE GAME HIGHS (regular season): Attempts—12 (December 16, 2001, vs. Kansas City); completions—7 (December 16, 2001, vs. Kansas City); yards—73 (December 16, 2001, vs. Kansas City); and touchdown passes—0.

			PASSING									RUSHING				TOTALS		
Year Team	G	GS	Att.	Cmp.	Pct.	Yds.	TD	Int.	Avg.	Skd.	Rat.	Att.	Yds.	Avg.	TD	TD	2pt.	Pts.
2000—Denver NFL	2	0	1	0	0.0	0	0	0	0.0	1	39.6	1	-1	-1.0	0	0	0	0
2001—Barcelona NFLE	...	...	223	125	56.1	1544	13	6	6.92	0	85.9	43	287	6.7	2	2	0	12
—Denver NFL	1	0	12	7	58.3	73	0	0	6.08	1	76.0	5	7	1.4	0	0	0	0
2002—Denver NFL	1	0	0	0	0.0	0	0	0	0.0	0	...	0	0	0.0	0	0	0	0
NFL Europe totals (1 year)	...	...	223	125	56.1	1544	13	6	6.92	0	85.9	43	287	6.7	2	2	0	12
NFL totals (3 years)	4	0	13	7	53.8	73	0	0	5.62	2	70.4	6	6	1.0	0	0	0	0
Pro totals (4 years)	...	...	236	132	55.9	1617	13	6	6.85	2	85.0	49	293	6.0	2	2	0	12

JACKSON, LADAIRIS   DE   REDSKINS

PERSONAL: Born June 16, 1979, in Denver. ... 6-2/261.
JUNIOR COLLEGE: El Camino College (Calif.).
COLLEGE: Oregon State.

TRANSACTIONS/CAREER NOTES: Signed as non-drafted free agent by Seattle Seahawks (April 27, 2001). ... Released by Seahawks (August 30, 2001). ... Signed by Washington Redskins (January 23, 2002). ... On injured reserve with knee injury (December 23, 2002-remainder of season).

Year Team	G	GS	TOTALS Tk.	Ast.	Sks.
2002—Washington NFL	15	0	12	4	2.5

JACKSON, TERRY   FB   49ERS

PERSONAL: Born January 10, 1976, in Gainesville, Fla. ... 6-0/232. ... Full name: Terrance Bernard Jackson. ... Brother of Willie Jackson Jr., wide receiver, with four NFL teams (1994-2001).
HIGH SCHOOL: P.K. Yonge (Gainesville, Fla.).
COLLEGE: Florida.
TRANSACTIONS/CAREER NOTES: Selected by San Francisco 49ers in fifth round (157th pick overall) of 1999 NFL draft. ... Signed by 49ers (July 26, 1999). ... Granted free agency (March 1, 2002). ... Re-signed by 49ers (July 22, 2002). ... On injured reserve with knee injury (October 16, 2002-remainder of season).
SINGLE GAME HIGHS (regular season): Attempts—5 (December 2, 2001, vs. Buffalo); yards—37 (December 2, 2001, vs. Buffalo); and rushing touchdowns—1 (January 6, 2002, vs. New Orleans).

Year Team	G	GS	RUSHING Att.	Yds.	Avg.	TD	RECEIVING No.	Yds.	Avg.	TD	KICKOFF RETURNS No.	Yds.	Avg.	TD	TOTALS TD	2pt.	Pts.	Fum.
1999—San Francisco NFL	16	0	15	75	5.0	0	3	6	2.0	0	0	0	0.0	0	0	0	0	1
2000—San Francisco NFL	15	1	5	6	1.2	1	5	48	9.6	1	1	9	9.0	0	2	1	14	0
2001—San Francisco NFL	16	1	22	138	6.3	1	12	91	7.6	2	0	0	0.0	0	3	0	18	1
2002—San Francisco NFL	5	0	0	0	0.0	0	0	0	0.0	0	4	67	16.8	0	0	0	0	0
Pro totals (4 years)	52	2	42	219	5.2	2	20	145	7.3	3	5	76	15.2	0	5	1	32	2

JACKSON, TYOKA   DT   RAMS

PERSONAL: Born November 22, 1971, in Washington, D.C. ... 6-2/280. ... Name pronounced tie-OH-kah.
HIGH SCHOOL: Bishop McNamara (Forestville, Md.).
COLLEGE: Penn State.
TRANSACTIONS/CAREER NOTES: Signed as non-drafted free agent by Atlanta Falcons (May 2, 1994). ... Released by Falcons (August 29, 1994). ... Re-signed by Falcons to practice squad (August 30, 1994). ... Signed by Miami Dolphins off Falcons practice squad (November 16, 1994). ... Released by Dolphins (August 27, 1995). ... Signed by Tampa Bay Buccaneers (December 27, 1995). ... Granted free agency (February 13, 1998). ... Re-signed by Buccaneers (June 22, 1998). ... Granted unconditional free agency (March 2, 2001). ... Signed by St. Louis Rams (May 1, 2001). ... Granted unconditional free agency (February 28, 2003). ... Re-signed by Rams (March 17, 2003).
CHAMPIONSHIP GAME EXPERIENCE: Member of Buccaneers for NFC championship game (1999 season); inactive. ... Played in NFC championship game (2001 season). ... Played in Super Bowl XXXVI (2001 season).

Year Team	G	GS	TOTALS Tk.	Ast.	Sks.
1994—Miami NFL	1	0	0	0	0.0
1995—			Did not play.		
1996—Tampa Bay NFL	13	2	9	2	0.0
1997—Tampa Bay NFL	12	0	5	2	2.5
1998—Tampa Bay NFL	16	12	21	6	3.0
1999—Tampa Bay NFL	6	1	5	2	1.0
2000—Tampa Bay NFL	16	1	4	3	2.0
2001—St. Louis NFL	16	0	12	7	3.0
2002—St. Louis NFL	16	0	14	3	3.5
Pro totals (8 years)	96	16	70	25	15.0

JACKSON, WAVERLY   G

PERSONAL: Born December 19, 1972, in South Hill, Va. ... 6-2/343.
HIGH SCHOOL: Park View (Sterling, Va.).
COLLEGE: Virginia Tech.
TRANSACTIONS/CAREER NOTES: Signed as non-drafted free agent by Carolina Panthers (April 19, 1997). ... Released by Panthers (August 25, 1997). ... Re-signed by Panthers to practice squad (August 26, 1997). ... Granted free agency after 1997 season. ... Signed by Indianapolis Colts (January 12, 1998). ... Granted free agency (March 2, 2001). ... Re-signed by Colts (March 7, 2001). ... Released by Colts (February 26, 2003).
PLAYING EXPERIENCE: Indianapolis NFL, 1998-2002. ... Games/Games started: 1998 (6/2), 1999 (16/16), 2000 (16/0), 2001 (16/0), 2002 (14/5). Total: 68/23.

JACKSON, WILLIE   WR

PERSONAL: Born August 16, 1971, in Gainesville, Fla. ... 6-1/212. ... Full name: Willie Bernard Jackson Jr. ... Brother of Terry Jackson, running back, San Francisco 49ers.
HIGH SCHOOL: P.K. Yonge (Gainesville, Fla.).
COLLEGE: Florida (degree in telecommunications, 1993).
TRANSACTIONS/CAREER NOTES: Selected by Dallas Cowboys in fourth round (109th pick overall) of 1994 NFL draft. ... Signed by Cowboys (July 16, 1994). ... Inactive for 16 games (1994). ... Selected by Jacksonville Jaguars from Cowboys in NFL expansion draft (February 15, 1995). ... Granted free agency (February 14, 1997). ... Re-signed by Jaguars (March 26, 1997). ... Released by Jaguars (August 30, 1998). ... Signed by Cincinnati Bengals (September 10, 1998). ... Granted unconditional free agency (February 11, 2000). ... Signed by New Orleans Saints (April 28, 2000) ... Granted unconditional free agency (March 2, 2001). ... Re-signed by Saints (April 24, 2001). ... Granted uncondi-

tional free agency (March 1, 2002). ... Signed by Atlanta Falcons (July 12, 2002). ... Released by Falcons (October 28, 2002). ... Signed by Washington Redskins (October 31, 2002). ... Released by Redskins (December 12, 2002).

CHAMPIONSHIP GAME EXPERIENCE: Member of Cowboys for NFC championship game (1994 season); inactive. ... Played in AFC championship game (1996 season).

SINGLE GAME HIGHS (regular season): Receptions—11 (November 11, 2001, vs. San Francisco); yards—167 (November 11, 2001, vs. San Francisco); and touchdown receptions—2 (November 19, 2000, vs. Oakland).

STATISTICAL PLATEAUS: 100-yard receiving games: 1995 (1), 1996 (1), 2001 (3). Total: 5.

Year Team	G	GS	RECEIVING				KICKOFF RETURNS				TOTALS			
			No.	Yds.	Avg.	TD	No.	Yds.	Avg.	TD	TD	2pt.	Pts.	Fum.
1994—Dallas NFL							Did not play.							
1995—Jacksonville NFL	14	10	53	589	11.1	5	19	404	21.3	0	5	1	32	2
1996—Jacksonville NFL	16	2	33	486	14.7	3	7	149	21.3	0	3	1	20	0
1997—Jacksonville NFL	16	1	17	206	12.1	2	32	653	20.4	0	2	1	14	1
1998—Cincinnati NFL	8	0	7	165	23.6	0	0	0	0.0	0	0	0	0	0
1999—Cincinnati NFL	16	2	31	369	11.9	2	6	179	29.8	0	2	†1	14	1
2000—New Orleans NFL	15	7	37	523	14.1	6	0	0	0.0	0	6	0	36	2
2001—New Orleans NFL	16	16	81	1046	12.9	5	0	0	0.0	0	5	1	32	0
2002—Atlanta NFL	7	1	18	199	11.1	0	0	0	0.0	0	0	0	0	1
—Washington NFL	5	0	7	58	8.3	1	3	47	15.7	0	1	0	6	1
Pro totals (8 years)	113	39	284	3641	12.8	24	67	1432	21.4	0	24	5	154	8

JACOX, KENDYL   C   SAINTS

PERSONAL: Born June 10, 1975, in Dallas. ... 6-2/330. ... Full name: Kendyl LaMarc Jacox. ... Name pronounced JAY-cox.
HIGH SCHOOL: Carter (Dallas).
COLLEGE: Kansas State.
TRANSACTIONS/CAREER NOTES: Signed as non-drafted free agent by San Diego Chargers (April 20, 1998). ... On injured reserve with knee injury (December 4, 1999-remainder of season). ... Granted free agency (March 2, 2001). ... Re-signed by Chargers (April 10, 2001). ... Granted unconditional free agency (March 1, 2002). ... Signed by New Orleans Saints (May 28, 2002).
PLAYING EXPERIENCE: San Diego NFL, 1998-2001; New Orleans NFL, 2002. ... Games/Games started: 1998 (16/6), 1999 (10/5), 2000 (15/3), 2001 (16/16), 2002 (16/16). Total: 73/46.

JAMES, CEDRIC   WR   VIKINGS

PERSONAL: Born March 19, 1979, in Fort Worth, Texas. ... 6-1/199.
HIGH SCHOOL: Kennedale (Texas).
COLLEGE: Texas Christian.
TRANSACTIONS/CAREER NOTES: Selected by Minnesota Vikings in fourth round (131st pick overall) of 2001 NFL draft. ... Signed by Vikings (July 26, 2001). ... On injured reserve with leg injury (September 6, 2001-entire season).
SINGLE GAME HIGHS (regular season): Receptions—1 (November 3, 2002, vs. Tampa Bay); yards—29 (November 3, 2002, vs. Tampa Bay); and touchdown receptions—0.

Year Team	G	GS	RECEIVING				KICKOFF RETURNS				TOTALS			
			No.	Yds.	Avg.	TD	No.	Yds.	Avg.	TD	TD	2pt.	Pts.	Fum.
2001—Minnesota NFL							Did not play.							
2002—Minnesota NFL	5	0	1	29	29.0	0	10	228	22.8	0	0	0	0	0
Pro totals (1 years)	5	0	1	29	29.0	0	10	228	22.8	0	0	0	0	0

JAMES, EDGERRIN   RB   COLTS

PERSONAL: Born August 1, 1978, in Immokalee, Fla. ... 6-0/214. ... Full name: Edgerrin Tyree James. ... Name pronounced EDGE-rin.
HIGH SCHOOL: Immokalee (Fla.).
COLLEGE: Miami (Fla.).
TRANSACTIONS/CAREER NOTES: Selected after junior season by Indianapolis Colts in first round (fourth pick overall) of 1999 NFL draft. ... Signed by Colts (August 12, 1999). ... On injured reserve with knee injury (November 21, 2001-remainder of season).
HONORS: Named NFL Rookie of the Year by THE SPORTING NEWS (1999). ... Named running back on THE SPORTING NEWS NFL All-Pro team (1999 and 2000). ... Played in Pro Bowl (1999 and 2000 seasons).
SINGLE GAME HIGHS (regular season): Attempts—38 (October 15, 2000, vs. Seattle); yards—219 (October 15, 2000, vs. Seattle); and rushing touchdowns—3 (December 11, 2000, vs. Buffalo).
STATISTICAL PLATEAUS: 100-yard rushing games: 1999 (10), 2000 (9), 2001 (5), 2002 (2). Total: 26.

Year Team	G	GS	RUSHING				RECEIVING				TOTALS			
			Att.	Yds.	Avg.	TD	No.	Yds.	Avg.	TD	TD	2pt.	Pts.	Fum.
1999—Indianapolis NFL	16	16	*369	*1553	4.2	▲13	62	586	9.5	4	†17	0	102	8
2000—Indianapolis NFL	16	16	387	*1709	4.4	13	63	594	9.4	5	§18	1	110	5
2001—Indianapolis NFL	6	6	151	662	4.4	3	24	193	8.0	0	3	1	20	3
2002—Indianapolis NFL	14	14	277	989	3.6	2	61	354	5.8	1	3	1	20	4
Pro totals (4 years)	52	52	1184	4913	4.1	31	210	1727	8.2	10	41	3	252	20

JAMES, JENO   G   PANTHERS

PERSONAL: Born January 12, 1977, in Montgomery, Ala. ... 6-3/310. ... Full name: Jenorris James.
HIGH SCHOOL: Sidney Lanier (Montgomery, Ala.).
COLLEGE: Auburn.
TRANSACTIONS/CAREER NOTES: Selected by Carolina Panthers in sixth round (182nd pick overall) of 2000 NFL draft. ... Signed by Panthers (June 19, 2000). ... Granted free agency (February 28, 2003). ... Re-signed by Panthers (June 3, 2003).
PLAYING EXPERIENCE: Carolina NFL, 2000-2002 ... Games/Games started: 2000 (16/4), 2001 (14/6), 2002 (9/2). Total: 39/12.

JAMES, TORY   CB   BENGALS

PERSONAL: Born May 18, 1973, in New Orleans. ... 6-2/190. ... Full name: Tory Steven James.
HIGH SCHOOL: Archbishop Shaw (Marrero, La.).
COLLEGE: Louisiana State.
TRANSACTIONS/CAREER NOTES: Selected by Denver Broncos in second round (44th pick overall) of 1996 NFL draft. ... Signed by Broncos (July 22, 1996). ... On injured reserve with knee injury (August 18, 1997-entire season). ... Granted unconditional free agency (February 11, 2000). ... Signed by Oakland Raiders (February 28, 2000). ... Released by Raiders (February 27, 2003). ... Signed by Cincinnati Bengals (March 10, 2003).
CHAMPIONSHIP GAME EXPERIENCE: Played in AFC championship game (1998, 2000 and 2002 seasons). ... Member of Super Bowl championship team (1998 season). ... Played in Super Bowl XXXVII (2002 season).

			TOTALS			INTERCEPTIONS			
Year Team	G	GS	Tk.	Ast.	Sks.	No.	Yds.	Avg.	TD
1996—Denver NFL	16	2	22	1	0.0	2	15	7.5	0
1997—Denver NFL				Did not play.					
1998—Denver NFL	16	0	10	1	0.0	0	0	0.0	0
1999—Denver NFL	16	4	32	1	0.0	5	59	11.8	0
2000—Oakland NFL	16	1	26	3	0.0	2	25	12.5	0
2001—Oakland NFL	16	2	33	3	0.0	5	72	14.4	0
2002—Oakland NFL	14	13	41	4	0.0	4	35	8.8	0
Pro totals (6 years)	94	22	164	13	0.0	18	206	11.4	0

JAMESON, MICHAEL   DB   BROWNS

PERSONAL: Born July 14, 1979, in Killeen, Texas. ... 5-11/192.
HIGH SCHOOL: Ellison (Killeen, Texas).
COLLEGE: Texas A&M.
TRANSACTIONS/CAREER NOTES: Selected by Cleveland Browns in sixth round (165th pick overall) of 2001 NFL draft. ... Signed by Browns (May 24, 2001). ... On injured reserve with ankle injury (August 27, 2001-entire season). ... Released by Browns (September 1, 2002). ... Re-signed by Browns to practice squad (September 4, 2002). ... Activated (October 9, 2002).

			TOTALS			INTERCEPTIONS			
Year Team	G	GS	Tk.	Ast.	Sks.	No.	Yds.	Avg.	TD
2002—Cleveland NFL	11	1	8	2	1.0	1	0	0.0	0

JAMMER, QUENTIN   CB   CHARGERS

PERSONAL: Born June 19, 1979, in Angleton, Texas. ... 5-11/204. ... Full name: Quentin T. Jammer. ... Cousin of Kevin Garrett, cornerback, St. Louis Rams.
HIGH SCHOOL: Angleton (Texas).
COLLEGE: Texas.
TRANSACTIONS/CAREER NOTES: Selected by San Diego Chargers in first round (fifth pick overall) of 2002 NFL draft. ... Signed by Chargers (September 11, 2002).
HONORS: Named cornerback on THE SPORTING NEWS college All-America first team (2001).

			TOTALS			INTERCEPTIONS			
Year Team	G	GS	Tk.	Ast.	Sks.	No.	Yds.	Avg.	TD
2002—San Diego NFL	14	4	56	8	0.0	0	0	0.0	0

JANIKOWSKI, SEBASTIAN   K   RAIDERS

PERSONAL: Born March 3, 1978, in Poland. ... 6-2/255.
HIGH SCHOOL: Seabreeze (Daytona, Fla.).
COLLEGE: Florida State.
TRANSACTIONS/CAREER NOTES: Selected after junior season by Oakland Raiders in first round (17th pick overall) of 2000 NFL draft. ... Signed by Raiders (July 20, 2000).
CHAMPIONSHIP GAME EXPERIENCE: Played in AFC championship game (2000 and 2002 seasons). ... Played in Super Bowl XXXVII (2002 season).
HONORS: Named kicker on THE SPORTING NEWS college All-America first team (1998 and 1999). ... Lou Groza Award winner (1998 and 1999).

		FIELD GOALS							TOTALS		
Year Team	G	1-29	30-39	40-49	50+	Tot.	Pct.	Lg.	XPM	XPA	Pts.
2000—Oakland NFL	14	7-7	6-7	8-14	1-4	22-32	68.8	▲54	46	46	112
2001—Oakland NFL	15	7-7	9-10	6-9	1-2	23-28	82.1	52	§42	▲42	111
2002—Oakland NFL	16	10-11	7-8	7-12	2-2	26-33	78.8	51	50	50	128
Pro totals (3 years)	45	24-25	22-25	21-35	4-8	71-93	76.3	54	138	138	351

JANSEN, JON   OT   REDSKINS

PERSONAL: Born January 28, 1976, in Clawson, Mich. ... 6-6/306. ... Full name: Jonathan Ward Jansen.
HIGH SCHOOL: Clawson (Mich.).
COLLEGE: Michigan.
TRANSACTIONS/CAREER NOTES: Selected by Washington Redskins in second round (37th pick overall) of 1999 NFL draft. ... Signed by Redskins (July 9, 1999).
PLAYING EXPERIENCE: Washington NFL, 1999-2002. ... Games/Games started: 1999 (16/16), 2000 (16/16), 2001 (16/16), 2002 (16/16). Total: 64/64.

JARRETT, CRAIG   P

PERSONAL: Born July 17, 1979, in Martinsville, Ind. ... 6-2/215.
HIGH SCHOOL: Martinsville (Ind.).
COLLEGE: Michigan State.
TRANSACTIONS/CAREER NOTES. Selected by Seattle Seahawks in sixth round (194th pick overall) of 2002 NFL draft. ... Signed by Seahawks (July 25, 2002). ... Released by Seahawks (September 1, 2002). ... Signed by San Francisco 49ers to practice squad (November 6, 2002). ... Released by 49ers (November 12, 2002). ... Signed by Washington Redskins to practice squad (November 20, 2002). ... Released by Redskins (November 26, 2002). ... Re-signed by Redskins (December 2, 2002). ... Released by Redskins (February 26, 2003).

			PUNTING				
Year Team	G	No.	Yds.	Avg.	Net avg.	In. 20	Blk.
2002—Washington NFL	4	20	771	38.6	30.5	5	1

JASPER, EDWARD   DT   FALCONS

PERSONAL: Born January 18, 1973, in Tyler, Texas. ... 6-2/293. ... Full name: Edward Vidal Jasper.
HIGH SCHOOL: Troup (Texas).
COLLEGE: Texas A&M.
TRANSACTIONS/CAREER NOTES: Selected by Philadelphia Eagles in sixth round (198th pick overall) of 1997 NFL draft. ... Signed by Eagles (July 16, 1997). ... Released by Eagles (August 30, 1998). ... Re-signed by Eagles (September 17, 1998). ... Released by Eagles (October 23, 1998). ... Re-signed by Eagles (December 9, 1998). ... Released by Eagles (February 12, 1999). ... Signed by Atlanta Falcons (March 5, 1999).

			TOTALS		
Year Team	G	GS	Tk.	Ast.	Sks.
1997—Philadelphia NFL	10	1	5	3	1.0
1998—Philadelphia NFL	7	0	11	2	0.0
1999—Atlanta NFL	13	0	23	5	0.0
2000—Atlanta NFL	15	15	30	12	3.5
2001—Atlanta NFL	16	1	20	5	3.5
2002—Atlanta NFL	16	16	29	6	2.0
Pro totals (6 years)	77	33	118	33	10.0

JEFFERSON, JOSEPH   CB   COLTS

PERSONAL: Born February 15, 1980, in Russelville, Ky. ... 6-1/207. ... Full name: Joseph Jefferson Jr.
HIGH SCHOOL: Logan County (Adairville, Ky.).
COLLEGE: Western Kentucky.
TRANSACTIONS/CAREER NOTES: Selected by Indianapolis Colts in third round (74th pick overall) of 2002 NFL draft. ... Signed by Colts (July 22, 2002).

			TOTALS			INTERCEPTIONS				PUNT RETURNS				KICKOFF RETURNS				TOTALS			
Year Team	G	GS	Tk.	Ast.	Sks.	No.	Yds.	Avg.	TD	No.	Yds.	Avg.	TD	No.	Yds.	Avg.	TD	TD	2pt.	Pts.	Fum.
2002—Indianapolis NFL	14	0	1	0	0.0	0	0	0.0	0	0	0	0.0	0	0	0	0.0	0	0	0	0	0

JEFFERSON, SHAWN   WR

PERSONAL: Born February 22, 1969, in Jacksonville. ... 5-11/185. ... Full name: Vanchi LaShawn Jefferson.
HIGH SCHOOL: Raines (Jacksonville).
COLLEGE: Central Florida.
TRANSACTIONS/CAREER NOTES: Selected by Houston Oilers in ninth round (240th pick overall) of 1991 NFL draft. ... Signed by Oilers (July 15, 1991). ... Traded to Oilers with first-round pick (DE Chris Mims) in 1992 draft to San Diego Chargers for DL Lee Williams (August 22, 1991). ... Granted free agency (March 1, 1993). ... Re-signed by Chargers (July 15, 1993). ... Granted free agency (February 17, 1994). ... Re-signed by Chargers (May 2, 1994). ... Released by Chargers (February 29, 1996). ... Signed by New England Patriots (March 14, 1996). ... Granted unconditional free agency (February 11, 2000). ... Signed by Atlanta Falcons (February 12, 2000). ... Released by Falcons (February 21, 2003). ... Signed by Lions (May 25, 2003).
CHAMPIONSHIP GAME EXPERIENCE: Played in AFC championship game (1994 and 1996 seasons). ... Played in Super Bowl XXIX (1994 season) and Super Bowl XXXI (1996 season).
SINGLE GAME HIGHS (regular season): Receptions—9 (November 10, 2002, vs. Pittsburgh); yards—148 (September 3, 2000, vs. San Francisco); and touchdown receptions—2 (October 31, 1999, vs. Arizona).
STATISTICAL PLATEAUS: 100-yard receiving games: 1995 (1), 1997 (1), 1998 (2), 1999 (1), 2000 (2), 2002 (1). Total: 8.

			RUSHING				RECEIVING				TOTALS			
Year Team	G	GS	Att.	Yds.	Avg.	TD	No.	Yds.	Avg.	TD	TD	2pt.	Pts.	Fum.
1991—San Diego NFL	16	3	1	27	27.0	0	12	125	10.4	1	1	0	6	0
1992—San Diego NFL	16	1	0	0	0.0	0	29	377	13.0	2	2	0	12	0
1993—San Diego NFL	16	4	5	53	10.6	0	30	391	13.0	2	2	0	12	0
1994—San Diego NFL	16	16	3	40	13.3	0	43	627	14.6	3	3	0	18	0
1995—San Diego NFL	16	15	2	1	0.5	0	48	621	12.9	2	2	0	12	0
1996—New England NFL	15	15	1	6	6.0	0	50	771	15.4	4	4	0	24	2
1997—New England NFL	16	14	0	0	0.0	0	54	841	15.6	2	2	0	12	2
1998—New England NFL	16	16	1	15	15.0	0	34	771	*22.7	2	2	0	12	0
1999—New England NFL	16	16	0	0	0.0	0	40	698	§17.5	6	6	0	36	0
2000—Atlanta NFL	16	14	1	1	1.0	0	60	822	13.7	2	2	0	12	1
2001—Atlanta NFL	16	6	0	0	0.0	0	37	539	14.6	2	2	1	14	0
2002—Atlanta NFL	13	7	0	0	0.0	0	27	394	14.6	1	1	0	6	0
Pro totals (12 years)	188	127	14	143	10.2	0	464	6977	15.0	29	29	1	176	5

JENKINS, BILLY S

PERSONAL: Born July 8, 1974, in Los Angeles. ... 5-10/211.
HIGH SCHOOL: Albuquerque (N.M.).
COLLEGE: Howard.
TRANSACTIONS/CAREER NOTES: Signed as non-drafted free agent by St. Louis Rams (April 29, 1997). ... Granted free agency (February 11, 2000). ... Re-signed by Rams (March 3, 2000). ... Traded by Rams to Denver Broncos for fifth-round pick (DL Brian Young) in 2000 draft and fifth-round pick (traded to Washington) in 2001 draft (March 7, 2000). ... Released by Broncos (October 23, 2001). ... Signed by Green Bay Packers (November 19, 2001). ... Released by Packers (November 27, 2001). ... Re-signed by Packers (December 7, 2001). ... Granted unconditional free agency (March 1, 2002). ... Signed by Buffalo Bills (April 5, 2002). ... Released by Bills (February 27, 2003).
CHAMPIONSHIP GAME EXPERIENCE: Played in NFC championship game (1999 season). ... Member of Super Bowl championship team (1999 season).

Year Team	G	GS	TOTALS			INTERCEPTIONS			
			Tk.	Ast.	Sks.	No.	Yds.	Avg.	TD
1997—St. Louis NFL	16	2	13	5	0.0	0	0	0.0	0
1998—St. Louis NFL	16	13	81	17	3.0	2	31	15.5	0
1999—St. Louis NFL	16	16	72	22	1.0	2	16	8.0	0
2000—Denver NFL	16	16	77	16	0.0	4	61	15.3	1
2001—Denver NFL	6	0	0	0	0.0	0	0	0.0	0
—Green Bay NFL	6	0	1	0	0.0	0	0	0.0	0
2002—Buffalo NFL	15	1	2	3	0.0	0	0	0.0	0
Pro totals (6 years)	91	48	246	63	4.0	8	108	13.5	1

JENKINS, J.R. K RAVENS

PERSONAL: Born January 31, 1979, in Springfield, Ill. ... 6-1/195. ... Full name: John Robert Jenkins.
HIGH SCHOOL: Loganville (W.Va.).
COLLEGE: Marshall.
TRANSACTIONS/CAREER NOTES: Signed as non-drafted free agent by Baltimore Ravens (April 26, 2002). ... Released by Ravens (November 12, 2002). ... Re-signed by Ravens to practice squad (November 14, 2002).

JENKINS, KERRY G BUCCANEERS

PERSONAL: Born September 6, 1973, in Tuscaloosa, Ala. ... 6-5/305.
HIGH SCHOOL: Holt (Ala.).
COLLEGE: Louisiana State, then Troy (Ala.) State.
TRANSACTIONS/CAREER NOTES: Signed as non-drafted free agent by Chicago Bears (April 25, 1997). ... Released by Bears (August 24, 1997). ... Re-signed by Bears to practice squad (August 27, 1997). ... Signed by New York Jets off Bears practice squad (December 3, 1997). ... Granted free agency (March 2, 2001). ... Re-signed by Jets (May 30, 2001). ... Granted unconditional free agency (March 1, 2002). ... Signed by Tampa Bay Buccaneers (March 6, 2002).
PLAYING EXPERIENCE: New York Jets NFL, 1997-2001; Tampa Bay NFL, 2002. ... Games/Games started: 1997 (2/2), 1998 (16/0), 1999 (16/16), 2000 (16/16), 2001 (16/16), 2002 (15/15). Total: 81/65.
CHAMPIONSHIP GAME EXPERIENCE: Played in AFC championship game (1998 season). ... Played in NFC championship game (2002 season). ... Member of Super Bowl championship team (2002 season).

JENKINS, KRIS DT PANTHERS

PERSONAL: Born August 3, 1979, in Ypsilanti, Mich. ... 6-4/315. ... Full name: Kristopher Rudy-Charles Jenkins.
HIGH SCHOOL: Belleville (Ypsilanti, Mich.).
COLLEGE: Maryland.
TRANSACTIONS/CAREER NOTES: Selected by Carolina Panthers in second round (44th pick overall) of 2001 NFL draft. ... Signed by Panthers (July 13, 2001).
HONORS: Played in Pro Bowl (2002 season).

Year Team	G	GS	TOTALS		
			Tk.	Ast.	Sks.
2001—Carolina NFL	16	11	27	7	2.0
2002—Carolina NFL	16	16	36	8	7.0
Pro totals (2 years)	32	27	63	15	9.0

JENKINS, MARTAY WR FALCONS

PERSONAL: Born February 28, 1975, in Waterloo, Iowa ... 6-0/206.
HIGH SCHOOL: Waterloo (Iowa) North.
JUNIOR COLLEGE: North Iowa Area Community College.
COLLEGE: Nebraska-Omaha (degree in sociology).
TRANSACTIONS/CAREER NOTES: Selected by Dallas Cowboys in sixth round (193rd pick overall) of 1999 NFL draft. ... Signed by Cowboys (July 27, 1999). ... Claimed on waivers by Arizona Cardinals (September 6, 1999). ... On injured reserve with shoulder injury (November 6, 2002-remainder of season). ... Granted unconditional free agency (February 28, 2003). ... Signed by Atlanta Falcons (March 28, 2003).
RECORDS: Holds NFL single-season record for most kickoff returns yards—2,186 (2000).
SINGLE GAME HIGHS (regular season): Receptions—6 (September 29, 2002, vs. New York Giants); yards—119 (October 7, 2001, vs. Philadelphia); and touchdown receptions—1 (September 22, 2002, vs. San Diego).
STATISTICAL PLATEAUS: 100-yard receiving games: 2001 (1).

Year Team	G	GS	RECEIVING				KICKOFF RETURNS				TOTALS			
			No.	Yds.	Avg.	TD	No.	Yds.	Avg.	TD	TD	2pt.	Pts.	Fum.
1999—Arizona NFL	3	0	0	0	0.0	0	0	0	0.0	0	0	0	0	0
2000—Arizona NFL	16	2	17	219	12.9	0	*82	*2186	26.7	0	1	0	6	3
2001—Arizona NFL	13	3	32	518	16.2	3	49	1120	22.9	0	3	0	18	5
2002—Arizona NFL	8	1	21	250	11.9	1	20	559	*28.0	1	2	0	12	0
Pro totals (4 years)	40	6	70	987	14.1	4	151	3865	25.6	2	6	0	36	8

JENKINS, RONNEY — RB/KR — RAIDERS

PERSONAL: Born May 25, 1977, in Los Angeles. ... 5-11/188. ... Full name: Ronney Gene Jenkins.
HIGH SCHOOL: Point Hueneme (Oxnard, Calif.).
COLLEGE: Northern Arizona.
TRANSACTIONS/CAREER NOTES: Signed as non-drafted free agent by San Diego Chargers (April 17, 2000). ... Granted free agency (February 28, 2003). ... Signed by Oakland Raiders (March 17, 2003).
SINGLE GAME HIGHS (regular season): Attempts—3 (October 29, 2000, vs. Oakland); yards—6 (October 1, 2000, vs. St. Louis); and rushing touchdowns—0.

Year Team	G	GS	KICKOFF RETURNS				TOTALS			
			No.	Yds.	Avg.	TD	TD	2pt.	Pts.	Fum.
2000—San Diego NFL	16	0	§67	1531	22.9	▲1	1	0	6	3
2001—San Diego NFL	16	0	§58	*1541	*26.6	†2	2	0	12	1
2002—San Diego NFL	13	0	40	925	23.1	0	0	0	0	0
Pro totals (3 years)	45	0	165	3997	24.2	3	3	0	18	4

JENNINGS, BRANDON — S — TEXANS

PERSONAL: Born July 15, 1978, in Houston. ... 6-0/190.
HIGH SCHOOL: Channelview (Houston).
COLLEGE: Texas A&M.
TRANSACTIONS/CAREER NOTES: Signed as non-drafted free agent by Oakland Raiders (April 23, 2001). ... Released by Raiders (September 29, 2001). ... Re-signed by Raiders to practice squad (October 2, 2001). ... Activated (October 9, 2001). ... Claimed on waivers by Cleveland Browns (October 15, 2001). ... Released by Browns (October 24, 2001). ... Signed by Raiders to practice squad (November 7, 2001). ... Activated (November 23, 2001). ... Released by Raiders (September 1, 2002). ... Signed by Green Bay Packers to practice squad (October 9, 2002). ... Released by Packers (October 15, 2002). ... Signed by Oakland Raiders to practice squad (October 24, 2002). ... Activated (October 26, 2002). ... Claimed on waivers by Houston Texans (January 27, 2003). ... Granted free agency (February 28, 2003). ... Re-signed by Texans (March 21, 2003).

Year Team	G	GS	TOTALS			INTERCEPTIONS			
			Tk.	Ast.	Sks.	No.	Yds.	Avg.	TD
2000—Oakland NFL	2	0	1	0	0.0	0	0	0.0	0
2001—Oakland NFL	8	0	0	0	0.0	0	0	0.0	0
2002—Oakland NFL	10	0	6	0	0.0	0	0	0.0	0
Pro totals (3 years)	20	0	7	0	0.0	0	0	0.0	0

JENNINGS, BRIAN — TE — 49ERS

PERSONAL: Born October 14, 1976, in Mesa, Ariz. ... 6-5/245. ... Full name: Brian Lewis Jennings.
HIGH SCHOOL: Red Mountain (Mesa, Ariz.).
COLLEGE: Arizona State.
TRANSACTIONS/CAREER NOTES: Selected by San Francisco 49ers in seventh round (230th pick overall) of 2000 NFL draft. ... Signed by 49ers (July 10, 2000). ... Granted free agency (February 28, 2003). ... Re-signed by 49ers (April 24, 2003).

Year Team	G	GS	RECEIVING			
			No.	Yds.	Avg.	TD
2000—San Francisco NFL	16	0	0	0	0.0	0
2001—San Francisco NFL	16	0	0	0	0.0	0
2002—San Francisco NFL	16	0	0	0	0.0	0
Pro totals (3 years)	48	0	0	0	0.0	0

JENNINGS, JONAS — OT — BILLS

PERSONAL: Born November 21, 1977, in College Park, Ga. ... 6-3/320.
HIGH SCHOOL: Tri-Cities (East Point, Ga.).
COLLEGE: Georgia.
TRANSACTIONS/CAREER NOTES: Selected by Buffalo Bills in third round (95th pick overall) of 2001 NFL draft. ... Signed by Bills (June 22, 2001).
PLAYING EXPERIENCE: Buffalo NFL, 2001-2002. ... Games/Games started: 2001 (12/12), 2002 (15/15). Total: 27/27.

JENNINGS, LIGARIUS — CB — BENGALS

PERSONAL: Born November 3, 1977, in Birmingham, Ala. ... 5-8/202.
HIGH SCHOOL: Wenonah (Ala.).
COLLEGE: Tennessee State.
TRANSACTIONS/CAREER NOTES: Signed as non-drafted free agent by Detroit Lions (April 27, 2000). ... Released by Lions (September 2, 2001). ... Re-signed by Lions to practice squad (September 4, 2001). ... Signed by Cincinnati Bengals off Lions practice squad (October 16,

2001). ... Assigned by Bengals to Amsterdam Admirals in 2002 NFL Europe enhancement allocation program (February 18, 2002). ... On injured reserve with knee injury (November 11, 2002-remainder of season).

			TOTALS			INTERCEPTIONS			
Year Team	G	GS	Tk.	Ast.	Sks.	No.	Yds.	Avg.	TD
2001—Cincinnati NFL	9	0	6	0	0.0	0	0	0.0	0
2002—Amsterdam NFLE	...	...	...	...	0.0	2	3	1.5	0
—Cincinnati NFL	9	0	1	2	0.0	0	0	0.0	0
NFL Europe totals (1 year)	...	...	...	...	0.0	2	3	1.5	0
NFL totals (2 years)	18	0	7	2	0.0	0	0	0.0	0
Pro totals (3 years)	...	...	...	...	0.0	2	3	1.5	0

JERMAN, GREG   OT   DOLPHINS

PERSONAL: Born January 24, 1979, in Hyannis, Mass. ... 6-5/300. ... Full name: Gregory Stephen Jerman.
HIGH SCHOOL: Franklin (El Paso, Texas).
COLLEGE: Baylor (degree in earth sciences).
TRANSACTIONS/CAREER NOTES: Signed as non-drafted free agent by Miami Dolphins (April 25, 2002).
PLAYING EXPERIENCE: Miami NFL, 2002. ... Games/games started: 2002 (2/0).

JERVEY, TRAVIS   RB   FALCONS

PERSONAL: Born May 5, 1972, in Columbia, S.C. ... 6-0/222. ... Full name: Travis Richard Jervey.
HIGH SCHOOL: Wando (Mount Pleasant, S.C.).
COLLEGE: The Citadel.
TRANSACTIONS/CAREER NOTES: Selected by Green Bay Packers in fifth round (170th pick overall) of 1995 NFL draft. ... Signed by Packers (May 23, 1995). ... Granted free agency (February 13, 1998). ... Re-signed by Packers (June 16, 1998). ... On injured reserve with knee and ankle injuries (November 11, 1998-remainder of season). ... Granted unconditional free agency (February 12, 1999). ... Signed by San Francisco 49ers (March 22, 1999). ... On physically unable to perform list with ankle injury (July 27-August 26, 1999). ... On suspended list for violating league substance abuse policy (October 21-November 26, 1999). ... On injured reserve with broken collarbone (October 30, 2000-remainder of season). ... Released by 49ers (March 19, 2001). ... Signed by Atlanta Falcons (May 1, 2001). ... Granted unconditional free agency (March 1, 2002). ... Re-signed by Falcons (April 9, 2002). ... On injured reserve with knee injury (October 22, 2002-remainder of season). ... Granted unconditional free agency (February 28, 2003). ... Re-signed by Falcons (March 7, 2003).
CHAMPIONSHIP GAME EXPERIENCE: Played in NFC championship game (1995-97 seasons). ... Member of Super Bowl championship team (1996 season). ... Played in Super Bowl XXXII (1997 season).
HONORS: Played in Pro Bowl (1997 season).
SINGLE GAME HIGHS (regular season): Attempts—29 (October 25, 1998, vs. Baltimore); yards—95 (November 1, 1998, vs. San Francisco; and rushing touchdowns—1 (January 3, 2000, vs. Atlanta).

			RUSHING				RECEIVING				KICKOFF RETURNS				TOTALS			
Year Team	G	GS	Att.	Yds.	Avg.	TD	No.	Yds.	Avg.	TD	No.	Yds.	Avg.	TD	TD	2pt.	Pts.	Fum.
1995—Green Bay NFL	16	0	0	0	0.0	0	0	0	0.0	0	8	165	20.6	0	0	0	0	0
1996—Green Bay NFL	16	0	26	106	4.1	0	0	0	0.0	0	1	17	17.0	0	0	0	0	4
1997—Green Bay NFL	16	0	0	0	0.0	0	0	0	0.0	0	0	0	0.0	0	0	0	0	0
1998—Green Bay NFL	8	5	83	325	3.9	1	9	33	3.7	0	0	0	0.0	0	1	0	6	0
1999—San Francisco NFL	8	0	6	49	8.2	1	1	2	2.0	0	8	191	23.9	0	1	0	6	0
2000—San Francisco NFL	8	0	1	0	0.0	0	0	0	0.0	0	8	209	26.1	0	0	0	0	0
2001—Atlanta NFL	16	0	3	6	2.0	0	0	0	0.0	0	0	0	0.0	0	0	0	0	0
2002—Atlanta NFL	6	0	10	17	1.7	0	0	0	0.0	0	4	143	35.8	0	0	0	0	1
Pro totals (8 years)	94	5	129	503	3.9	2	10	35	3.5	0	29	725	25.0	0	2	0	12	5

JETT, JAMES   WR   BILLS

PERSONAL: Born December 28, 1970, in Charlestown, W.Va. ... 5-10/170.
HIGH SCHOOL: Jefferson (Shenandoah Junction, W.Va.).
COLLEGE: West Virginia.
TRANSACTIONS/CAREER NOTES: Signed as non-drafted free agent by Los Angeles Raiders (May 1993). ... Raiders franchise moved to Oakland (July 21, 1995). ... Granted unconditional free agency (March 2, 2001). ... Re-signed by Raiders (March 2, 2001). ... Released by Raiders (February 27, 2003). ... Signed by Buffalo Bills (June 3, 2003).
CHAMPIONSHIP GAME EXPERIENCE: Played in AFC championship game (2000 season). ... Member of Raiders for AFC championship game (2002 season); inactive. ... Member of Raiders for Super Bowl XXXVII (2002 season); inactive.
SINGLE GAME HIGHS (regular season): Receptions—7 (October 13, 1996, vs. Detroit); yards—148 (September 21, 1997, vs. New York Jets); and touchdown receptions—2 (October 26, 1997, vs. Seattle).
STATISTICAL PLATEAUS: 100-yard receiving games: 1993 (2), 1996 (1), 1997 (1), 1998 (2). Total: 6.

			RECEIVING				TOTALS			
Year Team	G	GS	No.	Yds.	Avg.	TD	TD	2pt.	Pts.	Fum.
1993—Los Angeles Raiders NFL	16	1	33	771	*23.4	3	3	0	18	1
1994—Los Angeles Raiders NFL	16	1	15	253	16.9	0	0	0	0	0
1995—Oakland NFL	16	0	13	179	13.8	1	1	0	6	1
1996—Oakland NFL	16	16	43	601	14.0	4	4	0	24	0
1997—Oakland NFL	16	16	46	804	17.5	▲12	12	0	72	2
1998—Oakland NFL	16	16	45	882	19.6	6	6	0	36	0
1999—Oakland NFL	16	11	39	552	14.2	2	2	†1	14	0
2000—Oakland NFL	16	12	20	356	17.8	2	2	0	12	0
2001—Oakland NFL	10	0	2	19	9.5	0	0	0	0	0
2002—Oakland NFL	1	1	0	0	0.0	0	0	0	0	0
Pro totals (10 years)	139	74	256	4417	17.3	30	30	1	182	4

JETT, JOHN — P — LIONS

PERSONAL: Born November 11, 1968, in Richmond, Va. ... 6-0/197.
HIGH SCHOOL: Northumberland (Heathsville, Va.).
COLLEGE: East Carolina.
TRANSACTIONS/CAREER NOTES: Signed as non-drafted free agent by Minnesota Vikings (June 22, 1992). ... Released by Vikings (August 25, 1992). ... Signed by Dallas Cowboys (March 10, 1993). ... Granted unconditional free agency (February 16, 1996). ... Re-signed by Cowboys (April 15, 1996). ... Granted unconditional free agency (February 14, 1997). ... Signed by Detroit Lions (March 7, 1997). ... Granted unconditional free agency (February 11, 2000). ... Re-signed by Lions (February 21, 2000).
CHAMPIONSHIP GAME EXPERIENCE: Played in NFC championship game (1993-1995 seasons). ... Member of Super Bowl championship team (1993 and 1995 seasons).

				PUNTING			
Year Team	G	No.	Yds.	Avg.	Net avg.	In. 20	Blk.
1993—Dallas NFL	16	56	2342	41.8	37.7	22	0
1994—Dallas NFL	16	70	2935	41.9	35.3	26	0
1995—Dallas NFL	16	53	2166	40.9	34.5	17	0
1996—Dallas NFL	16	74	3150	42.6	36.7	22	0
1997—Detroit NFL	16	84	3576	42.6	35.6	24	†2
1998—Detroit NFL	14	66	2892	43.8	36.0	17	0
1999—Detroit NFL	16	86	3637	42.3	34.8	27	0
2000—Detroit NFL	16	‡93	‡4044	43.5	34.8	‡33	†2
2001—Detroit NFL	13	58	2512	43.3	35.5	16	0
2002—Detroit NFL	16	91	3838	42.2	38.0	29	0
Pro totals (10 years)	155	731	31092	42.5	35.9	233	4

JOHNSON, ALBERT — WR — JETS

PERSONAL: Born November 11, 1977, in Houston. ... 5-9/190. ... Full name: Albert Johnson III. ... Son of Albert Johnson Jr., defensive back with Houston Oilers (1972-78).
HIGH SCHOOL: Willowridge (Houston).
COLLEGE: Southern Methodist.
TRANSACTIONS/CAREER NOTES: Signed as non-drafted free agent by Miami Dolphins (January 11, 2001). ... On injured reserve with knee injury (August 9, 2001-entire season). ... On injured reserve with knee injury (October 1, 2002-remainder of season). ... Granted free agency (February 28, 2003). ... Signed by New York Jets (April 14, 2003).

			RECEIVING				PUNT RETURNS				KICKOFF RETURNS				TOTALS		
Year Team	G	GS	No.	Yds.	Avg.	TD	No.	Yds.	Avg.	TD	No.	Yds.	Avg.	TD	TD	2pt.	Pts. Fum.
2000—Winnipeg CFL	...	...	50	778	15.6	3	79	665	8.4	0	61	1505	24.7	1	0	0	0 0
2002—Miami NFL	4	0	0	0	0.0	0	8	69	8.6	0	12	330	27.5	0	0	0	0 1
CFL totals (1 year)	...	...	50	778	15.6	3	79	665	8.4	0	61	1505	24.7	1	0	0	0 0
NFL totals (1 year)	4	0	0	0	0.0	0	8	69	8.6	0	12	330	27.5	0	0	0	0 1
Pro totals (2 years)	...	...	50	778	15.6	3	87	734	8.4	0	73	1835	25.1	1	0	0	0 1

JOHNSON, BRAD — QB — BUCCANEERS

PERSONAL: Born September 13, 1968, in Marietta, Ga. ... 6-5/226. ... Full name: James Bradley Johnson.
HIGH SCHOOL: Charles D. Owen (Black Mountain, N.C.).
COLLEGE: Florida State (degree in physical education, 1991).
TRANSACTIONS/CAREER NOTES: Selected by Minnesota Vikings in ninth round (227th pick overall) of 1992 NFL draft. ... Signed by Vikings (July 17, 1992). ... Active for one game (1992); did not play. ... Inactive for all 16 games (1993). ... Granted free agency (February 17, 1995). ... Assigned by Vikings to London Monarchs in 1995 World League enhancement allocation program (February 20, 1995). ... Re-signed by Vikings (March 27, 1995). ... On injured reserve with neck injury (December 5, 1997-remainder of season). ... Traded by Vikings to Washington Redskins for first- (QB Daunte Culpepper) and third-round (traded to Pittsburgh) picks in 1999 draft and second-round pick (DE Michael Boireau) in 2000 draft (February 15, 1999). ... Granted unconditional free agency (March 2, 2001). ... Signed by Tampa Bay Buccaneers (March 6, 2001).
CHAMPIONSHIP GAME EXPERIENCE: Member of Vikings for NFC championship game (1998 season); did not play. ... Played in NFC championship game (2002 season). ... Member of Super Bowl championship team (2002 season).
HONORS: Played in Pro Bowl (1999 and 2002 seasons).
SINGLE GAME HIGHS (regular season): Attempts—56 (November 18, 2001, vs. Chicago); completions—40 (November 18, 2001, vs. Chicago); yards—471 (December 26, 1999, vs. San Francisco); and touchdown passes—5 (November 3, 2002, vs. Minnesota).
STATISTICAL PLATEAUS: 300-yard passing games: 1997 (2), 1998 (1), 1999 (4), 2001 (2), 2002 (1). Total: 10.
MISCELLANEOUS: Regular-season record as starting NFL quarterback: 51-28 (.646). ... Postseason record as starting NFL quarterback: 4-3 (.571).

			PASSING									RUSHING				TOTALS		
Year Team	G	GS	Att.	Cmp.	Pct.	Yds.	TD	Int.	Avg.	Skd.	Rat.	Att.	Yds.	Avg.	TD	TD	2pt.	Pts.
1992—Minnesota NFL							Did not play.											
1993—Minnesota NFL							Did not play.											
1994—Minnesota NFL	4	0	37	22	59.5	150	0	0	4.05	1	68.5	2	-2	-1.0	0	0	0	0
1995—London W.L.	...	...	328	194	59.1	2227	13	14	6.79	0	75.1	24	99	4.1	1	1	1	8
—Minnesota NFL	5	0	36	25	69.4	272	0	2	7.56	2	68.3	9	-9	-1.0	0	0	0	0
1996—Minnesota NFL	12	8	311	195	62.7	2258	17	10	7.26	15	89.4	34	90	2.6	1	1	0	6
1997—Minnesota NFL	13	13	452	275	60.8	3036	20	12	6.72	26	84.5	35	139	4.0	0	1	2	10
1998—Minnesota NFL	4	2	101	65	64.4	747	7	5	7.40	4	89.0	12	15	1.3	0	0	0	0
1999—Washington NFL	16	16	519	316	60.9	4005	24	13	7.72	29	90.0	26	31	1.2	2	2	0	12
2000—Washington NFL	12	11	365	228	62.5	2505	11	15	6.86	20	75.7	22	58	2.6	1	1	0	6
2001—Tampa Bay NFL	16	16	559	340	60.8	3406	13	11	6.09	44	77.7	39	120	3.1	3	3	0	18
2002—Tampa Bay NFL	13	13	451	281	62.3	3049	22	6	6.76	21	‡92.9	13	30	2.3	0	0	0	0
W.L. totals (1 year)	...	...	328	194	59.1	2227	13	14	6.79	0	75.1	24	99	4.1	1	1	1	8
NFL totals (9 years)	95	79	2831	1747	61.7	19428	114	74	6.86	162	84.6	192	472	2.5	7	8	2	52
Pro totals (10 years)	...	...	3159	1941	61.4	21655	127	88	6.86	162	83.6	216	571	2.6	8	9	3	60

JOHNSON, BRYAN   FB   REDSKINS

PERSONAL: Born January 18, 1978, in Pocatello, Idaho. ... 6-1/232.
HIGH SCHOOL: Highland (Pocatello, Idaho).
COLLEGE: Boise State.
TRANSACTIONS/CAREER NOTES: Signed as non-drafted free agent by Washington Redskins (April 18, 2000). ... Released by Redskins (August 27, 2000). ... Re-signed by Redskins to practice squad (August 28, 2000). ... Activated (December 18, 2000). ... Re-signed by Redskins (April 29, 2003).
SINGLE GAME HIGHS (regular season): Attempts—1 (October 6, 2002, vs. Tennessee); yards—0; and rushing touchdowns—0.

			RUSHING				RECEIVING				TOTALS		
Year Team	G	GS	Att.	Yds.	Avg.	TD	No.	Yds.	Avg.	TD	TD	2pt.	Pts.	Fum.
2000—Washington NFL	1	0	0	0	0.0	0	0	0	0.0	0	0	0	0	0
2001—Washington NFL	16	1	0	0	0.0	0	9	129	14.3	0	0	0	0	0
2002—Washington NFL	16	12	1	0	0.0	0	15	114	7.6	0	0	0	0	0
Pro totals (3 years)	33	13	1	0	0.0	0	24	243	10.1	0	0	0	0	0

JOHNSON, CHAD   WR   BENGALS

PERSONAL: Born January 9, 1978, in Los Angeles. ... 6-2/192.
HIGH SCHOOL: Miami Beach (Fla.).
JUNIOR COLLEGE: Santa Monica College (Calif.).
COLLEGE: Oregon State.
TRANSACTIONS/CAREER NOTES: Selected by Cincinnati Bengals in second round (36th pick overall) of 2001 NFL draft. ... Signed by Bengals (July 18, 2001).
SINGLE GAME HIGHS (regular season): Receptions—7 (November 24, 2002, vs. Pittsburgh); yards—152 (November 24, 2002, vs. Pittsburgh); and touchdown receptions—1 (December 1, 2002, vs. Baltimore).
STATISTICAL PLATEAUS: 100-yard receiving games: 2002 (5).

			RECEIVING			
Year Team	G	GS	No.	Yds.	Avg.	TD
2001—Cincinnati NFL	12	3	28	329	11.8	1
2002—Cincinnati NFL	16	14	69	1166	16.9	5
Pro totals (2 years)	28	17	97	1495	15.4	6

JOHNSON, CHARLES   WR   BILLS

PERSONAL: Born January 3, 1972, in San Bernardino, Calif. ... 6-0/205. ... Full name: Charles Everett Johnson.
HIGH SCHOOL: Cajon (San Bernardino, Calif.).
COLLEGE: Colorado (degree in marketing, 1993).
TRANSACTIONS/CAREER NOTES: Selected by Pittsburgh Steelers in first round (17th pick overall) of 1994 NFL draft. ... Signed by Steelers (July 21, 1994). ... On injured reserve with knee injury (December 23, 1995-remainder of season). ... Granted unconditional free agency (February 12, 1999). ... Signed by Philadelphia Eagles (February 16, 1999). ... On injured reserve with knee injury (December 3, 1999-remainder of season). ... Released by Eagles (April 24, 2001). ... Signed by New England Patriots (May 31, 2001). ... Released by Patriots (February 25, 2001). ... Signed by Buffalo Bills (June 21, 2002). ... Granted unconditional free agency (February 28, 2003). ... Re-signed by Bills (March 7, 2003).
CHAMPIONSHIP GAME EXPERIENCE: Played in AFC championship game (1994, 1997 and 2001 seasons). ... Member of Super Bowl championship team (2001 season).
HONORS: Named wide receiver on THE SPORTING NEWS college All-America second team (1993).
RECORDS: Shares NFL single-game record for most two-point converstions—2 (November 1, 1998).
SINGLE GAME HIGHS (regular season): Receptions—9 (November 1, 1998, vs. Tennessee); yards—165 (December 24, 1994, vs. San Diego); and touchdown receptions—3 (November 1, 1998, vs. Tennessee).
STATISTICAL PLATEAUS: 100-yard receiving games: 1994 (1), 1996 (4), 1997 (1), 1998 (1). Total: 7.

			RUSHING				RECEIVING				PUNT RETURNS				KICKOFF RETURNS				TOTALS		
Year Team	G	GS	Att.	Yds.	Avg.	TD	No.	Yds.	Avg.	TD	No.	Yds.	Avg.	TD	No.	Yds.	Avg.	TD	TD	2pt.	Pts.
1994—Pittsburgh NFL	16	9	4	-1	-0.3	0	38	577	15.2	3	15	90	6.0	0	16	345	21.6	0	3	0	18
1995—Pittsburgh NFL	15	10	1	-10	-10.0	0	38	432	11.4	0	0	0	0.0	0	2	47	23.5	0	0	0	0
1996—Pittsburgh NFL	16	12	0	0	0.0	0	60	1008	16.8	3	0	0	0.0	0	6	111	18.5	0	3	1	20
1997—Pittsburgh NFL	13	11	0	0	0.0	0	46	568	12.3	2	0	0	0.0	0	0	0	0.0	0	2	0	12
1998—Pittsburgh NFL	16	16	1	4	4.0	0	65	815	12.5	7	0	0	0.0	0	0	0	0.0	0	7	†2	46
1999—Philadelphia NFL	11	11	0	0	0.0	0	34	414	12.2	1	1	0	0.0	0	0	0	0.0	0	1	0	8
2000—Philadelphia NFL	16	15	5	18	3.6	0	56	642	11.5	7	0	0	0.0	0	0	0	0.0	0	7	0	42
2001—New England NFL	14	3	0	0	0.0	0	14	111	7.9	1	0	0	0.0	0	0	0	0.0	0	1	0	6
2002—Buffalo NFL	16	0	0	0	0.0	0	3	39	13.0	0	0	0	0.0	0	0	0	0.0	0	0	0	0
Pro totals (9 years)	133	87	11	11	1.0	0	354	4606	13.0	24	16	90	5.6	0	24	503	21.0	0	24	3	152

JOHNSON, DENNIS   DE   CARDINALS

PERSONAL: Born December 4, 1979, in Danville, Ky. ... 6-5/264. ... Full name: Dennis Alan Johnson.
HIGH SCHOOL: Harrodburg (Ky.).
COLLEGE: Kentucky.
TRANSACTIONS/CAREER NOTES: Selected after junior season by Arizona Cardinals in third round (98th pick overall) of 2002 NFL draft. ... Signed by Cardinals (June 12, 2002).

			TOTALS		
Year Team	G	GS	Tk.	Ast.	Sks.
2002—Arizona NFL	13	0	10	6	0.0

JOHNSON, DIRK   P   EAGLES

PERSONAL: Born June 1, 1975, in Hoxie, Kan. ... 6-0/205. ... Full name: Dirk R. Johnson.
HIGH SCHOOL: Montrose (Colo.).
COLLEGE: Northern Colorado.
TRANSACTIONS/CAREER NOTES: Signed as non-drafted free agent by San Diego Chargers (May 4, 2001). ... Released by Chargers (August 27, 2001). ... Signed by New Orleans Saints (February 18, 2002). ... Assigned by Saints to Rhein Fire in 2002 NFL Europe enhancement allocation program (February 18, 2002). ... Released by Saints (September 1, 2002). ... Re-signed by Saints (September 6, 2002). ... Released by Saints (September 9, 2002). ... Signed by Philadelphia Eagles (February 10, 2003).

			PUNTING			
Year Team	G	No.	Yds.	Avg.	Net avg.	In. 20	Blk.
2002—Rhein NFLE	...	56	2391	42.7	38.2	23	0
—New Orleans NFL	1	8	307	38.4	34.8	1	0
NFL Europe totals (1 year)	...	56	2391	42.7	38.2	23	0
NFL totals (1 year)	1	8	307	38.4	34.8	1	0
Pro totals (2 years)	...	64	2698	42.2	37.8	24	0

JOHNSON, DOUG   QB   FALCONS

PERSONAL: Born October 27, 1977, in Gainesville, Fla. ... 6-2/225.
HIGH SCHOOL: Buchholz (Gainesville, Fla.).
COLLEGE: Florida.
TRANSACTIONS/CAREER NOTES: Signed as non-drafted free agent by Atlanta Falcons (April 17, 2000). ... Granted free agency (February 28, 2003).
SINGLE GAME HIGHS (regular season): Attempts—33 (December 3, 2000, vs. Seattle); completions—19 (October 13, 2002, vs. New York Giants); yards—257 (October 13, 2002, vs. New York Giants); and touchdown passes—1 (November 24, 2002, vs. Carolina).
MISCELLANEOUS: Regular-season record as starting NFL quarterback: 1-2 (.333).

			PASSING								RUSHING				TOTALS		
Year Team	G	GS	Att.	Cmp.	Pct.	Yds.	TD	Int.	Avg.	Skd.	Rat.	Att.	Yds.	Avg.	TD	TD	2pt.	Pts.
2000—Atlanta NFL	5	2	67	36	53.7	406	2	3	6.06	13	63.4	3	11	3.7	0	0	0	0
2001—Atlanta NFL	3	0	5	3	60.0	23	1	0	4.60	2	110.8	5	12	2.4	0	0	0	0
2002—Atlanta NFL	6	1	57	37	64.9	448	2	3	7.86	3	78.7	8	16	2.0	1	1	0	6
Pro totals (3 years)	14	3	129	76	58.9	877	5	6	6.80	18	73.0	16	39	2.4	1	1	0	6

JOHNSON, DWIGHT   DE

PERSONAL: Born January 30, 1977, in Waco, Texas. ... 6-4/290. ... Full name: Dwight O'Neal Johnson.
HIGH SCHOOL: Waco (Texas).
COLLEGE: Baylor.
TRANSACTIONS/CAREER NOTES: Signed as non-drafted free agent by Philadelphia Eagles (April 19, 2000). ... Released by Eagles (October 31, 2000). ... Re-signed by Eagles to practice squad (November 1, 2000). ... Assigned by Eagles to Frankfurt Galaxy in 2001 NFL Europe enhancement allocation program (February 16, 2001). ... Released by Eagles (August 31, 2001). ... Signed by New York Giants to practice squad (November 21, 2001). ... Released by Giants (May 14, 2003).

			TOTALS		
Year Team	G	GS	Tk.	Ast.	Sks.
2000—Philadelphia NFL	4	0	0	0	0.0
2001—Frankfurt NFLE	...	...	...	...	0.5
2002—New York Giants NFL	10	2	8	2	0.0
NFL Europe totals (1 year)	...	...	...	...	0.5
NFL totals (2 years)	14	2	8	2	0.0
Pro totals (3 years)	...	...	...	...	0.5

JOHNSON, ELLIS   DT   FALCONS

PERSONAL: Born October 30, 1973, in Wildwood, Fla. ... 6-2/288. ... Full name: Ellis Bernard Johnson.
HIGH SCHOOL: Wildwood (Fla.).
COLLEGE: Florida.
TRANSACTIONS/CAREER NOTES: Selected by Indianapolis Colts in first round (15th pick overall) of 1995 NFL draft. ... Signed by Colts (June 7, 1995). ... On physically unable to perform list with knee injury (July 27-August 20, 2001). ... Released by Colts (August 28, 2002). ... Signed by Atlanta Falcons (September 1, 2002).
CHAMPIONSHIP GAME EXPERIENCE: Played in AFC championship game (1995 season).

			TOTALS			INTERCEPTIONS			
Year Team	G	GS	Tk.	Ast.	Sks.	No.	Yds.	Avg.	TD
1995—Indianapolis NFL	16	2	15	3	4.5	0	0	0.0	0
1996—Indianapolis NFL	12	6	14	8	0.0	0	0	0.0	0
1997—Indianapolis NFL	15	15	38	18	4.5	1	18	18.0	0
1998—Indianapolis NFL	16	16	38	17	8.0	0	0	0.0	0
1999—Indianapolis NFL	16	16	34	12	7.5	0	0	0.0	0
2000—Indianapolis NFL	13	13	29	11	5.0	1	-1	-1.0	0
2001—Indianapolis NFL	16	16	20	14	3.5	0	0	0.0	0
2002—Atlanta NFL	16	2	24	3	7.0	0	0	0.0	0
Pro totals (8 years)	120	86	212	86	40.0	2	17	8.5	0

JOHNSON, ERIC — TE — 49ERS

PERSONAL: Born September 15, 1979, in Needham, Mass. ... 6-3/256.
HIGH SCHOOL: Needham (Mass.).
COLLEGE: Yale.
TRANSACTIONS/CAREER NOTES: Selected by San Francisco 49ers in seventh round (224th pick overall) of 2001 NFL draft. ... Signed by 49ers (July 24, 2001).
SINGLE GAME HIGHS (regular season): Receptions—8 (December 15, 2002, vs. Green Bay); yards—69 (September 15, 2002, vs. Denver); and touchdown receptions—1 (December 16, 2001, vs. Miami).

				RECEIVING		
Year Team	G	GS	No.	Yds.	Avg.	TD
2001—San Francisco NFL	16	14	40	362	9.1	3
2002—San Francisco NFL	12	10	36	321	8.9	0
Pro totals (2 years)	28	24	76	683	9.0	3

JOHNSON, ERIC — S — RAIDERS

PERSONAL: Born April 30, 1976, in Phoenix, Ariz. ... 6-0/210.
HIGH SCHOOL: Alhambra (Arizona).
COLLEGE: Nebraska.
TRANSACTIONS/CAREER NOTES: Signed as non-drafted free agent by Oakland Raiders (March 23, 2000). ... On injured reserve with broken leg (November 7, 2001-remainder of season).
CHAMPIONSHIP GAME EXPERIENCE: Played in AFC championship game (2002 season). ... Played in Super Bowl XXXVII (2002 season).

			TOTALS			INTERCEPTIONS			
Year Team	G	GS	Tk.	Ast.	Sks.	No.	Yds.	Avg.	TD
2000—Oakland NFL	16	0	3	0	0.0	0	0	0.0	0
2001—Oakland NFL	7	0	0	0	0.0	0	0	0.0	0
2002—Oakland NFL	16	0	0	0	0.0	0	0	0.0	0
Pro totals (3 years)	39	0	3	0	0.0	0	0	0.0	0

JOHNSON, J.R. — LB — RAVENS

PERSONAL: Born June 20, 1979, in Los Angeles. ... 6-0/240. ... Full name: Charles A. Johnson Jr.
HIGH SCHOOL: Syracuse (N.Y.).
COLLEGE: Syracuse.
TRANSACTIONS/CAREER NOTES: Signed as non-drafted free agent by Baltimore Ravens (April 26, 2002). ... Claimed on waivers by New Orleans Saints (October 15, 2002). ... Claimed on waivers by Seattle Seahawks (December 9, 2002). ... Released by Seahawks (December 12, 2002).

			TOTALS			INTERCEPTIONS			
Year Team	G	GS	Tk.	Ast.	Sks.	No.	Yds.	Avg.	TD
2002—New Orleans NFL	1	0	0	0	0.0	0	0	0.0	0
—Baltimore NFL	4	0	0	0	0.0	0	0	0.0	0
Pro totals (1 years)	5	0	0	0	0.0	0	0	0.0	0

JOHNSON, JOE — DE — PACKERS

PERSONAL: Born July 11, 1972, in St. Louis. ... 6-4/275. ... Full name: Joe T. Johnson.
HIGH SCHOOL: Jennings (Mo.).
COLLEGE: Louisville.
TRANSACTIONS/CAREER NOTES: Selected after junior season by New Orleans Saints in first round (13th pick overall) of 1994 NFL draft. ... Signed by Saints (June 7, 1994). ... Designated by Saints as franchise player (February 13, 1998). ... Re-signed by Saints (September 2, 1998). ... On injured reserve with knee injury (August 31, 1999-entire season). ... Granted unconditional free agency (March 1, 2002). ... Signed by Green Bay Packers (March 21, 2002). ... On injured reserve with arm injury (October 9, 2002-remainder of season).
HONORS: Played in Pro Bowl (1998 and 2000 seasons).

			TOTALS		
Year Team	G	GS	Tk.	Ast.	Sks.
1994—New Orleans NFL	15	14	36	10	1.0
1995—New Orleans NFL	14	14	36	14	5.5
1996—New Orleans NFL	13	13	50	10	7.5
1997—New Orleans NFL	16	16	39	7	8.5
1998—New Orleans NFL	16	16	54	16	7.0
1999—New Orleans NFL			Did not play.		
2000—New Orleans NFL	16	15	38	10	12.0
2001—New Orleans NFL	16	16	53	11	9.0
2002—Green Bay NFL	5	5	6	4	2.0
Pro totals (8 years)	111	109	312	82	52.5

JOHNSON, KEVIN — WR — BROWNS

PERSONAL: Born July 15, 1976, in Trenton, N.J. ... 5-11/195. ... Full name: Kevin L. Johnson.
HIGH SCHOOL: Hamilton West (Trenton, N.J.).
COLLEGE: Syracuse.

J

TRANSACTIONS/CAREER NOTES: Selected by Cleveland Browns in second round (32nd pick overall) of 1999 NFL draft. ... Signed by Browns (July 22, 1999).

SINGLE GAME HIGHS (regular season): Receptions—9 (September 22, 2002, vs. Tennessee); yards—153 (October 14, 2001, vs. Cincinnati); and touchdown receptions—2 (December 2, 2001, vs. Tennessee).

STATISTICAL PLATEAUS: 100-yard receiving games: 1999 (2), 2000 (1), 2001 (2). Total: 5.

			RUSHING				RECEIVING				PUNT RETURNS				TOTALS			
Year Team	G	GS	Att.	Yds.	Avg.	TD	No.	Yds.	Avg.	TD	No.	Yds.	Avg.	TD	TD	2pt.	Pts.	Fum.
1999—Cleveland NFL	16	16	1	-6	-6.0	0	66	986	14.9	8	19	128	6.7	0	8	0	48	1
2000—Cleveland NFL	16	16	0	0	0.0	0	57	669	11.7	0	0	0	0.0	0	0	0	0	0
2001—Cleveland NFL	16	16	0	0	0.0	0	84	1097	13.1	9	14	117	8.4	0	9	0	54	2
2002—Cleveland NFL	16	15	0	0	0.0	0	67	703	10.5	4	0	0	0.0	0	4	0	24	0
Pro totals (4 years)	64	63	1	-6	-6.0	0	274	3455	12.6	21	33	245	7.4	0	21	0	126	3

JOHNSON, KEYSHAWN   WR   BUCCANEERS

PERSONAL: Born July 22, 1972, in Los Angeles. ... 6-4/212. ... Cousin of Chris Miller, wide receiver with Green Bay Packers (1997), Detroit Lions (1997) and Chicago Bears (1998); and cousin of Ed Gray, guard with Atlanta Hawks (1997-98 and 1998-99).

HIGH SCHOOL: Dorsey (Los Angeles).

JUNIOR COLLEGE: West Los Angeles College.

COLLEGE: Southern California (degree in history).

TRANSACTIONS/CAREER NOTES: Selected by New York Jets in first round (first pick overall) of 1996 NFL draft. ... Signed by Jets (August 6, 1996). ... Traded by Jets to Tampa Bay Buccaneers for two first-round picks (LB John Abraham and TE Anthony Becht) in 2000 draft (April 12, 2000).

CHAMPIONSHIP GAME EXPERIENCE: Played in AFC championship game (1998 season). ... Played in NFC championship game (2002 season). ... Member of Super Bowl championship team (2002 season).

HONORS: Named wide receiver on The Sporting News college All-America first team (1995). ... Played in Pro Bowl (1998, 1999 and 2001 seasons). ... Named co-Oustanding Player of Pro Bowl (1998 season).

SINGLE GAME HIGHS (regular season): Receptions—12 (November 18, 2001, vs. Chicago); yards—194 (September 12, 1999, vs. New England); and touchdown receptions—2 (November 3, 2002, vs. Minnesota).

STATISTICAL PLATEAUS: 100-yard receiving games: 1997 (1), 1998 (4), 1999 (2), 2000 (2), 2001 (4), 2002 (3). Total: 16.

			RECEIVING				TOTALS			
Year Team	G	GS	No.	Yds.	Avg.	TD	TD	2pt.	Pts.	Fum.
1996—New York Jets NFL	14	11	63	844	13.4	8	8	1	50	0
1997—New York Jets NFL	16	16	70	963	13.8	5	5	0	30	0
1998—New York Jets NFL	16	16	83	1131	13.6	▲10	11	0	66	0
1999—New York Jets NFL	16	16	89	1170	13.1	8	8	0	48	0
2000—Tampa Bay NFL	16	16	71	874	12.3	8	8	0	48	2
2001—Tampa Bay NFL	15	15	‡106	1266	11.9	1	1	0	6	2
2002—Tampa Bay NFL	16	16	76	1088	14.3	5	5	∞2	34	0
Pro totals (7 years)	109	106	558	7336	13.1	45	46	3	282	4

JOHNSON, LEE   P

PERSONAL: Born November 27, 1961, in Conroe, Texas. ... 6-2/202.

HIGH SCHOOL: McCullough (The Woodlands, Texas).

COLLEGE: Brigham Young.

TRANSACTIONS/CAREER NOTES: Selected by Houston Gamblers in ninth round (125th pick overall) of 1985 USFL draft. ... Selected by Houston Oilers in fifth round (138th pick overall) of 1985 NFL draft. ... Signed by Oilers (June 25, 1985). ... Crossed picket line during players strike (October 14, 1987). ... Claimed on waivers by Buffalo Bills (December 2, 1987). ... Claimed on waivers by Cleveland Browns (December 10, 1987). ... Claimed on waivers by Cincinnati Bengals (September 23, 1988). ... Granted free agency (February 1, 1991). ... Re-signed by Bengals (1991). ... Granted unconditional free agency (March 1, 1993). ... Re-signed by Bengals (May 10, 1993). ... Released by Bengals (December 7, 1998). ... Signed by New England Patriots (February 18, 1999). ... Released by Patriots (October 15, 2001). ... Signed by Minnesota Vikings (December 12, 2001). ... Granted unconditional free agency (March 1, 2002). ... Signed by Philadelphia Eagles (December 16, 2002). ... Granted unconditional free agency (February 28, 2003).

CHAMPIONSHIP GAME EXPERIENCE: Played in AFC championship game (1987 and 1988 seasons). ... Played in Super Bowl XXIII (1988 season). ... Played in NFC championship game (2002 season).

POST SEASON RECORDS: Holds Super Bowl record for longest punt—63 yards (January 22, 1989, vs. San Francisco).

		PUNTING						KICKING				TOTALS		
Year Team	G	No.	Yds.	Avg.	Net avg.	In. 20	Blk.	50+	Tot.	Pct.	Lg.	XPM	XPA	Pts.
1985—Houston NFL	16	83	3464	41.7	35.7	22	0	0-0	0-0	0.0	0	0	0	0
1986—Houston NFL	16	88	3623	41.2	35.7	26	0	0-0	0-0	0.0	0	0	0	0
1987—Houston NFL	9	41	1652	40.3	32.9	5	0	0-0	0-0	0.0	0	0	0	0
—Cleveland NFL	3	9	317	35.2	32.2	3	0	0-0	0-0	0.0	0	0	0	0
1988—Cleveland NFL	3	17	643	37.8	30.6	6	0	1-2	1-2	50.0	50	0	0	3
—Cincinnati NFL	12	14	594	42.4	36.7	4	0	0-0	0-0	0.0	0	0	0	0
1989—Cincinnati NFL	16	61	2446	40.1	30.1	14	2	0-0	0-0	0.0	0	0	1	0
1990—Cincinnati NFL	16	64	2705	42.3	34.2	12	0	0-1	0-1	0.0	0	0	0	0
1991—Cincinnati NFL	16	64	2795	43.7	34.7	15	0	1-3	1-3	33.3	53	0	0	3
1992—Cincinnati NFL	16	76	3196	42.1	35.8	15	0	0-1	0-1	0.0	0	0	0	0
1993—Cincinnati NFL	16	▲90	3954	43.9	36.6	24	0	0-0	0-0	0.0	0	0	0	0
1994—Cincinnati NFL	16	79	3461	43.8	35.2	19	1	0-0	0-0	0.0	0	0	0	0
1995—Cincinnati NFL	16	68	2861	42.1	38.6	26	0	0-0	0-0	0.0	0	0	0	0
1996—Cincinnati NFL	16	80	3630	45.4	34.3	16	1	0-0	0-0	0.0	0	0	0	0
1997—Cincinnati NFL	16	81	3471	42.9	35.9	27	0	0-0	0-0	0.0	0	0	0	0
1998—Cincinnati NFL	13	69	3083	44.7	35.6	14	1	0-0	0-0	0.0	0	0	0	0
1999—New England NFL	16	90	3735	41.5	34.6	23	0	0-0	0-0	0.0	0	0	0	0
2000—New England NFL	16	89	3798	42.7	36.8	31	▲1	0-0	0-0	0.0	0	0	0	0
2001—New England NFL	5	24	1045	43.5	38.3	3	0	0-0	0-0	0.0	0	0	0	0
—Minnesota NFL	4	25	983	39.3	34.4	9	0	0-0	0-0	0.0	0	0	0	0
2002—Philadelphia NFL	2	14	523	37.4	27.7	4	0	0-0	0-0	0.0	0	0	0	0
Pro totals (18 years)	259	1226	51979	42.4	35.2	318	6	2-7	2-7	28.6	53	0	1	6

JOHNSON, LEON   RB/KR   RAMS

PERSONAL: Born July 13, 1974, in Morganton, N.C... 6-0/222. ... Full name: William Leon Johnson.
HIGH SCHOOL: Freedom (Morganton, N.C.).
COLLEGE: North Carolina.
TRANSACTIONS/CAREER NOTES: Selected by New York Jets in fourth round (104th pick overall) of 1997 NFL draft. ... Signed by Jets (July 17, 1997). ... On injured reserve with rib injury (December 16, 1998-remainder of season). ... On injured reserve with knee injury (September 13, 1999-remainder of season). ... Granted free agency (February 11, 2000). ... Re-signed by Jets (May 8, 2000). ... Released by Jets (June 27, 2000). ... Re-signed by Jets (November 28, 2000). ... Released by Jets (February 19, 2001). ... Signed by Chicago Bears (October 9, 2001). ... Signed by St. Louis Rams (March 22, 2003).
SINGLE GAME HIGHS (regular season): Attempts—16 (December 22, 2002, vs. Carolina); yards—56 (December 15, 2002, vs. New York Jets); and rushing touchdowns—2 (September 20, 1998, vs Indianapolis).

			RUSHING				RECEIVING				PUNT RETURNS				KICKOFF RETURNS				TOTALS			
Year Team	G	GS	Att.	Yds.	Avg.	TD	No.	Yds.	Avg.	TD	No.	Yds.	Avg.	TD	No.	Yds.	Avg.	TD	TD	2pt.	Pts.	Fum.
1997—NYJ NFL	16	1	48	158	3.3	2	16	142	8.9	0	§51	*619	12.1	1	12	319	26.6	▲1	4	0	24	5
1998—NYJ NFL	12	2	41	185	4.5	2	13	222	17.1	2	29	203	7.0	0	16	366	22.9	0	4	0	24	3
1999—NYJ NFL	1	0	1	2	2.0	0	0	0	0.0	0	1	6	6.0	0	2	31	15.5	0	0	0	0	1
2000—NYJ NFL	3	0	0	0	0.0	0	0	0	0.0	0	10	62	6.2	0	6	117	19.5	0	0	0	0	0
2001—Chicago NFL	12	0	20	99	5.0	4	1	0	0.0	0	28	255	9.1	0	14	286	20.4	0	4	0	24	2
2002—Chicago NFL	16	4	103	329	3.2	1	16	125	7.8	0	28	288	10.3	0	21	418	19.9	0	1	0	6	3
Pro totals (6 yrs)	60	7	213	773	3.6	9	46	489	10.6	2	147	1433	9.7	1	71	1537	21.6	1	13	0	78	14

JOHNSON, PATRICK   WR   REDSKINS

PERSONAL: Born August 10, 1976, in Gainesville, Ga. ... 5-10/191. ... Full name: Patrick Jevon Johnson.
HIGH SCHOOL: Redlands (Calif.).
COLLEGE: Oregon.
TRANSACTIONS/CAREER NOTES: Selected by Baltimore Ravens in second round (42nd pick overall) of 1998 NFL draft. ... Signed by Ravens (June 24, 1998). ... Granted free agency (March 2, 2001). ... Signed by Jacksonville Jaguars (March 18, 2002). ... Granted unconditional free agency (February 28, 2003). ... Signed by Washington Redskins (March 11, 2003).
CHAMPIONSHIP GAME EXPERIENCE: Played in AFC championship game (2000 season). ... Member of Super Bowl championship team (2000 season).
HONORS: Named kick returner on THE SPORTING NEWS college All-America second team (1997).
SINGLE GAME HIGHS (regular season): Receptions—9 (January 2, 2000, vs. New England); yards—114 (January 2, 2000, vs. New England); and touchdown receptions—1 (September 15, 2002, vs. Kansas City).
STATISTICAL PLATEAUS: 100-yard receiving games: 1999 (1).

			RECEIVING				KICKOFF RETURNS				TOTALS			
Year Team	G	GS	No.	Yds.	Avg.	TD	No.	Yds.	Avg.	TD	TD	2pt.	Pts.	Fum.
1998—Baltimore NFL	13	0	12	159	13.3	1	16	399	24.9	▲1	2	0	12	1
1999—Baltimore NFL	10	6	29	526	18.1	3	0	0	0.0	0	3	0	18	1
2000—Baltimore NFL	12	9	12	156	13.0	2	0	0	0.0	0	2	0	12	0
2001—Baltimore NFL	4	0	5	57	11.4	1	2	39	19.5	0	1	0	6	1
2002—Jacksonville NFL	9	6	9	187	20.8	2	0	0	0.0	0	2	0	12	0
Pro totals (5 years)	48	21	67	1085	16.2	9	18	438	24.3	1	10	0	60	3

JOHNSON, RAYLEE   DE   CHARGERS

PERSONAL: Born June 1, 1970, in Chicago. ... 6-3/272. ... Full name: Raylee Terrell Johnson.
HIGH SCHOOL: Fordyce (Ark.).
COLLEGE: Arkansas.
TRANSACTIONS/CAREER NOTES: Selected by San Diego Chargers in fourth round (95th pick overall) of 1993 NFL draft. ... Signed by Chargers (July 15, 1993). ... Granted unconditional free agency (February 14, 1997). ... Re-signed by Chargers (March 11, 1997). ... On injured reserve with knee injury (August 22, 2000-entire season).
CHAMPIONSHIP GAME EXPERIENCE: Played in AFC championship game (1994 season). ... Played in Super Bowl XXIX (1994 season).

			TOTALS		
Year Team	G	GS	Tk.	Ast.	Sks.
1993—San Diego NFL	9	0	0	1	0.0
1994—San Diego NFL	15	0	4	2	1.5
1995—San Diego NFL	16	1	14	1	3.0
1996—San Diego NFL	16	1	15	3	3.0
1997—San Diego NFL	16	0	16	3	2.5
1998—San Diego NFL	16	3	23	6	5.5
1999—San Diego NFL	16	16	33	8	10.5
2000—San Diego NFL			Did not play.		
2001—San Diego NFL	16	16	28	10	9.5
2002—San Diego NFL	16	16	32	8	6.5
Pro totals (9 years)	136	53	165	42	42.0

JOHNSON, RIALL   LB   BENGALS

PERSONAL: Born April 20, 1978, in Lynnwood, Wash. ... 6-3/243. ... Brother of Teyo Johnson, wide receiver/tight end, Oakland Raiders.
HIGH SCHOOL: Mariner (Wash.).
COLLEGE: Stanford.
TRANSACTIONS/CAREER NOTES: Selected by Cincinnati Bengals in sixth round (168th pick overall) of 2001 NFL draft. ... Signed by Bengals (July 11, 2001). ... Released by Bengals (October 27, 2001). ... Re-signed by Bengals (October 30, 2001).

Year	Team	G	GS	TOTALS			INTERCEPTIONS			
				Tk.	Ast.	Sks.	No.	Yds.	Avg.	TD
2001—Cincinnati NFL		7	0	0	0	0.0	0	0	0.0	0
2002—Cincinnati NFL		12	0	0	0	0.0	0	0	0.0	0
Pro totals (2 years)		19	0	0	0	0.0	0	0	0.0	0

JOHNSON, ROB — QB — REDSKINS

PERSONAL: Born March 18, 1973, in Newport Beach, Calif. ... 6-4/212. ... Full name: Rob Garland Johnson. ... Brother of Bret Johnson, quarterback with Toronto Argonauts of CFL (1993); and cousin of Bart Johnson, pitcher with Chicago White Sox (1969-74, 1976 and 1977).
HIGH SCHOOL: El Toro (Calif.).
COLLEGE: Southern California.
TRANSACTIONS/CAREER NOTES: Selected by Jacksonville Jaguars in fourth round (99th pick overall) of 1995 NFL draft. ... Signed by Jaguars (June 1, 1995). ... Traded by Jaguars to Buffalo Bills for first- (RB Fred Taylor) and fourth-round (RB Tavian Banks) picks in 1998 draft (February 13, 1998). ... Released by Bills (February 28, 2002). ... Signed by Tampa Bay Buccaneers (March 10, 2002). ... Granted unconditional free agency (February 28, 2003). ... Signed by Washington Redskins (March 2, 2003).
CHAMPIONSHIP GAME EXPERIENCE: Member of Jaguars for AFC championship game (1996 season); did not play. ... Member of Buccaneers for NFC championship game (2002 season); did not play. ... Member of Super Bowl championship team (2002 season); did not play.
SINGLE GAME HIGHS (regular season): Attempts—47 (October 15, 2000, vs. San Diego); completions—29 (October 15, 2000, vs. San Diego); yards—321 (October 15, 2000, vs. San Diego); and touchdown passes—3 (September 10, 2000, vs. Green Bay).
STATISTICAL PLATEAUS: 300-yard passing games: 2000 (1), 2001 (1). Total: 2.
MISCELLANEOUS: Selected by Minnesota Twins organization in 16th round of free-agent draft (June 4, 1991); did not sign. ... Regular-season record as starting NFL quarterback: 12-17 (.414). ... Postseason record as starting NFL quarterback: 0-1.

Year	Team	G	GS	PASSING									RUSHING				TOTALS		
				Att.	Cmp.	Pct.	Yds.	TD	Int.	Avg.	Skd.	Rat.	Att.	Yds.	Avg.	TD	TD	2pt.	Pts.
1995—Jacksonville NFL		1	0	7	3	42.9	24	0	1	3.43	1	12.5	3	17	5.7	0	0	0	0
1996—Jacksonville NFL		2	0	0	0	0.0	0	0	0	0.0	0	...	0	0	0.0	0	0	0	0
1997—Jacksonville NFL		5	1	28	22	78.6	344	2	2	12.29	6	111.9	10	34	3.4	1	1	0	6
1998—Buffalo NFL		8	6	107	67	62.6	910	8	3	8.50	29	102.9	24	123	5.1	1	1	0	6
1999—Buffalo NFL		2	1	34	25	73.5	298	2	0	8.76	1	119.5	8	61	7.6	0	0	0	0
2000—Buffalo NFL		12	11	306	175	57.2	2125	12	7	6.94	49	82.2	42	307	7.3	1	1	0	6
2001—Buffalo NFL		8	8	216	134	62.0	1465	5	7	6.78	31	76.3	36	241	6.7	1	1	0	6
2002—Tampa Bay NFL		6	2	88	57	64.8	536	1	2	6.09	19	75.8	14	73	5.2	0	0	0	0
Pro totals (8 years)		44	29	786	483	61.5	5702	30	22	7.25	136	84.6	137	856	6.2	4	4	0	24

JOHNSON, RON — WR — RAVENS

PERSONAL: Born May 23, 1980, in Detroit. ... 6-2/225.
HIGH SCHOOL: Martin Luther King (Detroit).
COLLEGE: Minnesota.
TRANSACTIONS/CAREER NOTES: Selected by Baltimore Ravens in fourth round (123rd pick overall) of 2002 NFL draft. ... Signed by Ravens (July 26, 2002).
SINGLE GAME HIGHS (regular season): Receptions—3 (October 27, 2002, vs. Pittsburgh); yards—37 (October 20, 2002, vs. Jacksonville); and touchdown receptions—1 (September 8, 2002, vs. Carolina).

Year	Team	G	GS	RUSHING				RECEIVING				PUNT RETURNS				KICKOFF RETURNS				TOTALS		
				Att.	Yds.	Avg.	TD	No.	Yds.	Avg.	TD	No.	Yds.	Avg.	TD	No.	Yds.	Avg.	TD	TD	2pt.	Pts.
2002—Baltimore NFL		16	4	0	0	0.0	0	10	114	11.4	1	0	0	0.0	0	2	21	10.5	0	2	0	12

JOHNSON, RUDI — RB — BENGALS

PERSONAL: Born October 1, 1979, in Ettrick, Va. ... 5-10/220. ... Full name: Rudi Ali Johnson.
HIGH SCHOOL: Thomas Dale (Ettrick, Va.).
JUNIOR COLLEGE: Butler County Community College (Kan.).
COLLEGE: Auburn.
TRANSACTIONS/CAREER NOTES: Selected by Cincinnati Bengals in fourth round (100th pick overall) of 2001 NFL draft. ... Signed by Bengals (July 17, 2001).
HONORS: Named running back on THE SPORTING NEWS college All-America second team (2000).
SINGLE GAME HIGHS (regular season): Attempts—5 (December 8, 2002, vs. Carolina); yards—25 (December 29, 2002, vs. Buffalo); and rushing touchdowns—0.

Year	Team	G	GS	RUSHING				RECEIVING				KICKOFF RETURNS				TOTALS			
				Att.	Yds.	Avg.	TD	No.	Yds.	Avg.	TD	No.	Yds.	Avg.	TD	TD	2pt.	Pts.	Fum.
2001—Cincinnati NFL		2	0	0	0	0.0	0	0	0	0.0	0	4	79	19.8	0	0	0	0	0
2002—Cincinnati NFL		7	0	17	67	3.9	0	6	34	5.7	0	13	277	21.3	0	0	0	0	0
Pro totals (2 years)		9	0	17	67	3.9	0	6	34	5.7	0	17	356	20.9	0	0	0	0	0

JOHNSON, TED — LB — PATRIOTS

PERSONAL: Born December 4, 1972, in Alameda, Calif. ... 6-4/253. ... Full name: Ted Curtis Johnson.
HIGH SCHOOL: Carlsbad (Calif.).
COLLEGE: Colorado.
TRANSACTIONS/CAREER NOTES: Selected by New England Patriots in second round (57th pick overall) of 1995 NFL draft. ... Signed by Patriots (July 18, 1995). ... On injured reserve with bicep injury (December 11, 1998-remainder of season).
CHAMPIONSHIP GAME EXPERIENCE: Played in AFC championship game (1996 and 2001 seasons). ... Played in Super Bowl XXXI (1996 season). ... Member of Super Bowl championship team (2001 season).
HONORS: Named linebacker on THE SPORTING NEWS college All-America second team (1994).

Year Team	G	GS	TOTALS Tk.	Ast.	Sks.	INTERCEPTIONS No.	Yds.	Avg.	TD
1995—New England NFL	12	12	41	28	0.5	0	0	0.0	0
1996—New England NFL	16	16	87	28	0.0	1	0	0.0	0
1997—New England NFL	16	16	95	32	4.0	0	0	0.0	0
1998—New England NFL	13	13	64	33	2.0	0	0	0.0	0
1999—New England NFL	5	5	25	13	2.0	0	0	0.0	0
2000—New England NFL	13	11	51	22	0.5	0	0	0.0	0
2001—New England NFL	12	5	33	13	0.0	0	0	0.0	0
2002—New England NFL	14	11	63	33	1.5	0	0	0.0	0
Pro totals (8 years)	101	89	459	202	10.5	1	0	0.0	0

JOHNSON, TIM   LB   RAIDERS

J

PERSONAL: Born February 7, 1978, in Fairfield, Ala. ... 6-0/240.
HIGH SCHOOL: Fairfield (Ala.).
JUNIOR COLLEGE: East Mississippi Junior College.
COLLEGE: Youngstown State.
TRANSACTIONS/CAREER NOTES: Signed as non-drafted free agent by Baltimore Ravens (April 27, 2001). ... Released by Ravens (September 1, 2001). ... Re-signed by Ravens (September 5, 2001). ... Released by Ravens (September 10, 2001). ... Signed by Chicago Bears to practice squad (September 27, 2001). ... Released by Bears (October 30, 2001). ... Re-signed by Bears to practice squad (November 8, 2001). ... Assigned by Bears to Rhein Fire in 2002 NFL Europe enhancement allocation program (February 18, 2002). ... Released by Bears (September 1, 2002). ... Signed by Oakland Raiders to practice squad (September 3, 2002). ... Released by Raiders (September 18, 2002). ... Re-signed by Raiders to practice squad (September 24, 2002). ... Released by Raiders (October 9, 2002). ... Re-signed by Raiders to practice squad (October 31, 2002). ... Activated (November 24, 2002).
CHAMPIONSHIP GAME EXPERIENCE: Played in AFC championship game (2002 season). ... Played in Super Bowl XXXVII (2002 season).

Year Team	G	GS	TOTALS Tk.	Ast.	Sks.	INTERCEPTIONS No.	Yds.	Avg.	TD
2001—Baltimore NFL			Did not play.						
2002—Rhein NFLE	...	...	...	...	2.0	1	29	29.0	0
—Oakland NFL	6	0	0	0	0.0	0	0	0.0	0
NFL Europe totals (1 year)	...	...	...	...	2.0	1	29	29.0	0
NFL totals (2 years)	6	0	0	0	0.0	0	0	0.0	0
Pro totals (3 years)	...	...	...	...	2.0	1	29	29.0	0

JOHNSON, TRE'   G   REDSKINS

PERSONAL: Born August 30, 1971, in Manhattan, N.Y. ... 6-5/326. ... Full name: Edward Stanton Johnson III.
HIGH SCHOOL: Peekskill (N.Y.).
COLLEGE: Temple (degree in social administration, 1993).
TRANSACTIONS/CAREER NOTES: Selected by Washington Redskins in second round (31st pick overall) of 1994 NFL draft. ... Signed by Redskins (July 22, 1994). ... On injured reserve with shoulder injury (December 16, 1997-remainder of season). ... Granted unconditional free agency (February 13, 1998). ... Re-signed by Redskins (February 13, 1998). ... On injured reserve with knee injury (November 24, 1998-remainder of season). ... On injured reserve with knee injury (October 9, 2000-remainder of season). ... Released by Redskins (February 21, 2001). ... Signed by Cleveland Browns (May 24, 2001). ... On physically unable to perform list with knee injury (July 23-28, 2001). ... On injured reserve with knee injury (October 2, 2001-remainder of season). ... Granted unconditional free agency (March 1, 2002). ... Re-signed by Browns (March 26, 2002). ... Released by Browns (September 1, 2002). ... Signed by Redskins (October 22, 2002). ... Granted unconditional free agency (February 28, 2003). ... Re-signed by Redskins (March 3, 2003).
PLAYING EXPERIENCE: Washington NFL, 1994-2000; Cleveland NFL, 2001; Washington NFL, 2002. ... Games/Games started: 1994 (14/1), 1995 (10/9), 1996 (15/15), 1997 (11/11), 1998 (10/10), 1999 (16/16), 2000 (4/4), 2001 (3/3), 2002 (10/3). Total: 93/72.
HONORS: Played in Pro Bowl (1999 season).

JOHNSTONE, LANCE   DE   VIKINGS

PERSONAL: Born June 11, 1973, in Philadelphia. ... 6-4/253.
HIGH SCHOOL: Germantown (Philadelphia).
COLLEGE: Temple.
TRANSACTIONS/CAREER NOTES: Selected by Oakland Raiders in second round (57th pick overall) of 1996 NFL draft. ... Signed by Raiders for 1996 season. ... Granted unconditional free agency (March 2, 2001). ... Signed by Minnesota Vikings (March 30, 2001). ... Granted unconditional free agency (March 1, 2002). ... Re-signed by Vikings (March 28, 2002). ... Granted unconditional free agency (February 28, 2003). ... Re-signed by Vikings (March 20, 2003).
CHAMPIONSHIP GAME EXPERIENCE: Played in AFC championship game (2000 season).

Year Team	G	GS	TOTALS Tk.	Ast.	Sks.	INTERCEPTIONS No.	Yds.	Avg.	TD
1996—Oakland NFL	16	10	26	6	1.0	0	0	0.0	0
1997—Oakland NFL	14	6	20	11	3.5	0	0	0.0	0
1998—Oakland NFL	16	15	48	6	11.0	0	0	0.0	0
1999—Oakland NFL	16	16	45	7	10.0	1	0	0.0	0
2000—Oakland NFL	14	9	22	10	3.5	0	0	0.0	0
2001—Minnesota NFL	16	5	29	9	5.5	0	0	0.0	0
2002—Minnesota NFL	16	16	41	10	7.0	0	0	0.0	0
Pro totals (7 years)	108	77	231	59	41.5	1	0	0.0	0

JOLLEY, DOUG — TE — RAIDERS

PERSONAL: Born January 2, 1979, in St. George, Utah. ... 6-4/250.
HIGH SCHOOL: Dixie (St. George, Utah).
COLLEGE: Brigham Young.
TRANSACTIONS/CAREER NOTES: Selected by Oakland Raiders in second round (55th pick overall) of 2002 NFL draft. ... Signed by Raiders (July 23, 2002).
CHAMPIONSHIP GAME EXPERIENCE: Played in AFC championship game (2002 season). ... Played in Super Bowl XXXVII (2002 season).
SINGLE GAME HIGHS (regular season): Receptions—6 (December 8, 2002, vs. San Diego); yards—104 (December 8, 2002, vs. San Diego); and touchdown receptions—1 (December 28, 2002, vs. Kansas City).
STATISTICAL PLATEAUS: 100-yard receiving games: 2002 (1).

Year Team	G	GS	No.	Yds.	Avg.	TD
			RECEIVING			
2002—Oakland NFL	16	3	32	409	12.8	2

JONES, BOB — DE

PERSONAL: Born September 3, 1978, in Barberton, Ohio. ... 6-3/270. ... Full name: Robert Thomas Jones.
HIGH SCHOOL: Wadsworth (Ohio).
COLLEGE: Penn State.
TRANSACTIONS/CAREER NOTES: Signed as non-drafted free agent by Pittsburgh Steelers (April 22, 2002). ... Claimed on waivers by New York Giants (August 27, 2002). ... Released by Giants (November 30, 2002).

Year Team	G	GS	Tk.	Ast.	Sks.
			TOTALS		
2002—New York Giants NFL	11	0	0	0	0.0

JONES, DARYL — WR — GIANTS

PERSONAL: Born February 2, 1979, in Dallas. ... 5-9/175. ... Full name: Daryl Lawrence Jones.
HIGH SCHOOL: Carter (Dallas).
COLLEGE: Miami (Fla.).
TRANSACTIONS/CAREER NOTES: Selected by New York Giants in seventh round (226th pick overall) of 2002 NFL draft.
SINGLE GAME HIGHS (regular season): Receptions—3 (December 8, 2002, vs. Washington); yards—41 (December 8, 2002, vs. Washington); and touchdown receptions—0.

Year Team	G	GS	No.	Yds.	Avg.	TD	No.	Yds.	Avg.	TD	No.	Yds.	Avg.	TD	TD	2pt.	Pts.	Fum.
			RECEIVING				PUNT RETURNS				KICKOFF RETURNS				TOTALS			
2002—New York Giants NFL..	13	6	8	90	11.3	0	6	28	4.7	0	10	195	19.5	0	0	0	0	1

JONES, DHANI — LB — GIANTS

PERSONAL: Born February 22, 1978, in San Diego. ... 6-1/240. ... Full name: Dhani Makalani Jones.
HIGH SCHOOL: Winston Churchill (Potomac, Md.).
COLLEGE: Michigan.
TRANSACTIONS/CAREER NOTES: Selected by New York Giants in sixth round (177th pick overall) of 2000 NFL draft. ... Signed by Giants (July 18, 2000). ... On injured reserve with knee injury (August 20, 2000-entire season). ... Granted free agency (February 28, 2003). ... Re-signed by Giants (April 28, 2003).

Year Team	G	GS	Tk.	Ast.	Sks.	No.	Yds.	Avg.	TD
			TOTALS			INTERCEPTIONS			
2000—New York Giants NFL			Did not play.						
2001—New York Giants NFL	16	0	9	2	0.0	1	14	14.0	0
2002—New York Giants NFL	15	14	60	22	0.0	1	1	1.0	0
Pro totals (2 years)	31	14	69	24	0.0	2	15	7.5	0

JONES, FREDDIE — TE — CARDINALS

PERSONAL: Born September 16, 1974, in Cheverly, Md. ... 6-4/271. ... Full name: Freddie Ray Jones Jr.
HIGH SCHOOL: McKinley (Landover, Md.).
COLLEGE: North Carolina.
TRANSACTIONS/CAREER NOTES: Selected by San Diego Chargers in second round (45th pick overall) of 1997 NFL draft. ... Signed by Chargers (May 21, 1997). ... On injured reserve with leg injury (December 12, 1997-remainder of season). ... Granted free agency (February 11, 2000). ... Re-signed by Chargers (April 29, 2000). ... Released by Chargers (February 27, 2002). ... Signed by Arizona Cardinals (March 18, 2002).
SINGLE GAME HIGHS (regular season): Receptions—10 (October 29, 2000, vs. Oakland); yards—111 (October 29, 2000, vs. Oakland); and touchdown receptions—2 (November 26, 2000, vs. Kansas City).
STATISTICAL PLATEAUS: 100-yard receiving games: 2000 (1).

Year Team	G	GS	No.	Yds.	Avg.	TD	TD	2pt.	Pts.	Fum.
			RECEIVING				TOTALS			
1997—San Diego NFL	13	8	41	505	12.3	2	2	0	12	0
1998—San Diego NFL	16	16	57	602	10.6	3	3	1	20	1
1999—San Diego NFL	16	16	56	670	12.0	2	2	0	12	0
2000—San Diego NFL	16	16	71	766	10.8	5	5	0	30	3
2001—San Diego NFL	14	9	35	388	11.1	4	4	0	24	0
2002—Arizona NFL	16	16	44	358	8.1	1	1	0	6	0
Pro totals (6 years)	91	81	304	3289	10.8	17	17	1	104	4

JONES, GREG   LB   CARDINALS

PERSONAL: Born May 22, 1974, in Denver. ... 6-4/245. ... Full name: Greg Phillip Jones.

HIGH SCHOOL: John F. Kennedy (Denver).

COLLEGE: Colorado (degree in small business management, 1996).

TRANSACTIONS/CAREER NOTES: Selected by Washington Redskins in second round (51st pick overall) of 1997 NFL draft. ... Signed by Redskins (July 11, 1997). ... Granted unconditional free agency (March 2, 2001). ... Signed by Chicago Bears (May 8, 2001). ... Granted unconditional free agency (March 1, 2002). ... Signed by Houston Texans (March 15, 2002). ... Released by Texans (September 1, 2002). ... Signed by Arizona Cardinals (December 12, 2002). ... Granted unconditional free agency (February 28, 2003). ... Re-signed by Cardinals (March 14, 2003).

			TOTALS			INTERCEPTIONS			
Year Team	G	GS	Tk.	Ast.	Sks.	No.	Yds.	Avg.	TD
1997—Washington NFL	16	3	12	4	3.5	0	0	0.0	0
1998—Washington NFL	16	5	18	2	1.0	1	9	9.0	0
1999—Washington NFL	15	15	34	12	0.5	0	0	0.0	0
2000—Washington NFL	16	4	12	1	1.0	0	0	0.0	0
2001—Chicago NFL	16	0	3	0	0.0	0	0	0.0	0
2002—Arizona NFL	3	1	5	0	0.0	0	0	0.0	0
Pro totals (6 years)	82	28	84	19	6.0	1	9	9.0	0

JONES, HENRY   S

PERSONAL: Born December 29, 1967, in St. Louis. ... 6-0/200.

HIGH SCHOOL: St. Louis University High.

COLLEGE: Illinois (degree in psychology, 1990).

TRANSACTIONS/CAREER NOTES: Selected by Buffalo Bills in first round (26th pick overall) of 1991 NFL draft. ... Signed by Bills (August 30, 1991). ... Activated (September 7, 1991). ... Designated by Bills as transition player (February 15, 1994). ... On injured reserve with broken leg (October 9, 1996-remainder of season). ... Released by Bills (September 2, 2001). ... Signed by Minnesota Vikings (September 25, 2001). ... Released by Vikings (October 30, 2001). ... Signed by Atlanta Falcons (August 22, 2002). ... Granted unconditional free agency (February 28, 2003).

CHAMPIONSHIP GAME EXPERIENCE: Played in AFC championship game (1991-1993 seasons). ... Played in Super Bowl XXVI (1991 season), Super Bowl XXVII (1992 season) and Super Bowl XXVIII (1993 season).

HONORS: Named strong safety on THE SPORTING NEWS NFL All-Pro team (1992). ... Played in Pro Bowl (1992 season).

RECORDS: Shares NFL single-game record for most touchdowns scored by interception—2 (September 20, 1992, vs. Indianapolis).

			TOTALS			INTERCEPTIONS			
Year Team	G	GS	Tk.	Ast.	Sks.	No.	Yds.	Avg.	TD
1991—Buffalo NFL	15	0	8	0	0.0	0	0	0.0	0
1992—Buffalo NFL	16	16	75	17	0.0	†8	*263	32.9	▲2
1993—Buffalo NFL	16	16	67	16	2.0	2	92	46.0	▲1
1994—Buffalo NFL	16	16	61	20	1.0	2	45	22.5	0
1995—Buffalo NFL	13	13	57	21	0.0	1	10	10.0	0
1996—Buffalo NFL	5	5	19	6	0.0	0	0	0.0	0
1997—Buffalo NFL	15	15	64	17	2.0	0	0	0.0	0
1998—Buffalo NFL	16	16	57	14	0.0	3	0	0.0	0
1999—Buffalo NFL	16	16	63	12	0.0	0	0	0.0	0
2000—Buffalo NFL	16	16	45	25	0.0	2	45	22.5	1
2001—Minnesota NFL	5	5	21	7	0.0	0	0	0.0	0
2002—Atlanta NFL	9	0	15	4	0.0	0	0	0.0	0
Pro totals (12 years)	158	134	552	159	5.0	18	455	25.3	4

JONES, J.J.   LB   SAINTS

PERSONAL: Born June 7, 1978, in Little Rock, Ark. ... 6-1/230. ... Full name: Jerry Glen Jones.

HIGH SCHOOL: Magnolia (Ark.).

COLLEGE: Arkansas.

TRANSACTIONS/CAREER NOTES: Signed as non-drafted free agent by Dallas Cowboys (April 26, 2001). ... Released by Cowboys (August 28, 2001). ... Signed by New Orleans Saints (January 16, 2002). ... Released by Saints (September 1, 2002). ... Re-signed by Saints to practice squad (September 2, 2002). ... Activated (September 28, 2002).

			TOTALS			INTERCEPTIONS			
Year Team	G	GS	Tk.	Ast.	Sks.	No.	Yds.	Avg.	TD
2002—New Orleans NFL	13	0	0	0	0.0	0	0	0.0	0

JONES, JERMAINE   CB

PERSONAL: Born July 25, 1976, in Morgan City, La. ... 5-8/172.

HIGH SCHOOL: Central Catholic (Morgan City, La.).

COLLEGE: Northwestern (La.) State.

TRANSACTIONS/CAREER NOTES: Selected by New York Jets in fifth round (162nd pick overall) of 1999 NFL draft. ... Signed by Jets (July 7, 1999). ... Released by Jets (September 5, 1999). ... Re-signed by Jets to practice squad (September 6, 1999). ... Released by Jets (September 14, 1999). ... Signed by Chicago Bears to practice squad (September 21, 1999). ... Activated (December 1, 1999). ... Released by Bears (June 13, 2000). ... Signed by New York Giants (July 25, 2000). ... Released by Giants (July 29, 2000). ... Signed by Dallas Cowboys (January 31, 2001). ... Released by Cowboys (September 2, 2001). ... Signed by Edmonton Eskimos of CFL (September 14, 2001). ... Re-signed by Cowboys (December 12, 2002). ... Granted free agency (February 28, 2003).

Year Team	G	GS	TOTALS			INTERCEPTIONS			
			Tk.	Ast.	Sks.	No.	Yds.	Avg.	TD
1999—New York Jets NFL..	1	0	0	0	0.0	0	0	0.0	0
—Chicago NFL..	1	0	0	0	0.0	0	0	0.0	0
2001—Edmonton CFL..	8	0	0	0	0.0	0	0	0.0	0
2002—Dallas NFL..	2	0	0	0	0.0	0	0	0.0	0
CFL totals (1 year)	8	0	0	0	0.0	0	0	0.0	0
NFL totals (2 years)	4	0	0	0	0.0	0	0	0.0	0
Pro totals (3 years)	12	0	0	0	0.0	0	0	0.0	0

JONES, JOHN — TE — RAVENS

PERSONAL: Born April 4, 1975, in Cleveland. ... 6-4/255.
HIGH SCHOOL: Glen Mills (Concordville, Pa.).
COLLEGE: Indiana (Pa.).
TRANSACTIONS/CAREER NOTES: Signed as non-drafted free agent by Baltimore Ravens (April 28, 2000). ... On injured reserve with ankle injury (January 3, 2000-remainder of season). ... Granted free agency (February 28, 2003). ... Re-signed by Ravens (April 29, 2003).
SINGLE GAME HIGHS (regular season): Receptions—2 (October 27, 2002, vs. Pittsburgh); yards—24 (October 27, 2002, vs. Pittsburgh); and touchdown receptions—1 (October 27, 2002, vs. Pittsburgh).

Year Team	G	GS	RECEIVING			
			No.	Yds.	Avg.	TD
2000—Baltimore NFL..	8	0	0	0	0.0	0
2001—Baltimore NFL..	15	2	2	13	6.5	0
2002—Baltimore NFL..	15	4	6	47	7.8	1
Pro totals (3 years)	38	6	8	60	7.5	1

JONES, JULIAN — S — PANTHERS

PERSONAL: Born June 8, 1977, in Phoenix. ... 6-0/190.
HIGH SCHOOL: Carl Albert (Midwest City, Okla.).
COLLEGE: Missouri.
TRANSACTIONS/CAREER NOTES: Signed as non-drafted free agent by Philadelphia Eagles (April 23, 2001). ... On injured reserve with shoulder injury (August 16, 2001-entire season). ... Released by Eagles (September 1, 2002). ... Re-signed by Eagles to practice squad (September 3, 2002). ... Activated (September 26, 2002). ... Released by Eagles (October 8, 2002). ... Re-signed by Eagles to practice squad (October 9, 2002). ... Activated (November 1, 2002). ... Released by Eagles (November 6, 2002). ... Re-signed by Eagles to practice squad (November 7, 2002). ... Released by Eagles (November 19, 2002). ... Signed by Carolina Panthers to practice squad (November 26, 2002).

Year Team	G	GS	TOTALS			INTERCEPTIONS			
			Tk.	Ast.	Sks.	No.	Yds.	Avg.	TD
2002—Philadelphia NFL	2	0	0	0	0.0	0	0	0.0	0

JONES, KENYATTA — OL — PATRIOTS

PERSONAL: Born January 18, 1979, in Gainesville, Fla. ... 6-3/310. ... Full name: Kenyatta Lapoleon Jones.
HIGH SCHOOL: Eastside (Gainesville, Fla.).
COLLEGE: South Florida.
TRANSACTIONS/CAREER NOTES: Selected by New England Patriots in fourth round (96th pick overall) of 2001 NFL draft. ... Signed by Patriots (July 19, 2001).
PLAYING EXPERIENCE: New England NFL, 2001-2002. ... Games/Games started: 2001 (5/0), 2002 (13/12). Total: 18/12.
CHAMPIONSHIP GAME EXPERIENCE: Member of Patriots for AFC championship game (2001 season); inactive. ... Member of Super Bowl championship team (2001 season); inactive.

JONES, LENOY — LB

PERSONAL: Born September 25, 1974, in Marlin, Texas. ... 6-1/235.
HIGH SCHOOL: Groesbeck (Texas).
COLLEGE: Texas Christian.
TRANSACTIONS/CAREER NOTES: Signed as non-drafted free agent by Houston Oilers (April 23, 1996). ... Released by Oilers (August 20, 1996). ... Re-signed by Oilers to practice squad (August 26, 1996). ... Activated (October 9, 1996). ... Oilers franchise moved to Tennessee for 1997 season. ... Oilers franchise renamed Tennessee Titans for 1999 season (December 26, 1998). ... Selected by Cleveland Browns from Titans in NFL expansion draft (February 9, 1999). ... Granted free agency (February 12, 1999). ... Re-signed by Browns (May 26, 1999). ... Granted unconditional free agency (February 11, 2000). ... Re-signed by Browns (March 6, 2000). ... On injured reserve with knee injury (November 28, 2000-remainder of season). ... On physically unable to perform list with knee injury (July 23-November 9, 2001). ... Granted unconditional free agency (March 1, 2002). ... Re-signed by Browns (April 1, 2002). ... Released by Browns (August 27, 2002). ... Re-signed by Browns (November 26, 2002). ... Granted unconditional free agency (February 28, 2003).

Year Team	G	GS	TOTALS			INTERCEPTIONS			
			Tk.	Ast.	Sks.	No.	Yds.	Avg.	TD
1996—Houston NFL...	11	0	12	2	0.0	0	0	0.0	0
1997—Tennessee NFL..	16	0	22	5	1.0	0	0	0.0	0
1998—Tennessee NFL..	9	0	0	0	0.0	0	0	0.0	0
1999—Cleveland NFL...	16	1	8	3	0.0	1	3	3.0	0
2000—Cleveland NFL...	8	0	5	4	2.5	0	0	0.0	0
2001—Cleveland NFL...	7	1	3	5	0.0	0	0	0.0	0
2002—Cleveland NFL...	5	0	0	0	0.0	0	0	0.0	0
Pro totals (7 years)	72	2	50	19	3.5	1	3	3.0	0

JONES, LEVI   OT   BENGALS

PERSONAL: Born August 24, 1979, in Eloy, Ariz. ... 6-5/306. ... Full name: Levi J. Jones.
HIGH SCHOOL: Santa Cruz (Eloy, Ariz.).
COLLEGE: Arizona State.
TRANSACTIONS/CAREER NOTES: Selected by Cincinnati Bengals in first round (10th pick overall) of 2002 NFL draft. ... Signed by Bengals (July 25, 2002).
PLAYING EXPERIENCE: Cincinnati NFL, 2002. ... Games/games started: 2002 (16/14).

JONES, MARVIN   LB   JETS

PERSONAL: Born June 28, 1972, in Miami. ... 6-2/244. ... Full name: Marvin Maurice Jones.
HIGH SCHOOL: Miami Northwestern.
COLLEGE: Florida State.
TRANSACTIONS/CAREER NOTES: Selected after junior season by New York Jets in first round (fourth pick overall) of 1993 NFL draft. ... Signed by Jets (August 5, 1993). ... On injured reserve with hip injury (November 16, 1993-remainder of season). ... On injured reserve with knee injury (July 29, 1998-entire season). ... Released by Jets (February 26, 2002). ... Re-signed by Jets (March 6, 2002).
HONORS: Butkus Award winner (1992). ... Named College Football Player of the Year by THE SPORTING NEWS (1992). ... Named linebacker on THE SPORTING NEWS college All-America first team (1992).

| | | | TOTALS | | | INTERCEPTIONS | | | |
Year Team	G	GS	Tk.	Ast.	Sks.	No.	Yds.	Avg.	TD
1993—New York Jets NFL	9	0	22	8	0.0	0	0	0.0	0
1994—New York Jets NFL	15	11	60	26	0.5	0	0	0.0	0
1995—New York Jets NFL	10	10	59	33	1.5	0	0	0.0	0
1996—New York Jets NFL	12	12	75	28	1.0	0	0	0.0	0
1997—New York Jets NFL	16	16	87	40	3.0	0	0	0.0	0
1998—New York Jets NFL				Did not play.					
1999—New York Jets NFL	16	16	69	23	1.0	1	15	15.0	0
2000—New York Jets NFL	16	16	102	33	1.0	0	0	0.0	0
2001—New York Jets NFL	16	16	94	38	1.0	3	27	9.0	0
2002—New York Jets NFL	16	16	77	32	0.0	1	0	0.0	0
Pro totals (9 years)	126	113	645	261	9.0	5	42	8.4	0

JONES, MIKE   LB

PERSONAL: Born April 15, 1969, in Kansas City, Mo. ... 6-1/245. ... Full name: Michael Anthony Jones.
HIGH SCHOOL: Southwest (Kansas City, Mo.).
COLLEGE: Missouri.
TRANSACTIONS/CAREER NOTES: Signed as non-drafted free agent by Los Angeles Raiders (April 1991). ... Assigned by Raiders to Sacramento Surge in 1992 World League enhancement allocation program (February 20, 1992). ... Raiders franchise moved to Oakland (July 21, 1995). ... Granted unconditional free agency (February 14, 1997). ... Signed by St. Louis Rams (March 18, 1997). ... Granted unconditional free agency (March 2, 2001). ... Signed by Pittsburgh Steelers (April 20, 2001). ... Released by Steelers (June 3, 2002). ... Signed by Raiders (June 12, 2002). ... Released by Raiders (September 1, 2002). ... Re-signed by Raiders (October 9, 2002). ... Released by Raiders (October 31, 2002). ... Signed by Steelers (November 19, 2002). ... Granted unconditional free agency (February 28, 2003).
CHAMPIONSHIP GAME EXPERIENCE: Played in NFC championship game (1999 season). ... Member of Super Bowl championship team (1999 season). ... Played in AFC championship game (2001 season).

| | | | TOTALS | | | INTERCEPTIONS | | | |
Year Team	G	GS	Tk.	Ast.	Sks.	No.	Yds.	Avg.	TD
1991—Los Angeles Raiders NFL	16	0	0	0	0.0	0	0	0.0	0
1992—Sacramento W.L.	7	7	...	...	2.0	0	0	0.0	0
—Los Angeles Raiders NFL	16	0	0	0	0.0	0	0	0.0	0
1993—Los Angeles Raiders NFL	16	2	44	5	0.0	0	0	0.0	0
1994—Los Angeles Raiders NFL	16	1	23	3	0.0	0	0	0.0	0
1995—Oakland NFL	16	16	84	17	0.0	1	23	23.0	0
1996—Oakland NFL	15	15	82	15	1.0	0	0	0.0	0
1997—St. Louis NFL	16	16	70	19	2.0	1	0	0.0	0
1998—St. Louis NFL	16	15	67	17	3.0	2	13	6.5	0
1999—St. Louis NFL	16	16	53	14	1.0	4	96	24.0	†2
2000—St. Louis NFL	16	16	62	14	2.0	0	0	0.0	0
2001—Pittsburgh NFL	15	0	10	3	0.0	0	0	0.0	0
2002—Oakland NFL	3	0	0	0	0.0	0	0	0.0	0
—Pittsburgh NFL	6	1	7	2	0.0	0	0	0.0	0
W.L. totals (1 year)	7	7	...	...	2.0	0	0	0.0	0
NFL totals (12 years)	183	98	502	106	9.0	8	132	16.5	2
Pro totals (13 years)	190	105	...	...	11.0	8	132	16.5	2

JONES, TEBUCKY   S   SAINTS

PERSONAL: Born October 6, 1974, in New Britain, Conn. ... 6-2/218. ... Full name: Tebucky Shermaine Jones.
HIGH SCHOOL: New Britain (Conn.).
COLLEGE: Syracuse.
TRANSACTIONS/CAREER NOTES: Selected by New England Patriots in first round (22nd pick overall) of 1998 NFL draft. ... Signed by Patriots (July 18, 1998). ... On injured reserve with knee injury (December 31, 1999-remainder of season). ... Designated by Patriots as franchise player (February 20, 2003). ... Traded by Patriots to New Orleans Saints for third- (traded to Miami) and seventh-round picks (DE Tully Banta-Cain) in 2003 draft and fourth-round pick in 2004 draft (April 14, 2003).
CHAMPIONSHIP GAME EXPERIENCE: Played in AFC championship game (2001 season). ... Member of Super Bowl championship team (2001 season).

Year Team	G	GS	TOTALS			INTERCEPTIONS			
			Tk.	Ast.	Sks.	No.	Yds.	Avg.	TD
1998—New England NFL	16	0	10	3	0.0	0	0	0.0	0
1999—New England NFL	11	2	12	0	0.0	0	0	0.0	0
2000—New England NFL	15	9	42	13	0.0	2	20	10.0	0
2001—New England NFL	16	12	41	16	1.0	1	-4	-4.0	0
2002—New England NFL	14	12	38	12	1.5	1	0	0.0	0
Pro totals (5 years)	72	35	143	44	2.5	4	16	4.0	0

JONES, TERRY   TE   RAVENS

PERSONAL: Born December 3, 1979, in Tuscaloosa, Ala. ... 6-3/265. ... Full name: Terry Jones Jr..
HIGH SCHOOL: Central (Tuscaloosa, Ala.).
COLLEGE: Alabama.
TRANSACTIONS/CAREER NOTES: Selected by Baltimore Ravens in fifth round (155th pick overall) of 2002 NFL draft. ... Signed by Ravens (July 26, 2002).
SINGLE GAME HIGHS (regular season): Receptions—2 (December 15, 2002, vs. Houston); yards—35 (December 15, 2002, vs. Houston); and touchdown receptions—1 (December 8, 2002, vs. New Orleans).

Year Team	G	GS	RECEIVING			
			No.	Yds.	Avg.	TD
2002—Baltimore NFL	14	6	11	106	9.6	1

JONES, THOMAS   RB   CARDINALS

PERSONAL: Born August 19, 1978, in Big Stone Gap, Va. ... 5-10/220. ... Full name: Thomas Quinn Jones.
HIGH SCHOOL: Powell Valley (Big Stone Gap, Va.).
COLLEGE: Virginia (degree in psychology, 1999).
TRANSACTIONS/CAREER NOTES: Selected by Arizona Cardinals in first round (seventh pick overall) of 2000 NFL draft. ... Signed by Cardinals (July 21, 2000). ... On injured reserve with hand injury (November 26, 2002-remainder of season).
HONORS: Named running back on THE SPORTING NEWS college All-America first team (1999).
SINGLE GAME HIGHS (regular season): Attempts—24 (September 15, 2002, vs. Seattle); yards—173 (September 15, 2002, vs. Seattle); and rushing touchdowns—1 (October 27, 2002, vs. San Francisco).
STATISTICAL PLATEAUS: 100-yard rushing games: 2002 (1).

Year Team	G	GS	RUSHING				RECEIVING				TOTALS			
			Att.	Yds.	Avg.	TD	No.	Yds.	Avg.	TD	TD	2pt.	Pts.	Fum.
2000—Arizona NFL	14	4	112	373	3.3	2	32	208	6.5	0	2	0	12	4
2001—Arizona NFL	16	2	112	380	3.4	5	21	151	7.2	0	5	0	30	2
2002—Arizona NFL	9	9	138	511	3.7	2	20	113	5.7	0	2	0	12	3
Pro totals (3 years)	39	15	362	1264	3.5	9	73	472	6.5	0	9	0	54	9

JONES, WALTER   OT   SEAHAWKS

PERSONAL: Born January 19, 1974, in Aliceville, Ala. ... 6-5/308.
HIGH SCHOOL: Aliceville (Ala.).
JUNIOR COLLEGE: Holmes Junior College (Miss.).
COLLEGE: Florida State.
TRANSACTIONS/CAREER NOTES: Selected by Seattle Seahawks in first round (sixth pick overall) of 1997 NFL draft. ... Signed by Seahawks (August 6, 1997). ... Granted free agency (March 1, 2002). ... Re-signed by Seahawks (September 16, 2002). ... Designated by Seahawks as franchise player (February 20, 2003).
PLAYING EXPERIENCE: Seattle NFL, 1997-2002. ... Games/Games started: 1997 (12/12), 1998 (16/16), 1999 (16/16), 2000 (16/16), 2001 (16/16), 2002 (14/14). Total:90/90.
HONORS: Played in Pro Bowl (1999 and 2001 seasons). ... Named to play in Pro Bowl (2002 season); replaced by Chris Samuels due to injury.

JONES, WILLIE   OT   CHIEFS

PERSONAL: Born December 17, 1975, in Pahokee, Fla. ... 6-6/355.
HIGH SCHOOL: Glades (Belle Glade, Fla.).
COLLEGE: Grambling.
TRANSACTIONS/CAREER NOTES: Signed as non-drafted free agent by St. Louis Rams (April 30, 1999). ... On non-football injury list (November 24, 1999-remainder of season). ... Released by Rams (February 10, 2000). ... Signed by Miami Dolphins (March 23, 2000). ... Released by Dolphins (August 26, 2000). ... Signed by Kansas City Chiefs to practice squad (November 29, 2000). ... Granted free agency (March 1, 2002). ... Re-signed by Chiefs (April 8, 2002). ... On injured reserve with neck injury (November 20, 2002-remainder of season). ... Granted unconditional free agency (February 28, 2003). ... Re-signed by Chiefs (April 11, 2003).
PLAYING EXPERIENCE: Kansas City NFL, 2001-2002. ... Games/Games started: 2001 (12/0), 2002 (6/0).Total: 18/0.

JORDAN, JAMES   WR   49ERS

PERSONAL: Born June 11, 1978, in Los Angeles. ... 6-2/225. ... Full name: James Robert Jordan III.
HIGH SCHOOL: Bonnabel (New Orleans).
COLLEGE: Louisiana Tech.

TRANSACTIONS/CAREER NOTES: Signed as non-drafted free agent by San Francisco 49ers (April 27, 2001). ... Released by 49ers (August 28, 2001). ... Re-signed by 49ers (August 31, 2001). ... Released by 49ers (September 2, 2001). ... Re-signed by 49ers (January 23, 2002). ... Released by 49ers (September 1, 2002). ... Re-signed by 49ers to practice squad (September 2, 2002). ... Activated (October 14, 2002). ... Released by 49ers (November 12, 2002). ... Re-signed by 49ers to practice squad (November 13, 2002). ... Activated (November 25, 2002). ... Released by 49ers (December 3, 2002). ... Re-signed by 49ers to practice squad (December 4, 2002).

			RECEIVING			
Year Team	G	GS	No.	Yds.	Avg.	TD
2002—San Francisco NFL	6	0	0	0	0.0	0

JORDAN, LAMONT   RB   JETS

PERSONAL: Born November 11, 1978, in Forestville, Md. ... 5-10/230.
HIGH SCHOOL: Suitland (Forestville, Md.).
COLLEGE: Maryland.
TRANSACTIONS/CAREER NOTES: Selected by New York Jets in second round (49th pick overall) of 2001 NFL draft. ... Signed by Jets (July 25, 2001).
HONORS: Named running back on THE SPORTING NEWS college All-America third team (1999).
SINGLE GAME HIGHS (regular season): Attempts—13 (November 24, 2002, vs. Buffalo); yards—107 (November 3, 2002, vs. San Diego); and rushing touchdowns—1 (December 29, 2002, vs. Green Bay).
STATISTICAL PLATEAUS: 100-yard rushing games: 2002 (1).

			RUSHING				RECEIVING				KICKOFF RETURNS				TOTALS			
Year Team	G	GS	Att.	Yds.	Avg.	TD	No.	Yds.	Avg.	TD	No.	Yds.	Avg.	TD	TD	2pt.	Pts.	Fum.
2001—New York Jets NFL	16	0	39	292	7.5	1	7	44	6.3	1	3	62	20.7	0	2	0	12	0
2002—New York Jets NFL	14	0	84	316	3.8	3	17	160	9.4	0	5	112	22.4	0	3	0	18	4
Pro totals (2 years)	30	0	123	608	4.9	4	24	204	8.5	1	8	174	21.8	0	5	0	30	4

JORDAN, RANDY   RB

PERSONAL: Born June 6, 1970, in Manson, N.C. ... 5-11/220. ... Full name: Randy Loment Jordan.
HIGH SCHOOL: Warren County (Warrenton, N.C.).
COLLEGE: North Carolina.
TRANSACTIONS/CAREER NOTES: Signed as non-drafted free agent by Los Angeles Raiders (May 1993). ... Released by Raiders (August 25, 1993). ... Re-signed by Raiders to practice squad (August 31, 1993). ... Activated (October 30, 1993). ... Released by Raiders (August 28, 1994). ... Signed by Jacksonville Jaguars (December 15, 1994). ... Granted free agency (February 14, 1997). ... Re-signed by Jaguars (May 5, 1997). ... Released by Jaguars (August 19, 1997). ... Re-signed by Jaguars (September 24, 1997). ... Granted unconditional free agency (February 13, 1998). ... Signed by Oakland Raiders (June 2, 1998). ... Granted unconditional free agency (February 28, 2003).
CHAMPIONSHIP GAME EXPERIENCE: Played in AFC championship game (1996, 2000 and 2002 seasons). ... Played in Super Bowl XXXVII (2002 season).
SINGLE GAME HIGHS (regular season): Attempts—24 (December 20, 1998, vs. San Diego); yards—82 (December 20, 1998, vs. San Diego); and rushing touchdowns—2 (December 16, 2000, vs. Seattle).

			RUSHING				RECEIVING				KICKOFF RETURNS				TOTALS			
Year Team	G	GS	Att.	Yds.	Avg.	TD	No.	Yds.	Avg.	TD	No.	Yds.	Avg.	TD	TD	2pt.	Pts.	Fum.
1993—LA Raiders NFL	10	2	12	33	2.8	0	4	42	10.5	0	0	0	0.0	0	0	0	0	2
1994—Jacksonville NFL									Did not play.									
1995—Jacksonville NFL	12	3	21	62	3.0	0	5	89	17.8	1	2	41	20.5	0	1	0	6	0
1996—Jacksonville NFL	15	0	0	0	0.0	0	0	0	0.0	0	26	553	21.3	0	0	0	0	1
1997—Jacksonville NFL	7	0	1	2	2.0	0	0	0	0.0	0	0	0	0.0	0	0	0	0	0
1998—Oakland NFL	16	0	47	159	3.4	1	3	2	0.7	0	0	0	0.0	0	1	0	6	1
1999—Oakland NFL	16	0	9	32	3.6	2	8	82	10.3	0	10	207	20.7	0	2	0	12	2
2000—Oakland NFL	16	0	46	213	4.6	3	27	299	11.1	1	0	0	0.0	0	5	0	30	1
2001—Oakland NFL	16	0	13	59	4.5	0	9	63	7.0	0	0	0	0.0	0	0	0	0	0
2002—Oakland NFL	14	0	3	14	4.7	1	2	19	9.5	0	0	0	0.0	0	1	0	6	0
Pro totals (9 years)	122	5	152	574	3.8	7	58	596	10.3	2	38	801	21.1	0	10	0	60	7

JORDAN, RICHARD   LB

PERSONAL: Born December 1, 1974, in Holdenville, Okla. ... 6-1/260. ... Full name: Richard Lamont Jordan.
HIGH SCHOOL: Vian (Okla.).
COLLEGE: Missouri Southern.
TRANSACTIONS/CAREER NOTES: Selected by Detroit Lions in seventh round (239th pick overall) of 1997 NFL draft. ... Signed by Lions (May 22, 1997). ... Released by Lions (August 25, 1997). ... Re-signed by Lions to practice squad (August 27, 1997). ... Activated (September 27, 1997). ... On injured reserve with knee injury (November 17, 1999-remainder of season). ... Granted free agency (February 11, 2000). ... Re-signed by Lions (April 11, 2000). ... Released by Lions (August 27, 2000). ... Signed by Kansas City Chiefs (January 30, 2002). ... Released by Chiefs (September 1, 2002). ... Signed by Lions (October 2, 2002). ... On injured reserve with knee injury (October 22, 2002-remainder of season). ... Granted unconditional free agency (February 28, 2003).

			TOTALS			INTERCEPTIONS			
Year Team	G	GS	Tk.	Ast.	Sks.	No.	Yds.	Avg.	TD
1997—Detroit NFL	10	0	0	0	0.0	0	0	0.0	0
1998—Detroit NFL	16	3	25	14	0.0	1	4	4.0	0
1999—Detroit NFL	9	0	3	4	0.0	0	0	0.0	0
2002—Detroit NFL	1	0	1	0	0.0	0	0	0.0	0
Pro totals (4 years)	36	3	29	18	0.0	1	4	4.0	0

JOSEPH, ELVIS   RB   JAGUARS

PERSONAL: Born August 30, 1978, in St. Michaels, Barbados. ... 6-1/219.
HIGH SCHOOL: John Ehret (Marrara, La.).
COLLEGE: Southern.
TRANSACTIONS/CAREER NOTES: Signed as non-drafted free agent by Jacksonville Jaguars (April 23, 2001).
SINGLE GAME HIGHS (regular season): Attempts—12 (October 7, 2001, vs. Seattle); yards—86 (December 23, 2001, vs. Minnesota); and rushing touchdowns—0.

			RUSHING				RECEIVING				KICKOFF RETURNS				TOTALS		
Year Team	G	GS	Att.	Yds.	Avg.	TD	No.	Yds.	Avg.	TD	No.	Yds.	Avg.	TD	TD	2pt.	Pts. Fum.
2001—Jacksonville NFL	14	3	68	294	4.3	0	18	183	10.2	2	17	428	25.2	1	3	0	18	2
2002—Jacksonville NFL	15	0	0	0	0.0	0	0	0	0.0	0	27	562	20.8	0	0	0	0	0
Pro totals (2 years)	29	3	68	294	4.3	0	18	183	10.2	2	44	990	22.5	1	3	0	18	2

JOSEPH, RICOT   DB   REDSKINS

PERSONAL: Born March 13, 1980, in Haiti. ... 6-0/185.
HIGH SCHOOL: Lake Worth Community (Lake Worth, Fla.).
COLLEGE: Central Florida.
TRANSACTIONS/CAREER NOTES: Signed as non-drafted free agent by Washington Redskins (April 24, 2002). ... Released by Redskins (September 1, 2002). ... Re-signed by Redskins to practice squad (September 2, 2002). ... Activated (November 19, 2002).

			TOTALS			INTERCEPTIONS			
Year Team	G	GS	Tk.	Ast.	Sks.	No.	Yds.	Avg.	TD
2002—Washington NFL	6	0	0	0	0.0	0	0	0.0	0

JOYCE, DELVIN   RB   GIANTS

PERSONAL: Born September 21, 1978, in Martinsville, Va. ... 5-7/181.
HIGH SCHOOL: Fieldale-Collinsville (Va.).
COLLEGE: James Madison.
TRANSACTIONS/CAREER NOTES: Signed as non-drafted free agent by New York Giants (January 15, 2002).
SINGLE GAME HIGHS (regular season): Attempts—1 (October 28, 2002, vs. Philadelphia); yards—1 (October 28, 2002, vs. Philadelphia); and rushing touchdowns—0.

			RUSHING				RECEIVING				PUNT RETURNS				KICKOFF RETURNS				TOTALS		
Year Team	G	GS	Att.	Yds.	Avg.	TD	No.	Yds.	Avg.	TD	No.	Yds.	Avg.	TD	No.	Yds.	Avg.	TD	TD	2pt.	Pts. Fum.
2002—NYG NFL	12	0	2	2	1.0	0	1	5	5.0	0	25	210	8.4	0	33	776	23.5	0	0	0	0	3

JOYCE, ERIC   CB   BEARS

PERSONAL: Born January 21, 1978, in Nashville. ... 5-10/200. ... Full name: Eric Torezi Joyce.
HIGH SCHOOL: Whites Creek (Nashville).
COLLEGE: Tennessee State.
TRANSACTIONS/CAREER NOTES: Signed as non-drafted free agent by Arizona Cardinals (April 22, 2002). ... Released by Cardinals (August 27, 2002). ... Signed by Chicago Bears to practice squad (November 12, 2002). ... Released by Bears (December 3, 2002). ... Re-signed by Bears to practice squad (December 10, 2002). ... Activated (December 13, 2002).

			TOTALS			INTERCEPTIONS			
Year Team	G	GS	Tk.	Ast.	Sks.	No.	Yds.	Avg.	TD
2002—Chicago NFL	3	0	0	1	0.0	0	0	0.0	0

JOYCE, MATT   OT   LIONS

PERSONAL: Born March 30, 1972, in La Crosse, Wis. ... 6-7/300.
HIGH SCHOOL: New York Military Academy (Cornwall Hudson, N.Y.).
COLLEGE: Richmond (degree in health science, 1994).
TRANSACTIONS/CAREER NOTES: Signed as non-drafted free agent by Dallas Cowboys (May 2, 1994). ... Claimed on waivers by Cincinnati Bengals (August 28, 1994); released after failing physical. ... Signed by Cowboys to practice squad (September 5, 1994). ... Granted free agency after 1994 season. ... Signed by Seattle Seahawks (March 1, 1995). ... Released by Seahawks (August 25, 1996). ... Signed by Arizona Cardinals (December 3, 1996). ... Assigned by Cardinals to Scottish Claymores in 1997 World League enhancement allocation program (February 19, 1997). ... Granted free agency (February 12, 1999). ... Re-signed by Cardinals (April 1, 1999). ... Granted unconditional free agency (February 11, 2000). ... Re-signed by Cardinals (February 21, 2000). ... Released by Cardinals (March 16, 2001). ... Signed by Detriot Lions (April 26, 2001). ... On physically unable to perform list with shoulder injury (July 24-August 12, 2001). ... Granted unconditional free agency (March 1, 2002). ... Re-signed by Lions (March 14, 2002).
PLAYING EXPERIENCE: Seattle NFL, 1995; Scottish Claymores W.L., 1997; Arizona NFL, 1996-2000; Detroit NFL, 2001-2002. ... Games/Games started: 1995 (16/13), 1996 (2/0), W.L. 1997 (games played unavailable), NFL 1997 (9/6), 1998 (11/0), 1999 (15/15), 2000 (13/13), 2001 (16/12), 2002 (15/6). Total NFL: 86/65.

JUE, BHAWOH   CB/SS   PACKERS

PERSONAL: Born May 24, 1979, in Bhawoh Papi Je in Monrovia, Liberia. ... 6-0/200. ... Full name: Bhawoh Papi Jue.
HIGH SCHOOL: Chantilly (Va.).
COLLEGE: Penn State (degree in telecommunications).
TRANSACTIONS/CAREER NOTES: Selected by Green Bay Packers in third round (71st pick overall) of 2001 NFL draft. ... Signed by Packers (July 11, 2001). ... On injured reserve with hamstring injury (October 12, 2002-remainder of season).

J

Year Team	G	GS	TOTALS Tk.	Ast.	Sks.	INTERCEPTIONS No.	Yds.	Avg.	TD
2001—Green Bay NFL	15	7	31	12	0.0	2	35	17.5	0
2002—Green Bay NFL	4	0	0	0	0.0	0	0	0.0	0
Pro totals (2 years)	19	7	31	12	0.0	2	35	17.5	0

JULIEN, JARMAR   RB   CHIEFS

PERSONAL: Born December 11, 1979, in San Jose, Calif. ... 5-11/240. ... Full name: Jarmar Antwion Julien.
HIGH SCHOOL: Oak Grove (San Jose, Calif.).
COLLEGE: San Jose State.
TRANSACTIONS/CAREER NOTES: Signed as non-drafted free agent by Kansas City Chiefs (April 29, 2002). ... Released by Chiefs (August 27, 2002). ... Re-signed by Chiefs to practice squad (September 3, 2002). ... Activated (December 17, 2002).

Year Team	G	GS	RUSHING Att.	Yds.	Avg.	TD	TOTALS TD	2pt.	Pts.	Fum.
2002—Kansas City NFL	2	0	0	0	0.0	0	0	0	0	0

JUNKIN, TREY   TE

PERSONAL: Born January 23, 1961, in Conway, Ark. ... 6-2/247. ... Full name: Abner Kirk Junkin. ... Brother of Mike Junkin, linebacker with Cleveland Browns (1987 and 1988) and Kansas City Chiefs (1989).
HIGH SCHOOL: Northeast (North Little Rock, Ark.).
COLLEGE: Louisiana Tech.
TRANSACTIONS/CAREER NOTES: Selected by Buffalo Bills in fourth round (93rd pick overall) of 1983 NFL draft. ... Signed by Bills for 1983 season. ... Released by Bills (September 12, 1984). ... Signed by Washington Redskins (September 25, 1984). ... Rights relinquished by Redskins (February 1, 1985). ... Signed by Los Angeles Raiders (March 10, 1985). ... On injured reserve with knee injury (September 24, 1986-remainder of season). ... Released by Raiders (September 3, 1990). ... Signed by Seattle Seahawks (October 3, 1990). ... Granted unconditional free agency (February 1-April 1, 1991). ... Re-signed by Seahawks (July 9, 1991). ... Granted unconditional free agency (February 1-April 1, 1992). ... Re-signed by Seahawks for 1992 season. ... Granted unconditional free agency (March 1, 1993). ... Re-signed by Seahawks (March 11, 1993). ... Released by Seahawks (August 30, 1993). ... Re-signed by Seahawks (August 31, 1993). ... Granted unconditional free agency (February 17, 1994). ... Re-signed by Seahawks (May 31, 1994). ... Granted unconditional free agency (February 17, 1995). ... Re-signed by Seahawks (March 20, 1995). ... Granted unconditional free agency (February 16, 1996). ... Signed by Oakland Raiders (June 10, 1996). ... Claimed on waivers by Arizona Cardinals (October 14, 1996). ... Granted unconditional free agency (March 1, 2002). ... Signed by Dallas Cowboys (August 24, 2002). ... Released by Cowboys (September 1, 2002). ... Signed by New York Giants (December 31, 2002). ... Granted unconditional free agency (February 28, 2003).
SINGLE GAME HIGHS (regular season): Receptions—2 (November 22, 1992, vs. Kansas City); yards—38 (September 21, 1986, vs. New York Giants); and touchdown receptions—1 (September 25, 1994, vs. Pittsburgh).

Year Team	G	GS	RECEIVING No.	Yds.	Avg.	TD	TOTALS TD	2pt.	Pts.	Fum.
1983—Buffalo NFL	16	0	0	0	0.0	0	0	0	0	0
1984—Buffalo NFL	2	0	0	0	0.0	0	0	0	0	0
—Washington NFL	12	0	0	0	0.0	0	0	0	0	0
1985—Los Angeles Raiders NFL	16	0	2	8	4.0	1	1	0	6	0
1986—Los Angeles Raiders NFL	3	0	2	38	19.0	0	0	0	0	0
1987—Los Angeles Raiders NFL	12	1	2	15	7.5	0	0	0	0	0
1988—Los Angeles Raiders NFL	16	1	4	25	6.3	2	2	0	12	0
1989—Los Angeles Raiders NFL	16	0	3	32	10.7	2	2	0	12	0
1990—Seattle NFL	12	0	0	0	0.0	0	0	0	0	0
1991—Seattle NFL	16	0	0	0	0.0	0	0	0	0	0
1992—Seattle NFL	16	1	3	25	8.3	1	1	0	6	0
1993—Seattle NFL	16	1	0	0	0.0	0	0	0	0	0
1994—Seattle NFL	16	0	1	1	1.0	1	1	0	6	0
1995—Seattle NFL	16	0	0	0	0.0	0	0	0	0	0
1996—Oakland NFL	6	0	0	0	0.0	0	0	0	0	0
—Arizona NFL	10	0	0	0	0.0	0	0	0	0	0
1997—Arizona NFL	16	0	0	0	0.0	0	0	0	0	0
1998—Arizona NFL	16	0	0	0	0.0	0	0	0	0	0
1999—Arizona NFL	16	0	0	0	0.0	0	0	0	0	0
2000—Arizona NFL	16	0	0	0	0.0	0	0	0	0	0
2001—Arizona NFL	16	0	0	0	0.0	0	0	0	0	1
2002—					Did not play.					
Pro totals (19 years)	281	4	17	144	8.5	7	7	0	42	1

JUREVICIUS, JOE   WR   BUCCANEERS

PERSONAL: Born December 23, 1974, in Cleveland. ... 6-5/230. ... Full name: Joe Michael Jurevicius. ... Name pronounced jur-uh-VISH-us.
HIGH SCHOOL: Lake Catholic (Mentor, Ohio).
COLLEGE: Penn State.
TRANSACTIONS/CAREER NOTES: Selected by New York Giants in second round (55th pick overall) of 1998 NFL draft. ... Signed by Giants (July 28, 1998). ... Granted free agency (March 2, 2001). ... Re-signed by Giants for 2001 season. ... Granted unconditional free agency (March 1, 2002). ... Signed by Tampa Bay Buccaneers (April 9, 2002).
CHAMPIONSHIP GAME EXPERIENCE: Played in NFC championship game (2000 and 2002 seasons). ... Played in Super Bowl XXXV (2000 season). ... Member of Super Bowl championship team (2002 season).
SINGLE GAME HIGHS (regular season): Receptions—8 (December 8, 2002, vs. Atlanta); yards—100 (December 8, 2002, vs. Atlanta); and touchdown receptions—2 (December 8, 2002, vs. Atlanta).
STATISTICAL PLATEAUS: 100-yard receiving games: 2002 (1).

J

Year Team	G	GS	RECEIVING				TOTALS			
			No.	Yds.	Avg.	TD	TD	2pt.	Pts.	Fum.
1998—New York Giants NFL	14	1	9	146	16.2	0	0	0	0	0
1999—New York Giants NFL	16	1	18	318	17.7	1	1	0	6	1
2000—New York Giants NFL	14	3	24	272	11.3	1	1	0	6	1
2001—New York Giants NFL	14	9	51	706	13.8	3	3	0	18	0
2002—Tampa Bay NFL	15	3	37	423	11.4	4	4	0	24	1
Pro totals (5 years)	73	17	139	1865	13.4	9	9	0	54	3

KACYVENSKI, ISAIAH   LB   SEAHAWKS

PERSONAL: Born October 3, 1977, in Syracuse, N.Y. ... 6-1/252. ... Name pronounced kaz-uh-VEN-skee.
HIGH SCHOOL: Union Endicott (N.Y.).
COLLEGE: Harvard (degree in pre-med).
TRANSACTIONS/CAREER NOTES: Selected by Seattle Seahawks in fourth round (119th pick overall) of 2000 NFL draft. ... Signed by Seahawks (June 9, 2000). ... On injured reserve with ankle injury (December 4, 2002-remainder of season). ... Granted free agency (February 28, 2003). ... Re-signed by Seahawks (March 28, 2003).

Year Team	G	GS	TOTALS			INTERCEPTIONS			
			Tk.	Ast.	Sks.	No.	Yds.	Avg.	TD
2000—Seattle NFL	16	0	10	3	0.0	1	0	0.0	0
2001—Seattle NFL	16	0	9	2	0.0	1	22	22.0	0
2002—Seattle NFL	9	9	52	20	0.0	1	27	27.0	0
Pro totals (3 years)	41	9	71	25	0.0	3	49	16.3	0

KAESVIHARN, KEVIN   CB   BENGALS

PERSONAL: Born August 29, 1976, in Paramount, Calif. ... 6-1/190. ... Full name: Kevin Robert Kaesviharn.
HIGH SCHOOL: Lakeville (Minn.).
COLLEGE: Augustana (S.D.).
TRANSACTIONS/CAREER NOTES: Signed as non-drafted free agent by Green Bay Packers (April 25, 2001). ... Released by Packers (August 27, 2001). ... Signed by Cincinnati Bengals to practice squad (October 23, 2001). ... Activated (October 27, 2001). ... Released by Bengals (October 30, 2001). ... Re-signed by Bengals to practice squad (October 31, 2001). ... Activated (November 10, 2001).

Year Team	G	GS	TOTALS			INTERCEPTIONS			
			Tk.	Ast.	Sks.	No.	Yds.	Avg.	TD
2001—Cincinnati NFL	10	3	22	3	0.0	3	41	13.7	0
2002—Cincinnati NFL	16	6	43	7	0.0	2	17	8.5	0
Pro totals (2 years)	26	9	65	10	0.0	5	58	11.6	0

KALU, NDUKWE   DE   EAGLES

PERSONAL: Born August 3, 1975, in Baltimore. ... 6-3/265. ... Full name: Ndukwe Dike Kalu. ... Name pronounced EN-doo-kway ka-LOO.
HIGH SCHOOL: John Marshall (San Antonio).
COLLEGE: Rice.
TRANSACTIONS/CAREER NOTES: Selected by Philadelphia Eagles in fifth round (152nd pick overall) of 1997 NFL draft. ... Signed by Eagles (July 15, 1997). ... Released by Eagles (August 25, 1998). ... Signed by Washington Redskins (August 30, 1998). ... Granted free agency (February 11, 2000). ... Re-signed by Redskins (May 18, 2000). ... Granted unconditional free agency (March 2, 2001). ... Signed by Eagles (March 12, 2001).
CHAMPIONSHIP GAME EXPERIENCE: Played in NFC championship game (2001 and 2002 seasons).

Year Team	G	GS	TOTALS		
			Tk.	Ast.	Sks.
1997—Philadelphia NFL	3	0	0	1	0.0
1998—Washington NFL	13	1	7	7	3.0
1999—Washington NFL	12	0	11	3	3.5
2000—Washington NFL	15	0	4	3	1.0
2001—Philadelphia NFL	14	1	12	1	3.0
2002—Philadelphia NFL	16	0	18	5	8.0
Pro totals (6 years)	73	2	52	20	18.5

KAMPMAN, AARON   DT/DE   PACKERS

PERSONAL: Born November 30, 1979, in Kelsey, Iowa. ... 6-4/286.
HIGH SCHOOL: Aplington-Parkersburg (Parkersburg, Iowa).
COLLEGE: Iowa.
TRANSACTIONS/CAREER NOTES: Selected by Green Bay Packers in fifth round (156th pick overall) of 2002 NFL draft. ... Signed by Packers (July 25, 2002).

Year Team	G	GS	TOTALS			INTERCEPTIONS			
			Tk.	Ast.	Sks.	No.	Yds.	Avg.	TD
2002—Green Bay NFL	12	6	11	12	0.5	0	0	0.0	0

KASAY, JOHN   K   PANTHERS

PERSONAL: Born October 27, 1969, in Athens, Ga. ... 5-10/198. ... Full name: John David Kasay. ... Name pronounced CASEY.
HIGH SCHOOL: Clarke Central (Athens, Ga.).

COLLEGE: Georgia (degree in journalism, 1994).
TRANSACTIONS/CAREER NOTES: Selected by Seattle Seahawks in fourth round (98th pick overall) of 1991 NFL draft. ... Signed by Seahawks (July 19, 1991). ... Granted free agency (February 17, 1994). ... Re-signed by Seahawks (July 19, 1994). ... Granted unconditional free agency (February 17, 1995). ... Signed by Carolina Panthers (February 20, 1995). ... On injured reserve with knee injury (December 14, 1999-remainder of season). ... On injured reserve with knee injury (August 14, 2000-entire season). ... On injured reserve with hernia (September 21, 2002-remainder of season).
CHAMPIONSHIP GAME EXPERIENCE: Played in NFC championship game (1996 season).
HONORS: Played in Pro Bowl (1996 season).

			FIELD GOALS							TOTALS		
Year Team	G	1-29	30-39	40-49	50+	Tot.	Pct.	Lg.		XPM	XPA	Pts.
1991—Seattle NFL	16	6-7	11-14	6-7	2-3	25-31	80.6	54		27	28	102
1992—Seattle NFL	16	4-5	8-11	2-6	0-0	14-22	63.6	43		14	14	56
1993—Seattle NFL	16	6-6	10-11	4-6	3-5	23-28	82.1	55		29	29	98
1994—Seattle NFL	16	2-2	11-11	6-9	1-2	20-24	83.3	50		25	26	85
1995—Carolina NFL	16	6-6	10-14	9-12	1-1	26-33	78.8	52		27	28	105
1996—Carolina NFL	16	16-16	11-12	7-10	3-7	*37-*45	82.2	53		34	35	*145
1997—Carolina NFL	16	7-8	8-8	4-4	3-6	22-26	84.6	54		25 ·	25	91
1998—Carolina NFL	16	5-5	4-5	6-9	4-7	19-26	73.1	56		35	37	92
1999—Carolina NFL	13	9-9	6-6	5-6	2-4	22-25	88.0	52		33	33	99
2000—Carolina NFL					Did not play.							
2001—Carolina NFL	16	10-10	4-4	7-9	2-5	23-28	82.1	52		22	23	91
2002—Carolina NFL	2	2-2	0-0	0-2	0-1	2-5	40.0	27		5	5	11
Pro totals (11 years)	159	73-76	83-96	56-80	21-41	233-293	79.5	56		276	283	975

KASPER, KEVIN — WR — CARDINALS

K

PERSONAL: Born December 23, 1977, in Hinsdale, Ill. ... 6-0/193.
HIGH SCHOOL: Hinsdale South (Burr Ridge, Ill.).
COLLEGE: Iowa.
TRANSACTIONS/CAREER NOTES: Selected by Denver Broncos in sixth round (190th pick overall) of 2001 NFL draft. ... Signed by Broncos (May 17, 2001). ... Claimed on waivers by Seattle Seahawks (October 30, 2002). ... Claimed on waivers by Arizona Cardinals (November 23, 2002).
SINGLE GAME HIGHS (regular season): Receptions—4 (December 29, 2002, vs. Denver); yards—54 (December 15, 2002, vs. St. Louis); and touchdown receptions—2 (December 21, 2002, vs. San Francisco).

			RUSHING				RECEIVING				KICKOFF RETURNS				TOTALS			
Year Team	G	GS	Att.	Yds.	Avg.	TD	No.	Yds.	Avg.	TD	No.	Yds.	Avg.	TD	TD	2pt.	Pts.	Fum.
2001—Denver NFL	10	5	3	19	6.3	0	8	84	10.5	0	14	372	26.6	0	0	0	0	0
2002—Denver NFL	4	0	0	0	0.0	0	0	0	0.0	0	15	393	26.2	0	0	0	0	1
—Arizona NFL	6	4	3	19	6.3	0	15	180	12.0	3	32	722	22.6	0	3	0	18	0
—Seattle NFL	3	0	0	0	0.0	0	0	0	0.0	0	8	185	23.1	0	0	0	0	0
Pro totals (2 years)	23	9	6	38	6.3	0	23	264	11.5	3	69	1672	24.2	0	3	0	18	1

KASSELL, BRAD — LB — TITANS

PERSONAL: Born January 7, 1980, in Llano, Texas. ... 6-3/236.
HIGH SCHOOL: Llano (Texas).
COLLEGE: North Texas.
TRANSACTIONS/CAREER NOTES: Signed as non-drafted free agent by Tennessee Titans (April 22, 2002). ... Released by Titans (September 1, 2002). ... Re-signed by Titans to practice squad (September 3, 2002). ... Activated (November 1, 2002).
CHAMPIONSHIP GAME EXPERIENCE: Played in AFC championship game (2002 season).

			TOTALS			INTERCEPTIONS			
Year Team	G	GS	Tk.	Ast.	Sks.	No.	Yds.	Avg.	TD
2002—Tennessee NFL	9	0	0	0	0.0	0	0	0.0	0

KEARSE, JEVON — DE — TITANS

PERSONAL: Born September 3, 1976, in Fort Myers, Fla. ... 6-4/265. ... Name pronounced juh-VAUGHN CURSE.
HIGH SCHOOL: North Fort Myers (Fla.).
COLLEGE: Florida.
TRANSACTIONS/CAREER NOTES: Selected after junior season by Tennessee Titans in first round (16th pick overall) of 1999 NFL draft. ... Signed by Titans (July 27, 1999).
CHAMPIONSHIP GAME EXPERIENCE: Played in AFC championship game (1999 and 2002 seasons). ... Played in Super Bowl XXXIV (1999 season).
HONORS: Named outside linebacker on THE SPORTING NEWS college All-America second team (1998). ... Named defensive end on THE SPORTING NEWS NFL All-Pro team (1999). ... Played in Pro Bowl (1999-2001 seasons).
RECORDS: Holds NFL rookie-season record for most sacks—14.5 (1999).

			TOTALS		
Year Team	G	GS	Tk.	Ast.	Sks.
1999—Tennessee NFL	16	16	48	9	§14.5
2000—Tennessee NFL	16	16	37	16	11.5
2001—Tennessee NFL	16	16	25	11	10.0
2002—Tennessee NFL	4	1	3	1	2.0
Pro totals (4 years)	52	49	113	37	38.0

KEATHLEY, MICHAEL   G   CHARGERS

PERSONAL: Born March 9, 1978, in Glen Rose, Texas. ... 6-4/296.
HIGH SCHOOL: Glen Rose (Texas).
COLLEGE: Texas Christian.
TRANSACTIONS/CAREER NOTES: Signed as non-drafted free agent by San Diego Chargers (April 27, 2001). ... Re-signed by Chargers (April 16, 2003).
PLAYING EXPERIENCE: San Diego NFL, 2001-2002. ... Games/Games started: 2001 (16/0), 2002 (12/2). Totals: 28/2.

KEATON, CURTIS   RB/KR   SAINTS

PERSONAL: Born October 18, 1976, in Columbus, Ohio. ... 5-10/222. ... Full name: Curtis Isaiah Keaton.
HIGH SCHOOL: Beechcroft (Columbus, Ohio).
COLLEGE: West Virginia, then James Madison.
TRANSACTIONS/CAREER NOTES: Selected by Cincinnati Bengals in fourth round (97th pick overall) of 2000 NFL draft. ... Signed by Bengals (June 23, 2000). ... Traded by Bengals to New Orleans Saints for undisclosed pick in 2003 draft (September 1, 2002). ... Granted free agency (February 28, 2003). ... Re-signed by Saints (April 16, 2003).
SINGLE GAME HIGHS (regular season): Attempts—10 (November 24, 2002, vs. Cleveland); yards—44 (September 30, 2001, vs. San Diego); and rushing touchdowns—0.

				KICKOFF RETURNS				TOTALS		
Year Team	G	GS	No.	Yds.	Avg.	TD	TD	2pt.	Pts.	Fum.
2000—Cincinnati NFL	6	0	6	100	16.7	0	0	0	0	0
2001—Cincinnati NFL	13	0	42	891	21.2	0	0	0	0	0
2002—New Orleans NFL	6	0	0	0	0.0	0	0	0	0	1
Pro totals (3 years)	25	0	48	991	20.6	0	0	0	0	1

KEISEL, BRETT   DE   STEELERS

PERSONAL: Born September 19, 1978, in Provo, Utah. ... 6-5/269.
HIGH SCHOOL: Greybull (Wyo.).
JUNIOR COLLEGE: Snow College (Utah).
COLLEGE: Brigham Young.
TRANSACTIONS/CAREER NOTES: Selected by Pittsburgh Steelers in seventh round (242nd pick overall) of 2002 NFL draft. ... Signed by Steelers (July 17, 2002).

			TOTALS		
Year Team	G	GS	Tk.	Ast.	Sks.
2002—Pittsburgh NFL	5	0	0	0	0.0

KEITH, JOHN   S   49ERS

PERSONAL: Born February 4, 1977, in Newman, Ga. ... 6-0/207. ... Full name: John Martin Keith.
HIGH SCHOOL: East Coweta (Ga.).
COLLEGE: Furman.
TRANSACTIONS/CAREER NOTES: Selected by San Francisco 49ers in fourth round (108th pick overall) of 2000 NFL draft. ... Signed by 49ers (July 16, 2000). ... On injured reserve with broken arm (October 10, 2000-remainder of season). ... On injured reserve with knee injury (September 12, 2001-remainder of season). ... On physically unable to perform list with knee injury (July 22-23, 2002). ... Released by 49ers (August 27, 2002). ... Re-signed by 49ers to practice squad (September 2, 2002). ... Activated (November 6, 2002). ... Granted free agency (February 28, 2003). ... Re-signed by 49ers (March 28, 2003).

			TOTALS			INTERCEPTIONS			
Year Team	G	GS	Tk.	Ast.	Sks.	No.	Yds.	Avg.	TD
2000—San Francisco NFL	6	3	13	5	1.0	1	0	0.0	0
2001—San Francisco NFL	1	0	0	0	0.0	0	0	0.0	0
2002—San Francisco NFL	8	3	11	5	0.0	0	0	0.0	0
Pro totals (3 years)	15	6	24	10	1.0	1	0	0.0	0

KELLY, BEN   CB   PATRIOTS

PERSONAL: Born September 15, 1978, in Cleveland. ... 5-9/185. ... Full name: Ben O. Kelly.
HIGH SCHOOL: Mentor Lake (Cleveland).
COLLEGE: Colorado.
TRANSACTIONS/CAREER NOTES: Selected after junior season by Miami Dolphins in third round (84th pick overall) of 2000 NFL draft. ... Signed by Dolphins (July 24, 2000). ... On injured reserve with knee injury (September 26, 2000-remainder of season). ... Claimed on waivers by New England Patriots (November 2, 2001). ... On injured reserve with ankle injury (November 14, 2002-remainder of season). ... Granted free agency (February 28, 2003). ... Re-signed by Patriots (March 4, 2003).

			TOTALS			INTERCEPTIONS			
Year Team	G	GS	Tk.	Ast.	Sks.	No.	Yds.	Avg.	TD
2000—Miami NFL	2	0	0	0	0.0	0	0	0.0	0
2001—Miami NFL	2	0	0	1	0.0	0	0	0.0	0
—New England NFL	2	0	0	0	0.0	0	0	0.0	0
2002—New England NFL	7	0	3	1	0.0	0	0	0.0	0
Pro totals (3 years)	13	0	3	2	0.0	0	0	0.0	0

KELLY, BRIAN — CB — BUCCANEERS

PERSONAL: Born January 14, 1976, in Las Vegas, Nev. ... 5-11/193.
HIGH SCHOOL: Overland (Aurora, Colo.).
COLLEGE: Southern California.
TRANSACTIONS/CAREER NOTES: Selected by Tampa Bay Buccaneers in second round (45th pick overall) of 1998 NFL draft. ... Signed by Buccaneers (July 19, 1998). ... Granted free agency (March 2, 2001). ... Re-signed by Buccaneers (March 18, 2001). ... Granted unconditional free agency (March 1, 2002). ... Re-signed by Buccaneers (March 19, 2002).
CHAMPIONSHIP GAME EXPERIENCE: Played in NFC championship game (1999 and 2002 seasons). ... Member of Super Bowl championship team (2002 season).

			TOTALS			INTERCEPTIONS			
Year Team	G	GS	Tk.	Ast.	Sks.	No.	Yds.	Avg.	TD
1998—Tampa Bay NFL	16	3	25	2	0.0	1	4	4.0	0
1999—Tampa Bay NFL	16	3	29	5	0.0	1	26	26.0	0
2000—Tampa Bay NFL	16	3	44	4	0.0	1	9	9.0	1
2001—Tampa Bay NFL	16	11	40	10	1.5	0	0	0.0	0
2002—Tampa Bay NFL	16	16	58	8	1.0	†8	68	8.5	0
Pro totals (5 years)	80	36	196	29	2.5	11	107	9.7	1

KELLY, ERIC — CB — VIKINGS

PERSONAL: Born January 15, 1977, in Milwaukee. ... 5-10/197.
HIGH SCHOOL: Bay (Panama, Fla.).
COLLEGE: Kentucky.
TRANSACTIONS/CAREER NOTES: Selected by Minnesota Vikings in third round (64th pick overall) of 2001 NFL draft. ... Signed by Vikings (July 26, 2001).

			TOTALS			INTERCEPTIONS			
Year Team	G	GS	Tk.	Ast.	Sks.	No.	Yds.	Avg.	TD
2001—Minnesota NFL	16	11	59	15	0.0	2	-7	-3.5	0
2002—Minnesota NFL	16	12	59	5	0.0	1	0	0.0	0
Pro totals (2 years)	32	23	118	20	0.0	3	-7	-2.3	0

KELLY, JEFF — QB — SEAHAWKS

PERSONAL: Born September 7, 1979, in Deerpark, Ala. ... 6-1/212.
HIGH SCHOOL: Citronelle (Deerpark, Ark.).
COLLEGE: Southern Mississippi.
TRANSACTIONS/CAREER NOTES: Selected by Seattle Seahawks in seventh round (232nd pick overall) of 2002 NFL draft. ... Signed by Seahawks (July 8, 2002). ... Released by Seahawks (September 1, 2002). ... Re-signed by Seahawks to practice squad (September 2, 2002). ... Activated (September 24, 2002).

			PASSING								RUSHING				TOTALS		
Year Team	G	GS	Att.	Cmp.	Pct.	Yds.	TD	Int.	Avg.	Skd.	Rat.	Att.	Yds.	Avg.	TD	TD	2pt.	Pts.
2002—Seattle NFL	1	0	0	0	0.0	0	0	0	0.0	0	...	0	0	0.0	0	0	0	0

KELLY, JEFF — LB

PERSONAL: Born December 13, 1975, in La Grange, Texas. ... 5-11/242.
HIGH SCHOOL: La Grange (Texas).
JUNIOR COLLEGE: Garden City (Kan.) Community College.
COLLEGE: Stephen F. Austin State, then Kansas State.
TRANSACTIONS/CAREER NOTES: Selected by Atlanta Falcons in sixth round (198th pick overall) of 1999 NFL draft. ... Signed by Falcons (June 28, 1999). ... On injured reserve with knee injury (September 2, 2001-entire season). ... Granted free agency (March 1, 2002). ... Re-signed by Falcons ... Released by Falcons (September 14, 2002).
HONORS: Named inside linebacker on THE SPORTING NEWS college All-America second team (1998).

			TOTALS			INTERCEPTIONS			
Year Team	G	GS	Tk.	Ast.	Sks.	No.	Yds.	Avg.	TD
1999—Atlanta NFL	16	1	13	3	0.0	0	0	0.0	0
2000—Atlanta NFL	12	6	18	7	0.0	0	0	0.0	0
2002—Atlanta NFL	1	0	0	0	0.0	0	0	0.0	0
Pro totals (3 years)	29	7	31	10	0.0	0	0	0.0	0

KELLY, LEWIS — G — VIKINGS

PERSONAL: Born April 21, 1977, in Lithonia, Ga. ... 6-4/306.
HIGH SCHOOL: Henderson (Lithonia, Ga.).
COLLEGE: South Carolina State.
TRANSACTIONS/CAREER NOTES: Selected by Minnesota Vikings in seventh round (248th pick overall) of 2000 NFL draft. ... Signed by Vikings (April 27, 2000). ... On injured reserve with knee injury (August 22, 2000-entire season). ... On injured reserve with abdominal injury (December 16, 2002-remainder of season).
PLAYING EXPERIENCE: Minnesota NFL, 2001-2002. ... Games/Games started: 2001 (4/0), 2002 (7/5). Total: 11/5.

KELLY, REGGIE TE BENGALS

PERSONAL: Born February 22, 1977, in Aberdeen, Miss. ... 6-3/255. ... Full name: Reginald Kuta Kelly.
HIGH SCHOOL: Aberdeen (Miss.).
COLLEGE: Mississippi State.
TRANSACTIONS/CAREER NOTES: Selected by Atlanta Falcons in second round (42nd pick overall) of 1999 NFL draft. ... Signed by Falcons (June 25, 1999). ... Granted unconditional free agency (February 28, 2003). ... Signed by Cincinnati Bengals (March 13, 2003).
SINGLE GAME HIGHS (regular season): Receptions—4 (December 24, 2000, vs. Kansas City); yards—83 (September 24, 2000, vs. St. Louis); and touchdown receptions—1 (December 3, 2000, vs. Seattle).

			RECEIVING			
Year Team	G	GS	No.	Yds.	Avg.	TD
1999—Atlanta NFL	16	2	8	146	18.3	0
2000—Atlanta NFL	16	16	31	340	11.0	2
2001—Atlanta NFL	14	13	16	142	8.9	0
2002—Atlanta NFL	16	16	14	162	11.6	0
Pro totals (4 years)	62	47	69	790	11.4	2

KEMOEATU, MAAKE DT RAVENS

PERSONAL: Born January 10, 1979, in Tonga. ... 6-5/330. ... Full name: Maake Tu'Amelie Kemoeatu.
HIGH SCHOOL: Kahuku (Hawaii).
COLLEGE: Utah.
TRANSACTIONS/CAREER NOTES: Signed as non-drafted free agent by Baltimore Ravens (April 26, 2002).

			TOTALS		
Year Team	G	GS	Tk.	Ast.	Sks.
2002—Baltimore NFL	16	1	11	4	2.0

KENDALL, PETE G CARDINALS

PERSONAL: Born July 9, 1973, in Quincy, Mass. ... 6-5/288. ... Full name: Peter Marcus Kendall.
HIGH SCHOOL: Archbishop Williams (Weymouth, Mass.).
COLLEGE: Boston College (degree in marketing, 1995).
TRANSACTIONS/CAREER NOTES: Selected by Seattle Seahawks in first round (21st pick overall) of 1996 NFL draft. ... Signed by Seahawks (July 21, 1996). ... Granted unconditional free agency (March 2, 2001). ... Signed by Arizona Cardinals (March 12, 2001). ... On injured reserve with foot injury (December 26, 2001-remainder of season). ... On injured reserve with ankle injury (December 27, 2002-remainder of season).
PLAYING EXPERIENCE: Seattle NFL, 1996-2000; Seattle NFL, 2001-2002. ... Games/Games started: 1996 (12/11), 1997 (16/16), 1998 (16/16), 1999 (16/16), 2000 (16/16), 2001 (11/11), 2002 (12/12). Total: 99/98.

KENNEDY, KENOY S BRONCOS

PERSONAL: Born November 15, 1977, in Dallas. ... 6-1/215. ... Full name: Kenoy Wayne Kennedy.
HIGH SCHOOL: Terrell (Texas).
COLLEGE: Arkansas.
TRANSACTIONS/CAREER NOTES: Selected by Denver Broncos in second round (45th pick overall) of 2000 NFL draft. ... Signed by Broncos (June 1, 2000).

			TOTALS			INTERCEPTIONS			
Year Team	G	GS	Tk.	Ast.	Sks.	No.	Yds.	Avg.	TD
2000—Denver NFL	13	0	5	2	0.0	1	0	0.0	0
2001—Denver NFL	16	16	50	19	2.0	1	6	6.0	0
2002—Denver NFL	15	15	53	14	0.0	0	0	0.0	0
Pro totals (3 years)	44	31	108	35	2.0	2	6	3.0	0

KENNEDY, LINCOLN OT RAIDERS

PERSONAL: Born February 12, 1971, in York, Pa. ... 6-6/335. ... Full name: Tamerlane Lincoln Kennedy.
HIGH SCHOOL: Samuel F.B. Morse (San Diego).
COLLEGE: Washington (degree in speech and drama, 1993).
TRANSACTIONS/CAREER NOTES: Selected by Atlanta Falcons in first round (ninth pick overall) of 1993 NFL draft. ... Signed by Falcons (August 2, 1993). ... Granted free agency (February 16, 1996). ... Re-signed by Falcons (May 13, 1996). ... Traded by Falcons to Oakland Raiders for fifth-round pick (traded to Washington) in 1997 draft (May 13, 1996).
PLAYING EXPERIENCE: Atlanta NFL, 1993-1995; Oakland NFL, 1996-2002. ... Games/Games started: 1993 (16/16), 1994 (16/2), 1995 (16/4), 1996 (16/16), 1997 (16/16), 1998 (16/16), 1999 (15/15), 2000 (16/16), 2001 (15/15), 2002 (15/15). Total: 157/131.
CHAMPIONSHIP GAME EXPERIENCE: Played in AFC championship game (2000 and 2002 seasons). ... Played in Super Bowl XXXVII (2002 season).
HONORS: Named offensive tackle on THE SPORTING NEWS college All-America first team (1992). ... Played in Pro Bowl (2000-2002 seasons).

KENNISON, EDDIE WR CHIEFS

PERSONAL: Born January 20, 1973, in Lake Charles, La. ... 6-1/201. ... Full name: Eddie Joseph Kennison III.
HIGH SCHOOL: Washington-Marion (Lake Charles, La.).
COLLEGE: Louisiana State.

TRANSACTIONS/CAREER NOTES: Selected after junior season by St. Louis Rams in first round (18th pick overall) of 1996 NFL draft. ... Signed by Rams (July 27, 1996). ... Traded by Rams to New Orleans Saints for second-round pick (DB Dre' Bly) in 1999 draft (February 18, 1999). ... Traded by Saints to Chicago Bears for fifth-round pick (traded to Indianapolis) in 2000 draft (February 21, 2000). ... Granted unconditional free agency (March 2, 2001). ... Signed by Denver Broncos (April 5, 2001). ... Released by Broncos (November 14, 2001). ... Signed by Kansas City Chiefs (December 3, 2001).

SINGLE GAME HIGHS (regular season): Receptions—8 (November 10, 2002, vs. San Francisco); yards—226 (December 15, 1996, vs. Atlanta); and touchdown receptions—3 (December 15, 1996, vs. Atlanta).

STATISTICAL PLATEAUS: 100-yard receiving games: 1996 (2), 1999 (1), 2000 (1), 2001 (1), 2002 (2). Total: 7.

			RUSHING				RECEIVING				PUNT RETURNS				KICKOFF RETURNS				TOTALS		
Year Team	G	GS	Att.	Yds.	Avg.	TD	No.	Yds.	Avg.	TD	No.	Yds.	Avg.	TD	No.	Yds.	Avg.	TD	TD	2pt.	Pts.
1996—St. Louis NFL	15	14	0	0	0.0	0	54	924	17.1	9	29	423	14.6	2	23	454	19.7	0	11	0	66
1997—St. Louis NFL	14	9	3	13	4.3	0	25	404	16.2	0	34	247	7.3	0	1	14	14.0	0	0	0	0
1998—St. Louis NFL	16	13	2	9	4.5	0	17	234	13.8	1	40	415	10.4	1	0	0	0.0	0	2	0	12
1999—New Orleans NFL	16	16	3	20	6.7	0	61	835	13.7	4	35	258	7.4	0	0	0	0.0	0	4	†1	26
2000—Chicago NFL	16	10	3	72	24.0	0	55	549	10.0	2	0	0	0.0	0	0	0	0.0	0	2	0	12
2001—Denver NFL	8	6	3	9	3.0	0	15	169	11.3	1	0	0	0.0	0	0	0	0.0	0	1	0	6
—Kansas City NFL	5	1	2	13	6.5	0	16	322	20.1	0	0	0	0.0	0	0	0	0.0	0	0	1	2
2002—Kansas City NFL	16	14	7	58	8.3	0	53	906	17.1	2	0	0	0.0	0	0	0	0.0	0	2	0	12
Pro totals (7 years)	106	83	23	194	8.4	0	296	4343	14.7	19	138	1343	9.7	3	24	468	19.5	0	22	2	136

KERNEY, PATRICK   DE   FALCONS

K

PERSONAL: Born December 30, 1976, in Trenton, N.J. ... 6-5/273. ... Full name: Patrick Manning Kerney.

HIGH SCHOOL: Taft Prep (Watertown, Conn.).

COLLEGE: Virginia.

TRANSACTIONS/CAREER NOTES: Selected by Atlanta Falcons in first round (30th pick overall) of 1999 NFL draft. ... Signed by Falcons (June 25, 1999).

HONORS: Named defensive end on THE SPORTING NEWS college All-America second team (1998).

			TOTALS			INTERCEPTIONS			
Year Team	G	GS	Tk.	Ast.	Sks.	No.	Yds.	Avg.	TD
1999—Atlanta NFL	16	2	19	6	2.5	0	0	0.0	0
2000—Atlanta NFL	16	16	30	15	2.5	1	8	8.0	0
2001—Atlanta NFL	16	16	39	10	12.0	0	0	0.0	0
2002—Atlanta NFL	16	16	45	13	10.5	0	0	0.0	0
Pro totals (4 years)	64	50	133	44	27.5	1	8	8.0	0

KILLENS, TERRY   LB

PERSONAL: Born March 24, 1974, in Cincinnati. ... 6-1/235. ... Full name: Terry Deleon Killens.

HIGH SCHOOL: Purcell (Cincinnati).

COLLEGE: Penn State.

TRANSACTIONS/CAREER NOTES: Selected by Houston Oilers in third round (74th pick overall) of 1996 NFL draft. ... Signed by Oilers (July 20, 1996). ... Oilers franchise moved to Tennessee for 1997 season. ... Oilers franchise renamed Tennessee Titans for 1999 season (December 26, 1998). ... Granted free agency (February 12, 1999). ... Re-signed by Titans (June 2, 1999). ... Granted unconditional free agency (February 11, 2000). ... Re-signed by Titans (May 26, 2000). ... Released by Titans (March 1, 2001). ... Signed by San Francisco 49ers (August 2, 2001). ... Granted unconditional free agency (March 1, 2002). ... Signed by Denver Broncos (March 22, 2002). ... Released by Broncos (September 1, 2002). ... Signed by Seattle Seahawks (November 12, 2002). ... Released by Seahawks (December 9, 2002). ... Signed by San Francisco 49ers (January 8, 2003). ... Granted unconditional free agency (February 28, 2003).

CHAMPIONSHIP GAME EXPERIENCE: Played in AFC championship game (1999 season). ... Played in Super Bowl XXXIV (1999 season).

			TOTALS			INTERCEPTIONS			
Year Team	G	GS	Tk.	Ast.	Sks.	No.	Yds.	Avg.	TD
1996—Houston NFL	14	0	0	0	0.0	0	0	0.0	0
1997—Tennessee NFL	16	0	1	0	0.0	0	0	0.0	0
1998—Tennessee NFL	16	1	5	0	0.0	0	0	0.0	0
1999—Tennessee NFL	16	1	14	4	0.0	0	0	0.0	0
2000—Tennessee NFL	16	0	2	0	1.0	0	0	0.0	0
2001—San Francisco NFL	16	2	6	3	0.0	0	0	0.0	0
2002—Seattle NFL	3	0	0	0	0.0	0	0	0.0	0
Pro totals (7 years)	97	4	28	7	1.0	0	0	0.0	0

KING, ANDRE   WR   BROWNS

PERSONAL: Born November 26, 1973, in Fort Lauderdale, Fla. ... 5-11/195.

HIGH SCHOOL: Stranahan (Fla.).

COLLEGE: Miami.

TRANSACTIONS/CAREER NOTES: Selected by Cleveland Browns in seventh round (245th pick overall) of 2001 NFL draft. ... Signed by Browns (July 18, 2001).

SINGLE GAME HIGHS (regular season): Receptions—4 (December 16, 2001, vs. Jacksonville); yards—61 (December 30, 2001, vs. Tennessee); and touchdown receptions—0.

			RECEIVING				KICKOFF RETURNS				TOTALS			
Year Team	G	GS	No.	Yds.	Avg.	TD	No.	Yds.	Avg.	TD	TD	2pt.	Pts.	Fum.
2001—Cleveland NFL	7	0	11	149	13.5	0	14	279	19.9	0	0	0	0	1
2002—Cleveland NFL	11	1	5	41	8.2	0	8	155	19.4	0	0	0	0	0
Pro totals (2 years)	18	1	16	190	11.9	0	22	434	19.7	0	0	0	0	1

KING, ANDY   G   RAMS

PERSONAL: Born November 9, 1978, in Lincoln, Ill. ... 6-4/310. ... Full name: Andrew Joel King.
HIGH SCHOOL: Lincoln (Ill.).
COLLEGE: Illinois State.
TRANSACTIONS/CAREER NOTES: Signed as non-drafted free agent by St. Louis Rams (April 22, 2002). ... Released by Rams (September 1, 2002). ... Re-signed by Rams to practice squad (September 3, 2002). ... Activated (October 14, 2002). ... Released by Rams (November 19, 2002). ... Re-signed by Rams to practice squad (November 20, 2002). ... Activated (November 26, 2002).
PLAYING EXPERIENCE: St. Louis NFL, 2002. ... Games/games started: 2002 (5/0).

KING, LAMAR   DE   SEAHAWKS

PERSONAL: Born August 10, 1975, in Boston. ... 6-3/311.
HIGH SCHOOL: Chesapeake (Md.).
JUNIOR COLLEGE: Montgomery College (Md.).
COLLEGE: Saginaw Valley State (Mich.).
TRANSACTIONS/CAREER NOTES: Selected by Seattle Seahawks in first round (22nd pick overall) of 1999 NFL draft. ... Signed by Seahawks (August 12, 1999). ... On injured reserve with calf injury (January 4, 2001-remainder of season). ... On injured reserve with knee injury (December 13, 2002-remainder of season).

Year Team	G	GS	TOTALS		
			Tk.	Ast.	Sks.
1999—Seattle NFL	14	0	9	3	2.0
2000—Seattle NFL	14	14	42	6	6.0
2001—Seattle NFL	8	8	14	9	0.0
2002—Seattle NFL	12	12	17	9	1.0
Pro totals (4 years)	48	34	82	27	9.0

KING, SHAUN   QB   BUCCANEERS

PERSONAL: Born May 29, 1977, in St. Petersburg, Fla. ... 6-0/225. ... Full name: Shaun Earl King.
HIGH SCHOOL: Gibbs (St. Petersburg, Fla.).
COLLEGE: Tulane.
TRANSACTIONS/CAREER NOTES: Selected by Tampa Bay Buccaneers in second round (50th pick overall) of 1999 NFL draft. ... Signed by Buccaneers (August 1, 1999). ... Granted unconditional free agency (February 28, 2003). ... Re-signed by Buccaneers (April 4, 2003).
CHAMPIONSHIP GAME EXPERIENCE: Played in NFC championship game (1999 season). ... Member of Buccaneers for NFC championship game (2002 season); inactive. ... Member of Super Bowl championship team (2002 season); inactive.
SINGLE GAME HIGHS (regular season): Attempts—42 (December 24, 2000, vs. Green Bay); completions—26 (October 9, 2000, vs. Minnesota); passing yards—297 (December 12, 1999, vs. Detroit); and touchdown passes—4 (October 29, 2000, vs. Minnesota).
MISCELLANEOUS: Regular-season record as starting NFL quarterback: 14-8 (.636). ... Postseason record as starting NFL quarterback: 1-2 (.333).

Year Team	G	GS	PASSING								RUSHING				TOTALS		
			Att.	Cmp.	Pct.	Yds.	TD	Int.	Avg.	Skd.	Rat.	Att.	Yds.	Avg.	TD	TD	2pt.	Pts.
1999—Tampa Bay NFL	6	5	146	89	61.0	875	7	4	5.99	11	82.4	18	38	2.1	0	0	0	0
2000—Tampa Bay NFL	16	16	428	233	54.4	2769	18	13	6.47	37	75.8	73	353	4.8	5	5	1	32
2001—Tampa Bay NFL	3	0	31	21	67.7	210	0	1	6.77	3	73.3	5	-12	-2.4	0	0	1	2
2002—Tampa Bay NFL	3	1	27	10	37.0	80	0	1	2.96	1	30.0	4	25	6.3	0	0	0	0
Pro totals (4 years)	28	22	632	353	55.9	3934	25	19	6.22	52	75.2	100	404	4.0	5	5	2	34

KINNEY, ERRON   TE   TITANS

PERSONAL: Born July 28, 1977, in Richmond, Va. ... 6-5/285. ... Full name: Erron Quincy Kinney.
HIGH SCHOOL: Patrick Henry (Ashland, Va.).
COLLEGE: Florida.
TRANSACTIONS/CAREER NOTES: Selected by Tennessee Titans in third round (68th pick overall) of 2000 NFL draft. ... Signed by Titans (July 17, 2000). ... Granted free agency (February 28, 2003). ... Re-signed by Titans (May 12, 2003).
CHAMPIONSHIP GAME EXPERIENCE: Played in AFC championship game (2002 season).
SINGLE GAME HIGHS (regular season): Receptions—7 (October 7, 2001, vs. Baltimore); yards—75 (October 7, 2001, vs. Baltimore); and touchdown receptions—1 (September 9, 2001, vs. Miami).

Year Team	G	GS	RECEIVING			
			No.	Yds.	Avg.	TD
2000—Tennessee NFL	16	10	19	197	10.4	1
2001—Tennessee NFL	13	12	25	263	10.5	1
2002—Tennessee NFL	15	7	13	173	13.3	0
Pro totals (3 years)	44	29	57	633	11.1	2

KIRBY, TERRY   RB   BUCCANEERS

PERSONAL: Born January 20, 1970, in Hampton, Va. ... 6-1/225. ... Full name: Terry Gayle Kirby. ... Brother of Wayne Kirby, outfielder with three major league teams (1991-98); and cousin of Chris Slade, linebacker, with New England Patriots (1993-2000) and Carolina Panthers (2001).
HIGH SCHOOL: Tabb (Va.).
COLLEGE: Virginia (degree in psychology).

TRANSACTIONS/CAREER NOTES: Selected by Miami Dolphins in third round (78th pick overall) of 1993 NFL draft. ... Signed by Dolphins (July 19, 1993). ... On injured reserve with knee injury (September 26, 1994-remainder of season). ... Granted free agency (February 16, 1996). ... Traded by Dolphins to San Francisco 49ers for fourth-round pick (traded to Oakland) in 1997 draft (August 19, 1996). ... Released by 49ers (March 3, 1998). ... Re-signed by 49ers (September 23, 1998). ... Granted unconditional free agency (February 12, 1999). ... Signed by Cleveland Browns (March 9, 1999). ... Released by Browns (August 29, 2000). ... Signed by Oakland Raiders (November 21, 2000). ... On injured reserve with broken leg (October 21, 2002-remainder of season). ... Released by Raiders (February 27, 2003). ... Signed by Tampa Bay Buccaneers (June 3, 2003).

CHAMPIONSHIP GAME EXPERIENCE: Played in NFC championship game (1997 season). ... Played in AFC championship game (2000 season).

SINGLE GAME HIGHS (regular season): Attempts—22 (October 17, 1999, vs. Jacksonville); yards—105 (December 2, 1996, vs. Atlanta); and rushing touchdowns—2 (December 26, 1999, vs. Indianapolis).

STATISTICAL PLATEAUS: 100-yard rushing games: 1994 (1), 1996 (1). Total: 2. ... 100-yard receiving games: 1993 (2).

			RUSHING				RECEIVING				KICKOFF RETURNS				TOTALS		
Year Team	G	GS	Att.	Yds.	Avg.	TD	No.	Yds.	Avg.	TD	No.	Yds.	Avg.	TD	TD 2pt.	Pts.	Fum.
1993—Miami NFL	16	8	119	390	3.3	3	75	874	11.7	3	4	85	21.3	0	6 0	36	5
1994—Miami NFL	4	4	60	233	3.9	2	14	154	11.0	0	0	0	0.0	0	2 1	14	2
1995—Miami NFL	16	4	108	414	3.8	4	66	618	9.4	3	0	0	0.0	0	7 0	42	2
1996—San Francisco NFL	14	10	134	559	4.2	3	52	439	8.4	1	1	22	22.0	0	4 0	24	1
1997—San Francisco NFL	16	3	125	418	3.3	6	23	279	12.1	1	3	124	41.3	1	8 2	52	3
1998—San Francisco NFL	9	0	48	258	5.4	3	16	134	8.4	0	17	340	20.0	0	3 0	18	0
1999—Cleveland NFL.............	16	10	130	452	3.5	6	58	528	9.1	3	11	230	20.9	0	9 0	54	4
2000—Oakland NFL...............	2	0	11	51	4.6	0	3	19	6.3	0	0	0	0.0	0	0 0	0	0
2001—Oakland NFL...............	11	0	10	49	4.9	0	9	62	6.9	0	46	1066	23.2	1	1 0	6	1
2002—Oakland NFL...............	6	0	16	51	3.2	0	17	115	6.8	1	19	425	22.4	1	3 0	18	2
Pro totals (10 years)	110	39	761	2875	3.8	27	333	3222	9.7	12	101	2292	22.7	3	43 3	264	20

KIRKLAND, LEVON — LB
K

PERSONAL: Born February 16, 1969, in Lamar, S.C. ... 6-1/275. ... Full name: Lorenzo Levon Kirkland. ... Name pronounced luh-VON.

HIGH SCHOOL: Lamar (S.C.).

COLLEGE: Clemson.

TRANSACTIONS/CAREER NOTES: Selected by Pittsburgh Steelers in second round (38th pick overall) of 1992 NFL draft. ... Signed by Steelers (July 25, 1992). ... Released by Steelers (March 8, 2001). ... Signed by Seattle Seahawks (April 9, 2001). ... Released by Seahawks (July 12, 2002). ... Signed by Philadelphia Eagles (July 17, 2002). ... Granted unconditional free agency (February 28, 2003).

CHAMPIONSHIP GAME EXPERIENCE: Played in AFC championship game (1994, 1995 and 1997 seasons). ... Played in Super Bowl XXX (1995 season). ... Played in NFC championship game (2002 season).

HONORS: Named linebacker on THE SPORTING NEWS college All-America first team (1991). ... Played in Pro Bowl (1996 and 1997 seasons). ... Named inside linebacker on THE SPORTING NEWS NFL All-Pro team (1997).

			TOTALS			INTERCEPTIONS			
Year Team	G	GS	Tk.	Ast.	Sks.	No.	Yds.	Avg.	TD
1992—Pittsburgh NFL...	16	0	1	4	0.0	0	0	0.0	0
1993—Pittsburgh NFL...	16	13	64	39	1.0	0	0	0.0	0
1994—Pittsburgh NFL...	16	15	70	30	3.0	2	0	0.0	0
1995—Pittsburgh NFL...	16	16	58	30	1.0	0	0	0.0	0
1996—Pittsburgh NFL...	16	16	75	38	4.0	4	12	3.0	0
1997—Pittsburgh NFL...	16	16	95	31	5.0	2	14	7.0	0
1998—Pittsburgh NFL...	16	16	79	38	2.5	1	1	1.0	0
1999—Pittsburgh NFL...	16	16	89	22	2.0	1	23	23.0	0
2000—Pittsburgh NFL...	16	16	65	21	0.0	1	1	1.0	0
2001—Seattle NFL...	16	16	80	21	1.0	0	0	0.0	0
2002—Philadelphia NFL...	16	15	55	21	0.0	0	0	0.0	0
Pro totals (11 years)	176	155	731	295	19.5	11	51	4.6	0

KIRSCHKE, TRAVIS — DE
49ERS

PERSONAL: Born September 6, 1974, in Fullerton, Calif. ... 6-3/292.

HIGH SCHOOL: Esperanza (Anaheim, Calif.).

COLLEGE: UCLA.

TRANSACTIONS/CAREER NOTES: Signed as non-drafted free agent by Detroit Lions (April 24, 1997). ... Inactive for three games (1998). ... On injured reserve with abdominal injury (September 24, 1998-remainder of season). ... Granted free agency (February 11, 2000). ... Re-signed by Lions (April 25, 2000). ... Granted unconditional free agency (March 1, 2002). ... Re-signed by Lions (April 2, 2002). ... Granted unconditional free agency (February 28, 2003). ... Signed by San Francisco 49ers (April 8, 2003).

			TOTALS		
Year Team	G	GS	Tk.	Ast.	Sks.
1997—Detroit NFL	3	0	0	1	0.0
1999—Detroit NFL	15	7	12	8	2.0
2000—Detroit NFL	13	0	4	8	0.5
2001—Detroit NFL	16	2	11	8	0.0
2002—Detroit NFL	15	1	14	5	0.0
Pro totals (5 years)..	62	10	41	30	2.5

KITNA, JON — QB
BENGALS

PERSONAL: Born September 21, 1972, in Tacoma, Wash. ... 6-2/220.

HIGH SCHOOL: Lincoln (Tacoma, Wash.).

COLLEGE: Central Washington (degree in math education, 1995).

TRANSACTIONS/CAREER NOTES: Signed as non-drafted free agent by Seattle Seahawks (April 25, 1996) ... Released by Seahawks (August 19, 1996) ... Re-signed by Seahawks to practice squad (August 20, 1996). ... Assigned by Seahawks to Barcelona Dragons in 1997 World League enhancement allocation program (April 7, 1997). ... Granted free agency (February 11, 2000). ... Re-signed by Seahawks (March 15, 2000). ... Granted unconditional free agency (March 2, 2001). ... Signed by Cincinnati Bengals (March 8, 2001).
SINGLE GAME HIGHS (regular season): Attempts—68 (December 30, 2001, vs. Pittsburgh); completions—35 (December 30, 2001, vs. Pittsburgh); yards—411 (December 30, 2001, vs. Pittsburgh); and touchdown passes—4 (November 3, 2002, vs. Houston).
STATISTICAL PLATEAUS: 300-yard passing games: 2001 (3), 2002 (1). Total: 4.
MISCELLANEOUS: Regular-season record as starting NFL quarterback: 26-34 (.433). ... Postseason record as starting NFL quarterback: 0-1.

Year Team	G	GS	PASSING Att.	Cmp.	Pct.	Yds.	TD	Int.	Avg.	Skd.	Rat.	RUSHING Att.	Yds.	Avg.	TD	TOTALS TD	2pt.	Pts.
1997—Barcelona W.L.	10	...	317	171	53.9	2448	22	15	7.72	0	82.6	50	334	6.7	3	3	0	18
—Seattle NFL	3	1	45	31	68.9	371	1	2	8.24	3	82.7	10	9	0.9	1	1	0	6
1998—Seattle NFL	6	5	172	98	57.0	1177	7	8	6.84	11	72.3	20	67	3.4	1	1	0	6
1999—Seattle NFL	15	15	495	270	54.5	3346	23	16	6.76	32	77.7	35	56	1.6	0	0	0	0
2000—Seattle NFL	15	12	418	259	62.0	2658	18	19	6.36	33	75.6	48	127	2.6	1	1	0	6
2001—Cincinnati NFL	16	15	*581	313	53.9	3216	12	22	5.54	25	61.1	27	73	2.7	1	1	0	6
2002—Cincinnati NFL	14	12	473	294	62.2	3178	16	16	6.72	24	79.1	24	57	2.4	4	4	0	24
W.L. totals (1 year)	10	...	317	171	53.9	2448	22	15	7.72	0	82.6	50	334	6.7	3	3	0	18
NFL totals (6 years)	69	60	2184	1265	57.9	13946	77	83	6.39	128	72.9	164	389	2.4	8	8	0	48
Pro totals (7 years)	79	...	2501	1436	57.4	16394	99	98	6.55	128	74.1	214	723	3.4	11	11	0	66

K

KLEINSASSER, JIM — FB — VIKINGS

PERSONAL: Born January 31, 1977, in Carrington, N.D. ... 6-3/274.
HIGH SCHOOL: Carrington (N.D.).
COLLEGE: North Dakota.
TRANSACTIONS/CAREER NOTES: Selected by Minnesota Vikings in second round (44th pick overall) of 1999 NFL draft. ... Signed by Vikings (August 1, 1999). ... Designated by Vikings as franchise player (February 20, 2003). ... Re-signed by Vikings (March 23, 2003).
CHAMPIONSHIP GAME EXPERIENCE: Played in NFC championship game (2000 season).
SINGLE GAME HIGHS (regular season): Attempts—5 (October 21, 2001, vs. Green Bay); yards—20 (October 21, 2001, vs. Green Bay); and rushing touchdowns—1 (October 21, 2001, vs. Green Bay); receptions—8 (September 30, 2001, vs. Tampa Bay); yards—64 (November 3, 2002, vs. Tampa Bay); and touchdown receptions—1 (October 13, 2002, vs. Detroit).

Year Team	G	GS	RUSHING Att.	Yds.	Avg.	TD	RECEIVING No.	Yds.	Avg.	TD	TOTALS TD	2pt.	Pts.	Fum.
1999—Minnesota NFL	13	7	0	0	0.0	0	6	13	2.2	0	0	0	0	2
2000—Minnesota NFL	14	8	12	43	3.6	0	10	98	9.8	0	0	0	0	0
2001—Minnesota NFL	11	11	23	72	3.1	1	24	184	7.7	0	1	0	6	2
2002—Minnesota NFL	14	12	6	17	2.8	0	37	393	10.6	1	1	0	6	0
Pro totals (4 years)	52	38	41	132	3.2	1	77	688	8.9	1	2	0	12	4

KLEMM, ADRIAN — OT — PATRIOTS

PERSONAL: Born May 21, 1977, in Inglewood, Calif. ... 6-3/312. ... Full name: Adrian William Klemm.
HIGH SCHOOL: St. Monica (Santa Monica, Calif.).
COLLEGE: Hawaii.
TRANSACTIONS/CAREER NOTES: Selected by New England Patriots in second round (46th pick overall) of 2000 NFL draft. ... Signed by Patriots (July 12, 2000). ... On non-football injured list with knee injury (August 27-November 1, 2000). ... On injured reserve with leg injury (November 2, 2001-remainder of season).
PLAYING EXPERIENCE: New England NFL, 2000-2002. ... Games/Games started: 2000 (6/5), 2002 (16/3). Total: 22/8.

KNIGHT, BRYAN — LB — BEARS

PERSONAL: Born January 22, 1979, in Buffalo. ... 6-2/240. ... Full name: Bryan Jerome Knight.
HIGH SCHOOL: St. Joseph (Buffalo).
COLLEGE: Pittsburgh.
TRANSACTIONS/CAREER NOTES: Selected by Chicago Bears in fifth round (165th pick overall) of 2002 NFL draft. ... Signed by Bears (July 25, 2002).

Year Team	G	GS	TOTALS Tk.	Ast.	Sks.	INTERCEPTIONS No.	Yds.	Avg.	TD
2002—Chicago NFL	15	0	10	2	1.5	0	0	0.0	0

KNIGHT, MARCUS — WR — RAIDERS

PERSONAL: Born June 19, 1978, in Sylacauga, Ala. ... 6-1/180.
HIGH SCHOOL: Comer (Sylacauga, Ala.).
COLLEGE: Michigan.
TRANSACTIONS/CAREER NOTES: Signed as non-drafted free agent by Oakland Raiders (April 18, 2000) ... Released by Raiders (August 27, 2000). ... Re-signed by Raiders to practice squad (August 28, 2000). ... Assigned by Raiders to Amsterdam Admirals in 2002 NFL Europe enhancement allocation program (February 18, 2002).
CHAMPIONSHIP GAME EXPERIENCE: Played in AFC championship game (2002 season). ... Played in Super Bowl XXXVII (2002 season).
SINGLE GAME HIGHS (regular season): Receptions—1 (December 8, 2002, vs. San Diego); yards—12 (September 15, 2002, vs. Pittsburgh); and touchdown receptions—0.

Year Team	G	GS	RECEIVING No.	Yds.	Avg.	TD	PUNT RETURNS No.	Yds.	Avg.	TD	KICKOFF RETURNS No.	Yds.	Avg.	TD	TOTALS TD	2pt.	Pts.	Fum.
2001—Oakland NFL	5	1	0	0	0.0	0	0	0	0.0	0	0	0	0.0	0	0	0	0	0
2002—Amsterdam NFLE	...	...	40	546	13.7	5	3	34	11.3	0	0	0	0.0	0	5	0	30	0
—Oakland NFL	16	1	3	26	8.7	0	0	0	0.0	0	29	705	24.3	0	0	0	0	2
NFL Europe totals (1 year)	...	...	40	546	13.7	5	3	34	11.3	0	0	0	0.0	0	5	0	30	0
NFL totals (2 years)	21	2	3	26	8.7	0	0	0	0.0	0	29	705	24.3	0	0	0	0	2
Pro totals (3 years)	...	...	43	572	13.3	5	3	34	11.3	0	29	705	24.3	0	5	0	30	2

KNIGHT, ROGER — LB — SAINTS

PERSONAL: Born October 11, 1978, in St. Ann's, Jamaica. ... 6-0/245. ... Full name: Roger Oliver Knight.
HIGH SCHOOL: Brooklyn Tech (N.Y.).
COLLEGE: Wisconsin.
TRANSACTIONS/CAREER NOTES: Selected by Pittsburgh Steelers in sixth round (182nd pick overall) of 2001 NFL draft. ... Signed by Steelers (June 6, 2001). ... Released by Steelers (August 31, 2001). ... Signed by New Orleans Saints (December 4, 2001). ... On injured reserve with knee injury (December 12, 2001-remainder of season).

Year Team	G	GS	TOTALS Tk.	Ast.	Sks.	INTERCEPTIONS No.	Yds.	Avg.	TD
2001—New Orleans NFL	1	0	0	0	0.0	0	0	0.0	0
2002—New Orleans NFL	16	0	3	3	0.0	0	0	0.0	0
Pro totals (2 years)	17	0	3	3	0.0	0	0	0.0	0

KNIGHT, SAMMY — S — DOLPHINS

PERSONAL: Born September 10, 1975, in Fontana, Calif. ... 6-0/215.
HIGH SCHOOL: Rubidoux (Riverside, Calif.).
COLLEGE: Southern California.
TRANSACTIONS/CAREER NOTES: Signed as non-drafted free agent by New Orleans Saints (April 25, 1997). ... Granted unconditional free agency (February 28, 2003). ... Signed by Miami Dolphins (May 13, 2003).
HONORS: Played in Pro Bowl (2001 season).

Year Team	G	GS	TOTALS Tk.	Ast.	Sks.	INTERCEPTIONS No.	Yds.	Avg.	TD
1997—New Orleans NFL	16	12	67	17	0.0	5	75	15.0	0
1998—New Orleans NFL	14	13	62	13	0.0	6	171	28.5	2
1999—New Orleans NFL	16	16	75	27	0.0	1	0	0.0	0
2000—New Orleans NFL	16	16	74	26	2.0	5	68	13.6	‡2
2001—New Orleans NFL	16	16	80	18	1.0	6	114	19.0	0
2002—New Orleans NFL	16	16	82	25	2.0	5	36	7.2	0
Pro totals (6 years)	94	89	440	126	5.0	28	464	16.6	4

KNORR, MICAH — P — BRONCOS

PERSONAL: Born January 9, 1975, in Orange, Calif. ... 6-2/199.
HIGH SCHOOL: Orange (Calif.).
COLLEGE: Utah State.
TRANSACTIONS/CAREER NOTES: Signed as non-drafted free agent by Dallas Cowboys (April 18, 2000). ... Released by Cowboys (October 22, 2002). ... Signed by Denver Broncos (October 29, 2002).

Year Team	G	PUNTING No.	Yds.	Avg.	Net avg.	In. 20	Blk.
2000—Dallas NFL	14	58	2485	42.8	35.7	12	0
2001—Dallas NFL	16	78	3135	40.2	31.1	25	*3
2002—Dallas NFL	7	47	1928	41.0	35.1	11	0
—Denver NFL	8	24	906	37.8	34.1	8	0
Pro totals (3 years)	45	207	8454	40.8	33.6	56	3

KOLODZIEJ, ROSS — DT — 49ERS

PERSONAL: Born May 11, 1978, in Stevens Point, Wis. ... 6-2/295.
HIGH SCHOOL: Stevens Point (Wis.).
COLLEGE: Wisconsin.
TRANSACTIONS/CAREER NOTES: Selected by New York Giants in seventh round (230th pick overall) of 2001 NFL draft. ... Signed by Giants (July 26, 2001). ... Released by Giants (September 1, 2002). ... Signed by San Francisco 49ers (September 8, 2002). ... Released by 49ers (October 14, 2002). ... Re-signed by 49ers (October 16, 2002). ... Released by 49ers (October 22, 2002). ... Signed by Giants (December 4, 2002). ... Signed by 49ers (April 7, 2003).

Year Team	G	GS	TOTALS Tk.	Ast.	Sks.
2001—New York Giants NFL	9	1	3	1	0.0
2002—New York Giants NFL	1	0	0	0	0.0
Pro totals (2 years)	10	1	3	1	0.0

K

KONRAD, ROB   FB   DOLPHINS

PERSONAL: Born November 12, 1976, in Rochester, N.Y. ... 6-3/255. ... Full name: Robert L. Konrad.
HIGH SCHOOL: St. John's (Andover, Mass.).
COLLEGE: Syracuse.
TRANSACTIONS/CAREER NOTES: Selected by Miami Dolphins in second round (43rd pick overall) of 1999 NFL draft. ... Signed by Dolphins (July 27, 1999). ... On injured reserve with rib injury (January 12, 2002-remainder of 2001 playoffs). ... Granted unconditional free agency (February 28, 2003). ... Re-signed by Dolphins (March 1, 2003).
SINGLE GAME HIGHS (regular season): Attempts—7 (September 3, 2000, vs. Seattle); yards—19 (December 10, 2001, vs. Indianapolis); and rushing touchdowns—1 (December 10, 2001, vs. Indianapolis).

			RUSHING				RECEIVING				TOTALS		
Year Team	G	GS	Att.	Yds.	Avg.	TD	No.	Yds.	Avg.	TD	TD	2pt.	Pts.	Fum.
1999—Miami NFL	15	9	9	16	1.8	0	34	251	7.4	1	1	0	6	3
2000—Miami NFL	15	13	15	39	2.6	0	14	83	5.9	0	0	0	0	0
2001—Miami NFL	12	9	5	22	4.4	1	5	52	10.4	1	2	0	12	0
2002—Miami NFL	16	12	3	2	0.7	0	34	233	6.9	3	3	0	18	2
Pro totals (4 years)	58	43	32	79	2.5	1	87	619	7.1	5	6	0	36	5

KOSIER, KYLE   OT   49ERS

K

PERSONAL: Born January 27, 1978, in Peoria, Ariz. ... 6-5/293. ... Full name: Kyle Blaine Kosier.
HIGH SCHOOL: Cactus (Peoria, Ariz.).
COLLEGE: Arizona State.
TRANSACTIONS/CAREER NOTES: Selected by San Francisco 49ers in seventh round (248th pick overall) of 2002 NFL draft. ... Signed by 49ers (July 21, 2002).
PLAYING EXPERIENCE: San Francisco NFL, 2002. ... Games/games started: 2002 (15/1).

KOZLOWSKI, BRIAN   TE   FALCONS

PERSONAL: Born October 4, 1970, in Rochester, N.Y. ... 6-3/250. ... Full name: Brian Scott Kozlowski.
HIGH SCHOOL: Webster (N.Y.).
COLLEGE: Connecticut.
TRANSACTIONS/CAREER NOTES: Signed as non-drafted free agent by New York Giants (May 1, 1993). ... Released by Giants (August 16, 1993). ... Re-signed by Giants to practice squad (December 8, 1993). ... Granted unconditional free agency (February 14, 1997). ... Signed by Atlanta Falcons (March 21, 1997). ... Granted unconditional free agency (February 13, 1998). ... Re-signed by Falcons (March 4, 1998). ... Granted unconditional free agency (March 2, 2001). ... Re-signed by Falcons (April 5, 2001). ... Granted unconditional free agency (March 1, 2002). ... Re-signed by Falcons (April 3, 2002). ... Granted unconditional free agency (February 28, 2003). ... Re-signed by Falcons (March 17, 2003).
CHAMPIONSHIP GAME EXPERIENCE: Played in NFC championship game (1998 season). ... Played in Super Bowl XXXIII (1998 season).
SINGLE GAME HIGHS (regular season): Receptions—4 (September 23, 2001, vs. Carolina); yards—86 (September 23, 2001, vs. Carolina); and touchdown receptions—1 (November 11, 2001, vs. Dallas).

			RECEIVING				KICKOFF RETURNS				TOTALS		
Year Team	G	GS	No.	Yds.	Avg.	TD	No.	Yds.	Avg.	TD	TD	2pt.	Pts.	Fum.
1993—New York Giants NFL								Did not play.						
1994—New York Giants NFL	16	3	1	5	5.0	0	2	21	10.5	0	0	0	0	0
1995—New York Giants NFL	16	0	2	17	8.5	0	5	75	15.0	0	0	0	0	1
1996—New York Giants NFL	5	0	1	4	4.0	1	1	16	16.0	0	1	0	6	0
1997—Atlanta NFL	16	5	7	99	14.1	1	2	49	24.5	0	1	0	6	0
1998—Atlanta NFL	16	4	10	103	10.3	1	1	12	12.0	0	1	0	6	0
1999—Atlanta NFL	16	3	11	122	11.1	2	2	19	9.5	0	2	0	12	1
2000—Atlanta NFL	16	3	15	151	10.1	2	7	77	11.0	0	2	0	12	0
2001—Atlanta NFL	16	0	15	270	18.0	1	3	35	11.7	0	1	0	6	0
2002—Atlanta NFL	16	2	6	59	9.8	0	2	35	17.5	0	0	0	0	0
Pro totals (9 years)	133	20	68	830	12.2	8	25	339	13.6	0	8	0	48	2

KREIDER, DAN   FB   STEELERS

PERSONAL: Born March 11, 1977, in Lancaster, Pa. ... 5-11/246.
HIGH SCHOOL: Manheim Central (Pa.).
COLLEGE: New Hampshire.
TRANSACTIONS/CAREER NOTES: Signed as non-drafted free agent by Pittsburgh Steelers (April 21, 2000). ... On physically unable to perform list with calf injury (July 20-September 2, 2001). ... Granted free agency (February 28, 2003). ... Re-signed by Steelers (April 20, 2003).
CHAMPIONSHIP GAME EXPERIENCE: Played in AFC championship game (2001 season).
SINGLE GAME HIGHS (regular season): Attempts—2 (December 15, 2002, vs. Carolina); yards—24 (December 3, 2000, vs. Oakland); and rushing touchdowns—1 (December 16, 2001, vs. Baltimore).

			RUSHING				RECEIVING				TOTALS		
Year Team	G	GS	Att.	Yds.	Avg.	TD	No.	Yds.	Avg.	TD	TD	2pt.	Pts.	Fum.
2000—Pittsburgh NFL	10	7	2	24	12.0	0	5	42	8.4	0	0	0	0	0
2001—Pittsburgh NFL	13	1	7	29	4.1	1	2	5	2.5	0	1	0	6	0
2002—Pittsburgh NFL	16	13	6	16	2.7	0	18	122	6.8	1	1	1	8	1
Pro totals (3 years)	39	21	15	69	4.6	1	25	169	6.8	1	2	1	14	1

KREUTZ, OLIN   C   BEARS

PERSONAL: Born June 9, 1977, in Honolulu. ... 6-2/293.
HIGH SCHOOL: St. Louis (Honolulu).
COLLEGE: Washington.
TRANSACTIONS/CAREER NOTES: Selected after junior season by Chicago Bears in third round (64th pick overall) of 1998 NFL draft. ... Signed by Bears (July 20, 1998). ... On injured reserve with knee injury (November 21, 2000-remainder of season). ... Granted free agency (March 2, 2001). ... Re-signed by Bears (April 18, 2001). ... Granted unconditional free agency (March 1, 2002). ... Re-signed by Bears (March 4, 2002).
PLAYING EXPERIENCE: Chicago NFL, 1998-2002. ... Games/Games started: 1998 (9/1), 1999 (16/16), 2000 (7/7), 2001 (16/16), 2002 (15/15). Total: 63/55.
HONORS: Named center on THE SPORTING NEWS college All-America first team (1997). ... Played in Pro Bowl (2001 and 2002 seasons).

KRIEWALDT, CLINT   LB   STEELERS

PERSONAL: Born March 16, 1976, in Shiocton, Wis. ... 6-1/242.
HIGH SCHOOL: Shiocton (Wis.).
COLLEGE: Wisconsin-Stevens Point.
TRANSACTIONS/CAREER NOTES: Selected by Detroit Lions in sixth round (177th pick overall) of 1999 NFL draft. ... Signed by Lions (July 22, 1999). ... Granted free agency (March 1, 2002). ... Re-signed by Lions (April 16, 2002). ... Granted unconditional free agency (February 28, 2003). ... Signed by Pittsburgh Steelers (March 5, 2003).

			TOTALS			INTERCEPTIONS			
Year Team	G	GS	Tk.	Ast.	Sks.	No.	Yds.	Avg.	TD
1999—Detroit NFL	12	0	2	0	0.0	1	2	2.0	0
2000—Detroit NFL	13	1	4	1	0.0	0	0	0.0	0
2001—Detroit NFL	14	1	11	10	0.0	0	0	0.0	0
2002—Detroit NFL	10	0	5	6	0.0	0	0	0.0	0
Pro totals (4 years)	49	2	22	17	0.0	1	2	2.0	0

KUEHL, RYAN   DT   GIANTS

PERSONAL: Born January 18, 1972, in Washington, D.C. ... 6-5/290. ... Full name: Ryan Philip Kuehl.
HIGH SCHOOL: Walt Whitman (Bethesda, Md.).
COLLEGE: Virginia (degree in marketing, 1994).
TRANSACTIONS/CAREER NOTES: Signed as non-drafted free agent by San Francisco 49ers (April 26, 1995). ... Released by 49ers (August 19, 1995). ... Re-signed by Redskins to practice squad (August 26, 1995). ... Signed by Washington Redskins (February 16, 1996). ... Released by Redskins (August 25, 1996). ... Re-signed by Redskins to practice squad (August 26, 1996). ... Activated (October 19, 1996). ... Released by Redskins (November 6, 1996). ... Re-signed by Redskins to practice squad (November 7, 1996). ... Activated (November 11, 1996). ... Released by Redskins (August 23, 1997). ... Re-signed by Redskins (September 9, 1997). ... Released by Redskins (August 30, 1998). ... Signed by Cleveland Browns (February 11, 1999). ... Granted unconditional free agency (February 28, 2003). ... Signed by New York Giants (March 6, 2003).

			TOTALS		
Year Team	G	GS	Tk.	Ast.	Sks.
1996—Washington NFL	2	0	1	0	0.0
1997—Washington NFL	12	5	9	3	0.0
1999—Cleveland NFL	16	0	0	0	0.0
2000—Cleveland NFL	16	0	0	0	0.0
2001—Cleveland NFL	16	0	0	0	0.0
2002—Cleveland NFL	16	0	0	0	0.0
Pro totals (6 years)	78	5	10	3	0.0

KURPEIKIS, JUSTIN   LB   STEELERS

PERSONAL: Born July 17, 1977, in Allison Park, Pa. ... 6-3/254. ... Full name: Justin William Kurpeikis.
HIGH SCHOOL: Central Catholic (Pittsburgh).
COLLEGE: Penn State.
TRANSACTIONS/CAREER NOTES: Signed as non-drafted free agent by Pittsburgh Steelers (April 23, 2001). ... Released by Steelers (October 22, 2002). ... Re-signed by Steelers (November 5, 2002).
CHAMPIONSHIP GAME EXPERIENCE: Played in AFC championship game (2001 season).

			TOTALS			INTERCEPTIONS			
Year Team	G	GS	Tk.	Ast.	Sks.	No.	Yds.	Avg.	TD
2001—Pittsburgh NFL	3	0	1	1	0.0	0	0	0.0	0
2002—Pittsburgh NFL	6	0	0	0	0.0	0	0	0.0	0
Pro totals (2 years)	9	0	1	1	0.0	0	0	0.0	0

KYLE, JASON   LB   PANTHERS

PERSONAL: Born May 12, 1972, in Tempe, Ariz. ... 6-3/242. ... Full name: Jason C. Kyle.
HIGH SCHOOL: McClintock (Tempe, Ariz.).
COLLEGE: Arizona State.
TRANSACTIONS/CAREER NOTES: Selected by Seattle Seahawks in fourth round (126th pick overall) of 1995 NFL draft. ... Signed by Seahawks (July 16, 1995). ... On injured reserve with shoulder injury (August 18, 1997-entire season). ... Granted free agency (February 13, 1998). ... Re-signed by Seahawks (April 16, 1998). ... Selected by Cleveland Browns from Seahawks in NFL expansion draft (February 9, 1999). ... On physically unable to perform list with knee injury (August 26, 1999-entire season). ... Released by Browns (August 27, 2000). ... Signed by

K

St. Louis Rams (October 5, 2000). ... Released by Rams (October 16, 2000). ... Re-signed by Rams (October 24, 2000). ... Released by Rams (October 27, 2000). ... Signed by San Francisco 49ers (October 30, 2000). ... Granted unconditional free agency (March 2, 2001). ... Signed by Carolina Panthers (March 5, 2001).

				TOTALS			INTERCEPTIONS			
Year Team	G	GS	Tk.	Ast.	Sks.	No.	Yds.	Avg.	TD
1995—Seattle NFL	16	0	0	0	0.0	0	0	0.0	0
1996—Seattle NFL	16	0	1	0	0.0	0	0	0.0	0
1998—Seattle NFL	16	0	0	0	0.0	0	0	0.0	0
1999—Cleveland NFL				Did not play.					
2000—San Francisco NFL	2	0	2	0	0.0	0	0	0.0	0
2001—Carolina NFL	16	0	0	0	0.0	0	0	0.0	0
2002—Carolina NFL	16	0	1	1	0.0	0	0	0.0	0
Pro totals (6 years)	82	0	4	1	0.0	0	0	0.0	0

LACINA, CORBIN   G

PERSONAL: Born November 2, 1970, in Mankato, Minn. ... 6-4/314.
HIGH SCHOOL: Cretin-Derham Hall (St. Paul, Minn.).
COLLEGE: Augustana (S.D.).
TRANSACTIONS/CAREER NOTES: Selected by Buffalo Bills in sixth round (167th pick overall) of 1993 NFL draft. ... Signed by Bills (July 12, 1993). ... Released by Bills (August 30, 1993). ... Re-signed by Bills to practice squad (September 1, 1993). ... Activated (December 30, 1993); did not play. ... On injured reserve with foot injury (December 22, 1994-remainder of season). ... On injured reserve with groin injury (November 30, 1996-remainder of season). ... Granted free agency (February 14, 1997). ... Re-signed by Bills (June 12, 1997). ... Granted unconditional free agency (February 13, 1998). ... Signed by Carolina Panthers (February 26, 1998). ... Released by Panthers (June 16, 1999). ... Signed by Minnesota Vikings (June 18, 1999). ... Granted unconditional free agency (March 2, 2001). ... Re-signed by Vikings (June 19, 2001). ... Granted unconditional free agency (February 28, 2003).
PLAYING EXPERIENCE: Buffalo NFL, 1994-1997; Carolina NFL, 1998; Minnesota NFL, 1999-2002. ... Games/Games started: 1994 (11/10), 1995 (16/3), 1996 (12/2), 1997 (16/13), 1998 (10/10), 1999 (14/0), 2000 (15/15), 2001 (11/10), 2002 (16/16). Total: 121/79.
CHAMPIONSHIP GAME EXPERIENCE: Member of Bills for AFC championship game (1993 season); inactive. ... Member of Bills for Super Bowl XXVIII (1993 season); inactive. ... Played in NFC championship game (2000 season).

LAFLEUR, BILLY   P   49ERS

PERSONAL: Born February 25, 1976, in Superior, Neb. ... 6-0/204. ... Full name: William Lafleur.
HIGH SCHOOL: Norfolk Catholic (Norfolk, Neb.).
COLLEGE: Nebraska.
TRANSACTIONS/CAREER NOTES: Signed as non-drafted free agent by New Orleans Saints (April 18, 2000). ... Released by Saints (August 22, 2000). ... Re-signed by Saints (February 20, 2001). ... Released by Saints (September 1, 2001). ... Signed by San Diego Chargers (June 28, 2002). ... Released by Chargers (September 1, 2002). ... Re-signed by Chargers to practice squad (September 3, 2002). ... Signed by San Francisco 49ers off Chargers practice squad (November 27, 2002). ... Re-signed by 49ers (March 10, 2003).

			PUNTING				
Year Team	G	No.	Yds.	Avg.	Net avg.	In. 20	Blk.
2001—Barcelona NFLE	10	44	1702	38.7	31.5	17	0
2002—Barcelona NFLE	10	56	2220	39.6	31.2	17	0
—San Francisco NFL	5	22	805	36.6	30.8	5	1
NFL Europe totals (2 years)	20	100	3922	39.2	31.3	34	0
NFL totals (1 year)	5	22	805	36.6	30.8	5	1
Pro totals (3 years)	25	122	4727	38.7	31.2	39	1

LAKE, ANTWAN   DE   LIONS

PERSONAL: Born July 10, 1979, in Dorchester, Md. ... 6-4/285.
HIGH SCHOOL: Cambridge South (Dorchester, Md.).
COLLEGE: West Virginia.
TRANSACTIONS/CAREER NOTES: Signed as non-drafted free agent by Detroit Lions (April 26, 2002).

			TOTALS		
Year Team	G	GS	Tk.	Ast.	Sks.
2002—Detroit NFL	9	0	1	1	0.0

LAMAR, JASON   LB   TEXANS

PERSONAL: Born November 10, 1978, in Detroit. ... 6-0/228.
HIGH SCHOOL: Ypsilanti (Mich.).
COLLEGE: Toledo.
TRANSACTIONS/CAREER NOTES: Signed as non-drafted free agent by San Francisco 49ers (June 6, 2000). ... Released by 49ers (August 15, 2000). ... Signed by Hamilton Tiger-Cats of CFL (May 16, 2001). ... Signed by Houston Texans (January 22, 2002). ... On injured reserve with leg injury (October 30, 2002-remainder of season). ... Re-signed by Texans (March 21, 2003).

			TOTALS			INTERCEPTIONS			
Year Team	G	GS	Tk.	Ast.	Sks.	No.	Yds.	Avg.	TD
2001—Hamilton CFL	18	18	...	...	5.0	0	0	0.0	0
2002—Houston NFL	5	0	0	0	0.0	0	0	0.0	0
CFL totals (1 year)	18	18	...	...	5.0	0	0	0.0	0
NFL totals (1 year)	5	0	0	0	0.0	0	0	0.0	0
Pro totals (2 years)	23	18	...	...	5.0	0	0	0.0	0

PERSONAL: Born January 6, 1962, in Baltimore. ... 6-0/215. ... Full name: Sean Edward Landeta.
HIGH SCHOOL: Loch Raven (Baltimore).
COLLEGE: Towson State.
TRANSACTIONS/CAREER NOTES: Selected by Philadelphia Stars in 14th round (161st pick overall) of 1983 USFL draft. ... Signed by Stars (January 24, 1983). ... Stars franchise moved to Baltimore (November 1, 1984). ... Granted free agency (August 1, 1985). ... Signed by New York Giants (August 5, 1985). ... On injured reserve with back injury (September 7, 1988-remainder of season). ... Granted free agency (February 1, 1990). ... Re-signed by Giants (July 23, 1990). ... On injured reserve with knee injury (November 25, 1992-remainder of season). ... Granted unconditional free agency (March 1, 1993). ... Re-signed by Giants (March 18, 1993). ... Released by Giants (November 9, 1993). ... Signed by Los Angeles Rams (November 12, 1993). ... Granted unconditional free agency (February 17, 1994). ... Re-signed by Rams (May 10, 1994). ... Granted unconditional free agency (February 17, 1995). ... Rams franchise moved to St. Louis (April 12, 1995). ... Re-signed by Rams (May 8, 1995). ... Released by Rams (March 18, 1997). ... Signed by Tampa Bay Buccaneers (October 9, 1997). ... Granted unconditional free agency (February 13, 1998). ... Signed by Green Bay Packers (February 26, 1998). ... Granted unconditional free agency (February 12, 1999). ... Signed by Philadelphia Eagles (February 26, 1999). ... Granted unconditional free agency (March 1, 2002). ... Re-signed by Eagles (March 21, 2002). ... On injured reserve with calf injury (December 3, 2002-remainder of season). ... Granted unconditional free agency (February 28, 2003). ... Signed by Rams (March 18, 2003).
CHAMPIONSHIP GAME EXPERIENCE: Played in USFL championship game (1983-1985 seasons). ... Played in NFC championship game (1986, 1990 and 2001 seasons). ... Member of Super Bowl championship team (1986 and 1990 seasons).
HONORS: Named punter on THE SPORTING NEWS USFL All-Star team (1983 and 1984). ... Named punter on THE SPORTING NEWS NFL All-Pro team (1986, 1989 and 1990). ... Played in Pro Bowl (1986 and 1990 seasons).
RECORDS: Holds NFL career record for most punts—1,268.

Year Team	G	No.	Yds.	Avg.	Net avg.	In. 20	Blk.
			PUNTING				
1983—Philadelphia USFL	18	86	3601	41.9	36.5	31	0
1984—Philadelphia USFL	18	53	2171	41.0	*38.1	18	0
1985—Baltimore USFL	18	65	2718	41.8	33.2	18	0
—New York Giants NFL	16	81	3472	42.9	36.3	20	0
1986—New York Giants NFL	16	79	3539	‡44.8	‡37.1	24	0
1987—New York Giants NFL	12	65	2773	42.7	31.0	13	1
1988—New York Giants NFL	1	6	222	37.0	35.7	1	0
1989—New York Giants NFL	16	70	3019	43.1	*37.7	19	0
1990—New York Giants NFL	16	75	3306	‡44.1	37.2	†24	0
1991—New York Giants NFL	15	64	2768	43.3	35.2	16	0
1992—New York Giants NFL	11	53	2317	43.7	31.5	13	*2
1993—New York Giants NFL	8	33	1390	42.1	35.0	11	1
—Los Angeles Rams NFL	8	42	1825	43.5	32.8	7	0
1994—Los Angeles Rams NFL	16	78	3494	*44.8	34.2	23	0
1995—St. Louis NFL	16	83	3679	‡44.3	36.7	23	0
1996—St. Louis NFL	16	78	3491	44.8	36.1	23	0
1997—Tampa Bay NFL	10	54	2274	42.1	34.1	15	1
1998—Green Bay NFL	16	65	2788	42.9	37.1	30	0
1999—Philadelphia NFL	16	*107	‡4524	42.3	35.1	21	1
2000—Philadelphia NFL	16	86	3635	42.3	36.0	23	0
2001—Philadelphia NFL	16	‡97	4221	43.5	36.4	26	0
2002—Philadelphia NFL	12	52	2229	42.9	34.6	19	0
USFL totals (3 years)	54	204	8490	41.6	35.9	67	0
NFL totals (18 years)	253	1268	54966	43.3	35.4	351	6
Pro totals (21 years)	307	1472	63456	43.1	35.5	418	6

PERSONAL: Born January 31, 1975, in Orlando. ... 6-3/285. ... Full name: Kenard Dushun Lang.
HIGH SCHOOL: Maynard Evans (Orlando).
COLLEGE: Miami (Fla.).
TRANSACTIONS/CAREER NOTES: Selected by Washington Redskins in first round (17th pick overall) of 1997 NFL draft. ... Signed by Redskins (July 28, 1997). ... Granted unconditional free agency (March 1, 2002). ... Signed by Cleveland Browns (March 5, 2002).

Year Team	G	GS	TOTALS			INTERCEPTIONS			
			Tk.	Ast.	Sks.	No.	Yds.	Avg.	TD
1997—Washington NFL	11	11	26	9	1.5	0	0	0.0	0
1998—Washington NFL	16	16	46	8	7.0	0	0	0.0	0
1999—Washington NFL	16	9	34	3	6.0	0	0	0.0	0
2000—Washington NFL	16	0	16	0	3.0	0	0	0.0	0
2001—Washington NFL	16	16	52	15	4.0	1	14	14.0	0
2002—Cleveland NFL	15	14	33	13	5.5	1	71	71.0	0
Pro totals (6 years)	90	66	207	48	27.0	2	85	42.5	0

PERSONAL: Born December 3, 1969, in Hampton, Va. ... 6-0/207.
HIGH SCHOOL: Menchville (Newport News, Va.).
JUNIOR COLLEGE: Butler County Community College (Kan.).
COLLEGE: Kansas.
TRANSACTIONS/CAREER NOTES: Signed as non-drafted free agent by Arizona Cardinals (April 28, 1995). ... On injured reserve with ankle injury (October 5, 1995-remainder of season). ... Granted free agency (February 13, 1998). ... Re-signed by Cardinals (May 21, 1998). ... Granted unconditional free agency (February 12, 1999). ... Re-signed by Cardinals (March 9, 1999). ... Granted free agency (March 1, 2002). ... Re-signed by Cardinals (May 1, 2002). ... Granted unconditional free agency (February 28, 2003). ... Signed by San Diego Chargers (June 9, 2003).

Year Team	G	GS	TOTALS			INTERCEPTIONS			
			Tk.	Ast.	Sks.	No.	Yds.	Avg.	TD
1995—Arizona NFL	5	0	5	2	0.0	0	0	0.0	0
1996—Arizona NFL	14	0	13	3	0.0	1	20	20.0	0
1997—Arizona NFL	16	1	24	15	3.0	1	10	10.0	0
1998—Arizona NFL	16	6	40	15	0.0	‡8	80	10.0	0
1999—Arizona NFL	16	16	69	34	0.0	2	110	55.0	1
2000—Arizona NFL	16	16	63	31	0.0	1	11	11.0	0
2001—Arizona NFL	16	16	83	28	1.0	9	80	8.9	0
2002—Arizona NFL	16	16	59	29	0.0	2	7	3.5	0
Pro totals (8 years)	115	71	356	157	4.0	24	318	13.3	1

LAW, TY   CB   PATRIOTS

PERSONAL: Born February 10, 1974, in Aliquippa, Pa. ... 5-11/200. ... Full name: Tajuan Law.
HIGH SCHOOL: Aliquippa (Pa.).
COLLEGE: Michigan.
TRANSACTIONS/CAREER NOTES: Selected after junior season by New England Patriots in first round (23rd pick overall) of 1995 NFL draft. ... Signed by Patriots (July 20, 1995). ... On injured reserve with hand injury (December 29, 1999-remainder of season).
CHAMPIONSHIP GAME EXPERIENCE: Played in AFC championship game (1996 and 2001 seasons). ... Played in Super Bowl XXXI (1996 season). ... Member of Super Bowl championship team (2001 season).
HONORS: Named cornerback on THE SPORTING NEWS NFL All-Pro team (1998). ... Played in Pro Bowl (1998, 2001 and 2002 seasons). ... Named co-Oustanding Player of Pro Bowl (1998 season).
POST SEASON RECORDS: Shares Super Bowl single-game record for most interceptions returned for touchdown—1 (February 3, 2002 vs. St. Louis Rams).

Year Team	G	GS	TOTALS			INTERCEPTIONS			
			Tk.	Ast.	Sks.	No.	Yds.	Avg.	TD
1995—New England NFL	14	7	40	7	1.0	3	47	15.7	0
1996—New England NFL	13	12	56	6	0.0	3	45	15.0	1
1997—New England NFL	16	16	69	8	0.5	3	70	23.3	0
1998—New England NFL	16	16	60	10	0.0	*9	133	14.8	1
1999—New England NFL	13	13	50	9	0.5	2	20	10.0	1
2000—New England NFL	15	15	58	16	0.0	2	32	16.0	0
2001—New England NFL	16	16	60	10	1.0	3	91	30.3	†2
2002—New England NFL	16	16	60	17	1.0	4	33	8.3	0
Pro totals (8 years)	119	111	453	83	4.0	29	471	16.2	5

LAYNE, GEORGE   FB   FALCONS

PERSONAL: Born October 9, 1978, in Alvin, Texas. ... 6-0/245.
HIGH SCHOOL: Alvin (Texas).
COLLEGE: Texas Christian.
TRANSACTIONS/CAREER NOTES: Selected after junior season by Kansas City Chiefs in fourth round (108th pick overall) of 2001 NFL draft. ... Signed by Chiefs (July 23, 2001). ... Released by Chiefs (September 2, 2001). ... Re-signed by Chiefs to practice squad (September 4, 2001). ... Signed by Atlanta Falcons off Chiefs practice squad (October 2, 2001). ... Released by Falcons (September 1, 2002). ... Signed by Falcons (November 12, 2002).
SINGLE GAME HIGHS (regular season): Attempts—1 (December 22, 2002, vs. Detroit); yards—5 (December 22, 2002, vs. Detroit); and rushing touchdowns—0.

Year Team	G	GS	RUSHING				RECEIVING				TOTALS			
			Att.	Yds.	Avg.	TD	No.	Yds.	Avg.	TD	TD	2pt.	Pts.	Fum.
2001—Atlanta NFL	2	0	0	0	0.0	0	0	0	0.0	0	0	0	0	0
2002—Atlanta NFL	2	0	1	5	5.0	0	2	11	5.5	0	0	0	0	1
Pro totals (2 years)	4	0	1	5	5.0	0	2	11	5.5	0	0	0	0	1

LEACH, MIKE   FB   BRONCOS

PERSONAL: Born October 18, 1976, in Lake Hopatcong, N.J. ... 6-2/245.
HIGH SCHOOL: Jefferson Township (N.J.).
COLLEGE: Boston University, then William and Mary.
TRANSACTIONS/CAREER NOTES: Signed as non-drafted free agent by Tennessee Titans (April 20, 2000). ... Released by Titans (October 16, 2001). ... Signed by Chicago Bears (January 10, 2001). ... Released by Bears (August 26, 2002). ... Signed by Denver Broncos (November 4, 2002).

Year Team	G	GS	RUSHING				TOTALS			
			Att.	Yds.	Avg.	TD	TD	2pt.	Pts.	Fum.
2000—Tennessee NFL	15	0	0	0	0.0	0	0	0	0	0
2001—Tennessee NFL	4	0	0	0	0.0	0	0	0	0	0
2002—Denver NFL	8	0	0	0	0.0	0	0	0	0	0
Pro totals (3 years)	27	0	0	0	0.0	0	0	0	0	0

LEBER, BEN   LB   CHARGERS

PERSONAL: Born December 7, 1978, in Vermillion, S.D. ... 6-3/244.
HIGH SCHOOL: Vermillion (S.D.).
COLLEGE: Kansas State.
TRANSACTIONS/CAREER NOTES: Selected by San Diego Chargers in third round (71st pick overall) of 2002 NFL draft. ... Signed by Chargers (July 22, 2002).

Year Team	G	GS	TOTALS			INTERCEPTIONS			
			Tk.	Ast.	Sks.	No.	Yds.	Avg.	TD
2002—San Diego NFL	16	14	40	9	5.0	0	0	0.0	0

LECHLER, SHANE   P   RAIDERS

PERSONAL: Born August 7, 1976, in Sealy, Texas. ... 6-2/225. ... Full name: Edward Shane Lechler.
HIGH SCHOOL: East Bernard (Texas).
COLLEGE: Texas A&M.
TRANSACTIONS/CAREER NOTES: Selected by Oakland Raiders in fifth round (142nd pick overall) of 2000 NFL draft. ... Signed by Raiders (July 22, 2000).
CHAMPIONSHIP GAME EXPERIENCE: Played in AFC championship game (2000 and 2002 seasons). ... Played in Super Bowl XXXVII (2002 season).
HONORS: Named punter on THE SPORTING NEWS college All-America second team (1997). ... Named punter on THE SPORTING NEWS college All-America first team (1998). ... Named punter on THE SPORTING NEWS NFL All-Pro team (2000). ... Named punter on THE SPORTING NEWS college All-America third team (1999). ... Played in Pro Bowl (2001 season).

			PUNTING				
Year Team	G	No.	Yds.	Avg.	Net avg.	In. 20	Blk.
2000—Oakland NFL	16	65	2984	45.9	*38.0	24	▲1
2001—Oakland NFL	16	73	3375	§46.2	35.6	23	1
2002—Oakland NFL	14	53	2251	42.5	32.7	18	0
Pro totals (3 years)	46	191	8610	45.1	35.6	65	2

LEE, CHARLES   WR   BUCCANEERS

PERSONAL: Born November 19, 1977, in Miami. ... 6-2/210. ... Cousin of Harvey Clayton, defensive back with Pittsburgh Steelers (1983-86) and New York Giants (1987).
HIGH SCHOOL: Homestead (Fla.).
COLLEGE: Central Florida (degree in communications).
TRANSACTIONS/CAREER NOTES: Selected by Green Bay Packers in seventh round (242nd pick overall) of 2000 NFL draft. ... Signed by Packers (June 21, 2000). ... Released by Packers (September 1, 2002). ... Signed by Tampa Bay Buccaneers (October 1, 2002). ... Granted free agency (February 28, 2003). ... Re-signed by Buccaneers (May 22, 2003).
SINGLE GAME HIGHS (regular season): Receptions—3 (September 10, 2000, vs. Buffalo); yards—46 (October 8, 2000, vs. Detroit); and touchdown receptions—1 (October 21, 2001, vs. Minnesota).

			RECEIVING			
Year Team	G	GS	No.	Yds.	Avg.	TD
2000—Green Bay NFL	15	1	10	134	13.4	0
2001—Green Bay NFL	7	0	3	32	10.7	1
2002—Tampa Bay NFL	1	0	0	0	0.0	0
Pro totals (3 years)	23	1	13	166	12.8	1

LEGREE, LANCE   DT   GIANTS

PERSONAL: Born December 22, 1977, in Charleston, S.C. ... 6-1/300.
HIGH SCHOOL: St. Stephens (S.C.).
COLLEGE: Notre Dame.
TRANSACTIONS/CAREER NOTES: Signed as non-drafted free agent by New York Giants (April 27, 2001).

			TOTALS		
Year Team	G	GS	Tk.	Ast.	Sks.
2001—New York Giants NFL	13	2	15	4	0.0
2002—New York Giants NFL	15	10	18	12	0.0
Pro totals (2 years)	28	12	33	16	0.0

LEHR, MATT   G/OC   COWBOYS

PERSONAL: Born April 25, 1979, in Jacksonville. ... 6-2/304. ... Full name: Matthew Steven Lehr.
HIGH SCHOOL: Woodbridge (Va.).
COLLEGE: Virginia Tech.
TRANSACTIONS/CAREER NOTES: Selected by Dallas Cowboys in fifth round (137th pick overall) of 2001 NFL draft. ... Signed by Cowboys (July 21, 2001).
PLAYING EXPERIENCE: Dallas NFL, 2001-2002. ... Games/Games started: 2001 (8/0), 2002 (12/4). Total: 20/4.

LEIGEB, BRIAN   S

PERSONAL: Born October 2, 1978, in Midland, Mich. ... 6-2/207. ... Name pronounced LYE-geb.
HIGH SCHOOL: H.H. Dow (Midland, Mich.).
COLLEGE: Central Michigan.
TRANSACTIONS/CAREER NOTES: Signed as non-drafted free agent by Buffalo Bills (July 6, 2001). ... Released by Bills (September 3, 2001). ... Signed by Indianapolis Colts to practice squad (December 3, 2001). ... Released by Colts (November 4, 2002). ... Re-signed by Colts (November 15, 2002). ... Claimed on waivers by Cincinnati Bengals (March 2, 2003). ... Released by Bengals (March 11, 2003).

			TOTALS			INTERCEPTIONS			
Year Team	G	GS	Tk.	Ast.	Sks.	No.	Yds.	Avg.	TD
2002—Indianapolis NFL	15	0	3	1	0.0	0	0	0.0	0

LELIE, ASHLEY   WR   BRONCOS

PERSONAL: Born February 16, 1980, in Bellflower, Calif. ... 6-3/200.
HIGH SCHOOL: Radford (Honolulu, Hawaii).
COLLEGE: Hawaii.
TRANSACTIONS/CAREER NOTES: Selected after junior season by Denver Broncos in first round (19th pick overall) of 2002 NFL draft. ... Signed by Broncos (July 25, 2002).
HONORS: Named wide receiver on THE SPORTING NEWS college All-America third team (2001).
SINGLE GAME HIGHS (regular season): Receptions—8 (November 11, 2002, vs. Oakland); yards—106 (December 22, 2002, vs. Oakland); and touchdown receptions—1 (December 29, 2002, vs. Arizona).
STATISTICAL PLATEAUS: 100-yard receiving games: 2002 (1).

			RUSHING				RECEIVING				TOTALS			
Year Team	G	GS	Att.	Yds.	Avg.	TD	No.	Yds.	Avg.	TD	TD	2pt.	Pts.	Fum.
2002—Denver NFL	16	1	4	40	10.0	0	35	525	15.0	2	2	0	12	0

LENON, PARIS   LB   PACKERS

PERSONAL: Born November 26, 1977, in Lynchburg, Va. ... 6-2/232. ... Full name: Paris Michael Lenon.
HIGH SCHOOL: Heritage (Lynchburg, Va.).
COLLEGE: Richmond (degree in studio art).
TRANSACTIONS/CAREER NOTES: Signed as non-drafted free agent by Carolina Panthers (April 26, 2000). ... Released by Panthers (June 9, 2000). ... Signed by Green Bay Packers (April 26, 2001). ... Released by Packers (July 24, 2001). ... Signed by Seattle Seahawks (August 16, 2001). ... Released by Seahawks (August 27, 2001). ... Signed by Packers to practice squad (December 27, 2001). ... Assigned by Packers to Amsterdam Admirals in 2002 NFL Europe enhancement allocation program (February 12, 2002).

			TOTALS			INTERCEPTIONS			
Year Team	G	GS	Tk.	Ast.	Sks.	No.	Yds.	Avg.	TD
2002—Amsterdam NFLE	10	10	...	...	0.0	2	10	5.0	0
—Green Bay NFL	16	0	3	0	0.0	0	0	0.0	0
NFL Europe totals (1 year)	10	10	...	...	0.0	2	10	5.0	0
NFL totals (1 year)	16	0	3	0	0.0	0	0	0.0	0
Pro totals (2 years)	26	10	...	...	0.0	2	10	5.0	0

LEPSIS, MATT   OT   BRONCOS

PERSONAL: Born January 13, 1974, in Conroe, Texas. ... 6-4/290. ... Full name: Matthew Lepsis.
HIGH SCHOOL: Frisco (Texas).
COLLEGE: Colorado.
TRANSACTIONS/CAREER NOTES: Signed as non-drafted free agent by Denver Broncos (April 22, 1997). ... On non-football injury list with knee injury (July 16, 1997-entire season). ... Assigned by Broncos to Barcelona Dragons in 1998 NFL Europe enhancement allocation program (February 18, 1998). ... Granted free agency (March 2, 2001). ... Re-signed by Broncos (March 21, 2001).
PLAYING EXPERIENCE: Barcelona NFLE, 1998; Denver NFL, 1998-2002. ... Games/Games started: NFLE 1998 (games played unavailable), NFL 1998 (16/0), 1999 (16/16), 2000 (16/16), 2001 (16/16), 2002 (16/15). Total NFL: 80/63.
CHAMPIONSHIP GAME EXPERIENCE: Played in AFC championship game (1998 season). ... Member of Super Bowl championship team (1998 season).

LEVENS, DORSEY   RB   GIANTS

PERSONAL: Born May 21, 1970, in Syracuse, N.Y. ... 6-1/230. ... Full name: Herbert Dorsey Levens.
HIGH SCHOOL: Nottingham (Syracuse, N.Y.).
COLLEGE: Notre Dame, then Georgia Tech (degree in business management).
TRANSACTIONS/CAREER NOTES: Selected by Green Bay Packers in fifth round (149th pick overall) of 1994 NFL draft. ... Signed by Packers (June 9, 1994). ... Granted free agency (February 14, 1997). ... Re-signed by Packers (June 20, 1997). ... Designated by Packers as franchise player (February 13, 1998). ... Re-signed by Packers (August 30, 1998). ... Released by Packers (February 28, 2002). ... Signed by Philadelphia Eagles (July 11, 2002). ... Granted unconditional free agency (February 28, 2003). ... Signed by New York Giants (April 7, 2003).
CHAMPIONSHIP GAME EXPERIENCE: Played in NFC championship game (1995-97 and 2002 seasons). ... Member of Super Bowl championship team (1996 season). ... Played in Super Bowl XXXII (1997 season).
HONORS: Played in Pro Bowl (1997 season).
SINGLE GAME HIGHS (regular season): Attempts—33 (November 23, 1997, vs. Dallas); yards—190 (November 23, 1997, vs. Dallas); and rushing touchdowns—4 (January 2, 2000, vs. Arizona).
STATISTICAL PLATEAUS: 100-yard rushing games: 1997 (6), 1998 (1), 1999 (3). Total: 10.

			RUSHING				RECEIVING				KICKOFF RETURNS				TOTALS			
Year Team	G	GS	Att.	Yds.	Avg.	TD	No.	Yds.	Avg.	TD	No.	Yds.	Avg.	TD	TD	2pt.	Pts.	Fum.
1994—Green Bay NFL	14	0	5	15	3.0	0	1	9	9.0	0	2	31	15.5	0	0	0	0	0
1995—Green Bay NFL	15	12	36	120	3.3	3	48	434	9.0	4	0	0	0.0	0	7	0	42	0
1996—Green Bay NFL	16	1	121	566	4.7	5	31	226	7.3	5	5	84	16.8	0	10	0	60	2
1997—Green Bay NFL	16	16	329	1435	4.4	7	53	370	7.0	5	0	0	0.0	0	12	1	74	5
1998—Green Bay NFL	7	4	115	378	3.3	1	27	162	6.0	0	0	0	0.0	0	1	0	6	0
1999—Green Bay NFL	14	14	279	1034	3.7	9	71	573	8.1	1	0	0	0.0	0	10	0	60	5
2000—Green Bay NFL	5	5	77	224	2.9	3	16	146	9.1	0	0	0	0.0	0	3	0	18	0
2001—Green Bay NFL	15	1	44	165	3.8	0	24	159	6.6	1	14	362	25.9	0	1	0	6	0
2002—Philadelphia NFL	16	0	75	411	5.5	1	19	124	6.5	1	1	24	24.0	0	2	0	12	1
Pro totals (9 years)	118	53	1081	4348	4.0	29	290	2203	7.6	17	22	501	22.8	0	46	1	278	13

LEVERETTE, OTIS   DE   CHARGERS

PERSONAL: Born May 31, 1978, in Americus, Ga. ... 6-6/278. ... Full name: Otis Catrell Leverette.
HIGH SCHOOL: Americus (Ga.).
JUNIOR COLLEGE: Middle Georgia College.
COLLEGE: Alabama-Birmingham.
TRANSACTIONS/CAREER NOTES: Selected by Miami Dolphins in sixth round (187th pick overall) of 2001 NFL draft. ... Signed by Dolphins (July 12, 2001). ... Claimed on waivers by Washington Redskins (September 3, 2001). ... Claimed on waivers by San Diego Chargers (November 19, 2002).

				TOTALS			INTERCEPTIONS			
Year Team	G	GS	Tk.	Ast.	Sks.	No.	Yds.	Avg.	TD
2001—Washington NFL	4	0	0	0	0.0	1	1	1.0	0
2002—Washington NFL	1	0	1	0	0.0	0	0	0.0	0
Pro totals (2 years)	5	0	1	0	0.0	1	1	1.0	0

LEWIS, CHAD   TE   EAGLES

PERSONAL: Born October 5, 1971, in Fort Dix, N.J. ... 6-6/252. ... Full name: Chad Wayne Lewis.
HIGH SCHOOL: Orem (Utah).
COLLEGE: Brigham Young (degrees in communications and Chinese).
TRANSACTIONS/CAREER NOTES: Signed as non-drafted free agent by Philadelphia Eagles (April 23, 1997). ... Released by Eagles (September 15, 1998). ... Signed by St. Louis Rams (December 9, 1998). ... Inactive for three games with Rams (1998). ... Claimed on waivers by Eagles (November 16, 1999). ... Granted free agency (February 11, 2000). ... Re-signed by Eagles (March 17, 2000).
CHAMPIONSHIP GAME EXPERIENCE: Played in NFC championship game (2001 and 2002 seasons).
HONORS: Played in Pro Bowl (2000-2002 seasons).
SINGLE GAME HIGHS (regular season): Receptions—9 (December 24, 2000, vs. Cincinnati); yards—100 (December 10, 2000, vs. Cleveland); and touchdown receptions—2 (December 30, 2001, vs. New York Giants).
STATISTICAL PLATEAUS: 100-yard receiving games: 2000 (1).

			RECEIVING					TOTALS		
Year Team	G	GS	No.	Yds.	Avg.	TD	TD	2pt.	Pts.	Fum.
1997—Philadelphia NFL	16	3	12	94	7.8	4	4	0	24	0
1998—Philadelphia NFL	2	0	0	0	0.0	0	0	0	0	0
1999—St. Louis NFL	6	0	1	12	12.0	0	0	0	0	0
—Philadelphia NFL	6	4	7	76	10.9	3	3	0	18	0
2000—Philadelphia NFL	16	16	69	735	10.7	3	3	0	18	0
2001—Philadelphia NFL	15	15	41	422	10.3	6	6	0	36	2
2002—Philadelphia NFL	16	16	42	398	9.5	3	3	∞2	22	2
Pro totals (6 years)	77	54	172	1737	10.1	19	19	2	118	4

LEWIS, D.D.   LB   SEAHAWKS

PERSONAL: Born January 8, 1979, in Bermahaven, Germany. ... 6-1/241. ... Full name: De'Andre De'Wayne Lewis. ... Cousin of Rodney Thomas, running back with Houston/Tennessee Oilers (1995-97), Tennessee Titans (1998-2000) and Atlanta Falcons (2001).
HIGH SCHOOL: Aldine (Houston).
COLLEGE: Texas.
TRANSACTIONS/CAREER NOTES: Signed as non-drafted free agent by Seattle Seahawks (April 30, 2002).

				TOTALS			INTERCEPTIONS			
Year Team	G	GS	Tk.	Ast.	Sks.	No.	Yds.	Avg.	TD
2002—Seattle NFL	16	0	15	2	0.0	0	0	0.0	0

LEWIS, DAMIONE   DT   RAMS

PERSONAL: Born March 1, 1978, in Sulphur Springs, Texas. ... 6-2/301. ... Full name: Damione Ramon Lewis.
HIGH SCHOOL: Sulphur Springs (Texas).
COLLEGE: Miami.
TRANSACTIONS/CAREER NOTES: Selected by St. Louis Rams in first round (12th pick overall) of 2001 NFL draft. ... Signed by Rams (July 27, 2001). ... On injured reserve with foot injury (November 20, 2001-remainder of season).
HONORS: Named defensive tackle on THE SPORTING NEWS college All-America third team (2000).

			TOTALS		
Year Team	G	GS	Tk.	Ast.	Sks.
2001—St. Louis NFL	9	3	9	1	0.0
2002—St. Louis NFL	16	2	14	6	4.0
Pro totals (2 years)	25	5	23	7	4.0

LEWIS, DERRICK   WR   SAINTS

PERSONAL: Born October 30, 1975, in New Orleans. ... 6-2/185. ... Full name: Derrick Lamont Lewis.
HIGH SCHOOL: Joseph S. Clark (New Orleans).
JUNIOR COLLEGE: Sacramento City College.
COLLEGE: San Diego State.
TRANSACTIONS/CAREER NOTES: Signed as non-drafted free agent by New Orleans Saints (April 23, 2002). ... Released by Saints (August 26, 2002). ... Re-signed by Saints to practice squad (September 2, 2002). ... Released by Saints (September 11, 2002). ... Re-signed by Saints to practice squad (September 18, 2002). ... Activated (December 22, 2002).

			RECEIVING			
Year Team	G	GS	No.	Yds.	Avg.	TD
2002—New Orleans NFL	2	0	0	0	0.0	0

LEWIS, JAMAL　　　　　RB　　　　　RAVENS

PERSONAL: Born August 29, 1979, in Atlanta. ... 5-11/231. ... Full name: Jamal Lafitte Lewis.
HIGH SCHOOL: Douglass (Atlanta).
COLLEGE: Tennessee.
TRANSACTIONS/CAREER NOTES: Selected after junior season by Baltimore Ravens in first round (fifth pick overall) of 2000 NFL draft. ... Signed by Ravens (July 24, 2000). ... On injured reserve with knee injury (August 28, 2001-entire season). ... On suspended list for violating league substance abuse policy (November 17, 2001-present).
CHAMPIONSHIP GAME EXPERIENCE: Played in AFC championship game (2000 season). ... Member of Super Bowl championship team (2000 season).
HONORS: Named College Football Freshman of the Year by THE SPORTING NEWS (1997).
SINGLE GAME HIGHS (regular season): Attempts—30 (November 26, 2000, vs. Cleveland); yards—187 (October 6, 2002, vs. Cleveland); and rushing touchdowns—2 (November 10, 2002, vs. Cincinnati).
STATISTICAL PLATEAUS: 100-yard rushing games: 2000 (5), 2002 (5). Total: 10. ... 100-yard receiving games: 2002 (1).
MISCELLANEOUS: Holds Baltimore Ravens all-time records for most yards rushing (2,691) and rushing touchdowns (12).

			RUSHING				RECEIVING				TOTALS			
Year　Team	G	GS	Att.	Yds.	Avg.	TD	No.	Yds.	Avg.	TD	TD	2pt.	Pts.	Fum.
2000—Baltimore NFL	16	14	309	1364	4.4	6	27	296	11.0	0	6	1	38	6
2001—Baltimore NFL							Did not play.							
2002—Baltimore NFL	16	15	308	1327	4.3	6	47	442	9.4	1	7	0	42	8
Pro totals (2 years)	32	29	617	2691	4.4	12	74	738	10.0	1	13	1	80	14

LEWIS, JERMAINE　　　　　WR/PR　　　　　JAGUARS

PERSONAL: Born October 16, 1974, in Lanham, Md. ... 5-7/180. ... Full name: Jermaine Edward Lewis.
HIGH SCHOOL: Eleanor Roosevelt (Greenbelt, Md.).
COLLEGE: Maryland.
TRANSACTIONS/CAREER NOTES: Selected by Baltimore Ravens in fifth round (153rd pick overall) of 1996 NFL draft. ... Signed by Ravens (July 18, 1996). ... Selected by Houston Texans from Ravens in NFL expansion draft (February 18, 2002). ... Released by Texans (February 20, 2003). ... Signed by Jacksonville Jaguars (March 20, 2003).
CHAMPIONSHIP GAME EXPERIENCE: Played in AFC championship game (2000 season). ... Member of Super Bowl championship team (2000 season).
HONORS: Named punt returner on THE SPORTING NEWS NFL All-Pro team (1998 and 2001). ... Played in Pro Bowl (1998 and 2001 seasons).
RECORDS: Shares NFL single-game records for most touchdowns by punt returns—2; (December 7, 1997, vs. Seattle and also on December 24, 2000, vs. New York Jets) and most touchdowns by combined kick return—2 (December 7, 1997, vs. Seattle and also on December 24, 2000, vs. New York Jets).
SINGLE GAME HIGHS (regular season): Receptions—8 (September 21, 1997, vs. Tennessee); yards—124 (September 21, 1997, vs. Tennessee); and touchdown receptions—2 (December 5, 1999, vs. Tennessee).
STATISTICAL PLATEAUS: 100-yard receiving games: 1997 (2), 1998 (2). Total: 4.
MISCELLANEOUS: Holds Baltimore Ravens all-time record for most touchdowns (22).

			RUSHING				RECEIVING				PUNT RETURNS				KICKOFF RETURNS				TOTALS		
Year　Team	G	GS	Att.	Yds.	Avg.	TD	No.	Yds.	Avg.	TD	No.	Yds.	Avg.	TD	No.	Yds.	Avg.	TD	TD	2pt.	Pts.
1996—Baltimore NFL	16	1	1	-3	-3.0	0	5	78	15.6	1	36	339	9.4	0	41	883	21.5	0	1	0	6
1997—Baltimore NFL	14	7	3	35	11.7	0	42	648	15.4	6	28	437*15.6		2	41	905	22.1	0	8	0	48
1998—Baltimore NFL	13	13	5	20	4.0	0	41	784	19.1	6	32	405	12.7	†2	6	145	24.2	0	8	0	48
1999—Baltimore NFL	15	6	5	11	2.2	0	25	281	11.2	2	*57	452	7.9	0	8	158	19.8	0	2	0	12
2000—Baltimore NFL	15	1	3	38	12.7	0	19	161	8.5	1	36	578*16.1		†2	1	23	23.0	0	3	0	18
2001—Baltimore NFL	15	2	9	33	3.7	0	4	32	8.0	0	*42	*519	12.4	0	42	1039	24.7	0	0	0	0
2002—Houston NFL	12	2	3	8	2.7	0	2	41	20.5	0	36	280	7.8	0	46	961	20.9	0	0	0	0
Pro totals (7 years)	100	32	29	142	4.9	0	138	2025	14.7	16	267	3010	11.3	6	185	4114	22.2	0	22	0	132

LEWIS, KEVIN　　　　　LB　　　　　GIANTS

PERSONAL: Born October 6, 1978, in Orlando, Fla. ... 6-1/230.
HIGH SCHOOL: Jones (Orlando, Fla.).
COLLEGE: Duke.
TRANSACTIONS/CAREER NOTES: Signed by New York Giants as non-drafted free agent (April 20, 2000). ... Released by Giants (September 2, 2001). ... Re-signed by Giants to practice squad (September 3, 2001). ... Activated (November 4, 2001). ... Granted free agency (February 28, 2003). ... Re-signed by Giants (March 6, 2003).
CHAMPIONSHIP GAME EXPERIENCE: Member of Giants for Super Bowl XXXV (2000 season); inactive.

			TOTALS			INTERCEPTIONS			
Year　Team	G	GS	Tk.	Ast.	Sks.	No.	Yds.	Avg.	TD
2000—New York Giants NFL	6	0	1	0	0.0	0	0	0.0	0
2001—New York Giants NFL	9	0	0	0	0.0	0	0	0.0	0
2002—New York Giants NFL	15	2	10	3	1.0	0	0	0.0	0
Pro totals (3 years)	30	2	11	3	1.0	0	0	0.0	0

LEWIS, MICHAEL　　　　　WR　　　　　SAINTS

PERSONAL: Born November 14, 1971, in New Orleans. ... 5-8/165. ... Full name: Michael Lee Lewis.
HIGH SCHOOL: Grace King (Metairie, La.).
TRANSACTIONS/CAREER NOTES: Signed as non-drafted free agent by Philadelphia Eagles (July 14, 2000). ... Released by Eagles (August 21, 2000). ... Signed by New Orleans Saints (January 9, 2001). ... Assigned by Saints to Rhein Fire in 2001 NFL Europe enhancement allocation program (February 17, 2001). ... Released by Saints (October 30, 2001). ... Re-signed by Saints (December 21, 2001).

HONORS: Played in Pro Bowl (2002 season). ... Named kick returner on the THE SPORTING NEWS NFL All-Pro team (2002).
RECORDS: Holds NFL single-season record for most combined kick returns—114 (2002); and most yards from combined kick returns—2,432 (2002).
SINGLE GAME HIGHS (regular season): Receptions—3 (November 24, 2002, vs. Cleveland); yards—114 (November 24, 2002, vs. Cleveland); and touchdown receptions—0.
STATISTICAL PLATEAUS: 100-yard receiving games: 2002 (1).

			RECEIVING				PUNT RETURNS				KICKOFF RETURNS				TOTALS			
Year Team	G	GS	No.	Yds.	Avg.	TD	No.	Yds.	Avg.	TD	No.	Yds.	Avg.	TD	TD	2pt.	Pts.	Fum.
2001—Rhein NFLE	...	...	20	262	13.1	3	2	1	0.5	0	9	185	20.6	0	3	0	18	0
—New Orleans NFL	8	0	0	0	0.0	0	14	81	5.8	0	32	762	23.8	0	0	0	0	6
2002—New Orleans NFL	16	0	8	200	25.0	0	44	*625	14.2	1	*70	*1807	25.8	†2	3	0	18	6
NFL Europe totals (1 year)	...	...	20	262	13.1	3	2	1	0.5	0	9	185	20.6	0	3	0	18	0
NFL totals (2 years)	24	0	8	200	25.0	0	58	706	12.2	1	102	2569	25.2	2	3	0	18	12
Pro totals (3 years)	...	...	28	462	16.5	3	60	707	11.8	1	111	2754	24.8	2	6	0	36	12

LEWIS, MICHAEL   S   EAGLES

PERSONAL: Born April 29, 1980, in Houston. ... 6-1/211.
HIGH SCHOOL: Lamar Consolidated (Richmond, Texas).
COLLEGE: Colorado.
TRANSACTIONS/CAREER NOTES: Selected by Philadelphia Eagles in second round (58th pick overall) of 2002 NFL draft. ... Signed by Eagles (June 25, 2002).
CHAMPIONSHIP GAME EXPERIENCE: Played in NFC championship game (2002 season).
HONORS: Named safety on THE SPORTING NEWS college All-America third team (2001).

			TOTALS			INTERCEPTIONS			
Year Team	G	GS	Tk.	Ast.	Sks.	No.	Yds.	Avg.	TD
2002—Philadelphia NFL	14	4	33	5	1.0	1	0	0.0	0

LEWIS, MO   LB   JETS

PERSONAL: Born October 21, 1969, in Atlanta. ... 6-3/258. ... Full name: Morris C. Lewis.
HIGH SCHOOL: J.C. Murphy (Atlanta).
COLLEGE: Georgia.
TRANSACTIONS/CAREER NOTES: Selected by New York Jets in third round (62nd pick overall) of 1991 NFL draft. ... Signed by Jets (July 18, 1991). ... Designated by Jets as franchise player (February 11, 2000).
CHAMPIONSHIP GAME EXPERIENCE: Played in AFC championship game (1998 season).
HONORS: Played in Pro Bowl (1998-2000 seasons).

			TOTALS			INTERCEPTIONS			
Year Team	G	GS	Tk.	Ast.	Sks.	No.	Yds.	Avg.	TD
1991—New York Jets NFL	16	16	48	28	2.0	0	0	0.0	0
1992—New York Jets NFL	16	16	105	40	1.0	1	1	1.0	0
1993—New York Jets NFL	16	16	95	63	4.0	2	4	2.0	0
1994—New York Jets NFL	16	16	103	27	6.0	4	106	26.5	2
1995—New York Jets NFL	16	16	82	29	5.0	2	22	11.0	▲1
1996—New York Jets NFL	9	9	32	11	0.5	0	0	0.0	0
1997—New York Jets NFL	16	16	45	27	8.0	1	43	43.0	1
1998—New York Jets NFL	16	16	67	14	7.0	1	11	11.0	0
1999—New York Jets NFL	16	16	58	31	5.5	0	0	0.0	0
2000—New York Jets NFL	16	16	65	23	10.0	1	23	23.0	0
2001—New York Jets NFL	16	16	77	31	3.0	1	17	17.0	0
2002—New York Jets NFL	16	16	68	14	0.5	1	14	14.0	0
Pro totals (12 years)	185	185	845	338	52.5	14	241	17.2	4

LEWIS, RAY   LB   RAVENS

PERSONAL: Born May 15, 1975, in Bartow, Fla. ... 6-1/245. ... Full name: Ray Anthony Lewis.
HIGH SCHOOL: Kathleen (Lakeland, Fla.).
COLLEGE: Miami (Fla.).
TRANSACTIONS/CAREER NOTES: Selected after junior season by Baltimore Ravens in first round (26th pick overall) of 1996 NFL draft. ... Signed by Ravens (July 15, 1996). ... On injured reserve with shoulder injury (November 26, 2002-remainder of season).
CHAMPIONSHIP GAME EXPERIENCE: Played in AFC championship game (2000 season). ... Member of Super Bowl championship team (2000 season).
HONORS: Named linebacker on THE SPORTING NEWS college All-America second team (1995). ... Played in Pro Bowl (1997, 1998, 2000 and 2001 seasons). ... Named linebacker on THE SPORTING NEWS NFL All-Pro team (1998-2001). ... Named to play in Pro Bowl (1999 season); replaced by Junior Seau due to personal reasons. ... Named Most Valuable Player of Super Bowl XXXV (2000 season).

			TOTALS			INTERCEPTIONS			
Year Team	G	GS	Tk.	Ast.	Sks.	No.	Yds.	Avg.	TD
1996—Baltimore NFL	14	13	95	15	2.5	1	0	0.0	0
1997—Baltimore NFL	16	16	156	28	4.0	1	18	18.0	0
1998—Baltimore NFL	14	14	101	19	3.0	2	25	12.5	0
1999—Baltimore NFL	16	16	131	37	3.5	3	97	32.3	0
2000—Baltimore NFL	16	16	107	30	3.0	2	1	0.5	0
2001—Baltimore NFL	16	16	114	48	3.5	3	115	38.3	0
2002—Baltimore NFL	5	5	43	15	0.0	2	4	2.0	0
Pro totals (7 years)	97	96	747	192	19.5	14	260	18.6	0

LEYVA, VICTOR   G   BENGALS

PERSONAL: Born December 18, 1977, in Porteville, Calif. ... 6-4/315.
HIGH SCHOOL: Monache (Porterville, Calif.).
COLLEGE: Arizona State (degree in sociology).
TRANSACTIONS/CAREER NOTES: Selected by Cincinnati Bengals in fifth round (135th pick overall) of 2001 NFL draft. ... Signed by Bengals (July 10, 2001).
PLAYING EXPERIENCE: Cincinnati NFL, 2002. ... Games/games started: (10/0).

LIGHT, MATT   OT   PATRIOTS

PERSONAL: Born June 23, 1978, in Greenville, Ohio. ... 6-4/305. ... Full name: Matthew Charles Light.
HIGH SCHOOL: Greenville (Ohio).
COLLEGE: Purdue.
TRANSACTIONS/CAREER NOTES: Selected by New England Patriots in second round (48th pick overall) of 2001 NFL draft. ... Signed by Patriots (July 22, 2001).
PLAYING EXPERIENCE: New England NFL, 2001-2002. ... Games/Games started: 2001 (14/12), 2002 (16/16). Total: 30/28.
CHAMPIONSHIP GAME EXPERIENCE: Played in AFC championship game (2001 season). ... Member of Super Bowl championship team (2001 season).
HONORS: Named offensive tackle on THE SPORTING NEWS college All-America third team (2000).

LINDELL, RIAN   K   BILLS

PERSONAL: Born January 20, 1977, in Vancouver, Wash. ... 6-3/237. ... Full name: Rian David Lindell.
HIGH SCHOOL: Mountain View (Vancouver, Wash.).
COLLEGE: Washington State.
TRANSACTIONS/CAREER NOTES: Signed as non-drafted free agent by Seattle Seahawks (September 26, 2000). ... Granted free agency (February 28, 2003). ... Signed by Buffalo Bills (March 24, 2003).

				FIELD GOALS							TOTALS		
Year Team	G	1-29	30-39	40-49	50+	Tot.	Pct.	Lg.		XPM	XPA	Pts.
2000—Seattle NFL	12	4-5	1-1	7-8	3-3	15-17	88.2	52		25	25	70
2001—Seattle NFL	16	7-8	4-5	6-14	3-5	20-32	62.5	54		33	33	93
2002—Seattle NFL	16	10-10	8-10	4-5	1-4	23-29	79.3	52		38	38	107
Pro totals (3 years)	44	21-23	13-16	17-27	7-12	58-78	74.4	54		96	96	270

LINDSAY, EVERETT   OL   VIKINGS

PERSONAL: Born September 18, 1970, in Burlington, Iowa. ... 6-4/302. ... Full name: Everett Eric Lindsay.
HIGH SCHOOL: Millbrook (Raleigh, N.C.).
COLLEGE: Mississippi (degree in general business, 1992).
TRANSACTIONS/CAREER NOTES: Selected by Minnesota Vikings in fifth round (133rd pick overall) of 1993 NFL draft. ... Signed by Vikings (July 14, 1993). ... On injured reserve with shoulder injury (December 22, 1993-remainder of season). ... On injured reserve with shoulder injury (August 23, 1994-entire season). ... On physically unable to perform list with knee injury (July 22-August 20, 1996). ... On non-football injury list with knee injury (August 20, 1996-entire season). ... Assigned by Vikings to Barcelona Dragons in 1997 World League enhancement allocation program (February 19, 1997). ... Granted unconditional free agency (February 13, 1998). ... Re-signed by Vikings (February 17, 1998). ... Traded by Vikings to Baltimore Ravens for sixth-round pick (DE Talance Sawyer) in 1999 draft (April 17, 1999). ... Granted free agency (February 11, 2000). ... Signed by Cleveland Browns (February 15, 2000). ... Traded by Browns to Vikings for future draft pick (August 14, 2001).
PLAYING EXPERIENCE: Minnesota NFL, 1993, 1995, 1997 and 1998; Baltimore NFL, 1999; Cleveland NFL, 2000; Minnesota NFL, 2001-2002. ... Games/Games started: 1993 (12/12), 1995 (16/0), 1997 (16/3), 1998 (16/3), 1999 (16/16), 2000 (16/16), 2001 (16/8), 2002 (16/5). Total: 124/63.
CHAMPIONSHIP GAME EXPERIENCE: Played in NFC championship game (1998 season).
HONORS: Named offensive tackle on THE SPORTING NEWS college All-America second team (1992).

LITTLE, EARL   DB   BROWNS

PERSONAL: Born March 10, 1973, in Miami. ... 6-1/198. ... Full name: Earl Jerome Little.
HIGH SCHOOL: North Miami.
COLLEGE: Michigan, then Miami (Fla.).
TRANSACTIONS/CAREER NOTES: Signed as non-drafted free agent by Miami Dolphins (April 24, 1997). ... Released by Dolphins (August 24, 1997). ... Re-signed by Dolphins to practice squad (August 26, 1997). ... Released by Dolphins (August 29, 1997). ... Signed by New Orleans Saints to practice squad (October 1, 1997). ... Claimed on waivers by Cleveland Browns (October 25, 1999). ... Granted unconditional free agency (February 28, 2003). ... Re-signed by Browns (March 13, 2003).

			TOTALS			INTERCEPTIONS			
Year Team	G	GS	Tk.	Ast.	Sks.	No.	Yds.	Avg.	TD
1998—New Orleans NFL	16	0	0	0	0.0	0	0	0.0	0
1999—New Orleans NFL	1	0	0	0	0.0	0	0	0.0	0
—Cleveland NFL	9	0	5	0	0.0	1	0	0.0	0
2000—Cleveland NFL	16	0	24	2	0.0	1	7	7.0	0
2001—Cleveland NFL	16	16	65	17	1.0	5	33	6.6	0
2002—Cleveland NFL	13	9	42	19	0.0	4	17	4.3	0
Pro totals (5 years)	71	25	136	38	1.0	11	57	5.2	0

LITTLE, LEONARD   DE   RAMS

PERSONAL: Born October 19, 1974, in Asheville, N.C. ... 6-3/257. ... Full name: Leonard Antonio Little.
HIGH SCHOOL: Asheville (N.C.).
JUNIOR COLLEGE: Coffeyville (Kan.) Community College..
COLLEGE: Tennessee (degree in psychology, 1997).
TRANSACTIONS/CAREER NOTES: Selected by St. Louis Rams in third round (65th pick overall) of 1998 NFL draft. ... Signed by Rams (July 2, 1998). ... On non-football injury list for personal reasons (November 17, 1998-November 16, 1999). ... On suspended list for violating league substance abuse policy (July 16-November 9, 1999). ... Granted free agency (March 2, 2001). ... Re-signed by Rams (April 20, 2001). ... Granted unconditional free agency (March 1, 2002). ... Re-signed by Rams (March 3, 2002).
CHAMPIONSHIP GAME EXPERIENCE: Played in NFC championship game (1999 and 2001 seasons). ... Member of Super Bowl championship team (1999 season). ... Played in Super Bowl XXXVI (2001 season).

			TOTALS		
Year Team	G	GS	Tk.	Ast.	Sks.
1998—St. Louis NFL	6	0	1	1	0.5
1999—St. Louis NFL	6	0	1	0	0.0
2000—St. Louis NFL	14	0	13	4	5.0
2001—St. Louis NFL	13	0	23	3	14.5
2002—St. Louis NFL	16	15	37	7	12.0
Pro totals (5 years)	**55**	**15**	**75**	**15**	**32.0**

LITTLETON, JODY   LB

PERSONAL: Born October 23, 1974, in Brighton, Colo. ... 6-1/235.
HIGH SCHOOL: Brighton (Colo.).
COLLEGE: Baylor.
TRANSACTIONS/CAREER NOTES: Signed as non-drafted free agent by Atlanta Falcons (April 27, 1998). ... Released by Falcons (July 2, 1998). ... Signed by New York Giants (May 14, 2001). ... Released by Giants (August 27, 2001). ... Re-signed by Giants (January 15, 2002). ... Assigned by Giants to Frankfurt Galaxy in 2002 NFL Europe enhancement allocation program (February 12, 2002). ... Released by Giants (August 26, 2002). ... Signed by Chicago Bears (October 16, 2002). ... Released by Bears (October 29, 2002).

			TOTALS			INTERCEPTIONS			
Year Team	G	GS	Tk.	Ast.	Sks.	No.	Yds.	Avg.	TD
2002—Frankfurt NFLE	...	...	...	...	0.5	0	0	0.0	0
—Chicago NFL	2	0	0	0	0.0	0	0	0.0	0
NFL Europe totals (1 year)	...	...	...	...	0.5	0	0	0.0	0
NFL totals (1 year)	2	0	0	0	0.0	0	0	0.0	0
Pro totals (2 years)	...	...	...	...	0.5	0	0	0.0	0

LIWIENSKI, CHRIS   G   VIKINGS

PERSONAL: Born August 2, 1975, in Sterling Heights, Mich. ... 6-5/321. ... Name pronounced Loo-win-ski.
HIGH SCHOOL: Stevenson (Sterling Heights, Mich.).
COLLEGE: Indiana.
TRANSACTIONS/CAREER NOTES: Selected by Detroit Lions in seventh round (207th pick overall) of 1998 NFL draft. ... Signed by Lions (July 15, 1998). ... Released by Lions (August 24, 1998). ... Signed by Minnesota Vikings to practice squad (August 31, 1998). ... Activated (November 18, 1998). ... Released by Vikings (September 9, 1999). ... Re-signed by Vikings to practice squad (September 10, 1999). ... Activated (December 10, 1999); did not play.
PLAYING EXPERIENCE: Minnesota NFL, 1998, 2000-2002. ... Games/Games started: 1998 (1/0), 2000 (14/1), 2001 (16/16), 2002 (16/16). Total: 47/33.
CHAMPIONSHIP GAME EXPERIENCE: Member of Vikings for NFC championship game (1998 season); inactive. ... Played in NFC championship game (2000 season).

LOCKETT, KEVIN   WR   JAGUARS

PERSONAL: Born September 8, 1974, in Tulsa, Okla. ... 6-0/186.
HIGH SCHOOL: Washington (Okla.).
COLLEGE: Kansas State (degree in accounting).
TRANSACTIONS/CAREER NOTES: Selected by Kansas City Chiefs in second round (47th pick overall) of 1997 NFL draft. ... Signed by Chiefs (July 25, 1997). ... Granted free agency (February 11, 2000). ... Re-signed by Chiefs (May 3, 2000) ... Granted unconditional free agency (March 2, 2001). ... Signed by Washington Redskins (April 9, 2001). ... Claimed on waivers by Jacksonville Jaguars (November 3, 2002). ... Granted unconditional free agency (February 28, 2003). ... Re-signed by Jaguars (March 5, 2003).
SINGLE GAME HIGHS (regular season): Receptions—7 (November 5, 2000, vs. Oakland); yards—77 (October 29, 2000, vs. Seattle); and touchdown receptions—1 (December 15, 2002, vs. Cincinnati).

			RECEIVING				PUNT RETURNS				TOTALS			
Year Team	G	GS	No.	Yds.	Avg.	TD	No.	Yds.	Avg.	TD	TD	2pt.	Pts.	Fum.
1997—Kansas City NFL	9	0	1	35	35.0	0	0	0	0.0	0	0	0	0	0
1998—Kansas City NFL	13	3	19	281	14.8	0	7	36	5.1	0	0	0	0	2
1999—Kansas City NFL	16	1	34	426	12.5	2	1	10	10.0	0	2	0	12	0
2000—Kansas City NFL	16	2	33	422	12.8	2	26	208	8.0	0	2	0	12	3
2001—Washington NFL	16	0	22	293	13.3	0	5	14	2.8	0	0	0	0	1
2002—Washington NFL	6	2	11	129	11.7	2	0	0	0.0	0	2	0	12	1
—Jacksonville NFL	7	2	5	76	15.2	2	0	0	0.0	0	2	0	12	0
Pro totals (6 years)	**83**	**10**	**125**	**1662**	**13.3**	**8**	**39**	**268**	**6.9**	**0**	**8**	**0**	**48**	**7**

LOGAN, MIKE — S — STEELERS

PERSONAL: Born September 15, 1974, in Pittsburgh. ... 6-0/210. ... Full name: Michael V. Logan.
HIGH SCHOOL: McKeesport (Pa.).
COLLEGE: West Virginia.
TRANSACTIONS/CAREER NOTES: Selected by Jacksonville Jaguars in second round (50th pick overall) of 1997 NFL draft. ... Signed by Jaguars (May 23, 1997). ... On injured reserve with ankle injury (September 20, 1999-remainder of season). ... Granted free agency (February 11, 2000). ... Re-signed by Jaguars (March 10, 2000). ... Granted unconditional free agency (March 2, 2001). ... Signed by Pittsburgh Steelers (March 24, 2001). ... On injured reserve with knee injury (January 6, 2003-remainder of 2002 playoffs).
CHAMPIONSHIP GAME EXPERIENCE: Played in AFC championship game (2001 season).

Year Team	G	GS	TOTALS			INTERCEPTIONS				PUNT RETURNS				KICKOFF RETURNS				TOTALS			
			Tk.	Ast.	Sks.	No.	Yds.	Avg.	TD	No.	Yds.	Avg.	TD	No.	Yds.	Avg.	TD	TD	2pt.	Pts.	Fum.
1997—Jacksonville NFL	11	0	5	0	0.0	0	0	0.0	0	0	0	0.0	0	10	236	23.6	0	0	0	0	0
1998—Jacksonville NFL	15	0	13	5	0.0	0	0	0.0	0	2	26	13.0	0	18	414	23.0	0	0	0	0	1
1999—Jacksonville NFL	2	0	0	1	0.0	0	0	0.0	0	1	7	7.0	0	1	25	25.0	0	0	0	0	0
2000—Jacksonville NFL	15	11	48	6	1.0	2	14	7.0	0	0	0	0.0	0	0	0	0.0	0	0	0	0	0
2001—Pittsburgh NFL	16	1	20	3	2.0	2	2	1.0	0	0	0	0.0	0	1	9	9.0	0	0	0	0	0
2002—Pittsburgh NFL	14	0	29	7	0.5	1	46	46.0	0	0	0	0.0	0	0	0	0.0	0	0	0	0	0
Pro totals (6 years)	73	12	115	22	3.5	5	62	12.4	0	3	33	11.0	0	30	684	22.8	0	0	0	0	1

LONGWELL, RYAN — K — PACKERS

PERSONAL: Born August 16, 1974, in Seattle. ... 6-0/199. ... Full name: Ryan Walker Longwell.
HIGH SCHOOL: Bend (Ore.).
COLLEGE: California (degree in English).
TRANSACTIONS/CAREER NOTES: Signed as non-drafted free agent by San Francisco 49ers (April 28, 1997). ... Claimed on waivers by Green Bay Packers (July 10, 1997).
CHAMPIONSHIP GAME EXPERIENCE: Played in NFC championship game (1997 season). ... Played in Super Bowl XXXII (1997 season).

Year Team	G	FIELD GOALS							TOTALS		
		1-29	30-39	40-49	50+	Tot.	Pct.	Lg.	XPM	XPA	Pts.
1997—Green Bay NFL	16	11-12	10-13	2-4	1-1	24-30	80.0	50	*48	*48	120
1998—Green Bay NFL	16	7-7	13-15	9-10	0-1	29-33	87.9	45	41	43	128
1999—Green Bay NFL	16	8-9	8-9	8-10	1-2	25-30	83.3	50	38	38	113
2000—Green Bay NFL	16	7-8	10-10	13-15	3-5	‡33-‡38	86.8	52	32	32	131
2001—Green Bay NFL	16	3-4	9-10	7-14	1-3	20-31	64.5	54	44	45	104
2002—Green Bay NFL	16	9-10	12-13	7-10	0-1	28-34	82.4	49	‡44	‡44	128
Pro totals (6 years)	96	45-50	62-70	46-63	6-13	159-196	81.1	54	247	250	724

LOOKER, DANE — WR — RAMS

PERSONAL: Born May 5, 1976, in Puyallup, Wash. ... 6-0/194.
HIGH SCHOOL: Puyallup (Wash.).
COLLEGE: Washington.
TRANSACTIONS/CAREER NOTES: Signed as non-drafted free agent by St. Louis Rams (April 17, 2000). ... Traded by Rams to New England Patriots for undisclosed draft pick (August 7, 2000). ... Inactive for 10 games (2000). ... On injured reserve with leg injury (November 16, 2000-remainder of season). ... Released by Patriots (July 31, 2001). ... Signed by Rams (August 7, 2001). ... Released by Rams (August 27, 2001). ... Re-signed by Rams (February 12, 2002). ... Assigned by Rams to Berlin Thunder in 2002 NFL Europe enhancement allocation program (February 12, 2002). ... Released by Rams (September 1, 2002). ... Re-signed by Rams to practice squad (September 9, 2002). ... Activated (December 12, 2002).

Year Team	G	GS	RECEIVING				PUNT RETURNS				TOTALS			
			No.	Yds.	Avg.	TD	No.	Yds.	Avg.	TD	TD	2pt.	Pts.	Fum.
2002—Berlin NFLE	...	...	54	661	12.2	5	6	13	2.2	0	5	0	30	0
—St. Louis NFL	3	0	0	0	0.0	0	0	0	0.0	0	0	0	0	0
NFL Europe totals (1 year)	...	...	54	661	12.2	5	6	13	2.2	0	5	0	30	0
NFL totals (1 year)	3	0	0	0	0.0	0	0	0	0.0	0	0	0	0	0
Pro totals (2 years)	...	...	54	661	12.2	5	6	13	2.2	0	5	0	30	0

LOTT, ANDRE — CB — REDSKINS

PERSONAL: Born May 31, 1979, in Memphis, Tenn. ... 5-10/194. ... Full name: Andre Marquette Lott.
HIGH SCHOOL: Melrose (Memphis, Tenn.).
COLLEGE: Tennessee.
TRANSACTIONS/CAREER NOTES: Selected by Washington Redskins in fifth round (159th pick overall) of 2002 NFL draft. ... Signed by Redskins (July 12, 2002).

Year Team	G	GS	TOTALS			INTERCEPTIONS			
			Tk.	Ast.	Sks.	No.	Yds.	Avg.	TD
2002—Washington NFL	16	0	4	0	1.0	0	0	0.0	0

LOVE, CLARENCE — CB — RAIDERS

PERSONAL: Born June 16, 1976, in Jackson, Mich. ... 5-10/180. ... Full name: Clarence Eugene Love.
HIGH SCHOOL: Jackson (Mich.).
COLLEGE: Toledo.
TRANSACTIONS/CAREER NOTES: Selected by Philadelphia Eagles in fourth round (116th pick overall) of 1998 NFL draft. ... Signed by Eagles (July 14, 1998). ... Assigned by Eagles to Frankfurt Galaxy in 1999 NFL Europe enhancement allocation program (February 22, 1999). ... Released by Eagles (September 5, 1999). ... Signed by Jacksonville Jaguars to practice squad (September 21, 1999). ... Released by Jaguars

(November 23, 1999). ... Signed by Baltimore Ravens to practice squad (December 15, 1999). ... Activated (December 31, 1999); did not play. ... Released by Ravens (June 13, 2001). ... Signed by Oakland Raiders (February 11, 2002).

CHAMPIONSHIP GAME EXPERIENCE: Member of Ravens for AFC Championship game (2000 season); inactive. ... Member of Super Bowl championship team (2000 season); inactive. ... Played in AFC championship game (2002 season). ... Played in Super Bowl XXXVII (2002 season).

			TOTALS			INTERCEPTIONS			
Year Team	G	GS	Tk.	Ast.	Sks.	No.	Yds.	Avg.	TD
1998—Philadelphia NFL	6	0	2	1	0.0	0	0	0.0	0
2000—Baltimore NFL	1	0	0	0	0.0	0	0	0.0	0
2002—Oakland NFL	11	3	13	1	0.0	0	0	0.0	0
Pro totals (3 years)	18	3	15	2	0.0	0	0	0.0	0

LOVELADY, JOSH — OT — LIONS

PERSONAL: Born January 28, 1978, in Midfield, Texas. ... 6-3/320.
HIGH SCHOOL: Tidehaven (Midfield, Texas).
COLLEGE: Houston.
TRANSACTIONS/CAREER NOTES: Signed as non-drafted free agent by Detroit Lions (June 12, 2001). ... Released by Lions (September 2, 2001). ... Re-signed by Lions to practice squad (September 4, 2001). ... Activated (October 31, 2001); did not play. ... Assigned by Lions to Scottish Claymores in 2002 NFL Europe enhancement allocation program (February 12, 2002). ... Released by Lions (September 1, 2002). ... Re-signed by Lions to practice squad (September 2, 2002). ... Activated (December 3, 2002). ... Re-signed by Lions (March 25, 2003).
PLAYING EXPERIENCE: Detroit NFL, 2002. ... Games/games started: 2003 (3/0).

LOVERNE, DAVID — G — RAMS

PERSONAL: Born May 22, 1976, in San Ramon, Calif. ... 6-3/299. ... Name pronounced LAH-vern.
HIGH SCHOOL: De La Salle (Concord, Calif.).
COLLEGE: Idaho, then San Jose State.
TRANSACTIONS/CAREER NOTES: Selected by New York Jets in third round (90th pick overall) of 1999 NFL draft. ... Signed by Jets (July 1, 1999). ... Inactive for all 16 games (1999). ... Granted free agency (March 1, 2002). ... Re-signed by Jets (April 6, 2002). ... Traded by Jets with undisclosed draft pick to Washington Redskins for undisclosed draft pick (April 6, 2002). ... Traded by Redskins with fourth-round pick (DB DeJuan Groce) in 2003 draft to St. Louis Rams for RB Trung Canidate (February 28, 2003).
PLAYING EXPERIENCE: New York Jets NFL, 2000 and 2001; Washington NFL, 2002. ... Games/Games started: 2000 (16/0), 2001 (16/0), 2002 (15/11). Total: 47/11.

LOWE, OMARE — CB — DOLPHINS

PERSONAL: Born April 20, 1978, in Maple Valley, Wash. ... 6-1/196.
HIGH SCHOOL: Tacoma (Wash.).
COLLEGE: Washington.
TRANSACTIONS/CAREER NOTES: Selected by Miami Dolphins in fifth round (161st pick overall) of 2002 NFL draft. ... Signed by Dolphins (July 25, 2002).

			TOTALS			INTERCEPTIONS			
Year Team	G	GS	Tk.	Ast.	Sks.	No.	Yds.	Avg.	TD
2002—Miami NFL	1	0	0	0	0.0	0	0	0.0	0

LUCAS, JUSTIN — S — CARDINALS

PERSONAL: Born July 15, 1976, in Victoria, Texas. ... 5-10/198.
HIGH SCHOOL: Stroman (Victoria, Texas).
COLLEGE: Texas A&M, then Abilene Christian (degree in industrial technology).
TRANSACTIONS/CAREER NOTES: Signed as non-drafted free agent by Arizona Cardinals (April 23, 1999). ... Released by Cardinals (September 5, 1999). ... Re-signed by Cardinals to practice squad (September 7, 1999). ... Activated (October 17, 1999). ... Released by Cardinals (October 19, 1999). ... Re-signed by Cardinals to practice squad (October 20, 1999). ... Activated (December 31, 1999). ... Granted free agency (February 28, 2003). ... Re-signed by Cardinals (April 3, 2003).

			TOTALS			INTERCEPTIONS			
Year Team	G	GS	Tk.	Ast.	Sks.	No.	Yds.	Avg.	TD
1999—Arizona NFL	2	0	0	0	0.0	0	0	0.0	0
2000—Arizona NFL	16	0	12	8	0.0	0	0	0.0	0
2001—Arizona NFL	13	4	26	5	0.0	0	0	0.0	0
2002—Arizona NFL	16	4	27	9	0.0	2	80	40.0	2
Pro totals (4 years)	47	8	65	22	0.0	2	80	40.0	2

LUCAS, KEN — CB — SEAHAWKS

PERSONAL: Born January 23, 1979, in Cleveland, Miss. ... 6-0/205.
HIGH SCHOOL: East Side (Cleveland, Miss.).
COLLEGE: Mississippi.
TRANSACTIONS/CAREER NOTES: Selected by Seattle Seahawks in second round (40th pick overall) of 2001 NFL draft. ... Signed by Seahawks (July 26, 2001).

			TOTALS			INTERCEPTIONS			
Year Team	G	GS	Tk.	Ast.	Sks.	No.	Yds.	Avg.	TD
2001—Seattle NFL	16	8	42	5	0.0	1	0	0.0	0
2002—Seattle NFL	16	16	71	11	0.0	3	67	22.3	0
Pro totals (2 years)	32	24	113	16	0.0	4	67	16.8	0

LUCAS, RAY — QB

PERSONAL: Born August 6, 1972, in Harrison, N.J. ... 6-3/215.
HIGH SCHOOL: Harrison (N.J.).
COLLEGE: Rutgers.
TRANSACTIONS/CAREER NOTES: Signed as non-drafted free agent by New England Patriots (May 1, 1996). ... Released by Patriots (August 25, 1996). ... Re-signed by Patriots to practice squad (August 27, 1996). ... Activated (December 12, 1996). ... Claimed on waivers by New York Jets (August 19, 1997). ... Released by Jets (August 24, 1997). ... Re-signed by Jets to practice squad (August 26, 1997). ... Activated (November 22, 1997). ... Granted free agency (March 2, 2001). ... Tendered offer sheet by Miami Dolphins (March 9, 2001). ... Jets declined to match offer (March 16, 2001). ... Released by Dolphins (April 28, 2003).
CHAMPIONSHIP GAME EXPERIENCE: Played in AFC championship game (1996 season). ... Played in Super Bowl XXXI (1996 season). ... Member of Jets for AFC championship game (1998 season); did not play.
SINGLE GAME HIGHS (regular season): Attempts—48 (December 5, 1999, vs. New York Giants); completions—31 (December 5, 1999, vs. New York Giants); yards—284 (December 5, 1999, vs. New York Giants); and touchdown passes—4 (December 5, 1999, vs. New York Giants).
MISCELLANEOUS: Regular-season record as starting NFL quarterback: 8-7 (.533).

Year Team	G	GS	Att.	Cmp.	Pct.	Yds.	TD	Int.	Avg.	Skd.	Rat.	Att.	Yds.	Avg.	TD	TD	2pt.	Pts.
						PASSING							RUSHING				TOTALS	
1996—New England NFL	2	0	0	0	0.0	0	0	0	0.0	0	...	0	0	0.0	0	0	0	0
1997—New York Jets NFL	5	0	4	3	75.0	28	0	1	7.00	0	54.2	6	55	9.2	0	0	0	0
1998—New York Jets NFL	15	0	3	1	33.3	27	0	0	9.00	0	67.4	5	23	4.6	0	0	0	0
1999—New York Jets NFL	9	9	272	161	59.2	1678	14	6	6.17	11	85.1	41	144	3.5	1	1	0	6
2000—New York Jets NFL	6	0	41	21	51.2	206	0	4	5.02	6	26.1	6	42	7.0	0	0	0	0
2001—Miami NFL	10	0	3	2	66.7	45	0	0	15.00	0	109.7	8	6	0.8	1	1	0	6
2002—Miami NFL	7	6	160	92	57.5	1045	4	6	6.53	12	69.9	36	126	3.5	2	2	0	12
Pro totals (7 years)	54	15	483	280	58.0	3029	18	17	6.27	29	74.3	102	396	3.9	4	4	0	24

LUCHEY, NICOLAS — FB — PACKERS

PERSONAL: Born March 30, 1977, in Farmington Hills, Mich. ... 6-2/267. ... Full name: James Nicolas Luchey. ... Formerly known as Nick Williams.
HIGH SCHOOL: Harrison (Farmington Hills, Mich.).
COLLEGE: Miami (Fla.).
TRANSACTIONS/CAREER NOTES: Selected by Cincinnati Bengals in fifth round (135th pick overall) of 1999 NFL draft. ... Signed by Bengals (May 19, 1999). ... On physically unable to perform list with knee injury (July 22-November 27, 2001). ... Granted free agency (March 1, 2002). ... Re-signed by Bengals (April 23, 2002). ... Granted unconditional free agency (February 28, 2003). ... Signed by Green Bay Packers (March 11, 2003).
SINGLE GAME HIGHS (regular season): Attempts—12 (December 22, 2002, vs. New Orleans); yards—59 (December 22, 2002, vs. New Orleans); and rushing touchdowns—2 (December 22, 2002, vs. New Orleans).

Year Team	G	GS	Att.	Yds.	Avg.	TD	No.	Yds.	Avg.	TD	No.	Yds.	Avg.	TD	TD	2pt.	Pts.	Fum.
				RUSHING				RECEIVING				KICKOFF RETURNS				TOTALS		
1999—Cincinnati NFL	11	0	10	30	3.0	0	10	96	9.6	0	8	109	13.6	0	0	0	0	1
2000—Cincinnati NFL	14	4	10	54	5.4	0	7	84	12.0	0	2	12	6.0	0	0	0	0	2
2001—Cincinnati NFL	4	2	0	0	0.0	0	0	0	0.0	0	0	0	0.0	0	0	0	0	0
2002—Cincinnati NFL	16	3	12	59	4.9	2	7	46	6.6	0	3	40	13.3	0	2	0	12	0
Pro totals (4 years)	45	9	32	143	4.5	2	24	226	9.4	0	13	161	12.4	0	2	0	12	3

LUCKY, MIKE — TE

PERSONAL: Born November 23, 1975, in Antioch, Calif. ... 6-6/280. ... Full name: Michael Thomas Lucky.
HIGH SCHOOL: Antioch (Calif.).
COLLEGE: Arizona (degree in political science).
TRANSACTIONS/CAREER NOTES: Selected by Dallas Cowboys in seventh round (229th pick overall) of 1999 NFL draft. ... Signed by Cowboys (July 22, 1999). ... On injured reserve with knee injury (August 1, 2000-remainder of season). ... On physically unable to perform list with knee injury (July 22-August 14, 2001). ... Granted free agency (March 1, 2002). ... Re-signed by Cowboys (April 23, 2002). ... Granted unconditional free agency (February 28, 2003).
SINGLE GAME HIGHS (regular season): Receptions—2 (December 23, 2001, vs. Arizona); yards—29 (December 23, 2001, vs. Arizona); and touchdown receptions—1 (September 23, 2001, vs. San Diego).

Year Team	G	GS	No.	Yds.	Avg.	TD
			RECEIVING			
1999—Dallas NFL	14	4	5	25	5.0	0
2001—Dallas NFL	16	5	13	96	7.4	1
2002—Dallas NFL	16	0	1	22	22.0	0
Pro totals (3 years)	46	9	19	143	7.5	1

LUZAR, CHRIS — TE — JAGUARS

PERSONAL: Born February 12, 1979, in Newport News, Va. ... 6-7/260. ... Full name: Christopher Myers Luzar.
HIGH SCHOOL: Lafayette (Williamsburg, Va.).
COLLEGE: Virginia.
TRANSACTIONS/CAREER NOTES: Selected by Jacksonville Jaguars in fourth round (118th pick overall) of 2002 NFL draft. ... Signed by Jaguars (June 19, 2002).
SINGLE GAME HIGHS (regular season): Receptions—1 (September 29, 2002, vs. New York Jets); yards—5 (September 29, 2002, vs. New York Jets); and touchdown receptions—0.

Year Team	G	GS	No.	Yds.	Avg.	TD
			RECEIVING			
2002—Jacksonville NFL	12	0	1	5	5.0	0

LYGHT, TODD   CB

PERSONAL: Born February 9, 1969, in Kwajalein, Marshall Islands. ... 6-0/194. ... Full name: Todd William Lyght.
HIGH SCHOOL: Luke M. Powers Catholic (Flint, Mich.).
COLLEGE: Notre Dame.
TRANSACTIONS/CAREER NOTES: Selected by Los Angeles Rams in first round (fifth pick overall) of 1991 NFL draft. ... Signed by Rams (August 16, 1991). ... On injured reserve with shoulder injury (September 22-October 22, 1992). ... On injured reserve with knee injury (November 23, 1993-remainder of season). ... Designated by Rams as transition player (February 15, 1994). ... Rams franchise moved to St. Louis (April 12, 1995). ... Tendered offer sheet by Jacksonville Jaguars (April 12, 1996). ... Offer matched by Rams (April 15, 1996). ... Designated by Rams as transition player (February 11, 2000). ... Granted unconditional free agency (March 2, 2001). ... Signed by Detroit Lions (April 12, 2001). ... Announced retirement (December 30, 2002). ... Granted unconditional free agency (February 28, 2003).
CHAMPIONSHIP GAME EXPERIENCE: Played in NFC championship game (1999 season). ... Member of Super Bowl championship team (1999 season).
HONORS: Named defensive back on THE SPORTING NEWS college All-America first team (1989). ... Named defensive back on THE SPORTING NEWS college All-America second team (1990). ... Played in Pro Bowl (1999 season).

			TOTALS			INTERCEPTIONS			
Year Team	G	GS	Tk.	Ast.	Sks.	No.	Yds.	Avg.	TD
1991—Los Angeles Rams NFL	12	8	37	0	0.0	1	0	0.0	0
1992—Los Angeles Rams NFL	12	12	59	6	0.0	3	80	26.7	0
1993—Los Angeles Rams NFL	9	9	39	5	0.0	2	0	0.0	0
1994—Los Angeles Rams NFL	16	16	73	12	0.0	1	14	14.0	0
1995—St. Louis NFL	16	16	73	9	0.0	4	34	8.5	1
1996—St. Louis NFL	16	16	69	13	0.0	5	43	8.6	1
1997—St. Louis NFL	16	16	72	13	1.0	4	25	6.3	0
1998—St. Louis NFL	16	16	54	13	1.5	3	30	10.0	0
1999—St. Louis NFL	16	16	54	12	2.5	6	112	18.7	1
2000—St. Louis NFL	14	12	47	5	1.0	2	21	10.5	0
2001—Detroit NFL	16	16	53	6	0.0	4	72	18.0	1
2002—Detroit NFL	16	14	82	15	0.0	2	31	15.5	0
Pro totals (12 years)	**175**	**167**	**712**	**109**	**6.0**	**37**	**462**	**12.5**	**4**

LYLE, KEITH   S

L

PERSONAL: Born April 17, 1972, in Washington, D.C. ... 6-2/210. ... Full name: Keith Allen Lyle. ... Son of Garry Lyle, free safety/running back with Chicago Bears (1968-74).
HIGH SCHOOL: Mendon (N.Y.), then George C. Marshall (Falls Church, Va.).
COLLEGE: Virginia (degree in psychology, 1993).
TRANSACTIONS/CAREER NOTES: Selected by Los Angeles Rams in third round (71st pick overall) of 1994 NFL draft. ... Signed by Rams (July 8, 1994). ... Rams franchise moved to St. Louis (April 12, 1995). ... Granted free agency (February 14, 1997). ... Re-signed by Rams (April 15, 1997). ... Released by Rams (March 22, 2001). ... Signed by Washington Redskins (August 21, 2001). ... Granted unconditional free agency (March 1, 2002). ... Signed by Atlanta Falcons (April 8, 2002). ... Released by Falcons (August 31, 2002). ... Signed by San Diego Chargers (September 3, 2002). ... Granted unconditional free agency (February 28, 2003).
CHAMPIONSHIP GAME EXPERIENCE: Played in NFC championship game (1999 season). ... Member of Super Bowl championship team (1999 season).

			TOTALS			INTERCEPTIONS			
Year Team	G	GS	Tk.	Ast.	Sks.	No.	Yds.	Avg.	TD
1994—Los Angeles Rams NFL	16	0	13	2	0.0	2	1	0.5	0
1995—St. Louis NFL	16	16	73	18	0.0	3	42	14.0	0
1996—St. Louis NFL	16	16	63	16	0.0	†9	‡152	16.9	0
1997—St. Louis NFL	16	16	70	14	2.0	8	102	12.8	0
1998—St. Louis NFL	16	16	59	23	1.0	3	20	6.7	0
1999—St. Louis NFL	9	9	23	7	1.0	2	10	5.0	0
2000—St. Louis NFL	16	16	66	15	0.0	1	9	9.0	0
2001—Washington NFL	16	0	15	5	1.0	1	0	0.0	0
2002—San Diego NFL	15	6	23	4	0.0	2	26	13.0	0
Pro totals (9 years)	**136**	**95**	**405**	**104**	**5.0**	**31**	**362**	**11.7**	**0**

LYLE, RICK   DE/DT   PATRIOTS

PERSONAL: Born February 26, 1971, in Monroe, La. ... 6-5/285. ... Full name: Rick James Earl Lyle.
HIGH SCHOOL: Hickman Mills (Kansas City, Mo.).
COLLEGE: Missouri (degree in parks, recreation and tourism).
TRANSACTIONS/CAREER NOTES: Signed as non-drafted free agent by Cleveland Browns (May 2, 1994). ... On injured reserve with back injury (September 2, 1995-entire season). ... Browns franchise moved to Baltimore and renamed Ravens for 1996 season (March 11, 1996). ... Granted unconditional free agency (February 14, 1997). ... Signed by New York Jets (March 24, 1997). ... Granted unconditional free agency (March 2, 2001). ... Re-signed by Jets (May 14, 2001). ... Granted unconditional free agency (March 1, 2002). ... Signed by New England Patriots (March 12, 2002). ... Granted unconditional free agency (February 28, 2003). ... Re-signed by Patriots (March 5, 2003).
CHAMPIONSHIP GAME EXPERIENCE: Played in AFC championship game (1998 season).

			TOTALS		
Year Team	G	GS	Tk.	Ast.	Sks.
1994—Cleveland NFL	3	0	2	0	0.0
1995—Cleveland NFL			Did not play.		
1996—Baltimore NFL	11	3	6	1	1.0
1997—New York Jets NFL	16	16	30	12	3.0
1998—New York Jets NFL	16	16	29	12	1.5
1999—New York Jets NFL	16	16	27	18	1.0
2000—New York Jets NFL	14	14	40	8	1.0
2001—New York Jets NFL	16	3	27	13	3.5
2002—New England NFL	13	2	13	7	0.0
Pro totals (8 years)	**105**	**70**	**174**	**71**	**11.0**

LYMAN, DUSTIN TE BEARS

PERSONAL: Born August 5, 1976, in Boulder, Colo. ... 6-4/245.
HIGH SCHOOL: Fairview (Boulder, Colo.).
COLLEGE: Wake Forest.
TRANSACTIONS/CAREER NOTES: Selected by Chicago Bears in third round (87th pick overall) of 2000 NFL draft. ... Signed by Bears (June 15, 2000). ... On injured reserve with knee injury (December 10, 2002-remainder of season).
SINGLE GAME HIGHS (regular season): Receptions—7 (December 1, 2002, vs. Green Bay); yards—58 (December 1, 2002, vs. Green Bay); and touchdown receptions—2 (December 1, 2002, vs. Green Bay).

				RECEIVING		
Year Team	G	GS	No.	Yds.	Avg.	TD
2000—Chicago NFL	14	7	1	4	4.0	0
2001—Chicago NFL	4	0	0	0	0.0	0
2002—Chicago NFL	12	3	14	121	8.6	2
Pro totals (3 years)	30	10	15	125	8.3	2

LYNCH, BEN C

PERSONAL: Born November 18, 1972, in Santa Rosa, Calif. ... 6-4/295. ... Full name: Benjamin John Lynch.
HIGH SCHOOL: Analy (Sebastopol, Calif.).
COLLEGE: California.
TRANSACTIONS/CAREER NOTES: Selected by Kansas City Chiefs in seventh round (211th pick overall) of 1996 NFL draft. ... Signed by Chiefs (July 24, 1996). ... Released by Chiefs (August 20, 1996). ... Signed by Minnesota Vikings (February 10, 1997). ... Released by Vikings (August 18, 1997). ... Re-signed by Vikings to practice squad (December 11, 1997). ... Activated (December 30, 1997); did not play. ... Granted free agency (February 13, 1998). ... Selected by Frankfurt Galaxy in 1998 NFL Europe draft (February 18, 1998). ... Signed by Chicago Bears (July 1, 1998). ... On injured reserve with ankle injury (August 5-12, 1998). ... Released by Bears (August 12, 1998). ... Signed by San Francisco 49ers (May 4, 1999). ... Granted free agency (March 1, 2002). ... Re-signed by 49ers (August 8, 2002). ... Granted unconditional free agency (February 28, 2003).
PLAYING EXPERIENCE: Frankfurt NFLE, 1998; San Francisco NFL, 1999-2002. ... Games/Games started: 1998 (games played unavailable), 1999 (16/1), 2000 (11/0), 2001 (11/1), 2002 (16/0). Total: 54/2.

LYNCH, JOHN S BUCCANEERS

PERSONAL: Born September 25, 1971, in Hinsdale, Ill. ... 6-2/220. ... Full name: John Terrence Lynch. ... Son of John Lynch, linebacker with Pittsburgh Steelers (1969); brother-in-law of John Allred, tight end, with Chicago Bears (1997-2000); and brother of Ryan Lynch, pitcher in Baltimore Orioles organization.
HIGH SCHOOL: Torrey Pines (Encinitas, Calif.).
COLLEGE: Stanford.
TRANSACTIONS/CAREER NOTES: Selected by Tampa Bay Buccaneers in third round (82nd pick overall) of 1993 NFL draft. ... Signed by Buccaneers (June 1, 1993). ... On injured reserve with knee injury (December 12, 1995-remainder of season). ... Granted free agency (February 16, 1996). ... Re-signed by Buccaneers (July 13, 1996).
CHAMPIONSHIP GAME EXPERIENCE: Played in NFC championship game (1999 and 2002 seasons). ... Member of Super Bowl championship team (2002 season).
HONORS: Played in Pro Bowl (1997 and 1999-2002 seasons). ... Named safety on THE SPORTING NEWS NFL All-Pro team (1999 and 2000).

			TOTALS			INTERCEPTIONS			
Year Team	G	GS	Tk.	Ast.	Sks.	No.	Yds.	Avg.	TD
1993—Tampa Bay NFL	15	4	8	5	0.0	0	0	0.0	0
1994—Tampa Bay NFL	16	0	11	4	0.0	0	0	0.0	0
1995—Tampa Bay NFL	9	6	27	10	0.0	3	3	1.0	0
1996—Tampa Bay NFL	16	14	74	29	0.0	3	26	8.7	0
1997—Tampa Bay NFL	16	16	75	34	0.0	2	28	14.0	0
1998—Tampa Bay NFL	15	15	50	35	2.0	2	29	14.5	0
1999—Tampa Bay NFL	16	16	81	36	0.5	2	32	16.0	0
2000—Tampa Bay NFL	16	16	56	29	1.0	3	43	14.3	0
2001—Tampa Bay NFL	16	16	62	25	1.0	3	21	7.0	0
2002—Tampa Bay NFL	15	15	41	23	0.0	3	0	0.0	0
Pro totals (10 years)	150	118	485	230	5.5	21	182	8.7	0

LYON, BILLY DE/DT VIKINGS

PERSONAL: Born December 10, 1973, in Ashland, Ky. ... 6-5/295. ... Full name: William Morton Lyon.
HIGH SCHOOL: Lloyd (Erlanger, Ky.).
COLLEGE: Marshall (degree in occupational safety).
TRANSACTIONS/CAREER NOTES: Signed as non-drafted free agent by Kansas City Chiefs (April 28, 1997). ... Released by Chiefs (August 15, 1997). ... Signed by Green Bay Packers to practice squad (November 20, 1997) ... Granted unconditional free agency (February 28, 2003). ... Signed by Minnesota Vikings (March 4, 2003).

			TOTALS			INTERCEPTIONS			
Year Team	G	GS	Tk.	Ast.	Sks.	No.	Yds.	Avg.	TD
1998—Green Bay NFL	4	0	4	2	1.0	0	0	0.0	0
1999—Green Bay NFL	16	4	9	10	2.0	1	0	0.0	0
2000—Green Bay NFL	11	1	7	4	1.0	0	0	0.0	0
2001—Green Bay NFL	12	0	13	6	2.0	0	0	0.0	0
2002—Green Bay NFL	16	2	11	4	2.0	0	0	0.0	0
Pro totals (5 years)	59	7	44	26	8.0	1	0	0.0	0

MACHADO, J.P.   C/OG   JETS

PERSONAL: Born January 6, 1976, in Monmouth, Ill. ... 6-4/300.
HIGH SCHOOL: Monmouth (Ill.).
COLLEGE: Illinois.
TRANSACTIONS/CAREER NOTES: Selected by New York Jets in sixth round (197th pick overall) of 1999 NFL draft. ... Signed by Jets (July 27, 1999).
PLAYING EXPERIENCE: New York Jets NFL, 1999-2002. ... Games/Games started: 1999 (5/0), 2000 (16/0), 2001 (16/3), 2002 (16/12). Total: 53/15.

MACK, STACEY   FB   TEXANS

PERSONAL: Born June 26, 1975, in Orlando, Fla. ... 6-1/238. ... Full name: Stacey Lamar Mack.
HIGH SCHOOL: Boone (Orlando, Fla.).
JUNIOR COLLEGE: Southwest Mississippi College.
COLLEGE: Temple.
TRANSACTIONS/CAREER NOTES: Signed as non-drafted free agent by Jacksonville Jaguars (April 22, 1999). ... On injured reserve with finger injury (October 12, 2000-remainder of season). ... Granted free agency (March 1, 2002). ... Re-signed by Jaguars (March 1, 2002). ... Granted unconditional free agency (February 28, 2003). ... Signed by Houston Texans (April 9, 2003).
CHAMPIONSHIP GAME EXPERIENCE: Member of Jaguars for AFC championship game (1999 season); inactive.
SINGLE GAME HIGHS (regular season): Attempts—28 (December 16, 2001, vs. Cleveland); yards—125 (December 30, 2001, vs. Kansas City); and rushing touchdowns—3 (September 29, 2002, vs. New York Jets).
STATISTICAL PLATEAUS: 100-yard rushing games: 2001 (3).

			RUSHING				RECEIVING				KICKOFF RETURNS				TOTALS			
Year Team	G	GS	Att.	Yds.	Avg.	TD	No.	Yds.	Avg.	TD	No.	Yds.	Avg.	TD	TD	2pt.	Pts.	Fum.
1999—Jacksonville NFL	12	0	7	40	5.7	0	0	0	0.0	0	6	112	18.7	0	0	0	0	0
2000—Jacksonville NFL	6	2	54	145	2.7	1	0	0	0.0	0	6	104	17.3	0	1	0	6	3
2001—Jacksonville NFL	16	11	213	877	4.1	9	23	165	7.2	1	2	49	24.5	0	10	0	60	3
2002—Jacksonville NFL	16	0	98	436	4.4	9	11	79	7.2	0	12	234	19.5	0	9	0	54	0
Pro totals (4 years)	50	13	372	1498	4.0	19	34	244	7.2	1	26	499	19.2	0	20	0	120	6

MACKEY, LOUIS   LB   COWBOYS

PERSONAL: Born December 29, 1977, in Richmond, Calif. ... 6-1/225.
HIGH SCHOOL: Richmond (Calif.), then Albany (Calif.).
JUNIOR COLLEGE: Gavilan Junior College (Calif.).
COLLEGE: Akron.
TRANSACTIONS/CAREER NOTES: Signed by Dallas Cowboys (August 10, 2001). ... Released by Cowboys (September 2, 2001). ... Re-signed by Cowboys to practice squad (September 3, 2001). ... Activated (November 17, 2001). ... On injured reserve with knee injury (November 21, 2001-remainder of season). ... Released by Cowboys (August 27, 2002). ... Re-signed by Cowboys to practice squad (September 11, 2002). ... Activated (September 13, 2002). ... Re-signed by Cowboys (March 15, 2003).

			TOTALS			INTERCEPTIONS			
Year Team	G	GS	Tk.	Ast.	Sks.	No.	Yds.	Avg.	TD
2001—Dallas NFL	1	0	0	0	0.0	0	0	0.0	0
2002—Dallas NFL	15	0	3	0	0.0	0	0	0.0	0
Pro totals (2 years)	16	0	3	0	0.0	0	0	0.0	0

MACKLIN, DAVID   DB   COLTS

PERSONAL: Born July 14, 1978, in Newport News, Va. ... 5-9/196. ... Full name: David Thurman Macklin.
HIGH SCHOOL: Menchville (Newport News, Va.).
COLLEGE: Penn State.
TRANSACTIONS/CAREER NOTES: Selected by Indianapolis Colts in third round (91st pick overall) of 2000 NFL draft. ... Signed by Colts (July 13, 2000). ... Granted free agency (February 28, 2003). ... Re-signed by Colts (April 15, 2003).

			TOTALS			INTERCEPTIONS			
Year Team	G	GS	Tk.	Ast.	Sks.	No.	Yds.	Avg.	TD
2000—Indianapolis NFL	16	2	23	4	0.0	2	35	17.5	0
2001—Indianapolis NFL	16	16	53	9	0.5	3	15	5.0	0
2002—Indianapolis NFL	16	15	47	9	0.0	1	30	30.0	0
Pro totals (3 years)	48	33	123	22	0.5	6	80	13.3	0

MADDOX, TOMMY   QB   STEELERS

PERSONAL: Born September 2, 1971, in Shreveport, La. ... 6-4/220. ... Full name: Thomas Alfred Maddox.
HIGH SCHOOL: L.D. Bell (Hurst, Texas).
COLLEGE: UCLA.
TRANSACTIONS/CAREER NOTES: Selected after sophomore season by Denver Broncos in first round (25th pick overall) of 1992 NFL draft. ... Signed by Broncos (July 22, 1992). ... Traded by Broncos to Los Angeles Rams for fourth-round pick (LB Ken Brown) in 1995 draft (August 27, 1994). ... Granted free agency (February 17, 1995). ... Rams franchise moved to St. Louis (April 12, 1995). ... Re-signed by Rams (July 7, 1995). ... Released by Rams (August 27, 1995). ... Signed by New York Giants (August 30, 1995). ... Released by Giants (August 19, 1996). ... Signed by Atlanta Falcons (April 19, 1997). ... Released by Falcons (August 18, 1997). ... Signed by New Jersey Red Dogs of Arena League (November 9, 1999). ... Signed by Pittsburgh Steelers (June 12, 2001).
CHAMPIONSHIP GAME EXPERIENCE: Member of Steelers for AFC championship game (2001 season); did not play.
SINGLE GAME HIGHS (regular season): Attempts—57 (December 8, 2002, vs. Houston); completions—30 (December 8, 2002, vs. Houston); yards—473 (November 10, 2002 vs. Atlanta); and touchdown passes—4 (November 10, 2002, vs. Atlanta).
STATISTICAL PLATEAUS: 300-yard passing games: 2002 (2).
MISCELLANEOUS: Regular-season record as starting NFL quarterback: 7-7-1 (.500). ... Postseason record as starting NFL quarterback: 1-1 (.500).

M

Year Team	G	GS	Att.	Cmp.	Pct.	Yds.	TD	Int.	Avg.	Skd.	Rat.	Att.	Yds.	Avg.	TD	TD	2pt.	Pts.
												PASSING→RUSHING				TOTALS		
1992—Denver NFL	13	4	121	66	54.5	757	5	9	6.26	10	56.4	9	20	2.2	0	0	0	0
1993—Denver NFL	16	0	1	1	100.0	1	1	0	1.00	0	118.8	2	-2	-1.0	0	0	0	0
1994—L.A. Rams NFL	5	0	19	10	52.6	141	0	2	7.42	0	37.3	1	1	1.0	0	0	0	0
1995—N.Y. Giants NFL	16	0	23	6	26.1	49	0	3	2.13	2	0.0	1	4	4.0	0	0	0	0
1996—									Did not play.									
1997—									Did not play.									
1998—									Did not play.									
1999—									Did not play.									
2000—									Did not play.									
2001—Pittsburgh NFL	5	0	9	7	77.8	154	1	1	17.11	1	116.2	6	9	1.5	1	1	0	6
2002—Pittsburgh NFL	15	11	377	234	62.1	2836	20	16	7.52	26	85.2	19	43	2.3	0	0	0	0
Pro totals (6 years)	70	15	550	324	58.9	3938	27	31	7.16	39	73.9	38	75	2.0	1	1	0	6

MADISON, SAM   CB   DOLPHINS

PERSONAL: Born April 23, 1974, in Thomasville, Ga. ... 5-11/185. ... Full name: Samuel A. Madison Jr.
HIGH SCHOOL: Florida A&M High (Monticello, Fla.).
COLLEGE: Louisville.
TRANSACTIONS/CAREER NOTES: Selected by Miami Dolphins in second round (44th pick overall) of 1997 NFL draft. ... Signed by Dolphins (June 16, 1997).
HONORS: Named cornerback on THE SPORTING NEWS NFL All-Pro team (1999 and 2000). ... Played in Pro Bowl (1999, 2000 and 2002 seasons). ... Named to play in Pro Bowl (2001 season); replaced by Ryan McNeil due to injury.

			TOTALS			INTERCEPTIONS			
Year Team	G	GS	Tk.	Ast.	Sks.	No.	Yds.	Avg.	TD
1997—Miami NFL	14	3	16	5	0.0	1	21	21.0	0
1998—Miami NFL	16	16	31	13	1.0	8	114	14.3	0
1999—Miami NFL	16	16	38	8	0.0	†7	164	23.4	1
2000—Miami NFL	16	16	29	10	0.0	5	80	16.0	0
2001—Miami NFL	13	13	18	7	0.0	2	0	0.0	0
2002—Miami NFL	16	16	24	10	0.0	3	15	5.0	0
Pro totals (6 years)	91	80	156	53	1.0	26	394	15.2	1

MAESE, JOE   C   RAVENS

PERSONAL: Born December 2, 1978, in Morenci, Ariz. ... 6-0/241.
HIGH SCHOOL: Cortez (Ariz.).
JUNIOR COLLEGE: Phoenix College.
COLLEGE: New Mexico.
TRANSACTIONS/CAREER NOTES: Selected by Baltimore Ravens in sixth round (194th pick overall) in 2001 NFL draft. ... Signed by Ravens (June 14, 2001). ... On injured reserve with knee injury (January 3, 2002-remainder of season).
PLAYING EXPERIENCE: Baltimore NFL, 2001-2002. ... Games/Games started: 2001 (15/0), 2002 (16/0). Total: 31/0.

M

MAKOVICKA, JOEL   FB

PERSONAL: Born October 6, 1975, in Brainard, Neb. ... 5-11/251. ... Name pronounced mack-oh-VIK-uh.
HIGH SCHOOL: East Butler (Brainard, Neb.).
COLLEGE: Nebraska.
TRANSACTIONS/CAREER NOTES: Selected by Arizona Cardinals in fourth round (116th pick overall) of 1999 NFL draft. ... Signed by Cardinals (June 18, 1999). ... Granted free agency (March 1, 2002). ... Re-signed by Cardinals (May 2, 2002). ... Granted unconditional free agency (February 28, 2003).
SINGLE GAME HIGHS (regular season): Attempts—2 (December 8, 2002, vs. Detroit); yards—27 (December 8, 2002, vs. Detroit); and rushing touchdowns—0.

			RUSHING				RECEIVING				TOTALS			
Year Team	G	GS	Att.	Yds.	Avg.	TD	No.	Yds.	Avg.	TD	TD	2pt.	Pts.	Fum.
1999—Arizona NFL	16	10	8	7	0.9	0	10	70	7.0	1	1	0	6	1
2000—Arizona NFL	14	10	3	8	2.7	0	6	18	3.0	0	0	0	0	0
2001—Arizona NFL	16	14	1	19	19.0	0	16	95	5.9	1	1	0	6	1
2002—Arizona NFL	12	1	5	54	10.8	0	15	81	5.4	3	3	0	18	0
Pro totals (4 years)	58	35	17	88	5.2	0	47	264	5.6	5	5	0	30	2

MALLARD, JOSHUA   DE   COLTS

PERSONAL: Born March 21, 1979, in Savannah, Ga. ... 6-2/254. ... Full name: Joshua B. Mallard.
HIGH SCHOOL: Benedictine Military Academy (Ga.).
COLLEGE: Georgia.
TRANSACTIONS/CAREER NOTES: Selected by Indianapolis Colts in seventh round (220th pick overall) of 2002 NFL draft.

			TOTALS		
Year Team	G	GS	Tk.	Ast.	Sks.
2002—Indianapolis NFL	13	0	11	1	1.0

MALLARD, WESLY LB GIANTS

PERSONAL: Born November 21, 1978, in Hinesville, Ga. ... 6-1/221.
HIGH SCHOOL: Hardaway (Columbus, Ga.).
COLLEGE: Oregon.
TRANSACTIONS/CAREER NOTES: Selected by New York Giants in sixth round (188th pick overall) of 2002 NFL draft.

Year Team	G	GS	TOTALS Tk.	Ast.	Sks.	INTERCEPTIONS No.	Yds.	Avg.	TD
2002—New York Giants NFL	15	0	0	1	0.0	0	0	0.0	0

MANGUM, KRIS TE PANTHERS

PERSONAL: Born August 15, 1973, in Magee, Miss. ... 6-4/249. ... Full name: Kris Thomas Mangum. ... Son of John Mangum, defensive tackle with Boston Patriots (1966 and 1967) of AFL; and brother of John Mangum, cornerback with Chicago Bears (1990-98).
HIGH SCHOOL: Magee (Miss.).
COLLEGE: Mississippi.
TRANSACTIONS/CAREER NOTES: Selected by Carolina Panthers in seventh round (228th pick overall) of 1997 NFL draft. ... Signed by Panthers (May 20, 1997). ... Released by Panthers (September 2, 1997). ... Re-signed by Panthers to practice squad (September 4, 1997). ... Activated (December 5, 1997).
SINGLE GAME HIGHS (regular season): Receptions—4 (December 30, 2001, vs. Arizona); yards—56 (December 20, 1997, vs. St. Louis); and touchdown receptions—1 (December 9, 2001, vs. Buffalo).

Year Team	G	GS	RECEIVING No.	Yds.	Avg.	TD	TOTALS TD	2pt.	Pts.	Fum.
1997—Carolina NFL	2	1	4	56	14.0	0	0	0	0	0
1998—Carolina NFL	6	0	1	5	5.0	0	0	0	0	0
1999—Carolina NFL	11	0	1	6	6.0	0	0	0	0	0
2000—Carolina NFL	15	6	19	215	11.3	1	1	0	6	0
2001—Carolina NFL	16	10	15	89	5.9	2	2	0	12	0
2002—Carolina NFL	16	8	16	159	9.9	0	0	0	0	0
Pro totals (6 years)	66	25	56	530	9.5	3	3	0	18	0

MANNELLY, PATRICK OT BEARS

PERSONAL: Born April 18, 1975, in Atlanta. ... 6-5/269. ... Full name: James Patrick Mannelly.
HIGH SCHOOL: Marist (Atlanta).
COLLEGE: Duke.
TRANSACTIONS/CAREER NOTES: Selected by Chicago Bears in sixth round (189th pick overall) of 1998 NFL draft. ... Signed by Bears (June 11, 1998).
PLAYING EXPERIENCE: Chicago NFL, 1998-2002. ... Games/Games started: 1998 (16/0), 1999 (16/0), 2000 (16/0), 2001 (15/0), 2002 (14/0). Total: 77/0.

MANNING, PEYTON QB COLTS

M

PERSONAL: Born March 24, 1976, in New Orleans. ... 6-5/230. ... Full name: Peyton Williams Manning. ... Son of Archie Manning, quarterback with New Orleans Saints (1971-82), Houston Oilers (1982-83) and Minnesota Vikings (1983-84).
HIGH SCHOOL: Isidore Newman (New Orleans).
COLLEGE: Tennessee (degree in speech communication).
TRANSACTIONS/CAREER NOTES: Selected by Indianapolis Colts in first round (first pick overall) of 1998 NFL draft. ... Signed by Colts (July 28, 1998).
HONORS: Davey O'Brien Award winner (1997). ... Named College Player of the Year by THE SPORTING NEWS (1997). ... Named quarterback on THE SPORTING NEWS college All-America second team (1997). ... Played in Pro Bowl (1999, 2000 and 2002 seasons).
RECORDS: Holds NFL rookie-season records for most passes attempted—575 (1998); most passes completed—326 (1998); and most yards passing—3,739 (1998).
SINGLE GAME HIGHS (regular season): Attempts—54 (October 8, 2000, vs. New England); completions—37 (November 3, 2002, vs. Tennessee); yards—440 (September 25, 2000, vs. Jacksonville); and touchdown passes—4 (September 23, 2001, vs. Buffalo).
STATISTICAL PLATEAUS: 300-yard passing games: 1998 (4), 1999 (2), 2000 (5), 2001 (5), 2002 (4). Total: 20.
MISCELLANEOUS: Regular-season record as starting NFL quarterback: 42-38 (.525). ... Postseason record as starting NFL quarterback: 0-3.

Year Team	G	GS	PASSING Att.	Cmp.	Pct.	Yds.	TD	Int.	Avg.	Skd.	Rat.	RUSHING Att.	Yds.	Avg.	TD	TOTALS TD	2pt.	Pts.
1998—Indianapolis NFL	16	16	*575	§326	56.7	§3739	26	*28	6.50	22	71.2	15	62	4.1	0	0	0	0
1999—Indianapolis NFL	16	16	533	§331	§62.1	§4135	§26	15	§7.76	14	§90.7	35	73	2.1	2	2	0	12
2000—Indianapolis NFL	16	16	571	*357	62.5	*4413	†33	15	7.73	20	94.7	37	116	3.1	1	1	0	6
2001—Indianapolis NFL	16	16	547	343	62.7	§4131	26	23	7.55	29	84.1	35	157	4.5	4	4	0	24
2002—Indianapolis NFL	16	16	591	392	66.3	4200	27	§19	7.11	23	88.8	38	148	3.9	2	2	0	12
Pro totals (5 years)	80	80	2817	1749	62.1	20618	138	100	7.32	108	85.9	160	556	3.5	9	9	0	54

MANUEL, MARQUAND S BENGALS

PERSONAL: Born July 11, 1979, in Miami. ... 6-0/209. ... Full name: Marquand Alexander Manuel.
HIGH SCHOOL: Miami Senior (Fla.).
COLLEGE: Florida.
TRANSACTIONS/CAREER NOTES: Selected by Cincinnati Bengals in sixth round (181st pick overall) of 2002 NFL draft. ... Signed by Bengals (May 13, 2002).

Year Team	G	GS	TOTALS Tk.	Ast.	Sks.	INTERCEPTIONS No.	Yds.	Avg.	TD
2002—Cincinnati NFL	15	8	26	8	0.0	0	0	0.0	0

MANUMALEUNA, BRANDON — TE — RAMS

PERSONAL: Born January 4, 1980, in Torrance, Calif. ... 6-2/288. ... Full name: Brandon Michael Manumaleuna.
HIGH SCHOOL: Narbonne (Calif.).
COLLEGE: Arizona.
TRANSACTIONS/CAREER NOTES: Selected by St. Louis Rams in fourth round (129th pick overall) of 2001 NFL draft. ... Signed by Rams (June 21, 2001).
CHAMPIONSHIP GAME EXPERIENCE: Played in NFC championship game (2001 season). ... Played in Super Bowl XXXVI (2001 season).
SINGLE GAME HIGHS (regular season): Receptions—2 (December 8, 2002, vs. Kansas City); yards—38 (November 10, 2002, vs. San Diego); and touchdown receptions—1 (December 30, 2002, vs. San Francisco).

			RECEIVING			
Year Team	G	GS	No.	Yds.	Avg.	TD
2001—St. Louis NFL	16	0	1	1	1.0	1
2002—St. Louis NFL	16	10	8	106	13.3	1
Pro totals (2 years)	32	10	9	107	11.9	2

MARE, OLINDO — K — DOLPHINS

PERSONAL: Born June 6, 1973, in Hollywood, Fla. ... 5-10/195. ... Full name: Olindo Franco Mare. ... Name pronounced o-LEND-o MAR-ray.
HIGH SCHOOL: Cooper City (Fla.).
JUNIOR COLLEGE: Valencia Community College (Fla.).
COLLEGE: Syracuse.
TRANSACTIONS/CAREER NOTES: Signed as non-drafted free agent by New York Giants (May 2, 1996). ... Released by Giants (August 25, 1996). ... Re-signed by Giants to practice squad (August 27, 1996). ... Granted free agency after 1996 season. ... Signed by Miami Dolphins (February 27, 1997). ... Granted free agency (February 11, 2000). ... Re-signed by Dolphins (June 15, 2000). ... Granted unconditional free agency (March 2, 2001). ... Re-signed by Dolphins (March 2, 2001).
HONORS: Named kicker on THE SPORTING NEWS NFL All-Pro team (1999). ... Played in Pro Bowl (1999 season).
RECORDS: Holds NFL single-season record for most field goals made—39 (1999).

		PUNTING						KICKING						TOTALS		
Year Team	G	No.	Yds.	Avg.	Net avg.	In.20	Blk.	1-29	30-39	40-49	50+	Tot.	Pct.	Lg.	XPM	XPA	Pts.
1996—New York Giants NFL								Did not play.								
1997—Miami NFL	16	5	235	47.0	46.2	2	0	16-17	8-10	3-6	1-3	28-36	77.8	50	33	33	117
1998—Miami NFL	16	3	115	38.3	31.7	1	0	12-13	5-5	5-7	0-2	22-27	81.5	48	33	34	99
1999—Miami NFL	16	1	36	36.0	30.0	0	0	10-10	17-17	9-14	3-5	*39-*46	84.8	54	27	27	144
2000—Miami NFL	16	0	0	0.0	0	0	0	7-8	9-10	12-13	0-0	28-31	90.3	49	33	34	117
2001—Miami NFL	16	0	0	0.0	0	0	0	9-9	8-8	2-4	0-0	19-21	90.5	46	39	40	96
2002—Miami NFL	16	0	0	0.0	0	0	0	13-14	2-3	7-11	2-3	24-31	77.4	53	42	43	114
Pro totals (6 years)	96	9	386	42.9	39.6	3	0	67-71	49-53	38-55	6-13	160-192	83.3	54	207	211	687

MARION, BROCK — S — DOLPHINS

PERSONAL: Born June 11, 1970, in Bakersfield, Calif. ... 5-11/200. ... Full name: Brock Elliot Marion. ... Son of Jerry Marion, wide receiver with Pittsburgh Steelers (1967); and nephew of Brent McClanahan, running back with Minnesota Vikings (1973-79).
HIGH SCHOOL: West (Bakersfield, Calif.).
COLLEGE: Nevada.
TRANSACTIONS/CAREER NOTES: Selected by Dallas Cowboys in seventh round (196th overall) of 1993 NFL draft. ... Signed by Cowboys (July 14, 1993). ... Granted free agency (February 16, 1996). ... Re-signed by Cowboys (May 2, 1996). ... Granted unconditional free agency (February 14, 1997). ... Re-signed by Cowboys (April 7, 1997). ... Granted unconditional free agency (February 13, 1998). ... Signed by Miami Dolphins (March 3, 1998). ... Granted unconditional free agency (March 2, 2001). ... Re-signed by Dolphins (June 9, 2001). ... Released by Dolphins (February 28, 2002). ... Re-signed by Dolphins (March 10, 2002).
CHAMPIONSHIP GAME EXPERIENCE: Played in NFC championship game (1993-1995 seasons). ... Member of Super Bowl championship team (1993 and 1995 seasons).
HONORS: Played in Pro Bowl (2000 and 2002 seasons).

			TOTALS			INTERCEPTIONS				KICKOFF RETURNS				TOTALS			
Year Team	G	GS	Tk.	Ast.	Sks.	No.	Yds.	Avg.	TD	No.	Yds.	Avg.	TD	TD	2pt.	Pts.	Fum.
1993—Dallas NFL	15	0	11	5	0.0	1	2	2.0	0	0	0	0.0	0	0	0	0	0
1994—Dallas NFL	14	1	22	4	1.0	1	11	11.0	0	2	39	19.5	0	0	0	0	0
1995—Dallas NFL	16	16	64	16	0.0	6	40	6.7	1	1	16	16.0	0	1	0	6	0
1996—Dallas NFL	10	10	41	10	0.0	0	0	0.0	0	3	68	22.7	0	0	0	0	1
1997—Dallas NFL	16	16	100	17	0.0	0	0	0.0	0	10	311	31.1	0	0	0	0	0
1998—Miami NFL	16	16	71	27	0.0	0	0	0.0	0	6	109	18.2	0	0	0	0	0
1999—Miami NFL	16	16	53	33	1.0	2	30	15.0	0	*62	*1524	24.6	0	0	0	0	2
2000—Miami NFL	16	16	72	24	0.0	5	72	14.4	0	22	513	23.3	0	0	0	0	0
2001—Miami NFL	15	15	55	24	0.0	5	*227	45.4	†2	17	371	21.8	0	2	0	12	1
2002—Miami NFL	16	16	64	29	0.0	5	99	19.8	0	0	0	0.0	0	0	0	0	0
Pro totals (10 years)	150	122	553	189	2.0	25	481	19.2	3	123	2951	24.0	0	3	0	18	4

MARSHALL, LEMAR — LB — REDSKINS

PERSONAL: Born December 17, 1976, in Cincinnati. ... 6-2/228.
HIGH SCHOOL: St. Xavier (Cincinnati).
COLLEGE: Michigan State.
TRANSACTIONS/CAREER NOTES: Signed as non-drafted free agent by Tampa Bay Buccaneers (April 19, 1999). ... Released by Buccaneers (September 6, 1999). ... Re-signed by Eagles (January 12, 2000). ... Claimed on waivers by Buccaneers (August 22, 2000). ... Released by Buccaneers (August 28, 2000). ... Re-signed by Buccaneers to practice squad (November 22, 2000). ... Released by Buccaneers (December 14, 2000). ... Signed by Denver Broncos (January 29, 2001). ... Released by Broncos (September 1, 2001). ... Signed by Washington Redskins (December 26, 2001).

			TOTALS			INTERCEPTIONS			
Year Team	G	GS	Tk.	Ast.	Sks.	No.	Yds.	Avg.	TD
2002—Washington NFL	16	0	3	0	0.0	0	0	0.0	0

MARSHALL, TORRANCE   LB   PACKERS

PERSONAL: Born June 12, 1977, in Miami. ... 6-2/250.
HIGH SCHOOL: Sunset (Miami).
JUNIOR COLLEGE: Kemper Military Junior College (Mo.), then Miami-Dade Community College.
COLLEGE: Oklahoma.
TRANSACTIONS/CAREER NOTES: Selected by Green Bay Packers in third round (72nd pick overall) of 2001 NFL draft. ... Signed by Packers (July 24, 2001).
HONORS: Named linebacker on THE SPORTING NEWS college All-America third team (2000).

			TOTALS			INTERCEPTIONS			
Year Team	G	GS	Tk.	Ast.	Sks.	No.	Yds.	Avg.	TD
2001—Green Bay NFL	14	1	9	3	0.0	0	0	0.0	0
2002—Green Bay NFL	16	0	2	1	0.0	0	0	0.0	0
Pro totals (2 years)	30	1	11	4	0.0	0	0	0.0	0

MARTIN, CECIL   FB   RAIDERS

PERSONAL: Born July 8, 1975, in Chicago. ... 6-0/235.
HIGH SCHOOL: Evanston (Ill.).
COLLEGE: Wisconsin.
TRANSACTIONS/CAREER NOTES: Selected by Philadelphia Eagles in sixth round (172nd pick overall) of 1999 NFL draft. ... Signed by Eagles (July 25, 1999). ... Granted free agency (March 1, 2002). ... Re-signed by Eagles (April 26, 2002). ... Granted unconditional free agency (February 28, 2003). ... Signed by Oakland Raiders (March 19, 2003).
CHAMPIONSHIP GAME EXPERIENCE: Played in NFC championship game (2001 and 2002 seasons).
SINGLE GAME HIGHS (regular season): Attempts—5 (September 30, 2001, vs. Dallas); yards—28 (December 24, 2000, vs. Cincinnati); and rushing touchdowns—0.

			RUSHING				RECEIVING				TOTALS			
Year Team	G	GS	Att.	Yds.	Avg.	TD	No.	Yds.	Avg.	TD	TD	2pt.	Pts.	Fum.
1999—Philadelphia NFL	12	5	3	3	1.0	0	11	22	2.0	0	0	0	0	0
2000—Philadelphia NFL	16	10	13	77	5.9	0	31	219	7.1	0	0	0	0	1
2001—Philadelphia NFL	16	15	9	27	3.0	0	24	124	5.2	2	2	0	12	0
2002—Philadelphia NFL	16	9	1	-4	-4.0	0	15	126	8.4	0	0	0	0	1
Pro totals (4 years)	60	39	26	103	4.0	0	81	491	6.1	2	2	0	12	2

MARTIN, CURTIS   RB   JETS

M

PERSONAL: Born May 1, 1973, in Pittsburgh. ... 5-11/205.
HIGH SCHOOL: Taylor-Allderdice (Pittsburgh).
COLLEGE: Pittsburgh.
TRANSACTIONS/CAREER NOTES: Selected after junior season by New England Patriots in third round (74th pick overall) of 1995 NFL draft. ... Signed by Patriots (July 18, 1995). ... Granted free agency (February 13, 1998). ... Tendered offer sheet by New York Jets (March 20, 1998). ... Patriots declined to match offer (March 25, 1998).
CHAMPIONSHIP GAME EXPERIENCE: Played in AFC championship game (1996 and 1998 seasons). ... Played in Super Bowl XXXI (1996 season).
HONORS: Named NFL Rookie of the Year by THE SPORTING NEWS (1995). ... Played in Pro Bowl (1995, 1996, 1998 and 2001 seasons). ... Named running back on THE SPORTING NEWS NFL All-Pro team (2001).
SINGLE GAME HIGHS (regular season): Attempts—40 (September 14, 1997, vs. New York Jets); yards—203 (December 3, 2000, vs. Indianapolis); and rushing touchdowns—3 (November 11, 2001, vs. Kansas City).
STATISTICAL PLATEAUS: 100-yard rushing games: 1995 (9), 1996 (2), 1997 (3), 1998 (8), 1999 (6), 2000 (3), 2001 (7), 2002 (5). Total: 43.

			RUSHING				RECEIVING				TOTALS			
Year Team	G	GS	Att.	Yds.	Avg.	TD	No.	Yds.	Avg.	TD	TD	2pt.	Pts.	Fum.
1995—New England NFL	16	15	§368	§1487	4.0	14	30	261	8.7	1	15	1	92	5
1996—New England NFL	16	15	316	1152	3.6	§14	46	333	7.2	3	§17	1	104	4
1997—New England NFL	13	13	274	1160	4.2	4	41	296	7.2	1	5	0	30	3
1998—New York Jets NFL	15	15	369	1287	3.5	8	43	365	8.5	1	9	0	54	5
1999—New York Jets NFL	16	16	367	1464	4.0	5	45	259	5.8	0	5	0	30	2
2000—New York Jets NFL	16	16	316	1204	3.8	9	70	508	7.3	2	11	0	66	2
2001—New York Jets NFL	16	16	333	1513	4.5	10	53	320	6.0	0	10	0	60	2
2002—New York Jets NFL	16	16	261	1094	4.2	7	49	362	7.4	0	7	1	44	0
Pro totals (8 years)	124	122	2604	10361	4.0	71	377	2704	7.2	8	79	3	480	23

MARTIN, DAVID   TE   PACKERS

PERSONAL: Born March 13, 1979, in Fort Campbell, Va. ... 6-4/258. ... Full name: David Earl Martin.
HIGH SCHOOL: Norview (Norfolk, Va.).
COLLEGE: Tennessee.
TRANSACTIONS/CAREER NOTES: Selected by Green Bay Packers in sixth round (198th pick overall) of 2001 NFL draft. ... Signed by Packers (June 15, 2001).
SINGLE GAME HIGHS (regular season): Receptions—3 (October 20, 2002, vs. Washington); yards—33 (October 7, 2001, vs. Tampa Bay); and touchdown receptions—1 (September 8, 2002, vs. Atlanta).

			RECEIVING			
Year Team	G	GS	No.	Yds.	Avg.	TD
2001—Green Bay NFL	14	1	13	144	11.1	1
2002—Green Bay NFL	8	2	8	33	4.1	1
Pro totals (2 years)	22	3	21	177	8.4	2

MARTIN, JAMIE — QB

PERSONAL: Born February 8, 1970, in Orange, Calif. ... 6-2/205. ... Full name: Jamie Blane Martin.
HIGH SCHOOL: Arroyo Grande (Calif.).
COLLEGE: Weber State.
TRANSACTIONS/CAREER NOTES: Signed as non-drafted free agent by Los Angeles Rams (May 3, 1993). ... Released by Rams (August (24, 1993). ... Re-signed by Rams to practice squad (August 31, 1993). ... Activated (November 23, 1993). ... Inactive for five games (1993). ... Released by Rams (August 27, 1994). ... Re-signed by Rams (October 4, 1994). ... Released by Rams (October 12, 1994). ... Re-signed by Rams (November 15, 1994). ... Active for one game (1994); did not play. ... Assigned by Rams to Amsterdam Admirals of World Football League (1995). ... Rams franchise moved to St. Louis (April 12, 1995). ... On physically unable to perform list with broken collarbone (June 3, 1995-entire season). ... Released by Rams (August 17, 1997). ... Signed by Washington Redskins (December 2, 1997). ... Granted free agency (February 13, 1998). ... Signed by Jacksonville Jaguars (March 6, 1998). ... On injured reserve with knee injury (December 15, 1998-remainder of season). ... Granted unconditional free agency (February 12, 1999). ... Signed by Cleveland Browns (August 25, 1999). ... Granted unconditional free agency (February 11, 2000). ... Signed by Jaguars (February 22, 2000). ... Released by Jaguars (March 1, 2001). ... Re-signed by Jaguars (April 2, 2001). ... Released by Jaguars (September 2, 2001). ... Signed by Rams (September 3, 2001). ... Released by Rams (February 27, 2003).
CHAMPIONSHIP GAME EXPERIENCE: Member of Rams for NFC championship game (2001 season); did not play. ... Member of Rams for Super Bowl XXXVI (2001 season); did not play.
HONORS: Walter Payton Award winner (1991).
SINGLE GAME HIGHS (regular season): Attempts—48 (December 22, 2002, vs. Seattle); completions—31 (December 22, 2002, vs. Seattle); yards—262 (September 29, 2002, vs. Dallas); and touchdown passes—3 (December 30, 2002, vs. San Francisco).
MISCELLANEOUS: Regular-season record as starting NFL quarterback: 0-3.

					PASSING							RUSHING				TOTALS		
Year Team	G	GS	Att.	Cmp.	Pct.	Yds.	TD	Int.	Avg.	Skd.	Rat.	Att.	Yds.	Avg.	TD	TD	2pt.	Pts.
1993—L.A. Rams NFL...........									Did not play.									
1994—L.A. Rams NFL...........									Did not play.									
1995—Amsterdam W.L.	9	9	219	126	57.5	1433	11	6	6.54	0	82.6	0	0	0.0	0	0	0	0
—St. Louis NFL..........									Did not play.									
1996—St. Louis NFL..............	6	0	34	23	67.6	241	3	2	7.09	4	92.9	7	14	2.0	0	0	0	0
1997—Washington NFL									Did not play.									
1998—Jacksonville NFL.........	4	1	45	27	60.0	355	2	0	7.89	2	99.8	5	8	1.6	0	0	0	0
1999—Cleveland NFL									Did not play.									
2000—Jacksonville NFL.........	5	0	33	22	66.7	307	2	1	9.30	0	104.0	7	-6	-0.9	0	0	0	0
2001—St. Louis NFL..............	5	0	3	3	100.0	22	0	0	7.33	2	97.2	8	-9	-1.1	0	0	0	0
2002—St. Louis NFL..............	5	2	195	124	63.6	1216	7	10	6.24	10	71.7	5	6	1.2	0	0	0	0
W.L. totals (1 year)	9	9	219	126	57.5	1433	11	6	6.54	0	82.6	0	0	0.0	0	0	0	0
NFL totals (5 years)	25	3	310	199	64.2	2141	14	13	6.91	18	81.9	32	13	0.4	0	0	0	0
Pro totals (6 years)	34	12	529	325	61.4	3574	25	19	6.76	18	82.2	32	13	0.4	0	0	0	0

MARTIN, MATT — G — TITANS

M

PERSONAL: Born October 12, 1979, in Long Beach, Calif. ... 6-6/272. ... Full name: Matthew Stuart Martin.
HIGH SCHOOL: Edison (Calif.).
COLLEGE: Kansas State.
TRANSACTIONS/CAREER NOTES: Signed as non-drafted free agent by Tennessee Titans (April 22, 2002). ... Released by Titans (September 1, 2002). ... Re-signed by Titans to practice squad (September 3, 2002). ... Activated (December 20, 2002).
PLAYING EXPERIENCE: Tennessee NFL, 2002. ... Games/games started: 2002 (1/0).
CHAMPIONSHIP GAME EXPERIENCE: Member of Titans for AFC championship game (2002 season); inactive.

MARTIN, STEVE — DT

PERSONAL: Born May 31, 1974, in St. Paul, Minn. ... 6-4/320. ... Full name: Steven Albert Martin.
HIGH SCHOOL: Jefferson City (Mo.).
COLLEGE: Missouri.
TRANSACTIONS/CAREER NOTES: Selected by Indianapolis Colts in fifth round (151st pick overall) of 1996 NFL draft. ... Signed by Colts (July 5, 1996). ... Claimed on waivers by Philadelphia Eagles (October 23, 1998). ... Granted free agency (February 12, 1999). ... Re-signed by Eagles (April 9, 1999). ... Granted unconditional free agency (February 11, 2000). ... Signed by Kansas City Chiefs (February 24, 2000). ... Released by Chiefs (September 1, 2001). ... Signed by New York Jets (September 3, 2001). ... Granted unconditional free agency (March 1, 2002). ... Signed by New England Patriots (April 3, 2002). ... Released by Patriots (December 19, 2002).

			TOTALS		
Year Team	G	GS	Tk.	Ast.	Sks.
1996—Indianapolis NFL..	14	5	25	11	1.0
1997—Indianapolis NFL..	12	0	9	7	0.0
1998—Indianapolis NFL..	4	0	2	0	0.0
—Philadelphia NFL..	9	3	21	7	1.0
1999—Philadelphia NFL..	16	15	26	17	2.0
2000—Kansas City NFL	16	0	8	5	0.0
2001—New York Jets NFL	16	15	40	18	2.5
2002—New England NFL	14	6	13	4	0.0
Pro totals (7 years)..	101	44	144	69	6.5

MASLOWSKI, MIKE — LB

PERSONAL: Born July 11, 1974, in Thorp, Wis. ... 6-1/243. ... Full name: Michael John Maslowski.
HIGH SCHOOL: Thorp (Wis.).

COLLEGE: Wisconsin-La Crosse.

TRANSACTIONS/CAREER NOTES: Signed as non-drafted free agent by San Diego Chargers (April 21, 1997). ... Released by Chargers (August 1997). ... Played for San Jose Sabercats of Arena League (1998). ... Signed by Kansas City Chiefs (January 12, 1999). ... Assigned by Chiefs to Barcelona Dragons in 1999 NFL Europe enhancement allocation program (February 22, 1999). ... On injured reserve with knee injury (December 22, 2001-remainder of season). ... Granted free agency (March 1, 2002). ... Tendered offer sheet by New England Patriots (March 7, 2002). ... Offer matched by Chiefs (March 14, 2002). ... Granted unconditional free agency (February 28, 2003).

			TOTALS			INTERCEPTIONS			
Year Team	G	GS	Tk.	Ast.	Sks.	No.	Yds.	Avg.	TD
1999—Barcelona NFLE	...	...	...	...	2.0	4	56	14.0	1
—Kansas City NFL	15	0	0	0	0.0	0	0	0.0	0
2000—Kansas City NFL	16	5	29	12	2.0	0	0	0.0	0
2001—Kansas City NFL	8	0	5	1	1.0	0	0	0.0	0
2002—Kansas City NFL	16	16	94	32	1.0	3	28	9.3	0
NFL Europe totals (1 year)	...	...	...	...	2.0	4	56	14.0	1
NFL totals (4 years)	55	21	128	45	4.0	3	28	9.3	0
Pro totals (5 years)	...	...	...	...	6.0	7	84	12.0	1

MASON, DERRICK   WR   TITANS

PERSONAL: Born January 17, 1974, in Detroit. ... 5-10/192. ... Full name: Derrick James Mason.

HIGH SCHOOL: Mumford (Detroit).

COLLEGE: Michigan State.

TRANSACTIONS/CAREER NOTES: Selected by Houston Oilers in fourth round (98th pick overall) of 1997 NFL draft. ... Oilers franchise moved to Tennessee for 1997 season. ... Signed by Oilers (July 19, 1997). ... Oilers franchise renamed Tennessee Titans for 1999 season (December 26, 1998). ... Granted free agency (February 11, 2000). ... Re-signed by Titans (June 1, 2000). ... Granted unconditional free agency (March 2, 2001). ... Re-signed by Titans (March 2, 2001).

CHAMPIONSHIP GAME EXPERIENCE: Played in AFC championship game (1999 and 2002 seasons). ... Played in Super Bowl XXXIV (1999 season).

HONORS: Named kick returner on THE SPORTING NEWS NFL All-Pro team (2000). ... Played in Pro Bowl (2000 season).

RECORDS: Holds NFL single-season record for most combined net yards—2,690 (2000).

SINGLE GAME HIGHS (regular season): Receptions—12 (December 1, 2002, vs. New York Giants); yards—186 (January 6, 2002, vs. Cincinnati); and touchdown receptions—2 (October 27, 2002, vs. Cincinnati).

STATISTICAL PLATEAUS: 100-yard receiving games: 2000 (1), 2001 (4), 2002 (3). Total: 8.

			RECEIVING				PUNT RETURNS				KICKOFF RETURNS				TOTALS			
Year Team	G	GS	No.	Yds.	Avg.	TD	No.	Yds.	Avg.	TD	No.	Yds.	Avg.	TD	TD	2pt.	Pts.	Fum.
1997—Tennessee NFL	16	2	14	186	13.3	0	13	95	7.3	0	26	551	21.2	0	0	0	0	5
1998—Tennessee NFL	16	0	25	333	13.3	3	31	228	7.4	0	8	154	19.3	0	3	0	18	1
1999—Tennessee NFL	13	0	8	89	11.1	0	26	225	8.7	1	41	805	19.6	0	1	0	6	0
2000—Tennessee NFL	16	12	63	895	14.2	5	*51	*662	13.0	1	42	1132	§27.0	0	6	0	36	1
2001—Tennessee NFL	15	15	73	1128	15.5	9	20	128	6.4	0	34	748	22.0	1	10	1	62	2
2002—Tennessee NFL	14	14	79	1012	12.8	5	9	60	6.7	0	0	0	0.0	0	5	0	30	2
Pro totals (6 years)	90	43	262	3643	13.9	22	150	1398	9.3	2	151	3390	22.5	1	25	1	152	11

MASON, EDDIE   LB

M

PERSONAL: Born January 9, 1972, in Siler City, N.C. ... 6-0/232. ... Full name: Eddie Lee Mason.

HIGH SCHOOL: Jordan-Matthews (Siler City, N.C.).

COLLEGE: North Carolina.

TRANSACTIONS/CAREER NOTES: Selected by New York Jets in sixth round (178th pick overall) of 1995 NFL draft. ... Signed by Jets (June 14, 1995). ... On injured reserve with knee injury (August 20, 1996-entire season). ... Granted unconditional free agency (February 14, 1997). ... Signed by Tampa Bay Buccaneers (April 21, 1997). ... Released by Buccaneers (August 17, 1997). ... Signed by Carolina Panthers (March 4, 1998). ... Released by Panthers (August 24, 1998). ... Signed by Jacksonville Jaguars (December 2, 1998). ... Released by Jaguars (September 5, 1999). ... Signed by Washington Redskins (September 21, 1999). ... Granted free agency (February 11, 2000). ... Re-signed by Redskins (April 10, 2000). ... Released by Redskins (September 2, 2001). ... Re-signed by Redskins (September 25, 2001). ... Granted unconditional free agency (March 1, 2002). ... Re-signed by Redskins (April 8, 2002). ... Granted unconditional free agency (February 28, 2003).

			TOTALS			INTERCEPTIONS			
Year Team	G	GS	Tk.	Ast.	Sks.	No.	Yds.	Avg.	TD
1995—New York Jets NFL	15	0	0	1	0.0	0	0	0.0	0
1996—New York Jets NFL			Did not play.						
1997—			Did not play.						
1998—Jacksonville NFL	4	0	7	1	0.0	0	0	0.0	0
1999—Washington NFL	14	0	1	0	0.0	0	0	0.0	0
2000—Washington NFL	16	2	14	0	2.0	0	0	0.0	0
2001—Washington NFL	15	1	11	2	1.0	0	0	0.0	0
2002—Washington NFL	16	0	1	0	0.0	0	0	0.0	0
Pro totals (6 years)	80	3	34	4	3.0	0	0	0.0	0

MASSEY, CHRIS   C   RAMS

PERSONAL: Born August 21, 1979, in Charleston, W.Va. ... 6-0/245. ... Full name: Christopher Todd Massey.

HIGH SCHOOL: East Bank (W.Va.).

COLLEGE: Marshall.

TRANSACTIONS/CAREER NOTES: Selected by St. Louis Rams in seventh round (243rd pick overall) of 2002 NFL draft. ... Signed by Rams (June 28, 2002).

PLAYING EXPERIENCE: St. Louis NFL, 2002. ... Games/games started: 2002 (16/1).

MATHEWS, JASON   OT   TITANS

PERSONAL: Born February 9, 1971, in Orange, Texas. ... 6-5/284. ... Full name: Samuel Jason Mathews.
HIGH SCHOOL: Bridge City (Texas).
COLLEGE: Brigham Young, then Texas A&M.
TRANSACTIONS/CAREER NOTES: Selected by Indianapolis Colts in third round (67th pick overall) of 1994 NFL draft. ... Signed by Colts (July 23, 1994). ... Granted free agency (February 14, 1997). ... Re-signed by Colts (April 30, 1997). ... Granted unconditional free agency (February 13, 1998). ... Signed by Tampa Bay Buccaneers (May 7, 1998). ... Released by Buccaneers (August 30, 1998). ... Signed by Tennessee Oilers (September 1, 1998). ... Oilers franchise renamed Tennessee Titans for 1999 season (December 26, 1998).
PLAYING EXPERIENCE: Indianapolis NFL, 1994-1997; Tennessee NFL, 1998-2002. ... Games/Games started: 1994 (10/0), 1995 (16/16), 1996 (16/15), 1997 (16/0), 1998 (3/0), 1999 (5/0), 2000 (16/1), 2001 (16/2), 2002 (16/2). Total: 114/36.
CHAMPIONSHIP GAME EXPERIENCE: Played in AFC championship game (1995, 1999 and 2002 seasons). ... Member of Titans for Super Bowl XXXIV (1999 season); did not play.

MATHIS, KEVIN   CB   FALCONS

PERSONAL: Born April 29, 1974, in Gainesville, Texas. ... 5-9/185.
HIGH SCHOOL: Gainesville (Texas).
COLLEGE: East Texas State.
TRANSACTIONS/CAREER NOTES: Signed as non-drafted free agent by Dallas Cowboys (April 24, 1997). ... Granted free agency (February 11, 2000). ... Re-signed by Cowboys (April 26, 2000). ... Traded by Cowboys to New Orleans Saints for LB Chris Bordano (April 26, 2000). ... Granted unconditional free agency (March 2, 2001). ... Re-signed by Saints (March 2, 2001). ... Released by Saints (July 24, 2002). ... Signed by Atlanta Falcons (September 17, 2002). ... Granted unconditional free agency (February 28, 2003). ... Re-signed by Falcons (March 31, 2003).

			TOTALS			INTERCEPTIONS				PUNT RETURNS				KICKOFF RETURNS				TOTALS			
Year Team	G	GS	Tk.	Ast.	Sks.	No.	Yds.	Avg.	TD	No.	Yds.	Avg.	TD	No.	Yds.	Avg.	TD	TD	2pt.	Pts.	Fum.
1997—Dallas NFL	16	3	15	1	0.0	0	0	0.0	0	11	91	8.3	0	0	0	0.0	0	0	0	0	2
1998—Dallas NFL	13	4	28	4	1.0	2	0	0.0	0	2	3	1.5	0	25	621	24.8	0	0	0	0	2
1999—Dallas NFL	8	4	11	3	0.0	0	0	0.0	0	0	0	0.0	0	18	408	22.7	0	0	0	0	1
2000—New Orleans NFL	16	16	58	15	0.0	1	0	0.0	0	1	5	5.0	0	8	187	23.4	0	0	0	0	1
2001—New Orleans NFL	14	13	63	14	1.0	2	34	17.0	0	0	0	0.0	0	0	0	0.0	0	0	0	0	0
2002—Atlanta NFL	11	0	15	1	0.0	3	21	7.0	0	0	0	0.0	0	0	0	0.0	0	0	0	0	0
Pro totals (6 years)	78	40	190	38	2.0	8	55	6.9	0	14	99	7.1	0	51	1216	23.8	0	0	0	0	6

MATHIS, TERANCE   WR

M

PERSONAL: Born June 7, 1967, in Detroit. ... 5-10/185. ... Cousin of Jason Ferguson, defensive tackle, New York Jets.
HIGH SCHOOL: Redan (Stone Mountain, Ga.).
COLLEGE: New Mexico.
TRANSACTIONS/CAREER NOTES: Selected by New York Jets in sixth round (140th pick overall) of 1990 NFL draft. ... Signed by Jets (July 12, 1990). ... Granted unconditional free agency (February 17, 1994). ... Signed by Atlanta Falcons (May 3, 1994). ... Granted unconditional free agency (February 16, 1996). ... Re-signed by Falcons (April 30, 1996). ... Released by Falcons (February 25, 2002). ... Signed by Pittsburgh Steelers (June 13, 2002). ... Granted unconditional free agency (February 28, 2003).
CHAMPIONSHIP GAME EXPERIENCE: Played in NFC championship game (1998 season). ... Played in Super Bowl XXXIII (1998 season).
HONORS: Named wide receiver on THE SPORTING NEWS college All-America first team (1989). ... Played in Pro Bowl (1994 season).
RECORDS: Holds NFL career record for most two-point conversions—6.
SINGLE GAME HIGHS (regular season): Receptions—13 (September 18, 1994, vs. Kansas City); yards—198 (December 13, 1998, vs. New Orleans); and touchdown receptions—3 (November 19, 1995, vs. St. Louis).
STATISTICAL PLATEAUS: 100-yard receiving games: 1992 (1), 1994 (5), 1995 (2), 1996 (2), 1997 (1), 1998 (3), 1999 (1). Total: 15.
MISCELLANEOUS: Holds Atlanta Falcons all-time records for most receptions (573), most touchdown receptions (57), most touchdowns (57) and yards receiving (7,349).

			RUSHING				RECEIVING				PUNT RETURNS				KICKOFF RETURNS				TOTALS		
Year Team	G	GS	Att.	Yds.	Avg.	TD	No.	Yds.	Avg.	TD	No.	Yds.	Avg.	TD	No.	Yds.	Avg.	TD	TD	2pt.	Pts.
1990—N.Y. Jets NFL	16	1	2	9	4.5	0	19	245	12.9	0	11	165	15.0	†1	43	787	18.3	0	1	0	6
1991—N.Y. Jets NFL	16	0	1	19	19.0	0	28	329	11.8	1	23	157	6.8	0	29	599	20.7	0	1	0	6
1992—N.Y. Jets NFL	16	0	3	25	8.3	1	22	316	14.4	3	2	24	12.0	0	28	492	17.6	0	4	0	24
1993—N.Y. Jets NFL	16	3	2	20	10.0	1	24	352	14.7	0	14	99	7.1	0	7	102	14.6	0	1	0	6
1994—Atlanta NFL	16	16	0	0	0.0	0	111	1342	12.1	11	0	0	0.0	0	0	0	0.0	0	11	∞2	70
1995—Atlanta NFL	14	12	0	0	0.0	0	78	1039	13.3	9	0	0	0.0	0	0	0	0.0	0	9	*3	60
1996—Atlanta NFL	16	16	0	0	0.0	0	69	771	11.2	7	3	19	6.3	0	0	0	0.0	0	7	1	44
1997—Atlanta NFL	16	16	3	35	11.7	0	62	802	12.9	6	0	0	0.0	0	0	0	0.0	0	6	0	36
1998—Atlanta NFL	16	16	1	-6	-6.0	0	64	1136	17.8	11	1	0	0.0	0	0	0	0.0	0	11	0	66
1999—Atlanta NFL	16	16	1	0	0.0	0	81	1016	12.5	6	0	0	0.0	0	0	0	0.0	0	6	0	36
2000—Atlanta NFL	16	16	1	-5	-5.0	0	57	679	11.9	5	0	0	0.0	0	0	0	0.0	0	5	0	30
2001—Atlanta NFL	16	16	0	0	0.0	0	51	564	11.1	2	0	0	0.0	0	0	0	0.0	0	2	0	12
2002—Pittsburgh NFL	16	0	0	0	0.0	0	23	218	9.5	2	0	0	0.0	0	0	0	0.0	0	2	0	12
Pro totals (13 years)	206	128	14	97	6.9	2	689	8809	12.8	63	54	464	8.6	1	107	1980	18.5	0	66	6	408

MATTHEWS, SHANE   QB   BENGALS

PERSONAL: Born June 1, 1970, in Pascagoula, Miss. ... 6-3/196. ... Full name: Michael Shane Matthews.
HIGH SCHOOL: Pascagoula (Miss.).
COLLEGE: Florida.
TRANSACTIONS/CAREER NOTES: Signed as non-drafted free agent by Chicago Bears (April 29, 1993). ... Released by Bears (August 30, 1993). ... Re-signed by Bears to practice squad (September 1, 1993). ... Activated (October 8, 1993); did not play. ... Active for two games

(1994); did not play. ... Released by Bears (September 15, 1995). ... Re-signed by Bears (February 12, 1996). ... Released by Bears (June 7, 1996). ... Re-signed by Bears (October 9, 1996). ... Granted unconditional free agency (February 14, 1997). ... Assigned by Bears to Rhein Fire in 1997 World League enhancement allocation program (February 19, 1997). ... Signed by Carolina Panthers (August 25, 1997). ... Released by Panthers (September 17, 1997). ... Re-signed by Panthers (October 16, 1997). ... Active for two games (1997); did not play. ... Granted unconditional free agency (February 13, 1998). ... Re-signed by Panthers (March 19, 1998). ... Active for 12 games (1998); did not play. ... Granted unconditional free agency (February 12, 1999). ... Signed by Bears (April 3, 1999). ... Granted unconditional free agency (February 11, 2000). ... Re-signed by Bears (July 18, 2000). ... Granted unconditional free agency (March 2, 2001). ... Re-signed by Bears (March 14, 2001). ... Released by Bears (October 13, 2001). ... Re-signed by Bears (October 13, 2001). ... Released by Bears (April 24, 2002). ... Signed by Washington Redskins (April 29, 2002). ... Granted unconditional free agency (February 28, 2003). ... Signed by Tampa Bay Buccaneers (March 14, 2003). ... Released by Buccaneers (April 28, 2003). ... Signed by Cincinnati Bengals (June 1, 2003).

SINGLE GAME HIGHS (regular season): Attempts—50 (November 10, 2002, vs. Jacksonville); completions—30 (November 4, 2001, vs. Cleveland); yards—357 (November 4, 2001, vs. Cleveland); and touchdown passes—3 (September 8, 2002, vs. Arizona).

STATISTICAL PLATEAUS: 300-yard passing games: 2001 (1), 2002 (1). Total: 2.

MISCELLANEOUS: Regular-season record as starting NFL quarterback: 11-11 (.500).

Year Team	G	GS	PASSING Att.	Cmp.	Pct.	Yds.	TD	Int.	Avg.	Skd.	Rat.	RUSHING Att.	Yds.	Avg.	TD	TOTALS TD	2pt.	Pts.
1993—Chicago NFL											Did not play.							
1994—Chicago NFL											Did not play.							
1995—											Did not play.							
1996—Chicago NFL	2	0	17	13	76.5	158	1	0	9.29	1	124.1	1	2	2.0	1	1	0	6
1997—Carolina NFL											Did not play.							
1998—Carolina NFL											Did not play.							
1999—Chicago NFL	8	7	275	167	60.7	1645	10	6	5.98	13	80.6	14	31	2.2	0	0	0	0
2000—Chicago NFL	6	5	178	102	57.3	964	3	6	5.42	5	64.0	10	35	3.5	0	0	0	0
2001—Chicago NFL	5	3	129	84	65.1	694	5	6	5.38	6	72.3	4	5	1.3	0	0	0	0
2002—Washington NFL	8	7	237	124	52.3	1251	11	6	5.28	9	72.6	12	31	2.6	0	0	0	0
Pro totals (5 years)	29	22	836	490	58.6	4712	30	24	5.64	34	74.4	41	104	2.5	1	1	0	6

MAWAE, KEVIN — C — JETS

PERSONAL: Born January 23, 1971, in Savannah, Ga. ... 6-4/289. ... Full name: Kevin James Mawae. ... Name pronounced ma-WHY.

HIGH SCHOOL: Leesville (La.).

COLLEGE: Louisiana State (degree in general studies).

TRANSACTIONS/CAREER NOTES: Selected by Seattle Seahawks in second round (36th pick overall) of 1994 NFL draft. ... Signed by Seahawks (July 21, 1994). ... Granted free agency (February 14, 1997). ... Re-signed by Seahawks (May 5, 1997). ... Granted unconditional free agency (February 13, 1998). ... Signed by New York Jets (February 19, 1998).

PLAYING EXPERIENCE: Seattle NFL, 1994-1997; New York Jets NFL, 1998-2002. ... Games/Games started: 1994 (14/11), 1995 (16/16), 1996 (16/16), 1997 (16/16), 1998 (16/16), 1999 (16/16), 2000 (16/16), 2001 (16/16), 2002 (16/16). Total: 142/139.

CHAMPIONSHIP GAME EXPERIENCE: Played in AFC championship game (1998 season).

HONORS: Named center on THE SPORTING NEWS NFL All-Pro team (1999, 2001 and 2002). ... Played in Pro Bowl (1999-2002 seasons).

MAYBERRY, JERMANE — G/OT — EAGLES

M

PERSONAL: Born August 29, 1973, in Floresville, Texas. ... 6-4/325. ... Full name: Jermane Timothy Mayberry.

HIGH SCHOOL: Floresville (Texas).

JUNIOR COLLEGE: Navarro College (Texas).

COLLEGE: Texas A&M-Kingsville.

TRANSACTIONS/CAREER NOTES: Selected by Philadelphia Eagles in first round (25th pick overall) of 1996 NFL draft. ... Signed by Eagles (June 13, 1996).

PLAYING EXPERIENCE: Philadelphia NFL, 1996-2002. ... Games/Games started: 1996 (3/1), 1997 (16/16), 1998 (15/10), 1999 (13/5), 2000 (16/16), 2001 (16/15), 2002 (16/16). Total: 95/79.

CHAMPIONSHIP GAME EXPERIENCE: Played in NFC championship game (2001 and 2002 seasons).

HONORS: Played in Pro Bowl (2002 season).

MAYNARD, BRAD — P — BEARS

PERSONAL: Born February 9, 1974, in Tipton, Ind. ... 6-1/186. ... Full name: Bradley Alan Maynard.

HIGH SCHOOL: Sheridan (Ind.).

COLLEGE: Ball State.

TRANSACTIONS/CAREER NOTES: Selected by New York Giants in third round (95th pick overall) of 1997 NFL draft. ... Signed by Giants (July 19, 1997). ... Granted free agency (February 11, 2000). ... Re-signed by Giants (June 8, 2000). ... Granted unconditional free agency (March 2, 2001). ... Signed by Chicago Bears (March 3, 2001).

CHAMPIONSHIP GAME EXPERIENCE: Played in NFC championship game (2000 season). ... Played in Super Bowl XXXV (2000 season).

HONORS: Named punter on THE SPORTING NEWS college All-America second team (1996).

Year Team	G	PUNTING No.	Yds.	Avg.	Net avg.	In. 20	Blk.
1997—New York Giants NFL	16	*111	*4531	40.8	34.6	*33	1
1998—New York Giants NFL	16	101	*4566	45.2	37.8	∞33	0
1999—New York Giants NFL	16	89	3651	41.0	35.1	‡31	0
2000—New York Giants NFL	16	79	3210	40.6	33.7	26	1
2001—Chicago NFL	16	87	3709	42.6	37.0	*36	0
2002—Chicago NFL	16	87	3679	42.3	37.4	26	0
Pro totals (6 years)	96	554	23346	42.1	36.0	185	2

MAYS, LEE — WR — STEELERS

PERSONAL: Born September 18, 1978, in Houston. ... 6-2/192.
HIGH SCHOOL: Westfield (Houston).
COLLEGE: Texas-El Paso.
TRANSACTIONS/CAREER NOTES: Selected by Pittsburgh Steelers in sixth round (202nd pick overall) of 2002 NFL draft. ... Signed by Steelers (July 18, 2002).

Year Team	G	GS	RUSHING				RECEIVING				KICKOFF RETURNS				TOTALS			
			Att.	Yds.	Avg.	TD	No.	Yds.	Avg.	TD	No.	Yds.	Avg.	TD	TD	2pt.	Pts.	Fum.
2002—Pittsburgh NFL	16	0	0	0	0.0	0	0	0	0.0	0	32	671	21.0	0	0	0	0	0

McADDLEY, JASON — WR — CARDINALS

PERSONAL: Born July 28, 1979, in Oak Ridge, Tenn. ... 6-2/204.
HIGH SCHOOL: Oak Ridge (Tenn.).
COLLEGE: Alabama.
TRANSACTIONS/CAREER NOTES: Selected by Arizona Cardinals in fifth round (149th pick overall) of 2002 NFL draft. ... Signed by Cardinals (June 5, 2002).
SINGLE GAME HIGHS (regular season): Receptions—5 (December 8, 2002, vs. Detroit); yards—113 (November 10, 2002, vs. Seattle); and touchdown receptions—1 (November 17, 2002, vs. Philadelphia).
STATISTICAL PLATEAUS: 100-yard receiving games: 2002 (1).

Year Team	G	GS	RUSHING				RECEIVING				KICKOFF RETURNS				TOTALS			
			Att.	Yds.	Avg.	TD	No.	Yds.	Avg.	TD	No.	Yds.	Avg.	TD	TD	2pt.	Pts.	Fum.
2002—Arizona NFL	9	8	0	0	0.0	0	25	362	14.5	1	2	45	22.5	0	1	0	6	0

McAFEE, FRED — RB — SAINTS

PERSONAL: Born June 20, 1968, in Philadelphia, Miss. ... 5-10/193. ... Full name: Fred Lee McAfee.
HIGH SCHOOL: Philadelphia (Miss.).
COLLEGE: Mississippi College (degree in mass communications, 1990).
TRANSACTIONS/CAREER NOTES: Selected by New Orleans Saints in sixth round (154th pick overall) of 1991 NFL draft. ... Signed by Saints (July 14, 1991). ... Released by Saints (August 26, 1991). ... Re-signed by Saints to practice squad (August 28, 1991). ... Activated (October 18, 1991). ... On injured reserve with shoulder injury (December 15, 1992-remainder of season). ... Granted free agency (February 17, 1994). ... Signed by Arizona Cardinals (August 2, 1994). ... Released by Cardinals (October 31, 1994). ... Signed by Pittsburgh Steelers (November 9, 1994). ... Granted unconditional free agency (February 16, 1996). ... Re-signed by Steelers (April 12, 1996). ... Granted unconditional free agency (February 12, 1999). ... Signed by Kansas City Chiefs (July 30, 1999). ... Released by Chiefs (August 31, 1999). ... Signed by Tampa Bay Buccaneers (December 28, 1999). ... Granted unconditional free agency (February 11, 2000). ... Signed by Saints (October 2, 2000). ... Granted unconditional free agency (March 2, 2001). ... Re-signed by Saints (June 6, 2001). ... Granted unconditional free agency (February 28, 2003). ... Re-signed by Saints (March 19, 2003).
CHAMPIONSHIP GAME EXPERIENCE: Played in AFC championship game (1994, 1995 and 1997 seasons). ... Played in Super Bowl XXX (1995 season). ... Played in NFC championship game (1999 season).
HONORS: Played in Pro Bowl (2002 season).
SINGLE GAME HIGHS (regular season): Attempts—28 (November 24, 1991, vs. Atlanta); yards—138 (November 24, 1991, vs. Atlanta); and rushing touchdowns—1 (September 10, 1995, vs. Houston).
STATISTICAL PLATEAUS: 100-yard rushing games: 1991 (1).

Year Team	G	GS	RUSHING				RECEIVING				KICKOFF RETURNS				TOTALS			
			Att.	Yds.	Avg.	TD	No.	Yds.	Avg.	TD	No.	Yds.	Avg.	TD	TD	2pt.	Pts.	Fum.
1991—New Orleans NFL	9	0	109	494	4.5	2	1	8	8.0	0	1	14	14.0	0	2	0	12	2
1992—New Orleans NFL	14	1	39	114	2.9	1	1	16	16.0	0	19	393	20.7	0	1	0	6	0
1993—New Orleans NFL	15	4	51	160	3.1	1	1	3	3.0	0	28	580	20.7	0	1	0	6	3
1994—Arizona NFL	7	0	2	-5	-2.5	0	1	4	4.0	0	7	113	16.1	0	1	0	6	1
—Pittsburgh NFL	6	0	16	56	3.5	1	0	0	0.0	0	0	0	0.0	0	1	0	6	0
1995—Pittsburgh NFL	16	1	39	156	4.0	1	15	88	5.9	0	5	56	11.2	0	1	0	6	0
1996—Pittsburgh NFL	14	0	7	17	2.4	0	5	21	4.2	0	0	0	0.0	0	0	0	0	0
1997—Pittsburgh NFL	14	0	13	41	3.2	0	2	44	22.0	0	0	0	0.0	0	0	0	0	1
1998—Pittsburgh NFL	14	0	18	111	6.2	0	9	27	3.0	0	1	10	10.0	0	1	0	6	0
1999—Tampa Bay NFL	1	0	0	0	0.0	0	0	0	0.0	0	0	0	0.0	0	0	0	0	0
2000—New Orleans NFL	12	0	2	37	18.5	0	0	0	0.0	0	10	251	25.1	0	0	0	0	0
2001—New Orleans NFL	16	0	1	2	2.0	0	0	0	0.0	0	6	144	24.0	0	0	0	0	0
2002—New Orleans NFL	11	0	1	11	11.0	0	0	0	0.0	0	2	69	34.5	0	0	0	0	0
Pro totals (12 years)	149	6	298	1194	4.0	7	35	211	6.0	0	79	1630	20.6	0	8	0	48	7

McALISTER, CHRIS — CB — RAVENS

PERSONAL: Born June 14, 1977, in Pasedena, Calif. ... 6-1/206. ... Full name: Christopher James McAlister. ... Son of James McAlister, running back with Philadelphia Eagles (1975 and 1976) and New England Patriots (1978).
HIGH SCHOOL: Pasadena (Calif.).
JUNIOR COLLEGE: Mt. San Antonio College (Calif.).
COLLEGE: Arizona.
TRANSACTIONS/CAREER NOTES: Selected by Baltimore Ravens in first round (10th pick overall) of 1999 NFL draft. ... Signed by Ravens (July 23, 1999). ... Designated by Ravens as franchise player (February 20, 2003).
CHAMPIONSHIP GAME EXPERIENCE: Played in AFC championship game (2000 season). ... Member of Super Bowl championship team (2000 season).
HONORS: Named cornerback on THE SPORTING NEWS college All-America third team (1997). ... Named cornerback on THE SPORTING NEWS college All-America first team (1998).

Year Team	G	GS	TOTALS			INTERCEPTIONS				PUNT RETURNS				TOTALS			
			Tk.	Ast.	Sks.	No.	Yds.	Avg.	TD	No.	Yds.	Avg.	TD	TD	2pt.	Pts.	Fum.
1999—Baltimore NFL	16	12	45	2	0.0	5	28	5.6	0	0	0	0.0	0	0	0	0	0
2000—Baltimore NFL	16	16	35	6	0.0	4	*165	41.3	1	0	0	0.0	0	1	0	6	0
2001—Baltimore NFL	16	16	63	8	0.0	1	0	0.0	0	5	44	8.8	0	0	0	0	0
2002—Baltimore NFL	13	12	48	5	0.0	1	0	0.0	1	17	122	7.2	0	1	0	6	2
Pro totals (4 years)	61	56	191	21	0.0	11	193	17.5	2	22	166	7.5	0	2	0	12	2

McALLISTER, DEUCE   RB   SAINTS

PERSONAL: Born December 27, 1978, in Morton, Miss. ... 6-1/221. ... Full name: Dulymus James McAllister.
HIGH SCHOOL: Morton (Miss.).
COLLEGE: Mississippi.
TRANSACTIONS/CAREER NOTES: Selected by New Orleans Saints in first round (23rd pick overall) of 2001 NFL draft. ... Signed by Saints (August 4, 2001).
HONORS: Played in Pro Bowl (2002 season).
SINGLE GAME HIGHS (regular season): Attempts—32 (December 8, 2002, vs. Baltimore); yards—139 (October 20, 2002, vs. San Francisco); and rushing touchdowns—3 (December 8, 2002, vs. Baltimore).
STATISTICAL PLATEAUS: 100-yard rushing games: 2002 (8).

Year Team	G	GS	RUSHING				RECEIVING				PUNT RETURNS				KICKOFF RETURNS				TOTALS			
			Att.	Yds.	Avg.	TD	No.	Yds.	Avg.	TD	No.	Yds.	Avg.	TD	No.	Yds.	Avg.	TD	TD	2pt.	Pts.	Fum.
2001—NO NFL	16	4	16	91	5.7	1	15	166	11.1	1	4	24	6.0	0	45	1091	24.2	0	2	0	12	1
2002—NO NFL	15	15	‡325	‡1388	4.3	13	47	352	7.5	3	0	0	0.0	0	0	0	0.0	0	16	0	96	4
Pro totals (2 yrs)	31	19	341	1479	4.3	14	62	518	8.4	4	4	24	6.0	0	45	1091	24.2	0	18	0	108	5

McBRIDE, TOD   CB   FALCONS

PERSONAL: Born January 26, 1976, in Los Angeles. ... 6-1/208. ... Full name: Tod Anthony McBride.
HIGH SCHOOL: Walnut (Calif.).
COLLEGE: UCLA.
TRANSACTIONS/CAREER NOTES: Signed as non-drafted free agent by Seattle Seahawks (April 23, 1999). ... Claimed on waivers by Green Bay Packers (June 23, 1999). ... Granted free agency (March 1, 2002). ... Re-signed by Packers (April 24, 2002). ... Granted unconditional free agency (February 28, 2003). ... Signed by Atlanta Falcons (March 24, 2003).

Year Team	G	GS	TOTALS			INTERCEPTIONS			
			Tk.	Ast.	Sks.	No.	Yds.	Avg.	TD
1999—Green Bay NFL	15	0	4	1	0.0	0	0	0.0	0
2000—Green Bay NFL	15	6	43	11	0.0	2	43	21.5	0
2001—Green Bay NFL	16	0	29	7	2.0	0	0	0.0	0
2002—Green Bay NFL	15	4	35	7	0.0	1	0	0.0	0
Pro totals (4 years)	61	10	111	26	2.0	3	43	14.3	0

McBURROWS, GERALD   S   FALCONS

PERSONAL: Born October 7, 1973, in Detroit. ... 5-11/208. ... Full name: Gerald Lance McBurrows.
HIGH SCHOOL: Martin Luther King (Detroit).
COLLEGE: Kansas.
TRANSACTIONS/CAREER NOTES: Selected by St. Louis Rams in seventh round (214th pick overall) of 1995 NFL draft. ... Signed by Rams (June 16, 1995). ... On injured reserve with knee injury (October 29, 1997-remainder of season). ... Re-signed by Rams (February 13, 1998). ... Re-signed by Rams (April 24, 1998). ... On injured reserve with knee injury (November 17, 1998-remainder of season). ... Granted unconditional free agency (February 12, 1999). ... Signed by Atlanta Falcons (March 2, 1999). ... Granted unconditional free agency (March 2, 2001). ... Re-signed by Falcons (March 21, 2001).

Year Team	G	GS	TOTALS			INTERCEPTIONS			
			Tk.	Ast.	Sks.	No.	Yds.	Avg.	TD
1995—St. Louis NFL	14	3	23	4	1.0	0	0	0.0	0
1996—St. Louis NFL	16	7	55	7	0.0	1	3	3.0	0
1997—St. Louis NFL	8	3	16	3	0.0	0	0	0.0	0
1998—St. Louis NFL	10	0	3	0	0.0	0	0	0.0	0
1999—Atlanta NFL	16	4	28	12	1.0	2	64	32.0	0
2000—Atlanta NFL	16	4	29	7	2.0	0	0	0.0	0
2001—Atlanta NFL	14	8	41	6	0.0	0	0	0.0	0
2002—Atlanta NFL	15	14	39	10	0.5	2	36	18.0	0
Pro totals (8 years)	109	43	234	49	4.5	5	103	20.6	0

McCADAM, KEVIN   S   FALCONS

PERSONAL: Born March 6, 1979, in La Mesa, Calif. ... 6-1/219. ... Full name: Kevin Edward McCadam.
HIGH SCHOOL: El Capitan (Calif.).
JUNIOR COLLEGE: Grossmont College.
COLLEGE: Colorado State, Virginia Tech.
TRANSACTIONS/CAREER NOTES: Selected by Atlanta Falcons in fifth round (148th pick overall) of 2002 NFL draft. ... Signed by Falcons (June 19, 2002).

Year Team	G	GS	TOTALS			INTERCEPTIONS				PUNT RETURNS				KICKOFF RETURNS				TOTALS			
			Tk.	Ast.	Sks.	No.	Yds.	Avg.	TD	No.	Yds.	Avg.	TD	No.	Yds.	Avg.	TD	TD	2pt.	Pts.	Fum.
2002—Atlanta NFL	11	1	3	0	0.0	0	0	0.0	0	0	0	0.0	0	0	0	0.0	0	0	0	0	0

M

McCAFFREY, ED   WR   BRONCOS

PERSONAL: Born August 17, 1968, in Waynesboro, Pa. ... 6-5/215. ... Full name: Edward McCaffrey.
HIGH SCHOOL: Allentown (Pa.) Central Catholic.
COLLEGE: Stanford.
TRANSACTIONS/CAREER NOTES: Selected by New York Giants in third round (83rd pick overall) of 1991 NFL draft. ... Signed by Giants (July 23, 1991). ... Granted free agency (February 17, 1994). ... Signed by San Francisco 49ers (July 24, 1994). ... Granted unconditional free agency (February 17, 1995). ... Signed by Denver Broncos (March 7, 1995). ... On injured reserve with leg injury (September 12, 2001-remainder of season).
CHAMPIONSHIP GAME EXPERIENCE: Played in NFC championship game (1994 season). ... Member of Super Bowl championship team (1994, 1997 and 1998 seasons). ... Played in AFC championship game (1997 and 1998 seasons).
HONORS: Named wide receiver on THE SPORTING NEWS college All-America second team (1990). ... Played in Pro Bowl (1998 season).
SINGLE GAME HIGHS (regular season): Receptions—10 (November 19, 2000, vs. San Diego); yards—148 (November 19, 2000, vs. San Diego); and touchdown receptions—3 (September 13, 1999, vs. Miami).
STATISTICAL PLATEAUS: 100-yard receiving games: 1992 (1), 1997 (1), 1998 (4), 1999 (4), 2000 (5), 2002 (4). Total: 19.

Year Team	G	GS	RECEIVING				TOTALS			
			No.	Yds.	Avg.	TD	TD	2pt.	Pts.	Fum.
1991—New York Giants NFL	16	0	16	146	9.1	0	0	0	0	0
1992—New York Giants NFL	16	3	49	610	12.4	5	5	0	30	2
1993—New York Giants NFL	16	1	27	335	12.4	2	2	0	12	0
1994—San Francisco NFL	16	0	11	131	11.9	2	2	0	12	0
1995—Denver NFL	16	5	39	477	12.2	2	2	1	14	1
1996—Denver NFL	15	15	48	553	11.5	7	7	0	42	0
1997—Denver NFL	15	15	45	590	13.1	8	8	0	48	0
1998—Denver NFL	15	15	64	1053	16.5	▲10	10	1	62	1
1999—Denver NFL	15	15	71	1018	14.3	7	7	0	42	0
2000—Denver NFL	16	16	101	1317	13.0	9	9	1	56	0
2001—Denver NFL	1	1	6	94	15.7	1	1	0	6	0
2002—Denver NFL	16	16	69	903	13.1	2	2	0	12	1
Pro totals (12 years)	173	102	546	7227	13.2	55	55	3	336	5

McCANTS, DARNERIAN   WR   REDSKINS

PERSONAL: Born August 1, 1977, in Odenton, Md. ... 6-3/210. ... Full name: Damerien McCants.
HIGH SCHOOL: Arundel (Md.).
COLLEGE: Delaware State.
TRANSACTIONS/CAREER NOTES: Selected by Washington Redskins in fifth round (154th pick overall) of 2001 NFL draft. ... Signed by Redskins (July 25, 2001).
SINGLE GAME HIGHS (regular season): Receptions—6 (December 29, 2002, vs. Dallas); yards—60 (December 29, 2002, vs. Dallas); and touchdown receptions—1 (November 3, 2002, vs. Seattle).

Year Team	G	GS	RECEIVING			
			No.	Yds.	Avg.	TD
2002—Washington NFL	9	1	21	256	12.2	2

McCARDELL, KEENAN   WR   BUCCANEERS

PERSONAL: Born January 6, 1970, in Houston. ... 6-1/191. ... Full name: Keenan Wayne McCardell. ... Name pronounced mc-CAR-dell.
HIGH SCHOOL: Waltrip (Houston).
COLLEGE: UNLV (degree in business management, 1991).
TRANSACTIONS/CAREER NOTES: Selected by Washington Redskins in 12th round (326th pick overall) of 1991 NFL draft. ... Signed by Redskins for 1991 season. ... On injured reserve with knee injury (August 20, 1991-entire season). ... Granted unconditional free agency (February 1, 1992). ... Signed by Cleveland Browns (March 24, 1992). ... Released by Browns (September 1, 1992). ... Re-signed by Browns to practice squad (September 3, 1992). ... Activated (October 6, 1992). ... Released by Browns (October 13, 1992). ... Re-signed by Browns to practice squad (October 14, 1992). ... Activated (November 14, 1992). ... Released by Browns (November 19, 1992). ... Re-signed by Browns to practice squad (November 20, 1992). ... Activated (December 26, 1992). ... Released by Browns (September 22, 1993). ... Signed by Chicago Bears to practice squad (November 2, 1993). ... Signed by Browns off Bears practice squad (November 24, 1993). ... Granted free agency (February 17, 1994). ... Re-signed by Browns (March 4, 1994). ... Granted unconditional free agency (February 16, 1996). ... Signed by Jacksonville Jaguars (March 2, 1996). ... Released by Jaguars (June 3, 2002). ... Signed by Tampa Bay Buccaneers (June 8, 2002).
CHAMPIONSHIP GAME EXPERIENCE: Played in AFC championship game (1996 and 1999 seasons). ... Played in NFC championship game (2002 season). ... Member of Super Bowl championship team (2002 season).
HONORS: Played in Pro Bowl (1996 season).
SINGLE GAME HIGHS (regular season): Receptions—16 (October 20, 1996, vs. St. Louis); yards—232 (October 20, 1996, vs. St. Louis); and touchdown receptions—2 (December 8, 2002, vs. Atlanta).
STATISTICAL PLATEAUS: 100-yard receiving games: 1995 (1), 1996 (3), 1997 (4), 1998 (2), 1999 (3), 2000 (5), 2001 (2), 2002 (2). Total: 22.

Year Team	G	GS	RECEIVING				TOTALS			
			No.	Yds.	Avg.	TD	TD	2pt.	Pts.	Fum.
1991—Washington NFL					Did not play.					
1992—Cleveland NFL	2	0	1	8	8.0	0	0	0	0	0
1993—Cleveland NFL	6	3	13	234	18.0	4	4	0	24	0
1994—Cleveland NFL	13	3	10	182	18.2	0	0	0	0	0
1995—Cleveland NFL	16	5	56	709	12.7	4	4	0	24	0
1996—Jacksonville NFL	16	15	85	1129	13.3	3	3	2	22	1
1997—Jacksonville NFL	16	16	85	1164	13.7	5	5	0	30	0
1998—Jacksonville NFL	15	15	64	892	13.9	6	6	1	38	0
1999—Jacksonville NFL	16	15	78	891	11.4	5	5	†1	32	1
2000—Jacksonville NFL	16	16	94	1207	12.8	5	5	0	30	3
2001—Jacksonville NFL	16	16	93	1110	11.9	6	6	0	38	1
2002—Tampa Bay NFL	14	14	61	670	11.0	6	6	0	36	1
Pro totals (11 years)	146	118	640	8196	12.8	44	44	5	274	7

M

McCAREINS, JUSTIN   WR   TITANS

PERSONAL: Born December 11, 1978, in Naperville, Ill. ... 6-2/218.
HIGH SCHOOL: Naperville (Ill.) North.
COLLEGE: Northern Illinois.
TRANSACTIONS/CAREER NOTES: Selected by Tennessee Titans in fourth round (124th pick overall) of 2001 NFL draft. ... Signed by Titans (July 9, 2001).
CHAMPIONSHIP GAME EXPERIENCE: Played in AFC championship game (2002 season).
SINGLE GAME HIGHS (regular season): Receptions—4 (December 1, 2002, vs. New York Giants); yards—70 (October 14, 2001, vs. Tampa Bay); and touchdown receptions—1 (September 29, 2002, vs. Oakland).

			RECEIVING				PUNT RETURNS				KICKOFF RETURNS				TOTALS		
Year Team	G	GS	No.	Yds.	Avg.	TD	No.	Yds.	Avg.	TD	No.	Yds.	Avg.	TD	TD	2pt.	Pts. Fum.
2001—Tennessee NFL	4	1	3	88	29.3	0	2	29	14.5	0	4	70	17.5	0	0	0	0 0
2002—Tennessee NFL	16	1	19	301	15.8	2	6	44	7.3	0	13	300	23.1	0	2	0	12 0
Pro totals (2 years)	20	2	22	389	17.7	2	8	73	9.1	0	17	370	21.8	0	2	0	12 0

McCLAIN, JIMMY   LB   TEXANS

PERSONAL: Born July 23, 1980 ... 6-0/231.
HIGH SCHOOL: Enterprise (Ala.).
COLLEGE: Troy State.
TRANSACTIONS/CAREER NOTES: Signed as non-drafted free agent by Houston Texans (April 25, 2002).

McCLEON, DEXTER   CB   CHIEFS

PERSONAL: Born October 9, 1973, in Meridian, Miss. ... 5-10/195. ... Full name: Dexter Keith McCleon.
HIGH SCHOOL: Meridian (Miss.).
COLLEGE: Clemson (degree in management, 1996).
TRANSACTIONS/CAREER NOTES: Selected by St. Louis Rams in second round (40th pick overall) of 1997 NFL draft. ... Signed by Rams (July 3, 1997). ... Granted free agency (February 11, 2000). ... Re-signed by Rams (June 13, 2000). ... Released by Rams (February 27, 2003). ... Signed by Kansas City Chiefs (March 5, 2003).
CHAMPIONSHIP GAME EXPERIENCE: Played in NFC championship game (1999 and 2001 seasons). ... Member of Super Bowl championship team (1999 season). ... Played in Super Bowl XXXVI (2001 season).
MISCELLANEOUS: Selected by Minnesota Twins organization in 13th round of free-agent baseball draft (June 3, 1993); did not sign.

			TOTALS			INTERCEPTIONS			
Year Team	G	GS	Tk.	Ast.	Sks.	No.	Yds.	Avg.	TD
1997—St. Louis NFL	16	1	13	0	1.0	1	0	0.0	0
1998—St. Louis NFL	15	6	28	1	0.0	2	29	14.5	0
1999—St. Louis NFL	15	15	41	4	1.5	4	17	4.3	0
2000—St. Louis NFL	16	16	49	5	2.0	8	28	3.5	0
2001—St. Louis NFL	16	16	59	6	0.0	4	66	16.5	0
2002—St. Louis NFL	13	4	17	4	0.0	1	0	0.0	0
Pro totals (6 years)	91	58	207	20	4.5	20	140	7.0	0

M

McCLURE, TODD   C   FALCONS

PERSONAL: Born February 16, 1977, in Baton Rouge, La. ... 6-1/286.
HIGH SCHOOL: Central (Baton Rouge, La.).
COLLEGE: Louisiana State.
TRANSACTIONS/CAREER NOTES: Selected by Atlanta Falcons in seventh round (237th pick overall) of 1999 NFL draft. ... Signed by Falcons (June 25, 1999). ... On injured reserve with knee injury (August 30, 1999-entire season). ... Granted free agency (March 1, 2002). ... Re-signed by Falcons (May 28, 2002). ... Granted unconditional free agency (February 28, 2003). ... Re-signed by Falcons (April 16, 2003).
PLAYING EXPERIENCE: Atlanta NFL, 2000-2002. ... Games/Games started: 2000 (9/7), 2001 (15/15), 2002 (16/16). Total:40/38.

McCOLLUM, ANDY   G   RAMS

PERSONAL: Born June 2, 1970, in Akron, Ohio. ... 6-4/300. ... Full name: Andrew Jon McCollum. ... Name pronounced Mc-COL-umn.
HIGH SCHOOL: Revere (Richfield, Ohio).
COLLEGE: Toledo.
TRANSACTIONS/CAREER NOTES: Played with Milwaukee Mustangs of Arena League (1994). ... Signed as non-drafted free agent by Cleveland Browns (June 1994). ... Released by Browns (August 28, 1994). ... Re-signed by Browns to practice squad (August 30, 1994). ... Signed by New Orleans Saints off Browns practice squad (November 15, 1994). ... Inactive for five games (1994). ... Assigned by Saints to Barcelona Dragons in 1995 World League enhancement allocation program (February 20, 1995). ... Granted unconditional free agency (February 12, 1999). ... Signed by St. Louis Rams (April 13, 1999). ... Granted unconditional free agency (February 11, 2000). ... Re-signed by Rams (February 22, 2000). ... Granted unconditional free agency (February 28, 2003). ... Re-signed by Rams (April 4, 2003).
PLAYING EXPERIENCE: Barcelona W.L., 1995; New Orleans NFL, 1995-1998; St. Louis NFL, 1999-2002. ... Games/Games started: W.L. 1995 (games played unavailable), NFL 1995 (11/9), 1996 (16/16), 1997 (16/16), 1998 (16/5), 1999 (16/2), 2000 (16/16), 2001 (16/16), 2002 (16/16). Total NFL: 123/96.
CHAMPIONSHIP GAME EXPERIENCE: Played in NFC championship game (1999 and 2001 seasons). ... Member of Super Bowl championship team (1999 season). ... Played in Super Bowl XXXVI (2001 season).

McCORD, QUENTIN　　　　WR　　　　FALCONS

PERSONAL: Born June 26, 1978, in Troup County, Ga. ... 5-10/188.
HIGH SCHOOL: La Grange (Ga.).
COLLEGE: Kentucky.
TRANSACTIONS/CAREER NOTES: Selected by Atlanta Falcons in seventh round (236th pick overall) of 2001 NFL draft. ... Signed by Falcons (June 20, 2001). ... Released by Falcons (September 1, 2002). ... Re-signed by Falcons to practice squad (September 3, 2002). ... Activated (October 28, 2002).
SINGLE GAME HIGHS (regular season): Receptions—7 (December 22, 2002, vs. Detroit); yards—182 (December 22, 2002, vs. Detroit); and touchdown receptions—1 (December 22, 2002, vs. Detroit).
STATISTICAL PLATEAUS: 100-yard receiving games: 2002 (1).

Year　Team	G	GS	RUSHING Att.	Yds.	Avg.	TD	RECEIVING No.	Yds.	Avg.	TD	TOTALS TD	2pt.	Pts.	Fum.
2001—Atlanta NFL	7	0	2	11	5.5	0	3	53	17.7	0	0	0	0	0
2002—Atlanta NFL	9	0	0	0	0.0	0	11	253	23.0	1	1	0	6	0
Pro totals (2 years)	16	0	2	11	5.5	0	14	306	21.9	1	1	0	6	0

McCOWN, JOSH　　　　QB　　　　CARDINALS

PERSONAL: Born July 4, 1979, in Jacksonville, Texas. ... 6-4/220. ... Full name: Joshua McCown.
HIGH SCHOOL: Jacksonville (Texas).
COLLEGE: Southern Methodist, then Sam Houston State.
TRANSACTIONS/CAREER NOTES: Selected by Arizona Cardinals in third round (81st pick overall) of 2002 NFL draft. ... Signed by Cardinals (July 25, 2002).
SINGLE GAME HIGHS (regular season): Attempts—12 (December 1, 2002, vs. Kansas City); completions—4 (December 1, 2002, vs. Kansas City); yards—45 (December 1, 2002, vs. Kansas City); and touchdown passes—0.

Year　Team	G	GS	PASSING Att.	Cmp.	Pct.	Yds.	TD	Int.	Avg.	Skd.	Rat.	RUSHING Att.	Yds.	Avg.	TD	TOTALS TD	2pt.	Pts.
2002—Arizona NFL	2	0	18	7	38.9	66	0	2	3.67	5	10.2	1	20	20.0	0	0	0	0

McCRARY, FRED　　　　FB　　　　PATRIOTS

PERSONAL: Born September 19, 1972, in Naples, Fla. ... 6-0/245. ... Full name: Freddy Demetrius McCrary.
HIGH SCHOOL: Naples (Fla.).
COLLEGE: Mississippi State.
TRANSACTIONS/CAREER NOTES: Selected by Philadelphia Eagles in sixth round (208th pick overall) of 1995 NFL draft. ... Signed by Eagles (June 27, 1995). ... Released by Eagles (August 25, 1996). ... Signed by New Orleans Saints (March 5, 1997). ... Released by Saints (August 24, 1998). ... Signed by San Diego Chargers (March 26, 1999). ... Granted free agency (February 11, 2000). ... Re-signed by Chargers (May 22, 2000). ... Released by Chargers (February 27, 2003). ... Signed by New England Patriots (March 24, 2003).
SINGLE GAME HIGHS (regular season): Attempts—5 (September 24, 2000, vs. Seattle); yards—13 (November 23, 1997, vs. Atlanta); and rushing touchdowns—1 (September 10, 1995, vs. Arizona).

M

Year　Team	G	GS	RUSHING Att.	Yds.	Avg.	TD	RECEIVING No.	Yds.	Avg.	TD	TOTALS TD	2pt.	Pts.	Fum.
1995—Philadelphia NFL	13	4	3	1	0.3	1	9	60	6.7	0	1	0	6	0
1996—							Did not play.							
1997—New Orleans NFL	7	0	8	15	1.9	0	4	17	4.3	0	0	0	0	0
1998—							Did not play.							
1999—San Diego NFL	16	14	0	0	0.0	0	37	201	5.4	1	1	0	6	0
2000—San Diego NFL	15	12	7	8	1.1	0	18	141	7.8	2	2	0	12	1
2001—San Diego NFL	16	12	2	3	1.5	0	13	71	5.5	0	0	0	0	0
2002—San Diego NFL	16	16	2	1	0.5	0	22	96	4.4	3	3	0	18	1
Pro totals (6 years)	83	58	22	28	1.3	1	103	586	5.7	6	7	0	42	2

McCRARY, MICHAEL　　　　DE　　　　RAVENS

PERSONAL: Born July 7, 1970, in Vienna, Va. ... 6-4/260. ... Full name: Michael Curtis McCrary.
HIGH SCHOOL: George C. Marshall (Falls Church, Va.).
COLLEGE: Wake Forest.
TRANSACTIONS/CAREER NOTES: Selected by Seattle Seahawks in seventh round (170th pick overall) of 1993 NFL draft. ... Signed by Seahawks (July 13, 1993). ... Granted free agency (February 16, 1996). ... Re-signed by Seahawks (June 6, 1996). ... Granted unconditional free agency (February 14, 1997). ... Signed by Baltimore Ravens (April 7, 1997). ... On injured reserve with knee injury (November 28, 2001-remainder of season). ... On physically unable to perform list with knee injury (July 26-August 25, 2002). ... On injured reserve with knee injury (December 3, 2002-remainder of season).
CHAMPIONSHIP GAME EXPERIENCE: Played in AFC championship game (2000 season). ... Member of Super Bowl championship team (2000 season).
HONORS: Named defensive end on The Sporting News NFL All-Pro team (1998). ... Played in Pro Bowl (1998 and 1999 seasons).

Year　Team	G	GS	TOTALS Tk.	Ast.	Sks.	INTERCEPTIONS No.	Yds.	Avg.	TD
1993—Seattle NFL	15	0	7	1	4.0	0	0	0.0	0
1994—Seattle NFL	16	0	9	2	1.5	0	0	0.0	0
1995—Seattle NFL	11	0	7	2	1.0	0	0	0.0	0
1996—Seattle NFL	16	13	57	19▲13.5		0	0	0.0	0
1997—Baltimore NFL	15	15	56	13	9.0	0	0	0.0	0
1998—Baltimore NFL	16	16	66	6	14.5	0	0	0.0	0

Year Team	G	GS	TOTALS Tk.	Ast.	Sks.	INTERCEPTIONS No.	Yds.	Avg.	TD
1999—Baltimore NFL	16	16	43	16	11.5	0	0	0.0	0
2000—Baltimore NFL	16	16	35	9	6.5	0	0	0.0	0
2001—Baltimore NFL	10	10	34	17	7.5	1	1	1.0	0
2002—Baltimore NFL	5	2	3	2	2.0	0	0	0.0	0
Pro totals (10 years)	136	88	317	87	71.0	1	1	1.0	0

McCREE, MARLON S JAGUARS

PERSONAL: Born March 17, 1977, in Orlando, Fla. ... 5-11/198. ... Full name: Marlon Tarron McCree.
HIGH SCHOOL: Atlantic (Daytona, Fla.).
COLLEGE: Kentucky (degree in finance).
TRANSACTIONS/CAREER NOTES: Selected by Jacksonville Jaguars in seventh round (233rd pick overall) of 2001 NFL draft. ... Signed by Jaguars (May 30, 2001).

Year Team	G	GS	TOTALS Tk.	Ast.	Sks.	INTERCEPTIONS No.	Yds.	Avg.	TD
2001—Jacksonville NFL	13	11	33	13	1.0	1	10	10.0	0
2002—Jacksonville NFL	16	16	56	15	1.0	6	129	21.5	0
Pro totals (2 years)	29	27	89	28	2.0	7	139	19.9	0

McCUTCHEON, DAYLON CB BROWNS

PERSONAL: Born December 9, 1976, in Walnut, Calif. ... 5-10/185. ... Son of Lawrence McCutcheon, Director of Scouting, St. Louis Rams, and former running back with four NFL teams (1972-81). ... Name pronounced mc-CUTCH-in.
HIGH SCHOOL: Bishop Amat (La Puente, Calif.).
COLLEGE: Southern California.
TRANSACTIONS/CAREER NOTES: Selected by Cleveland Browns in third round (62nd pick overall) of 1999 NFL draft. ... Signed by Browns (July 22, 1999). ... Granted free agency (March 1, 2002). ... Re-signed by Browns (June 11, 2002).
HONORS: Named cornerback on THE SPORTING NEWS college All-America second team (1998).

Year Team	G	GS	TOTALS Tk.	Ast.	Sks.	INTERCEPTIONS No.	Yds.	Avg.	TD
1999—Cleveland NFL	16	15	74	5	1.0	1	12	12.0	0
2000—Cleveland NFL	15	15	56	3	4.0	1	20	20.0	0
2001—Cleveland NFL	16	15	67	6	2.0	4	62	15.5	1
2002—Cleveland NFL	13	11	40	2	0.0	1	24	24.0	0
Pro totals (4 years)	60	56	237	16	7.0	7	118	16.9	1

McDANIEL, EMMANUEL CB PANTHERS

M

PERSONAL: Born July 27, 1972, in Griffin, Ga. ... 5-9/180.
HIGH SCHOOL: Jonesboro (Ga.).
COLLEGE: East Carolina.
TRANSACTIONS/CAREER NOTES: Selected by Carolina Panthers in fourth round (111th pick overall) of 1996 NFL draft. ... Signed by Panthers (July 20, 1996). ... Released by Panthers (August 26, 1997). ... Signed by Indianapolis Colts (November 27, 1997). ... Released by Colts (August 24, 1998). ... Re-signed by Colts (September 3, 1998). ... Inactive for one game with Colts (1998). ... Released by Colts (September 9, 1998). ... Signed by Miami Dolphins (October 8, 1998). ... Inactive for one game with Dolphins (1998). ... Released by Dolphins (October 14, 1998). ... Re-signed by Dolphins to practice squad (October 15, 1998). ... Activated (January 7, 1999). ... Claimed on waivers by New York Giants (September 1, 1999). ... Released by Giants (September 5, 1999). ... Re-signed by Giants to practice squad (September 6, 1999). ... Activated (November 15, 1999). ... Granted free agency (March 2, 2001). ... Re-signed by Giants (April 19, 2001). ... Granted unconditional free agency (March 1, 2002). ... Signed by Cleveland Browns (June 14, 2002). ... Released by Browns (August 27, 2002). ... Signed by Panthers (August 28, 2002).
CHAMPIONSHIP GAME EXPERIENCE: Member of Panthers for NFC championship game (1996 season); inactive. ... Played in NFC championship game (2000 season). ... Played in Super Bowl XXXV (2000 season).

Year Team	G	GS	TOTALS Tk.	Ast.	Sks.	INTERCEPTIONS No.	Yds.	Avg.	TD
1996—Carolina NFL	2	0	0	1	0.0	0	0	0.0	0
1997—Indianapolis NFL	3	0	0	0	0.0	0	0	0.0	0
1999—New York Giants NFL	7	2	18	1	0.0	0	0	0.0	0
2000—New York Giants NFL	16	3	37	3	1.0	6	30	5.0	0
2001—New York Giants NFL	16	0	10	2	0.0	0	0	0.0	0
2002—Carolina NFL	16	5	23	5	0.0	2	13	6.5	0
Pro totals (6 years)	60	10	88	12	1.0	8	43	5.4	0

McDERMOTT, SEAN C TEXANS

PERSONAL: Born December 5, 1976, in Lufkin, Texas. ... 6-4/250.
HIGH SCHOOL: Fort Worth Arlington Heights (Texas).
COLLEGE: Kansas.
TRANSACTIONS/CAREER NOTES: Signed as non-drafted free agent by Tampa Bay Buccaneers (June 4, 2001). ... Selected by Houston Texans from Buccaneers in NFL expansion draft (February 18, 2002). ... Re-signed by Texans (March 24, 2003).
PLAYING EXPERIENCE: Tampa Bay NFL, 2001; Houston NFL, 2002 ... Games/Games started: 2001 (16/0), 2002 (16/0). Total: 32/0.

McDONNELL, BRADY   TE   BILLS

PERSONAL: Born July 24, 1977, in Rapid City, S.D. ... 6-4/265. ... Full name: Brady Joe McDonnell.
HIGH SCHOOL: Wall (Quinn, S.D.).
COLLEGE: Colorado.
TRANSACTIONS/CAREER NOTES: Signed as non-drafted free agent by New York Giants (April 27, 2001). ... On injured reserve with knee injury (August 14, 2001-entire season). ... Released by Giants (February 21, 2002). ... Signed by Buffalo Bills (April 3, 2002). ... Released by Bills (September 1, 2002). ... Re-signed by Bills to practice squad (September 2, 2002). ... Activated (November 20, 2002).

			RECEIVING		
Year Team	G	GS	No.	Yds.	Avg.	TD
2002—Buffalo NFL	6	0	0	0	0.0	0

McDOUGLE, STOCKAR   OT   LIONS

PERSONAL: Born January 11, 1977, in Deerfield Beach, Fla. ... 6-6/367. ... Brother of Jerome McDougle, defensive end, Philadelphia Eagles.
HIGH SCHOOL: Deerfield Beach (Fla.).
JUNIOR COLLEGE: Navarro College (Texas).
COLLEGE: Oklahoma.
TRANSACTIONS/CAREER NOTES: Selected by Detroit Lions in first round (20th pick overall) of 2000 NFL draft. ... Signed by Lions (July 15, 2000).
PLAYING EXPERIENCE: Detroit NFL, 2000-2002. ... Games/Games started: 2000 (8/8), 2001 (9/3), 2002 (12/11). Total: 29/22.

McFADDEN, MARQUES   OL   COWBOYS

PERSONAL: Born September 12, 1978, in St. Louis. ... 6-4/317. ... Full name: Marques Arthur McFadden.
HIGH SCHOOL: Capital (Boise, Idaho).
COLLEGE: Arizona.
TRANSACTIONS/CAREER NOTES: Signed as non-drafted free agent by Green Bay Packers (April 30, 2001). ... Released by Packers (August 27, 2001). ... Signed by Atlanta Falcons (January 29, 2002). ... Assigned by Falcons to Amsterdam Admirals in 2002 NFL Europe enhancement allocation program (February 12, 2002). ... Released by Falcons (September 1, 2002). ... Re-signed by Falcons to practice squad (September 3, 2002). ... Signed by Dallas Cowboys off Falcons practice squad (September 18, 2002). ... On injured reserve with shoulder injury (October 23, 2002-remainder of season).
PLAYING EXPERIENCE: Dallas NFL, 2002. ... Games/games started: 2002 (4/0).

McFARLAND, ANTHONY   DT   BUCCANEERS

M

PERSONAL: Born December 18, 1977, in Winnsboro, La. ... 6-0/300. ... Full name: Anthony Darelle McFarland.
HIGH SCHOOL: Winnsboro (La.).
COLLEGE: Louisiana State.
TRANSACTIONS/CAREER NOTES: Selected by Tampa Bay Buccaneers in first round (15th pick overall) of 1999 NFL draft. ... Signed by Buccaneers (August 3, 1999). ... On injured reserve with foot injury (December 17, 2002-remainder of season).
CHAMPIONSHIP GAME EXPERIENCE: Played in NFC championship game (1999 season).
HONORS: Named defensive tackle on THE SPORTING NEWS college All-America second team (1998).

			TOTALS		
Year Team	G	GS	Tk.	Ast.	Sks.
1999—Tampa Bay NFL	14	0	9	5	1.0
2000—Tampa Bay NFL	16	16	31	19	6.5
2001—Tampa Bay NFL	14	14	24	17	3.5
2002—Tampa Bay NFL	10	10	12	8	1.5
Pro totals (4 years)	54	40	76	49	12.5

McGARRAHAN, SCOTT   S   DOLPHINS

PERSONAL: Born February 12, 1974, in Arlington, Texas. ... 6-1/200. ... Full name: John Scott McGarrahan. ... Name pronounced ma-GAIR-a-han.
HIGH SCHOOL: Lamar (Arlington, Texas).
COLLEGE: New Mexico.
TRANSACTIONS/CAREER NOTES: Selected by Green Bay Packers in sixth round (156th pick overall) of 1998 NFL draft. ... Signed by Packers (July 17, 1998). ... On injured reserve with hamstring injury (December 29, 1999-remainder of season). ... Granted free agency (March 2, 2001). ... Re-signed by Packers (May 8, 2001). ... Released by Packers (September 1, 2001). ... Signed by Miami Dolphins (September 5, 2001). ... Granted unconditional free agency (March 1, 2002). ... Re-signed by Dolphins (March 21, 2002).

			TOTALS			INTERCEPTIONS			
Year Team	G	GS	Tk.	Ast.	Sks.	No.	Yds.	Avg.	TD
1998—Green Bay NFL	15	0	8	3	0.0	0	0	0.0	0
1999—Green Bay NFL	13	0	2	0	0.0	0	0	0.0	0
2000—Green Bay NFL	16	0	8	1	0.5	0	0	0.0	0
2001—Miami NFL	16	0	0	0	0.0	0	0	0.0	0
2002—Miami NFL	14	0	1	1	1.0	0	0	0.0	0
Pro totals (5 years)	74	0	19	5	1.5	0	0	0.0	0

PERSONAL: Born April 21, 1971, in Terre Haute, Ind. ... 6-4/241.

HIGH SCHOOL: Terre Haute (Ind.) South.

COLLEGE: Michigan (degree in communications).

TRANSACTIONS/CAREER NOTES: Selected by Cincinnati Bengals in second round (37th pick overall) of 1993 NFL draft. ... Signed by Bengals (July 20, 1993). ... Granted free agency (February 16, 1996). ... Re-signed by Bengals for 1996 season. ... On injured reserve with broken ankle (December 14, 2000-remainder of season). ... On injured reserve with ankle injury (December 3, 2001-remainder of season). ... Released by Bengals (April 25, 2002). ... Signed by Dallas Cowboys (April 28, 2002).

SINGLE GAME HIGHS (regular season): Receptions—8 (December 22, 1996, vs. Indianapolis); yards—118 (September 3, 1995, vs. Indianapolis); and touchdown receptions—2 (November 9, 1997, vs. Indianapolis).

STATISTICAL PLATEAUS: 100-yard receiving games: 1993 (1), 1995 (2). Total: 3.

			RECEIVING				TOTALS			
Year Team	G	GS	No.	Yds.	Avg.	TD	TD	2pt.	Pts.	Fum.
1993—Cincinnati NFL	15	15	44	525	11.9	0	0	0	0	1
1994—Cincinnati NFL	16	16	40	492	12.3	1	1	0	6	0
1995—Cincinnati NFL	16	16	55	754	13.7	4	4	0	24	2
1996—Cincinnati NFL	16	16	38	446	11.7	4	4	0	24	0
1997—Cincinnati NFL	16	16	34	414	12.2	6	6	1	38	0
1998—Cincinnati NFL	16	16	22	363	16.5	1	1	0	6	0
1999—Cincinnati NFL	16	16	26	344	13.2	2	2	0	12	0
2000—Cincinnati NFL	14	14	26	309	11.9	1	1	0	6	0
2001—Cincinnati NFL	11	9	14	148	10.6	1	1	0	6	0
2002—Dallas NFL	16	16	23	294	12.8	1	1	0	6	0
Pro totals (10 years)	152	150	322	4089	12.7	21	21	1	128	3

PERSONAL: Born December 11, 1971, in Long Beach, Calif. ... 6-5/270. ... Full name: William Lee McGinest Jr.

HIGH SCHOOL: Polytechnic (Pasadena, Calif.).

COLLEGE: Southern California.

TRANSACTIONS/CAREER NOTES: Selected by New England Patriots in first round (fourth pick overall) of 1994 NFL draft. ... Signed by Patriots (May 17, 1994). ... Granted unconditional free agency (February 13, 1998). ... Re-signed by Patriots (February 12, 1998).

CHAMPIONSHIP GAME EXPERIENCE: Played in AFC championship game (1996 and 2001 seasons). ... Played in Super Bowl XXXI (1996 season). ... Member of Super Bowl championship team (2001 season).

			TOTALS			INTERCEPTIONS			
Year Team	G	GS	Tk.	Ast.	Sks.	No.	Yds.	Avg.	TD
1994—New England NFL	16	7	29	14	4.5	0	0	0.0	0
1995—New England NFL	16	16	70	18	11.0	0	0	0.0	0
1996—New England NFL	16	16	49	18	9.5	1	46	46.0	1
1997—New England NFL	11	11	25	10	2.0	0	0	0.0	0
1998—New England NFL	9	8	21	8	3.5	0	0	0.0	0
1999—New England NFL	16	16	51	25	9.0	0	0	0.0	0
2000—New England NFL	14	14	45	18	6.0	0	0	0.0	0
2001—New England NFL	11	5	25	8	6.0	0	0	0.0	0
2002—New England NFL	16	9	42	21	5.5	1	2	2.0	0
Pro totals (9 years)	125	102	357	140	57.0	2	48	24.0	1

M

PERSONAL: Born September 16, 1969, in Whiteville, N.C. ... 6-4/334.

HIGH SCHOOL: Whiteville (N.C.).

COLLEGE: Clemson.

TRANSACTIONS/CAREER NOTES: Selected after junior season by Los Angeles Raiders in first round (16th pick overall) of 1992 NFL draft. ... Signed by Raiders for 1992 season. ... On injured reserve (January 11, 1994-remainder of 1993 playoffs). ... Raiders franchise moved to Oakland (July 21, 1995). ... Designated by Raiders as franchise player (February 12, 1998). ... Tendered offer sheet by Kansas City Chiefs (April 10, 1998). ... Raiders declined to match offer (April 17, 1998). ... Released by Chiefs (February 28, 2001). ... Signed by Denver Broncos (April 10, 2001). ... Released by Broncos (February 25, 2003).

HONORS: Named defensive tackle on THE SPORTING NEWS NFL All-Pro team (1994). ... Played in Pro Bowl (1994-1997 seasons).

			TOTALS			INTERCEPTIONS			
Year Team	G	GS	Tk.	Ast.	Sks.	No.	Yds.	Avg.	TD
1992—Los Angeles Raiders NFL	10	0	18	0	3.0	0	0	0.0	0
1993—Los Angeles Raiders NFL	16	16	63	15	7.0	1	19	19.0	0
1994—Los Angeles Raiders NFL	16	16	48	14	9.5	0	0	0.0	0
1995—Oakland NFL	16	16	47	8	7.5	0	0	0.0	0
1996—Oakland NFL	16	16	59	4	8.0	0	0	0.0	0
1997—Oakland NFL	16	16	54	10	4.5	0	0	0.0	0
1998—Kansas City NFL	10	9	23	4	1.0	0	0	0.0	0
1999—Kansas City NFL	16	16	30	12	1.5	1	30	30.0	0
2000—Kansas City NFL	15	15	34	6	4.5	0	0	0.0	0
2001—Denver NFL	16	16	34	5	1.0	2	17	8.5	0
2002—Denver NFL	16	15	32	5	2.5	0	0	0.0	0
Pro totals (11 years)	163	151	442	83	50.0	4	66	16.5	0

McGRAW, JON   S   JETS

PERSONAL: Born April 2, 1979, in Manhattan, Kan. ... 6-3/206.
HIGH SCHOOL: Riley County (Manhattan, Kan.).
COLLEGE: Kansas State.
TRANSACTIONS/CAREER NOTES: Selected by New York Jets in second round (57th pick overall) of 2002 NFL draft. ... Signed by Jets (July 26, 2002).

Year Team	G	GS	TOTALS Tk.	Ast.	Sks.	INTERCEPTIONS No.	Yds.	Avg.	TD
2002—New York Jets NFL	15	1	20	8	0.0	1	0	0.0	0

McGREW, REGGIE   DT   JAGUARS

PERSONAL: Born December 16, 1976, in Mayo, Fla. ... 6-1/312. ... Full name: Reginald Gerard McGrew.
HIGH SCHOOL: Lafayette (Mayo, Fla.).
COLLEGE: Florida.
TRANSACTIONS/CAREER NOTES: Selected after junior season by San Francisco 49ers in first round (24th pick overall) of 1999 NFL draft. ... Signed by 49ers (July 26, 1999). ... Inactive for four games (1999). ... On injured reserve with triceps injury (October 4, 1999-remainder of season). ... Released by 49ers (August 31, 2002). ... Signed by Atlanta Falcons (September 17, 2002). ... Released by Falcons (November 25, 2002). ... Signed by Jacksonville Jaguars (January 30, 2003).

Year Team	G	GS	TOTALS Tk.	Ast.	Sks.
1999—San Francisco NFL			Did not play.		
2000—San Francisco NFL	10	0	2	1	0.0
2001—San Francisco NFL	12	0	7	0	1.0
2002—Atlanta NFL	2	0	0	0	0.0
Pro totals (3 years)	24	0	9	1	1.0

McINTOSH, DAMION   OT   CHARGERS

PERSONAL: Born March 25, 1977, in Kingston, Jamaica. ... 6-4/325. ... Full name: Damion Alexis McIntosh.
HIGH SCHOOL: McArthur (Hollywood, Fla.).
COLLEGE: Kansas State.
TRANSACTIONS/CAREER NOTES: Selected by San Diego Chargers in third round (83rd pick overall) of 2000 NFL draft. ... Signed by Chargers (July 20, 2000). ... Granted free agency (February 28, 2003). ... Re-signed by Chargers (April 16, 2003).
PLAYING EXPERIENCE: San Diego NFL, 2000-2002. ... Games/Games started: 2000 (3/0), 2001 (15/14), 2002 (10/10). Total: 28/24.

McKENZIE, KAREEM   OT   JETS

PERSONAL: Born May 24, 1979, in Willingboro, N.J. ... 6-6/327. ... Full name: Kareem Michael McKenzie.
HIGH SCHOOL: Willingboro (N.J.).
COLLEGE: Penn State.
TRANSACTIONS/CAREER NOTES: Selected by New York Jets in third round (79th pick overall) of 2001 NFL draft. ... Signed by Jets (July 25, 2001).
PLAYING EXPERIENCE: New York Jets NFL, 2001-2002. ... Games/Games started: 2001 (8/0), 2002 (16/16). Total: 24/16.

McKENZIE, KEITH   DL   BILLS

PERSONAL: Born October 17, 1973, in Detroit. ... 6-3/273. ... Full name: Keith Derrick McKenzie.
HIGH SCHOOL: Highland Park (Mich.).
COLLEGE: Ball State (degree in history).
TRANSACTIONS/CAREER NOTES: Selected by Green Bay Packers in seventh round (252nd pick overall) of 1996 NFL draft. ... Signed by Packers (July 15, 1996). ... Granted free agency (February 12, 1999). ... Re-signed by Packers (June 1, 1999). ... Granted unconditional free agency (February 11, 2000). ... Signed by Cleveland Browns (February 24, 2000). ... On injured reserve with ankle injury (November 9, 2001-remainder of season). ... Granted unconditional free agency (March 1, 2002). ... Signed by Chicago Bears (May 30, 2002). ... Released by Bears (October 16, 2002). ... Signed by Packers (Novemebr 20, 2002). ... Released by Packers (January 1, 2003). ... Signed by Buffalo Bills (February 25, 2003).
CHAMPIONSHIP GAME EXPERIENCE: Member of Super Bowl championship team (1996 season). ... Played in NFC championship game (1996 and 1997 seasons). ... Played in Super Bowl XXXII (1997 season).

Year Team	G	GS	TOTALS Tk.	Ast.	Sks.	INTERCEPTIONS No.	Yds.	Avg.	TD
1996—Green Bay NFL	10	0	3	3	1.0	0	0	0.0	0
1997—Green Bay NFL	16	0	2	1	1.5	0	0	0.0	0
1998—Green Bay NFL	16	0	19	9	8.0	1	33	33.0	1
1999—Green Bay NFL	16	2	21	11	8.0	0	0	0.0	0
2000—Cleveland NFL	16	16	50	8	8.0	0	0	0.0	0
2001—Cleveland NFL	7	6	12	2	3.0	0	0	0.0	0
2002—Chicago NFL	4	3	4	0	0.0	0	0	0.0	0
—Green Bay NFL	4	0	3	2	0.0	0	0	0.0	0
Pro totals (7 years)	89	27	114	36	29.5	1	33	33.0	1

McKENZIE, MIKE — CB — PACKERS

PERSONAL: Born April 26, 1976, in Miami. ... 6-0/194. ... Full name: Michael Terrance McKenzie.
HIGH SCHOOL: Norland (Miami).
COLLEGE: Memphis.
TRANSACTIONS/CAREER NOTES: Selected after junior season by Green Bay Packers in third round (87th pick overall) of 1999 NFL draft. ... Signed by Packers (July 8, 1999).

Year Team	G	GS	TOTALS			INTERCEPTIONS			
			Tk.	Ast.	Sks.	No.	Yds.	Avg.	TD
1999—Green Bay NFL	16	16	53	12	0.0	6	4	0.7	0
2000—Green Bay NFL	10	8	30	3	0.0	1	26	26.0	0
2001—Green Bay NFL	16	16	54	10	0.0	2	38	19.0	0
2002—Green Bay NFL	13	13	47	19	1.0	2	0	0.0	0
Pro totals (4 years)	55	53	184	44	1.0	11	68	6.2	1

McKIE, JASON — FB — COWBOYS

PERSONAL: Born May 22, 1980, in Gulf Breeze, Fla. ... 5-11/239.
HIGH SCHOOL: Gulf Breeze (Fla.).
COLLEGE: Temple (degree in communications).
TRANSACTIONS/CAREER NOTES: Signed as non-drafted free agent by Philadelphia Eagles (April 23, 2002). ... Released by Eagles (September 1, 2002). ... Re-signed by Eagles to practice squad (September 3, 2002). ... Released by Eagles (September 17, 2002). ... Re-signed by Eagles to practice squad (September 25, 2002). ... Signed by Dallas Cowboys off Eagles practice squad (December 7, 2002).

Year Team	G	GS	RUSHING				TOTALS			
			Att.	Yds.	Avg.	TD	TD	2pt.	Pts.	Fum.
2002—Dallas NFL	1	1	0	0	0.0	0	0	0	0	0

McKINLEY, ALVIN — DT — BROWNS

PERSONAL: Born June 9, 1978, in Kosciusko, Miss. ... 6-3/292. ... Full name: Alvin Jerome McKinley.
HIGH SCHOOL: Weir (Miss.).
JUNIOR COLLEGE: Holmes Junior College (Miss.).
COLLEGE: Mississippi State.
TRANSACTIONS/CAREER NOTES: Selected by Carolina Panthers in fourth round (120th pick overall) of 2000 NFL draft. ... Signed by Panthers (June 21, 2000). ... Claimed on waivers by Cleveland Browns (August 29, 2001). ... Released by Browns (September 1, 2001). ... Re-signed by Browns to practice squad (September 3, 2001). ... Activated (October 9, 2001). ... Granted free agency (February 28, 2003). ... Re-signed by Browns (March 7, 2003).

Year Team	G	GS	TOTALS		
			Tk.	Ast.	Sks.
2000—Carolina NFL	7	0	9	0	0.0
2001—Cleveland NFL	7	0	6	6	0.0
2002—Cleveland NFL	13	0	7	4	0.0
Pro totals (3 years)	27	0	22	10	0.0

McKINLEY, DENNIS — FB — CARDINALS

PERSONAL: Born November 3, 1976, in Kosciusko, Miss. ... 6-2/247. ... Full name: Dennis L. McKinley.
HIGH SCHOOL: Weir (Miss.) Attendance Center.
COLLEGE: Mississippi State (degree in educational psychology).
TRANSACTIONS/CAREER NOTES: Selected by Arizona Cardinals in sixth round (206th pick overall) of 1999 NFL draft. ... Signed by Cardinals (June 14, 1999). ... Granted free agency (March 1, 2002). ... Re-signed by Cardinals (April 12, 2002). ... Granted unconditional free agency (February 28, 2003). ... Re-signed by Cardinals (March 12, 2003).
SINGLE GAME HIGHS (regular season): Attempts—1 (December 30, 2001, vs. Carolina); yards—1 (December 30, 2001, vs. Carolina); and rushing touchdowns—0.

Year Team	G	GS	RUSHING				TOTALS			
			Att.	Yds.	Avg.	TD	TD	2pt.	Pts.	Fum.
1999—Arizona NFL	16	0	0	0	0.0	0	0	0	0	0
2000—Arizona NFL	16	0	0	0	0.0	0	0	0	0	0
2001—Arizona NFL	14	0	1	1	1.0	0	0	0	0	0
2002—Arizona NFL	12	1	0	0	0.0	0	0	0	0	0
Pro totals (4 years)	58	1	1	1	1.0	0	0	0	0	0

McKINNEY, JEREMY — G

PERSONAL: Born January 6, 1976, in Huntington Park, Calif. ... 6-6/301. ... Full name: Jeremy Adam McKinney.
HIGH SCHOOL: Horizon (Brighton, Colo.).
COLLEGE: Iowa.
TRANSACTIONS/CAREER NOTES: Signed as non-drafted free agent by St. Louis Rams (April 20, 1998). ... Released by Rams (August 31, 1998). ... Re-signed by Rams to practice squad (September 1, 1998). ... Activated (December 19, 1998; did not play. ... Released by Rams (September 7, 1998). ... Signed by Detroit Lions to practice squad (October 12, 1999). ... Released by Lions (November 9, 1999). ... Signed by Rams to practice squad (November 24, 1999). ... Signed off Rams practice squad by Cleveland Browns (December 16, 1999). ... On injured reserve with knee injury (August 16, 2000-remainder of season). ... Selected by Houston Texans from Browns in NFL expansion draft (February 18, 2002). ... Released by Texans (September 1, 2002). ... Re-signed by Texans (September 6, 2002). ... Released by Texans (September 10, 2002). ... Signed by Dallas Cowboys (October 18, 2002). ... On non-football illness list with heart condition (November 12, 2002-remainder of season). ... Released by Cowboys (February 20, 2003).
PLAYING EXPERIENCE: Cleveland NFL, 2001; Dallas NFL, 2002. ... Games/Games started: 2001 (15/9), 2002 (3/2). Total: 18/11.

McKINNEY, SETH   C   DOLPHINS

PERSONAL: Born June 12, 1979, in Austin, Texas. ... 6-3/305.
HIGH SCHOOL: Westlake (Austin, Texas).
JUNIOR COLLEGE: Lackawanna Junior College (Pa.).
COLLEGE: Texas A&M.
TRANSACTIONS/CAREER NOTES: Selected by Miami Dolphins in third round (90th pick overall) of 2002 NFL draft. ... Signed by Dolphins (July 28, 2002).
PLAYING EXPERIENCE: Miami NFL, 2002. ... Games/games started: 2002 (16/2).
HONORS: Named center on THE SPORTING NEWS college All-America second team (2001).

McKINNEY, STEVE   C   TEXANS

PERSONAL: Born October 15, 1975, in Galveston, Texas. ... 6-4/295. ... Full name: Stephen Michael McKinney.
HIGH SCHOOL: Clear Lake (Houston).
COLLEGE: Texas A&M.
TRANSACTIONS/CAREER NOTES: Selected by Indianapolis Colts in fourth round (93rd pick overall) of 1998 NFL draft. ... Signed by Colts (July 23, 1998). ... Granted free agency (March 2, 2001). ... Re-signed by Colts (May 9, 2001). ... Granted unconditional free agency (March 1, 2002). ... Signed by Houston Texans (March 6, 2002).
PLAYING EXPERIENCE: Indianapolis NFL, 1998-2001; Houston NFL, 2002. ... Games/Games started: 1998 (16/16), 1999 (15/14), 2000 (16/16), 2001 (14/14), 2002 (16/16). Total: 77/76.

McKINNIE, BRYANT   OT   VIKINGS

PERSONAL: Born September 23, 1979, in Woodbury, N.J. ... 6-8/343. ... Full name: Bryant Douglas McKinnie.
HIGH SCHOOL: Woodbury (N.J.).
JUNIOR COLLEGE: Lackawanna Junior College (Pa.).
COLLEGE: Miami.
TRANSACTIONS/CAREER NOTES: Selected by Minnesota Vikings in first round (seventh pick overall) of 2002 NFL draft. ... Signed by Vikings (November 2, 2002).
PLAYING EXPERIENCE: Minnesota NFL, 2002. ... Games/games started: 2002 (8/7).
HONORS: Named offensive tackle on THE SPORTING NEWS college All-America first team (2001). ... Outland Trophy winner (2001).

McKINNON, RONALD   LB   CARDINALS

PERSONAL: Born September 20, 1973, in Fort Rucker Army Base, Ala. ... 6-0/248.
HIGH SCHOOL: Elba (Ala.).
COLLEGE: North Alabama.
TRANSACTIONS/CAREER NOTES: Signed as non-drafted free agent by Arizona Cardinals (April 23, 1996). ... Granted free agency (February 12, 1999). ... Re-signed by Cardinals (June 14, 1999). ... Granted unconditional free agency (February 11, 2000). ... Re-signed by Cardinals (February 24, 2000).
HONORS: Harlon Hill Trophy winner (1995).

			TOTALS			INTERCEPTIONS			
Year Team	G	GS	Tk.	Ast.	Sks.	No.	Yds.	Avg.	TD
1996—Arizona NFL	16	0	6	1	0.0	0	0	0.0	0
1997—Arizona NFL	16	16	61	36	1.0	3	40	13.3	0
1998—Arizona NFL	13	13	66	29	2.0	5	25	5.0	0
1999—Arizona NFL	16	16	94	47	1.0	1	0	0.0	0
2000—Arizona NFL	16	16	119	38	4.0	0	0	0.0	0
2001—Arizona NFL	16	16	98	49	2.0	1	24	24.0	1
2002—Arizona NFL	16	16	67	41	0.0	0	0	0.0	0
Pro totals (7 years)	109	93	511	241	10.0	10	89	8.9	1

McKNIGHT, JAMES   WR   DOLPHINS

PERSONAL: Born June 17, 1972, in Orlando, Fla. ... 6-1/198.
HIGH SCHOOL: Apopka (Fla.).
COLLEGE: Liberty (Va.).
TRANSACTIONS/CAREER NOTES: Signed as non-drafted free agent by Seattle Seahawks (April 29, 1994). ... Released by Seahawks (August 28, 1994). ... Re-signed by Seahawks to practice squad (August 29, 1994). ... Activated (November 19, 1994). ... Granted unconditional free agency (February 13, 1998). ... Re-signed by Seahawks (February 17, 1998). ... Traded by Seahawks to Dallas Cowboys for third-round pick (WR Darrell Jackson) in 2000 draft (June 24, 1999). ... On injured reserve with knee injury (August 27, 1999-entire season). ... Granted unconditional free agency (March 2, 2001). ... Signed by Miami Dolphins (March 16, 2001).
SINGLE GAME HIGHS (regular season): Receptions—9 (November 18, 2001, vs. New York Jets); yards—164 (November 12, 2000, vs. Cincinnati); and touchdown receptions—1 (December 29, 2002, vs. New England).
STATISTICAL PLATEAUS: 100-yard receiving games: 1997 (1), 1998 (1), 2000 (3), 2002 (1). Total: 6.

			RUSHING				RECEIVING				TOTALS			
Year Team	G	GS	Att.	Yds.	Avg.	TD	No.	Yds.	Avg.	TD	TD	2pt.	Pts.	Fum.
1994—Seattle NFL	2	0	0	0	0.0	0	1	25	25.0	1	1	0	6	0
1995—Seattle NFL	16	0	0	0	0.0	0	6	91	15.2	0	0	0	0	1
1996—Seattle NFL	16	0	0	0	0.0	0	1	73	73.0	0	0	0	0	0
1997—Seattle NFL	12	6	0	0	0.0	0	34	637	*18.7	6	6	0	36	1
1998—Seattle NFL	14	3	0	0	0.0	0	21	346	16.5	2	2	0	12	0
1999—Dallas NFL							Did not play.							
2000—Dallas NFL	16	15	0	0	0.0	0	52	926	17.8	2	2	0	12	1
2001—Miami NFL	16	15	6	39	6.5	0	55	684	12.4	3	3	1	20	3
2002—Miami NFL	15	9	7	58	8.3	0	29	528	18.2	2	2	0	12	2
Pro totals (8 years)	107	48	13	97	7.5	0	199	3310	16.6	16	16	1	98	8

McMAHON, MIKE — QB — LIONS

PERSONAL: Born February 8, 1979, in Wexford, Pa. ... 6-2/208. ... Full name: Michael Edward McMahon.
HIGH SCHOOL: North Allegheny (Pa.).
COLLEGE: Rutgers.
TRANSACTIONS/CAREER NOTES: Selected by Detroit Lions in fifth round (149th pick overall) of 2001 NFL draft. ... Signed by Lions (June 7, 2001).
SINGLE GAME HIGHS (regular season): Attempts—44 (December 29, 2002, vs. Minnesota); completions—19 (December 29, 2002, vs. Minnesota); yards—293 (December 29, 2002, vs. Minnesota); and touchdown passes—3 (December 29, 2002, vs. Minnesota).
MISCELLANEOUS: Regular-season record as starting NFL quarterback: 1-6 (.143).

Year Team	G	GS	Att.	Cmp.	Pct.	Yds.	TD	Int.	Avg.	Skd.	Rat.	Att.	Yds.	Avg.	TD	TD	2pt.	Pts.
						PASSING							**RUSHING**				**TOTALS**	
2001—Detroit NFL	8	3	115	53	46.1	671	3	1	5.83	21	69.9	27	145	5.4	1	1	1	8
2002—Detroit NFL	8	4	147	62	42.2	874	7	9	5.95	12	52.4	14	96	6.9	3	3	0	18
Pro totals (2 years)	16	7	262	115	43.9	1545	10	10	5.90	33	60.1	41	241	5.9	4	4	1	26

McMICHAEL, RANDY — TE — DOLPHINS

PERSONAL: Born June 28, 1979, in Fort Valley, Ga. ... 6-3/247.
HIGH SCHOOL: Peach County (Fort Valley, Ga.).
COLLEGE: Georgia.
TRANSACTIONS/CAREER NOTES: Selected by Miami Dolphins in fourth round (114th pick overall) of 2002 NFL draft. ... Signed by Dolphins (July 25, 2002).
SINGLE GAME HIGHS (regular season): Receptions—5 (October 13, 2002, vs. Denver); yards—79 (September 22, 2002, vs. New York Jets); and touchdown receptions—1 (October 20, 2002, vs. Buffalo).

Year Team	G	GS	No.	Yds.	Avg.	TD
			RECEIVING			
2002—Miami NFL	16	16	39	485	12.4	4

McMILLON, TODD — CB — BEARS

PERSONAL: Born September 26, 1974, in Bellflower, Calif. ... 5-11/188.
HIGH SCHOOL: Cerritus (Bellflower, Calif.).
COLLEGE: Northern Arizona.
TRANSACTIONS/CAREER NOTES: Signed as non-drafted free agent by Chicago Bears (February 16, 2000). ... Released by Bears (August 22, 2000). ... Re-signed by Bears to practice squad (August 29, 2000). ... Activated (November 15, 2000). ... Assigned by Bears to Frankfurt Galaxy in 2001 NFL Europe enhancement allocation program (February 19, 2001). ... Released by Bears (September 3, 2001). ... Re-signed by Bears to practice squad (September 5, 2001). ... Activated (November 13, 2001). ... On injured reserve with thumb injury (November 19, 2002-remainder of season). ... Granted free agency (February 28, 2003). ... Re-signed by Bears (April 22, 2003).

Year Team	G	GS	Tk.	Ast.	Sks.	No.	Yds.	Avg.	TD
			TOTALS			**INTERCEPTIONS**			
2000—Chicago NFL	3	0	3	0	0.0	0	0	0.0	0
2001—Frankfurt NFLE	...	...	...	...	1.0	1	12	12.0	0
—Chicago NFL	8	0	1	0	0.0	0	0	0.0	0
2002—Chicago NFL	10	1	22	2	0.0	0	0	0.0	0
NFL Europe totals (1 year)	...	...	...	...	1.0	1	12	12.0	0
NFL totals (3 years)	21	1	26	2	0.0	0	0	0.0	0
Pro totals (4 years)	...	...	...	...	1.0	1	12	12.0	0

M

McNABB, DONOVAN — QB — EAGLES

PERSONAL: Born November 25, 1976, in Chicago. ... 6-2/226. ... Full name: Donovan Jamal McNabb.
HIGH SCHOOL: Mount Carmel (Ill.).
COLLEGE: Syracuse (degree in speech communications).
TRANSACTIONS/CAREER NOTES: Selected by Philadelphia Eagles in first round (second pick overall) of 1999 NFL draft. ... Signed by Eagles (July 30, 1999).
CHAMPIONSHIP GAME EXPERIENCE: Played in NFC championship game (2001 and 2002 seasons).
HONORS: Played in Pro Bowl (2000-2002 seasons).
SINGLE GAME HIGHS (regular season): Attempts—55 (November 12, 2000, vs. Pittsburgh); completions—32 (September 9, 2001, vs. St. Louis); passing yards—390 (December 10, 2000, vs. Cleveland); and touchdown passes—4 (November 17, 2002, vs. Arizona).
STATISTICAL PLATEAUS: 300-yard passing games: 2000 (2), 2001 (1). Total: 3. ... 100-yard rushing games: 2000 (1), 2002 (2). Total: 3.
MISCELLANEOUS: Regular-season record as starting NFL quarterback: 31-17 (.646). ... Postseason record as starting NFL quarterback: 4-3 (.571).

Year Team	G	GS	Att.	Cmp.	Pct.	Yds.	TD	Int.	Avg.	Skd.	Rat.	Att.	Yds.	Avg.	TD	TD	2pt.	Pts.
						PASSING							**RUSHING**				**TOTALS**	
1999—Philadelphia NFL	12	6	216	106	49.1	948	8	7	4.39	28	60.1	47	313	6.7	0	0	†1	2
2000—Philadelphia NFL	16	16	569	330	58.0	3365	21	13	5.91	45	77.8	86	629	7.3	6	6	0	36
2001—Philadelphia NFL	16	16	493	285	57.8	3233	25	12	6.56	39	84.3	82	482	5.9	2	2	0	12
2002—Philadelphia NFL	10	10	361	211	58.4	2289	17	6	6.34	28	86.0	63	460	7.3	6	6	0	36
Pro totals (4 years)	54	48	1639	932	56.9	9835	71	38	6.00	140	79.3	278	1884	6.8	14	14	1	86

McNAIR, STEVE   QB   TITANS

PERSONAL: Born February 14, 1973, in Mount Olive, Miss. ... 6-2/229. ... Full name: Steve LaTreal McNair. ... Brother of Fred McNair, quarterback with Carolina Cobras of Arena League.
HIGH SCHOOL: Mount Olive (Miss.).
COLLEGE: Alcorn State.
TRANSACTIONS/CAREER NOTES: Selected by Houston Oilers in first round (third pick overall) of 1995 NFL draft. ... Signed by Oilers (July 25, 1995). ... Oilers franchise moved to Tennessee for 1997 season. ... Oilers franchise renamed Tennessee Titans for 1999 season (December 26, 1998).
CHAMPIONSHIP GAME EXPERIENCE: Played in AFC championship game (1999 and 2002 seasons). ... Played in Super Bowl XXXIV (1999 season).
HONORS: Walter Payton Award winner (1994). ... Named to play in Pro Bowl (2000 season); replaced by Elvis Grbac due to injury.
SINGLE GAME HIGHS (regular season): Attempts—49 (December 20, 1998, vs. Green Bay); completions—32 (September 29, 2002, vs. Oakland); yards—398 (September 29, 2002, vs. Oakland); and touchdown passes—5 (December 26, 1999, vs. Jacksonville).
STATISTICAL PLATEAUS: 300-yard passing games: 1996 (1), 1999 (1), 2001 (2), 2002 (2). Total: 6.
MISCELLANEOUS: Regular-season record as starting NFL quarterback: 59-36 (.621). ... Postseason record as starting NFL quarterback: 4-3 (.571).

			PASSING									RUSHING				TOTALS		
Year Team	G	GS	Att.	Cmp.	Pct.	Yds.	TD	Int.	Avg.	Skd.	Rat.	Att.	Yds.	Avg.	TD	TD	2pt.	Pts.
1995—Houston NFL	4	2	80	41	51.3	569	3	1	7.11	6	81.7	11	38	3.5	0	0	0	0
1996—Houston NFL	9	4	143	88	61.5	1197	6	4	8.37	9	90.6	31	169	5.5	2	2	0	12
1997—Tennessee NFL	16	16	415	216	52.0	2665	14	13	6.42	31	70.4	101	674	*6.7	8	8	0	48
1998—Tennessee NFL	16	16	492	289	58.7	3228	15	10	6.56	33	80.1	77	559	7.3	4	4	0	24
1999—Tennessee NFL	11	11	331	187	56.5	2179	12	8	6.58	16	78.6	72	337	4.7	8	8	0	48
2000—Tennessee NFL	16	15	396	248	62.6	2847	15	13	7.19	24	83.2	72	403	5.6	0	0	0	0
2001—Tennessee NFL	15	15	431	264	61.3	3350	21	12	§7.77	37	90.2	75	414	5.5	5	5	0	30
2002—Tennessee NFL	16	16	492	301	61.2	3387	22	15	6.88	21	84.0	82	440	5.4	3	3	1	20
Pro totals (8 years)	103	95	2780	1634	58.8	19422	108	76	6.99	177	81.7	521	3034	5.8	30	30	1	182

McNEIL, RYAN   S   CHARGERS

PERSONAL: Born October 4, 1970, in Fort Pierce, Fla. ... 6-2/210. ... Full name: Ryan Darrell McNeil.
HIGH SCHOOL: Westwood Christian (Miami).
COLLEGE: Miami, Fla. (degree in psychology, 1992).
TRANSACTIONS/CAREER NOTES: Selected by Detroit Lions in second round (33rd pick overall) of 1993 NFL draft. ... Signed by Lions (August 25, 1993). ... Granted unconditional free agency (February 14, 1997). ... Signed by St. Louis Rams (July 7, 1997). ... Designated by Rams as franchise player (February 13, 1998). ... Re-signed by Rams (August 31, 1998). ... Granted unconditional free agency (February 12, 1999). ... Signed by Cleveland Browns (August 1, 1999). ... Granted unconditional free agency (February 11, 2000). ... Signed by Dallas Cowboys (March 2, 2000). ... Released by Cowboys (February 28, 2001). ... Signed by San Diego Chargers (March 6, 2001).
HONORS: Named defensive back on THE SPORTING NEWS college All-America second team (1992). ... Played in Pro Bowl (2001 season).

			TOTALS			INTERCEPTIONS			
Year Team	G	GS	Tk.	Ast.	Sks.	No.	Yds.	Avg.	TD
1993—Detroit NFL	16	2	29	4	0.0	2	19	9.5	0
1994—Detroit NFL	14	13	51	7	0.0	1	14	14.0	0
1995—Detroit NFL	16	16	69	17	0.0	2	26	13.0	0
1996—Detroit NFL	16	16	68	18	0.0	5	14	2.8	0
1997—St. Louis NFL	16	16	62	9	0.0	*9	127	14.1	1
1998—St. Louis NFL	16	12	43	5	0.0	1	37	37.0	1
1999—Cleveland NFL	16	14	64	17	1.0	0	0	0.0	0
2000—Dallas NFL	16	16	68	9	0.0	2	4	2.0	0
2001—San Diego NFL	16	16	64	12	0.0	8	55	6.9	0
2002—San Diego NFL	15	15	72	7	0.0	1	16	16.0	0
Pro totals (10 years)	157	136	590	105	1.0	31	312	10.1	2

McQUARTERS, R.W.   CB   BEARS

PERSONAL: Born December 21, 1976, in Tulsa, Okla. ... 5-10/198. ... Full name: Robert William McQuarters II.
HIGH SCHOOL: Washington (Okla.).
COLLEGE: Oklahoma State.
TRANSACTIONS/CAREER NOTES: Selected after junior season by San Francisco 49ers in first round (28th pick overall) of 1998 NFL draft. ... Signed by 49ers (July 28, 1998). ... On injured reserve with shoulder injury (November 30, 1999-remainder of season). ... Traded by 49ers to Chicago Bears for sixth-round pick (WR Cedrick Wilson) in 2001 draft (June 5, 2000).

			TOTALS			INTERCEPTIONS				PUNT RETURNS				KICKOFF RETURNS				TOTALS			
Year Team	G	GS	Tk.	Ast.	Sks.	No.	Yds.	Avg.	TD	No.	Yds.	Avg.	TD	No.	Yds.	Avg.	TD	TD	2pt.	Pts.	Fum.
1998—San Francisco NFL	16	7	45	4	0.0	0	0	0.0	0	*47	406	8.6	1	17	339	19.9	0	1	0	6	4
1999—San Francisco NFL	11	4	25	3	0.0	1	25	25.0	0	18	90	5.0	0	26	568	21.8	0	0	0	0	1
2000—Chicago NFL	15	2	22	7	1.0	1	61	61.0	1	0	0	0.0	0	0	0	0.0	0	1	0	6	0
2001—Chicago NFL	16	16	65	14	1.0	3	47	15.7	0	12	96	8.0	0	0	0	0.0	0	1	0	6	0
2002—Chicago NFL	9	9	35	8	0.0	1	33	33.0	0	0	0	0.0	0	0	0	0.0	0	0	0	0	0
Pro totals (5 years)	67	38	192	36	2.0	6	166	27.7	1	77	592	7.7	1	43	907	21.1	0	3	0	18	5

MEADOWS, ADAM   OT   COLTS

PERSONAL: Born January 25, 1974, in Powder Springs, Ga. ... 6-5/290. ... Full name: Adam Jonathon Meadows.
HIGH SCHOOL: McEachern (Powder Springs, Ga.).
COLLEGE: Georgia.

TRANSACTIONS/CAREER NOTES: Selected by Indianapolis Colts in second round (48th pick overall) of 1997 NFL draft. ... Signed by Colts (July 8, 1997). ... Granted free agency (February 11, 2000). ... Re-signed by Colts (March 1, 2000).
PLAYING EXPERIENCE: Indianapolis NFL, 1997-2002. ... Games/Games started: 1997 (16/16), 1998 (14/14), 1999 (16/16), 2000 (16/16), 2001 (15/15), 2002 (14/14). Total: 91/91.

MEALEY, RONDELL   RB

PERSONAL: Born February 24, 1977, in New Orleans. ... 6-0/224. ... Full name: Rondell Christopher Mealey.
HIGH SCHOOL: Destrehan (La.).
COLLEGE: Louisiana State (degree in sports administration).
TRANSACTIONS/CAREER NOTES: Selected by Green Bay Packers in seventh round (252nd pick overall) of 2000 NFL draft. ... Signed by Packers (June 29, 2000). ... On injured reserve with knee injury (August 18, 2000-entire season). ... On injured reserve with broken leg (December 12, 2001-remainder of season). ... Released by Packers (September 26, 2002).
SINGLE GAME HIGHS (regular season): Attempts—7 (September 30, 2001, vs. Carolina); yards—30 (September 8, 2002, vs. Atlanta); and rushing touchdowns—1 (September 8, 2002, vs. Atlanta).

			RUSHING				RECEIVING				KICKOFF RETURNS				TOTALS			
Year Team	G	GS	Att.	Yds.	Avg.	TD	No.	Yds.	Avg.	TD	No.	Yds.	Avg.	TD	TD	2pt.	Pts.	Fum.
2000—Green Bay NFL									Did not play.									
2001—Green Bay NFL	11	0	11	37	3.4	0	2	31	15.5	0	4	63	15.8	0	1	0	6	0
2002—Green Bay NFL	3	1	11	36	3.3	1	7	45	6.4	0	0	0	0.0	0	1	0	6	0
Pro totals (2 years)	14	1	22	73	3.3	1	9	76	8.4	0	4	63	15.8	0	2	0	12	0

MEESTER, BRAD   G/OC   JAGUARS

PERSONAL: Born March 23, 1977, in Iowa Falls, Iowa. ... 6-3/295. ... Full name: Brad Ley Meester.
HIGH SCHOOL: Aplington-Parkersburg (Aplington, Iowa).
COLLEGE: Northern Iowa (degree in business management, 1999).
TRANSACTIONS/CAREER NOTES: Selected by Jacksonville Jaguars in second round (60th pick overall) of 2000 NFL draft. ... Signed by Jaguars (May 16, 2000).
PLAYING EXPERIENCE: Jacksonville NFL, 2000-2002. ... Games/Games started: 2000 (16/16), 2001 (16/16), 2002 (16/16). Total:48/48.

MEIER, ROB   DE   JAGUARS

PERSONAL: Born August 29, 1977, in Vancouver, B.C. ... 6-5/293. ... Full name: Robert Jack Daniel Meier.
HIGH SCHOOL: Sentinel (West Vancouver, B.C.).
COLLEGE: Washington State (degree in business).
TRANSACTIONS/CAREER NOTES: Selected by Jacksonville Jaguars in seventh round (241st pick overall) of 2000 NFL draft. ... Signed by Jaguars (May 17, 2000).

			TOTALS		
Year Team	G	GS	Tk.	Ast.	Sks.
2000—Jacksonville NFL	16	0	10	1	0.5
2001—Jacksonville NFL	16	0	12	3	0.0
2002—Jacksonville NFL	16	7	20	3	2.0
Pro totals (3 years)	48	7	42	7	2.5

M

MEIER, SHAD   TE   TITANS

PERSONAL: Born June 7, 1978, in Pittsburgh, Kan. ... 6-4/256.
HIGH SCHOOL: Pittsburgh (Kan.).
COLLEGE: Kansas State.
TRANSACTIONS/CAREER NOTES: Selected by Tennessee Titans in third round (90th pick overall) of 2001 NFL draft. ... Signed by Titans (July 24, 2001).
CHAMPIONSHIP GAME EXPERIENCE: Played in AFC championship game (2002 season).
SINGLE GAME HIGHS (regular season): Receptions—2 (November 4, 2001, vs. Jacksonville); yards—27 (November 4, 2001, vs. Jacksonville); and touchdown receptions—1 (November 10, 2002, vs. Houston).

			RECEIVING		
Year Team	G	GS	No.	Yds.	Avg.	TD
2001—Tennessee NFL	11	1	3	31	10.3	0
2002—Tennessee NFL	12	0	1	17	17.0	1
Pro totals (2 years)	23	1	4	48	12.0	1

MERCER, GIRADIE   DT   JETS

PERSONAL: Born March 19, 1976, in Washington, D.C. ... 6-2/285. ... Full name: Girardie Mercer.
HIGH SCHOOL: Woodson (Washington, D.C.).
COLLEGE: Marshall.
TRANSACTIONS/CAREER NOTES: Signed as non-drafted free agent by Carolina Panthers (April 17, 2000). ... Released by Panthers (June 8, 2000). ... Signed by Philadelphia Eagles (July 18, 2000). ... On injured reserve with arm injury (August 17, 2000-entire season). ... Released by Eagles (July 27, 2001). ... Signed by New England Patriots (July 31, 2001). ... Claimed on waivers by Green Bay Packers (August 21, 2001). ... Released by Packers (August 26, 2001). ... Signed by New York Jets to practice squad (September 3, 2001). ... Activated (November 7, 2001). ... Released by Jets (October 14, 2002). ... Re-signed by Jets to practice squad (October 17, 2002).

			TOTALS		
Year Team	G	GS	Tk.	Ast.	Sks.
2002—New York Jets NFL	2	0	0	0	0.0

MERRITT, AHMAD   WR   BEARS

PERSONAL: Born February 5, 1977, in Chicago. ... 5-10/193.
HIGH SCHOOL: St. Rita (Chicago).
COLLEGE: Wisconsin.
TRANSACTIONS/CAREER NOTES: Signed as non-drafted free agent by Chicago Bears (May 22, 2000). ... Released by Bears (August 22, 2000). ... Re-signed by Bears to practice squad (December 6, 2000). ... Assigned by Bears to Berlin Thunder in 2001 NFL Europe enhancement allocation program (February 19, 2001). ... Released by Bears (September 2, 2001). ... Re-signed by Bears to practice squad (September 3, 2001).
SINGLE GAME HIGHS (regular season): Receptions—4 (December 29, 2002, vs. Tampa Bay); yards—30 (November 3, 2002, vs. Philadelphia); and touchdown receptions—0.

			RUSHING				RECEIVING				PUNT RETURNS				KICKOFF RETURNS				TOTALS		
Year Team	G	GS	Att.	Yds.	Avg.	TD	No.	Yds.	Avg.	TD	No.	Yds.	Avg.	TD	No.	Yds.	Avg.	TD	TD	2pt.	Pts.
2001—Berlin NFLE.........	...	...	4	26	6.5	0	39	582	14.9	6	1	2	2.0	0	6	126	21.0	0	6	0	36
—Chicago NFL.......	2	0	0	0	0.0	0	2	20	10.0	0	0	0	0.0	0	0	0	0.0	0	0	0	0
2002—Chicago NFL.......	12	3	1	5	5.0	0	14	100	7.1	0	10	71	7.1	0	45	1029	22.9	0	0	0	0
NFL Europe totals (1 year)	...	...	4	26	6.5	0	39	582	14.9	6	1	2	2.0	0	6	126	21.0	0	6	0	36
NFL totals (2 years)........	14	3	1	5	5.0	0	16	120	7.5	0	10	71	7.1	0	45	1029	22.9	0	0	0	0
Pro totals (3 years)........			5	31	6.2	0	55	702	12.8	6	11	73	6.6	0	51	1155	22.6	0	6	0	36

METCALF, ERIC   WR

PERSONAL: Born January 23, 1968, in Seattle. ... 5-10/188. ... Full name: Eric Quinn Metcalf. ... Son of Terry Metcalf, running back with St. Louis Cardinals (1973-77), Toronto Argonauts of CFL (1978-80) and Washington Redskins (1981); and cousin of Ray Hall, defensive tackle with Jacksonville Jaguars (1995).
HIGH SCHOOL: Bishop Denis J. O'Connell (Arlington, Va.).
COLLEGE: Texas (degree in liberal arts, 1990).
TRANSACTIONS/CAREER NOTES: Selected by Cleveland Browns in first round (13th pick overall) of 1989 NFL draft. ... Signed by Browns (August 20, 1989). ... Granted free agency (February 1, 1991). ... Re-signed by Browns for 1991 season. ... On injured reserve with shoulder injury (November 2, 1991-remainder of season). ... Granted free agency (February 1, 1992). ... Re-signed by Browns (August 30, 1992). ... Granted roster exemption (August 30-September 5, 1992). ... Traded by Browns with first-round pick (DB Devin Bush) in 1995 draft to Atlanta Falcons for first-round pick (traded to San Francisco) in 1995 draft (March 25, 1995). ... Granted unconditional free agency (February 14, 1997). ... Signed by San Diego Chargers (May 8, 1997). ... Traded by Chargers with first- (DE Andre Wadsworth) and second-round (CB Corey Chavous) picks in 1998 draft, first-round pick (WR David Boston) in 1999 draft and LB Patrick Sapp to Arizona Cardinals for first-round pick (QB Ryan Leaf) in 1998 draft (March 12, 1998). ... Granted unconditional free agency (February 12, 1999). ... Signed by Baltimore Ravens (July 2, 1999). ... Released by Ravens (September 5, 1999). ... Signed by Carolina Panthers (September 7, 1999). ... Granted unconditional free agency (February 11, 2000). ... Signed by Oakland Raiders (February 6, 2001). ... Released by Raiders (September 2, 2001). ... Signed by Washington Redskins (October 24, 2001). ... Granted unconditional free agency (March 1, 2002). ... Signed by Green Bay Packers (December 24, 2002). ... Granted unconditional free agency (February 28, 2003).
CHAMPIONSHIP GAME EXPERIENCE: Played in AFC championship game (1989 season).
HONORS: Named all-purpose player on THE SPORTING NEWS college All-America second team (1987). ... Named punt returner on THE SPORTING NEWS NFL All-Pro team (1993 and 1994). ... Played in Pro Bowl (1993, 1994 and 1997 seasons).
RECORDS: Holds NFL career record for most touchdowns by punt return—10. ... Shares NFL single-game record for most touchdowns by punt return—2 (October 24, 1993, vs. Pittsburgh and November 2, 1997, vs. Cincinnati).
POST SEASON RECORDS: Shares NFL postseason single-game record for most touchdowns by kickoff return—1 (January 6, 1990, vs. Buffalo).
SINGLE GAME HIGHS (regular season): Receptions—11 (September 17, 1995, vs. New Orleans); yards—177 (September 20, 1992, vs. Los Angeles Raiders); and touchdown receptions—3 (September 20, 1992, vs. Los Angeles Raiders).
STATISTICAL PLATEAUS: 100-yard receiving games: 1992 (1), 1993 (1), 1995 (2), 1996 (1), 1997 (1). Total: 6.

			RUSHING				RECEIVING				PUNT RETURNS				KICKOFF RETURNS				TOTALS		
Year Team	G	GS	Att.	Yds.	Avg.	TD	No.	Yds.	Avg.	TD	No.	Yds.	Avg.	TD	No.	Yds.	Avg.	TD	TD	2pt.	Pts.
1989—Cleveland NFL.....	16	11	187	633	3.4	6	54	397	7.4	4	0	0	0.0	0	31	718	23.2	0	10	0	60
1990—Cleveland NFL.....	16	10	80	248	3.1	1	57	452	7.9	1	0	0	0.0	0	*52	*1052	20.2	*2	4	0	24
1991—Cleveland NFL.....	8	3	30	107	3.6	0	29	294	10.1	0	12	100	8.3	0	23	351	15.3	0	0	0	0
1992—Cleveland NFL.....	16	5	73	301	4.1	1	47	614	13.1	5	*44	§429	9.8	1	9	157	17.4	0	7	0	42
1993—Cleveland NFL.....	16	9	129	611	4.7	1	63	539	8.6	2	36	464§12.9		†2	15	318	21.2	0	5	0	30
1994—Cleveland NFL.....	16	8	93	329	3.5	2	47	436	9.3	3	35	348	9.9	†2	9	210	23.3	0	7	0	42
1995—Atlanta NFL	16	15	28	133	4.8	1	104	1189	11.4	8	39	383	9.8	†1	12	278	23.2	0	10	0	60
1996—Atlanta NFL	16	11	3	8	2.7	0	54	599	11.1	6	27	296	11.0	0	49	1034	21.1	0	6	0	36
1997—San Diego NFL.....	16	1	3	-5	-1.7	0	40	576	14.4	2	45	489	10.9	†3	16	355	22.2	0	5	0	30
1998—Arizona NFL	16	3	0	0	0.0	0	31	324	10.5	0	43	295	6.9	0	57	1218	21.4	0	0	0	0
1999—Carolina NFL	16	1	2	20	10.0	0	11	133	12.1	0	34	238	7.0	0	4	56	14.0	0	0	0	0
2000—									Did not play.												
2001—Washington NFL .	10	0	0	0	0.0	0	4	19	4.8	0	33	412	12.5	∞1	1	25	25.0	0	1	0	6
2002—Green Bay NFL.....	1	0	2	7	3.5	0	0	0	0.0	0	3	-1	-0.3	0	2	41	20.5	0	0	0	0
Pro totals (13 years)......	179	77	630	2392	3.8	12	541	5572	10.3	31	351	3453	9.8	10	280	5813	20.8	2	55	0	330

METCALF, TERRENCE   OT/OG   BEARS

PERSONAL: Born January 28, 1978, in Clarksdale, Miss. ... 6-3/320. ... Full name: Terrence Orlando Metcalf.
HIGH SCHOOL: Clarksdale (Miss.).
COLLEGE: Mississippi.
TRANSACTIONS/CAREER NOTES: Selected by Chicago Bears in third round (93rd pick overall) of 2002 NFL draft. ... Signed by Bears (July 12, 2002).
PLAYING EXPERIENCE: Chicago NFL, 2002. ... Games/games started: 2002 (5/0).
HONORS: Named guard ON THE SPORTING NEWS college All-America second team (1999). ... Named offensive tackle on THE SPORTING NEWS college All-America third team (2001).

M

MICKENS, RAY   CB   JETS

PERSONAL: Born January 4, 1973, in Frankfurt, West Germany. ... 5-8/180.
HIGH SCHOOL: Andress (El Paso, Texas).
COLLEGE: Texas A&M.
TRANSACTIONS/CAREER NOTES: Selected by New York Jets in third round (62nd pick overall) of 1996 NFL draft. ... Signed by Jets (July 13, 1996). ... Granted free agency (February 12, 1999). ... Re-signed by Jets (April 9, 1999).
CHAMPIONSHIP GAME EXPERIENCE: Played in AFC championship game (1998 season).
HONORS: Named defensive back on THE SPORTING NEWS college All-America second team (1995).

			TOTALS			INTERCEPTIONS			
Year Team	G	GS	Tk.	Ast.	Sks.	No.	Yds.	Avg.	TD
1996—New York Jets NFL	15	10	37	7	0.0	0	0	0.0	0
1997—New York Jets NFL	16	0	25	1	1.0	4	2	0.5	0
1998—New York Jets NFL	16	4	30	4	0.0	3	10	3.3	0
1999—New York Jets NFL	15	5	34	7	2.0	2	2	1.0	0
2000—New York Jets NFL	16	0	19	3	0.0	0	0	0.0	0
2001—New York Jets NFL	16	4	52	10	1.0	0	0	0.0	0
2002—New York Jets NFL	16	1	29	7	2.0	0	0	0.0	0
Pro totals (7 years)	110	24	226	39	6.0	9	14	1.6	0

MIDDLEBROOKS, WILLIE   CB   BRONCOS

PERSONAL: Born February 12, 1979, in Miami. ... 6-1/200.
HIGH SCHOOL: Homestead (Fla.).
COLLEGE: Minnesota.
TRANSACTIONS/CAREER NOTES: Selected after junior season by Denver Broncos in first round (24th pick overall) of 2001 NFL draft. ... Signed by Broncos (July 27, 2001).

			TOTALS			INTERCEPTIONS			
Year Team	G	GS	Tk.	Ast.	Sks.	No.	Yds.	Avg.	TD
2001—Denver NFL	8	0	1	0	0.0	0	0	0.0	0
2002—Denver NFL	15	0	0	0	0.0	0	0	0.0	0
Pro totals (2 years)	23	0	1	0	0.0	0	0	0.0	0

MIDDLETON, FRANK   G   RAIDERS

PERSONAL: Born October 25, 1974, in Beaumont, Texas. ... 6-4/330. ... Full name: Frank Middleton Jr.
HIGH SCHOOL: West Brook (Beaumont, Texas).
JUNIOR COLLEGE: Fort Scott (Kan.) Community College.
COLLEGE: Arizona.
TRANSACTIONS/CAREER NOTES: Selected by Tampa Bay Buccaneers in third round (63rd pick overall) of 1997 NFL draft. ... Signed by Buccaneers (July 20, 1997). ... Granted free agency (February 11, 2000). ... Re-signed by Buccanners (May 2, 2000). ... Granted unconditional free agency (March 2, 2001). ... Signed by Oakland Raiders (April 26, 2001).
PLAYING EXPERIENCE: Tampa Bay NFL, 1997-2000; Oakland NFL, 2001-2002. ... Games/Games started: 1997 (15/2), 1998 (16/16), 1999 (16/16), 2000 (16/16), 2001 (13/12), 2002 (16/16). Total: 90/78.
CHAMPIONSHIP GAME EXPERIENCE: Played in NFC championship game (1999 season). ... Played in AFC championship game (2002 season). ... Played in Super Bowl XXXVII (2002 season).

MILI, ITULA   TE   SEAHAWKS

PERSONAL: Born April 20, 1973, in Kahuku, Hawaii. ... 6-4/260. ... Name pronounced EE-too-la MEE-lee.
HIGH SCHOOL: Kahuku (Hawaii).
COLLEGE: Brigham Young.
TRANSACTIONS/CAREER NOTES: Selected by Seattle Seahawks in sixth round (174th pick overall) of 1997 NFL draft. ... Signed by Seahawks (June 11, 1997). ... On physically unable to perform list with knee injury (August 18, 1997-entire season). ... On injured reserve with knee injury (December 25, 1998-remainder of season). ... Granted free agency (March 2, 2001). ... Re-signed by Seahawks (April 13, 2001). ... Granted unconditional free agency (March 1, 2002). ... Re-signed by Seahawks (March 14, 2002).
SINGLE GAME HIGHS (regular season): Receptions—7 (December 29, 2002, vs. San Diego); yards—119 (December 29, 2002, vs. San Diego); and touchdown receptions—1 (September 15. 2002, vs. Arizona).
STATISTICAL PLATEAUS: 100-yard receiving games: 2002 (1).

			RECEIVING				TOTALS			
Year Team	G	GS	No.	Yds.	Avg.	TD	TD	2pt.	Pts.	Fum.
1997—Seattle NFL						Did not play.				
1998—Seattle NFL	7	0	1	20	20.0	0	0	0	0	0
1999—Seattle NFL	16	1	5	28	5.6	1	1	0	6	1
2000—Seattle NFL	16	6	28	288	10.3	3	3	0	18	1
2001—Seattle NFL	16	5	8	98	12.3	2	2	0	12	0
2002—Seattle NFL	16	12	43	508	11.8	2	2	0	12	1
Pro totals (5 years)	71	24	85	942	11.1	8	8	0	48	3

MILLER, BILLY   TE   TEXANS

PERSONAL: Born April 24, 1977, in Los Angeles. ... 6-3/230. ... Full name: Billy RoShawn Miller.
HIGH SCHOOL: Westlake (Westlake Village, Calif.).

M

COLLEGE: Southern California.

TRANSACTIONS/CAREER NOTES: Selected by Denver Broncos in seventh round (218th pick overall) of 1999 NFL draft. ... Signed by Broncos (July 20, 1999). ... Released by Broncos (September 5, 1999). ... Re-signed by Broncos to practice squad (September 6, 1999). ... Activated (October 19, 1999). ... Released by Broncos (September 2, 2001). ... Signed by Houston Texans (February 8, 2002). ... Granted free agency (February 28, 2003).

SINGLE GAME HIGHS (regular season): Receptions—8 (December 15, 2002, vs. Baltimore); yards—78 (October 27, 2002, vs. Jacksonville); and touchdown receptions—1 (October 27, 2002, vs. Jacksonville).

MISCELLANEOUS: Holds Houston Texans all-time records for most receptions (51).

			RECEIVING		
Year Team	G	GS	No.	Yds.	Avg.	TD
1999—Denver NFL	10	0	5	59	11.8	0
2000—Denver NFL	12	0	1	7	7.0	0
2002—Houston NFL	16	7	51	613	12.0	3
Pro totals (3 years)	38	7	57	679	11.9	3

MILLER, FRED OT TITANS

PERSONAL: Born February 6, 1973, in Houston. ... 6-7/315. ... Full name: Fred J. Miller Jr.

HIGH SCHOOL: Aldine Eisenhower (Houston).

COLLEGE: Baylor (degree in sociology, 1995).

TRANSACTIONS/CAREER NOTES: Selected by St. Louis Rams in fifth round (141st pick overall) of 1996 NFL draft. ... Signed by Rams (July 15, 1996). ... Granted free agency (February 12, 1999). ... Re-signed by Rams (May 24, 1999). ... Granted unconditional free agency (February 11, 2000). ... Signed by Tennessee Titans (February 16, 2000).

PLAYING EXPERIENCE: St. Louis NFL, 1996-1999; Tennessee NFL, 2000-2002. ... Games/Games started: 1996 (14/0), 1997 (15/7), 1998 (15/15), 1999 (16/16), 2000 (16/16), 2001 (16/16), 2002 (16/16). Total: 108/86.

CHAMPIONSHIP GAME EXPERIENCE: Played in NFC championship game (1999 season). ... Member of Super Bowl championship team (1999 season). ... Played in AFC championship game (2002 season).

MILLER, JAMIR LB

PERSONAL: Born November 19, 1973, in Philadelphia. ... 6-5/266. ... Full name: Jamir Malik Miller. ... Cousin of Mark Gunn, defensive lineman with New York Jets (1991-94 and 1996) and Philadelphia Eagles (1995 and 1996). ... Name pronounced JA-meer.

HIGH SCHOOL: El Cerrito (Calif.).

COLLEGE: UCLA.

TRANSACTIONS/CAREER NOTES: Selected after junior season by Arizona Cardinals in first round (10th pick overall) of 1994 NFL draft. ... Signed by Cardinals (August 12, 1994). ... On suspended list for violating league substance abuse policy (September 4-October 3, 1995). ... Granted unconditional free agency (February 12, 1999). ... Signed by Cleveland Browns (May 13, 1999). ... On injured reserve with Achilles' injury (August 12, 2002-entire season). ... Released by Browns (February 27, 2003). ... Retired (May 15, 2003).

HONORS: Named linebacker on THE SPORTING NEWS college All-America first team (1993). ... Named linebacker on THE SPORTING NEWS NFL All-Pro team (2001). ... Played in Pro Bowl (2001 season).

			TOTALS			INTERCEPTIONS			
Year Team	G	GS	Tk.	Ast.	Sks.	No.	Yds.	Avg.	TD
1994—Arizona NFL	16	0	16	3	3.0	0	0	0.0	0
1995—Arizona NFL	10	9	29	23	1.0	0	0	0.0	0
1996—Arizona NFL	16	16	55	37	1.0	0	0	0.0	0
1997—Arizona NFL	16	16	58	33	5.5	0	0	0.0	0
1998—Arizona NFL	16	16	82	31	3.0	0	0	0.0	0
1999—Cleveland NFL	15	15	93	23	4.5	0	0	0.0	0
2000—Cleveland NFL	16	16	64	21	5.0	1	0	0.0	0
2001—Cleveland NFL	16	16	83	18	13.0	1	0	0.0	0
2002—Cleveland NFL					Did not play.				
Pro totals (8 years)	121	104	480	189	36.0	2	0	0.0	0

MILLER, JIM QB BUCCANEERS

PERSONAL: Born February 9, 1971, in Grosse Pointe, Mich. ... 6-2/225. ... Full name: James Donald Miller.

HIGH SCHOOL: Kettering (Detroit).

COLLEGE: Michigan State (degree in financial administration).

TRANSACTIONS/CAREER NOTES: Selected by Pittsburgh Steelers in sixth round (178th pick overall) of 1994 NFL draft. ... Signed by Steelers (May 12, 1994). ... Inactive for all 16 games (1994). ... Assigned by Steelers to Frankfurt Galaxy in 1995 World League enhancement allocation program (February 20, 1995). ... Released by Steelers (August 23, 1997). ... Signed by Jacksonville Jaguars (September 2, 1997). ... Released by Jaguars (September 23, 1997). ... Signed by Atlanta Falcons (October 27, 1997). ... Granted unconditional free agency (February 13, 1998). ... Signed by Detroit Lions (March 2, 1998). ... Released by Lions (August 24, 1998). ... Signed by Dallas Cowboys (September 8, 1998). ... Released by Cowboys (October 1998). ... Signed by Chicago Bears (December 1, 1998). ... Active for four games (1998); did not play. ... On suspended list for violating league substance abuse policy (December 1, 1999-remainder of season). ... Granted unconditional free agency (February 11, 2000). ... Re-signed by Bears (February 17, 2000). ... On injured reserve with torn Achilles' tendon (November 13, 2000-remainder of season). ... Granted unconditional free agency (March 1, 2002). ... Re-signed by Bears (March 1, 2002). ... On injured reserve with knee injury (December 20, 2002-remainder of season). ... Released by Bears (February 26, 2003). ... Signed by Tampa Bay Buccaneers (March 31, 2003).

CHAMPIONSHIP GAME EXPERIENCE: Member of Steelers for AFC championship game (1994 and 1995 seasons); inactive. ... Member of Steelers for Super Bowl XXX (1995 season); inactive.

SINGLE GAME HIGHS (regular season): Attempts—49 (October 7, 2002, vs. Green Bay); completions—34 (November 14, 1999, vs. Minnesota); yards—422 (November 14, 1999, vs. Minnesota); and touchdown passes—3 (October 7, 2002, vs. Green Bay).

STATISTICAL PLATEAUS: 300-yard passing games: 1999 (2), 2002 (1). Total: 3.

MISCELLANEOUS: Regular-season record as starting NFL quarterback: 15-12 (.556). ... Postseason record as starting NFL quarterback: 0-1.

Year	Team	G	GS	PASSING									RUSHING				TOTALS		
				Att.	Cmp.	Pct.	Yds.	TD	Int.	Avg.	Skd.	Rat.	Att.	Yds.	Avg.	TD	TD	2pt.	Pts.
1994—Pittsburgh NFL............									Did not play.										
1995—Frankfurt W.L..............		...	...	43	23	53.5	236	1	1	5.49	0	67.6	3	-2	-0.7	0	0	0	0
—Pittsburgh NFL		3	0	56	32	57.1	397	2	5	7.09	2	53.9	1	2	2.0	0	0	0	0
1996—Pittsburgh NFL...........		2	1	25	13	52.0	123	0	0	4.92	2	65.9	2	-4	-2.0	0	0	0	0
1997—Atlanta NFL									Did not play.										
—Jacksonville NFL........									Did not play.										
1998—Chicago NFL...............									Did not play.										
1999—Chicago NFL..............		5	3	174	110	63.2	1242	7	6	7.14	7	83.5	3	9	3.0	0	0	0	0
2000—Chicago NFL..............		3	2	82	47	57.3	382	1	1	4.66	2	68.2	7	5	0.7	0	0	0	0
2001—Chicago NFL..............		14	13	395	228	57.7	2299	13	10	5.82	11	74.9	29	-19	-0.7	0	0	0	0
2002—Chicago NFL..............		10	8	314	180	57.3	1944	13	9	6.19	16	77.5	13	11	0.8	0	0	0	0
W.L. totals (1 year)		...	...	43	23	53.5	236	1	1	5.49	0	67.6	3	-2	-0.7	0	0	0	0
NFL totals (5 years)		37	27	1046	610	58.3	6387	36	31	6.11	40	75.2	55	4	0.1	0	0	0	0
Pro totals (6 years)		...	...	1089	633	58.1	6623	37	32	6.08	40	74.9	58	2	0.0	0	0	0	0

MILLER, JOSH — P — STEELERS

PERSONAL: Born July 14, 1970, in Rockway, N.Y. ... 6-4/220.
HIGH SCHOOL: East Brunswick (N.J.).
JUNIOR COLLEGE: Scottsdale (Ariz.) Community College.
COLLEGE: Arizona (degree in communications, 1993).
TRANSACTIONS/CAREER NOTES: Signed as non-drafted free agent by Green Bay Packers (April 1993). ... Released by Packers before 1993 season. ... Signed by Baltimore Stallions of CFL (June 1994). ... Signed by Seattle Seahawks (May 29, 1996). ... Released by Seahawks (August 13, 1996). ... Signed by Pittsburgh Steelers (August 15, 1996). ... On injured reserve with shoulder injury (December 20, 2002-remainder of season).
CHAMPIONSHIP GAME EXPERIENCE: Played in Grey Cup, CFL championship game (1994). ... Played in AFC championship game (1997 and 2001 seasons).
HONORS: Named punter on THE SPORTING NEWS college All-America first team (1992).

Year	Team	G	PUNTING					
			No.	Yds.	Avg.	Net avg.	In. 20	Blk.
1994—Baltimore CFL		18	117	5024	42.9	36.9	0	0
1995—Baltimore CFL		18	118	5629	47.7	42.2	0	0
1996—Pittsburgh NFL		12	55	2256	41.0	33.6	18	0
1997—Pittsburgh NFL		16	64	2729	42.6	35.0	17	0
1998—Pittsburgh NFL		16	81	3530	43.6	36.8	*34	0
1999—Pittsburgh NFL		16	84	3795	45.2	38.1	27	0
2000—Pittsburgh NFL		16	90	3944	43.8	37.5	*34	▲1
2001—Pittsburgh NFL		16	59	2505	42.5	34.9	23	1
2002—Pittsburgh NFL		14	55	2267	41.2	32.5	14	1
CFL totals (2 years)		36	235	10653	45.3	39.6	0	0
NFL totals (7 years)		106	488	21026	43.1	35.8	167	3
Pro totals (9 years)		142	723	31679	43.8	37.1	167	3

M

MILLER, KEITH — LB — SEAHAWKS

PERSONAL: Born July 9, 1976, in San Diego ... 6-1/238.
HIGH SCHOOL: Mt. Carmel (San Diego).
COLLEGE: California.
TRANSACTIONS/CAREER NOTES: Signed as non-drafted free agent by St. Louis Rams (April 18, 2000). ... Assigned by Rams to Scottish Claymores in 2001 NFL Europe enhancement allocation program (February 19, 2001). ... Released by Rams (July 2, 2001). ... Signed by Tennessee Titans (July 18, 2001). ... Released by Titans (August 31, 2001). ... Signed by Seattle Seahawks (January 17, 2002). ... Released by Seahawks (August 26, 2002). ... Re-signed by Seahawks (November 12, 2002).

Year	Team	G	GS	TOTALS			INTERCEPTIONS			
				Tk.	Ast.	Sks.	No.	Yds.	Avg.	TD
2000—St. Louis NFL		16	0	3	1	0.0	0	0	0.0	0
2001—Scottish NFLE		...	...	...	...	2.0	0	0	0.0	0
2002—Seattle NFL...		7	0	1	0	0.0	0	0	0.0	0
NFL Europe totals (1 year)		...	...	...	...	2.0	0	0	0.0	0
NFL totals (2 years)		23	0	4	0	0.0	0	0	0.0	0
Pro totals (3 years)		...	...	...	...	2.0	0	0	0.0	0

MILLOY, LAWYER — S — PATRIOTS

PERSONAL: Born November 14, 1973, in St. Louis. ... 6-0/210.
HIGH SCHOOL: Lincoln (Tacoma, Wash.).
COLLEGE: Washington.
TRANSACTIONS/CAREER NOTES: Selected after junior season by New England Patriots in second round (36th pick overall) of 1996 NFL draft. ... Signed by Patriots (June 5, 1996).
CHAMPIONSHIP GAME EXPERIENCE: Played in AFC championship game (1996 and 2001 seasons). ... Played in Super Bowl XXXI (1996 season). ... Member of Super Bowl championship team (2001 season).
HONORS: Named defensive back on THE SPORTING NEWS college All-America first team (1995). ... Played in Pro Bowl (1998, 1999, 2001 and 2002 seasons). ... Named safety on THE SPORTING NEWS NFL All-Pro team (1999).

Year Team	G	GS	TOTALS Tk.	Ast.	Sks.	INTERCEPTIONS No.	Yds.	Avg.	TD
1996—New England NFL	16	10	54	30	1.0	2	14	7.0	0
1997—New England NFL	16	16	82	30	0.0	3	15	5.0	0
1998—New England NFL	16	16	79	41	1.0	6	54	9.0	1
1999—New England NFL	16	16	91	29	2.0	4	17	4.3	0
2000—New England NFL	16	16	90	31	0.0	2	2	1.0	0
2001—New England NFL	16	16	77	36	3.0	2	21	10.5	0
2002—New England NFL	16	16	61	30	0.0	0	0	0.0	0
Pro totals (7 years)	112	106	534	227	7.0	19	123	6.5	1

MILLS, JAVOR　　　　DE　　　　JAGUARS

PERSONAL: Born May 11, 1979, in Wilmington, Del. ... 6-5/271. ... Full name: Javor Irvin Mills.
HIGH SCHOOL: Concord (Wilmington, Del.).
JUNIOR COLLEGE: Holmes Community College (Miss.).
COLLEGE: Auburn.
TRANSACTIONS/CAREER NOTES: Signed as non-drafted free agent by Jacksonville Jaguars (April 21, 2002). ... Re-signed by Jaguars (March 24, 2003)

Year Team	G	GS	TOTALS Tk.	Ast.	Sks.
2002—Jacksonville NFL	8	0	0	0	0.0

MINNIS, MARVIN　　　　WR　　　　CHIEFS

PERSONAL: Born February 6, 1977, in Miami. ... 6-1/172.
HIGH SCHOOL: Nortwestern (Miami).
COLLEGE: Florida State.
TRANSACTIONS/CAREER NOTES: Selected by Kansas City Chiefs in third round (77th pick overall) of 2001 NFL draft. ... Signed by Chiefs (May 25, 2001). ... On physically unable to perform list with hand injury (September 1-November 6, 2002).
HONORS: Named wide receiver on THE SPORTING NEWS college All-America first team (2000).
SINGLE GAME HIGHS (regular season): Receptions—6 (December 23, 2001, vs. San Diego); yards—89 (December 16, 2001, vs. Denver); and touchdown receptions—1 (September 9, 2001, vs. Oakland).

Year Team	G	GS	RECEIVING No.	Yds.	Avg.	TD
2001—Kansas City NFL	13	11	33	511	15.5	1
2002—Kansas City NFL	2	0	1	4	4.0	0
Pro totals (2 years)	15	11	34	515	15.1	1

MINOR, KORY　　　　LB

M

PERSONAL: Born December 14, 1976, in Inglewood, Calif. ... 6-1/247. ... Full name: Kory DeShaun Minor.
HIGH SCHOOL: Bishop Amat (La Puente, Calif.).
COLLEGE: Notre Dame.
TRANSACTIONS/CAREER NOTES: Selected by San Francisco 49ers in seventh round (234th pick overall) of 1999 NFL draft. ... Signed by 49ers (July 26, 1999). ... Released by 49ers (September 5, 1999). ... Signed by Carolina Panthers to practice squad (September 14, 1999). ... Activated (December 28, 1999); did not play. ... On injured reserve with knee injury (December 19, 2000-remainder of season). ... Released by Panthers (September 1, 2002). ... Re-signed by Panthers (November 26, 2002). ... Granted free agency (February 28, 2003).

Year Team	G	GS	TOTALS Tk.	Ast.	Sks.	INTERCEPTIONS No.	Yds.	Avg.	TD
2000—Carolina NFL	15	0	0	1	0.0	0	0	0.0	0
2001—Carolina NFL	11	2	13	4	0.0	0	0	0.0	0
2002—Carolina NFL	4	0	0	0	0.0	0	0	0.0	0
Pro totals (3 years)	30	2	13	5	0.0	0	0	0.0	0

MINOR, TRAVIS　　　　RB　　　　DOLPHINS

PERSONAL: Born June 30, 1979, in New Orleans. ... 5-10/205. ... Full name: Travis D. Minor.
HIGH SCHOOL: Catholic (Baton, La.).
COLLEGE: Florida State.
TRANSACTIONS/CAREER NOTES: Selected by Miami Dolphins in third round (85th pick overall) of 2001 NFL draft. ... Signed by Dolphins (July 23, 2001).
SINGLE GAME HIGHS (regular season): Attempts—11 (September 8, 2002, vs. Detroit); yards—71 (November 11, 2001, vs. Indianapolis); and rushing touchdowns—1 (December 15, 2002, vs. Oakland).

Year Team	G	GS	RUSHING Att.	Yds.	Avg.	TD	RECEIVING No.	Yds.	Avg.	TD	KICKOFF RETURNS No.	Yds.	Avg.	TD	TOTALS TD	2pt.	Pts.	Fum.
2001—Miami NFL	16	0	59	281	4.8	2	29	263	9.1	1	0	0	0.0	0	4	0	24	0
2002—Miami NFL	16	0	44	180	4.1	2	0	0	0.0	0	46	1071	23.3	0	2	0	12	0
Pro totals (2 years)	32	0	103	461	4.5	4	29	263	9.1	1	46	1071	23.3	0	6	0	36	0

MINTER, MIKE　　　　S　　　　PANTHERS

PERSONAL: Born January 15, 1974, in Cleveland. ... 5-10/188. ... Full name: Michael Christopher Minter.
HIGH SCHOOL: Lawton (Okla.).
COLLEGE: Nebraska (degree in engineering, 1996).
TRANSACTIONS/CAREER NOTES: Selected by Carolina Panthers in second round (56th pick overall) of 1997 NFL draft. ... Signed by Panthers (June 12, 1997). ... Granted unconditional free agency (March 2, 2001). ... Re-signed by Panthers (March 3, 2001).

Year Team	G	GS	TOTALS Tk.	Ast.	Sks.	INTERCEPTIONS No.	Yds.	Avg.	TD
1997—Carolina NFL	16	11	53	16	3.5	0	0	0.0	0
1998—Carolina NFL	6	4	19	7	0.0	1	7	7.0	0
1999—Carolina NFL	16	16	63	20	1.0	3	69	23.0	0
2000—Carolina NFL	16	16	86	30	2.0	2	38	19.0	1
2001—Carolina NFL	14	14	64	14	0.0	2	32	16.0	0
2002—Carolina NFL	16	16	62	20	1.0	4	125	31.3	1
Pro totals (6 years)	84	77	347	107	7.5	12	271	22.6	2

MIRER, RICK — QB — RAIDERS

PERSONAL: Born March 19, 1970, in Elkhart, Ind. ... 6-3/212. ... Full name: Rick F. Mirer.
HIGH SCHOOL: Goshen (Ind.).
COLLEGE: Notre Dame.
TRANSACTIONS/CAREER NOTES: Selected by Seattle Seahawks in first round (second pick overall) of 1993 NFL draft. ... Signed by Seahawks (August 2, 1993). ... On injured reserve with thumb injury (December 20, 1994-remainder of season). ... Traded by Seahawks with fourth-round pick (RB Darnell Autry) in 1997 draft to Chicago Bears for first-round pick (traded to Atlanta) in 1997 draft (February 18, 1997). ... Released by Bears (August 30, 1998). ... Signed by Green Bay Packers (September 2, 1998). ... Active for four games (1998); did not play. ... Traded by Packers to New York Jets for fourth-round pick (traded to San Francisco) in 2000 draft (August 20, 1999). ... Released by Jets (February 2, 2000). ... Signed by San Francisco 49ers (June 13, 2000). ... Granted unconditional free agency (March 2, 2001). ... Re-signed by 49ers (June 5, 2001). ... Released by 49ers (September 4, 2001). ... Re-signed by 49ers (October 31, 2001). ... Granted unconditional free agency (March 1, 2002). ... Signed by Oakland Raiders (March 24, 2002). ... Granted unconditional free agency (February 28, 2003). ... Re-signed by Raiders (March 19, 2003).
CHAMPIONSHIP GAME EXPERIENCE: Member of Raiders for AFC championship game (2002 season); inactive. ... Member of Raiders for Super Bowl XXXVII (2002 season); inactive.
SINGLE GAME HIGHS (regular season): Attempts—43 (October 24, 1993, vs. New England); completions—25 (October 3, 1993, vs. San Diego); yards—287 (December 5, 1993, vs. Kansas City); and touchdown passes—3 (September 11, 1994, vs. Los Angeles Raiders).
MISCELLANEOUS: Regular-season record as starting NFL quarterback: 22-38 (.367).

Year Team	G	GS	PASSING Att.	Cmp.	Pct.	Yds.	TD	Int.	Avg.	Skd.	Rat.	RUSHING Att.	Yds.	Avg.	TD	TOTALS TD	2pt.	Pts.
1993—Seattle NFL	16	16	486	274	56.4	2833	12	17	5.83	*47	67.0	68	343	5.0	3	3	0	18
1994—Seattle NFL	13	13	381	195	51.2	2151	11	7	5.65	27	70.2	34	153	4.5	0	0	0	0
1995—Seattle NFL	15	13	391	209	53.5	2564	13	§20	6.56	42	63.7	43	193	4.5	1	1	0	6
1996—Seattle NFL	11	9	265	136	51.3	1546	5	12	5.83	22	56.6	33	191	5.8	2	2	0	12
1997—Chicago NFL	7	3	103	53	51.5	420	0	6	4.08	16	37.7	20	78	3.9	1	1	1	8
1998—Green Bay NFL									Did not play.									
1999—New York Jets NFL	8	6	176	95	54.0	1062	5	9	6.03	22	60.4	21	89	4.2	1	1	0	6
2000—San Francisco NFL	3	0	20	10	50.0	126	1	0	6.30	1	86.7	3	0	0.0	0	0	0	0
2001—San Francisco NFL									Did not play.									
2002—Oakland NFL									Did not play.									
Pro totals (7 years)	73	60	1822	972	53.3	10702	47	71	5.87	177	63.4	222	1047	4.7	8	8	1	50

MITCHELL, ANTHONY — S — RAVENS

M

PERSONAL: Born December 13, 1974, in Youngstown, Ohio. ... 6-1/211. ... Full name: Anthony Maurice Mitchell.
HIGH SCHOOL: West Lake (Atlanta, Ga.).
COLLEGE: Tuskegee.
TRANSACTIONS/CAREER NOTES: Signed as non-drafted free agent by Jacksonville Jaguars (April 26, 1999). ... Released by Jaguars (September 1, 1999). ... Signed by Baltimore Ravens to practice squad (September 7, 1999). ... Activated (December 7, 1999). ... Granted free agency (February 28, 2003).
CHAMPIONSHIP GAME EXPERIENCE: Member of Super Bowl championship team (2000 season).

Year Team	G	GS	TOTALS Tk.	Ast.	Sks.	INTERCEPTIONS No.	Yds.	Avg.	TD
2000—Baltimore NFL	16	0	0	1	0.0	0	0	0.0	0
2001—Baltimore NFL	16	0	5	2	0.0	0	0	0.0	0
2002—Baltimore NFL	16	6	20	14	0.0	3	62	20.7	0
Pro totals (3 years)	48	6	25	17	0.0	3	62	20.7	0

MITCHELL, BRANDON — DE — SEAHAWKS

PERSONAL: Born June 19, 1975, in Abbeville, La. ... 6-3/290. ... Full name: Brandon Pete Mitchell.
HIGH SCHOOL: Abbeville (La.).
COLLEGE: Texas A&M.
TRANSACTIONS/CAREER NOTES: Selected by New England Patriots in second round (59th pick overall) of 1997 NFL draft. ... Signed by Patriots (June 6, 1997). ... On injured reserve with ankle injury (October 30, 1998-remainder of season). ... Granted free agency (February 11, 2000). ... Re-signed by Patriots (July 16, 2000). ... On injured reserve with leg injury (December 6, 2000-remainder of season). ... Granted unconditional free agency (March 2, 2001). ... Re-signed by Patriots (April 16, 2001). ... Granted unconditional free agency (March 1, 2002). ... Signed by Seattle Seahawks (April 10, 2002). ... On injured reserve with calf injury (October 30, 2002-remainder of season).
CHAMPIONSHIP GAME EXPERIENCE: Played in AFC championship game (2001 season). ... Member of Super Bowl championship team (2001 season).

Year Team	G	GS	TOTALS Tk.	Ast.	Sks.
1997—New England NFL	11	0	6	3	0.0
1998—New England NFL	7	1	14	7	2.0
1999—New England NFL	16	16	23	25	3.0
2000—New England NFL	11	9	13	16	0.0
2001—New England NFL	16	11	26	17	1.0
2002—Seattle NFL	5	2	5	3	1.0
Pro totals (6 years)	66	39	87	71	7.0

MITCHELL, BRIAN — RB/KR — GIANTS

PERSONAL: Born August 18, 1968, in Fort Polk, La. ... 5-10/221. ... Full name: Brian Keith Mitchell.

HIGH SCHOOL: Plaquemine (La.).

COLLEGE: Southwestern Louisiana.

TRANSACTIONS/CAREER NOTES: Selected by Washington Redskins in fifth round (130th pick overall) of 1990 NFL draft. ... Signed by Redskins (July 22, 1990). ... Granted free agency (February 1, 1992). ... Re-signed by Redskins for 1992 season. ... Granted unconditional free agency (February 17, 1994). ... Re-signed by Redskins (May 24, 1994). ... Granted free agency (February 17, 1995). ... Re-signed by Redskins (March 27, 1995). ... Granted unconditional free agency (February 13, 1998). ... Re-signed by Redskins (February 12, 1998). ... Released by Redskins (June 1, 2000). ... Signed by Philadelphia Eagles (June 9, 2000). ... Granted unconditional free agency (March 1, 2002). ... Re-signed by Eagles (March 27, 2002). ... Granted unconditional free agency (February 28, 2003). ... Signed by New York Giants (March 3, 2003).

CHAMPIONSHIP GAME EXPERIENCE: Played in NFC championship game (1991, 2001 and 2002 seasons). ... Member of Super Bowl championship team (1991 season).

HONORS: Named punt returner on THE SPORTING NEWS NFL All-Pro team (1995). ... Played in Pro Bowl (1995 season).

RECORDS: Holds NFL career record for most punt returns—434; most combined kick returns—986; most yards by combined kick returns—17,742; most yards gained by punt return—4,845; most kickoff returns—552; most yards gained by kick return—12,897; and most touchdowns by combined kick returns—13. ... Holds NFL career record for most fair catches—217 (1990-2002). ... Holds NFL single-season record for most fair catches—33 (2000).

SINGLE GAME HIGHS (regular season): Attempts—21 (September 6, 1993, vs. Dallas); yards—116 (September 6, 1993, vs. Dallas); and rushing touchdowns—2 (September 6, 1993, vs. Dallas).

STATISTICAL PLATEAUS: 100-yard rushing games: 1993 (1), 2000 (1). Total: 2.

			RUSHING				RECEIVING				PUNT RETURNS				KICKOFF RETURNS				TOTALS		
Year Team	G	GS	Att.	Yds.	Avg.	TD	No.	Yds.	Avg.	TD	No.	Yds.	Avg.	TD	No.	Yds.	Avg.	TD	TD	2pt.	Pts.
1990—Washington NFL	15	0	15	81	5.4	1	2	5	2.5	0	12	107	8.9	0	18	365	20.3	0	1	0	6
1991—Washington NFL	16	0	3	14	4.7	0	0	0	0.0	0	45	*600	13.3	*2	29	583	20.1	0	2	0	12
1992—Washington NFL	16	0	6	70	11.7	0	3	30	10.0	0	29	271	9.3	1	23	492	21.4	0	1	0	6
1993—Washington NFL	16	4	63	246	3.9	3	20	157	7.9	0	29	193	6.7	0	33	678	20.5	0	3	0	18
1994—Washington NFL	16	7	78	311	4.0	0	26	236	9.1	1	32	‡452	*14.1	†2	58	1478	25.5	0	3	1	20
1995—Washington NFL	16	1	46	301	6.5	1	38	324	8.5	1	25	315	12.6	†1	55	1408	‡25.6	0	3	0	18
1996—Washington NFL	16	2	39	193	4.9	0	32	286	8.9	0	23	258	11.2	0	56	1258	22.5	0	0	0	0
1997—Washington NFL	16	1	23	107	4.7	1	36	438	12.2	1	38	442	11.6	∞1	47	1094	23.3	1	4	0	24
1998—Washington NFL	16	0	39	208	5.3	2	44	306	7.0	0	44	‡506	11.5	0	59	1337	22.7	1	3	0	18
1999—Washington NFL	16	0	40	220	5.5	1	31	305	9.8	0	40	332	8.3	0	43	893	20.8	0	1	0	6
2000—Philadelphia NFL	16	1	25	187	7.5	2	13	89	6.8	1	32	335	10.5	1	47	1124	23.9	1	5	0	30
2001—Philadelphia NFL	16	0	7	9	1.3	0	6	122	20.3	0	39	‡467	12.0	0	41	1025	25.0	1	1	0	6
2002—Philadelphia NFL	16	0	0	0	0.0	0	0	0	0.0	0	46	567	12.3	1	43	1162	27.0	0	1	0	6
Pro totals (13 years)	207	16	384	1947	5.1	11	251	2298	9.2	4	434	4845	11.2	9	552	12897	23.4	4	28	1	170

MITCHELL, DONALD — CB — COWBOYS

PERSONAL: Born December 14, 1976, in Beaumont, Texas. ... 5-10/182. ... Full name: Donald Roosevelt Mitchell.

HIGH SCHOOL: Central (Beaumont, Texas).

COLLEGE: Southern Methodist.

TRANSACTIONS/CAREER NOTES: Selected by Tennessee Titans in fourth round (117th pick overall) of 1999 NFL draft. ... Signed by Titans (July 27, 1999). ... On injured reserve with knee injury (August 22, 2000-entire season). ... Granted unconditional free agency (February 28, 2003). ... Signed by Dallas Cowboys (March 20, 2003).

CHAMPIONSHIP GAME EXPERIENCE: Played in AFC championship game (1999 and 2002 seasons). ... Played in Super Bowl XXXIV (1999 season).

			TOTALS			INTERCEPTIONS			
Year Team	G	GS	Tk.	Ast.	Sks.	No.	Yds.	Avg.	TD
1999—Tennessee NFL	16	0	7	1	0.0	1	42	42.0	1
2001—Tennessee NFL	12	3	22	4	0.0	0	0	0.0	0
2002—Tennessee NFL	16	9	39	10	0.0	1	-2	-2.0	0
Pro totals (3 years)	44	12	68	15	0.0	2	40	20.0	1

MITCHELL, FREDDIE — WR — EAGLES

PERSONAL: Born November 28, 1978, in Lakeland, Fla. ... 5-11/184. ... Full name: Freddie Lee Mitchell II.

HIGH SCHOOL: Kathleen (Lakeland, Fla.).

COLLEGE: UCLA.

TRANSACTIONS/CAREER NOTES: Selected after junior season by Philadelphia Eagles in first round (25th pick overall) of 2001 NFL draft. ... Signed by Eagles (July 26, 2001).

CHAMPIONSHIP GAME EXPERIENCE: Played in NFC championship game (2001 and 2002 seasons).

HONORS: Named wide receiver on THE SPORTING NEWS college All-America first team (2000).

SINGLE GAME HIGHS (regular season): Receptions—4 (December 28, 2002, vs. New York Giants); yards—62 (November 4, 2001, vs. Arizona); and touchdown receptions—1 (December 16, 2001, vs. Washington).

			RECEIVING			
Year Team	G	GS	No.	Yds.	Avg.	TD
2001—Philadelphia NFL	15	1	21	283	13.5	1
2002—Philadelphia NFL	16	1	12	105	8.8	0
Pro totals (2 years)	31	2	33	388	11.8	1

MITCHELL, JEFF   C   PANTHERS

PERSONAL: Born January 29, 1974, in Dallas. ... 6-4/300. ... Full name: Jeffrey Clay Mitchell. ... Brother of Clint Mitchell, defensive end, Denver Broncos.
HIGH SCHOOL: Countryside (Clearwater, Fla.).
COLLEGE: Florida.
TRANSACTIONS/CAREER NOTES: Selected by Baltimore Ravens in fifth round (134th pick overall) of 1997 NFL draft. ... Signed by Ravens (July 10, 1997). ... On injured reserve with knee injury (August 18, 1997-entire season). ... Granted free agency (February 11, 2000). ... Re-signed by Ravens (April 17, 2000) ... Granted unconditional free agency (March 2, 2001). ... Signed by Carolina Panthers (March 12, 2001).
PLAYING EXPERIENCE: Baltimore NFL, 1998-2000; Carolina NFL, 2001-2002. ... Games/Games started: 1998 (11/10), 1999 (16/16), 2000 (14/14), 2001 (15/15), 2002 (16/16). Total: 72/71.
CHAMPIONSHIP GAME EXPERIENCE: Played in AFC championship game (2000 season). ... Member of Super Bowl championship team (2000 season).

MITCHELL, KEITH   LB   JAGUARS

PERSONAL: Born July 24, 1974, in Garland, Texas ... 6-2/245. ... Full name: Clarence Marquis Mitchell.
HIGH SCHOOL: Lakeview (Garland, Texas).
COLLEGE: Texas A&M.
TRANSACTIONS/CAREER NOTES: Signed as non-drafted free agent by New Orleans Saints (April 25, 1997). ... Released by Saints (June 4, 2002). ... Signed by Houston Texans (July 20, 2002). ... Granted unconditional free agency (February 28, 2003). ... Signed by Jacksonville Jaguars (March 14, 2003).
HONORS: Named outside linebacker on THE SPORTING NEWS college All-America second team (1996). ... Played in Pro Bowl (2000 season).

Year Team	G	GS	TOTALS Tk.	Ast.	Sks.	INTERCEPTIONS No.	Yds.	Avg.	TD
1997—New Orleans NFL	16	2	20	4	4.0	0	0	0.0	0
1998—New Orleans NFL	16	15	42	24	2.5	0	0	0.0	0
1999—New Orleans NFL	16	16	76	28	3.5	3	22	7.3	0
2000—New Orleans NFL	16	16	60	25	6.5	1	40	40.0	1
2001—New Orleans NFL	15	14	63	27	2.0	0	0	0.0	0
2002—Houston NFL	11	7	21	7	1.0	0	0	0.0	0
Pro totals (6 years)	90	70	282	115	19.5	4	62	15.5	1

MITCHELL, KEVIN   LB   REDSKINS

PERSONAL: Born January 1, 1971, in Harrisburg, Pa. ... 6-1/257. ... Full name: Kevin Danyelle Mitchell. ... Cousin of Troy Drayton, tight end, Kansas City Chiefs.
HIGH SCHOOL: Harrisburg (Pa.).
COLLEGE: Syracuse (degree in sociology).
TRANSACTIONS/CAREER NOTES: Selected by San Francisco 49ers in second round (53rd pick overall) of 1994 NFL draft. ... Signed by 49ers (July 20, 1994). ... Granted free agency (February 14, 1997). ... Re-signed by 49ers (April 24, 1997). ... Granted free agency (February 13, 1998). ... Signed by New Orleans Saints (February 19, 1998). ... Granted unconditional free agency (February 11, 2000). ... Signed by Washington Redskins (February 29, 2000). ... Granted unconditional free agency (March 2, 2001). ... Re-signed by Redskins (March 29, 2001). ... On injured reserve with ankle injury (December 26, 2001-remainder of season). ... Granted unconditional free agency (February 28, 2003). ... Re-signed by Redskins (April 24, 2003).
CHAMPIONSHIP GAME EXPERIENCE: Played in NFC championship game (1994 and 1997 seasons). ... Member of Super Bowl championship team (1994 season).
HONORS: Named defensive lineman on THE SPORTING NEWS college All-America second team (1992 and 1993).

Year Team	G	GS	TOTALS Tk.	Ast.	Sks.	INTERCEPTIONS No.	Yds.	Avg.	TD
1994—San Francisco NFL	16	0	6	0	0.0	0	0	0.0	0
1995—San Francisco NFL	15	0	4	0	0.0	0	0	0.0	0
1996—San Francisco NFL	12	3	15	1	1.0	0	0	0.0	0
1997—San Francisco NFL	16	0	4	2	0.0	0	0	0.0	0
1998—New Orleans NFL	8	8	31	25	2.5	0	0	0.0	0
1999—New Orleans NFL	16	1	14	1	0.0	0	0	0.0	0
2000—Washington NFL	16	0	4	0	1.0	1	0	0.0	0
2001—Washington NFL	13	13	69	13	2.0	0	0	0.0	0
2002—Washington NFL	16	4	20	4	0.0	1	7	7.0	0
Pro totals (9 years)	128	29	167	46	6.5	2	7	3.5	0

MITCHELL, MEL   CB   SAINTS

PERSONAL: Born February 10, 1979, in Rockledge, Fla. ... 6-1/220. ... Full name: Melvin Mitchell III.
HIGH SCHOOL: Rockledge (Fla.).
COLLEGE: Western Kentucky.
TRANSACTIONS/CAREER NOTES: Selected by New Orleans Saints in fifth round (150th pick overall) of 2002 NFL draft. ... Signed by Saints (July 25, 2002).

Year Team	G	GS	TOTALS Tk.	Ast.	Sks.	INTERCEPTIONS No.	Yds.	Avg.	TD	KICKOFF RETURNS No.	Yds.	Avg.	TD	TOTALS TD	2pt.	Pts.	Fum.
2002—New Orleans NFL	16	0	0	0	0.0	0	0	0.0	0	0	0	0.0	0	0	0	0	0

M

MITCHELL, PETE TE

PERSONAL: Born October 9, 1971, in Royal Oak, Mich. ... 6-2/243. ... Full name: Peter Clark Mitchell.
HIGH SCHOOL: Brother Rice (Bloomfield Hills, Mich.).
COLLEGE: Boston College (degree in communications, 1994).
TRANSACTIONS/CAREER NOTES: Selected by Miami Dolphins in fourth round (122nd pick overall) of 1995 NFL draft. ... Signed by Dolphins (July 14, 1995). ... Traded by Dolphins to Jacksonville Jaguars for WR Mike Williams (August 27, 1995). ... Granted free agency (February 13, 1998). ... Re-signed by Jaguars (April 13, 1998). ... Designated by Jaguars as transition player (February 12, 1999). ... Free agency status changed from transition to unconditional (February 18, 1999). ... Signed by New York Giants (March 23, 1999). ... Granted unconditional free agency (March 2, 2001). ... Signed by Detriot Lions (April 26, 2000). ... Released by Lions (November 14, 2001). ... Signed by Jaguars (March 22, 2002). ... Granted unconditional free agency (February 28, 2003).
CHAMPIONSHIP GAME EXPERIENCE: Played in AFC championship game (1996 season). ... Played in NFC championship game (2000 season). ... Played in Super Bowl XXXV (2000 season).
HONORS: Named tight end on THE SPORTING NEWS college All-America first team (1993 and 1994).
SINGLE GAME HIGHS (regular season): Receptions—10 (November 19, 1995, vs. Tampa Bay); yards—161 (November 19, 1995, vs. Tampa Bay); and touchdown receptions—1 (December 15, 2002, vs. Cincinnati).
STATISTICAL PLATEAUS: 100-yard receiving games: 1995 (1).

| | | | RECEIVING | | | | TOTALS | | | |
Year Team	G	GS	No.	Yds.	Avg.	TD	TD	2pt.	Pts.	Fum.
1995—Jacksonville NFL	16	5	41	527	12.9	2	2	0	12	0
1996—Jacksonville NFL	16	7	52	575	11.1	1	1	0	6	1
1997—Jacksonville NFL	16	12	35	380	10.9	4	4	0	24	0
1998—Jacksonville NFL	16	16	38	363	9.6	2	2	0	12	0
1999—New York Giants NFL	15	6	58	520	9.0	3	3	0	18	1
2000—New York Giants NFL	14	5	25	245	9.8	1	1	0	6	1
2001—Detroit NFL	5	1	5	29	5.8	0	0	0	0	0
2002—Jacksonville NFL	16	11	25	246	9.8	2	2	0	12	0
Pro totals (8 years)	114	63	279	2885	10.3	15	15	0	90	3

MITRIONE, MATT DT GIANTS

PERSONAL: Born July 15, 1978, in Springfield, Ill. ... 6-2/295. ... Full name: Matthew Steven Mitrione.
HIGH SCHOOL: Sacred Heart-Griffin (Springfield, Ill.).
COLLEGE: Purdue.
TRANSACTIONS/CAREER NOTES: Signed as non-drafted free agent by New York Giants (April 26, 2002).

| | | | TOTALS | | |
Year Team	G	GS	Tk.	Ast.	Sks.
2002—New York Giants NFL	9	0	2	2	0.0

MIXON, KENNY DE VIKINGS

M

PERSONAL: Born May 31, 1975, in Sun Valley, Calif. ... 6-4/275. ... Full name: Kenneth Jermaine Mixon.
HIGH SCHOOL: Pineville (La.).
COLLEGE: Louisiana State.
TRANSACTIONS/CAREER NOTES: Selected by Miami Dolphins in second round (49th pick overall) of 1998 NFL draft. ... Signed by Dolphins (July 21, 1998). ... Granted unconditional free agency (March 1, 2002). ... Signed by Minnesota Vikings (March 10, 2002).

| | | | TOTALS | | | INTERCEPTIONS | | | |
Year Team	G	GS	Tk.	Ast.	Sks.	No.	Yds.	Avg.	TD
1998—Miami NFL	16	16	22	13	2.0	0	0	0.0	0
1999—Miami NFL	11	2	4	6	0.0	0	0	0.0	0
2000—Miami NFL	16	16	25	19	2.5	0	0	0.0	0
2001—Miami NFL	16	16	26	18	2.0	1	56	56.0	1
2002—Minnesota NFL	16	16	45	26	4.5	1	6	6.0	0
Pro totals (5 years)	75	66	122	82	11.0	2	62	31.0	1

MOBLEY, JOHN LB BRONCOS

PERSONAL: Born October 10, 1973, in Chester, Pa. ... 6-1/236. ... Full name: John Ulysses Mobley.
HIGH SCHOOL: Chichester (Marcus Hook, Pa.).
COLLEGE: Kutztown (Pa.) University.
TRANSACTIONS/CAREER NOTES: Selected by Denver Broncos in first round (15th pick overall) of 1996 NFL draft. ... Signed by Broncos (July 23, 1996). ... On injured reserve with knee injury (September 22, 1999-remainder of season). ... Granted unconditional free agency (March 2, 2001). ... Re-signed by Broncos (March 2, 2001).
CHAMPIONSHIP GAME EXPERIENCE: Played in AFC championship game (1997 and 1998 seasons). ... Member of Super Bowl championship team (1997 and 1998 seasons).
HONORS: Named outside linebacker on THE SPORTING NEWS NFL All-Pro team (1997).

| | | | TOTALS | | | INTERCEPTIONS | | | |
Year Team	G	GS	Tk.	Ast.	Sks.	No.	Yds.	Avg.	TD
1996—Denver NFL	16	16	49	12	1.5	1	8	8.0	0
1997—Denver NFL	16	16	96	36	4.0	1	13	13.0	1
1998—Denver NFL	16	15	93	19	1.0	1	-2	-2.0	0
1999—Denver NFL	2	2	7	3	0.0	0	0	0.0	0
2000—Denver NFL	15	14	69	16	2.0	1	9	9.0	0
2001—Denver NFL	16	16	76	13	1.0	1	17	17.0	0
2002—Denver NFL	16	16	70	27	1.0	0	0	0.0	0
Pro totals (7 years)	97	95	460	126	10.5	5	45	9.0	1

MOHR, CHRIS   P   FALCONS

PERSONAL: Born May 11, 1966, in Atlanta. ... 6-5/215. ... Full name: Christopher Garrett Mohr.
HIGH SCHOOL: Briarwood Academy (Warrenton, Ga.).
COLLEGE: Alabama (degree in criminal justice).
TRANSACTIONS/CAREER NOTES: Selected by Tampa Bay Buccaneers in sixth round (146th pick overall) of 1989 NFL draft. ... Signed by Buccaneers (July 15, 1989). ... Released by Buccaneers (September 2, 1990). ... Signed by WLAF (January 31, 1991). ... Selected by Montreal Machine in first round (eighth punter) of 1991 WLAF positional draft.·... Signed by Buffalo Bills (June 6, 1991). ... Granted unconditional free agency (February 17, 1994). ... Re-signed by Bills (March 3, 1994). ... Granted unconditional free agency (February 14, 1997). ... Re-signed by Bills (March 4, 1997). ... Released by Bills (February 22, 2001). ... Signed by Atlanta Falcons (March 13, 2001). ... Re-signed by Falcons (March 13, 2003).
CHAMPIONSHIP GAME EXPERIENCE: Played in AFC championship game (1991-1993 seasons). ... Played in Super Bowl XXVI (1991 season), Super Bowl XXVII (1992 season) and Super Bowl XXVIII (1993 season).
HONORS: Named punter on All-World League team (1991).

				PUNTING			
Year Team	G	No.	Yds.	Avg.	Net avg.	In. 20	Blk.
1989—Tampa Bay NFL	16	∞84	3311	39.4	32.1	10	2
1990—			Did not play.				
1991—Montreal W.L.	10	57	2436	*42.7	34.0	13	2
—Buffalo NFL	16	54	2085	38.6	36.1	12	0
1992—Buffalo NFL	15	60	2531	42.2	36.7	12	0
1993—Buffalo NFL	16	74	2991	40.4	36.0	19	0
1994—Buffalo NFL	16	67	2799	41.8	36.0	13	0
1995—Buffalo NFL	16	86	3473	40.4	36.2	23	0
1996—Buffalo NFL	16	§101	§4194	41.5	36.5	§27	0
1997—Buffalo NFL	16	90	3764	41.8	36.0	24	1
1998—Buffalo NFL	16	69	2882	41.8	33.2	18	0
1999—Buffalo NFL	16	73	2840	38.9	33.9	20	0
2000—Buffalo NFL	16	95	3661	38.5	31.4	19	▲1
2001—Atlanta NFL	16	69	2680	38.8	36.1	25	0
2002—Atlanta NFL	16	67	2804	41.9	*38.7	21	0
W.L. totals (1 year)	10	57	2436	42.7	34.0	13	2
NFL totals (13 years)	207	989	40015	40.5	35.2	243	4
Pro totals (14 years)	217	1046	42451	40.6	35.1	256	6

MOLDEN, ALEX   CB   REDSKINS

PERSONAL: Born August 4, 1973, in Detroit. ... 5-10/190. ... Full name: Alex M. Molden.
HIGH SCHOOL: Sierra (Colorado Springs, Colo.).
COLLEGE: Oregon.
TRANSACTIONS/CAREER NOTES: Selected by New Orleans Saints in first round (11th pick overall) of 1996 NFL draft. ... Signed by Saints (July 21, 1996). ... Granted unconditional free agency (March 2, 2001). ... Signed by San Diego Chargers (March 7, 2001). ... On injured reserve with ankle injury (December 14, 2001-remainder of season). ... Released by Chargers (February 27, 2003). ... Signed by Washington Redskins (May 2, 2003),
HONORS: Named defensive back on THE SPORTING NEWS college All-America second team (1995).

			TOTALS			INTERCEPTIONS			
Year Team	G	GS	Tk.	Ast.	Sks.	No.	Yds.	Avg.	TD
1996—New Orleans NFL	14	2	17	4	2.0	2	2	1.0	0
1997—New Orleans NFL	16	15	57	11	4.0	0	0	0.0	0
1998—New Orleans NFL	16	15	54	8	0.0	2	35	17.5	0
1999—New Orleans NFL	13	0	13	2	0.0	1	2	2.0	0
2000—New Orleans NFL	15	6	24	9	0.0	3	24	8.0	0
2001—San Diego NFL	6	3	18	1	0.0	1	0	0.0	0
2002—San Diego NFL	16	16	68	11	2.0	3	9	3.0	0
Pro totals (7 years)	96	57	251	46	8.0	12	72	6.0	0

M

MONK, QUINCY   LB   GIANTS

PERSONAL: Born January 30, 1979, in Jacksonville, N.C. ... 6-3/250. ... Full name: Quincy Omar Monk.
HIGH SCHOOL: White Oak (Jacksonville, N.C.).
COLLEGE: North Carolina.
TRANSACTIONS/CAREER NOTES: Selected by New York Giants in seventh round (245th pick overall) of 2002 NFL draft.

			TOTALS			INTERCEPTIONS			
Year Team	G	GS	Tk.	Ast.	Sks.	No.	Yds.	Avg.	TD
2002—New York Giants NFL	9	0	1	0	0.0	0	0	0.0	0

MONTGOMERY, JOE   RB

PERSONAL: Born June 8, 1976, in Robbins, Ill. ... 5-10/230.
HIGH SCHOOL: Richards (Oak Lawn, Ill.).
COLLEGE: Ohio State.
TRANSACTIONS/CAREER NOTES: Selected by New York Giants in second round (49th pick overall) of 1999 NFL draft. ... Signed by Giants (July 29, 1999). ... On injured reserve with Achilles' injury (August 27, 2001-entire season). ... Claimed on waivers by Carolina Panthers (March 1, 2002). ... Released by Panthers (September 1, 2002). ... Re-signed by Panthers to practice squad (September 3, 2002). ... Released by Panthers (September 19, 2002). ... Re-signed by Panthers to practice squad (September 25, 2002). ... Activated (December 4, 2002). ... Granted free agency (February 28, 2003).

CHAMPIONSHIP GAME EXPERIENCE: Played in NFC championship game (2000 season). ... Played in Super Bowl XXXV (2000 season).
SINGLE GAME HIGHS (regular season): Attempts—38 (December 5, 1999, vs. New York Jets); yards—111 (December 5, 1999, vs. New York Jets); and rushing touchdowns—1 (October 29, 2000, vs. Philadelphia).
STATISTICAL PLATEAUS: 100-yard rushing games: 1999 (1).

| Year   Team | G | GS | RUSHING | | | | TOTALS | | | |
			Att.	Yds.	Avg.	TD	TD	2pt.	Pts.	Fum.
1999—New York Giants NFL	7	5	115	348	3.0	3	3	†1	20	2
2000—New York Giants NFL	2	0	1	4	4.0	1	1	0	6	0
2002—Carolina NFL	3	0	7	20	2.9	0	0	0	0	0
Pro totals (3 years)	12	5	123	372	3.0	4	4	1	26	2

MONTGOMERY, SCOTTIE WR RAIDERS

PERSONAL: Born May 26, 1978, in Shelby, N.C. ... 6-1/195. ... Full name: Scottie Austin Montgomery.
HIGH SCHOOL: Burns (Cherryville, N.C.).
COLLEGE: Duke.
TRANSACTIONS/CAREER NOTES: Signed as non-drafted free agent by Carolina Panthers (April 27, 2000). ... Released by Panthers (August 27, 2000). ... Signed by Denver Broncos to practice squad (September 13, 2000). ... Activated (October 21, 2000). ... Released by Broncos (September 2, 2001). ... Re-signed by Broncos to practice squad (September 4, 2001). ... Activated (October 23, 2001). ... Granted free agency (February 28, 2003). ... Signed by Oakland Raiders (March 25, 2003).
SINGLE GAME HIGHS (regular season): Receptions—4 (December 30, 2001, vs. Oakland); yards—34 (December 30, 2001, vs. Oakland); and touchdown receptions—1 (September 15, 2002, vs. San Francisco).

| Year   Team | G | GS | RUSHING | | | | RECEIVING | | | | KICKOFF RETURNS | | | | TOTALS | | | |
			Att.	Yds.	Avg.	TD	No.	Yds.	Avg.	TD	No.	Yds.	Avg.	TD	TD	2pt.	Pts.	Fum.
2000—Denver NFL	4	0	0	0	0.0	0	1	10	10.0	0	0	0	0.0	0	0	0	0	0
2001—Denver NFL	8	0	1	5	5.0	0	11	99	9.0	0	0	0	0.0	0	0	0	0	0
2002—Denver NFL	15	0	4	27	6.8	0	4	51	12.8	1	15	370	24.7	0	1	0	6	0
Pro totals (3 years)	27	0	5	32	6.4	0	16	160	10.0	1	15	370	24.7	0	1	0	6	0

MOORE, BRANDON LB 49ERS

PERSONAL: Born January 16, 1979, in East Meadow, N.Y. ... 6-1/242. ... Full name: Brandon T. Moore. ... Brother of Rob Moore, wide receiver with New York Jets (1990-95) and Arizona Cardinals (1996-2001).
HIGH SCHOOL: Baldwin (N.Y.).
COLLEGE: Oklahoma.
TRANSACTIONS/CAREER NOTES: Signed as non-drafted free agent by San Francisco 49ers (April 26, 2002). ... Released by 49ers (September 2, 2002). ... Signed by New England Patriots to practice squad (September 3, 2002). ... Signed by 49ers off Patriots practice squad (September 24, 2002).

| Year   Team | G | GS | TOTALS | | | INTERCEPTIONS | | | |
			Tk.	Ast.	Sks.	No.	Yds.	Avg.	TD
2002—San Francisco NFL	13	2	7	1	0.0	0	0	0.0	0

MOORE, DAMON S

PERSONAL: Born September 15, 1976, in Fostoria, Ohio. ... 5-11/215.
HIGH SCHOOL: Fostoria (Ohio).
COLLEGE: Ohio State.
TRANSACTIONS/CAREER NOTES: Selected by Philadelphia Eagles in fourth round (128th pick overall) of 1999 NFL draft. ... Signed by Eagles (July 28, 1999). ... Granted free agency (March 1, 2002). ... Signed by Chicago Bears (June 4, 2002). ... On physically unable to perform list with knee injury (August 30-November 1, 2002). ... On suspended list for violating league substance abuse policy (September 12-30, 2002). ... Released by Bears (April 29, 2003).
CHAMPIONSHIP GAME EXPERIENCE: Played in NFC championship game (2001 season).
HONORS: Named strong safety on THE SPORTING NEWS college All-America first team (1998).

| Year   Team | G | GS | TOTALS | | | INTERCEPTIONS | | | |
			Tk.	Ast.	Sks.	No.	Yds.	Avg.	TD
1999—Philadelphia NFL	16	1	19	4	0.0	1	28	28.0	0
2000—Philadelphia NFL	16	16	56	10	0.0	2	24	12.0	0
2001—Philadelphia NFL	16	16	58	20	1.0	2	2	1.0	0
2002—Chicago NFL	6	1	5	3	0.0	1	35	35.0	0
Pro totals (4 years)	54	34	138	37	1.0	6	89	14.8	0

MOORE, DAVE TE BILLS

PERSONAL: Born November 11, 1969, in Morristown, N.J. ... 6-2/250. ... Full name: David Edward Moore.
HIGH SCHOOL: Roxbury (Succasunna, N.J.).
COLLEGE: Pittsburgh (degree in justice administration, 1991).
TRANSACTIONS/CAREER NOTES: Selected by Miami Dolphins in seventh round (191st pick overall) of 1992 NFL draft. ... Signed by Dolphins (July 15, 1992). ... Released by Dolphins (August 31, 1992). ... Re-signed by Dolphins to practice squad (September 1, 1992). ... Released by Dolphins (September 16, 1992). ... Re-signed by Dolphins to practice squad (October 21, 1992). ... Activated (October 24, 1992). ... Released by Dolphins (October 28, 1992). ... Re-signed by Dolphins to practice squad (October 28, 1992). ... Released by Dolphins (November 18, 1992). ... Signed by Tampa Bay Buccaneers to practice squad (November 24, 1992). ... Activated (December 4, 1992). ... Granted free agency (February 16, 1996). ... Re-signed by Buccaneers (May 31, 1996). ... Granted unconditional free agency (February 14, 1997). ... Re-signed by Buccaneers (February 18, 1997). ... Granted unconditional free agency (February 11, 2000). ... Re-signed by Buccaneers (March 20, 2000). ... Released by Buccaneers (February 27, 2002). ... Signed by Buffalo Bills (March 11, 2002).

CHAMPIONSHIP GAME EXPERIENCE: Played in NFC championship game (1999 season).
SINGLE GAME HIGHS (regular season): Receptions—6 (November 2, 1997, vs. Indianapolis); yards—62 (November 3, 1996, vs. Chicago); and touchdown receptions—1 (October 6, 2002, vs. Oakland).

Year Team	G	GS	No.	Yds.	Avg.	TD	TD	2pt.	Pts.	Fum.
				RECEIVING				**TOTALS**		
1992—Miami NFL	1	0	0	0	0.0	0	0	0	0	0
—Tampa Bay NFL	4	2	1	10	10.0	0	0	0	0	0
1993—Tampa Bay NFL	15	1	4	47	11.8	1	1	0	6	0
1994—Tampa Bay NFL	15	5	4	57	14.3	0	0	0	0	0
1995—Tampa Bay NFL	16	8	13	102	7.8	0	0	0	0	0
1996—Tampa Bay NFL	16	8	27	237	8.8	3	3	0	18	0
1997—Tampa Bay NFL	16	7	19	217	11.4	4	4	0	24	0
1998—Tampa Bay NFL	16	16	24	255	10.6	4	4	0	24	1
1999—Tampa Bay NFL	16	16	23	276	12.0	5	5	0	30	0
2000—Tampa Bay NFL	16	16	29	288	9.9	3	3	0	18	0
2001—Tampa Bay NFL	16	16	35	285	8.1	4	4	0	24	0
2002—Buffalo NFL	14	5	16	141	8.8	2	2	0	12	0
Pro totals (11 years)	161	100	195	1915	9.8	26	26	0	156	1

MOORE, HERMAN — WR

PERSONAL: Born October 20, 1969, in Danville, Va. ... 6-4/218. ... Full name: Herman Joseph Moore.
HIGH SCHOOL: George Washington (Danville, Va.).
COLLEGE: Virginia (degree in rhetoric and communication studies, 1991).
TRANSACTIONS/CAREER NOTES: Selected after junior season by Detroit Lions in first round (10th pick overall) of 1991 NFL draft. ... Signed by Lions (July 19, 1991). ... On injured reserve with quadricep injury (September 11-October 9, 1992). ... On practice squad (October 9-14, 1992). ... Designated by Lions as transition player (February 25, 1993). ... On injured reserve with hip injury (October 17, 2001-remainder of season). ... Released by Lions (June 3, 2002). ... Signed by New York Giants (November 13, 2002). ... Announced retirement (December 4, 2002).
CHAMPIONSHIP GAME EXPERIENCE: Played in NFC championship game (1991 season).
HONORS: Named wide receiver on THE SPORTING NEWS college All-America first team (1990). ... Played in Pro Bowl (1994-1997 seasons). ... Named wide receiver on THE SPORTING NEWS NFL All-Pro team (1995-1997).
SINGLE GAME HIGHS (regular season): Receptions—14 (December 4, 1995, vs. Chicago); yards—183 (December 4, 1995, vs. Chicago); and touchdown receptions—3 (October 29, 1995, vs. Green Bay).
STATISTICAL PLATEAUS: 100-yard receiving games: 1992 (3), 1993 (3), 1994 (3), 1995 (10), 1996 (5), 1997 (6), 1998 (4). Total: 34.
MISCELLANEOUS: Holds Detroit Lions all-time records for most yards receiving (9,174), most receptions (670), and most touchdown receptions (62).

Year Team	G	GS	No.	Yds.	Avg.	TD	TD	2pt.	Pts.	Fum.
				RECEIVING				**TOTALS**		
1991—Detroit NFL	13	1	11	135	12.3	0	0	0	0	0
1992—Detroit NFL	12	11	51	966	‡18.9	4	4	0	24	0
1993—Detroit NFL	15	15	61	935	15.3	6	6	0	36	2
1994—Detroit NFL	16	16	72	1173	16.3	11	11	0	66	1
1995—Detroit NFL	16	16	*123	1686	13.7	14	14	0	84	2
1996—Detroit NFL	16	16	106	1296	12.2	9	9	1	56	0
1997—Detroit NFL	16	16	†104	1293	12.4	8	8	1	50	0
1998—Detroit NFL	15	15	82	983	12.0	5	5	0	30	0
1999—Detroit NFL	8	4	16	197	12.3	2	2	0	12	0
2000—Detroit NFL	15	11	40	434	10.9	3	3	0	18	0
2001—Detroit NFL	3	1	4	76	19.0	0	0	0	0	0
2002—New York Giants NFL	1	0	0	0	0.0	0	0	0	0	0
Pro totals (12 years)	146	122	670	9174	13.7	62	62	2	376	5

MOORE, JASON — S — BROWNS

PERSONAL: Born January 15, 1976, in San Bernardino, Calif. ... 5-10/195. ... Full name: Jason Dwayne Moore.
HIGH SCHOOL: Pacific (San Bernardino, Calif.).
COLLEGE: San Diego State.
TRANSACTIONS/CAREER NOTES: Signed as non-drafted free agent by Cincinnati Bengals (April 19, 1998). ... Released by Bengals (August 24, 1998). ... Signed by Denver Broncos (March 12, 1999). ... Released by Broncos (August 31, 1999). ... Re-signed by Broncos to practice squad (September 14, 1999). ... Activated (November 18, 1999). ... Released by Broncos (August 27, 2000). ... Signed by Green Bay Packers to practice squad (September 6, 2000). ... Activated (September 16, 2000). ... Released by Packers (September 30, 2000). ... Re-signed by Packers to practice squad (October 3, 2000). ... Activated (October 5, 2000). ... Released by Packers (October 9, 2000). ... Signed by 49ers (October 10, 2000). ... Released by 49ers (November 14, 2000). ... Re-signed by 49ers to practice squad (November 15, 2000). ... Activated (December 21, 2000). ... Released by 49ers (March 21, 2001). ... Signed by Miami Dolphins (July 29, 2002). ... Released by Dolphins (September 1, 2002). ... Signed by 49ers (September 17, 2002). ... Released by 49ers (November 5, 2002). ... Re-signed by 49ers (November 26, 2002). ... Released by 49ers (January 8, 2003). ... Signed by Cleveland Browns (February 10, 2003).

Year Team	G	GS	Tk.	Ast.	Sks.	No.	Yds.	Avg.	TD
				TOTALS			**INTERCEPTIONS**		
1999—Denver NFL	6	0	0	0	0.0	0	0	0.0	0
2000—Green Bay NFL	3	0	0	0	0.0	0	0	0.0	0
—San Francisco NFL	5	0	0	0	0.0	0	0	0.0	0
2002—Barcelona NFLE	...	...	...	...	0.0	2	81	40.5	0
—San Francisco NFL	9	0	4	0	0.0	0	0	0.0	0
NFL Europe totals (1 year)	...	...	...	...	0.0	2	81	40.5	0
NFL totals (3 years)	23	0	4	0	0.0	0	0	0.0	0
Pro totals (4 years)	...	...	...	...	0.0	2	81	40.5	0

MOORE, LARRY   C   REDSKINS

PERSONAL: Born June 1, 1975, in San Diego. ... 6-2/302. ... Full name: Larry Maceo Moore.
HIGH SCHOOL: Monte Vista (Spring Valley, Calif.).
JUNIOR COLLEGE: Grossmont College (Calif.).
COLLEGE: Brigham Young.
TRANSACTIONS/CAREER NOTES: Signed as non-drafted free agent by Seattle Seahawks (April 25, 1997). ... Released by Seahawks (August 17, 1997). ... Signed by Washington Redskins to practice squad (August 26, 1997). ... Released by Redskins (September 3, 1997). ... Signed by Indianapolis Colts (January 29, 1998). ... Granted free agency (March 2, 2001). ... Re-signed by Colts (April 21, 2001). ... Granted unconditional free agency (March 1, 2002). ... Signed by Redskins (March 13, 2002).
PLAYING EXPERIENCE: Indianapolis NFL, 1998-2001; Washington NFL, 2002. ... Games/Games started: 1998 (6/5), 1999 (16/16), 2000 (16/16), 2001 (16/11), 2002 (16/16). Total: 70/64.

MOORMAN, BRIAN   P   BILLS

PERSONAL: Born February 4, 1976, in Segdwick, Kan. ... 6-0/180.
HIGH SCHOOL: Segdwick (Kan.).
COLLEGE: Pittsburgh State.
TRANSACTIONS/CAREER NOTES: Signed as non-drafted free agent by Seattle Seahawks (February 24, 1999). ... Released by Seahawks (August 30, 1999). ... Re-signed by Seahawks (February 17, 2000). ... Assigned by Seahawks to Berlin Thunder in 2000 NFL Europe enhancement allocation program (February 18, 2000). ... Released by Seahawks (August 27, 2000). ... Signed by Buffalo Bills (July 20, 2001).

Year Team	G	No.	Yds.	Avg.	Net avg.	In. 20	Blk.
2001—Berlin NFLE	...	38	1645	43.3	37.0	7	0
—Buffalo NFL	16	80	3262	40.8	33.8	16	0
2002—Buffalo NFL	16	66	2844	43.1	36.0	18	1
NFL Europe totals (1 year)	...	38	1645	43.3	37.0	7	0
NFL totals (2 years)	32	146	6106	41.8	34.8	34	1
Pro totals (3 years)	...	184	7751	42.1	35.3	41	1

(Header: PUNTING spans No., Yds., Avg., Net avg., In. 20, Blk.)

MORAN, SEAN   DE   49ERS

PERSONAL: Born June 5, 1973, in Aurora, Colo. ... 6-4/275. ... Full name: Sean Farrell Moran.
HIGH SCHOOL: Overland (Aurora, Colo.).
COLLEGE: Colorado State.
TRANSACTIONS/CAREER NOTES: Selected by Buffalo Bills in fourth round (120th pick overall) of 1996 NFL draft. ... Signed by Bills (July 9, 1996). ... Granted free agency (February 12, 1999). ... Re-signed by Bills (April 1, 1999). ... Granted unconditional free agency (February 11, 2000). ... Signed by St. Louis Rams (March 15, 2000). ... Granted unconditional free agency (March 1, 2002). ... Signed by San Francisco 49ers (April 4, 2002).
CHAMPIONSHIP GAME EXPERIENCE: Played in NFC championship game (2001 season). ... Played in Super Bowl XXXVI (2001 season).

Year Team	G	GS	Tk.	Ast.	Sks.	No.	Yds.	Avg.	TD
1996—Buffalo NFL	16	0	4	1	0.0	0	0	0.0	0
1997—Buffalo NFL	16	7	24	13	4.5	2	12	6.0	0
1998—Buffalo NFL	9	2	0	0	0.0	0	0	0.0	0
1999—Buffalo NFL	16	0	7	4	0.5	0	0	0.0	0
2000—St. Louis NFL	15	3	6	3	2.0	0	0	0.0	0
2001—St. Louis NFL	16	1	11	5	2.0	0	0	0.0	0
2002—San Francisco NFL	16	0	6	3	0.0	0	0	0.0	0
Pro totals (7 years)	104	13	58	29	9.0	2	12	6.0	0

(Headers: TOTALS spans Tk., Ast., Sks.; INTERCEPTIONS spans No., Yds., Avg., TD)

MORENO, ZEKE   LB   CHARGERS

PERSONAL: Born October 10, 1978, in Chula Vista, Calif. ... 6-2/246. ... Full name: Ezekiel Aaron Moreno.
HIGH SCHOOL: Castle Park (Chula Vista, Calif.).
COLLEGE: Southern California.
TRANSACTIONS/CAREER NOTES: Selected by San Diego Chargers in fifth round (139th pick overall) of 2001 NFL draft. ... Signed by Chargers (July 19, 2001).

Year Team	G	GS	Tk.	Ast.	Sks.	No.	Yds.	Avg.	TD
2001—San Diego NFL	16	0	5	1	1.0	0	0	0.0	0
2002—San Diego NFL	16	3	28	4	0.0	1	8	8.0	0
Pro totals (2 years)	32	3	33	5	1.0	1	8	8.0	0

(Headers: TOTALS spans Tk., Ast., Sks.; INTERCEPTIONS spans No., Yds., Avg., TD)

MORGAN, DAN   LB   PANTHERS

PERSONAL: Born December 19, 1978, in Coral Springs, Fla. ... 6-2/233. ... Full name: Daniel Thomas Morgan Jr..
HIGH SCHOOL: Taravella (Coral Springs, Fla.).
COLLEGE: Miami.
TRANSACTIONS/CAREER NOTES: Selected by Carolina Panthers in first round (11th pick overall) of 2001 NFL draft. ... Signed by Panthers (July 21, 2001). ... On injured reserve with shoulder injury (December 12, 2002-remainder of season).
HONORS: Named linebacker on The Sporting News college All-America first team (2000). ... Butkus Award winner (2000). ... Bronko Nagurski Award winner (2000).

Year	Team	G	GS	TOTALS			INTERCEPTIONS			
				Tk.	Ast.	Sks.	No.	Yds.	Avg.	TD
2001—Carolina NFL		11	11	45	22	1.0	1	10	10.0	0
2002—Carolina NFL		8	8	39	15	1.0	2	26	13.0	0
Pro totals (2 years)		19	19	84	37	2.0	3	36	12.0	0

MORGAN, DON — S

PERSONAL: Born September 18, 1975, in Stockton, Calif. ... 5-11/202.
HIGH SCHOOL: Manteca (Calif.).
COLLEGE: Nevada-Reno.
TRANSACTIONS/CAREER NOTES: Signed as non-drafted free agent by Minnesota Vikings (April 19, 1999). ... Released by Vikings (September 5, 1999). ... Re-signed by Vikings to practice squad (September 6, 1999). ... Activated (December 23, 1999). ... Released by Vikings (August 27, 2000). ... Re-signed by Vikings to practice squad (August 28, 2000). ... Activated (December 5, 2000). ... Released by Vikings (December 19, 2000). ... Re-signed by Vikings to practice squad (December 20, 2000). ... Activated (January 10, 2001). ... Released by Vikings (June 6, 2002). ... Signed by Arizona Cardinals (July 26, 2002). ... Released by Cardinals (November 23, 2002). ... Re-signed by Cardinals (November 26, 2002). ... Released by Cardinals (December 4, 2002).
CHAMPIONSHIP GAME EXPERIENCE: Played in NFC championship game (2000 season).

Year	Team	G	GS	TOTALS			INTERCEPTIONS			
				Tk.	Ast.	Sks.	No.	Yds.	Avg.	TD
1999—Minnesota NFL		2	0	0	0	0.0	0	0	0.0	0
2000—Minnesota NFL		2	0	2	0	0.0	0	0	0.0	0
2001—Minnesota NFL		16	2	5	0	0.0	0	0	0.0	0
2002—Arizona NFL		7	0	1	2	0.0	0	0	0.0	0
Pro totals (4 years)		27	2	8	2	0.0	0	0	0.0	0

MORGAN, QUINCY — WR — BROWNS

PERSONAL: Born September 23, 1977, in Garland, Texas. ... 6-1/209.
HIGH SCHOOL: South Garland (Texas).
COLLEGE: Kansas State.
TRANSACTIONS/CAREER NOTES: Selected by Cleveland Browns in second round (33rd pick overall) of 2001 NFL draft. ... Signed by Browns (July 23, 2001).
HONORS: Named wide receiver on THE SPORTING NEWS college All-America third team (2000).
SINGLE GAME HIGHS (regular season): Receptions—9 (September 8, 2002, vs. Kansas City); yards—151 (September 8, 2002, vs. Kansas City); and touchdown receptions—2 (December 8, 2002, vs. Jacksonville).
STATISTICAL PLATEAUS: 100-yard receiving games: 2002 (2).

Year	Team	G	GS	RUSHING				RECEIVING				KICKOFF RETURNS				TOTALS			
				Att.	Yds.	Avg.	TD	No.	Yds.	Avg.	TD	No.	Yds.	Avg.	TD	TD	2pt.	Pts.	Fum.
2001—Cleveland NFL		16	10	2	27	13.5	0	30	432	14.4	2	7	175	25.0	0	2	0	12	3
2002—Cleveland NFL		16	16	3	7	2.3	0	56	964	*17.2	7	0	0	0.0	0	7	1	44	2
Pro totals (2 years)		32	26	5	34	6.8	0	86	1396	16.2	9	7	175	25.0	0	9	1	56	5

M

MORRIS, ARIC — S — PATRIOTS

PERSONAL: Born July 22, 1977, in Winston-Salem, N.C. ... 5-10/212.
HIGH SCHOOL: Berkley (Mich.).
COLLEGE: Michigan State.
TRANSACTIONS/CAREER NOTES: Selected by Tennessee Titans in fifth round (135th pick overall) of 2000 NFL draft. ... Signed by Titans (July 5, 2000). ... Granted free agency (February 28, 2003). ... Released by Titans (March 23, 2003). ... Signed by New England Patriots (May 9, 2003).
CHAMPIONSHIP GAME EXPERIENCE: Played in AFC championship game (2002 season).

Year	Team	G	GS	TOTALS			INTERCEPTIONS			
				Tk.	Ast.	Sks.	No.	Yds.	Avg.	TD
2000—Tennessee NFL		15	0	1	0	0.0	0	0	0.0	0
2001—Tennessee NFL		16	10	33	14	1.5	0	0	0.0	0
2002—Tennessee NFL		16	0	7	2	0.0	0	0	0.0	0
Pro totals (3 years)		47	10	41	16	1.5	0	0	0.0	0

MORRIS, MAURICE — RB — SEAHAWKS

PERSONAL: Born December 1, 1979, in Chester, S.C. ... 5-11/202. ... Full name: Maurice Autora Morris.
HIGH SCHOOL: Chester (S.C.).
JUNIOR COLLEGE: Fresno City College.
COLLEGE: Oregon.
TRANSACTIONS/CAREER NOTES: Selected by Seattle Seahawks in second round (54th pick overall) of 2002 NFL draft. ... Signed by Seahawks (July 25, 2002).
SINGLE GAME HIGHS (regular season): Attempts—15 (November 10, 2002, vs. Arizona); yards—72 (November 10, 2002, vs. Arizona); and rushing touchdowns—0.

Year	Team	G	GS	RUSHING				RECEIVING				KICKOFF RETURNS				TOTALS			
				Att.	Yds.	Avg.	TD	No.	Yds.	Avg.	TD	No.	Yds.	Avg.	TD	TD	2pt.	Pts.	Fum.
2002—Seattle NFL		11	0	32	153	4.8	0	3	25	8.3	0	34	821	24.1	1	1	0	6	1

MORRIS, ROB   LB   COLTS

PERSONAL: Born January 18, 1975, in Nampa, Idaho. ... 6-2/243. ... Full name: Robert Samuel Morris.
HIGH SCHOOL: Nampa (Idaho).
COLLEGE: Brigham Young.
TRANSACTIONS/CAREER NOTES: Selected by Indianapolis Colts in first round (28th pick overall) of 2000 NFL draft. ... Signed by Colts (July 26, 2000). ... On injured reserve with knee injury (October 25, 2000-remainder of season).
HONORS: Named linebacker on The Sporting News college All-America second team (1999).

				TOTALS			INTERCEPTIONS			
Year Team	G	GS	Tk.	Ast.	Sks.	No.	Yds.	Avg.	TD
2000—Indianapolis NFL	7	0	8	3	0.0	0	0	0.0	0
2001—Indianapolis NFL	14	14	84	30	1.0	0	0	0.0	0
2002—Indianapolis NFL	16	16	76	24	3.0	0	0	0.0	0
Pro totals (3 years)	37	30	168	57	4.0	0	0	0.0	0

MORRIS, SAMMY   RB   BILLS

PERSONAL: Born March 23, 1977, in San Antonio. ... 6-0/225. ... Full name: Samuel Morris III.
HIGH SCHOOL: John Jay (San Antonio).
COLLEGE: Texas Tech.
TRANSACTIONS/CAREER NOTES: Selected by Buffalo Bills in fifth round (156th pick overall) of 2000 NFL draft. ... Signed by Bills (June 21, 2000). ... Granted free agency (February 28, 2003). ... Re-signed by Bills (April 17, 2003).
SINGLE GAME HIGHS (regular season): Attempts—19 (October 29, 2000, vs. New York Jets); yards—60 (October 15, 2000, vs. San Diego); and rushing touchdowns—1 (December 11, 2000, vs. Indianapolis).

			RUSHING				RECEIVING				TOTALS			
Year Team	G	GS	Att.	Yds.	Avg.	TD	No.	Yds.	Avg.	TD	TD	2pt.	Pts.	Fum.
2000—Buffalo NFL	12	8	93	341	3.7	5	37	268	7.2	1	6	0	36	2
2001—Buffalo NFL	16	1	20	72	3.6	0	7	36	5.1	0	0	0	0	1
2002—Buffalo NFL	16	0	2	5	2.5	0	3	48	16.0	0	0	0	0	0
Pro totals (3 years)	44	9	115	418	3.6	5	47	352	7.5	1	6	0	36	3

MORRIS, SYLVESTER   WR   CHIEFS

PERSONAL: Born October 6, 1977, in New Orleans. ... 6-3/216.
HIGH SCHOOL: McDonogh 35 (New Orleans).
COLLEGE: Jackson State.
TRANSACTIONS/CAREER NOTES: Selected by Kansas City Chiefs in first round (21st pick overall) of 2000 NFL draft. ... Signed by Chiefs (August 9, 2000). ... On physically unable to perform list with knee injury (August 28, 2001-entire season). ... On injured reserve with knee injury (September 1, 2002-entire season).
SINGLE GAME HIGHS (regular season): Receptions—6 (November 5, 2000, vs. Oakland); yards—112 (September 17, 2000, vs. San Diego); and touchdown receptions—3 (September 17, 2000, vs. San Diego).
STATISTICAL PLATEAUS: 100-yard receiving games: 2000 (2).

			RECEIVING			
Year Team	G	GS	No.	Yds.	Avg.	TD
2000—Kansas City NFL	15	14	48	678	14.1	3
2001—Kansas City NFL				Did not play.		
2002—Kansas City NFL				Did not play.		
Pro totals (1 years)	15	14	48	678	14.1	3

MORROW, HAROLD   FB   RAVENS

PERSONAL: Born February 24, 1973, in Maplesville, Ala. ... 5-11/232. ... Full name: Harold Morrow Jr. ... Cousin of Tommie Agee, fullback with Seattle Seahawks (1988), Kansas City Chiefs (1989) and Dallas Cowboys (1990-94).
HIGH SCHOOL: Maplesville (Ala.).
COLLEGE: Auburn.
TRANSACTIONS/CAREER NOTES: Signed as non-drafted free agent by Dallas Cowboys (April 25, 1996). ... Claimed on waivers by Minnesota Vikings (August 26, 1996). ... Granted free agency (February 12, 1999). ... Re-signed by Vikings (April 23, 1999). ... Granted unconditional free agency (February 11, 2000). ... Re-signed by Vikings (March 7, 2000). ... Granted unconditional free agency (March 1, 2002). ... Re-signed by Vikings (March 6, 2002). ... Released by Vikings (February 27, 2003). ... Signed by Baltimore Ravens (March 6, 2003).
CHAMPIONSHIP GAME EXPERIENCE: Played in NFC championship game (1998 and 2000 seasons).
SINGLE GAME HIGHS (regular season): Attempts—5 (January 7, 2002, vs. Baltimore); yards—24 (December 30, 2001, vs. Green Bay); and rushing touchdowns—0.

			RUSHING				TOTALS			
Year Team	G	GS	Att.	Yds.	Avg.	TD	TD	2pt.	Pts.	Fum.
1996—Minnesota NFL	8	0	0	0	0.0	0	0	0	0	0
1997—Minnesota NFL	16	0	0	0	0.0	0	0	0	0	0
1998—Minnesota NFL	11	0	3	7	2.3	0	0	0	0	0
1999—Minnesota NFL	16	0	2	1	0.5	0	0	0	0	0
2000—Minnesota NFL	16	0	0	0	0.0	0	0	0	0	0
2001—Minnesota NFL	16	2	12	67	5.6	0	0	0	0	1
2002—Minnesota NFL	16	0	0	0	0.0	0	0	0	0	0
Pro totals (7 years)	99	2	17	75	4.4	0	0	0	0	1

PERSONAL: Born April 4, 1977, in Torrance, Calif. ... 5-8/186. ... Brother of Johnnie Morton, wide receiver, Kansas City Chiefs; and half brother of Michael Morton, running back with Tampa Bay Buccaneers (1982-84), Washington Redskins (1985) and Seattle Seahawks (1987).
HIGH SCHOOL: South Torrance (Calif.).
COLLEGE: Southern California.
TRANSACTIONS/CAREER NOTES: Selected by New Orleans Saints in fifth round (166th pick overall) of 2000 NFL draft. ... Signed by Saints (July 11, 2000). ... Traded by Saints to New York Jets for CB Earthwind Moreland and sixth-round pick (TE John Gilmore) in 2002 draft (August 23, 2001). ... Granted free agency (February 28, 2003). ... Tendered offer sheet by Washington Redskins (March 6, 2003). ... Jets ruled not to have matched offer sheet by arbitrator (April 7, 2003).
RECORDS: Shares NFL single-game record for most kickoff return touchdowns—2 (September 8, 2002, New York Jets at Buffalo).
SINGLE GAME HIGHS (regular season): Attempts—12 (November 26, 2000, vs. St. Louis); yards—45 (November 19, 2000, vs. Oakland); and rushing touchdowns—0.

Year Team	G	GS	RUSHING				RECEIVING				PUNT RETURNS				KICKOFF RETURNS				TOTALS			
			Att.	Yds.	Avg.	TD	No.	Yds.	Avg.	TD	No.	Yds.	Avg.	TD	No.	Yds.	Avg.	TD	TD	2pt.	Pts.	Fum.
2000—NO NFL	16	3	36	136	3.8	0	30	213	7.1	0	30	278	9.3	0	44	1029	23.4	0	0	0	0	2
2001—NYJ NFL	9	0	0	0	0.0	0	0	0	0.0	0	13	113	8.7	0	12	247	20.6	0	0	0	0	0
2002—NYJ NFL	16	0	4	8	2.0	0	3	19	6.3	0	4	51	12.8	0	58§1509		26.0	†2	2	0	12	1
Pro totals (3 years)	41	3	40	144	3.6	0	33	232	7.0	0	47	442	9.4	0	114	2785	24.4	2	2	0	12	3

PERSONAL: Born October 7, 1971, in Inglewood, Calif. ... 6-0/190. ... Full name: Johnnie James Morton. ... Brother of Chad Morton, running back, New York Jets; half brother of Michael Morton, running back with Tampa Bay Buccaneers (1982-84), Washington Redskins (1985) and Seattle Seahawks (1987).
HIGH SCHOOL: South Torrance (Calif.).
COLLEGE: Southern California (degree in communications).
TRANSACTIONS/CAREER NOTES: Selected by Detroit Lions in first round (21st pick overall) of 1994 NFL draft. ... Signed by Lions (July 18, 1994). ... Released by Lions (March 14, 2002). ... Signed by Kansas City Chiefs (March 29, 2002).
HONORS: Named wide receiver on THE SPORTING NEWS college All-America first team (1993).
SINGLE GAME HIGHS (regular season): Receptions—10 (January 2, 2000, vs. Minnesota); yards—174 (September 22, 1996, vs. Chicago); and touchdown receptions—2 (January 2, 2000, vs. Minnesota).
STATISTICAL PLATEAUS: 100-yard receiving games: 1995 (1), 1996 (2), 1997 (3), 1998 (3), 1999 (5), 2001 (4). Total: 18.

Year Team	G	GS	RUSHING				RECEIVING				KICKOFF RETURNS				TOTALS			
			Att.	Yds.	Avg.	TD	No.	Yds.	Avg.	TD	No.	Yds.	Avg.	TD	TD	2pt.	Pts.	Fum.
1994—Detroit NFL	14	0	0	0	0.0	0	3	39	13.0	1	4	143	35.8	1	2	0	12	1
1995—Detroit NFL	16	13	3	33	11.0	0	44	590	13.4	8	18	390	21.7	0	8	0	48	1
1996—Detroit NFL	16	15	9	35	3.9	0	55	714	13.0	6	0	0	0.0	0	6	0	36	1
1997—Detroit NFL	16	16	3	33	11.0	0	80	1057	13.2	6	0	0	0.0	0	6	0	36	2
1998—Detroit NFL	16	16	1	11	11.0	0	69	1028	14.9	2	0	0	0.0	0	2	0	12	0
1999—Detroit NFL	16	12	0	0	0.0	0	80	1129	14.1	5	1	22	22.0	0	5	0	30	0
2000—Detroit NFL	16	16	4	25	6.3	0	61	788	12.9	3	0	0	0.0	0	3	1	20	1
2001—Detroit NFL	16	16	1	6	6.0	0	77	1154	15.0	4	1	4	4.0	0	4	0	24	1
2002—Kansas City NFL	14	14	10	124	12.4	0	29	397	13.7	1	0	0	0.0	0	1	0	6	0
Pro totals (9 years)	140	118	31	267	8.6	0	498	6896	13.8	36	24	559	23.3	1	37	1	224	7

PERSONAL: Born September 12, 1979, in Waterloo, Iowa. ... 5-9/178. ... Full name: Jerry James Moses Jr.
HIGH SCHOOL: Waterloo (Iowa).
COLLEGE: Iowa State.
TRANSACTIONS/CAREER NOTES: Signed as non-drafted free agent by Kansas City Chiefs (April 26, 2001). ... Released by Chiefs (August 27, 2001). ... Signed by Green Bay Packers to practice squad (September 26, 2001). ... Released by Packers (October 3, 2001). ... Signed by Chiefs to practice squad (November 21, 2001). ... Assigned by Chiefs to Scottish Claymores in 2002 NFL Europe enhancement allocation program (February 12, 2002). ... Released by Chiefs (September 1, 2002). ... Signed by Packers to practice squad (November 13, 2002). ... Released by Packers (November 28, 2002). ... Re-signed by Packers to practice squad (December 2, 2002). ... Activated (December 15, 2002). ... Released by Packers (December 24, 2002).

Year Team	G	GS	RECEIVING				PUNT RETURNS				KICKOFF RETURNS				TOTALS			
			No.	Yds.	Avg.	TD	No.	Yds.	Avg.	TD	No.	Yds.	Avg.	TD	TD	2pt.	Pts.	Fum.
2002—Scottish NFLE	10	2	11	94	8.5	0	25	280	11.2	0	14	344	24.6	0	0	0	0	0
—Green Bay NFL	2	0	0	0	0.0	0	5	12	2.4	0	4	69	17.3	0	0	0	0	1
NFL Europe totals (1 year)	10	2	11	94	8.5	0	25	280	11.2	0	14	344	24.6	0	0	0	0	0
NFL totals (1 year)	2	0	0	0	0.0	0	5	12	2.4	0	4	69	17.3	0	0	0	0	1
Pro totals (2 years)	12	2	11	94	8.5	0	30	292	9.7	0	18	413	22.9	0	0	0	0	1

PERSONAL: Born September 3, 1976, in Hartsville, S.C. ... 6-0/239.
HIGH SCHOOL: Hartsville (S.C.).
COLLEGE: Wake Forest.
TRANSACTIONS/CAREER NOTES: Signed as non-drafted free agent by New York Jets (April 27, 2000). ... Released by Jets (August 21, 2000). ... Re-signed by Jets (January 3, 2001). ... Assigned by Jets to Frankfurt Galaxy in 2001 NFL Europe enhancement allocation program (February 19, 2001). ... Re-signed by Jets (April 2, 2003).

M

Year Team	G	GS	TOTALS Tk.	Ast.	Sks.	INTERCEPTIONS No.	Yds.	Avg.	TD
2001—Frankfurt NFLE	...	...	...	...	3.0	0	0	0.0	0
—New York Jets NFL	16	0	2	2	0.0	0	0	0.0	0
2002—New York Jets NFL	16	0	4	0	0.0	0	0	0.0	0
NFL Europe totals (1 year)	...	...	...	...	3.0	0	0	0.0	0
NFL totals (2 years)	32	0	6	2	0.0	0	0	0.0	0
Pro totals (3 years)	...	...	...	...	3.0	0	0	0.0	0

MOSS, RANDY · WR · VIKINGS

PERSONAL: Born February 13, 1977, in Rand, W.Va. ... 6-4/204. ... Half brother of Eric Moss, offensive lineman with Minnesota Vikings (1997-99).
HIGH SCHOOL: DuPont (Belle, W.Va.).
COLLEGE: Florida State (did not play football), then Marshall.
TRANSACTIONS/CAREER NOTES: Selected after sophomore season by Minnesota Vikings in first round (21st pick overall) of 1998 NFL draft. ... Signed by Minnesota Vikings (July 26, 1998).
CHAMPIONSHIP GAME EXPERIENCE: Played in NFC championship game (1998 and 2000 seasons).
HONORS: Fred Biletnikoff Award winner (1997). ... Named wide receiver on THE SPORTING NEWS college All-America first team (1997). ... Named NFL Rookie of the Year by THE SPORTING NEWS (1998). ... Named wide receiver on THE SPORTING NEWS NFL All-Pro team (1998 and 2000). ... Played in Pro Bowl (1998 and 1999 seasons). ... Named Outstanding Player of the Pro Bowl (1999). ... Named to play in Pro Bowl (2000 season); replaced by Joe Horn due to injury. ... Named to play in Pro Bowl (2002 season); replaced by Donald Driver due to injury.
RECORDS: Holds NFL rookie-season record for most receiving touchdowns—17 (1998).
SINGLE GAME HIGHS (regular season): Receptions—12 (November 14, 1999, vs. Chicago); yards—204 (November 14, 1999, vs. Chicago); and touchdown receptions—3 (November 19, 2001, vs. New York Giants).
STATISTICAL PLATEAUS: 100-yard receiving games: 1998 (4), 1999 (7), 2000 (8), 2001 (4), 2002 (7). Total: 30.

Year Team	G	GS	RECEIVING No.	Yds.	Avg.	TD	PUNT RETURNS No.	Yds.	Avg.	TD	TOTALS TD	2pt.	Pts.	Fum.
1998—Minnesota NFL	16	11	69	1313	‡19.0	*17	1	0	0.0	0	‡17	†2	106	2
1999—Minnesota NFL	16	16	80	‡1413	17.7	11	17	162	9.5	∞1	12	0	72	3
2000—Minnesota NFL	16	16	77	1437	18.7	*15	0	0	0.0	0	15	1	92	2
2001—Minnesota NFL	16	16	82	1233	15.0	10	0	0	0.0	0	10	0	60	0
2002—Minnesota NFL	16	16	‡106	‡1347	12.7	7	0	0	0.0	0	7	0	42	1
Pro totals (5 years)	80	75	414	6743	16.3	60	18	162	9.0	1	61	3	372	8

MOSS, SANTANA · WR/PR · JETS

PERSONAL: Born June 1, 1979, in Miami. ... 5-10/185. ... Full name: Santana Terrell Moss.
HIGH SCHOOL: Carol City (Miami).
COLLEGE: Miami (Fla.).
TRANSACTIONS/CAREER NOTES: Selected by New York Jets in first round (16th pick overall) of 2001 NFL draft. ... Signed by Jets (July 28, 2001).
HONORS: Named kick returner on THE SPORTING NEWS college All-America first team (2000). ... Named punt returner on the THE SPORTING NEWS NFL All-Pro team (2002).
SINGLE GAME HIGHS (regular season): Receptions—5 (October 20, 2002, vs. Minnesota); yards—111 (October 20, 2002, vs. Minnesota); and touchdown receptions—1 (December 29, 2002, vs. Green Bay).
STATISTICAL PLATEAUS: 100-yard receiving games: 2002 (1).

Year Team	G	GS	RECEIVING No.	Yds.	Avg.	TD	PUNT RETURNS No.	Yds.	Avg.	TD	TOTALS TD	2pt.	Pts.	Fum.
2001—New York Jets NFL	5	0	2	40	20.0	0	6	82	13.7	0	0	0	0	0
2002—New York Jets NFL	15	3	30	433	14.4	4	25	§413	§16.5	†2	6	0	36	2
Pro totals (2 years)	20	3	32	473	14.8	4	31	495	16.0	2	6	0	36	2

MOULDS, ERIC · WR · BILLS

PERSONAL: Born July 17, 1973, in Lucedale, Miss. ... 6-2/204. ... Full name: Eric Shannon Moulds.
HIGH SCHOOL: George County (Lucedale, Miss.).
COLLEGE: Mississippi State.
TRANSACTIONS/CAREER NOTES: Selected by Buffalo Bills in first round (24th pick overall) of 1996 NFL draft. ... Signed by Bills (July 16, 1996).
HONORS: Played in Pro Bowl (1998, 2000-2002 seasons).
POST SEASON RECORDS: Holds NFL postseason single-game record for most yards receiving—240 (January 2, 1999, vs. Miami).
SINGLE GAME HIGHS (regular season): Receptions—12 (October 22, 2000, vs. Minnesota); yards—196 (November 25, 2001, vs. Miami); and touchdown receptions—2 (December 8, 2002, vs. New England).
STATISTICAL PLATEAUS: 100-yard receiving games: 1998 (4), 1999 (3), 2000 (7), 2001 (2), 2002 (5). Total: 21.

Year Team	G	GS	RUSHING Att.	Yds.	Avg.	TD	RECEIVING No.	Yds.	Avg.	TD	KICKOFF RETURNS No.	Yds.	Avg.	TD	TOTALS TD	2pt.	Pts.	Fum.
1996—Buffalo NFL	16	5	12	44	3.7	0	20	279	14.0	2	52	1205	23.2	▲1	3	0	18	1
1997—Buffalo NFL	16	8	4	59	14.8	0	29	294	10.1	0	43	921	21.4	0	0	1	2	3
1998—Buffalo NFL	16	15	0	0	0.0	0	67	§1368	20.4	9	0	0	0.0	0	9	0	54	0
1999—Buffalo NFL	14	14	1	1	1.0	0	65	994	15.3	7	0	0	0.0	0	7	0	42	0
2000—Buffalo NFL	16	16	2	24	12.0	0	94	1326	14.1	5	0	0	0.0	0	5	0	30	1
2001—Buffalo NFL	16	16	3	3	1.0	0	67	904	13.5	5	0	0	0.0	0	5	1	32	1
2002—Buffalo NFL	16	15	1	7	7.0	0	100	1292	12.9	10	0	0	0.0	0	10	0	60	1
Pro totals (7 years)	110	89	23	138	6.0	0	442	6457	14.6	38	95	2126	22.4	1	39	2	238	8

MUHAMMAD, MUHSIN   WR   PANTHERS

PERSONAL: Born May 5, 1973, in Lansing, Mich. ... 6-2/217. ... Full name: Muhsin Muhammad II. ... Name pronounced moo-SIN moo-HAH-med.
HIGH SCHOOL: Waverly (Lansing, Mich.).
COLLEGE: Michigan State.
TRANSACTIONS/CAREER NOTES: Selected by Carolina Panthers in second round (43rd pick overall) of 1996 NFL draft. ... Signed by Panthers (July 23, 1996).
CHAMPIONSHIP GAME EXPERIENCE: Played in NFC championship game (1996 season).
HONORS: Played in Pro Bowl (1999 season).
SINGLE GAME HIGHS (regular season): Receptions—11 (November 27, 2000, vs. Green Bay); yards—192 (September 13, 1998, vs. New Orleans); and touchdown receptions—3 (December 18, 1999, vs. San Francisco).
STATISTICAL PLATEAUS: 100-yard receiving games: 1998 (3), 1999 (5), 2000 (5), 2001 (2), 2002 (3). Total: 18.
MISCELLANEOUS: Holds Carolina Panthers all-time records for most receiving yards (5,509) and most receptions (431).

			RUSHING				RECEIVING				TOTALS		
Year Team	G	GS	Att.	Yds.	Avg.	TD	No.	Yds.	Avg.	TD	TD	2pt.	Pts.	Fum.
1996—Carolina NFL	9	5	1	-1	-1.0	0	25	407	16.3	1	1	0	6	0
1997—Carolina NFL	13	5	0	0	0.0	0	27	317	11.7	0	0	1	2	0
1998—Carolina NFL	16	16	0	0	0.0	0	68	941	13.8	6	6	1	38	2
1999—Carolina NFL	15	15	0	0	0.0	0	‡96	1253	13.1	8	8	0	48	1
2000—Carolina NFL	16	16	2	12	6.0	0	†102	1183	11.6	6	6	0	36	1
2001—Carolina NFL	11	11	0	0	0.0	0	50	585	11.7	1	1	0	6	2
2002—Carolina NFL	14	14	3	40	13.3	0	63	823	13.1	3	3	0	18	0
Pro totals (7 years)	94	82	6	51	8.5	0	431	5509	12.8	25	25	2	154	6

MULITALO, EDWIN   G   RAVENS

PERSONAL: Born September 1, 1974, in Daly City, Calif. ... 6-3/340. ... Full name: Edwin Moliki Mulitalo. ... Name pronounced moo-lih-TAHL-oh.
HIGH SCHOOL: Jefferson (Daly City, Calif.).
JUNIOR COLLEGE: Ricks College (Idaho).
COLLEGE: Arizona.
TRANSACTIONS/CAREER NOTES: Selected by Baltimore Ravens in fourth round (129th pick overall) of 1999 NFL draft. ... Signed by Ravens (July 29, 1999). ... Granted free agency (March 1, 2002). ... Re-signed by Ravens (June 17, 2002).
PLAYING EXPERIENCE: Baltimore NFL, 1999-2002. ... Games/Games started: 1999 (10/8), 2000 (16/16), 2001 (14/14), 2002 (16/15). Total: 56/53.
CHAMPIONSHIP GAME EXPERIENCE: Played in AFC championship game (2000 season). ... Member of Super Bowl championship team (2000 season).

MUNGRO, JAMES   RB   COLTS

PERSONAL: Born February 13, 1978, in East Stroudsburg, Pa. ... 5-9/214. ... Full name: James Alevia Mungro II.
HIGH SCHOOL: East Stroudsburg (Pa.).
COLLEGE: Syracuse.
TRANSACTIONS/CAREER NOTES: Signed as non-drafted free agent by Detroit Lions (April 26, 2002). ... Claimed on waivers by Indianapolis Colts (September 3, 2002).
SINGLE GAME HIGHS (regular season): Attempts—28 (November 10, 2002, vs. Philadelphia); yards—114 (November 10, 2002, vs. Philadelphia); and rushing touchdowns—2 (December 15, 2002, vs. Cleveland).
STATISTICAL PLATEAUS: 100-yard rushing games: 2002 (1).

			RUSHING				RECEIVING				TOTALS		
Year Team	G	GS	Att.	Yds.	Avg.	TD	No.	Yds.	Avg.	TD	TD	2pt.	Pts.	Fum.
2002—Indianapolis NFL	9	1	97	336	3.5	8	13	81	6.2	0	8	0	48	3

MURPHY, FRANK   WR   TEXANS

PERSONAL: Born February 11, 1977, in Jacksonville, Fla. ... 6-0/200.
HIGH SCHOOL: West Nassau (Callahan, Fla.).
JUNIOR COLLEGE: Itawamba Community College (Miss.), then Garden City (Kan.) Commmunity College.
COLLEGE: Kansas State.
TRANSACTIONS/CAREER NOTES: Selected by Chicago Bears in sixth round (170th pick overall) of 2000 NFL draft. ... Signed by Bears (May 31, 2000). ... Released by Bears (August 27, 2000). ... Signed by Tampa Bay Buccaneers to practice squad (August 28, 2000). ... Activated (November 22, 2000). ... Released by Buccaneers (September 1, 2002). ... Signed by Houston Texans (November 26, 2002). ... Re-signed by Texans (March 24, 2003).
SINGLE GAME HIGHS (regular season): Receptions—3 (January 6, 2002, vs. Philadelphia); yards—25 (January 6, 2002, vs. Philadelphia); and touchdown receptions—1 (October 21, 2001, vs. Pittsburgh).

			RECEIVING				KICKOFF RETURNS				TOTALS		
Year Team	G	GS	No.	Yds.	Avg.	TD	No.	Yds.	Avg.	TD	TD	2pt.	Pts.	Fum.
2000—Tampa Bay NFL	1	0	0	0	0.0	0	2	24	12.0	0	0	0	0	0
2001—Tampa Bay NFL	11	0	8	71	8.9	1	20	445	22.3	0	1	0	6	2
2002—Houston NFL	5	0	0	0	0.0	0	1	0	0.0	0	0	0	0	1
Pro totals (3 years)	17	0	8	71	8.9	1	23	469	20.4	0	1	0	6	3

MURPHY, MATT — TE — LIONS

PERSONAL: Born February 23, 1980, in New Haven, Mich. ... 6-5/253.
HIGH SCHOOL: New Haven (Mich.).
COLLEGE: Maryland.
TRANSACTIONS/CAREER NOTES: Selected by Detroit Lions in seventh round (252nd pick overall) of 2002 NFL draft. ... Signed by Lions (July 18, 2002).
SINGLE GAME HIGHS (regular season): Receptions—1 (December 29, 2002, vs. Minnesota); yards—8 (December 29, 2002, vs. Minnesota); and touchdown receptions—0.

				RECEIVING		
Year Team	G	GS	No.	Yds.	Avg.	TD
2002—Detroit NFL	3	0	1	8	8.0	0

MURPHY, ROB — G — COLTS

PERSONAL: Born January 18, 1977, in Cincinnati. ... 6-5/310. ... Full name: Robert Donald Murphy.
HIGH SCHOOL: Moeller (Cincinnati).
COLLEGE: Ohio State.
TRANSACTIONS/CAREER NOTES: Signed as non-drafted free agent by Cincinnati Bengals (July 9, 1999). ... Released by Bengals (August 30, 1999). ... Signed by Kansas City Chiefs (January 11, 2000). ... Allocated by Chiefs to Frankfurt Galaxy in 2000 NFL Europe enhancement allocation program (February 18, 2000). ... Released by Chiefs (September 18, 2000). ... Signed by Indianapolis Colts (April 22, 2001). ... Released by Colts (September 1, 2001). ... Re-signed by Colts to practice squad (September 3, 2001). ... Re-signed by Colts (March 23, 2003).
PLAYING EXPERIENCE: Indianapolis NFL, 2002. ... Games/games started: 2002 (9/0).

MURPHY, YO — WR

PERSONAL: Born May 11, 1973, in San Pedro, Calif. ... 5-10/187. ... Full name: Llewellyan Murphy.
HIGH SCHOOL: Idaho Falls (Idaho).
COLLEGE: Idaho.
TRANSACTIONS/CAREER NOTES: Signed by B.C. Lions of CFL (April 1993). ... Granted free agency (February 16, 1996). ... Re-signed by Lions (August 20, 1996). ... Released by Lions (August 26, 1996). ... Signed as non-drafted free agent by Minnesota Vikings (February 7, 1998). ... Released by Vikings (August 24, 1998). ... Selected by Scottish Claymores in NFL Europe draft (February 22, 1999). ... Signed by Tampa Bay Buccaneers (July 12, 1999). ... Claimed on waivers by Vikings (December 2, 1999). ... Released by Vikings (January 11, 1999). ... Signed by Buccaneers (February 2, 2000). ... Released by Buccaneers (August 27, 2000). ... Re-signed by Buccaneers to practice squad (October 5, 2000). ... Granted free agency after 2000 season. ... Signed by St. Louis Rams (July 23, 2001). ... Released by Rams (November 27, 2002). ... Signed by Kansas City Chiefs (December 17, 2002). ... Released by Chiefs (December 26, 2002).
CHAMPIONSHIP GAME EXPERIENCE: Member of Grey Cup championship team (1994). ... Played in NFC championship game (2001 season). ... Played in Super Bowl XXXVI (2001 season).
SINGLE GAME HIGHS (regular season): Receptions—4 (October 31, 1999, vs. Detroit); yards—28 (October 31, 1999, vs. Detroit); and touchdown receptions—0.

			RECEIVING				PUNT RETURNS				KICKOFF RETURNS				TOTALS			
Year Team	G	GS	No.	Yds.	Avg.	TD	No.	Yds.	Avg.	TD	No.	Yds.	Avg.	TD	TD	2pt.	Pts.	Fum.
1993—British Columbia CFL ..	1	...	0	0	0.0	0	0	0	0.0	0	0	0	0.0	0	0	0	0	0
1994—British Columbia CFL ..	7	...	14	127	9.1	0	0	0	0.0	0	0	0	0.0	0	0	0	0	0
1995—British Columbia CFL ..	10	...	31	510	16.5	2	0	0	0.0	0	0	0	0.0	0	2	0	12	0
1996—									Did not play.									
1997—									Did not play.									
1998—									Did not play.									
1999—Scottish NFLE	...	...	45	752	16.7	4	7	65	9.3	0	23	600	26.1	1	5	0	30	0
—Tampa Bay NFL	7	0	4	28	7.0	0	0	0	0.0	0	14	307	21.9	0	0	0	0	0
—Minnesota NFL	1	0	0	0	0.0	0	3	14	4.7	0	4	80	20.0	0	0	0	0	1
2000—Tampa Bay NFL									Did not play.									
2001—St. Louis NFL	16	0	0	0	0.0	0	0	0	0.0	0	8	174	21.8	0	0	0	0	0
2002—St. Louis NFL	11	1	5	23	4.6	0	0	0	0.0	0	1	21	21.0	0	0	0	0	0
NFL Europe totals (1 year)	...	...	45	752	16.7	4	7	65	9.3	0	23	600	26.1	1	5	0	30	0
CFL totals (3 years)	18	...	45	637	14.2	2	0	0	0.0	0	0	0	0.0	0	2	0	12	0
NFL totals (3 years)	35	1	9	51	5.7	0	3	14	4.7	0	27	582	21.6	0	0	0	0	1
Pro totals (7 years)	...	...	99	1440	14.5	6	10	79	7.9	0	50	1182	23.6	1	7	0	42	1

MYERS, LEONARD — CB — PATRIOTS

PERSONAL: Born December 18, 1978, in Fort Lauderdale, Fla. ... 5-10/198. ... Full name: Leonard Bernard Myers.
HIGH SCHOOL: Dillard (Fort Lauderdale, Fla.).
COLLEGE: Miami.
TRANSACTIONS/CAREER NOTES: Selected by New England Patriots in sixth round (200th pick overall) of 2001 NFL draft. ... Signed by Patriots (July 2, 2001). ... On physically unable to perform list with groin injury (September 1-November 10, 2002).
CHAMPIONSHIP GAME EXPERIENCE: Member of Patriots for AFC championship game (2001 season); inactive. ... Member of Super Bowl championship team (2001 season); inactive.

			TOTALS			INTERCEPTIONS			
Year Team	G	GS	Tk.	Ast.	Sks.	No.	Yds.	Avg.	TD
2001—New England NFL	7	0	3	2	0.0	0	0	0.0	0
2002—New England NFL	8	1	11	1	0.0	0	0	0.0	0
Pro totals (2 years)	15	1	14	3	0.0	0	0	0.0	0

MYERS, MICHAEL   DL   COWBOYS

PERSONAL: Born January 20, 1976, in Vicksburg, Miss. ... 6-2/292.
HIGH SCHOOL: Vicksburg (Miss.).
JUNIOR COLLEGE: Hinds Community College (Miss.).
COLLEGE: Alabama.
TRANSACTIONS/CAREER NOTES: Selected by Dallas Cowboys in fourth round (100th pick overall) of 1998 NFL draft. ... Signed by Cowboys (July 10, 1998). ... Granted free agency (March 2, 2001). ... Re-signed by Cowboys (May 3, 2001). ... Granted unconditional free agency (March 1, 2002). ... Re-signed by Cowboys (April 19, 2002). ... Granted unconditional free agency (February 28, 2003). ... Re-signed by Cowboys (May 1, 2003).
HONORS: Named defensive tackle on The Sporting News college All-America first team (1996).

Year Team	G	GS	TOTALS Tk.	Ast.	Sks.
1998—Dallas NFL	16	1	10	5	3.0
1999—Dallas NFL	6	0	4	4	0.0
2000—Dallas NFL	13	7	28	7	0.0
2001—Dallas NFL	16	16	37	18	3.5
2002—Dallas NFL	16	0	22	13	1.0
Pro totals (5 years)	67	24	101	47	7.5

MYLES, REGGIE   CB   BENGALS

PERSONAL: Born October 10, 1979, in Pascagoula, Miss. ... 5-11/185.
HIGH SCHOOL: Pascagoula (Miss.).
COLLEGE: Alabama.
TRANSACTIONS/CAREER NOTES: Signed as non-drafted free agent by Cincinnati Bengals (April 23, 2002). ... Released by Bengals (September 1, 2002). ... Re-signed by Bengals to practice squad (September 2, 2002). ... Activated (November 2, 2002).

Year Team	G	GS	TOTALS Tk.	Ast.	Sks.	INTERCEPTIONS No.	Yds.	Avg.	TD
2002—Cincinnati NFL	9	0	4	0	0.0	0	0	0.0	0

NAEOLE, CHRIS   G   JAGUARS

PERSONAL: Born December 25, 1974, in Kailua, Hawaii. ... 6-3/314. ... Full name: Chris Kealoha Naeole. ... Name pronounced NAY-oh-lee.
HIGH SCHOOL: Kahuka (Kaaava, Hawaii).
COLLEGE: Colorado.
TRANSACTIONS/CAREER NOTES: Selected by New Orleans Saints in first round (10th pick overall) of 1997 NFL draft. ... Signed by Saints (July 17, 1997). ... On injured reserve with ankle injury (October 17, 1997-remainder of season). ... Granted unconditional free agency (March 1, 2002). ... Signed by Jacksonville Jaguars (April 5, 2002).
PLAYING EXPERIENCE: New Orleans NFL, 1997-2001; Jacksonville NFL, 2002. ... Games/Games started: 1997 (4/0), 1998 (16/16), 1999 (15/15), 2000 (16/16), 2001 (16/16), 2002 (16/16). Total: 83/79.
HONORS: Named guard on The Sporting News college All-America second team (1996).

NAILS, JAMIE   G   DOLPHINS

PERSONAL: Born June 3, 1975, in Baxley, Ga. ... 6-6/335. ... Full name: Jamie Marcellus Nails.
HIGH SCHOOL: Appling County (Baxley, Ga.).
COLLEGE: Florida A&M.
TRANSACTIONS/CAREER NOTES: Selected by Buffalo Bills in fourth round (120th pick overall) of 1997 NFL draft. ... Signed by Bills (July 2, 1997). ... Granted free agency (February 11, 2000). ... Re-signed by Bills (April 28, 2000) ... Granted unconditional free agency (March 2, 2001). ... Signed by Miami Dolphins (August 15, 2001). ... Released by Dolphins (September 2, 2001). ... Re-signed by Dolphins (March 5, 2002). ... On injured reserve with Achilles' injury (December 17, 2002-remainder of season).
PLAYING EXPERIENCE: Buffalo NFL, 1997-2000; Miami NFL, 2002. ... Games/Games started: 1997 (2/0), 1998 (15/3), 1999 (16/3), 2000 (16/16), 2002 (14/14). Total: 63/36.

NALEN, TOM   C   BRONCOS

PERSONAL: Born May 13, 1971, in Foxboro, Mass. ... 6-3/286. ... Full name: Thomas Andrew Nalen.
HIGH SCHOOL: Foxboro (Mass.).
COLLEGE: Boston College.
TRANSACTIONS/CAREER NOTES: Selected by Denver Broncos in seventh round (218th pick overall) of 1994 NFL draft. ... Signed by Broncos (July 15, 1994). ... Released by Broncos (September 2, 1994). ... Re-signed by Broncos to practice squad (September 6, 1994). ... Activated (October 7, 1994). ... On injured reserve with knee injury (October 23, 2002-remainder of season).
PLAYING EXPERIENCE: Denver NFL, 1994-2002. ... Games/Games started: 1994 (7/1), 1995 (15/15), 1996 (16/16), 1997 (16/16), 1998 (16/16), 1999 (16/16), 2000 (16/16), 2001 (16/16), 2002 (7/7). Total: 119/119.
CHAMPIONSHIP GAME EXPERIENCE: Played in AFC championship game (1997 and 1998 seasons). ... Member of Super Bowl championship team (1997 and 1998 seasons).
HONORS: Played in Pro Bowl (1997-1999 seasons). ... Named center on The Sporting News NFL All-Pro team (1999 and 2000). ... Named to play in Pro Bowl (2000 season); replaced by Tim Ruddy due to injury.

M
N

NAVIES, HANNIBAL LB PACKERS

PERSONAL: Born July 19, 1977, in Chicago. ... 6-2/240. ... Full name: Hannibal Carter Navies. ... Name pronounced NAY-vees.
HIGH SCHOOL: St. Patrick (Chicago), then Berkeley (Oakland).
COLLEGE: Colorado.
TRANSACTIONS/CAREER NOTES: Selected by Carolina Panthers in fourth round (100th pick overall) of 1999 NFL draft. ... Signed by Panthers (July 21, 1999). ... On injured reserve with broken arm (October 23, 2001-remainder of season). ... Granted free agency (March 1, 2002). ... Re-signed by Panthers (May 10, 2002). ... Granted unconditional free agency (February 28, 2003). ... Signed by Green Bay Packers (March 19, 2003).

			TOTALS			INTERCEPTIONS			
Year Team	G	GS	Tk.	Ast.	Sks.	No.	Yds.	Avg.	TD
1999—Carolina NFL	9	0	3	0	0.0	0	0	0.0	0
2000—Carolina NFL	13	1	19	1	2.0	1	0	0.0	0
2001—Carolina NFL	5	5	17	4	0.0	0	0	0.0	0
2002—Carolina NFL	12	9	21	11	0.0	0	0	0.0	0
Pro totals (4 years)	39	15	60	16	2.0	1	0	0.0	0

NEAL, LORENZO FB CHARGERS

PERSONAL: Born December 27, 1970, in Hanford, Calif. ... 5-11/245. ... Full name: Lorenzo LaVonne Neal.
HIGH SCHOOL: Lemoore (Calif.).
COLLEGE: Fresno State.
TRANSACTIONS/CAREER NOTES: Selected by New Orleans Saints in fourth round (89th pick overall) of 1993 NFL draft. ... Signed by Saints (July 15, 1993). ... On injured reserve with ankle injury (September 15, 1993-remainder of season). ... Granted free agency (February 16, 1996). ... Re-signed by Saints (July 1, 1996). ... Granted unconditional free agency (February 14, 1997). ... Signed by New York Jets (March 31, 1997). ... Traded by Jets to Tampa Bay Buccaneers for fifth-round pick (TE Blake Spence) in 1998 draft (March 12, 1998). ... Released by Buccaneers (February 11, 1999). ... Signed by Tennessee Titans (March 2, 1999). ... Released by Titans (March 1, 2001). ... Signed by Cincinnati Bengals (May 7, 2001). ... Granted unconditional free agency (February 28, 2003). ... Signed by San Diego Chargers (February 28, 2003).
CHAMPIONSHIP GAME EXPERIENCE: Played in AFC championship game (1999 season). ... Played in Super Bowl XXXIV (1999 season).
HONORS: Played in Pro Bowl (2002 season).
SINGLE GAME HIGHS (regular season): Attempts—14 (October 9, 1994, vs. Chicago); yards—89 (September 5, 1993, vs. Houston); and rushing touchdowns—1 (October 10, 1999, vs. Baltimore).

			RUSHING				RECEIVING				KICKOFF RETURNS				TOTALS			
Year Team	G	GS	Att.	Yds.	Avg.	TD	No.	Yds.	Avg.	TD	No.	Yds.	Avg.	TD	TD	2pt.	Pts.	Fum.
1993—New Orleans NFL	2	2	21	175	8.3	1	0	0	0.0	0	0	0	0.0	0	1	0	6	1
1994—New Orleans NFL	16	7	30	90	3.0	1	2	9	4.5	0	1	17	17.0	0	1	0	6	1
1995—New Orleans NFL	16	7	5	3	0.6	0	12	123	10.3	1	2	28	14.0	0	1	0	6	2
1996—New Orleans NFL	16	11	21	58	2.8	1	31	194	6.3	1	0	0	0.0	0	2	0	12	1
1997—New York Jets NFL	16	10	10	28	2.8	0	8	40	5.0	1	2	22	11.0	0	1	0	6	0
1998—Tampa Bay NFL	16	1	5	25	5.0	0	5	14	2.8	1	0	0	0.0	0	1	0	6	0
1999—Tennessee NFL	16	14	2	1	0.5	1	7	27	3.9	2	2	15	7.5	0	3	0	18	0
2000—Tennessee NFL	16	5	1	-2	-2.0	0	9	31	3.4	2	1	15	15.0	0	2	0	12	0
2001—Cincinnati NFL	16	10	5	10	2.0	0	19	101	5.3	1	0	0	0.0	0	1	0	6	0
2002—Cincinnati NFL	16	8	9	31	3.4	0	21	133	6.3	1	5	52	10.4	0	1	0	6	0
Pro totals (10 years)	146	75	109	419	3.8	4	114	672	5.9	10	13	149	11.5	0	14	0	84	5

NEAL, STEPHEN OL PATRIOTS

PERSONAL: Born October 9, 1976, in San Diego. ... 6-4/305.
HIGH SCHOOL: San Diego (Calif.).
COLLEGE: Cal State-Bakersfield.
TRANSACTIONS/CAREER NOTES: Signed as non-drafted free agent by New England Patriots (July 23, 2001). ... Released by Patriots (August 26, 2001). ... Signed by Philadelphia Eagles to practice squad (September 4, 2001). ... Signed by Patriots off Eagles practice squad (December 12, 2001). ... Inactive for three games (2001). ... On injured reserve with shoulder injury (October 23, 2002-remainder of season).
PLAYING EXPERIENCE: New England NFL, 2002. ... Games/Games started: 2002 (2/1).

NECE, RYAN LB BUCCANEERS

PERSONAL: Born February 24, 1979, in San Bernardino, Calif. ... 6-3/224. ... Full name: Ryan Clint Nece. ... Son of Ronnie Lott, Hall of Fame safety with San Francisco 49ers (1981-90), Los Angeles Raiders (1991-92) and New York Jets (1993-94).
HIGH SCHOOL: Pacific (San Bernardino, Calif.).
COLLEGE: UCLA.
TRANSACTIONS/CAREER NOTES: Signed as non-drafted free agent by Tampa Bay Buccaneers (April 22, 2002). ... On injured reserve with knee injury (October 29, 2002-remainder of season).

			TOTALS			INTERCEPTIONS			
Year Team	G	GS	Tk.	Ast.	Sks.	No.	Yds.	Avg.	TD
2002—Tampa Bay NFL	8	0	1	1	0.0	0	0	0.0	0

NEDNEY, JOE K TITANS

PERSONAL: Born March 22, 1973, in San Jose, Calif. ... 6-5/225. ... Full name: Joseph Thomas Nedney. ... Name pronounced NED-nee.
HIGH SCHOOL: Santa Teresa (San Jose, Calif.).
COLLEGE: San Jose State (degree in recreation administration, 1998).
TRANSACTIONS/CAREER NOTES: Signed as non-drafted free agent by Green Bay Packers (April 1995). ... Released by Packers (August 27, 1995). ... Signed by Oakland Raiders to practice squad (August 29, 1995). ... Released by Raiders (September 6, 1995). ... Signed by Miami Dolphins to practice squad (September 21, 1995). ... Claimed on waivers by New York Jets (August 12, 1997). ... Released by Jets (August

N

25, 1997). ... Signed by Dolphins (October 3, 1997). ... Released by Dolphins (October 6, 1997). ... Signed by Arizona Cardinals (October 15, 1997). ... On injured reserve with knee injury (December 1, 1998-remainder of season). ... Released by Cardinals (February 12, 1999). ... Re-signed by Cardinals (March 31, 1999). ... Claimed on waivers by Baltimore Ravens (October 6, 1999). ... Inactive for four games with Ravens (1999). ... Released by Ravens (November 9, 1999). ... Signed by Raiders (December 14, 1999). ... Released by Raiders (August 27, 2000). ... Signed by Denver Broncos (September 12, 2000). ... Released by Broncos (October 2, 2000). ... Signed by Carolina Panthers (October 3, 2000). ... Granted unconditional free agency (March 2, 2001). ... Signed by Tennessee Titans (March 9, 2001).

CHAMPIONSHIP GAME EXPERIENCE: Played in AFC championship game (2002 season).

Year Team	G	FIELD GOALS							TOTALS		
		1-29	30-39	40-49	50+	Tot.	Pct.	Lg.	XPM	XPA	Pts.
1995—Miami NFL		Did not play.									
1996—Miami NFL	16	8-8	7-11	3-8	0-2	18-29	62.1	44	35	36	89
1997—Arizona NFL	10	4-4	4-4	3-7	0-2	11-17	64.7	45	19	19	52
1998—Arizona NFL	12	6-6	1-1	5-8	1-4	13-19	68.4	53	30	30	69
1999—Arizona NFL	1	0-0	0-0	0-0	0-0	0-0	0.0	0	0	0	0
—Oakland NFL	3	2-2	2-2	0-1	1-2	5-7	71.4	52	13	13	28
2000—Denver NFL	3	6-6	1-1	1-2	0-1	8-10	80.0	43	4	4	28
—Carolina NFL	12	11-11	6-7	7-8	2-2	26-28	92.9	52	20	20	98
2001—Tennessee NFL	16	6-6	5-5	8-15	1-2	20-28	71.4	51	34	35	94
2002—Tennessee NFL	16	9-9	10-12	5-8	1-2	25-31	80.6	53	36	36	111
Pro totals (7 years)	89	52-52	36-43	32-57	6-17	126-169	74.6	53	191	193	569

NEIL, DAN   G   BRONCOS

PERSONAL: Born October 21, 1973, in Houston. ... 6-2/285. ... Full name: Daniel Neil.
HIGH SCHOOL: Cypress Creek (Houston).
COLLEGE: Texas.
TRANSACTIONS/CAREER NOTES: Selected by Denver Broncos in third round (67th pick overall) of 1997 NFL draft. ... Signed by Broncos (July 17, 1997). ... Granted free agency (February 11, 2000). ... Re-signed by Broncos (April 28, 2000) ... Granted unconditional free agency (March 2, 2001). ... Re-signed by Broncos (March 2, 2001).
PLAYING EXPERIENCE: Denver NFL, 1997-2002. ... Games/Games started: 1997 (3/0), 1998 (16/16), 1999 (15/15), 2000 (16/16), 2001 (15/15), 2002 (16/16). Total: 81/78.
CHAMPIONSHIP GAME EXPERIENCE: Member of Broncos for AFC championship game (1997 season); inactive. ... Member of Super Bowl championship team (1997 season); inactive. ... Played in AFC championship game (1998 season). ... Member of Super Bowl championship team (1998 season).
HONORS: Named guard on THE SPORTING NEWS college All-America first team (1996).

NELSON, JIM   LB   COLTS

PERSONAL: Born April 16, 1975, in Riverside, Calif. ... 6-1/234. ... Full name: James Robert Nelson.
HIGH SCHOOL: McDonough (Waldorf, Md.).
COLLEGE: Penn State (degree in criminal justice).
TRANSACTIONS/CAREER NOTES: Signed as non-drafted free agent by San Francisco 49ers (April 24, 1998). ... Claimed on waivers by Green Bay Packers (July 20, 1998). ... Released by Packers (August 25, 1998). ... Re-signed by Packers to practice squad (September 14, 1998). ... Activated (December 29, 1998; did not play. ... Claimed on waivers by Minnesota Vikings (August 28, 2000). ... Granted free agency (March 1, 2002). ... Re-signed by Vikings (April 23, 2002). ... Granted unconditional free agency (February 28, 2003). ... Signed by Indianapolis Colts (March 22, 2003).
CHAMPIONSHIP GAME EXPERIENCE: Played in NFC championship game (2000 season).

Year Team	G	GS	TOTALS			INTERCEPTIONS			
			Tk.	Ast.	Sks.	No.	Yds.	Avg.	TD
1998—Green Bay NFL			Did not play.						
1999—Green Bay NFL	16	0	7	1	0.0	1	0	0.0	0
2000—Minnesota NFL	16	0	3	3	0.0	0	0	0.0	0
2001—Minnesota NFL	16	2	21	16	0.0	0	0	0.0	0
2002—Minnesota NFL	16	2	7	2	0.0	0	0	0.0	0
Pro totals (4 years)	64	4	38	22	0.0	1	0	0.0	0

N

NESBIT, JAMAR   G   JAGUARS

PERSONAL: Born December 17, 1976, in Summerville, S.C. ... 6-4/330. ... Full name: Jamar Kendric Nesbit.
HIGH SCHOOL: Summerville (S.C.).
COLLEGE: South Carolina.
TRANSACTIONS/CAREER NOTES: Signed as non-drafted free agent by Carolina Panthers (April 18, 1999). ... Granted free agency (March 1, 2002). ... Re-signed by Panthers (June 21, 2002). ... Granted unconditional free agency (February 28, 2003). ... Signed by Jacksonville Jaguars (May 5, 2003).
PLAYING EXPERIENCE: Carolina NFL, 1999-2002. ... Games/Games started: 1999 (7/0), 2000 (16/16), 2001 (16/16), 2002 (14/13). Total: 53/45.

NEWBERRY, JEREMY   C   49ERS

PERSONAL: Born March 23, 1976, in Antioch, Calif. ... 6-5/310. ... Full name: Jeremy David Newberry.
HIGH SCHOOL: Antioch (Calif.).
COLLEGE: California.
TRANSACTIONS/CAREER NOTES: Selected by after junior season San Francisco 49ers in second round (58th pick overall) of 1998 NFL draft. ... Signed by San Francisco 49ers (July 18, 1998). ... On physically unable to perform list with knee injury (July 17-November 7, 1998). ... Active for one game (1998); did not play. ... Granted unconditional free agency (March 1, 2002). ... Re-signed by 49ers (March 12, 2002).
PLAYING EXPERIENCE: San Francisco NFL, 1999-2002. ... Games/Games started: 1999 (16/16), 2000 (16/16), 2001 (15/15), 2002 (16/16). Total: 63/63.
HONORS: Played in Pro Bowl (2001 and 2002 seasons).

NEWMAN, KEITH — LB — FALCONS

PERSONAL: Born January 19, 1977, in Tampa. ... 6-2/248. ... Full name: Keith Anthony Newman.
HIGH SCHOOL: Thomas Jefferson (Tampa).
COLLEGE: North Carolina.
TRANSACTIONS/CAREER NOTES: Selected by Buffalo Bills in fourth round (119th pick overall) of 1999 NFL draft. ... Signed by Bills (July 27, 1999). ... Granted free agency (March 1, 2002). ... Re-signed by Bills (May 21, 2002). ... Granted unconditional free agency (February 28, 2003). ... Signed by Atlanta Falcons (March 17, 2003).

Year Team	G	GS	TOTALS Tk.	Ast.	Sks.	INTERCEPTIONS No.	Yds.	Avg.	TD
1999—Buffalo NFL	3	0	0	1	0.0	0	0	0.0	0
2000—Buffalo NFL	16	16	44	18	8.0	0	0	0.0	0
2001—Buffalo NFL	16	16	62	21	3.5	0	0	0.0	0
2002—Buffalo NFL	16	10	21	13	3.0	0	0	0.0	0
Pro totals (4 years)	51	42	127	53	14.5	0	0	0.0	0

NEWSON, TONY — LB — CHIEFS

PERSONAL: Born September 11, 1979, in Las Vegas. ... 6-0/247. ... Full name: Tony Roderick Newson.
HIGH SCHOOL: Cheyenne (Las Vegas).
COLLEGE: Utah State.
TRANSACTIONS/CAREER NOTES: Signed as non-drafted free agent by Kansas City Chiefs (April 23, 2002). ... Released by Chiefs (September 1, 2002). ... Re-signed by Chiefs to practice squad (September 3, 2002). ... Activated (December 4, 2002).

Year Team	G	GS	TOTALS Tk.	Ast.	Sks.	INTERCEPTIONS No.	Yds.	Avg.	TD
2002—Kansas City NFL	4	0	0	0	0.0	0	0	0.0	0

NGUYEN, DAT — LB — COWBOYS

PERSONAL: Born September 25, 1975, in Fulton, Texas. ... 5-11/243. ... Name pronounced WIN.
HIGH SCHOOL: Rockport-Fulton (Rockport, Texas).
COLLEGE: Texas A&M (degree in agricultural development).
TRANSACTIONS/CAREER NOTES: Selected by Dallas Cowboys in third round (85th pick overall) of 1999 NFL draft. ... Signed by Cowboys (July 26, 1999). ... Granted free agency (March 1, 2002). ... Re-signed by Cowboys (April 16, 2002).
HONORS: Lombardi Award winner (1998). ... Named inside linebacker on THE SPORTING NEWS college All-America first team (1998).

Year Team	G	GS	TOTALS Tk.	Ast.	Sks.	INTERCEPTIONS No.	Yds.	Avg.	TD
1999—Dallas NFL	16	0	26	5	1.0	1	6	6.0	0
2000—Dallas NFL	10	5	42	6	0.0	2	31	15.5	0
2001—Dallas NFL	16	16	91	22	0.0	0	0	0.0	0
2002—Dallas NFL	8	8	42	10	1.0	0	0	0.0	0
Pro totals (4 years)	50	29	201	43	2.0	3	37	12.3	0

NICKERSON, HARDY — LB

N

PERSONAL: Born September 1, 1965, in Compton, Calif. ... 6-2/230. ... Full name: Hardy Otto Nickerson.
HIGH SCHOOL: Verbum Dei (Los Angeles).
COLLEGE: California (degree in sociology, 1986).
TRANSACTIONS/CAREER NOTES: Selected by Pittsburgh Steelers in fifth round (122nd pick overall) of 1987 NFL draft. ... Signed by Steelers (July 26, 1987). ... On injured reserve with ankle and knee injuries (November 3-December 16, 1989). ... Granted free agency (February 1, 1992). ... Re-signed by Steelers (June 15, 1992). ... Granted unconditional free agency (March 1, 1993). ... Signed by Tampa Bay Buccaneers (March 18, 1993). ... Granted unconditional free agency (February 16, 1996). ... Re-signed by Buccaneers (February 22, 1996). ... On injured reserve with heart problems (November 25, 1998-remainder of season). ... Granted unconditional free agency (February 11, 2000). ... Signed by Jacksonville Jaguars (February 22, 2000). ... On injured reserve with knee injury (December 5, 2000-remainder of season). ... Released by Jaguars (June 3, 2002). ... Signed by Green Bay Packers (June 12, 2002). ... Granted unconditional free agency (February 28, 2003).
CHAMPIONSHIP GAME EXPERIENCE: Played in NFC championship game (1999 season).
HONORS: Named linebacker on THE SPORTING NEWS college All-America second team (1985). ... Named inside linebacker on THE SPORTING NEWS NFL All-Pro team (1993). ... Played in Pro Bowl (1993 and 1996-1999 seasons).

Year Team	G	GS	TOTALS Tk.	Ast.	Sks.	INTERCEPTIONS No.	Yds.	Avg.	TD
1987—Pittsburgh NFL	12	0	10	7	0.0	0	0	0.0	0
1988—Pittsburgh NFL	15	10	73	26	3.5	1	0	0.0	0
1989—Pittsburgh NFL	10	8	26	9	1.0	0	0	0.0	0
1990—Pittsburgh NFL	16	14	58	9	2.0	0	0	0.0	0
1991—Pittsburgh NFL	16	14	70	24	1.0	0	0	0.0	0
1992—Pittsburgh NFL	15	15	68	46	2.0	0	0	0.0	0
1993—Tampa Bay NFL	16	16	124	90	1.0	1	6	6.0	0
1994—Tampa Bay NFL	14	14	86	36	1.0	2	9	4.5	0
1995—Tampa Bay NFL	16	16	89	54	1.5	2	24	12.0	0
1996—Tampa Bay NFL	16	16	76	44	3.0	2	24	12.0	0
1997—Tampa Bay NFL	16	16	105	42	1.0	0	0	0.0	0
1998—Tampa Bay NFL	10	10	45	25	1.0	0	0	0.0	0
1999—Tampa Bay NFL	16	16	65	45	0.5	2	18	9.0	0
2000—Jacksonville NFL	6	6	27	4	1.0	1	10	10.0	0
2001—Jacksonville NFL	15	14	89	28	0.0	3	4	1.3	0
2002—Green Bay NFL	16	15	49	37	1.5	0	0	0.0	0
Pro totals (16 years)	225	200	1060	526	21.0	12	71	5.9	0

NIX, JOHN　　　　　DT　　　　　COWBOYS

PERSONAL: Born November 24, 1976, in Lucendale, Miss. ... 6-1/313.
HIGH SCHOOL: George County (Miss.).
COLLEGE: Southern Mississippi.
TRANSACTIONS/CAREER NOTES: Selected by Dallas Cowboys in seventh round (240th pick overall) of 2001 NFL draft. ... Signed by Cowboys (July 20, 2001).

			TOTALS		
Year　Team	G	GS	Tk.	Ast.	Sks.
2001—Dallas NFL	16	0	10	1	0.0
2002—Dallas NFL	14	0	7	3	0.0
Pro totals (2 years)	30	0	17	4	0.0

NOBLE, BRANDON　　　　　DT　　　　　REDSKINS

PERSONAL: Born April 10, 1974, in San Rafael, Calif. ... 6-2/312. ... Full name: Brandon Patrick Noble.
HIGH SCHOOL: First Colonial (Virginia Beach, Va.).
COLLEGE: Penn State.
TRANSACTIONS/CAREER NOTES: Signed as non-drafted free agent by San Francisco 49ers (April 29, 1997). ... Released by 49ers (August 19, 1997). ... Re-signed by 49ers to practice squad (November 12, 1997). ... Released by 49ers (November 19, 1997). ... Re-signed by 49ers (January 13, 1998). ... Assigned by 49ers to Barcelona Dragons in 1998 NFL Europe enhancement allocation program (February 18, 1998). ... Released by 49ers (August 25, 1998). ... Re-signed by 49ers to practice squad (December 3, 1998). ... Granted free agency after 1998 season. ... Signed by Dallas Cowboys (February 2, 1999). ... Assigned by Cowboys to Barcelona Dragons in 1999 NFL Europe enhancement allocation program (February 22, 1999). ... Granted free agency (March 1, 2002). ... Re-signed by Cowboys (April 15, 2002). ... Granted unconditional free agency (February 28, 2003). ... Signed by Washington Redskins (March 1, 2003).

			TOTALS			INTERCEPTIONS			
Year　Team	G	GS	Tk.	Ast.	Sks.	No.	Yds.	Avg.	TD
1998—Barcelona NFLE	...	...	...	...	2.0	1	0	0.0	0
1999—Barcelona NFLE	...	...	...	...	5.0	0	0	0.0	0
—Dallas NFL	16	0	15	8	3.0	0	0	0.0	0
2000—Dallas NFL	16	9	36	7	1.0	0	0	0.0	0
2001—Dallas NFL	16	16	27	10	3.5	0	0	0.0	0
2002—Dallas NFL	16	16	23	8	0.0	0	0	0.0	0
NFL Europe totals (2 years)	...	...	...	...	7.0	1	0	0.0	0
NFL totals (4 years)	64	41	101	33	7.5	0	0	0.0	0
Pro totals (6 years)	...	...	...	...	14.5	1	0	0.0	0

NORMAN, JOSH　　　　　TE　　　　　CHARGERS

PERSONAL: Born July 27, 1980, in Midland, Texas. ... 6-2/236.
HIGH SCHOOL: Robert E. Lee (Midland, Texas).
COLLEGE: Oklahoma.
TRANSACTIONS/CAREER NOTES: Signed as non-drafted free agent by San Diego Chargers (April 26, 2002).
SINGLE GAME HIGHS (regular season): Receptions—4 (December 29, 2002, vs. Seattle); yards—62 (December 29, 2002, vs. Seattle); and touchdown receptions—1 (September 8, 2002, vs. Cincinnati).

			RECEIVING			
Year　Team	G	GS	No.	Yds.	Avg.	TD
2002—San Diego NFL	11	1	16	201	12.6	1

NORRIS, MORAN　　　　　FB　　　　　TEXANS

N

PERSONAL: Born June 16, 1978, in Houston. ... 6-1/250. ... Full name: Torrance Moran Norris.
HIGH SCHOOL: James Madison (Houston).
COLLEGE: Kansas.
TRANSACTIONS/CAREER NOTES: Selected by New Orleans Saints in fourth round (115th pick overall) of 2001 NFL draft. ... Signed by Saints (July 27, 2001). ... Claimed on waivers by Houston Texans (September 18, 2002).

			RUSHING				KICKOFF RETURNS				TOTALS			
Year　Team	G	GS	Att.	Yds.	Avg.	TD	No.	Yds.	Avg.	TD	TD	2pt.	Pts.	Fum.
2001—New Orleans NFL	5	0	0	0	0.0	0	0	0	0.0	0	0	0	0	0
2002—Houston NFL	13	0	0	0	0.0	0	2	11	5.5	0	0	0	0	0
Pro totals (2 years)	18	0	0	0	0.0	0	2	11	5.5	0	0	0	0	0

NORTHCUTT, DENNIS　　　　　WR　　　　　BROWNS

PERSONAL: Born December 22, 1977, in Los Angeles. ... 5-11/175.
HIGH SCHOOL: Dorsey (Los Angeles).
COLLEGE: Arizona.
TRANSACTIONS/CAREER NOTES: Selected by Cleveland Browns in second round (32nd pick overall) of 2000 NFL draft. ... Signed by Browns (July 19, 2000). ... On non-football injury list with shoulder injury (July 23-September 30, 2001).
HONORS: Named wide receiver on The Sporting News college All-America second team (1999).
SINGLE GAME HIGHS (regular season): Receptions—8 (October 6, 2002, vs. Baltimore); yards—165 (October 6, 2002, vs. Baltimore); and touchdown receptions—2 (October 6, 2002, vs. Baltimore).
STATISTICAL PLATEAUS: 100-yard receiving games: 2002 (1).

Year Team	G	GS	RECEIVING				PUNT RETURNS				TOTALS			
			No.	Yds.	Avg.	TD	No.	Yds.	Avg.	TD	TD	2pt.	Pts.	Fum.
2000—Cleveland NFL	15	8	39	422	10.8	0	27	289	10.7	0	0	0	0	1
2001—Cleveland NFL	12	7	18	211	11.7	0	15	86	5.7	0	0	0	0	3
2002—Cleveland NFL	13	0	38	601	15.8	5	25	367	14.7	†2	8	1	50	2
Pro totals (3 years)	40	15	95	1234	13.0	5	67	742	11.1	2	8	1	50	6

NUGENT, DAVID — DE — RAVENS

PERSONAL: Born October 27, 1977, in Cincinnati. ... 6-4/295. ... Full name: David Michael Nugent.
HIGH SCHOOL: Houston (Germantown, Tenn.).
COLLEGE: Purdue.
TRANSACTIONS/CAREER NOTES: Selected by New England Patriots in sixth round (201st pick overall) of 2000 NFL draft. ... Signed by Patriots (July 12, 2000). ... Released by Patriots (September 2, 2001). ... Re-signed by Patriots to practice squad (September 4, 2001). ... Activated (October 15, 2001). ... Released by Patriots (September 1, 2002). ... Signed by Baltimore Ravens (October 29, 2002). ... Granted free agency (February 28, 2003). ... Re-signed by Ravens (April 24, 2003).
CHAMPIONSHIP GAME EXPERIENCE: Member of Patriots for AFC championship game (2001 season); inactive. ... Member of Super Bowl championship team (2001 season); inactive.

Year Team	G	GS	TOTALS		
			Tk.	Ast.	Sks.
2000—New England NFL	6	0	1	0	0.0
2001—New England NFL	9	1	3	1	0.0
2002—Baltimore NFL	9	0	5	4	0.0
Pro totals (3 years)	24	1	9	5	0.0

NUTTEN, TOM — G — JETS

PERSONAL: Born June 8, 1971, in Magog, Quebec. ... 6-5/310. ... Full name: Thomas Nutten. ... Name pronounced NEW-ton.
HIGH SCHOOL: Champlain Regional (Lennoxville, Quebec).
COLLEGE: Western Michigan (degree in marketing, 1994).
TRANSACTIONS/CAREER NOTES: Selected by Hamilton Tiger-Cats in first round (first pick overall) of 1995 CFL draft. ... Selected by Buffalo Bills in seventh round (221st pick overall) of 1995 NFL draft. ... Signed by Bills (June 12, 1995). ... Released by Bills (August 27, 1995). ... Re-signed by Bills to practice squad (August 29, 1995). ... Activated (October 10, 1995). ... Released by Bills (August 26, 1996). ... Signed by Denver Broncos (January 14, 1997). ... Released by Broncos (July 16, 1997). ... Signed by Tiger-Cats of CFL (July 28, 1997). ... Signed by St. Louis Rams (January 16, 1998). ... Assigned by Rams to Amsterdam Admirals in 1998 NFL Europe enhancement allocation program (February 18, 1998). ... On injured reserve with neck injury (November 17, 1998-remainder of season). ... Granted free agency (February 11, 2000). ... Re-signed by Rams (February 12, 2000). ... On injured reserve with broken leg (November 27, 2002-remainder of season). ... Granted unconditional free agency (February 28, 2003). ... Signed by New York Jets (March 7, 2003).
PLAYING EXPERIENCE: Buffalo NFL, 1995; Hamilton CFL, 1997; Amsterdam NFLE, 1998; St. Louis NFL, 1998-2002. ... Games/Games started: 1995 (1/0), 1997 (13/games started unavailable), NFLE 1998 (games played unavailable), NFL 1998 (4/2), 1999 (14/14), 2000 (16/16), 2001 (15/14), 2002 (11/11). Total NFL: 61/57. Total CFL: 13/-.
CHAMPIONSHIP GAME EXPERIENCE: Played in NFC championship game (1999 and 2001 seasons). ... Member of Super Bowl championship team (1999 season). ... Played in Super Bowl XXXVI (2001 season).

NWOKORIE, CHUKIE — DE — PACKERS

PERSONAL: Born July 10, 1975, in Tuskegee, Ala. ... 6-3/280. ... Full name: Chijioke Obinna Nwokorie. ... Name pronounced CHEW-key wuh-CORE-e.
HIGH SCHOOL: Lafayette-Jefferson (Lafayette, Ind.).
COLLEGE: Purdue.
TRANSACTIONS/CAREER NOTES: Signed as non-drafted free agent by Indianapolis Colts (April 20, 1999). ... Released by Colts (October 25, 2000). ... Re-signed by Colts to practice squad (October 26, 2000). ... Activated (December 22, 2000). ... Granted free agency (March 1, 2002). ... Re-signed by Colts (May 21, 2002). ... On physically unable to perform list with back injury (August 26-November 6, 2002). ... Granted unconditional free agency (February 28, 2003). ... Signed by Green Bay Packers (April 8, 2003).

Year Team	G	GS	TOTALS		
			Tk.	Ast.	Sks.
1999—Indianapolis NFL	1	0	0	0	0.0
2000—Indianapolis NFL	1	0	0	0	0.0
2001—Indianapolis NFL	16	5	32	9	5.0
2002—Indianapolis NFL	3	0	1	1	0.0
Pro totals (4 years)	21	5	33	10	5.0

O'DONNELL, NEIL — QB

PERSONAL: Born July 3, 1966, in Morristown, N.J. ... 6-3/228. ... Full name: Neil Kennedy O'Donnell.
HIGH SCHOOL: Madison-Boro (Madison, N.J.).
COLLEGE: Maryland (degree in economics, 1990).
TRANSACTIONS/CAREER NOTES: Selected by Pittsburgh Steelers in third round (70th pick overall) of 1990 NFL draft. ... Signed by Steelers (August 8, 1990). ... Active for three games (1990); did not play. ... Granted free agency (March 1, 1993). ... Tendered offer sheet by Tampa Bay Buccaneers (April 2, 1993). ... Offer matched by Steelers (April 12, 1993). ... Granted unconditional free agency (February 16, 1996). ... Signed by New York Jets (February 29, 1996). ... Released by Jets (June 24, 1998). ... Signed by Cincinnati Bengals (July 7, 1998). ... On injured reserve with hand injury (December 9, 1998-remainder of season). ... Released by Bengals (April 19, 1999). ... Signed by Tennessee Titans (July 23, 1999). ... Granted unconditional free agency (February 11, 2000). ... Re-signed by Titans (April 25, 2000). ... Released by Titans (February 20, 2003).

CHAMPIONSHIP GAME EXPERIENCE: Played in AFC championship game (1994, 1995 and 1999 seasons). ... Played in Super Bowl XXX (1995 season). ... Member of Titans for Super Bowl XXXIV (1999 season); did not play. ... Member of Titans for AFC championship game (2002); did not play.
HONORS: Played in Pro Bowl (1992 season).
RECORDS: Holds NFL career record for lowest interception percentage—2.09.
POST SEASON RECORDS: Holds NFL postseason single-game record for most passes attempted without an interception—54 (January 15, 1995, vs. San Diego).
SINGLE GAME HIGHS (regular season): Attempts—55 (December 24, 1995, vs. Green Bay); completions—34 (November 5, 1995, vs. Chicago); yards—377 (November 19, 1995, vs. Cincinnati); and touchdown passes—5 (August 31, 1997, vs. Seattle).
STATISTICAL PLATEAUS: 300-yard passing games: 1991 (1), 1993 (1), 1995 (4), 1996 (2), 1997 (1), 1998 (1), 1999 (2). Total: 12.
MISCELLANEOUS: Regular-season record as starting NFL quarterback: 54-45 (.545). ... Postseason record as starting NFL quarterback: 3-4 (.429).

Year Team	G	GS	PASSING Att.	Cmp.	Pct.	Yds.	TD	Int.	Avg.	Skd.	Rat.	RUSHING Att.	Yds.	Avg.	TD	TOTALS TD	2pt.	Pts.
1990—Pittsburgh NFL											Did not play.							
1991—Pittsburgh NFL	12	8	286	156	54.5	1963	11	7	6.86	30	78.8	18	82	4.6	1	1	0	6
1992—Pittsburgh NFL	12	12	313	185	59.1	2283	13	9	7.29	27	83.6	27	5	0.2	1	1	0	6
1993—Pittsburgh NFL	16	15	486	270	55.6	3208	14	7	6.60	41	79.5	26	111	4.3	0	0	0	0
1994—Pittsburgh NFL	14	14	370	212	57.3	2443	13	9	6.60	35	78.9	31	80	2.6	1	1	0	6
1995—Pittsburgh NFL	12	12	416	246	59.1	2970	17	7	7.14	15	87.7	24	45	1.9	0	0	0	0
1996—New York Jets NFL	6	6	188	110	58.5	1147	4	7	6.10	18	67.8	6	30	5.0	0	0	0	0
1997—New York Jets NFL	15	14	460	259	56.3	2796	17	7	6.08	45	80.3	32	36	1.1	1	1	0	6
1998—Cincinnati NFL	13	11	343	212	§61.8	2216	15	4	6.46	30	90.2	13	34	2.6	0	0	0	0
1999—Tennessee NFL	8	5	195	116	59.5	1382	10	5	7.09	9	87.6	19	1	0.1	0	0	0	0
2000—Tennessee NFL	5	1	64	36	56.3	530	2	3	8.28	3	74.3	9	-2	-0.2	0	0	0	0
2001—Tennessee NFL	5	1	76	42	55.3	496	2	2	6.53	6	73.1	6	28	4.7	0	0	0	0
2002—Tennessee NFL	4	0	5	3	60.0	24	0	0	4.80	0	72.1	3	-3	-1.0	0	0	0	0
Pro totals (12 years)	122	99	3202	1847	57.7	21458	118	67	6.70	259	81.6	214	447	2.1	4	4	0	24

O'DWYER, MATT　　　　G　　　　BENGALS

PERSONAL: Born September 1, 1972, in Lincolnshire, Ill. ... 6-5/310. ... Full name: Matthew Phillip O'Dwyer.
HIGH SCHOOL: Adlai E. Stevenson (Prairie View, Ill.).
COLLEGE: Northwestern.
TRANSACTIONS/CAREER NOTES: Selected by New York Jets in second round (33rd pick overall) of 1995 NFL draft. ... Signed by Jets (July 20, 1995). ... Granted unconditional free agency (February 12, 1999). ... Signed by Cincinnati Bengals (June 19, 1999). ... Suspended two games by NFL for involvement in bar fight (March 14, 2000). ... On injured reserve with broken ankle (November 20, 2000-remainder of season). ... Granted unconditional free agency (March 2, 2001). ... Re-signed by Bengals (March 2, 2001).
PLAYING EXPERIENCE: New York Jets NFL, 1995-1998; Cincinnati NFL, 1999-2002. ... Games/Games started: 1995 (12/2), 1996 (16/16), 1997 (16/16), 1998 (16/16), 1999 (16/16), 2000 (10/10), 2001 (12/12), 2002 (16/16). Total: 114/104.
CHAMPIONSHIP GAME EXPERIENCE: Played in AFC championship game (1998 season).

O'HARA, SHAUN　　　　C　　　　BROWNS

PERSONAL: Born June 23, 1977, in Hillsborough, N.J. ... 6-3/306.
HIGH SCHOOL: Hillsborough (N.J.).
COLLEGE: Rutgers.
TRANSACTIONS/CAREER NOTES: Signed as non-drafted free agent by Cleveland Browns (April 17, 2000). ... Granted free agency (February 28, 2003).
PLAYING EXPERIENCE: Cleveland NFL, 2000-2002. ... Games/Games started: 2000 (9/4), 2001 (16/4), 2002 (16/16). Total: 41/24.

O'LEARY, DAN　　　　TE　　　　GIANTS

PERSONAL: Born September 1, 1977, in Cleveland. ... 6-3/252. ... Full name: Daniel Edward O'Leary.
HIGH SCHOOL: St. Ignatius (Ohio).
COLLEGE: Notre Dame.
TRANSACTIONS/CAREER NOTES: Selected by Buffalo Bills in sixth round (195th pick overall) of 2001 NFL draft. ... Signed by Bills (June 12, 2001). ... On injured reserve with wrist injury (November 21, 2001-remainder of season). ... Released by Bills (August 27, 2002). ... Signed by Tennessee Titans to practice squad (September 11, 2002). ... Signed by Pittsburgh Steelers off Titans practice squad (September 24, 2002). ... Released by Steelers (November 19, 2002). ... Signed by New York Giants to practice squad (November 27, 2002). ... Activated (November 30, 2002).

Year Team	G	GS	RECEIVING No.	Yds.	Avg.	TD
2001—Buffalo NFL	8	0	0	0	0.0	0
2002—New York Giants NFL	5	0	0	0	0.0	0
—Pittsburgh NFL	4	0	0	0	0.0	0
Pro totals (2 years)	17	0	0	0	0.0	0

O'NEAL, DELTHA　　　　CB/PR　　　　BRONCOS

PERSONAL: Born January 30, 1977, in Palo Alto, Calif. ... 5-10/196. ... Full name: Deltha Lee O'Neal III.
HIGH SCHOOL: West (Milpitas, Calif.).
COLLEGE: California.

TRANSACTIONS/CAREER NOTES: Selected by Denver Broncos in first round (15th pick overall) of 2000 NFL draft. ... Signed by Broncos (July 21, 2000).
HONORS: Named kick returner on THE SPORTING NEWS college All-America first team (1999). ... Named cornerback on THE SPORTING NEWS college All-America second team (1999). ... Played in Pro Bowl (2001 season).

Year Team	G	GS	TOTALS			INTERCEPTIONS				PUNT RETURNS				KICKOFF RETURNS				TOTALS			
			Tk.	Ast.	Sks.	No.	Yds.	Avg.	TD	No.	Yds.	Avg.	TD	No.	Yds.	Avg.	TD	TD	2pt.	Pts.	Fum.
2000—Denver NFL	16	0	3	0	0.0	0	0	0.0	0	34	354	10.4	0	46	1102	24.0 ▲1	1	1	0	6	6
2001—Denver NFL	16	16	63	7	0.0	9	115	12.8	0	31	405	13.1	1	0	0	0.0	0	1	0	6	2
2002—Denver NFL	16	14	59	10	0.0	5	70	14.0	▲2	30	251	8.4	0	1	15	15.0	0	2	0	12	2
Pro totals (3 years)	48	30	125	17	0.0	14	185	13.2	2	95	1010	10.6	1	47	1117	23.8	1	4	0	24	10

O'SULLIVAN, DENNIS   C   JETS

PERSONAL: Born January 28, 1976, in Stony Point, N.Y. ... 6-3/300.
HIGH SCHOOL: North Rockland (Stony Point, N.Y.).
COLLEGE: Tulane.
TRANSACTIONS/CAREER NOTES: Signed as non-drafted free agent by San Francisco 49ers (April 20, 1999). ... Released by 49ers (September 5, 1999). ... Signed by New York Jets to practice squad (October 6, 1999). ... Activated (December 29, 1999); did not play. ... Released by Jets (August 26, 2000). ... Re-signed by Jets (December 26, 2000). ... Assigned by Jets to Amsterdam Admirals in 2001 NFL Europe enhancement allocation program (February 18, 2001). ... Released by Jets (September 2, 2001). ... Signed by San Diego Chargers (September 3, 2001). ... Released by Chargers (September 9, 2001). ... Signed by Jets to practice squad (October 4, 2001). ... Activated (January 8, 2002); did not play. ... Re-signed by Jets (April 2, 2003).
PLAYING EXPERIENCE: New York Jets NFL, 2002. ... Games/games started: 2002 (3/0).

OBEN, ROMAN   OT   BUCCANEERS

PERSONAL: Born October 9, 1972, in Cameroon, West Africa. ... 6-4/305. ... Name pronounced OH-bin.
HIGH SCHOOL: Gonzaga (Washington, D.C.), then Fork Union (Va.) Military Academy.
COLLEGE: Louisville (degree in economics).
TRANSACTIONS/CAREER NOTES: Selected by New York Giants in third round (66th pick overall) of 1996 NFL draft. ... Signed by Giants (July 20, 1996). ... Granted free agency (February 12, 1999). ... Re-signed by Giants (July 28, 1999). ... Granted unconditional free agency (February 11, 2000). ... Signed by Cleveland Browns (March 9, 2000). ... Released by Browns (February 25, 2002). ... Signed by Tampa Bay Buccaneers (May 20, 2002). ... Granted unconditional free agency (February 28, 2003). ... Re-signed by Buccaneers (March 31, 2003).
PLAYING EXPERIENCE: New York Giants NFL, 1996-1999; Cleveland NFL, 2000 and 2001. Tampa Bay NFL, 2002. ... Games/Games started: 1996 (2/0), 1997 (16/16), 1998 (16/16), 1999 (16/16), 2000 (16/16), 2001 (16/14), 2002 (16/16). Total: 98/94.
CHAMPIONSHIP GAME EXPERIENCE: Played in NFC championship game (2002 season). ... Member of Super Bowl championship team (2002 season).

OFFICE, KENDRICK   DE

PERSONAL: Born August 2, 1978, in Butler, Ala. ... 6-5/270. ... Full name: Kendrick LaShawn Office.
HIGH SCHOOL: Choctaw (Ala.).
COLLEGE: West Alabama.
TRANSACTIONS/CAREER NOTES: Signed as non-drafted free agent by Buffalo Bills (April 24, 2001). ... Claimed on waivers by Cleveland Browns (August 29, 2001). ... Released by Browns (September 2, 2001). ... Signed by Bills to practice squad (September 4, 2001). ... Activated (October 3, 2001). ... Granted free agency (February 28, 2003).

Year Team	G	GS	TOTALS		
			Tk.	Ast.	Sks.
2001—Buffalo NFL	7	1	11	5	3.0
2002—Buffalo NFL	10	1	4	9	0.0
Pro totals (2 years)	17	2	15	14	3.0

OFFORD, WILLIE   S   VIKINGS

PERSONAL: Born December 22, 1978, in Palatka, Fla. ... 6-1/215.
HIGH SCHOOL: Palatka (Fla.).
COLLEGE: South Carolina.
TRANSACTIONS/CAREER NOTES: Selected by Minnesota Vikings in third round (70th pick overall) of 2002 NFL draft. ... Signed by Vikings (July 25, 2002).

Year Team	G	GS	TOTALS			INTERCEPTIONS			
			Tk.	Ast.	Sks.	No.	Yds.	Avg.	TD
2002—Minnesota NFL	12	6	23	4	0.0	1	6	6.0	0

OGBOGU, ERIC   DE

PERSONAL: Born July 18, 1975, in Irvington, N.Y. ... 6-4/270. ... Name pronounced a-BAH-goo.
HIGH SCHOOL: Archbishop Stepinac (White Plains, N.Y.).
COLLEGE: Maryland.
TRANSACTIONS/CAREER NOTES: Selected by New York Jets in sixth round (163rd pick overall) of 1998 NFL draft. ... Signed by Jets (July 2, 1998). ... On injured reserve with shoulder injury (August 7, 2000-entire season). ... Granted unconditional free agency (March 1, 2002). ... Signed by Cincinnati Bengals (April 29, 2002). ... Released by Bengals (May 27, 2003).
CHAMPIONSHIP GAME EXPERIENCE: Played in AFC championship game (1998 season).

Year Team	G	GS	TOTALS Tk.	Ast.	Sks.
1998—New York Jets NFL	12	0	5	3	0.0
1999—New York Jets NFL	14	0	9	4	1.0
2000—New York Jets NFL			Did not play.		
2001—New York Jets NFL	15	0	15	3	0.0
2002—Cincinnati NFL	12	0	1	2	0.0
Pro totals (4 years)	**53**	**0**	**30**	**12**	**1.0**

OGDEN, JEFF   WR

PERSONAL: Born February 22, 1975, in Snohomish, Wash. ... 6-0/190. ... Full name: Jeffery Ogden.
HIGH SCHOOL: Snohomish (Wash.).
COLLEGE: Eastern Washington.
TRANSACTIONS/CAREER NOTES: Signed as non-drafted free agent by Dallas Cowboys (April 21, 1998). ... Assigned by Cowboys to Rhein Fire in 2000 NFL Europe enhancement allocation program (February 18, 2000). ... Traded by Cowboys to Miami Dolphins for future seventh-round pick (August 22, 2000). ... Granted free agency (March 2, 2001). ... Re-signed by Dolphins (April 20, 2001). ... Granted unconditional free agency (March 1, 2002). ... Re-signed by Dolphins (April 3, 2002). ... Released by Dolphins (September 1, 2002). ... Signed by Baltimore Ravens (September 10, 2002). ... Granted unconditional free agency (February 28, 2003).
SINGLE GAME HIGHS (regular season): Receptions—4 (November 22, 1998, vs. Seattle); yards—28 (December 22, 2001, vs. New England); and touchdown receptions—1 (December 22, 2001, vs. New England).

Year Team	G	GS	RECEIVING No.	Yds.	Avg.	TD	PUNT RETURNS No.	Yds.	Avg.	TD	TOTALS TD	2pt.	Pts.	Fum.
1998—Dallas NFL	16	0	8	63	7.9	0	0	0	0.0	0	0	0	0	1
1999—Dallas NFL	16	0	12	144	12.0	0	4	28	7.0	0	0	0	0	0
2000—Rhein NFLE	...	...	44	635	14.4	7	4	28	7.0	0	0	0	0	0
—Miami NFL	16	0	2	24	12.0	0	19	323	17.0	1	1	0	6	1
2001—Miami NFL	16	0	6	73	12.2	1	32	377	11.8	0	1	0	6	3
2002—Baltimore NFL	3	0	0	0	0.0	0	2	21	10.5	0	0	0	0	0
NFL Europe totals (1 year)	...	...	44	635	14.4	7	4	28	7.0	0	0	0	0	0
NFL totals (5 years)	67	0	28	304	10.9	1	57	749	13.1	1	2	0	12	5
Pro totals (6 years)	...	...	72	939	13.0	8	61	777	12.7	1	2	0	12	5

OGDEN, JONATHAN   OT   RAVENS

PERSONAL: Born July 31, 1974, in Washington, D.C. ... 6-9/340. ... Full name: Jonathan Phillip Ogden. ... Brother of Marques Ogden, offensive tackle, Jacksonville Jaguars.
HIGH SCHOOL: St. Alban's (Washington, D.C.).
COLLEGE: UCLA.
TRANSACTIONS/CAREER NOTES: Selected by Baltimore Ravens in first round (fourth pick overall) of 1996 NFL draft. ... Signed by Ravens (July 15, 1996).
PLAYING EXPERIENCE: Baltimore NFL, 1996-2002. ... Games/Games started: 1996 (16/16), 1997 (16/16), 1998 (13/13), 1999 (16/16), 2000 (15/15), 2001 (16/16), 2002 (16/16). Total: 108/108.
CHAMPIONSHIP GAME EXPERIENCE: Played in AFC championship game (2000 season). ... Member of Super Bowl championship team (2000 season).
HONORS: Outland Trophy winner (1995). ... Named offensive lineman on THE SPORTING NEWS college All-America first team (1995). ... Named offensive tackle on the THE SPORTING NEWS NFL All-Pro team (1997 and 2000-2002). ... Played in Pro Bowl (1997-2002 seasons).

OGUNLEYE, ADEWALE   DE   DOLPHINS

PERSONAL: Born August 9, 1977, in Brooklyn, N.Y. ... 6-4/255.
HIGH SCHOOL: Tottenville (Staten Island, N.Y.).
COLLEGE: Indiana.
TRANSACTIONS/CAREER NOTES: Signed as non-drafted free agent by Miami Dolphins (April 25, 2000). ... On non-football injury list with knee injury (August 22, 2000-entire season).

Year Team	G	GS	TOTALS Tk.	Ast.	Sks.
2001—Miami NFL	7	0	1	2	0.5
2002—Miami NFL	16	16	33	12	9.5
Pro totals (2 years)	**23**	**16**	**34**	**14**	**10.0**

OHALETE, IFEANYI   S   REDSKINS

PERSONAL: Born May 22, 1979, in Los Alamitos, Calif. ... 6-2/220.
HIGH SCHOOL: Los Alamitos (Calif.).
COLLEGE: Southern California.
TRANSACTIONS/CAREER NOTES: Signed as non-drafted free agent by Washington Redskins (April 25, 2001). ... Re-signed by Redskins (March 11, 2003).

Year Team	G	GS	TOTALS Tk.	Ast.	Sks.	INTERCEPTIONS No.	Yds.	Avg.	TD
2001—Washington NFL	16	0	0	0	0.0	1	12	12.0	0
2002—Washington NFL	16	10	44	15	1.0	3	109	36.3	1
Pro totals (2 years)	**32**	**10**	**44**	**15**	**1.0**	**4**	**121**	**30.3**	**1**

O

OKEAFOR, CHIKE   DE   SEAHAWKS

PERSONAL: Born March 27, 1976, in Grand Rapids, Mich. ... 6-4/265. ... Full name: Chikeze Russell Okeafor. ... Name pronounced chee-KAY oh-KEY-fer.
HIGH SCHOOL: West Lafayette (Ind.).
COLLEGE: Purdue.
TRANSACTIONS/CAREER NOTES: Selected by San Francisco 49ers in third round (89th pick overall) of 1999 NFL draft. ... Signed by 49ers (July 27, 1999). ... On non-football injury list with back injury (July 27-September 5, 1999). ... Granted free agency (March 1, 2002). ... Re-signed by 49ers (April 20, 2002). ... Granted unconditional free agency (February 28, 2003). ... Signed by Seattle Seahawks (April 4, 2003).

				TOTALS	
Year Team	G	GS	Tk.	Ast.	Sks.
1999—San Francisco NFL	12	0	10	0	1.0
2000—San Francisco NFL	15	0	22	9	2.0
2001—San Francisco NFL	14	3	23	10	2.5
2002—San Francisco NFL	16	16	32	11	6.0
Pro totals (4 years)	57	19	87	30	11.5

OKOBI, CHUKKY   C   STEELERS

PERSONAL: Born November 18, 1978, in Pittsburgh. ... 6-1/310. ... Full name: Chukwunweze Sonume Okobi.
HIGH SCHOOL: Trinity Prawling (N.Y.).
COLLEGE: Purdue.
TRANSACTIONS/CAREER NOTES: Selected by Pittsburgh Steelers in fifth round (146th pick overall) of 2001 NFL draft. ... Signed by Steelers (May 17, 2001). ... On physically unable to perform list with leg injury (July 20-August 14, 2001).
PLAYING EXPERIENCE: Pittsburgh NFL, 2001-2002. ... Games/Games started: 2001 (1/0), 2002 (13/5). Total: 14/5.
CHAMPIONSHIP GAME EXPERIENCE: Member of Steelers for AFC championship game (2001 season); inactive.

OLSON, BENJI   G   TITANS

PERSONAL: Born June 5, 1975, in Bremerton, Wash. ... 6-4/315. ... Full name: Benji Dempsey Olson.
HIGH SCHOOL: South Kitsap (Port Orchard, Wash.).
COLLEGE: Washington.
TRANSACTIONS/CAREER NOTES: Selected after junior season by Tennessee Oilers in fifth round (139th pick overall) of 1998 NFL draft. ... Signed by Oilers (June 29, 1998). ... Oilers franchise renamed Tennessee Titans for 1999 season (December 26, 1998). ... Granted free agency (March 2, 2001). ... Re-signed by Titans (July 25, 2001).
PLAYING EXPERIENCE: Tennessee NFL, 1998-2002. ... Games/Games started: 1998 (13/1), 1999 (16/16), 2000 (16/16), 2001 (16/16), 2002 (16/16). Total: 77/65.
CHAMPIONSHIP GAME EXPERIENCE: Played in AFC championship game (1999 and 2002 seasons). ... Played in Super Bowl XXXIV (1999 season).
HONORS: Named guard on THE SPORTING NEWS college All-America first team (1996).

OSIKA, CRAIG   C   49ERS

PERSONAL: Born December 4, 1979, in Merriville, Ind. ... 6-3/293.
HIGH SCHOOL: Hobart (Ind.).
COLLEGE: Indiana.
TRANSACTIONS/CAREER NOTES: Signed as non-drafted free agent by San Diego Chargers (April 26, 2002). ... Released by Chargers (September 1, 2002). ... Re-signed by Chargers to practice squad (September 3, 2002). ... Signed by San Francisco 49ers off Chargers practice squad (September 25, 2002). ... Assigned by 49ers to Amsterdam Admirals in 2003 NFL Europe enhancement allocation program (February 4, 2003).
PLAYING EXPERIENCE: San Francisco NFL, 2002. ... Games/games started: 2002 (1/0).

OURS, WES   RB   STEELERS

PERSONAL: Born December 30, 1977, in Rawlings, Md. ... 6-0/284.
HIGH SCHOOL: Westmar (Rawlings, Md.).
COLLEGE: West Virginia.
TRANSACTIONS/CAREER NOTES: Signed as non-drafted free agent by Indianapolis Colts (April 27, 2001). ... Claimed on waivers by Tennessee Titans (September 26, 2001). ... Claimed on waivers by Colts (November 21, 2001). ... Released by Colts (September 1, 2002). ... Signed by Pittsburgh Steelers (January 23, 2003). ... Assigned by Steelers to Amsterdam Admirals in 2003 NFL Europe enhancement allocation program (February 4, 2003).

			RUSHING				TOTALS			
Year Team	G	GS	Att.	Yds.	Avg.	TD	TD	2pt.	Pts.	Fum.
2001—Tennessee NFL	3	1	0	0	0.0	0	0	0	0	0
2002—						Did not play.				
Pro totals (1 years)	3	1	0	0	0.0	0	0	0	0	0

OVERHAUSER, CHAD   OT

PERSONAL: Born June 17, 1975, in Sacramento. ... 6-4/314. ... Full name: Chad Michael Overhauser.
HIGH SCHOOL: Rio Americano (Sacramento).
COLLEGE: UCLA.

TRANSACTIONS/CAREER NOTES: Selected by Chicago Bears in seventh round (217th pick overall) of 1998 NFL draft. ... Signed by Bears (June 16, 1998). ... Inactive for all 16 games (1998). ... On injured reserve with hamstring injury (August 31, 1999-remainder of season). ... Assigned by Bears to Amsterdam Admirals in 2000 NFL Europe enhancement allocation program (February 18, 2000). ... Traded by Bears to Seattle Seahawks for undisclosed pick in 2001 draft (August 27, 2000). ... Released by Seahawks (September 2, 2001). ... Signed by Atlanta Falcons to practice squad (October 22, 2001). ... Granted free agency following 2001 season. ... Signed by Houston Texans (January 15, 2002). ... Released by Texans (September 23, 2002). ... Re-signed by Texans to practice squad (September 24, 2002). ... Released by Texans (October 14, 2002).

PLAYING EXPERIENCE: Houston NFL, 2002. ... Games/games started: 2002 (3/0).

HONORS: Named offensive tackle on THE SPORTING NEWS college All-America first team (1997).

OVERSTREET, WILL   LB   FALCONS

PERSONAL: Born October 7, 1979, in Jackson, Miss. ... 6-2/259. ... Full name: William Sparkman Overstreet.
HIGH SCHOOL: Jackson (Miss.) Prep.
COLLEGE: Tennessee.
TRANSACTIONS/CAREER NOTES: Selected by Atlanta Falcons in third round (80th pick overall) of 2002 NFL draft. ... Signed by Falcons (July 22, 2002). ... On injured reserve with shoulder injury (October 14, 2002-remainder of season).

			TOTALS			INTERCEPTIONS			
Year Team	G	GS	Tk.	Ast.	Sks.	No.	Yds.	Avg.	TD
2002—Atlanta NFL	2	0	2	0	0.0	0	0	0.0	0

OWENS, JOHN   TE   LIONS

PERSONAL: Born January 10, 1980, in Washington, D.C. ... 6-3/266. ... Full name: John Wesley Owens.
HIGH SCHOOL: DeMatha (Hyattsville, Md.).
COLLEGE: Notre Dame.
TRANSACTIONS/CAREER NOTES: Selected by Detroit Lions in fifth round (138th pick overall) of 2002 NFL draft. ... Signed by Lions (July 22, 2002).
SINGLE GAME HIGHS (regular season): Receptions—2 (October 20, 2002, vs. Chicago); yards—19 (October 20, 2002, vs. Chicago); and touchdown receptions—0.

			RECEIVING			
Year Team	G	GS	No.	Yds.	Avg.	TD
2002—Detroit NFL	15	8	5	49	9.8	0

OWENS, RICH   DE

PERSONAL: Born May 22, 1972, in Philadelphia. ... 6-6/287.
HIGH SCHOOL: Lincoln (Philadelphia).
COLLEGE: Lehigh.
TRANSACTIONS/CAREER NOTES: Selected by Washington Redskins in fifth round (152nd pick overall) of 1995 NFL draft. ... Signed by Redskins (May 23, 1995). ... Granted free agency (February 13, 1998). ... Re-signed by Redskins (May 7, 1998). ... On injured reserve with knee injury (August 25, 1998-entire season). ... Granted unconditional free agency (February 12, 1999). ... Signed by Miami Dolphins (March 16, 1999). ... Granted unconditional free agency (March 2, 2001). ... Signed by Kansas City Chiefs (April 6, 2001). ... Granted unconditional free agency (March 1, 2002). ... Re-signed by Chiefs (April 30, 2002). ... Claimed on waivers by Seattle Seahawks (December 11, 2002). ... Granted unconditional free agency (February 28, 2003).

			TOTALS		
Year Team	G	GS	Tk.	Ast.	Sks.
1995—Washington NFL	10	3	15	5	3.0
1996—Washington NFL	16	16	35	11	11.0
1997—Washington NFL	16	15	28	12	2.5
1998—Washington NFL			Did not play.		
1999—Miami NFL	16	14	37	20	8.5
2000—Miami NFL	12	3	15	9	0.5
2001—Kansas City NFL	16	1	15	4	3.0
2002—Kansas City NFL	8	0	6	0	0.0
—Seattle NFL	3	0	0	0	0.0
Pro totals (7 years)	97	52	151	61	28.5

OWENS, TERRELL   WR   49ERS   O

PERSONAL: Born December 7, 1973, in Alexander City, Ala. ... 6-3/226. ... Full name: Terrell Eldorado Owens. ... Name pronounced TARE-el.
HIGH SCHOOL: Benjamin Russell (Alexander City, Ala.).
COLLEGE: Tennessee-Chattanooga.
TRANSACTIONS/CAREER NOTES: Selected by San Francisco 49ers in third round (89th pick overall) of 1996 NFL draft. ... Signed by 49ers (July 18, 1996). ... On physically unable to perform list with foot injury (July 17-August 11, 1997). ... Designated by 49ers as franchise player (February 12, 1999). ... Re-signed by 49ers (June 4, 1999).
CHAMPIONSHIP GAME EXPERIENCE: Played in NFC championship game (1997 season).
HONORS: Played in Pro Bowl (2000-2002 seasons). ... Named wide receiver on THE SPORTING NEWS NFL All-Pro team (2001 and 2002).
RECORDS: Holds NFL record for most receptions in a game—20 (December 17, 2000).
POST SEASON RECORDS: Holds NFL single-game and career record for two-point conversions—2 (January 5, 2003 v. New York Giants).
SINGLE GAME HIGHS (regular season): Receptions—20 (December 17, 2000, vs. Chicago); yards—283 (December 17, 2000, vs. Chicago); and touchdown receptions—3 (October 14, 2001, vs. Atlanta).
STATISTICAL PLATEAUS: 100-yard receiving games: 1996 (1), 1998 (2), 1999 (2), 2000 (5), 2001 (6), 2002 (5). Total: 21.

Year Team	G	GS	RUSHING Att.	Yds.	Avg.	TD	RECEIVING No.	Yds.	Avg.	TD	TOTALS TD	2pt.	Pts.	Fum.
1996—San Francisco NFL	16	10	0	0	0.0	0	35	520	14.9	4	4	0	24	1
1997—San Francisco NFL	16	15	0	0	0.0	0	60	936	15.6	8	8	0	48	1
1998—San Francisco NFL	16	10	4	53	13.3	1	67	1097	16.4	14	15	1	92	1
1999—San Francisco NFL	14	14	0	0	0.0	0	60	754	12.6	4	4	0	24	1
2000—San Francisco NFL	14	13	3	11	3.7	0	97	1451	15.0	13	13	1	80	3
2001—San Francisco NFL	16	16	4	21	5.3	0	93	1412	15.2	*16	16	0	96	0
2002—San Francisco NFL	14	14	7	79	11.3	1	100	1300	13.0	*13	14	0	84	0
Pro totals (7 years)	106	92	18	164	9.1	2	512	7470	14.6	72	74	2	448	7

PACE, ORLANDO — OT — RAMS

PERSONAL: Born November 4, 1975, in Sandusky, Ohio. ... 6-7/325. ... Full name: Orlando Lamar Pace.
HIGH SCHOOL: Sandusky (Ohio).
COLLEGE: Ohio State.
TRANSACTIONS/CAREER NOTES: Selected after junior season by St. Louis Rams in first round (first pick overall) of 1997 NFL draft. ... Signed by Rams (August 16, 1997). ... Designated by Rams as franchise player (February 20, 2003).
PLAYING EXPERIENCE: St. Louis NFL, 1997-2002. ... Games/Games started: 1997 (13/9), 1998 (16/16), 1999 (16/16), 2000 (16/16), 2001 (16/16), 2002 (10/10). Total: 87/83.
CHAMPIONSHIP GAME EXPERIENCE: Played in NFC championship game (1999 and 2001 seasons). ... Member of Super Bowl championship team (1999 season). ... Played in Super Bowl XXXVI (2001 season).
HONORS: Lombardi Award winner (1995 and 1996). ... Named offensive tackle on The Sporting News college All-America first team (1995 and 1996). ... Outland Trophy winner (1996). ... Named offensive tackle on The Sporting News NFL All-Pro team (1999-2001). ... Played in Pro Bowl (1999 and 2000 seasons). ... Named to play in Pro Bowl (2001 season); replaced by Tra Thomas due to injury. ... Named to play in Pro Bowl (2002 season); replaced by Jon Runyan due to injury.

PAGE, SOLOMON — G

PERSONAL: Born February 27, 1976, in Pittsburgh. ... 6-5/325.
HIGH SCHOOL: Brashear (Pittsburgh).
COLLEGE: West Virginia.
TRANSACTIONS/CAREER NOTES: Selected after junior season by Dallas Cowboys in second round (55th pick overall) of 1999 NFL draft. ... Signed by Cowboys (July 28, 1999). ... On injured reserve with knee injury (December 24, 2001-remainder of season). ... Granted unconditional free agency (February 28, 2003).
PLAYING EXPERIENCE: Dallas NFL, 1999-2002. ... Games/Games started: 1999 (14/6), 2000 (16/16), 2001 (14/14), 2002 (15/15). Total: 59/51.

PALEPOI, ANTON — DE — SEAHAWKS

PERSONAL: Born November 19, 1978, in American Samoa. ... 6-3/283. ... Full name: Anton Charles Palepoi.
HIGH SCHOOL: Hunter (Salt Lake City, Utah).
JUNIOR COLLEGE: Dixie College (Utah).
COLLEGE: UNLV.
TRANSACTIONS/CAREER NOTES: Selected by Seattle Seahawks in second round (60th pick overall) of 2002 NFL draft. ... Signed by Seahawks (July 25, 2002).

Year Team	G	GS	TOTALS Tk.	Ast.	Sks.
2002—Seattle NFL	13	1	10	7	1.0

PALMER, JESSE — QB — GIANTS

PERSONAL: Born October 5, 1978, in Toronto. ... 6-2/225. ... Full name: Jesse James Palmer.
HIGH SCHOOL: St. Pius X (Ottawa).
COLLEGE: Florida.
TRANSACTIONS/CAREER NOTES: Selected by New York Giants in fourth round (125th pick overall) of 2001 NFL draft. ... Signed by Giants (July 26, 2001). ... Inactive for all 16 games (2001).
SINGLE GAME HIGHS (regular season): Attempts—4 (December 15, 2002, vs. Dallas); completions—3 (December 15, 2002, vs. Dallas); yards—30 (December 15, 2002, vs. Dallas); and touchdown passes—0.

Year Team	G	GS	PASSING Att.	Cmp.	Pct.	Yds.	TD	Int.	Avg.	Skd.	Rat.	RUSHING Att.	Yds.	Avg.	TD	TOTALS TD	2pt.	Pts.
2001—N.Y. Giants NFL									Did not play.									
2002—N.Y. Giants NFL	2	0	4	3	75.0	30	0	0	7.50	0	95.8	1	-3	-3.0	0	0	0	0
Pro totals (1 years)	2	0	4	3	75.0	30	0	0	7.50	0	95.8	1	-3	-3.0	0	0	0	0

P — PARKER, ERIC — WR — CHARGERS

PERSONAL: Born April 14, 1979, in Shorewood, Ill. ... 6-0/172. ... Full name: Eric Samuel Parker.
HIGH SCHOOL: Joliet Township (Shorewood, Ill.).
COLLEGE: Tennessee (degree in sociology).

TRANSACTIONS/CAREER NOTES: Signed as non-drafted free agent by Houston Texans (April 25, 2002). ... Released by Texans (July 13, 2002). ... Signed by San Diego Chargers (July 23, 2002). ... Released by Chargers (September 1, 2002). ... Re-signed by Chargers to practice squad (September 3, 2002). ... Activated (September 26, 2002). ... Released by Chargers (October 12, 2002). ... Re-signed by Chargers (October 15, 2002). ... Re-signed by Chargers (April 4, 2003).

SINGLE GAME HIGHS (regular season): Receptions—7 (December 8, 2002, vs. Oakland); yards—96 (December 8, 2002, vs. Oakland); and touchdown receptions—1 (December 29, 2002, vs. Seattle).

				RECEIVING		
Year Team	G	GS	No.	Yds.	Avg.	TD
2002—San Diego NFL	9	2	17	268	15.8	1

PARKER, RIDDICK   DE   RAVENS

PERSONAL: Born November 20, 1972, in Emporia, Va. ... 6-3/295.
HIGH SCHOOL: Southampton (Courtland, Va.).
COLLEGE: North Carolina.
TRANSACTIONS/CAREER NOTES: Signed as non-drafted free agent by San Diego Chargers (April 28, 1995). ... Released by Chargers (August 22, 1995). ... Signed by Seattle Seahawks (July 8, 1996). ... Released by Seahawks (August 24, 1996). ... Re-signed by Seahawks to practice squad (August 26, 1996). ... Granted free agency (February 11, 2000). ... Re-signed by Seahawks (May 12, 2000). ... Granted unconditional free agency (March 2, 2001). ... Signed by New England Patriots (June 5, 2001). ... Granted unconditional free agency (March 1, 2002). ... Signed by New York Jets (April 22, 2002). ... Released by Jets (July 17, 2002). ... Signed by Patriots (July 26, 2002). ... Released by Patriots (September 1, 2002). ... Signed by Baltimore Ravens (October 15, 2002). ... Granted unconditional free agency (February 28, 2003). ... Re-signed by Ravens (March 11, 2003).
CHAMPIONSHIP GAME EXPERIENCE: Played in AFC championship game (2001 season). ... Member of Super Bowl championship team (2001 season); did not play.

			TOTALS		
Year Team	G	GS	Tk.	Ast.	Sks.
1997—Seattle NFL	12	0	2	1	0.0
1998—Seattle NFL	8	0	5	2	1.0
1999—Seattle NFL	16	3	15	9	2.0
2000—Seattle NFL	16	16	32	16	0.0
2001—New England NFL	13	0	7	3	1.0
2002—Baltimore NFL	11	0	15	4	1.0
Pro totals (6 years)	76	19	76	35	5.0

PARKER, VAUGHN   OT   CHARGERS

PERSONAL: Born June 5, 1971, in Buffalo. ... 6-3/300. ... Full name: Vaughn Antoine Parker.
HIGH SCHOOL: Saint Joseph's Collegiate Institute (Buffalo).
COLLEGE: UCLA.
TRANSACTIONS/CAREER NOTES: Selected by San Diego Chargers in second round (63rd pick overall) of 1994 NFL draft. ... Signed by Chargers (July 12, 1994). ... Granted free agency (February 14, 1997). ... Re-signed by Chargers (June 6, 1997). ... On injured reserve with leg injury (December 12, 1998-remainder of season). ... Granted unconditional free agency (February 11, 2000). ... Re-signed by Chargers (February 11, 2000).
PLAYING EXPERIENCE: San Diego NFL, 1994-2002. ... Games/Games started: 1994 (6/0), 1995 (14/7), 1996 (16/16), 1997 (16/16), 1998 (6/6), 1999 (15/15), 2000 (16/16), 2001 (16/16), 2002 (12/12). Total: 117/104.
CHAMPIONSHIP GAME EXPERIENCE: Played in AFC championship game (1994 season). ... Played in Super Bowl XXIX (1994 season).

PARRELLA, JOHN   DT   RAIDERS

PERSONAL: Born November 22, 1969, in Topeka, Kan. ... 6-3/300. ... Full name: John Lorin Parrella.
HIGH SCHOOL: Grand Island (Neb.) Central Catholic.
COLLEGE: Nebraska.
TRANSACTIONS/CAREER NOTES: Selected by Buffalo Bills in second round (55th pick overall) of 1993 NFL draft. ... Signed by Bills (July 12, 1993). ... Released by Bills (August 28, 1994). ... Signed by San Diego Chargers (September 12, 1994). ... Granted free agency (February 16, 1996). ... Re-signed by Chargers (June 14, 1996). ... Granted unconditional free agency (March 1, 2002). ... Signed by Oakland Raiders (March 7, 2002).
CHAMPIONSHIP GAME EXPERIENCE: Member of Bills for AFC championship game (1993 season); inactive. ... Member of Bills for Super Bowl XXVIII (1993 season); inactive. ... Played in AFC championship game (1994 and 2002 seasons). ... Played in Super Bowl XXIX (1994 season). ... Played in Super Bowl XXXVII (2002 season).

			TOTALS		
Year Team	G	GS	Tk.	Ast.	Sks.
1993—Buffalo NFL	10	0	1	1	1.0
1994—San Diego NFL	13	1	4	3	1.0
1995—San Diego NFL	16	1	9	4	2.0
1996—San Diego NFL	16	9	31	7	2.0
1997—San Diego NFL	16	16	32	7	3.5
1998—San Diego NFL	16	16	30	7	1.5
1999—San Diego NFL	16	16	45	9	5.5
2000—San Diego NFL	16	16	54	11	7.0
2001—San Diego NFL	16	16	61	6	2.0
2002—Oakland NFL	16	15	36	8	1.0
Pro totals (10 years)	151	106	303	63	26.5

P

PARRISH, TONY — S — 49ERS

PERSONAL: Born November 23, 1975, in Huntington Beach, Calif. ... 6-0/210.
HIGH SCHOOL: Marina (Huntington Beach, Calif.).
COLLEGE: Washington.
TRANSACTIONS/CAREER NOTES: Selected by Chicago Bears in second round (35th pick overall) of 1998 NFL draft. ... Signed by Bears (July 20, 1998). ... Granted unconditional free agency (March 1, 2002). ... Signed by San Francisco 49ers (April 4, 2002).

			TOTALS			INTERCEPTIONS			
Year Team	G	GS	Tk.	Ast.	Sks.	No.	Yds.	Avg.	TD
1998—Chicago NFL	16	16	65	13	1.0	1	8	8.0	0
1999—Chicago NFL	16	16	87	13	0.0	1	41	41.0	0
2000—Chicago NFL	16	16	63	20	2.0	3	81	27.0	1
2001—Chicago NFL	16	16	56	11	1.0	3	36	12.0	0
2002—San Francisco NFL	16	16	63	9	0.0	7	204	29.1	0
Pro totals (5 years)	80	80	334	66	4.0	15	370	24.7	1

PASS, PATRICK — RB — PATRIOTS

PERSONAL: Born December 31, 1977, in Scottsdale, Ga. ... 5-10/217. ... Full name: Patrick D. Pass.
HIGH SCHOOL: Tucker (Ga.).
COLLEGE: Georgia.
TRANSACTIONS/CAREER NOTES: Selected by New England Patriots in seventh round (239th pick overall) of 2000 NFL draft. ... Signed by Patriots (June 29, 2000). ... Released by Patriots (August 27, 2000). ... Re-signed by Patriots to practice squad (August 29, 2000). ... Activated (September 16, 2000). ... Granted free agency (February 28, 2003). ... Re-signed by Patriots (May 22, 2003).
CHAMPIONSHIP GAME EXPERIENCE: Played in AFC championship game (2001 season). ... Member of Super Bowl championship team (2001 season).
SINGLE GAME HIGHS (regular season): Attempts—12 (November 19, 2000, vs. Cincinnati); yards—39 (November 19, 2000, vs. Cincinnati); and rushing touchdowns—0.
MISCELLANEOUS: Selected by Florida Marlins organization in 44th round of free-agent draft (June 4, 1996).

			RUSHING				RECEIVING				KICKOFF RETURNS				TOTALS			
Year Team	G	GS	Att.	Yds.	Avg.	TD	No.	Yds.	Avg.	TD	No.	Yds.	Avg.	TD	TD	2pt.	Pts.	Fum.
2000—New England NFL	5	2	18	58	3.2	0	4	17	4.3	0	0	0	0.0	0	0	0	0	0
2001—New England NFL	16	0	1	7	7.0	0	6	66	11.0	1	10	222	22.2	0	1	0	6	0
2002—New England NFL	15	0	4	27	6.8	0	0	0	0.0	0	7	123	17.6	0	0	0	0	0
Pro totals (3 years)	36	2	23	92	4.0	0	10	83	8.3	1	17	345	20.3	0	1	0	6	0

PATHON, JEROME — WR — SAINTS

PERSONAL: Born December 16, 1975, in Capetown, South Africa. ... 6-0/182. ... Name pronounced PAY-thin.
HIGH SCHOOL: Carson Graham Secondary School (North Vancouver).
COLLEGE: Acadia (Nova Scotia), then Washington.
TRANSACTIONS/CAREER NOTES: Selected by Indianapolis Colts in second round (32nd pick overall) of 1998 NFL draft. ... Signed by Colts (July 26, 1998). ... On injured reserve with foot injury (November 19, 2001-remainder of season). ... Granted unconditional free agency (March 1, 2002). ... Signed by New Orleans Saints (April 15, 2002).
HONORS: Named wide receiver on THE SPORTING NEWS college All-America second team (1997).
SINGLE GAME HIGHS (regular season): Receptions—9 (September 23, 2001, vs. Buffalo); yards—168 (September 23, 2001, vs. Buffalo); and touchdown receptions—1 (October 6, 2002, vs. Pittsburgh).
STATISTICAL PLATEAUS: 100-yard receiving games: 2001 (1).

			RECEIVING				TOTALS			
Year Team	G	GS	No.	Yds.	Avg.	TD	TD	2pt.	Pts.	Fum.
1998—Indianapolis NFL	16	15	50	511	10.2	1	1	0	6	0
1999—Indianapolis NFL	12	2	14	163	11.6	0	0	0	0	0
2000—Indianapolis NFL	16	10	50	646	12.9	3	3	0	18	0
2001—Indianapolis NFL	4	3	24	330	13.8	2	2	0	12	0
2002—New Orleans NFL	14	13	43	523	12.2	4	4	0	24	0
Pro totals (5 years)	62	43	181	2173	12.0	10	10	0	60	0

PATMON, DEWAYNE — S

PERSONAL: Born April 25, 1979, in San Diego. ... 6-0/202.
HIGH SCHOOL: Patrick Henry (San Diego).
COLLEGE: Michigan.
TRANSACTIONS/CAREER NOTES: Signed as non-drafted free agent by New York Giants (April 27, 2001). ... Released by Giants (March 12, 2003).

			TOTALS			INTERCEPTIONS			
Year Team	G	GS	Tk.	Ast.	Sks.	No.	Yds.	Avg.	TD
2001—New York Giants NFL	7	0	0	0	0.0	0	0	0.0	0
2002—New York Giants NFL	15	0	3	3	0.0	0	0	0.0	0
Pro totals (2 years)	22	0	3	3	0.0	0	0	0.0	0

P

PATTEN, DAVID — WR — PATRIOTS

PERSONAL: Born August 19, 1974, in Columbia, S.C. ... 5-10/190.
HIGH SCHOOL: Lower Richland (Hopkins, S.C.).
COLLEGE: Western Carolina.

TRANSACTIONS/CAREER NOTES: Played for Albany Firebirds of Arena League (1996). ... Signed as non-drafted free agent by New York Giants (March 24, 1997). ... Released by Giants (August 24, 1997). ... Re-signed by Giants to practice squad (August 25, 1997). ... Activated (August 27, 1997). ... On injured reserve with knee injury (December 16, 1998-remainder of season). ... Granted free agency (February 11, 2000). ... Signed by Cleveland Browns (March 16, 2000). ... Granted unconditional free agency (March 2, 2001). ... Signed by New England Patriots (April 2, 2001).

CHAMPIONSHIP GAME EXPERIENCE: Played in AFC championship game (2001 season). ... Member of Super Bowl championship team (2001 season).

SINGLE GAME HIGHS (regular season): Receptions—7 (September 29, 2002, vs. San Diego); yards—117 (October 21, 2001, vs. Indianapolis); and touchdown receptions—2 (October 6, 2002, vs. Miami).

STATISTICAL PLATEAUS: 100-yard receiving games: 2000 (2), 2001 (1), 2002 (2). Total: 5.

			RECEIVING				KICKOFF RETURNS				TOTALS		
Year Team	G	GS	No.	Yds.	Avg.	TD	No.	Yds.	Avg.	TD	TD	2pt.	Pts.	Fum.
1997—New York Giants NFL	16	3	13	226	17.4	2	8	123	15.4	0	2	0	12	2
1998—New York Giants NFL	12	0	11	119	10.8	1	43	928	21.6	1	2	0	12	0
1999—New York Giants NFL	16	0	9	115	12.8	0	33	673	20.4	0	0	0	0	0
2000—Cleveland NFL	14	11	38	546	14.4	1	22	469	21.3	0	1	0	6	2
2001—New England NFL	16	14	51	749	14.7	4	2	44	22.0	0	5	0	30	1
2002—New England NFL	16	14	61	824	13.5	5	0	0	0.0	0	5	0	30	0
Pro totals (6 years)	90	42	183	2579	14.1	13	108	2237	20.7	1	15	0	90	5

PATTON, MARVCUS   LB   CHIEFS

PERSONAL: Born May 1, 1967, in Los Angeles. ... 6-2/241. ... Full name: Marvcus Raymond Patton.
HIGH SCHOOL: Leuzinger (Lawndale, Calif.).
COLLEGE: UCLA (degree in political science, 1990).
TRANSACTIONS/CAREER NOTES: Selected by Buffalo Bills in eighth round (208th pick overall) of 1990 NFL draft. ... Signed by Bills (July 27, 1990). ... On injured reserve with broken leg (January 26, 1991-remainder of 1990 playoffs). ... Granted free agency (February 1, 1992). ... Re-signed by Bills (July 23, 1992). ... Granted unconditional free agency (February 17, 1995). ... Signed by Washington Redskins (February 22, 1995). ... Granted unconditional free agency (February 12, 1999). ... Signed by Kansas City Chiefs (April 27, 1999).
CHAMPIONSHIP GAME EXPERIENCE: Played in AFC championship game (1991-1993 seasons). ... Played in Super Bowl XXVI (1991 season), Super Bowl XXVII (1992 season) and Super Bowl XXVIII (1993 season).

			TOTALS			INTERCEPTIONS			
Year Team	G	GS	Tk.	Ast.	Sks.	No.	Yds.	Avg.	TD
1990—Buffalo NFL	16	0	8	4	0.5	0	0	0.0	0
1991—Buffalo NFL	16	2	9	1	0.0	0	0	0.0	0
1992—Buffalo NFL	16	4	20	5	2.0	0	0	0.0	0
1993—Buffalo NFL	16	16	76	42	1.0	2	0	0.0	0
1994—Buffalo NFL	16	16	62	33	0.0	2	8	4.0	0
1995—Washington NFL	16	16	94	19	2.0	2	7	3.5	0
1996—Washington NFL	16	16	96	19	2.0	2	26	13.0	0
1997—Washington NFL	16	16	98	37	4.5	2	5	2.5	0
1998—Washington NFL	16	16	115	28	3.0	0	0	0.0	0
1999—Kansas City NFL	16	16	89	16	6.5	1	0	0.0	0
2000—Kansas City NFL	16	15	88	23	1.0	2	39	19.5	1
2001—Kansas City NFL	16	15	99	15	3.0	2	5	2.5	0
2002—Kansas City NFL	16	15	71	21	2.0	2	29	14.5	0
Pro totals (13 years)	208	163	925	263	27.5	17	119	7.0	1

PAXTON, LONIE   TE   PATRIOTS

PERSONAL: Born March 13, 1978, in Anaheim, Calif. ... 6-2/260. ... Full name: Leonidas E. Paxton.
HIGH SCHOOL: Centennial (Carona, Calif.).
COLLEGE: Sacramento State.
TRANSACTIONS/CAREER NOTES: Signed as non-drafted free agent by New England Patriots (April 19, 2000). ... Granted free agency (February 28, 2003). ... Re-signed by Patriots (February 28, 2003).
CHAMPIONSHIP GAME EXPERIENCE: Played in AFC championship game (2001 season). ... Member of Super Bowl championship team (2001 season).

			RECEIVING			
Year Team	G	GS	No.	Yds.	Avg.	TD
2000—New England NFL	16	0	0	0	0.0	0
2001—New England NFL	16	0	0	0	0.0	0
2002—New England NFL	16	0	0	0	0.0	0
Pro totals (3 years)	48	0	0	0	0.0	0

PAYNE, SETH   DT   TEXANS

PERSONAL: Born February 12, 1975, in Clifton Springs, N.Y. ... 6-4/303. ... Full name: Seth Copeland Payne.
HIGH SCHOOL: Victor (N.Y.) Central.
COLLEGE: Cornell.
TRANSACTIONS/CAREER NOTES: Selected by Jacksonville Jaguars in fourth round (114th pick overall) of 1997 NFL draft. ... Signed by Jaguars (May 23, 1997). ... On injured reserve with shoulder injury (November 17, 1998-remainder of season). ... Selected by Houston Texans from Jaguars in NFL expansion draft (February 18, 2002).
CHAMPIONSHIP GAME EXPERIENCE: Played in AFC championship game (1999 season).

P

Year Team	G	GS	TOTALS		
			Tk.	Ast.	Sks.
1997—Jacksonville NFL	12	5	12	2	0.0
1998—Jacksonville NFL	6	1	7	4	0.0
1999—Jacksonville NFL	16	16	13	11	1.5
2000—Jacksonville NFL	16	14	22	11	2.0
2001—Jacksonville NFL	16	16	41	14	5.0
2002—Houston NFL	16	16	54	11	1.0
Pro totals (6 years)	82	68	149	53	9.5

PEARSON, KALVIN   DB   BROWNS

PERSONAL: Born October 22, 1978, in Town Creek, Ala. ... 5-10/190. ... Cousin of Antonio Langham, cornerback with four NFL teams (1994-2000).
HIGH SCHOOL: Hazelwood (Ala.).
COLLEGE: Morehouse College, then Grambling State.
TRANSACTIONS/CAREER NOTES: Signed as non-drafted free agent by Cleveland Browns (April 26, 2002). ... Released by Browns (October 8, 2002). ... Re-signed by Browns to practice squad (October 9, 2002). ... Assigned by Browns to Frankfurt Galaxy in 2003 NFL Europe enhancement allocation program (February 4, 2003).

Year Team	G	GS	TOTALS			INTERCEPTIONS			
			Tk.	Ast.	Sks.	No.	Yds.	Avg.	TD
2002—Cleveland NFL	5	0	5	0	0.0	0	0	0.0	0

PEARSON, MIKE   OT   JAGUARS

PERSONAL: Born August 2, 1980, in Tampa, Fla. ... 6-7/303. ... Full name: Michael Wayne Pearson.
HIGH SCHOOL: Armwood (Seffner, Fla.).
COLLEGE: Florida.
TRANSACTIONS/CAREER NOTES: Selected after junior season by Jacksonville Jaguars in second round (40th pick overall) of 2002 NFL draft. ... Signed by Jaguars (July 24, 2002).
PLAYING EXPERIENCE: Jacksonville NFL, 2002. ... Games/games started: 2002 (16/11).
HONORS: Named offensive tackle on THE SPORTING NEWS college All-America first team (2001).

PEDERSON, DOUG   QB   PACKERS

PERSONAL: Born January 31, 1968, in Bellingham, Wash. ... 6-3/220. ... Full name: Douglas Irvin Pederson.
HIGH SCHOOL: Ferndale (Wash.).
COLLEGE: Northeast Louisiana (degree in business management).
TRANSACTIONS/CAREER NOTES: Signed as non-drafted free agent by Miami Dolphins (April 30, 1991). ... Released by Dolphins (August 16, 1991). ... Selected by New York/New Jersey Knights in fifth round (49th pick overall) of 1992 World League draft. ... Re-signed by Dolphins (June 1, 1992). ... Released by Dolphins (August 31, 1992). ... Re-signed by Dolphins to practice squad (September 1, 1992). ... Released by Dolphins (October 7, 1992). ... Re-signed by Dolphins (March 3, 1993). ... Released by Dolphins (August 30, 1993). ... Re-signed by Dolphins to practice squad (August 31, 1993). ... Activated (October 22, 1993). ... Released by Dolphins (December 15, 1993). ... Re-signed by Dolphins (April 15, 1994). ... Inactive for all 16 games (1994). ... Selected by Carolina Panthers from Dolphins in NFL expansion draft (February 15, 1995). ... Released by Panthers (May 22, 1995). ... Signed by Dolphins (July 11, 1995). ... Released by Dolphins (August 21, 1995). ... Re-signed by Dolphins (October 10, 1995). ... Inactive for two games with Dolphins (1995). ... Released by Dolphins (October 25, 1995). ... Signed by Green Bay Packers (November 22, 1995). ... Inactive for five games with Packers (1995). ... Granted unconditional free agency (February 14, 1997). ... Re-signed by Packers (February 20, 1997). ... Granted unconditional free agency (February 12, 1999). ... Signed by Philadelphia Eagles (February 17, 1999). ... Released by Eagles (August 27, 2000). ... Signed by Cleveland Browns (September 1, 2000). ... Released by Browns (February 22, 2001). ... Signed by Packers (March 13, 2001). ... Granted unconditional free agency (March 1, 2002). ... Re-signed by Packers (April 2, 2002). ... Granted unconditional free agency (February 28, 2003). ... Re-signed by Packers (April 29, 2003).
CHAMPIONSHIP GAME EXPERIENCE: Member of Packers for NFC championship game (1995-97 seasons); inactive. ... Member of Super Bowl championship team (1996 season); inactive. ... Member of Packers for Super Bowl XXXII (1997 season); inactive.
SINGLE GAME HIGHS (regular season): Attempts—40 (December 10, 2000, vs. Philadelphia); completions—29 (December 10, 2000, vs. Philadelphia); yards—309 (December 10, 2000, vs. Philadelphia); and touchdown passes—2 (October 17, 1999, vs. Chicago).
STATISTICAL PLATEAUS: 300-yard passing games: 2000 (1).
MISCELLANEOUS: Regular-season record as starting NFL quarterback: 3-14 (.176).

Year Team	G	GS	PASSING									RUSHING				TOTALS		
			Att.	Cmp.	Pct.	Yds.	TD	Int.	Avg.	Skd.	Rat.	Att.	Yds.	Avg.	TD	TD	2pt.	Pts.
1992—NY/New Jersey W.L.	7	1	128	70	54.7	1077	8	3	8.41	0	93.8	15	46	3.1	0	0	0	0
1993—Miami NFL	7	0	8	4	50.0	41	0	0	5.13	1	65.1	2	-1	-0.5	0	0	0	0
1994—Miami NFL									Did not play.									
1995—Miami NFL									Did not play.									
—Green Bay NFL									Did not play.									
1996—Green Bay NFL	1	0	0	0	0.0	0	0	0	0.0	0	...	0	0	0.0	0	0	0	0
1997—Green Bay NFL	1	0	0	0	0.0	0	0	0	0.0	0	...	3	-4	-1.3	0	0	0	0
1998—Green Bay NFL	12	0	24	14	58.3	128	2	0	5.33	1	100.7	8	-4	-0.5	0	0	0	0
1999—Philadelphia NFL	16	9	227	119	52.4	1276	7	9	5.62	20	62.9	20	33	1.7	0	0	0	0
2000—Cleveland NFL	11	8	210	117	55.7	1047	2	8	4.99	17	56.6	18	68	3.8	0	0	0	0
2001—Green Bay NFL	16	0	0	0	0.0	0	0	0	0.0	0	...	1	-1	-1.0	0	0	0	0
2002—Green Bay NFL	16	0	28	19	67.9	134	1	0	4.79	1	90.5	1	-1	-1.0	0	0	0	0
W.L. totals (1 year)	7	1	128	70	54.7	1077	8	3	8.41	0	93.8	15	46	3.1	0	0	0	0
NFL totals (8 years)	80	17	497	273	54.9	2626	12	17	5.28	40	63.7	53	90	1.7	0	0	0	0
Pro totals (9 years)	87	18	625	343	54.9	3703	20	20	5.92	40	69.8	68	136	2.0	0	0	0	0

P

PEELLE, JUSTIN — TE — CHARGERS

PERSONAL: Born March 15, 1979, in Fresno, Calif. ... 6-4/255. ... Full name: Justin Morris Peelle.
HIGH SCHOOL: Dublin (Calif.).
COLLEGE: Oregon.
TRANSACTIONS/CAREER NOTES: Selected by San Diego Chargers in fourth round (103rd pick overall) of 2002 NFL draft. ... Signed by Chargers (July 18, 2002).
SINGLE GAME HIGHS (regular season): Receptions—1 (December 15, 2002, vs. Buffalo); yards—10 (December 15, 2002, vs. Buffalo); and touchdown receptions—0.

			RECEIVING			
Year Team	G	GS	No.	Yds.	Avg.	TD
2002—San Diego NFL	15	2	3	15	5.0	0

PEETE, RODNEY — QB — PANTHERS

PERSONAL: Born March 16, 1966, in Mesa, Ariz. ... 6-0/230. ... Son of Willie Peete, former running backs coach and scout with Chicago Bears; cousin of Calvin Peete, professional golfer.
HIGH SCHOOL: Sahuaro (Tucson, Ariz.), then Shawnee Mission South (Overland Park, Kan.).
COLLEGE: Southern California (degree in communications, 1989).
TRANSACTIONS/CAREER NOTES: Selected by Detroit Lions in sixth round (141st pick overall) of 1989 NFL draft. ... Signed by Lions (July 13, 1989). ... On injured reserve with Achilles' tendon injury (October 30, 1991-remainder of season). ... Granted free agency (February 1, 1992). ... Re-signed by Lions (July 30, 1992). ... Granted unconditional free agency (February 17, 1994). ... Signed by Dallas Cowboys (May 4, 1994). ... Granted unconditional free agency (February 17, 1995). ... Signed by Philadelphia Eagles (April 22, 1995). ... Granted unconditional free agency (February 16, 1996). ... Re-signed by Eagles (March 14, 1996). ... On injured reserve with knee injury (October 3, 1996-remainder of season). ... Granted unconditional free agency (February 14, 1997). ... Re-signed by Eagles (April 1, 1997). ... Traded by Eagles to Washington Redskins for sixth-round pick (C John Romero) in 2000 draft (April 28, 1999). ... Released by Redskins (April 18, 2000). ... Signed by Oakland Raiders (July 13, 2000). ... Released by Raiders (September 2, 2001). ... Re-signed by Raiders (September 29, 2001). ... Granted unconditional free agency (March 1, 2002). ... Signed by Carolina Panthers (March 28, 2002). ... Granted unconditional free agency (February 28, 2003). ... Re-signed by Panthers (March 5, 2003).
CHAMPIONSHIP GAME EXPERIENCE: Member of Cowboys for NFC championship game (1994 season); did not play. ... Member of Raiders for AFC Championship game (2000 season); inactive.
HONORS: Named quarterback on THE SPORTING NEWS college All-America second team (1988).
SINGLE GAME HIGHS (regular season): Attempts—45 (October 8, 1995, vs. Washington); completions—30 (October 8, 1995, vs. Washington); yards—323 (September 27, 1992, vs. Tampa Bay); and touchdown passes—4 (December 16, 1990, vs. Chicago).
STATISTICAL PLATEAUS: 300-yard passing games: 1990 (1), 1992 (1), 2002 (3). Total: 5.
MISCELLANEOUS: Selected by Toronto Blue Jays organization in 30th round of free-agent baseball draft (June 4, 1984); did not sign. ... Selected by Oakland Athletics organization in 14th round of free-agent baseball draft (June 1, 1988); did not sign. ... Selected by Athletics organization in 13th round of free-agent baseball draft (June 5, 1989); did not sign. ... Regular-season record as starting NFL quarterback: 44-42 (.512). ... Postseason record as starting NFL quarterback: 1-1 (.500).

						PASSING						RUSHING				TOTALS		
Year Team	G	GS	Att.	Cmp.	Pct.	Yds.	TD	Int.	Avg.	Skd.	Rat.	Att.	Yds.	Avg.	TD	TD	2pt.	Pts.
1989—Detroit NFL	8	8	195	103	52.8	1479	5	9	7.58	27	67.0	33	148	4.5	4	4	0	24
1990—Detroit NFL	11	11	271	142	52.4	1974	13	8	7.28	27	79.8	47	363	7.7	6	6	0	36
1991—Detroit NFL	8	8	194	116	59.8	1339	5	9	6.90	11	69.9	25	125	5.0	2	2	0	12
1992—Detroit NFL	10	10	213	123	57.7	1702	9	9	7.99	28	80.0	21	83	4.0	0	0	0	0
1993—Detroit NFL	10	10	252	157	62.3	1670	6	14	6.63	34	66.4	45	165	3.7	1	1	0	6
1994—Dallas NFL	7	1	56	33	58.9	470	4	1	8.39	4	102.5	9	-2	-0.2	0	0	0	0
1995—Philadelphia NFL	15	12	375	215	57.3	2326	8	14	6.20	33	67.3	32	147	4.6	1	1	0	6
1996—Philadelphia NFL	5	5	134	80	59.7	992	3	5	7.40	11	74.6	20	31	1.6	1	1	0	6
1997—Philadelphia NFL	5	3	118	68	57.6	869	4	4	7.36	17	78.0	8	37	4.6	0	0	0	0
1998—Philadelphia NFL	5	4	129	71	55.0	758	2	4	5.88	16	64.7	5	30	6.0	1	1	0	6
1999—Washington NFL	3	0	17	8	47.1	107	2	1	6.29	2	82.2	2	-1	-0.5	0	0	0	0
2000—Oakland NFL								Did not play.										
2001—Oakland NFL	1	0	0	0	0.0	0	0	0	0.0	0	—	0	0	0.0	0	0	0	0
2002—Carolina NFL	14	14	381	223	58.5	2630	15	14	6.90	31	77.4	22	14	0.6	0	0	0	0
Pro totals (13 years)	102	86	2335	1339	57.3	16316	76	92	6.99	241	73.4	269	1140	4.2	16	16	0	96

PENNINGTON, CHAD — QB — JETS

PERSONAL: Born June 26, 1976, in Knoxville, Tenn. ... 6-3/225. ... Full name: James Chad Pennington.
HIGH SCHOOL: Webb (Knoxville, Tenn.).
COLLEGE: Marshall.
TRANSACTIONS/CAREER NOTES: Selected by New York Jets in first round (18th pick overall) of 2000 NFL draft. ... Signed by Jets (July 13, 2000).
HONORS: Named quarterback on THE SPORTING NEWS college All-America third team (1999).
SINGLE GAME HIGHS (regular season): Attempts—37 (November 3, 2002, vs. San Diego); completions—28 (November 3, 2002, vs. San Diego); yards—324 (October 20, 2002, vs. Minnesota); and touchdown passes—4 (December 29, 2002, vs. Green Bay).
STATISTICAL PLATEAUS: 300-yard passing games: 2002 (1).
MISCELLANEOUS: Regular-season record as starting NFL quarterback: 8-4 (.667). ... Postseason record as starting NFL quarterback: 1-1 (.500).

						PASSING						RUSHING				TOTALS		
Year Team	G	GS	Att.	Cmp.	Pct.	Yds.	TD	Int.	Avg.	Skd.	Rat.	Att.	Yds.	Avg.	TD	TD	2pt.	Pts.
2000—New York Jets NFL	2	0	5	2	40.0	67	1	0	13.40	1	127.1	1	0	0.0	0	0	0	0
2001—New York Jets NFL	2	0	20	10	50.0	92	1	0	4.60	1	79.6	1	11	11.0	0	0	0	0
2002—New York Jets NFL	15	12	399	275	*68.9	3120	22	6	7.82	22	*104.2	29	49	1.7	2	2	0	12
Pro totals (3 years)	19	12	424	287	67.7	3279	24	6	7.73	24	103.7	31	60	1.9	2	2	0	12

P

PEPPERS, JULIUS　　　　　　DE　　　　　　PANTHERS

PERSONAL: Born January 18, 1980, in Wilson, N.C. ... 6-6/283. ... Full name: Julius Frazier Peppers.
HIGH SCHOOL: Southern Nash (Bailey, N.C.).
COLLEGE: North Carolina.
TRANSACTIONS/CAREER NOTES: Selected after junior season by Carolina Panthers in first round (second pick overall) of 2002 NFL draft. ... Signed by Panthers (July 22, 2002). ... On suspended list for violating league substance abuse policy (December 4, 2002-remainder of season).
HONORS: Lombardi Award winner (2001). ... Named defensive end on THE SPORTING NEWS college All-America first team (2001).

			TOTALS			INTERCEPTIONS			
Year　Team	G	GS	Tk.	Ast.	Sks.	No.	Yds.	Avg.	TD
2002—Carolina NFL	12	12	29	7	12.0	1	21	21.0	0

PERRY, ED　　　　　　TE　　　　　　DOLPHINS

PERSONAL: Born September 1, 1974, in Richmond, Va. ... 6-4/270. ... Full name: Edward Lewis Perry.
HIGH SCHOOL: Highlands Springs (Va.).
COLLEGE: James Madison.
TRANSACTIONS/CAREER NOTES: Selected by Miami Dolphins in sixth round (177th pick overall) of 1997 NFL draft. ... Signed by Dolphins (June 13, 1997). ... Granted free agency (February 11, 2000). ... Re-signed by Dolphins (April 28, 2000). ... On injured reserve with shoulder injury (November 23, 2000-remainder of season). ... Granted unconditional free agency (March 2, 2001). ... Re-signed by Dolphins (March 16, 2001).
SINGLE GAME HIGHS (regular season): Receptions—4 (September 13, 1998, vs. Buffalo); yards—59 (November 23, 1998, vs. New England); and touchdown receptions—1 (December 27, 1999, vs. New York Jets).

			RECEIVING				TOTALS			
Year　Team	G	GS	No.	Yds.	Avg.	TD	TD	2pt.	Pts.	Fum.
1997—Miami NFL	16	4	11	45	4.1	1	1	0	6	0
1998—Miami NFL	14	5	25	255	10.2	0	0	0	0	0
1999—Miami NFL	16	1	3	8	2.7	1	1	0	6	0
2000—Miami NFL	10	0	0	0	0.0	0	0	0	0	0
2001—Miami NFL	16	0	0	0	0.0	0	0	0	0	1
2002—Miami NFL	16	0	0	0	0.0	0	0	0	0	0
Pro totals (6 years)	88	10	39	308	7.9	2	2	0	12	1

PERRY, JASON　　　　　　S

PERSONAL: Born August 1, 1976, in Passaic, N.J. ... 6-0/200. ... Full name: Jason Robert Perry.
HIGH SCHOOL: Paterson (N.J.) Catholic.
COLLEGE: North Carolina State.
TRANSACTIONS/CAREER NOTES: Selected by San Diego Chargers in fourth round (104th pick overall) of 1999 NFL draft. ... Signed by Chargers (July 22, 1999). ... On injured reserve with knee injury (September 26, 2000-remainder of season). ... Granted free agency (March 1, 2002). ... Re-signed by Chargers (April 2, 2002). ... Released by Chargers (September 3, 2002). ... Signed by Minnesota Vikings (October 3, 2002). ... Claimed on waivers by Cincinnati Bengals (December 17, 2002). ... Granted unconditional free agency (February 28, 2003).

			TOTALS			INTERCEPTIONS			
Year　Team	G	GS	Tk.	Ast.	Sks.	No.	Yds.	Avg.	TD
1999—San Diego NFL	16	5	21	5	0.0	0	0	0.0	0
2000—San Diego NFL	1	0	0	0	0.0	0	0	0.0	0
2001—San Diego NFL	14	3	20	4	0.0	2	37	18.5	1
2002—Cincinnati NFL	2	0	2	2	0.0	0	0	0.0	0
—Minnesota NFL	3	0	1	1	0.0	0	0	0.0	0
Pro totals (4 years)	36	8	44	12	0.0	2	37	18.5	1

PERRY, TODD　　　　　　G　　　　　　DOLPHINS

PERSONAL: Born November 28, 1970, in Elizabethtown, Ky. ... 6-5/310. ... Full name: Todd Joseph Perry.
HIGH SCHOOL: North Hardin (Radcliff, Ky.).
COLLEGE: Kentucky.
TRANSACTIONS/CAREER NOTES: Selected by Chicago Bears in fourth round (97th pick overall) of 1993 NFL draft. ... Signed by Bears (June 16, 1993). ... On injured reserve with back injury (December 19, 1997-remainder of season). ... Granted unconditional free agency (February 11, 2000). ... Re-signed by Bears (May 4, 2000). ... Granted unconditional free agency (March 2, 2001). ... Signed by Miami Dolphins (March 3, 2001).
PLAYING EXPERIENCE: Chicago NFL, 1993-2000; Miami NFL, 2001-2002. ... Games/Games started: 1993 (13/3), 1994 (15/4), 1995 (15/15), 1996 (16/16), 1997 (11/11), 1998 (16/16), 1999 (16/16), 2000 (16/16), 2001 (16/16), 2002 (16/16). Total: 150/129.

PERRYMAN, RAYMOND　　　　　　DB　　　　　　RAVENS

P

PERSONAL: Born November 27, 1978, in Phoenix. ... 6-0/204.
HIGH SCHOOL: South Mountain (Phoenix).
COLLEGE: Northern Arizona.
TRANSACTIONS/CAREER NOTES: Selected by Oakland Raiders in fifth round (158th pick overall) of 2001 NFL draft. ... Signed by Raiders (July 21, 2001). ... Released by Raiders (September 2, 2001). ... Re-signed by Raiders to practice squad (September 4, 2001). ... Activated (January 17, 2002). ... Assigned by Raiders to Amsterdam Admirals in 2002 NFL Europe enhancement allocation program (February 12, 2002). ... Released by Raiders (September 1, 2002). ... Signed by Baltimore Ravens to practice squad (November 19, 2002). ... Activated (November 27, 2002). ... Re-signed by Ravens (March 23, 2003).

Year Team	G	GS	TOTALS Tk.	Ast.	Sks.	INTERCEPTIONS No.	Yds.	Avg.	TD
2002—Amsterdam NFLE	...	...	...	...	0.0	2	39	19.5	0
—Baltimore NFL	2	0	0	0	0.0	0	0	0.0	0
NFL Europe totals (1 year)	...	...	...	...	0.0	2	39	19.5	0
NFL totals (1 year)	2	0	0	0	0.0	0	0	0.0	0
Pro totals (2 years)	...	...	...	...	0.0	2	39	19.5	0

PETER, CHRISTIAN   DT

PERSONAL: Born October 5, 1972, in Locust, N.J. ... 6-2/292. ... Brother of Jason Peter, defensive end, with Carolina Panthers (1998-2001).
HIGH SCHOOL: Middletown South (Middleton, N.J.), then Milford (Conn.) Academy.
COLLEGE: Nebraska.
TRANSACTIONS/CAREER NOTES: Selected by New England Patriots in fifth round (149th pick overall) of 1996 NFL draft. ... Patriots released rights (April 24, 1996). ... Signed by New York Giants (January 22, 1997). ... Granted free agency (February 11, 2000). ... Re-signed by Giants (April 12, 2000). ... Granted unconditional free agency (March 2, 2001). ... Signed by Indianapolis Colts (April 21, 2001). ... On injured reserve with neck injury (January 4, 2002-remainder of season). ... Released by Colts (February 28, 2002). ... Signed by Chicago Bears (July 12, 2002). ... Granted unconditional free agency (February 28, 2003).
CHAMPIONSHIP GAME EXPERIENCE: Played in NFC championship game (2000 season). ... Played in Super Bowl XXXV (2000 season).

Year Team	G	GS	TOTALS Tk.	Ast.	Sks.
1997—New York Giants NFL	7	0	1	1	0.5
1998—New York Giants NFL	16	6	22	10	1.0
1999—New York Giants NFL	16	10	19	7	0.0
2000—New York Giants NFL	16	15	23	14	1.0
2001—Indianapolis NFL	14	0	7	6	1.0
2002—Chicago NFL	12	3	12	6	0.0
Pro totals (6 years)	81	34	84	44	3.5

PETERSON, ADRIAN   RB   BEARS

PERSONAL: Born July 1, 1979, in Gainesville, Fla. ... 5-10/208.
HIGH SCHOOL: Sante Fe (Alachua, Fla.).
COLLEGE: Georgia Southern.
TRANSACTIONS/CAREER NOTES: Selected by Chicago Bears in sixth round (199th pick overall) of 2002 NFL draft. ... Signed by Bears (July 25, 2002).
SINGLE GAME HIGHS (regular season): Attempts—7 (December 29, 2002, vs. Tampa Bay); yards—42 (December 29, 2002, vs. Tampa Bay); and rushing touchdowns—1 (December 15, 2002, vs. New York Jets).

Year Team	G	GS	RUSHING Att.	Yds.	Avg.	TD	RECEIVING No.	Yds.	Avg.	TD	KICKOFF RETURNS No.	Yds.	Avg.	TD	TOTALS TD	2pt.	Pts.	Fum.
2002—Chicago NFL	9	0	19	101	5.3	1	3	18	6.0	0	2	37	18.5	0	1	0	6	0

PETERSON, JULIAN   LB   49ERS

PERSONAL: Born July 28, 1978, in Hillcrest Heights, Md. ... 6-3/235. ... Full name: Julian Thomas Peterson.
HIGH SCHOOL: Crossland (Temple Hills, Md.).
JUNIOR COLLEGE: Valley Forge Junior College (Pa.).
COLLEGE: Michigan State.
TRANSACTIONS/CAREER NOTES: Selected by San Francisco 49ers in first round (16th pick overall) of 2000 NFL draft. ... Signed by 49ers (July 27, 2000).
HONORS: Played in Pro Bowl (2002 season).

Year Team	G	GS	TOTALS Tk.	Ast.	Sks.	INTERCEPTIONS No.	Yds.	Avg.	TD
2000—San Francisco NFL	13	7	29	17	4.0	2	33	16.5	0
2001—San Francisco NFL	14	14	37	15	3.0	0	0	0.0	0
2002—San Francisco NFL	16	16	78	18	2.0	1	2	2.0	0
Pro totals (3 years)	43	37	144	50	9.0	3	35	11.7	0

PETERSON, MIKE   LB   JAGUARS

PERSONAL: Born June 17, 1976, in Gainesville, Fla. ... 6-1/234. ... Full name: Porter Michael Peterson. ... Couson of Freddie Solomon, wide receiver with Philadelphia Eagles (1995-98).
HIGH SCHOOL: Santa Fe (Alachua, Fla.).
COLLEGE: Florida.
TRANSACTIONS/CAREER NOTES: Selected by Indianapolis Colts in second round (36th pick overall) of 1999 NFL draft. ... Signed by Colts (July 28, 1999). ... Granted unconditional free agency (February 28, 2003). ... Signed by Jacksonville Jaguars (March 13, 2003).
HONORS: Named outside linebacker on THE SPORTING NEWS college All-America first team (1998).

Year Team	G	GS	TOTALS Tk.	Ast.	Sks.	INTERCEPTIONS No.	Yds.	Avg.	TD
1999—Indianapolis NFL	16	13	71	21	3.0	0	0	0.0	0
2000—Indianapolis NFL	16	16	103	55	0.0	2	8	4.0	0
2001—Indianapolis NFL	9	9	46	19	1.5	2	18	9.0	0
2002—Indianapolis NFL	16	16	103	33	0.0	3	96	32.0	0
Pro totals (4 years)	57	54	323	128	4.5	7	122	17.4	0

P

PETERSON, TODD — K

PERSONAL: Born February 4, 1970, in Washington, D.C. ... 5-10/177. ... Full name: Joseph Todd Peterson.
HIGH SCHOOL: Valdosta (Ga.) State.
COLLEGE: Navy, then Georgia (degree in finance, 1992).
TRANSACTIONS/CAREER NOTES: Selected by New York Giants in seventh round (177th pick overall) of 1993 NFL draft. ... Signed by Giants (July 19, 1993). ... Released by Giants (August 24, 1993). ... Signed by New England Patriots to practice squad (November 30, 1993). ... Released by Patriots (December 6, 1993). ... Signed by Atlanta Falcons (May 3, 1994). ... Released by Falcons (August 29, 1994). ... Signed by Arizona Cardinals (October 12, 1994). ... Released by Cardinals (October 24, 1994). ... Signed by Seattle Seahawks (January 17, 1995). ... Granted free agency (February 13, 1998). ... Re-signed by Seahawks for 1998 season. ... Granted unconditional free agency (February 12, 1999). ... Re-signed by Seahawks (March 2, 1999). ... Released by Seahawks (August 27, 2000). ... Signed by Kansas City Chiefs (October 11, 2000). ... Granted unconditional free agency (March 1, 2002). ... Signed by Pittsburgh Steelers (March 25, 2002). ... On injured reserve with rib injury (November 19, 2002-remainder of season). ... Released by Steelers (February 27, 2003).

				FIELD GOALS						TOTALS		
Year Team	G	1-29	30-39	40-49	50+	Tot.	Pct.	Lg.		XPM	XPA	Pts.
1993—New England NFL					Did not play.							
1994—Arizona NFL	2	1-1	1-1	0-2	0-0	2-4	50.0	35		4	4	10
1995—Seattle NFL	16	6-6	9-10	8-10	0-2	23-28	82.1	49		§40	§40	109
1996—Seattle NFL	16	11-13	7-7	8-11	2-3	28-34	82.4	54		27	27	111
1997—Seattle NFL	16	9-9	7-10	5-7	1-2	22-28	78.6	52		37	37	103
1998—Seattle NFL	16	7-7	4-5	5-5	3-7	19-24	79.2	51		41	41	98
1999—Seattle NFL	16	11-11	8-11	14-16	1-2	34-40	85.0	51		32	32	134
2000—Kansas City NFL	11	6-6	7-9	2-5	0-0	15-20	75.0	42		25	25	70
2001—Kansas City NFL	16	9-11	9-10	8-12	1-2	27-35	77.1	51		27	28	108
2002—Pittsburgh NFL	10	3-4	6-10	3-7	0-0	12-21	57.1	46		25	26	61
Pro totals (9 years)	119	63-68	58-73	53-75	8-18	182-234	77.8	54		258	260	804

PETERSON, WILL — CB — GIANTS

PERSONAL: Born June 15, 1979, in Uniontown, Pa. ... 6-0/200. ... Full name: William James Peterson Jr..
HIGH SCHOOL: Laurel Highlands (Pa.).
COLLEGE: Michigan, then Western Illinois.
TRANSACTIONS/CAREER NOTES: Selected by New Yorks Giants in third round (78th pick overall) of 2001 NFL draft. ... Signed by Giants (July 26, 2001).

			TOTALS			INTERCEPTIONS			
Year Team	G	GS	Tk.	Ast.	Sks.	No.	Yds.	Avg.	TD
2001—New York Giants NFL	16	5	47	5	0.0	1	0	0.0	0
2002—New York Giants NFL	12	12	36	4	0.0	2	1	0.5	0
Pro totals (2 years)	28	17	83	9	0.0	3	1	0.3	0

PETITGOUT, LUKE — OT — GIANTS

PERSONAL: Born June 16, 1976, in Milford, Del. ... 6-6/310. ... Full name: Lucas George Petitgout. ... Name pronounced pet-ee-GOO.
HIGH SCHOOL: Sussex Central (Georgetown, Del.).
COLLEGE: Notre Dame.
TRANSACTIONS/CAREER NOTES: Selected by New York Giants in first round (19th pick overall) of 1999 NFL draft. ... Signed by Giants (July 29, 1999). ... Granted unconditional free agency (February 28, 2003). ... Re-signed by Giants (February 28, 2003).
PLAYING EXPERIENCE: New York Giants NFL, 1999-2002. ... Games/Games started: 1999 (15/8), 2000 (16/16), 2001 (16/16), 2002 (16/16). Total: 73/56.
CHAMPIONSHIP GAME EXPERIENCE: Played in NFC championship game (2000 season). ... Played in Super Bowl XXXV (2000 season).

PHIFER, ROMAN — LB — PATRIOTS

PERSONAL: Born March 5, 1968, in Plattsburgh, N.Y. ... 6-2/248. ... Full name: Roman Zubinsky Phifer.
HIGH SCHOOL: South Mecklenburg (Charlotte).
COLLEGE: UCLA.
TRANSACTIONS/CAREER NOTES: Selected by Los Angeles Rams in second round (31st pick overall) of 1991 NFL draft. ... Signed by Rams (July 19, 1991). ... On injured reserve with broken leg (November 26, 1991-remainder of season). ... Granted unconditional free agency (February 17, 1995). ... Re-signed by Rams (March 22, 1995). ... Rams franchise moved to St. Louis (April 12, 1995). ... Granted unconditional free agency (February 12, 1999). ... Signed by New York Jets (March 9, 1999). ... Released by Jets (February 22, 2001). ... Signed by New England Patriots (August 3, 2001). ... Granted unconditional free agency (March 1, 2002). ... Re-signed by Patriots (June 21, 2002).
CHAMPIONSHIP GAME EXPERIENCE: Played in AFC championship game (2001 season). ... Member of Super Bowl championship team (2001 season).

			TOTALS			INTERCEPTIONS			
Year Team	G	GS	Tk.	Ast.	Sks.	No.	Yds.	Avg.	TD
1991—Los Angeles Rams NFL	12	5	21	3	2.0	0	0	0.0	0
1992—Los Angeles Rams NFL	16	14	51	15	0.0	1	3	3.0	0
1993—Los Angeles Rams NFL	16	16	96	21	0.0	0	0	0.0	0
1994—Los Angeles Rams NFL	16	15	79	17	1.5	2	7	3.5	0
1995—St. Louis NFL	16	16	87	28	3.0	3	52	17.3	0
1996—St. Louis NFL	15	15	104	18	1.5	0	0	0.0	0
1997—St. Louis NFL	16	15	57	17	2.0	0	0	0.0	0
1998—St. Louis NFL	13	13	57	14	6.5	1	41	41.0	0
1999—New York Jets NFL	16	12	36	14	4.5	2	20	10.0	0
2000—New York Jets NFL	16	10	32	13	4.0	0	0	0.0	0
2001—New England NFL	16	16	71	21	2.0	1	14	14.0	0
2002—New England NFL	14	14	69	40	0.5	0	0	0.0	0
Pro totals (12 years)	182	161	760	222	27.5	10	137	13.7	0

P

PHILLIPS, JERMAINE S BUCCANEERS

PERSONAL: Born March 27, 1979, in Roswell, Ga. ... 6-1/214.
HIGH SCHOOL: Roswell (Ga.).
COLLEGE: Georgia.
TRANSACTIONS/CAREER NOTES: Selected by Tampa Bay Buccaneers in fifth round (157th pick overall) of 2002 NFL draft. ... Signed by Buccaneers (July 22, 2002).
CHAMPIONSHIP GAME EXPERIENCE: Played in NFC championship game (2002 season). ... Member of Super Bowl championship team (2002 season).

Year Team	G	GS	TOTALS Tk.	Ast.	Sks.	INTERCEPTIONS No.	Yds.	Avg.	TD
2002—Tampa Bay NFL	16	0	0	1	0.0	0	0	0.0	0

PICKETT, RYAN DT RAMS

PERSONAL: Born October 8, 1979, in Zephyrhills, Fla. ... 6-2/310.
HIGH SCHOOL: Zephyrhills (Fla.).
COLLEGE: Ohio State.
TRANSACTIONS/CAREER NOTES: Selected after junior season by St. Louis Rams in first round (29th pick overall) of 2001 NFL draft. ... Signed by Rams (July 29, 2001).
CHAMPIONSHIP GAME EXPERIENCE: Played in NFC championship game (2001 season). ... Played in Super Bowl XXXVI (2001 season).

Year Team	G	GS	TOTALS Tk.	Ast.	Sks.
2001—St. Louis NFL	11	0	10	9	0.5
2002—St. Louis NFL	16	14	45	22	0.5
Pro totals (2 years)	27	14	55	31	1.0

PIERCE, ANTONIO LB REDSKINS

PERSONAL: Born October 26, 1978, in Ontario, Calif. ... 6-1/237.
HIGH SCHOOL: Paramount (Calif.).
JUNIOR COLLEGE: Mount San Antonio College (Calif.).
COLLEGE: Arizona.
TRANSACTIONS/CAREER NOTES: Signed as non-drafted free agent by Washington Redskins (April 25, 2001). ... Re-signed by Redskins (April 25, 2003).

Year Team	G	GS	TOTALS Tk.	Ast.	Sks.	INTERCEPTIONS No.	Yds.	Avg.	TD
2001—Washington NFL	16	7	42	8	1.0	1	0	0.0	0
2002—Washington NFL	8	2	8	4	0.0	0	0	0.0	0
Pro totals (2 years)	24	9	50	12	1.0	1	0	0.0	0

PIERSON, PETE OT

PERSONAL: Born February 4, 1971, in Portland, Ore. ... 6-5/315. ... Full name: Peter Samuel Pierson.
HIGH SCHOOL: David Douglas (Portland, Ore.).
COLLEGE: Washington (degree in political science, 1994).
TRANSACTIONS/CAREER NOTES: Selected by Tampa Bay Buccaneers in fifth round (136th pick overall) of 1994 NFL draft. ... Signed by Buccaneers (July 6, 1994). ... Released by Buccaneers (August 28, 1994). ... Re-signed by Buccaneers to practice squad (September 2, 1994). ... Activated (November 22, 1994). ... Released by Buccaneers (August 18, 1996). ... Re-signed by Buccaneers (September 10, 1996). ... Granted free agency (February 13, 1998). ... Re-signed by Buccaneers (June 11, 1998). ... Granted unconditional free agency (March 1, 2002). ... Re-signed by Buccaneers (May 23, 2002). ... Released by Buccaneers (September 1, 2002). ... Signed by Indianapolis Colts (November 6, 2002). ... Released by Colts (December 4, 2002).
PLAYING EXPERIENCE: Tampa Bay NFL, 1995-2001; Indianapolis NFL, 2002. ... Games/Games started: 1995 (12/4), 1996 (11/2), 1997 (15/0), 1998 (16/0), 1999 (15/0), 2000 (15/15), 2001 (16/0), 2002 (1/0). Total: 101/21.
CHAMPIONSHIP GAME EXPERIENCE: Played in NFC championship game (1999 season).

PILLER, ZACH G TITANS

PERSONAL: Born May 2, 1976, in St. Petersburg, Fla. ... 6-5/315. ... Full name: Zachary Paul Piller.
HIGH SCHOOL: Lincoln (Tallahassee, Fla.).
COLLEGE: Georgia Tech, then Florida.
TRANSACTIONS/CAREER NOTES: Selected by Tennessee Titans in third round (81st pick overall) of 1999 NFL draft. ... Signed by Titans (July 22, 1999). ... Granted unconditional free agency (February 28, 2003). ... Re-signed by Titans (March 3, 2003).
PLAYING EXPERIENCE: Tennessee NFL, 1999-2002. ... Games/Games started: 1999 (8/0), 2000 (16/0), 2001 (14/9), 2002 (13/13). Total: 51/22.
CHAMPIONSHIP GAME EXPERIENCE: Member of Titans for AFC championship game (1999 season); inactive. ... Member of Titans for Super Bowl XXXIV (1999 season); inactive. ... Played in AFC championship game (2002 season).

PINKSTON, TODD WR EAGLES

PERSONAL: Born April 23, 1977, in Forest, Miss. ... 6-2/174.
HIGH SCHOOL: Forest (Miss.).
COLLEGE: Southern Mississippi.

P

TRANSACTIONS/CAREER NOTES: Selected by Philadelphia Eagles in second round (36th pick overall) of 2000 NFL draft. ... Signed by Eagles (July 16, 2000).
CHAMPIONSHIP GAME EXPERIENCE: Played in NFC championship game (2001 and 2002 seasons).
SINGLE GAME HIGHS (regular season): Receptions—7 (December 8, 2002, vs. Seattle); yards—99 (September 9, 2001, vs. St. Louis); and touchdown receptions—2 (September 22, 2002, vs. Dallas).

			RECEIVING			
Year Team	G	GS	No.	Yds.	Avg.	TD
2000—Philadelphia NFL	16	1	10	181	18.1	0
2001—Philadelphia NFL	15	15	42	586	14.0	4
2002—Philadelphia NFL	15	15	60	798	13.3	7
Pro totals (3 years)	46	31	112	1565	14.0	11

PITTMAN, KAVIKA　　　　　DE

PERSONAL: Born October 9, 1974, in Frankfurt, West Germany. ... 6-6/273. ... Name pronounced kuh-VEE-kuh.
HIGH SCHOOL: Leesville (La.).
COLLEGE: McNeese State.
TRANSACTIONS/CAREER NOTES: Selected by Dallas Cowboys in second round (37th pick overall) of 1996 NFL draft. ... Signed by Cowboys (July 16, 1996). ... Granted unconditional free agency (February 11, 2000). ... Signed by Denver Broncos (February 22, 2000). ... On injured reserve with calf injury (December 19, 2001-remainder of season). ... Released by Broncos (February 25, 2003).

			TOTALS		
Year Team	G	GS	Tk.	Ast.	Sks.
1996—Dallas NFL	15	0	2	0	0.0
1997—Dallas NFL	15	0	4	1	1.0
1998—Dallas NFL	15	15	37	4	6.0
1999—Dallas NFL	16	16	33	10	3.0
2000—Denver NFL	15	15	26	2	7.0
2001—Denver NFL	14	14	28	6	1.0
2002—Denver NFL	16	15	29	9	0.0
Pro totals (7 years)	106	75	159	32	18.0

PITTMAN, MICHAEL　　　　　RB　　　　　BUCCANEERS

PERSONAL: Born August 14, 1975, in New Orleans. ... 6-0/218.
HIGH SCHOOL: Mira Mesa (San Diego).
COLLEGE: Fresno State.
TRANSACTIONS/CAREER NOTES: Selected by Arizona Cardinals in fourth round (95th pick overall) of 1998 NFL draft. ... Signed by Cardinals (May 20, 1998). ... Granted free agency (March 2, 2001). ... Re-signed by Cardinals (May 11, 2001). ... On suspended list (September 9-23, 2001). ... Granted unconditional free agency (March 1, 2002). ... Signed by Tampa Bay Buccaneers (March 25, 2002).
CHAMPIONSHIP GAME EXPERIENCE: Played in NFC championship game (2002 season). ... Member of Super Bowl championship team (2002 season).
SINGLE GAME HIGHS (regular season): Attempts—26 (October 21, 2001, vs. Kansas City); yards—133 (November 14, 1999, vs. Detroit); and rushing touchdowns—1 (December 15, 2002, vs. Detroit).
STATISTICAL PLATEAUS: 100-yard rushing games: 1999 (1), 2000 (1). Total: 2.

			RUSHING				RECEIVING				PUNT RETURNS				KICKOFF RETURNS				TOTALS		
Year Team	G	GS	Att.	Yds.	Avg.	TD	No.	Yds.	Avg.	TD	No.	Yds.	Avg.	TD	No.	Yds.	Avg.	TD	TD	2pt.	Pts.Fum.
1998—Ari. NFL	15	0	29	91	3.1	0	0	0	0.0	0	0	0	0.0	0	4	84	21.0	0	0	0	0　1
1999—Ari. NFL	10	2	64	289	4.5	2	16	196	12.3	0	4	16	4.0	0	2	31	15.5	0	2	0	12　3
2000—Ari. NFL	16	12	184	719	3.9	4	73	579	7.9	2	0	0	0.0	0	0	0	0.0	0	6	0	36　5
2001—Ari. NFL	15	14	241	846	3.5	5	42	264	6.3	0	0	0	0.0	0	6	161	26.8	0	5	0	30　5
2002—TB NFL	16	15	204	718	3.5	1	59	477	8.1	0	0	0	0.0	0	0	0	0.0	0	1	0	6　3
Pro totals (5 years)	72	43	722	2663	3.7	12	190	1516	8.0	2	4	16	4.0	0	12	276	23.0	0	14	0	84　17

PITTS, CHESTER　　　　　G　　　　　TEXANS

PERSONAL: Born June 26, 1979, in Inglewood, Calif. ... 6-4/320. ... Full name: Chester Morise Pitts II.
HIGH SCHOOL: California Academy for Math and Science (Los Angeles).
COLLEGE: San Diego State.
TRANSACTIONS/CAREER NOTES: Selected by Houston Texans in second round (50th pick overall) of 2002 NFL draft. ... Signed by Texans (July 16, 2002).
PLAYING EXPERIENCE: Houston NFL, 2002. ... Games/games started: 2002 (16/16).

PLAYER, SCOTT　　　　　P　　　　　CARDINALS

PERSONAL: Born December 17, 1969, in St. Augustine, Fla. ... 6-1/221.
HIGH SCHOOL: St. Augustine (Fla.).
JUNIOR COLLEGE: Florida Community College.
COLLEGE: Flagler College (Fla.), then Florida State (degree in education).
TRANSACTIONS/CAREER NOTES: Played with Birmingham Barracudas of CFL (1995). ... Granted free agency (March 7, 1996). ... Signed as non-drafted free agent by Arizona Cardinals (April 23, 1996). ... Released by Cardinals (August 19, 1996). ... Signed by New York Giants (February 14, 1997). ... Assigned by Giants to Frankfurt Galaxy in 1997 World League enhancement allocation program (February 18, 1997). ... Released by Giants (August 24, 1997). ... Signed by New York Jets to practice squad (August 26, 1997). ... Released by Jets (August 28, 1997). ... Re-signed by Cardinals (March 3, 1998). ... Granted free agency (March 2, 2001). ... Re-signed by Cardinals (July 13, 2001).
HONORS: Played in Pro Bowl (2000 season).

P

Year Team	G		No.	Yds.	Avg.	Net avg.	In. 20	Blk.
					PUNTING			
1995—Birmingham CFL	18		143	6247	43.7	36.5	0	0
1996—					Did not play.			
1997—Frankfurt W.L.	...		60	2617	43.6	34.3	17	1
1998—Arizona NFL	16		81	3378	41.7	35.9	12	∞1
1999—Arizona NFL	16		94	3948	42.0	36.7	18	0
2000—Arizona NFL	16		65	2871	44.2	37.3	17	0
2001—Arizona NFL	12		67	2779	41.5	33.8	17	0
2002—Arizona NFL	16		88	3864	43.9	35.0	28	1
W.L. totals (1 year)	...		60	2617	43.6	34.3	17	1
CFL totals (1 year)	18		143	6247	43.7	36.5	0	0
NFL totals (5 years)	76		395	16840	42.6	35.8	92	2
Pro totals (7 years)	...		598	25704	43.0	35.8	109	3

PLEASANT, ANTHONY   DE   PATRIOTS

PERSONAL: Born January 27, 1968, in Century, Fla. ... 6-5/280. ... Full name: Anthony Devon Pleasant.
HIGH SCHOOL: Century (Fla.).
COLLEGE: Tennessee State.
TRANSACTIONS/CAREER NOTES: Selected by Cleveland Browns in third round (73rd pick overall) of 1990 NFL draft. ... Signed by Browns (July 22, 1990). ... Browns franchise moved to Baltimore and renamed Ravens for 1996 season (March 11, 1996). ... Granted unconditional free agency (February 14, 1997). ... Signed by Atlanta Falcons (June 21, 1997). ... Released by Falcons (February 11, 1998). ... Signed by New York Jets (March 12, 1998). ... Granted unconditional free agency (February 11, 2000). ... Signed by San Francisco 49ers (July 19, 2000). ... Granted unconditional free agency (March 2, 2001). ... Signed by New England Patriots (March 22, 2001).
CHAMPIONSHIP GAME EXPERIENCE: Played in AFC championship game (1998 and 2001 seasons). ... Member of Super Bowl championship team (2001 season).

Year Team	G	GS	TOTALS			INTERCEPTIONS			
			Tk.	Ast.	Sks.	No.	Yds.	Avg.	TD
1990—Cleveland NFL	16	7	38	12	3.5	0	0	0.0	0
1991—Cleveland NFL	16	7	12	9	2.5	0	0	0.0	0
1992—Cleveland NFL	16	14	35	16	4.0	0	0	0.0	0
1993—Cleveland NFL	16	13	43	23	11.0	0	0	0.0	0
1994—Cleveland NFL	14	14	44	14	4.5	0	0	0.0	0
1995—Cleveland NFL	16	16	41	10	8.0	0	0	0.0	0
1996—Baltimore NFL	12	12	22	3	4.0	0	0	0.0	0
1997—Atlanta NFL	11	0	9	1	0.5	0	0	0.0	0
1998—New York Jets NFL	16	15	34	12	6.0	0	0	0.0	0
1999—New York Jets NFL	16	16	41	11	2.0	0	0	0.0	0
2000—San Francisco NFL	16	16	17	5	2.0	0	0	0.0	0
2001—New England NFL	16	16	35	8	6.0	2	0	0.0	0
2002—New England NFL	14	11	20	15	3.0	0	0	0.0	0
Pro totals (13 years)	195	157	391	139	57.0	2	0	0.0	0

PLUMMER, AHMED   CB   49ERS

PERSONAL: Born March 26, 1976, in Wyoming, Ohio. ... 6-0/191. ... Full name: Ahmed Kamil Plummer.
HIGH SCHOOL: Wyoming (Ohio).
COLLEGE: Ohio State.
TRANSACTIONS/CAREER NOTES: Selected by San Francisco 49ers in first round (24th pick overall) of 2000 NFL draft. ... Signed by 49ers (July 15, 2000).

Year Team	G	GS	TOTALS			INTERCEPTIONS			
			Tk.	Ast.	Sks.	No.	Yds.	Avg.	TD
2000—San Francisco NFL	16	15	66	9	0.0	0	0	0.0	0
2001—San Francisco NFL	15	15	58	6	0.0	7	45	6.4	0
2002—San Francisco NFL	15	15	52	11	0.0	1	0	0.0	0
Pro totals (3 years)	46	45	176	26	0.0	8	45	5.6	0

PLUMMER, JAKE   QB   BRONCOS

PERSONAL: Born December 19, 1974, in Boise, Idaho. ... 6-2/212. ... Full name: Jason Steven Plummer.
HIGH SCHOOL: Capital (Boise, Idaho).
COLLEGE: Arizona State.
TRANSACTIONS/CAREER NOTES: Selected by Arizona Cardinals in second round (42nd pick overall) of 1997 NFL draft. ... Signed by Cardinals (July 14, 1997). ... Granted unconditional free agency (February 28, 2003). ... Signed by Denver Broncos (March 5, 2003).
HONORS: Named quarterback on THE SPORTING NEWS college All-America second team (1996).
SINGLE GAME HIGHS (regular season): Attempts—57 (January 2, 2000, vs. Green Bay); completions—35 (January 2, 2000, vs. Green Bay); yards—465 (November 15, 1998, vs. Dallas); and touchdown passes—4 (November 18, 2001, vs. Detroit).
STATISTICAL PLATEAUS: 300-yard passing games: 1997 (2), 1998 (2), 1999 (1), 2000 (1), 2001 (1). Total: 7.
MISCELLANEOUS: Regular-season record as starting NFL quarterback: 30-52 (.366). ... Postseason record as starting NFL quarterback: 1-1 (.500).

Year Team	G	GS	PASSING									RUSHING				TOTALS		
			Att.	Cmp.	Pct.	Yds.	TD	Int.	Avg.	Skd.	Rat.	Att.	Yds.	Avg.	TD	TD	2pt.	Pts.
1997—Arizona NFL	10	9	296	157	53.0	2203	15	15	7.44	‡52	73.1	39	216	5.5	2	2	1	14
1998—Arizona NFL	16	16	547	324	59.2	3737	17	20	6.83	†49	75.0	51	217	4.3	4	4	0	24
1999—Arizona NFL	12	11	381	201	52.8	2111	9	*24	5.54	27	50.8	39	121	3.1	2	2	0	12
2000—Arizona NFL	14	14	475	270	56.8	2946	13	‡21	6.20	22	66.0	37	183	4.9	0	0	0	0
2001—Arizona NFL	16	16	525	304	57.9	3653	18	14	6.96	29	79.6	35	163	4.7	0	0	1	2
2002—Arizona NFL	16	16	530	284	53.6	2972	18	20	5.61	36	65.7	46	283	6.2	2	2	0	12
Pro totals (6 years)	84	82	2754	1540	55.9	17622	90	114	6.40	215	69.0	247	1183	4.8	10	10	2	64

P

POLK, CARLOS   LB   CHARGERS

PERSONAL: Born February 22, 1977, in Memphis, Tenn. ... 6-2/250. ... Full name: Carlos Devonn Polk.
HIGH SCHOOL: Guilford (Rockford, Ill.).
COLLEGE: Nebraska (degree in sociology).
TRANSACTIONS/CAREER NOTES: Selected by San Diego Chargers in fourth round (112th pick overall) of 2001 NFL draft. ... Signed by Chargers (June 20, 2001). ... On injured reserve with shoulder injury (November 14, 2001-remainder of season).
HONORS: Named linebacker on THE SPORTING NEWS college All-America third team.

Year	Team	G	GS	TOTALS Tk.	Ast.	Sks.	INTERCEPTIONS No.	Yds.	Avg.	TD
2001—San Diego NFL		6	0	0	0	0.0	0	0	0.0	0
2002—San Diego NFL		15	0	3	1	1.0	0	0	0.0	0
Pro totals (2 years)		21	0	3	1	1.0	0	0	0.0	0

POLK, DASHON   LB   BILLS

PERSONAL: Born March 13, 1977, in Pacoima, Calif. ... 6-2/240. ... Full name: DaShon Lamor Polk.
HIGH SCHOOL: Taft (Woodlands Hills, Calif.).
COLLEGE: Arizona.
TRANSACTIONS/CAREER NOTES: Selected by Buffalo Bills in seventh round (251st pick overall) of 2000 NFL draft. ... Signed by Bills (June 22, 2000). ... Granted free agency (February 28, 2003). ... Re-signed by Bills (April 10, 2003).

Year	Team	G	GS	TOTALS Tk.	Ast.	Sks.	INTERCEPTIONS No.	Yds.	Avg.	TD
2000—Buffalo NFL		5	0	0	0	0.0	0	0	0.0	0
2001—Buffalo NFL		16	1	13	6	0.0	0	0	0.0	0
2002—Buffalo NFL		16	0	8	10	0.0	0	0	0.0	0
Pro totals (3 years)		37	1	21	16	0.0	0	0	0.0	0

POLLARD, MARCUS   TE   COLTS

PERSONAL: Born February 8, 1972, in Valley, Ala. ... 6-3/247. ... Full name: Marcus LaJuan Pollard.
HIGH SCHOOL: Valley (Ala.).
JUNIOR COLLEGE: Seward County Community College, Kan. (did not play football).
COLLEGE: Bradley (did not play football).
TRANSACTIONS/CAREER NOTES: Signed as non-drafted free agent by Indianapolis Colts (January 24, 1995). ... Released by Colts (August 22, 1995). ... Re-signed by Colts to practice squad (August 28, 1995). ... Activated (October 10, 1995). ... Granted free agency (February 13, 1998). ... Tendered offer sheet by Philadelphia Eagles (March 4, 1998). ... Offer matched by Colts (March 9, 1998). ... Designated by Colts as franchise player (February 22, 2001).
CHAMPIONSHIP GAME EXPERIENCE: Played in AFC championship game (1995 season).
SINGLE GAME HIGHS (regular season): Receptions—7 (November 3, 2002, vs. Tennessee); yards—216 (November 18, 2001, vs. New Orleans); and touchdown receptions—2 (October 10, 1999, vs. Miami).
STATISTICAL PLATEAUS: 100-yard receiving games: 2001 (2).

Year	Team	G	GS	RECEIVING No.	Yds.	Avg.	TD	TOTALS TD	2pt.	Pts.	Fum.
1995—Indianapolis NFL		8	0	0	0	0.0	0	0	0	0	0
1996—Indianapolis NFL		16	4	6	86	14.3	1	1	0	6	0
1997—Indianapolis NFL		16	6	10	116	11.6	0	0	1	2	0
1998—Indianapolis NFL		16	11	24	309	12.9	4	4	†2	28	0
1999—Indianapolis NFL		16	10	34	374	11.0	4	4	0	24	2
2000—Indianapolis NFL		16	14	30	439	14.6	3	3	1	20	0
2001—Indianapolis NFL		16	16	47	739	15.7	8	8	0	48	0
2002—Indianapolis NFL		15	15	43	478	11.1	6	6	1	38	1
Pro totals (8 years)		119	76	194	2541	13.1	26	26	5	166	3

POLLEY, TOMMY   LB   RAMS

PERSONAL: Born January 11, 1978, in Baltimore. ... 6-3/240.
HIGH SCHOOL: Dunbar (Baltimore).
COLLEGE: Florida State.
TRANSACTIONS/CAREER NOTES: Selected by St. Louis Rams in second round (42nd pick overall) of 2001 NFL draft. ... Signed by Rams (July 23, 2001).
CHAMPIONSHIP GAME EXPERIENCE: Played in NFC championship game (2001 season). ... Played in Super Bowl XXXVI (2001 season).
HONORS: Named linebacker on THE SPORTING NEWS college All-America third team (2000).

Year	Team	G	GS	TOTALS Tk.	Ast.	Sks.	INTERCEPTIONS No.	Yds.	Avg.	TD
2001—St. Louis NFL		16	11	61	17	0.0	0	0	0.0	0
2002—St. Louis NFL		12	11	42	15	0.0	0	0	0.0	0
Pro totals (2 years)		28	22	103	32	0.0	0	0	0.0	0

POOLE, NATHAN   WR   CARDINALS

PERSONAL: Born February 1, 1977, in Danville, Va. ... 6-2/212.
HIGH SCHOOL: George Washington (Danville, Va.).
COLLEGE: Marshall.
TRANSACTIONS/CAREER NOTES: Signed as non-drafted free agent by Arizona Cardinals (April 23, 2001). ... Released by Cardinals (September 1, 2001). ... Re-signed by Cardinals to practice squad (December 3, 2001). ... Released by Cardinals (August 26, 2002). ... Re-signed by Cardinals to practice squad (October 30, 2002). ... Activated (November 6, 2002). ... Re-signed by Cardinals (April 2, 2003).

P

SINGLE GAME HIGHS (regular season): Receptions—6 (December 8, 2002, vs. Detroit); yards—41 (December 8, 2002, vs. Detroit); and touchdown receptions—1 (December 8, 2002, vs. Detroit).

					RECEIVING		
Year Team	G	GS	No.	Yds.	Avg.	TD	
2002—Arizona NFL	5	1	13	108	8.3	1	

POOLE, TYRONE — DB — PATRIOTS

PERSONAL: Born February 3, 1972, in La Grange, Ga. ... 5-8/188.
HIGH SCHOOL: La Grange (Ga.).
COLLEGE: Fort Valley (Ga.) State.
TRANSACTIONS/CAREER NOTES: Selected by Carolina Panthers in first round (22nd pick overall) of 1995 NFL draft. ... Signed by Panthers (July 15, 1995). ... Traded by Panthers to Indianapolis Colts for second-round pick (OT Chris Terry) in 1999 draft (July 22, 1998). ... Released by Colts (March 1, 2001). ... Signed by Denver Broncos (May 22, 2001). ... On reserve/left squad list (August 9, 2001-February 27, 2002). ... Granted unconditional free agency (February 28, 2003). ... Signed by New England Patriots (March 4, 2003).
CHAMPIONSHIP GAME EXPERIENCE: Played in NFC championship game (1996 season).

			TOTALS			INTERCEPTIONS				PUNT RETURNS				TOTALS			
Year Team	G	GS	Tk.	Ast.	Sks.	No.	Yds.	Avg.	TD	No.	Yds.	Avg.	TD	TD	2pt.	Pts.	Fum.
1995—Carolina NFL	16	13	59	9	2.0	2	8	4.0	0	0	0	0.0	0	0	0	0	0
1996—Carolina NFL	15	15	57	11	0.0	1	35	35.0	0	3	26	8.7	0	0	0	0	0
1997—Carolina NFL	16	16	48	4	1.0	2	0	0.0	0	26	191	7.3	0	0	0	0	3
1998—Indianapolis NFL	15	15	52	9	0.0	1	0	0.0	0	12	107	8.9	0	0	0	0	0
1999—Indianapolis NFL	15	14	34	5	1.0	3	85	28.3	0	0	0	0.0	0	0	0	0	0
2000—Indianapolis NFL	15	12	38	12	0.0	1	1	1.0	0	0	0	0.0	0	0	0	0	0
2002—Denver NFL	16	4	41	10	1.0	0	0	0.0	0	4	24	6.0	0	0	0	0	1
Pro totals (7 years)	108	89	329	60	5.0	10	129	12.9	0	45	348	7.7	0	0	0	0	4

POPE, MONSANTO — DT — BRONCOS

PERSONAL: Born January 27, 1978, in Norfolk, Va. ... 6-3/300.
HIGH SCHOOL: Hopewell (Va.).
COLLEGE: Virginia.
TRANSACTIONS/CAREER NOTES: Selected by Denver Broncos in seventh round (231st pick overall) of 2002 NFL draft. ... Signed by Broncos (June 14, 2002).

			TOTALS		
Year Team	G	GS	Tk.	Ast.	Sks.
2002—Denver NFL	14	1	15	3	4.0

PORCHER, ROBERT — DE — LIONS

PERSONAL: Born July 30, 1969, in Wando, S.C. ... 6-3/266. ... Full name: Robert Porcher III. ... Name pronounced por-SHAY.
HIGH SCHOOL: Cainhoy (Huger, S.C.).
COLLEGE: Tennessee State, then South Carolina State (degree in criminal justice).
TRANSACTIONS/CAREER NOTES: Selected by Detroit Lions in first round (26th pick overall) of 1992 NFL draft. ... Signed by Lions (July 25, 1992). ... Granted unconditional free agency (February 16, 1996). ... Re-signed by Lions (March 29, 1996). ... Granted unconditional free agency (February 14, 1997). ... Re-signed by Lions (March 4, 1997). ... Designated by Lions as franchise player (February 10, 2000).
HONORS: Played in Pro Bowl (1999 and 2001 seasons).
MISCELLANEOUS: Holds Detroit Lions all-time record for most sacks (91).

			TOTALS			INTERCEPTIONS			
Year Team	G	GS	Tk.	Ast.	Sks.	No.	Yds.	Avg.	TD
1992—Detroit NFL	16	1	11	10	1.0	0	0	0.0	0
1993—Detroit NFL	16	4	37	10	8.5	0	0	0.0	0
1994—Detroit NFL	15	15	47	22	3.0	0	0	0.0	0
1995—Detroit NFL	16	16	29	22	5.0	0	0	0.0	0
1996—Detroit NFL	16	16	45	21	10.0	0	0	0.0	0
1997—Detroit NFL	16	15	40	32	12.5	1	5	5.0	0
1998—Detroit NFL	16	16	41	21	11.5	0	0	0.0	0
1999—Detroit NFL	15	14	32	16	15.0	0	0	0.0	0
2000—Detroit NFL	16	16	30	6	8.0	0	0	0.0	0
2001—Detroit NFL	16	16	45	7	11.0	0	0	0.0	0
2002—Detroit NFL	15	15	30	15	5.5	0	0	0.0	0
Pro totals (11 years)	173	144	387	182	91.0	1	5	5.0	0

PORTER, ALVIN — DB — RAVENS

PERSONAL: Born May 10, 1977, in Shreveport, La. ... 5-11/175. ... Full name: Alvin Guy Porter.
HIGH SCHOOL: Adamson (Dallas).
COLLEGE: Oklahoma State.
TRANSACTIONS/CAREER NOTES: Signed as non-drafted free agent by Baltimore Ravens (April 27, 2001).

			TOTALS			INTERCEPTIONS			
Year Team	G	GS	Tk.	Ast.	Sks.	No.	Yds.	Avg.	TD
2001—Baltimore NFL	16	0	5	0	0.0	1	-3	-3.0	0
2002—Baltimore NFL	16	5	27	5	0.0	0	0	0.0	0
Pro totals (2 years)	32	5	32	5	0.0	1	-3	-3.0	0

P

PORTER, JERRY — WR — RAIDERS

PERSONAL: Born July 14, 1978, in Washington, D.C. ... 6-2/220.
HIGH SCHOOL: Coolidge (Washington, D.C.).
COLLEGE: West Virginia.
TRANSACTIONS/CAREER NOTES: Selected by Oakland Raiders in second round (47th pick overall) of 2000 NFL draft. ... Signed by Raiders (July 22, 2000).
CHAMPIONSHIP GAME EXPERIENCE: Played in AFC championship game (2000 and 2002 seasons). ... Played in Super Bowl XXXVII (2002 season).
SINGLE GAME HIGHS (regular season): Receptions—7 (October 6, 2002, vs. Buffalo); yards—117 (October 6, 2002, vs. Buffalo); and touchdown receptions—2 (November 24, 2002, vs. Arizona).
STATISTICAL PLATEAUS: 100-yard receiving games: 2002 (1).

			RUSHING				RECEIVING				TOTALS			
Year Team	G	GS	Att.	Yds.	Avg.	TD	No.	Yds.	Avg.	TD	TD	2pt.	Pts.	Fum.
2000—Oakland NFL	12	0	0	0	0.0	0	1	6	6.0	0	0	0	0	0
2001—Oakland NFL	15	1	2	13	6.5	0	19	220	11.6	0	0	0	0	0
2002—Oakland NFL	16	14	4	6	1.5	0	51	688	13.5	9	9	2	58	0
Pro totals (3 years)	43	15	6	19	3.2	0	71	914	12.9	9	9	2	58	0

PORTER, JOEY — LB — STEELERS

PERSONAL: Born March 22, 1977, in Bakersfield, Calif. ... 6-2/248. ... Full name: Joey Eugene Porter.
HIGH SCHOOL: Foothills (Calif.).
COLLEGE: Colorado State.
TRANSACTIONS/CAREER NOTES: Selected by Pittsburgh Steelers in third round (73rd pick overall) of 1999 NFL draft. ... Signed by Steelers (July 30, 1999). ... Granted free agency (March 1, 2002). ... Re-signed by Steelers (April 29, 2002).
CHAMPIONSHIP GAME EXPERIENCE: Played in AFC championship game (2001 season).
HONORS: Played in Pro Bowl (2002 season). ... Named linebacker on the THE SPORTING NEWS NFL All-Pro team (2002).

			TOTALS			INTERCEPTIONS			
Year Team	G	GS	Tk.	Ast.	Sks.	No.	Yds.	Avg.	TD
1999—Pittsburgh NFL	16	0	10	0	2.0	0	0	0.0	0
2000—Pittsburgh NFL	16	16	41	18	10.5	1	0	0.0	0
2001—Pittsburgh NFL	15	15	47	14	9.0	0	0	0.0	0
2002—Pittsburgh NFL	16	16	61	28	9.0	4	153	38.3	0
Pro totals (4 years)	63	47	159	60	30.5	5	153	30.6	0

PORTIS, CLINTON — RB — BRONCOS

PERSONAL: Born September 1, 1981, in Gainesville, Fla. ... 5-11/205. ... Full name: Clinton Earl Portis.
HIGH SCHOOL: Gainesville (Fla.).
COLLEGE: Miami (Fla.).
TRANSACTIONS/CAREER NOTES: Selected after junior season by Denver Broncos in second round (51st pick overall) of 2002 NFL draft. ... Signed by Broncos (July 25, 2002).
HONORS: Named NFL Rookie of the Year by THE SPORTING NEWS (2002).
SINGLE GAME HIGHS (regular season): Attempts—26 (October 27, 2002, vs. New England); yards—228 (December 29, 2002, vs. Arizona); and rushing touchdowns—3 (December 15, 2002, vs. Kansas City).
STATISTICAL PLATEAUS: 100-yard rushing games: 2002 (8).

			RUSHING				RECEIVING				TOTALS			
Year Team	G	GS	Att.	Yds.	Avg.	TD	No.	Yds.	Avg.	TD	TD	2pt.	Pts.	Fum.
2002—Denver NFL	16	12	273	1508	§5.5	15	33	364	11.0	2	17	0	102	5

POSEY, JEFF — DE — BILLS

PERSONAL: Born August 14, 1975, in Bassfield, Miss. ... 6-4/249.
HIGH SCHOOL: Greenville (Miss.).
JUNIOR COLLEGE: Pearl River Community College (Miss.).
COLLEGE: Southern Mississippi.
TRANSACTIONS/CAREER NOTES: Signed as non-drafted free agent by San Francisco 49ers (May 2, 1997) ... Released by 49ers (August 19, 1997). ... Re-signed by 49ers to practice squad (August 25, 1997). ... Granted free agency (March 2, 2001). ... Signed by Philadelphia Eagles (June 18, 2001). ... Released by Eagles (August 31, 2001). ... Signed by Carolina Panthers (October 23, 2001). ... Claimed on waivers by Jacksonville Jaguars (November 21, 2001). ... Granted unconditional free agency (March 1, 2002). ... Signed by Houston Texans (April 19, 2002). ... Granted unconditional free agency (February 28, 2003). ... Signed by Buffalo Bills (February 28, 2003).
MISCELLANEOUS: Holds Houston Texans all-time record for most sacks (8).

			TOTALS			INTERCEPTIONS			
Year Team	G	GS	Tk.	Ast.	Sks.	No.	Yds.	Avg.	TD
1998—San Francisco NFL	16	0	7	2	0.5	0	0	0.0	0
1999—San Francisco NFL	16	6	10	5	2.0	0	0	0.0	0
2000—San Francisco NFL	16	8	22	11	0.5	0	0	0.0	0
2001—Carolina NFL	4	0	2	0	0.0	0	0	0.0	0
—Jacksonville NFL	7	5	5	1	0.0	0	0	0.0	0
2002—Houston NFL	16	9	45	15	8.0	1	0	0.0	0
Pro totals (5 years)	75	28	91	34	11.0	1	0	0.0	0

P

POTEAT, HANK — CB — STEELERS

PERSONAL: Born August 30, 1977, in Philadelphia. ... 5-9/192. ... Full name: Henry Major Poteat II.
HIGH SCHOOL: Harrisburg (Pa.).
COLLEGE: Pittsburgh.
TRANSACTIONS/CAREER NOTES: Selected by Pittsburgh Steelers in third round (77th pick overall) of 2000 NFL draft. ... Signed by Steelers (July 21, 2000). ... Granted free agency (February 28, 2003).
CHAMPIONSHIP GAME EXPERIENCE: Member of Steelers for AFC championship game (2001 season); inactive.

			TOTALS			INTERCEPTIONS				PUNT RETURNS				KICKOFF RETURNS				TOTALS			
Year Team	G	GS	Tk.	Ast.	Sks.	No.	Yds.	Avg.	TD	No.	Yds.	Avg.	TD	No.	Yds.	Avg.	TD	TD	2pt.	Pts.	Fum.
2000—Pittsburgh NFL	15	0	0	0	0.0	0	0	0.0	0	36	467	13.0	1	24	465	19.4	0	1	0	6	3
2001—Pittsburgh NFL	13	0	1	0	0.0	0	0	0.0	0	36	292	8.1	0	16	250	15.6	0	0	0	0	4
2002—Pittsburgh NFL	13	0	8	0	0.0	0	0	0.0	0	4	29	7.3	0	5	103	20.6	0	0	0	0	1
Pro totals (3 years)	41	0	9	0	0.0	0	0	0.0	0	76	788	10.4	1	45	818	18.2	0	1	0	6	8

POWELL, CARL — DT — BENGALS

PERSONAL: Born January 4, 1974, in Detroit. ... 6-2/273. ... Full name: Carl Demetris Powell.
HIGH SCHOOL: Northern (Detroit).
JUNIOR COLLEGE: Grand Rapids (Mich.) Community College.
COLLEGE: Louisville.
TRANSACTIONS/CAREER NOTES: Selected by Indianapolis Colts in fifth round (156th pick overall) of 1997 NFL draft. ... Signed by Colts (July 3, 1997). ... Released by Colts (August 28, 1998). ... Selected by Rhein Fire in 1999 NFL Europe draft (February 23, 1999). ... Signed by Baltimore Ravens (July 21, 2000). ... Released by Ravens (November 13, 2000). ... Signed by Chicago Bears (March 5, 2001). ... Granted unconditional free agency (March 1, 2002). ... Signed by Washington Redskins (March 28, 2002). ... Granted unconditional free agency (February 28, 2003). ... Signed by Cincinnati Bengals (March 2, 2003).

			TOTALS		
Year Team	G	GS	Tk.	Ast.	Sks.
1997—Indianapolis NFL	11	0	3	0	0.0
1998—	Did not play.				
1999—Rhein NFLE	...	...	...	...	3.0
2000—Barcelona NFLE	...	...	...	...	1.0
—Baltimore NFL	2	0	0	0	0.0
2001—Chicago NFL	16	0	8	1	0.0
2002—Washington NFL	15	5	21	10	3.0
NFL Europe totals (2 years)	...	...	...	...	4.0
NFL totals (3 years)	44	5	32	11	3.0
Pro totals (5 years)	...	...	...	...	7.0

PRENTICE, TRAVIS — RB — CARDINALS

PERSONAL: Born December 8, 1976, in Louisville, Ky. ... 5-11/221. ... Full name: Travis Jason Prentice.
HIGH SCHOOL: Manual (Louisville, Ky.).
COLLEGE: Miami of Ohio.
TRANSACTIONS/CAREER NOTES: Selected by Cleveland Browns in third round (63rd pick overall) of 2000 NFL draft. ... Signed by Browns (July 16, 2000). ... Traded by Browns with QB Spergon Wynn to Minnesota Vikings for pick in 2002 draft (LB Andra Davis) and pick in 2003 draft (September 2, 2001). ... Claimed on waivers by Houston Texans (May 2, 2002). ... Released by Texans (September 1, 2002). ... Signed by Arizona Cardinals (December 4, 2002). ... Re-signed by Cardinals (March 12, 2003).
HONORS: Named running back on THE SPORTING NEWS college All-America second team (1998 and 1999).
SINGLE GAME HIGHS (regular season): Attempts—28 (Ocotober 8, 2000, vs. Arizona); yards—97 (October 8, 2000, vs. Arizona); and rushing touchdowns—3 (October 8, 2000, vs. Arizona).

			RUSHING				RECEIVING				TOTALS			
Year Team	G	GS	Att.	Yds.	Avg.	TD	No.	Yds.	Avg.	TD	TD	2pt.	Pts.	Fum.
2000—Cleveland NFL	16	11	173	512	3.0	7	37	191	5.2	1	8	0	48	2
2001—Minnesota NFL	14	0	14	13	0.9	2	1	10	10.0	0	2	0	12	1
2002—Arizona NFL	Did not play.													
Pro totals (2 years)	30	11	187	525	2.8	9	38	201	5.3	1	10	0	60	3

PRICE, MARCUS — OT — BILLS

PERSONAL: Born March 3, 1972, in Port Arthur, Texas. ... 6-4/314. ... Full name: Marcus Raymond Price.
HIGH SCHOOL: Lincoln (Port Arthur, Texas).
COLLEGE: Louisiana State.
TRANSACTIONS/CAREER NOTES: Selected by Jacksonville Jaguars in sixth round (172nd pick overall) of 1995 NFL draft. ... Signed by Jaguars (June 1, 1995). ... On injured reserve with ankle injury (August 19, 1995-entire season). ... Released by Jaguars (August 25, 1996). ... Signed by Denver Broncos to practice squad (December 3, 1996). ... Released by Broncos (December 30, 1996). ... Signed by Jaguars (January 31, 1997). ... Released by Jaguars (August 19, 1997). ... Re-signed by Jaguars to practice squad (October 28, 1997). ... Signed by San Diego Chargers off Jaguars practice squad (November 26, 1997). ... Released by Chargers (September 21, 1999). ... Signed by New Orleans Saints (March 23, 2000). ... Released by Saints (December 3, 2000). ... Re-signed by Saints (December 5, 2000). ... Granted unconditional free agency (March 1, 2002). ... Signed by Buffalo Bills (March 13, 2002).
PLAYING EXPERIENCE: San Diego NFL, 1997 and 1998; New Orleans NFL, 2000-2001; Buffalo NFL, 2002. ... Games/Games started: 1997 (2/0), 1998 (10/0), 2000 (7/0), 2001 (12/0), 2002 (16/3). Total: 47/3.

P

PRICE, PEERLESS   WR   FALCONS

PERSONAL: Born October 27, 1976, in Dayton, Ohio. ... 5-11/190. ... Full name: Peerless LeCross Price.
HIGH SCHOOL: Meadowdale (Dayton, Ohio).
COLLEGE: Tennessee.
TRANSACTIONS/CAREER NOTES: Selected by Buffalo Bills in second round (53rd pick overall) of 1999 NFL draft. ... Signed by Bills (July 30, 1999). ... Designated by Bills as franchise player (February 19, 2003). ... Traded by Bills to Atlanta Falcons for first-round pick (RB Willis McGahee) in 2003 draft (March 7, 2003).
SINGLE GAME HIGHS (regular season): Receptions—13 (September 15, 2002, vs. Minnesota); yards—185 (September 15, 2002, vs. Minnesota); and touchdown receptions—2 (December 1, 2002, vs. Miami).
STATISTICAL PLATEAUS: 100-yard receiving games: 1999 (1), 2000 (1), 2001 (3), 2002 (5). Total: 10.

			RUSHING				RECEIVING				PUNT RETURNS				KICKOFF RETURNS				TOTALS		
Year Team	G	GS	Att.	Yds.	Avg.	TD	No.	Yds.	Avg.	TD	No.	Yds.	Avg.	TD	No.	Yds.	Avg.	TD	TD	2pt.	Pts.
1999—Buffalo NFL	16	4	1	-7	-7.0	0	31	393	12.7	3	1	16	16.0	0	1	27	27.0	0	3	0	18
2000—Buffalo NFL	16	16	2	32	16.0	0	52	762	14.7	3	5	27	5.4	0	0	0	0.0	0	3	0	18
2001—Buffalo NFL	16	16	6	97	16.2	0	55	895	16.3	7	19	110	5.8	0	0	0	0.0	0	7	0	42
2002—Buffalo NFL	16	16	3	-13	-4.3	0	94	1252	13.3	9	0	0	0.0	0	0	0	0.0	0	9	0	54
Pro totals (4 years)	64	52	12	109	9.1	0	232	3302	14.2	22	25	153	6.1	0	1	27	27.0	0	22	0	132

PRICE, SHAWN   DE

PERSONAL: Born March 28, 1970, in Van Nuys, Calif. ... 6-4/290. ... Full name: Shawn Sterling Price.
HIGH SCHOOL: North Tahoe (Nev.).
JUNIOR COLLEGE: Sierra College (Calif.).
COLLEGE: Pacific.
TRANSACTIONS/CAREER NOTES: Signed as non-drafted free agent by Tampa Bay Buccaneers (April 29, 1993). ... Released by Buccaneers (August 30, 1993). ... Re-signed by Buccaneers to practice squad (August 31, 1993). ... Activated (November 5, 1993). ... Selected by Carolina Panthers from Buccaneers in NFL expansion draft (February 15, 1995). ... Granted unconditional free agency (February 16, 1996). ... Signed by Buffalo Bills (April 12, 1996). ... Granted unconditional free agency (February 13, 1998). ... Re-signed by Bills (March 9, 1998). ... Granted unconditional free agency (March 2, 2001). ... Re-signed by Bills (April 27, 2001). ... On injured reserve with knee injury (January 4, 2002-remainder of season). ... Granted unconditional free agency (March 1, 2002). ... Re-signed by Bills (August 16, 2002). ... Released by Bills (September 1, 2002). ... Signed by San Diego Chargers (December 4, 2002). ... Granted unconditional free agency (February 28, 2003).

			TOTALS		
Year Team	G	GS	Tk.	Ast.	Sks.
1993—Tampa Bay NFL	9	6	11	14	3.0
1994—Tampa Bay NFL	6	0	2	0	0.0
1995—Carolina NFL	16	0	14	1	1.0
1996—Buffalo NFL	15	0	5	3	0.0
1997—Buffalo NFL	10	0	12	9	0.0
1998—Buffalo NFL	14	2	17	5	5.0
1999—Buffalo NFL	15	1	13	3	2.5
2000—Buffalo NFL	13	6	14	12	1.0
2001—Buffalo NFL	11	11	18	16	2.0
2002—San Diego NFL	2	0	0	0	0.0
Pro totals (10 years)	111	26	106	63	14.5

PRIOLEAU, PIERSON   S   BILLS

PERSONAL: Born August 6, 1977, in Alvin, S.C. ... 5-11/190. ... Full name: Pierson Olin Prioleau. ... Name pronounced pray-LOW.
HIGH SCHOOL: Macedonia (Saint Stephens, S.C.).
COLLEGE: Virginia Tech.
TRANSACTIONS/CAREER NOTES: Selected by San Francisco 49ers in fourth round (110th pick overall) of 1999 NFL draft. ... Signed by 49ers (July 27, 1999). ... Released by 49ers (September 2, 2001). ... Signed by Buffalo Bills (November 7, 2001). ... Granted free agency (March 1, 2002). ... Re-signed by Bills (April 16, 2002).
HONORS: Named strong safety on The Sporting News college All-America third team (1997).

			TOTALS			INTERCEPTIONS			
Year Team	G	GS	Tk.	Ast.	Sks.	No.	Yds.	Avg.	TD
1999—San Francisco NFL	14	5	32	8	0.0	0	0	0.0	0
2000—San Francisco NFL	13	5	36	10	0.0	1	13	13.0	0
2001—Buffalo NFL	6	2	23	8	1.0	0	0	0.0	0
2002—Buffalo NFL	16	16	64	22	1.0	0	0	0.0	0
Pro totals (4 years)	49	28	155	48	2.0	1	13	13.0	0

PRITCHETT, KELVIN   DT   LIONS

PERSONAL: Born October 24, 1969, in Atlanta. ... 6-3/322. ... Full name: Kelvin Bratodd Pritchett.
HIGH SCHOOL: Therrell (Atlanta).
COLLEGE: Mississippi.
TRANSACTIONS/CAREER NOTES: Selected by Dallas Cowboys in first round (20th pick overall) of 1991 NFL draft. ... Rights traded by Cowboys to Detroit Lions for second- (LB Dixon Edwards), third- (G James Richards) and fourth-round (DE Tony Hill) picks in 1991 draft (April 21, 1991). ... Granted free agency (February 17, 1994). ... Re-signed by Lions (August 12, 1994). ... Granted unconditional free agency (February 17, 1995). ... Signed by Jacksonville Jaguars (March 11, 1995). ... On injured reserve with knee injury (November 4, 1997-remainder of season). ... Granted unconditional free agency (February 12, 1999). ... Signed by Lions (April 22, 1999). ... Granted unconditional free agency (February 11, 2000). ... Re-signed by Lions (May 12, 2000). ... Granted unconditional free agency (March 2, 2001). ... Re-signed by

Lions (July 11, 2001). ... Granted unconditional free agency (March 1, 2002). ... Re-signed by Lions (March 26, 2002). ... Granted unconditional free agency (February 28, 2003). ... Re-signed by Lions (March 13, 2003).
CHAMPIONSHIP GAME EXPERIENCE: Played in NFC championship game (1991 season). ... Played in AFC championship game (1996 season).

Year Team	G	GS	TOTALS			INTERCEPTIONS			
			Tk.	Ast.	Sks.	No.	Yds.	Avg.	TD
1991—Detroit NFL	16	0	20	6	1.5	0	0	0.0	0
1992—Detroit NFL	16	15	38	21	6.5	0	0	0.0	0
1993—Detroit NFL	16	5	33	9	4.0	0	0	0.0	0
1994—Detroit NFL	16	15	41	33	5.5	0	0	0.0	0
1995—Jacksonville NFL	16	16	41	22	1.5	0	0	0.0	0
1996—Jacksonville NFL	13	4	16	7	2.0	0	0	0.0	0
1997—Jacksonville NFL	8	5	20	12	3.0	0	0	0.0	0
1998—Jacksonville NFL	15	9	25	8	3.0	0	0	0.0	0
1999—Detroit NFL	16	2	16	4	1.0	0	0	0.0	0
2000—Detroit NFL	15	0	8	8	2.5	1	78	78.0	0
2001—Detroit NFL	16	1	10	7	0.0	0	0	0.0	0
2002—Detroit NFL	16	4	28	14	0.0	0	0	0.0	0
Pro totals (12 years)	179	76	296	151	30.5	1	78	78.0	0

PRITCHETT, STANLEY   FB   BEARS

PERSONAL: Born December 22, 1973, in Atlanta. ... 6-2/250. ... Full name: Stanley Jerome Pritchett.
HIGH SCHOOL: Frederick Douglass (College Park, Ga.).
COLLEGE: South Carolina.
TRANSACTIONS/CAREER NOTES: Selected by Miami Dolphins in fourth round (118th pick overall) of 1996 NFL draft. ... Signed by Dolphins (July 10, 1996). ... Granted free agency (February 12, 1999). ... Re-signed by Dolphins (April 13, 1999). ... Granted unconditional free agency (February 11, 2000). ... Signed by Philadelphia Eagles (March 9, 2000). ... Released by Eagles (September 2, 2001). ... Signed by Chicago Bears (October 17, 2001). ... Granted unconditional free agency (February 28, 2003). ... Re-signed by Bears (March 1, 2003).
SINGLE GAME HIGHS (regular season): Attempts—17 (December 12, 1999, vs. New York Jets); yards—68 (December 12, 1999, vs. New York Jets); and rushing touchdowns—1 (October 15, 2000, vs. Arizona).

Year Team	G	GS	RUSHING				RECEIVING				TOTALS			
			Att.	Yds.	Avg.	TD	No.	Yds.	Avg.	TD	TD	2pt.	Pts.	Fum.
1996—Miami NFL	16	16	7	27	3.9	0	33	354	10.7	2	2	0	12	3
1997—Miami NFL	6	5	3	7	2.3	0	5	35	7.0	0	0	0	0	0
1998—Miami NFL	16	12	6	19	3.2	1	17	97	5.7	0	1	0	6	0
1999—Miami NFL	14	7	47	158	3.4	1	43	312	7.3	4	5	0	30	0
2000—Philadelphia NFL	16	2	58	225	3.9	0	25	193	7.7	0	1	0	6	1
2001—Chicago NFL	7	0	0	0	0.0	0	0	0	0.0	0	0	0	0	0
2002—Chicago NFL	16	2	1	2	2.0	0	19	165	8.7	1	1	0	6	0
Pro totals (7 years)	91	44	122	438	3.6	3	142	1156	8.1	7	10	0	60	4

PROEHL, RICKY   WR   PANTHERS

PERSONAL: Born March 7, 1968, in Bronx, N.Y. ... 6-0/190. ... Full name: Richard Scott Proehl.
HIGH SCHOOL: Hillsborough (Belle Mead, N.J.).
COLLEGE: Wake Forest.
TRANSACTIONS/CAREER NOTES: Selected by Phoenix Cardinals in third round (58th pick overall) of 1990 NFL draft. ... Signed by Cardinals (July 23, 1990). ... Granted free agency (March 1, 1993). ... Tendered offer sheet by New England Patriots (April 13, 1993). ... Offer matched by Cardinals (April 19, 1993). ... Cardinals franchise renamed Arizona Cardinals for 1994 season. ... Traded by Cardinals to Seattle Seahawks for fourth-round pick (traded to New York Jets) in 1995 draft (April 3, 1995). ... Released by Seahawks (March 7, 1997). ... Signed by Chicago Bears (April 10, 1997). ... Granted unconditional free agency (February 13, 1998). ... Signed by St. Louis Rams (February 25, 1998). ... Granted unconditional free agency (March 1, 2002). ... Re-signed by Rams (April 9, 2002). ... Granted unconditional free agency (February 28, 2003). ... Signed by Carolina Panthers (March 17, 2003).
CHAMPIONSHIP GAME EXPERIENCE: Played in NFC championship game (1999 and 2001 seasons). ... Member of Super Bowl championship team (1999 season). ... Played in Super Bowl XXXVI (2001 season).
SINGLE GAME HIGHS (regular season): Receptions—11 (November 16, 1997, vs. New York Jets); yards—164 (November 27, 1997, vs. Detroit); and touchdown receptions—2 (January 6, 2002, vs. Atlanta).
STATISTICAL PLATEAUS: 100-yard receiving games: 1990 (2), 1991 (1), 1992 (3), 1993 (1), 1997 (3), 1998 (1), 2001 (1). Total: 12.

Year Team	G	GS	RUSHING				RECEIVING				TOTALS			
			Att.	Yds.	Avg.	TD	No.	Yds.	Avg.	TD	TD	2pt.	Pts.	Fum.
1990—Phoenix NFL	16	2	1	4	4.0	0	56	802	14.3	4	4	0	24	0
1991—Phoenix NFL	16	16	3	21	7.0	0	55	766	13.9	2	2	0	12	0
1992—Phoenix NFL	16	15	3	23	7.7	0	60	744	12.4	3	3	0	18	5
1993—Phoenix NFL	16	16	8	47	5.9	0	65	877	13.5	7	7	0	42	1
1994—Arizona NFL	16	16	0	0	0.0	0	51	651	12.8	5	5	0	30	2
1995—Seattle NFL	8	0	0	0	0.0	0	5	29	5.8	0	0	0	0	0
1996—Seattle NFL	16	7	0	0	0.0	0	23	309	13.4	2	2	0	12	0
1997—Chicago NFL	15	10	0	0	0.0	0	58	753	13.0	7	7	1	44	2
1998—St. Louis NFL	16	11	1	14	14.0	0	60	771	12.9	3	3	1	20	0
1999—St. Louis NFL	15	2	0	0	0.0	0	33	349	10.6	0	0	0	0	0
2000—St. Louis NFL	12	4	0	0	0.0	0	31	441	14.2	4	4	0	24	0
2001—St. Louis NFL	16	3	1	5	5.0	0	40	563	14.1	5	5	1	32	0
2002—St. Louis NFL	16	2	0	0	0.0	0	43	466	10.8	4	4	0	24	0
Pro totals (13 years)	194	104	17	114	6.7	0	580	7521	13.0	46	46	3	282	10

P

PRYCE, TREVOR — DT — BRONCOS

PERSONAL: Born August 3, 1975, in Brooklyn, N.Y. ... 6-5/295.
HIGH SCHOOL: Lake Howell (Casselberry, Fla.).
COLLEGE: Clemson.
TRANSACTIONS/CAREER NOTES: Selected by Denver Broncos in first round (28th pick overall) of 1997 NFL draft. ... Signed by Broncos (July 24, 1997).
CHAMPIONSHIP GAME EXPERIENCE: Played in AFC championship game (1997 and 1998 seasons). ... Member of Super Bowl championship team (1997 and 1998 seasons).
HONORS: Played in Pro Bowl (1999, 2000 and 2002 seasons). ... Named to play in Pro Bowl (2001 season); replaced by Gary Walker due to injury.

			TOTALS			INTERCEPTIONS			
Year Team	G	GS	Tk.	Ast.	Sks.	No.	Yds.	Avg.	TD
1997—Denver NFL	8	3	16	8	2.0	0	0	0.0	0
1998—Denver NFL	16	15	31	12	8.5	1	1	1.0	0
1999—Denver NFL	15	15	33	13	13.0	1	0	0.0	0
2000—Denver NFL	16	16	34	12	12.0	0	0	0.0	0
2001—Denver NFL	16	16	34	7	7.0	0	0	0.0	0
2002—Denver NFL	16	16	40	6	9.0	0	0	0.0	0
Pro totals (6 years)	87	81	188	58	51.5	2	1	0.5	0

PUGH, DAVID — DT — COLTS

PERSONAL: Born July 24, 1979, in Madison Heights, Va. ... 6-2/270. ... Full name: David Winston Pugh Jr..
HIGH SCHOOL: Amerherst County (Va.).
COLLEGE: Virginia Tech.
TRANSACTIONS/CAREER NOTES: Selected by Indianapolis Colts in sixth round (182nd pick overall) of 2002 NFL draft. ... Signed by Colts (July 8, 2002).
HONORS: Named defensive tackle on THE SPORTING NEWS college All-America third team (2001).

			TOTALS			INTERCEPTIONS			
Year Team	G	GS	Tk.	Ast.	Sks.	No.	Yds.	Avg.	TD
2002—Indianapolis NFL	4	1	0	1	0.0	0	0	0.0	0

PUTZIER, JEB — TE — BRONCOS

PERSONAL: Born January 20, 1979, in Eagle, Idaho. ... 6-4/256.
HIGH SCHOOL: Eagle (Idaho).
COLLEGE: Boise State.
TRANSACTIONS/CAREER NOTES: Selected by Denver Broncos in sixth round (191st pick overall) of 2002 NFL draft. ... Signed by Broncos (June 14, 2002).

			RECEIVING			
Year Team	G	GS	No.	Yds.	Avg.	TD
2002—Denver NFL	3	1	0	0	0.0	0

QUARLES, SHELTON — LB — BUCCANEERS

PERSONAL: Born September 11, 1971, in Nashville. ... 6-1/225. ... Full name: Shelton Eugene Quarles.
HIGH SCHOOL: Whites Creek (Tenn.).
COLLEGE: Vanderbilt (degree in human and organized development).
TRANSACTIONS/CAREER NOTES: Signed as non-drafted free agent by Miami Dolphins (April 29, 1994). ... Released by Dolphins (August 15, 1994). ... Signed by B.C. Lions of CFL (December 1, 1994). ... Granted free agency (February 16, 1997). ... Signed by Tampa Bay Buccaneers (March 21, 1997). ... Granted unconditional free agency (February 28, 2003). ... Re-signed by Buccaneers (March 7, 2003).
CHAMPIONSHIP GAME EXPERIENCE: Played in NFC championship game (1999 and 2002 seasons). ... Member of Super Bowl championship team (2002 season).
HONORS: Played in Pro Bowl (2002).

			TOTALS			INTERCEPTIONS			
Year Team	G	GS	Tk.	Ast.	Sks.	No.	Yds.	Avg.	TD
1997—Tampa Bay NFL	16	0	1	3	0.0	0	0	0.0	0
1998—Tampa Bay NFL	16	0	9	3	1.0	0	0	0.0	0
1999—Tampa Bay NFL	16	14	23	12	0.0	0	0	0.0	0
2000—Tampa Bay NFL	14	13	35	15	2.0	1	5	5.0	0
2001—Tampa Bay NFL	16	16	28	16	2.0	1	98	98.0	1
2002—Tampa Bay NFL	16	16	74	39	1.0	2	29	14.5	1
Pro totals (6 years)	94	59	170	88	6.0	4	132	33.0	2

QUINN, JONATHAN — QB — CHIEFS

PERSONAL: Born February 27, 1975, in Turlock, Calif. ... 6-6/243. ... Full name: Jonathan Ryan Quinn.
HIGH SCHOOL: McGavock (Nashville).
COLLEGE: Tulane, then Middle Tennessee State (degree in business administration, 1997).
TRANSACTIONS/CAREER NOTES: Selected by Jacksonville Jaguars in third round (86th pick overall) of 1998 NFL draft. ... Signed by Jaguars (May 19, 1998). ... Active for one game (1999); did not play. ... Assigned by Jaguars to Berlin Thunder in 2001 NFL Europe enhancement allocation program (February 19, 2001). ... Granted unconditional free agency (March 1, 2002). ... Signed by Kansas City Chiefs (May 1, 2002).

CHAMPIONSHIP GAME EXPERIENCE: Member of Jaguars for AFC championship game (1999 season); inactive.
SINGLE GAME HIGHS (regular season): Attempts—31 (November 18, 2001, vs. Pittsburgh); completions—17 (November 18, 2001, vs. Pittsburgh); yards—225 (November 18, 2001, vs. Pittsburgh); and touchdown passes—1 (September 30, 2001, vs. Cleveland).
MISCELLANEOUS: Regular-season record as starting NFL quarterback: 1-2 (.333).

			PASSING									RUSHING				TOTALS		
Year Team	G	GS	Att.	Cmp.	Pct.	Yds.	TD	Int.	Avg.	Skd.	Rat.	Att.	Yds.	Avg.	TD	TD	2pt.	Pts.
1998—Jacksonville NFL	4	2	64	34	53.1	387	2	3	6.05	9	62.4	11	77	7.0	1	1	0	6
1999—Jacksonville NFL									Did not play.									
2000—Jacksonville NFL	2	0	0	0	0.0	0	0	0	0.0	0	...	2	-2	-1.0	0	0	0	0
2001—Berlin NFLE	...	...	296	167	56.4	2257	24	9	7.63	0	95.2	33	112	3.4	0	0	0	0
—Jacksonville NFL	6	1	61	32	52.5	361	1	1	5.92	6	69.1	8	42	5.3	0	0	0	0
2002—Kansas City NFL	1	0	0	0	0.0	0	0	0	0.0	0	...	1	-1	-1.0	0	0	0	0
NFL Europe totals (1 year)	...	...	296	167	56.4	2257	24	9	7.63	0	95.2	33	112	3.4	0	0	0	0
NFL totals (4 years)	13	3	125	66	52.8	748	3	4	5.98	15	65.7	22	116	5.3	1	1	0	6
Pro totals (5 years)	...	...	421	233	55.3	3005	27	13	7.14	15	86.5	55	228	4.1	1	1	0	6

RABACH, CASEY — C — RAVENS

PERSONAL: Born September 24, 1977, in Sturgeon Bay, Wis. ... 6-4/301.
HIGH SCHOOL: Sturgeon Bay (Wis.).
COLLEGE: Wisconsin.
TRANSACTIONS/CAREER NOTES: Selected by Baltimore Ravens in third round (92nd pick overall) of 2001 NFL draft. ... Signed by Ravens (July 21, 2001). ... Active for two games (2001); did not play.
PLAYING EXPERIENCE: Baltimore NFL, 2002. ... Games/games started: 2002 (12/5).

RACKERS, NEIL — K — BENGALS

PERSONAL: Born August 16, 1976, in Florissant, Mo. ... 6-0/205. ... Full name: Neil W. Rackers.
HIGH SCHOOL: Aquinas-Mercy (Florissant, Mo.).
COLLEGE: Illinois (degree in speech communication.).
TRANSACTIONS/CAREER NOTES: Selected by Cincinnati Bengals in sixth round (169th pick overall) of 2000 NFL draft. ... Signed by Bengals (July 21, 2000). ... Granted free agency (February 28, 2003). ... Re-signed by Bengals (April 15, 2003).

		FIELD GOALS							TOTALS		
Year Team	G	1-29	30-39	40-49	50+	Tot.	Pct.	Lg.	XPM	XPA	Pts.
2000—Cincinnati NFL	16	5-5	5-9	2-7	0-0	12-21	57.1	45	21	21	57
2001—Cincinnati NFL	16	4-6	8-11	4-9	1-2	17-28	60.7	52	23	24	74
2002—Cincinnati NFL	16	7-7	3-3	3-5	2-3	15-18	83.3	54	30	32	75
Pro totals (3 years)	48	16-18	16-23	9-21	3-5	44-67	65.7	54	74	77	206

RACKLEY, DEREK — TE — FALCONS

PERSONAL: Born July 18, 1977, in Apple Valley, Minn. ... 6-4/250.
HIGH SCHOOL: Apple Valley (Minn.).
COLLEGE: Minnesota.
TRANSACTIONS/CAREER NOTES: Signed as non-drafted free agent by Atlanta Falcons (April 17, 2000). ... Granted free agency (February 28, 2003). ... Re-signed by Falcons (March 25, 2003).
SINGLE GAME HIGHS (regular season): Receptions—1 (December 30, 2001, vs. Miami); yards—1 (December 30, 2001, vs. Miami); and touchdown receptions—1 (December 30, 2001, vs. Miami).

			RECEIVING			
Year Team	G	GS	No.	Yds.	Avg.	TD
2000—Atlanta NFL	16	0	0	0	0.0	0
2001—Atlanta NFL	16	0	1	1	1.0	1
2002—Atlanta NFL	16	0	0	0	0.0	0
Pro totals (3 years)	48	0	1	1	1.0	1

RAINER, WALI — LB — LIONS

PERSONAL: Born April 19, 1977, in Rockingham, N.C. ... 6-2/247. ... Full name: Wali Rashid Rainer.
HIGH SCHOOL: West Charlotte (N.C.).
COLLEGE: Virginia.
TRANSACTIONS/CAREER NOTES: Selected by Cleveland Browns in fourth round (124th pick overall) of 1999 NFL draft. ... Signed by Browns (July 22, 1999). ... Granted free agency (March 1, 2002). ... Re-signed by Browns (April 20, 2002). ... Traded by Browns with third-round pick (traded to Washington) in 2002 draft to Jacksonville Jaguars for third-round pick (C Melvin Fowler) in 2002 draft (April 20, 2002). ... Granted unconditional free agency (February 28, 2003). ... Signed by Detroit Lions (April 7, 2003).

			TOTALS			INTERCEPTIONS			
Year Team	G	GS	Tk.	Ast.	Sks.	No.	Yds.	Avg.	TD
1999—Cleveland NFL	16	15	108	29	1.0	0	0	0.0	0
2000—Cleveland NFL	16	16	86	33	1.0	1	5	5.0	0
2001—Cleveland NFL	14	14	50	28	1.0	0	0	0.0	0
2002—Jacksonville NFL	16	14	66	20	1.0	0	0	0.0	0
Pro totals (4 years)	62	59	310	110	4.0	1	5	5.0	0

RAIOLA, DOMINIC   C   LIONS

PERSONAL: Born December 30, 1978, in Honolulu, Hawaii. ... 6-1/295.
HIGH SCHOOL: St. Louis (Honolulu, Hawaii).
COLLEGE: Nebraska (degree in communication studies).
TRANSACTIONS/CAREER NOTES: Selected by Detroit Lions in second round (50th pick overall) of 2001 NFL draft. ... Signed by Lions (July 23, 2001).
PLAYING EXPERIENCE: Detroit NFL, 2001-2002. ... Games/Games started: 2001 (16/0), 2002 (16/16). Total: 32/16.
HONORS: Named center on THE SPORTING NEWS college All-America second team (2000).

RAMBO, KEN-YON   WR   COWBOYS

PERSONAL: Born October 4, 1978, in Cerritos, Calif. ... 6-1/195.
HIGH SCHOOL: Polytechnic (Long Beach, Calif.).
COLLEGE: Ohio State.
TRANSACTIONS/CAREER NOTES: Selected by Oakland Raiders in seventh round (229th pick overall) of 2001 NFL draft. ... Signed by Raiders (July 21, 2001). ... Released by Raiders (August 28, 2001). ... Signed by Dallas Cowboys (September 5, 2001). ... Re-signed by Cowboys (March 23, 2003).
SINGLE GAME HIGHS (regular season): Receptions—3 (September 15, 2002, vs. Tennessee); yards—65 (November 24, 2002, vs. Jacksonville); and touchdown receptions—0.

			RECEIVING				PUNT RETURNS				KICKOFF RETURNS				TOTALS			
Year Team	G	GS	No.	Yds.	Avg.	TD	No.	Yds.	Avg.	TD	No.	Yds.	Avg.	TD	TD	2pt.	Pts.	Fum.
2001—Dallas NFL	13	0	3	28	9.3	0	2	15	7.5	0	2	30	15.0	0	0	0	0	0
2002—Dallas NFL	16	0	14	211	15.1	0	5	3	0.6	0	7	127	18.1	0	0	0	0	3
Pro totals (2 years)	29	0	17	239	14.1	0	7	18	2.6	0	9	157	17.4	0	0	0	0	3

RAMSEY, PATRICK   QB   REDSKINS

PERSONAL: Born February 14, 1979, in Ruston, La. ... 6-2/217. ... Full name: Patrick Allen Ramsey.
HIGH SCHOOL: Ruston (La.).
COLLEGE: Tulane.
TRANSACTIONS/CAREER NOTES: Selected by Washington Redskins in first round (32nd pick overall) of 2002 NFL draft. ... Signed by Redskins (August 7, 2002).
SINGLE GAME HIGHS (regular season): Attempts—43 (October 13, 2002, vs. New Orleans); completions—23 (December 15, 2002, vs. Philadelphia); yards—320 (October 13, 2002, vs. New Orleans); and touchdown passes—3 (December 15, 2002, vs. Philadelphia).
STATISTICAL PLATEAUS: 300-yard passing games: 2002 (1).
MISCELLANEOUS: Regular-season record as starting NFL quarterback: 2-3 (.400).

			PASSING									RUSHING				TOTALS		
Year Team	G	GS	Att.	Cmp.	Pct.	Yds.	TD	Int.	Avg.	Skd.	Rat.	Att.	Yds.	Avg.	TD	TD	2pt.	Pts.
2002—Washington NFL	10	5	227	117	51.5	1539	9	8	6.78	18	71.8	13	-1	-0.1	1	1	0	6

RANDLE, JOHN   DT   SEAHAWKS

PERSONAL: Born December 12, 1967, in Hearne, Texas. ... 6-1/287. ... Brother of Ervin Randle, linebacker with Tampa Bay Buccaneers (1985-90) and Kansas City Chiefs (1991 and 1992).
HIGH SCHOOL: Hearne (Texas).
JUNIOR COLLEGE: Trinity Valley Community College (Texas).
COLLEGE: Texas A&I.
TRANSACTIONS/CAREER NOTES: Signed as non-drafted free agent by Minnesota Vikings (May 4, 1990). ... Designated by Vikings as transition player (January 15, 1994). ... Designated by Vikings as transition player (February 13, 1998). ... Tendered offer sheet by Miami Dolphins (February 16, 1998). ... Offer matched by Vikings (February 18, 1998). ... Released by Vikings (March 1, 2001). ... Signed by Seattle Seahawks (March 3, 2001).
CHAMPIONSHIP GAME EXPERIENCE: Played in NFC championship game (1998 and 2000 seasons).
HONORS: Played in Pro Bowl (1993-1998 and 2001 seasons). ... Named defensive tackle on THE SPORTING NEWS NFL All-Pro team (1994-1998).

			TOTALS			INTERCEPTIONS			
Year Team	G	GS	Tk.	Ast.	Sks.	No.	Yds.	Avg.	TD
1990—Minnesota NFL	16	0	12	9	1.0	0	0	0.0	0
1991—Minnesota NFL	16	8	32	26	9.5	0	0	0.0	0
1992—Minnesota NFL	16	14	45	11	11.5	0	0	0.0	0
1993—Minnesota NFL	16	16	54	5	12.5	0	0	0.0	0
1994—Minnesota NFL	16	16	30	12∞13.5		0	0	0.0	0
1995—Minnesota NFL	16	16	33	11	10.5	0	0	0.0	0
1996—Minnesota NFL	16	16	35	11	11.5	0	0	0.0	0
1997—Minnesota NFL	16	16	47	11	*15.5	0	0	0.0	0
1998—Minnesota NFL	16	16	27	14	10.5	0	0	0.0	0
1999—Minnesota NFL	16	16	29	9	10.0	1	1	1.0	0
2000—Minnesota NFL	16	16	25	1	8.0	0	0	0.0	0
2001—Seattle NFL	15	14	26	9	11.0	0	0	0.0	0
2002—Seattle NFL	12	12	13	2	7.0	0	0	0.0	0
Pro totals (13 years)	203	176	408	131	132.0	1	1	1.0	0

RANDLE EL, ANTWAAN   WR   STEELERS

PERSONAL: Born August 17, 1979, in Markham, Ill. ... 5-10/184.
HIGH SCHOOL: Thornton (Riverdale, Ill.).
COLLEGE: Indiana.
TRANSACTIONS/CAREER NOTES: Selected by Pittsburgh Steelers in second round (62nd pick overall) of 2002 NFL draft. ... Signed by Steelers (July 23, 2002).
POST SEASON RECORDS: Shares NFL career and single-game record for most punt returns for touchdown—1 (January 5, 2003, vs. Cleveland).
SINGLE GAME HIGHS (regular season): Receptions—8 (December 8, 2002, vs. Houston); yards—88 (December 8, 2002, vs. Houston); and touchdown receptions—1 (December 29, 2002, vs. Baltimore).

			RUSHING				RECEIVING				PUNT RETURNS				KICKOFF RETURNS				TOTALS	
Year Team	G	GS	Att.	Yds.	Avg.	TD	No.	Yds.	Avg.	TD	No.	Yds.	Avg.	TD	No.	Yds.	Avg.	TD	TD	2pt.	Pts.
2002—Pittsburgh NFL....	16	0	19	134	7.1	0	47	489	10.4	2	§37	257	6.9	0	32	733	22.9	1	3	0	18

RANSOM, DERRICK   DT   CHIEFS

PERSONAL: Born September 13, 1976, in Indianapolis. ... 6-3/306. ... Full name: Derrick Wayne Ransom Jr.
HIGH SCHOOL: Lawrence Central (Indianapolis).
COLLEGE: Cincinnati (degree in finance).
TRANSACTIONS/CAREER NOTES: Selected by Kansas City Chiefs in sixth round (181st pick overall) of 1998 NFL draft. ... Signed by Chiefs (June 3, 1998). ... Granted free agency (March 2, 2001). ... Re-signed by Chiefs (April 3, 2001). ... Granted unconditional free agency (March 1, 2002). ... Re-signed by Chiefs (April 3, 2002).

			TOTALS		
Year Team	G	GS	Tk.	Ast.	Sks.
1998—Kansas City NFL	7	0	1	0	0.0
1999—Kansas City NFL	10	0	1	0	1.0
2000—Kansas City NFL	10	0	2	0	0.0
2001—Kansas City NFL	16	16	41	13	3.0
2002—Kansas City NFL	13	10	20	5	0.0
Pro totals (5 years)	56	26	65	18	4.0

RASBY, WALTER   TE   CARDINALS

PERSONAL: Born September 7, 1972, in Washington, D.C. ... 6-3/252. ... Full name: Walter Herbert Rasby.
HIGH SCHOOL: Washington (N.C.).
COLLEGE: Wake Forest.
TRANSACTIONS/CAREER NOTES: Signed as non-drafted free agent by Pittsburgh Steelers (April 29, 1994). ... Released by Steelers (August 27, 1995). ... Signed by Carolina Panthers (October 17, 1995). ... Granted free agency (February 14, 1997). ... Re-signed by Panthers (June 3, 1997). ... On injured reserve with knee injury (December 10, 1997-remainder of season). ... Granted unconditional free agency (February 13, 1998). ... Signed by Detroit Lions (April 13, 1998). ... Granted unconditional free agency (March 2, 2001). ... Signed by Washington Redskins (April 10, 2001). ... Released by Redskins (February 26, 2003).
CHAMPIONSHIP GAME EXPERIENCE: Played in AFC championship game (1994 season). ... Played in NFC championship game (1996 season).
SINGLE GAME HIGHS (regular season): Receptions—5 (October 4, 1998, vs. Chicago); yards—45 (January 6, 2002, vs. Arizona); and touchdown receptions—1 (January 6, 2002, vs. Arizona).

			RECEIVING				TOTALS			
Year Team	G	GS	No.	Yds.	Avg.	TD	TD	2pt.	Pts.	Fum.
1994—Pittsburgh NFL	2	0	0	0	0.0	0	0	0	0	0
1995—Carolina NFL	9	2	5	47	9.4	0	0	1	2	0
1996—Carolina NFL	16	1	0	0	0.0	0	0	0	0	0
1997—Carolina NFL	14	2	1	1	1.0	0	0	0	0	0
1998—Detroit NFL	16	16	15	119	7.9	1	1	0	6	0
1999—Detroit NFL	16	6	3	19	6.3	1	1	0	6	0
2000—Detroit NFL	16	8	10	78	7.8	1	1	0	6	0
2001—Washington NFL	16	11	10	128	12.8	2	2	0	12	0
2002—Washington NFL	13	10	9	85	9.4	0	0	0	0	0
Pro totals (9 years)	118	56	53	477	9.0	5	5	1	32	0

RASHEED, SALEEM   LB   49ERS

PERSONAL: Born June 15, 1981, in Birmingham, Ala. ... 6-2/229.
HIGH SCHOOL: Shades Valley (Birmingham, Ala.).
COLLEGE: Alabama.
TRANSACTIONS/CAREER NOTES: Selected after junior season by San Francisco in third round (69th pick overall) of 2002 NFL draft. ... Signed by 49ers (July 21, 2002).

			TOTALS			INTERCEPTIONS			
Year Team	G	GS	Tk.	Ast.	Sks.	No.	Yds.	Avg.	TD
2002—San Francisco NFL	6	0	6	0	1.0	0	0	0.0	0

RASMUSSEN, KEMP   DE   PANTHERS

PERSONAL: Born May 25, 1979, in Hadley, Mich. ... 6-3/255. ... Full name: Kemp Alan Rasmussen.
HIGH SCHOOL: Lampeer West (Hadley, Mich.).
COLLEGE: Indiana.
TRANSACTIONS/CAREER NOTES: Signed as non-drafted free agent by Carolina Panthers (April 29, 2002).

			TOTALS		
Year Team	G	GS	Tk.	Ast.	Sks.
2002—Carolina NFL	10	0	2	1	0.0

RATTAY, TIM   QB   49ERS

PERSONAL: Born March 15, 1977, in Elyria, Ohio. ... 6-0/200.
HIGH SCHOOL: Phoenix (Ariz.) Christian.
JUNIOR COLLEGE: Scottsdale (Ariz.) Community College.
COLLEGE: Louisiana Tech.
TRANSACTIONS/CAREER NOTES: Selected by San Francisco 49ers in seventh round (212th pick overall) of 2000 NFL draft. ... Signed by 49ers (July 16, 2000). ... Granted free agency (February 28, 2003). ... Re-signed by 49ers (April 7, 2003).
SINGLE GAME HIGHS (regular season): Attempts—21 (December 30, 2002, vs. St. Louis); completions—14 (December 30, 2002, vs. St. Louis); yards—138 (December 30, 2002, vs. St. Louis); and touchdown passes—2 (December 30, 2002, vs. St. Louis).

					PASSING							RUSHING				TOTALS		
Year Team	G	GS	Att.	Cmp.	Pct.	Yds.	TD	Int.	Avg.	Skd.	Rat.	Att.	Yds.	Avg.	TD	TD	2pt.	Pts.
2000—San Francisco NFL	1	0	1	1	100.0	-4	0	0	-4.00	0	79.2	2	-1	-0.5	0	0	0	0
2001—San Francisco NFL	3	0	2	2	100.0	21	0	0	10.50	0	110.4	5	-3	-0.6	0	0	0	0
2002—San Francisco NFL	4	0	43	26	60.5	232	2	0	5.40	5	90.5	5	0	0.0	0	0	0	0
Pro totals (3 years)	8	0	46	29	63.0	249	2	0	5.41	5	91.7	12	-4	-0.3	0	0	0	0

RAYMER, CORY   C   CHARGERS

PERSONAL: Born March 3, 1973, in Fond du Lac, Wis. ... 6-3/300.
HIGH SCHOOL: Goodrich (Fond du Lac, Wis.).
COLLEGE: Wisconsin.
TRANSACTIONS/CAREER NOTES: Selected by Washington Redskins in second round (37th pick overall) of 1995 NFL draft. ... Signed by Redskins (July 24, 1995). ... On injured reserve with back injury (November 25, 1996-remainder of season). ... Granted unconditional free agency (February 12, 1999). ... Re-signed by Redskins (March 16, 1999). ... Granted unconditional free agency (February 11, 2000). ... Re-signed by Redskins (February 26, 2000). ... On injured reserve with knee injury (September 28, 2000-remainder of season). ... Granted unconditional free agency (March 1, 2002). ... Signed by San Diego Chargers (March 8, 2002). ... On injured reserve with Achilles' injury (September 26, 2002-remainder of season).
PLAYING EXPERIENCE: Washington NFL, 1995-1999 and 2001; San Diego NFL, 2002. ... Games/Games started: 1995 (3/2), 1996 (6/5), 1997 (6/3), 1998 (16/16), 1999 (16/16), 2001 (16/16), 2002 (3/3). Total: 66/61.
HONORS: Named offensive lineman on THE SPORTING NEWS college All-America first team (1994).

REAGOR, MONTAE   DE

PERSONAL: Born June 29, 1977, in Waxahachie, Texas. ... 6-3/285. ... Full name: Willie Montae Reagor. ... Name pronounced MON-tay RAY-ger.
HIGH SCHOOL: Waxahachie (Texas).
COLLEGE: Texas Tech (degree in exercise and sports sciences).
TRANSACTIONS/CAREER NOTES: Selected by Denver Broncos in second round (58th pick overall) of 1999 NFL draft. ... Signed by Broncos (July 13, 1999). ... Granted unconditional free agency (February 28, 2003).
HONORS: Named defensive end on THE SPORTING NEWS college All-America second team (1997). ... Named defensive end on THE SPORTING NEWS college All-America first team (1998).

			TOTALS			INTERCEPTIONS			
Year Team	G	GS	Tk.	Ast.	Sks.	No.	Yds.	Avg.	TD
1999—Denver NFL	9	0	9	1	0.0	0	0	0.0	0
2000—Denver NFL	13	0	8	1	2.0	0	0	0.0	0
2001—Denver NFL	8	0	4	0	1.0	0	0	0.0	0
2002—Denver NFL	15	1	12	8	1.0	1	31	31.0	0
Pro totals (4 years)	45	1	33	10	4.0	1	31	31.0	0

REDMAN, CHRIS   QB   RAVENS

PERSONAL: Born July 7, 1977, in Louisville, Ky. ... 6-3/223.
HIGH SCHOOL: Male (Louisville, Ky.).
COLLEGE: Louisville.
TRANSACTIONS/CAREER NOTES: Selected by Baltimore Ravens in third round (75th pick overall) of 2000 NFL draft. ... Signed by Ravens (July 24, 2000). ... Inactive for 14 games (2001). ... Granted free agency (February 28, 2003). ... Re-signed by Ravens (May 20, 2003).
CHAMPIONSHIP GAME EXPERIENCE: Member of Ravens for AFC Championship game (2000 season); inactive. ... Member of Super Bowl championship team (2000 season); inactive.
SINGLE GAME HIGHS (regular season): Attempts—38 (September 15, 2002, vs. Tampa Bay); completions—20 (September 8, 2002, vs.Carolina); yards—218 (September 8, 2002, vs. Carolina); and touchdown passes—2 (October 20, 2002, vs. Jacksonville).
MISCELLANEOUS: Regular-season record as starting NFL quarterback: 3-3 (.500).

					PASSING							RUSHING				TOTALS		
Year Team	G	GS	Att.	Cmp.	Pct.	Yds.	TD	Int.	Avg.	Skd.	Rat.	Att.	Yds.	Avg.	TD	TD	2pt.	Pts.
2000—Baltimore NFL	2	0	3	2	66.7	19	0	0	6.33	0	84.0	1	0	0.0	0	0	0	0
2001—Baltimore NFL									Did not play.									
2002—Baltimore NFL	6	6	182	97	53.3	1034	7	3	5.68	11	76.1	10	8	0.8	0	0	0	0
Pro totals (2 years)	8	6	185	99	53.5	1053	7	3	5.69	11	76.3	11	8	0.7	0	0	0	0

REDMOND, J.R.   RB   PATRIOTS

PERSONAL: Born September 28, 1977, in Los Angeles. ... 5-11/215. ... Full name: Joseph Robert Redmond.
HIGH SCHOOL: Carson (Calif.).

COLLEGE: Arizona State.
TRANSACTIONS/CAREER NOTES: Selected by New England Patriots in third round (76th pick overall) of 2000 NFL draft. ... Signed by Patriots (July 23, 2000).
CHAMPIONSHIP GAME EXPERIENCE: Played in AFC championship game (2001 season). ... Member of Super Bowl championship team (2001 season).
SINGLE GAME HIGHS (regular season): Attempts—24 (November 5, 2000, vs. Buffalo); yards—97 (October 22, 2000, vs. Indianapolis); and rushing touchdowns—1 (November 5, 2000 vs. Buffalo).

			RUSHING				RECEIVING				TOTALS			
Year Team	G	GS	Att.	Yds.	Avg.	TD	No.	Yds.	Avg.	TD	TD	2pt.	Pts.	Fum.
2000—New England NFL	12	5	125	406	3.2	1	20	126	6.3	2	3	0	18	2
2001—New England NFL	12	0	35	119	3.4	0	13	132	10.2	0	0	0	0	0
2002—New England NFL	9	0	4	2	0.5	0	2	5	2.5	0	0	0	0	0
Pro totals (3 years)	33	5	164	527	3.2	1	35	263	7.5	2	3	0	18	2

REDMOND, JIMMY   WR   JAGUARS

PERSONAL: Born August 18, 1977, in Kansas City, Mo. ... 6-0/192. ... Full name: James Louis Redmond III.
HIGH SCHOOL: South (Blue Springs, Mo.).
COLLEGE: Ohio State, then McNeese State.
TRANSACTIONS/CAREER NOTES: Signed as non-drafted free agent by Tennessee Titans (April 27, 2001). ... Released by Jaguars (August 26, 2001). ... Signed by Jacksonville Jaguars to practice squad (December 11, 2001). ... Assigned by Jaguars to Frankfurt Galaxy in 2002 NFL Europe enhancement allocation program (February 12, 2002). ... Re-signed by Jaguars (March 24, 2003).

			RECEIVING				KICKOFF RETURNS				TOTALS			
Year Team	G	GS	No.	Yds.	Avg.	TD	No.	Yds.	Avg.	TD	TD	2pt.	Pts.	Fum.
2002—Frankfurt NFLE	...	...	32	493	15.4	0	8	119	14.9	0	0	0	0	0
—Jacksonville NFL	14	0	0	0	0.0	0	1	32	32.0	0	0	0	0	0
NFL Europe totals (1 year)	0	0	32	493	15.4	0	8	119	14.9	0	0	0	0	0
NFL totals (1 year)	14	0	0	0	0.0	0	1	32	32.0	0	0	0	0	0
Pro totals (2 years)	...	...	32	493	15.4	0	9	151	16.8	0	0	0	0	0

REED, EDWARD   S   RAVENS

PERSONAL: Born September 11, 1978, in St. Rose, La. ... 5-11/205. ... Full name: Edward Earl Reed.
HIGH SCHOOL: Destrehan (St. Rose, La.).
COLLEGE: Miami (Fla.).
TRANSACTIONS/CAREER NOTES: Selected by Baltimore Ravens in first round (24th pick overall) of 2002 NFL draft. ... Signed by Ravens (August 3, 2002).
HONORS: Named free safety on The Sporting News college All-America first team (2001).

			TOTALS			INTERCEPTIONS				PUNT RETURNS				TOTALS			
Year Team	G	GS	Tk.	Ast.	Sks.	No.	Yds.	Avg.	TD	No.	Yds.	Avg.	TD	TD	2pt.	Pts.	Fum.
2002—Baltimore NFL	16	16	67	13	1.0	5	167	33.4	0	0	0	0.0	0	1	0	6	1

REED, JAKE   WR

PERSONAL: Born September 28, 1967, in Covington, Ga. ... 6-3/213. ... Full name: Willis Reed. ... Brother of Dale Carter, cornerback, New Orleans Saints.
HIGH SCHOOL: Newton County (Covington, Ga.).
COLLEGE: Grambling (degree in criminal justice, 1990).
TRANSACTIONS/CAREER NOTES: Selected by Minnesota Vikings in third round (68th pick overall) of 1991 NFL draft. ... Signed by Vikings (July 22, 1991). ... On injured reserve with ankle injury (November 2, 1991-remainder of season). ... Granted free agency (February 17, 1994). ... Re-signed by Vikings (May 6, 1994). ... Granted unconditional free agency (February 17, 1995). ... Re-signed by Vikings (February 28, 1995). ... Released by Vikings (February 10, 2000). ... Signed by New Orleans Saints (February 21, 2000). ... Released by Saints (March 1, 2001). ... Signed by Vikings (March 27, 2001). ... Granted unconditional free agency (March 1, 2002). ... Signed by Saints (March 12, 2002). ... Granted unconditional free agency (February 28, 2003).
CHAMPIONSHIP GAME EXPERIENCE: Member of Vikings for NFC championship game (1998 season); inactive.
SINGLE GAME HIGHS (regular season): Receptions—12 (September 7, 1997, vs. Chicago); yards—157 (November 6, 1994, vs. New Orleans); and touchdown receptions—2 (November 1, 1998, vs. Tampa Bay).
STATISTICAL PLATEAUS: 100-yard receiving games: 1994 (3), 1995 (3), 1996 (4), 1997 (5), 1998 (1), 1999 (2). Total: 18.

			RECEIVING				TOTALS			
Year Team	G	GS	No.	Yds.	Avg.	TD	TD	2pt.	Pts.	Fum.
1991—Minnesota NFL	1	0	0	0	0.0	0	0	0	0	0
1992—Minnesota NFL	16	0	6	142	23.7	0	0	0	0	0
1993—Minnesota NFL	10	1	5	65	13.0	0	0	0	0	0
1994—Minnesota NFL	16	16	85	1175	13.8	4	4	0	24	3
1995—Minnesota NFL	16	16	72	1167	16.2	9	9	0	54	1
1996—Minnesota NFL	16	15	72	1320	18.3	7	7	0	42	0
1997—Minnesota NFL	16	16	68	1138	16.7	6	6	0	36	0
1998—Minnesota NFL	11	11	34	474	13.9	4	4	0	24	0
1999—Minnesota NFL	16	8	44	643	14.6	2	2	0	12	0
2000—New Orleans NFL	7	6	16	206	12.9	0	0	0	0	0
2001—Minnesota NFL	16	0	27	309	11.4	1	1	1	8	0
2002—New Orleans NFL	14	1	21	360	17.1	3	3	0	18	1
Pro totals (12 years)	155	90	450	6999	15.6	36	36	1	218	5

REED, JAMES — DT — JETS

PERSONAL: Born February 3, 1977, in Saginaw, Mich. ... 6-0/286. ... Full name: James Reed Jr..
HIGH SCHOOL: Saginaw (Mich.).
COLLEGE: Iowa State.
TRANSACTIONS/CAREER NOTES: Selected by New York Jets in seventh round (206th pick overall) of 2001 NFL draft. ... Signed by Jets (June 28, 2001). ... Re-signed by Jets (April 2, 2003).

Year Team	G	GS	TOTALS Tk.	Ast.	Sks.
2001—New York Jets NFL	16	2	19	9	1.0
2002—New York Jets NFL	16	0	12	4	0.0
Pro totals (2 years)	32	2	31	13	1.0

REED, JEFF — K — STEELERS

PERSONAL: Born April 9, 1979, in Kansas City, Mo. ... 5-10/212. ... Full name: Jeffrey Montgomery Reed.
HIGH SCHOOL: East Mecklenburg (Charlotte, N.C.).
COLLEGE: North Carolina.
TRANSACTIONS/CAREER NOTES: Signed as non-drafted free agent by New Orleans Saints (April 23, 2002). ... Released by Saints (August 26, 2002). ... Signed by Pittsburgh Steelers (November 19, 2002).

Year Team	G	1-29	30-39	FIELD GOALS 40-49	50+	Tot.	Pct.	Lg.	XPM	TOTALS XPA	Pts.
2002—Pittsburgh NFL	6	5-5	5-5	6-7	1-2	17-19	89.5	50	10	11	61

REED, JOSH — WR — BILLS

PERSONAL: Born May 1, 1980, in Lafayette, La. ... 5-10/203. ... Full name: Joshua Blake Reed.
HIGH SCHOOL: Rayne (La.).
COLLEGE: Louisiana State.
TRANSACTIONS/CAREER NOTES: Selected after junior season by Buffalo Bills in second round (36th pick overall) of 2002 NFL draft. ... Signed by Bills (July 25, 2002).
HONORS: Named wide receiver on THE SPORTING NEWS college All-America first team (2001). ... Fred Biletnikoff Award winner (2001).
SINGLE GAME HIGHS (regular season): Receptions—8 (September 15, 2002, vs. Minnesota); yards—110 (September 15, 2002, vs. Minnesota); and touchdown receptions—1 (September 22, 2002, vs. Denver).
STATISTICAL PLATEAUS: 100-yard receiving games: 2002 (1).

Year Team	G	GS	RUSHING Att.	Yds.	Avg.	TD	RECEIVING No.	Yds.	Avg.	TD	PUNT RETURNS No.	Yds.	Avg.	TD	KICKOFF RETURNS No.	Yds.	Avg.	TD	TOTALS TD	2pt.	Pts.
2002—Buffalo NFL	16	2	0	0	0.0	0	37	509	13.8	2	0	0	0.0	0	0	0	0.0	0	2	0	12

REESE, IKE — LB — EAGLES

PERSONAL: Born October 16, 1973, in Jacksonville, N.C. ... 6-2/222. ... Full name: Isaiah Reese.
HIGH SCHOOL: Woodward (Cincinnati), then Aiken (Cincinnati).
COLLEGE: Michigan State.
TRANSACTIONS/CAREER NOTES: Selected by Philadelphia Eagles in fifth round (142nd pick overall) of 1998 NFL draft. ... Signed by Eagles (July 14, 1998). ... Granted free agency (March 2, 2001). ... Re-signed by Eagles (March 20, 2001).
CHAMPIONSHIP GAME EXPERIENCE: Member of Eagles for NFC championship game (2001 season); inactive. ... Played in NFC championship game (2002 season).

Year Team	G	GS	TOTALS Tk.	Ast.	Sks.	INTERCEPTIONS No.	Yds.	Avg.	TD
1998—Philadelphia NFL	16	0	3	1	0.0	0	0	0.0	0
1999—Philadelphia NFL	16	0	15	6	3.0	0	0	0.0	0
2000—Philadelphia NFL	16	0	4	1	0.0	0	0	0.0	0
2001—Philadelphia NFL	16	0	13	5	0.0	0	0	0.0	0
2002—Philadelphia NFL	16	3	42	7	1.5	0	0	0.0	0
Pro totals (5 years)	80	3	77	20	4.5	0	0	0.0	0

REESE, IZELL — S — BILLS

PERSONAL: Born May 7, 1974, in Dothan, Ala. ... 6-2/190.
HIGH SCHOOL: Northview (Dothan, Ala.).
COLLEGE: Alabama-Birmingham.
TRANSACTIONS/CAREER NOTES: Selected by Dallas Cowboys in sixth round (188th pick overall) of 1998 NFL draft. ... Signed by Cowboys (July 15, 1998). ... On injured reserve with neck injury (November 19, 1999-remainder of season). ... Granted free agency (March 2, 2001). ... Re-signed by Cowboys (April 30, 2001). ... Granted unconditional free agency (March 1, 2002). ... Signed by Denver Broncos (April 1, 2002). ... Granted unconditional free agency (February 28, 2003). ... Signed by Buffalo Bills (March 21, 2003).

Year Team	G	GS	TOTALS Tk.	Ast.	Sks.	INTERCEPTIONS No.	Yds.	Avg.	TD
1998—Dallas NFL	16	0	4	0	0.0	1	6	6.0	0
1999—Dallas NFL	8	4	17	5	0.0	3	28	9.3	0
2000—Dallas NFL	16	7	32	15	0.0	2	60	30.0	0
2001—Dallas NFL	16	4	24	1	3.0	1	42	42.0	0
2002—Denver NFL	15	15	41	10	0.5	0	0	0.0	0
Pro totals (5 years)	71	30	118	31	3.5	7	136	19.4	0

REHBERG, SCOTT   G   BENGALS

PERSONAL: Born November 17, 1973, in Kalamazoo, Mich. ... 6-8/325. ... Full name: Scott Joseph Rehberg. ... Name pronounced RAY-berg.
HIGH SCHOOL: Central (Kalamazoo, Mich.).
COLLEGE: Central Michigan.
TRANSACTIONS/CAREER NOTES: Selected by New England Patriots in seventh round (230th pick overall) of 1997 NFL draft. ... Signed by Patriots (June 19, 1997). ... Selected by Cleveland Browns from Patriots in NFL expansion draft (February 9, 1999). ... Granted free agency (February 11, 2000). ... Signed by Cincinnati Bengals (March 2, 2000).
PLAYING EXPERIENCE: New England NFL, 1997 and 1998; Cleveland NFL, 1999; Cincinnati NFL, 2000-2002. ... Games/Games started: 1997 (6/0), 1998 (2/0), 1999 (15/13), 2000 (10/6), 2001 (15/4), 2002 (16/3). Total: 60/26.

REYNOLDS, JAMAL   DE   PACKERS

PERSONAL: Born February 20, 1979, in Aiken, S.C. ... 6-3/265.
HIGH SCHOOL: Aiken (S.C.).
COLLEGE: Florida State.
TRANSACTIONS/CAREER NOTES: Selected by Green Bay Packers in first round (10th pick overall) of 2001 NFL draft. ... Signed by Packers (July 25, 2001).
HONORS: Named defensive end on THE SPORTING NEWS college All-America first team (2000). ... Lombardi Trophy winner (2000).

			TOTALS		
Year Team	G	GS	Tk.	Ast.	Sks.
2001—Green Bay NFL	6	0	4	0	2.0
2002—Green Bay NFL	7	0	5	3	1.0
Pro totals (2 years)	13	0	9	3	3.0

RHINEHART, COBY   CB   CARDINALS

PERSONAL: Born February 7, 1977, in Dallas. ... 5-11/196. ... Full name: Jacoby M. Rhinehart.
HIGH SCHOOL: Tyler Street Christian Academy (Dallas).
COLLEGE: Southern Methodist.
TRANSACTIONS/CAREER NOTES: Selected by Arizona Cardinals in sixth round (190th pick overall) of 1999 NFL draft. ... Signed by Cardinals (June 18, 1999). ... On injured reserve with knee injury (August 22, 2000-entire season). ... Granted free agency (March 1, 2002). ... Re-signed by Cardinals (May 2, 2002). ... Granted unconditional free agency (February 28, 2003). ... Re-signed by Cardinals (March 20, 2003).

			TOTALS			INTERCEPTIONS			
Year Team	G	GS	Tk.	Ast.	Sks.	No.	Yds.	Avg.	TD
1999—Arizona NFL	16	0	2	0	0.0	0	0	0.0	0
2001—Arizona NFL	13	0	5	2	0.0	0	0	0.0	0
2002—Arizona NFL	16	2	15	1	0.0	1	0	0.0	0
Pro totals (3 years)	45	2	22	3	0.0	1	0	0.0	0

RHODES, DOMINIC   RB   COLTS

PERSONAL: Born January 17, 1979, in Waco, Texas. ... 5-9/208. ... Full name: Dominic Dondrell Rhodes.
HIGH SCHOOL: Cooper (Texas).
JUNIOR COLLEGE: Tyler Junior College.
COLLEGE: Midwestern State.
TRANSACTIONS/CAREER NOTES: Signed as non-drafted free agent by Indianapolis Colts (April 22, 2001). ... On injured reserve with knee injury (August 26, 2002-entire season).
SINGLE GAME HIGHS (regular season): Attempts—34 (November 4, 2001, vs. Buffalo); yards—177 (December 16, 2001, vs. Atlanta); and rushing touchdowns—2 (December 16, 2001, vs. Atlanta).
STATISTICAL PLATEAUS: 100-yard rushing games: 2001 (5).

			RUSHING				RECEIVING				KICKOFF RETURNS				TOTALS			
Year Team	G	GS	Att.	Yds.	Avg.	TD	No.	Yds.	Avg.	TD	No.	Yds.	Avg.	TD	TD	2pt.	Pts.	Fum.
2001—Indianapolis NFL	15	10	233	1104	4.7	9	34	224	6.6	0	14	356	25.4	1	10	0	60	6
2002—Indianapolis NFL								Did not play.										
Pro totals (1 year)	15	10	233	1104	4.7	9	34	224	6.6	0	14	356	25.4	1	10	0	60	6

RICARD, ALAN   FB   RAVENS

PERSONAL: Born January 17, 1977, in Independence, La. ... 5-11/237.
HIGH SCHOOL: Amite (La.).
COLLEGE: Northeast Louisiana.
TRANSACTIONS/CAREER NOTES: Signed as non-drafted free agent by Dallas Cowboys (April 30, 1999). ... Released by Cowboys (August 4, 1999). ... Signed by Baltimore Ravens (July 21, 2000). ... Released by Ravens (August 26, 2000). ... Re-signed by Ravens to practice squad (August 29, 2000).

			RUSHING				RECEIVING				TOTALS			
Year Team	G	GS	Att.	Yds.	Avg.	TD	No.	Yds.	Avg.	TD	TD	2pt.	Pts.	Fum.
2001—Baltimore NFL	5	0	0	0	0.0	0	0	0	0.0	0	0	0	0	0
2002—Baltimore NFL	16	8	14	58	4.1	2	10	60	6.0	0	3	0	18	0
Pro totals (2 years)	21	8	14	58	4.1	2	10	60	6.0	0	3	0	18	0

PERSONAL: Born October 13, 1962, in Starkville, Miss. ... 6-2/200. ... Full name: Jerry Lee Rice.

HIGH SCHOOL: Crawford MS Moor (Crawford, Miss.).

COLLEGE: Mississippi Valley State.

TRANSACTIONS/CAREER NOTES: Selected by Birmingham Stallions in first round (first pick overall) of 1985 USFL draft. ... Selected by San Francisco 49ers in first round (16th pick overall) of 1985 NFL draft. ... Signed by 49ers (July 23, 1985). ... Granted free agency (February 1, 1992). ... Re-signed by 49ers (August 25, 1992). ... On injured reserve with knee injury (December 23, 1997-remainder of season). ... Released by 49ers (June 4, 2001). ... Signed by Oakland Raiders (June 5, 2001).

CHAMPIONSHIP GAME EXPERIENCE: Played in NFC championship game (1988-1990 and 1992-1994 seasons). ... Member of Super Bowl championship team (1988, 1989 and 1994 seasons). ... Played in AFC championship game (2002 season). ... Played in Super Bowl XXXVII (2002 season).

HONORS: Named wide receiver on The Sporting News college All-America first team (1984). ... Named wide receiver on The Sporting News NFL All-Pro team (1986-1996). ... Played in Pro Bowl (1986, 1987, 1989-1993, 1995, 1998 and 2002 seasons). ... Named NFL Player of the Year by The Sporting News (1987 and 1990). ... Named Most Valuable Player of Super Bowl XXIII (1988 season). ... Named to play in Pro Bowl (1988 season); replaced by J.T. Smith due to injury. ... Named to play in Pro Bowl (1994 season); replaced by Herman Moore due to injury. ... Named Outstanding Player of Pro Bowl (1995 season). ... Named to play in Pro Bowl (1996 season); replaced by Irving Fryar due to injury.

RECORDS: Holds NFL career records for most touchdowns—203; most touchdown receptions—192; most receiving yards—21,597; most pass receptions—1,456; most seasons with 1,000 or more yards receiving—14; most games with 100 or more yards receiving—73; most combined net yards—22,248; most consecutive games with one or more reception—257 (December 9, 1985-present); most consecutive games with one or more touchdown reception—13 (December 19, 1986-December 27, 1987); and most seasons with 50 or more receptions—16. ... Holds NFL single-season record for most yards receiving—1,848 (1995); and most touchdown receptions—22 (1987). ... Shares NFL single-game record for most touchdown receptions—5 (October 14, 1990, at Atlanta).

POST SEASON RECORDS: Holds Super Bowl career records for most points—48; most touchdowns—8; most touchdown receptions—8; most receptions—33; most combined yards—604; and most yards receiving—589. ... Holds Super Bowl single-game records for most touchdowns—3 (January 28, 1990, vs. Denver and January 29, 1995, vs. San Diego); and most yards receiving—215 (January 22, 1989, vs. Cincinnati). ... Shares Super Bowl single-game records for most points—18 (January 28, 1990, vs. Denver and January 29, 1995, vs. San Diego); most touchdowns—3 (January 28, 1990, vs. Denver and January 29, 1995, vs. San Diego); and most receptions—11 (January 22, 1989, vs. Cincinnati). ... Holds NFL postseason career records for most touchdowns—22; most touchdown receptions—22; most receptions—151; most yards receiving—2,245; most games with 100 or more yards receiving—8; and most points by a non-kicker—132. ... Holds NFL postseason record for most consecutive games with one or more receptions—28 (1985-present). ... Shares NFL postseason career record for most consecutive games with 100 or more yards receiving—3 (1988-89). ... Shares NFL postseason single-game record for most touchdown receptions—3 (January 28, 1990, vs. Denver; January 1, 1989, vs. Minnesota; and January 29, 1995, vs. San Diego).

SINGLE GAME HIGHS (regular season): Receptions—16 (November 20, 1994, vs. Los Angeles Rams); yards—289 (December 18, 1995, vs. Minnesota); and touchdown receptions—5 (October 14, 1990, vs. Atlanta).

STATISTICAL PLATEAUS: 100-yard receiving games: 1985 (2), 1986 (6), 1987 (4), 1988 (5), 1989 (8), 1990 (7), 1991 (4), 1992 (3), 1993 (5), 1994 (5), 1995 (9), 1996 (3), 1998 (3), 1999 (2), 2001 (2), 2002 (5). Total: 73.

MISCELLANEOUS: Active NFL leader for career receptions (1,456), receiving yards (21,597), touchdown receptions (192) and touchdowns (203). ... Holds San Francisco 49ers all-time records for most yards receiving (19,247), most touchdowns (187), most receptions (1,281) and most touchdown receptions (176).

			RUSHING				RECEIVING				TOTALS			
Year Team	G	GS	Att.	Yds.	Avg.	TD	No.	Yds.	Avg.	TD	TD	2pt.	Pts.	Fum.
1985—San Francisco NFL	16	4	6	26	4.3	1	49	927	18.9	3	4	0	24	1
1986—San Francisco NFL	16	15	10	72	7.2	1	‡86	*1570	18.3	*15	16	0	96	2
1987—San Francisco NFL	12	12	8	51	6.4	1	65	1078	16.6	*22	*23	0	*138	2
1988—San Francisco NFL	16	16	13	107	8.2	1	64	1306	20.4	9	10	0	60	2
1989—San Francisco NFL	16	16	5	33	6.6	0	82	*1483	18.1	*17	17	0	102	0
1990—San Francisco NFL	16	16	2	0	0.0	0	*100	*1502	15.0	*13	13	0	78	1
1991—San Francisco NFL	16	16	1	2	2.0	0	80	1206	15.1	*14	14	0	84	1
1992—San Francisco NFL	16	16	9	58	6.4	1	84	1201	14.3	10	11	0	66	2
1993—San Francisco NFL	16	16	3	69	23.0	1	98	*1503	15.3	†15	*16	0	96	3
1994—San Francisco NFL	16	16	7	93	13.3	2	112	*1499	13.4	13	15	1	92	1
1995—San Francisco NFL	16	16	5	36	7.2	1	122	*1848	15.1	15	17	1	104	3
1996—San Francisco NFL	16	16	11	77	7.0	1	*108	1254	11.6	8	9	0	54	0
1997—San Francisco NFL	2	1	1	-10	-10.0	0	7	78	11.1	1	1	0	6	0
1998—San Francisco NFL	16	16	0	0	0.0	0	82	1157	14.1	9	9	†2	58	2
1999—San Francisco NFL	16	16	2	13	6.5	0	67	830	12.4	5	5	0	30	0
2000—San Francisco NFL	16	16	1	-2	-2.0	0	75	805	10.7	7	7	0	42	3
2001—Oakland NFL	16	15	0	0	0.0	0	83	1139	13.7	9	9	0	54	1
2002—Oakland NFL	16	16	3	20	6.7	0	92	1211	13.2	7	7	0	42	1
Pro totals (18 years)	270	255	87	645	7.4	10	1456	21597	14.8	192	203	4	1226	25

RICE, SIMEON   DE   BUCCANEERS

PERSONAL: Born February 24, 1974, in Chicago. ... 6-5/268. ... Name pronounced simm-ee-ON.

HIGH SCHOOL: Mount Carmel (Chicago).

COLLEGE: Illinois (degree in speech communications, 1996).

TRANSACTIONS/CAREER NOTES: Selected by Arizona Cardinals in first round (third pick overall) of 1996 NFL draft. ... Signed by Cardinals (August 19, 1996). ... Designated by Cardinals as franchise player (February 11, 2000). ... Re-signed by Cardinals (September 7, 2000). ... Granted unconditional free agency (March 2, 2001). ... Signed by Tampa Bay Buccaneers (March 23, 2001).

CHAMPIONSHIP GAME EXPERIENCE: Played in NFC championship game (2002 season). ... Member of Super Bowl championship team (2002 season).

HONORS: Played in Pro Bowl (1999 and 2002 seasons). ... Named linebacker on The Sporting News college All-America second team (1995). ... Named defensive end of THE SPORTING NFL All-Pro team (2002).

Year Team	G	GS	TOTALS			INTERCEPTIONS			
			Tk.	Ast.	Sks.	No.	Yds.	Avg.	TD
1996—Arizona NFL	16	15	42	10	12.5	0	0	0.0	0
1997—Arizona NFL	16	15	33	14	5.0	1	0	0.0	0
1998—Arizona NFL	16	16	34	5	10.0	0	0	0.0	0
1999—Arizona NFL	16	16	38	11	16.5	0	0	0.0	0
2000—Arizona NFL	15	11	30	3	7.5	0	0	0.0	0
2001—Tampa Bay NFL	16	16	39	5	11.0	0	0	0.0	0
2002—Tampa Bay NFL	16	16	41	9	‡15.5	1	30	30.0	0
Pro totals (7 years)	111	105	257	57	78.0	2	30	15.0	0

RICHARD, KRIS   CB   SEAHAWKS

PERSONAL: Born October 28, 1978, in Carson, Calif. ... 5-11/190.
HIGH SCHOOL: Serra (Gardena, Calif.).
COLLEGE: Southern California.
TRANSACTIONS/CAREER NOTES: Selected by Seattle Seahawks in third round (85th pick overall) of 2002 NFL draft. ... Signed by Seahawks (July 25, 2002). ... On injured reserve with hernia (December 17, 2002-remainder of season).

Year Team	G	GS	TOTALS			INTERCEPTIONS				PUNT RETURNS				TOTALS			
			Tk.	Ast.	Sks.	No.	Yds.	Avg.	TD	No.	Yds.	Avg.	TD	TD	2pt.	Pts.	Fum.
2002—Seattle NFL	7	0	3	0	0.0	0	0	0.0	0	0	0	0.0	0	0	0	0	0

RICHARDSON, DAMIEN   S   PANTHERS

PERSONAL: Born April 3, 1976, in Los Angeles. ... 6-1/210. ... Full name: Damien A. Richardson.
HIGH SCHOOL: Clovis West (Fresno, Calif.).
COLLEGE: Arizona State.
TRANSACTIONS/CAREER NOTES: Selected by Carolina Panthers in sixth round (165th pick overall) of 1998 NFL draft. ... Signed by Panthers (July 24, 1998). ... Granted free agency (March 2, 2001). ... Re-signed by Panthers (March 2, 2001). ... Granted unconditional free agency (March 1, 2002). ... Re-signed by Panthers (March 25, 2002).

Year Team	G	GS	TOTALS			INTERCEPTIONS			
			Tk.	Ast.	Sks.	No.	Yds.	Avg.	TD
1998—Carolina NFL	14	7	37	10	0.0	0	0	0.0	0
1999—Carolina NFL	15	0	11	0	1.0	1	27	27.0	0
2000—Carolina NFL	16	1	3	0	0.0	0	0	0.0	0
2001—Carolina NFL	16	2	8	1	0.0	0	0	0.0	0
2002—Carolina NFL	16	0	5	1	0.0	0	0	0.0	0
Pro totals (5 years)	77	10	64	12	1.0	1	27	27.0	0

RICHARDSON, KYLE   P   EAGLES

PERSONAL: Born March 2, 1973, in Farmington, Mo. ... 6-2/210. ... Full name: Kyle Davis Richardson.
HIGH SCHOOL: Farmington (Mo.).
COLLEGE: Arkansas State.
TRANSACTIONS/CAREER NOTES: Played for Rhein Fire of World League (1996). ... Signed as non-drafted free agent by Miami Dolphins (September 3, 1997). ... Released by Dolphins (September 8, 1997). ... Re-signed by Dolphins (September 18, 1997). ... Released by Dolphins (October 7, 1997). ... Signed by Seattle Seahawks (November 12, 1997). ... Released by Seahawks (November 25, 1997). ... Signed by Baltimore Ravens (March 25, 1998). ... Granted free agency (March 2, 2001). ... Re-signed by Ravens for 2001 season. ... Granted unconditional free agency (March 1, 2002). ... Signed by Minnesota Vikings (April 21, 2002). ... Granted unconditional free agency (February 28, 2003). ... Signed by Philadelphia Eagles (May 12, 2003).
CHAMPIONSHIP GAME EXPERIENCE: Played in AFC championship game (2000 season). ... Member of Super Bowl championship team (2000 season).

Year Team	G	PUNTING					
		No.	Yds.	Avg.	Net avg.	In. 20	Blk.
1996—Rhein W.L.				Statistics unavailable.			
1997—Miami NFL	3	11	480	43.6	33.1	0	0
—Seattle NFL	2	8	324	40.5	23.8	2	†2
1998—Baltimore NFL	16	90	3948	43.9	38.3	25	*2
1999—Baltimore NFL	16	103	4355	42.3	35.5	*39	1
2000—Baltimore NFL	16	86	3457	40.2	33.9	*35	0
2001—Baltimore NFL	16	85	3309	38.9	33.6	§29	§2
2002—Minnesota NFL	16	62	2474	39.9	35.3	21	1
NFL totals (6 years)	85	445	18347	41.2	35.1	151	8

RICHARDSON, TONY   FB   CHIEFS

PERSONAL: Born December 17, 1971, in Frankfurt, West Germany. ... 6-1/232. ... Full name: Antonio Richardson.
HIGH SCHOOL: Daleville (Ala.).
COLLEGE: Auburn.
TRANSACTIONS/CAREER NOTES: Signed as non-drafted free agent by Dallas Cowboys (April 28, 1994). ... Released by Cowboys (August 28, 1994). ... Re-signed by Cowboys to practice squad (August 30, 1994). ... Granted free agency after 1994 season. ... Signed by Kansas City Chiefs (February 28, 1995). ... On injured reserve with wrist injury (December 11, 1996-remainder of season). ... On injured reserve with shoulder injury (December 17, 2002-remainder of season).

SINGLE GAME HIGHS (regular season): Attempts—23 (December 17, 2000, vs. Denver); yards—156 (December 17, 2000, vs. Denver); and rushing touchdowns—2 (November 4, 2001, vs. San Diego).
STATISTICAL PLATEAUS: 100-yard rushing games: 2000 (1).

Year Team	G	GS	RUSHING				RECEIVING				TOTALS			
			Att.	Yds.	Avg.	TD	No.	Yds.	Avg.	TD	TD	2pt.	Pts.	Fum.
1995—Kansas City NFL	14	1	8	18	2.3	0	0	0	0.0	0	0	0	0	0
1996—Kansas City NFL	13	0	4	10	2.5	0	2	18	9.0	1	1	0	6	0
1997—Kansas City NFL	14	0	2	11	5.5	0	3	6	2.0	3	3	0	18	0
1998—Kansas City NFL	14	1	20	45	2.3	2	2	13	6.5	0	2	0	12	0
1999—Kansas City NFL	16	16	84	387	4.6	1	24	141	5.9	0	1	0	6	1
2000—Kansas City NFL	16	16	147	697	4.7	3	58	468	8.1	3	6	0	36	3
2001—Kansas City NFL	14	7	66	191	2.9	7	30	265	8.8	0	7	0	42	0
2002—Kansas City NFL	14	12	22	81	3.7	2	18	125	6.9	1	3	0	18	1
Pro totals (8 years)	115	53	353	1440	4.1	15	137	1036	7.6	8	23	0	138	5

RICHEY, WADE — K

PERSONAL: Born May 19, 1976, in Lafayette, La. ... 6-3/205. ... Full name: Wade Edward Richey.
HIGH SCHOOL: Carencro (Lafayette, La.).
COLLEGE: Louisiana State.
TRANSACTIONS/CAREER NOTES: Signed as non-drafted free agent by Seattle Seahawks (April 21, 1998). ... Claimed on waivers by San Francisco 49ers (August 26, 1998). ... Granted free agency (March 2, 2001). ... Tendered offer sheet by San Diego Chargers (April 13, 2001). ... 49ers declined to match offer (April 18, 2001). ... Released by Chargers (December 2, 2002).

Year Team	G	FIELD GOALS						TOTALS		
		1-29	30-39	40-49	50+	Tot.	Pct.	Lg.	XPM	XPA	Pts.
1998—San Francisco NFL	16	9-10	3-4	6-13	0-0	18-27	66.7	46	49	51	103
1999—San Francisco NFL	16	8-8	7-8	5-6	1-1	21-23	91.3	52	30	31	93
2000—San Francisco NFL	16	6-7	6-8	3-6	0-1	15-22	68.2	47	43	∞45	88
2001—San Diego NFL	16	13-15	4-7	3-7	1-3	21-32	65.6	51	26	26	89
2002—San Diego NFL	12	0-0	0-0	0-0	0-0	0-0	0.0	0	0	0	0
Pro totals (5 years)	76	36-40	20-27	17-32	2-5	75-104	72.1	52	148	153	373

RICKS, MIKHAEL — TE — LIONS

PERSONAL: Born November 14, 1974, in Galveston, Texas. ... 6-5/252. ... Full name: Mikhael Roy Ricks. ... Name pronounced Michael.
HIGH SCHOOL: Anahuac (Texas).
COLLEGE: Stephen F. Austin State.
TRANSACTIONS/CAREER NOTES: Selected by San Diego Chargers in second round (59th pick overall) of 1998 NFL draft. ... Signed by Chargers (July 23, 1998). ... Released by Chargers (October 3, 2000). ... Signed by Kansas City Chiefs (October 11, 2000). ... Granted unconditional free agency (March 1, 2002). ... Signed by Detroit Lions (April 17, 2002). ... Granted unconditional free agency (February 28, 2003). ... Re-signed by Lions (February 28, 2003).
SINGLE GAME HIGHS (regular season): Receptions—6 (October 24, 1999,vs. Green Bay); yards—86 (September 19, 1999, vs. Cincinnati); and touchdown receptions—1 (December 8, 2002, vs. Arizona).

Year Team	G	GS	RECEIVING				TOTALS			
			No.	Yds.	Avg.	TD	TD	2pt.	Pts.	Fum.
1998—San Diego NFL	16	9	30	450	15.0	2	2	0	12	1
1999—San Diego NFL	16	15	40	429	10.7	0	0	†1	2	0
2000—San Diego NFL	3	1	3	35	11.7	0	0	0	0	0
—Kansas City NFL	1	0	0	0	0.0	0	0	0	0	0
2001—Kansas City NFL	16	0	18	252	14.0	1	1	0	8	0
2002—Detroit NFL	14	12	27	339	12.6	3	3	0	18	0
Pro totals (5 years)	66	37	118	1505	12.8	6	6	1	40	1

RIEMERSMA, JAY — TE — STEELERS

PERSONAL: Born May 17, 1973, in Evansville, Ind. ... 6-5/252. ... Full name: Allen Jay Riemersma. ... Name pronounced REEM-urz-muh.
HIGH SCHOOL: Zeeland (Mich.).
COLLEGE: Michigan.
TRANSACTIONS/CAREER NOTES: Selected by Buffalo Bills in seventh round (244th pick overall) of 1996 NFL draft. ... Signed by Bills (July 9, 1996). ... Released by Bills (August 25, 1996). ... Re-signed by Bills to practice squad (August 26, 1996). ... Activated (October 15, 1996); did not play. ... Granted free agency (February 12, 1999). ... Re-signed by Bills (April 26, 1999). ... Granted unconditional free agency (February 11, 2000). ... Re-signed by Bills (February 15, 2000). ... On physically unable to perform list with hamstring injury (July 25-28, 2002). ... Released by Bills (February 27, 2003). ... Signed by Pittsburgh Steelers (March 19, 2003).
SINGLE GAME HIGHS (regular season): Receptions—8 (December 30, 2001, vs. New York Jets); yards—86 (November 7, 1999, vs. Washington); and touchdown receptions—2 (September 10, 2000, vs. Green Bay).

Year Team	G	GS	RECEIVING				TOTALS			
			No.	Yds.	Avg.	TD	TD	2pt.	Pts.	Fum.
1996—Buffalo NFL					Did not play.					
1997—Buffalo NFL	16	8	26	208	8.0	2	2	1	14	1
1998—Buffalo NFL	16	4	25	288	11.5	6	6	0	36	0
1999—Buffalo NFL	14	11	37	496	13.4	4	4	0	24	0
2000—Buffalo NFL	12	12	31	372	12.0	5	5	0	30	1
2001—Buffalo NFL	16	15	53	590	11.1	3	3	0	18	0
2002—Buffalo NFL	16	15	32	350	10.9	0	0	0	0	0
Pro totals (6 years)	90	65	204	2304	11.3	20	20	1	122	2

RILEY, KARON   LB/DE   FALCONS

PERSONAL: Born August 23, 1978, in Detroit. ... 6-2/268.
HIGH SCHOOL: Martin Luther King (Detroit).
COLLEGE: Southern Methodist, then Minnesota.
TRANSACTIONS/CAREER NOTES: Selected by Chicago Bears in fourth round (103rd pick overall) of 2001 NFL draft. ... Signed by Bears (June 18, 2001). ... Released by Bears (September 1, 2002). ... Signed by Atlanta Falcons to practice squad (September 3, 2002). ... Activated (October 14, 2002). ... Released by Falcons (November 12, 2002). ... Re-signed by Falcons to practice squad (November 13, 2002). ... Activated (November 25, 2002).
HONORS: Named defensive end on THE SPORTING NEWS college All-America third team (2000).

| | | | | TOTALS | |
Year Team	G	GS	Tk.	Ast.	Sks.
2001—Chicago NFL	5	0	1	0	0.0
2002—Atlanta NFL	3	0	0	0	0.0
Pro totals (2 years)	8	0	1	0	0.0

RILEY, VICTOR   OT   SAINTS

PERSONAL: Born November 4, 1974, in Swansea, S.C. ... 6-5/328. ... Full name: Victor Allan Riley.
HIGH SCHOOL: Swansea (S.C.).
COLLEGE: Auburn.
TRANSACTIONS/CAREER NOTES: Selected by Kansas City Chiefs in first round (27th pick overall) of 1998 NFL draft. ... Signed by Chiefs (July 2, 1998). ... Granted unconditional free agency (March 1, 2002). ... Signed by New Orleans Saints (April 4, 2002).
PLAYING EXPERIENCE: Kansas City NFL, 1998-2001; New Orleans NFL, 2002. ... Games/Games started: 1998 (16/15), 1999 (16/16), 2000 (16/16), 2001 (7/5), 2002 (14/2). Total: 69/54.

RITCHIE, JON   RB   EAGLES

PERSONAL: Born September 4, 1974, in Mechanicsburg, Pa. ... 6-1/250.
HIGH SCHOOL: Cumberland Valley (Mechanicsburg, Pa.).
COLLEGE: Michigan, then Stanford.
TRANSACTIONS/CAREER NOTES: Selected by Oakland Raiders in third round (63rd pick overall) of 1998 NFL draft. ... Signed by Raiders (July 18, 1998). ... Granted unconditional free agency (February 28, 2003). ... Signed by Philadelphia Eagles (March 7, 2003).
CHAMPIONSHIP GAME EXPERIENCE: Played in AFC championship game (2000 and 2002 seasons). ... Played in Super Bowl XXXVII (2002 season).
SINGLE GAME HIGHS (regular season): Attempts—2 (September 12, 1999, vs. Green Bay); yards—14 (November 15, 1998, vs. Seattle; and rushing touchdowns—0.

| | | | RUSHING | | | | RECEIVING | | | | | TOTALS | | |
Year Team	G	GS	Att.	Yds.	Avg.	TD	No.	Yds.	Avg.	TD	TD	2pt.	Pts.	Fum.
1998—Oakland NFL	15	10	9	23	2.6	0	29	225	7.8	0	0	0	0	2
1999—Oakland NFL	16	14	5	12	2.4	0	45	408	9.1	1	1	0	6	0
2000—Oakland NFL	13	12	0	0	0.0	0	26	173	6.7	0	0	0	0	0
2001—Oakland NFL	15	10	0	0	0.0	0	19	154	8.1	2	2	0	12	0
2002—Oakland NFL	16	2	0	0	0.0	0	10	66	6.6	1	1	0	6	1
Pro totals (5 years)	75	48	14	35	2.5	0	129	1026	8.0	4	4	0	24	3

RIVERA, MARCO   G   PACKERS

PERSONAL: Born April 26, 1972, in Brooklyn, N.Y. ... 6-4/308. ... Full name: Marco Anthony Rivera.
HIGH SCHOOL: Elmont (N.Y.) Memorial.
COLLEGE: Penn State (degree in administration of justice).
TRANSACTIONS/CAREER NOTES: Selected by Green Bay Packers in sixth round (208th pick overall) of 1996 NFL draft. ... Signed by Packers (July 15, 1996). ... Inactive for all 16 games (1996). ... Assigned by Packers to Scottish Claymores in 1997 World League enhancement allocation program (February 19, 1997). ... Granted free agency (February 12, 1999). ... Re-signed by Packers (March 24, 1999).
PLAYING EXPERIENCE: Scottish W.L., 1997, Green Bay NFL, 1997-2002. ... Games/Games started: W.L. 1997 (10/10), NFL 1997 (14/0), 1998 (15/15), 1999 (16/16), 2000 (16/16), 2001 (16/16), 2002 (16/16). Total W.L.:10/10. Total NFL: 93/79. Total Pro: 103/83.
CHAMPIONSHIP GAME EXPERIENCE: Member of Packers for NFC championship game (1996 season); inactive. ... Member of Super Bowl championship team (1996 season); inactive. ... Played in NFC championship game (1997 season). ... Played in Super Bowl XXXII (1997 season).
HONORS: Played in Pro Bowl (2002 season).

RIVERS, MARCELLUS   TE   GIANTS

PERSONAL: Born October 26, 1978, in Oklahoma City, Okla. ... 6-4/255.
HIGH SCHOOL: Douglass (Oklahoma City, Okla.).
COLLEGE: Oklahoma State.
TRANSACTIONS/CAREER NOTES: Signed as non-drafted free agent by New York Giants (April 27, 2001).
SINGLE GAME HIGHS (regular season): Receptions—1 (October 28, 2002, vs. Philadelphia); yards—17 (October 6, 2002, vs. Dallas); and touchdown receptions—1 (October 6, 2002, vs. Dallas).

| | | | RECEIVING | | | |
Year Team	G	GS	No.	Yds.	Avg.	TD
2001—New York Giants NFL	16	0	3	11	3.7	2
2002—New York Giants NFL	15	0	2	25	12.5	1
Pro totals (2 years)	31	0	5	36	7.2	3

ROAF, WILLIE   OT   CHIEFS

PERSONAL: Born April 18, 1970, in Pine Bluff, Ark. ... 6-5/315. ... Full name: William Layton Roaf.
HIGH SCHOOL: Pine Bluff (Ark.).
COLLEGE: Louisiana Tech.
TRANSACTIONS/CAREER NOTES: Selected by New Orleans Saints in first round (eighth pick overall) of 1993 NFL draft. ... Signed by Saints (July 15, 1993). ... Designated by Saints as transition player (February 15, 1994). ... On injured reserve with knee injury (November 28, 2001-remainder of season). ... Traded by Saints to Kansas City Chiefs for fourth-round pick in 2003 (March 26, 2002).
PLAYING EXPERIENCE: New Orleans NFL, 1993-2001; Kansas City NFL, 2002. ... Games/Games started: 1993 (16/16), 1994 (16/16), 1995 (16/16), 1996 (13/13), 1997 (16/16), 1998 (15/15), 1999 (16/16), 2000 (16/16), 2001 (7/7), 2002 (16/16). Total: 147/147.
HONORS: Named offensive tackle on THE SPORTING NEWS college All-America second team (1992). ... Named offensive tackle on THE SPORTING NEWS NFL All-Pro team (1994-1996). ... Played in Pro Bowl (1994-1997, 1999, 2000 and 2002 seasons). ... Named to play in Pro Bowl (1998 season); replaced by Bob Whitfield due to injury.

ROBBINS, BARRET   C   RAIDERS

PERSONAL: Born August 26, 1973, in Houston. ... 6-3/320.
HIGH SCHOOL: Sharpstown (Houston).
COLLEGE: Texas Christian.
TRANSACTIONS/CAREER NOTES: Selected by Los Angeles Raiders in second round (49th pick overall) of 1995 NFL draft. ... Signed by Raiders (June 20, 1995). ... Raiders franchise moved to Oakland (July 21, 1995). ... On injured reserve with knee injury (September 26, 2001-remainder of season).
PLAYING EXPERIENCE: Oakland NFL, 1995-2001. ... Games/Games started: 1995 (16/0), 1996 (14/14), 1997 (16/16), 1998 (16/16), 1999 (16/16), 2000 (16/16), 2001 (2/2), 2002 (16/16). Total: 112/96.
CHAMPIONSHIP GAME EXPERIENCE: Played in AFC championship game (2000 and 2002 seasons). ... Member of Raiders for Super Bowl XXXVII (2002 season); inactive.
HONORS: Named to play in Pro Bowl (2002 season); replaced by Damien Woody due to injury.

ROBBINS, FRED   DT   VIKINGS

PERSONAL: Born March 25, 1977, in Pensacola, Fla. ... 6-4/313. ... Full name: Fredrick Robbins.
HIGH SCHOOL: Tate (Gonzalez, Fla.).
COLLEGE: Wake Forest.
TRANSACTIONS/CAREER NOTES: Selected by Minnesota Vikings in second round (55th pick overall) of 2000 NFL draft. ... Signed by Vikings (July 21, 2000).
CHAMPIONSHIP GAME EXPERIENCE: Member of Vikings for NFC championship game (2000 season); inactive.

			TOTALS		
Year Team	G	GS	Tk.	Ast.	Sks.
2000—Minnesota NFL	8	0	1	2	1.0
2001—Minnesota NFL	16	12	17	10	2.0
2002—Minnesota NFL	16	14	19	14	0.0
Pro totals (3 years)	40	26	37	26	3.0

ROBERG, MIKE   TE   COLTS

PERSONAL: Born September 18, 1977, in Kent, Wash. ... 6-4/263.
HIGH SCHOOL: University (Spokane, Wash.).
COLLEGE: Idaho.
TRANSACTIONS/CAREER NOTES: Selected by Carolina Panthers in seventh round (227th pick overall) of 2001 NFL draft. ... Signed by Panthers (June 21, 2001). ... Claimed on waivers by Tampa Bay Buccaneers (August 29, 2001). ... Released by Buccaneers (September 2, 2001). ... Re-signed by Buccaneers to practice squad (September 3, 2001). ... Activated (December 4, 2001). ... Released by Buccaneers (August 25, 2002). ... Signed by Indianapolis Colts (September 11, 2002).
SINGLE GAME HIGHS (regular season): Receptions—1 (November 3, 2002, vs. Tennessee); yards—15 (October 21, 2002, vs. Pittsburgh); and touchdown receptions—1 (November 3, 2002, vs. Tennessee).

			RECEIVING			
Year Team	G	GS	No.	Yds.	Avg.	TD
2001—Tampa Bay NFL	1	0	0	0	0.0	0
2002—Indianapolis NFL	12	1	2	17	8.5	1
Pro totals (2 years)	13	1	2	17	8.5	1

ROBERTSON, BERNARD   OT   BEARS

PERSONAL: Born June 9, 1979, in New Orleans. ... 6-3/310. ... Full name: Bernard Robertson Jr..
HIGH SCHOOL: Karr (New Orleans).
COLLEGE: Tulane.
TRANSACTIONS/CAREER NOTES: Selected by Chicago Bears in fifth round (138th pick overall) of 2001 NFL draft. ... Signed by Bears (July 17, 2001). ... Active for one game (2001); did not play.
PLAYING EXPERIENCE: Chicago NFL, 2002. ... Games/games started: 2002 (15/5).

ROBERTSON, JAMAL   RB   49ERS

PERSONAL: Born January 10, 1977, in Washington, D.C. ... 5-10/210.
HIGH SCHOOL: Stebbins (Dayton, Ohio).
COLLEGE: Ohio Northern.
TRANSACTIONS/CAREER NOTES: Signed by Calgary Stampeders of CFL (June 7, 2001). ... Released by Stampeders (June 23, 2001). ... Re-signed by Stampeders to practice squad (June 24, 2001). ... Signed as non-drafted free agent by San Francisco 49ers (January 23, 2002). ...

Assigned by 49ers to Rhein Fire in 2002 NFL Europe enhancement allocation program (February 12, 2002). ... On injured reserve with hamstring injury (December 30, 2002-remainder of season).

Year Team	G	GS	RUSHING				KICKOFF RETURNS				TOTALS			
			Att.	Yds.	Avg.	TD	No.	Yds.	Avg.	TD	TD	2pt.	Pts.	Fum.
2002—Rhein NFLE	...	...	151	792	5.2	8	0	0	0.0	0	8	0	48	0
—San Francisco NFL	6	0	0	0	0.0	0	11	242	22.0	0	0	0	0	0
NFL Europe totals (1 year)	...	...	151	792	5.2	8	0	0	0.0	0	8	0	48	0
NFL totals (1 year)	6	0	0	0	0.0	0	11	242	22.0	0	0	0	0	0
Pro totals (2 years)	...	...	151	792	5.2	8	11	242	22.0	0	8	0	48	0

ROBERTSON, MARCUS   S

PERSONAL: Born October 2, 1969, in Pasadena, Calif. ... 5-11/206. ... Full name: Marcus Aaron Robertson.
HIGH SCHOOL: John Muir (Pasadena, Calif.).
COLLEGE: Iowa State.
TRANSACTIONS/CAREER NOTES: Selected by Houston Oilers in fourth round (102nd pick overall) of 1991 NFL draft. ... Signed by Oilers (July 16, 1991). ... On injured reserve with knee injury (December 30, 1993-remainder of season). ... Granted free agency (February 17, 1994). ... Re-signed by Oilers (July 11, 1994). ... On injured reserve with knee injury (November 30, 1995-remainder of season). ... Oilers franchise moved to Tennessee for 1997 season. ... Oilers franchise renamed Tennessee Titans for 1999 season (December 26, 1998). ... Granted unconditional free agency (February 11, 2000). ... Re-signed by Titans (February 22, 2000). ... Released by Titans (March 1, 2001). ... Signed by Seattle Seahawks (April 12, 2001). ... Released by Seahawks (February 28, 2003).
CHAMPIONSHIP GAME EXPERIENCE: Played in AFC championship game (1999 season). ... Member of Titans for Super Bowl XXXIV (1999 season); inactive.
HONORS: Named free safety on THE SPORTING NEWS NFL All-Pro team (1993).

Year Team	G	GS	TOTALS			INTERCEPTIONS			
			Tk.	Ast.	Sks.	No.	Yds.	Avg.	TD
1991—Houston NFL	16	0	28	5	1.0	0	0	0.0	0
1992—Houston NFL	16	14	44	35	0.0	1	27	27.0	0
1993—Houston NFL	13	13	62	20	0.0	7	137	19.6	0
1994—Houston NFL	16	16	80	31	0.0	3	90	30.0	0
1995—Houston NFL	2	2	2	0	0.0	0	0	0.0	0
1996—Houston NFL	16	16	57	25	0.0	4	44	11.0	0
1997—Tennessee NFL	14	14	44	18	0.0	5	127	25.4	0
1998—Tennessee NFL	12	12	35	8	0.0	1	0	0.0	0
1999—Tennessee NFL	15	15	49	28	0.5	1	3	3.0	0
2000—Tennessee NFL	15	15	62	10	0.0	0	0	0.0	0
2001—Seattle NFL	12	12	48	15	0.0	2	30	15.0	0
2002—Seattle NFL	15	15	67	22	0.0	0	0	0.0	0
Pro totals (12 years)	162	144	578	217	1.5	24	458	19.1	0

ROBINSON, BRYAN   DE   BEARS

PERSONAL: Born June 22, 1974, in Toledo, Ohio. ... 6-4/294. ... Full name: Bryan Keith Robinson.
HIGH SCHOOL: Woodward (Cincinnati).
JUNIOR COLLEGE: College of the Desert (Palm Desert, Calif.).
COLLEGE: Fresno State.
TRANSACTIONS/CAREER NOTES: Signed as non-drafted free agent by St. Louis Rams (April 29, 1997). ... Claimed on waivers by Chicago Bears (August 31, 1998). ... Granted free agency (February 11, 2000). ... Re-signed by Bears (April 19, 2000). ... Designated by Bears as transition player (February 22, 2001).

Year Team	G	GS	TOTALS		
			Tk.	Ast.	Sks.
1997—St. Louis NFL	11	0	10	0	1.0
1998—Chicago NFL	11	5	11	7	0.5
1999—Chicago NFL	16	16	38	4	5.0
2000—Chicago NFL	16	16	42	9	4.5
2001—Chicago NFL	16	16	38	10	4.5
2002—Chicago NFL	15	13	28	6	1.0
Pro totals (6 years)	85	66	167	36	16.5

ROBINSON, DAMIEN   S   SEAHAWKS

PERSONAL: Born December 23, 1973, in Dallas. ... 6-2/223. ... Full name: Damien Dion Robinson.
HIGH SCHOOL: Hillcrest (Dallas).
COLLEGE: Iowa.
TRANSACTIONS/CAREER NOTES: Selected by Philadelphia Eagles in fourth round (119th pick overall) of 1997 NFL draft. ... Signed by Eagles (June 4, 1997). ... Released by Eagles (August 25, 1997). ... Re-signed by Eagles to practice squad (August 27, 1997). ... Signed by Tampa Bay Buccaneers off Eagles practice squad (September 17, 1997). ... Inactive for 13 games (1997). ... On injured reserve with arm injury (October 27, 1998-remainder of season). ... Granted free agency (February 11, 2000). ... Re-signed by Buccaneers (May 15, 2000). ... Granted unconditional free agency (March 2, 2001). ... Signed by New York Jets (April 25, 2001). ... Released by Jets (February 20, 2003). ... Signed by Seattle Seahawks (March 11, 2003).
CHAMPIONSHIP GAME EXPERIENCE: Played in NFC championship game (1999 season).

Year Team	G	GS	TOTALS			INTERCEPTIONS			
			Tk.	Ast.	Sks.	No.	Yds.	Avg.	TD
1998—Tampa Bay NFL	7	0	6	6	0.0	0	0	0.0	0
1999—Tampa Bay NFL	16	16	50	22	0.5	2	36	18.0	0
2000—Tampa Bay NFL	16	16	51	20	0.0	6	1	0.2	0
2001—New York Jets NFL	14	14	38	18	0.0	2	58	29.0	0
2002—New York Jets NFL	15	15	55	18	0.0	2	12	6.0	0
Pro totals (5 years)	68	61	200	84	0.5	12	107	8.9	0

ROBINSON, EDDIE　　LB

PERSONAL: Born April 13, 1970, in New Orleans. ... 6-1/243. ... Full name: Eddie Joseph Robinson Jr.
HIGH SCHOOL: Brother Martin (New Orleans).
COLLEGE: Alabama State (degree in chemistry, 1993).
TRANSACTIONS/CAREER NOTES: Selected by Houston Oilers in second round (50th pick overall) of 1992 NFL draft. ... Signed by Oilers (July 16, 1992). ... Granted free agency (February 17, 1995). ... Re-signed by Oilers (July 1995). ... Granted unconditional free agency (February 16, 1996). ... Signed by Jacksonville Jaguars (March 1, 1996). ... Released by Jaguars (August 30, 1998). ... Signed by Tennessee Oilers (September 1, 1998). ... Oilers franchise renamed Tennessee Titans for 1999 season (December 26, 1998). ... Granted unconditional free agency (February 12, 1999). ... Re-signed by Titans (March 1, 1999). ... Released by Titans (February 28, 2002). ... Signed by Buffalo Bills (April 17, 2002). ... Released by Bills (March 20, 2003).
CHAMPIONSHIP GAME EXPERIENCE: Played in AFC championship game (1996 and 1999 seasons). ... Played in Super Bowl XXXIV (1999 season).

				TOTALS			INTERCEPTIONS			
Year　Team	G	GS	Tk.	Ast.	Sks.	No.	Yds.	Avg.	TD
1992—Houston NFL	16	11	39	25	1.0	0	0	0.0	0
1993—Houston NFL	16	15	42	15	1.0	0	0	0.0	0
1994—Houston NFL	15	15	41	25	0.0	0	0	0.0	0
1995—Houston NFL	16	16	48	24	3.5	1	49	49.0 ▲1
1996—Jacksonville NFL	16	15	57	30	1.0	0	0	0.0	0
1997—Jacksonville NFL	16	13	55	20	2.0	1	0	0.0	0
1998—Tennessee NFL	16	16	72	18	3.5	1	11	11.0	0
1999—Tennessee NFL	16	16	68	15	6.0	0	0	0.0	0
2000—Tennessee NFL	16	16	49	11	4.0	0	0	0.0	0
2001—Tennessee NFL	16	16	51	18	1.0	2	13	6.5	0
2002—Buffalo NFL	16	15	49	33	0.0	1	21	21.0	0
Pro totals (11 years)	175	164	571	234	23.0	6	94	15.7	1

ROBINSON, JEFF　　TE　　COWBOYS

PERSONAL: Born February 20, 1970, in Kennewick, Wash. ... 6-4/275. ... Full name: Jeffrey William Robinson.
HIGH SCHOOL: Joel E. Ferris (Spokane, Wash.).
COLLEGE: Idaho (degree in finance, 1992).
TRANSACTIONS/CAREER NOTES: Selected by Denver Broncos in fourth round (98th pick overall) of 1993 NFL draft. ... Signed by Broncos (July 13, 1993). ... Granted free agency (February 16, 1996). ... Re-signed by Broncos (March 28, 1996). ... Granted unconditional free agency (February 14, 1997). ... Signed by St. Louis Rams (March 14, 1997). ... Granted unconditional free agency (March 1, 2002). ... Signed by Dallas Cowboys (March 5, 2002). ... On injured reserve with knee injury (August 27, 2002-entire season).
CHAMPIONSHIP GAME EXPERIENCE: Played in NFC championship game (1999 and 2001 seasons). ... Member of Super Bowl championship team (1999 season). ... Played in Super Bowl XXXVI (2001 season).
SINGLE GAME HIGHS (regular season): Receptions—2 (November 18, 2001, vs. New England); yards—34 (December 10, 2000, vs. Minnesota); and touchdown receptions—1 (September 23, 2001, vs. San Francisco).
MISCELLANEOUS: Played defensive line (1993-98).

			RECEIVING				TOTALS		
Year　Team	G	GS	No.	Yds.	Avg.	TD	Tk.	Ast.	Sks.
1993—Denver NFL	16	0	0	0	0.0	0	7	6	3.5
1994—Denver NFL	16	0	0	0	0.0	0	7	1	1.0
1995—Denver NFL	16	0	0	0	0.0	0	6	1	1.0
1996—Denver NFL	16	0	0	0	0.0	0	0	1	0.5
1997—St. Louis NFL	16	0	0	0	0.0	0	4	2	0.5
1998—St. Louis NFL	16	0	1	4	4.0	1	1	0	0.0
1999—St. Louis NFL	16	9	6	76	12.7	2	0	0	0.0
2000—St. Louis NFL	16	2	5	52	10.4	0	0	0	0.0
2001—St. Louis NFL	16	6	11	108	9.8	1	0	0	0.0
2002—Dallas NFL					Did not play.				
Pro totals (9 years)	144	17	23	240	10.4	4	25	11	6.5

ROBINSON, KOREN　　WR　　SEAHAWKS

PERSONAL: Born March 19, 1980, in Belmont, N.C. ... 6-1/205.
HIGH SCHOOL: South Point (N.C.).
COLLEGE: North Carolina State.
TRANSACTIONS/CAREER NOTES: Selected after sophomore season by Seattle Seahawks in first round (ninth pick overall) of 2001 NFL draft. ... Signed by Seahawks (July 27, 2001).
SINGLE GAME HIGHS (regular season): Receptions—9 (December 29, 2002, vs. San Diego); yards—168 (November 24, 2002, vs. Kansas City); and touchdown receptions—1 (December 29, 2002, vs. San Diego).
STATISTICAL PLATEAUS: 100-yard receiving games: 2002 (5).

			RUSHING				RECEIVING				TOTALS			
Year　Team	G	GS	Att.	Yds.	Avg.	TD	No.	Yds.	Avg.	TD	TD	2pt.	Pts.	Fum.
2001—Seattle NFL	16	13	4	13	3.3	0	39	536	13.7	1	1	0	6	2
2002—Seattle NFL	16	16	8	56	7.0	0	78	1240	15.9	5	5	0	30	2
Pro totals (2 years)	32	29	12	69	5.8	0	117	1776	15.2	6	6	0	36	4

ROBINSON, MARCUS　　WR　　RAVENS

PERSONAL: Born February 27, 1975, in Fort Valley, Ga. ... 6-3/215.
HIGH SCHOOL: Peach County (Fort Valley, Ga.).
COLLEGE: South Carolina.
TRANSACTIONS/CAREER NOTES: Selected by Chicago Bears in fourth round (108th pick overall) of 1997 NFL draft. ... Signed by Bears (July 11, 1997). ... Inactive for four games (1997). ... On injured reserve with thumb injury (September 24, 1997-remainder of season). ... Assigned

by Bears to Rhein Fire in 1998 NFL Europe enhancement allocation program (February 18, 1998). ... On injured reserve with back injury (December 4, 2000-remainder of season). ... On injured reserve with knee injury (October 23, 2001-remainder of season). ... Released by Bears (April 16, 2003). ... Signed by Baltimore Ravens (May 1, 2003).
SINGLE GAME HIGHS (regular season): Receptions—11 (December 19, 1999, vs. Detroit); yards—170 (December 19, 1999, vs. Detroit); and touchdown receptions—3 (December 19, 1999, vs. Detroit).
STATISTICAL PLATEAUS: 100-yard receiving games: 1999 (5), 2000 (1), 2001 (1). Total: 7.

Year Team	G	GS	RECEIVING No.	Yds.	Avg.	TD	TOTALS TD	2pt.	Pts.	Fum.
1997—Chicago NFL							Did not play.			
1998—Rhein NFLE	...	...	39	811	20.8	5	5	0	30	0
—Chicago NFL	3	0	4	44	11.0	1	1	0	6	0
1999—Chicago NFL	16	11	84	1400	16.7	9	9	0	54	0
2000—Chicago NFL	11	11	55	738	13.4	5	5	0	30	1
2001—Chicago NFL	5	4	23	269	11.7	2	2	0	12	0
2002—Chicago NFL	16	2	21	244	11.6	3	3	0	18	0
NFL Europe totals (1 year)	...	...	39	811	20.8	5	5	0	30	0
NFL totals (4 years)	51	28	187	2695	14.4	20	20	0	120	1
Pro totals (5 years)	...	...	226	3506	15.5	25	25	0	150	1

ROBINSON-RANDALL, GREG   OT   TEXANS

PERSONAL: Born June 23, 1978, in Galveston, Texas. ... 6-5/322.
HIGH SCHOOL: La Marque (Texas).
JUNIOR COLLEGE: Coffeyville (Kan.) Community College.
COLLEGE: Michigan State.
TRANSACTIONS/CAREER NOTES: Selected by New England Patriots in fourth round (127th pick overall) of 2000 NFL draft. ... Signed by Patriots (July 12, 2000). ... Traded by Patriots to Houston Texans for fifth-round pick (traded to Tennessee) in 2003 draft (March 6, 2003).
PLAYING EXPERIENCE: New England NFL, 2000-2002. ... Games/Games started: 2000 (12/4), 2001 (16/16), 2002 (7/2). Total: 35/22.
CHAMPIONSHIP GAME EXPERIENCE: Played in AFC championship game (2001 season). ... Member of Super Bowl championship team (2001 season).

RODGERS, DERRICK   LB   SAINTS

PERSONAL: Born October 14, 1971, in Memphis, Tenn. ... 6-1/230. ... Full name: Derrick Andre Rodgers.
HIGH SCHOOL: St. Augustine (New Orleans).
JUNIOR COLLEGE: Riverside (Calif.) Community College.
COLLEGE: Arizona State.
TRANSACTIONS/CAREER NOTES: Selected by Miami Dolphins in third round (92nd pick overall) of 1997 NFL draft. ... Signed by Dolphins (July 8, 1997). ... Granted free agency (February 11, 2000). ... Re-signed by Dolphins (April 28, 2000). ... Granted unconditional free agency (March 2, 2001). ... Re-signed by Dolphins (March 3, 2001). ... On injured reserve with shoulder injury (December 27, 2001-remainder of season). ... Traded by Dolphins to New Orleans Saints for seventh-round pick in 2004 draft (May 27, 2003).

Year Team	G	GS	TOTALS Tk.	Ast.	Sks.	INTERCEPTIONS No.	Yds.	Avg.	TD
1997—Miami NFL	15	14	56	24	5.0	0	0	0.0	0
1998—Miami NFL	16	16	26	21	2.5	0	0	0.0	0
1999—Miami NFL	16	15	21	15	0.0	1	5	5.0	0
2000—Miami NFL	16	14	52	23	0.5	0	0	0.0	0
2001—Miami NFL	14	14	40	26	1.0	0	0	0.0	0
2002—Miami NFL	16	15	45	29	0.0	2	28	14.0	0
Pro totals (6 years)	93	88	240	138	9.0	3	33	11.0	0

ROGERS, CHARLIE   KR/PR   DOLPHINS

PERSONAL: Born June 19, 1976, in Cliffwood, N.J. ... 5-9/177. ... Full name: John Edward Rogers.
HIGH SCHOOL: Matawan Regional (Aberdeen, N.J.).
COLLEGE: Georgia Tech.
TRANSACTIONS/CAREER NOTES: Selected by Seattle Seahawks in fifth round (152nd pick overall) of 1999 NFL draft. ... Signed by Seahawks (July 29, 1999). ... Selected by Houston Texans from Seahawks in NFL expansion draft (February 18, 2002). ... Granted free agency (March 1, 2002). ... Re-signed by Texans (April 17, 2002). ... Traded by Texans to Buffalo Bills for LB Jay Foreman (April 17, 2002). ... Granted unconditional free agency (February 28, 2003). ... Signed by Miami Dolphins (April 11, 2003).

Year Team	G	GS	PUNT RETURNS No.	Yds.	Avg.	TD	KICKOFF RETURNS No.	Yds.	Avg.	TD	TOTALS TD	2pt.	Pts.	Fum.
1999—Seattle NFL	12	0	22	318	*14.5	1	18	465	25.8	0	1	0	6	3
2000—Seattle NFL	15	0	26	363	14.0	0	66	§1629	24.7	▲1	1	0	6	5
2001—Seattle NFL	13	0	25	244	9.8	0	50	1120	22.4	0	0	0	0	2
2002—Buffalo NFL	16	0	26	137	5.3	0	§64	1280	20.0	1	1	0	6	1
Pro totals (4 years)	56	0	99	1062	10.7	1	198	4494	22.7	2	3	0	18	11

ROGERS, NICK   LB   VIKINGS

PERSONAL: Born May 31, 1979, in East Point, Ga. ... 6-2/251. ... Full name: Nicholas Quixote Rogers.
HIGH SCHOOL: St. Pius X (East Point, Ga.).
COLLEGE: Georgia Tech.
TRANSACTIONS/CAREER NOTES: Selected by Minnesota Vikings in sixth round (177th pick overall) of 2002 NFL draft. ... Signed by Vikings (July 16, 2002).

Year Team	G	GS	TOTALS Tk.	Ast.	Sks.	INTERCEPTIONS No.	Yds.	Avg.	TD
2002—Minnesota NFL	16	11	33	9	2.0	0	0	0.0	0

ROGERS, SAM   LB   FALCONS

PERSONAL: Born May 30, 1970, in Pontiac, Mich. ... 6-3/245. ... Full name: Sammy Lee Rogers.
HIGH SCHOOL: Saint Mary's Preparatory (Orchard Lake, Mich.).
JUNIOR COLLEGE: West Hills College (Calif.), then West Los Angeles College.
COLLEGE: Colorado.
TRANSACTIONS/CAREER NOTES: Selected by Buffalo Bills in second round (64th pick overall) of 1994 NFL draft. ... Signed by Bills (July 12, 1994). ... Granted free agency (February 14, 1997). ... Re-signed by Bills (June 12, 1997). ... Granted unconditional free agency (February 13, 1998). ... Re-signed by Bills (February 15, 1998). ... Released by Bills (March 1, 2001). ... Signed by San Diego Chargers (May 23, 2001). ... Released by Chargers (June 6, 2002). ... Signed by Atlanta Falcons (August 12, 2002). ... Granted unconditional free agency (February 28, 2003). ... Re-signed by Falcons (May 13, 2003).

			TOTALS			INTERCEPTIONS			
Year Team	G	GS	Tk.	Ast.	Sks.	No.	Yds.	Avg.	TD
1994—Buffalo NFL	14	0	0	0	0.0	0	0	0.0	0
1995—Buffalo NFL	16	8	32	13	2.0	0	0	0.0	0
1996—Buffalo NFL	14	14	38	20	3.5	0	0	0.0	0
1997—Buffalo NFL	15	15	39	14	3.5	0	0	0.0	0
1998—Buffalo NFL	15	15	39	19	4.5	0	0	0.0	0
1999—Buffalo NFL	16	16	52	16	3.0	1	24	24.0	0
2000—Buffalo NFL	11	11	28	12	5.0	1	10	10.0	0
2001—San Diego NFL	15	0	4	0	1.0	0	0	0.0	0
2002—Atlanta NFL	15	13	32	9	6.5	0	0	0.0	0
Pro totals (9 years)	131	92	264	103	29.0	2	34	17.0	0

ROGERS, SHAUN   DT   LIONS

PERSONAL: Born March 12, 1979, in Houston. ... 6-4/357.
HIGH SCHOOL: LaPorte (Texas).
COLLEGE: Texas.
TRANSACTIONS/CAREER NOTES: Selected by Detroit Lions in second round (61st pick overall) of 2001 NFL draft. ... Signed by Lions (July 23, 2001). ... On physically unable to perfrom list with ankle injury (July 24-August 6, 2001). ... On physically unable to perform list with thumb injury (July 25-August 19, 2002).

			TOTALS		
Year Team	G	GS	Tk.	Ast.	Sks.
2001—Detroit NFL	16	16	62	19	3.0
2002—Detroit NFL	14	12	26	22	2.5
Pro totals (2 years)	30	28	88	41	5.5

ROGERS, TYRONE   DE   BROWNS

PERSONAL: Born March 9, 1974, in Montgomery, Ala. ... 6-5/250.
HIGH SCHOOL: Robert E. Lee (Montgomery, Ala.).
COLLEGE: Alabama State.
TRANSACTIONS/CAREER NOTES: Signed as non-drafted free agent by Cleveland Browns (April 23, 1999). ... Released by Browns (September 5, 1999). ... Re-signed by Browns to practice squad (September 6, 1999). ... Activated (November 23, 1999).

			TOTALS		
Year Team	G	GS	Tk.	Ast.	Sks.
1999—Cleveland NFL	3	0	3	0	0.0
2000—Cleveland NFL	16	0	9	4	2.0
2001—Cleveland NFL	16	10	31	9	6.0
2002—Cleveland NFL	14	5	19	7	3.0
Pro totals (4 years)	49	15	62	20	11.0

ROLLE, SAMARI   CB   TITANS

PERSONAL: Born August 10, 1976, in Miami. ... 6-0/175. ... Full name: Samari Toure Rolle. ... Name pronounced suh-MARI ROLL.
HIGH SCHOOL: Miami Beach.
COLLEGE: Florida State.
TRANSACTIONS/CAREER NOTES: Selected by Tennessee Oilers in second round (46th pick overall) of 1998 NFL draft. ... Signed by Oilers (July 24, 1998). ... Oilers franchise renamed Tennessee Titans for 1999 season (December 26, 1998). ... Granted free agency (March 2, 2001). ... Re-signed by Titans (July 28, 2001). ... On physically unable to perform list with knee injury (July 28-August 14, 2001).
CHAMPIONSHIP GAME EXPERIENCE: Played in AFC championship game (1999 and 2002 seasons). ... Played in Super Bowl XXXIV (1999 season).
HONORS: Named cornerback on The Sporting News NFL All-Pro team (2000). ... Played in Pro Bowl (2000 season).

			TOTALS			INTERCEPTIONS			
Year Team	G	GS	Tk.	Ast.	Sks.	No.	Yds.	Avg.	TD
1998—Tennessee NFL	15	1	22	3	2.0	0	0	0.0	0
1999—Tennessee NFL	16	16	59	10	3.0	4	65	16.3	0
2000—Tennessee NFL	15	15	35	4	1.5	▲7	140	20.0	1
2001—Tennessee NFL	14	14	51	5	2.0	3	3	1.0	0
2002—Tennessee NFL	16	16	39	9	0.0	2	0	0.0	0
Pro totals (5 years)	76	62	206	31	8.5	16	208	13.0	1

ROMAN, MARK   S   BENGALS

PERSONAL: Born March 26, 1977, in New Iberia, La. ... 5-11/189. ... Full name: Mark Emery Roman.
HIGH SCHOOL: New Iberia (La.).
COLLEGE: Louisiana State.
TRANSACTIONS/CAREER NOTES: Selected by Cincinnati Bengals in second round (34th pick overall) of 2000 NFL draft. ... Signed by Bengals (August 7, 2000). ... On injured reserve with finger injury (December 20, 2001-remainder of season). ... On injured reserve with knee injury (December 23, 2002-remainder of season).

				TOTALS			INTERCEPTIONS			
Year Team	G	GS	Tk.	Ast.	Sks.	No.	Yds.	Avg.	TD	
2000—Cincinnati NFL	8	2	15	1	0.0	0	0	0.0	0	
2001—Cincinnati NFL	13	8	44	7	2.0	1	0	0.0	0	
2002—Cincinnati NFL	13	1	23	7	0.0	0	0	0.0	0	
Pro totals (3 years)	34	11	82	15	2.0	1	0	0.0	0	

ROMANOWSKI, BILL   LB   RAIDERS

PERSONAL: Born April 2, 1966, in Vernon, Conn. ... 6-4/245. ... Full name: William Thomas Romanowski.
HIGH SCHOOL: Rockville (Vernon, Conn.).
COLLEGE: Boston College (degree in general management, 1988).
TRANSACTIONS/CAREER NOTES: Selected by San Francisco 49ers in third round (80th pick overall) of 1988 NFL draft. ... Signed by 49ers (July 15, 1988). ... Granted free agency (February 1, 1991). ... Re-signed by 49ers (July 17, 1991). ... Granted unconditional free agency (March 1, 1993). ... Re-signed by 49ers (March 23, 1993). ... Traded by 49ers to Philadelphia Eagles for third-(traded to Los Angeles Rams) and sixth-round (traded to Green Bay) picks in 1994 draft (April 24, 1994). ... Granted unconditional free agency (February 16, 1996). ... Signed by Denver Broncos (February 23, 1996). ... Released by Broncos (February 21, 2002). ... Signed by Oakland Raiders (February 27, 2002).
CHAMPIONSHIP GAME EXPERIENCE: Played in NFC championship game (1988-1990, 1992 and 1993 seasons). ... Member of Super Bowl championship team (1988, 1989, 1997 and 1998 seasons). ... Played in AFC championship game (1997, 1998 and 2002 seasons). ... Played in Super Bowl XXXVII (2002 season).
HONORS: Played in Pro Bowl (1996 and 1998 seasons).

				TOTALS			INTERCEPTIONS			
Year Team	G	GS	Tk.	Ast.	Sks.	No.	Yds.	Avg.	TD	
1988—San Francisco NFL	16	8	38	15	0.0	0	0	0.0	0	
1989—San Francisco NFL	16	4	47	6	1.0	1	13	13.0	0	
1990—San Francisco NFL	16	16	68	11	1.0	0	0	0.0	0	
1991—San Francisco NFL	16	16	67	9	1.0	1	7	7.0	0	
1992—San Francisco NFL	16	16	65	15	1.0	0	0	0.0	0	
1993—San Francisco NFL	16	16	81	23	3.0	0	0	0.0	0	
1994—Philadelphia NFL	16	15	49	17	2.5	2	8	4.0	0	
1995—Philadelphia NFL	16	16	50	13	1.0	2	5	2.5	0	
1996—Denver NFL	16	16	56	21	3.0	3	1	0.3	0	
1997—Denver NFL	16	16	56	14	2.0	1	7	7.0	0	
1998—Denver NFL	16	16	55	17	7.5	2	22	11.0	0	
1999—Denver NFL	16	16	55	18	0.0	3	35	11.7	1	
2000—Denver NFL	16	16	62	10	3.5	2	0	0.0	0	
2001—Denver NFL	16	16	55	14	7.0	0	0	0.0	0	
2002—Oakland NFL	16	16	65	26	4.0	1	0	0.0	0	
Pro totals (15 years)	240	219	869	229	37.5	18	98	5.4	1	

ROSENFELS, SAGE   QB   DOLPHINS

PERSONAL: Born March 6, 1978, in Maquoketa, Iowa. ... 6-4/216.
HIGH SCHOOL: Maquoketa (Iowa).
COLLEGE: Iowa State.
TRANSACTIONS/CAREER NOTES: Selected by Washington Redskins in fourth round (109th pick overall) of 2001 NFL draft. ... Signed by Redskins (July 26, 2001). ... Traded by Redskins to Miami Dolphins for undisclosed pick in 2003 draft (August 22, 2002).
SINGLE GAME HIGHS (regular season): Attempts—3 (November 4, 2002, vs. Green Bay); completions—0; yards—0; and touchdown passes—0.

				PASSING							RUSHING				TOTALS		
Year Team	G	GS	Att.	Cmp.	Pct.	Yds.	TD	Int.	Avg.	Skd.	Rat.	Att.	Yds.	Avg.	TD	TD	2pt.	Pts.
2002—Miami NFL	4	0	3	0	0.0	0	0	0	0.0	0	39.6	2	-9	-4.5	0	0	0	0

ROSENTHAL, MIKE   G   VIKINGS

PERSONAL: Born June 10, 1977, in Pittsburgh. ... 6-7/315. ... Full name: Michael Paul Rosenthal.
HIGH SCHOOL: Penn (Mishawaka, Ind.).
COLLEGE: Notre Dame.
TRANSACTIONS/CAREER NOTES: Selected by New York Giants in fifth round (149th pick overall) of 1999 NFL draft. ... Signed by Giants (July 26, 1999). ... Granted free agency (March 1, 2002). ... Re-signed by Giants (April 24, 2002). ... Granted unconditional free agency (February 28, 2003). ... Signed by Minnesota Vikings (March 20, 2003).
PLAYING EXPERIENCE: New York Giants NFL, 1999-2001. ... Games/Games started: 1999 (9/7), 2000 (8/2), 2001 (7/0), 2002 (16/16). Total: 40/25.
CHAMPIONSHIP GAME EXPERIENCE: Played in NFC championship game (2000 season). ... Played in Super Bowl XXXV (2000 season).

ROSS, ADRIAN   LB   BENGALS

PERSONAL: Born February 19, 1975, in Santa Clara, Calif. ... 6-2/251. ... Full name: Adrian Lamont Ross.
HIGH SCHOOL: Elk Grove (Calif.).
COLLEGE: Colorado State.
TRANSACTIONS/CAREER NOTES: Signed as non-drafted free agent by Cincinnati Bengals (April 21, 1998). ... Granted free agency (March 2, 2001). ... Re-signed by Bengals (May 1, 2001).

			TOTALS			INTERCEPTIONS			
Year Team	G	GS	Tk.	Ast.	Sks.	No.	Yds.	Avg.	TD
1998—Cincinnati NFL	14	1	11	2	0.0	1	11	11.0	0
1999—Cincinnati NFL	16	10	15	3	1.0	0	0	0.0	0
2000—Cincinnati NFL	13	4	31	2	1.0	0	0	0.0	0
2001—Cincinnati NFL	16	1	4	5	1.0	0	0	0.0	0
2002—Cincinnati NFL	16	6	17	3	0.0	0	0	0.0	0
Pro totals (5 years)	75	22	78	15	3.0	1	11	11.0	0

ROSS, DEREK   CB   COWBOYS

PERSONAL: Born January 5, 1980, in Rock Hill, S.C. ... 5-10/197.
HIGH SCHOOL: Northwestern (Rock Hill, S.C.).
COLLEGE: Ohio State.
TRANSACTIONS/CAREER NOTES: Selected after junior season by Dallas Cowboys in third round (75th pick overall) of 2002 NFL draft. ... Signed by Cowboys (July 26, 2002).

			TOTALS			INTERCEPTIONS				PUNT RETURNS				TOTALS			
Year Team	G	GS	Tk.	Ast.	Sks.	No.	Yds.	Avg.	TD	No.	Yds.	Avg.	TD	TD	2pt.	Pts.	Fum.
2002—Dallas NFL	14	9	51	5	0.0	5	17	3.4	0	0	0	0.0	0	0	0	0	0

ROSS, MICAH   WR   JAGUARS

PERSONAL: Born January 13, 1976, in Jacksonville. ... 6-2/219. ... Full name: Micah David Ross.
HIGH SCHOOL: Andrew Jackson (Fla.).
COLLEGE: Jacksonville.
TRANSACTIONS/CAREER NOTES: Signed as non-drafted free agent by Jacksonville Jaguars (August 17, 2001). ... Released by Jaguars (August 28, 2001). ... Re-signed by Jaguars to practice squad (October 31, 2001). ... Activated (December 8, 2001). ... Re-signed by Jaguars (March 24, 2003).

			RECEIVING			
Year Team	G	GS	No.	Yds.	Avg.	TD
2001—Jacksonville NFL	5	0	0	0	0.0	0
2002—Jacksonville NFL	16	0	0	0	0.0	0
Pro totals (2 years)	21	0	0	0	0.0	0

ROSS, OLIVER   OT   STEELERS

PERSONAL: Born September 27, 1974, in Los Angeles. ... 6-5/314.
HIGH SCHOOL: Washington (Los Angeles).
JUNIOR COLLEGE: Southwestern College (Calif.).
COLLEGE: Iowa State.
TRANSACTIONS/CAREER NOTES: Selected by Dallas Cowboys in fifth round (138th pick overall) of 1998 NFL draft. ... Signed by Cowboys (July 16, 1998). ... Assigned by Cowboys to Rhein Fire in 1999 NFL Europe enhancement allocation program (February 22, 1999). ... Released by Cowboys (September 5, 1999). ... Signed by Philadelphia Eagles to practice squad (September 8, 1999). ... Activated (September 14, 1999); did not play. ... Assigned by Eagles to Amsterdam Admirals in 2000 NFL Europe enhancement allocation program (February 18, 2000). ... Released by Eagles (August 27, 2000). ... Signed by Chicago Bears to practice squad (September 4, 2000). ... Released by Bears (September 7, 2000). ... Signed by Steelers to practice squad (November 22, 2000). ... Activated (December 13, 2000). ... Granted free agency (March 1, 2002). ... Tendered offer sheet by Cleveland Browns (March 13, 2002). ... Offer matched by Steelers (March 15, 2002).
PLAYING EXPERIENCE: Dallas NFL, 1998; Rhein NFLE, 1999; Amsterdam NFLE, 2000; Pittsburgh NFL, 2001-2002. ... Games/Games started: 1998 (2/0), NFLE 1999 (games played unavailable), NFLE 2000 (-), 2001 (16/7), 2002 (16/1). Total: 34/8.
CHAMPIONSHIP GAME EXPERIENCE: Played in AFC championship game (2001 season).

ROSSUM, ALLEN   KR   FALCONS

PERSONAL: Born October 22, 1975, in Dallas. ... 5-8/178.
HIGH SCHOOL: Skyline (Dallas).
COLLEGE: Notre Dame.
TRANSACTIONS/CAREER NOTES: Selected by Philadelphia Eagles in third round (85th pick overall) of 1998 NFL draft. ... Signed by Eagles (July 14, 1998). ... Traded by Eagles to Green Bay Packers for fifth-round pick (TE Tony Stewart) in 2001 draft (August 21, 2000). ... Granted free agency (March 2, 2001). ... Re-signed by Packers (April 23, 2001). ... Granted unconditional free agency (March 1, 2002). ... Signed by Atlanta Falcons (March 13, 2002).

			PUNT RETURNS				KICKOFF RETURNS				TOTALS			
Year Team	G	GS	No.	Yds.	Avg.	TD	No.	Yds.	Avg.	TD	TD	2pt.	Pts.	Fum.
1998—Philadelphia NFL	15	2	22	187	8.5	0	44	1080	24.5	0	0	0	0	4
1999—Philadelphia NFL	16	0	28	250	8.9	0	54	1347	24.9	1	1	0	6	6
2000—Green Bay NFL	16	0	29	248	8.6	0	50	1288	25.8	1	1	0	6	0
2001—Green Bay NFL	6	0	11	109	9.9	∞1	23	431	18.7	0	1	0	6	0
2002—Atlanta NFL	14	0	24	288	12.0	0	53	1164	22.0	1	1	0	6	1
Pro totals (5 years)	67	2	114	1082	9.5	1	224	5310	23.7	3	4	0	24	15

ROUEN, TOM   P

PERSONAL: Born June 9, 1968, in Hinsdale, Ill. ... 6-3/225. ... Full name: Thomas Francis Rouen Jr. ... Name pronounced RUIN.
HIGH SCHOOL: Heritage (Littleton, Colo.).
COLLEGE: Colorado State, then Colorado.
TRANSACTIONS/CAREER NOTES: Signed as non-drafted free, agent by New York Giants (April 29, 1991). ... Released by Giants (August 19, 1991). ... Selected by Ohio Glory in fourth round (44th pick overall) of 1992 World League draft. ... Signed by Los Angeles Rams (July 1992). ... Released by Rams (August 24, 1992). ... Signed by Denver Broncos (April 29, 1993). ... Granted unconditional free agency (February 14, 1997). ... Re-signed by Broncos (March 6, 1997). ... Granted unconditional free agency (February 11, 2000). ... Re-signed by Broncos (February 24, 2000). ... Released by Broncos (October 29, 2002). ... Signed by Giants (November 1, 2002). ... Released by Giants (November 19, 2002). ... Signed by Pittsburgh Steelers (December 20, 2002). ... Granted unconditional free agency (February 28, 2003).
CHAMPIONSHIP GAME EXPERIENCE: Played in AFC championship game (1997 and 1998 seasons). ... Member of Super Bowl championship team (1997 and 1998 seasons).
HONORS: Named punter on THE SPORTING NEWS college All-America second team (1989).

		PUNTING					
Year Team	G	No.	Yds.	Avg.	Net avg.	In. 20	Blk.
1992—Ohio W.L.	10	48	1992	41.5	36.1	14	1
1993—Denver NFL	16	67	3017	45.0	37.1	17	1
1994—Denver NFL	16	76	3258	42.9	*37.1	23	0
1995—Denver NFL	16	52	2192	42.2	37.6	22	1
1996—Denver NFL	16	65	2714	41.8	36.2	16	0
1997—Denver NFL	16	60	2598	43.3	38.1	22	0
1998—Denver NFL	16	66	3097	46.9	37.6	14	1
1999—Denver NFL	16	84	3908	*46.5	35.6	19	0
2000—Denver NFL	16	61	2455	40.2	32.3	18	▲1
2001—Denver NFL	16	81	3668	45.3	36.5	25	1
2002—Denver NFL	8	29	1239	42.7	31.7	6	2
—New York Giants NFL	2	8	333	41.6	33.0	1	0
—Pittsburgh NFL	2	7	316	45.1	38.7	1	0
W.L. totals (1 year)	10	48	1992	41.5	36.1	14	1
NFL totals (10 years)	156	656	28795	43.9	36.2	184	7
Pro totals (11 years)	166	704	30787	43.7	36.2	198	8

ROUNDTREE, RALEIGH   G/OT   CARDINALS

PERSONAL: Born August 31, 1975, in Augusta, Ga. ... 6-4/295. ... Full name: Raleigh Cito Roundtree.
HIGH SCHOOL: Josey (Augusta, Ga.).
COLLEGE: South Carolina State.
TRANSACTIONS/CAREER NOTES: Selected by San Diego Chargers in fourth round (109th pick overall) of 1997 NFL draft. ... Signed by Chargers (July 14, 1997). ... Inactive for all 16 games (1997). ... Granted free agency (February 11, 2000). ... Re-signed by Chargers (May 30, 2000). ... Granted unconditional free agency (March 2, 2001). ... Re-signed by Chargers (May 4, 2001). ... Granted unconditional free agency (March 1, 2002). ... Signed by Jacksonville Jaguars (June 13, 2002). ... Released by Jaguars (September 3, 2002). ... Signed by Arizona Cardinals (September 9, 2002). ... Granted unconditional free agency (February 28, 2003). ... Re-signed by Cardinals (March 14, 2003).
PLAYING EXPERIENCE: San Diego NFL, 1998-2001; Arizona NFL, 2002. ... Games/Games started: 1998 (15/5), 1999 (15/5), 2000 (16/15), 2001 (16/16), 2002: (10/6). Total: 72/47.

ROYALS, MARK   P   DOLPHINS

PERSONAL: Born June 22, 1965, in Hampton, Va. ... 6-5/225. ... Full name: Mark Alan Royals.
HIGH SCHOOL: Mathews (Va.).
JUNIOR COLLEGE: Chowan College (N.C.).
COLLEGE: Appalachian State (degree in political science).
TRANSACTIONS/CAREER NOTES: Signed as non-drafted free agent by Dallas Cowboys (June 6, 1986). ... Released by Cowboys (August 8, 1986). ... Signed as replacement player by St. Louis Cardinals (September 30, 1987). ... Released by Cardinals (October 7, 1987). ... Signed as replacement player by Philadelphia Eagles (October 14, 1987). ... Released by Eagles (November 1987). ... Signed by Cardinals (December 12, 1987). ... Released by Cardinals (July 27, 1988). ... Signed by Miami Dolphins (May 2, 1989). ... Released by Dolphins (August 28, 1989). ... Signed by Tampa Bay Buccaneers (April 24, 1990). ... Granted unconditional free agency (February 1, 1992). ... Signed by Pittsburgh Steelers (March 15, 1992). ... Granted unconditional free agency (February 17, 1995). ... Signed by Detroit Lions (April 26, 1995). ... Granted free agency (February 16, 1996). ... Re-signed by Lions (June 19, 1996). ... Granted unconditional free agency (February 14, 1997). ... Signed by New Orleans Saints (April 25, 1997). ... Released by Saints (June 29, 1999). ... Signed by Buccaneers (August 4, 1999). ... Granted unconditional free agency (February 11, 2000). ... Re-signed by Buccaneers (March 24, 2000). ... Released by Buccaneers (February 26, 2002). ... Signed by Miami Dolphins (April 14, 2002). ... Granted unconditional free agency (February 28, 2003). ... Re-signed by Dolphins (March 4, 2003).
CHAMPIONSHIP GAME EXPERIENCE: Played in AFC championship game (1994 season). ... Played in NFC championship game (1999 season).

		PUNTING					
Year Team	G	No.	Yds.	Avg.	Net avg.	In. 20	Blk.
1987—St. Louis NFL	1	6	222	37.0	17.2	2	0
—Philadelphia NFL	1	5	209	41.8	30.6	1	0
1988—				Did not play.			
1989—				Did not play.			
1990—Tampa Bay NFL	16	72	2902	40.3	34.0	8	0
1991—Tampa Bay NFL	16	84	3389	40.3	32.3	22	0
1992—Pittsburgh NFL	16	73	3119	42.7	35.6	22	1
1993—Pittsburgh NFL	16	89	3781	42.5	34.2	§28	0
1994—Pittsburgh NFL	16	§97	3849	39.7	35.7	†35	0
1995—Detroit NFL	16	57	2393	42.0	31.0	15	2
1996—Detroit NFL	16	69	3020	43.8	33.4	11	1
1997—New Orleans NFL	16	88	4038	*45.9	34.9	21	0

Year Team	G	No.	Yds.	Avg.	Net avg.	In. 20	Blk.
PUNTING header spans No./Yds./Avg./Net avg./In. 20/Blk.

Year Team	G	No.	Yds.	Avg.	Net avg.	In. 20	Blk.
1998—New Orleans NFL	16	88	4017	‡45.6	36.0	26	0
1999—Tampa Bay NFL	16	90	3882	43.1	37.4	23	0
2000—Tampa Bay NFL	16	85	3551	41.8	35.1	17	0
2001—Tampa Bay NFL	16	83	3382	40.7	34.2	26	0
2002—Miami NFL	16	69	2772	40.2	34.5	15	0
Pro totals (14 years)	210	1055	44526	42.2	34.5	272	4

ROYE, ORPHEUS — DL — BROWNS

PERSONAL: Born January 21, 1973, in Miami. ... 6-4/313. ... Full name: Orpheus Michael Roye. ... Name pronounced OR-fee-us ROY.
HIGH SCHOOL: Miami Springs.
JUNIOR COLLEGE: Jones County Junior College (Miss.).
COLLEGE: Florida State.
TRANSACTIONS/CAREER NOTES: Selected by Pittsburgh Steelers in sixth round (200th pick overall) of 1996 NFL draft. ... Signed by Steelers (July 16, 1996). ... Granted free agency (February 12, 1999). ... Re-signed by Steelers (April 23, 1999). ... Granted unconditional free agency (February 11, 2000). ... Signed by Cleveland Browns (February 12, 2000). ... On injured reserve with knee injury (December 11, 2001-remainder of season).
CHAMPIONSHIP GAME EXPERIENCE: Played in AFC championship game (1997 season).

Year Team	G	GS	Tk.	Ast.	Sks.	No.	Yds.	Avg.	TD
			TOTALS			INTERCEPTIONS			
1996—Pittsburgh NFL	13	1	1	2	0.0	0	0	0.0	0
1997—Pittsburgh NFL	16	0	3	1	1.0	0	0	0.0	0
1998—Pittsburgh NFL	16	9	29	13	3.5	0	0	0.0	0
1999—Pittsburgh NFL	16	16	41	17	4.5	1	2	2.0	0
2000—Cleveland NFL	16	16	42	13	2.0	0	0	0.0	0
2001—Cleveland NFL	12	10	18	7	0.0	1	0	0.0	0
2002—Cleveland NFL	16	16	38	17	0.5	0	0	0.0	0
Pro totals (7 years)	105	68	172	70	11.5	2	2	1.0	0

RUCKER, MIKE — DE — PANTHERS

PERSONAL: Born February 28, 1975, in St. Joseph, Mo. ... 6-5/275. ... Full name: Michael Dean Rucker.
HIGH SCHOOL: Benton (St. Joseph, Mo.).
COLLEGE: Nebraska (degree in sociology).
TRANSACTIONS/CAREER NOTES: Selected by Carolina Panthers in second round (38th pick overall) of 1999 NFL draft. ... Signed by Panthers (July 13, 1999).

Year Team	G	GS	Tk.	Ast.	Sks.
			TOTALS		
1999—Carolina NFL	16	0	24	6	3.0
2000—Carolina NFL	16	1	33	6	2.5
2001—Carolina NFL	16	16	44	12	9.0
2002—Carolina NFL	16	15	58	10	10.0
Pro totals (4 years)	64	32	159	34	24.5

RUDD, DWAYNE — LB — BUCCANEERS

PERSONAL: Born February 3, 1976, in Batesville, Miss. ... 6-2/235. ... Full name: Dwayne Dupree Rudd.
HIGH SCHOOL: South Panola (Batesville, Miss.).
COLLEGE: Alabama.
TRANSACTIONS/CAREER NOTES: Selected by Minnesota Vikings in first round (20th pick overall) of 1997 NFL draft. ... Signed by Vikings (July 18, 1997). ... Granted unconditional free agency (March 2, 2001). ... Signed by Cleveland Browns (March 3, 2001). ... Released by Browns (February 26, 2003). ... Signed by Tampa Bay Buccaneers (April 8, 2003).
CHAMPIONSHIP GAME EXPERIENCE: Played in NFC championship game (1998 and 2000 seasons).
RECORDS: Shares NFL single-season records for most touchdowns by fumble recovery—2 (1998); most touchdowns by recovery of opponents' fumbles—2 (1998).

Year Team	G	GS	Tk.	Ast.	Sks.	No.	Yds.	Avg.	TD
			TOTALS			INTERCEPTIONS			
1997—Minnesota NFL	16	2	31	15	5.0	0	0	0.0	0
1998—Minnesota NFL	15	15	79	14	2.0	0	0	0.0	0
1999—Minnesota NFL	16	16	88	29	3.0	0	0	0.0	0
2000—Minnesota NFL	14	13	52	17	0.0	0	0	0.0	0
2001—Cleveland NFL	16	16	69	27	0.5	1	0	0.0	0
2002—Cleveland NFL	16	15	50	12	1.0	0	0	0.0	0
Pro totals (6 years)	93	77	369	114	11.5	1	0	0.0	0

RUDDY, TIM — C — DOLPHINS

PERSONAL: Born April 27, 1972, in Scranton, Pa. ... 6-3/295. ... Full name: Timothy Daniel Ruddy.
HIGH SCHOOL: Dunmore (Pa.).
COLLEGE: Notre Dame (degree in mechanical engineering).
TRANSACTIONS/CAREER NOTES: Selected by Miami Dolphins in second round (65th pick overall) of 1994 NFL draft. ... Signed by Dolphins (July 18, 1994). ... Granted unconditional free agency (February 11, 2000). ... Re-signed by Dolphins (February 24, 2000).
PLAYING EXPERIENCE: Miami NFL, 1994-2002, ... Games/Games started: 1994 (16/0), 1995 (16/16), 1996 (16/16), 1997 (15/15), 1998 (16/16), 1999 (16/16), 2000 (16/16), 2001 (15/15), 2002 (16/16). Total: 142/126.
HONORS: Played in Pro Bowl (2000 season).

RUEGAMER, GREY　　　　　G　　　　　PACKERS

PERSONAL: Born June 1, 1976, in Las Vegas, Nev. ... 6-5/302. ... Full name: Christopher Grey Ruegamer.
HIGH SCHOOL: Bishop Gorman (Las Vegas, Nev.).
COLLEGE: Arizona State.
TRANSACTIONS/CAREER NOTES: Selected by Miami Dolphins in third round (72nd pick overall) of 1999 NFL draft. ... Signed by Dolphins (July 27, 1999). ... Active for one game (1999); did not play. ... Released by Dolphins (August 27, 2000). ... Signed by Pittsburgh Steelers to practice squad (August 29, 2000). ... Signed by New England Patriots off Steelers practice squad (November 16, 2000). ... Granted free agency (March 1, 2002). ... Re-signed by Patriots (April 19, 2002). ... Granted unconditional free agency (February 28, 2003). ... Signed by Green Bay Packers (April 8, 2003).
PLAYING EXPERIENCE: New England NFL, 2000-2002. ... Games/Games started: 2000 (6/0), 2001 (14/1), 2002 (13/2). Total: 33/3.
CHAMPIONSHIP GAME EXPERIENCE: Played in AFC championship game (2001 season). ... Member of Super Bowl championship team (2001 season).

RUFF, ORLANDO　　　　　LB　　　　　SAINTS

PERSONAL: Born September 28, 1976, in Charleston, S.C. ... 6-3/247. ... Full name: Orlando Bernarda Ruff.
HIGH SCHOOL: Fairfield Central (Winnsboro, S.C.).
COLLEGE: Furman.
TRANSACTIONS/CAREER NOTES: Signed as non-drafted free agent by San Diego Chargers (April 20, 1999). ... Granted free agency (March 1, 2002). ... Re-signed by Chargers (April 3, 2002). ... Granted unconditional free agency (February 28, 2003). ... Signed by New Orleans Saints (March 3, 2003).

| | | | TOTALS | | | INTERCEPTIONS | | | |
Year　Team	G	GS	Tk.	Ast.	Sks.	No.	Yds.	Avg.	TD
1999—San Diego NFL	14	0	5	2	0.0	0	0	0.0	0
2000—San Diego NFL	16	14	54	14	0.0	1	18	18.0	0
2001—San Diego NFL	16	15	59	15	1.0	0	0	0.0	0
2002—San Diego NFL	16	0	4	0	0.0	0	0	0.0	0
Pro totals (4 years)	62	29	122	31	1.0	1	18	18.0	0

RUMPH, MIKE　　　　　CB　　　　　49ERS

PERSONAL: Born November 8, 1979, in Delray Beach, Fla. ... 6-2/205. ... Full name: Michael Jamaine Rumph.
HIGH SCHOOL: Atlantic (Delray Beach, Fla.).
COLLEGE: Miami (Fla.).
TRANSACTIONS/CAREER NOTES: Selected by San Francisco 49ers in first round (27th pick overall) of 2002 NFL draft. ... Signed by 49ers (July 23, 2002).

| | | | TOTALS | | | INTERCEPTIONS | | | |
Year　Team	G	GS	Tk.	Ast.	Sks.	No.	Yds.	Avg.	TD
2002—San Francisco NFL	16	1	36	5	0.0	0	0	0.0	0

RUNYAN, JON　　　　　OT　　　　　EAGLES

PERSONAL: Born November 27, 1973, in Flint, Mich. ... 6-7/330. ... Full name: Jon Daniel Runyan.
HIGH SCHOOL: Carman-Ainsworth (Flint, Mich.).
COLLEGE: Michigan.
TRANSACTIONS/CAREER NOTES: Selected after junior season by Houston Oilers in fourth round (109th pick overall) of 1996 NFL draft. ... Signed by Oilers (July 20, 1996). ... Oilers franchise moved to Tennessee for 1997 season. ... Oilers franchise renamed Tennessee Titans for 1999 season (December 26, 1998). ... Granted free agency (February 12, 1999). ... Re-signed by Titans (June 23, 1999). ... Granted unconditional free agency (February 11, 2000). ... Signed by Philadelphia Eagles (February 14, 2000).
PLAYING EXPERIENCE: Houston NFL, 1996; Tennessee NFL, 1997-1999; Philadelphia NFL, 2000-2002. ... Games/Games started: 1996 (10/0), 1997 (16/16), 1998 (16/16), 1999 (16/16), 2000 (16/16), 2001 (16/16), 2002 (16/16). Total: 106/96.
CHAMPIONSHIP GAME EXPERIENCE: Played in AFC championship game (1999 season). ... Played in Super Bowl XXXIV (1999 season). ... Played in NFC championship game (2001 and 2002 seasons).
HONORS: Named offensive lineman on THE SPORTING NEWS college All-America second team (1995). ... Played in Pro Bowl (2002 season).

RUSSELL, BRIAN　　　　　S　　　　　VIKINGS

PERSONAL: Born February 5, 1978, in West Covina, Calif. ... 6-2/204. ... Full name: Brian William Russell.
HIGH SCHOOL: Bishop Amat (West Covina, Calif.).
COLLEGE: Pennsylvania, then San Diego State.
TRANSACTIONS/CAREER NOTES: Signed as non-drafted free by Minnesota Vikings (April 23, 2001). ... Released by Vikings (September 1, 2001). ... Re-signed by Vikings to practice squad (September 3, 2001).

| | | | TOTALS | | | INTERCEPTIONS | | | |
Year　Team	G	GS	Tk.	Ast.	Sks.	No.	Yds.	Avg.	TD
2002—Minnesota NFL	16	2	10	4	0.0	1	18	18.0	0

RUSSELL, TWAN　　　　　LB　　　　　FALCONS

PERSONAL: Born April 25, 1974, in Fort Lauderdale, Fla. ... 6-1/230. ... Full name: Twan Sanchez Russell.
HIGH SCHOOL: St. Thomas Aquinas (Fort Lauderdale, Fla.).
COLLEGE: Miami, Fla. (degree in broadcasting, 1996).

TRANSACTIONS/CAREER NOTES: Selected by Washington Redskins in fifth round (148th pick overall) of 1997 NFL draft. ... Signed by Redskins (May 9, 1997). ... On injured reserve with foot and knee injuries (September 23, 1998-remainder of season). ... On injured reserve with knee injury (November 16, 1999-remainder of season). ... Granted free agency (February 11, 2000). ... Signed by Miami Dolphins (March 23, 2000). ... Granted unconditional free agency (March 2, 2001). ... Re-signed by Dolphins (March 6, 2001). ... On injured reserve with knee injury (November 13, 2002-remainder of season). ... Released by Dolphins (February 26, 2003). ... Signed by Atlanta Falcons (March 24, 2003).

			TOTALS			INTERCEPTIONS			
Year Team	G	GS	Tk.	Ast.	Sks.	No.	Yds.	Avg.	TD
1997—Washington NFL	15	0	3	0	0.0	0	0	0.0	0
1998—Washington NFL	3	0	0	0	0.0	0	0	0.0	0
1999—Washington NFL	9	0	2	0	0.0	0	0	0.0	0
2000—Miami NFL	16	2	3	0	0.0	0	0	0.0	0
2001—Miami NFL	16	2	4	6	0.0	0	0	0.0	0
2002—Miami NFL	3	0	0	0	0.0	0	0	0.0	0
Pro totals (6 years)	62	4	12	6	0.0	0	0	0.0	0

RUTLEDGE, JOHNNY   LB

PERSONAL: Born January 4, 1977, in Belle Glade, Fla. ... 6-3/239. ... Full name: Johnny Boykins Rutledge III.
HIGH SCHOOL: Glades Central (Belle Glade, Fla.).
COLLEGE: Florida.
TRANSACTIONS/CAREER NOTES: Selected by Arizona Cardinals in second round (51st pick overall) of 1999 NFL draft. ... Signed by Cardinals (July 29, 1999). ... Granted unconditional free agency (February 28, 2003).

			TOTALS			INTERCEPTIONS			
Year Team	G	GS	Tk.	Ast.	Sks.	No.	Yds.	Avg.	TD
1999—Arizona NFL	6	0	1	1	0.0	0	0	0.0	0
2000—Arizona NFL	11	3	16	7	0.0	0	0	0.0	0
2001—Arizona NFL	14	0	1	0	0.0	0	0	0.0	0
2002—Arizona NFL	9	0	0	0	0.0	0	0	0.0	0
Pro totals (4 years)	40	3	18	8	0.0	0	0	0.0	0

RUTLEDGE, ROD   TE   TEXANS

PERSONAL: Born August 12, 1975, in Birmingham, Ala. ... 6-5/265. ... Full name: Rodrick Almar Rutledge.
HIGH SCHOOL: Erwin (Birmingham, Ala.).
COLLEGE: Alabama.
TRANSACTIONS/CAREER NOTES: Selected by New England Patriots in second round (54th pick overall) of 1998 NFL draft. ... Signed by Patriots (June 15, 1998). ... Granted unconditional free agency (March 1, 2002). ... Signed by Houston Texans (April 10, 2002). ... On injured reserve with foot injury (November 26, 2002-remainder of season).
CHAMPIONSHIP GAME EXPERIENCE: Played in AFC championship game (2001 season). ... Member of Super Bowl championship team (2001 season).
SINGLE GAME HIGHS (regular season): Receptions—4 (November 23, 2000, vs. Detroit); yards—27 (December 4, 2000, vs. Kansas City); and touchdown receptions—1 (November 12, 2000, vs. Cleveland).

			RECEIVING			
Year Team	G	GS	No.	Yds.	Avg.	TD
1998—New England NFL	16	4	0	0	0.0	0
1999—New England NFL	16	2	7	66	9.4	0
2000—New England NFL	16	11	15	103	6.9	1
2001—New England NFL	15	14	5	35	7.0	0
2002—Houston NFL	7	5	0	0	0.0	0
Pro totals (5 years)	70	36	27	204	7.6	1

SALAAM, EPHRAIM   OT   BRONCOS

PERSONAL: Born June 19, 1976, in Chicago. ... 6-7/295. ... Full name: Ephraim Mateen Salaam. ... Name pronounced EFF-rum sah-LAHM.
HIGH SCHOOL: Florin (Sacramento).
COLLEGE: San Diego State.
TRANSACTIONS/CAREER NOTES: Selected by Atlanta Falcons in seventh round (199th pick overall) of 1998 NFL draft. ... Signed by Falcons (June 3, 1998). ... Granted free agency (March 2, 2001). ... Re-signed by Falcons (April 6, 2001). ... Granted unconditional free agency (March 1, 2002). ... Signed by Denver Broncos (April 15, 2002).
PLAYING EXPERIENCE: Atlanta NFL, 1998-2002. ... Games/Games started: 1998 (16/16), 1999 (16/16), 2000 (14/10), 2001 (14/13), 2002 (16/16). Total: 76/71.
CHAMPIONSHIP GAME EXPERIENCE: Played in NFC championship game (1998 season). ... Played in Super Bowl XXXIII (1998 season).

SAMUELS, CHRIS   OT   REDSKINS

PERSONAL: Born July 28, 1977, in Mobile, Ala. ... 6-5/303.
HIGH SCHOOL: Shaw (Mobile, Ala.).
COLLEGE: Alabama.
TRANSACTIONS/CAREER NOTES: Selected by Washington Redskins in first round (third pick overall) of 2000 NFL draft. ... Signed by Redskins (July 18, 2000).
PLAYING EXPERIENCE: Washington NFL, 2000-2002. ... Games/Games started: 2000 (16/16), 2001 (16/16), 2002 (15/15). Total: 47/47.
HONORS: Outland Trophy winner (1999). ... Named offensive tackle on THE SPORTING NEWS college All-America first team (1999). ... Played in Pro Bowl (2001 and 2002 seasons).

SANCHEZ, DAVIS   DB

PERSONAL: Born August 7, 1974, in Vancouver. ... 5-10/190.
HIGH SCHOOL: North Delta (British Columbia).
JUNIOR COLLEGE: Butte Junior College.
COLLEGE: Oregon.
TRANSACTIONS/CAREER NOTES: Selected by Montreal Alouettes in first round (sixth pick overall) in 1999 CFL draft. ... Announced retirement (December 20, 1999). ... Signed as non-drafted free agent by San Diego Chargers (February 17, 2001). ... Granted free agency (February 28, 2003).

			TOTALS			INTERCEPTIONS			
Year Team	G	GS	Tk.	Ast.	Sks.	No.	Yds.	Avg.	TD
1999—Montreal CFL	17	...	...	...	0.0	3	0	0.0	0
2000—Montreal CFL	...	...	...	...	0.0	9	163	18.1	2
2001—San Diego NFL	12	2	14	0	0.0	0	0	0.0	0
2002—San Diego NFL	10	0	4	0	0.0	0	0	0.0	0
CFL totals (2 years)	...	...	...	...	0.0	12	163	13.6	2
NFL totals (2 years)	22	2	18	0	0.0	0	0	0.0	0
Pro totals (4 years)	...	...	...	...	0.0	12	163	13.6	2

SANDERS, DARNELL   TE   BROWNS

S

PERSONAL: Born March 16, 1979, in Warrensville Heights, Ohio. ... 6-6/267.
HIGH SCHOOL: Warrensville Heights (Ohio).
COLLEGE: Ohio State.
TRANSACTIONS/CAREER NOTES: Selected after junior season by Cleveland Browns in fourth round (122nd pick overall) of 2002 NFL draft. ... Signed by Browns (July 8, 2002).
SINGLE GAME HIGHS (regular season): Receptions—1 (November 24, 2002, vs. New Orleans); yards—14 (November 17, 2002, vs. Cincinnati); and touchdown receptions—1 (November 17, 2002, vs. Cincinnati).

			RECEIVING			
Year Team	G	GS	No.	Yds.	Avg.	TD
2002—Cleveland NFL	10	3	3	23	7.7	1

SANDERS, FRANK   WR   RAVENS

PERSONAL: Born February 17, 1973, in Fort Lauderdale, Fla. ... 6-2/215. ... Full name: Frank Vondel Sanders.
HIGH SCHOOL: Dillard (Fort Lauderdale, Fla.).
COLLEGE: Auburn.
TRANSACTIONS/CAREER NOTES: Selected by Arizona Cardinals in second round (47th pick overall) of 1995 NFL draft. ... Signed by Cardinals (July 17, 1995). ... Granted free agency (February 13, 1998). ... Re-signed by Cardinals (March 13, 1998). ... On injured reserve with foot injury (December 27, 2002-remainder of season). ... Granted unconditional free agency (February 28, 2003). ... Signed by Baltimore Ravens (April 16, 2003).
HONORS: Named wide receiver on THE SPORTING NEWS college All-America second team (1994).
SINGLE GAME HIGHS (regular season): Receptions—13 (January 2, 2000, vs. Green Bay); yards—190 (November 15, 1998, vs. Dallas); and touchdown receptions—2 (October 8, 2000, vs. Cleveland).
STATISTICAL PLATEAUS: 100-yard receiving games: 1995 (2), 1997 (2), 1998 (5), 1999 (2), 2001 (1). Total: 12.

			RECEIVING				TOTALS			
Year Team	G	GS	No.	Yds.	Avg.	TD	TD	2pt.	Pts.	Fum.
1995—Arizona NFL	16	15	52	883	17.0	2	2	2	16	0
1996—Arizona NFL	16	16	69	813	11.8	4	4	0	24	1
1997—Arizona NFL	16	16	75	1017	13.6	4	4	1	26	3
1998—Arizona NFL	16	16	‡89	1145	12.9	3	3	0	18	3
1999—Arizona NFL	16	16	79	954	12.1	1	1	0	6	2
2000—Arizona NFL	16	16	54	749	13.9	6	6	0	36	0
2001—Arizona NFL	15	13	41	618	15.1	2	2	0	12	1
2002—Arizona NFL	12	12	34	400	11.8	2	2	1	14	0
Pro totals (8 years)	123	120	493	6579	13.3	24	24	4	152	10

SANDERS, LEWIS   DB   BROWNS

PERSONAL: Born June 22, 1978, in Staten Island, N.Y. ... 6-1/200. ... Full name: Lewis Lindell Sanders.
HIGH SCHOOL: St. Peter's (Staten Island, N.Y.).
COLLEGE: Maryland.
TRANSACTIONS/CAREER NOTES: Selected after junior season by Cleveland Browns in fourth round (95th pick overall) of 2000 NFL draft. ... Signed by Browns (June 3, 2000). ... On injured reserve with leg injury (August 27, 2001-entire season). ... Granted free agency (February 28, 2003). ... Re-signed by Browns (March 26, 2003).
HONORS: Named cornerback on THE SPORTING NEWS college All-America third team (1999).

			TOTALS			INTERCEPTIONS			
Year Team	G	GS	Tk.	Ast.	Sks.	No.	Yds.	Avg.	TD
2000—Cleveland NFL	11	2	9	6	0.0	1	0	0.0	0
2002—Cleveland NFL	16	2	26	1	1.0	1	25	25.0	0
Pro totals (2 years)	27	4	35	7	1.0	2	25	12.5	0

SANDERSON, SCOTT   G/OT   SAINTS

PERSONAL: Born July 25, 1974, in Walnut Creek, Calif. ... 6-6/295. ... Full name: Scott Michael Sanderson.
HIGH SCHOOL: Clayton Valley (Concord, Calif.).
COLLEGE: Washington State.
TRANSACTIONS/CAREER NOTES: Selected by Houston Oilers in third round (81st pick overall) of 1997 NFL draft. ... Oilers franchise moved to Tennessee for 1997 season. ... Signed by Oilers (July 17, 1997). ... Oilers franchise renamed Tennessee Titans for 1999 season (December 26, 1998). ... On injured reserve with back injury (October 9, 1999-remainder of season). ... Granted free agency (February 11, 2000). ... Re-signed by Titans (March 24, 2000). ... Granted unconditional free agency (March 2, 2001). ... Signed by Cleveland Browns (July 29, 2001). ... Released by Browns (September 3, 2001). ... Signed by New Orleans Saints (November 28, 2001). ... Granted unconditional free agency (February 28, 2003). ... Re-signed by Saints (April 1, 2003).
PLAYING EXPERIENCE: Tennessee NFL, 1997-2000; New Orleans NFL, 2002. ... Games/Games started: 1997 (10/0), 1998 (15/3), 1999 (3/3), 2000 (9/0), 2002 (6/0). Total: 43/6.
HONORS: Named offensive tackle on THE SPORTING NEWS college All-America first team (1996).

SANTIAGO, O.J.   TE   RAIDERS

PERSONAL: Born April 4, 1974, in Whitby, Ont. ... 6-7/264. ... Full name: Otis Jason Santiago.
HIGH SCHOOL: St. Michael's (Toronto).
COLLEGE: Kent.
TRANSACTIONS/CAREER NOTES: Selected by Atlanta Falcons in third round (70th pick overall) of 1997 NFL draft. ... Signed by Falcons (July 11, 1997). ... On injured reserved with leg injury (November 20, 1997-remainder of season). ... Granted free agency (February 11, 2000). ... Re-signed by Falcons (June 5, 2000). ... Traded by Falcons to Dallas Cowboys for fourth round pick (LB Matt Stewart) in 2001 draft and seventh-round pick (WR Michael Coleman) in 2002 draft (August 27, 2000). ... Claimed on waivers by Cleveland Browns (November 22, 2000). ... Granted unconditional free agency (March 2, 2001). ... Re-signed by Browns (March 26, 2001). ... Granted unconditional free agency (March 1, 2002). ... Signed by Minnesota Vikings (July 15, 2002). ... Released by Vikings (August 27, 2002). ... Signed by Oakland Raiders (March 8, 2003).
CHAMPIONSHIP GAME EXPERIENCE: Played in NFC championship game (1998 season). ... Played in Super Bowl XXXIII (1998 season).
SINGLE GAME HIGHS (regular season): Reception—5 (September 14, 1997, vs. Oakland); yards—65 (December 27, 1998, vs. Miami); and touchdown receptions—2 (December 27, 1998, vs. Miami).

			RECEIVING				TOTALS			
Year Team	G	GS	No.	Yds.	Avg.	TD	TD	2pt.	Pts.	Fum.
1997—Atlanta NFL	11	11	17	217	12.8	2	2	0	12	1
1998—Atlanta NFL	16	16	27	428	15.9	5	5	0	30	1
1999—Atlanta NFL	14	14	15	174	11.6	0	0	0	0	0
2000—Dallas NFL	11	0	0	0	0.0	0	0	0	0	0
2001—Cleveland NFL	14	12	17	153	9.0	2	2	0	12	0
2002—					Did not play.					
Pro totals (5 years)	66	53	76	972	12.8	9	9	0	54	2

SAPP, WARREN   DT   BUCCANEERS

PERSONAL: Born December 19, 1972, in Orlando. ... 6-2/303. ... Full name: Warren Carlos Sapp.
HIGH SCHOOL: Apopka (Fla.).
COLLEGE: Miami (Fla.).
TRANSACTIONS/CAREER NOTES: Selected after junior season by Tampa Bay Buccaneers in first round (12th pick overall) of 1995 NFL draft. ... Signed by Buccaneers (April 27, 1995).
CHAMPIONSHIP GAME EXPERIENCE: Played in NFC championship game (1999 and 2002 seasons). ... Member of Super Bowl championship team (2002 season).
HONORS: Lombardi Award winner (1994). ... Bronko Nagurski Award winner (1994). ... Named defensive lineman on THE SPORTING NEWS college All-America first team (1994). ... Played in Pro Bowl (1997-2000 seasons). ... Named defensive tackle on THE SPORTING NEWS NFL All-Pro team (1999-2002). ... Named to play in Pro Bowl (2001 season); replaced by Ted Washington due to injury. ... Named to play in Pro Bowl (2002 season); replaced by Kris Jenkins due to injury.

			TOTALS			INTERCEPTIONS			
Year Team	G	GS	Tk.	Ast.	Sks.	No.	Yds.	Avg.	TD
1995—Tampa Bay NFL	16	8	17	10	3.0	1	5	5.0	1
1996—Tampa Bay NFL	15	14	41	10	9.0	0	0	0.0	0
1997—Tampa Bay NFL	15	15	47	11	10.5	0	0	0.0	0
1998—Tampa Bay NFL	16	16	28	17	7.0	0	0	0.0	0
1999—Tampa Bay NFL	15	15	27	14	12.5	0	0	0.0	0
2000—Tampa Bay NFL	16	15	43	9	16.5	0	0	0.0	0
2001—Tampa Bay NFL	16	16	28	8	6.0	0	0	0.0	0
2002—Tampa Bay NFL	16	16	40	7	7.5	2	0	0.0	0
Pro totals (8 years)	125	115	271	86	72.0	3	5	1.7	1

SATURDAY, JEFF   C   COLTS

PERSONAL: Born June 8, 1975, in Atlanta. ... 6-2/291. ... Full name: Jeffrey Bryant Saturday.
HIGH SCHOOL: Shamrock (Tucker, Ga.).
COLLEGE: North Carolina.
TRANSACTIONS/CAREER NOTES: Signed as non-drafted free agent by Baltimore Ravens (April 27, 1998). ... Released by Ravens (June 12, 1998). ... Signed by Indianapolis Colts (January 7, 1999). ... Granted free agency (March 1, 2002). ... Re-signed by Colts (April 3, 2002). ... Granted unconditional free agency (February 28, 2003). ... Re-signed by Colts (February 28, 2003).
PLAYING EXPERIENCE: Indianapolis NFL, 1999-2002. ... Games/Games started: 1999 (11/2), 2000 (16/16), 2001 (16/16), 2002 (16/16). Total: 59/50.

SAUERBRUN, TODD — P — PANTHERS

PERSONAL: Born January 4, 1973, in Setauket, N.Y. ... 5-10/211. ... Name pronounced SOUR-brun.
HIGH SCHOOL: Ward Melville (Setauket, N.Y.).
COLLEGE: West Virginia.
TRANSACTIONS/CAREER NOTES: Selected by Chicago Bears in second round (56th pick overall) of 1995 NFL draft. ... Signed by Bears (July 20, 1995). ... Granted free agency (February 13, 1998). ... Re-signed by Bears (May 19, 1998). ... On injured reserve with knee injury (September 23, 1998-remainder of season). ... Granted unconditional free agency (February 11, 2000). ... Signed by Kansas City Chiefs (March 27, 2000). ... Released by Chiefs (March 13, 2001). ... Signed by Carolina Panthers (April 24, 2001). ... Designated by Panthers as franchise player (February 19, 2003). ... Re-signed by Panthers (April 25, 2003).
HONORS: Named punter on THE SPORTING NEWS college All-America first team (1994). ... Named punter on THE SPORTING NEWS NFL All-Pro team (2001 and 2002). ... Played in Pro Bowl (2001 and 2002 seasons).

		PUNTING					
Year Team	G	No.	Yds.	Avg.	Net avg.	In. 20	Blk.
1995—Chicago NFL	15	55	2080	37.8	31.1	16	0
1996—Chicago NFL	16	78	3491	44.8	34.9	15	0
1997—Chicago NFL	16	95	4059	42.7	32.8	26	0
1998—Chicago NFL	3	15	741	49.4	42.1	6	0
1999—Chicago NFL	16	85	3478	40.9	35.4	20	0
2000—Kansas City NFL	16	82	3656	44.6	35.8	28	0
2001—Carolina NFL	16	93	*4419	*47.5	*38.9	35	1
2002—Carolina NFL	16	‡104	*4735	*45.5	37.5	‡31	1
Pro totals (8 years)	114	607	26659	43.9	35.7	177	2

SAUTER, CORY — QB — BEARS

S

PERSONAL: Born November 21, 1974, in Hutchinson, Minn. ... 6-4/216. ... Name pronounced SAW-ter.
HIGH SCHOOL: Hutchinson (Minn.).
COLLEGE: Minnesota.
TRANSACTIONS/CAREER NOTES: Signed as non-drafted free agent by Arizona Cardinals (April 23, 1998). ... Released by Cardinals (August 25, 1998). ... Re-signed by Cardinals to practice squad (August 31, 1998). ... Granted free agency after 1998 season. ... Signed by Detroit Lions (March 1, 1999). ... Inactive for all 16 games (1999). ... Assigned by Lions to Barcelona Dragons in 2000 NFL Europe enhancement allocation program (February 18, 2000). ... Released by Lions (August 27, 2001). ... Signed by Indianapolis Colts to practice squad (November 23, 2001). ... Claimed on waivers by Chicago Bears (November 12. 2002). ... Granted free agency (February 28, 2003). ... Re-signed by Bears (March 18, 2003).
SINGLE GAME HIGHS (regular season): Attempts—9 (December 29, 2002, vs. Tampa Bay); completions—6 (December 29, 2002, vs. Tampa Bay); yards—59 (December 29, 2002, vs. Tampa Bay); and touchdown passes—0.

			PASSING								RUSHING				TOTALS		
Year Team	G	GS	Att.	Cmp.	Pct.	Yds.	TD	Int.	Avg.	Skd.	Rat.	Att.	Yds.	Avg.	TD	TD	2pt.	Pts.
1998—Arizona NFL										Did not play.								
1999—Detroit NFL										Did not play.								
2000—Barcelona NFLE	...	...	163	102	62.6	916	6	2	5.62	0	84.8	18	104	5.8	0	0	0	0
2002—Chicago NFL	1	0	9	6	66.7	59	0	0	6.56	0	85.0	2	8	4.0	0	0	0	0
NFL Europe totals (1 year)	...	...	163	102	62.6	916	6	2	5.62	0	84.8	18	104	5.8	0	0	0	0
NFL totals (1 year)	1	0	9	6	66.7	59	0	0	6.56	0	85.0	2	8	4.0	0	0	0	0
Pro totals (2 years)	...	...	172	108	62.8	975	6	2	5.67	0	84.8	20	112	5.6	0	0	0	0

SAWYER, TALANCE — DE

PERSONAL: Born June 14, 1976, in Bastrop, La. ... 6-2/270.
HIGH SCHOOL: Bastrop (La.).
COLLEGE: UNLV.
TRANSACTIONS/CAREER NOTES: Selected by Minnesota Vikings in sixth round (185th pick overall) of 1999 NFL draft. ... Signed by Vikings (June 4, 1999). ... Granted free agency (March 1, 2002). ... Re-signed by Vikings (April 22, 2002). ... On injured reserve with knee and ankle injuries (October 29, 2002-remainder of season). ... Granted unconditional free agency (February 28, 2003).
CHAMPIONSHIP GAME EXPERIENCE: Played in NFC championship game (2000 season).

			TOTALS			INTERCEPTIONS			
Year Team	G	GS	Tk.	Ast.	Sks.	No.	Yds.	Avg.	TD
1999—Minnesota NFL	2	0	0	0	0.0	0	0	0.0	0
2000—Minnesota NFL	16	16	27	10	6.0	0	0	0.0	0
2001—Minnesota NFL	16	16	35	22	5.0	1	2	2.0	0
2002—Minnesota NFL	2	0	1	0	0.0	0	0	0.0	0
Pro totals (4 years)	36	32	63	32	11.0	1	2	2.0	0

SCHAU, RYAN — OT/OG — TEXANS

PERSONAL: Born December 30, 1976, in Hammond, Ind. ... 6-6/300. ... Twin brother of Thomas Schau, center, Buffalo Bills.
HIGH SCHOOL: Bloomington (Ill.).
COLLEGE: Illinois.
TRANSACTIONS/CAREER NOTES: Signed as non-drafted free agent by Philadelphia Eagles (April 19, 1999). ... Selected by Houston Texans from Eagles in NFL expansion draft (February 18, 2002). ... Granted free agency (March 1, 2002). ... Re-signed by Texans (April 22, 2002). ... On injured reserve with foot injury (November 4, 2002-remainder of season). ... Granted unconditional free agency (February 28, 2003). ... Re-signed by Texans (April 25, 2003).
PLAYING EXPERIENCE: Philadelphia NFL, 1999-2001; Houston NFL, 2002. ... Games/Games started: 1999 (1/0), 2000 (10/0), 2001 (2/1), 2002 (4/4). Total: 17/5.
CHAMPIONSHIP GAME EXPERIENCE: Member of Eagles for NFC championship game (2001 season); inactive.

SCHLESINGER, CORY   FB   LIONS

PERSONAL: Born June 23, 1972, in Columbus, Neb. ... 6-0/247.
HIGH SCHOOL: Columbus (Neb.).
COLLEGE: Nebraska (degree in indusrial technology education).
TRANSACTIONS/CAREER NOTES: Selected by Detroit Lions in sixth round (192nd pick overall) of 1995 NFL draft. ... Signed by Lions (July 19, 1995). ... Granted unconditional free agency (March 2, 2001). ... Re-signed by Lions (March 2, 2001).
SINGLE GAME HIGHS (regular season): Attempts—10 (September 12, 1999, vs. Seattle); yards—50 (September 12, 1999, vs. Seattle); and rushing touchdowns—1 (September 22, 2002, vs. Green Bay).

			RUSHING				RECEIVING				TOTALS			
Year Team	G	GS	Att.	Yds.	Avg.	TD	No.	Yds.	Avg.	TD	TD	2pt.	Pts.	Fum.
1995—Detroit NFL	16	2	1	1	1.0	0	1	2	2.0	0	0	0	0	0
1996—Detroit NFL	16	1	0	0	0.0	0	0	0	0.0	0	0	0	0	0
1997—Detroit NFL	16	2	7	11	1.6	0	5	69	13.8	1	1	0	6	0
1998—Detroit NFL	15	2	5	17	3.4	0	3	16	5.3	1	1	0	6	0
1999—Detroit NFL	16	11	43	124	2.9	0	21	151	7.2	1	1	0	6	4
2000—Detroit NFL	16	8	1	3	3.0	0	12	73	6.1	0	0	0	0	0
2001—Detroit NFL	16	13	47	154	3.3	3	60	466	7.8	0	3	0	18	1
2002—Detroit NFL	16	14	49	139	2.8	2	35	263	7.5	0	2	0	12	2
Pro totals (8 years)	127	53	153	449	2.9	5	137	1040	7.6	3	8	0	48	7

SCHNECK, MIKE   C   STEELERS

PERSONAL: Born August 4, 1977, in Whitefish Bay, Wis. ... 6-0/246. ... Full name: Mike Louis Schneck.
HIGH SCHOOL: Whitefish Bay (Wis.).
COLLEGE: Wisconsin.
TRANSACTIONS/CAREER NOTES: Signed as non-drafted free agent by Pittsburgh Steelers (April 23, 1999); contract voided by NFL because he did not meet eligibility requirements. ... Re-signed by Steelers (July 12, 1999). ... Granted free agency (March 1, 2002). ... Re-signed by Steelers (April 23, 2002).
PLAYING EXPERIENCE: Pittsburgh NFL, 1999-2002. ... Games/Games started: 1999 (16/0), 2000 (16/0), 2001 (16/0), 2002 (12/0). Total: 60/0.
CHAMPIONSHIP GAME EXPERIENCE: Played in AFC championship game (2001 season).

SCHOBEL, AARON   DE   BILLS

PERSONAL: Born April 1, 1977, in Columbus, Texas. ... 6-4/265.
HIGH SCHOOL: Columbus (Texas).
COLLEGE: Texas Christian.
TRANSACTIONS/CAREER NOTES: Selected by Buffalo Bills in second round (46th pick overall) of 2001 NFL draft. ... Signed by Bills (July 26, 2001).
HONORS: Named defensive end on THE SPORTING NEWS college All-America second team (2000).

			TOTALS		
Year Team	G	GS	Tk.	Ast.	Sks.
2001—Buffalo NFL	16	11	31	11	6.5
2002—Buffalo NFL	16	16	34	18	8.5
Pro totals (2 years)	32	27	65	29	15.0

SCHOBEL, MATT   TE   BENGALS

PERSONAL: Born November 4, 1978, in Columbus, Texas. ... 6-5/263. ... Full name: Matthew Thomas Schobel.
HIGH SCHOOL: Columbus (Texas).
COLLEGE: Texas A&M. then Texas Christian.
TRANSACTIONS/CAREER NOTES: Selected by Cincinnati Bengals in third round (67th pick overall) of 2002 NFL draft. ... Signed by Bengals (May 10, 2002).
SINGLE GAME HIGHS (regular season): Receptions—4 (December 1, 2002, vs. Baltimore); yards—41 (November 3, 2002, vs. Houston); and touchdown receptions—1 (November 24, 2002, vs. Pittsburgh).

			RECEIVING			
Year Team	G	GS	No.	Yds.	Avg.	TD
2002—Cincinnati NFL	16	10	27	212	7.9	2

SCHROEDER, BILL   WR   LIONS

PERSONAL: Born January 9, 1971, in Eau Claire, Wis. ... 6-3/200. ... Full name: William Fredrich Schroeder. ... Name pronounced SHRAY-der.
HIGH SCHOOL: Sheboygan (Wis.) South.
COLLEGE: Wisconsin-La Crosse (degree in physical education/teaching).
TRANSACTIONS/CAREER NOTES: Selected by Green Bay Packers in sixth round (181st pick overall) of 1994 NFL draft. ... Signed by Packers (May 10, 1994). ... Released by Packers (August 28, 1994). ... Re-signed by Packers to practice squad (August 30, 1994). ... Activated (December 29, 1994). ... Traded by Packers with TE Jeff Wilner to New England Patriots for C Mike Arthur (August 11, 1995). ... On injured reserve with foot injury (August 27, 1995-entire season). ... Released by Patriots (August 14, 1996). ... Signed by Packers to practice squad (August 28, 1996). ... Assigned by Packers to Rhein Fire in 1997 World League enhancement allocation program (February 19, 1997). ... On injured reserve with broken collarbone (December 9, 1998-remainder of season). ... Granted unconditional free agency (March 1, 2002). ... Signed by Detroit Lions (March 14, 2002).
CHAMPIONSHIP GAME EXPERIENCE: Member of Packers for NFC championship game (1997 season); inactive. ... Member of Packers for Super Bowl XXXII (1997 season); inactive.
SINGLE GAME HIGHS (regular season): Receptions—8 (December 17, 2000, vs. Minnesota); yards—158 (October 10, 1999, vs. Tampa Bay); and touchdown receptions—2 (November 17, 2002, vs. New York Jets).
STATISTICAL PLATEAUS: 100-yard receiving games: 1998 (1), 1999 (1), 2000 (3), 2001 (5), 2002 (1). Total: 11.

Year Team	G	GS	RECEIVING				PUNT RETURNS				KICKOFF RETURNS				TOTALS			
			No.	Yds.	Avg.	TD	No.	Yds.	Avg.	TD	No.	Yds.	Avg.	TD	TD	2pt.	Pts.	Fum.
1994—Green Bay NFL............							Did not play.											
1995—New England NFL.......							Did not play.											
1996—Green Bay NFL..........							Did not play.											
1997—Rhein W.L.	...	...	43	702	16.3	6	0	0	0.0	0	1	20	20.0	0	6	0	36	0
—Green Bay NFL	15	1	2	15	7.5	1	33	342	10.4	0	24	562	23.4	0	1	0	6	4
1998—Green Bay NFL...........	13	3	31	452	14.6	1	2	5	2.5	0	0	0	0.0	0	1	0	6	1
1999—Green Bay NFL...........	16	16	74	1051	14.2	5	0	0	0.0	0	1	10	10.0	0	5	0	30	3
2000—Green Bay NFL...........	16	16	65	999	15.4	4	0	0	0.0	0	0	0	0.0	0	4	0	24	1
2001—Green Bay NFL............	14	14	53	918	‡17.3	9	0	0	0.0	0	0	0	0.0	0	9	0	54	1
2002—Detroit NFL................	14	13	36	595	16.5	5	0	0	0.0	0	0	0	0.0	0	5	1	32	0
W.L. totals (1 year)	...	...	43	702	16.3	6	0	0	0.0	0	1	20	20.0	0	6	0	36	0
NFL totals (5 years)	88	63	261	4030	15.4	25	35	347	9.9	0	25	572	22.9	0	25	1	152	10
Pro totals (6 years)	...	...	304	4732	15.6	31	35	347	9.9	0	26	592	22.8	0	31	1	188	10

SCHULTERS, LANCE   S   TITANS

PERSONAL: Born May 27, 1975, in Guyana. ... 6-2/207.
HIGH SCHOOL: Canarsie (Brooklyn, N.Y.).
JUNIOR COLLEGE: Nassau Community College (N.Y.).
COLLEGE: Hofstra.
TRANSACTIONS/CAREER NOTES: Selected by San Francisco 49ers in fourth round (119th pick overall) of 1998 NFL draft. ... Signed by 49ers (July 18, 1998). ... On injured reserve with knee injury (December 21, 2000-remainder of season). ... Granted free agency (March 2, 2001). ... Re-signed by 49ers (March 2, 2001). ... On physically unable to perform list with knee injury (July 29-August 6, 2001). ... Granted unconditional free agency (March 1, 2002). ... Signed by Tennessee Titans (April 11, 2002).
CHAMPIONSHIP GAME EXPERIENCE: Played in AFC championship game (2002 season).
HONORS: Played in Pro Bowl (1999 season).

Year Team	G	GS	TOTALS			INTERCEPTIONS			
			Tk.	Ast.	Sks.	No.	Yds.	Avg.	TD
1998—San Francisco NFL....................	15	0	12	3	0.0	0	0	0.0	0
1999—San Francisco NFL....................	13	13	53	9	0.0	6	127	21.2	1
2000—San Francisco NFL....................	12	12	61	30	0.5	0	0	0.0	0
2001—San Francisco NFL....................	16	16	52	9	1.0	3	0	0.0	0
2002—Tennessee NFL........................	16	16	71	13	2.0	6	56	9.3	0
Pro totals (5 years)	72	57	249	64	3.5	15	183	12.2	1

SCIOLI, BRAD   DE   COLTS

PERSONAL: Born September 6, 1976, in Bridgeport, Pa. ... 6-3/280. ... Full name: Brad Elliott Scioli. ... Name pronounced SHE-o-lee.
HIGH SCHOOL: Upper Merion (King of Prussia, Pa.).
COLLEGE: Penn State.
TRANSACTIONS/CAREER NOTES: Selected by Indianapolis Colts in fifth round (138th pick overall) of 1999 NFL draft. ... Signed by Colts (July 22, 1999). ... Granted free agency (March 1, 2002). ... Re-signed by Colts (April 16, 2002). ... Granted unconditional free agency (February 28, 2003). ... Re-signed by Colts (March 9, 2003).

Year Team	G	GS	TOTALS		
			Tk.	Ast.	Sks.
1999—Indianapolis NFL...	10	0	1	0	0.0
2000—Indianapolis NFL...	16	2	7	3	2.0
2001—Indianapolis NFL...	13	12	22	10	4.0
2002—Indianapolis NFL...	16	13	39	11	7.0
Pro totals (4 years)..	55	27	69	24	13.0

SCOTT, BART   LB   RAVENS

PERSONAL: Born August 18, 1980, in Detroit. ... 6-2/235. ... Full name: Bart Edward Scott.
HIGH SCHOOL: Southeastern (Detroit).
COLLEGE: Southern Illinois.
TRANSACTIONS/CAREER NOTES: Signed as non-drafted free agent by Baltimore Ravens (April 25, 2002).

Year Team	G	GS	TOTALS			INTERCEPTIONS			
			Tk.	Ast.	Sks.	No.	Yds.	Avg.	TD
2002—Baltimore NFL	16	0	2	2	0.0	1	0	0.0	0

SCOTT, CAREY   CB   VIKINGS

PERSONAL: Born August 11, 1978, in Savannah, Ga. ... 5-11/207.
HIGH SCHOOL: Beach (Ga.).
COLLEGE: Kentucky State.
TRANSACTIONS/CAREER NOTES: Selected by Minnesota Vikings in sixth round (189th pick overall) of 2001 NFL draft. ... Signed by Vikings (July 30, 2001). ... On injured reserve with stomach injury (September 2, 2001-entire season). ... Released by Vikings (September 1, 2002). ... Re-signed by Vikings to practice squad (September 3, 2002). ... Released by Vikings (October 15, 2002). ... Signed by Oakland Raiders to practice squad (October 30, 2002). ... Released by Raiders (December 14, 2002). ... Signed by Vikings (December 16, 2002).

Year Team	G	GS	TOTALS			INTERCEPTIONS			
			Tk.	Ast.	Sks.	No.	Yds.	Avg.	TD
2001—Minnesota NFL..................................			Did not play.						
2002—Oakland NFL.....................................	1	0	0	0	0.0	0	0	0.0	0
—Minnesota NFL...................................	1	0	0	0	0.0	0	0	0.0	0
Pro totals (1 years)...................................	2	0	0	0	0.0	0	0	0.0	0

SCOTT, CEDRIC   DE   BROWNS

PERSONAL: Born October 19, 1977, in Gulfport, Miss. ... 6-5/290.
HIGH SCHOOL: Gulfport (Miss.).
COLLEGE: Southern Mississippi (degree in exercise physiology).
TRANSACTIONS/CAREER NOTES: Selected by New York Giants in fourth round (114th pick overall) of 2001 NFL draft. ... Signed by Giants (July 26, 2001). ... Released by Giants (September 1, 2002). ... Signed by Cleveland Browns (November 11, 2002).

			TOTALS		
Year Team	G	GS	Tk.	Ast.	Sks.
2001—New York Giants NFL	9	0	1	2	0.0
2002—Cleveland NFL	4	0	0	0	0.0
Pro totals (2 years)	13	0	1	2	0.0

SCOTT, CHAD   CB   STEELERS

PERSONAL: Born September 6, 1974, in Capitol Heights, Md. ... 6-1/201. ... Full name: Chad Oliver Scott.
HIGH SCHOOL: Suitland (Forestville, Md.).
COLLEGE: Towson State, then Maryland.
TRANSACTIONS/CAREER NOTES: Selected by Pittsburgh Steelers in first round (24th pick overall) of 1997 NFL draft. ... Signed by Steelers (July 16, 1997). ... On injured reserve with knee injury (July 20, 1998-entire season).
CHAMPIONSHIP GAME EXPERIENCE: Played in AFC championship game (1997 and 2001 seasons).

			TOTALS			INTERCEPTIONS			
Year Team	G	GS	Tk.	Ast.	Sks.	No.	Yds.	Avg.	TD
1997—Pittsburgh NFL	13	9	45	2	0.0	2	-4	-2.0	0
1998—Pittsburgh NFL				Did not play.					
1999—Pittsburgh NFL	13	12	49	1	0.0	1	16	16.0	0
2000—Pittsburgh NFL	16	16	64	6	0.0	5	49	9.8	0
2001—Pittsburgh NFL	15	15	71	9	0.0	5	204	40.8	†2
2002—Pittsburgh NFL	15	15	64	17	0.0	2	30	15.0	1
Pro totals (5 years)	72	67	293	35	0.0	15	295	19.7	3

SCOTT, DARNAY   WR

PERSONAL: Born July 7, 1972, in St. Louis. ... 6-1/204.
HIGH SCHOOL: Kearny (San Diego).
COLLEGE: San Diego State.
TRANSACTIONS/CAREER NOTES: Selected after junior season by Cincinnati Bengals in second round (30th pick overall) of 1994 NFL draft. ... Signed by Bengals (July 18, 1994). ... Granted free agency (February 14, 1997). ... Re-signed by Bengals (June 16, 1997). ... On injured reserve with fractured leg (August 2, 2000-entire season). ... Released by Bengals (July 9, 2002). ... Signed by Jacksonville Jaguars (July 22, 2002). ... Released by Jaguars (September 1, 2002). ... Signed by Dallas Cowboys (September 9, 2002). ... Granted unconditional free agency (February 28, 2003).
SINGLE GAME HIGHS (regular season): Receptions—9 (January 6, 2002, vs. Tennessee); yards—157 (November 6, 1994, vs. Seattle); and touchdown receptions—2 (November 21, 1999, vs. Baltimore).
STATISTICAL PLATEAUS: 100-yard receiving games: 1994 (2), 1995 (1), 1996 (1), 1997 (2), 1998 (2), 1999 (2), 2001 (3). Total: 13.

			RUSHING				RECEIVING				KICKOFF RETURNS				TOTALS			
Year Team	G	GS	Att.	Yds.	Avg.	TD	No.	Yds.	Avg.	TD	No.	Yds.	Avg.	TD	TD	2pt.	Pts.	Fum.
1994—Cincinnati NFL	16	12	10	106	10.6	0	46	866	§18.8	5	15	342	22.8	0	5	0	30	0
1995—Cincinnati NFL	16	16	5	11	2.2	0	52	821	15.8	5	0	0	0.0	0	5	0	30	0
1996—Cincinnati NFL	16	16	3	4	1.3	0	58	833	14.4	5	0	0	0.0	0	5	0	30	0
1997—Cincinnati NFL	16	15	1	6	6.0	0	54	797	14.8	5	0	0	0.0	0	5	0	30	0
1998—Cincinnati NFL	13	13	2	10	5.0	0	51	817	16.0	7	0	0	0.0	0	7	0	42	0
1999—Cincinnati NFL	16	16	0	0	0.0	0	68	1022	15.0	7	0	0	0.0	0	7	0	42	0
2000—Cincinnati NFL								Did not play.										
2001—Cincinnati NFL	16	15	0	0	0.0	0	57	819	14.4	2	0	0	0.0	0	2	0	12	0
2002—Dallas NFL	15	1	1	14	14.0	0	22	218	9.9	1	0	0	0.0	0	1	0	6	0
Pro totals (8 years)	124	104	22	151	6.9	0	408	6193	15.2	37	15	342	22.8	0	37	0	222	0

SCOTT, DEQUINCY   DT   CHARGERS

PERSONAL: Born April 19, 1978, in LaPlace, La. ... 6-1/280.
HIGH SCHOOL: East St. John (LaPlace, La.).
COLLEGE: Southern Mississippi.
TRANSACTIONS/CAREER NOTES: Signed as non-drafted free agent by San Diego Chargers (April 24, 2001). ... Released by Chargers (September 2, 2001). ... Re-signed by Chargers to practice squad (September 3, 2001).

			TOTALS		
Year Team	G	GS	Tk.	Ast.	Sks.
2002—San Diego NFL	10	0	8	0	2.0

SCOTT, GREGORY   DE   REDSKINS

PERSONAL: Born October 2, 1979, in Courtland, Va. ... 6-4/258. ... Full name: Greg Scott.
HIGH SCHOOL: Southampton (Courtland, Va.).
COLLEGE: Hampton.
TRANSACTIONS/CAREER NOTES: Selected by Washington Redskins in seventh round (234th pick overall) of 2002 NFL draft. ... Signed by Redskins (July 16, 2002).

			TOTALS			INTERCEPTIONS			
Year Team	G	GS	Tk.	Ast.	Sks.	No.	Yds.	Avg.	TD
2002—Washington NFL	2	0	0	0	0.0	0	0	0.0	0

SCOTT, LYNN   S   COWBOYS

PERSONAL: Born June 23, 1977, in Turpin, Okla. ... 6-0/221.
HIGH SCHOOL: Turpin (Okla.).
COLLEGE: Northwestern Oklahoma.
TRANSACTIONS/CAREER NOTES: Signed as non-drafted free agent by Dallas Cowboys (April 27, 2001). ... Re-signed by Cowboys (March 13, 2003).

			TOTALS			INTERCEPTIONS			
Year Team	G	GS	Tk.	Ast.	Sks.	No.	Yds.	Avg.	TD
2001—Dallas NFL	14	0	2	0	0.0	0	0	0.0	0
2002—Dallas NFL	14	0	6	4	0.0	0	0	0.0	0
Pro totals (2 years)	28	0	8	4	0.0	0	0	0.0	0

SEARS, COREY   DE   TEXANS

PERSONAL: Born April 15, 1973, in San Antonio. ... 6-3/319. ... Full name: Corey Alexander Sears.
HIGH SCHOOL: Judson (Converse, Texas).
JUNIOR COLLEGE: Navarro College (Texas).
COLLEGE: Mississippi State.
TRANSACTIONS/CAREER NOTES: Signed as non-drafted free agent by Baltimore Ravens (April 29, 1996). ... On injured reserve with knee injury (August 20-November 6, 1996). ... Released by Ravens (November 6, 1996). ... Signed by St. Louis Rams (April 24, 1998). ... Claimed on waivers by San Francisco 49ers (August 26, 1998). ... Released by 49ers (August 28, 1998). ... Signed by Rams to practice squad (September 1, 1998). ... Activated (November 30, 1998). ... Claimed on waivers by Arizona Cardinals (September 6, 1999). ... Released by Cardinals (February 19, 2001). ... Signed by Houston Texans (February 8, 2002). ... Granted unconditional free agency (February 28, 2003). ... Re-signed by Texans (March 11, 2003).

			TOTALS		
Year Team	G	GS	Tk.	Ast.	Sks.
1998—St. Louis NFL	4	0	4	0	0.0
1999—Arizona NFL	9	1	6	2	0.0
2000—Arizona NFL	8	2	9	9	0.0
2002—Houston NFL	16	0	13	8	1.0
Pro totals (4 years)	37	3	32	19	1.0

SEAU, JUNIOR   LB   DOLPHINS

PERSONAL: Born January 19, 1969, in San Diego. ... 6-3/250. ... Full name: Tiaina Seau Jr. ... Name pronounced SAY-ow.
HIGH SCHOOL: Oceanside (Calif.).
COLLEGE: Southern California.
TRANSACTIONS/CAREER NOTES: Selected after junior season by San Diego Chargers in first round (fifth pick overall) of 1990 NFL draft. ... Signed by Chargers (August 27, 1990). ... Traded by Chargers to Miami Dolphins for conditional pick in 2004 draft (April 16, 2003).
CHAMPIONSHIP GAME EXPERIENCE: Played in AFC championship game (1994 season). ... Played in Super Bowl XXIX (1994 season).
HONORS: Named linebacker on THE SPORTING NEWS college All-America first team (1989). ... Played in Pro Bowl (1991-2001 seasons). ... Named inside linebacker on THE SPORTING NEWS NFL All-Pro team (1992-1996, 1998 and 2000). ... Named to play in Pro Bowl (2002 season); replaced by Jason Gildon due to injury.

			TOTALS			INTERCEPTIONS			
Year Team	G	GS	Tk.	Ast.	Sks.	No.	Yds.	Avg.	TD
1990—San Diego NFL	16	15	61	24	1.0	0	0	0.0	0
1991—San Diego NFL	16	16	111	18	7.0	0	0	0.0	0
1992—San Diego NFL	15	15	79	23	4.5	2	51	25.5	0
1993—San Diego NFL	16	16	108	21	0.0	2	58	29.0	0
1994—San Diego NFL	16	16	124	31	5.5	0	0	0.0	0
1995—San Diego NFL	16	16	111	19	2.0	2	5	2.5	0
1996—San Diego NFL	15	15	110	28	7.0	2	18	9.0	0
1997—San Diego NFL	15	15	84	13	7.0	2	33	16.5	0
1998—San Diego NFL	16	16	92	23	3.5	0	0	0.0	0
1999—San Diego NFL	14	14	75	24	3.5	1	16	16.0	0
2000—San Diego NFL	16	16	103	20	3.5	2	2	1.0	0
2001—San Diego NFL	16	16	84	11	1.0	1	2	2.0	0
2002—San Diego NFL	13	13	60	24	1.5	1	25	25.0	0
Pro totals (13 years)	200	199	1202	279	47.0	15	210	14.0	0

SEDER, TIM   K

PERSONAL: Born September 17, 1974, in Ashland, Ohio. ... 5-9/185.
HIGH SCHOOL: Lucas (Ashland, Ohio).
COLLEGE: Ashland.
TRANSACTIONS/CAREER NOTES: Signed as non-drafted free agent by Dallas Cowboys (April 6, 2000). ... On injured reserve with ankle injury (November 14, 2001-remainder of season). ... Claimed on waivers by Minnesota Vikings (September 2, 2002). ... Released by Vikings (September 3, 2002). ... Signed by Jacksonville Jaguars (October 23, 2002). ... Released by Jaguars (November 26, 2002).

		FIELD GOALS							TOTALS		
Year Team	G	1-29	30-39	40-49	50+	Tot.	Pct.	Lg.	XPM	XPA	Pts.
2000—Dallas NFL	15	7-8	9-11	9-13	0-1	25-33	75.8	48	27	27	108
2001—Dallas NFL	8	5-5	3-5	3-6	0-1	11-17	64.7	46	12	12	51
2002—Jacksonville NFL	5	4-4	2-3	2-4	0-1	8-12	66.7	43	11	11	35
Pro totals (3 years)	28	16-17	14-19	14-23	0-3	44-62	71.0	48	50	50	194

SEHORN, JASON   CB   RAMS

PERSONAL: Born April 15, 1971, in Sacramento. ... 6-2/213.
HIGH SCHOOL: Mt. Shasta (Calif.).
JUNIOR COLLEGE: Shasta College (Calif.).
COLLEGE: Southern California.
TRANSACTIONS/CAREER NOTES: Selected by New York Giants in second round (59th pick overall) of 1994 NFL draft. ... Signed by Giants (July 17, 1994). ... Granted free agency (February 14, 1997). ... Re-signed by Giants (August 9, 1997). ... On injured reserve with knee injury (August 25, 1998-entire season). ... Granted unconditional free agency (March 2, 2001). ... Re-signed by Giants (March 2, 2001). ... On injured reserve with knee injury (January 2, 2002-remainder of season). ... Released by Giants (March 7, 2003). ... Signed by St. Louis Rams (May 19, 2003).
CHAMPIONSHIP GAME EXPERIENCE: Played in NFC championship game (2000 season). ... Played in Super Bowl XXXV (2000 season).

| | | | TOTALS | | | INTERCEPTIONS | | | |
Year Team	G	GS	Tk.	Ast.	Sks.	No.	Yds.	Avg.	TD
1994—New York Giants NFL	8	0	1	0	0.0	0	0	0.0	0
1995—New York Giants NFL	14	0	4	2	0.0	0	0	0.0	0
1996—New York Giants NFL	16	15	83	14	3.0	5	61	12.2	1
1997—New York Giants NFL	16	16	75	11	1.5	6	74	12.3	1
1998—New York Giants NFL			Did not play.						
1999—New York Giants NFL	10	10	37	8	0.0	1	-4	-4.0	0
2000—New York Giants NFL	14	14	60	13	0.0	2	32	16.0	0
2001—New York Giants NFL	13	13	57	6	1.0	3	34	11.3	1
2002—New York Giants NFL	16	5	43	4	0.0	2	31	15.5	1
Pro totals (8 years)	107	73	360	58	5.5	19	228	12.0	4

S

SEMPLE, TONY   G   LIONS

PERSONAL: Born December 20, 1970, in Springfield, Ill. ... 6-5/305. ... Full name: Anthony Lee Semple.
HIGH SCHOOL: Lincoln (Ill.) Community.
COLLEGE: Memphis State (degree in sports administration).
TRANSACTIONS/CAREER NOTES: Selected by Detroit Lions in fifth round (154th pick overall) of 1994 NFL draft. ... Signed by Lions (July 21, 1994). ... On injured reserve with knee injury (August 19, 1994-entire season). ... Granted free agency (February 14, 1997). ... Re-signed by Lions (June 13, 1997). ... Granted unconditional free agency (February 13, 1998). ... Re-signed by Lions (February 21, 1998). ... Granted unconditional free agency (March 2, 2001). ... Re-signed by Lions (June 7, 2001). ... Granted unconditional free agency (March 1, 2002). ... Re-signed by Lions (April 1, 2002). ... On injured reserve with shoulder injury (December 3, 2002-remainder of season).
PLAYING EXPERIENCE: Detroit NFL, 1995-2002. ... Games/Games started: 1995 (16/0), 1996 (15/1), 1997 (16/1), 1998 (16/3), 1999 (12/12), 2000 (11/8), 2001 (15/12), 2002 (10/10). Total: 111/47.

SERWANGA, KATO   CB   GIANTS

PERSONAL: Born July 23, 1976, in Kampala, Uganda, Africa. ... 6-0/200. ... Twin brother of Wasswa Serwanga, cornerback, with San Francisco 49ers (1999) and Minnesota Vikings (2000 and 2001). ... Name pronounced kah-TOE ser-WAN-guh.
HIGH SCHOOL: Sacramento (Calif.).
COLLEGE: Sacramento State, then Pacific, then California.
TRANSACTIONS/CAREER NOTES: Signed as non-drafted free agent by New England Patriots (April 24, 1998). ... Released by Patriots (August 30, 1998). ... Re-signed by Patriots to practice squad (August 31, 1998). ... Activated (December 12, 1998); did not play. ... Assigned by Patriots to Scottish Claymores in 2001 NFL Europe enhancement allocation program (February 19, 2001). ... Released by Patriots (September 2, 2001). ... Signed by Washington Redskins (October 16, 2001). ... Granted free agency (March 1, 2002). ... Re-signed by Redskins (April 11, 2002). ... On injured reserve with knee injury (September 1-November 27, 2002). ... Released by Redskins (November 27, 2002). ... Signed by Giants (December 4, 2002). ... Granted unconditional free agency (February 28, 2003). ... Re-signed by Giants (March 4, 2003).

| | | | TOTALS | | | INTERCEPTIONS | | | |
Year Team	G	GS	Tk.	Ast.	Sks.	No.	Yds.	Avg.	TD
1998—New England NFL			Did not play.						
1999—New England NFL	16	3	37	7	1.0	3	2	0.7	0
2000—New England NFL	15	0	20	3	2.0	0	0	0.0	0
2001—Scottish NFLE			Statistics unavailable.						
—Washington NFL	11	0	0	0	0.0	0	0	0.0	0
2002—New York Giants NFL	3	0	2	0	0.0	0	0	0.0	0
NFL totals (4 years)	45	3	59	10	3.0	3	2	0.7	0

SETZER, BOBBY   DE   BEARS

PERSONAL: Born June 16, 1976, in Walnut Creek, Calif. ... 6-4/280. ... Full name: Robert Kelley Setzer Jr..
HIGH SCHOOL: South Salem (Kelso, Wash.).
JUNIOR COLLEGE: Walla Walla Community College.
COLLEGE: Boise State.
TRANSACTIONS/CAREER NOTES: Signed as non-drafted free agent by New York Giants (February 7, 2000). ... Released by Giants (February 9, 2000). ... Signed by New Orleans Saints (March 23, 2000). ... Released by Saints (August 27, 2000). ... Re-signed by Saints to practice squad (August 29, 2000). ... Released by Saints (September 2, 2001). ... Signed by San Francisco 49ers (September 5, 2001). ... Released by 49ers (August 31, 2002). ... Released by 49ers (October 22, 2002). ... Signed by Chicago Bears (November 12, 2002).

| | | | TOTALS | | |
Year Team	G	GS	Tk.	Ast.	Sks.
2001—San Francisco NFL	14	0	3	2	1.0
2002—Chicago NFL	2	0	2	0	0.0
Pro totals (2 years)	16	0	5	2	1.0

SEUBERT, RICH　　　　　　　　G　　　　　　　　GIANTS

PERSONAL: Born March 30, 1979, in Stratford, Wis. ... 6-5/305.
HIGH SCHOOL: Marsfield Columbus (Stratford, Wis.).
COLLEGE: Western Illinois.
TRANSACTIONS/CAREER NOTES: Signed as non-drafted free agent by New York Giants (April 27, 2001). ... Re-signed by Giants (May 13, 2003).
PLAYING EXPERIENCE: New York Giants NFL, 2001-2002. ... Games/Games started: 2001 (2/0), 2002 (16/16). Total: 18/16.

SEYMOUR, RICHARD　　　　　DT　　　　　PATRIOTS

PERSONAL: Born October 6, 1979, in Gadsden, S.C. ... 6-6/310.
HIGH SCHOOL: Lower Richland (S.C.).
COLLEGE: Georgia.
TRANSACTIONS/CAREER NOTES: Selected by New England Patriots in first round (sixth pick overall) of 2001 NFL draft. ... Signed by Patriots (July 24, 2001).
CHAMPIONSHIP GAME EXPERIENCE: Played in AFC championship game (2001 season). ... Member of Super Bowl championship team (2001 season).
HONORS: Named defensive tackle on THE SPORTING NEWS college All-America second team (2000). ... Played in Pro Bowl (2002 season).

			TOTALS			INTERCEPTIONS			
Year　Team	G	GS	Tk.	Ast.	Sks.	No.	Yds.	Avg.	TD
2001—New England NFL	13	10	25	20	3.0	0	0	0.0	0
2002—New England NFL	16	16	33	23	5.5	1	6	6.0	0
Pro totals (2 years)	29	26	58	43	8.5	1	6	6.0	0

SHADE, SAM　　　　　　　　S

PERSONAL: Born June 14, 1973, in Birmingham, Ala. ... 6-0/211.
HIGH SCHOOL: Wenonah (Birmingham, Ala.).
COLLEGE: Alabama.
TRANSACTIONS/CAREER NOTES: Selected by Cincinnati Bengals in fourth round (102nd pick overall) of 1995 NFL draft. ... Signed by Bengals (July 18, 1995). ... Granted free agency (February 13, 1998). ... Re-signed by Bengals (June 15, 1998). ... Granted unconditional free agency (February 12, 1999). ... Signed by Washington Redskins (February 18, 1999). ... On injured reserve with neck injury (November 18, 2002-remainder of season). ... Released by Redskins (February 26, 2003).

			TOTALS			INTERCEPTIONS			
Year　Team	G	GS	Tk.	Ast.	Sks.	No.	Yds.	Avg.	TD
1995—Cincinnati NFL	16	2	14	2	0.0	0	0	0.0	0
1996—Cincinnati NFL	12	0	5	2	0.0	0	0	0.0	0
1997—Cincinnati NFL	16	12	81	15	4.0	1	21	21.0	0
1998—Cincinnati NFL	16	15	60	18	1.0	3	33	11.0	0
1999—Washington NFL	16	16	86	26	1.5	2	7	3.5	0
2000—Washington NFL	16	14	81	15	7.5	2	15	7.5	0
2001—Washington NFL	16	15	71	13	0.0	2	9	4.5	0
2002—Washington NFL	9	3	18	6	1.0	0	0	0.0	0
Pro totals (8 years)	117	77	416	97	8.5	10	85	8.5	0

SHAFFER, KEVIN　　　　　OT　　　　　FALCONS

PERSONAL: Born March 2, 1980, in Salisbury, Md. ... 6-5/290.
HIGH SCHOOL: Conestoga (Md.).
COLLEGE: Tulsa.
TRANSACTIONS/CAREER NOTES: Selected by Atlanta Falcons in seventh round (244th pick overall) of 2002 NFL draft. ... Signed by Falcons (June 14, 2002).
PLAYING EXPERIENCE: Atlanta NFL, 2002. ... Games/Games started: 2002 (6/0).

SHARPE, SHANNON　　　　　TE　　　　　BRONCOS

PERSONAL: Born June 26, 1968, in Chicago. ... 6-2/228. ... Brother of Sterling Sharpe, wide receiver with Green Bay Packers (1988-94).
HIGH SCHOOL: Glennville (Ga.).
COLLEGE: Savannah (Ga.) State.
TRANSACTIONS/CAREER NOTES: Selected by Denver Broncos in seventh round (192nd pick overall) of 1990 NFL draft. ... Signed by Broncos (July 1990). ... Granted free agency (February 1, 1992). ... Re-signed by Broncos (July 31, 1992). ... Designated by Broncos as transition player (February 15, 1994). ... On injured reserve with broken collarbone (November 30, 1999-remainder of season). ... Granted unconditional free agency (February 11, 2000). ... Signed by Baltimore Ravens (February 16, 2000). ... Released by Ravens (February 27, 2002). ... Signed by Broncos (April 12, 2002).
CHAMPIONSHIP GAME EXPERIENCE: Played in AFC championship game (1991, 1997, 1998 and 2000 seasons). ... Member of Super Bowl championship team (1997, 1998 and 2000 seasons).
HONORS: Played in Pro Bowl (1992, 1993, 1995-1997 and 2001 seasons). ... Named tight end on THE SPORTING NEWS NFL All-Pro team (1993 and 1996-1998). ... Named to play in Pro Bowl (1994 season); replaced by Eric Green due to injury. ... Named to play in Pro Bowl (1998 season); replaced by Frank Wycheck due to injury.
POST SEASON RECORDS: Shares NFL postseason single-game record for most receptions—13 (January 9, 1994, vs. Los Angeles Raiders).
SINGLE GAME HIGHS (regular season): Receptions—13 (October 6, 1996, vs. San Diego); yards—214 (October 20, 2002, vs. Kansas City); and touchdown receptions—3 (October 6, 1996, vs. San Diego).

STATISTICAL PLATEAUS: 100-yard receiving games: 1992 (2), 1993 (2), 1994 (1), 1995 (2), 1996 (3), 1997 (4), 2000 (2), 2002 (2). Total: 18.
MISCELLANEOUS: Holds Denver Broncos all-time records for most receptions (613).

Year Team	G	GS	RECEIVING				TOTALS			
			No.	Yds.	Avg.	TD	TD	2pt.	Pts.	Fum.
1990—Denver NFL	16	2	7	99	14.1	1	1	0	6	1
1991—Denver NFL	16	9	22	322	14.6	1	1	0	6	0
1992—Denver NFL	16	11	53	640	12.1	2	2	0	12	1
1993—Denver NFL	16	12	81	995	12.3	§9	9	0	54	1
1994—Denver NFL	15	13	87	1010	11.6	4	4	2	28	1
1995—Denver NFL	13	12	63	756	12.0	4	4	0	24	1
1996—Denver NFL	15	15	80	1062	13.3	10	10	0	60	1
1997—Denver NFL	16	16	72	1107	15.4	3	3	1	20	1
1998—Denver NFL	16	16	64	768	12.0	▲10	10	0	60	0
1999—Denver NFL	5	5	23	224	9.7	0	0	0	0	0
2000—Baltimore NFL	16	15	67	810	12.1	5	5	0	30	0
2001—Baltimore NFL	16	15	73	811	11.1	2	2	0	12	1
2002—Denver NFL	13	13	61	686	11.2	3	3	0	18	0
Pro totals (13 years)	189	154	753	9290	12.3	54	54	3	330	8

SHARPER, DARREN   S   PACKERS

PERSONAL: Born November 3, 1975, in Richmond, Va. ... 6-2/210. ... Full name: Darren Mallory Sharper. ... Brother of Jamie Sharper, line-backer, Houston Texans.
HIGH SCHOOL: Hermitage (Richmond, Va.).
COLLEGE: William & Mary.
TRANSACTIONS/CAREER NOTES: Selected by Green Bay Packers in second round (60th pick overall) of 1997 NFL draft. ... Signed by Packers (July 11, 1997).
CHAMPIONSHIP GAME EXPERIENCE: Played in NFC championship game (1997 season). ... Played in Super Bowl XXXII (1997 season).
HONORS: Named safety on The Sporting News NFL All-Pro team (2000 and 2002). ... Played in Pro Bowl (2000 and 2002 seasons).

Year Team	G	GS	TOTALS			INTERCEPTIONS				PUNT RETURNS				TOTALS			
			Tk.	Ast.	Sks.	No.	Yds.	Avg.	TD	No.	Yds.	Avg.	TD	TD	2pt.	Pts.	Fum.
1997—Green Bay NFL	14	0	12	1	0.0	2	70	35.0	∞2	7	32	4.6	0	3	0	18	1
1998—Green Bay NFL	16	16	53	20	0.0	0	0	0.0	0	0	0	0.0	0	0	0	0	0
1999—Green Bay NFL	16	16	84	29	1.0	3	12	4.0	0	0	0	0.0	0	0	0	0	0
2000—Green Bay NFL	16	16	72	20	1.0	*9	109	12.1	0	0	0	0.0	0	0	0	0	0
2001—Green Bay NFL	16	16	71	24	2.0	6	78	13.0	0	1	18	18.0	0	0	0	0	1
2002—Green Bay NFL	13	13	51	17	0.0	7	*233	33.3	1	1	0	0.0	0	1	0	6	0
Pro totals (6 years)	91	77	343	111	4.0	27	502	18.6	3	9	50	5.6	0	4	0	24	2

SHARPER, JAMIE   LB   TEXANS

PERSONAL: Born November 23, 1974, in Richmond, Va. ... 6-3/240. ... Full name: Harry Jamie Sharper Jr. ... Brother of Darren Sharper, safe-ty, Green Bay Packers.
HIGH SCHOOL: Hermitage (Richmond, Va.).
COLLEGE: Virginia (degree in psychology, 1996).
TRANSACTIONS/CAREER NOTES: Selected by Baltimore Ravens in second round (34th pick overall) of 1997 NFL draft. ... Signed by Ravens (July 23, 1997). ... Granted free agency (February 11, 2000). ... Re-signed by Ravens (June 16, 2000). ... Granted unconditional free agency (March 2, 2001). ... Re-signed by Ravens (April 3, 2001). ... Selected by Houston Texans from Ravens in NFL expansion draft (February 18, 2002).
CHAMPIONSHIP GAME EXPERIENCE: Played in AFC championship game (2000 season). ... Member of Super Bowl championship team (2000 season).

Year Team	G	GS	TOTALS			INTERCEPTIONS			
			Tk.	Ast.	Sks.	No.	Yds.	Avg.	TD
1997—Baltimore NFL	16	15	52	14	3.0	1	4	4.0	0
1998—Baltimore NFL	16	16	45	9	1.0	0	0	0.0	0
1999—Baltimore NFL	16	16	69	17	4.0	0	0	0.0	0
2000—Baltimore NFL	16	16	59	13	0.0	1	45	45.0	0
2001—Baltimore NFL	16	16	77	31	6.0	0	0	0.0	0
2002—Houston NFL	16	16	95	42	5.5	0	0	0.0	0
Pro totals (6 years)	96	95	397	126	19.5	2	49	24.5	0

SHAW, BOBBY   WR   BILLS

PERSONAL: Born April 23, 1975, in San Francisco. ... 6-0/183.
HIGH SCHOOL: Galileo (San Francisco).
COLLEGE: California.
TRANSACTIONS/CAREER NOTES: Selected by Seattle Seahawks in sixth round (169th pick overall) of 1998 NFL draft. ... Signed by Seahawks (June 5, 1998). ... Released by Seahawks (August 30, 1998). ... Re-signed by Seahawks to practice squad (August 31, 1998). ... Activated (November 4, 1998); did not play. ... Released by Seahawks (November 18, 1998). ... Signed by Pittsburgh Steelers (November 20, 1998). ... Granted free agency (March 2, 2001). ... Re-signed by Steelers (March 2, 2001). ... Granted unconditional free agency (March 1, 2002). ... Signed by Jacksonville Jaguars (April 3, 2002). ... Granted unconditional free agency (February 28, 2003). ... Signed by Buffalo Bills (March 17, 2003).
CHAMPIONSHIP GAME EXPERIENCE: Played in AFC championship game (2001 season).
HONORS: Named wide receiver on The Sporting News college All-America first team (1997).
SINGLE GAME HIGHS (regular season): Receptions—7 (January 2, 2000, vs. Tennessee); yards—131 (January 2, 2000, vs. Tennessee); and touchdown receptions—1 (November 3, 2002, vs. New York Giants).
STATISTICAL PLATEAUS: 100-yard receiving games: 1999 (1), 2001 (1). Total: 2.

Year Team	G	GS	RUSHING				RECEIVING				PUNT RETURNS				KICKOFF RETURNS				TOTALS		
			Att.	Yds.	Avg.	TD	No.	Yds.	Avg.	TD	No.	Yds.	Avg.	TD	No.	Yds.	Avg.	TD	TD	2pt.	Pts.
1998—Seattle NFL..........										Did not play.										
1999—Pittsburgh NFL....	15	1	0	0	0.0	0	28	387	13.8	3	4	53	13.3	0	0	0	0.0	0	3	0	18
2000—Pittsburgh NFL....	16	0	0	0	0.0	0	40	672	16.8	4	2	17	8.5	0	0	-8	0.0	0	4	0	24
2001—Pittsburgh NFL....	16	0	0	0	0.0	0	24	409	17.0	2	4	45	11.3	0	1	2	2.0	0	2	0	12
2002—Jacksonville NFL.	16	10	0	0	0.0	0	44	525	11.9	1	25	310	12.4	1	3	53	17.7	0	2	0	12
Pro totals (4 years)	63	11	0	0	0.0	0	136	1993	14.7	10	35	425	12.1	1	4	47	11.8	0	11	0	66

SHAW, JOSH — DT — 49ERS

PERSONAL: Born September 7, 1979, in Fort Lauderdale, Fla. ... 6-3/279.
HIGH SCHOOL: Dillard (Fort Lauderdale, Fla.).
COLLEGE: Michigan State.
TRANSACTIONS/CAREER NOTES: Selected by San Francisco 49ers in fifth round (172nd pick overall) of 2002 NFL draft. ... Signed by 49ers (July 26, 2002). ... On non-football injury list with knee injury (August 27-November 12, 2002).

Year Team	G	GS	TOTALS			INTERCEPTIONS			
			Tk.	Ast.	Sks.	No.	Yds.	Avg.	TD
2002—San Francisco NFL..	3	0	3	0	1.0	0	0	0.0	0

SHAW, TERRANCE — CB — RAIDERS

PERSONAL: Born January 11, 1973, in Alameda, Calif. ... 6-0/200. ... Full name: Terrance Bernard Shaw.
HIGH SCHOOL: Marshall (Texas).
COLLEGE: Stephen F. Austin.
TRANSACTIONS/CAREER NOTES: Selected by San Diego Chargers in second round (34th pick overall) of 1995 NFL draft. ... Signed by Chargers (June 15, 1995). ... Released by Chargers (March 21, 2000). ... Signed by Miami Dolphins (June 13, 2000). ... Granted unconditional free agency (March 2, 2001). ... Signed by New England Patriots (March 22, 2001). ... Released by Patriots (February 25, 2002). ... Signed by Oakland Raiders (March 21, 2002).
CHAMPIONSHIP GAME EXPERIENCE: Played in AFC championship game (2001 and 2002 seasons). ... Member of Super Bowl championship team (2001 season). ... Played in Super Bowl XXXVII (2002 season).

Year Team	G	GS	TOTALS			INTERCEPTIONS			
			Tk.	Ast.	Sks.	No.	Yds.	Avg.	TD
1995—San Diego NFL...	16	14	53	5	0.0	1	31	31.0	0
1996—San Diego NFL...	16	16	72	13	0.0	3	78	26.0	0
1997—San Diego NFL...	16	16	66	5	0.0	1	11	11.0	0
1998—San Diego NFL...	13	13	35	5	0.0	2	0	0.0	0
1999—San Diego NFL...	8	8	21	3	0.0	0	0	0.0	0
2000—Miami NFL..	11	3	15	3	0.0	1	0	0.0	0
2001—New England NFL...	13	2	19	2	0.0	0	0	0.0	0
2002—Oakland NFL..	16	7	30	4	0.0	2	-2	-1.0	0
Pro totals (8 years)	109	79	311	40	0.0	10	118	11.8	0

SHEA, AARON — TE/FB — BROWNS

PERSONAL: Born December 5, 1976, in Ottawa, Ill. ... 6-3/250. ... Full name: Aaron T. Shea.
HIGH SCHOOL: Ottawa (Ill.).
COLLEGE: Michigan.
TRANSACTIONS/CAREER NOTES: Selected by Cleveland Browns in fourth round (110th pick overall) of 2000 NFL draft. ... Signed by Browns (July 13, 2000). ... On injured reserve with shoulder injury (December 27, 2001-remainder of season). ... On injured reserve with ankle injury (November 19, 2002-remainder of season). ... Granted free agency (February 28, 2003). ... Re-signed by Browns (April 25, 2003).
SINGLE GAME HIGHS (regular season): Receptions—6 (December 2, 2001, vs. Tennessee); yards—76 (October 15, 2000, vs. Denver); and touchdown receptions—1 (November 12, 2000, vs. New England).

Year Team	G	GS	RECEIVING				TOTALS			
			No.	Yds.	Avg.	TD	TD	2pt.	Pts.	Fum.
2000—Cleveland NFL	15	8	30	302	10.1	2	2	0	12	1
2001—Cleveland NFL	12	5	14	86	6.1	0	0	0	0	0
2002—Cleveland NFL	7	3	7	49	7.0	0	0	0	0	0
Pro totals (3 years)	34	16	51	437	8.6	2	2	0	12	1

SHELTON, DAIMON — FB — BEARS

PERSONAL: Born September 15, 1972, in Duarte, Calif. ... 6-0/262.
HIGH SCHOOL: Duarte (Calif.).
JUNIOR COLLEGE: Fresno (Calif.) City College.
COLLEGE: Cal State Sacramento.
TRANSACTIONS/CAREER NOTES: Selected by Jacksonville Jaguars in sixth round (184th pick overall) of 1997 NFL draft. ... Signed by Jaguars (May 23, 1997). ... Granted free agency (February 11, 2000). ... Re-signed by Jaguars (March 21, 2000). ... Granted unconditional free agency (March 2, 2001). ... Signed by Chicago Bears (May 23, 2001). ... Granted unconditional free agency (March 1, 2002). ... Re-signed by Bears (April 2, 2002). ... On suspended list for violating league substance abuse policy (September 1-27, 2002).
CHAMPIONSHIP GAME EXPERIENCE: Played in AFC championship game (1999 season).
SINGLE GAME HIGHS (regular season): Attempts—13 (October 18, 1998, vs. Buffalo); yards —44 (October 18, 1998, vs. Buffalo); and rushing touchdowns—1 (November 1, 1998, vs. Baltimore).

Year Team	G	GS	RUSHING				RECEIVING				TOTALS			
			Att.	Yds.	Avg.	TD	No.	Yds.	Avg.	TD	TD	2pt.	Pts.	Fum.
1997—Jacksonville NFL	13	0	6	4	0.7	0	0	0	0.0	0	0	0	0	1
1998—Jacksonville NFL	14	8	30	95	3.2	1	10	79	7.9	0	1	0	6	0
1999—Jacksonville NFL	16	9	1	2	2.0	0	12	87	7.3	0	0	0	0	0
2000—Jacksonville NFL	16	9	2	3	1.5	0	4	48	12.0	0	0	0	0	0
2001—Chicago NFL	16	9	0	0	0.0	0	12	76	6.3	1	1	0	6	2
2002—Chicago NFL	12	8	0	0	0.0	0	7	34	4.9	0	0	0	0	0
Pro totals (6 years)	87	43	39	104	2.7	1	45	324	7.2	1	2	0	12	3

SHELTON, L.J. OT CARDINALS

PERSONAL: Born March 21, 1976, in Rochester Hills, Mich. ... 6-6/335. ... Full name: Lonnie Jewel Shelton. ... Son of Lonnie Shelton, forward with New York Knicks (1976-77 and 1977-78), Seattle SuperSonics (1978-79 through 1982-83) and Cleveland Cavaliers (1983-84 through 1985-86).
HIGH SCHOOL: Rochester (Rochester Hills, Mich.).
COLLEGE: Eastern Michigan.
TRANSACTIONS/CAREER NOTES: Selected by Arizona Cardinals in first round (21st pick overall) of 1999 NFL draft. ... Signed by Cardinals (September 24, 1999).
PLAYING EXPERIENCE: Arizona NFL, 1999-2002. ... Games/Games started: 1999 (9/7), 2000 (14/14), 2001 (16/16), 2002 (16/16). Total: 55/53.

SHEPPARD, LITO CB EAGLES

PERSONAL: Born April 8, 1981, in Jacksonville. ... 5-10/194. ... Full name: Lito Decorian Sheppard.
HIGH SCHOOL: Raines (Jacksonville).
COLLEGE: Florida.
TRANSACTIONS/CAREER NOTES: Selected after junior season by Philadelphia Eagles in first round (26th pick overall) of 2002 NFL draft. ... Signed by Eagles (July 24, 2002).
CHAMPIONSHIP GAME EXPERIENCE: Member of Eagles for NFC championship game (2002 season); inactive.
HONORS: Named cornerback on THE SPORTING NEWS college All-America second team (2000 and 2001).

Year Team	G	GS	TOTALS			INTERCEPTIONS				PUNT RETURNS				KICKOFF RETURNS				TOTALS			
			Tk.	Ast.	Sks.	No.	Yds.	Avg.	TD	No.	Yds.	Avg.	TD	No.	Yds.	Avg.	TD	TD	2pt.	Pts.	Fum.
2002—Philadelphia NFL	12	0	5	2	0.0	0	0	0.0	0	0	0	0.0	0	0	0	0.0	0	0	0	0	0

SHIELDS, WILL G CHIEFS

PERSONAL: Born September 15, 1971, in Fort Riley, Kan. ... 6-3/315. ... Full name: Will Herthie Shields.
HIGH SCHOOL: Lawton (Okla.).
COLLEGE: Nebraska (degree in communications).
TRANSACTIONS/CAREER NOTES: Selected by Kansas City Chiefs in the third round (74th pick overall) of 1993 NFL draft. ... Signed by Chiefs (May 3, 1993). ... Designated by Chiefs as franchise player (February 11, 2000).
PLAYING EXPERIENCE: Kansas City NFL, 1993-2002. ... Games/Games started: 1993 (16/15), 1994 (16/16), 1995 (16/16), 1996 (16/16), 1997 (16/16), 1998 (16/16), 1999 (16/16), 2000 (16/16), 2001 (16/16), 2002 (16/16). Total: 160/159.
CHAMPIONSHIP GAME EXPERIENCE: Played in AFC championship game (1993 season).
HONORS: Named guard on THE SPORTING NEWS college All-America second team (1991). ... Named guard on THE SPORTING NEWS college All-America first team (1992). ... Named guard on THE SPORTING NEWS NFL All-Pro team (1999 and 2002). ... Played in Pro Bowl (1995-2002 seasons).

SHIPP, MARCEL RB CARDINALS

PERSONAL: Born August 8, 1978, in Paterson, N.J. ... 5-11/226.
HIGH SCHOOL: Milford (Conn.), then Passaic (N.J.).
COLLEGE: Massachusetts.
TRANSACTIONS/CAREER NOTES: Signed as non-drafted free agent by Arizona Cardinals (April 23, 2001).
SINGLE GAME HIGHS (regular season): Attempts—26 (December 15, 2002, vs. St. Louis); yards—135 (November 24, 2002, vs. Oakland); and rushing touchdowns—2 (December 15, 2002, vs. St. Louis).
STATISTICAL PLATEAUS: 100-yard rushing games: 2002 (1).

Year Team	G	GS	RUSHING				RECEIVING				KICKOFF RETURNS				TOTALS			
			Att.	Yds.	Avg.	TD	No.	Yds.	Avg.	TD	No.	Yds.	Avg.	TD	TD	2pt.	Pts.	Fum.
2001—Arizona NFL	11	0	0	0	0.0	0	0	0	0.0	0	6	118	19.7	0	0	0	0	0
2002—Arizona NFL	15	6	188	834	4.4	6	38	413	10.9	3	6	120	20.0	0	9	0	54	4
Pro totals (2 years)	26	6	188	834	4.4	6	38	413	10.9	3	12	238	19.8	0	9	0	54	4

SHOCKEY, JEREMY TE GIANTS

PERSONAL: Born August 18, 1980, in Ada, Okla. ... 6-5/252. ... Full name: Jeremy Charles Shockey.
HIGH SCHOOL: Ada (Okla.).
JUNIOR COLLEGE: Northeastern A&M Community College (Okla.).
COLLEGE: Miami (Fla.).
TRANSACTIONS/CAREER NOTES: Selected after junior season by New York Giants in first round (14th pick overall) of 2002 NFL draft. ... Signed by Giants (July 29, 2002).
HONORS: Played in Pro Bowl (2002 season).
SINGLE GAME HIGHS (regular season): Receptions—11 (November 17, 2002, vs. Washington); yards—116 (December 22, 2002, vs. Indianapolis); and touchdown receptions—1 (December 28, 2002, vs. Philadelphia).
STATISTICAL PLATEAUS: 100-yard receiving games: 2002 (2).

Year	Team		G	GS	RECEIVING			
					No.	Yds.	Avg.	TD
2002—New York Giants NFL			15	13	74	894	12.1	2

SHORT, BRANDON — LB — GIANTS

PERSONAL: Born July 11, 1977, in McKeesport, Pa. ... 6-3/253. ... Full name: Brandon Darnell Short.
HIGH SCHOOL: McKeesport (Pa.).
COLLEGE: Penn State (degree in marketing, 1999).
TRANSACTIONS/CAREER NOTES: Selected by New York Giants in fourth round (105th pick overall) of 2000 NFL draft. ... Signed by Giants (July 25, 2000). ... Granted free agency (February 28, 2003).
CHAMPIONSHIP GAME EXPERIENCE: Played in NFC championship game (2000 season). ... Played in Super Bowl XXXV (2000 season).
HONORS: Named linebacker on THE SPORTING NEWS college All-America second team (1999).

Year	Team	G	GS	TOTALS			INTERCEPTIONS			
				Tk.	Ast.	Sks.	No.	Yds.	Avg.	TD
2000—New York Giants NFL		11	0	3	0	0.0	0	0	0.0	0
2001—New York Giants NFL		16	16	45	15	1.0	1	21	21.0	0
2002—New York Giants NFL		16	15	62	25	3.0	1	32	32.0	0
Pro totals (3 years)		43	31	110	40	4.0	2	53	26.5	0

SIDNEY, DAINON — CB — BILLS

PERSONAL: Born May 30, 1975, in Atlanta. ... 6-0/188. ... Full name: Dainon Tarquinius Sidney. ... Name pronounced DAY-nun.
HIGH SCHOOL: Riverdale (Ga.).
COLLEGE: East Tennessee State, then Alabama-Birmingham.
TRANSACTIONS/CAREER NOTES: Selected by Tennessee Oilers in third round (77th pick overall) of 1998 NFL draft. ... Signed by Oilers (July 21, 1998). ... Oilers franchise renamed Tennessee Titans for 1999 season (December 26, 1998). ... Granted free agency (March 2, 2001). ... On injured reserve with knee injury (September 26, 2001-remainder of season). ... Granted unconditional free agency (March 1, 2002). ... Re-signed by Titans (March 12, 2002). ... Granted unconditional free agency (February 28, 2003). ... Signed by Buffalo Bills (April 10, 2003).
CHAMPIONSHIP GAME EXPERIENCE: Played in AFC championship game (1999 and 2002 seasons). ... Played in Super Bowl XXXIV (1999 season).

Year	Team	G	GS	TOTALS			INTERCEPTIONS			
				Tk.	Ast.	Sks.	No.	Yds.	Avg.	TD
1998—Tennessee NFL		16	1	15	1	0.0	0	0	0.0	0
1999—Tennessee NFL		16	2	33	5	0.0	3	12	4.0	0
2000—Tennessee NFL		11	2	16	3	0.0	3	19	6.3	0
2001—Tennessee NFL		1	1	0	0	0.0	0	0	0.0	0
2002—Tennessee NFL		4	0	0	0	0.0	0	0	0.0	0
Pro totals (5 years)		48	6	64	9	0.0	6	31	5.2	0

SIMMONS, ANTHONY — LB — SEAHAWKS

PERSONAL: Born June 20, 1976, in Spartanburg, S.C. ... 6-0/242.
HIGH SCHOOL: Spartanburg (S.C.).
COLLEGE: Clemson (degree in marketing, 1998).
TRANSACTIONS/CAREER NOTES: Selected after junior season by Seattle Seahawks in first round (15th pick overall) of 1998 NFL draft. ... Signed by Seahawks (July 18, 1998). ... Granted unconditional free agency (February 28, 2003). ... Re-signed by Seahawks (March 4, 2003).
HONORS: Named inside linebacker on THE SPORTING NEWS college All-America first team (1996 and 1997).

Year	Team	G	GS	TOTALS			INTERCEPTIONS			
				Tk.	Ast.	Sks.	No.	Yds.	Avg.	TD
1998—Seattle NFL		12	4	31	10	0.0	1	36	36.0	1
1999—Seattle NFL		16	16	57	35	0.0	0	0	0.0	0
2000—Seattle NFL		16	16	119	28	4.0	2	15	7.5	0
2001—Seattle NFL		16	16	103	20	2.0	0	0	0.0	0
2002—Seattle NFL		7	7	35	11	1.0	2	19	9.5	0
Pro totals (5 years)		67	59	345	104	7.0	5	70	14.0	1

SIMMONS, BRIAN — LB — BENGALS

PERSONAL: Born June 21, 1975, in New Bern, N.C. ... 6-3/248. ... Full name: Brian Eugene Simmons.
HIGH SCHOOL: New Bern (N.C.).
COLLEGE: North Carolina.
TRANSACTIONS/CAREER NOTES: Selected by Cincinnati Bengals in first round (17th pick overall) of 1998 NFL draft. ... Signed by Bengals (July 27, 1998). ... On injured reserve with knee injury (November 9, 2000-remainder of season).
HONORS: Named outside linebacker on THE SPORTING NEWS college All-America second team (1996). ... Named outside linebacker on THE SPORTING NEWS college All-America third team (1997).

Year	Team	G	GS	TOTALS			INTERCEPTIONS			
				Tk.	Ast.	Sks.	No.	Yds.	Avg.	TD
1998—Cincinnati NFL		14	12	62	16	3.0	1	18	18.0	0
1999—Cincinnati NFL		16	16	90	20	3.0	0	0	0.0	0
2000—Cincinnati NFL		1	1	7	2	1.0	0	0	0.0	0
2001—Cincinnati NFL		16	16	52	32	6.5	1	5	5.0	0
2002—Cincinnati NFL		16	15	65	21	3.0	1	51	51.0	1
Pro totals (5 years)		63	60	276	91	16.5	3	74	24.7	1

S

SIMMONS, JASON — CB — TEXANS

PERSONAL: Born March 30, 1976, in Inglewood, Calif. ... 5-9/198. ... Full name: Jason Lawrence Simmons.
HIGH SCHOOL: Leuzinger (Lawndale, Calif.).
COLLEGE: Arizona State.
TRANSACTIONS/CAREER NOTES: Selected by Pittsburgh Steelers in fifth round (137th pick overall) of 1998 NFL draft. ... Signed by Steelers (July 14, 1998). ... Granted free agency (March 2, 2001). ... Re-signed by Steelers (April 26, 2001). ... Granted unconditional free agency (March 1, 2002). ... Signed by Houston Texans (April 8, 2002). ... Granted unconditional free agency (February 28, 2003). ... Re-signed by Texans (March 21, 2003).
CHAMPIONSHIP GAME EXPERIENCE: Played in AFC championship game (2001 season).

Year Team	G	GS	Tk.	Ast.	Sks.	No.	Yds.	Avg.	TD
			TOTALS			**INTERCEPTIONS**			
1998—Pittsburgh NFL	6	0	7	1	0.0	0	0	0.0	0
1999—Pittsburgh NFL	16	0	3	1	0.0	0	0	0.0	0
2000—Pittsburgh NFL	15	0	12	1	0.0	0	0	0.0	0
2001—Pittsburgh NFL	12	0	4	1	0.0	0	0	0.0	0
2002—Houston NFL	15	0	7	1	1.0	0	0	0.0	0
Pro totals (5 years)	64	0	33	5	1.0	0	0	0.0	0

SIMMONS, KENDALL — G — STEELERS

PERSONAL: Born March 11, 1979, in Ripley, Miss. ... 6-3/313. ... Full name: Henry Alexander Kendall Simmons.
HIGH SCHOOL: Ripley (Miss.).
COLLEGE: Auburn.
TRANSACTIONS/CAREER NOTES: Selected by Pittsburgh Steelers in first round (30th pick overall) of 2002 NFL draft. ... Signed by Steelers (July 26, 2002).
PLAYING EXPERIENCE: Pittsburgh NFL, 2002. ... Games/Games started: 2002 (14/14).

SIMMONS, TERRANCE — OL — PANTHERS

PERSONAL: Born May 3, 1976, in Prichard, Ala. ... 6-8/310.
HIGH SCHOOL: Vigor-Prichard (Ala.).
COLLEGE: Alabama State.
TRANSACTIONS/CAREER NOTES: Signed as non-drafted free agent by Washington Redskins (April 16, 2000). ... Released by Redskins (August 24, 2000). ... Re-signed by Redskins (December 28, 2000). ... Assigned by Redskins to Frankfurt Galaxy in 2001 NFL Europe enhancement allocation program (February 18, 2001). ... Released by Redskins (September 3, 2001). ... Re-signed by Redskins to practice squad (September 3, 2001). ... Released by Redskins (December 5, 2001). ... Re-signed by Redskins (December 27, 2001); did not play. ... Granted free agency (March 1, 2002). ... Signed by Carolina Panthers (August 1, 2002). ... Released by Panthers (September 1, 2002). ... Re-signed by Panthers to practice squad (September 3, 2002). ... Activated (October 16, 2002). ... Released by Panthers (November 27, 2002). ... Re-signed by Panthers to practice squad (December 4, 2002). ... Released by Panthers (December 26, 2002). ... Re-signed by Panthers (April 14, 2003).
PLAYING EXPERIENCE: Carolina NFL, 2002. ... Games/Games started: 2002 (2/0).

SIMMONS, TONY — WR

PERSONAL: Born December 8, 1974, in Chicago. ... 6-1/212. ... Full name: Tony Angelo Simmons.
HIGH SCHOOL: St. Rita (Chicago).
COLLEGE: Wisconsin (degree in construction administration).
TRANSACTIONS/CAREER NOTES: Selected by New England Patriots in second round (52nd pick overall) of 1998 NFL draft. ... Signed by Patriots (July 18, 1998). ... Assigned by Patriots to Barcelona Dragons in 2001 NFL Europe enhancement allocation program (February 19, 2001). ... Claimed on waivers by Cleveland Browns (September 3, 2001). ... Released by Browns (October 2, 2001). ... Signed by Indianapolis Colts (October 8, 2001). ... Released by Colts (November 7, 2001). ... Re-signed by Colts (November 21, 2001). ... Granted unconditional free agency (March 1, 2002). ... Signed by Houston Texans (March 26, 2002). ... Released by Texans (September 1, 2002). ... Signed by New York Giants (November 13, 2002). ... Released by Giants (November 16, 2002). ... Re-signed by Giants (November 19, 2002). ... Granted unconditional free agency (February 28, 2003).
SINGLE GAME HIGHS (regular season): Receptions—7 (October 10, 1999, vs. Kansas City); yards—109 (November 1, 1998, vs. Indianapolis); and touchdown receptions—1 (October 8, 2000, vs. Indianapolis).
STATISTICAL PLATEAUS: 100-yard receiving games: 1998 (1), 1999 (1). Total: 2.

Year Team	G	GS	No.	Yds.	Avg.	TD	TD	2pt.	Pts.	Fum.
			RECEIVING				**TOTALS**			
1998—New England NFL	11	6	23	474	20.6	3	3	0	18	0
1999—New England NFL	15	1	19	276	14.5	2	2	0	12	1
2000—New England NFL	12	2	14	231	16.5	1	1	0	6	0
2001—Barcelona NFLE	...	...	32	538	16.8	7	7	0	42	0
—Cleveland NFL	1	0	0	0	0.0	0	0	0	0	0
—Indianapolis NFL	6	0	2	17	8.5	0	0	0	0	0
2002—New York Giants NFL	3	0	0	0	0.0	0	0	0	0	0
NFL Europe totals (1 year)	...	...	32	538	16.8	7	7	0	42	0
NFL totals (5 years)	48	9	58	998	17.2	6	6	0	36	1
Pro totals (6 years)	...	...	90	1536	17.1	13	13	0	78	1

SIMON, COREY — DT — EAGLES

PERSONAL: Born March 2, 1977, in Boynton Beach, Fla. ... 6-2/293.
HIGH SCHOOL: Ely (Pompano Beach, Fla.).
COLLEGE: Florida State.

TRANSACTIONS/CAREER NOTES: Selected by Philadelphia Eagles in first round (sixth pick overall) of 2000 NFL draft. ... Signed by Eagles (July 28, 2000).
CHAMPIONSHIP GAME EXPERIENCE: Played in NFC championship game (2001 and 2002 seasons).
HONORS: Named defensive tackle on THE SPORTING NEWS college All-America first team (1999).

Year Team	G	GS	TOTALS Tk.	Ast.	Sks.
2000—Philadelphia NFL	16	16	38	13	9.5
2001—Philadelphia NFL	16	16	39	11	7.5
2002—Philadelphia NFL	14	14	32	7	2.0
Pro totals (3 years)	46	46	109	31	19.0

SIMON, JOHN   RB   TITANS

PERSONAL: Born December 11, 1978, in Baton Rouge, La. ... 5-11/202. ... Full name: John Ray Simon Jr.
HIGH SCHOOL: Lab (Baton Rouge, La.).
COLLEGE: Louisiana Tech.
TRANSACTIONS/CAREER NOTES: Signed as non-drafted free agent by Tennessee Titans (April 22, 2002).
CHAMPIONSHIP GAME EXPERIENCE: Played in AFC championship game (2002 season).
SINGLE GAME HIGHS (regular season): Attempts—4 (September 29, 2002, vs. Oakland); yards—11 (September 29, 2002, vs. Oakland); and rushing touchdowns—1 (September 29, 2002, vs. Oakland).

Year Team	G	GS	RUSHING Att.	Yds.	Avg.	TD	RECEIVING No.	Yds.	Avg.	TD	PUNT RETURNS No.	Yds.	Avg.	TD	KICKOFF RETURNS No.	Yds.	Avg.	TD	TOTALS TD	2pt.	Pts.Fum.
2002—Ten NFL	12	0	9	18	2.0	1	16	167	10.4	3	13	113	8.7	0	20	371	18.6	0	4	0	24 1

SIMONEAU, MARK   LB   FALCONS

PERSONAL: Born January 16, 1977, in Phillipsburg, Kan. ... 6-0/234.
HIGH SCHOOL: Smith Center (Kan.).
COLLEGE: Kansas State.
TRANSACTIONS/CAREER NOTES: Selected by Atlanta Falcons in third round (67th pick overall) of 2000 NFL draft. ... Signed by Falcons (May 17, 2000). ... Granted free agency (February 28, 2003). ... Traded by Falcons to Philadelphia Eagles for sixth-round pick (DB Waine Bacon) in 2003 draft and fourth-round pick in 2004 draft (March 4, 2003).
HONORS: Named linebacker on THE SPORTING NEWS college All-America first team (1999).

Year Team	G	GS	TOTALS Tk.	Ast.	Sks.	INTERCEPTIONS No.	Yds.	Avg.	TD
2000—Atlanta NFL	14	4	36	11	0.5	0	0	0.0	0
2001—Atlanta NFL	16	5	25	6	0.0	0	0	0.0	0
2002—Atlanta NFL	15	0	6	1	0.0	0	0	0.0	0
Pro totals (3 years)	45	9	67	18	0.5	0	0	0.0	0

SIMS, BARRY   G/OT   RAIDERS

PERSONAL: Born December 1, 1974, in Park City, Utah. ... 6-5/300.
HIGH SCHOOL: Park City (Utah).
JUNIOR COLLEGE: Dixie College (Utah).
COLLEGE: Utah.
TRANSACTIONS/CAREER NOTES: Selected by Scottish Claymores in 1999 NFL Europe draft (February 23, 1999). ... Signed as non-drafted free agent by Oakland Raiders (July, 1999).
PLAYING EXPERIENCE: Scottish NFLE, 1999; Oakland NFL, 1999-2002. ... Games/Games started: NFLE 1999 (games played unavailable), NFL 1999 (16/10), 2000 (16/8), 2001 (15/15), 2002 (15/15). Total NFL: 62/48.
CHAMPIONSHIP GAME EXPERIENCE: Played in AFC championship game (2000 and 2002 seasons). ... Played in Super Bowl XXXVII (2002 season).

SIMS, RYAN   DT   CHIEFS

PERSONAL: Born May 4, 1980, in Spartanburg, S.C. ... 6-4/315. ... Full name: Ryan O'Neal Sims.
HIGH SCHOOL: Paul M. Dorman (Spartanburg, S.C.).
COLLEGE: North Carolina.
TRANSACTIONS/CAREER NOTES: Selected by Kansas City Chiefs in first round (sixth pick overall) of 2002 NFL draft. ... Signed by Chiefs (August 28, 2002). ... On injured reserve with elbow injury (October 17, 2002-remainder of season).

Year Team	G	GS	TOTALS Tk.	Ast.	Sks.
2002—Kansas City NFL	6	2	5	1	0.0

SINCLAIR, MICHAEL   DE

PERSONAL: Born January 31, 1968, in Galveston, Texas. ... 6-4/275. ... Full name: Michael Glenn Sinclair.
HIGH SCHOOL: Charlton-Pollard (Beaumont, Texas).
COLLEGE: Eastern New Mexico (degree in physical education).
TRANSACTIONS/CAREER NOTES: Selected by Seattle Seahawks in sixth round (155th pick overall) of 1991 NFL draft. ... Signed by Seahawks (July 18, 1991). ... Released by Seahawks (August 26, 1991). ... Re-signed by Seahawks to practice squad (August 28, 1991). ... Activated (November 30, 1991). ... On injured reserve with back injury (December 14, 1991-remainder of season). ... Active for two games (1991); did

not play. ... Assigned by Seahawks to Sacramento Surge in 1992 World League enhancement allocation program (February 20, 1992). ... On injured reserve with ankle injury (September 1-October 3, 1992). ... On injured reserve with thumb injury (November 10, 1993-remainder of season). ... Granted free agency (February 17, 1995). ... Re-signed by Seahawks (May 24, 1995). ... Granted unconditional free agency (February 16, 1996). ... Re-signed by Seahawks (February 17, 1996). ... Released by Seahawks (February 22, 2002). ... Signed by Denver Broncos (July 25, 2002). ... Released by Broncos (September 1, 2002). ... Signed by Philadelphia Eagles (September 10, 2002). ... Released by Eagles (October 22, 2002).

HONORS: Named defensive end on All-World League team (1992). ... Played in Pro Bowl (1996-1998 seasons).

Year Team	G	GS	TOTALS Tk.	Ast.	Sks.
1991—Seattle NFL			Did not play.		
1992—Sacramento W.L.	10	10	...	...	10.0
—Seattle NFL	12	1	9	1	1.0
1993—Seattle NFL	9	1	12	0	8.0
1994—Seattle NFL	12	2	10	2	4.5
1995—Seattle NFL	16	15	37	9	5.5
1996—Seattle NFL	16	16	39	8	13.0
1997—Seattle NFL	16	16	35	10	12.0
1998—Seattle NFL	16	16	42	13	*16.5
1999—Seattle NFL	15	15	29	7	6.0
2000—Seattle NFL	16	16	35	13	3.5
2001—Seattle NFL	16	16	25	15	3.5
2002—Philadelphia NFL	4	0	0	1	0.0
W.L. totals (1 year)	10	10	...	...	10.0
NFL totals (10 years)	148	114	273	79	73.5
Pro totals (11 years)	158	124	...	...	83.5

SINGLETON, ALSHERMOND LB COWBOYS

PERSONAL: Born August 7, 1975, in Newark, N.J. ... 6-2/228. ... Full name: Alshermond Glendale Singleton.
HIGH SCHOOL: Irvington (N.J.).
COLLEGE: Temple (degree in sports recreation management).
TRANSACTIONS/CAREER NOTES: Selected by Tampa Bay Buccaneers in fourth round (128th pick overall) of 1997 NFL draft. ... Signed by Buccaneers (July 17, 1997). ... Granted unconditional free agency (February 28, 2003). ... Signed by Dallas Cowboys (March 13, 2003).
CHAMPIONSHIP GAME EXPERIENCE: Member of Buccaneers for NFC championship game (1999 season); inactive. ... Played in NFC championship game (2002 season). ... Member of Super Bowl championship team (2002 season).

Year Team	G	GS	TOTALS Tk.	Ast.	Sks.	INTERCEPTIONS No.	Yds.	Avg.	TD
1997—Tampa Bay NFL	12	0	0	0	0.0	0	0	0.0	0
1998—Tampa Bay NFL	15	0	11	4	0.0	0	0	0.0	0
1999—Tampa Bay NFL	15	0	13	8	0.5	1	7	7.0	0
2000—Tampa Bay NFL	13	1	16	6	0.0	0	0	0.0	0
2001—Tampa Bay NFL	16	0	17	4	1.0	0	0	0.0	0
2002—Tampa Bay NFL	16	14	40	18	1.0	1	0	0.0	0
Pro totals (6 years)	87	15	97	40	2.5	2	7	3.5	0

SIRMON, PETER LB TITANS

PERSONAL: Born February 18, 1977, in Wenatchee, Wash. ... 6-2/240. ... Full name: Peter Anton Sirmon.
HIGH SCHOOL: Walla Walla (Wash.).
COLLEGE: Oregon.
TRANSACTIONS/CAREER NOTES: Selected by Tennessee Titans in fourth round (128th pick overall) of 2000 NFL draft. ... Signed by Titans (July 11, 2000). ... Granted free agency (February 28, 2003). ... Re-signed by Titans (April 17, 2003).
CHAMPIONSHIP GAME EXPERIENCE: Played in AFC championship game (2002 season).

Year Team	G	GS	TOTALS Tk.	Ast.	Sks.	INTERCEPTIONS No.	Yds.	Avg.	TD
2000—Tennessee NFL	5	0	0	0	0.0	0	0	0.0	0
2001—Tennessee NFL	16	0	0	0	0.0	0	0	0.0	0
2002—Tennessee NFL	16	12	72	21	2.0	3	88	29.3	1
Pro totals (3 years)	37	12	72	21	2.0	3	88	29.3	1

SKAGGS, JUSTIN WR REDSKINS

PERSONAL: Born April 22, 1979, in Wentzville, Mo. ... 6-2/200.
HIGH SCHOOL: St. Clair (Wentzville, Mo.).
COLLEGE: Evangel (Mo.).
TRANSACTIONS/CAREER NOTES: Singed as non-drafted free agent by Washington Redskins (April 25, 2001). ... Released by Redskins (September 2, 2001). ... Re-signed by Redskins to practice squad (September 3, 2001). ... Activated (December 26, 2001; did not play. ... Released by Redskins (September 1, 2002). ... Re-signed by Redskins to practice squad (September 3, 2002). ... Activated (November 12, 2002). ... Assigned by Redskins to Amsterdam Admirals in 2003 NFL Europe enhancement allocation program (February 4, 2003).

Year Team	G	GS	RECEIVING No.	Yds.	Avg.	TD
2001—Washington NFL			Did not play.			
2002—Washington NFL	1	0	0	0	0.0	0
Pro totals (1 years)	1	0	0	0	0.0	0

SLAUGHTER, T.J.   LB   JAGUARS

PERSONAL: Born February 20, 1977, in Birmingham, Ala. ... 6-0/233. ... Full name: Tavaris Jermell Slaughter.
HIGH SCHOOL: John Carroll (Birmingham, Ala.).
COLLEGE: Southern Mississippi.
TRANSACTIONS/CAREER NOTES: Selected by Jacksonville Jaguars in third round (92nd pick overall) of 2000 NFL draft. ... Signed by Jaguars (May 16, 2000). ... On suspended list for violating league substance abuse policy (September 6-October 7, 2002). ... On injured reserve with knee injury (December 8, 2001-remainder of season). ... Granted free agency (February 28, 2003). ... Re-signed by Jaguars (May 15, 2003).

			TOTALS			INTERCEPTIONS			
Year Team	G	GS	Tk.	Ast.	Sks.	No.	Yds.	Avg.	TD
2000—Jacksonville NFL	16	7	38	16	0.0	0	0	0.0	0
2001—Jacksonville NFL	9	8	41	13	1.0	0	0	0.0	0
2002—Jacksonville NFL	11	11	39	20	0.0	0	0	0.0	0
Pro totals (3 years)	36	26	118	49	1.0	0	0	0.0	0

SLECHTA, JEREMY   DT   EAGLES

PERSONAL: Born May 12, 1980, in LaVista, Neb. ... 6-6/285.
HIGH SCHOOL: Papillion-LaVista (LaVista, Neb.).
COLLEGE: Nebraska.
TRANSACTIONS/CAREER NOTES: Signed as non-drafted free agent by Philadelphia Eagles (April 23, 2002). ... Released by Eagles (September 1, 2002). ... Re-signed by Eagles to practice squad (September 3, 2002). ... Activated (September 26, 2002).
CHAMPIONSHIP GAME EXPERIENCE: Played in NFC championship game (2002 season).

			TOTALS		
Year Team	G	GS	Tk.	Ast.	Sks.
2002—Philadelphia NFL	13	0	2	2	0.0

S

SLOAN, DAVID   TE   SAINTS

PERSONAL: Born June 8, 1972, in Fresno, Calif. ... 6-6/260. ... Full name: David Lyle Sloan.
HIGH SCHOOL: Sierra Joint Union (Tollhouse, Calif.).
JUNIOR COLLEGE: Fresno (Calif.) City College.
COLLEGE: New Mexico.
TRANSACTIONS/CAREER NOTES: Selected by Detroit Lions in third round (70th pick overall) of 1995 NFL draft. ... Signed by Lions (July 20, 1995). ... Granted free agency (February 13, 1998). ... Re-signed by Lions (June 10, 1998). ... On physically unable to perform list with knee injury (August 25-October 23, 1998). ... Granted unconditional free agency (February 12, 1999). ... Re-signed by Lions (March 24, 1999). ... Granted unconditional free agency (March 1, 2002). ... Signed by New Orleans Saints (April 3, 2002).
HONORS: Played in Pro Bowl (1999 season).
SINGLE GAME HIGHS (regular season): Receptions—7 (November 14, 1999, vs. Arizona); yards—88 (November 14, 1999, vs. Arizona); and touchdown receptions—2 (December 23, 2001, vs. Pittsburgh).

			RECEIVING				TOTALS			
Year Team	G	GS	No.	Yds.	Avg.	TD	TD	2pt.	Pts.	Fum.
1995—Detroit NFL	16	7	17	184	10.8	1	1	0	6	0
1996—Detroit NFL	4	4	7	51	7.3	0	0	0	0	0
1997—Detroit NFL	14	12	29	264	9.1	0	0	0	0	0
1998—Detroit NFL	10	2	11	146	13.3	1	1	0	6	0
1999—Detroit NFL	16	15	47	591	12.6	4	4	0	24	0
2000—Detroit NFL	15	10	32	379	11.8	2	2	0	12	0
2001—Detroit NFL	15	15	37	409	11.1	7	7	0	42	0
2002—New Orleans NFL	16	14	12	127	10.6	0	0	0	0	0
Pro totals (8 years)	106	79	192	2151	11.2	15	15	0	90	0

SMART, ROD   RB   PANTHERS

PERSONAL: Born January 9, 1977, in Lakeland, Fla. ... 5-11/201.
HIGH SCHOOL: Lakeland (Fla.).
COLLEGE: Western Kentucky.
TRANSACTIONS/CAREER NOTES: Signed as non-drafted free agent by San Diego Chargers (May 19, 2000). ... Released by Chargers (June 9, 2000). ... Signed by Philadelphia Eagles to practice squad (October 2, 2001). ... Activated (November 19, 2001). ... On injured reserve with foot injury (January 8, 2002-remainder of season). ... Claimed on waivers by Carolina Panthers (September 2, 2002).
SINGLE GAME HIGHS (regular season): Attempts—2 (January 6, 2002, vs. Tampa Bay); yards—6 (January 6, 2002, vs. Tampa Bay); and rushing touchdowns—0.

			RUSHING				TOTALS			
Year Team	G	GS	Att.	Yds.	Avg.	TD	TD	2pt.	Pts.	Fum.
2001—Philadelphia NFL	6	0	2	6	3.0	0	0	0	0	0
2002—Carolina NFL	16	0	1	2	2.0	0	0	0	0	0
Pro totals (2 years)	22	0	3	8	2.7	0	0	0	0	0

SMITH, AARON   DE   STEELERS

PERSONAL: Born April 9, 1976, in Colorado Springs, Colo. ... 6-5/300. ... Full name: Aaron Douglas Smith.
HIGH SCHOOL: Sierra (Colorado Springs, Colo.).
COLLEGE: Northern Colorado.

TRANSACTIONS/CAREER NOTES: Selected by Pittsburgh Steelers in fourth round (109th pick overall) of 1999 NFL draft. ... Signed by Steelers (August 3, 1999). ... Granted free agency (March 1, 2002). ... Re-signed by Steelers (July 25, 2002).

CHAMPIONSHIP GAME EXPERIENCE: Played in AFC championship game (2001 season).

Year Team	G	GS	TOTALS Tk.	Ast.	Sks.
1999—Pittsburgh NFL	6	0	1	1	0.0
2000—Pittsburgh NFL	16	15	27	15	4.0
2001—Pittsburgh NFL	16	16	23	6	8.0
2002—Pittsburgh NFL	16	16	53	17	5.5
Pro totals (4 years)	54	47	104	39	17.5

SMITH, AKILI — QB

PERSONAL: Born August 21, 1975, in San Diego. ... 6-3/220. ... Full name: Kabisa Akili Maradu Smith. ... Cousin of Marquis Smith, defensive back, Cleveland Browns. ... Name pronounced uh-KEE-lee.

HIGH SCHOOL: Lincoln (San Diego).

JUNIOR COLLEGE: Grossmont College (Calif.).

COLLEGE: Oregon.

TRANSACTIONS/CAREER NOTES: Selected by Cincinnati Bengals in first round (third pick overall) of 1999 NFL draft. ... Signed by Bengals (August 24, 1999). ... On injured reserve with hamstring injury (December 18, 2001-remainder of season). ... Released by Bengals (June 1, 2003).

SINGLE GAME HIGHS (regular season): Attempts—43 (September 10, 2000, vs. Cleveland); completions—25 (October 10, 1999, vs. Cleveland); passing yards—250 (September 10, 2000, vs. Cleveland); and touchdown passes—2 (October 10, 1999, vs. Cleveland).

MISCELLANEOUS: Regular-season record as starting NFL quarterback: 3-14 (.176).

Year Team	G	GS	PASSING Att.	Cmp.	Pct.	Yds.	TD	Int.	Avg.	Skd.	Rat.	RUSHING Att.	Yds.	Avg.	TD	TOTALS TD	2pt.	Pts.
1999—Cincinnati NFL	7	4	153	80	52.3	805	2	6	5.26	19	55.6	19	114	6.0	1	1	0	6
2000—Cincinnati NFL	12	11	267	118	44.2	1253	3	6	4.69	36	52.8	41	232	5.7	0	0	0	0
2001—Cincinnati NFL	2	1	8	5	62.5	37	0	0	4.63	1	73.4	6	20	3.3	0	0	0	0
2002—Cincinnati NFL	1	1	33	12	36.4	117	0	1	3.55	3	34.5	4	5	1.3	0	0	0	0
Pro totals (4 years)	22	17	461	215	46.6	2212	5	13	4.80	59	52.8	70	371	5.3	1	1	0	6

SMITH, ANTOWAIN — RB — PATRIOTS

PERSONAL: Born March 14, 1972, in Millbrook, Ala. ... 6-2/232. ... Full name: Antowain Drurell Smith. ... Name pronounced AN-twan.

HIGH SCHOOL: Elmore (Ala.).

JUNIOR COLLEGE: East Mississippi Junior College.

COLLEGE: Houston.

TRANSACTIONS/CAREER NOTES: Selected by Buffalo Bills in first round (23rd pick overall) of 1997 NFL draft. ... Signed by Bills (July 11, 1997). ... Released by Bills (May 18, 2001). ... Signed by New England Patriots (June 7, 2001). ... Granted unconditional free agency (March 1, 2002). ... Re-signed by Patriots (March 1, 2002).

CHAMPIONSHIP GAME EXPERIENCE: Played in AFC championship game (2001 season). ... Member of Super Bowl championship team (2001 season).

SINGLE GAME HIGHS (regular season): Attempts—31 (October 11, 1998, vs. Indianapolis); yards—156 (December 22, 2001, vs. Miami); and rushing touchdowns—3 (December 23, 2000, vs. Seattle).

STATISTICAL PLATEAUS: 100-yard rushing games: 1997 (1), 1998 (3), 1999 (2), 2000 (1), 2001 (4), 2002 (1). Total: 12.

Year Team	G	GS	RUSHING Att.	Yds.	Avg.	TD	RECEIVING No.	Yds.	Avg.	TD	TOTALS TD	2pt.	Pts.	Fum.
1997—Buffalo NFL	16	0	194	840	4.3	8	28	177	6.3	0	8	0	48	4
1998—Buffalo NFL	16	14	300	1124	3.7	8	5	11	2.2	0	8	0	48	5
1999—Buffalo NFL	14	11	165	614	3.7	6	2	32	16.0	0	6	0	36	4
2000—Buffalo NFL	11	3	101	354	3.5	4	3	20	6.7	0	4	0	24	1
2001—New England NFL	16	15	287	1157	4.0	12	19	192	10.1	1	13	0	78	4
2002—New England NFL	16	15	252	982	3.9	6	31	243	7.8	2	8	1	50	2
Pro totals (6 years)	89	58	1299	5071	3.9	44	88	675	7.7	3	47	1	284	20

SMITH, BRADY — DE — FALCONS

PERSONAL: Born June 5, 1973, in Royal Oak, Mich. ... 6-5/274. ... Full name: Brady McKay Smith. ... Son of Steve Smith, offensive tackle with four NFL teams (1966-74).

HIGH SCHOOL: Barrington (Ill.).

COLLEGE: Colorado State (degree in liberal arts).

TRANSACTIONS/CAREER NOTES: Selected by New Orleans Saints in third round (70th pick overall) of 1996 NFL draft. ... Signed by Saints (July 12, 1996). ... Granted free agency (February 12, 1999). ... Re-signed by Saints (April 14, 1999). ... Granted unconditional free agency (February 11, 2000). ... Signed by Atlanta Falcons (February 19, 2000).

Year Team	G	GS	TOTALS Tk.	Ast.	Sks.
1996—New Orleans NFL	16	4	15	2	2.0
1997—New Orleans NFL	16	2	22	8	5.0
1998—New Orleans NFL	14	5	10	2	0.0
1999—New Orleans NFL	16	16	26	7	6.0
2000—Atlanta NFL	15	14	29	5	4.5
2001—Atlanta NFL	15	15	26	8	8.0
2002—Atlanta NFL	14	14	26	13	6.5
Pro totals (7 years)	106	70	154	45	32.0

SMITH, BRUCE   DE   REDSKINS

PERSONAL: Born June 18, 1963, in Norfolk, Va. ... 6-4/265. ... Full name: Bruce Bernard Smith.
HIGH SCHOOL: Booker T. Washington (Norfolk, Va.).
COLLEGE: Virginia Tech.
TRANSACTIONS/CAREER NOTES: Selected by Baltimore Stars in 1985 USFL territorial draft. ... Signed by Buffalo Bills (February 28, 1985). ... Selected officially by Bills in first round (first pick overall) of 1985 NFL draft. ... On non-football injury list with substance abuse problem (September 2-28, 1988). ... Granted free agency (February 1, 1989). ... Tendered offer sheet by Denver Broncos (March 23, 1989). ... Offer matched by Bills (March 29, 1989). ... On injured reserve with knee injury (October 12-November 30, 1991). ... Released by Bills (February 10, 2000). ... Signed by Washington Redskins (February 14, 2000).
CHAMPIONSHIP GAME EXPERIENCE: Played in AFC championship game (1988 and 1990-1993 seasons). ... Played in Super Bowl XXV (1990 season), Super Bowl XXVI (1991 season), Super Bowl XXVII (1992 season) and Super Bowl XXVIII (1993 season).
HONORS: Named defensive lineman on THE SPORTING NEWS college All-America second team (1983 and 1984). ... Outland Trophy winner (1984). ... Named defensive end on THE SPORTING NEWS NFL All-Pro team (1987, 1988, 1990 and 1992-1997). ... Played in Pro Bowl (1987-1990, 1994, 1995, 1997 and 1998 seasons). ... Named Outstanding Player of Pro Bowl (1987 season). ... Named to play in Pro Bowl (1992 season); replaced by Howie Long due to injury. ... Named to play in Pro Bowl (1993 season); replaced by Sean Jones due to injury. ... Named to play in Pro Bowl (1996 season); replaced by Willie McGinest due to injury.
POST SEASON RECORDS: Shares Super Bowl single-game record for most safeties—1 (January 27, 1991, vs. New York Giants). ... Holds NFL postseason career record for most sacks—14.5. ... Shares NFL postseason single-game record for most safeties—1 (January 27, 1991, vs. New York Giants).
MISCELLANEOUS: Active NFL leader for career sacks (195). ... Holds Buffalo Bills all-time record for most sacks (171).

Year Team	G	GS	TOTALS Tk.	Ast.	Sks.	INTERCEPTIONS No.	Yds.	Avg.	TD
1985—Buffalo NFL	16	13	32	16	6.5	0	0	0.0	0
1986—Buffalo NFL	16	15	36	27	15.0	0	0	0.0	0
1987—Buffalo NFL	12	12	60	18	12.0	0	0	0.0	0
1988—Buffalo NFL	12	12	39	17	11.0	0	0	0.0	0
1989—Buffalo NFL	16	16	66	22	13.0	0	0	0.0	0
1990—Buffalo NFL	16	16	82	19	19.0	0	0	0.0	0
1991—Buffalo NFL	5	5	13	5	1.5	0	0	0.0	0
1992—Buffalo NFL	15	15	66	23	14.0	0	0	0.0	0
1993—Buffalo NFL	16	16	87	21	14.0	1	0	0.0	0
1994—Buffalo NFL	15	15	57	24	10.0	1	0	0.0	0
1995—Buffalo NFL	15	15	52	22	10.5	0	0	0.0	0
1996—Buffalo NFL	16	16	69	21▲13.5		0	0	0.0	0
1997—Buffalo NFL	16	16	49	16 §14.0		0	0	0.0	0
1998—Buffalo NFL	15	15	35	15	10.0	0	0	0.0	0
1999—Buffalo NFL	16	16	30	15	7.0	0	0	0.0	0
2000—Washington NFL	16	16	50	8	10.0	0	0	0.0	0
2001—Washington NFL	14	14	31	11	5.0	0	0	0.0	0
2002—Washington NFL	16	16	37	12	9.0	0	0	0.0	0
Pro totals (18 years)	263	259	891	312 195.0		2	0	0.0	0

SMITH, COREY   DE   BUCCANEERS

PERSONAL: Born November 2, 1979, in Richmond, Va. ... 6-2/250. ... Full name: Corey Dominique Smith.
HIGH SCHOOL: John Marshall (Richmond, Va.).
COLLEGE: North Carolina State.
TRANSACTIONS/CAREER NOTES: Signed as non-drafted free agent by Tampa Bay Buccaneers (April 22, 2002). ... On injured reserve with knee injury (November 28, 2002-remainder of season).

Year Team	G	GS	TOTALS Tk.	Ast.	Sks.
2002—Tampa Bay NFL	6	0	1	0	1.0

SMITH, DARRIN   LB   SAINTS

PERSONAL: Born April 15, 1970, in Miami. ... 6-1/236. ... Full name: Darrin Andrew Smith.
HIGH SCHOOL: Miami Norland.
COLLEGE: Miami (Fla.) (degree in business management, 1991; master's degree in business administration, 1993).
TRANSACTIONS/CAREER NOTES: Selected by Dallas Cowboys in second round (54th pick overall) of 1993 NFL draft. ... On reserve/did not report list (July 20-October 14, 1995). ... Granted free agency (February 16, 1996). ... Re-signed by Cowboys (June 17, 1996). ... Granted unconditional free agency (February 14, 1997). ... Signed by Philadelphia Eagles (April 19, 1997). ... On injured reserve with ankle injury (November 19, 1997-remainder of season). ... Granted unconditional free agency (February 13, 1998). ... Signed by Seattle Seahawks (February 19, 1998). ... Released by Seahawks (February 10, 2000). ... Signed by New Orleans Saints (July 16, 2000). ... Granted unconditional free agency (March 2, 2001). ... Re-signed by Saints (April 10, 2001).
CHAMPIONSHIP GAME EXPERIENCE: Played in NFC championship game (1993 and 1995 seasons). ... Member of Super Bowl championship team (1993 and 1995 seasons).

Year Team	G	GS	TOTALS Tk.	Ast.	Sks.	INTERCEPTIONS No.	Yds.	Avg.	TD
1993—Dallas NFL	16	13	49	44	1.0	0	0	0.0	0
1994—Dallas NFL	16	16	46	21	4.0	2	13	6.5	1
1995—Dallas NFL	9	9	40	6	3.0	0	0	0.0	0
1996—Dallas NFL	16	16	54	27	1.0	0	0	0.0	0
1997—Philadelphia NFL	7	7	9	4	1.0	0	0	0.0	0
1998—Seattle NFL	13	12	59	21	5.0	3	56	18.7 ▲2
1999—Seattle NFL	15	15	65	25	1.0	1	0	0.0	0
2000—New Orleans NFL	16	11	61	30	2.0	2	56	28.0	1
2001—New Orleans NFL	16	16	49	17	1.5	0	0	0.0	0
2002—New Orleans NFL	15	15	63	33	3.5	2	21	10.5	0
Pro totals (10 years)	139	130	495	228	23.0	10	146	14.6	4

SMITH, DEREK — LB — 49ERS

PERSONAL: Born January 18, 1975, in American Fork, Utah. ... 6-2/245. ... Full name: Derek Mecham Smith.
HIGH SCHOOL: American Fork (Utah).
JUNIOR COLLEGE: Snow College (Utah).
COLLEGE: Arizona State.
TRANSACTIONS/CAREER NOTES: Selected by Washington Redskins in third round (80th pick overall) of 1997 NFL draft. ... Signed by Redskins (July 11, 1997). ... Granted free agency (February 11, 2000). ... Re-signed by Redskins (April 11, 2000). ... Granted unconditional free agency (March 2, 2001). ... Signed by San Francisco 49ers (March 23, 2001).

				TOTALS			INTERCEPTIONS			
Year Team	G	GS	Tk.	Ast.	Sks.	No.	Yds.	Avg.	TD
1997—Washington NFL	16	16	59	28	2.0	0	0	0.0	0
1998—Washington NFL	16	15	78	25	0.5	0	0	0.0	0
1999—Washington NFL	16	16	66	28	1.0	1	0	0.0	0
2000—Washington NFL	16	14	71	17	1.0	0	0	0.0	0
2001—San Francisco NFL	14	14	78	30	3.0	1	0	0.0	0
2002—San Francisco NFL	16	16	83	29	1.0	0	0	0.0	0
Pro totals (6 years)	**94**	**91**	**435**	**157**	**8.5**	**2**	**0**	**0.0**	**0**

SMITH, DETRON — FB — COLTS

S

PERSONAL: Born February 25, 1974, in Dallas. ... 5-10/229. ... Full name: Detron Negil Smith. ... Name pronounced DEE-tron.
HIGH SCHOOL: Lake Highlands (Dallas).
COLLEGE: Texas A&M.
TRANSACTIONS/CAREER NOTES: Selected by Denver Broncos in third round (65th pick overall) of 1996 NFL draft. ... Signed by Broncos (July 20, 1996). ... Released by Broncos (February 27, 2002). ... Signed by Jacksonville Jaguars (April 8, 2002). ... Released by Jaguars (September 1, 2002). ... Signed by Indianapolis Colts (September 3, 2002).
CHAMPIONSHIP GAME EXPERIENCE: Played in AFC championship game (1997 and 1998 seasons). ... Member of Super Bowl championship team (1997 and 1998 seasons).
HONORS: Played in Pro Bowl (1999 season).
SINGLE GAME HIGHS (regular season): Attempts—2 (December 21, 1997, vs. San Diego); yards—11 (December 21, 1997, vs. San Diego); and rushing touchdowns—0.

			RUSHING				TOTALS			
Year Team	G	GS	Att.	Yds.	Avg.	TD	TD	2pt.	Pts.	Fum.
1996—Denver NFL	13	0	0	0	0.0	0	0	0	0	0
1997—Denver NFL	16	0	4	10	2.5	0	1	0	6	0
1998—Denver NFL	15	2	0	0	0.0	0	0	0	0	0
1999—Denver NFL	16	0	1	7	7.0	0	0	0	0	0
2000—Denver NFL	16	0	0	0	0.0	0	1	0	6	0
2001—Denver NFL	15	0	0	0	0.0	0	0	0	0	0
2002—Indianapolis NFL	11	2	0	0	0.0	0	0	0	0	0
Pro totals (7 years)	**102**	**4**	**5**	**17**	**3.4**	**0**	**2**	**0**	**12**	**0**

SMITH, DWIGHT — CB — BUCCANEERS

PERSONAL: Born August 13, 1978, in Detroit. ... 5-10/201.
HIGH SCHOOL: Central (Detroit).
COLLEGE: Akron.
TRANSACTIONS/CAREER NOTES: Selected by Tampa Bay Buccaneers in third round (84th pick overall) of 2001 NFL draft. ... Signed by Buccaneers (July 17, 2001).
CHAMPIONSHIP GAME EXPERIENCE: Played in NFC championship game (2002 season). ... Member of Super Bowl championship team (2002 season).
HONORS: Named cornerback on THE SPORTING NEWS college All-America third team (2000).
POST SEASON RECORDS: Holds single-game Super Bowl record for most interceptions returned for touchdown—2 (January 26, 2003, vs. Tampa Bay Buccaneers). ... Shares NFL single-game record for most interceptions returned for touchdown—2 (January 26, 2003, vs. Tampa Bay Buccaneers).

			TOTALS			INTERCEPTIONS				KICKOFF RETURNS				TOTALS			
Year Team	G	GS	Tk.	Ast.	Sks.	No.	Yds.	Avg.	TD	No.	Yds.	Avg.	TD	TD	2pt.	Pts.	Fum.
2001—Tampa Bay NFL	15	0	4	1	0.0	0	0	0.0	0	16	355	22.2	0	0	0	0	2
2002—Tampa Bay NFL	16	2	24	2	0.0	4	39	9.8	0	4	93	23.3	0	0	0	0	1
Pro totals (2 years)	**31**	**2**	**28**	**3**	**0.0**	**4**	**39**	**9.8**	**0**	**20**	**448**	**22.4**	**0**	**0**	**0**	**0**	**3**

SMITH, EMMITT — RB — CARDINALS

PERSONAL: Born May 15, 1969, in Pensacola, Fla. ... 5-9/212. ... Full name: Emmitt J. Smith III.
HIGH SCHOOL: Escambia (Pensacola, Fla.).
COLLEGE: Florida (degree in public recreation, 1996).
TRANSACTIONS/CAREER NOTES: Selected after junior season by Dallas Cowboys in first round (17th pick overall) of 1990 NFL draft. ... Signed by Cowboys (September 4, 1990). ... Granted roster exemption (September 4-8, 1990). ... Granted free agency (March 1, 1993). ... Re-signed by Cowboys (September 16, 1993). ... Released by Cowboys (February 27, 2003). ... Signed by Arizona Cardinals (March 26, 2003).
CHAMPIONSHIP GAME EXPERIENCE: Played in NFC championship game (1992-1995 seasons). ... Member of Super Bowl championship team (1992, 1993 and 1995 seasons).
HONORS: Named running back on THE SPORTING NEWS college All-America first team (1989). ... Played in Pro Bowl (1990-1992, 1995, 1998 and 1999 seasons). ... Named running back on THE SPORTING NEWS NFL All-Pro team (1992-1995). ... Named NFL Player of the Year by THE SPORTING NEWS (1993). ... Named Most Valuable Player of Super Bowl XXVIII (1993 season). ... Named to play in Pro Bowl (1993 season); replaced by Rodney Hampton due to injury. ... Named Sportsman of the Year by THE SPORTING NEWS (1994). ... Named to play in Pro Bowl (1994 season); replaced by Ricky Watters due to injury.

RECORDS: Holds NFL career record for most rushing attempts—4,052; most yards rushing—17,162; most rushing touchdowns—153; most consecutive seasons with 1,000 or more yards rushing—11 (1991-2001); and most seasons with 1,000 or more yards rushing—11 (1991-2001). ... Holds NFL single-season record for most touchdowns—25 (1995).

POST SEASON RECORDS: Holds NFL postseason career record for most rushing touchdowns—19. ... Holds NFL postseason career record for most yards rushing—1,586. ... Shares NFL postseason career record for most games with 100 or more yards rushing—7. ... Holds Super Bowl career record for most rushing touchdowns—5.

SINGLE GAME HIGHS (regular season): Attempts—35 (November 7, 1994, vs. New York Giants); yards—237 (October 31, 1993, vs. Philadelphia); and touchdowns—4 (September 4, 1995, vs. New York Giants).

STATISTICAL PLATEAUS: 100-yard rushing games: 1990 (3), 1991 (8), 1992 (7), 1993 (7), 1994 (6), 1995 (11), 1996 (4), 1997 (2), 1998 (7), 1999 (9), 2000 (6), 2001 (4), 2002 (2). Total: 76. ... 100-yard receiving games: 1990 (1), 1993 (1). Total: 2.

MISCELLANEOUS: Active NFL leader for career rushing yards (17,162) and rushing touchdowns (153). ... Holds Dallas Cowboys all-time records for most yards rushing (17,162), most touchdowns (164) and most rushing touchdowns (153).

Year Team	G	GS	RUSHING				RECEIVING				TOTALS			
			Att.	Yds.	Avg.	TD	No.	Yds.	Avg.	TD	TD	2pt.	Pts.	Fum.
1990—Dallas NFL	16	15	241	937	3.9	11	24	228	9.5	0	11	0	66	7
1991—Dallas NFL	16	16	*365	*1563	4.3	12	49	258	5.3	1	13	0	78	8
1992—Dallas NFL	16	16	‡373	*1713	4.6	*18	59	335	5.7	1	*19	0	114	4
1993—Dallas NFL	14	13	283	*1486	*5.3	9	57	414	7.3	1	10	0	60	4
1994—Dallas NFL	15	15	*368	1484	4.0	*21	50	341	6.8	1	*22	0	132	1
1995—Dallas NFL	16	16	*377	*1773	4.7	*25	62	375	6.0	0	*25	0	*150	7
1996—Dallas NFL	15	15	327	1204	3.7	12	47	249	5.3	3	15	0	90	5
1997—Dallas NFL	16	16	261	1074	4.1	4	40	234	5.9	0	4	1	26	1
1998—Dallas NFL	16	16	319	1332	4.2	13	27	175	6.5	2	15	0	90	3
1999—Dallas NFL	15	15	‡329	1397	4.2	11	27	119	4.4	2	13	0	78	5
2000—Dallas NFL	16	16	294	1203	4.1	9	11	79	7.2	0	9	0	54	6
2001—Dallas NFL	14	14	261	1021	3.9	3	17	116	6.8	0	3	0	18	1
2002—Dallas NFL	16	16	254	975	3.8	5	16	89	5.6	0	5	0	30	3
Pro totals (13 years)	201	199	4052	17162	4.2	153	486	3012	6.2	11	164	1	986	55

SMITH, HUNTER   P   COLTS

PERSONAL: Born August 9, 1977, in Sherman, Texas. ... 6-2/204. ... Full name: Hunter Dwight Smith.
HIGH SCHOOL: Sherman (Texas).
COLLEGE: Notre Dame.
TRANSACTIONS/CAREER NOTES: Selected by Indianapolis Colts in seventh round (210th pick overall) of 1999 NFL draft. ... Signed by Colts (July 22, 1999). ... Granted free agency (March 1, 2002). ... Re-signed by Colts (May 21, 2002). ... Granted unconditional free agency (February 28, 2003). ... Re-signed by Colts (March 16, 2003).

Year Team	G	PUNTING					
		No.	Yds.	Avg.	Net avg.	In. 20	Blk.
1999—Indianapolis NFL	16	58	2467	42.5	30.6	16	†2
2000—Indianapolis NFL	16	65	2906	44.7	36.4	20	0
2001—Indianapolis NFL	16	68	3023	44.5	33.8	12	0
2002—Indianapolis NFL	16	66	2672	40.5	34.9	26	1
Pro totals (4 years)	64	257	11068	43.1	34.0	74	3

SMITH, JIMMY   WR   JAGUARS

PERSONAL: Born February 9, 1969, in Detroit. ... 6-1/213. ... Full name: Jimmy Lee Smith Jr.
HIGH SCHOOL: Callaway (Jackson, Miss.).
COLLEGE: Jackson State (degree in business management, 1992).
TRANSACTIONS/CAREER NOTES: Selected by Dallas Cowboys in second round (36th pick overall) of 1992 NFL draft. ... Signed by Cowboys (April 26, 1992). ... On injured reserve with fibula injury (September 2-October 7, 1992); on practice squad (September 28-October 7, 1992). ... On non-football injury list with appendicitis (September 2, 1993-entire season). ... Released by Cowboys (July 11, 1994). ... Signed by Philadelphia Eagles (July 19, 1994). ... Released by Eagles (August 29, 1994). ... Signed by Jacksonville Jaguars (February 28, 1995). ... Granted free agency (February 16, 1996). ... Re-signed by Jaguars (May 28, 1996). ... On reserve/did not report list (July 25-September 1, 2002).

CHAMPIONSHIP GAME EXPERIENCE: Played in NFC championship game (1992 season). ... Member of Super Bowl championship team (1992 season). ... Played in AFC championship game (1996 and 1999 seasons).

HONORS: Played in Pro Bowl (1997-2000 seasons). ... Named to play in Pro Bowl (2001 season); replaced by Hines Ward due to injury.

SINGLE GAME HIGHS (regular season): Receptions—15 (September 10, 2000, vs. Baltimore); yards—291 (September 10, 2000, vs. Baltimore); and touchdown receptions—3 (September 10, 2000, vs. Baltimore).

STATISTICAL PLATEAUS: 100-yard receiving games: 1996 (4), 1997 (6), 1998 (5), 1999 (9), 2000 (5), 2001 (6), 2002 (2). Total: 37.

MISCELLANEOUS: Holds Jacksonville Jaguars all-time record for most receptions (664), most yards receiving (9,287), most touchdowns (53) and most touchdown receptions (51).

Year Team	G	GS	RECEIVING				KICKOFF RETURNS				TOTALS			
			No.	Yds.	Avg.	TD	No.	Yds.	Avg.	TD	TD	2pt.	Pts.	Fum.
1992—Dallas NFL	7	0	0	0	0.0	0	0	0	0.0	0	0	0	0	0
1993—Dallas NFL							Did not play.							
1994—							Did not play.							
1995—Jacksonville NFL	16	4	22	288	13.1	3	24	540	22.5	1	5	0	30	2
1996—Jacksonville NFL	16	9	83	§1244	15.0	7	2	49	24.5	0	7	0	42	1
1997—Jacksonville NFL	16	16	82	1324	16.1	4	0	0	0.0	0	4	0	24	1
1998—Jacksonville NFL	16	15	78	1182	15.2	8	0	0	0.0	0	8	0	48	2
1999—Jacksonville NFL	16	16	*116	1636	14.1	6	0	0	0.0	0	6	†1	38	1
2000—Jacksonville NFL	15	14	91	1213	13.3	8	0	0	0.0	0	8	0	48	1
2001—Jacksonville NFL	16	16	112	1373	12.3	8	0	0	0.0	0	8	0	48	1
2002—Jacksonville NFL	16	16	80	1027	12.8	7	0	0	0.0	0	7	1	44	0
Pro totals (9 years)	134	106	664	9287	14.0	51	26	589	22.7	1	53	2	322	9

SMITH, JUSTIN — DE — BENGALS

PERSONAL: Born September 30, 1979, in Jefferson City, Mo. ... 6-4/270.
HIGH SCHOOL: Jefferson City (Mo.).
COLLEGE: Missouri.
TRANSACTIONS/CAREER NOTES: Selected after junior season by Cincinnati Bengals in first round (fourth pick overall) of 2001 NFL draft. ... Signed by Bengals (September 8, 2001).
HONORS: Named defensive end on THE SPORTING NEWS college All-America third team (2000).

			TOTALS			INTERCEPTIONS			
Year Team	G	GS	Tk.	Ast.	Sks.	No.	Yds.	Avg.	TD
2001—Cincinnati NFL	15	11	41	13	8.5	2	28	14.0	0
2002—Cincinnati NFL	16	16	48	13	6.5	0	0	0.0	0
Pro totals (2 years)	31	27	89	26	15.0	2	28	14.0	0

SMITH, KENNY — DT — SAINTS

PERSONAL: Born September 8, 1977, in Meridian, Miss. ... 6-4/295.
HIGH SCHOOL: Meridian (Miss.).
COLLEGE: Alabama.
TRANSACTIONS/CAREER NOTES: Selected by New Orleans Saints in third round (81st pick overall) of 2001 NFL draft. ... Signed by Saints (July 28, 2001).

			TOTALS		
Year Team	G	GS	Tk.	Ast.	Sks.
2001—New Orleans NFL	6	0	7	1	0.0
2002—New Orleans NFL	9	1	17	2	3.5
Pro totals (2 years)	15	1	24	3	3.5

SMITH, LAMAR — RB — PACKERS

PERSONAL: Born November 29, 1970, in Fort Wayne, Ind. ... 5-11/224.
HIGH SCHOOL: South Side (Fort Wayne, Ind.).
COLLEGE: Houston.
TRANSACTIONS/CAREER NOTES: Selected by Seattle Seahawks in third round (73rd pick overall) of 1994 NFL draft. ... Signed by Seahawks (July 19, 1994). ... On non-football injury list with back injury (December 14, 1994-remainder of season). ... Granted free agency (February 14, 1997). ... Re-signed by Seahawks (February 1997). ... Granted unconditional free agency (February 13, 1998). ... Signed by New Orleans Saints (February 28, 1998). ... Released by Saints (February 24, 2000). ... Signed by Miami Dolphins (March 15, 2000). ... Granted unconditional free agency (March 1, 2002). ... Signed by Carolina Panthers (March 25, 2002). ... On injured reserve with shoulder injury (December 18, 2002-remainder of season). ... Released by Panthers (March 5, 2003). ... Signed by Green Bay Packers (June 2, 2003).
SINGLE GAME HIGHS (regular season): Attempts—33 (November 17, 1996, vs. Detroit); yards—158 (January 6, 2002, vs. Buffalo); and rushing touchdowns—2 (September 29, 2002, vs. Green Bay).
STATISTICAL PLATEAUS: 100-yard rushing games: 1996 (1), 1998 (1), 2000 (4), 2001 (3), 2002 (1). Total: 10.

			RUSHING				RECEIVING				TOTALS			
Year Team	G	GS	Att.	Yds.	Avg.	TD	No.	Yds.	Avg.	TD	TD	2pt.	Pts.	Fum.
1994—Seattle NFL	2	0	2	-1	-0.5	0	0	0	0.0	0	0	0	0	0
1995—Seattle NFL	12	0	36	215	6.0	0	1	10	10.0	0	0	0	0	1
1996—Seattle NFL	16	2	153	680	4.4	8	9	58	6.4	0	8	*3	54	4
1997—Seattle NFL	12	2	91	392	4.3	2	23	183	8.0	0	2	1	14	0
1998—New Orleans NFL	14	9	138	457	3.3	1	24	249	10.4	2	3	0	18	4
1999—New Orleans NFL	13	2	60	205	3.4	0	20	151	7.6	1	1	0	6	1
2000—Miami NFL	15	15	309	1139	3.7	14	31	201	6.5	2	16	0	96	3
2001—Miami NFL	16	16	313	968	3.1	6	30	234	7.8	2	8	0	48	6
2002—Carolina NFL	11	11	209	737	3.5	7	20	167	8.4	0	7	0	42	2
Pro totals (9 years)	111	57	1311	4792	3.7	38	158	1253	7.9	7	45	4	278	21

SMITH, LARRY — DT — JAGUARS

PERSONAL: Born December 4, 1974, in Kingsland, Ga. ... 6-5/300. ... Full name: Larry Smith Jr.
HIGH SCHOOL: Charlton County (Folkston, Ga.), then Valley Forge (Pa.).
COLLEGE: Florida State.
TRANSACTIONS/CAREER NOTES: Selected after junior season by Jacksonville Jaguars in second round (56th pick overall) of 1999 NFL draft. ... Signed by Jaguars (April 26, 1999). ... Granted unconditional free agency (February 28, 2003). ... Re-signed by Jaguars (May 5, 2003).
CHAMPIONSHIP GAME EXPERIENCE: Played in AFC championship game (1999 season).

			TOTALS		
Year Team	G	GS	Tk.	Ast.	Sks.
1999—Jacksonville NFL	15	0	11	1	3.0
2000—Jacksonville NFL	14	4	15	5	0.0
2001—Jacksonville NFL	7	0	3	0	0.0
2002—Jacksonville NFL	15	3	15	3	1.0
Pro totals (4 years)	51	7	44	9	4.0

SMITH, MARK — DT

PERSONAL: Born August 28, 1974, in Vicksburg, Miss. ... 6-3/302. ... Full name: Mark Anthony Smith.

HIGH SCHOOL: Vicksburg (Miss.).
JUNIOR COLLEGE: Navarro College (Texas), then Hinds Community College (Miss.).
COLLEGE: Auburn.
TRANSACTIONS/CAREER NOTES: Selected by Arizona Cardinals in seventh round (212th pick overall) of 1997 NFL draft. ... Signed by Cardinals (May 5, 1997). ... On injured reserve with knee injury (November 1, 1999-remainder of season). ... Granted free agency (February 11, 2000). ... Re-signed by Cardinals (June 27, 2000). ... Granted unconditional free agency (March 2, 2001). ... Signed by Cleveland Browns (March 13, 2001). ... Granted unconditional free agency (March 1, 2002). ... Re-signed by Browns (March 20, 2002). ... Released by Browns (October 21, 2002).

Year Team	G	GS	Tk.	Ast.	Sks.
			TOTALS		
1997—Arizona NFL	16	4	26	12	6.0
1998—Arizona NFL	14	13	52	20	9.0
1999—Arizona NFL	2	0	4	0	0.0
2000—Arizona NFL	14	7	26	7	3.0
2001—Cleveland NFL	16	11	27	12	2.0
2002—Cleveland NFL	5	0	2	0	0.0
Pro totals (6 years)	67	35	137	51	20.0

SMITH, MARQUIS — DB — PANTHERS

PERSONAL: Born January 13, 1975, in San Diego. ... 6-2/213. ... Cousin of Akili Smith, quarterback, Cincinnati Bengals. ... Name pronounced mar-KEYS.
HIGH SCHOOL: Patrick Henry (San Diego).
COLLEGE: California.
TRANSACTIONS/CAREER NOTES: Selected by Cleveland Browns in third round (76th pick overall) of 1999 NFL draft. ... Signed by Browns (July 15, 1999). ... Granted free agency (March 1, 2002). ... Re-signed by Browns (April 20, 2002). ... Released by Browns (August 27, 2002). ... Signed by Carolina Panthers (March 24, 2003).

Year Team	G	GS	Tk.	Ast.	Sks.	No.	Yds.	Avg.	TD
			TOTALS			**INTERCEPTIONS**			
1999—Cleveland NFL	16	2	24	4	0.0	0	0	0.0	0
2000—Cleveland NFL	16	16	67	17	1.0	0	0	0.0	0
2001—Cleveland NFL	14	2	5	3	0.0	0	0	0.0	0
2002—					Did not play.				
Pro totals (3 years)	46	20	96	24	1.0	0	0	0.0	0

SMITH, MARVEL — OT — STEELERS

PERSONAL: Born August 6, 1978, in Oakland. ... 6-5/308. ... Full name: Marvel Amos Smith.
HIGH SCHOOL: Skyline (Oakland).
COLLEGE: Arizona State.
TRANSACTIONS/CAREER NOTES: Selected after junior season by Pittsburgh Steelers in second round (38th pick overall) of 2000 NFL draft. ... Signed by Steelers (July 16, 2000).
PLAYING EXPERIENCE: Pittsburgh NFL, 2000-2002. ... Games/Games started: 2000 (12/9), 2001 (16/16), 2002 (16/16). Total: 44/41.
CHAMPIONSHIP GAME EXPERIENCE: Played in AFC championship game (2001 season).
HONORS: Named offensive tackle on THE SPORTING NEWS college All-America third team (1999).

SMITH, MAURICE — RB

PERSONAL: Born September 7, 1976, in Palmyra, North Carolina. ... 6-0/235.
HIGH SCHOOL: S.E. Halifax (N.C.).
COLLEGE: North Carolina A & T.
TRANSACTIONS/CAREER NOTES: Signed as non-drafted free agent by Atlanta Falcons (April 17, 2000). ... Released by Falcons (August 31, 2002). ... Signed by Green Bay Packers (September 18, 2002). ... Released by Packers (September 24, 2002). ... Signed by Falcons (October 22, 2002). ... Released by Falcons (November 21, 2002). ... Signed by Packers (December 11, 2002). ... Released by Packers (December 22, 2002).
SINGLE GAME HIGHS (regular season): Attempts—27 (November 11, 2001, vs. Dallas); yards—148 (November 11, 2001, vs. Dallas); and rushing touchdowns—1 (December 30, 2001, vs. Miami).
STATISTICAL PLATEAUS: 100-yard rushing games: 2001 (1). ... 100-yard receiving games: 2001 (1).

Year Team	G	GS	Att.	Yds.	Avg.	TD	No.	Yds.	Avg.	TD	TD	2pt.	Pts.	Fum.
			RUSHING				**RECEIVING**				**TOTALS**			
2000—Atlanta NFL	11	0	19	69	3.6	0	1	5	5.0	0	0	0	0	0
2001—Atlanta NFL	16	12	237	760	3.2	5	19	230	12.1	1	6	0	36	1
2002—Atlanta NFL	2	0	0	0	0.0	0	0	0	0.0	0	0	0	0	0
—Green Bay NFL							Did not play.							
Pro totals (3 years)	29	12	256	829	3.2	5	20	235	11.8	1	6	0	36	1

SMITH, OMAR — OL — GIANTS

PERSONAL: Born September 8, 1977, in Spanish Town, Jamaica. ... 6-2/296. ... Full name: Omar Dave Smith.
HIGH SCHOOL: Nova (Davie, Fla.).
COLLEGE: Kentucky. (degree in social work).
TRANSACTIONS/CAREER NOTES: Signed as non-drafted free agent by St. Louis Rams (April 25, 2001). ... Released by Rams (August 27, 2001). ... Signed by New York Giants (January 15, 2002). ... Released by Giants (October 3, 2002). ... Re-signed by Giants to practice squad (October 7, 2002). ... Activated (October 31, 2002).
PLAYING EXPERIENCE: New York Giants NFL, 2002. ... Games/Games started: 2002 (7/0).

S

SMITH, OTIS · CB · PATRIOTS

PERSONAL: Born October 22, 1965, in New Orleans. ... 5-11/198. ... Full name: Otis Smith III.
HIGH SCHOOL: East Jefferson (Metairie, La.).
JUNIOR COLLEGE: Taft (Calif.) College.
COLLEGE: Missouri.
TRANSACTIONS/CAREER NOTES: Signed as non-drafted free agent by Philadelphia Eagles (April 25, 1990). ... On physically unable to perform list with appendectomy (August 2, 1990-entire season). ... Granted free agency (February 1, 1992). ... Re-signed by Eagles (August 11, 1992). ... Granted unconditional free agency (February 17, 1994). ... Re-signed by Eagles (April 25, 1994). ... Released by Eagles (March 22, 1995). ... Signed by New York Jets (April 13, 1995). ... Released by Jets (September 24, 1996). ... Signed by New England Patriots (October 9, 1996). ... Granted unconditional free agency (February 14, 1997). ... Re-signed by Jets (May 20, 1997). ... Granted unconditional free agency (February 13, 1998). ... Re-signed by Jets (April 9, 1998). ... On injured reserve with broken collarbone (October 5, 1999-remainder of season). ... Released by Jets (August 20, 2000). ... Signed by Patriots (August 23, 2000). ... On injured reserve with shoulder injury (December 19, 2002-remainder of season).
CHAMPIONSHIP GAME EXPERIENCE: Played in AFC championship game (1996, 1998 and 2001 seasons). ... Played in Super Bowl XXXI (1996 season). ... Member of Super Bowl championship team (2001 season).

Year Team	G	GS	TOTALS Tk.	Ast.	Sks.	INTERCEPTIONS No.	Yds.	Avg.	TD
1990—Philadelphia NFL			Did not play.						
1991—Philadelphia NFL	15	1	7	3	0.0	2	74	37.0	∞1
1992—Philadelphia NFL	16	1	16	8	0.0	1	0	0.0	0
1993—Philadelphia NFL	15	0	3	2	0.0	1	0	0.0	0
1994—Philadelphia NFL	16	2	19	1	1.0	0	0	0.0	0
1995—New York Jets NFL	11	10	34	7	0.0	6	101	16.8	▲1
1996—New York Jets NFL	2	0	0	0	0.0	0	0	0.0	0
—New England NFL	11	6	26	5	1.0	2	20	10.0	0
1997—New York Jets NFL	16	16	57	13	0.0	6	158	26.3	†3
1998—New York Jets NFL	16	16	57	13	0.0	2	34	17.0	0
1999—New York Jets NFL	1	1	3	0	0.0	0	0	0.0	0
2000—New England NFL	16	14	59	10	0.0	1	56	56.0	0
2001—New England NFL	15	15	50	7	2.0	5	181	36.2	†2
2002—New England NFL	14	13	44	7	0.0	2	21	10.5	0
Pro totals (12 years)	164	95	375	76	4.0	28	645	23.0	7

SMITH, PAUL · RB · 49ERS

PERSONAL: Born January 31, 1978, in El Paso, Texas. ... 5-11/234.
HIGH SCHOOL: Andress (El Paso, Texas).
COLLEGE: Texas-El Paso.
TRANSACTIONS/CAREER NOTES: Selected by San Francisco 49ers in fifth round (132nd pick overall) of 2000 NFL draft. ... Signed by 49ers (July 21, 2000).
SINGLE GAME HIGHS (regular season): Attempts—13 (December 8, 2002, vs. Dallas); yards—40 (December 8, 2002, vs. Dallas); and rushing touchdowns—1 (December 2, 2001, vs. Buffalo).

Year Team	G	GS	RUSHING Att.	Yds.	Avg.	TD	RECEIVING No.	Yds.	Avg.	TD	KICKOFF RETURNS No.	Yds.	Avg.	TD	TOTALS TD	2pt.	Pts.	Fum.
2000—San Francisco NFL	10	0	18	72	4.0	0	2	55	27.5	0	9	167	18.6	0	0	0	0	2
2001—San Francisco NFL	15	0	4	27	6.8	1	0	0	0.0	0	3	37	12.3	0	1	0	6	1
2002—San Francisco NFL	11	0	18	90	5.0	0	5	33	6.6	0	7	107	15.3	0	0	0	0	0
Pro totals (3 years)	36	0	40	189	4.7	1	7	88	12.6	0	19	311	16.4	0	1	0	6	3

SMITH, ROBAIRE · DE/DT · TITANS

PERSONAL: Born November 15, 1977, in Flint, Mich. ... 6-4/280. ... Full name: Robaire Freddick Smith. ... Brother of Fernando Smith, defensive end, with four NFL teams (1994-2000).
HIGH SCHOOL: Flint (Mich.).
COLLEGE: Michigan State.
TRANSACTIONS/CAREER NOTES: Selected by Tennessee Titans in sixth round (197th pick overall) of 2000 NFL draft. ... Signed by Titans (July 5, 2000). ... Granted free agency (February 28, 2003). ... Re-signed by Titans (May 9, 2003).
CHAMPIONSHIP GAME EXPERIENCE: Played in AFC championship game (2002 season).
HONORS: Named defensive end on THE SPORTING NEWS college All-America second team (1999).

Year Team	G	GS	TOTALS Tk.	Ast.	Sks.
2000—Tennessee NFL	7	0	5	1	2.5
2001—Tennessee NFL	10	0	5	2	2.0
2002—Tennessee NFL	16	2	25	9	2.5
Pro totals (3 years)	33	2	35	12	7.0

SMITH, ROD · WR · BRONCOS

PERSONAL: Born May 15, 1970, in Texarkana, Ark. ... 6-0/200.
HIGH SCHOOL: Texarkana (Ark.).
COLLEGE: Missouri Southern.
TRANSACTIONS/CAREER NOTES: Signed as non-drafted free agent by Denver Broncos (March 23, 1995).
CHAMPIONSHIP GAME EXPERIENCE: Played in AFC championship game (1997 and 1998 seasons). ... Member of Super Bowl championship team (1997 and 1998 seasons).
HONORS: Played in Pro Bowl (2000 season). ... Named to play in Pro Bowl (2001 season); replaced by Troy Brown due to injury.

SINGLE GAME HIGHS (regular season): Receptions—14 (September 23, 2001, vs. Arizona); yards—187 (November 19, 2000, vs. San Diego); and touchdown receptions—3 (October 15, 2000, vs. Cleveland).
STATISTICAL PLATEAUS: 100-yard receiving games: 1997 (6), 1998 (4), 1999 (3), 2000 (8), 2001 (5). Total: 26.
MISCELLANEOUS: Holds Denver Broncos all-time records for most yards receiving (7,783) and most touchdown receptions (49).

			RUSHING				RECEIVING				PUNT RETURNS				KICKOFF RETURNS				TOTALS		
Year Team	G	GS	Att.	Yds.	Avg.	TD	No.	Yds.	Avg.	TD	No.	Yds.	Avg.	TD	No.	Yds.	Avg.	TD	TD	2pt.	Pts.
1995—Denver NFL	16	1	0	0	0.0	0	6	152	25.3	1	0	0	0.0	0	4	54	13.5	0	1	0	6
1996—Denver NFL	10	1	1	1	1.0	0	16	237	14.8	2	23	283	12.3	0	1	29	29.0	0	2	0	12
1997—Denver NFL	16	16	5	16	3.2	0	70	1180	16.9▲12		1	12	12.0	0	0	0	0.0	0	12	0	72
1998—Denver NFL	16	16	6	63	10.5	0	86	1222	14.2	6	0	0	0.0	0	0	0	0.0	0	7	0	42
1999—Denver NFL	15	15	0	0	0.0	0	79	1020	12.9	4	0	0	0.0	0	1	10	10.0	0	4	0	24
2000—Denver NFL	16	16	6	99	16.5	1	100	§1602	16.0	8	0	0	0.0	0	0	0	0.0	0	9	0	54
2001—Denver NFL	15	14	3	27	9.0	0	*113	1343	11.9	11	0	0	0.0	0	0	0	0.0	0	11	1	68
2002—Denver NFL	16	16	6	9	1.5	0	89	1027	11.5	5	0	0	0.0	0	0	0	0.0	0	5	0	30
Pro totals (8 years)	120	95	27	215	8.0	1	559	7783	13.9	49	24	295	12.3	0	6	93	15.5	0	51	1	308

SMITH, RON — DT — BENGALS

PERSONAL: Born August 18, 1978, in St. Louis. ... 6-3/310.
HIGH SCHOOL: Gateway Tech (St. Louis).
COLLEGE: Baylor, then Lane College.
TRANSACTIONS/CAREER NOTES: Signed as non-drafted free agent by Seattle Seahawks (January 17, 2002). ... Claimed on waivers by Cincinnati Bengals (August 27, 2002). ... Released by Bengals (September 1, 2002). ... Re-signed by Bengals to practice squad (September 2, 2002). ... Activated (November 14, 2002).

			TOTALS		
Year Team	G	GS	Tk.	Ast.	Sks.
2002—Cincinnati NFL	5	0	0	0	0.0

SMITH, STEVE — WR — PANTHERS

PERSONAL: Born May 12, 1979, in Lynwood, Calif. ... 5-9/179. ... Full name: Stevonne Smith.
HIGH SCHOOL: University (Los Angeles).
JUNIOR COLLEGE: Santa Monica Junior College.
COLLEGE: Utah.
TRANSACTIONS/CAREER NOTES: Selected by Carolina Panthers in third round (74th pick overall) of 2001 NFL draft. ... Signed by Panthers (June 19, 2001). ... On suspended list (November 20-25, 2002).
HONORS: Named kick returner on THE SPORTING NEWS NFL All-Pro team (2001). ... Played in Pro Bowl (2001 season).
RECORDS: Shares NFL single-game records for most touchdowns by punt returns—2; and most touchdowns by combined kick return—2 (December 8, 2002, vs. Cincinnati).
SINGLE GAME HIGHS (regular season): Receptions—5 (December 15, 2002, vs. Pittsburgh); yards—144 (December 8, 2002, vs. Cincinnati); and touchdown receptions—1 (December 8, 2002, vs. Cincinnati).
STATISTICAL PLATEAUS: 100-yard receiving games: 2002 (2).

			RECEIVING				PUNT RETURNS				KICKOFF RETURNS				TOTALS			
Year Team	G	GS	No.	Yds.	Avg.	TD	No.	Yds.	Avg.	TD	No.	Yds.	Avg.	TD	TD	2pt.	Pts.	Fum.
2001—Carolina NFL	15	1	10	154	15.4	0	34	364	10.7	†1	56	1431	‡25.6	†2	3	0	18	8
2002—Carolina NFL	15	13	54	872	16.1	3	*55	470	8.5	†2	26	571	22.0	0	5	0	30	5
Pro totals (2 years)	30	14	64	1026	16.0	3	89	834	9.4	3	82	2002	24.4	2	8	0	48	13

SMITH, STEVE — CB

PERSONAL: Born June 28, 1979, in Torrance, Calif. ... 6-1/190. ... Full name: Steven Michael Smith.
HIGH SCHOOL: San Pedro (Calif.).
COLLEGE: Oregon.
TRANSACTIONS/CAREER NOTES: Selected by Jacksonville Jaguars in seventh round (246th pick overall) of 2002 NFL draft. ... Signed by Jaguars (July 17, 2002). ... Released by Jaguars (September 1, 2002). ... Re-signed by Jaguars to practice squad (September 3, 2002). ... Activated (December 4, 2002). ... Re-signed by Jaguars (March 27, 2003). ... Released by Jaguars (May 19, 2003).

			TOTALS			INTERCEPTIONS			
Year Team	G	GS	Tk.	Ast.	Sks.	No.	Yds.	Avg.	TD
2002—Jacksonville NFL	4	0	0	0	0.0	0	0	0.0	0

SMITH, TERRELLE — FB — SAINTS

PERSONAL: Born March 12, 1978, in West Covina, Calif. ... 6-0/246. ... Full name: Terrelle Vernon Smith.
HIGH SCHOOL: Canyon Springs (Moreno Valley, Calif.).
COLLEGE: Arizona State.
TRANSACTIONS/CAREER NOTES: Selected by New Orleans Saints in fourth round (96th pick overall) of 2000 NFL draft. ... Signed by Saints (July 11, 2000). ... Granted free agency (February 28, 2003). ... Re-signed by Saints (April 22, 2003).
SINGLE GAME HIGHS (regular season): Attempts—6 (December 10, 2000, vs. San Francisco); yards—42 (November 19, 2000, vs. Oakland); and rushing touchdowns—0.

			RUSHING				RECEIVING				TOTALS			
Year Team	G	GS	Att.	Yds.	Avg.	TD	No.	Yds.	Avg.	TD	TD	2pt.	Pts.	Fum.
2000—New Orleans NFL	14	9	29	131	4.5	0	12	65	5.4	0	0	0	0	1
2001—New Orleans NFL	14	9	5	8	1.6	0	4	30	7.5	2	2	0	12	1
2002—New Orleans NFL	16	9	5	11	2.2	0	9	30	3.3	0	0	0	0	1
Pro totals (3 years)	44	27	39	150	3.8	0	25	125	5.0	2	2	0	12	3

S

SMITH, TRAVIAN   LB   RAIDERS

PERSONAL: Born August 26, 1975, in Good Shepard, Texas. ... 6-4/240.
HIGH SCHOOL: Tatum (Texas).
COLLEGE: Oklahoma.
TRANSACTIONS/CAREER NOTES: Selected by Oakland Raiders in fifth round (152nd pick overall) of 1998 NFL draft. ... Signed by Raiders (July 6, 1998). ... Released by Raiders (August 26, 1998). ... Re-signed by Raiders to practice squad (August 31, 1998). ... Activated (December 15, 1998).
CHAMPIONSHIP GAME EXPERIENCE: Played in AFC championship game (2000 and 2002 seasons). ... Played in Super Bowl XXXVII (2002 season).

			TOTALS			INTERCEPTIONS			
Year Team	G	GS	Tk.	Ast.	Sks.	No.	Yds.	Avg.	TD
1998—Oakland NFL	2	0	0	0	0.0	0	0	0.0	0
1999—Oakland NFL	16	1	6	1	0.0	0	0	0.0	0
2000—Oakland NFL	16	0	2	0	0.0	0	0	0.0	0
2001—Oakland NFL	16	2	14	11	2.5	1	9	9.0	0
2002—Oakland NFL	16	2	23	7	5.0	0	0	0.0	0
Pro totals (5 years)	66	5	45	19	7.5	1	9	9.0	0

SMOOT, FRED   CB   REDSKINS

PERSONAL: Born April 17, 1979, in Jackson, Miss. ... 5-11/168. ... Full name: Fredrick D. Smoot.
HIGH SCHOOL: Provine (Jackson, Miss.).
JUNIOR COLLEGE: Hinds Community College (Miss.).
COLLEGE: Mississippi State.
TRANSACTIONS/CAREER NOTES: Selected by Washington Redskins in second round (45th pick overall) of 2001 NFL draft. ... Signed by Redskins (July 31, 2001).
HONORS: Named cornerback on THE SPORTING NEWS college All-America first team (2000).

			TOTALS			INTERCEPTIONS			
Year Team	G	GS	Tk.	Ast.	Sks.	No.	Yds.	Avg.	TD
2001—Washington NFL	14	13	30	3	0.0	5	36	7.2	0
2002—Washington NFL	16	16	49	12	0.0	4	12	3.0	0
Pro totals (2 years)	30	29	79	15	0.0	9	48	5.3	0

SNOW, JUSTIN   TE   COLTS

PERSONAL: Born December 21, 1976, in Ft. Worth, Texas. ... 6-3/232.
HIGH SCHOOL: Cooper (Abilene, Texas.).
COLLEGE: Baylor.
TRANSACTIONS/CAREER NOTES: Signed as non-drafted free agent by Indianapolis Colts (April 20, 2000).

			RECEIVING			
Year Team	G	GS	No.	Yds.	Avg.	TD
2000—Indianapolis NFL	16	0	0	0	0.0	0
2001—Indianapolis NFL	16	0	0	0	0.0	0
2002—Indianapolis NFL	16	0	0	0	0.0	0
Pro totals (3 years)	48	0	0	0	0.0	0

SOLIDAY, JAKE   WR   CARDINALS

PERSONAL: Born November 16, 1978, in Mansfield, Ohio. ... 6-1/195.
HIGH SCHOOL: Mansfield (Ohio).
COLLEGE: Northern Iowa.
TRANSACTIONS/CAREER NOTES: Signed as non-drafted free agent by Arizona Cardinals (April 22, 2002). ... Released by Cardinals (August 27, 2002). ... Re-signed by Cardinals to practice squad (September 2, 2002). ... Activated (October 30, 2002).
SINGLE GAME HIGHS (regular season): Receptions—2 (November 17, 2002, vs. Philadelphia); yards—20 (November 17, 2002, vs. Philadelphia); and touchdown receptions—0.

			RECEIVING			
Year Team	G	GS	No.	Yds.	Avg.	TD
2002—Arizona NFL	4	0	4	39	9.8	0

SOLWOLD, MIKE   C

PERSONAL: Born September 30, 1977, in Hartland, Wis. ... 6-6/244.
HIGH SCHOOL: Arrowhead (Wis.).
COLLEGE: Wisconsin.
TRANSACTIONS/CAREER NOTES: Signed as non-drafted free agent by Minnesota Vikings (April 22, 2001). ... Claimed on waivers by Dallas Cowboys (August 28, 2001). ... Released by Cowboys (September 3, 2001). ... Re-signed by Cowboys (November 14, 2001). ... Released by Cowboys (April 18, 2002). ... Signed by Tampa Bay Buccaneers (May 1, 2002). ... On injured reserve with foot injury (October 1, 2002-remainder of season). ... Granted free agency (February 28, 2003).
PLAYING EXPERIENCE: Dallas NFL, 2001; Tampa Bay NFL, 2002. ... Games/Games started: 2001 (8/0), 2002 (4/0).Total: 12/0.

SORENSEN, NICK — S — RAMS

PERSONAL: Born July 31, 1978, in Winter Haven, Fla. ... 6-2/205. ... Full name: Nicholas Carl Sorensen.
HIGH SCHOOL: George C. Marshall (Vienna, Va.).
COLLEGE: Virginia Tech.
TRANSACTIONS/CAREER NOTES: Signed as non-drafted free agent by Miami Dolphins (April 26, 2001). ... Released by Dolphins (August 26, 2001). ... Signed by St. Louis Rams to practice squad (October 16, 2001). ... Activated (November 16, 2001). ... Released by Rams (November 24, 2001). ... Re-signed by Rams (November 27, 2001).
CHAMPIONSHIP GAME EXPERIENCE: Played in NFC championship game (2001 season). ... Played in Super Bowl XXXVI (2001 season).

			TOTALS			INTERCEPTIONS			
Year Team	G	GS	Tk.	Ast.	Sks.	No.	Yds.	Avg.	TD
2001—St. Louis NFL	7	0	1	0	0.0	0	0	0.0	0
2002—St. Louis NFL	16	0	1	0	0.0	0	0	0.0	0
Pro totals (2 years)	23	0	2	0	0.0	0	0	0.0	0

SOWELL, JERALD — FB — JETS

PERSONAL: Born January 21, 1974, in Baton Rouge, La. ... 6-0/237. ... Full name: Jerald Monye Sowell.
HIGH SCHOOL: Baker (La.).
COLLEGE: Tulane (degree in exercise science/kinesiology).
TRANSACTIONS/CAREER NOTES: Selected by Green Bay Packers in seventh round (231st pick overall) of 1997 NFL draft. ... Signed by Packers (July 10, 1997). ... Claimed on waivers by New York Jets (August 25, 1997). ... Granted free agency (February 11, 2000). ... Re-signed by Jets (April 25, 2000). ... Granted unconditional free agency (February 28, 2003). ... Re-signed by Jets (March 3, 2003).
CHAMPIONSHIP GAME EXPERIENCE: Member of Jets for AFC championship game (1998 season); inactive.
SINGLE GAME HIGHS (regular season): Attempts—14 (November 8, 1998, vs. Buffalo); yards—82 (September 20, 1998, vs. Indianapolis); and rushing touchdowns—0.

			RUSHING				RECEIVING				TOTALS			
Year Team	G	GS	Att.	Yds.	Avg.	TD	No.	Yds.	Avg.	TD	TD	2pt.	Pts.	Fum.
1997—New York Jets NFL	9	0	7	35	5.0	0	1	8	8.0	0	0	0	0	0
1998—New York Jets NFL	16	2	40	164	4.1	0	10	59	5.9	0	0	0	0	2
1999—New York Jets NFL	16	0	3	5	1.7	0	0	0	0.0	0	0	0	0	0
2000—New York Jets NFL	16	0	2	0	0.0	0	6	84	14.0	0	0	0	0	0
2001—New York Jets NFL	16	0	4	9	2.3	0	1	19	19.0	0	0	0	0	0
2002—New York Jets NFL	16	0	1	0	0.0	0	9	85	9.4	1	1	0	6	0
Pro totals (6 years)	89	2	57	213	3.7	0	27	255	9.4	1	1	0	6	2

SPEARMAN, ARMEGIS — LB — BENGALS

PERSONAL: Born April 5, 1978, in Bruce, Miss. ... 6-1/251.
HIGH SCHOOL: Bruce (Miss.).
COLLEGE: Mississippi.
TRANSACTIONS/CAREER NOTES: Signed as non-drafted free agent by Cincinnati Bengals (April 27, 2000). ... On injured reserve with torn pectoral muscle (September 2, 2001-remainder of season). ... On injured reserve with ankle injury (November 1, 2002-remainder of season). ... Granted free agency (February 28, 2003). ... Tendered offer sheet by Green Bay Packers (March 10, 2003). ... Offer matched by Bengals (March 17, 2003).

			TOTALS			INTERCEPTIONS			
Year Team	G	GS	Tk.	Ast.	Sks.	No.	Yds.	Avg.	TD
2000—Cincinnati NFL	15	11	46	24	1.0	0	0	0.0	0
2002—Cincinnati NFL	7	0	0	0	0.0	0	0	0.0	0
Pro totals (2 years)	22	11	46	24	1.0	0	0	0.0	0

SPEARS, MARCUS — G/OT — CHIEFS

PERSONAL: Born September 28, 1971, in Baton Rouge, La. ... 6-4/320. ... Full name: Marcus DeWayne Spears.
HIGH SCHOOL: Belaire (Baton Rouge, La.).
COLLEGE: Northwestern State (La.).
TRANSACTIONS/CAREER NOTES: Selected by Chicago Bears in second round (39th pick overall) of 1994 NFL draft. ... Signed by Bears (July 16, 1994). ... Inactive for all 16 games (1994). ... Active for five games (1995); did not play. ... Assigned by Bears to Amsterdam Admirals in 1996 World League enhancement allocation program (February 19, 1996). ... Granted unconditional free agency (February 14, 1997). ... Signed by Green Bay Packers (March 12, 1997). ... Released by Packers (August 19, 1997). ... Signed by Kansas City Chiefs (September 16, 1997). ... On injured reserve with hand injury (December 9, 1998-remainder of season). ... Granted unconditional free agency (February 12, 1999). ... Re-signed by Chiefs (February 16, 1999). ... On injured reserve with arm injury (December 15, 2000-remainder of season). ... Granted unconditional free agency (March 1, 2002). ... Re-signed by Chiefs (May 6, 2002).
PLAYING EXPERIENCE: Amsterdam W.L., 1996; Chicago NFL, 1996; Kansas City NFL, 1997-2002. ... Games/Games started: W.L. 1996 (games played unavailable), NFL 1996 (9/0), 1997 (3/0), 1998 (12/0), 1999 (10/2), 2000 (13/0), 2001 (16/16), 2002 (9/0). Total NFL: 72/18.
HONORS: Named offensive lineman on THE SPORTING NEWS college All-America second team (1993).

SPENCER, JIMMY — CB — BRONCOS

PERSONAL: Born March 29, 1969, in Manning, S.C. ... 5-9/188. ... Full name: James Arthur Spencer Jr.
HIGH SCHOOL: Glades Central (Belle Glade, Fla.).
COLLEGE: Florida.
TRANSACTIONS/CAREER NOTES: Selected by Washington Redskins in eighth round (215th pick overall) of 1991 NFL draft. ... Signed by Redskins for 1991 season. ... Released by Redskins (August 26, 1991). ... Signed by New Orleans Saints (April 2, 1992). ... Granted unconditional free agency (February 16, 1996). ... Signed by Cincinnati Bengals (March 21, 1996). ... Released by Bengals (August 25, 1998). ...

Signed by San Diego Chargers (September 1, 1998). ... Granted unconditional free agency (February 12, 1999). ... Re-signed by Chargers (April 7, 1999). ... On injured reserve with broken arm (December 20, 1999-remainder of season). ... Released by Chargers (February 10, 2000). ... Signed by Denver Broncos (March 6, 2000). ... Released by Broncos (February 25, 2003). ... Re-signed by Broncos (February 26, 2003).

				TOTALS			INTERCEPTIONS			
Year Team	G	GS	Tk.	Ast.	Sks.	No.	Yds.	Avg.	TD
1992—New Orleans NFL	16	4	37	6	0.0	0	0	0.0	0
1993—New Orleans NFL	16	3	15	5	0.0	0	0	0.0	0
1994—New Orleans NFL	16	16	56	7	0.0	5	24	4.8	0
1995—New Orleans NFL	16	15	59	7	0.0	4	11	2.8	0
1996—Cincinnati NFL	15	14	55	8	0.0	5	48	9.6	0
1997—Cincinnati NFL	16	9	36	2	0.0	1	-2	-2.0	0
1998—San Diego NFL	15	4	29	0	0.0	1	0	0.0	0
1999—San Diego NFL	14	7	40	8	0.0	4	1	0.3	0
2000—Denver NFL	16	6	37	3	1.0	3	102	34.0	2
2001—Denver NFL	16	1	27	1	0.0	3	25	8.3	0
2002—Denver NFL	5	0	4	0	0.0	0	0	0.0	0
Pro totals (11 years)	161	79	395	47	1.0	26	209	8.0	2

SPICER, PAUL   DE   JAGUARS

PERSONAL: Born August 18, 1975, in Indianapolis. ... 6-4/292.
HIGH SCHOOL: Northwestern (Indianapolis).
COLLEGE: College of DuPage (III.), then Saginaw Valley State (Mich.).
TRANSACTIONS/CAREER NOTES: Signed as non-drafted free agent by Seattle Seahawks (April 20, 1998). ... Released by Seahawks (August 24, 1998). ... Signed by Sasketchewan Roughriders of CFL (September 26, 1998). ... Signed by Detroit Lions (February 24, 1999). ... Released by Lions (September 5, 1999). ... Re-signed by Lions to practice squad (September 7, 1999). ... Activated (October 8, 1999). ... Released by Lions (November 6, 1999). ... Re-signed by Lions to practice squad (November 10, 1999). ... Released by Lions (August 22, 2000). ... Signed by Jacksonville Jaguars to practice squad (August 30, 2000). ... Activated (October 4, 2000). ... Assigned by Jaguars to Frankfurt Galaxy in 2001 NFL Europe enhancement allocation program (February 19, 2001). ... Granted free agency (February 28, 2003). ... Re-signed by Jaguars (April 23, 2003).

			TOTALS		
Year Team	G	GS	Tk.	Ast.	Sks.
1998—Saskatchewan CFL	7	...	...	...	4.0
1999—Detroit NFL	2	0	0	0	0.0
2000—Jacksonville NFL	3	0	4	1	1.0
2001—Frankfurt NFLE	...	...	...	...	3.5
—Jacksonville NFL	16	4	23	5	2.0
2002—Jacksonville NFL	16	4	35	2	4.0
NFL Europe totals (1 year)	...	...	...	...	3.5
CFL totals (1 year)	7	...	...	...	4.0
NFL totals (4 years)	37	8	62	8	7.0
Pro totals (6 years)	...	...	...	...	14.5

SPIKES, CAMERON   G   CARDINALS

PERSONAL: Born November 6, 1976, in Madisonville, Texas. ... 6-2/323. ... Full name: Cameron Wade Spikes.
HIGH SCHOOL: Bryan (Texas).
COLLEGE: Texas A&M.
TRANSACTIONS/CAREER NOTES: Selected by St. Louis Rams in fifth round (145th pick overall) of 1999 NFL draft. ... Signed by Rams (July 19, 1999). ... Granted free agency (March 1, 2002). ... Re-signed by Rams (April 17, 2002). ... Claimed on waivers by Houston Texans (August 26, 2002). ... Granted unconditional free agency (February 28, 2003). ... Signed by Arizona Cardinals (March 28, 2003).
PLAYING EXPERIENCE: St. Louis NFL, 1999-2001; Houston NFL, 2002. ... Games/Games started: 1999 (5/0), 2000 (9/0), 2001 (5/0), 2002 (12/5). Total:31/5.
CHAMPIONSHIP GAME EXPERIENCE: Member of Rams for NFC championship game (1999 and 2001 seasons); inactive. ... Member of Super Bowl championship team (1999 season); inactive. ... Played in Super Bowl XXXVI (2001 season).

SPIKES, TAKEO   LB   BILLS

PERSONAL: Born December 17, 1976, in Sandersville, Ga. ... 6-2/245. ... Full name: Takeo Gerard Spikes. ... Name pronounced tuh-KEE-oh.
HIGH SCHOOL: Washington County (Sandersville, Ga.).
COLLEGE: Auburn.
TRANSACTIONS/CAREER NOTES: Selected after junior season by Cincinnati Bengals in first round (13th pick overall) of 1998 NFL draft. ... Signed by Bengals (July 25, 1998). ... Designated by Bengals as transition player (February 20, 2003). ... Tendered offer sheet by Buffalo Bills (March 10, 2003). ... Bengals declined to match offer (March 11, 2003).
HONORS: Named inside linebacker on THE SPORTING NEWS college All-America first team (1997).

			TOTALS			INTERCEPTIONS			
Year Team	G	GS	Tk.	Ast.	Sks.	No.	Yds.	Avg.	TD
1998—Cincinnati NFL	16	16	95	17	2.0	0	0	0.0	0
1999—Cincinnati NFL	16	16	82	23	3.0	2	7	3.5	0
2000—Cincinnati NFL	16	16	109	19	2.0	2	12	6.0	0
2001—Cincinnati NFL	15	15	80	29	6.0	1	66	66.0	1
2002—Cincinnati NFL	16	16	81	32	1.5	0	0	0.0	0
Pro totals (5 years)	79	79	447	120	14.5	5	85	17.0	1

SPIRES, GREG   DE   BUCCANEERS

PERSONAL: Born August 12, 1974, in Mariana, Fla. ... 6-1/265. ... Full name: Greg Tyrone Spires.
HIGH SCHOOL: Mariner (Cape Coral, Fla.).
COLLEGE: Florida State.
TRANSACTIONS/CAREER NOTES: Selected by New England Patriots in third round (83rd pick overall) of 1998 NFL draft. ... Signed by Patriots (July 16, 1998). ... On injured reserve with knee injury (December 15, 1999-remainder of season). ... Granted free agency (March 2, 2001). ... Re-signed by Patriots (April 30, 2001). ... Claimed on waivers by Cleveland Browns (September 4, 2001). ... Granted unconditional free agency (March 1, 2002). ... Signed by Tampa Bay Buccaneers (March 22, 2002).
CHAMPIONSHIP GAME EXPERIENCE: Played in NFC championship game (2002 season). ... Member of Super Bowl championship team (2002 season).

				TOTALS	
Year Team	G	GS	Tk.	Ast.	Sks.
1998—New England NFL	15	1	18	6	3.0
1999—New England NFL	11	1	6	1	0.5
2000—New England NFL	16	2	12	5	6.0
2001—Cleveland NFL	16	4	23	8	4.0
2002—Tampa Bay NFL	16	16	27	10	3.5
Pro totals (5 years)	74	24	86	30	17.0

SPRAGAN, DONNIE   LB   BRONCOS

PERSONAL: Born July 12, 1976, in Oakland. ... 6-3/239.
HIGH SCHOOL: Logan (Union City, Calif.).
COLLEGE: Pacific, then Stanford.
TRANSACTIONS/CAREER NOTES: Signed as non-drafted free agent by New Orleans Saints (April 23, 1999). ... On injured reserve with knee injury (September 6, 1999-entire season). ... Released by Saints (August 22, 2000). ... Signed by Green Bay Packers (July 19, 2001). ... Released by Packers (September 1, 2001). ... Signed by Cleveland Browns to practice squad (October 2, 2001). ... Released by Browns (October 31, 2001). ... Signed by Denver Broncos to practice squad (December 11, 2001).

			TOTALS			INTERCEPTIONS			
Year Team	G	GS	Tk.	Ast.	Sks.	No.	Yds.	Avg.	TD
2002—Denver NFL	16	0	0	0	0.0	0	0	0.0	0

SPRIGGS, MARCUS   OT   PACKERS

PERSONAL: Born May 30, 1974, in Hattiesburg, Miss. ... 6-4/310. ... Full name: Thomas Marcus Spriggs.
HIGH SCHOOL: Byram (Jackson, Miss.).
JUNIOR COLLEGE: Hinds Community College (Miss.).
COLLEGE: Houston.
TRANSACTIONS/CAREER NOTES: Selected by Buffalo Bills in sixth round (185th pick overall) of 1997 NFL draft. ... Signed by Bills (June 13, 1997). ... Granted free agency (February 11, 2000). ... Re-signed by Bills (April 10, 2000). ... Granted unconditional free agency (March 2, 2001). ... Signed by Miami Dolphins (April 19, 2001). ... On injured reserve with knee injury (September 11, 2001-remainder of season) ... Granted unconditional free agency (February 28, 2003). ... Signed by Green Bay Packers (June 3, 2003).
PLAYING EXPERIENCE: Buffalo NFL, 1997-2000; Miami NFL, 2001-2002. ... Games/Games started: 1997 (2/0), 1998 (1/0), 1999 (11/2), 2000 (16/11), 2001 (1/1), 2002 (16/4). Total: 47/18.

SPRINGS, SHAWN   CB   SEAHAWKS

PERSONAL: Born March 11, 1975, in Williamsburg, W.Va. ... 6-0/204. ... Son of Ron Springs, running back with Dallas Cowboys (1979-84) and Tampa Bay Buccaneers (1985 and 1986).
HIGH SCHOOL: Springbrook (Silver Spring, Md.).
COLLEGE: Ohio State.
TRANSACTIONS/CAREER NOTES: Selected by Seattle Seahawks in first round (third pick overall) of 1997 NFL draft. ... Signed by Seahawks (August 4, 1997). ... On suspended list for violating league substance abuse policy (November 27-January 4, 2001).
HONORS: Named cornerback on THE SPORTING NEWS college All-America second team (1996). ... Played in Pro Bowl (1998 season).

			TOTALS			INTERCEPTIONS			
Year Team	G	GS	Tk.	Ast.	Sks.	No.	Yds.	Avg.	TD
1997—Seattle NFL	10	10	34	5	0.0	1	0	0.0	0
1998—Seattle NFL	16	16	61	14	0.0	7	142	20.3	▲2
1999—Seattle NFL	16	16	63	10	0.0	5	77	15.4	0
2000—Seattle NFL	16	16	72	13	0.0	2	8	4.0	0
2001—Seattle NFL	8	7	16	4	0.0	1	0	0.0	0
2002—Seattle NFL	15	15	54	5	0.0	3	0	0.0	0
Pro totals (6 years)	81	80	300	51	0.0	19	227	11.9	2

ST. CLAIR, JOHN   OT   RAMS

PERSONAL: Born July 15, 1977, in Roanoke, Va. ... 6-4/320. ... Full name: John Bradley St. Clair.
HIGH SCHOOL: William Fleming (Roanoke, Va.).
COLLEGE: Virginia.
TRANSACTIONS/CAREER NOTES: Selected by St. Louis Rams in third round (94th pick overall) of 2000 NFL draft. ... Signed by Rams (July 20, 2000). ... Granted free agency (February 28, 2003). ... Re-signed by Rams (April 23, 2003).
PLAYING EXPERIENCE: St. Louis NFL, 2002. ... Games/Games started: 2002 (16/16).
CHAMPIONSHIP GAME EXPERIENCE: Member of Rams for NFC championship game (2001 season); inactive. ... Member of Rams for Super Bowl XXXVI (2001 season); inactive.

ST. LOUIS, BRAD   TE   BENGALS

PERSONAL: Born August 19, 1976, in Waverly, Mo. ... 6-3/247. ... Full name: Brad Allen St. Louis.
HIGH SCHOOL: Belton (Mo.).
COLLEGE: Southwest Missouri State.
TRANSACTIONS/CAREER NOTES: Selected by Cincinnati Bengals in seventh round (210th pick overall) of 2000 NFL draft. ... Signed by Bengals (July 20, 2000). ... On injured reserve with leg injury (December 5, 2001-remainder of season). ... Granted free agency (February 28, 2003). ... Re-signed by Bengals (March 17, 2003).

| | | | RECEIVING | | |
Year Team	G	GS	No.	Yds.	Avg.	TD
2000—Cincinnati NFL	16	0	0	0	0.0	0
2001—Cincinnati NFL	11	0	0	0	0.0	0
2002—Cincinnati NFL	16	0	0	0	0.0	0
Pro totals (3 years)	43	0	0	0	0.0	0

STACKHOUSE, CHARLES   FB   GIANTS

PERSONAL: Born April 11, 1980, in West Memphis, Ark. ... 6-2/252.
HIGH SCHOOL: West Memphis (Ark.).
COLLEGE: Mississippi.
TRANSACTIONS/CAREER NOTES: Signed as non-drafted free agent by New York Giants (April 26, 2002).

| | | | RUSHING | | | | RECEIVING | | | | TOTALS | | |
Year Team	G	GS	Att.	Yds.	Avg.	TD	No.	Yds.	Avg.	TD	TD	2pt.	Pts.	Fum.
2002—New York Giants NFL	16	3	0	0	0.0	0	13	88	6.8	3	3	0	18	1

STAI, BRENDEN   G

PERSONAL: Born March 30, 1972, in Phoenix. ... 6-4/318. ... Full name: Brenden Michael Stai. ... Name pronounced STY.
HIGH SCHOOL: Anaheim High.
COLLEGE: Nebraska.
TRANSACTIONS/CAREER NOTES: Selected by Pittsburgh Steelers in third round (91st pick overall) of 1995 NFL draft. ... Signed by Steelers (July 18, 1995). ... Granted free agency (February 13, 1998). ... Re-signed by Steelers (June 9, 1998). ... Released by Steelers (March 14, 2000). ... Signed by Kansas City Chiefs (May 4, 2000). ... Traded by Chiefs to Jacksonville Jaguars for fourth-round pick (RB George Layne) in 2001 draft (August 16, 2000). ... Released by Jaguars (March 1, 2001). ... Signed by Detroit Lions (March 12, 2001). ... Traded by Lions to Washington Redskins for undisclosed draft pick (August 22, 2002). ... On injured reserve with knee injury (December 23, 2002-remainder of season). ... Released by Redskins (March 3, 2003).
PLAYING EXPERIENCE: Pittsburgh NFL, 1995-1999; Jacksonville NFL, 2000; Detroit NFL, 2001; Washington NFL, 2002. ... Games/Games started: 1995 (16/9), 1996 (9/9), 1997 (11/9), 1998 (16/16), 1999 (16/16), 2000 (16/16), 2001 (16/16), 2002 (5/5). Total: 105/96.
CHAMPIONSHIP GAME EXPERIENCE: Played in AFC championship game (1995 and 1997 seasons). ... Played in Super Bowl XXX (1995 season).
HONORS: Named offensive lineman on THE SPORTING NEWS college All-America second team (1994).

STALEY, DUCE   RB   EAGLES

PERSONAL: Born February 27, 1975, in Columbia, S.C. ... 5-11/220. ... Name pronounced DEUCE.
HIGH SCHOOL: Airport (Columbia, S.C.).
JUNIOR COLLEGE: Itawamba Community College (Miss.).
COLLEGE: South Carolina.
TRANSACTIONS/CAREER NOTES: Selected by Philadelphia Eagles in third round (71st pick overall) of 1997 NFL draft. ... Signed by Eagles (June 12, 1997). ... On injured reserve with foot injury (October 10, 2000-remainder of season).
CHAMPIONSHIP GAME EXPERIENCE: Played in NFC championship game (2001 and 2002 seasons).
SINGLE GAME HIGHS (regular season): Attempts—31 (November 17, 2002, vs. Arizona); yards—201 (September 3, 2000, vs. Dallas); and rushing touchdowns—2 (September 29, 2002, vs. Houston).
STATISTICAL PLATEAUS: 100-yard rushing games: 1998 (1), 1999 (5), 2000 (1), 2001 (2), 2002 (4). Total: 13. ... 100-yard receiving games: 2001 (1).

| | | | RUSHING | | | | RECEIVING | | | | KICKOFF RETURNS | | | | TOTALS | | |
Year Team	G	GS	Att.	Yds.	Avg.	TD	No.	Yds.	Avg.	TD	No.	Yds.	Avg.	TD	TD	2pt.	Pts.	Fum.
1997—Philadelphia NFL	16	0	7	29	4.1	0	2	22	11.0	0	47	1139	24.2	0	0	0	0	0
1998—Philadelphia NFL	16	13	258	1065	4.1	5	57	432	7.6	1	1	19	19.0	0	6	0	36	2
1999—Philadelphia NFL	16	16	325	1273	3.9	4	41	294	7.2	2	0	0	0.0	0	6	0	36	5
2000—Philadelphia NFL	5	5	79	344	4.4	1	25	201	8.0	0	0	0	0.0	0	1	0	6	3
2001—Philadelphia NFL	13	10	166	604	3.6	2	63	626	9.9*	2	0	0	0.0	0	4	0	24	3
2002—Philadelphia NFL	16	16	269	1029	3.8	5	51	541	10.6	3	0	0	0.0	0	8	1	50	3
Pro totals (6 years)	82	60	1104	4344	3.9	17	239	2116	8.9	8	48	1158	24.1	0	25	1	152	16

STALLWORTH, DONTE'   WR   SAINTS

PERSONAL: Born November 10, 1980, in Sacramento, Calif. ... 6-0/197. ... Full name: Donte' Lamar Stallworth.
HIGH SCHOOL: Grant (Sacramento, Calif.).
COLLEGE: Tennessee.
TRANSACTIONS/CAREER NOTES: Selected after junior season by New Orleans Saints in first round (13th pick overall) of 2002 NFL draft. ... Signed by Saints (July 29, 2002).
SINGLE GAME HIGHS (regular season): Receptions—6 (December 22, 2002, vs. Cincinnati); yards—111 (December 22, 2002, vs. Cincinnati); and touchdown receptions—1 (December 22, 2002, vs. Cincinnati).
STATISTICAL PLATEAUS: 100-yard receiving games: 2002 (1).

| | | | RUSHING | | | | RECEIVING | | | | PUNT RETURNS | | | | TOTALS | | |
Year Team	G	GS	Att.	Yds.	Avg.	TD	No.	Yds.	Avg.	TD	No.	Yds.	Avg.	TD	TD	2pt.	Pts.	Fum.
2002—New Orleans NFL	13	7	2	2	1.0	0	42	594	14.1	8	0	0	0.0	0	8	0	48	0

STAMPER, JOHN   DE   BEARS

PERSONAL: Born August 30, 1978, in Andrews, S.C. ... 6-4/265.
HIGH SCHOOL: Andrews (S.C.).
COLLEGE: South Carolina.
TRANSACTIONS/CAREER NOTES: Selected by Tampa Bay Buccaneers in sixth round (193rd pick overall) of 2002 NFL draft. ... Signed by Buccaneers (July 26, 2002). ... Released by Buccaneers (August 27, 2002). ... Signed by Chicago Bears to practice squad (October 30, 2002). ... Activated (November 29, 2002).

Year Team	G	GS	TOTALS Tk.	Ast.	Sks.
2002—Chicago NFL	4	0	0	0	0.0

STANLEY, CHAD   P   TEXANS

PERSONAL: Born January 29, 1976, in Ore City, Texas. ... 6-3/205. ... Full name: Benjamin Chadwick Stanley.
HIGH SCHOOL: Ore City (Texas).
COLLEGE: Stephen F. Austin State.
TRANSACTIONS/CAREER NOTES: Signed as non-drafted free agent by San Francisco 49ers (April 23, 1999). ... Released by 49ers (September 1, 2001). ... Signed by Arizona Cardinals (November 6, 2001). ... Released by Cardinals (December 5, 2001). ... Signed by Houston Texans (February 6, 2002). ... Granted free agency (February 28, 2003). ... Re-signed by Texans (June 1, 2003).
RECORDS: Shares NFL single-season record for most punts—114 (2002).

Year Team	G	No.	Yds.	PUNTING Avg.	Net avg.	In. 20	Blk.
1999—San Francisco NFL	16	69	2737	39.7	30.7	20	†2
2000—San Francisco NFL	16	69	2727	39.5	32.2	15	1
2001—Arizona NFL	4	19	751	39.5	34.2	4	0
2002—Houston NFL	16	*114	§4720	41.4	36.8	*36	2
Pro totals (4 years)	52	271	10935	40.4	33.9	75	5

STANSBURY, ED   FB

PERSONAL: Born May 3, 1979, in El Paso, Texas. ... 6-0/257. ... Full name: Edmund Elisala Ieremia- Stansbury.
HIGH SCHOOL: Irvin (El Paso, Texas).
COLLEGE: UCLA.
TRANSACTIONS/CAREER NOTES: Signed as non-drafted free agent by Houston Texans (April 25, 2002). ... Released by Texans (September 10, 2002). ... Re-signed by Texans to practice squad (September 11, 2002). ... Released by Texans (September 24, 2002).

Year Team	G	GS	RUSHING Att.	Yds.	Avg.	TD	TOTALS TD	2pt.	Pts.	Fum.
2002—Houston NFL	1	0	0	0	0.0	0	0	0	0	0

STARKEY, JASON   C   CARDINALS

PERSONAL: Born July 15, 1977, in Barboursville, W.Va. ... 6-4/297.
HIGH SCHOOL: Cabell-Midland (W.Va.).
COLLEGE: Marshall.
TRANSACTIONS/CAREER NOTES: Signed as non-drafted free agent by Arizona Cardinals (June 1, 2000). ... Released by Cardinals (August 27, 2000). ... Re-signed by Cardinals to practice squad (August 28, 2000). ... Activated (September 8, 2000). ... Released by Cardinals (September 11, 2000). ... Re-signed by Cardinals to practice squad (September 13, 2000). ... Granted free agency (February 28, 2003). ... Re-signed by Cardinals (March 20, 2003).
PLAYING EXPERIENCE: Arizona NFL, 2000-2002. ... Games/Games started: 2000 (2/0), 2001 (12/1), 2002 (16/8). Total: 30/9.

STARKS, DUANE   CB   CARDINALS

PERSONAL: Born May 23, 1974, in Miami. ... 5-10/172. ... Full name: Duane Lonell Starks.
HIGH SCHOOL: Miami Beach Senior.
JUNIOR COLLEGE: Holmes Junior College (Miss.).
COLLEGE: Miami (Fla.).
TRANSACTIONS/CAREER NOTES: Selected by Baltimore Ravens in first round (10th pick overall) of 1998 NFL draft. ... Signed by Ravens (August 5, 1998). ... Granted unconditional free agency (March 1, 2002). ... Signed by Arizona Cardinals (March 18, 2002).
CHAMPIONSHIP GAME EXPERIENCE: Played in AFC championship game (2000 season). ... Member of Super Bowl championship team (2000 season).
MISCELLANEOUS: Shares Baltimore Ravens all-time record for most interceptions (20).

Year Team	G	GS	TOTALS Tk.	Ast.	Sks.	INTERCEPTIONS No.	Yds.	Avg.	TD
1998—Baltimore NFL	16	8	49	4	0.0	5	3	0.6	0
1999—Baltimore NFL	16	6	39	3	0.0	5	59	11.8	1
2000—Baltimore NFL	15	15	45	4	0.0	6	125	20.8	0
2001—Baltimore NFL	15	15	54	5	0.0	4	9	2.3	0
2002—Arizona NFL	10	10	47	8	0.0	2	3	1.5	0
Pro totals (5 years)	72	54	234	24	0.0	22	199	9.0	1

S

STECKER, AARON   RB   BUCCANEERS

PERSONAL: Born November 13, 1975, in Green Bay. ... 5-10/205.
HIGH SCHOOL: Ashwaubenon (Green Bay).
COLLEGE: Western Illinois.
TRANSACTIONS/CAREER NOTES: Signed as non-drafted free agent by Chicago Bears (April 18, 1999). ... Released by Bears (August 30, 1999). ... Signed by Tampa Bay Buccaneers to practice squad (October 20, 1999). ... Granted free agency (February 28, 2003). ... Re-signed by Buccaneers (April 10, 2003).
CHAMPIONSHIP GAME EXPERIENCE: Played in NFC championship game (2002 season). ... Member of Super Bowl championship team (2002 season).
SINGLE GAME HIGHS (regular season): Attempts—12 (January 6, 2002, vs. Philadelphia); yards—59 (November 3, 2002, vs. Minnesota); and rushing touchdowns—1 (January 6, 2002, vs. Philadelphia).

			RUSHING				RECEIVING				KICKOFF RETURNS				TOTALS		
Year Team	G	GS	Att.	Yds.	Avg.	TD	No.	Yds.	Avg.	TD	No.	Yds.	Avg.	TD	TD 2pt.	Pts. Fum.	
2000—Tampa Bay NFL	10	0	12	31	2.6	0	1	15	15.0	0	29	663	22.9	0	0	0	0	1
2001—Tampa Bay NFL	13	0	24	72	3.0	1	10	101	10.1	1	9	259	28.8	0	2	0	12	0
2002—Tampa Bay NFL	16	1	28	174	6.2	0	13	69	5.3	0	37	934	25.2	0	0	0	0	3
Pro totals (3 years)	39	1	64	277	4.3	1	24	185	7.7	1	75	1856	24.7	0	2	0	12	4

STEELE, GLEN   DT   BENGALS

PERSONAL: Born October 4, 1974, in Ligonier, Ind. ... 6-4/300. ... Full name: James Lendale Steele Jr.
HIGH SCHOOL: West Noble (Ligonier, Ind.).
COLLEGE: Michigan.
TRANSACTIONS/CAREER NOTES: Selected by Cincinnati Bengals in fourth round (105th pick overall) of 1998 NFL draft. ... Signed by Bengals (July 14, 1998). ... On injured reserve with ankle injury (December 15, 1998-remainder of season).

			TOTALS		
Year Team	G	GS	Tk.	Ast.	Sks.
1998—Cincinnati NFL	10	0	6	1	0.0
1999—Cincinnati NFL	16	1	13	1	0.0
2000—Cincinnati NFL	16	1	13	4	2.0
2001—Cincinnati NFL	16	1	5	5	1.0
2002—Cincinnati NFL	16	7	15	13	0.0
Pro totals (5 years)	74	10	52	24	3.0

STEELE, MARKUS   LB   COWBOYS

PERSONAL: Born July 24, 1979, in Cleveland. ... 6-3/240.
HIGH SCHOOL: Chanel (New Bedford, Ohio).
JUNIOR COLLEGE: Long Beach City College.
COLLEGE: Southern California.
TRANSACTIONS/CAREER NOTES: Selected by Dallas Cowboys in fourth round (122nd pick overall) of 2001 NFL draft. ... Signed by Cowboys (July 20, 2001).

			TOTALS			INTERCEPTIONS			
Year Team	G	GS	Tk.	Ast.	Sks.	No.	Yds.	Avg.	TD
2001—Dallas NFL	15	10	32	4	0.0	0	0	0.0	0
2002—Dallas NFL	13	1	13	5	0.0	0	0	0.0	0
Pro totals (2 years)	28	11	45	9	0.0	0	0	0.0	0

STEMKE, KEVIN   P   DOLPHINS

PERSONAL: Born November 23, 1978, in Green Bay, Wis. ... 6-3/190.
HIGH SCHOOL: Preble (Green Bay, Wis.).
COLLEGE: Wisconsin.
TRANSACTIONS/CAREER NOTES: Signed as non-drafted free agent by Green Bay Packers (April 27, 2001). ... Released by Packers (August 26, 2001). ... Signed by St. Louis Rams (January 10, 2002). ... Released by Rams (August 12, 2002). ... Signed by Oakland Raiders (August 16, 2002). ... Released by Raiders (September 25, 2002). ... Signed by Miami Dolphins (January 24, 2003). ... Assigned by Dolphins to Scottish Claymores in 2003 NFL Europe enhancement allocation program (February 4, 2003)

		PUNTING					
Year Team	G	No.	Yds.	Avg.	Net avg.	In. 20	Blk.
2002—Oakland NFL	2	5	212	42.4	31.8	1	1

STEPHENS, LEONARD   TE   REDSKINS

PERSONAL: Born July 9, 1978, in Miami. ... 6-3/249.
HIGH SCHOOL: West Windsor (Princeton, N.J.).
COLLEGE: Howard.
TRANSACTIONS/CAREER NOTES: Signed as non-drafted free agent by San Diego Chargers (April 17, 2000). ... Released by Chargers (July 19, 2000). ... Signed by Detroit Lions (February 14, 2001). ... Assigned by Lions to Scottish Claymores in 2001 NFL Europe enhancement allocation program (February 18, 2001). ... Released by Lions (July 14, 2001). ... Signed by Washington Redskins (April 24, 2002). ... Re-signed by Redskins (March 25, 2003).
SINGLE GAME HIGHS (regular season): Receptions—1 (October 27, 2002, vs. Indianapolis); yards—13 (October 27, 2002, vs. Indianapolis); and touchdown receptions—0.

			RECEIVING			
Year Team	G	GS	No.	Yds.	Avg.	TD
2002—Washington NFL	5	0	1	13	13.0	0

STEPHENS, REGGIE   CB

PERSONAL: Born February 21, 1975, in Dallas. ... 5-9/200.
HIGH SCHOOL: Santa Cruz (Calif.).
JUNIOR COLLEGE: Cabrillo College (Calif.).
COLLEGE: Rutgers.
TRANSACTIONS/CAREER NOTES: Signed as non-drafted free agent by New York Giants (April 27, 1999). ... Released by Giants (September 5, 1999). ... Re-signed by Giants to practice squad (November 16, 1999). ... Activated (December 10, 1999). ... Released by Giants (December 14, 1999). ... Re-signed by Giants to practice squad (December 15, 1999). ... Released by Giants (May 15, 2001). ... Signed by Kansas City Chiefs (January 21, 2002). ... Released by Chiefs (August 26, 2002). ... Signed by Giants (October 8, 2002).
CHAMPIONSHIP GAME EXPERIENCE: Member of Giants for NFC championship game (2000 season); inactive. ... Member of Giants for Super Bowl XXXV (2000 season); inactive.

Year Team	G	GS	TOTALS			INTERCEPTIONS			
			Tk.	Ast.	Sks.	No.	Yds.	Avg.	TD
1999—New York Giants NFL	1	0	0	0	0.0	0	0	0.0	0
2000—New York Giants NFL	15	0	8	0	0.0	3	4	1.3	0
2002—New York Giants NFL	8	0	5	0	0.0	0	0	0.0	0
Pro totals (3 years)	24	0	13	0	0.0	3	4	1.3	0

STEPHENS, TRAVIS   RB   BUCCANEERS

PERSONAL: Born June 26, 1978, in Clarksville, Tenn. ... 5-8/194. ... Full name: Travis Tremaine Stephens.
HIGH SCHOOL: Northeast (Clarksville, Tenn.).
COLLEGE: Tennessee.
TRANSACTIONS/CAREER NOTES: Selected by Tampa Bay Buccaneers in fourth round (118th pick overall) of 2002 NFL draft. ... Signed by Buccaneers (July 26, 2002). ... On injured reserve with toe injury (November 15, 2002-remainder of season).
HONORS: Named running back on THE SPORTING NEWS college All-America second team (2001).

Year Team	G	GS	RUSHING				RECEIVING				KICKOFF RETURNS				TOTALS			
			Att.	Yds.	Avg.	TD	No.	Yds.	Avg.	TD	No.	Yds.	Avg.	TD	TD	2pt.	Pts.	Fum.
2002—Tampa Bay NFL	1	0	0	0	0.0	0	1	6	6.0	0	0	0	0.0	0	0	0	0	0

STEUSSIE, TODD   OT   PANTHERS

PERSONAL: Born December 1, 1970, in Canoga Park, Calif. ... 6-6/308. ... Full name: Todd Edward Steussie. ... Name pronounced STEW-see.
HIGH SCHOOL: Agoura (Calif.).
COLLEGE: California.
TRANSACTIONS/CAREER NOTES: Selected by Minnesota Vikings in first round (19th pick overall) of 1994 NFL draft. ... Signed by Vikings (July 13, 1994). ... Released by Vikings (March 14, 2001). ... Signed by Carolina Panthers (March 29, 2001).
PLAYING EXPERIENCE: Minnesota NFL, 1994-2000; Carolina NFL, 2001-2002. ... Games/Games started: 1994 (16/16), 1995 (16/16), 1996 (16/16), 1997 (16/16), 1998 (15/15), 1999 (16/16), 2000 (16/16), 2001 (16/16), 2002 (16/16). Total: 143/143.
CHAMPIONSHIP GAME EXPERIENCE: Played in NFC championship game (1998 and 2000 seasons).
HONORS: Named offensive lineman on THE SPORTING NEWS college All-America second team (1993). ... Played in Pro Bowl (1997 and 1998 seasons).

STEVENS, JERRAMY   TE   SEAHAWKS

PERSONAL: Born November 13, 1979, in Boise, Idaho. ... 6-7/265.
HIGH SCHOOL: River Ridge (Olympia, Wash.).
COLLEGE: Washington.
TRANSACTIONS/CAREER NOTES: Selected after junior season by Seattle Seahawks in first round (28th pick overall) of 2002 NFL draft. ... Signed by Seahawks (July 30, 2002).
SINGLE GAME HIGHS (regular season): Receptions—4 (December 29, 2002, vs. San Diego); yards—70 (December 22, 2002, vs. St. Louis); and touchdown receptions—1 (December 15, 2002, vs. Atlanta).

Year Team	G	GS	RECEIVING			
			No.	Yds.	Avg.	TD
2002—Seattle NFL	12	1	26	252	9.7	3

STEVENS, MATT   S   TEXANS

PERSONAL: Born June 14, 1973, in Chapel Hill, N.C. ... 6-0/205. ... Full name: Matthew Brian Stevens.
HIGH SCHOOL: Chapel Hill (N.C.).
COLLEGE: Appalachian State.
TRANSACTIONS/CAREER NOTES: Selected by Buffalo Bills in third round (87th pick overall) of 1996 NFL draft. ... Signed by Bills (July 15, 1996). ... Claimed on waivers by Philadelphia Eagles (August 25, 1997). ... On suspended list for anabolic steroid use (August 27-September 29, 1997). ... Claimed on waivers by Washington Redskins (December 8, 1998). ... Granted free agency (February 12, 1999). ... Re-signed by Redskins (April 23, 1999). ... Granted unconditional free agency (February 11, 2000). ... Re-signed by Redskins (May 12, 2000). ... Claimed on waivers by New England Patriots (December 20, 2000). ... Granted unconditional free agency (March 2, 2001). ... Re-signed by Patriots (March 16, 2001). ... Selected by Houston Texans from Patriots in NFL expansion draft (February 18, 2002). ... Released by Texans (February 27, 2003). ... Re-signed by Texans (March 21, 2003).
CHAMPIONSHIP GAME EXPERIENCE: Played in AFC championship game (2001 season). ... Member of Super Bowl championship team (2001 season).

Year Team	G	GS	TOTALS Tk.	Ast.	Sks.	INTERCEPTIONS No.	Yds.	Avg.	TD
1996—Buffalo NFL	13	11	26	7	0.0	2	0	0.0	0
1997—Philadelphia NFL	11	0	10	0	0.0	1	0	0.0	0
1998—Philadelphia NFL	7	1	6	5	0.0	0	0	0.0	0
—Washington NFL	3	0	0	0	0.0	0	0	0.0	0
1999—Washington NFL	15	1	30	6	1.0	6	61	10.2	0
2000—Washington NFL	15	4	26	10	0.0	1	0	0.0	0
—New England NFL	1	0	0	0	0.0	0	0	0.0	0
2001—New England NFL	15	4	24	13	0.0	1	9	9.0	0
2002—Houston NFL	16	16	60	23	0.0	1	0	0.0	0
Pro totals (7 years)	96	37	182	64	1.0	12	70	5.8	0

STEVENSON, DOMINIQUE — LB — BILLS

PERSONAL: Born December 28, 1977, in Gaffney, S.C. ... 6-0/231. ... Full name: Antone Dominique Stevenson.
HIGH SCHOOL: Gaffney (S.C.).
COLLEGE: Tennessee.
TRANSACTIONS/CAREER NOTES: Selected by Buffalo Bills in seventh round (260th pick overall) of 2002 NFL draft.. ... Signed by Bills (July 3, 2002). ... Released by Bills (September 3, 2002). ... Re-signed by Bills to practice squad (September 4, 2002). ... Activated (October 2, 2002).

Year Team	G	GS	TOTALS Tk.	Ast.	Sks.	INTERCEPTIONS No.	Yds.	Avg.	TD
2002—Buffalo NFL	4	0	0	0	0.0	0	0	0.0	0

STEWART, JAMES — RB — LIONS

PERSONAL: Born December 27, 1971, in Morristown, Tenn. ... 6-1/224. ... Full name: James Ottis Stewart III.
HIGH SCHOOL: Morristown-Hamblen West (Morristown, Tenn.).
COLLEGE: Tennessee.
TRANSACTIONS/CAREER NOTES: Selected by Jacksonville Jaguars in first round (19th pick overall) of 1995 NFL draft. ... Signed by Jaguars (June 1, 1995). ... On injured reserve with knee injury (September 22, 1998-remainder of season). ... Granted unconditional free agency (February 11, 2000). ... Signed by Detroit Lions (February 14, 2000).
CHAMPIONSHIP GAME EXPERIENCE: Played in AFC championship game (1996 and 1999 seasons).
SINGLE GAME HIGHS (regular season): Attempts—37 (December 17, 2000, vs. New York Jets); yards—172 (October 20, 2002, vs. Chicago); and rushing touchdowns—5 (October 12, 1997, vs. Philadelphia).
STATISTICAL PLATEAUS: 100-yard rushing games: 1996 (1), 1997 (1), 1998 (2), 1999 (2), 2000 (3), 2001 (2), 2002 (2). Total: 13.

Year Team	G	GS	RUSHING Att.	Yds.	Avg.	TD	RECEIVING No.	Yds.	Avg.	TD	TOTALS TD	2pt.	Pts.	Fum.
1995—Jacksonville NFL	14	8	137	525	3.8	2	21	190	9.0	1	3	0	18	1
1996—Jacksonville NFL	13	11	190	723	3.8	8	30	177	5.9	2	10	0	60	2
1997—Jacksonville NFL	16	5	136	555	4.1	8	41	336	8.2	1	9	0	54	0
1998—Jacksonville NFL	3	3	53	217	4.1	2	6	42	7.0	1	3	0	18	2
1999—Jacksonville NFL	14	7	249	931	3.7	▲13	21	108	5.1	0	13	0	78	4
2000—Detroit NFL	16	16	‡339	1184	3.5	10	32	287	9.0	1	11	3	72	4
2001—Detroit NFL	11	10	143	685	4.8	1	23	242	10.5	1	2	0	12	0
2002—Detroit NFL	14	9	231	1021	4.4	4	46	333	7.2	2	6	0	36	0
Pro totals (8 years)	101	69	1478	5841	4.0	48	220	1715	7.8	9	57	3	348	13

STEWART, KORDELL — QB — BEARS

PERSONAL: Born October 16, 1972, in New Orleans. ... 6-1/217.
HIGH SCHOOL: John Ehret (Marrero, La.).
COLLEGE: Colorado.
TRANSACTIONS/CAREER NOTES: Selected by Pittsburgh Steelers in second round (60th pick overall) of 1995 NFL draft. ... Signed by Steelers (July 17, 1995). ... Released by Steelers (February 26, 2003). ... Signed by Chicago Bears (March 13, 2003).
CHAMPIONSHIP GAME EXPERIENCE: Played in AFC championship game (1995, 1997 and 2001 seasons). ... Played in Super Bowl XXX (1995 season).
HONORS: Played in Pro Bowl (2001 season).
SINGLE GAME HIGHS (regular season): Attempts—48 (December 13, 1997, vs. New England); completions—26 (December 13, 1997, vs. New England); yards—333 (December 16, 2001, vs. Baltimore); and touchdown passes—3 (December 30, 2001, vs. Cincinnati).
STATISTICAL PLATEAUS: 300-yard passing games: 1997 (2), 2001 (1). Total: 3. ... 100-yard rushing games: 1996 (1), 1998 (1). Total: 2.
MISCELLANEOUS: Regular-season record as starting NFL quarterback: 46-29 (.613). ... Postseason record as starting NFL quarterback: 2-2 (.500). ... Started two games at wide receiver (1995). ... Started two games at wide receiver (1996). ... Started one game at wide receiver (1999).

Year Team	G	GS	PASSING Att.	Cmp.	Pct.	Yds.	TD	Int.	Avg.	Rat.	RUSHING Att.	Yds.	Avg.	TD	RECEIVING No.	Yds.	Avg.	TD	TOTALS TD	2pt.	Pts.
1995—Pittsburgh NFL	10	2	7	5	71.4	60	1	0	8.57		15	86	5.7	1	14	235	16.8	1	2	0	12
1996—Pittsburgh NFL	16	2	30	11	36.7	100	0	2	3.33		39	171	4.4	5	17	293	17.2	3	8	0	48
1997—Pittsburgh NFL	16	16	440	236	53.6	3020	21	§17	6.86		88	476	5.4	11	0	0	0.0	0	11	0	66
1998—Pittsburgh NFL	16	16	458	252	55.0	2560	11	18	5.59		81	406	5.0	2	1	17	17.0	0	2	0	12
1999—Pittsburgh NFL	16	12	275	160	58.2	1464	6	10	5.32		56	258	4.6	2	9	113	12.6	1	3	0	18
2000—Pittsburgh NFL	16	11	289	151	52.2	1860	11	8	6.44		78	436	5.6	7	0	0	0.0	0	7	0	42
2001—Pittsburgh NFL	16	16	442	266	60.2	3109	14	11	7.03		96	537	5.6	5	0	0	0.0	0	5	0	30
2002—Pittsburgh NFL	8	5	166	109	65.7	1155	6	6	6.96		43	191	4.4	2	0	0	0.0	0	2	0	12
Pro totals (8 years)	114	80	2107	1190	56.5	13328	70	72	6.33		496	2561	5.2	35	41	658	16.0	5	40	0	240

STEWART, MATT　　　　　LB　　　　　FALCONS

PERSONAL: Born August 31, 1979, in Columbus, Ohio. ... 6-3/232.
HIGH SCHOOL: DeSales (Columbus, Ohio).
COLLEGE: Vanderbilt.
TRANSACTIONS/CAREER NOTES: Selected by Atlanta Falcons in fourth round (102nd pick overall) of 2001 NFL draft. ... Signed by Falcons (May 30, 2001).

			TOTALS			INTERCEPTIONS			
Year Team	G	GS	Tk.	Ast.	Sks.	No.	Yds.	Avg.	TD
2001—Atlanta NFL	15	0	9	3	0.0	0	0	0.0	0
2002—Atlanta NFL	16	13	48	5	3.0	0	0	0.0	0
Pro totals (2 years)	31	13	57	8	3.0	0	0	0.0	0

STEWART, QUINCY　　　　　LB　　　　　BRONCOS

PERSONAL: Born March 27, 1978, in Tyler, Texas. ... 6-1/234. ... Full name: Quincy Jermaine Stewart.
HIGH SCHOOL: John Tyler (Texas).
COLLEGE: Louisiana Tech.
TRANSACTIONS/CAREER NOTES: Signed as non-drafted free agent by San Francisco 49ers (April 25, 2001). ... Granted free agency (February 28, 2003). ... Signed by Denver Broncos (April 2, 2003).

			TOTALS			INTERCEPTIONS			
Year Team	G	GS	Tk.	Ast.	Sks.	No.	Yds.	Avg.	TD
2001—San Francisco NFL	16	0	0	0	0.0	0	0	0.0	0
2002—San Francisco NFL	15	0	3	1	0.0	1	0	0.0	0
Pro totals (2 years)	31	0	3	1	0.0	1	0	0.0	0

STEWART, TONY　　　　　TE　　　　　BENGALS

PERSONAL: Born August 9, 1979, in Lohne, Germany. ... 6-5/260. ... Full name: Tony Alexander Stewart.
HIGH SCHOOL: Allentown Central (Pa.).
COLLEGE: Penn State.
TRANSACTIONS/CAREER NOTES: Selected by Philadelphia Eagles in fifth round (147th pick overall) of 2001 NFL draft. ... Signed by Eagles (May 22, 2001). ... Released by Eagles (September 10, 2002). ... Re-signed by Eagles to practice squad (September 12, 2002). ... Signed by Cincinnati Bengals off Eagles practice squad (November 23, 2002).
CHAMPIONSHIP GAME EXPERIENCE: Member of Eagles for NFC championship game (2001 season); inactive.
SINGLE GAME HIGHS (regular season): Receptions—3 (January 6, 2002, vs. Tampa Bay); yards—41 (January 6, 2002, vs. Tampa Bay); and touchdown receptions—1 (November 29, 2001, vs. Kansas City).

			RECEIVING			
Year Team	G	GS	No.	Yds.	Avg.	TD
2001—Philadelphia NFL	3	1	5	52	10.4	1
2002—Cincinnati NFL	3	0	1	6	6.0	0
Pro totals (2 years)	6	1	6	58	9.7	1

STILLS, GARY　　　　　LB

PERSONAL: Born July 11, 1974, in Trenton, N.J. ... 6-2/244.
HIGH SCHOOL: Valley Forge (Pa.) Military Academy.
COLLEGE: West Virginia.
TRANSACTIONS/CAREER NOTES: Selected by Kansas City Chiefs in third round (75th pick overall) of 1999 NFL draft. ... Signed by Chiefs (July 26, 1999). ... Assigned by Chiefs to Frankfurt Galaxy in 2001 NFL Europe enhancement allocation program (February 19, 2001). ... Granted free agency (March 1, 2002). ... Re-signed by Chiefs (April 20, 2002). ... Granted unconditional free agency (February 28, 2003).

			TOTALS			INTERCEPTIONS			
Year Team	G	GS	Tk.	Ast.	Sks.	No.	Yds.	Avg.	TD
1999—Kansas City NFL	2	0	0	0	0.0	0	0	0.0	0
2000—Kansas City NFL	11	0	0	0	0.0	0	0	0.0	0
2001—Frankfurt NFLE	...	...	...	...	9.5	1	0	0.0	0
—Kansas City NFL	10	0	1	0	0.0	0	0	0.0	0
2002—Kansas City NFL	16	1	18	3	2.0	0	0	0.0	0
NFL Europe totals (1 year)	...	...	...	...	9.5	1	0	0.0	0
NFL totals (4 years)	39	1	19	3	2.0	0	0	0.0	0
Pro totals (5 years)	...	...	...	...	11.5	1	0	0.0	0

STINCHCOMB, MATT　　　　　OT　　　　　RAIDERS

PERSONAL: Born June 3, 1977, in Lilburn, Ga. ... 6-6/310. ... Full name: Matthew Douglass Stinchcomb. ... Brother of Jon Stinchcomb, offensive tackle, New Orleans Saints.
HIGH SCHOOL: Parkview (Lilburn, Ga.).
COLLEGE: Georgia.
TRANSACTIONS/CAREER NOTES: Selected by Oakland Raiders in first round (18th pick overall) of 1999 NFL draft. ... Signed by Raiders (July 22, 1999). ... Inactive for three games (1999). ... On injured reserve with shoulder injury (October 1, 1999-remainder of season).
PLAYING EXPERIENCE: Oakland NFL, 2000-2002. ... Games/Games started: 2000 (13/9), 2001 (14/1), 2002 (16/6). Total: 43/16.
CHAMPIONSHIP GAME EXPERIENCE: Member of Raiders for AFC Championship game (2000 season); did not play. ... Played in AFC championship game (2002 season). ... Played in Super Bowl XXXVII (2002 season).
HONORS: Named offensive tackle on THE SPORTING NEWS college All-America second team (1997 and 1998).

STITH, SHYRONE   RB

PERSONAL: Born April 2, 1978, in Portsmouth, Va. ... 5-8/205. ... Full name: Shyrone Orenthal Stith.
HIGH SCHOOL: Western Branch (Chesapeake, Va.).
COLLEGE: Virginia Tech.
TRANSACTIONS/CAREER NOTES: Selected after junior season by Jacksonville Jaguars in seventh round (243rd pick overall) of 2000 NFL draft. ... Signed by Jaguars (May 17, 2000). ... Released by Jaguars (September 3, 2001). ... Signed by Indianapolis Colts (November 7, 2001). ... On injured reserve with knee injury (September 11-December 9, 2002). ... Released by Colts (December 9, 2002).
SINGLE GAME HIGHS (regular season): Attempts—11 (December 3, 2000, vs. Cleveland); yards—27 (December 3, 2000, vs. Cleveland); and rushing touchdowns—1 (December 3, 2000, vs. Cleveland).

			RUSHING				KICKOFF RETURNS				TOTALS		
Year Team	G	GS	Att.	Yds.	Avg.	TD	No.	Yds.	Avg.	TD	TD	2pt.	Pts.	Fum.
2000—Jacksonville NFL	14	0	20	55	2.8	1	33	785	23.8	0	1	0	6	1
2002—Indianapolis NFL	1	0	0	0	0.0	0	0	0	0.0	0	0	0	0	0
Pro totals (2 years)	15	0	20	55	2.8	1	33	785	23.8	0	1	0	6	1

STOERNER, CLINT   QB   COWBOYS

PERSONAL: Born December 29, 1977, in Baytown, Texas. ... 6-2/210.
HIGH SCHOOL: Lee (Baytown, Texas).
COLLEGE: Arkansas.
TRANSACTIONS/CAREER NOTES: Signed as non-drafted free agent by Dallas Cowboys (May 5, 2000). ... Released by Cowboys (August 27, 2000). ... Re-signed by Cowboys to practice squad (August 29, 2000). ... Activated (September 8, 2000). ... Released by Cowboys (October 10, 2000). ... Re-signed by Cowboys to practice squad (October 11, 2000). ... Activated (November 1, 2000). ... Released by Cowboys (November 21, 2000). ... Re-signed by Cowboys to practice squad (November 27, 2000). ... Activated (December 13, 2000). ... Assigned by Cowboys to Scottish Claymores in 2001 NFL Europe enhancement allocation program (February 12, 2001). ... Granted free agency (February 28, 2003). ... Re-signed by Cowboys (April 5, 2003).
SINGLE GAME HIGHS (regular season): Attempts—23 (November 4, 2001, vs. New York Giants); completions—13 (November 4, 2001, vs. New York Giants); passing yards—177 (November 4, 2001, vs. New York Giants); and touchdown passes—2 (September 30, 2001, vs. Philadelphia).
MISCELLANEOUS: Regular-season record as starting NFL quarterback: 1-1 (.500).

			PASSING									RUSHING				TOTALS		
Year Team	G	GS	Att.	Cmp.	Pct.	Yds.	TD	Int.	Avg.	Skd.	Rat.	Att.	Yds.	Avg.	TD	TD	2pt.	Pts.
2000—Dallas NFL	2	0	5	3	60.0	53	1	0	10.60	2	135.8	0	0	0.0	0	0	0	0
2001—Scottish NFLE	...	...	307	171	55.7	1866	10	8	6.08	...	73.8	31	101	3.3	0	0	0	0
—Dallas NFL	4	2	49	26	53.1	314	3	5	6.41	5	53.8	9	27	3.0	1	1	0	6
2002—Dallas NFL									Did not play.									
NFL Europe totals (1 year)	...	...	307	171	55.7	1866	10	8	6.08	...	73.8	31	101	3.3	0	0	0	0
NFL totals (2 years)	6	2	54	29	53.7	367	4	5	6.80	7	61.3	9	27	3.0	1	1	0	6
Pro totals (3 years)	...	...	361	200	55.4	2233	14	13	6.19	...	71.9	40	128	3.2	1	1	0	6

STOKES, BARRY   OT/OG   BROWNS

PERSONAL: Born December 20, 1973, in Flint, Mich. ... 6-4/310. ... Full name: Barry Wade Stokes.
HIGH SCHOOL: Davison (Mich.).
COLLEGE: Eastern Michigan.
TRANSACTIONS/CAREER NOTES: Signed as non-drafted free agent by Detroit Lions (April 26, 1996). ... Released by Lions (August 14, 1996). ... Signed by Jacksonville Jaguars to practice squad (October 23, 1996). ... Granted free agency after 1996 season. ... Signed by Atlanta Falcons (January 30, 1997). ... Released by Falcons (August 1997). ... Signed by St. Louis Rams to practice squad (August 26, 1997). ... Released by Rams (October 6, 1997). ... Signed by Miami Dolphins to practice squad (November 26, 1997). ... Assigned by Dolphins to Scottish Claymores in 1998 NFL Europe enhancement allocation program (February 18, 1998). ... Released by Dolphins (August 25, 1998). ... Re-signed by Dolphins (November 4, 1998). ... Assigned by Dolphins to Scottish Claymores in 1999 NFL Europe enhancement allocation program (February 22, 1999). ... Released by Dolphins (September 4, 1999). ... Signed by Green Bay Packers (September 8, 1999). ... Released by Packers (September 21, 1999). ... Re-signed by Packers (October 20, 1999). ... Inactive for five games (1999). ... Released by Packers (November 9, 1999). ... Signed by Oakland Raiders (January 2, 2000). ... Released by Raiders (July 21, 2000). ... Signed by Packers (July 22, 2000). ... Released by Packers (September 27, 2000). ... Re-signed by Packers (October 23, 2000). ... Granted unconditional free agency (March 1, 2002). ... Signed by Cleveland Browns (April 1, 2002).
PLAYING EXPERIENCE: Scottish NFLE, 1998; Miami NFL, 1998; Green Bay NFL, 2000 and 2001; Cleveland NFL, 2002. ... Games/Games started: NFLE 1998 (10/10), NFL 1998 (3/0), 2000 (8/0), 2001 (16/3), 2002 (16/16). Total NFL: 43/19. Total Pro: 53/29.

STOKES, J.J.   WR

PERSONAL: Born October 6, 1972, in San Diego. ... 6-4/225. ... Full name: Jerel Jamal Stokes.
HIGH SCHOOL: Point Loma (San Diego).
COLLEGE: UCLA (degree in sociology, 1994).
TRANSACTIONS/CAREER NOTES: Selected by San Francisco 49ers in first round (10th pick overall) of 1995 NFL draft. ... Signed by 49ers (July 27, 1995). ... On injured reserve with wrist injury (October 26, 1996-remainder of season). ... Granted unconditional free agency (February 12, 1999). ... Re-signed by 49ers (March 8, 1999). ... Released by 49ers (June 1, 2003).
CHAMPIONSHIP GAME EXPERIENCE: Played in NFC championship game (1997 season).
HONORS: Named wide receiver on THE SPORTING NEWS college All-America first team (1993).
SINGLE GAME HIGHS (regular season): Receptions—9 (October 18, 1998, vs. Indianapolis); yards—130 (January 3, 2000, vs. Atlanta); and touchdown receptions—2 (December 30, 2001, vs. Dallas).
STATISTICAL PLATEAUS: 100-yard receiving games: 1995 (1), 1998 (2), 1999 (1). Total: 4.

Year Team	G	GS	RECEIVING				TOTALS			
			No.	Yds.	Avg.	TD	TD	2pt.	Pts.	Fum.
1995—San Francisco NFL	12	2	38	517	13.6	4	4	0	24	0
1996—San Francisco NFL	6	6	18	249	13.8	0	0	0	0	0
1997—San Francisco NFL	16	16	58	733	12.6	4	4	0	24	1
1998—San Francisco NFL	16	11	63	770	12.2	8	8	0	48	0
1999—San Francisco NFL	16	4	34	429	12.6	3	3	†1	20	1
2000—San Francisco NFL	16	3	30	524	17.5	3	3	1	20	0
2001—San Francisco NFL	16	16	54	585	10.8	7	7	0	42	0
2002—San Francisco NFL	13	8	32	332	10.4	1	1	0	6	0
Pro totals (8 years)	111	66	327	4139	12.7	30	30	2	184	2

STOKLEY, BRANDON   WR   COLTS

PERSONAL: Born June 23, 1976, in Blacksburg, Va. ... 5-11/197.
HIGH SCHOOL: Comeaux (Lafayette, La.).
COLLEGE: Southwestern Louisiana.
TRANSACTIONS/CAREER NOTES: Selected by Baltimore Ravens in fourth round (105th pick overall) of 1999 NFL draft. ... Signed by Ravens (July 28, 1999). ... On injured reserve with shoulder injury (October 25, 1999-remainder of season). ... Granted free agency (March 1, 2002). ... Re-signed by Ravens (April 16, 2002). ... On injured reserve with foot injury (November 26, 2002-remainder of season). ... Granted unconditional free agency (February 28, 2003). ... Signed by Indianapolis Colts (March 13, 2003).
CHAMPIONSHIP GAME EXPERIENCE: Played in AFC championship game (2000 season). ... Member of Super Bowl championship team (2000 season).
SINGLE GAME HIGHS (regular season): Receptions—6 (September 8, 2002, vs. Carolina); yards—83 (September 8, 2002, vs. Carolina); and touchdown receptions—2 (October 6, 2002, vs. Cleveland).

Year Team	G	GS	RUSHING				RECEIVING				TOTALS			
			Att.	Yds.	Avg.	TD	No.	Yds.	Avg.	TD	TD	2pt.	Pts.	Fum.
1999—Baltimore NFL	2	0	0	0	0.0	0	1	28	28.0	1	1	0	6	0
2000—Baltimore NFL	7	1	1	6	6.0	0	11	184	16.7	2	2	0	12	0
2001—Baltimore NFL	16	5	1	1	1.0	0	24	344	14.3	2	2	0	12	1
2002—Baltimore NFL	8	5	6	31	5.2	0	24	357	14.9	2	2	0	12	1
Pro totals (4 years)	33	11	8	38	4.8	0	60	913	15.2	7	7	0	42	2

STONE, MICHAEL   CB   CARDINALS

PERSONAL: Born February 13, 1978, in Southfield, Mich. ... 5-11/197. ... Full name: Michael Ahmed Stone.
HIGH SCHOOL: Southfield-Lathrup (Southfield, Mich.).
COLLEGE: Memphis.
TRANSACTIONS/CAREER NOTES: Selected by Arizona Cardinals in second round (54th pick overall) of 2001 NFL draft. ... Signed by Cardinals (July 16, 2001).

Year Team	G	GS	TOTALS			INTERCEPTIONS			
			Tk.	Ast.	Sks.	No.	Yds.	Avg.	TD
2001—Arizona NFL	7	0	0	0	0.0	0	0	0.0	0
2002—Arizona NFL	16	0	1	2	0.0	0	0	0.0	0
Pro totals (2 years)	23	0	1	2	0.0	0	0	0.0	0

STONE, RON   G   49ERS

PERSONAL: Born July 20, 1971, in West Roxbury, Mass. ... 6-5/325.
HIGH SCHOOL: West Roxbury (Mass.).
COLLEGE: Boston College.
TRANSACTIONS/CAREER NOTES: Selected by Dallas Cowboys in fourth round (96th pick overall) of 1993 NFL draft. ... Signed by Cowboys (July 16, 1993). ... Active for four games with Cowboys (1993); did not play. ... Granted free agency (February 16, 1996). ... Tendered offer sheet by New York Giants (March 1, 1996). ... Cowboys declined to match offer (March 7, 1996). ... Granted unconditional free agency (March 1, 2002). ... Signed by San Francisco 49ers (April 12, 2002).
PLAYING EXPERIENCE: Dallas NFL, 1994 and 1995; New York Giants NFL, 1996-2001; San Francisco NFL, 2002. ... Games/Games started: 1994 (16/0), 1995 (16/1), 1996 (16/16), 1997 (16/16), 1998 (14/14), 1999 (16/16), 2000 (15/15), 2001 (15/15), 2002 (15/15). Total: 139/108.
CHAMPIONSHIP GAME EXPERIENCE: Member of Cowboys for NFC championship game (1993 season); inactive. ... Member of Super Bowl championship team (1993 and 1995 seasons). ... Played in NFC championship game (1994, 1995 and 2000 seasons). ... Played in Super Bowl XXXV (2000 season).
HONORS: Played in Pro Bowl (2000-2002 seasons).

STOUTMIRE, OMAR   S   GIANTS

PERSONAL: Born July 9, 1974, in Pensacola, Fla. ... 5-11/203.
HIGH SCHOOL: Polytechnic (Pasadena, Calif.).
COLLEGE: Fresno State.
TRANSACTIONS/CAREER NOTES: Selected by Dallas Cowboys in seventh round (224th pick overall) of 1997 NFL draft. ... Signed by Cowboys (July 14, 1997). ... Claimed on waivers by Cleveland Browns (September 6, 1999). ... Inactive for two games with Browns (1999). ... Released by Browns (September 21, 1999). ... Signed by New York Jets (October 6, 1999). ... Granted free agency (February 11, 2000). ... Re-signed by Jets (April 18, 2000). ... Released by Jets (August 27, 2000). ... Signed by New York Giants (August 30, 2000). ... Granted unconditional free agency (March 2, 2001). ... Re-signed by Giants (May 14, 2001). ... Granted unconditional free agency (February 28, 2003). ... Re-signed by Giants (March 20, 2003).
CHAMPIONSHIP GAME EXPERIENCE: Played in NFC championship game (2000 season). ... Played in Super Bowl XXXV (2000 season).

Year Team	G	GS	Tk.	Ast.	Sks.	No.	Yds.	Avg.	TD
1997—Dallas NFL	16	2	38	8	2.0	2	8	4.0	0
1998—Dallas NFL	16	12	36	16	1.0	0	0	0.0	0
1999—New York Jets NFL	12	5	25	4	1.0	2	97	48.5	1
2000—New York Giants NFL	16	0	1	0	0.0	0	0	0.0	0
2001—New York Giants NFL	16	0	2	0	0.0	0	0	0.0	0
2002—New York Giants NFL	16	16	63	18	0.0	0	0	0.0	0
Pro totals (6 years)	92	35	165	46	4.0	4	105	26.3	1

STOVER, MATT — K — RAVENS

PERSONAL: Born January 27, 1968, in Dallas. ... 5-11/178. ... Full name: John Matthew Stover.
HIGH SCHOOL: Lake Highlands (Dallas).
COLLEGE: Louisiana Tech (degree in marketing, 1991).
TRANSACTIONS/CAREER NOTES: Selected by New York Giants in 12th round (329th pick overall) of 1990 NFL draft. ... Signed by Giants (July 23, 1990). ... On injured reserve with leg injury (September 4, 1990-entire season). ... Granted unconditional free agency (February 1, 1991). ... Signed by Cleveland Browns (March 15, 1991). ... Granted free agency (March 1, 1993). ... Re-signed by Browns (July 24, 1993). ... Released by Browns (August 30, 1993). ... Re-signed by Browns (August 31, 1993). ... Granted unconditional free agency (February 17, 1994). ... Re-signed by Browns (March 4, 1994). ... Browns franchise moved to Baltimore and renamed Ravens for 1996 season (March 11, 1996).
CHAMPIONSHIP GAME EXPERIENCE: Played in AFC championship game (2000 season). ... Member of Super Bowl championship team (2000 season).
HONORS: Named kicker on THE SPORTING NEWS NFL All-Pro team (2000). ... Played in Pro Bowl (2000 season).
RECORDS: Holds NFL record for most consecutive games with one or more field goals made—38 (October 31, 1999-December 2, 2001).

		FIELD GOALS							TOTALS		
Year Team	G	1-29	30-39	40-49	50+	Tot.	Pct.	Lg.	XPM	XPA	Pts.
1990—New York Giants NFL				Did not play.							
1991—Cleveland NFL	16	3-5	8-9	3-6	2-2	16-22	72.7	§55	33	34	81
1992—Cleveland NFL	16	12-12	6-8	2-6	1-3	21-29	72.4	51	29	30	92
1993—Cleveland NFL	16	4-4	6-8	6-8	1-4	16-22	72.7	53	36	36	84
1994—Cleveland NFL	16	8-8	10-11	8-8	0-1	26-28	92.9	45	32	32	110
1995—Cleveland NFL	16	13-13	9-10	7-9	0-1	29-33	87.9	47	26	26	113
1996—Baltimore NFL	16	8-8	5-6	5-10	1-1	19-25	76.0	50	34	35	91
1997—Baltimore NFL	16	8-9	12-12	6-11	0-2	26-34	76.5	49	32	32	110
1998—Baltimore NFL	16	6-6	5-5	10-17	0-0	21-28	75.0	48	24	24	87
1999—Baltimore NFL	16	13-13	6-8	7-7	2-5	28-33	84.8	50	32	32	116
2000—Baltimore NFL	16	11-11	12-13	10-12	2-3	*35-*39	89.7	51	30	30	§135
2001—Baltimore NFL	16	16-16	9-10	5-9	0-0	30-35	85.7	49	25	25	115
2002—Baltimore NFL	15	9-9	4-5	7-10	1-1	21-25	84.0	51	33	33	96
Pro totals (12 years)	191	111-114	91-103	76-113	10-23	288-353	81.6	55	366	369	1230

STRAHAN, MICHAEL — DE — GIANTS

PERSONAL: Born November 21, 1971, in Houston. ... 6-5/275. ... Full name: Michael Anthony Strahan. ... Nephew of Art Strahan, defensive tackle with Atlanta Falcons (1968). ... Name pronounced STRAY-han.
HIGH SCHOOL: Westbury (Houston), then Mannheim (West Germany) American.
COLLEGE: Texas Southern.
TRANSACTIONS/CAREER NOTES: Selected by New York Giants in second round (40th pick overall) of 1993 NFL draft. ... Signed by Giants (July 25, 1993). ... On injured reserve with foot injury (January 13, 1994-remainder of playoffs). ... Granted free agency (February 16, 1996). ... Re-signed by Giants (July 8, 1996).
CHAMPIONSHIP GAME EXPERIENCE: Played in NFC championship game (2000 season). ... Played in Super Bowl XXXV (2000 season).
HONORS: Named defensive end on THE SPORTING NEWS NFL All-Pro team (1997 and 2001). ... Played in Pro Bowl (1997-1999, 2001 and 2002 seasons).
RECORDS: Holds NFL single-season record for most sacks—22 1/2 (2001).

			TOTALS			INTERCEPTIONS			
Year Team	G	GS	Tk.	Ast.	Sks.	No.	Yds.	Avg.	TD
1993—New York Giants NFL	9	0	1	2	1.0	0	0	0.0	0
1994—New York Giants NFL	15	15	27	13	4.5	0	0	0.0	0
1995—New York Giants NFL	15	15	48	10	7.5	2	56	28.0	0
1996—New York Giants NFL	16	16	54	9	5.0	0	0	0.0	0
1997—New York Giants NFL	16	16	49	19	14.0	0	0	0.0	0
1998—New York Giants NFL	16	15	53	14	15.0	1	24	24.0	1
1999—New York Giants NFL	16	16	43	15	5.5	1	44	44.0	1
2000—New York Giants NFL	16	16	51	15	9.5	0	0	0.0	0
2001—New York Giants NFL	16	16	62	11	*22.5	0	0	0.0	0
2002—New York Giants NFL	16	16	57	14	11.0	0	0	0.0	0
Pro totals (10 years)	151	141	445	122	95.5	4	124	31.0	2

STREETS, TAI — WR — 49ERS

PERSONAL: Born April 20, 1977, in Matteson, Ill. ... 6-2/206.
HIGH SCHOOL: Thornton Township (Harvey, Ill.).
COLLEGE: Michigan.
TRANSACTIONS/CAREER NOTES: Selected by San Francisco 49ers in sixth round (171st pick overall) of 1999 NFL draft. ... Signed by 49ers (July 30, 1999). ... On non-football injury list with Achilles' tendon injury (July 30-November 30, 1999). ... Granted free agency (February 28, 2003). ... Re-signed by 49ers (May 16, 2003).

SINGLE GAME HIGHS (regular season): Receptions—8 (December 21, 2002, vs. Arizona); yards—90 (December 21, 2002, vs. Arizona); and touchdown receptions—2 (December 30, 2002, vs. St. Louis).

				RECEIVING		
Year Team	G	GS	No.	Yds.	Avg.	TD
1999—San Francisco NFL	2	0	2	25	12.5	0
2000—San Francisco NFL	15	1	19	287	15.1	0
2001—San Francisco NFL	16	3	28	345	12.3	1
2002—San Francisco NFL	16	14	72	756	10.5	5
Pro totals (4 years)	49	18	121	1413	11.7	6

STRONG, FRANK — LB — 49ERS

PERSONAL: Born January 14, 1980, in Stockton, Calif. ... 6-1/232.
HIGH SCHOOL: Franklin (Stockton, Calif.).
COLLEGE: Southern California.
TRANSACTIONS/CAREER NOTES: Signed as non-drafted free agent by San Francisco 49ers (April 24, 2002). ... On injured reserve with shoulder injury (October 25, 2002-remainder of season).

			TOTALS			INTERCEPTIONS			
Year Team	G	GS	Tk.	Ast.	Sks.	No.	Yds.	Avg.	TD
2002—San Francisco NFL	6	0	1	0	0.0	0	0	0.0	0

STRONG, MACK — FB — SEAHAWKS

PERSONAL: Born September 11, 1971, in Fort Benning, Ga. ... 6-0/245.
HIGH SCHOOL: Brookstone (Columbus, Ga.).
COLLEGE: Georgia.
TRANSACTIONS/CAREER NOTES: Signed as non-drafted free agent by Seattle Seahawks (April 28, 1993). ... Released by Seahawks (September 4, 1993). ... Re-signed by Seahawks to practice squad (September 6, 1993). ... Released by Seahawks (February 10, 2000). ... Re-signed by Seahawks (February 14, 2000). ... Granted unconditional free agency (March 1, 2002). ... Re-signed by Seahawks (May 1, 2002). ... Granted unconditional free agency (February 28, 2003). ... Re-signed by Seahawks (April 8, 2003).
SINGLE GAME HIGHS (regular season): Attempts—10 (December 11, 1994, vs. Houston); yards—44 (December 11, 1994, vs. Houston); rushing touchdowns—1 (November 12, 1995, vs. Jacksonville).

			RUSHING				RECEIVING				TOTALS			
Year Team	G	GS	Att.	Yds.	Avg.	TD	No.	Yds.	Avg.	TD	TD	2pt.	Pts.	Fum.
1993—Seattle NFL							Did not play.							
1994—Seattle NFL	8	1	27	114	4.2	2	3	3	1.0	0	2	0	12	1
1995—Seattle NFL	16	2	8	23	2.9	1	12	117	9.8	3	4	0	24	2
1996—Seattle NFL	14	8	5	8	1.6	0	9	78	8.7	0	0	0	0	0
1997—Seattle NFL	16	9	4	8	2.0	0	13	91	7.0	2	2	0	12	0
1998—Seattle NFL	16	5	15	47	3.1	0	8	48	6.0	2	2	0	12	2
1999—Seattle NFL	14	1	1	0	0.0	0	1	5	5.0	0	0	0	0	0
2000—Seattle NFL	16	12	3	9	3.0	0	23	141	6.1	1	1	0	6	0
2001—Seattle NFL	16	13	17	55	3.2	0	17	141	8.3	0	0	0	0	0
2002—Seattle NFL	16	12	23	94	4.1	0	22	120	5.5	2	2	0	12	0
Pro totals (9 years)	132	63	103	358	3.5	3	108	744	6.9	10	13	0	78	5

STROUD, MARCUS — DT — JAGUARS

PERSONAL: Born June 25, 1978, in Thomasville, Ga. ... 6-6/322.
HIGH SCHOOL: Brooks County (Barney, Ga.).
COLLEGE: Georgia.
TRANSACTIONS/CAREER NOTES: Selected by Jacksonville Jaguars in first round (13th pick overall) of 2001 draft. ... Signed by Jaguars (July 26, 2001).

			TOTALS		
Year Team	G	GS	Tk.	Ast.	Sks.
2001—Jacksonville NFL	16	0	21	4	0.0
2002—Jacksonville NFL	16	16	41	7	6.5
Pro totals (2 years)	32	16	62	11	6.5

STRYZINSKI, DAN — P — JETS

PERSONAL: Born May 15, 1965, in Vincennes, Ind. ... 6-2/205. ... Full name: Daniel Thomas Stryzinski. ... Name pronounced stra-ZIN-ski.
HIGH SCHOOL: Lincoln (Vincennes, Ind.).
COLLEGE: Indiana (bachelor of science degree in public finance and management, 1988).
TRANSACTIONS/CAREER NOTES: Signed as non-drafted free agent by Indianapolis Colts (July 1988). ... Released by Colts (August 23, 1988). ... Signed by Cleveland Browns (August 25, 1988). ... Released by Browns (August 30, 1988). ... Re-signed by Browns for 1989 season. ... Released by Browns (August 30, 1989). ... Signed by New Orleans Saints to developmental squad (October 11, 1989). ... Granted free agency following 1989 season. ... Signed by Pittsburgh Steelers (March 14, 1990). ... Granted unconditional free agency (February 1, 1992). ... Signed by Tampa Bay Buccaneers (February 21, 1992). ... Granted unconditional free agency (February 17, 1995). ... Signed by Atlanta Falcons (February 20, 1995). ... Granted unconditional free agency (March 2, 2001). ... Signed by Kansas City Chiefs (March 9, 2001). ... Released by Chiefs (February 28, 2003). ... Signed by New York Jets (March 24, 2003).
CHAMPIONSHIP GAME EXPERIENCE: Played in NFC championship game (1998 season). ... Played in Super Bowl XXXIII (1998 season).

Year Team	G	No.	Yds.	Avg.	Net avg.	In. 20	Blk.
				PUNTING			
1990—Pittsburgh NFL	16	65	2454	37.8	34.1	18	1
1991—Pittsburgh NFL	16	74	2996	40.5	36.2	10	1
1992—Tampa Bay NFL	16	74	3015	40.7	36.2	15	0
1993—Tampa Bay NFL	16	*93	3772	40.6	35.2	24	1
1994—Tampa Bay NFL	16	72	2800	38.9	35.8	20	0
1995—Atlanta NFL	16	67	2759	41.2	36.2	21	0
1996—Atlanta NFL	16	75	3152	42.0	35.5	22	0
1997—Atlanta NFL	16	89	3498	39.3	36.7	20	0
1998—Atlanta NFL	16	74	2963	40.0	36.6	25	0
1999—Atlanta NFL	16	80	3163	39.5	37.1	27	0
2000—Atlanta NFL	16	84	3447	41.0	‡37.9	27	1
2001—Kansas City NFL	16	73	2976	40.8	35.6	27	0
2002—Kansas City NFL	16	64	2422	37.8	31.2	15	1
Pro totals (13 years)	208	984	39417	40.1	35.8	271	5

STUBBLEFIELD, DANA — DT — RAIDERS

PERSONAL: Born November 14, 1970, in Cleves, Ohio. ... 6-2/290. ... Full name: Dana William Stubblefield.
HIGH SCHOOL: Taylor (North Bend, Ohio).
COLLEGE: Kansas.
TRANSACTIONS/CAREER NOTES: Selected by San Francisco 49ers in first round (26th pick overall) of 1993 NFL draft. ... Signed by 49ers (July 14, 1993). ... Granted unconditional free agency (February 13, 1998). ... Signed by Washington Redskins (February 23, 1998). ... Released by Redskins (March 1, 2001). ... Signed by 49ers (April 25, 2001). ... Released by 49ers (February 26, 2003). ... Signed by Oakland Raiders (March 12, 2003).
CHAMPIONSHIP GAME EXPERIENCE: Played in NFC championship game (1993, 1994 and 1997 seasons). ... Member of Super Bowl championship team (1994 season).
HONORS: Played in Pro Bowl (1994, 1995 and 1997 seasons). ... Named defensive tackle on THE SPORTING NEWS NFL All-Pro team (1997).

Year Team	G	GS	Tk.	Ast.	Sks.	No.	Yds.	Avg.	TD
			TOTALS			**INTERCEPTIONS**			
1993—San Francisco NFL	16	14	55	9	10.5	0	0	0.0	0
1994—San Francisco NFL	14	14	34	4	8.5	0	0	0.0	0
1995—San Francisco NFL	16	16	27	7	4.5	1	12	12.0	0
1996—San Francisco NFL	15	15	26	7	1.0	1	15	15.0	0
1997—San Francisco NFL	16	16	48	13	15.0	0	0	0.0	0
1998—Washington NFL	7	7	26	6	1.5	0	0	0.0	0
1999—Washington NFL	16	16	30	14	3.0	0	0	0.0	0
2000—Washington NFL	15	14	31	9	2.5	0	0	0.0	0
2001—San Francisco NFL	16	16	25	7	4.0	0	0	0.0	0
2002—San Francisco NFL	15	15	29	9	3.0	0	0	0.0	0
Pro totals (10 years)	146	143	331	85	53.5	2	27	13.5	0

SULFSTED, ALEX — OT — REDSKINS

PERSONAL: Born December 21, 1977, in Lebanon, Ohio. ... 6-3/320.
HIGH SCHOOL: Mariemont (Ohio).
COLLEGE: Miami (Ohio).
TRANSACTIONS/CAREER NOTES: Selected by Kansas City Chiefs in sixth round (176th pick overall) of 2001 NFL draft. ... Signed by Chiefs (July 18, 2001). ... Released by Chiefs (September 1, 2001). ... Signed by Cincinnati Bengals to practice squad (September 4, 2001). ... Signed by Washington Redskins off Bengals practice squad (October 26, 2001). ... Re-signed by Redskins (March 31, 2003).
PLAYING EXPERIENCE: Washington NFL, 2002. ... Games/Games started: 2002 (14/3).

SULLIVAN, MARQUES — OT — BILLS

PERSONAL: Born February 2, 1978, in Oak Park, Ill. ... 6-5/320.
HIGH SCHOOL: Fenwick (Oak Park, Ill.).
COLLEGE: Illinois.
TRANSACTIONS/CAREER NOTES: Selected by Buffalo Bills in fifth round (144th pick overall) of 2001 NFL draft. ... Signed by Bills (June 11, 2001).
PLAYING EXPERIENCE: Buffalo NFL, 2001-2002. ... Games/Games started: 2001 (10/2), 2002 (16/6). Total: 26/18.

SURTAIN, PATRICK — CB — DOLPHINS

PERSONAL: Born June 19, 1976, in New Orleans. ... 5-11/192. ... Full name: Patrick Frank Surtain. ... Name pronounced sir-TANE.
HIGH SCHOOL: Edna Karr (New Orleans).
COLLEGE: Southern Mississippi.
TRANSACTIONS/CAREER NOTES: Selected by Miami Dolphins in second round (44th pick overall) of 1998 NFL draft. ... Signed by Dolphins (July 21, 1998).
HONORS: Named cornerback on THE SPORTING NEWS college All-America second team (1997). ... Named to play in Pro Bowl (2002 season); replaced by Sam Madison due to injury. ... Named cornerback on the THE SPORTING NEWS NFL All-Pro team (2002).

Year Team	G	GS	Tk.	Ast.	Sks.	No.	Yds.	Avg.	TD
			TOTALS			**INTERCEPTIONS**			
1998—Miami NFL	16	0	23	5	0.0	2	1	0.5	0
1999—Miami NFL	16	6	32	5	2.0	2	28	14.0	0
2000—Miami NFL	16	16	44	9	1.0	5	55	11.0	0
2001—Miami NFL	16	16	43	10	1.0	3	74	24.7	1
2002—Miami NFL	14	14	39	19	1.5	6	79	13.2	1
Pro totals (5 years)	78	52	181	48	5.5	18	237	13.2	2

SUTHERLAND, VINNY — WR/KR

PERSONAL: Born April 22, 1978, in West Palm Beach, Fla. ... 5-8/188. ... Full name: Vincent Joseph Sutherland.
HIGH SCHOOL: Palm Beach Lakes (Fla.).
COLLEGE: Purdue.
TRANSACTIONS/CAREER NOTES: Selected by Atlanta Falcons in fifth round (136th pick overall) of 2001 NFL draft. ... Signed by Falcons (May 29, 2001). ... Released by Falcons (August 27, 2001). ... Signed by San Francisco 49ers (September 3, 2001). ... Released by 49ers (August 27, 2002). ... Signed by Chicago Bears (October 3, 2002). ... Released by Bears (October 25, 2002). ... Signed by 49ers (January 2, 2003). ... Granted free agency (February 28, 2003).
SINGLE GAME HIGHS (regular season): Receptions—1 (December 30, 2001, vs. Dallas); yards—5 (December 30, 2001, vs. Dallas); and touchdown receptions—0.

			RUSHING				RECEIVING				PUNT RETURNS				KICKOFF RETURNS				TOTALS		
Year Team	G	GS	Att.	Yds.	Avg.	TD	No.	Yds.	Avg.	TD	No.	Yds.	Avg.	TD	No.	Yds.	Avg.	TD	TD	2pt.	Pts.
2001—San Fran. NFL	15	0	1	16	16.0	0	1	5	5.0	0	21	147	7.0	0	50	1140	22.8	0	0	0	0
2002—Chicago NFL	1	0	0	0	0.0	0	0	0	0.0	0	0	0	0.0	0	3	49	16.3	0	0	0	0
Pro totals (2 years)	16	0	1	16	16.0	0	1	5	5.0	0	21	147	7.0	0	53	1189	22.4	0	0	0	0

SWAYNE, KEVIN — WR — JETS

PERSONAL: Born January 17, 1975, in Banning, Calif. ... 6-1/191.
HIGH SCHOOL: Banning (Calif.).
COLLEGE: Wayne State.
TRANSACTIONS/CAREER NOTES: Signed as non-drafted free agent by Chicago Bears (April 25, 1997). ... Released by Bears prior to 1997 season. ... Signed by Philadelphia Eagles to practice squad (November 17, 1999). ... Granted free agency after 1999 season. ... Signed by San Diego Chargers (February 10, 2000). ... Released by Chargers (August 23, 2000). ... Signed by New York Jets (May 30, 2001). ... Re-signed by Jets (April 2, 2003).
SINGLE GAME HIGHS (regular season): Receptions—4 (December 16, 2001, vs. Cincinnati); yards—74 (December 16, 2001, vs. Cincinnati); and touchdown receptions—0.

			RECEIVING			
Year Team	G	GS	No.	Yds.	Avg.	TD
2001—New York Jets NFL	15	1	13	203	15.6	0
2002—New York Jets NFL	15	0	5	78	15.6	0
Pro totals (2 years)	30	1	18	281	15.6	0

SWIFT, JUSTIN — TE — TEXANS

PERSONAL: Born August 14, 1975, in Kansas City, Kan. ... 6-3/265. ... Full name: Justin Charles Swift.
HIGH SCHOOL: Blue Valley (Overland Park, Kan.).
COLLEGE: Kansas State.
TRANSACTIONS/CAREER NOTES: Selected by Denver Broncos in seventh round (238th pick overall) of 1999 NFL draft. ... Signed by Broncos (July 20, 1999). ... Released by Broncos (August 27, 1999). ... Signed by Philadelphia Eagles (September 14, 1999). ... Released by Eagles (September 28, 1999). ... Signed by Broncos to practice squad (October 19, 1999). ... Released by Broncos (November 2, 1999). ... Signed by San Francisco 49ers to practice squad (November 15, 1999). ... Released by 49ers (February 10, 2000). ... Re-signed by 49ers (February 18, 2000). ... Assigned by 49ers to Frankfurt Galaxy in 2000 NFL Europe enhancement allocation program (February 18, 2000). ... Granted free agency (February 28, 2003). ... Signed by Houston Texans (June 1, 2003).
SINGLE GAME HIGHS (regular season): Receptions—3 (November 10, 2002, vs. Kansas City); yards—18 (November 10, 2002, vs. Kansas City); and touchdown receptions—1 (October 28, 2001, vs. Chicago).

			RECEIVING			
Year Team	G	GS	No.	Yds.	Avg.	TD
1999—Philadelphia NFL	1	0	0	0	0.0	0
2000—Frankfurt NFLE	...	...	27	260	9.6	2
—San Francisco NFL	16	1	1	8	8.0	0
2001—San Francisco NFL	16	2	11	66	6.0	1
2002—San Francisco NFL	16	4	10	63	6.3	0
NFL Europe totals (1 year)	...	...	27	260	9.6	2
NFL totals (4 years)	49	7	22	137	6.2	1
Pro totals (5 years)	...	...	49	397	8.1	3

SWINEY, ERWIN — CB — PACKERS

PERSONAL: Born October 8, 1978, in Dallas. ... 6-0/192. ... Full name: Erwin Bernard Swiney.
HIGH SCHOOL: Northeast (Lincoln, Neb.).
COLLEGE: Nebraska (degree in sociology).
TRANSACTIONS/CAREER NOTES: Signed as non-drafted free agent by Green Bay Packers (April 25, 2002). ... Released by Packers (September 1, 2002). ... Re-signed by Packers to practice squad (September 3, 2002). ... Released by Packers (September 5, 2002). ... Re-signed by Packers to practice squad (September 10, 2002). ... Activated (October 12, 2002). ... Released by Packers (October 16, 2002). ... Re-signed by Packers to practice squad (October 17, 2002). ... Released by Packers (October 22, 2002). ... Re-signed by Packers to practice squad (October 31, 2002). ... Activated (December 22, 2002).

			TOTALS			INTERCEPTIONS			
Year Team	G	GS	Tk.	Ast.	Sks.	No.	Yds.	Avg.	TD
2002—Green Bay NFL	3	0	0	0	0.0	0	0	0.0	0

SWINTON, REGGIE   WR   COWBOYS

PERSONAL: Born July 24, 1975, in Little Rock, Ark. ... 6-0/186.
HIGH SCHOOL: Central (Ark.).
COLLEGE: Murray State.
TRANSACTIONS/CAREER NOTES: Signed as non-drafted free agent by Jacksonville Jaguars (April 18, 1998). ... Released by Jaguars (August 25, 1998). ... Signed by Toronto Argonauts of the CFL (February 19, 1999). ... Traded by Argonauts to Winnipeg Blue Bombers for Eric Blount and RB Mitch Running (March 1, 1999). ... Released by Blue Bombers (August 16, 1999). ... Signed by Edmonton Eskimos of CFL (September 13, 1999). ... Released by Eskimos (October 12, 1999). ... Signed by Seattle Seahawks (February 24, 2000). ... Released by Seahawks (August 27, 2000). ... Signed by Dallas Cowboys (August 6, 2001). ... Re-signed by Cowboys (March 7, 2003).
SINGLE GAME HIGHS (regular season): Receptions—3 (September 22, 2002, vs. Philadelphia); yards—72 (December 23, 2001, vs. Arizona); and touchdown receptions—1 (December 23, 2001, vs. Arizona).

			RECEIVING				PUNT RETURNS				KICKOFF RETURNS				TOTALS		
Year Team	G	GS	No.	Yds.	Avg.	TD	No.	Yds.	Avg.	TD	No.	Yds.	Avg.	TD	TD 2pt.	Pts.	Fum.
1999—Winnipeg CFL	4	...	11	162	14.7	1	7	235	33.6	1	5	18	3.6	0	2 0	12	0
—Toronto CFL	3	...	3	22	7.3	0	9	178	19.8	0	3	33	11.0	0	0 0	0	0
2000—									Did not play.								
2001—Dallas NFL	15	1	7	117	16.7	1	31	414	13.4	†1	56	1327	23.7	0	2 0	12	4
2002—Dallas NFL	14	0	7	63	9.0	0	19	141	7.4	0	28	697	24.9	1	1 0	6	1
CFL totals (1 year)	7	...	14	184	13.1	1	16	413	25.8	1	8	51	6.4	0	2 0	12	0
NFL totals (2 years)	29	1	14	180	12.9	1	50	555	11.1	1	84	2024	24.1	1	3 0	18	5
Pro totals (3 years)	36	...	28	364	13.0	2	66	968	14.7	2	92	2075	22.6	1	5 0	30	5

SWORD, SAM   LB

PERSONAL: Born December 4, 1974, in Saginaw, Mich. ... 6-1/244. ... Full name: Sam Lee-Arthur Sword.
HIGH SCHOOL: Arthur Hill (Saginaw, Mich.).
COLLEGE: Michigan.
TRANSACTIONS/CAREER NOTES: Signed as non-drafted free agent by Oakland Raiders (April 22, 1999). ... Released by Raiders (August 27, 2000). ... Signed by Indianapolis Colts (October 25, 2000). ... Released by Colts (November 24, 2000). ... Re-signed by Colts (November 30, 2000). ... Granted free agency (March 1, 2002). ... Re-signed by Colts (May 16, 2002). ... Granted unconditional free agency (February 28, 2003).

			TOTALS			INTERCEPTIONS			
Year Team	G	GS	Tk.	Ast.	Sks.	No.	Yds.	Avg.	TD
1999—Oakland NFL	10	5	16	6	1.0	0	0	0.0	0
2000—Indianapolis NFL	4	0	0	0	0.0	0	0	0.0	0
2001—Indianapolis NFL	16	2	22	5	1.0	0	0	0.0	0
2002—Indianapolis NFL	16	1	10	2	0.0	0	0	0.0	0
Pro totals (4 years)	46	8	48	13	2.0	0	0	0.0	0

SZOTT, DAVE   G   JETS

PERSONAL: Born December 12, 1967, in Passaic, N.J. ... 6-4/289. ... Full name: David Andrew Szott. ... Name pronounced ZOT.
HIGH SCHOOL: Clifton (N.J.).
COLLEGE: Penn State (degree in political science).
TRANSACTIONS/CAREER NOTES: Selected by Kansas City Chiefs in seventh round (180th pick overall) of 1990 NFL draft. ... Signed by Chiefs (July 25, 1990). ... Re-signed by Chiefs for 1993 season. ... On injured reserve with arm injury (December 2, 1998-remainder of season). ... On injured reserve with arm injury (October 11, 2000-remainder of season). ... Granted unconditional free agency (March 2, 2001). ... Signed by Washington Redskins (August 19, 2001). ... Granted unconditional free agency (March 1, 2002). ... Signed by New York Jets (March 21, 2002). ... On physically unable to perform list with knee injury (August 27-November 18, 2002).
PLAYING EXPERIENCE: Kansas City NFL, 1990-2000; Washington NFL, 2001; New York Jets NFL, 2002. ... Games/Games started: 1990 (16/11), 1991 (16/16), 1992 (16/16), 1993 (14/13), 1994 (16/16), 1995 (16/16), 1996 (16/16), 1997 (16/16), 1998 (1/1), 1999 (14/14), 2000 (1/1), 2001 (16/16), 2002 (4/4). Total: 162/156.
CHAMPIONSHIP GAME EXPERIENCE: Played in AFC championship game (1993 season).

TAFOYA, JOE   DE   BEARS

PERSONAL: Born September 6, 1977, in Pittsburg, Calif. ... 6-4/278. ... Full name: Joseph Peter Tafoya.
HIGH SCHOOL: Pittsburg (Calif.).
COLLEGE: Arizona.
TRANSACTIONS/CAREER NOTES: Selected by Tampa Bay Buccaneers in seventh round (234th pick overall) of 2001 NFL draft. ... Signed by Buccaneers (July 18, 2001). ... Released by Buccaneers (September 2, 2001). ... Signed by Chicago Bears to practice squad (October 9, 2001). ... Activated (October 23, 2001).

			TOTALS		
Year Team	G	GS	Tk.	Ast.	Sks.
2001—Chicago NFL	5	0	0	0	0.0
2002—Chicago NFL	14	1	5	3	0.5
Pro totals (2 years)	19	1	5	3	0.5

TAIT, JOHN   OT   CHIEFS

PERSONAL: Born January 26, 1975, in Phoenix. ... 6-6/323.
HIGH SCHOOL: McClintock (Tempe, Ariz.).
COLLEGE: Brigham Young (degree in communications).
TRANSACTIONS/CAREER NOTES: Selected after junior season by Kansas City Chiefs in first round (14th pick overall) of 1999 NFL draft. ... Signed by Chiefs (September 9, 1999).
PLAYING EXPERIENCE: Kansas City NFL, 1999-2002. ... Games/Games started: 1999 (12/3), 2000 (15/15), 2001 (16/16), 2002 (16/16). Total: 59/50.

S
T

TANNER, BARRON — DT — CARDINALS

PERSONAL: Born September 14, 1973, in Athens, Texas. ... 6-3/346. ... Full name: Barron Keith Tanner.
HIGH SCHOOL: Athens (Texas).
COLLEGE: Oklahoma.
TRANSACTIONS/CAREER NOTES: Selected by Miami Dolphins in fifth round (149th pick overall) of 1997 NFL draft. ... Signed by Dolphins (July 8, 1997). ... Traded by Dolphins to Washington Redskins for seventh-round pick (traded to San Francisco) in 2001 draft (September 4, 1999). ... Inactive for all 16 games (1999). ... Granted free agency (February 11, 2000). ... Re-signed by Redskins (June 6, 2000). ... Released by Redskins (August 27, 2000). ... Signed by Arizona Cardinals (November 6, 2000). ... Granted unconditional free agency (February 28, 2003). ... Re-signed by Cardinals (March 5, 2003).

			TOTALS			INTERCEPTIONS			
Year Team	G	GS	Tk.	Ast.	Sks.	No.	Yds.	Avg.	TD
1997—Miami NFL	16	0	16	6	0.0	0	0	0.0	0
1998—Miami NFL	13	0	5	4	0.0	0	0	0.0	0
1999—Washington NFL			Did not play.						
2000—Arizona NFL	4	0	5	0	0.0	0	0	0.0	0
2001—Arizona NFL	16	16	24	13	0.0	0	0	0.0	0
2002—Arizona NFL	15	8	17	9	2.0	1	17	17.0	0
Pro totals (5 years)	64	24	67	32	2.0	1	17	17.0	0

TATE, ROBERT — CB

PERSONAL: Born October 19, 1973, in Harrisburg, Pa. ... 5-10/193.
HIGH SCHOOL: John Harris (Harrisburg, Pa.), then Milford (Conn.) Academy.
COLLEGE: Cincinnati.
TRANSACTIONS/CAREER NOTES: Selected by Minnesota Vikings in sixth round (183rd pick overall) of 1997 NFL draft. ... Signed by Vikings (June 17, 1997). ... On injured reserve with ankle injury (October 8, 1997-remainder of season). ... Released by Vikings (August 21, 2002). ... Signed by Baltimore Ravens (August 22, 2002). ... Granted unconditional free agency (February 28, 2003).
CHAMPIONSHIP GAME EXPERIENCE: Member of Vikings for NFC championship game (1998 season); inactive. ... Played in NFC championship game (2000 season).
SINGLE GAME HIGHS (regular season): Receptions—1 (October 3, 1999, vs. Tampa Bay); yards—17 (December 3, 1999, vs. Tampa Bay); and touchdown receptions—0.

			TOTALS			INTERCEPTIONS				KICKOFF RETURNS				TOTALS			
Year Team	G	GS	Tk.	Ast.	Sks.	No.	Yds.	Avg.	TD	No.	Yds.	Avg.	TD	TD	2pt.	Pts.	Fum.
1997—Minnesota NFL	4	0	0	0	0.0	0	0	0.0	0	10	196	19.6	0	0	0	0	0
1998—Minnesota NFL	15	1	0	0	0.0	0	0	0.0	0	2	43	21.5	0	0	0	0	0
1999—Minnesota NFL	16	1	14	1	0.0	1	18	18.0	0	25	627	25.1	1	1	0	6	1
2000—Minnesota NFL	16	16	57	12	0.0	2	12	6.0	0	0	0	0.0	0	0	0	0	0
2001—Minnesota NFL	16	5	34	7	0.0	0	0	0.0	0	0	0	0.0	0	0	0	0	0
2002—Baltimore NFL	13	1	11	1	0.0	0	0	0.0	0	17	356	20.9	0	0	0	0	2
Pro totals (6 years)	80	24	116	21	0.0	3	30	10.0	0	54	1222	22.6	1	1	0	6	3

TAUSCHER, MARK — OT/OG — PACKERS

PERSONAL: Born June 17, 1977, in Marshfield, Wis. ... 6-4/320. ... Full name: Mark Gerald Tauscher.
HIGH SCHOOL: Auburndale (Wis.).
COLLEGE: Wisconsin.
TRANSACTIONS/CAREER NOTES: Selected by Green Bay Packers in seventh round (224th pick overall) of 2000 NFL draft. ... Signed by Packers (June 21, 2000). ... On injured reserve with knee injury (September 18, 2002-remainder of season).
PLAYING EXPERIENCE: Green Bay NFL, 2000-2002. ... Games/Games started: 2000 (16/14), 2001 (16/16), 2002 (2/2). Total: 34/32.

TAYLOR, BEN — LB — BROWNS

PERSONAL: Born August 31, 1978, in Bellaire, Ohio. ... 6-2/240. ... Full name: Benjamin Frazier Taylor.
HIGH SCHOOL: Bellaire (Ohio).
COLLEGE: Virginia Tech.
TRANSACTIONS/CAREER NOTES: Selected by Cleveland Browns in fourth round (111th pick overall) of 2002 NFL draft. ... Signed by Browns (July 19, 2002). ... On injured reserve with hamstring injury (November 25, 2002-remainder of season).
HONORS: Named linebacker on THE SPORTING NEWS college All-America third team (2001).

			TOTALS			INTERCEPTIONS			
Year Team	G	GS	Tk.	Ast.	Sks.	No.	Yds.	Avg.	TD
2002—Cleveland NFL	7	0	1	2	0.0	0	0	0.0	0

TAYLOR, BOBBY — CB — EAGLES

PERSONAL: Born December 28, 1973, in Houston. ... 6-3/216. ... Full name: Robert Taylor. ... Son of Robert Taylor, silver medalist in 100-meter dash and member of gold-medal winning 400-meter relay team at 1972 Summer Olympics.
HIGH SCHOOL: Longview (Texas).
COLLEGE: Notre Dame.
TRANSACTIONS/CAREER NOTES: Selected after junior season by Philadelphia Eagles in second round (49th pick overall) of 1995 NFL draft. ... Signed by Eagles (July 19, 1995). ... On injured reserve with knee injury (October 17, 1997-remainder of season). ... Granted free agency (February 13, 1998). ... Re-signed by Eagles (June 11, 1998). ... On injured reserve with fractured jaw (December 28, 1999-remainder of season).

CHAMPIONSHIP GAME EXPERIENCE: Played in NFC championship game (2001 and 2002 seasons).
HONORS: Named defensive back on THE SPORTING NEWS college All-America first team (1993 and 1994). ... Played in Pro Bowl (2002 season).

Year Team	G	GS	TOTALS Tk.	Ast.	Sks.	INTERCEPTIONS No.	Yds.	Avg.	TD
1995—Philadelphia NFL	16	12	47	5	0.0	2	52	26.0	0
1996—Philadelphia NFL	16	16	55	7	1.0	3	-1	-0.3	0
1997—Philadelphia NFL	6	5	14	4	2.0	0	0	0.0	0
1998—Philadelphia NFL	11	10	22	9	0.0	0	0	0.0	0
1999—Philadelphia NFL	15	14	39	7	0.0	4	59	14.8	1
2000—Philadelphia NFL	16	15	39	7	0.0	3	64	21.3	0
2001—Philadelphia NFL	16	14	36	3	1.0	1	5	5.0	0
2002—Philadelphia NFL	16	16	47	11	0.0	5	43	8.6	1
Pro totals (8 years)	112	102	299	53	4.0	18	222	12.3	2

TAYLOR, CHESTER · RB · RAVENS

PERSONAL: Born September 22, 1979, in River Rouge, Mich. ... 5-11/213. ... Full name: Chester Lamar Taylor.
HIGH SCHOOL: River Rouge (Mich.).
COLLEGE: Toledo.
TRANSACTIONS/CAREER NOTES: Selected by Baltimore Ravens in sixth round (207th pick overall) of 2002 NFL draft. ... Signed by Ravens (July 24, 2002).
SINGLE GAME HIGHS (regular season): Attempts—5 (December 29, 2002, vs. Pittsburgh); yards—25 (November 10, 2002, vs. Cincinnati); and rushing touchdowns—0.

Year Team	G	GS	RUSHING Att.	Yds.	Avg.	TD	RECEIVING No.	Yds.	Avg.	TD	KICKOFF RETURNS No.	Yds.	Avg.	TD	TOTALS TD	2pt.	Pts.	Fum.
2002—Baltimore NFL	15	2	33	122	3.7	0	14	129	9.2	2	10	236	23.6	0	2	1	14	1

TAYLOR, FRED · RB · JAGUARS

PERSONAL: Born January 27, 1976, in Pahokee, Fla. ... 6-1/232. ... Full name: Frederick Antwon Taylor.
HIGH SCHOOL: Glades Central (Belle Glade, Fla.).
COLLEGE: Florida.
TRANSACTIONS/CAREER NOTES: Selected by Jacksonville Jaguars in first round (ninth pick overall) of 1998 NFL draft. ... Signed by Jaguars (July 6, 1998).
CHAMPIONSHIP GAME EXPERIENCE: Played in AFC championship game (1999 season).
HONORS: Named running back on THE SPORTING NEWS college All-America third team (1997).
SINGLE GAME HIGHS (regular season): Attempts—32 (December 17, 2000, vs. Cincinnati); yards—234 (November 19, 2000, vs. Pittsburgh); and rushing touchdowns—3 (December 3, 2000, vs. Cleveland).
STATISTICAL PLATEAUS: 100-yard rushing games: 1998 (6), 1999 (3), 2000 (9), 2002 (5). Total: 23.
MISCELLANEOUS: Holds Jacksonville Jaguars all-time record for most yards rushing (4,784) and most rushing touchdowns (40).

Year Team	G	GS	RUSHING Att.	Yds.	Avg.	TD	RECEIVING No.	Yds.	Avg.	TD	TOTALS TD	2pt.	Pts.	Fum.
1998—Jacksonville NFL	15	12	264	1223	4.6	14	44	421	9.6	3	17	0	102	3
1999—Jacksonville NFL	10	9	159	732	4.6	6	10	83	8.3	0	6	0	36	0
2000—Jacksonville NFL	13	13	292	1399	4.8	12	36	240	6.7	2	14	0	84	4
2001—Jacksonville NFL	2	2	30	116	3.9	0	2	13	6.5	0	0	0	0	1
2002—Jacksonville NFL	16	16	287	1314	4.6	8	49	408	8.3	0	8	2	52	3
Pro totals (5 years)	56	52	1032	4784	4.6	40	141	1165	8.3	5	45	2	274	11

TAYLOR, JASON · DE · DOLPHINS

PERSONAL: Born September 1, 1974, in Pittsburgh. ... 6-6/260. ... Full name: Jason Paul Taylor.
HIGH SCHOOL: Woodland Hills (Pittsburgh).
COLLEGE: Akron.
TRANSACTIONS/CAREER NOTES: Selected by Miami Dolphins in third round (73rd pick overall) of 1997 NFL draft. ... Signed by Dolphins (July 9, 1997). ... On injured reserve with broken collarbone (December 29, 1998-remainder of playoffs). ... Granted free agency (February 11, 2000). ... Re-signed by Dolphins (April 13, 2000). ... Designated by Dolphins as franchise player (February 22, 2001).
HONORS: Named defensive end on THE SPORTING NEWS NFL All-Pro team (2000 and 2002). ... Played in Pro Bowl (2000 and 2002 seasons).

Year Team	G	GS	TOTALS Tk.	Ast.	Sks.	INTERCEPTIONS No.	Yds.	Avg.	TD
1997—Miami NFL	13	11	30	12	5.0	0	0	0.0	0
1998—Miami NFL	16	15	34	18	9.0	0	0	0.0	0
1999—Miami NFL	15	15	24	16	2.5	1	0	0.0	0
2000—Miami NFL	16	16	35	28	14.5	1	2	2.0	0
2001—Miami NFL	16	16	48	23	8.5	1	4	4.0	0
2002—Miami NFL	16	16	46	23	*18.5	0	0	0.0	0
Pro totals (6 years)	92	89	217	120	58.0	3	6	2.0	0

TAYLOR, SHANNON · LB · TEXANS

PERSONAL: Born February 16, 1975, in Roanoke, Va. ... 6-3/247. ... Full name: Shannon Andre Taylor.
HIGH SCHOOL: Patrick Henry (Roanoke, Va.).
COLLEGE: Virginia.

TRANSACTIONS/CAREER NOTES: Selected by San Diego Chargers in sixth round (184th pick overall) of 2000 NFL draft. ... Signed by Chargers (June 21, 2000). ... Released by Chargers (August 27, 2000). ... Re-signed by Chargers to practice squad (August 29, 2000). ... Activated (October 4, 2000). ... Released by Chargers (August 27, 2001). ... Signed by Baltimore Ravens (September 9, 2001). ... On injured reserve with shoulder injury (January 10, 2002-remainder of season). ... Granted free agency (February 28, 2003). ... Signed by Houston Texans (April 1, 2003).

				TOTALS			INTERCEPTIONS			
Year Team	G	GS	Tk.	Ast.	Sks.	No.	Yds.	Avg.	TD	
2000—San Diego NFL	11	0	3	0	0.0	0	0	0.0	0	
2001—Baltimore NFL	11	0	3	1	1.0	0	0	0.0	0	
2002—Baltimore NFL	16	2	6	3	0.0	0	0	0.0	0	
Pro totals (3 years)	38	2	12	4	1.0	0	0	0.0	0	

TAYLOR, TRAVIS   WR   RAVENS

PERSONAL: Born March 30, 1978, in Fernadina Beach, Fla. ... 6-1/200. ... Full name: Travis Lamont Taylor.
HIGH SCHOOL: Camden County (Ga.), then Jean Ribault (Jacksonville).
COLLEGE: Florida.
TRANSACTIONS/CAREER NOTES: Selected after junior season by Baltimore Ravens in first round (10th pick overall) of 2000 NFL draft. ... Signed by Ravens (August 1, 2000). ... On injured reserve with broken clavicle (November 8, 2000-remainder of season).
SINGLE GAME HIGHS (regular season): Receptions—7 (November 10, 2002, vs. Cincinnati); yards—127 (November 3, 2002, vs. Atlanta); and touchdown receptions—2 (September 10, 2000, vs. Jacksonville).
STATISTICAL PLATEAUS: 100-yard receiving games: 2002 (1).

			RUSHING				RECEIVING				TOTALS			
Year Team	G	GS	Att.	Yds.	Avg.	TD	No.	Yds.	Avg.	TD	TD	2pt.	Pts.	Fum.
2000—Baltimore NFL	9	8	2	11	5.5	0	28	276	9.9	3	3	0	18	1
2001—Baltimore NFL	16	13	5	46	9.2	0	42	560	13.3	3	3	0	18	0
2002—Baltimore NFL	16	15	11	105	9.5	0	61	869	14.2	6	6	0	36	0
Pro totals (3 years)	41	36	18	162	9.0	0	131	1705	13.0	12	12	0	72	1

TEAGUE, TREY   OT   BILLS

PERSONAL: Born December 27, 1974, in Jackson, Tenn. ... 6-5/292. ... Full name: Fred Everette Teague III. ... Name pronounced TEEG.
HIGH SCHOOL: University (Jackson, Tenn).   ·
COLLEGE: Tennessee.
TRANSACTIONS/CAREER NOTES: Selected by Denver Broncos in seventh round (200th pick overall) of 1998 NFL draft. ... Signed by Broncos (July 23, 1998). ... Inactive for all 16 games (1998). ... On injured reserve with knee injury (September 12, 2000-remainder of season). ... Granted free agency (March 2, 2001). ... Re-signed by Broncos (May 3, 2001). ... Granted unconditional free agency (March 1, 2002). ... Signed by Buffalo Bills (March 27, 2002).
PLAYING EXPERIENCE: Denver NFL, 1999-2001; Buffalo NFL, 2002. ... Games/Games started: 1999 (16/4), 2000 (2/0), 2001 (16/16), 2002 (16/16). Total: 50/36.
CHAMPIONSHIP GAME EXPERIENCE: Member of Broncos for AFC championship game (1998 season); inactive. ... Member of Super Bowl championship team (1998 season); inactive.

TERRELL, DARYL   OT   JAGUARS

PERSONAL: Born January 25, 1975, in Vossburg, Miss. ... 6-5/296.
HIGH SCHOOL: Heidelberg (Miss.).
JUNIOR COLLEGE: Jones County Junior College (Miss.).
COLLEGE: Southern Mississippi.
TRANSACTIONS/CAREER NOTES: Signed as non-drafted free agent by Baltimore Ravens (June 3, 1997). ... Released by Ravens (July 8, 1997). ... Signed by New Orleans Saints (April 27, 1998). ... Released by Saints (August 24, 1998). ... Re-signed by Saints to practice squad (September 2, 1998). ... Assigned by Saints to Amsterdam Admirals in 1999 NFL Europe enhancement allocation program (February 22, 1999). ... Granted free agency (March 1, 2002). ... Signed by Jacksonville Jaguars (June 5, 2002). ... Re-signed by Jaguars (March 3, 2003).
PLAYING EXPERIENCE: Amsterdam NFLE, 1999; New Orleans NFL, 1999-2001; Jacksonville NFL, 2002. ... Games/Games started: NFLE 1999 (games played unavailable), NFL 1999 (12/1), 2000 (16/0), 2001 (16/10), 2002 (9/0). Total NFL: 43/11.

TERRELL, DAVID   WR   BEARS

PERSONAL: Born March 13, 1979, in Richmond, Va. ... 6-3/215.
HIGH SCHOOL: Huguenot (Richmond, Va.).
COLLEGE: Michigan.
TRANSACTIONS/CAREER NOTES: Selected after junior season by Chicago Bears in first round (eighth pick overall) of 2001 NFL draft. ... Signed by Bears (July 31, 2001). ... On injured reserve with foot injury (November 12, 2002-remainder of season).
HONORS: Named wide receiver on THE SPORTING NEWS college All-America second team (2000).
SINGLE GAME HIGHS (regular season): Receptions—7 (October 21, 2001, vs. Cincinnati); yards—94 (December 16, 2001, vs. Tampa Bay); and touchdown receptions—2 (October 28, 2001, vs. San Francisco).

			RECEIVING				TOTALS			
Year Team	G	GS	No.	Yds.	Avg.	TD	TD	2pt.	Pts.	Fum.
2001—Chicago NFL	16	6	34	415	12.2	4	4	0	24	0
2002—Chicago NFL	5	1	9	127	14.1	3	3	0	18	0
Pro totals (2 years)	21	7	43	542	12.6	7	7	0	42	0

TERRELL, DAVID   CB   REDSKINS

PERSONAL: Born July 8, 1975, in Floyada, Texas. ... 6-0/188.
HIGH SCHOOL: Sweetwater (Texas).
COLLEGE: Texas-El Paso.
TRANSACTIONS/CAREER NOTES: Selected by Washington Redskins in seventh round (191st pick overall) of 1998 NFL draft. ... Signed by Redskins (May 13, 1998). ... Released by Redskins (August 25, 1998). ... Selected by Rhein Fire in 1999 NFL Europe draft (February 23, 1999). ... Released by Redskins (September 4, 1999). ... Re-signed by Redskins to practice squad (September 14, 1999). ... Granted free agency (February 28, 2003). ... Re-signed by Redskins (April 22, 2003).

			TOTALS			INTERCEPTIONS			
Year Team	G	GS	Tk.	Ast.	Sks.	No.	Yds.	Avg.	TD
1999—Rhein NFLE	...	...	...	...	0.5	1	0	0.0	0
2000—Washington NFL	16	0	3	0	0.0	0	0	0.0	0
2001—Washington NFL	16	16	61	10	1.0	2	0	0.0	0
2002—Washington NFL	16	16	48	15	0.0	2	41	20.5	0
NFL Europe totals (1 year)	...	...	...	...	0.5	1	0	0.0	0
NFL totals (3 years)	48	32	112	25	1.0	4	41	10.3	0
Pro totals (4 years)	...	...	...	...	1.5	5	41	8.2	0

TERRY, CHRIS   OT   SEAHAWKS

PERSONAL: Born August 8, 1975, in Jacksonville. ... 6-5/295. ... Full name: Christopher Alexander Terry.
HIGH SCHOOL: Jean Ribault (Jacksonville).
COLLEGE: Georgia.
TRANSACTIONS/CAREER NOTES: Selected by Carolina Panthers in second round (34th pick overall) of 1999 NFL draft. ... Signed by Panthers (May 24, 1999). ... Claimed on waivers by Seattle Seahawks (November 21, 2002).
PLAYING EXPERIENCE: Carolina NFL, 1999-2001; Carolina (10)-Seattle (5) NFL, 2002. ... Games/Games started: 1999 (16/16), 2000 (16/16), 2001 (15/15), 2002 (Sea.-5/5; Car.-10/10. Total: 15/15). Total: 62/62.

TERRY, TIM   LB   SEAHAWKS

PERSONAL: Born July 26, 1974, in Hempstead, N.Y. ... 6-2/240.
HIGH SCHOOL: Hempstead (N.Y.).
COLLEGE: Temple.
TRANSACTIONS/CAREER NOTES: Signed as non-drafted free agent by Cincinnati Bengals (April 25, 1997). ... Released by Bengals (August 24, 1997). ... Re-signed by Bengals to practice squad (August 26, 1997). ... Activated (September 27, 1997). ... On injured reserve with knee injury (December 8, 1997-remainder of season). ... Released by Bengals (August 19, 1998). ... Re-signed by Bengals to practice squad (December 16, 1998). ... Claimed on waivers by Kansas City Chiefs (August 10, 1999). ... Released by Chiefs (August 31, 1999). ... Re-signed by Chiefs (March 6, 2000). ... Released by Chiefs (August 27, 2000). ... Signed by Seattle Seahawks to practice squad (August 30, 2000). ... Activated (November 10, 2000). ... Granted free agency (March 1, 2002). ... Re-signed by Seahawks (May 2, 2002).

			TOTALS			INTERCEPTIONS			
Year Team	G	GS	Tk.	Ast.	Sks.	No.	Yds.	Avg.	TD
1997—Cincinnati NFL	5	0	2	1	0.0	0	0	0.0	0
2000—Seattle NFL	6	0	0	0	0.0	0	0	0.0	0
2001—Seattle NFL	16	0	9	1	2.5	0	0	0.0	0
2002—Seattle NFL	16	8	31	11	1.0	0	0	0.0	0
Pro totals (4 years)	43	8	42	13	3.5	0	0	0.0	0

TESTAVERDE, VINNY   QB   JETS

PERSONAL: Born November 13, 1963, in Brooklyn, N.Y. ... 6-5/235. ... Full name: Vincent Frank Testaverde. ... Name pronounced TESS-tuh-VER-dee.
HIGH SCHOOL: Sewanhaka (Floral Park, N.Y.), then Fork Union (Va.) Military Academy.
COLLEGE: Miami (Fla.).
TRANSACTIONS/CAREER NOTES: Signed by Tampa Bay Buccaneers (April 3, 1987). ... Selected officially by Buccaneers in first round (first pick overall) of 1987 NFL draft. ... On injured reserve with ankle injury (December 20, 1989-remainder of season). ... Granted unconditional free agency (March 1, 1993). ... Signed by Cleveland Browns (March 31, 1993). ... Browns franchise moved to Baltimore and renamed Ravens for 1996 season (March 11, 1996). ... Released by Ravens (June 2, 1998). ... Signed by New York Jets (June 24, 1998). ... Granted free agency (February 12, 1999). ... Re-signed by Jets (March 1, 1999). ... On injured reserve with torn Achilles' tendon (September 13, 1999-remainder of season).
CHAMPIONSHIP GAME EXPERIENCE: Played in AFC championship game (1998 season).
HONORS: Named quarterback on THE SPORTING NEWS college All-America second team (1985). ... Heisman Trophy winner (1986). ... Named College Football Player of the Year by THE SPORTING NEWS (1986). ... Maxwell Award winner (1986). ... Davey O'Brien Award winner (1986). ... Named quarterback on THE SPORTING NEWS college All-America first team (1986). ... Played in Pro Bowl (1996 and 1998 seasons).
SINGLE GAME HIGHS (regular season): Attempts—69 (December 24, 2000, vs. Baltimore); completions—42 (December 6, 1998, vs. Seattle); yards—481 (December 24, 2000, vs. Baltimore); and touchdown passes—5 (October, 23, 2000, vs. Miami).
STATISTICAL PLATEAUS: 300-yard passing games: 1987 (1), 1988 (4), 1989 (4), 1990 (1), 1991 (1), 1992 (1), 1993 (1), 1995 (2), 1996 (5), 1997 (3), 1998 (1), 2000 (2). Total: 26. ... 100-yard rushing games: 1990 (1).
MISCELLANEOUS: Regular-season record as starting NFL quarterback: 80-101-1 (.442). ... Postseason record as starting NFL quarterback: 2-3 (.400). ... Holds Tampa Bay Buccaneers all-time records for most yards passing (14,820) and most touchdown passes (77). ... Holds Baltimore Ravens all-time records for most yards passing (7,148) and most touchdown passes (51).

Year Team	G	GS	PASSING Att.	Cmp.	Pct.	Yds.	TD	Int.	Avg.	Skd.	Rat.	RUSHING Att.	Yds.	Avg.	TD	TOTALS TD	2pt.	Pts.
1987—Tampa Bay NFL	6	4	165	71	43.0	1081	5	6	6.55	18	60.2	13	50	3.8	1	1	0	6
1988—Tampa Bay NFL	15	15	466	222	47.6	3240	13	*35	6.95	33	48.8	28	138	4.9	1	1	0	6
1989—Tampa Bay NFL	14	14	480	258	53.8	3133	20	†22	6.53	38	68.9	25	139	5.6	0	0	0	0
1990—Tampa Bay NFL	14	13	365	203	55.6	2818	17	∞18	‡7.72	38	75.6	38	280	7.4	1	1	0	6
1991—Tampa Bay NFL	13	12	326	166	50.9	1994	8	15	6.12	‡35	59.0	32	101	3.2	0	0	0	0
1992—Tampa Bay NFL	14	14	358	206	57.5	2554	14	16	7.13	35	74.2	36	197	5.5	2	2	0	12
1993—Cleveland NFL	10	6	230	130	56.5	1797	14	9	‡7.81	17	85.7	18	74	4.1	0	0	0	0
1994—Cleveland NFL	14	13	376	207	55.1	2575	16	18	6.85	12	70.7	21	37	1.8	2	2	0	12
1995—Cleveland NFL	13	12	392	241	61.5	2883	17	10	7.35	17	87.8	18	62	3.4	2	2	0	12
1996—Baltimore NFL	16	16	549	325	59.2	4177	§33	19	7.61	34	88.7	34	188	5.5	2	2	1	14
1997—Baltimore NFL	13	13	470	271	57.7	2971	18	15	6.32	20	75.9	34	138	4.1	0	0	0	0
1998—New York Jets NFL	14	13	421	259	61.5	3256	§29	7	7.73	19	§101.6	24	104	4.3	1	1	0	6
1999—New York Jets NFL	1	1	15	10	66.7	96	1	1	6.40	0	78.8	0	0	0.0	0	0	0	0
2000—New York Jets NFL	16	16	*590	328	55.6	3732	21	*25	6.33	13	69.0	25	32	1.3	0	0	0	0
2001—New York Jets NFL	16	16	441	260	59.0	2752	15	14	6.24	18	75.3	31	25	0.8	0	0	0	0
2002—New York Jets NFL	5	4	83	54	65.1	499	3	3	6.01	9	78.3	2	23	11.5	0	0	0	0
Pro totals (16 years)	194	182	5727	3211	56.1	39558	244	233	6.91	356	74.8	379	1588	4.2	12	12	1	74

THIERRY, JOHN — DE

PERSONAL: Born September 4, 1971, in Houston. ... 6-4/262. ... Full name: John Fitzgerald Thierry. ... Name pronounced Theory.
HIGH SCHOOL: Plaisance (Opelousas, La.).
COLLEGE: Alcorn State.
TRANSACTIONS/CAREER NOTES: Selected by Chicago Bears in first round (11th pick overall) of 1994 NFL draft. ... Signed by Bears (June 21, 1994). ... On injured reserve with knee injury (November 5, 1997-remainder of season). ... Granted unconditional free agency (February 12, 1999). ... Signed by Cleveland Browns (February 26, 1999). ... Granted unconditional free agency (February 11, 2000). ... Signed by Green Bay Packers (February 17, 2000). ... On injured reserve with knee injury (January 2, 2002-remainder of season). ... Released by Packers (February 27, 2002). ... Signed by Atlanta Falcons (March 27, 2002). ... Granted unconditional free agency (February 28, 2003).

Year Team	G	GS	TOTALS Tk.	Ast.	Sks.	INTERCEPTIONS No.	Yds.	Avg.	TD
1994—Chicago NFL	16	1	3	2	0.0	0	0	0.0	0
1995—Chicago NFL	16	7	20	5	4.0	0	0	0.0	0
1996—Chicago NFL	16	2	10	3	2.0	0	0	0.0	0
1997—Chicago NFL	9	9	9	6	3.0	0	0	0.0	0
1998—Chicago NFL	16	9	20	10	3.5	1	14	14.0	0
1999—Cleveland NFL	16	10	33	6	7.0	1	8	8.0	0
2000—Green Bay NFL	16	16	32	8	6.5	0	0	0.0	0
2001—Green Bay NFL	12	12	20	6	3.5	0	0	0.0	0
2002—Atlanta NFL	14	4	12	3	4.0	0	0	0.0	0
Pro totals (9 years)	131	70	159	49	33.5	2	22	11.0	0

THOMAS, ADALIUS — DE — RAVENS

PERSONAL: Born August 17, 1977, in Equality, Ala. ... 6-2/270. ... Full name: Adalius Donquail Thomas.
HIGH SCHOOL: Central Coosa (Equality, Ala.).
COLLEGE: Southern Mississippi.
TRANSACTIONS/CAREER NOTES: Selected by Baltimore Ravens in sixth round (186th pick overall) of 2000 NFL draft. ... Signed by Ravens (July 6, 2000). ... Granted free agency (February 28, 2003).
CHAMPIONSHIP GAME EXPERIENCE: Played in AFC championship game (2000 season). ... Member of Super Bowl championship team (2000 season); inactive.
HONORS: Named defensive end on THE SPORTING NEWS college All-America second team (1999).

Year Team	G	GS	TOTALS Tk.	Ast.	Sks.	INTERCEPTIONS No.	Yds.	Avg.	TD
2000—Baltimore NFL	3	0	0	1	0.0	0	0	0.0	0
2001—Baltimore NFL	16	2	22	6	3.5	0	0	0.0	0
2002—Baltimore NFL	16	12	30	11	3.0	2	57	28.5	1
Pro totals (3 years)	35	14	52	18	6.5	2	57	28.5	1

THOMAS, ANTHONY — RB — BEARS

PERSONAL: Born November 11, 1977, in Winnfield, La. ... 6-2/228. ... Full name: Anthony Jermaine Thomas.
HIGH SCHOOL: Winnfield (La.).
COLLEGE: Michigan (degree in sports management and communications).
TRANSACTIONS/CAREER NOTES: Selected by Chicago Bears in second round (38th pick overall) of 2001 NFL draft. ... Signed by Bears (July 20, 2001). ... On injured reserve with finger injury (December 10, 2002-remainder of season).
HONORS: Named running back to THE SPORTING NEWS college All-America third team (2000).
SINGLE GAME HIGHS (regular season): Attempts—33 (January 6, 2002, vs. Jacksonville); yards—188 (October 21, 2001, vs. Cincinnati); and rushing touchdowns—1 (November 18, 2002, vs. St. Louis).
STATISTICAL PLATEAUS: 100-yard rushing games: 2001 (4), 2002 (1). Total: 5.

Year Team	G	GS	RUSHING Att.	Yds.	Avg.	TD	RECEIVING No.	Yds.	Avg.	TD	TOTALS TD	2pt.	Pts.	Fum.
2001—Chicago NFL	14	10	278	1183	4.3	7	22	178	8.1	0	7	1	44	0
2002—Chicago NFL	12	12	214	721	3.4	6	24	163	6.8	0	6	0	36	5
Pro totals (2 years)	26	22	492	1904	3.9	13	46	341	7.4	0	13	1	80	5

THOMAS, BRYAN   DE   JETS

PERSONAL: Born June 7, 1979, in Birmingham, Ala. ... 6-4/266.
HIGH SCHOOL: Minor (Birmingham, Ala.).
COLLEGE: Alabama-Birmingham.
TRANSACTIONS/CAREER NOTES: Selected by New York Jets in first round (22nd pick overall) of 2002 NFL draft. ... Signed by Jets (June 19, 2002).

			TOTALS		
Year Team	G	GS	Tk.	Ast.	Sks.
2002—New York Jets NFL	15	0	5	4	0.5

THOMAS, EDWARD   LB

PERSONAL: Born September 27, 1974, in Thomasville, Ga. ... 6-1/228. ... Full name: Edward Tervin Thomas.
HIGH SCHOOL: C.L. Harper (Atlanta).
COLLEGE: Georgia Southern.
TRANSACTIONS/CAREER NOTES: Signed by Montreal Alouettes of CFL (May 9, 1997). ... Released by Alouettes (June 20, 1997). ... Re-signed by Alouettes (July 14, 1997). ... Signed as non-drafted free agent by San Francisco 49ers (June 7, 2000). ... Released by 49ers (September 19, 2000). ... Re-signed by 49ers to practice squad (September 21, 2001). ... Activated (October 14, 2000). ... Released by 49ers (November 2, 2000). ... Re-signed by 49ers to practice squad (November 7, 2000). ... Released by 49ers (November 14, 2000). ... Signed by Jacksonville Jaguars to practice squad (November 21, 2000). ... Activated (November 29, 2000). ... Released by Jaguars (March 1, 2001). ... Re-signed by Jaguars (March 25, 2001). ... Released by Jaguars (October 16, 2002).

			TOTALS			INTERCEPTIONS			
Year Team	G	GS	Tk.	Ast.	Sks.	No.	Yds.	Avg.	TD
1997—Montreal CFL	7	...	...	...	1.0	1	0	0.0	0
1998—Montreal CFL	3	...	...	...	0.0	0	0	0.0	0
1999—Montreal CFL	12	...	...	...	2.0	0	0	0.0	0
2000—San Francisco NFL	4	0	2	0	0.0	0	0	0.0	0
—Jacksonville NFL	4	0	0	0	0.0	0	0	0.0	0
2001—Jacksonville NFL	16	4	12	6	0.0	0	0	0.0	0
2002—Jacksonville NFL	4	0	0	0	0.0	0	0	0.0	0
CFL totals (3 years)	22	...	...	...	3.0	1	0	0.0	0
NFL totals (3 years)	28	4	14	6	0.0	0	0	0.0	0
Pro totals (6 years)	50	...	...	6	3.0	1	0	0.0	0

THOMAS, FRED   CB   SAINTS

PERSONAL: Born September 11, 1973, in Bruce, Miss. ... 5-9/184.
HIGH SCHOOL: Bruce (Miss.).
JUNIOR COLLEGE: Northwest Mississippi Community College.
COLLEGE: Mississippi Valley State (did not play football), then Mississippi, then Tennessee-Martin.
TRANSACTIONS/CAREER NOTES: Selected by Seattle Seahawks in second round (47th pick overall) of 1996 NFL draft. ... Signed by Seahawks (July 19, 1996). ... Granted free agency (February 12, 1999). ... Re-signed by Seahawks (May 27, 1999). ... On injured reserve with broken leg (September 17, 1999-remainder of season). ... Granted unconditional free agency (February 11, 2000). ... Signed by New Orleans Saints (February 14, 2000).

			TOTALS			INTERCEPTIONS			
Year Team	G	GS	Tk.	Ast.	Sks.	No.	Yds.	Avg.	TD
1996—Seattle NFL	15	0	4	1	0.0	0	0	0.0	0
1997—Seattle NFL	16	3	24	4	0.0	0	0	0.0	0
1998—Seattle NFL	15	2	32	7	0.0	0	0	0.0	0
1999—Seattle NFL	1	0	0	0	0.0	0	0	0.0	0
2000—New Orleans NFL	11	0	16	0	0.0	0	0	0.0	0
2001—New Orleans NFL	16	16	51	13	0.0	1	0	0.0	0
2002—New Orleans NFL	15	14	69	11	1.0	5	80	16.0	0
Pro totals (7 years)	89	35	196	36	1.0	6	80	13.3	0

THOMAS, HOLLIS   DT   EAGLES

PERSONAL: Born January 10, 1974, in Abilene, Texas. ... 6-0/306.
HIGH SCHOOL: Sumner (St. Louis).
COLLEGE: Northern Illinois.
TRANSACTIONS/CAREER NOTES: Signed as non-drafted free agent by Philadelphia Eagles (April 26, 1996). ... On injured reserve with arm/shoulder injury (December 2, 1998-remainder of season). ... On injured reserve with foot injury (December 31, 2001-remainder of season). ... On injured reserve with foot injury (August 27, 2002-entire season).

			TOTALS		
Year Team	G	GS	Tk.	Ast.	Sks.
1996—Philadelphia NFL	16	5	32	10	1.0
1997—Philadelphia NFL	16	16	39	22	2.5
1998—Philadelphia NFL	12	12	34	8	5.0
1999—Philadelphia NFL	16	16	36	13	1.0
2000—Philadelphia NFL	16	16	46	14	4.0
2001—Philadelphia NFL	14	14	43	9	0.0
2002—Philadelphia NFL			Did not play.		
Pro totals (6 years)	90	79	230	76	13.5

THOMAS, JASON   G   RAVENS

PERSONAL: Born July 10, 1977, in Savannah, Ga. ... 6-3/300.
HIGH SCHOOL: A.E. Beach (Savannah, Ga.).
COLLEGE: South Carolina, then Hampton.
TRANSACTIONS/CAREER NOTES: Selected by San Diego Chargers in seventh round (222nd pick overall) of 2000 NFL draft. ... Signed by Chargers (July 19, 2000). ... Released by Chargers (August 27, 2000). ... Re-signed by Chargers to practice squad (August 29, 2000). ... Activated (December 23, 2000); did not play. ... Released by Chargers (September 2, 2001). ... Re-signed by Chargers to practice squad (September 4, 2001). ... Signed by Baltimore Ravens off Chargers practice squad (November 21, 2001); did not play.
PLAYING EXPERIENCE: Baltimore NFL, 2002. ... Games/Games started: (13/0).

THOMAS, JUQUA   DE   TITANS

PERSONAL: Born May 15, 1978, in Houston. ... 6-2/252. ... Full name: Juqua Demail Thomas.
HIGH SCHOOL: Aldine (Texas).
JUNIOR COLLEGE: Northeastern Oklahoma.
COLLEGE: Oklahoma State.
TRANSACTIONS/CAREER NOTES: Signed as non-drafted free agent by Tennessee Titans (April 27, 2001). ... Re-signed by Titans (April 2, 2003).
CHAMPIONSHIP GAME EXPERIENCE: Member of Titans for AFC championship game (2002 season); inactive.

Year Team	G	GS	TOTALS		
			Tk.	Ast.	Sks.
2001—Tennessee NFL	7	0	4	1	0.0
2002—Tennessee NFL	9	0	9	0	1.0
Pro totals (2 years)	16	0	13	1	1.0

THOMAS, KEVIN   CB   BILLS

PERSONAL: Born July 28, 1978, in Phoenix. ... 5-11/180. ... Full name: Marvin Kevin Thomas.
HIGH SCHOOL: Foothill (Calif.).
COLLEGE: UNLV.
TRANSACTIONS/CAREER NOTES: Selected by Buffalo Bills in sixth round (176th pick overall) of 2002 NFL draft. ... Signed by Bills (July 23, 2002).

Year Team	G	GS	TOTALS			INTERCEPTIONS			
			Tk.	Ast.	Sks.	No.	Yds.	Avg.	TD
2002—Buffalo NFL	6	1	8	0	0.0	1	31	31.0	0

THOMAS, KIWAUKEE   CB   JAGUARS

PERSONAL: Born June 19, 1977, in Warner Robins, Ga. ... 5-11/189. ... Full name: Kiwaukee Sanchez Thomas. ... Name pronounced kee-WA-kee.
HIGH SCHOOL: Perry (Ga.).
COLLEGE: Georgia Southern.
TRANSACTIONS/CAREER NOTES: Selected by Jacksonville Jaguars in fifth round (159th pick overall) of 2000 NFL draft. ... Signed by Jaguars (May 25, 2000). ... Granted free agency (February 28, 2003). ... Re-signed by Jaguars (April 23, 2003).

Year Team	G	GS	TOTALS			INTERCEPTIONS			
			Tk.	Ast.	Sks.	No.	Yds.	Avg.	TD
2000—Jacksonville NFL	16	3	17	1	0.0	0	0	0.0	0
2001—Jacksonville NFL	16	5	40	2	3.0	0	0	0.0	0
2002—Jacksonville NFL	16	0	23	2	0.0	0	0	0.0	0
Pro totals (3 years)	48	8	80	5	3.0	0	0	0.0	0

THOMAS, RANDY   G   REDSKINS

PERSONAL: Born January 19, 1976, in East Point, Ga. ... 6-4/301.
HIGH SCHOOL: Tri-Cities (East Point, Ga.).
JUNIOR COLLEGE: Copiah-Lincoln Junior College (Miss.).
COLLEGE: Mississippi State.
TRANSACTIONS/CAREER NOTES: Selected by New York Jets in second round (57th pick overall) of 1999 NFL draft. ... Signed by Jets (July 20, 1999). ... Granted unconditional free agency (February 28, 2003). ... Signed by Washington Redskins (March 1, 2003).
PLAYING EXPERIENCE: New York Jets NFL, 1999-2002. ... Games/Games started: 1999 (16/16), 2000 (16/16), 2001 (13/13), 2002 (16/16). Total: 61/61.
HONORS: Named offensive guard on The Sporting News college All-America second team (1998).

THOMAS, ROBERT   LB   RAMS

PERSONAL: Born July 17, 1980, in El Centro, Calif. ... 6-0/229. ... Full name: Robert W. Thomas.
HIGH SCHOOL: Imperial (Calif.).
COLLEGE: UCLA.
TRANSACTIONS/CAREER NOTES: Selected by St. Louis Rams in first round (31st pick overall) of 2002 NFL draft. ... Signed by Rams (July 23, 2002).
HONORS: Named linebacker on The Sporting News college All-America first team (2001).

Year Team	G	GS	TOTALS			INTERCEPTIONS			
			Tk.	Ast.	Sks.	No.	Yds.	Avg.	TD
2002—St. Louis NFL	16	10	34	3	0.0	0	0	0.0	0

THOMAS, ROBERT — FB

PERSONAL: Born December 1, 1974, in Jacksonville, Ark. ... 6-1/273.
HIGH SCHOOL: Jacksonville (Ark.).
COLLEGE: Henderson State (Ark.).
TRANSACTIONS/CAREER NOTES: Signed as non-drafted free agent by Dallas Cowboys (February 24, 1998). ... Assigned by Cowboys to Rhein Fire in 1999 NFL Europe enhancement allocation program (February 22, 1999). ... Granted free agency (March 2, 2001). ... Re-signed by Cowboys (March 21, 2001). ... On injured reserve with ankle injury (October 22, 2001-remainder of season). ... Released by Cowboys (February 20, 2003).
SINGLE GAME HIGHS (regular season): Attempts—4 (December 19, 1999, vs. New York Jets); yards—28 (September 9, 2001, vs. Tampa Bay); and rushing touchdowns—0.
MISCELLANEOUS: Played linebacker (1998 and 1999).

| | | | RUSHING | | | | RECEIVING | | | | TOTALS | | | |
Year Team	G	GS	Att.	Yds.	Avg.	TD	No.	Yds.	Avg.	TD	TD	2pt.	Pts.	Fum.
1998—Dallas NFL	16	0	0	0	0.0	0	0	0	0.0	0	0	0	0	0
1999—Rhein NFLE	...	...	0	0	0.0	0	0	0	0.0	0	0	0	0	0
—Dallas NFL	16	7	8	35	4.4	0	10	64	6.4	0	0	0	0	0
2000—Dallas NFL	16	15	15	51	3.4	0	23	117	5.1	2	2	0	12	2
2001—Dallas NFL	5	5	6	40	6.7	0	5	19	3.8	1	1	0	6	0
2002—Dallas NFL	15	9	10	31	3.1	0	12	80	6.7	0	0	0	0	0
NFL Europe totals (1 year)	...	...	0	0	0.0	0	0	0	0.0	0	0	0	0	0
NFL totals (5 years)	68	36	39	157	4.0	0	50	280	5.6	3	3	0	18	2
Pro totals (6 years)	...	...	39	157	4.0	0	50	280	5.6	3	3	0	18	2

THOMAS, TRA — OT — EAGLES

PERSONAL: Born November 20, 1974, in De Land, Fla. ... 6-7/349. ... Full name: William Thomas III. ... Name pronounced TRAY.
HIGH SCHOOL: De Land (Fla.).
COLLEGE: Florida State.
TRANSACTIONS/CAREER NOTES: Selected by Philadelphia Eagles in first round (11th pick overall) of 1998 NFL draft. ... Signed by Eagles (June 19, 1998).
PLAYING EXPERIENCE: Philadelphia NFL, 1998-2002. ... Games/Games started: 1998 (16/16), 1999 (16/15), 2000 (16/16), 2001 (15/15), 2002 (16/16). Total: 79/78.
CHAMPIONSHIP GAME EXPERIENCE: Played in NFC championship game (2001 and 2002 seasons).
HONORS: Played in Pro Bowl (2001 and 2002 seasons). ... Named offensive tackle on the THE SPORTING NEWS NFL All-Pro team (2002).

THOMAS, ZACH — LB — DOLPHINS

PERSONAL: Born September 1, 1973, in Pampa, Texas. ... 5-11/235. ... Full name: Zach Michael Thomas.
HIGH SCHOOL: White Deer (Texas), then Pampa (Texas).
COLLEGE: Texas Tech.
TRANSACTIONS/CAREER NOTES: Selected by Miami Dolphins in fifth round (154th pick overall) of 1996 NFL draft. ... Signed by Dolphins (July 10, 1996). ... Granted free agency (February 12, 1999). ... Re-signed by Dolphins (February 12, 1999).
HONORS: Named linebacker on THE SPORTING NEWS college All-America second team (1994). ... Named linebacker on THE SPORTING NEWS college All-America first team (1995). ... Played in Pro Bowl (1999, 2000 and 2002 seasons). ... Named to play in Pro Bowl (2001 season); replaced by Al Wilson due to injury.

| | | | TOTALS | | | INTERCEPTIONS | | | |
Year Team	G	GS	Tk.	Ast.	Sks.	No.	Yds.	Avg.	TD
1996—Miami NFL	16	16	120	34	2.0	3	64	21.3	1
1997—Miami NFL	15	15	78	50	0.5	1	10	10.0	0
1998—Miami NFL	16	16	86	51	2.0	3	21	7.0	▲2
1999—Miami NFL	16	16	80	53	1.0	1	0	0.0	0
2000—Miami NFL	11	11	56	43	1.5	1	0	0.0	0
2001—Miami NFL	15	15	96	59	3.0	2	51	25.5	1
2002—Miami NFL	16	16	100	56	0.5	1	7	7.0	0
Pro totals (7 years)	105	105	616	346	10.5	12	153	12.8	4

THOMASON, JEFF — TE

PERSONAL: Born December 30, 1969, in San Diego. ... 6-5/255. ... Full name: Jeffrey David Thomason.
HIGH SCHOOL: Corona Del Mar (Newport Beach, Calif.).
COLLEGE: Oregon (degree in psychology).
TRANSACTIONS/CAREER NOTES: Signed as non-drafted free agent by Cincinnati Bengals (April 29, 1992). ... On injured reserve with sprained knee (September 1- December 5, 1992). ... Released by Bengals (August 30, 1993). ... Re-signed by Bengals (September 15, 1993). ... Claimed on waivers by Green Bay Packers (August 2, 1994). ... Released by Packers (August 21, 1994). ... Re-signed by Packers (January 20, 1995). ... Granted unconditional free agency (February 13, 1998). ... Re-signed by Packers (March 17, 1998). ... Traded by Packers to Philadelphia Eagles for TE Kaseem Sinceno (March 16, 2000). ... Granted unconditional free agency (March 2, 2001). ... Re-signed by Eagles (May 25, 2001). ... Granted unconditional free agency (February 28, 2003).
CHAMPIONSHIP GAME EXPERIENCE: Played in NFC championship game (1995-1997, 2001 and 2002 seasons). ... Member of Super Bowl championship team (1996 season). ... Played in Super Bowl XXXII (1997 season).
SINGLE GAME HIGHS (regular season): Receptions—5 (September 1, 1997, vs. Chicago); yards—58 (September 1, 1997, vs. Chicago); and touchdown receptions—1 (November 10, 2002, vs. Indianapolis).

Year Team	G	GS	RECEIVING No.	Yds.	Avg.	TD	TOTALS TD	2pt.	Pts.	Fum.
1992—Cincinnati NFL	4	0	2	14	7.0	0	0	0	0	0
1993—Cincinnati NFL	3	0	2	8	4.0	0	0	0	0	0
1994—					Did not play.					
1995—Green Bay NFL	16	1	3	32	10.7	0	0	0	0	0
1996—Green Bay NFL	16	1	3	45	15.0	0	0	0	0	0
1997—Green Bay NFL	13	1	9	115	12.8	1	1	0	6	1
1998—Green Bay NFL	16	2	9	89	9.9	0	0	0	0	0
1999—Green Bay NFL	14	2	14	140	10.0	2	2	0	12	0
2000—Philadelphia NFL	16	5	10	46	4.6	5	5	0	30	0
2001—Philadelphia NFL	14	0	5	33	6.6	0	0	0	0	0
2002—Philadelphia NFL	16	3	10	128	12.8	2	2	0	12	0
Pro totals (10 years)	128	15	67	650	9.7	10	10	0	60	1

THOMPSON, DERRIUS — WR — DOLPHINS

PERSONAL: Born July 5, 1977, in Dallas. ... 6-2/216. ... Full name: Derrius Damon Thompson. ... Cousin of Reyna Thompson, cornerback with Miami Dolphins (1986-88), New York Giants (1989-92) and New England Patriots (1993-94).
HIGH SCHOOL: Cedar Hill (Texas).
COLLEGE: Baylor.
TRANSACTIONS/CAREER NOTES: Signed as non-drafted free agent by Washington Redskins (April 21, 1999). ... Released by Redskins (September 4, 1999). ... Re-signed by Redskins to practice squad (September 6, 1999). ... Activated (November 16, 1999). ... Released by Redskins (August 27, 2000). ... Re-signed by Redskins to practice squad (August 28, 2000). ... Activated (September 8, 2000). ... Released by Redskins (September 18, 2000). ... Re-signed by Redskins to practice squad (November 16, 2000). ... Activated (December 18, 2000). ... Granted free agency (March 1, 2002). ... Re-signed by Redskins (June 14, 2002). ... Granted unconditional free agency (February 28, 2003). ... Signed by Miami Dolphins (March 9, 2003).
SINGLE GAME HIGHS (regular season): Receptions—7 (December 15, 2002, vs. Philadelphia); yards—122 (December 8, 2002, vs. New York Giants); and touchdown receptions—1 (December 22, 2002, vs. Houston).
STATISTICAL PLATEAUS: 100-yard receiving games: 2002 (1).

Year Team	G	GS	RUSHING Att.	Yds.	Avg.	TD	RECEIVING No.	Yds.	Avg.	TD	KICKOFF RETURNS No.	Yds.	Avg.	TD	TOTALS TD	2pt.	Pts.	Fum.
1999—Washington NFL	1	0	0	0	0.0	0	0	0	0.0	0	0	0	0.0	0	0	0	0	0
2000—Washington NFL	4	0	0	0	0.0	0	0	0	0.0	0	0	0	0.0	0	0	0	0	0
2001—Washington NFL	16	0	0	0	0.0	0	3	52	17.3	1	3	17	5.7	0	1	0	6	0
2002—Washington NFL	16	14	10	77	7.7	0	53	773	14.6	4	6	91	15.2	0	4	0	24	2
Pro totals (4 years)	37	14	10	77	7.7	0	56	825	14.7	5	9	108	12.0	0	5	0	30	2

THOMPSON, DONNEL — LB — COLTS

PERSONAL: Born February 17, 1978, in Madison, Wis. ... 6-0/237.
HIGH SCHOOL: West (Madison, Wis.).
COLLEGE: Wisconsin.
TRANSACTIONS/CAREER NOTES: Signed as non-drafted free agent by Pittsburgh Steelers (April 21, 2000). ... Released by Steelers (September 2, 2001). ... Signed by Indianapolis Colts to practice squad (September 3, 2001). ... Activated (December 15, 2001). ... Granted free agency (February 28, 2003). ... Re-signed by Colts (March 26, 2003).

Year Team	G	GS	TOTALS Tk.	Ast.	Sks.	INTERCEPTIONS No.	Yds.	Avg.	TD
2000—Pittsburgh NFL	8	0	0	0	0.0	0	0	0.0	0
2001—Indianapolis NFL	4	0	0	0	0.0	0	0	0.0	0
2002—Indianapolis NFL	16	0	0	0	0.0	0	0	0.0	0
Pro totals (3 years)	28	0	0	0	0.0	0	0	0.0	0

THOMPSON, LAMONT — S — BENGALS

PERSONAL: Born July 30, 1978, in Richmond, Calif. ... 6-1/220. ... Full name: Lamont Darnell Thompson.
HIGH SCHOOL: El Cerrito (Richmond, Calif.).
COLLEGE: Washington State.
TRANSACTIONS/CAREER NOTES: Selected by Cincinnati Bengals in second round (41st pick overall) of 2002 NFL draft. ... Signed by Bengals (July 25, 2002). ... On injured reserve with knee injury (December 12, 2002-remainder of season).
HONORS: Named free safety on THE SPORTING NEWS college All-America second team (2001).

Year Team	G	GS	TOTALS Tk.	Ast.	Sks.	INTERCEPTIONS No.	Yds.	Avg.	TD
2002—Cincinnati NFL	13	0	10	0	0.0	1	4	4.0	0

THOMPSON, MICHAEL — OT — SEAHAWKS

PERSONAL: Born February 11, 1977, in Savannah, Ga. ... 6-4/295. ... Full name: Michael Anthony Thompson.
HIGH SCHOOL: Windsor Forest (Savannah, Ga.).
COLLEGE: Tennessee State.
TRANSACTIONS/CAREER NOTES: Selected by Atlanta Falcons in fourth round (100th pick overall) of 2000 NFL draft. ... Signed by Falcons (May 16, 2000). ... On injured reserve with torn Achilles' tendon (October 10, 2000-remainder of season). ... Granted free agency (February 28, 2003). ... Re-signed by Falcons (April 10, 2003). ... Traded by Falcons to Seattle Seahawks for undisclosed pick in 2004 draft (April 10, 2003).
PLAYING EXPERIENCE: Atlanta NFL, 2000-2002. ... Games/Games started: 2000 (3/2), 2001 (2/1), 2002 (8/1). Total: 13/4.

THOMPSON, RAYNOCH   LB   CARDINALS

PERSONAL: Born November 21, 1977, in Los Angeles. ... 6-3/217. ... Full name: Raynoch Joseph Thompson.
HIGH SCHOOL: St. Augustine (New Orleans).
COLLEGE: Tennessee.
TRANSACTIONS/CAREER NOTES: Selected by Arizona Cardinals in second round (41st pick overall) of 2000 NFL draft. ... Signed by Cardinals (June 21, 2000). ... On injured reserve with knee injury (December 15, 2000-remainder of season).

				TOTALS			INTERCEPTIONS			
Year Team	G	GS	Tk.	Ast.	Sks.	No.	Yds.	Avg.	TD
2000—Arizona NFL	11	9	30	13	0.0	0	0	0.0	0
2001—Arizona NFL	14	14	62	21	0.5	0	0	0.0	0
2002—Arizona NFL	16	16	73	31	3.0	0	0	0.0	0
Pro totals (3 years)	41	39	165	65	3.5	0	0	0.0	0

THORNHILL, JOSH   LB   LIONS

PERSONAL: Born January 19, 1980, in Lansing, Mich. ... 6-2/243.
HIGH SCHOOL: Eastern (Lansing, Mich.).
COLLEGE: Michigan State.
TRANSACTIONS/CAREER NOTES: Signed as non-drafted free agent by Detroit Lions (April 26, 2002). ... Released by Lions (September 1, 2002). ... Re-signed by Lions to practice squad (September 2, 2002). ... Activated (September 28, 2002). ... Released by Lions (October 2, 2002). ... Re-signed by Lions to practice squad (October 3, 2002). ... Activated (October 22, 2002). ... Re-signed by Lions (March 23, 2003).

				TOTALS			INTERCEPTIONS			
Year Team	G	GS	Tk.	Ast.	Sks.	No.	Yds.	Avg.	TD
2002—Detroit NFL	7	0	0	0	0.0	0	0	0.0	0

THORNTON, DAVID   LB   COLTS

PERSONAL: Born November 1, 1978, in Goldsboro, N.C. ... 6-2/230. ... Full name: David Dontay Thornton.
HIGH SCHOOL: Goldsboro (N.C.).
COLLEGE: North Carolina.
TRANSACTIONS/CAREER NOTES: Selected by Indianapolis Colts in fourth round (106th pick overall) of 2002 NFL draft. ... Signed by Colts (July 10, 2002).

				TOTALS			INTERCEPTIONS			
Year Team	G	GS	Tk.	Ast.	Sks.	No.	Yds.	Avg.	TD
2002—Indianapolis NFL	15	0	27	6	0.0	0	0	0.0	0

THORNTON, JOHN   DT   BENGALS

PERSONAL: Born October 2, 1976, in Philadelphia. ... 6-2/292. ... Full name: John Jason Thornton.
HIGH SCHOOL: Scotland (Pa.) School for Veterans' Children.
COLLEGE: West Virginia.
TRANSACTIONS/CAREER NOTES: Selected by Tennessee Titans in second round (52nd pick overall) of 1999 NFL draft. ... Signed by Titans (July 26, 1999). ... On injured reserve with shoulder injury (November 8, 2001-remainder of season). ... Granted free agency (March 1, 2002). ... Re-signed by Titans (March 28, 2002). ... Granted unconditional free agency (February 28, 2003). ... Signed by Cincinnati Bengals (May 5, 2003).
CHAMPIONSHIP GAME EXPERIENCE: Played in AFC championship game (1999 and 2002 seasons). ... Played in Super Bowl XXXIV (1999 season).

			TOTALS		
Year Team	G	GS	Tk.	Ast.	Sks.
1999—Tennessee NFL	16	3	16	4	4.5
2000—Tennessee NFL	16	16	19	9	4.0
2001—Tennessee NFL	3	0	0	0	0.0
2002—Tennessee NFL	16	16	15	5	2.0
Pro totals (4 years)	51	35	50	18	10.5

THRASH, JAMES   WR   EAGLES

PERSONAL: Born April 28, 1975, in Denver. ... 6-0/200.
HIGH SCHOOL: Wewoka (Okla.).
COLLEGE: Missouri Southern.
TRANSACTIONS/CAREER NOTES: Signed as non-drafted free agent by Philadelphia Eagles (April 22, 1997). ... Released by Eagles (July 8, 1997). ... Signed by Washington Redskins (July 11, 1997). ... On injured reserve with shoulder injury (December 8, 1998-remainder of season). ... Granted free agency (February 11, 2000). ... Re-signed with Redskins (April 21, 2000). ... Granted unconditional free agency (March 2, 2001). ... Signed by Eagles (March 9, 2001).
CHAMPIONSHIP GAME EXPERIENCE: Played in NFC championship game (2001 and 2002 seasons).
SINGLE GAME HIGHS (regular season): Receptions—10 (September 23, 2001, vs. Seattle); yards—165 (September 23, 2001, vs. Seattle); and touchdown receptions—2 (November 11, 2001, vs. Minnesota).
STATISTICAL PLATEAUS: 100-yard receiving games: 2000 (2), 2001 (2), 2002 (1). Total: 5.

			RUSHING				RECEIVING				KICKOFF RETURNS				TOTALS			
Year Team	G	GS	Att.	Yds.	Avg.	TD	No.	Yds.	Avg.	TD	No.	Yds.	Avg.	TD	TD	2pt.	Pts.	Fum.
1997—Washington NFL	4	0	0	0	0.0	0	2	24	12.0	0	0	0	0.0	0	0	0	0	0
1998—Washington NFL	10	1	0	0	0.0	0	10	163	16.3	1	6	129	21.5	0	1	0	6	0
1999—Washington NFL	16	0	1	37	37.0	0	3	44	14.7	0	14	355	25.4	1	1	0	6	0
2000—Washington NFL	16	8	10	82	8.2	0	50	653	13.1	2	45	1000	22.2	0	2	0	12	1
2001—Philadelphia NFL	15	15	6	57	9.5	0	63	833	13.2	8	5	101	20.2	0	8	0	48	1
2002—Philadelphia NFL	16	16	18	126	7.0	2	52	635	12.2	6	0	0	0.0	0	8	0	48	1
Pro totals (6 years)	77	40	35	302	8.6	2	180	2352	13.1	17	70	1585	22.6	1	20	0	120	3

TIMMERMAN, ADAM   G   RAMS

PERSONAL: Born August 14, 1971, in Cherokee, Iowa. ... 6-4/310. ... Full name: Adam Larry Timmerman.
HIGH SCHOOL: Washington (Cherokee, Iowa).
COLLEGE: South Dakota State (degree in agriculture business).
TRANSACTIONS/CAREER NOTES: Selected by Green Bay Packers in seventh round (230th pick overall) of 1995 NFL draft. ... Signed by Packers (June 2, 1995). ... Granted free agency (February 13, 1998). ... Re-signed by Packers (April 15, 1998). ... Granted unconditional free agency (February 12, 1999). ... Signed by St. Louis Rams (February 15, 1999).
PLAYING EXPERIENCE: Green Bay NFL, 1995-1998; St. Louis NFL, 1999-2002. ... Games/Games started: 1995 (13/0), 1996 (16/16), 1997 (16/16), 1998 (16/16), 1999 (16/16), 2000 (16/15), 2001 (16/16), 2002 (16/16). Total: 125/111.
CHAMPIONSHIP GAME EXPERIENCE: Played in NFC championship game (1995-97, 1999 and 2001 seasons). ... Member of Super Bowl championship team (1996 and 1999 seasons). ... Played in Super Bowl XXXII (1997 season). ... Played in Super Bowl XXXVI (2001 season).
HONORS: Played in Pro Bowl (1999 and 2001 seasons).

TOBECK, ROBBIE   C/OG   SEAHAWKS

PERSONAL: Born March 6, 1970, in Tarpon Springs, Fla. ... 6-4/297. ... Full name: Robert L. Tobeck.
HIGH SCHOOL: New Port Richey (Fla.).
COLLEGE: Washington State.
TRANSACTIONS/CAREER NOTES: Signed as non-drafted free agent by Atlanta Falcons (May 7, 1993). ... Released by Falcons (August 30, 1993). ... Re-signed by Falcons to practice squad (August 31, 1993). ... Activated (January 1, 1994). ... Granted unconditional free agency (February 11, 2000). ... Signed by Seattle Seahawks (March 20, 2000). ... On physically unable to perform list with knee injury (August 20-October 14, 2000).
PLAYING EXPERIENCE: Atlanta NFL, 1994-1999; Seattle NFL, 2000-2002. ... Games/Games started: 1994 (5/0), 1995 (16/16), 1996 (16/16), 1997 (16/15), 1998 (16/16), 1999 (15/15), 2000 (4/0), 2001 (16/16), 2002 (16/16). Total: 120/110.
CHAMPIONSHIP GAME EXPERIENCE: Played in NFC championship game (1998 season). ... Played in Super Bowl XXXIII (1998 season).

TOMICH, JARED   DE

PERSONAL: Born April 24, 1974, in St. John, Ind. ... 6-3/283. ... Full name: Jared James Tomich.
HIGH SCHOOL: Lake Central (St. John, Ind.).
COLLEGE: Nebraska.
TRANSACTIONS/CAREER NOTES: Selected by New Orleans Saints in second round (39th pick overall) of 1997 NFL draft. ... Signed by Saints (July 17, 1997). ... On injured reserve with ankle injury (December 24, 1999-remainder of season). ... Granted free agency (February 11, 2000). ... Re-signed by Saints (June 9, 2000). ... Signed by Arizona Cardinals (July 25, 2001). ... Released by Cardinals (August 27, 2001). ... Signed by Green Bay Packers (January 2, 2002). ... Released by Packers (September 1, 2002). ... Re-signed by Packers (November 6, 2002). ... Released by Packers (November 21, 2002).

| | | | TOTALS | | |
Year Team	G	GS	Tk.	Ast.	Sks.
1997—New Orleans NFL	16	1	11	1	1.0
1998—New Orleans NFL	16	11	21	5	6.0
1999—New Orleans NFL	8	6	11	5	3.0
2000—New Orleans NFL	14	0	0	1	0.0
2002—Green Bay NFL	2	0	1	0	0.0
Pro totals (5 years)	56	18	44	12	10.0

TOMLINSON, LADAINIAN   RB   CHARGERS

PERSONAL: Born June 23, 1979, in Rosebud, Texas. ... 5-10/221.
HIGH SCHOOL: Waco University (Texas).
COLLEGE: Texas Christian.
TRANSACTIONS/CAREER NOTES: Selected by San Diego Chargers in first round (fifth pick overall) of 2001 draft. ... Signed by Chargers (August 23, 2001).
HONORS: Named running back on THE SPORTING NEWS college All-America third team (1999). ... Named running back on THE SPORTING NEWS college All-America first team (2000). ... Doak Walker Award winner (2000). ... Played in Pro Bowl (2002 season).
SINGLE GAME HIGHS (regular season): Attempts—39 (October 20, 2002, vs. Oakland); yards—220 (December 1, 2002, vs. Denver); and rushing touchdowns—3 (December 1, 2002, vs. Denver).
STATISTICAL PLATEAUS: 100-yard rushing games: 2001 (4), 2002 (7). Total: 11.

| | | | RUSHING | | | | RECEIVING | | | | TOTALS | | | |
Year Team	G	GS	Att.	Yds.	Avg.	TD	No.	Yds.	Avg.	TD	TD	2pt.	Pts.	Fum.
2001—San Diego NFL	16	16	339	1236	3.6	10	59	367	6.2	0	10	0	60	8
2002—San Diego NFL	16	16	372	1683	4.5	14	79	489	6.2	1	15	0	90	3
Pro totals (2 years)	32	32	711	2919	4.1	24	138	856	6.2	1	25	0	150	11

TONGUE, REGGIE   S   SEAHAWKS

PERSONAL: Born April 11, 1973, in Baltimore. ... 6-0/204. ... Full name: Reginald Clinton Tongue.
HIGH SCHOOL: Lathrop (Fairbanks, Alaska).
COLLEGE: Oregon State.
TRANSACTIONS/CAREER NOTES: Selected by Kansas City Chiefs in second round (58th pick overall) of 1996 NFL draft. ... Signed by Chiefs (July 26, 1996). ... Granted unconditional free agency (February 11, 2000). ... Signed by Seattle Seahawks (February 22, 2000).

Year Team	G	GS	TOTALS Tk.	Ast.	Sks.	INTERCEPTIONS No.	Yds.	Avg.	TD
1996—Kansas City NFL	16	0	4	0	0.0	0	0	0.0	0
1997—Kansas City NFL	16	16	67	21	2.5	1	0	0.0	0
1998—Kansas City NFL	15	15	78	20	2.0	0	0	0.0	0
1999—Kansas City NFL	16	16	66	10	2.0	1	80	80.0	1
2000—Seattle NFL	16	6	31	9	0.0	0	0	0.0	0
2001—Seattle NFL	16	16	56	20	1.0	3	67	22.3	1
2002—Seattle NFL	16	16	68	25	0.0	5	118	23.6	1
Pro totals (7 years)	111	85	370	105	7.5	10	265	26.5	3

TOOMER, AMANI   WR   GIANTS

PERSONAL: Born September 8, 1974, in Berkely, Calif. ... 6-3/208. ... Name pronounced uh-MAHN-ee.
HIGH SCHOOL: De La Salle Catholic (Concord, Calif.).
COLLEGE: Michigan.
TRANSACTIONS/CAREER NOTES: Selected by New York Giants in second round (34th pick overall) of 1996 NFL draft. ... Signed by Giants (July 21, 1996). ... On injured reserve with knee injury (October 31, 1996-remainder of season). ... Granted free agency (February 12, 1999). ... Re-signed by Giants (July 31, 1999).
CHAMPIONSHIP GAME EXPERIENCE: Played in NFC championship game (2000 season). ... Played in Super Bowl XXXV (2000 season).
SINGLE GAME HIGHS (regular season): Receptions—10 (December 22, 2002, vs. Indianapolis); yards—204 (December 22, 2002, vs. Indianapolis); and touchdown receptions—3 (December 22, 2002, vs. Indianapolis).
STATISTICAL PLATEAUS: 100-yard receiving games: 1999 (4), 2000 (5), 2001 (2), 2002 (5). Total: 16.

Year Team	G	GS	RECEIVING No.	Yds.	Avg.	TD	PUNT RETURNS No.	Yds.	Avg.	TD	KICKOFF RETURNS No.	Yds.	Avg.	TD	TOTALS TD	2pt.	Pts.	Fum.
1996—New York Giants NFL	7	1	1	12	12.0	0	18	298	16.6	2	11	191	17.4	0	2	0	12	1
1997—New York Giants NFL	16	0	16	263	16.4	1	47	455	9.7	∞1	0	0	0.0	0	2	0	12	0
1998—New York Giants NFL	16	0	27	360	13.3	5	35	252	7.2	0	4	66	16.5	0	5	0	30	0
1999—New York Giants NFL	16	16	79	1183	15.0	6	1	14	14.0	0	0	0	0.0	0	6	0	36	0
2000—New York Giants NFL	16	15	78	1094	14.0	7	0	0	0.0	0	0	0	0.0	0	8	0	48	1
2001—New York Giants NFL	16	14	72	1054	14.6	5	8	41	5.1	0	0	0	0.0	0	5	0	30	2
2002—New York Giants NFL	16	16	82	1343	16.4	8	0	0	0.0	0	0	0	0.0	0	8	0	48	0
Pro totals (7 years)	103	62	355	5309	15.0	32	109	1060	9.7	3	15	257	17.1	0	36	0	216	4

TOTTEN, ERIK   S   STEELERS

PERSONAL: Born January 21, 1980, in Renton, Wash. ... 5-9/194. ... Full name: Erik Terry Totten.
HIGH SCHOOL: Tacoma (Kent, Wash.).
COLLEGE: Western Washington.
TRANSACTIONS/CAREER NOTES: Signed as non-drafted free agent by Pittsburgh Steelers (April 22, 2002). ... Released by Steelers (September 1, 2002). ... Re-signed by Steelers to practice squad (September 3, 2002). ... Released by Steelers (October 22, 2002). ... Re-signed by Steelers to practice squad (November 5, 2002). ... Activated (November 21, 2002). ... Released by Steelers (November 28, 2002). ... Re-signed by Steelers to practice squad (November 30, 2002). ... Activated (January 6, 2003).

Year Team	G	GS	TOTALS Tk.	Ast.	Sks.	INTERCEPTIONS No.	Yds.	Avg.	TD
2002—Pittsburgh NFL	1	0	0	0	0.0	0	0	0.0	0

TOWNS, LESTER   LB   PANTHERS

PERSONAL: Born August 28, 1977, in Pasadena, Calif. ... 6-1/252. ... Full name: Lester Towns III.
HIGH SCHOOL: Pasadena (Calif.).
COLLEGE: Washington.
TRANSACTIONS/CAREER NOTES: Selected by Carolina Panthers in seventh round (221st pick overall) of 2000 NFL draft. ... Signed by Panthers (July 14, 2000). ... On injured reserve with foot injury (November 21, 2002-remainder of season). ... Granted free agency (February 28, 2003).

Year Team	G	GS	TOTALS Tk.	Ast.	Sks.	INTERCEPTIONS No.	Yds.	Avg.	TD
2000—Carolina NFL	16	14	79	14	0.0	0	0	0.0	0
2001—Carolina NFL	16	15	61	25	0.0	1	0	0.0	0
2002—Carolina NFL	8	0	2	1	0.0	0	0	0.0	0
Pro totals (3 years)	40	29	142	40	0.0	1	0	0.0	0

TOWNSEND, DESHEA   CB   STEELERS

PERSONAL: Born September 8, 1975, in Batesville, Miss. ... 5-9/191. ... Full name: Trevor Deshea Townsend.
HIGH SCHOOL: South Panola (Batesville, Miss.).
COLLEGE: Alabama.
TRANSACTIONS/CAREER NOTES: Selected by Pittsburgh Steelers in fourth round (117th pick overall) of 1998 NFL draft. ... Signed by Steelers (July 6, 1998). ... Granted free agency (March 2, 2001). ... Re-signed by Steelers (March 2, 2001). ... Granted unconditional free agency (March 1, 2002). ... Re-signed by Steelers (April 2, 2002).
CHAMPIONSHIP GAME EXPERIENCE: Played in AFC championship game (2001 season).

Year Team	G	GS	TOTALS Tk.	Ast.	Sks.	INTERCEPTIONS No.	Yds.	Avg.	TD
1998—Pittsburgh NFL	12	0	9	2	0.0	0	0	0.0	0
1999—Pittsburgh NFL	16	4	27	4	0.0	0	0	0.0	0
2000—Pittsburgh NFL	16	0	20	5	3.5	0	0	0.0	0
2001—Pittsburgh NFL	16	1	20	4	2.0	2	7	3.5	0
2002—Pittsburgh NFL	16	3	28	6	0.0	3	3	1.0	0
Pro totals (5 years)	76	8	104	21	5.5	5	10	2.0	0

TRAPP, JAMES   CB   JAGUARS

PERSONAL: Born December 28, 1969, in Greenville, S.C. ... 6-0/190. ... Full name: James Harold Trapp.
HIGH SCHOOL: Lawton (Okla.).
COLLEGE: Clemson.
TRANSACTIONS/CAREER NOTES: Selected by Los Angeles Raiders in third round (72nd pick overall) of 1993 NFL draft. ... Signed by Raiders (July 13, 1993). ... Raiders franchise moved to Oakland (July 21, 1995). ... Granted free agency (February 16, 1996). ... Re-signed by Raiders (March 30, 1996). ... Granted unconditional free agency (February 12, 1999). ... Signed by Baltimore Ravens (April 23, 1999). ... Granted unconditional free agency (February 11, 2000). ... Re-signed by Ravens (March 16, 2000). ... On injured reserve with groin injury (January 16, 2002-remainder of 2001 playoffs). ... Granted unconditional free agency (March 1, 2002). ... Re-signed by Ravens (May 20, 2002). ... Granted unconditional free agency (February 28, 2003). ... Signed by Jacksonville Jaguars (May 5, 2003).
CHAMPIONSHIP GAME EXPERIENCE: Played in AFC championship game (2000 season). ... Member of Super Bowl championship team (2000 season).

				TOTALS			INTERCEPTIONS			
Year Team	G	GS	Tk.	Ast.	Sks.	No.	Yds.	Avg.	TD
1993—Los Angeles Raiders NFL	14	2	19	2	0.0	1	7	7.0	0
1994—Los Angeles Raiders NFL	16	2	23	6	1.0	0	0	0.0	0
1995—Oakland NFL	14	2	23	2	0.0	0	0	0.0	0
1996—Oakland NFL	12	4	21	2	0.0	1	23	23.0	0
1997—Oakland NFL	16	16	82	21	0.0	2	24	12.0	0
1998—Oakland NFL	16	0	7	6	0.0	0	0	0.0	0
1999—Baltimore NFL	16	0	1	2	1.0	0	0	0.0	0
2000—Baltimore NFL	16	1	19	2	2.0	0	0	0.0	0
2001—Baltimore NFL	10	4	22	5	1.0	1	15	15.0	0
2002—Baltimore NFL	14	1	23	3	1.0	3	26	8.7	0
Pro totals (10 years)	144	32	240	51	6.0	8	95	11.9	0

TRAYLOR, KEITH   DT   BEARS

PERSONAL: Born September 3, 1969, in Little Rock, Ark. ... 6-2/340. ... Full name: Byron Keith Traylor. ... Cousin of Isaac Davis, guard with San Diego Chargers (1994-97) and New Orleans Saints (1997).
HIGH SCHOOL: Malvern (Ark.).
JUNIOR COLLEGE: Coffeyville (Kan.) Community College.
COLLEGE: Oklahoma, then Central Oklahoma.
TRANSACTIONS/CAREER NOTES: Selected by Denver Broncos in third round (61st pick overall) of 1991 NFL draft. ... Signed by Broncos for 1991 season. ... Released by Broncos (June 7, 1993). ... Signed by Los Angeles Raiders (June 1993). ... Released by Raiders (August 30, 1993). ... Signed by Green Bay Packers (September 14, 1993). ... Released by Packers (November 9, 1993). ... Signed by Kansas City Chiefs (January 7, 1994). ... Released by Chiefs (January 14, 1994). ... Re-signed by Chiefs (May 18, 1994). ... Released by Chiefs (August 28, 1994). ... Re-signed by Chiefs (February 28, 1995). ... Granted unconditional free agency (February 14, 1997). ... Signed by Broncos (March 10, 1997). ... Released by Broncos (March 14, 2001). ... Signed by Chicago Bears (March 24, 2001).
CHAMPIONSHIP GAME EXPERIENCE: Played in AFC championship game (1991, 1997 and 1998 seasons). ... Member of Super Bowl championship team (1997 and 1998 seasons).

				TOTALS			INTERCEPTIONS			
Year Team	G	GS	Tk.	Ast.	Sks.	No.	Yds.	Avg.	TD
1991—Denver NFL	16	2	12	15	0.0	0	0	0.0	0
1992—Denver NFL	16	3	21	18	1.0	0	0	0.0	0
1993—Green Bay NFL	5	0	0	1	0.0	0	0	0.0	0
1994—			Did not play.						
1995—Barcelona W.L.	8	3	...	...	0.0	0	0	0.0	0
—Kansas City NFL	16	0	9	2	1.5	0	0	0.0	0
1996—Kansas City NFL	15	1	21	6	1.0	0	0	0.0	0
1997—Denver NFL	16	16	28	11	2.0	1	62	62.0	1
1998—Denver NFL	15	14	24	8	2.0	0	0	0.0	0
1999—Denver NFL	15	15	25	7	1.5	0	0	0.0	0
2000—Denver NFL	16	16	32	5	1.0	0	0	0.0	0
2001—Chicago NFL	16	15	29	4	2.0	1	67	67.0	0
2002—Chicago NFL	15	15	26	5	1.0	0	0	0.0	0
W.L. totals (1 year)	8	3	...	...	0.0	0	0	0.0	0
NFL totals (11 years)	161	97	227	82	13.0	2	129	64.5	1
Pro totals (12 years)	169	100	...	...	13.0	2	129	64.5	1

TREJO, STEPHEN   FB   LIONS

PERSONAL: Born November 20, 1977, in Mesa, Ariz. ... 6-2/254. ... Full name: Stephen Nicholas Trejo.
HIGH SCHOOL: Casa Grande (Ariz.).
COLLEGE: Arizona State.
TRANSACTIONS/CAREER NOTES: Signed as non-drafted free agent by Detroit Lions (April 27, 2001).
SINGLE GAME HIGHS (regular season): Attempts—1 (September 15, 2002, vs. Carolina); yards—0; and rushing touchdowns—0.

			RUSHING				TOTALS			
Year Team	G	GS	Att.	Yds.	Avg.	TD	TD	2pt.	Pts.	Fum.
2001—Detroit NFL	14	0	0	0	0.0	0	0	0	0	0
2002—Detroit NFL	16	0	1	0	0.0	0	0	0	0	0
Pro totals (2 years)	30	0	1	0	0.0	0	0	0	0	0

TREU, ADAM — C — RAIDERS

PERSONAL: Born June 24, 1974, in Lincoln, Neb. ... 6-5/300. ... Name pronounced TRUE.
HIGH SCHOOL: Pius X (Lincoln, Neb.).
COLLEGE: Nebraska.
TRANSACTIONS/CAREER NOTES: Selected by Oakland Raiders in third round (72nd pick overall) of 1997 NFL draft. ... Signed by Raiders for 1997 season.
PLAYING EXPERIENCE: Oakland NFL, 1997-2002. ... Games/Games started: 1997 (16/0), 1998 (16/0), 1999 (16/0), 2000 (16/0), 2001 (16/14), 2002 (16/0). Total: 96/14.
CHAMPIONSHIP GAME EXPERIENCE: Played in AFC championship game (2000 and 2002 seasons). ... Played in Super Bowl XXXVII (2002 season).

TRIPPLETT, LARRY — DT — COLTS

PERSONAL: Born January 18, 1979, in Los Angeles. ... 6-2/314.
HIGH SCHOOL: Westchester (Los Angeles).
COLLEGE: Washington.
TRANSACTIONS/CAREER NOTES: Selected by Indianapolis Colts in second round (42nd pick overall) of 2002 NFL draft. ... Signed by Colts (July 26, 2002).
HONORS: Named defensive tackle on THE SPORTING NEWS college All-America second team (2000). ... Named defensive tackle on THE SPORTING NEWS college All-America third team (2001).

Year Team	G	GS	TOTALS Tk.	Ast.	Sks.
2002—Indianapolis NFL	13	10	18	3	0.0

TROTTER, JEREMIAH — LB — REDSKINS

PERSONAL: Born January 20, 1977, in Hooks, Texas. ... 6-1/262.
HIGH SCHOOL: Hooks (Texas).
COLLEGE: Stephen F. Austin State.
TRANSACTIONS/CAREER NOTES: Selected after junior season by Philadelphia Eagles in third round (72nd pick overall) of 1998 NFL draft. ... Signed by Eagles (July 14, 1998). ... Granted free agency (March 2, 2001). ... Re-signed by Eagles (April 27, 2001). ... Designated by Eagles as franchise player (February 21, 2002). ... Granted unconditional free agency (April 5, 2002). ... Signed by Washington Redskins (April 22, 2002). ... On injured reserve with knee injury (December 2, 2002-remainder of season).
CHAMPIONSHIP GAME EXPERIENCE: Played in NFC championship game (2001 season).
HONORS: Played in Pro Bowl (2000 and 2001 seasons).

Year Team	G	GS	TOTALS Tk.	Ast.	Sks.	INTERCEPTIONS No.	Yds.	Avg.	TD
1998—Philadelphia NFL	8	0	3	0	0.0	0	0	0.0	0
1999—Philadelphia NFL	16	16	91	31	2.5	2	30	15.0	0
2000—Philadelphia NFL	16	16	99	21	3.0	1	27	27.0	1
2001—Philadelphia NFL	16	16	93	22	3.5	2	64	32.0	1
2002—Washington NFL	12	12	58	33	0.0	1	2	2.0	0
Pro totals (5 years)	68	60	344	107	9.0	6	123	20.5	2

TRULUCK, R-KAL — DE — CHIEFS

PERSONAL: Born September 30, 1974, in Brooklyn, N.Y. ... 6-4/255. ... Full name: R-Kal K-Quan Truluck.
HIGH SCHOOL: Spring Valley (Rockland County, N.Y.).
COLLEGE: Southern University of New York-Cortland (degree in health sciences).
TRANSACTIONS/CAREER NOTES: Signed as non-drafted free agent by Washington Redskins (April 27, 1997). ... Released by Redskins (August 20, 1997). ... Signed by Saskatchewan Roughriders of CFL (May 1998). ... Signed by St. Louis Rams (April 16, 2001). ... Released by Rams (April 26, 2001). ... Signed by Redskins to practice squad (August 26, 2001). ... Released by Redskins (September 2, 2001). ... Played with Detroit Fury of Arena League (2001-02). ... Signed by Kansas City Chiefs (August 6, 2002). ... Released by Chiefs (September 1, 2002). ... Re-signed by Chiefs to practice squad (September 3, 2002). ... Activated (November 20, 2002).

Year Team	G	GS	TOTALS Tk.	Ast.	Sks.
1998—Saskatchewan CFL	3	...	...	...	4.0
1999—Saskatchewan CFL	18	...	...	...	7.0
2000—Saskatchewan CFL	17	...	...	...	1.0
2002—Kansas City NFL	6	0	6	2	0.5
CFL totals (3 years)	38	...	...	...	12.0
NFL totals (1 year)	6	0	6	2	0.5
Pro totals (4 years)	44	...	...	...	12.5

TUCKER, REX — G — BEARS

PERSONAL: Born December 20, 1976, in Midland, Texas. ... 6-5/315. ... Full name: Rex Truman Tucker. ... Brother of Ryan Tucker, offensive tackle, Cleveland Browns.
HIGH SCHOOL: Robert E. Lee (Midland, Texas).
COLLEGE: Texas A&M.
TRANSACTIONS/CAREER NOTES: Selected in third round by Chicago Bears (66th pick overall) of 1999 NFL draft. ... Signed by Bears (July 21, 1999). ... Granted free agency (March 1, 2002). ... Re-signed by Bears (April 19, 2002). ... On injured reserve with ankle injury (October 9, 2002-remainder of season).
PLAYING EXPERIENCE: Chicago NFL, 1999-2002. ... Games/Games started: 1999 (2/1), 2000 (6/0), 2001 (16/16), 2002 (5/5). Total: 29/22.

TUCKER, ROSS G COWBOYS

PERSONAL: Born March 2, 1979, in Wyomissing, Pa. ... 6-4/316.
HIGH SCHOOL: Wyomissing (Pa.).
COLLEGE: Princeton.
TRANSACTIONS/CAREER NOTES: Singed as non-drafted free agent by Washington Redskins (April 25, 2001). ... Claimed on waivers by Dallas Cowboys (October 23, 2002). ... Re-signed by Cowboys (March 23, 2003).
PLAYING EXPERIENCE: Washington NFL, 2001; Washington (3)-Dallas (7) NFL, 2002. ... Games/Games started: 2001 (3/0), 2002 (Dal.-7/7; Was.-3/0; Total: 10/7). Total: 13/7.

TUCKER, RYAN OT BROWNS

PERSONAL: Born June 12, 1975, in Midland, Texas. ... 6-5/305. ... Full name: Ryan Huey Tucker. ... Brother of Rex Tucker, guard, Chicago Bears.
HIGH SCHOOL: Robert E. Lee (Midland, Texas).
COLLEGE: Texas Christian.
TRANSACTIONS/CAREER NOTES: Selected by St. Louis Rams in fourth round (112th pick overall) of 1997 NFL draft. ... Signed by Rams (July 3, 1997). ... On physically unable to perform list with knee injury (August 19-October 29, 1997). ... Granted free agency (February 11, 2000). ... Tendered offer sheet by Miami Dolphins (February 17, 2000). ... Offer matched by Rams (February 22, 2000). ... Released by Rams (February 28, 2002). ... Signed by Cleveland Browns (March 7, 2002).
PLAYING EXPERIENCE: St. Louis NFL, 1997-2001; Cleveland NFL, 2002. ... Games/Games started: 1997 (7/0), 1998 (5/0), 1999 (16/0), 2000 (16/16), 2001 (15/15), 2002 (14/14). Total: 63/45.
CHAMPIONSHIP GAME EXPERIENCE: Played in NFC championship game (1999 and 2001 seasons). ... Member of Super Bowl championship team (1999 season). ... Played in Super Bowl XXXVI (2001 season).

TUIASOSOPO, MARQUES QB RAIDERS

PERSONAL: Born March 22, 1979, in Woodinville, Wash. ... 6-1/220.
HIGH SCHOOL: Woodinville (Wash.).
COLLEGE: Washington.
TRANSACTIONS/CAREER NOTES: Selected by Oakland Raiders in second round (59th pick overall) of 2001 NFL draft. ... Signed by Raiders (July 21, 2001).
CHAMPIONSHIP GAME EXPERIENCE: Member of Raiders for AFC championship game (2002 season); did not play. ... Member of Raiders for Super Bowl XXXVII (2002 season); did not play.
SINGLE GAME HIGHS (regular season): Attempts—4 (September 30, 2001, vs. Seattle); completions—3 (September 30, 2001, vs. Seattle); yards—34 (September 30, 2001, vs. Seattle); and touchdown passes—0.

			PASSING								RUSHING			TOTALS		
Year Team	G	GS	Att.	Cmp.	Pct.	Yds.	TD	Int.	Avg.	Skd.	Rat.	Att.	Yds.	Avg.	TD	TD	2pt.	Pts.
2001—Oakland NFL	1	0	4	3	75.0	34	0	0	8.50	0	100.0	1	1	1.0	0	0	0	0
2002—Oakland NFL	3	0	0	0	0.0	0	0	0	0.0	0	...	2	-3	-1.5	0	0	0	0
Pro totals (2 years)	4	0	4	3	75.0	34	0	0	8.50	0	100.0	3	-2	-0.7	0	0	0	0

TUIPALA, JOE LB JAGUARS

PERSONAL: Born September 13, 1976, in Honolulu, Hawaii. ... 6-1/248. ... Full name: Joseph Lafaele Tuipala.
HIGH SCHOOL: Burroughs (Ridgecrest, Calif.).
COLLEGE: San Diego State.
TRANSACTIONS/CAREER NOTES: Signed as non-drafted free agent by Detroit Lions (May 5, 1999). ... Released by Lions (August 31, 1999). ... Signed by New Orleans Saints to practice squad (December 15, 1999). ... Activated (December 23, 1999); did not play. ... Released by Saints (August 27, 2000). ... Signed by Jacksonville Jaguars (April 20, 2001). ... Re-signed by Jaguars (March 6, 2003).

			TOTALS			INTERCEPTIONS			
Year Team	G	GS	Tk.	Ast.	Sks.	No.	Yds.	Avg.	TD
2001—Jacksonville NFL	12	0	3	4	0.0	0	0	0.0	0
2002—Jacksonville NFL	15	0	0	0	0.0	0	0	0.0	0
Pro totals (2 years)	27	0	3	4	0.0	0	0	0.0	0

TUITELE, MAUGAULA LB PATRIOTS

PERSONAL: Born May 26, 1978, in Torrance, Calif. ... 6-1/255. ... Full name: Maugaula Norman Tuitele.
HIGH SCHOOL: Pacific (Calif.).
COLLEGE: Colorado State.
TRANSACTIONS/CAREER NOTES: Signed as non-drafted free agent by New England Patriots (April 19, 2000). ... Released by Patriots (August 28, 2001). ... Re-signed by Patriots to practice squad (September 25, 2001). ... Released by Patriots (September 26, 2001). ... Re-signed by Patriots to practice squad (November 20, 2001). ... Activated (December 2, 2001). ... Released by Patriots (December 5, 2001). ... Re-signed by Patriots to practice squad (December 6, 2001). ... Released by Patriots (December 27, 2001). ... Signed by Tampa Bay Buccaneers to practice squad (December 27, 2001). ... Granted free agency after 2001 season. ... Signed by Patriots (February 11, 2002). ... Assigned by Patriots to Rhein Fire in NFL Europe enhancement allocation program (February 12, 2002). ... Claimed on waivers by Buffalo Bills (September 3, 2002). ... Released by Bills (November 18, 2002). ... Signed by Patriots (December 11, 2002). ... Re-signed by Patriots (March 25, 2003).

			TOTALS			INTERCEPTIONS			
Year Team	G	GS	Tk.	Ast.	Sks.	No.	Yds.	Avg.	TD
2000—New England NFL	1	0	0	1	0.0	0	0	0.0	0
2001—New England NFL	1	0	0	0	0.0	0	0	0.0	0
2002—Rhein NFLE	...	...	...	...	1.0	0	0	0.0	0
—Buffalo NFL	9	0	0	0	0.0	0	0	0.0	0
—New England NFL	3	0	0	0	0.0	0	0	0.0	0
NFL Europe totals (1 year)	...	...	...	...	1.0	0	0	0.0	0
NFL totals (3 years)	14	0	0	1	0.0	0	0	0.0	0
Pro totals (4 years)	...	...	...	...	1.0	0	0	0.0	0

TUMAN, JERAME — TE

PERSONAL: Born March 24, 1976, in Liberal, Kan. ... 6-4/270. ... Full name: Jerame Dean Tuman. ... Name pronounced Jeremy TOO-man.
HIGH SCHOOL: Liberal (Kan.).
COLLEGE: Michigan.
TRANSACTIONS/CAREER NOTES: Selected by Pittsburgh Steelers in fifth round (136th pick overall) of 1999 NFL draft. ... Signed by Steelers (July 19, 1999). ... On injured reserve with knee injury (October 27, 1999-remainder of season). ... Granted free agency (March 1, 2002). ... Re-signed by Steelers (April 10, 2002). ... Granted unconditional free agency (February 28, 2003). ... Re-signed by Steelers (February 28, 2003).
CHAMPIONSHIP GAME EXPERIENCE: Played in AFC championship game (2001 season).
HONORS: Named tight end on THE SPORTING NEWS college All-America third team (1997).
SINGLE GAME HIGHS (regular season): Receptions—1 (December 29, 2002, vs. Baltimore); yards—32 (October 21, 2001, vs. Tampa Bay); and touchdown receptions—1 (November 10, 2002, vs. Atlanta).

			RECEIVING			
Year Team	G	GS	No.	Yds.	Avg.	TD
1999—Pittsburgh NFL	7	0	0	0	0.0	0
2000—Pittsburgh NFL	16	1	0	0	0.0	0
2001—Pittsburgh NFL	16	7	7	96	13.7	1
2002—Pittsburgh NFL	13	8	4	63	15.8	1
Pro totals (4 years)	52	16	11	159	14.5	2

TUPA, TOM — P /QB

PERSONAL: Born February 6, 1966, in Cleveland. ... 6-4/225. ... Full name: Thomas Joseph Tupa Jr.
HIGH SCHOOL: Brecksville (Broadview Heights, Ohio).
COLLEGE: Ohio State.
TRANSACTIONS/CAREER NOTES: Selected by Phoenix Cardinals in third round (68th pick overall) of 1988 NFL draft. ... Signed by Cardinals (July 12, 1988). ... Granted free agency (February 1, 1991). ... Re-signed by Cardinals (July 17, 1991). ... Granted unconditional free agency (February 1, 1992). ... Signed by Indianapolis Colts (March 31, 1992). ... Released by Colts (August 30, 1993). ... Signed by Cleveland Browns (November 9, 1993). ... Released by Browns (November 24, 1993). ... Re-signed by Browns (March 30, 1994). ... Granted unconditional free agency (February 16, 1996). ... Signed by New England Patriots (March 15, 1996). ... Granted unconditional free agency (February 12, 1999). ... Signed by New York Jets (February 15, 1999). ... Released by Jets (February 25, 2002). ... Signed by Tampa Bay Buccaneers (May 10, 2002). ... Granted unconditional free agency (February 28, 2003).
CHAMPIONSHIP GAME EXPERIENCE: Played in AFC championship game (1996 season). ... Played in Super Bowl XXXI (1996 season). ... Played in NFC championship game (2002 season). ... Member of Super Bowl championship team (2002 season).
HONORS: Played in Pro Bowl (1999 season).
STATISTICAL PLATEAUS: 300-yard passing games: 1991 (1).
MISCELLANEOUS: Regular-season starting record as starting NFL quarterback: 4-9 (.308).

				PUNTING			
Year Team	G	No.	Yds.	Avg.	Net avg.	In. 20	Blk.
1988—Phoenix NFL	2	0	0	0.0	.0	0	0
1989—Phoenix NFL	14	6	280	46.7	39.7	2	0
1990—Phoenix NFL	15	0	0	0.0	.0	0	0
1991—Phoenix NFL	11	0	0	0.0	.0	0	0
1992—Indianapolis NFL	3	0	0	0.0	.0	0	0
1993—Cleveland NFL				Did not play.			
1994—Cleveland NFL	16	80	3211	40.1	35.3	27	0
1995—Cleveland NFL	16	65	2831	43.6	36.2	18	0
1996—New England NFL	16	63	2739	43.5	36.0	14	0
1997—New England NFL	16	78	3569	§45.8	36.1	24	1
1998—New England NFL	16	74	3294	44.5	35.4	13	0
1999—New York Jets NFL	16	81	3659	45.2	38.2	25	0
2000—New York Jets NFL	16	83	3714	44.7	33.2	18	0
2001—New York Jets NFL	15	67	2575	38.4	32.0	21	0
2002—Tampa Bay NFL	16	90	3856	42.8	35.4	30	0
Pro totals (14 years)	188	687	29728	43.3	35.4	192	1

TURK, MATT — P

PERSONAL: Born June 16, 1968, in Greenfield, Wis. ... 6-5/250. ... Brother of Dan Turk, center with five NFL teams (1985-99).
HIGH SCHOOL: Greenfield (Wis.).
COLLEGE: Wisconsin-Whitewater.
TRANSACTIONS/CAREER NOTES: Signed as non-drafted free agent by Green Bay Packers (July 13, 1993). ... Released by Packers (August 4, 1993). ... Signed by Los Angeles Rams (April 1994). ... Released by Rams (August 22, 1994). ... Signed by Washington Redskins (April 5, 1995). ... Traded by Redskins to Miami Dolphins for sevnth-round pick (traded to San Francisco) in 2001 draft (March 9, 2000). ... Granted unconditional free agency (March 1, 2002). ... Signed by New York Jets (April 23, 2002). ... Released by Jets (March 7, 2003).
HONORS: Played in Pro Bowl (1996-1998 seasons). ... Named punter on THE SPORTING NEWS NFL All-Pro team (1997).

				PUNTING			
Year Team	G	No.	Yds.	Avg.	Net avg.	In. 20	Blk.
1995—Washington NFL	16	74	3140	42.4	37.7	†29	0
1996—Washington NFL	16	75	3386	*45.1	*39.2	24	0
1997—Washington NFL	16	84	3788	45.1	*39.2	32	1
1998—Washington NFL	16	93	4103	44.1	‡39.0	∞33	∞1
1999—Washington NFL	14	62	2564	41.4	35.6	16	0
2000—Miami NFL	16	92	3870	42.1	36.2	25	0
2001—Miami NFL	16	81	3321	41.0	37.6	28	0
2002—New York Jets NFL	16	63	2584	41.0	34.9	13	0
Pro totals (8 years)	126	624	26756	42.9	37.6	200	2

TURLEY, KYLE   OT   RAMS

PERSONAL: Born September 24, 1975, in Provo, Utah. ... 6-5/300. ... Full name: Kyle John Turley.
HIGH SCHOOL: Valley View (Moreno Valley, Calif.).
COLLEGE: San Diego State.
TRANSACTIONS/CAREER NOTES: Selected by New Orleans Saints in first round (seventh pick overall) of 1998 NFL draft. ... Signed by Saints (July 23, 1998). ... Traded by Saints to St. Louis Rams for second-round pick in 2004 draft (March 21, 2003).
PLAYING EXPERIENCE: New Orleans NFL, 1998-2002. ... Games/Games started: 1998 (15/15), 1999 (16/16), 2000 (16/16), 2001 (16/16), 2002 (16/16). Total: 79/79.
HONORS: Named offensive tackle on THE SPORTING NEWS college All-America first team (1997).

TUTEN, MELVIN   OT   PANTHERS

PERSONAL: Born November 11, 1971, in Washington, D.C. ... 6-7/320. ... Full name: Melvin Eugene Tuten Jr.
HIGH SCHOOL: Woodrow Wilson (Washington, D.C.).
COLLEGE: Syracuse.
TRANSACTIONS/CAREER NOTES: Selected by Cincinnati Bengals in third round (69th pick overall) of 1995 NFL draft. ... Signed by Bengals (July 18, 1995). ... Released by Bengals (August 18, 1997). ... Signed by Denver Broncos (February 5, 1998). ... Released by Broncos (August 25, 1998). ... Re-signed by Broncos (December 30, 1998). ... Assigned by Broncos to Barcelona Dragons in 1999 NFL Europe enhancement allocation program (February 22, 1999). ... Released by Broncos (September 5, 1999). ... Re-signed by Broncos (November 10, 1999). ... Released by Broncos (August 27, 2000). ... Re-signed by Broncos (September 12, 2000). ... Released by Broncos (October 14, 2000). ... Re-signed by Broncos (October 16, 2000). ... Claimed on waivers by Carolina Panthers (October 23, 2000).
PLAYING EXPERIENCE: Cincinnati NFL, 1995 and 1996; Barcelona NFLE, 1999; Denver NFL, 1999; Carolina NFL, 2000-2002. ... Games/Games started: 1995 (16/2), 1996 (16/7), NFLE 1999 (games played unavailable), NFL 1999 (2/0), 2000 (2/0), 2001 (15/1), 2002 (14/7). Total NFL: 65/17.

TUTHILL, JAMES   K   JAGUARS

PERSONAL: Born March 25, 1976, in Upland, Calif. ... 6-2/250. ... Full name: James Joseph Tuthill.
HIGH SCHOOL: Upland (Calif.).
COLLEGE: Cal Poly.
TRANSACTIONS/CAREER NOTES: Signed as non-drafted free agent by San Francisco 49ers (July 5, 2000). ... Released by 49ers (August 21, 2000). ... Re-signed by 49ers (February 20, 2001). ... Released by 49ers (July 10, 2001). ... Signed by Green Bay Packers (November 15, 2001). ... Released by Packers (November 19, 2001). ... Signed by Houston Texans (January 22, 2002). ... Claimed on waivers by Washington Redskins (August 21, 2002). ... Released by Redskins (September 1, 2002). ... Re-signed by Redskins (September 10, 2002). ... Claimed on waivers by San Diego Chargers (December 3, 2002). ... Released by Chargers (December 21, 2002). ... Signed by Jacksonville Jaguars (April 10, 2003).

		PUNTING					KICKING						TOTALS		
Year Team	G	No.	Yds.	Avg.Net avg.In. 20		Blk.	1-29	30-39	40-49	50+	Tot.	Pct.	Lg.	XPM	XPA	Pts.
2002—San Diego NFL	1	0	0	0.0	0	0	0-0	0-0	0-0	0-0	0-0	0.0	0	0	0	0
—Washington NFL	11	4	160	40.0	27.5	0	0	3-3	4-7	2-5	1-1	10-16	62.5	∞53	20	21	50
Pro totals (1 years)	12	4	160	40.0	27.5	0	0	3-3	4-7	2-5	1-1	10-16	62.5	53	20	21	50

ULBRICH, JEFF   LB   49ERS

PERSONAL: Born February 17, 1977, in San Jose, Calif. ... 6-0/249.
HIGH SCHOOL: Live Oak (Morgan Hill, Calif.).
JUNIOR COLLEGE: Gavilan College (Calif.).
COLLEGE: San Jose State, then Hawaii.
TRANSACTIONS/CAREER NOTES: Selected by San Francisco 49ers in third round (86th pick overall) of 2000 NFL draft. ... Signed by 49ers (July 13, 2000). ... On injured reserve with shoulder injury (November 20, 2000-remainder of season).

			TOTALS			INTERCEPTIONS			
Year Team	G	GS	Tk.	Ast.	Sks.	No.	Yds.	Avg.	TD
2000—San Francisco NFL	4	0	0	1	0.0	0	0	0.0	0
2001—San Francisco NFL	14	14	62	44	0.5	0	0	0.0	0
2002—San Francisco NFL	14	13	46	22	1.5	0	0	0.0	0
Pro totals (3 years)	32	27	108	47	2.0	0	0	0.0	0

ULMER, ARTIE   LB   FALCONS

PERSONAL: Born July 30, 1973, in Rincon, Ga. ... 6-3/247. ... Full name: Charles Artie Ulmer.
HIGH SCHOOL: Effingham County (Springfield, Ga.).
COLLEGE: Georgia Southern, then Valdosta (Ga.) State.
TRANSACTIONS/CAREER NOTES: Selected by Minnesota Vikings in seventh round (220th pick overall) of 1997 NFL draft. ... On suspended list for violating league substance abuse policy (August 19-September 23, 1997). ... Signed by Vikings (June 17, 1997). ... Assigned by Vikings to Frankfurt Galaxy in 1998 NFL Europe enhancement allocation program (February 18, 1998). ... Released by Vikings (August 24, 1998). ... Signed by Denver Broncos (January 14, 1999). ... On injured reserve with knee injury (November 4, 1999-remainder of season). ... Granted free agency (February 11, 2000). ... Signed by San Francisco 49ers to practice squad (September 14, 2000). ... Activated (September 19, 2000). ... Released by 49ers (February 19, 2001). ... Signed by Atlanta Falcons (April 16, 2001). ... Granted unconditional free agency (March 1, 2002). ... Re-signed by Falcons (March 22, 2002). ... Granted unconditional free agency (February 28, 2003). ... Re-signed by Falcons (April 1, 2003).

Year Team	G	GS	TOTALS Tk.	Ast.	Sks.	INTERCEPTIONS No.	Yds.	Avg.	TD
1998—Frankfurt NFLE	...	...	...	...	3.0	0	0	0.0	0
1999—Denver NFL	7	0	0	0	0.0	0	0	0.0	0
2000—San Francisco NFL	12	2	6	6	1.0	0	0	0.0	0
2001—Atlanta NFL	15	0	3	1	0.0	0	0	0.0	0
2002—Atlanta NFL	15	0	2	0	0.0	0	0	0.0	0
NFL Europe totals (1 year)	...	...	...	...	3.0	0	0	0.0	0
NFL totals (4 years)	49	2	11	7	1.0	0	0	0.0	0
Pro totals (5 years)	...	...	...	...	4.0	0	0	0.0	0

UNUTOA, MORRIS   C

PERSONAL: Born March 10, 1971, in Torrance, Calif. ... 6-2/289. ... Full name: Morris Taua Unutoa. ... Name pronounced oo-nuh-TOE-uh.
HIGH SCHOOL: Carson (Calif.).
COLLEGE: Brigham Young.
TRANSACTIONS/CAREER NOTES: Signed as non-drafted free agent by Philadelphia Eagles (April 26, 1996). ... Granted free agency (February 12, 1999). ... Re-signed by Eagles (March 24, 1999). ... Released by Eagles (September 8, 1999). ... Signed by Tampa Bay Buccaneers (October 5, 1999). ... Granted unconditional free agency (March 2, 2001). ... Signed by Buffalo Bills (November 16, 2001). ... Granted unconditional free agency (March 1, 2002). ... Signed by New York Giants (August 19, 2002). ... Released by Giants (August 27, 2002). ... Signed by Tampa Bay Buccaneers (October 1, 2002). ... Released by Buccaneers (October 14, 2002).
PLAYING EXPERIENCE: Philadelphia NFL, 1996-1998; Tampa Bay NFL, 1999 and 2000; Buffalo NFL, 2001; Tampa Bay NFL, 2002. ... Games/Games started: 1996 (16/0), 1997 (16/0), 1998 (16/0), 1999 (12/0), 2000 (16/0), 2001 (8/0), 2002 (2/0). Total: 86/0.
CHAMPIONSHIP GAME EXPERIENCE: Played in NFC championship game (1999 season).

UPSHAW, REGAN   DE   REDSKINS

PERSONAL: Born August 12, 1975, in Barrien Springs, Mich. ... 6-4/260. ... Full name: Regan Charles Upshaw.
HIGH SCHOOL: Pittsburg (Calif.).
COLLEGE: California.
TRANSACTIONS/CAREER NOTES: Selected after junior season by Tampa Bay Buccaneers in first round (12th pick overall) of 1996 NFL draft. ... Signed by Buccaneers (July 21, 1996). ... Traded by Buccaneers to Jacksonville Jaguars for sixth-round pick (RB Jameel Cook) in 2001 draft (October 19, 1999). ... Granted unconditional free agency (February 11, 2000). ... Signed by Oakland Raiders (March 1, 2000). ... On physically unable to perform list with knee injury (August 26-November 20, 2002). ... Released by Raiders (February 27, 2003). ... Signed by Washington Redskins (March 1, 2003).
CHAMPIONSHIP GAME EXPERIENCE: Played in AFC championship game (1999, 2000 and 2002 seasons). ... Played in Super Bowl XXXVII (2002 season).

Year Team	G	GS	TOTALS Tk.	Ast.	Sks.	INTERCEPTIONS No.	Yds.	Avg.	TD
1996—Tampa Bay NFL	16	15	20	5	4.0	0	0	0.0	0
1997—Tampa Bay NFL	15	15	23	5	7.5	0	0	0.0	0
1998—Tampa Bay NFL	16	16	23	6	7.0	1	26	26.0	0
1999—Tampa Bay NFL	1	0	0	1	0.0	0	0	0.0	0
—Jacksonville NFL	6	0	6	0	0.0	0	0	0.0	0
2000—Oakland NFL	16	7	17	5	6.0	0	0	0.0	0
2001—Oakland NFL	16	15	24	8	7.0	0	0	0.0	0
2002—Oakland NFL	5	1	2	1	2.0	0	0	0.0	0
Pro totals (7 years)	91	69	115	31	33.5	1	26	26.0	0

URLACHER, BRIAN   LB   BEARS

PERSONAL: Born May 25, 1978, in Pasco, Wash. ... 6-4/254. ... Full name: Brian Keith Urlacher.
HIGH SCHOOL: Lovington (N.M.).
COLLEGE: New Mexico.
TRANSACTIONS/CAREER NOTES: Selected by Chicago Bears in first round (ninth pick overall) of 2000 NFL draft. ... Signed by Bears (June 16, 2000).
HONORS: Named strong safety on THE SPORTING NEWS college All-America second team (1999). ... Named NFL Rookie of the Year by THE SPORTING NEWS (2000). ... Played in Pro Bowl (2000-2002 seasons). ... Named linebacker on THE SPORTING NEWS NFL All-Pro team (2001 and 2002).

Year Team	G	GS	TOTALS Tk.	Ast.	Sks.	INTERCEPTIONS No.	Yds.	Avg.	TD
2000—Chicago NFL	16	14	97	26	8.0	2	19	9.5	0
2001—Chicago NFL	16	16	90	27	6.0	3	60	20.0	0
2002—Chicago NFL	16	16	116	36	4.5	1	0	0.0	0
Pro totals (3 years)	48	46	303	89	18.5	6	79	13.2	0

VAN PELT, ALEX   QB   BILLS

PERSONAL: Born May 1, 1970, in Pittsburgh. ... 6-1/218. ... Full name: Gregory Alexander Van Pelt.
HIGH SCHOOL: Grafton (W.Va.), then Winston Churchill (San Antonio).
COLLEGE: Pittsburgh.
TRANSACTIONS/CAREER NOTES: Selected by Pittsburgh Steelers in eighth round (216th pick overall) of 1993 NFL draft. ... Signed by Steelers for 1993 season. ... Released by Steelers (August 30, 1993). ... Signed by Kansas City Chiefs to practice squad (November 3, 1993). ... Activated (November 8, 1993); did not play. ... Released by Chiefs (November 17, 1993). ... Re-signed by Chiefs (May 18, 1994). ... Released by Chiefs (August 23, 1994). ... Signed by Buffalo Bills to practice squad (December 14, 1994). ... Activated (December 17, 1994); did not

play. ... Granted unconditional free agency (February 11, 2000). ... Re-signed by Bills (July 31, 2000). ... Granted unconditional free agency (March 2, 2001). ... Re-signed by Bills (March 19, 2001).

SINGLE GAME HIGHS (regular season): Attempts—44 (December 16, 2001, vs. New England); completions—28 (November 18, 2001, vs. Seattle); yards—316 (November 18, 2001, vs. Seattle); and touchdown passes—3 (November 25, 2001, vs. Miami).

STATISTICAL PLATEAUS: 300-yard passing games: 2001 (2).

MISCELLANEOUS: Regular-season record as starting NFL quarterback: 3-8 (.273).

			PASSING									RUSHING				TOTALS		
Year Team	G	GS	Att.	Cmp.	Pct.	Yds.	TD	Int.	Avg.	Skd.	Rat.	Att.	Yds.	Avg.	TD	TD	2pt.	Pts.
1993—Kansas City NFL									Did not play.									
1994—Buffalo NFL									Did not play.									
1995—Buffalo NFL	1	0	18	10	55.6	106	2	0	5.89	0	110.0	0	0	0.0	0	0	0	0
1996—Buffalo NFL	1	0	5	2	40.0	9	0	0	1.80	0	47.9	3	-5	-1.7	0	0	0	0
1997—Buffalo NFL	6	3	124	60	48.4	684	2	10	5.52	4	37.2	11	33	3.0	1	1	0	6
1998—Buffalo NFL	1	0	0	0	0.0	0	0	0	0.0	0	...	1	-1	-1.0	0	0	0	0
1999—Buffalo NFL	1	0	1	1	100.0	9	0	0	9.00	0	104.2	1	-1	-1.0	0	0	0	0
2000—Buffalo NFL	2	0	8	4	50.0	67	0	0	8.38	0	78.6	0	0	0.0	0	0	0	0
2001—Buffalo NFL	12	8	307	178	58.0	2056	12	11	6.70	14	76.4	12	33	2.8	0	0	0	0
2002—Buffalo NFL	2	0	2	2	100.0	5	0	0	2.50	0	79.2	0	0	0.0	0	0	0	0
Pro totals (8 years)	26	11	465	257	55.3	2936	16	21	6.31	18	67.1	28	59	2.1	1	1	0	6

VANCE, ERIC   S

PERSONAL: Born July 14, 1975, in Tampa. ... 6-2/218.

HIGH SCHOOL: L.D. Bell (Hurst, Texas).

COLLEGE: Vanderbilt.

TRANSACTIONS/CAREER NOTES: Signed as non-drafted free agent by Carolina Panthers (April 25, 1997). ... Released by Panthers (September 1, 1997). ... Signed by San Diego Chargers to practice squad (December 3, 1997). ... Granted free agency after 1997 season. ... Signed by Tampa Bay Buccaneers (December 30, 1997). ... Released by Buccaneers (August 25, 1998). ... Signed by Indianapolis Colts to practice squad (August 31, 1998). ... Signed by Buccaneers off Colts practice squad (October 28, 1998). ... On injured reserve with foot injury (November 10-December 7, 1999). ... Released by Buccaneers (December 7, 1999). ... Signed by San Diego Chargers (February 22, 2000). ... Released by Chargers (August 27, 2000). ... Signed by Buccaneers (August 28, 2000). ... On injured reserve with knee injury (December 27, 2001-remainder of season). ... Released by Buccaneers (February 26, 2002). ... Signed by Indianapolis Colts (December 4, 2002). ... Granted unconditional free agency (February 28, 2003).

			TOTALS			INTERCEPTIONS			
Year Team	G	GS	Tk.	Ast.	Sks.	No.	Yds.	Avg.	TD
1998—Tampa Bay NFL	3	1	7	3	0.0	0	0	0.0	0
1999—Tampa Bay NFL	6	0	0	0	0.0	0	0	0.0	0
2000—Tampa Bay NFL	14	0	1	0	0.0	0	0	0.0	0
2001—Tampa Bay NFL	10	0	1	0	0.0	0	0	0.0	0
2002—Indianapolis NFL	2	0	0	0	0.0	0	0	0.0	0
Pro totals (5 years)	35	1	9	3	0.0	0	0	0.0	0

VANDEN BOSCH, KYLE   DE   CARDINALS

PERSONAL: Born November 17, 1978, in Larchwood, Iowa. ... 6-4/263.

HIGH SCHOOL: West Lyon (Larchwood, Iowa).

COLLEGE: Nebraska (degree in finance).

TRANSACTIONS/CAREER NOTES: Selected by Arizona Cardinals in second round (34th pick overall) of 2001 NFL draft. ... Signed by Cardinals (July 12, 2001). ... On injured reserve with knee injury (October 25, 2001-remainder of season).

			TOTALS		
Year Team	G	GS	Tk.	Ast.	Sks.
2001—Arizona NFL	3	3	12	1	0.5
2002—Arizona NFL	16	16	37	13	3.5
Pro totals (2 years)	19	19	49	14	4.0

V

VANDERJAGT, MIKE   K   COLTS

PERSONAL: Born March 24, 1970, in Oakville, Ont. ... 6-5/211. ... Name pronounced vander-JAT.

HIGH SCHOOL: White Oaks (Ont.).

JUNIOR COLLEGE: Allan Hancock College (Calif.).

COLLEGE: West Virginia.

TRANSACTIONS/CAREER NOTES: Signed by Saskatchewan Roughriders prior to 1993 season. ... Signed by Toronto Argonauts of CFL (February 15, 1994). ... Released by Argonauts (June 13, 1994). ... Signed by Hamilton Tiger-Cats of CFL (June 24, 1994). ... Released by Tiger-Cats (July 11, 1994). ... Signed by Argonauts of CFL (March 16, 1995). ... Released by Argonauts (June 25, 1995). ... Re-signed by Argonauts of CFL (May 10, 1996). ... Signed as non-drafted free agent by Indianapolis Colts (March 4, 1998).

CHAMPIONSHIP GAME EXPERIENCE: Member of CFL Championship team (1996 and 1997).

HONORS: Named Most Outstanding Canadian Player in Grey Cup (1996). ... Named to CFL All-Star team (1997).

RECORDS: Holds NFL career record for highest field-goal percentage—85.09.

			PUNTING						KICKING							
Year Team	G	No.	Yds.	Avg.	Net avg.	In. 20	Blk.	1-29	30-39	40-49	50+	Tot.	Pct.	Lg.	XPM	XPA	Pts.
1993—Saskatchewan CFL	2	17	672	39.5	32.1	...	...	...	...	...	...	0-0	0.0	0	0	0	0
1994—								Did not play.									
1995—								Did not play.									
1996—Toronto CFL	18	103	4459	43.3	35.1	...	...	...	...	...	...	40-56	71.4	51	59	59	179
1997—Toronto CFL	18	118	5303	44.9	37.4	...	...	...	...	...	...	33-43	76.7	51	77	77	176

Year Team	G	No.	Yds.	Avg.	Net avg.	In. 20	Blk.	1-29	30-39	40-49	50+	Tot.	Pct.	Lg.	XPM	XPA	Pts.
1998—Indianapolis NFL.....	14	0	0	0.0	.0	0	0	9-9	4-4	8-9	6-9	27-31	87.1	53	23	23	104
1999—Indianapolis NFL.....	16	0	0	0.0	.0	0	0	12-12	11-13	10-11	1-2	34-38	89.5	53	43	43	*145
2000—Indianapolis NFL.....	16	0	0	0.0	.0	0	0	7-7	13-13	5-6	0-1	25-27	92.6	48	46	46	121
2001—Indianapolis NFL.....	16	0	0	0.0	.0	0	0	7-8	6-6	12-16	3-4	28-34	82.4	52	41▲	42	§125
2002—Indianapolis NFL.....	16	0	0	0.0	.0	0	0	8-9	6-7	6-12	3-3	23-31	74.2	54	34	34	103
CFL totals (3 years)	38	238	10434	43.8	36.0	...	...	...	...	...	...	73-99	73.7	51	136	136	355
NFL totals (5 years)	78	0	0	0.0	0.0	0	0	43-45	40-43	41-54	13-19	137-161	85.1	54	187	188	598
Pro totals (8 years)	116	238	10434	43.8	36.0	...	...	...	...	...	...	210-260	80.8	54	323	324	953

VANOVER, TAMARICK — WR/KR

PERSONAL: Born February 25, 1974, in Tallahassee, Fla. ... 6-0/220. ... Name pronounced tom-ARE-ik.
HIGH SCHOOL: Leon (Tallahassee, Fla.).
COLLEGE: Florida State.
TRANSACTIONS/CAREER NOTES: Signed after sophomore season with Las Vegas Posse of CFL (February 13, 1994). ... Selected by Kansas City Chiefs in third round (81st pick overall) of 1995 NFL draft. ... Signed by Chiefs for 1995 season. ... Released by Chiefs (April 14, 2000). ... Signed by San Diego Chargers (May 6, 2002). ... Released by Chargers (November 12, 2002).
HONORS: Named kick returner on THE SPORTING NEWS college All-America first team (1992). ... Named kick returner on THE SPORTING NEWS college All-America second team (1993).
SINGLE GAME HIGHS (regular season): Receptions—7 (September 1, 1996, vs. Houston); yards—85 (November 23, 1995, vs. Dallas); and touchdown receptions—1 (September 1, 1996, vs. Houston).

			RUSHING				RECEIVING				PUNT RETURNS				KICKOFF RETURNS				TOTALS		
Year Team	G	GS	Att.	Yds.	Avg.	TD	No.	Yds.	Avg.	TD	No.	Yds.	Avg.	TD	No.	Yds.	Avg.	TD	TD	2pt.	Pts.
1994—Las Vegas CFL	15	...	1	6	6.0	0	23	385	16.7	3	36	341	9.5	1	31	718	23.2	1	5	1	32
1995—Kansas City NFL..	15	0	6	31	5.2	0	11	231	21.0	2	§51	*540	10.6	†1	43	1095	25.5	†2	5	0	30
1996—Kansas City NFL..	13	6	4	6	1.5	0	21	241	11.5	1	17	116	6.8	0	33	854	§25.9	▲1	2	0	12
1997—Kansas City NFL..	16	0	5	50	10.0	0	7	92	13.1	0	35	383	10.9	1	51	1308	25.6	▲1	2	1	14
1998—Kansas City NFL..	12	0	2	1	0.5	0	0	0	0.0	0	27	264	9.8	0	41	956	23.3	0	0	0	0
1999—Kansas City NFL..	14	0	0	0	0.0	0	0	0	0.0	0	51	*627	12.3	†2	44	886	20.1	0	2	0	12
2002—San Diego NFL....	7	0	0	0	0.0	0	0	0	0.0	0	16	86	5.4	0	14	323	23.1	0	0	0	0
CFL totals (1 year)	15	...	1	6	6.0	0	23	385	16.7	3	36	341	9.5	1	31	718	23.2	1	5	1	32
NFL totals (6 years)	77	6	17	88	5.2	0	39	564	14.5	3	197	2016	10.2	4	226	5422	24.0	4	11	1	68
Pro totals (7 years)	92	...	18	94	5.2	0	62	949	15.3	6	233	2357	10.1	5	257	6140	23.9	5	16	2	100

VAUGHN, DARRICK — CB/KR — TEXANS

PERSONAL: Born October 2, 1978, in Houston. ... 5-11/193.
HIGH SCHOOL: Aldine Nimitz (Houston).
COLLEGE: Southwest Texas State.
TRANSACTIONS/CAREER NOTES: Selected by Atlanta Falcons in seventh round (211th pick overall) of 2000 NFL draft. ... Signed by Falcons (May 17, 2000). ... Released by Falcons (September 1, 2002). ... Signed by Houston Texans (January 14, 2003).

			TOTALS			INTERCEPTIONS				KICKOFF RETURNS				TOTALS			
Year Team	G	GS	Tk.	Ast.	Sks.	No.	Yds.	Avg.	TD	No.	Yds.	Avg.	TD	TD	2pt.	Pts.	Fum.
2000—Atlanta NFL	16	0	10	1	0.0	0	0	0.0	0	39	1082	*27.7	*3	3	0	18	1
2001—Atlanta NFL	16	0	20	4	0.0	1	0	0.0	0	*61	‡1491	24.4	1	1	0	6	3
2002—								Did not play.									
Pro totals (2 years)	32	0	30	5	0.0	1	0	0.0	0	100	2573	25.7	4	4	0	24	4

VERBA, ROSS — OL — BROWNS

V

PERSONAL: Born October 31, 1973, in Des Moines, Iowa. ... 6-4/308. ... Full name: Ross Robert Verba.
HIGH SCHOOL: Dowling (West Des Moines, Iowa).
COLLEGE: Iowa.
TRANSACTIONS/CAREER NOTES: Selected by Green Bay Packers in first round (30th pick overall) of 1997 NFL draft. ... Signed by Packers (July 31, 1997). ... Granted unconditional free agency (March 2, 2001). ... Signed by Cleveland Browns (March 23, 2001). ... On physically unable to perform list with back injury (July 23-August 13, 2001).
PLAYING EXPERIENCE: Green Bay NFL, 1997-2001; Cleveland NFL, 2002. ... Games/Games started: 1997 (16/11), 1998 (16/16), 1999 (11/10), 2000 (16/16), 2001 (15/15), 2002 (16/16). Total: 90/84.
CHAMPIONSHIP GAME EXPERIENCE: Played in NFC championship game (1997 season). ... Played in Super Bowl XXXII (1997 season).

VICK, MICHAEL — QB — FALCONS

PERSONAL: Born June 26, 1980, in Newport News, Va. ... 6-0/215. ... Full name: Michael Dwayne Vick.
HIGH SCHOOL: Warwick (Newport News, Va.).
COLLEGE: Virginia Tech.
TRANSACTIONS/CAREER NOTES: Selected after sophomore season by Atlanta Falcons in first round (first pick overall) of 2001 draft. ... Signed by Falcons (May 9, 2001).
HONORS: Named College Football Freshman of the Year by THE SPORTING NEWS (1999). ... Named quarterback on THE SPORTING NEWS college All-America first team (1999). ... Named to play in Pro Bowl (2002 season); replaced by Brad Johnson due to injury.
SINGLE GAME HIGHS (regular season): Attempts—46 (November 10, 2002, vs. Pittsburgh); completions—24 (November 10, 2002, vs. Pittsburgh); yards—337 (December 22, 2002, vs. Detroit); and touchdown passes—2 (December 22, 2002, vs. Detroit).
STATISTICAL PLATEAUS: 300-yard passing games: 2002 (1). ... 100-yard rushing games: 2002 (1).
MISCELLANEOUS: Regular-season record as starting NFL quarterback: 9-7-1 (.559). ... Postseason record as starting NFL quarterback: 1-1 (.500).

Year	Team	G	GS	PASSING Att.	Cmp.	Pct.	Yds.	TD	Int.	Avg.	Skd.	Rat.	RUSHING Att.	Yds.	Avg.	TD	TOTALS TD	2pt.	Pts.
2001—Atlanta NFL	....	8	2	113	50	44.2	785	2	3	6.95	21	62.7	31	289	9.3	1	1	0	6
2002—Atlanta NFL	....	15	15	421	231	54.9	2936	16	8	6.97	33	81.6	113	777	*6.9	8	8	0	48
Pro totals (2 years)	....	23	17	534	281	52.6	3721	18	11	6.97	54	77.6	144	1066	7.4	9	9	0	54

VICKERS, KIPP   OL

PERSONAL: Born August 27, 1969, in Tarpon Springs, Fla. ... 6-2/300. ... Full name: Kipp Emmanuel Vickers.
HIGH SCHOOL: Tarpon Springs (Holiday, Fla.).
COLLEGE: Miami (Fla.).
TRANSACTIONS/CAREER NOTES: Signed as non-drafted free agent by Indianapolis Colts (April 30, 1993). ... Released by Colts (August 30, 1993). ... Re-signed by Colts to practice squad (September 1, 1993). ... Activated (December 21, 1993); did not play. ... Released by Colts (August 28, 1994). ... Re-signed by Colts to practice squad (August 31, 1994). ... Released by Colts (November 1, 1994). ... Re-signed by Colts to practice squad (November 16, 1994). ... Assigned by Colts to Frankfurt Galaxy in 1995 World League enhancement allocation program (February 20, 1995). ... Released by Colts (February 4, 1997). ... Re-signed by Colts for 1997 season. ... Granted free agency (February 13, 1998). ... Re-signed by Colts (February 24, 1998). ... Released by Colts (August 24, 1998). ... Signed by Washington Redskins (November 24, 1998). ... Inactive for five games (1998). ... Granted free agency (February 12, 1999). ... Re-signed by Redskins (February 23, 1999). ... Granted unconditional free agency (February 11, 2000). ... Signed by Baltimore Ravens (February 17, 2000). ... Released by Ravens (February 27, 2002). ... Signed by Redskins (June 4, 2002). ... Granted unconditional free agency (February 28, 2003).
PLAYING EXPERIENCE: Frankfurt W.L., 1995; Indianapolis NFL, 1995-1997; Washington NFL, 1999; Baltimore NFL, 2000 and 2001; Washington NFL, 2002. ... Games/Games started: W.L. 1995 (games played unavailable), NFL 1995 (9/0), 1996 (10/6), 1997 (9/0), 1999 (11/0), 2000 (12/2), 2001 (16/14), 2002 (5/2). Total NFL: 71/24.
CHAMPIONSHIP GAME EXPERIENCE: Played in AFC championship game (1995 and 2000 seasons). ... Member of Super Bowl championship team (2000 season).

VILLARRIAL, CHRIS   G   BEARS

PERSONAL: Born June 9, 1973, in Hummelstown, Pa. ... 6-3/310. ... Name pronounced vuh-LAR-ree-uhl.
HIGH SCHOOL: Hershey (Pa.).
COLLEGE: Indiana University (Pa.).
TRANSACTIONS/CAREER NOTES: Selected by Chicago Bears in fifth round (152nd pick overall) of 1996 NFL draft. ... Signed by Bears (July 11, 1996). ... Granted free agency (February 12, 1999). ... Re-signed by Bears (April 16, 1999).
PLAYING EXPERIENCE: Chicago NFL, 1996-2002. ... Games/Games started: 1996 (14/8), 1997 (11/11), 1998 (16/16), 1999 (15/15), 2000 (16/15), 2001 (16/16), 2002 (15/15). Total: 103/96.

VINATIERI, ADAM   K   PATRIOTS

PERSONAL: Born December 28, 1972, in Yankton, S.D. ... 6-0/202. ... Full name: Adam Matthew Vinatieri. ... Name pronounced VIN-a-TERRY.
HIGH SCHOOL: Rapid City (S.D.) Central.
COLLEGE: South Dakota State (degree in fitness and wellness).
TRANSACTIONS/CAREER NOTES: Signed by Amsterdam Admirals of World League for 1996 season. ... Signed as non-drafted free agent by New England Patriots (June 28, 1996). ... Granted free agency (February 12, 1999). ... Re-signed by Patriots (March 12, 1999). ... Granted free agency (March 1, 2002). ... Re-signed by Patriots (March 15, 2002).
CHAMPIONSHIP GAME EXPERIENCE: Played in AFC championship game (1996 and 2001 seasons). ... Played in Super Bowl XXXI (1996 season). ... Member of Super Bowl championship team (2001 season).
HONORS: Played in Pro Bowl (2002 season).

Year	Team	G	FIELD GOALS 1-29	30-39	40-49	50+	Tot.	Pct.	Lg.	TOTALS XPM	XPA	Pts.
1996—Amsterdam W.L.	....	10	...	...	...	...	9-10	90.0	43	4	4	31
—New England NFL	....	16	10-11	8-8	8-14	1-2	27-35	77.1	50	39	42	120
1997—New England NFL	....	16	11-11	7-9	6-8	1-1	25-29	86.2	52	40	40	115
1998—New England NFL	....	16	11-11	9-14	9-12	2-2	31-39	79.5	55	32	32	127
1999—New England NFL	....	16	15-15	5-7	5-9	1-2	26-33	78.8	51	29	30	107
2000—New England NFL	....	16	11-13	8-9	7-8	1-3	27-33	81.8	53	25	25	106
2001—New England NFL	....	16	9-9	7-8	7-12	1-1	24-30	80.0	54	41	▲42	113
2002—New England NFL	....	16	6-6	12-12	8-10	1-2	§27-30	90.0	*57	36	36	117
W.L. totals (1 year)	....	10	...	...	...	...	9-10	90.0	43	4	4	31
NFL totals (7 years)	....	112	73-76	56-67	50-73	8-13	187-229	81.7	57	242	247	805
Pro totals (8 years)	....	122	...	...	...	...	196-239	82.0	57	246	251	834

VINCENT, KEYDRICK   G   STEELERS

PERSONAL: Born April 13, 1978, in Bartow, Fla. ... 6-5/330. ... Full name: Keydrick Trepell Vincent.
HIGH SCHOOL: Lake Gibson (Fla.).
COLLEGE: Mississippi.
TRANSACTIONS/CAREER NOTES: Signed as non-drafted free agent by Pittsburgh Steelers (April 23, 2001).
PLAYING EXPERIENCE: Pittsburgh NFL, 2001-2002. ... Games/Games started: 2001 (5/1), 2002 (7/1). Totals: 12/2.
CHAMPIONSHIP GAME EXPERIENCE: Played in AFC championship game (2001 season).

VINCENT, TROY   CB   EAGLES

PERSONAL: Born June 8, 1971, in Trenton, N.J. ... 6-1/200. ... Full name: Troy D. Vincent. ... Nephew of Steve Luke, safety with Green Bay Packers (1975-80).

HIGH SCHOOL: Pennsbury (Fairless Hills, Pa.).

COLLEGE: Wisconsin.

TRANSACTIONS/CAREER NOTES: Selected by Miami Dolphins in first round (seventh pick overall) of 1992 NFL draft. ... Signed by Dolphins (August 8, 1992). ... Designated by Dolphins as transition player (February 25, 1993). ... On injured reserve with knee injury (December 15, 1993-remainder of season). ... Tendered offer sheet by Philadelphia Eagles (February 24, 1996). ... Dolphins declined to match offer (March 3, 1996).

CHAMPIONSHIP GAME EXPERIENCE: Played in AFC championship game (1992 season). ... Played in NFC championship game (2001 and 2002 seasons).

HONORS: Named defensive back on THE SPORTING NEWS college All-America first team (1991). ... Played in Pro Bowl (1999, 2000 and 2002 seasons). ... Named to play in Pro Bowl (2001 season); replaced by Champ Bailey due to injury.

			TOTALS			INTERCEPTIONS			
Year Team	G	GS	Tk.	Ast.	Sks.	No.	Yds.	Avg.	TD
1992—Miami NFL	15	14	56	21	0.0	2	47	23.5	0
1993—Miami NFL	13	13	58	10	0.0	2	29	14.5	0
1994—Miami NFL	13	12	41	11	0.0	5	113	22.6	1
1995—Miami NFL	16	16	52	10	0.0	5	95	19.0	▲1
1996—Philadelphia NFL	16	16	45	7	0.0	3	144	*48.0	1
1997—Philadelphia NFL	16	16	50	15	0.0	3	14	4.7	0
1998—Philadelphia NFL	13	13	42	8	1.0	2	29	14.5	0
1999—Philadelphia NFL	14	14	62	20	1.0	†7	91	13.0	0
2000—Philadelphia NFL	16	16	64	13	1.0	5	34	6.8	0
2001—Philadelphia NFL	15	15	58	11	1.5	3	0	0.0	0
2002—Philadelphia NFL	15	15	55	12	0.0	2	1	0.5	0
Pro totals (11 years)	162	160	583	138	4.5	39	597	15.3	3

VOLLERS, KURT   G   COWBOYS

PERSONAL: Born April 4, 1979, in San Gabriel, Calif. ... 6-7/317.

HIGH SCHOOL: Servite (Whittier, Calif.).

COLLEGE: Notre Dame.

TRANSACTIONS/CAREER NOTES: Signed as non-drafted free agent by Indianapolis Colts (April 20, 2002). ... Released by Colts (September 1, 2002). ... Re-signed by Colts to practice squad (September 3, 2002). ... Claimed on waivers by Dallas Cowboys (October 23, 2002).

PLAYING EXPERIENCE: Dallas NFL, 2002. ... Games/Games started: 2002 (1/0).

VON OELHOFFEN, KIMO   DE   STEELERS

PERSONAL: Born January 30, 1971, in Kaunakaki, Hawaii. ... 6-4/300. ... Full name: Kimo K. von Oelhoffen. ... Name pronounced KEE-moe von OHL-hoffen.

HIGH SCHOOL: Molokai (Hoolehua, Hawaii).

JUNIOR COLLEGE: Walla Walla (Wash.) Community College.

COLLEGE: Hawaii, then Boise State.

TRANSACTIONS/CAREER NOTES: Selected by Cincinnati Bengals in sixth round (162nd pick overall) of 1994 NFL draft. ... Signed by Bengals (May 9, 1994). ... Granted unconditional free agency (February 11, 2000). ... Signed by Pittsburgh Steelers (February 14, 2000).

CHAMPIONSHIP GAME EXPERIENCE: Played in AFC championship game (2001 season).

			TOTALS		
Year Team	G	GS	Tk.	Ast.	Sks.
1994—Cincinnati NFL	7	0	2	0	0.0
1995—Cincinnati NFL	16	1	7	1	0.0
1996—Cincinnati NFL	11	1	11	4	1.0
1997—Cincinnati NFL	13	13	32	10	0.0
1998—Cincinnati NFL	16	16	36	9	0.0
1999—Cincinnati NFL	16	5	24	2	4.0
2000—Pittsburgh NFL	16	16	29	15	1.0
2001—Pittsburgh NFL	15	15	20	8	4.0
2002—Pittsburgh NFL	16	16	12	10	3.0
Pro totals (9 years)	126	83	173	59	13.0

V

VRABEL, MIKE   LB   PATRIOTS

PERSONAL: Born August 14, 1975, in Akron, Ohio. ... 6-4/261. ... Full name: Michael George Vrabel.

HIGH SCHOOL: Walsh Jesuit (Cuyahoga Falls, Ohio).

COLLEGE: Ohio State.

TRANSACTIONS/CAREER NOTES: Selected by Pittsburgh Steelers in third round (91st pick overall) of 1997 NFL draft. ... Signed by Steelers (July 15, 1997). ... Granted free agency (February 11, 2000). ... Re-signed by Steelers (April 20, 2000). ... Granted unconditional free agency (March 2, 2001). ... Signed by New England Patriots (March 16, 2001).

CHAMPIONSHIP GAME EXPERIENCE: Played in AFC championship game (1997 and 2001 seasons). ... Member of Super Bowl championship team (2001 season).

Year Team	G	GS	TOTALS			INTERCEPTIONS			
			Tk.	Ast.	Sks.	No.	Yds.	Avg.	TD
1997—Pittsburgh NFL	15	0	14	3	1.5	0	0	0.0	0
1998—Pittsburgh NFL	11	0	6	3	2.5	0	0	0.0	0
1999—Pittsburgh NFL	10	0	4	1	2.0	0	0	0.0	0
2000—Pittsburgh NFL	15	0	3	2	1.0	0	0	0.0	0
2001—New England NFL	16	12	37	23	3.0	2	27	13.5	0
2002—New England NFL	16	13	51	24	4.5	1	0	0.0	0
Pro totals (6 years)	83	25	115	56	14.5	3	27	9.0	0

WADE, JOHN   C   BUCCANEERS

PERSONAL: Born January 25, 1975, in Harrisonburg, Va. ... 6-5/299. ... Full name: John Robert Wade.
HIGH SCHOOL: Harrisonburg (Va.).
COLLEGE: Marshall (degree in business management, 1997).
TRANSACTIONS/CAREER NOTES: Selected by Jacksonville Jaguars in fifth round (148th pick overall) of 1998 NFL draft. ... Signed by Jaguars (June 1, 1998). ... On injured reserve with broken foot (September 27, 2000-remainder of season). ... On physically unable to perform list with foot injury (July 27-September 2, 2001). ... Granted unconditional free agency (March 1, 2002). ... Re-signed by Jaguars (March 13, 2002). ... Granted unconditional free agency (February 28, 2003). ... Signed by Tampa Bay Buccaneers (March 12, 2003).
PLAYING EXPERIENCE: Jacksonville NFL, 1998-2002. ... Games/Games started: 1998 (5/0), 1999 (16/16), 2000 (2/2), 2001 (15/0), 2002 (16/16). Total: 54/34.
CHAMPIONSHIP GAME EXPERIENCE: Played in AFC championship game (1999 season).

WADE, TODD   OT   DOLPHINS

PERSONAL: Born October 30, 1976, in Greenwood, Miss. ... 6-8/325. ... Full name: Todd McLaurin Wade.
HIGH SCHOOL: Jackson (Miss.) Prep.
COLLEGE: Mississippi.
TRANSACTIONS/CAREER NOTES: Selected by Miami Dolphins in second round (53rd pick overall) of 2000 NFL draft. ... Signed by Dolphins (July 24, 2000).
PLAYING EXPERIENCE: Miami NFL, 2000-2002. ... Games/Games started: 2000 (16/16), 2001 (15/15), 2002 (16/16). Total: 47/47.

WAHLE, MIKE   G   PACKERS

PERSONAL: Born March 29, 1977, in Portland, Ore. ... 6-6/307. ... Full name: Michael James Wahle. ... Name pronounced WALL.
HIGH SCHOOL: Rim of the World (Lake Arrowhead, Calif.).
COLLEGE: Navy.
TRANSACTIONS/CAREER NOTES: Selected by Green Bay Packers in second round of 1998 supplemental draft (July 9, 1998). ... Signed by Packers (August 6, 1998). ... Granted free agency (March 2, 2001). ... Re-signed by Packers (May 31, 2001). ... Granted unconditional free agency (March 1, 2002). ... Re-signed by Packers (March 8, 2002).
PLAYING EXPERIENCE: Green Bay NFL, 1998-2002. ... Games/Games started: 1998 (1/0), 1999 (16/13), 2000 (16/6), 2001 (16/16), 2002 (16/16). Total: 65/51.

WAKEFIELD, FRED   DE   CARDINALS

PERSONAL: Born September 17, 1978, in Tuscola, Ill. ... 6-7/288.
HIGH SCHOOL: Tuscola (Ill.).
COLLEGE: Illinois.
TRANSACTIONS/CAREER NOTES: Signed as non-drafted free agent by Arizona Cardinals (April 23, 2001).

Year Team	G	GS	TOTALS			INTERCEPTIONS			
			Tk.	Ast.	Sks.	No.	Yds.	Avg.	TD
2001—Arizona NFL	16	12	28	6	2.5	1	20	20.0	1
2002—Arizona NFL	16	14	21	10	3.0	0	0	0.0	0
Pro totals (2 years)	32	26	49	16	5.5	1	20	20.0	1

WALKER, BRACEY   S   LIONS

PERSONAL: Born October 28, 1970, in Portsmouth, Va. ... 6-0/205. ... Full name: Bracey Wordell Walker.
HIGH SCHOOL: Pine Forest (Fayetteville, N.C.).
COLLEGE: North Carolina.
TRANSACTIONS/CAREER NOTES: Selected by Kansas City Chiefs in fourth round (127th pick overall) of 1994 NFL draft. ... Signed by Chiefs (July 20, 1994). ... Claimed on waivers by Cincinnati Bengals (October 12, 1994). ... Granted free agency (February 14, 1997). ... Re-signed by Bengals (April 18, 1997). ... Claimed on waivers by Miami Dolphins (August 20, 1997). ... On injured reserve with leg injury (December 2, 1997-remainder of season). ... Granted unconditional free agency (February 13, 1998). ... Re-signed by Dolphins (April 27, 1998). ... Released by Dolphins (August 19, 1998). ... Signed by Chiefs (November 3, 1998). ... Granted unconditional free agency (February 11, 2000). ... Re-signed by Chiefs (February 24, 2000). ... Granted unconditional free agency (March 2, 2002). ... Signed by Detroit Lions (April 15, 2002). ... On injured reserve with liver injury (December 18, 2002-remainder of season).
HONORS: Named defensive back on THE SPORTING NEWS college All-America second team (1993).

Year Team	G	GS	TOTALS			INTERCEPTIONS			
			Tk.	Ast.	Sks.	No.	Yds.	Avg.	TD
1994—Kansas City NFL	2	0	0	0	0.0	0	0	0.0	0
—Cincinnati NFL	7	0	1	1	0.0	0	0	0.0	0
1995—Cincinnati NFL	14	14	60	25	0.0	4	56	14.0	0
1996—Cincinnati NFL	16	16	57	13	0.0	2	35	17.5	0
1997—Miami NFL	12	0	2	0	0.0	0	0	0.0	0
1998—Kansas City NFL	8	0	1	0	0.0	0	0	0.0	0
1999—Kansas City NFL	16	1	8	0	0.0	0	0	0.0	0
2000—Kansas City NFL	15	0	0	0	0.0	0	0	0.0	0
2001—Kansas City NFL	15	0	1	0	0.0	0	0	0.0	0
2002—Detroit NFL	14	1	24	12	1.0	0	0	0.0	0
Pro totals (9 years)	119	32	154	51	1.0	6	91	15.2	0

W

WALKER, BRIAN   S   LIONS

PERSONAL: Born May 31, 1972, in Colorado Springs, Colo. ... 6-1/205.
HIGH SCHOOL: Widefield (Colorado Springs, Colo.).
JUNIOR COLLEGE: Snow College (Utah).
COLLEGE: Washington State.
TRANSACTIONS/CAREER NOTES: Signed as non-drafted free agent by Washington Redskins (May 1, 1996). ... Released by Redskins (October 9, 1997). ... Signed by Miami Dolphins (December 9, 1997). ... Active for two games with Dolphins (1997); did not play. ... Claimed on waivers by Seattle Seahawks (September 6, 1999). ... Released by Seahawks (September 14, 1999). ... Re-signed by Seahawks (September 30, 1999). ... On injured reserve with hamstring injury (January 8, 2000-remainder of playoffs). ... Granted unconditional free agency (February 11, 2000). ... Signed by Dolphins (February 16, 2000). ... Granted unconditional free agency (March 1, 2002). ... Signed by Detroit Lions (March 5, 2002).

| | | | TOTALS | | | INTERCEPTIONS | | | |
Year Team	G	GS	Tk.	Ast.	Sks.	No.	Yds.	Avg.	TD
1996—Washington NFL	16	4	29	9	1.0	0	0	0.0	0
1997—Washington NFL	5	0	0	0	0.0	0	0	0.0	0
1998—Miami NFL	16	0	12	3	0.0	4	12	3.0	0
1999—Seattle NFL	5	0	8	1	0.0	1	21	21.0	0
2000—Miami NFL	16	16	60	28	2.0	▲7	80	11.4	0
2001—Miami NFL	13	13	52	25	0.0	1	0	0.0	0
2002—Detroit NFL	10	8	32	12	1.0	0	0	0.0	0
Pro totals (7 years)	81	41	193	78	4.0	13	113	8.7	0

WALKER, DARWIN   DT   EAGLES

PERSONAL: Born June 15, 1977, in Walterboro, S.C. ... 6-3/294. ... Full name: Darwin Jamar Walker.
HIGH SCHOOL: Walterboro (S.C.).
COLLEGE: North Carolina State, then Tennessee.
TRANSACTIONS/CAREER NOTES: Selected by Arizona Cardinals in third round (71st pick overall) of 2000 NFL draft. ... Signed by Cardinals (June 19, 2000). ... Claimed on waivers by Philadelphia Eagles (September 12, 2000).
CHAMPIONSHIP GAME EXPERIENCE: Played in NFC championship game (2001 and 2002 seasons).
HONORS: Named defensive tackle on THE SPORTING NEWS college All-America second team (1999).

| | | | TOTALS | | |
Year Team	G	GS	Tk.	Ast.	Sks.
2000—Arizona NFL	1	0	0	0	0.0
2001—Philadelphia NFL	10	0	4	1	1.0
2002—Philadelphia NFL	16	16	29	6	7.5
Pro totals (3 years)	27	16	33	7	8.5

WALKER, DENARD   CB   VIKINGS

PERSONAL: Born August 9, 1973, in Dallas. ... 6-1/190. ... Full name: Denard Antuan Walker.
HIGH SCHOOL: South Garland (Texas), than Harlingen (Texas) Military Institute.
COLLEGE: Louisiana State.
TRANSACTIONS/CAREER NOTES: Selected by Houston Oilers in third round (75th pick overall) of 1997 NFL draft. ... Oilers franchise moved to Tennessee for 1997 season. ... Signed by Oilers (July 18, 1997). ... Oilers franchise renamed Tennessee Titans for 1999 season (December 26, 1998). ... Granted free agency (February 11, 2000). ... Re-signed by Titans (June 3, 2000). ... On suspended list (September 3-5, 2000). ... Granted unconditional free agency (March 2, 2001). ... Signed by Denver Broncos (March 19, 2001). ... Released by Broncos (February 25, 2003). ... Signed by Minnesota Vikings (March 12, 2003).
CHAMPIONSHIP GAME EXPERIENCE: Played in AFC championship game (1999 season). ... Played in Super Bowl XXXIV (1999 season).

| | | | TOTALS | | | INTERCEPTIONS | | | |
Year Team	G	GS	Tk.	Ast.	Sks.	No.	Yds.	Avg.	TD
1997—Tennessee NFL	15	11	56	12	0.0	2	53	26.5	1
1998—Tennessee NFL	16	16	68	15	0.0	2	6	3.0	0
1999—Tennessee NFL	15	14	39	8	0.0	1	27	27.0	0
2000—Tennessee NFL	15	14	44	1	0.0	2	4	2.0	0
2001—Denver NFL	16	15	51	5	0.0	3	60	20.0	1
2002—Denver NFL	16	16	56	8	0.0	1	8	8.0	0
Pro totals (6 years)	93	86	314	49	0.0	11	158	14.4	2

WALKER, GARY   DT   TEXANS

PERSONAL: Born February 28, 1973, in Royston, Ga. ... 6-2/305. ... Full name: Gary Lamar Walker.
HIGH SCHOOL: Franklin County (Carnesville, Ga.).
JUNIOR COLLEGE: Hinds Community College (Miss.).
COLLEGE: Auburn.
TRANSACTIONS/CAREER NOTES: Selected by Houston Oilers in fifth round (159th pick overall) of 1995 NFL draft. ... Signed by Oilers (July 10, 1995). ... Oilers franchise moved to Tennessee for 1997 season. ... Granted free agency (February 13, 1998). ... Re-signed by Oilers (July 15, 1998). ... Granted unconditional free agency (February 12, 1999). ... Signed by Jacksonville Jaguars (February 15, 1999). ... Selected by Houston Texans from Jaguars in NFL expansion draft (February 18, 2002).
CHAMPIONSHIP GAME EXPERIENCE: Played in AFC championship game (1999 season).
HONORS: Played in Pro Bowl (2001 and 2002 seasons).

W

Year Team	G	GS	Tk.	TOTALS Ast.	Sks.
1995—Houston NFL	15	9	22	10	2.5
1996—Houston NFL	16	16	30	15	5.5
1997—Tennessee NFL	15	15	31	13	7.0
1998—Tennessee NFL	16	16	31	16	1.0
1999—Jacksonville NFL	16	16	46	8	10.0
2000—Jacksonville NFL	15	14	40	3	5.0
2001—Jacksonville NFL	16	16	35	8	7.5
2002—Houston NFL	16	16	37	15	6.5
Pro totals (8 years)	**125**	**118**	**272**	**88**	**45.0**

WALKER, JAVON — WR — PACKERS

PERSONAL: Born October 14, 1978, in Lafayette, La. ... 6-3/215.
HIGH SCHOOL: St. Thomas More (Lafayette, La.).
JUNIOR COLLEGE: Jones Junior College (Miss.).
COLLEGE: Florida State.
TRANSACTIONS/CAREER NOTES: Selected by Green Bay Packers in first round (20th pick overall) of 2002 NFL draft. ... Signed by Packers (July 23, 2002).
SINGLE GAME HIGHS (regular season): Receptions—4 (September 8, 2002, vs. Atlanta); yards—56 (September 8, 2002, vs. Atlanta); and touchdown receptions—1 (September 8, 2002, vs. Atlanta).

Year Team	G	GS	RUSHING Att.	Yds.	Avg.	TD	RECEIVING No.	Yds.	Avg.	TD	KICKOFF RETURNS No.	Yds.	Avg.	TD	TOTALS TD	2pt.	Pts.	Fum.
2002—Green Bay NFL	15	2	1	11	11.0	0	23	319	13.9	1	35	769	22.0	0	1	0	6	1

WALKER, JOE — S

PERSONAL: Born March 19, 1977, in Memphis, Tenn. ... 5-10/204.
HIGH SCHOOL: Arlington-Lamar (Texas).
COLLEGE: Nebraska.
TRANSACTIONS/CAREER NOTES: Signed as non-drafted free agent by Tennessee Titans (April 27, 2001). ... Released by Titans (August 26, 2002). ... Signed by Indianapolis Colts (September 24, 2002). ... Released by Colts (October 5, 2002). ... Re-signed by Colts (November 20, 2002). ... Released by Colts (February 26, 2003).

Year Team	G	GS	TOTALS Tk.	Ast.	Sks.	INTERCEPTIONS No.	Yds.	Avg.	TD	PUNT RETURNS No.	Yds.	Avg.	TD	KICKOFF RETURNS No.	Yds.	Avg.	TD	TOTALS TD	2pt.	Pts.	Fum.
2001—Tennessee NFL	16	3	5	8	0.0	0	0	0.0	0	14	125	8.9	0	3	33	11.0	0	0	0	0	1
2002—Indianapolis NFL	5	0	0	0	0.0	0	0	0.0	0	2	6	3.0	0	3	50	16.7	0	0	0	0	0
Pro totals (2 years)	**21**	**3**	**5**	**8**	**0.0**	**0**	**0**	**0.0**	**0**	**16**	**131**	**8.2**	**0**	**6**	**83**	**13.8**	**0**	**0**	**0**	**0**	**1**

WALKER, KENYATTA — OT — BUCCANEERS

PERSONAL: Born February 1, 1979, in Meridian, Miss. ... 6-5/302. ... Full name: Idrees Kenyatta Walker.
HIGH SCHOOL: Meridian (Miss.).
COLLEGE: Florida.
TRANSACTIONS/CAREER NOTES: Selected after junior season by Tampa Bay Buccaneers in first round (14th pick overall) of 2001 draft. ... Signed by Buccaneers (July 26, 2001).
PLAYING EXPERIENCE: Tampa Bay NFL, 2001-2002. ... Games/Games started: 2001 (16/16), 2002 (13/13). Total: 29/29.
CHAMPIONSHIP GAME EXPERIENCE: Played in NFC championship game (2002 season). ... Member of Super Bowl championship team (2002 season).

WALKER, LANGSTON — OT — RAIDERS

PERSONAL: Born September 3, 1979, in Oakland. ... 6-8/345.
HIGH SCHOOL: Bishop O'Dowd (Calif.).
COLLEGE: California.
TRANSACTIONS/CAREER NOTES: Selected by Oakland Raiders in second round (53rd pick overall) of 2002 NFL draft. ... Signed by Raiders (July 19, 2002).
PLAYING EXPERIENCE: Oakland NFL, 2002. ... Games/Games started: 2002 (12/2).
CHAMPIONSHIP GAME EXPERIENCE: Played in AFC championship game (2002 season). ... Played in Super Bowl XXXVII (2002 season).

WALKER, RAMON — S — TEXANS

PERSONAL: Born November 8, 1979, in Akron, Ohio. ... 6-0/197. ... Full name: Ramon D. Walker.
HIGH SCHOOL: John R. Buchtel (Akron, Ohio).
COLLEGE: Pittsburgh.
TRANSACTIONS/CAREER NOTES: Selected after junior season by Houston Texans in fifth round (153rd pick overall) of 2002 NFL draft. ... Signed by Texans (July 17, 2002). ... On injured reserve with knee injury (December 24, 2002-remainder of season).

Year Team	G	GS	TOTALS Tk.	Ast.	Sks.	INTERCEPTIONS No.	Yds.	Avg.	TD
2002—Houston NFL	9	1	4	0	0.0	0	0	0.0	0

W

WALKER, ROD   DT   PACKERS

PERSONAL: Born February 4, 1976, in Milton, Fla. ... 6-3/319. ... Full name: Roderick Dion Walker.
HIGH SCHOOL: Milton (Fla.).
COLLEGE: Troy State.
TRANSACTIONS/CAREER NOTES: Signed as non-drafted free agent by Washington Redskins (April 21, 1999). ... Released by Redskins (August 30, 1999). ... Re-signed by Redskins (September 2, 1999). ... Released by Redskins (September 4, 1999). ... Signed by Tennessee Titans to practice squad (October 26, 1999). ... Released by Titans (August 26, 2000). ... Re-signed by Titans to practice squad (August 30, 2000). ... Activated (December 1, 2000); did not play. ... Traded by Titans to Green Bay Packers for future draft pick (September 2, 2001).

			TOTALS		
Year Team	G	GS	Tk.	Ast.	Sks.
2001—Green Bay NFL	11	0	5	2	0.0
2002—Green Bay NFL	13	5	10	8	0.0
Pro totals (2 years)	24	5	15	10	0.0

WALLACE, AL   DE   PANTHERS

PERSONAL: Born March 25, 1974, in Delray Beach, Fla. ... 6-5/258. ... Full name: Alonzo Dwight Wallace.
HIGH SCHOOL: Spanish River (Boca Raton, Fla.).
COLLEGE: Maryland (degree in health education, 1997).
TRANSACTIONS/CAREER NOTES: Signed as non-drafted free agent by Jacksonville Jaguars (April 21, 1997). ... Released by Jaguars (August 19, 1997). ... Re-signed by Jaguars to practice squad (August 25, 1997). ... Signed by Philadelphia Eagles off Jaguars practice squad (December 2, 1997). ... On injured reserve with ankle injury (September 5, 1999-entire season). ... Released by Eagles (August 27, 2000). ... Signed by Chicago Bears (December 20, 2000). ... Released by Bears (August 28, 2001). ... Signed by Miami Dolphins (January 15, 2002). ... Traded by Dolphins with fourth-round pick (DB Colin Branch) in 2003 draft to Carolina Panthers for DE Jay Williams (July 19, 2002).

			TOTALS		
Year Team	G	GS	Tk.	Ast.	Sks.
1997—Philadelphia NFL	1	0	0	0	0.0
1998—Philadelphia NFL	15	0	14	4	6.0
1999—Philadelphia NFL			Did not play.		
2002—Carolina NFL	16	4	22	4	3.0
Pro totals (3 years)	32	4	36	8	9.0

WALLS, LENNY   CB   BRONCOS

PERSONAL: Born September 26, 1979, in San Francisco. ... 6-4/192.
HIGH SCHOOL: Galileo (San Francisco).
JUNIOR COLLEGE: City College of San Francisco.
COLLEGE: Boston College.
TRANSACTIONS/CAREER NOTES: Signed as non-drafted free agent by Denver Broncos (April 22, 2002).

			TOTALS			INTERCEPTIONS			
Year Team	G	GS	Tk.	Ast.	Sks.	No.	Yds.	Avg.	TD
2002—Denver NFL	13	0	0	0	0.0	0	0	0.0	0

WALLS, RAYMOND   CB   BROWNS

PERSONAL: Born July 24, 1979, in Kentwood, La. ... 5-10/176. ... Full name: Raymond Omoncial Tyshone Walls.
HIGH SCHOOL: Kentwood (La.).
COLLEGE: Southern Mississippi.
TRANSACTIONS/CAREER NOTES: Selected by Indianapolis Colts in fifth round (152nd pick overall) of 2001 NFL draft. ... Signed by Colts (June 13, 2001). ... Released by Colts (September 1, 2001). ... Re-signed by Colts to practice squad (September 3, 2001). ... Activated (October 8, 2001). ... Released by Colts (August 28, 2002). ... Signed by Cleveland Browns to practice squad (September 25, 2002). ... Activated (October 23, 2002). ... Released by Browns (November 14, 2002). ... Re-signed by Browns to practice squad (November 14, 2002). ... Activated (November 26, 2002).

			TOTALS			INTERCEPTIONS			
Year Team	G	GS	Tk.	Ast.	Sks.	No.	Yds.	Avg.	TD
2001—Indianapolis NFL	4	0	3	0	0.0	1	0	0.0	0
2002—Cleveland NFL	4	0	0	0	0.0	0	0	0.0	0
Pro totals (2 years)	8	0	3	0	0.0	1	0	0.0	0

W

WALLS, WESLEY   TE

PERSONAL: Born February 26, 1966, in Pontotoc, Miss. ... 6-5/250. ... Full name: Charles Wesley Walls.
HIGH SCHOOL: Pontotoc (Miss.).
COLLEGE: Mississippi.
TRANSACTIONS/CAREER NOTES: Selected by San Francisco 49ers in second round (56th pick overall) of 1989 NFL draft. ... Signed by 49ers (July 26, 1989). ... Granted free agency (February 1, 1992). ... Re-signed by 49ers (July 18, 1992). ... On injured reserve with shoulder injury (September 1, 1992-January 16, 1993). ... On injured reserve with shoulder injury (October 27, 1993-remainder of season). ... Granted unconditional free agency (February 17, 1994). ... Signed by New Orleans Saints (April 27, 1994). ... Granted unconditional free agency (February 16, 1996). ... Signed by Carolina Panthers (February 21, 1996). ... On injured reserve with knee injury (October 31, 2000-remainder of season). ... Released by Panthers (February 26, 2003).
CHAMPIONSHIP GAME EXPERIENCE: Played in NFC championship game (1989, 1990 and 1996 seasons). ... Member of Super Bowl championship team (1989 season).
HONORS: Named tight end on THE SPORTING NEWS college All-America second team (1988). ... Played in Pro Bowl (1996-1999 seasons). ... Named to play in Pro Bowl (2001 season); replaced by Byron Chamberlain due to injury.

SINGLE GAME HIGHS (regular season): Receptions—10 (October 7, 2001, vs. San Francisco); yards—147 (September 7, 1997, vs. Atlanta); and touchdown receptions—2 (January 2, 2000, vs. New Orleans).
STATISTICAL PLATEAUS: 100-yard receiving games: 1997 (2), 2000 (1). Total: 3.
MISCELLANEOUS: Holds Carolina Panthers all-time records for most touchdown receptions (44) and most touchdowns (44).

Year Team	G	GS	RECEIVING No.	Yds.	Avg.	TD	TOTALS TD	2pt.	Pts.	Fum.
1989—San Francisco NFL	16	0	4	16	4.0	1	1	0	6	1
1990—San Francisco NFL	16	0	5	27	5.4	0	0	0	0	0
1991—San Francisco NFL	15	0	2	24	12.0	0	0	0	0	0
1992—San Francisco NFL						Did not play.				
1993—San Francisco NFL	6	0	0	0	0.0	0	0	0	0	0
1994—New Orleans NFL	15	7	38	406	10.7	4	4	1	26	0
1995—New Orleans NFL	16	11	57	694	12.2	4	4	1	26	1
1996—Carolina NFL	16	15	61	713	11.7	10	10	0	60	0
1997—Carolina NFL	15	15	58	746	12.9	6	6	0	36	0
1998—Carolina NFL	14	14	49	506	10.3	5	5	0	30	0
1999—Carolina NFL	16	16	63	822	13.0	12	12	0	72	1
2000—Carolina NFL	8	8	31	422	13.6	2	2	0	12	0
2001—Carolina NFL	14	14	43	452	10.5	5	5	0	30	0
2002—Carolina NFL	15	14	19	241	12.7	4	4	0	24	0
Pro totals (13 years)	182	114	430	5069	11.8	53	53	2	322	3

WALSH, CHRIS   WR

PERSONAL: Born December 12, 1968, in Cleveland. ... 6-1/199. ... Full name: Christopher Lee Walsh.
HIGH SCHOOL: Ygnacio Valley (Concord, Calif.).
COLLEGE: Stanford (degree in quantitative economics, 1991).
TRANSACTIONS/CAREER NOTES: Selected by Buffalo Bills in ninth round (251st pick overall) of 1992 NFL draft. ... Signed by Bills (July 22, 1992). ... Released by Bills (August 31, 1992). ... Re-signed by Bills to practice squad (September 1, 1992). ... Activated (September 19, 1992). ... Released by Bills (October 2, 1992). ... Re-signed by Bills to practice squad (October 2, 1992). ... Released by Bills (March 10, 1994). ... Signed by Minnesota Vikings (May 6, 1994). ... Granted unconditional free agency (February 16, 1996). ... Re-signed by Vikings (March 4, 1996). ... Granted unconditional free agency (February 13, 1998). ... Re-signed by Vikings (March 4, 1998). ... Granted unconditional free agency (March 2, 2001). ... Re-signed by Vikings (June 11, 2001). ... Granted unconditional free agency (February 28, 2003).
CHAMPIONSHIP GAME EXPERIENCE: Member of Bills for AFC championship game (1993 season); inactive. ... Member of Bills for Super Bowl XXVIII (1993 season); inactive. ... Played in NFC championship game (1998 and 2000 seasons).
SINGLE GAME HIGHS (regular season): Receptions—4 (December 24, 2000, vs. Indianapolis); yards—44 (December 17, 2000, vs. Green Bay); and touchdown receptions—1 (September 22, 2002, vs. Carolina).

Year Team	G	GS	RECEIVING No.	Yds.	Avg.	TD	TOTALS TD	2pt.	Pts.	Fum.
1992—Buffalo NFL	2	0	0	0	0.0	0	0	0	0	0
1993—Buffalo NFL	3	0	0	0	0.0	0	0	0	0	0
1994—Minnesota NFL	10	0	0	0	0.0	0	0	0	0	0
1995—Minnesota NFL	16	0	7	66	9.4	0	0	0	0	0
1996—Minnesota NFL	15	0	4	39	9.8	1	1	1	8	0
1997—Minnesota NFL	14	0	11	114	10.4	1	1	0	6	0
1998—Minnesota NFL	15	0	2	46	23.0	0	0	0	0	0
1999—Minnesota NFL	16	1	2	24	12.0	1	1	0	6	0
2000—Minnesota NFL	16	0	18	191	10.6	0	0	0	0	0
2001—Minnesota NFL	16	0	9	67	7.4	0	0	0	0	0
2002—Minnesota NFL	16	3	14	172	12.3	1	1	0	6	0
Pro totals (11 years)	139	4	67	719	10.7	4	4	1	26	0

WALTER, KEN   P   PATRIOTS

PERSONAL: Born August 15, 1972, in Cleveland. ... 6-1/207. ... Full name: Kenneth Matthew Walter Jr.
HIGH SCHOOL: Euclid (Ohio).
COLLEGE: Kent.
TRANSACTIONS/CAREER NOTES: Signed as non-drafted free agent by Carolina Panthers (April 14, 1997). ... Released by Panthers (April 24, 2001). ... Signed by New England Patriots (October 16, 2001).
CHAMPIONSHIP GAME EXPERIENCE: Played in AFC championship game (2001 season). ... Member of Super Bowl championship team (2001 season).

Year Team	G	PUNTING No.	Yds.	Avg.	Net avg.	In. 20	Blk.
1997—Carolina NFL	16	85	3604	42.4	36.4	29	0
1998—Carolina NFL	16	77	3131	40.7	38.1	20	0
1999—Carolina NFL	16	65	2562	39.4	36.7	18	0
2000—Carolina NFL	16	64	2459	38.4	33.8	19	†2
2001—New England NFL	11	49	1964	40.1	§38.1	24	0
2002—New England NFL	16	70	2723	38.9	33.3	19	1
Pro totals (6 years)	91	410	16443	40.1	36.0	129	3

WALTER, TYSON   OT   COWBOYS

PERSONAL: Born March 17, 1978, in Bainbridge, Ohio. ... 6-5/310.
HIGH SCHOOL: Kenston (Ohio).
COLLEGE: Ohio State.
TRANSACTIONS/CAREER NOTES: Selected by Dallas Cowboys in sixth round (179th pick overall) of 2002 NFL draft. ... Signed by Cowboys (July 24, 2002).
PLAYING EXPERIENCE: Dallas NFL, 2002. ... Games/Games started: 2002 (12/8).

W

WALTERS, TROY — WR/KR — COLTS

PERSONAL: Born December 15, 1976, in College Station, Texas. ... 5-7/172. ... Full name: Troy M. Walters.
HIGH SCHOOL: A&M Consolidated (College Station, Texas).
COLLEGE: Stanford.
TRANSACTIONS/CAREER NOTES: Selected by Minnesota Vikings in fifth round (165th pick overall) of 2000 NFL draft. ... Signed by Vikings (July 12, 2000). ... Claimed on waivers by Indianapolis Colts (February 24, 2002).
CHAMPIONSHIP GAME EXPERIENCE: Played in NFC championship game (2000 season).
HONORS: Named wide receiver on THE SPORTING NEWS college All-America first team (1999). ... Fred Biletnikoff Award winner (1999).
SINGLE GAME HIGHS (regular season): Receptions—7 (November 17, 2002, vs. Dallas); yards—91 (November 17, 2002, vs. Dallas); and touchdown receptions—0.

			RUSHING				RECEIVING				PUNT RETURNS				KICKOFF RETURNS				TOTALS		
Year Team	G	GS	Att.	Yds.	Avg.	TD	No.	Yds.	Avg.	TD	No.	Yds.	Avg.	TD	No.	Yds.	Avg.	TD	TD	2pt.	Pts.
2000—Minnesota NFL....	12	0	1	3	3.0	0	1	5	5.0	0	15	217	14.5	0	30	692	23.1	0	0	0	0
2001—Minnesota NFL....	6	0	0	0	0.0	0	0	0	0.0	0	11	69	6.3	0	18	425	23.6	0	0	0	0
2002—Indianapolis NFL.	16	1	2	33	16.5	0	18	207	11.5	0	35	270	7.7	0	53	1150	21.7	0	0	0	0
Pro totals (3 years)	34	1	3	36	12.0	0	19	212	11.2	0	61	556	9.1	0	101	2267	22.4	0	0	0	0

WANSLEY, TIM — CB — BUCCANEERS

PERSONAL: Born November 11, 1978, in Buford, Ga. ... 5-8/180.
HIGH SCHOOL: Buford (Ga.).
COLLEGE: Georgia.
TRANSACTIONS/CAREER NOTES: Selected by Tampa Bay Buccaneers in seventh round (233rd pick overall) of 2002 NFL draft. ... Signed by Buccaneers (July 24, 2002).
CHAMPIONSHIP GAME EXPERIENCE: Member of Buccaneers for NFC championship game (2002 season); inactive. ... Member of Super Bowl championship team (2002 season); inactive.

			TOTALS			INTERCEPTIONS				PUNT RETURNS				TOTALS			
Year Team	G	GS	Tk.	Ast.	Sks.	No.	Yds.	Avg.	TD	No.	Yds.	Avg.	TD	TD	2pt.	Pts.	Fum.
2002—Tampa Bay NFL..................................	1	0	0	0	0.0	0	0	0.0	0	0	0	0.0	0	0	0	0	0

WARD, DEDRIC — WR/KR — PATRIOTS

PERSONAL: Born September 29, 1974, in Cedar Rapids, Iowa. ... 5-9/185. ... Full name: Dedric Lamar Ward. ... Name pronounced DEE-drick.
HIGH SCHOOL: Washington (Cedar Rapids, Iowa).
COLLEGE: Northern Iowa (degree in psychology).
TRANSACTIONS/CAREER NOTES: Selected by New York Jets in third round (88th pick overall) of 1997 NFL draft. ... Signed by Jets (July 17, 1997). ... Granted free agency (February 11, 2000). ... Re-signed by Jets (May 3, 2000). ... Granted unconditional free agency (March 2, 2001). ... Signed by Miami Dolphins (April 18, 2001). ... Released by Dolphins (February 26, 2003). ... Signed by New England Patriots (May 22, 2003).
CHAMPIONSHIP GAME EXPERIENCE: Played in AFC championship game (1998 season).
SINGLE GAME HIGHS (regular season): Receptions—8 (December 24, 2000, vs. Baltimore); yards—147 (December 24, 2000, vs. Baltimore); and touchdown receptions—1 (December 24, 2000, vs. Baltimore).
STATISTICAL PLATEAUS: 100-yard receiving games: 1997 (1), 2000 (3). Total: 4.

			RECEIVING				PUNT RETURNS				KICKOFF RETURNS				TOTALS			
Year Team	G	GS	No.	Yds.	Avg.	TD	No.	Yds.	Avg.	TD	No.	Yds.	Avg.	TD	TD	2pt.	Pts.	Fum.
1997—New York Jets NFL......	11	0	18	212	11.8	1	8	55	6.9	0	2	10	5.0	0	1	0	6	1
1998—New York Jets NFL......	16	2	25	477	19.1	4	8	72	9.0	0	3	60	20.0	0	4	0	24	0
1999—New York Jets NFL......	16	10	22	325	14.8	3	38	288	7.6	0	0	0	0.0	0	3	0	18	2
2000—New York Jets NFL......	16	16	54	801	14.8	3	27	214	7.9	0	0	0	0.0	0	3	0	18	1
2001—Miami NFL	13	1	21	209	10.0	0	9	88	9.8	0	0	0	0.0	0	0	0	0	1
2002—Miami NFL	16	1	19	172	9.1	0	16	169	10.6	0	0	0	0.0	0	0	0	0	1
Pro totals (6 years)	88	30	159	2196	13.8	11	106	886	8.4	0	5	70	14.0	0	11	0	66	6

WARD, HINES — WR — STEELERS

PERSONAL: Born March 8, 1976, in Forest Park, Ga. ... 6-0/200. ... Full name: Hines Ward Jr.
HIGH SCHOOL: Forest Park (Ga.).
COLLEGE: Georgia.
TRANSACTIONS/CAREER NOTES: Selected by Pittsburgh Steelers in third round (92nd pick overall) of 1998 NFL draft. ... Signed by Steelers (July 20, 1998). ... Granted free agency (March 2, 2001). ... Re-signed by Steelers (July 1, 2001).
CHAMPIONSHIP GAME EXPERIENCE: Played in AFC championship game (2001 season).
HONORS: Played in Pro Bowl (2001-2002 seasons).
SINGLE GAME HIGHS (regular season): Receptions—11 (November 10, 2002, vs. Atlanta); yards—168 (November 17, 2002, vs. Tennessee; and touchdown receptions—2 (November 17, 2002, vs. Tennessee).
STATISTICAL PLATEAUS: 100-yard receiving games: 2001 (2), 2002 (4). Total: 6.

			RUSHING				RECEIVING				TOTALS			
Year Team	G	GS	Att.	Yds.	Avg.	TD	No.	Yds.	Avg.	TD	TD	2pt.	Pts.	Fum.
1998—Pittsburgh NFL	16	0	1	13	13.0	0	15	246	16.4	0	0	0	0	0
1999—Pittsburgh NFL	16	14	2	-2	-1.0	0	61	638	10.5	7	7	†1	44	1
2000—Pittsburgh NFL	16	15	4	53	13.3	0	48	672	14.0	4	4	0	24	2
2001—Pittsburgh NFL	16	16	10	83	8.3	0	94	1003	10.7	4	4	0	24	1
2002—Pittsburgh NFL	16	16	12	142	11.8	0	112	1329	11.9	§12	12	*3	78	1
Pro totals (5 years)	80	61	29	289	10.0	0	330	3888	11.8	27	27	4	170	5

W

WARFIELD, ERIC   CB   CHIEFS

PERSONAL: Born March 3, 1976, in Vicksburg, Miss. ... 6-0/200. ... Full name: Eric Andrew Warfield.
HIGH SCHOOL: Arkansas (Texarkana, Ark.).
COLLEGE: Nebraska.
TRANSACTIONS/CAREER NOTES: Selected by Kansas City Chiefs in seventh round (216th pick overall) of 1998 NFL draft. ... Signed by Chiefs (May 27, 1998). ... Granted unconditional free agency (March 1, 2002). ... Re-signed by Chiefs (March 4, 2002).

			TOTALS			INTERCEPTIONS			
Year Team	G	GS	Tk.	Ast.	Sks.	No.	Yds.	Avg.	TD
1998—Kansas City NFL	12	0	0	0	0.0	0	0	0.0	0
1999—Kansas City NFL	16	1	25	4	0.0	3	0	0.0	0
2000—Kansas City NFL	13	4	19	2	0.0	0	0	0.0	0
2001—Kansas City NFL	16	16	64	6	0.0	4	61	15.3	1
2002—Kansas City NFL	16	16	56	8	0.0	4	30	7.5	0
Pro totals (5 years)	73	37	164	20	0.0	11	91	8.3	1

WARNER, KURT   QB   RAMS

PERSONAL: Born June 22, 1971, in Burlington, Iowa. ... 6-2/220. ... Full name: Kurtis Eugene Warner.
HIGH SCHOOL: Regis (Cedar Rapids, Iowa).
COLLEGE: Northern Iowa (degree in communications).
TRANSACTIONS/CAREER NOTES: Signed as non-drafted free agent by Green Bay Packers (April 28, 1994). ... Released by Packers prior to 1994 season. ... Played for Iowa Barnstormers of Arena Football League (1995-97). ... Signed by St. Louis Rams (December 26, 1997). ... Assigned by Rams to Amsterdam Admirals in 1998 NFL Europe enhancement allocation program (February 18, 1998). ... On injured reserve with hand injury (December 12, 2002-remaider of season).
CHAMPIONSHIP GAME EXPERIENCE: Played in NFC championship game (1999 and 2001 seasons). ... Member of Super Bowl championship team (1999 season). ... Played in Super Bowl XXXVI (2001 season).
HONORS: Named NFL Player of the Year by THE SPORTING NEWS (1999). ... Named quarterback on THE SPORTING NEWS NFL All-Pro team (1999 and 2001). ... Named Most Valuable Player of Super Bowl XXXIV (1999 season). ... Played in Pro Bowl (1999 and 2001 seasons). ... Named to play in Pro Bowl (2000 season); replaced by Donovan McNabb due to injury.
RECORDS: Holds NFL career record for highest passer rating—98.2; and most yards per attempt—8.68. ... Shares NFL record for most consecutive games with 300 or more yards passing—6 (September 4-October 15, 2000).
POST SEASON RECORDS: Holds Super Bowl single-game record for most yards passing—414 (January 30, 2000, vs. Tennessee).
SINGLE GAME HIGHS (regular season): Attempts—49 (November 24, 2002, vs. Washington); completions—35 (September 10, 2000, vs. Seattle); yards—441 (September 4, 2000, vs. Denver); and touchdown passes—5 (October 10, 1999, vs. San Francisco).
STATISTICAL PLATEAUS: 300-yard passing games: 1999 (9), 2000 (8), 2001 (9), 2002 (3). Total: 29.
MISCELLANEOUS: Regular-season record as starting NFL quarterback: 35-14 (.714). ... Postseason record as starting NFL quarterback: 5-2 (.714).

			PASSING								RUSHING				TOTALS		
Year Team	G	GS	Att.	Cmp.	Pct.	Yds.	TD	Int.	Avg.	Skd.	Rat.	Att.	Yds.	Avg.	TD	TD	2pt.	Pts.
1998—Amsterdam W.L.	10	...	326	165	50.6	2101	15	6	6.44	0	78.8	19	17	0.9	1	1	0	6
—St. Louis NFL	1	0	11	4	36.4	39	0	0	3.55	0	47.2	0	0	0.0	0	0	0	0
1999—St. Louis NFL	16	16	499	325	*65.1	4353	*41	13	*8.72	29	*109.2	23	92	4.0	1	1	0	6
2000—St. Louis NFL	11	11	347	235	*67.7	3429	21	18	*9.88	20	98.3	18	17	0.9	0	0	0	0
2001—St. Louis NFL	16	16	546	*375	*68.7	*4830	*36	∞22	*8.85	38	*101.4	28	60	2.1	0	0	0	0
2002—St. Louis NFL	7	6	220	144	65.5	1431	3	11	6.50	21	67.4	8	33	4.1	0	0	0	0
NFL Europe totals (1 year)	10	...	326	165	50.6	2101	15	6	6.44	0	78.8	19	17	0.9	1	1	0	6
NFL totals (5 years)	51	49	1623	1083	66.7	14082	101	64	8.68	108	98.2	77	202	2.6	1	1	0	6
Pro totals (6 years)	61	...	1949	1248	64.0	16183	116	70	8.30	108	94.9	96	219	2.3	2	2	0	12

WARNER, RON   DE   BUCCANEERS

PERSONAL: Born September 26, 1975, in Independence, Kan. ... 6-2/248.
HIGH SCHOOL: Independence (Kan.).
JUNIOR COLLEGE: Independence (Kan.) Community College..
COLLEGE: Kansas.
TRANSACTIONS/CAREER NOTES: Selected by New Orleans Saints in seventh round (239th pick overall) of 1998 NFL draft. ... Signed by Saints (July 23, 1998). ... On non-football injury list with knee injury (August 25-November 4, 1998). ... Released by Saints (September 5, 1999). ... Signed by Washington Redskins to practice (September 14, 1999). ... Released by Redskins (November 24, 1999). ... Signed by Chicago Bears to practice squad (December 22, 1999). ... Granted free agency following 1999 season. ... Signed by Buccaneers (March 4, 2001). ... Released by Buccaneers (September 8, 2001). ... Re-signed by Buccaneers to practice squad (September 10, 2001). ... On suspended list (September 1-30, 2002). ... Released by Buccaneers (October 7, 2002). ... Re-signed by Buccaneers (November 28, 2002). ... Re-signed by Buccaneers (March 20, 2003).
CHAMPIONSHIP GAME EXPERIENCE: Played in NFC championship game (2002 season). ... Member of Super Bowl championship team (2002 season).
HONORS: Named outside linebacker on THE SPORTING NEWS college All-America second team (1997).

			TOTALS		
Year Team	G	GS	Tk.	Ast.	Sks.
1998—New Orleans NFL	1	0	2	2	0.0
2002—Barcelona NFLE	...	...	...	...	6.0
—Tampa Bay NFL	4	0	0	0	0.0
NFL Europe totals (1 year)	...	...	...	...	6.0
NFL totals (2 years)	5	0	2	2	0.0
Pro totals (3 years)	...	...	...	...	6.0

W

WARREN, GERARD   DT   BROWNS

PERSONAL: Born July 25, 1978, in Lake City, Fla. ... 6-4/320. ... Full name: Gerard T. Warren.
HIGH SCHOOL: Union City (Raiford, Fla.).
COLLEGE: Florida.
TRANSACTIONS/CAREER NOTES: Selected by Cleveland Browns in first round (third pick overall) of 2001 draft. ... Signed by Browns (August 1, 2001).

				TOTALS	
Year Team	G	GS	Tk.	Ast.	Sks.
2001—Cleveland NFL	15	15	48	13	5.0
2002—Cleveland NFL	16	16	30	10	2.0
Pro totals (2 years)	31	31	78	23	7.0

WARREN, LAMONT   RB

PERSONAL: Born January 4, 1973, in Indianapolis. ... 5-11/211. ... Full name: Lamont Allen Warren.
HIGH SCHOOL: Dorsey (Los Angeles).
COLLEGE: Colorado.
TRANSACTIONS/CAREER NOTES: Selected after junior season by Indianapolis Colts in sixth round (164th pick overall) of 1994 NFL draft. ... Signed by Colts (July 13, 1994). ... Released by Colts (April 12, 1999). ... Signed by New England Patriots (April 17, 1999). ... Released by Patriots (February 22, 2000). ... Signed by Detroit Lions (February 14, 2001). ... On injured reserve with shoulder injury (September 28, 2002-remainder of season). ... Granted unconditional free agency (February 28, 2003).
CHAMPIONSHIP GAME EXPERIENCE: Played in AFC championship game (1995 season).
SINGLE GAME HIGHS (regular season): Attempts—22 (December 23, 1995, vs. New England); yards—90 (December 23, 1995, vs. New England); and rushing touchdowns—1 (November 22, 2001, vs. Green Bay).

			RUSHING				RECEIVING				KICKOFF RETURNS				TOTALS			
Year Team	G	GS	Att.	Yds.	Avg.	TD	No.	Yds.	Avg.	TD	No.	Yds.	Avg.	TD	TD	2pt.	Pts.	Fum.
1994—Indianapolis NFL	11	0	18	80	4.4	0	3	47	15.7	0	2	56	28.0	0	0	0	0	0
1995—Indianapolis NFL	12	1	47	152	3.2	1	17	159	9.4	0	15	315	21.0	0	1	0	6	1
1996—Indianapolis NFL	13	3	67	230	3.4	1	22	174	7.9	0	3	54	18.0	0	1	0	6	3
1997—Indianapolis NFL	13	0	28	80	2.9	2	20	192	9.6	0	1	19	19.0	0	2	0	12	0
1998—Indianapolis NFL	12	2	25	61	2.4	1	11	44	4.0	1	8	152	19.0	0	2	0	12	0
1999—New England NFL	16	2	35	120	3.4	0	29	262	9.0	1	2	25	12.5	0	1	0	6	0
2000—									Did not play.									
2001—Detroit NFL	16	3	61	191	3.1	3	40	336	8.4	1	0	0	0.0	0	4	1	26	1
2002—Detroit NFL	3	1	6	8	1.3	0	4	56	14.0	2	0	0	0.0	0	2	0	12	0
Pro totals (8 years)	96	12	287	922	3.2	8	146	1270	8.7	5	31	621	19.9	0	13	1	80	5

WARREN, STEVE   DT   PACKERS

PERSONAL: Born January 22, 1978, in Lawton, Okla. ... 6-1/302. ... Full name: Steven Jerome Warren.
HIGH SCHOOL: Kickapoo (Springfield, Mo.).
COLLEGE: Nebraska.
TRANSACTIONS/CAREER NOTES: Selected by Green Bay Packers in third round (74th pick overall) of 2000 NFL draft. ... Signed by Packers (June 5, 2000). ... On physically unable to perform list with thigh injury (August 28-December 4, 2001). ... On injured reserve with thigh injury (December 4, 2001-remainder of season).

				TOTALS	
Year Team	G	GS	Tk.	Ast.	Sks.
2000—Green Bay NFL	13	0	5	1	0.0
2002—Green Bay NFL	12	0	11	3	1.0
Pro totals (2 years)	25	0	16	4	1.0

WARRICK, PETER   WR/PR   BENGALS

PERSONAL: Born June 19, 1977, in Bradenton, Fla. ... 5-11/195.
HIGH SCHOOL: Southeast (Bradenton, Fla.).
COLLEGE: Florida State.
TRANSACTIONS/CAREER NOTES: Selected by Cincinnati Bengals in first round (fourth pick overall) of 2000 NFL draft. ... Signed by Bengals (June 4, 2000).
HONORS: Named wide receiver on THE SPORTING NEWS college All-America first team (1998 and 1999).
SINGLE GAME HIGHS (regular season): Receptions—10 (December 30, 2001, vs. Pittsburgh); yards—109 (December 30, 2001, vs. Pittsburgh); and touchdown receptions—2 (December 8, 2002, vs. Carolina).
STATISTICAL PLATEAUS: 100-yard receiving games: 2001 (1).

			RUSHING				RECEIVING				PUNT RETURNS				TOTALS			
Year Team	G	GS	Att.	Yds.	Avg.	TD	No.	Yds.	Avg.	TD	No.	Yds.	Avg.	TD	TD	2pt.	Pts.	Fum.
2000—Cincinnati NFL	16	16	16	148	9.3	2	51	592	11.6	4	7	123	17.6	1	7	0	42	2
2001—Cincinnati NFL	16	14	8	14	1.8	0	70	667	9.5	1	18	116	6.4	0	1	0	6	3
2002—Cincinnati NFL	15	10	8	22	2.8	0	53	606	11.4	6	4	14	3.5	0	6	0	36	2
Pro totals (3 years)	47	40	32	184	5.8	2	174	1865	10.7	11	29	253	8.7	1	14	0	84	7

WASHINGTON, DAMON   RB

PERSONAL: Born February 20, 1977, in Lockney, Texas. ... 5-11/205. ... Full name: Damon Keane Washington.
HIGH SCHOOL: Southwest (San Diego, Calif.).
COLLEGE: Colorado State.

W

			RUSHING				KICKOFF RETURNS				TOTALS		
Year Team	G	GS	Att.	Yds.	Avg.	TD	No.	Yds.	Avg.	TD	TD	2pt.	Pts.	Fum.
2000—New York Giants NFL	3	0	0	0	0.0	0	0	0	0.0	0	0	0	0	0
2001—New York Giants NFL	10	0	28	89	3.2	0	6	99	16.5	0	0	0	0	2
2002—New York Giants NFL	12	0	0	0	0.0	0	4	77	19.3	0	0	0	0	0
Pro totals (3 years)	25	0	28	89	3.2	0	10	176	17.6	0	0	0	0	2

WASHINGTON, DEWAYNE   CB   STEELERS

PERSONAL: Born December 27, 1972, in Durham, N.C. ... 6-0/193. ... Full name: Dewayne Neron Washington.
HIGH SCHOOL: Northern (Durham, N.C.).
COLLEGE: North Carolina State.
TRANSACTIONS/CAREER NOTES: Selected by Minnesota Vikings in first round (18th pick overall) of 1994 NFL draft. ... Signed by Vikings (July 14, 1994). ... Granted unconditional free agency (February 13, 1998). ... Signed by Pittsburgh Steelers (February 25, 1998).
CHAMPIONSHIP GAME EXPERIENCE: Played in AFC championship game (2001 season).
HONORS: Was a high school All-America selection by THE SPORTING NEWS (1989).

			TOTALS			INTERCEPTIONS			
Year Team	G	GS	Tk.	Ast.	Sks.	No.	Yds.	Avg.	TD
1994—Minnesota NFL	16	16	68	7	0.0	3	135	45.0	2
1995—Minnesota NFL	15	14	54	8	0.0	1	25	25.0	0
1996—Minnesota NFL	16	16	69	6	0.0	2	27	13.5	1
1997—Minnesota NFL	16	16	74	10	0.0	4	71	17.8	0
1998—Pittsburgh NFL	16	16	79	14	0.0	5	§178	35.6	▲2
1999—Pittsburgh NFL	16	16	50	2	0.0	4	1	0.3	0
2000—Pittsburgh NFL	16	16	69	9	0.0	5	59	11.8	0
2001—Pittsburgh NFL	16	16	66	11	1.0	1	15	15.0	0
2002—Pittsburgh NFL	16	16	45	9	0.0	3	51	17.0	0
Pro totals (9 years)	143	142	574	76	1.0	28	562	20.1	5

WASHINGTON, KEITH   DE   GIANTS

PERSONAL: Born December 18, 1972, in Dallas. ... 6-4/275. ... Full name: Keith L. Washington.
HIGH SCHOOL: Wilmer-Hutchins (Dallas).
COLLEGE: UNLV.
TRANSACTIONS/CAREER NOTES: Signed as non-drafted free agent by Minnesota Vikings (April 9, 1995). ... Released by Vikings (August 27, 1995). ... Re-signed by Vikings to practice squad (August 28, 1995). ... Activated (October 9, 1995); did not play. ... On injured reserve with ankle injury (November 15, 1995-remainder of season). ... Released by Vikings (August 25, 1996). ... Signed by Detroit Lions (August 26, 1996). ... Released by Lions (August 26, 1997). ... Signed by Baltimore Ravens (October 15, 1997). ... Granted free agency (February 13, 1998). ... Re-signed by Ravens (April 14, 1998). ... Granted unconditional free agency (February 11, 2000). ... Re-signed by Ravens (March 31, 2000). ... Released by Ravens (March 13, 2001). ... Signed by Denver Broncos (April 6, 2001). ... Released by Broncos (February 25, 2003). ... Signed by New York Giants (March 28, 2003).
CHAMPIONSHIP GAME EXPERIENCE: Played in AFC championship game (2000 season). ... Member of Super Bowl championship team (2000 season).

			TOTALS			INTERCEPTIONS			
Year Team	G	GS	Tk.	Ast.	Sks.	No.	Yds.	Avg.	TD
1996—Detroit NFL	12	0	7	0	0.0	0	0	0.0	0
1997—Baltimore NFL	10	1	14	4	2.0	0	0	0.0	0
1998—Baltimore NFL	16	0	13	2	1.0	0	0	0.0	0
1999—Baltimore NFL	16	0	9	2	1.0	0	0	0.0	0
2000—Baltimore NFL	16	0	11	7	0.0	0	0	0.0	0
2001—Denver NFL	16	16	27	9	4.0	0	0	0.0	0
2002—Denver NFL	10	0	9	0	0.0	1	-2	-2.0	0
Pro totals (7 years)	96	17	90	24	8.0	1	-2	-2.0	0

WASHINGTON, MARCUS   LB   COLTS

W

PERSONAL: Born October 17, 1977, in Auburn, Ala. ... 6-3/247. ... Full name: Marcus Cornelius Washington.
HIGH SCHOOL: Auburn (Ala.).
COLLEGE: Auburn.
TRANSACTIONS/CAREER NOTES: Selected by Indianapolis Colts in second round (59th pick overall) of 2000 NFL draft. ... Signed by Colts (July 13, 2000).

			TOTALS			INTERCEPTIONS			
Year Team	G	GS	Tk.	Ast.	Sks.	No.	Yds.	Avg.	TD
2000—Indianapolis NFL	16	0	6	5	2.0	1	1	1.0	0
2001—Indianapolis NFL	16	16	74	20	8.0	0	0	0.0	0
2002—Indianapolis NFL	15	15	47	19	2.0	1	40	40.0	1
Pro totals (3 years)	47	31	127	44	12.0	2	41	20.5	1

WASHINGTON, PATRICK   FB

PERSONAL: Born March 4, 1978, in Washington, D.C. ... 6-2/244. ... Full name: Patrick Orlando Washington Jr.
HIGH SCHOOL: St. Albans (Washington, D.C.).
COLLEGE: Virginia.
TRANSACTIONS/CAREER NOTES: Signed as non-drafted free agent by Jacksonville Jaguars (April 23, 2001). ... On injured reserve with knee injury (December 17, 2002-remainder of season). ... Re-signed by Jaguars (March 12, 2003). ... Released by Jaguars (May 1, 2003).

			RUSHING				RECEIVING				KICKOFF RETURNS				TOTALS		
Year Team	G	GS	Att.	Yds.	Avg.	TD	No.	Yds.	Avg.	TD	No.	Yds.	Avg.	TD	TD 2pt.	Pts. Fum.
2001—Jacksonville NFL........	16	6	0	0	0.0	0	5	36	7.2	0	0	0	0.0	0	0 0	0 0
2002—Jacksonville NFL........	14	3	0	0	0.0	0	1	5	5.0	0	5	35	7.0	0	0 0	0 0
Pro totals (2 years)..............	30	9	0	0	0.0	0	6	41	6.8	0	5	35	7.0	0	0 0	0 0

WASHINGTON, TED   DT   BEARS

PERSONAL: Born April 13, 1968, in Tampa. ... 6-5/365. ... Full name: Theodore Washington. ... Son of Ted Washington, linebacker with New York Jets (1973) and Houston Oilers (1974-82).
HIGH SCHOOL: Tampa Bay Vocational Tech Senior.
COLLEGE: Louisville.
TRANSACTIONS/CAREER NOTES: Selected by San Francisco 49ers in first round (25th pick overall) of 1991 NFL draft. ... Signed by 49ers (July 10, 1991). ... Traded by 49ers to Denver Broncos for fifth-round pick (traded to Green Bay) in 1994 draft (April 19, 1994). ... Granted unconditional free agency (February 17, 1995). ... Signed by Buffalo Bills (February 25, 1995). ... Designated by Bills as franchise player (February 13, 1998). ... Free agency status changed from franchise to transitional (February 27, 1998). ... Re-signed by Bills (March 2, 1998). ... Released by Bills (February 22, 2001). ... Signed by Chicago Bears (April 10, 2001). ... On injured reserve with leg injury (November 29, 2002-remainder of season).
CHAMPIONSHIP GAME EXPERIENCE: Played in NFC championship game (1992 and 1993 seasons).
HONORS: Played in Pro Bowl (1997, 1998, 2000 and 2001 seasons). ... Named defensive tackle on THE SPORTING NEWS NFL All-Pro team (2001).

			TOTALS			INTERCEPTIONS			
Year Team	G	GS	Tk.	Ast.	Sks.	No.	Yds.	Avg.	TD
1991—San Francisco NFL..	16	0	20	1	1.0	0	0	0.0	0
1992—San Francisco NFL..	16	6	27	8	2.0	0	0	0.0	0
1993—San Francisco NFL..	12	12	36	5	3.0	0	0	0.0	0
1994—Denver NFL...	15	15	44	12	2.5	1	5	5.0	0
1995—Buffalo NFL...	16	15	42	11	2.5	0	0	0.0	0
1996—Buffalo NFL...	16	16	70	22	3.5	0	0	0.0	0
1997—Buffalo NFL...	16	16	63	17	4.0	0	0	0.0	0
1998—Buffalo NFL...	16	16	35	15	4.5	1	0	0.0	0
1999—Buffalo NFL...	16	16	35	10	2.5	0	0	0.0	0
2000—Buffalo NFL...	16	16	37	21	2.5	0	0	0.0	0
2001—Chicago NFL...	16	15	26	8	1.5	0	0	0.0	0
2002—Chicago NFL...	2	2	4	1	0.0	0	0	0.0	0
Pro totals (12 years)...	173	145	439	131	29.5	2	5	2.5	0

WASHINGTON, TODD   C/OG   TEXANS

PERSONAL: Born July 19, 1976, in Nassawadox, Va. ... 6-3/310. ... Full name: Todd Page Washington.
HIGH SCHOOL: Nandua (Onley, Va.).
COLLEGE: Virginia Tech (degree in physical education and health, 1998).
TRANSACTIONS/CAREER NOTES: Selected by Tampa Bay Buccaneers in fourth round (104th pick overall) of 1998 NFL draft. ... Signed by Buccaneers (June 11, 1998). ... Granted free agency (March 2, 2001). ... Re-signed by Buccaneers (March 14, 2001). ... Granted unconditional free agency (March 1, 2002). ... Re-signed by Buccaneers (March 18, 2002). ... Signed by Houston Texans (March 24, 2003).
PLAYING EXPERIENCE: Tampa Bay NFL, 1998-2002. ... Games/Games started: 1998 (4/0), 1999 (6/0), 2000 (9/0), 2001 (15/1), 2002 (16/2). Total: 50/3.
CHAMPIONSHIP GAME EXPERIENCE: Played in NFC championship game (1999 and 2002 seasons). ... Member of Super Bowl championship team (2002).

WATERS, BRIAN   G   CHIEFS

PERSONAL: Born February 18, 1977, in Waxahachie, Texas. ... 6-3/318. ... Full name: Brian Demond Waters.
HIGH SCHOOL: Waxahachie (Texas).
COLLEGE: North Texas.
TRANSACTIONS/CAREER NOTES: Signed as non-drafted free agent by Dallas Cowboys (April 23, 1999). ... Released by Cowboys (September 5, 1999). ... Signed by Kansas City Chiefs (January 11, 2000).
PLAYING EXPERIENCE: Kansas City NFL, 2000-2002. ... Games/Games started: 2000 (6/0), 2001 (16/8), 2002 (16/16). Total: 38/24.

WATSON, CHRIS   CB   LIONS

PERSONAL: Born June 30, 1977, in Chicago. ... 6-1/188.
HIGH SCHOOL: Leo (Chicago).
COLLEGE: Eastern Illinois.
TRANSACTIONS/CAREER NOTES: Selected by Denver Broncos in third round (67th pick overall) of 1999 NFL draft. ... Signed by Broncos (June 15, 1999). ... Traded by Broncos to Buffalo Bills for fourth-round pick (traded back to Buffalo) in 2001 draft (August 27, 2000). ... Granted free agency (March 1, 2002). ... Re-signed by Bills (March 27, 2002). ... Released by Bills (April 29, 2003). ... Signed by Detroit Lions (May 4, 2003).

Year Team	G	GS	TOTALS			INTERCEPTIONS				PUNT RETURNS				KICKOFF RETURNS				TOTALS			
			Tk.	Ast.	Sks.	No.	Yds.	Avg.	TD	No.	Yds.	Avg.	TD	No.	Yds.	Avg.	TD	TD	2pt.	Pts.	Fum.
1999—Denver NFL	14	1	5	0	0.0	0	0	0.0	0	44	334	7.6	1	48	1138	23.7	0	1	0	6	5
2000—Buffalo NFL	16	5	24	6	0.0	0	0	0.0	0	33	163	4.9	0	44	894	20.3	0	0	0	0	4
2001—Buffalo NFL	14	0	9	3	0.0	1	23	23.0	0	0	0	0.0	0	5	96	19.2	0	0	0	0	1
2002—Buffalo NFL	14	8	37	7	0.0	1	0	0.0	0	0	0	0.0	0	0	0	0.0	0	0	0	0	0
Pro totals (4 years)	58	14	75	16	0.0	2	23	11.5	0	77	497	6.5	1	97	2128	21.9	0	1	0	6	10

WATSON, KENNY — RB — REDSKINS

PERSONAL: Born March 13, 1978, in Harrisburg, Pa. ... 5-11/214.
HIGH SCHOOL: Harrisburg (Pa.).
COLLEGE: Penn State.
TRANSACTIONS/CAREER NOTES: Signed as non-drafted free agent by Washington Redskins (April 23, 2001). ... Released by Redskins (October 16, 2001). ... Re-signed by Redskins to practice squad (October 18, 2001).
SINGLE GAME HIGHS (regular season): Attempts—23 (November 3, 2002, vs. Seattle); yards—110 (December 22, 2002, vs. Houston); and rushing touchdowns—1 (December 29, 2002, vs. Dallas).
STATISTICAL PLATEAUS: 100-yard rushing games: 2002 (2).

Year Team	G	GS	RUSHING				RECEIVING				KICKOFF RETURNS				TOTALS			
			Att.	Yds.	Avg.	TD	No.	Yds.	Avg.	TD	No.	Yds.	Avg.	TD	TD	2pt.	Pts.	Fum.
2002—Washington NFL	16	4	116	534	4.6	1	32	253	7.9	1	23	496	21.6	0	2	0	12	0

WAYNE, NATE — LB — EAGLES

PERSONAL: Born January 12, 1975, in Chicago. ... 6-0/237.
HIGH SCHOOL: Noxubee County (Macon, Miss.).
COLLEGE: Mississippi.
TRANSACTIONS/CAREER NOTES: Selected by Denver Broncos in seventh round (219th pick overall) of 1998 NFL draft. ... Signed by Broncos (June 9, 1998). ... Assigned by Broncos to Barcelona Dragons in 1999 NFL Europe enhancement allocation program (February 22, 1999). ... Released by Broncos (September 19, 1999). ... Re-signed by Broncos to practice squad (September 21, 1999). ... Activated (September 22, 1999). ... Traded by Broncos to Green Bay Packers for conditional future draft pick (August 15, 2000). ... Released by Packers (March 10, 2003). ... Signed by Philadelphia Eagles (March 14, 2003).
CHAMPIONSHIP GAME EXPERIENCE: Member of Broncos for AFC championship game (1998 season); inactive. ... Member of Super Bowl championship team (1998 season); inactive.

Year Team	G	GS	TOTALS			INTERCEPTIONS			
			Tk.	Ast.	Sks.	No.	Yds.	Avg.	TD
1998—Denver NFL	1	0	0	0	0.0	0	0	0.0	0
1999—Barcelona NFLE	...	...	...	...	1.0	1	31	31.0	0
—Denver NFL	15	0	8	2	2.0	0	0	0.0	0
2000—Green Bay NFL	16	13	75	26	2.0	0	0	0.0	0
2001—Green Bay NFL	12	12	60	26	5.5	3	55	18.3	0
2002—Green Bay NFL	16	15	70	41	2.5	3	32	10.7	0
NFL Europe totals (1 year)	...	...	...	...	1.0	1	31	31.0	0
NFL totals (5 years)	60	40	213	95	12.0	6	87	14.5	0
Pro totals (6 years)	...	...	...	...	13.0	7	118	16.9	0

WAYNE, REGGIE — WR — COLTS

PERSONAL: Born November 17, 1978, in New Orleans. ... 6-0/203.
HIGH SCHOOL: Ehret (La.).
COLLEGE: Miami (Fla.).
TRANSACTIONS/CAREER NOTES: Selected by Indianapolis Colts in first round (30th pick overall) of 2001 NFL draft. ... Signed by Colts (July 26, 2001).
SINGLE GAME HIGHS (regular season): Receptions—6 (December 22, 2002, vs. New York Giants); yards—121 (November 10, 2002, vs. Philadelphia); and touchdown receptions—2 (December 22, 2002, vs. New York Giants).
STATISTICAL PLATEAUS: 100-yard receiving games: 2002 (3).

Year Team	G	GS	RECEIVING			
			No.	Yds.	Avg.	TD
2001—Indianapolis NFL	13	9	27	345	12.8	0
2002—Indianapolis NFL	16	7	49	716	14.6	4
Pro totals (2 years)	29	16	76	1061	14.0	4

W

WEARY, FRED — G — TEXANS

PERSONAL: Born September 30, 1977, in Montgomery, Ala. ... 6-4/308. ... Full name: Fred Edward Weary Jr..
HIGH SCHOOL: Robert E. Lee (Montgomery, Ala.).
COLLEGE: Tennessee.
TRANSACTIONS/CAREER NOTES: Selected by Houston Texans in third round (66th pick overall) of 2002 NFL draft. ... Signed by Texans (July 17, 2002).
PLAYING EXPERIENCE: Houston NFL, 2002. ... Games/Games started: 2002 (16/12).
HONORS: Named guard on THE SPORTING NEWS college All-America second team (2001).

WEARY, FRED   CB

PERSONAL: Born April 12, 1974, in Jacksonville. ... 5-10/181. ... Full name: Joseph Fredrick Weary.
HIGH SCHOOL: Mandarin (Jacksonville).
COLLEGE: Florida.
TRANSACTIONS/CAREER NOTES: Selected by New Orleans Saints in fourth round (97th pick overall) of 1998 NFL draft. ... Signed by Saints (July 10, 1998). ... On injured reserve with knee injury (November 29, 2000-remainder of season). ... Granted free agency (March 2, 2001). ... Re-signed by Saints (March 30, 2001). ... Granted unconditional free agency (March 1, 2002). ... Signed by Atlanta Falcons (April 9, 2002). ... Granted unconditional free agency (February 28, 2003).
HONORS: Named cornerback on THE SPORTING NEWS college All-America first team (1997).

			TOTALS			INTERCEPTIONS			
Year Team	G	GS	Tk.	Ast.	Sks.	No.	Yds.	Avg.	TD
1998—New Orleans NFL	14	1	28	6	0.0	2	64	32.0	1
1999—New Orleans NFL	16	11	57	8	0.0	2	49	24.5	0
2000—New Orleans NFL	12	12	48	7	2.0	2	27	13.5	0
2001—New Orleans NFL	14	1	14	2	0.0	0	0	0.0	0
2002—Atlanta NFL	16	0	18	2	0.0	1	14	14.0	0
Pro totals (5 years)	72	25	165	25	2.0	7	154	22.0	1

WEATHERINGTON, COLSTON   DE   COWBOYS

PERSONAL: Born October 29, 1977, in Graceville, Fla. ... 6-5/289.
HIGH SCHOOL: Graceville (Fla.).
JUNIOR COLLEGE: Fort Scott (Kan.), then Northwest Mississippi.
COLLEGE: Central Missouri State.
TRANSACTIONS/CAREER NOTES: Selected by Dallas Cowboys in seventh round (207th pick overall) of 2001 NFL draft. ... Signed by Cowboys (July 20, 2001). ... Released by Cowboys (September 2, 2001). ... Re-signed by Cowboys to practice squad (September 3, 2001). ... Re-signed by Cowboys (March 7, 2003).

			TOTALS		
Year Team	G	GS	Tk.	Ast.	Sks.
2002—Dallas NFL	3	0	1	0	0.0

WEAVER, ANTHONY   DE   RAVENS

PERSONAL: Born July 28, 1980, in Saratoga Springs, N.Y. ... 6-3/300. ... Full name: Anthony Lee Weaver.
HIGH SCHOOL: Saratoga Springs (N.Y.).
COLLEGE: Notre Dame.
TRANSACTIONS/CAREER NOTES: Selected by Baltimore Ravens in second round (52nd pick overall) of 2002 NFL draft. ... Signed by Ravens (July 27, 2002).

			TOTALS			INTERCEPTIONS			
Year Team	G	GS	Tk.	Ast.	Sks.	No.	Yds.	Avg.	TD
2002—Baltimore NFL	16	16	27	4	3.5	0	0	0.0	0

WEAVER, JED   TE   49ERS

PERSONAL: Born August 11, 1976, in Bend, Ore. ... 6-4/258. ... Full name: Timothy Jed Weaver. ... Cousin of Jeff Weaver, pitcher, New York Yankees.
HIGH SCHOOL: Redmond (Ore.).
COLLEGE: Oregon.
TRANSACTIONS/CAREER NOTES: Selected by Philadelphia Eagles in seventh round (208th pick overall) of 1999 NFL draft. ... Signed by Eagles (July 16, 1999). ... Claimed on waivers by Miami Dolphins (August 23, 2000). ... Granted free agency (March 1, 2002). ... Re-signed by Dolphins (April 1, 2002). ... Granted unconditional free agency (February 28, 2003). ... Signed by San Francisco 49ers (March 11, 2003).
SINGLE GAME HIGHS (regular season): Receptions—5 (December 24, 2000, vs. New England); yards—63 (December 24, 2000, vs. New England); and touchdown receptions—1 (December 21, 2002, vs. Minnesota).

			RECEIVING				TOTALS			
Year Team	G	GS	No.	Yds.	Avg.	TD	TD	2pt.	Pts.	Fum.
1999—Philadelphia NFL	16	10	11	91	8.3	0	0	†1	2	0
2000—Miami NFL	16	0	10	179	17.9	0	0	0	0	1
2001—Miami NFL	16	7	18	215	11.9	2	2	0	12	1
2002—Miami NFL	16	4	6	75	12.5	3	3	0	18	0
Pro totals (4 years)	64	21	45	560	12.4	5	5	1	32	2

WEBB, RICHMOND   OT

PERSONAL: Born January 11, 1967, in Dallas. ... 6-6/325. ... Full name: Richmond Jewel Webb Jr.
HIGH SCHOOL: Franklin D. Roosevelt (Dallas).
COLLEGE: Texas A&M (degree in industrial distribution).
TRANSACTIONS/CAREER NOTES: Selected by Miami Dolphins in first round (ninth pick overall) of 1990 NFL draft. ... Signed by Dolphins (July 27, 1990). ... Designated by Dolphins as franchise player (February 12, 1999). ... Designated by Dolphins as franchise player (February 11, 2000). ... Granted unconditional free agency (March 2, 2001). ... Signed by Cincinnati Bengals (April 30, 2001). ... On injured reserve with chest injury (October 1, 2002-remainder of season). ... Released by Bengals (February 20, 2003).
PLAYING EXPERIENCE: Miami NFL, 1990-2000; Cincinnati NFL, 2001-2002. ... Games/Games started: 1990 (16/16), 1991 (14/14), 1992 (16/16), 1993 (16/16), 1994 (16/16), 1995 (16/16), 1996 (16/16), 1997 (16/16), 1998 (9/9), 1999 (15/14), 2000 (14/14), 2001 (16/16), 2002 (4/4). Total: 184/183.

W

CHAMPIONSHIP GAME EXPERIENCE: Played in AFC championship game (1992 season).
HONORS: Named NFL Rookie of the Year by THE SPORTING NEWS (1990). ... Played in Pro Bowl (1990-1996 seasons). ... Named offensive tackle on THE SPORTING NEWS NFL All-Pro team (1992 and 1994).

WEBSTER, JASON   CB   49ERS

PERSONAL: Born September 8, 1977, in Houston. ... 5-10/187. ... Full name: Jason Richmond Webster.
HIGH SCHOOL: Willowridge (Houston).
COLLEGE: Texas A&M.
TRANSACTIONS/CAREER NOTES: Selected by San Francisco 49ers in second round (48th pick overall) of 2000 NFL draft. ... Signed by 49ers (July 18, 2000).

| | | | TOTALS | | | INTERCEPTIONS | | | |
Year Team	G	GS	Tk.	Ast.	Sks.	No.	Yds.	Avg.	TD
2000—San Francisco NFL	16	10	41	14	0.0	2	78	39.0	1
2001—San Francisco NFL	16	16	69	7	0.5	3	61	20.3	0
2002—San Francisco NFL	16	16	71	14	0.0	1	37	37.0	1
Pro totals (3 years)	48	42	181	35	0.5	6	176	29.3	2

WEBSTER, LARRY   DT

PERSONAL: Born January 18, 1969, in Elkton, Md. ... 6-5/315. ... Full name: Larry Melvin Webster Jr.
HIGH SCHOOL: Elkton (Md.).
COLLEGE: Maryland.
TRANSACTIONS/CAREER NOTES: Selected by Miami Dolphins in third round (70th pick overall) of 1992 NFL draft. ... Signed by Dolphins (July 10, 1992). ... Granted free agency (February 17, 1995). ... Signed by Cleveland Browns (May 4, 1995). ... On suspended list for violating league substance abuse policy (September 4-26, 1995). ... Browns franchise moved to Baltimore and renamed Ravens for 1996 season (March 11, 1996). ... On suspended list for violating league substance abuse policy (August 20, 1996-July 13, 1997). ... Granted unconditional free agency (February 13, 1998). ... Re-signed by Ravens (February 16, 1998). ... Granted unconditional free agency (February 11, 2000). ... Re-signed by Ravens (February 16, 2000). ... On suspended list for violating league substance abuse policy (July 6-November 13, 2000). ... Released by Ravens (February 27, 2002). ... Signed by New York Jets (April 29, 2002). ... Granted unconditional free agency (February 28, 2003).
CHAMPIONSHIP GAME EXPERIENCE: Played in AFC championship game (1992 and 2000 seasons). ... Member of Super Bowl championship team (2000 season).

| | | | TOTALS | | |
Year Team	G	GS	Tk.	Ast.	Sks.
1992—Miami NFL	16	0	7	6	1.5
1993—Miami NFL	13	9	18	12	0.0
1994—Miami NFL	16	7	15	10	0.0
1995—Cleveland NFL	10	0	20	1	0.0
1996—Baltimore NFL			Did not play.		
1997—Baltimore NFL	16	3	18	6	0.0
1998—Baltimore NFL	15	0	8	1	0.0
1999—Baltimore NFL	16	16	24	8	2.0
2000—Baltimore NFL	5	0	4	1	0.0
2001—Baltimore NFL	15	0	12	5	0.5
2002—New York Jets NFL	14	0	6	1	0.0
Pro totals (10 years)	136	35	132	51	4.0

WEBSTER, NATE   LB   BUCCANEERS

PERSONAL: Born November 29, 1977, in Miami. ... 6-0/230. ... Full name: Nathaniel Webster Jr.
HIGH SCHOOL: Northwestern (Miami).
COLLEGE: Miami (Fla.).
TRANSACTIONS/CAREER NOTES: Selected after junior season by Tampa Bay Buccaneers in third round (90th pick overall) of 2000 NFL draft. ... Signed by Buccaneers (July 11, 2000). ... Granted free agency (February 28, 2003). ... Re-signed by Buccaneers (April 24, 2003).
CHAMPIONSHIP GAME EXPERIENCE: Played in NFC championship game (2002 season). ... Member of Super Bowl championship team (2002 season).
HONORS: Named linebacker on THE SPORTING NEWS college All-America second team (1999).

| | | | TOTALS | | | INTERCEPTIONS | | | |
Year Team	G	GS	Tk.	Ast.	Sks.	No.	Yds.	Avg.	TD
2000—Tampa Bay NFL	16	0	17	3	0.0	0	0	0.0	0
2001—Tampa Bay NFL	16	1	25	11	0.0	0	0	0.0	0
2002—Tampa Bay NFL	16	0	14	9	0.0	0	0	0.0	0
Pro totals (3 years)	48	1	56	23	0.0	0	0	0.0	0

WEDDERBURN, FLOYD   OT

PERSONAL: Born May 5, 1976, in Kingston, Jamaica. ... 6-5/333. ... Full name: Floyd E. Wedderburn.
HIGH SCHOOL: Upper Darby (Drexel Hill, Pa.).
COLLEGE: Penn State.
TRANSACTIONS/CAREER NOTES: Selected by Seattle Seahawks in fifth round (140th pick overall) of 1999 NFL draft. ... Signed by Seahawks (July 29, 1999). ... Active for five games (1999); did not play. ... Granted free agency (March 1, 2002). ... Re-signed by Seahawks (May 2, 2002). ... Granted unconditional free agency (February 28, 2003).
PLAYING EXPERIENCE: Seattle NFL, 2000-2002. ... Games/Games started: 2000 (16/16), 2001 (16/0), 2002 (14/10). Total: 46/26.

WEINER, TODD   OT   FALCONS

PERSONAL: Born September 16, 1975, in Bristol, Pa. ... 6-4/297.
HIGH SCHOOL: Taravella (Coral Springs, Fla.).
COLLEGE: Kansas State.
TRANSACTIONS/CAREER NOTES: Selected by Seattle Seahawks in second round (47th pick overall) of 1998 NFL draft. ... Signed by Seahawks (July 15, 1998). ... Granted unconditional free agency (March 1, 2002). ... Signed by Atlanta Falcons (March 6, 2002).
PLAYING EXPERIENCE: Seattle NFL, 1998-2001; Atlanta NFL, 2002. ... Games/Games started: 1998 (6/0), 1999 (11/1), 2000 (16/6), 2001 (16/13), 2002 (16/15). Total: 65/35.
HONORS: Named offensive tackle on THE SPORTING NEWS college All-America second team (1997).

WEINKE, CHRIS   QB   PANTHERS

PERSONAL: Born July 31, 1972, in St. Paul, Minn. ... 6-4/232.
HIGH SCHOOL: Cretin-Derham (St. Paul, Minn.).
COLLEGE: Florida State (degree in sports management).
TRANSACTIONS/CAREER NOTES: Selected by Carolina Panthers in fourth round (106th pick overall) of 2001 NFL draft. ... Signed by Panthers (July 21, 2001).
HONORS: Named quarterback on THE SPORTING NEWS college All-America second team (2000). ... Heisman Trophy winner (2000). ... Davey O'Brien Award winner (2000).
SINGLE GAME HIGHS (regular season): Attempts—63 (December 30, 2001, vs. Arizona); completions—36 (December 30, 2001, vs. Arizona); yards—312 (December 23, 2001, vs. St. Louis); and touchdown passes—2 (November 18, 2001, vs. San Francisco).
STATISTICAL PLATEAUS: 300-yard passing games: 2001 (1).
MISCELLANEOUS: Regular-season record as starting NFL quarterback: 1-15 (.063).

Year Team	G	GS	Att.	Cmp.	Pct.	Yds.	TD	Int.	Avg.	Skd.	Rat.	Att.	Yds.	Avg.	TD	TD	2pt.	Pts.
					PASSING								RUSHING				TOTALS	
2001—Carolina NFL	15	15	540	293	54.3	2931	11	19	5.43	26	62.0	37	128	3.5	6	6	0	36
2002—Carolina NFL	6	1	38	17	44.7	180	0	3	4.74	6	26.2	5	9	1.8	0	0	0	0
Pro totals (2 years)	21	16	578	310	53.6	3111	11	22	5.38	32	59.7	42	137	3.3	6	6	0	36

WELBOURN, JOHN   OT/OG   EAGLES

PERSONAL: Born March 30, 1976, in Torrance, Calif. ... 6-5/318. ... Full name: John R. Welbourn.
HIGH SCHOOL: Palos Verdes Peninsula (Rolling Hills Estate, Calif.).
COLLEGE: California (degree in rhetoric).
TRANSACTIONS/CAREER NOTES: Selected by Philadelphia Eagles in fourth round (97th pick overall) of 1999 NFL draft. ... Signed by Eagles (July 25, 1999). ... On injured reserve with knee injury (September 13, 1999-remainder of season).
PLAYING EXPERIENCE: Philadelphia NFL, 1999-2002. ... Games/Games started: 1999 (1/1), 2000 (16/16), 2001 (15/15), 2002 (11/11). Total: 43/43.
CHAMPIONSHIP GAME EXPERIENCE: Played in NFC championship game (2001 and 2002 seasons).

WELLS, JONATHAN   RB   TEXANS

PERSONAL: Born July 21, 1979, in River Ridge, La. ... 6-1/243.
HIGH SCHOOL: John Curtis (River Ridge, La.).
COLLEGE: Ohio State.
TRANSACTIONS/CAREER NOTES: Selected by Houston Texans in fourth round (99th pick overall) of 2002 NFL draft. ... Signed by Texans (July 19, 2002).
SINGLE GAME HIGHS (regular season): Attempts—24 (November 24, 2002, vs. New York Giants); yards—93 (September 22, 2002, vs. Indianapolis); and rushing touchdowns—1 (December 15, 2002, vs. Baltimore).
MISCELLANEOUS: Holds Houston Texans all-time record for most yards rushing (529). ... Shares Houston Texans all-time record for most rushing touchdowns (3).

Year Team	G	GS	Att.	Yds.	Avg.	TD	No.	Yds.	Avg.	TD	No.	Yds.	Avg.	TD	TD	2pt.	Pts.	Fum.
				RUSHING				RECEIVING				KICKOFF RETURNS				TOTALS		
2002—Houston NFL	16	11	197	529	2.7	3	9	48	5.3	0	0	0	0.0	0	3	0	18	3

WESLEY, DANTE   CB   PANTHERS

PERSONAL: Born April 5, 1979, in Pine Bluff, Ark. ... 6-1/211.
HIGH SCHOOL: Watson Chapel (Pine Bluff, Ark.).
COLLEGE: Arkansas-Pine Bluff.
TRANSACTIONS/CAREER NOTES: Selected by Carolina Panthers in fourth round (100th pick overall) of 2002 NFL draft. ... Signed by Panthers (July 15, 2002).

Year Team	G	GS	Tk.	Ast.	Sks.	No.	Yds.	Avg.	TD
			TOTALS			INTERCEPTIONS			
2002—Carolina NFL	13	1	15	3	0.0	0	0	0.0	0

WESLEY, GREG   S   CHIEFS

PERSONAL: Born March 19, 1976, in Little Rock, Ark. ... 6-2/203. ... Full name: Gregory Lashon Wesley.
HIGH SCHOOL: England (Ark.).

COLLEGE: Arkansas-Pine Bluff.
TRANSACTIONS/CAREER NOTES: Selected by Kansas City Chiefs in third round (85th pick overall) of 2000 NFL draft. ... Signed by Chiefs (June 6, 2000). ... Granted free agency (February 28, 2003). ... Re-signed by Chiefs (May 16, 2003).

			TOTALS			INTERCEPTIONS			
Year Team	G	GS	Tk.	Ast.	Sks.	No.	Yds.	Avg.	TD
2000—Kansas City NFL	16	16	69	16	1.0	2	28	14.0	0
2001—Kansas City NFL	16	16	72	11	2.0	2	44	22.0	0
2002—Kansas City NFL	13	13	54	10	1.0	6	170	28.3	0
Pro totals (3 years)	45	45	195	37	4.0	10	242	24.2	0

WEST, LYLE   S   CHIEFS

PERSONAL: Born December 20, 1976, in Columbus, Ga. ... 6-0/210.
HIGH SCHOOL: Washington (Fremont, Calif.).
JUNIOR COLLEGE: Chabot College (Calif.).
COLLEGE: San Jose State.
TRANSACTIONS/CAREER NOTES: Selected by New York Giants in sixth round (189th pick overall) of 1999 NFL draft. ... Signed by Giants (July 29, 1999). ... On suspended list for violating league substance abuse policy (November 23-December 20, 1999). ... Released by Giants (May 14, 2001). ... Signed by Kansas City Chiefs (August 1, 2001). ... Released by Chiefs (August 28, 2001). ... Re-signed by Chiefs (February 21, 2002).
CHAMPIONSHIP GAME EXPERIENCE: Played in NFC championship game (2000 season). ... Played in Super Bowl XXXV (2000 season).

			TOTALS			INTERCEPTIONS			
Year Team	G	GS	Tk.	Ast.	Sks.	No.	Yds.	Avg.	TD
1999—New York Giants NFL	7	0	0	0	0.0	0	0	0.0	0
2000—New York Giants NFL	16	2	8	0	0.0	0	0	0.0	0
2002—Kansas City NFL	16	0	3	0	0.0	0	0	0.0	0
Pro totals (3 years)	39	2	11	0	0.0	0	0	0.0	0

WESTBROOK, BRIAN   RB   EAGLES

PERSONAL: Born September 2, 1979, in Washington, D.C. ... 5-8/200.
HIGH SCHOOL: DeMantha (Ft. Washington, Md.).
COLLEGE: Villanova.
TRANSACTIONS/CAREER NOTES: Selected by Philadelphia Eagles in third round (91st pick overall) of 2002 NFL draft. ... Signed by Eagles (July 11, 2002).
CHAMPIONSHIP GAME EXPERIENCE: Played in NFC championship game (2002 season).
HONORS: Walter Payton Award winner (2001).
SINGLE GAME HIGHS (regular season): Attempts—8 (December 21, 2002, vs. Dallas); yards—55 (December 21, 2002, vs. Dallas); and rushing touchdowns—0.

			RUSHING				RECEIVING				TOTALS			
Year Team	G	GS	Att.	Yds.	Avg.	TD	No.	Yds.	Avg.	TD	TD	2pt.	Pts.	Fum.
2002—Philadelphia NFL	15	3	46	193	4.2	0	9	86	9.6	0	0	0	0	2

WESTBROOK, BRYANT   CB   PACKERS

PERSONAL: Born December 19, 1974, in Charlotte. ... 6-0/190. ... Full name: Bryant Antoine Westbrook.
HIGH SCHOOL: El Camino (Oceanside, Calif.).
COLLEGE: Texas.
TRANSACTIONS/CAREER NOTES: Selected by Detroit Lions in first round (fifth pick overall) of 1997 NFL draft. ... Signed by Lions (August 9, 1997). ... On injured reserve with Achilles' injury (December 4, 2000-remainder of season). ... Granted unconditional free agency (March 2, 2002). ... Signed by Dallas Cowboys (March 22, 2002). ... Released by Cowboys (September 13, 2002). ... Signed by Green Bay Packers (October 9, 2002). ... Granted unconditional free agency (February 28, 2003). ... Re-signed by Packers (March 1, 2003).

			TOTALS			INTERCEPTIONS			
Year Team	G	GS	Tk.	Ast.	Sks.	No.	Yds.	Avg.	TD
1997—Detroit NFL	15	14	41	4	0.0	2	64	32.0	1
1998—Detroit NFL	16	16	59	15	0.0	3	49	16.3	1
1999—Detroit NFL	10	8	32	3	0.0	0	0	0.0	0
2000—Detroit NFL	13	13	36	13	0.0	6	126	21.0	1
2001—Detroit NFL	10	3	19	1	0.0	1	0	0.0	0
2002—Dallas NFL	1	1	3	0	0.0	0	0	0.0	0
—Green Bay NFL	6	0	3	0	0.0	1	0	0.0	0
Pro totals (6 years)	71	55	193	36	0.0	13	239	18.4	3

WESTBROOK, MICHAEL   WR

PERSONAL: Born July 7, 1972, in Detroit. ... 6-3/221.
HIGH SCHOOL: Chadsey (Detroit).
COLLEGE: Colorado.
TRANSACTIONS/CAREER NOTES: Selected by Washington Redskins in first round (fourth pick overall) of 1995 NFL draft. ... Signed by Redskins (August 14, 1995). ... On injured reserve with neck injury (December 8, 1998-remainder of season). ... On injured reserve with knee injury (September 12, 2000-remainder of season). ... Granted unconditional free agency (March 1, 2002). ... Signed by Cincinnati Bengals (July 2, 2002). ... Released by Bengals (November 27, 2002).
HONORS: Named wide receiver on THE SPORTING NEWS college All-America first team (1994).

W

SINGLE GAME HIGHS (regular season): Receptions—10 (November 22, 1998, vs. Arizona); yards—159 (September 12, 1999, vs. Dallas); and touchdown receptions—3 (November 22, 1998, vs. Arizona).

STATISTICAL PLATEAUS: 100-yard receiving games: 1996 (1), 1997 (1), 1998 (4), 1999 (5), 2001 (1). Total: 12.

				RUSHING				RECEIVING				TOTALS		
Year Team	G	GS	Att.	Yds.	Avg.	TD	No.	Yds.	Avg.	TD	TD	2pt.	Pts.	Fum.
1995—Washington NFL	11	9	6	114	19.0	1	34	522	15.4	1	2	0	12	0
1996—Washington NFL	11	6	2	2	1.0	0	34	505	14.9	1	1	0	6	0
1997—Washington NFL	13	9	3	-11	-3.7	0	34	559	16.4	3	3	0	18	0
1998—Washington NFL	11	10	1	11	11.0	0	44	736	16.7	6	6	0	36	0
1999—Washington NFL	16	16	7	35	5.0	0	65	1191	18.3	9	9	†1	56	3
2000—Washington NFL	2	2	0	0	0.0	0	9	103	11.4	0	0	0	0	0
2001—Washington NFL	16	16	2	8	4.0	0	57	664	11.6	4	4	0	24	0
2002—Cincinnati NFL	9	4	1	1	1.0	0	8	94	11.8	2	2	0	12	0
Pro totals (8 years)	89	72	22	160	7.3	1	285	4374	15.3	26	27	1	164	3

WESTMORELAND, ERIC   LB   JAGUARS

PERSONAL: Born March 11, 1977, in Jasper, Tenn. ... 6-0/233. ... Full name: Eric Lebron Westmoreland.
HIGH SCHOOL: Marion County (Tenn.).
COLLEGE: Tennessee.
TRANSACTIONS/CAREER NOTES: Selected by Jacksonville Jaguars in third round (73rd pick overall) of 2001 NFL draft. ... Signed by Jaguars (June 4, 2001).

			TOTALS			INTERCEPTIONS			
Year Team	G	GS	Tk.	Ast.	Sks.	No.	Yds.	Avg.	TD
2001—Jacksonville NFL	11	2	15	4	1.0	0	0	0.0	0
2002—Jacksonville NFL	15	2	21	7	1.0	0	0	0.0	0
Pro totals (2 years)	26	4	36	11	2.0	0	0	0.0	0

WHALEN, JAMES   TE   COWBOYS

PERSONAL: Born December 11, 1977, in Portland, Ore. ... 6-2/244. ... Full name: James Patrick Whalen Jr.
HIGH SCHOOL: La Salle (Portland, Ore.).
JUNIOR COLLEGE: Shasta College (Calif.).
COLLEGE: Kentucky.
TRANSACTIONS/CAREER NOTES: Selected by Tampa Bay Buccaneers in fifth round (157th pick overall) of 2000 NFL draft. ... Signed by Buccaneers (July 10, 2000). ... Released by Buccaneers (August 27, 2000). ... Signed by Dallas Cowboys to practice squad (August 30, 2000). ... Activated (December 7, 2000). ... Assigned by Cowboys to Scottish Claymores in 2001 NFL Europe enhancement allocation program (February 12, 2001). ... On injured reserve with Achilles' tendon injury (September 22, 2001-remainder of season).
HONORS: Named tight end on THE SPORTING NEWS college All-America third team (1999).
SINGLE GAME HIGHS (regular season): Receptions—5 (September 29, 2002, vs. St. Louis); yards—38 (September 29, 2002, vs. St. Louis); and touchdown receptions—0.

			RECEIVING			
Year Team	G	GS	No.	Yds.	Avg.	TD
2000—Dallas NFL	3	0	0	0	0.0	0
2001—Scottish NFLE	...	...	66	691	10.5	3
2002—Dallas NFL	16	5	17	152	8.9	0
NFL Europe totals (1 year)	...	...	66	691	10.5	3
NFL totals (2 years)	19	5	17	152	8.9	0
Pro totals (3 years)	...	...	83	843	10.2	3

WHEATLEY, TYRONE   RB   RAIDERS

PERSONAL: Born January 19, 1972, in Inkster, Mich. ... 6-0/235.
HIGH SCHOOL: Robichaud (Dearborn Heights, Mich.).
COLLEGE: Michigan.
TRANSACTIONS/CAREER NOTES: Selected by New York Giants in first round (17th pick overall) of 1995 NFL draft. ... Signed by Giants (August 9, 1995). ... Traded by Giants to Miami Dolphins for seventh-round pick (LB O.J. Childress) in 1999 draft (February 12, 1999). ... Released by Dolphins (August 3, 1999). ... Signed by Oakland Raiders (August 4, 1999). ... Granted unconditional free agency (February 28, 2003). ... Re-signed by Raiders (March 25, 2003).
CHAMPIONSHIP GAME EXPERIENCE: Played in AFC championship game (2000 and 2002 seasons). ... Played in Super Bowl XXXVII (2002 season).
SINGLE GAME HIGHS (regular season): Attempts—26 (December 16, 2000, vs. Seattle); yards—156 (October 22, 2000, vs. Seattle); and rushing touchdowns—2 (October 7, 2001, vs. Dallas).
STATISTICAL PLATEAUS: 100-yard rushing games: 1997 (1), 1999 (2), 2000 (3). Total: 6.

			RUSHING				RECEIVING				KICKOFF RETURNS				TOTALS		
Year Team	G	GS	Att.	Yds.	Avg.	TD	No.	Yds.	Avg.	TD	No.	Yds.	Avg.	TD	TD	2pt.	Pts.	Fum.
1995—New York Giants NFL	13	1	78	245	3.1	3	5	27	5.4	0	10	186	18.6	0	3	0	18	2
1996—New York Giants NFL	14	0	112	400	3.6	1	12	51	4.3	2	23	503	21.9	0	3	0	18	6
1997—New York Giants NFL	14	7	152	583	3.8	4	16	140	8.8	0	0	0	0.0	0	4	0	24	3
1998—New York Giants NFL	5	0	14	52	3.7	0	0	0	0.0	0	1	16	16.0	0	0	0	0	0
1999—Oakland NFL	16	9	242	936	3.9	8	21	196	9.3	3	0	0	0.0	0	11	0	66	3
2000—Oakland NFL	14	14	232	1046	4.5	9	20	156	7.8	1	0	0	0.0	0	10	0	60	0
2001—Oakland NFL	11	2	88	276	3.1	5	12	61	5.1	0	0	0	0.0	0	6	0	36	3
2002—Oakland NFL	14	0	108	419	3.9	2	12	71	5.9	0	0	0	0.0	0	2	0	12	1
Pro totals (8 years)	101	33	1026	3957	3.9	32	98	702	7.2	7	34	705	20.7	0	39	0	234	22

W

WHIGHAM, LARRY   S

PERSONAL: Born June 23, 1972, in Hattiesburg, Miss. ... 6-2/218. ... Full name: Larry Jerome Whigham.
HIGH SCHOOL: Hattiesburg (Miss.).
JUNIOR COLLEGE: Pearl River Community College (Poplarville, Miss.).
COLLEGE: Northeast Louisiana (degree in criminal justice).
TRANSACTIONS/CAREER NOTES: Selected by Seattle Seahawks in fourth round (110th pick overall) of 1994 NFL draft. ... Signed by Seahawks (June 9, 1994). ... Released by Seahawks (August 28, 1994). ... Re-signed by Seahawks to practice squad (August 29, 1994). ... Signed by New England Patriots off Seahawks practice squad (September 13, 1994). ... Granted free agency (February 14, 1997). ... Re-signed by Patriots (May 1, 1997). ... Granted unconditional free agency (February 12, 1999). ... Re-signed by Patriots (April 14, 1999). ... Released by Patriots (March 13, 2001). ... Signed by Chicago Bears (April 18, 2001). ... Granted unconditional free agency (February 28, 2003).
CHAMPIONSHIP GAME EXPERIENCE: Played in AFC championship game (1996 season). ... Played in Super Bowl XXXI (1996 season).
HONORS: Played in Pro Bowl (1997 and 2001 seasons).

				TOTALS			INTERCEPTIONS			
Year Team	G	GS	Tk.	Ast.	Sks.	No.	Yds.	Avg.	TD
1994—New England NFL	12	0	2	0	0.0	1	21	21.0	0
1995—New England NFL	16	0	4	0	0.0	0	0	0.0	0
1996—New England NFL	16	1	9	6	0.0	0	0	0.0	0
1997—New England NFL	16	0	15	4	2.0	2	60	30.0	1
1998—New England NFL	16	0	22	3	0.0	1	0	0.0	0
1999—New England NFL	16	0	16	5	3.0	0	0	0.0	0
2000—New England NFL	14	4	20	8	0.0	0	0	0.0	0
2001—Chicago NFL	14	0	0	0	0.0	0	0	0.0	0
2002—Chicago NFL	16	1	8	4	0.0	0	0	0.0	0
Pro totals (9 years)	136	6	96	30	5.0	4	81	20.3	1

WHITE, DEZ   WR   BEARS

PERSONAL: Born August 23, 1979, in Orange Park, Fla. ... 6-1/215. ... Full name: Edward Dezmon White. ... Nephew of Adrian White, defensive back with New York Giants (1987-89 and 1991), Green Bay Packers (1992) and New England Patriots (1993).
HIGH SCHOOL: Bolles (Orange Park, Fla.).
COLLEGE: Georgia Tech.
TRANSACTIONS/CAREER NOTES: Selected after junior season by Chicago Bears in third round (69th pick overall) of 2000 NFL draft. ... Signed by Bears (July 19, 2000). ... Granted free agency (February 28, 2003). ... Re-signed by Bears (April 25, 2003).
SINGLE GAME HIGHS (regular season): Receptions—8 (November 24, 2002, vs. Detroit); yards—106 (November 24, 2002, vs. Detroit); and touchdown receptions—2 (December 22, 2002, vs. Carolina).
STATISTICAL PLATEAUS: 100-yard receiving games: 2002 (1).

			RUSHING				RECEIVING				KICKOFF RETURNS				TOTALS			
Year Team	G	GS	Att.	Yds.	Avg.	TD	No.	Yds.	Avg.	TD	No.	Yds.	Avg.	TD	TD	2pt.	Pts.	Fum.
2000—Chicago NFL	15	0	0	0	0.0	0	10	87	8.7	1	0	0	0.0	0	1	0	6	1
2001—Chicago NFL	14	6	0	0	0.0	0	45	428	9.5	0	0	0	0.0	0	0	0	0	0
2002—Chicago NFL	16	14	3	11	3.7	0	51	656	12.9	4	2	47	23.5	0	4	0	24	1
Pro totals (3 years)	45	20	3	11	3.7	0	106	1171	11.0	5	2	47	23.5	0	5	0	30	2

WHITE, JAMEL   RB   BROWNS

PERSONAL: Born February 11, 1978, in Los Angeles. ... 5-9/208.
HIGH SCHOOL: Palmdale (Calif.).
COLLEGE: South Dakota.
TRANSACTIONS/CAREER NOTES: Signed as non-drafted free agent by Indianapolis Colts (April 20, 2000). ... Released by Colts (August 27, 2000). ... Signed by Cleveland Browns (August 29, 2000). ... Granted free agency (February 28, 2003). ... Re-signed by Browns (April 20, 2003).
SINGLE GAME HIGHS (regular season): Attempts—23 (September 30, 2001, vs. Jacksonville); yards—131 (December 23, 2001, vs. Green Bay); and rushing touchdowns—2 (December 30, 2001, vs. Tennessee).
STATISTICAL PLATEAUS: 100-yard rushing games: 2001 (1), 2002 (1). Total: 2.

			RUSHING				RECEIVING				KICKOFF RETURNS				TOTALS			
Year Team	G	GS	Att.	Yds.	Avg.	TD	No.	Yds.	Avg.	TD	No.	Yds.	Avg.	TD	TD	2pt.	Pts.	Fum.
2000—Cleveland NFL	13	0	47	145	3.1	0	13	100	7.7	0	43	935	21.7	0	0	0	0	0
2001—Cleveland NFL	16	7	126	443	3.5	5	44	418	9.5	1	9	189	21.0	0	6	1	38	1
2002—Cleveland NFL	14	6	106	470	4.4	3	63	452	7.2	0	2	21	10.5	0	3	0	18	0
Pro totals (3 years)	43	13	279	1058	3.8	8	120	970	8.1	1	54	1145	21.2	0	9	1	56	1

WHITE, STEVE   DE

PERSONAL: Born October 25, 1973, in Memphis, Tenn. ... 6-2/271. ... Full name: Stephen Gregory White.
HIGH SCHOOL: Westwood (Memphis, Tenn.).
COLLEGE: Tennessee (degree in psychology, 1996).
TRANSACTIONS/CAREER NOTES: Selected by Philadelphia Eagles in sixth round (194th pick overall) of 1996 NFL draft. ... Signed by Eagles (July 17, 1996). ... Released by Eagles (August 20, 1996). ... Signed by Tampa Bay Buccaneers to practice squad (August 27, 1996). ... Activated (October 15, 1996). ... Released by Buccaneers (November 9, 1996). ... Re-signed by Buccaneers (November 12, 1996). ... Granted unconditional free agency (March 1, 2002). ... Signed by New York Jets (March 7, 2002). ... Released by Jets (February 20, 2003).
CHAMPIONSHIP GAME EXPERIENCE: Played in NFC championship game (1999 season).

W

Year Team	G	GS	TOTALS Tk.	Ast.	Sks.
1996—Tampa Bay NFL	4	0	1	0	0.0
1997—Tampa Bay NFL	15	1	6	2	0.0
1998—Tampa Bay NFL	16	0	14	4	2.0
1999—Tampa Bay NFL	13	13	16	0	2.0
2000—Tampa Bay NFL	15	0	15	7	2.0
2001—Tampa Bay NFL	16	1	15	10	5.0
2002—New York Jets NFL	15	0	5	7	0.5
Pro totals (7 years)	94	15	72	30	11.5

WHITEHEAD, WILLIE — DE — SAINTS

PERSONAL: Born January 26, 1973, in Tuskegee, Ala. ... 6-3/285. ... Full name: William Whitehead.
HIGH SCHOOL: Tuskegee (Ala.) Institute.
COLLEGE: Auburn.
TRANSACTIONS/CAREER NOTES: Signed as non-drafted free agent by San Francisco 49ers (April 26, 1995). ... Released by 49ers (July 16, 1995). ... Signed by Baltimore Stallions of CFL (August 1995). ... Signed by Montreal Alouettes of CFL to practice squad (1996). ... Signed by Hamilton Tiger-Cats of CFL (May 14, 1997). ... Signed by Detroit Lions (February 11, 1998). ... Released by Lions (August 25, 1998). ... Signed by New Orleans Saints (January 27, 1999). ... Assigned by Saints to Frankfurt Galaxy in 1999 NFL Europe enhancement allocation program (February 22, 1999). ... Granted free agency (March 1, 2002). ... Re-signed by Saints (April 4, 2002). ... Granted unconditional free agency (February 28, 2003). ... Re-signed by Saints (April 25, 2003).

Year Team	G	GS	TOTALS Tk.	Ast.	Sks.
1995—Baltimore CFL	1	...	...	...	0.0
1996—Montreal CFL			Did not play.		
1997—Hamilton CFL	15	...	...	...	13.0
1998—			Did not play.		
1999—Frankfurt NFLE	...	...	...	...	2.0
—New Orleans NFL	16	3	24	6	7.0
2000—New Orleans NFL	16	2	17	10	5.5
2001—New Orleans NFL	14	0	18	3	2.0
2002—New Orleans NFL	12	10	24	10	3.0
NFL Europe totals (1 year)	...	...	...	...	2.0
CFL totals (2 years)	16	...	...	...	13.0
NFL totals (4 years)	58	15	83	29	17.5
Pro totals (7 years)	...	...	...	...	32.5

WHITFIELD, BOB — OT — FALCONS

PERSONAL: Born October 18, 1971, in Carson, Calif. ... 6-5/310. ... Full name: Bob Whitfield Jr..
HIGH SCHOOL: Banning (Los Angeles).
COLLEGE: Stanford.
TRANSACTIONS/CAREER NOTES: Selected after junior season by Atlanta Falcons in first round (eighth pick overall) of 1992 NFL draft. ... Signed by Falcons (September 4, 1992). ... Granted roster exemption for one game (September 1992).
PLAYING EXPERIENCE: Atlanta NFL, 1992-2002. ... Games/Games started: 1992 (11/0), 1993 (16/16), 1994 (16/16), 1995 (16/16), 1996 (16/16), 1997 (16/16), 1998 (16/16), 1999 (16/16), 2000 (15/15), 2001 (16/16), 2002 (16/16). Total: 170/159.
CHAMPIONSHIP GAME EXPERIENCE: Played in NFC championship game (1998 season). ... Played in Super Bowl XXXIII (1998 season).
HONORS: Named offensive tackle on THE SPORTING NEWS college All-America first team (1991). ... Played in Pro Bowl (1998 season).

WHITING, BRANDON — DT/DE — EAGLES

PERSONAL: Born July 30, 1976, in Santa Rosa, Calif. ... 6-3/285. ... Name pronounced WHITE-ing.
HIGH SCHOOL: Polytechnic (Pasadena, Calif.).
COLLEGE: California.
TRANSACTIONS/CAREER NOTES: Selected by Philadelphia Eagles in fourth round (112th pick overall) of 1998 NFL draft. ... Signed by Eagles (July 14, 1998). ... Granted free agency (March 2, 2001). ... Re-signed by Eagles (March 20, 2001).
CHAMPIONSHIP GAME EXPERIENCE: Played in NFC championship game (2001 and 2002 seasons).

Year Team	G	GS	TOTALS Tk.	Ast.	Sks.	INTERCEPTIONS No.	Yds.	Avg.	TD
1998—Philadelphia NFL	16	5	14	4	1.5	0	0	0.0	0
1999—Philadelphia NFL	13	2	9	7	1.0	1	22	22.0	1
2000—Philadelphia NFL	16	11	23	11	3.5	0	0	0.0	0
2001—Philadelphia NFL	13	12	15	11	2.5	0	0	0.0	0
2002—Philadelphia NFL	16	15	23	16	6.0	0	0	0.0	0
Pro totals (5 years)	74	45	84	49	14.5	1	22	22.0	1

WHITING, TEAG — G — CARDINALS

PERSONAL: Born April 16, 1979, in Burley, Idaho. ... 6-3/320.
HIGH SCHOOL: Brighton (Salt Lake City).
JUNIOR COLLEGE: Ricks College (Idaho).
COLLEGE: Brigham Young.

WHITLEY, JAMES   CB   RAMS

PERSONAL: Born May 13, 1979, in Decatur, Ill. ... 5-11/190. ... Full name: James LaVell Whitley.
HIGH SCHOOL: Norview (Va.).
COLLEGE: Michigan State.
TRANSACTIONS/CAREER NOTES: Signed by Montreal Alouettes of CFL (2001). ... Signed as non-drafted free agent by St. Louis Rams (February 26, 2002).

			TOTALS			INTERCEPTIONS			
Year Team	G	GS	Tk.	Ast.	Sks.	No.	Yds.	Avg.	TD
2001—Montreal CFL	14	5	...	...	1.0	2	18	9.0	0
2002—St. Louis NFL	13	1	26	1	3.0	0	0	0.0	0
CFL totals (1 year)	14	5	...	...	1.0	2	18	9.0	0
NFL totals (1 year)	13	1	26	1	3.0	0	0	0.0	0
Pro totals (2 years)	27	6	...	...	4.0	2	18	9.0	0

WHITTED, ALVIS   WR   RAIDERS

PERSONAL: Born September 4, 1974, in Durham, N.C. ... 6-0/186. ... Full name: Alvis James Whitted.
HIGH SCHOOL: Orange (Hillsborough, N.C.).
COLLEGE: North Carolina State.
TRANSACTIONS/CAREER NOTES: Selected by Jacksonville Jaguars in seventh round (192nd pick overall) of 1998 NFL draft. ... Signed by Jaguars (May 19, 1998). ... Released by Jaguars (December 4, 2001). ... Signed by Atlanta Falcons (January 10, 2002). ... Released by Falcons (August 31, 2002). ... Signed by Oakland Raiders (September 25, 2002).
CHAMPIONSHIP GAME EXPERIENCE: Played in AFC championship game (1999 and 2002 seasons). ... Played in Super Bowl XXXVII (2002 season).
SINGLE GAME HIGHS (regular season): Receptions—4 (December 23, 2000, vs. New York Giants); yards—55 (October 29, 2000, vs. Dallas); and touchdown receptions—2 (October 29, 2000, vs. Dallas).

			RUSHING				RECEIVING				KICKOFF RETURNS				TOTALS			
Year Team	G	GS	Att.	Yds.	Avg.	TD	No.	Yds.	Avg.	TD	No.	Yds.	Avg.	TD	TD	2pt.	Pts.	Fum.
1998—Jacksonville NFL	16	0	3	13	4.3	0	2	61	30.5	0	0	0	0.0	0	1	0	6	0
1999—Jacksonville NFL	14	1	1	9	9.0	0	0	0	0.0	0	8	187	23.4	▲1	1	0	6	0
2000—Jacksonville NFL	16	3	0	0	0.0	0	13	137	10.5	3	4	67	16.8	0	3	0	18	1
2001—Jacksonville NFL	11	0	1	4	4.0	0	2	17	8.5	0	0	0	0.0	0	0	0	0	0
2002—Oakland NFL	9	0	0	0	0.0	0	0	0	0.0	0	4	50	12.5	0	0	0	0	0
Pro totals (5 years)	66	4	5	26	5.2	0	17	215	12.6	3	16	304	19.0	1	5	0	30	1

WHITTINGTON, BERNARD   DT

PERSONAL: Born August 20, 1971, in St. Louis. ... 6-5/291. ... Full name: Bernard Maurice Whittington.
HIGH SCHOOL: Hazelwood East (St. Louis).
COLLEGE: Indiana (degree in sports management).
TRANSACTIONS/CAREER NOTES: Signed as non-drafted free agent by Indianapolis Colts (May 5, 1994). ... Granted free agency (February 14, 1997). ... Re-signed by Colts (June 13, 1997). ... Granted unconditional free agency (March 2, 2001). ... Signed by Cincinnati Bengals (July 12, 2001). ... Granted unconditional free agency (February 28, 2003).
CHAMPIONSHIP GAME EXPERIENCE: Played in AFC championship game (1995 season).

			TOTALS		
Year Team	G	GS	Tk.	Ast.	Sks.
1994—Indianapolis NFL	13	8	22	14	0.0
1995—Indianapolis NFL	16	13	32	16	2.0
1996—Indianapolis NFL	16	14	46	20	3.0
1997—Indianapolis NFL	15	6	35	10	0.0
1998—Indianapolis NFL	15	11	39	10	4.0
1999—Indianapolis NFL	15	15	27	6	1.0
2000—Indianapolis NFL	15	12	31	11	1.0
2001—Cincinnati NFL	16	5	17	4	0.0
2002—Cincinnati NFL	16	11	22	14	1.0
Pro totals (9 years)	137	95	271	105	12.0

WHITTLE, JASON   G   BUCCANEERS

PERSONAL: Born March 7, 1975, in Springfield, Mo. ... 6-4/305.
HIGH SCHOOL: Camdenton (Mo.).
COLLEGE: Southwest Missouri State.
TRANSACTIONS/CAREER NOTES: Signed as non-drafted free agent by New York Giants (April 24, 1998). ... Released by Giants (August 30, 1998). ... Re-signed by Giants to practice squad (September 1, 1998). ... Activated (December 16, 1998). ... Granted free agency (March 1, 2002). ... Re-signed by Giants (April 24, 2002). ... Granted unconditional free agency (February 28, 2003). ... Signed by Tampa Bay Buccaneers (March 7, 2003).
PLAYING EXPERIENCE: New York Giants NFL, 1998-2002. ... Games/Games started: 1998 (1/0), 1999 (16/1), 2000 (16/2), 2001 (16/2), 2002 (14/14). Total: 53/19.
CHAMPIONSHIP GAME EXPERIENCE: Played in NFC championship game (2000 season). ... Played in Super Bowl XXXV (2000 season).

W

WIEGERT, ZACH   OT   TEXANS

PERSONAL: Born August 16, 1972, in Fremont, Neb. ... 6-5/309. ... Full name: Zach Allen Wiegert. ... Name pronounced WEE-gert.
HIGH SCHOOL: Fremont (Neb.) Bergan.
COLLEGE: Nebraska.
TRANSACTIONS/CAREER NOTES: Selected by St. Louis Rams in second round (38th pick overall) of 1995 NFL draft. ... Signed by Rams (July 18, 1995). ... Granted free agency (February 13, 1998). ... Re-signed by Rams (June 17, 1998). ... Designated by Rams as transition player (February 12, 1999). ... Re-signed by Rams (March 24, 1999). ... Released by Rams (April 28, 1999). ... Signed by Jacksonville Jaguars (May 5, 1999). ... On injured reserve with knee injury (October 25, 2000-remainder of season). ... On injured reserve with knee injury (November 6, 2002-remainder of season). ... Granted unconditional free agency (February 28, 2003). ... Signed by Houston Texans (March 1, 2003).
PLAYING EXPERIENCE: St. Louis NFL, 1995-1998; Jacksonville NFL, 1999-2002. ... Games/Games started: 1995 (5/2), 1996 (16/16), 1997 (15/15), 1998 (13/13), 1999 (16/12), 2000 (8/8), 2001 (16/16), 2002 (7/7). Total: 96/89.
CHAMPIONSHIP GAME EXPERIENCE: Played in AFC championship game (1999 season).
HONORS: Outland Trophy Award winner (1994). ... Named offensive lineman on THE SPORTING NEWS college All-America first team (1994).

WIEGMANN, CASEY   C   CHIEFS

PERSONAL: Born July 20, 1973, in Waterloo, Iowa. ... 6-2/285. ... Name pronounced WEG-man.
HIGH SCHOOL: Parkersburg (Iowa).
COLLEGE: Iowa.
TRANSACTIONS/CAREER NOTES: Signed as non-drafted free agent by Indianapolis Colts (April 26, 1996). ... Released by Colts (August 25, 1996). ... Re-signed by Colts to practice squad (August 27, 1996). ... Activated (September 10, 1996); did not play. ... Released by Colts (September 22, 1996). ... Re-signed by Colts to practice squad (September 23, 1996). ... Activated (October 15, 1996); did not play. ... Claimed on waivers by New York Jets (October 29, 1996). ... Released by Jets (September 21, 1997). ... Signed by Chicago Bears (September 24, 1997). ... Granted free agency (February 12, 1999). ... Tendered offer sheet by Miami Dolphins (April 5, 1999). ... Offer matched by Bears (April 8, 1999). ... Granted unconditional free agency (March 2, 2001). ... Signed by Kansas City Chiefs (March 15, 2001).
PLAYING EXPERIENCE: New York Jets (3)-Chicago (1) NFL, 1997; Chicago NFL, 1998-2000; Kansas City NFL, 2001-2002. ... Games/Games started: 1997 (NYJ-3/0; Chi.-1/0; Total: 4/0), 1998 (16/15), 1999 (16/0), 2000 (16/10), 2001 (15/15), 2002 (16/16). Total: 83/57.

WIGGINS, JERMAINE   TE   PANTHERS

PERSONAL: Born January 18, 1975, in East Boston, Mass. ... 6-2/255.
HIGH SCHOOL: East Boston.
COLLEGE: Georgia.
TRANSACTIONS/CAREER NOTES: Signed by New York Jets as non-drafted free agent (April 19, 1999). ... Released by Jets (August 23, 1999). ... Re-signed by Jets to practice squad (August 28, 1999). ... Claimed on waivers by New England Patriots (November 28, 2000). ... Released by Patriots (May 2, 2002). ... Signed by Indianapolis Colts (May 14, 2002). ... Released by Colts (September 24, 2002). ... Signed by Carolina Panthers (October 8, 2002). ... Granted free agency (February 28, 2003). ... Re-signed by Panthers (May 2, 2003).
CHAMPIONSHIP GAME EXPERIENCE: Played in AFC championship game (2001 season). ... Member of Super Bowl championship team (2001 season).
SINGLE GAME HIGHS (regular season): Receptions—5 (December 4, 2000, vs. Kansas City); yards—81 (December 24, 2000, vs. Miami); and touchdown receptions—1 (November 10, 2002, vs. New Orleans).

| | | | RECEIVING | | | |
Year Team	G	GS	No.	Yds.	Avg.	TD
2000—New York Jets NFL	11	0	2	4	2.0	1
—New England NFL	4	2	16	203	12.7	1
2001—New England NFL	16	6	14	133	9.5	4
2002—Indianapolis NFL	3	0	2	17	8.5	0
—Carolina NFL	11	1	8	45	5.6	1
Pro totals (3 years)	45	9	42	402	9.6	7

WILEY, CHUCK   DE   VIKINGS

PERSONAL: Born March 6, 1975, in Baton Rouge, La. ... 6-5/277. ... Full name: Samuel Charles Wiley Jr. ... Cousin of Doug Williams, quarterback with Tampa Bay Buccaneers (1978-82), Oklahoma Outlaws of USFL (1984), Arizona Outlaws of USFL (1985) and Washington Redskins (1986-89).
HIGH SCHOOL: Southern University Lab (Baton Rouge, La.).
COLLEGE: Louisiana State (degree in pre-physical therapy).
TRANSACTIONS/CAREER NOTES: Selected by Carolina Panthers in third round (62nd pick overall) of 1998 NFL draft. ... Signed by Panthers (June 10, 1998). ... On injured reserve with heel injury (August 30, 1998-entire season). ... Claimed on waivers Atlanta Falcons (August 28, 2000). ... Granted unconditional free agency (March 1, 2002). ... Signed by Minnesota Vikings (May 2, 2002).

| | | | TOTALS | | | INTERCEPTIONS | | | |
Year Team	G	GS	Tk.	Ast.	Sks.	No.	Yds.	Avg.	TD
1998—Carolina NFL			Did not play.						
1999—Carolina NFL	16	16	32	4	0.0	0	0	0.0	0
2000—Atlanta NFL	16	0	25	14	4.0	0	0	0.0	0
2001—Atlanta NFL	16	1	12	5	1.0	1	1	1.0	0
2002—Minnesota NFL	16	0	7	3	0.0	0	0	0.0	0
Pro totals (4 years)	64	17	76	26	5.0	1	1	1.0	0

WILEY, MARCELLUS   DE   CHARGERS

PERSONAL: Born November 30, 1974, in Compton, Calif. ... 6-4/275. ... Full name: Marcellus Vernon Wiley.
HIGH SCHOOL: Santa Monica (Calif.).
COLLEGE: Columbia (degree in sociology, 1997).

W

Year Team	G	GS	TOTALS			INTERCEPTIONS			
			Tk.	Ast.	Sks.	No.	Yds.	Avg.	TD
1997—Buffalo NFL	16	0	12	4	0.0	0	0	0.0	0
1998—Buffalo NFL	16	3	17	7	3.5	0	0	0.0	0
1999—Buffalo NFL	16	1	18	8	5.0	1	52	52.0	0
2000—Buffalo NFL	16	15	40	25	10.5	0	0	0.0	0
2001—San Diego NFL	14	14	38	10	13.0	0	0	0.0	0
2002—San Diego NFL	14	14	31	5	6.0	1	40	40.0	0
Pro totals (6 years)	92	47	156	59	38.0	2	92	46.0	0

WILEY, MICHAEL RB COWBOYS

PERSONAL: Born January 5, 1978, in Spring Valley, Calif. ... 5-11/203. ... Full name: Michael Deshawn Wiley.
HIGH SCHOOL: Monte Vista (Spring Valley, Calif.).
COLLEGE: Ohio State.
TRANSACTIONS/CAREER NOTES: Selected by Dallas Cowboys in fifth round (143rd pick overall) of 2000 NFL draft. ... Signed by Cowboys (July 14, 2000). ... Granted unconditional free agency (February 28, 2003). ... Re-signed by Cowboys (April 4, 2003).
SINGLE GAME HIGHS (regular season): Attempts—11 (December 10, 2000, vs. Washington); yards—85 (November 11, 2001, vs. Atlanta); and rushing touchdowns—1 (September 8, 2002, vs. Houston).

Year Team	G	GS	RUSHING				RECEIVING				KICKOFF RETURNS				TOTALS			
			Att.	Yds.	Avg.	TD	No.	Yds.	Avg.	TD	No.	Yds.	Avg.	TD	TD	2pt.	Pts.	Fum.
2000—Dallas NFL	10	0	24	88	3.7	0	14	72	5.1	1	13	303	23.3	0	1	0	6	3
2001—Dallas NFL	16	0	34	247	7.3	0	16	99	6.2	1	4	90	22.5	0	1	0	6	1
2002—Dallas NFL	16	1	22	168	7.6	1	13	144	11.1	0	4	62	15.5	0	1	0	6	0
Pro totals (3 years)	42	1	80	503	6.3	1	43	315	7.3	2	21	455	21.7	0	3	0	18	4

WILKINS, JEFF K RAMS

PERSONAL: Born April 19, 1972, in Youngstown, Ohio. ... 6-2/205. ... Full name: Jeff Allen Wilkins.
HIGH SCHOOL: Austintown Fitch (Youngstown, Ohio).
COLLEGE: Youngstown State (degree in communications, 1993).
TRANSACTIONS/CAREER NOTES: Signed as non-drafted free agent by Dallas Cowboys (April 28, 1994). ... Released by Cowboys (July 18, 1994). ... Signed by Philadelphia Eagles (November 14, 1994). ... Released by Eagles (August 14, 1995). ... Signed by San Francisco 49ers (November 8, 1995). ... Granted unconditional free agency (February 14, 1997). ... Signed by St. Louis Rams (March 6, 1997). ... Granted unconditional free agency (March 2, 2001). ... Re-signed by Rams (March 2, 2001).
CHAMPIONSHIP GAME EXPERIENCE: Played in NFC championship game (1999 and 2001 seasons). ... Member of Super Bowl championship team (1999 season). ... Played in Super Bowl XXXVI (2001 season).
RECORDS: Holds NFL single-season record for most PATs without a miss—64 (1999).

Year Team	G	FIELD GOALS							TOTALS		
		1-29	30-39	40-49	50+	Tot.	Pct.	Lg.	XPM	XPA	Pts.
1994—Philadelphia NFL	6	0-0	0-0	0-0	0-0	0-0	0.0	0	0	0	0
1995—San Francisco NFL	7	6-6	5-5	1-2	0-0	12-13	92.3	40	27	29	63
1996—San Francisco NFL	16	16-16	7-8	7-10	0-0	30-34	88.2	49	40	40	130
1997—St. Louis NFL	16	8-9	8-12	7-14	2-2	25-∞37	67.6	52	32	32	107
1998—St. Louis NFL	16	4-5	8-8	5-7	3-6	20-26	76.9	‡57	25	26	§85
1999—St. Louis NFL	16	6-6	6-7	7-11	1-4	20-28	71.4	51	*64	*64	‡124
2000—St. Louis NFL	11	7-7	6-6	3-3	1-1	17-17	100.0	51	38	38	89
2001—St. Louis NFL	16	11-11	5-5	6-12	1-1	23-29	79.3	54	*58	*58	127
2002—St. Louis NFL	16	5-5	8-10	6-9	0-1	19-25	76.0	47	37	37	94
Pro totals (9 years)	120	63-65	53-61	42-68	8-15	166-209	79.4	57	321	324	819

WILKINS, MARCUS LB PACKERS

PERSONAL: Born January 2, 1980, in Austin, Texas. ... 6-2/231. ... Full name: Marcus Wesley Wilkins.
HIGH SCHOOL: Westwood (Austin, Texas).
COLLEGE: Texas.
TRANSACTIONS/CAREER NOTES: Signed as non-drafted free agent by Green Bay Packers (April 25, 2002).

Year Team	G	GS	TOTALS			INTERCEPTIONS			
			Tk.	Ast.	Sks.	No.	Yds.	Avg.	TD
2002—Green Bay NFL	5	0	1	1	0.0	0	0	0.0	0

W

WILKINS, TERRENCE WR/KR RAMS

PERSONAL: Born July 29, 1975, in Washington, D.C. ... 5-10/180. ... Full name: Terrence Olondo Wilkins.
HIGH SCHOOL: Bishop Denis J O'Connell (Arlington, Va.).
COLLEGE: Virginia.
TRANSACTIONS/CAREER NOTES: Signed as non-drafted free agent by Indianapolis Colts (April 22, 1999). ... Granted free agency (March 1, 2002). ... Re-signed by Colts (April 15, 2002). ... Traded by Colts to St. Louis Rams for undisclosed draft pick (April 15, 2002).
SINGLE GAME HIGHS (regular season): Receptions—9 (September 25, 2000, vs. Jacksonville); yards—148 (September 25, 2000, vs. Jacksonville); and touchdown receptions—1 (December 3, 2000, vs. New York Jets).
STATISTICAL PLATEAUS: 100-yard receiving games: 1999 (1), 2000 (2). Total: 3.

			RUSHING				RECEIVING				PUNT RETURNS				KICKOFF RETURNS				TOTALS	
Year Team	G	GS	Att.	Yds.	Avg.	TD	No.	Yds.	Avg.	TD	No.	Yds.	Avg.	TD	No.	Yds.	Avg.	TD	TD	2pt.	Pts.
1999—Indianapolis NFL.	16	11	1	2	2.0	0	42	565	13.5	4	41	388	9.5	1	51	1134	22.2	▲1	7	0	42
2000—Indianapolis NFL.	14	7	3	8	2.7	0	43	569	13.2	3	29	240	8.3	0	15	279	18.6	0	3	0	18
2001—Indianapolis NFL.	11	4	0	0	0.0	0	34	332	9.8	0	21	219	10.4	1	44	1007	22.9	0	1	0	6
2002—St. Louis NFL	13	0	6	56	9.3	0	5	31	6.2	0	25	242	9.7	0	47	1074	22.9	0	0	0	0
Pro totals (4 years)	54	22	10	66	6.6	0	124	1497	12.1	7	116	1089	9.4	2	157	3494	22.3	1	11	0	66

WILKINSON, DAN — DT — REDSKINS

PERSONAL: Born March 13, 1973, in Dayton, Ohio. ... 6-4/353. ... Nickname: Big Daddy.

HIGH SCHOOL: Paul L. Dunbar (Dayton, Ohio).

COLLEGE: Ohio State.

TRANSACTIONS/CAREER NOTES: Selected after sophomore season by Cincinnati Bengals in first round (first pick overall) of 1994 NFL draft. ... Signed by Bengals (May 5, 1994). ... Designated by Bengals as franchise player (February 11, 1998). ... Tendered offer sheet by Washington Redskins (February 25, 1998). ... Bengals declined to match offer (February 26, 1998); Bengals received first-(LB Brian Simmons) and third-round (G Mike Goff) picks as compensation. ... On injured reserve with calf injury (December 5, 2002-remainder of season).

HONORS: Named defensive lineman on THE SPORTING NEWS college All-America first team (1993).

			TOTALS			INTERCEPTIONS			
Year Team	G	GS	Tk.	Ast.	Sks.	No.	Yds.	Avg.	TD
1994—Cincinnati NFL	16	14	37	7	5.5	0	0	0.0	0
1995—Cincinnati NFL	14	14	30	10	8.0	0	0	0.0	0
1996—Cincinnati NFL	16	16	37	7	6.5	1	7	7.0	0
1997—Cincinnati NFL	15	15	24	10	5.0	0	0	0.0	0
1998—Washington NFL	16	16	38	7	7.5	1	4	4.0	0
1999—Washington NFL	16	16	23	9	8.0	1	88	88.0	1
2000—Washington NFL	16	16	15	5	3.5	0	0	0.0	0
2001—Washington NFL	16	16	19	6	4.0	2	0	0.0	0
2002—Washington NFL	12	11	12	4	0.0	0	0	0.0	0
Pro totals (9 years)	137	134	235	65	48.0	5	99	19.8	1

WILLIAMS, AENEAS — CB — RAMS

PERSONAL: Born January 29, 1968, in New Orleans. ... 5-11/200. ... Full name: Aeneas Demetrius Williams. ... Name pronounced uh-NEE-us.

HIGH SCHOOL: Fortier (New Orleans).

COLLEGE: Southern (degree in accounting, 1990).

TRANSACTIONS/CAREER NOTES: Selected by Phoenix Cardinals in third round (59th pick overall) of 1991 NFL draft. ... Signed by Cardinals (July 26, 1991). ... Granted free agency (February 17, 1994). ... Cardinals franchise renamed Arizona Cardinals for 1994 season. ... Re-signed by Cardinals (June 1, 1994). ... Granted unconditional free agency (February 16, 1996). ... Re-signed by Cardinals (February 27, 1996). ... Designated by Cardinals as franchise player (February 22, 2001). ... Re-signed by Cardinals (April 21, 2001). ... Traded by Cardinals to St. Louis Rams for second- (DB Michael Stone) and fourth-round (DT Marcus Bell) picks in 2001 draft (April 21, 2001). ... On injured reserve with broken ankle (October 21, 2002-remainder of season). ... Released by Rams (February 27, 2003). ... Re-signed by Rams (March 1, 2003).

CHAMPIONSHIP GAME EXPERIENCE: Played in NFC championship game (2001 season). ... Played in Super Bowl XXXVI (2001 season).

HONORS: Named cornerback on THE SPORTING NEWS NFL All-Pro team (1995, 1997 and 2001). ... Played in Pro Bowl (1994-1999 and 2001 seasons).

RECORDS: Shares NFL record for longest fumble recovery return for touchdown—104 yards (November 5, 2002, Arizona v. Washington).

POST SEASON RECORDS: Shares NFL single-game postseason record for most interceptions returned for touchdown—2 (January 20, 2002, vs. Green Bay Packers). ... Holds NFL postseason record for most consecutive postseason games with an interceptions—4 (1998-2001).

			TOTALS			INTERCEPTIONS			
Year Team	G	GS	Tk.	Ast.	Sks.	No.	Yds.	Avg.	TD
1991—Phoenix NFL	16	15	38	10	0.0	∞6	60	10.0	0
1992—Phoenix NFL	16	16	40	8	0.0	3	25	8.3	0
1993—Phoenix NFL	16	16	37	5	0.0	2	87	43.5	1
1994—Arizona NFL	16	16	40	1	0.0	†9	89	9.9	0
1995—Arizona NFL	16	16	52	10	0.0	6	86	14.3	†2
1996—Arizona NFL	16	16	65	12	1.0	6	89	14.8	1
1997—Arizona NFL	16	16	49	14	0.0	6	95	15.8	∞2
1998—Arizona NFL	16	16	57	13	1.0	1	15	15.0	0
1999—Arizona NFL	16	16	49	7	0.0	2	5	2.5	0
2000—Arizona NFL	16	16	48	14	0.0	5	102	20.4	0
2001—St. Louis NFL	16	16	56	17	0.0	4	69	17.3	†2
2002—St. Louis NFL	6	6	23	6	0.0	1	3	3.0	0
Pro totals (12 years)	182	181	554	117	2.0	51	725	14.2	8

W

WILLIAMS, BOBBIE — G — EAGLES

PERSONAL: Born September 25, 1976, in Jefferson, Texas. ... 6-3/320.

HIGH SCHOOL: Jefferson (Texas).

COLLEGE: Arkansas.

TRANSACTIONS/CAREER NOTES: Selected by Philadelphia Eagles in second round (61st pick overall) of 2000 NFL draft. ... Signed by Eagles (July 17, 2000). ... Inactive for all 16 games (2000).

PLAYING EXPERIENCE: Philadelphia NFL, 2001-2002. ... Games/Games started: 2001 (1/1), 2002 (16/0). Total: 17/1.

CHAMPIONSHIP GAME EXPERIENCE: Member of Eagles for NFC championship game (2001 season); inactive. ... Played in NFC championship game (2002 season).

WILLIAMS, BOO   TE   SAINTS

PERSONAL: Born June 22, 1979, in Tallahassee, Fla. ... 6-4/245. ... Full name: Eddie Lee Williams. ... Cousin of Tamarick Vanover, wide receiver, San Diego Chargers.
HIGH SCHOOL: Lincoln (Tallahassee, Fla.).
JUNIOR COLLEGE: Coffeyville (Kan.) Community College.
COLLEGE: Arkansas.
TRANSACTIONS/CAREER NOTES: Signed as non-drafted free agent by New Orleans Saints (April 26, 2000). ... Released by Saints (September 2, 2001). ... Re-signed by Saints to practice squad (September 3, 2001). ... Activated (October 27, 2001).

			RECEIVING			
Year Team	G	GS	No.	Yds.	Avg.	TD
2001—New Orleans NFL	11	4	20	202	10.1	3
2002—New Orleans NFL	16	3	13	143	11.0	2
Pro totals (2 years)	27	7	33	345	10.5	5

WILLIAMS, BRIAN   CB   VIKINGS

PERSONAL: Born July 2, 1979, in High Point, N.C. ... 5-11/207.
HIGH SCHOOL: Southwest Guilford (N.C.).
COLLEGE: North Carolina State.
TRANSACTIONS/CAREER NOTES: Selected by Minnesota Vikings in fourth round (105th pick overall) of 2002 NFL draft. ... Signed by Vikings (July 24, 2002).

			TOTALS			INTERCEPTIONS				PUNT RETURNS				TOTALS			
Year Team	G	GS	Tk.	Ast.	Sks.	No.	Yds.	Avg.	TD	No.	Yds.	Avg.	TD	TD	2pt.	Pts.	Fum.
2002—Minnesota NFL	16	7	32	5	0.0	1	2	2.0	0	0	0	0.0	0	0	0	0	0

WILLIAMS, BRIAN   LB   LIONS

PERSONAL: Born December 17, 1972, in Dallas. ... 6-1/243. ... Full name: Brian Marcee Williams.
HIGH SCHOOL: Bishop Dunne (Dallas).
COLLEGE: Southern California (degree in public administration).
TRANSACTIONS/CAREER NOTES: Selected by Green Bay Packers in third round (73rd pick overall) of 1995 NFL draft. ... Signed by Packers (May 9, 1995). ... Granted free agency (February 13, 1998). ... Re-signed by Packers (February 17, 1998). ... On injured reserve with knee injury (November 9, 1999-remainder of season). ... On injured reserve with knee injury (December 15, 2000-remainder of season). ... Released by Packers (February 22, 2001). ... Aigned by Jacksonville Jaguars (April 23, 2001). ... Released by Jaguars (July 18, 2001). ... Signed by New Orleans Saints (July 28, 2001). ... Claimed on waivers by Detroit Lions (December 5, 2001). ... Granted unconditional free agency (March 1, 2002). ... Re-signed by Lions (June 3, 2002). ... On physically unable to perform list with knee injury (July 25-August 11, 2002). ... On injured reserve with broken leg (October 19, 2002-remainder of season). ... Granted unconditional free agency (February 28, 2003). ... Re-signed by Lions (March 14, 2003).
CHAMPIONSHIP GAME EXPERIENCE: Played in NFC championship game (1995-97 seasons). ... Member of Super Bowl championship team (1996 season). ... Played in Super Bowl XXXII (1997 season).

			TOTALS			INTERCEPTIONS			
Year Team	G	GS	Tk.	Ast.	Sks.	No.	Yds.	Avg.	TD
1995—Green Bay NFL	13	0	0	0	0.0	0	0	0.0	0
1996—Green Bay NFL	16	16	52	31	0.5	0	0	0.0	0
1997—Green Bay NFL	16	16	62	38	1.0	2	30	15.0	0
1998—Green Bay NFL	16	15	77	31	2.0	0	0	0.0	0
1999—Green Bay NFL	7	7	44	24	2.0	2	60	30.0	0
2000—Green Bay NFL	4	3	17	8	0.5	0	0	0.0	0
2001—New Orleans NFL	4	0	0	0	0.0	0	0	0.0	0
—Detroit NFL	2	1	15	2	0.0	0	0	0.0	0
2002—Detroit NFL	3	3	8	3	0.0	0	0	0.0	0
Pro totals (8 years)	81	61	275	137	6.0	4	90	22.5	0

WILLIAMS, CHAD   S   RAVENS

PERSONAL: Born January 22, 1979, in Birmingham, Ala. ... 5-9/207.
HIGH SCHOOL: Wenonah (Birmingham, Ala.).
COLLEGE: Southern Mississippi.
TRANSACTIONS/CAREER NOTES: Selected by Baltimore Ravens in sixth round (209th pick overall) of 2002 NFL draft. ... Signed by Ravens (July 25, 2002).

			TOTALS			INTERCEPTIONS				PUNT RETURNS				KICKOFF RETURNS				TOTALS			
Year Team	G	GS	Tk.	Ast.	Sks.	No.	Yds.	Avg.	TD	No.	Yds.	Avg.	TD	No.	Yds.	Avg.	TD	TD	2pt.	Pts.	Fum.
2002—Baltimore NFL	16	0	29	3	0.0	3	98	32.7	1	0	0	0.0	0	0	0	0.0	0	1	0	6	0

WILLIAMS, GRANT   OT   RAMS

PERSONAL: Born May 10, 1974, in Hattiesburg, Miss. ... 6-7/320.
HIGH SCHOOL: Clinton (Miss.).
JUNIOR COLLEGE: Hinds Community College (Miss.).
COLLEGE: Louisiana Tech (degree in biology, 1995).
TRANSACTIONS/CAREER NOTES: Signed as non-drafted free agent by Seattle Seahawks (April 22, 1996). ... Granted unconditional free agency (February 11, 2000). ... Signed by New England Patriots (March 17, 2000). ... Granted unconditional free agency (March 1, 2002). ...

W

Re-signed by Patriots (April 19, 2002). ... Traded by Patriots to St. Louis Rams for seventh-round pick (traded to Tennessee) in 2003 draft (August 19, 2002). ... On injured reserve with ankle injury (October 15, 2002-remainder of season). ... Granted unconditional free agency (February 28, 2003). ... Re-signed by Rams (April 16, 2003).

PLAYING EXPERIENCE: Seattle NFL, 1996-1999; New England NFL, 2000 and 2001; St. Louis NFL, 2002. ... Games/Games started: 1996 (8/0), 1997 (16/8), 1998 (16/0), 1999 (16/15), 2000 (16/9), 2001 (14/4), 2002 (5/3). Total: 91/39.

CHAMPIONSHIP GAME EXPERIENCE: Played in AFC championship game (2001 season). ... Member of Super Bowl championship team (2001 season).

WILLIAMS, JAMAL   DT   CHARGERS

PERSONAL: Born April 28, 1976, in Washington, D.C. ... 6-3/305.
HIGH SCHOOL: Archbishop Carroll (Washington, D.C.).
COLLEGE: Oklahoma State.
TRANSACTIONS/CAREER NOTES: Selected by San Diego Chargers in second round of 1998 supplemental draft (July 9, 1998). ... Signed by Chargers (August 7, 1998). ... Granted free agency (March 2, 2001). ... Re-signed by Chargers (May 11, 2001). ... On injured reserve with knee injury (October 3, 2001-remainder of season). ... On injured reserve with ankle injury (December 2, 2002-remainder of season).

			TOTALS			INTERCEPTIONS			
Year Team	G	GS	Tk.	Ast.	Sks.	No.	Yds.	Avg.	TD
1998—San Diego NFL	9	0	5	1	0.0	1	14	14.0	1
1999—San Diego NFL	16	2	22	4	1.0	0	0	0.0	0
2000—San Diego NFL	16	16	46	7	1.0	0	0	0.0	0
2001 San Diego NFL	3	3	2	0	0.0	0	0	0.0	0
2002—San Diego NFL	12	10	20	4	2.5	0	0	0.0	0
Pro totals (5 years)	56	31	95	16	4.5	1	14	14.0	1

WILLIAMS, JAMES   WR   SEAHAWKS

PERSONAL: Born March 6, 1978, in Vicksburg, Miss. ... 5-10/186. ... Full name: James L. Williams.
HIGH SCHOOL: Warren Central (Vicksburg, Miss.).
JUNIOR COLLEGE: Hinds Community College (Miss.).
COLLEGE: Marshall.
TRANSACTIONS/CAREER NOTES: Selected by Seattle Seahawks in sixth round (175th pick overall) of 2000 NFL draft. ... Signed by Seahawks (June 22, 2000). ... Granted free agency (February 28, 2003). ... Re-signed by Seahawks (April 2, 2003).
SINGLE GAME HIGHS (regular season): Receptions—4 (December 30, 2001, vs. San Diego); yards—101 (December 30, 2001, vs. San Diego); and touchdown receptions—1 (December 30, 2001, vs. San Diego).
STATISTICAL PLATEAUS: 100-yard receiving games: 2001 (1).

			RECEIVING				KICKOFF RETURNS				TOTALS			
Year Team	G	GS	No.	Yds.	Avg.	TD	No.	Yds.	Avg.	TD	TD	2pt.	Pts.	Fum.
2000—Seattle NFL	10	0	8	99	12.4	0	3	76	25.3	0	0	0	2	0
2001—Seattle NFL	6	2	12	212	17.7	1	9	175	19.4	0	1	0	6	1
2002—Seattle NFL	13	2	9	99	11.0	0	21	354	16.9	0	0	0	0	0
Pro totals (3 years)	29	4	29	410	14.1	1	33	605	18.3	0	1	0	8	1

WILLIAMS, JAMES   OT

PERSONAL: Born March 29, 1968, in Pittsburgh. ... 6-7/332. ... Full name: James Otis Williams.
HIGH SCHOOL: Allderdice (Pittsburgh).
COLLEGE: Cheyney (Pa.) State.
TRANSACTIONS/CAREER NOTES: Signed as non-drafted free agent by Chicago Bears (April 25, 1991). ... Granted free agency (February 16, 1996). ... Re-signed by Bears (March 15, 1996). ... Released by Bears (February 26, 2003).
PLAYING EXPERIENCE: Chicago NFL, 1991-2002. ... Games/Games started: 1991 (14/0), 1992 (5/0), 1993 (3/0), 1994 (16/15), 1995 (16/16), 1996 (16/16), 1997 (16/16), 1998 (16/16), 1999 (16/16), 2000 (16/16), 2001 (16/16), 2002 (16/16). Total: 166/143.
HONORS: Played in Pro Bowl (2001 season).
MISCELLANEOUS: Switched from defensive line to offensive line during the 1992 season.

WILLIAMS, JAY   DE   DOLPHINS

W

PERSONAL: Born October 13, 1971, in Washington, D.C. ... 6-3/280. ... Full name: Jay Omar Williams.
HIGH SCHOOL: St. John's (Washington, D.C.).
COLLEGE: Wake Forest.
TRANSACTIONS/CAREER NOTES: Signed as non-drafted free agent by Miami Dolphins (April 28, 1994). ... Released by Dolphins (August 28, 1994). ... Signed by Los Angeles Rams to practice squad (September 27, 1994). ... Activated (December 7, 1994); did not play. ... Rams franchise moved from Los Angeles to St. Louis (April 12, 1995). ... On physically unable to perform list with forearm injury (July 31-November 18, 1996). ... Released by Rams (November 20, 1996). ... Re-signed by Rams (December 11, 1996). ... Granted free agency (February 12, 1999). ... Re-signed by Rams (May 4, 1999). ... Granted unconditional free agency (February 11, 2000). ... Signed by Carolina Panthers (February 16, 2000). ... Traded by Panthers to Miami Dolphins for DE Al Wallace and fourth-round pick (DB Colin Branch) in 2003 draft (July 19, 2002).
CHAMPIONSHIP GAME EXPERIENCE: Played in NFC championship game (1999 season). ... Member of Super Bowl championship team (1999 season).

Year Team	G	GS	TOTALS			INTERCEPTIONS			
			Tk.	Ast.	Sks.	No.	Yds.	Avg.	TD
1994—Los Angeles Rams NFL			Did not play.						
1995—St. Louis NFL	7	0	0	0	0.0	0	0	0.0	0
1996—St. Louis NFL	2	0	0	0	0.0	0	0	0.0	0
1997—St. Louis NFL	16	2	4	3	1.0	0	0	0.0	0
1998—St. Louis NFL	16	1	10	4	1.0	0	0	0.0	0
1999—St. Louis NFL	16	0	13	1	4.0	0	0	0.0	0
2000—Carolina NFL	16	14	21	6	6.0	0	0	0.0	0
2001—Carolina NFL	16	13	27	12	1.0	1	0	0.0	0
2002—Miami NFL	16	0	17	5	6.0	0	0	0.0	0
Pro totals (8 years)	105	30	92	31	19.0	1	0	0.0	0

WILLIAMS, JIMMY　　　　CB　　　　49ERS

PERSONAL: Born March 10, 1979, in Baton Rouge, La. ... 5-11/190.
HIGH SCHOOL: Episcopal (Baton Rouge, La.).
COLLEGE: Vanderbilt.
TRANSACTIONS/CAREER NOTES: Selected by Buffalo Bills in sixth round (196th pick overall) of 2001 NFL draft. ... Signed by Bills (June 13, 2001). ... Released by Bills (September 2, 2001). ... Signed by San Francisco 49ers to practice squad (September 5, 2001). ... Activated (October 16, 2001). ... On injured reserve with knee injury (December 10, 2002-remainder of season). ... Re-signed by 49ers (May 6, 2003).

Year Team	G	GS	TOTALS			INTERCEPTIONS				PUNT RETURNS				KICKOFF RETURNS				TOTALS			
			Tk.	Ast.	Sks.	No.	Yds.	Avg.	TD	No.	Yds.	Avg.	TD	No.	Yds.	Avg.	TD	TD	2pt.	Pts.	Fum.
2001—San Francisco NFL	10	0	0	0	0.0	0	0	0.0	0	0	0	0.0	0	0	0	0.0	0	0	0	0	0
2002—San Francisco NFL	13	0	0	0	0.0	0	0	0.0	0	20	336	*16.8	1	35	765	21.9	0	1	0	6	2
Pro totals (2 years)	23	0	0	0	0.0	0	0	0.0	0	20	336	16.8	1	35	765	21.9	0	1	0	6	2

WILLIAMS, JOSH　　　　DT　　　　COLTS

PERSONAL: Born August 9, 1976, in Denver. ... 6-3/285. ... Full name: Josh Sinclair Williams.
HIGH SCHOOL: Cypress Creek (Houston).
COLLEGE: Michigan.
TRANSACTIONS/CAREER NOTES: Selected by Indianapolis Colts in fourth round (122nd pick overall) of 2000 NFL draft. ... Signed by Colts (June 27, 2000). ... Granted free agency (February 28, 2003). ... Re-signed by Colts (April 15, 2003).

Year Team	G	GS	TOTALS		
			Tk.	Ast.	Sks.
2000—Indianapolis NFL	14	7	26	16	3.0
2001—Indianapolis NFL	16	16	30	19	3.0
2002—Indianapolis NFL	7	3	10	4	1.0
Pro totals (3 years)	37	26	66	39	7.0

WILLIAMS, KARL　　　　WR　　　　BUCCANEERS

PERSONAL: Born April 10, 1971, in Albion, Mich. ... 5-10/177.
HIGH SCHOOL: Garland (Texas).
COLLEGE: Texas A&M-Kingsville.
TRANSACTIONS/CAREER NOTES: Signed as non-drafted free agent by Tampa Bay Buccaneers (April 23, 1996). ... Granted unconditional free agency (March 1, 2002). ... Re-signed by Buccaneers (April 17, 2002).
CHAMPIONSHIP GAME EXPERIENCE: Played in NFC championship game (1999 and 2002 seasons). ... Member of Super Bowl championship team (2002 season).
SINGLE GAME HIGHS (regular season): Receptions—6 (September 13, 1998, vs. Green Bay); yards—87 (December 7, 1997, vs. Green Bay); and touchdown receptions—2 (November 2, 1997, vs. Indianapolis).

Year Team	G	GS	RECEIVING				PUNT RETURNS				KICKOFF RETURNS				TOTALS			
			No.	Yds.	Avg.	TD	No.	Yds.	Avg.	TD	No.	Yds.	Avg.	TD	TD	2pt.	Pts.	Fum.
1996—Tampa Bay NFL..........	16	0	22	246	11.2	0	13	274	21.1	1	14	383	27.4	0	1	0	6	2
1997—Tampa Bay NFL..........	16	7	33	486	14.7	4	46	‡597	13.0	∞1	15	277	18.5	0	5	0	30	5
1998—Tampa Bay NFL..........	13	6	21	252	12.0	1	10	83	8.3	0	0	0	0.0	0	1	0	6	0
1999—Tampa Bay NFL..........	13	4	21	176	8.4	0	20	153	7.7	0	1	15	15.0	0	0	0	0	2
2000—Tampa Bay NFL..........	13	0	2	35	17.5	0	31	286	9.2	1	19	453	23.8	0	1	0	6	2
2001—Tampa Bay NFL..........	15	3	24	314	13.1	1	35	366	10.5	†1	2	35	17.5	0	2	0	12	3
2002—Tampa Bay NFL..........	16	2	7	77	11.0	1	43	410	9.5	1	3	49	16.3	0	2	0	12	0
Pro totals (7 years)	102	22	130	1586	12.2	7	198	2169	11.0	5	54	1212	22.4	0	12	0	72	14

W

WILLIAMS, KEVIN　　　　S

PERSONAL: Born August 4, 1975, in Pine Bluff, Ark. ... 6-0/192.
HIGH SCHOOL: Watson Chapel (Pine Bluff, Ark.).
COLLEGE: Oklahoma State.
TRANSACTIONS/CAREER NOTES: Selected by New York Jets in third round (87th pick overall) of 1998 NFL draft. ... Signed by Jets (July 20, 1998). ... On non-football illness list with viral infection (October 18, 1999-remainder of season). ... Released by Jets (November 7, 2000). ... Signed by Miami Dolphins (November 28, 2000). ... Released by Dolphins (July 11, 2001). ... Signed by Philadelphia Eagles (July 29, 2001). ... Released by Eagles (August 24, 2001). ... Signed by Houston Texans (December 29, 2001). ... Released by Texans (September 23, 2002). ... Re-signed by Texans (October 22, 2002). ... Granted unconditional free agency (February 28, 2003). ... Re-signed by Texans (March 11, 2003). ... Released by Texans (May 8, 2003).
CHAMPIONSHIP GAME EXPERIENCE: Played in AFC championship game (1998 season).

Year Team	G	GS	TOTALS			INTERCEPTIONS				KICKOFF RETURNS				TOTALS			
			Tk.	Ast.	Sks.	No.	Yds.	Avg.	TD	No.	Yds.	Avg.	TD	TD	2pt.	Pts.	Fum.
1998—New York Jets NFL	15	6	27	5	0.0	1	34	34.0	0	11	230	20.9	0	0	0	0	0
1999—New York Jets NFL	4	0	2	0	0.0	0	0	0.0	0	6	166	27.7	0	0	0	0	1
2000—New York Jets NFL	9	7	7	7	0.0	0	0	0.0	0	21	551	26.2 ▲1	1	1	0	6	0
—Miami NFL	2	0	0	0	0.0	0	0	0.0	0	3	64	21.3	0	0	0	0	0
2002—Houston NFL	13	0	18	6	0.0	0	0	0.0	0	0	0	0.0	0	1	0	6	0
Pro totals (4 years)	43	13	54	18	0.0	1	34	34.0	0	41	1011	24.7	1	2	0	12	1

WILLIAMS, LOUIS — C — PANTHERS

PERSONAL: Born April 11, 1979, in Fort Walton Beach, Fla. ... 6-4/291. ... Full name: Louis Randall Williams Jr..
HIGH SCHOOL: Choctawhatchee (Fla.).
COLLEGE: Louisiana State.
TRANSACTIONS/CAREER NOTES: Selected by Carolina Panthers in seventh round (211th pick overall) of 2001 NFL draft. ... Signed by Panthers (July 13, 2001).
PLAYING EXPERIENCE: Carolina NFL, 2002. ... Games/Games started: 2002 (2/0).

WILLIAMS, MARCUS — TE — RAIDERS

PERSONAL: Born December 12, 1977, in Oakland. ... 6-5/230.
HIGH SCHOOL: Berkeley (Calif.).
JUNIOR COLLEGE: Laney Junior College (Calif.).
COLLEGE: Washington State.
TRANSACTIONS/CAREER NOTES: Signed as non-drafted free agent by Indianapolis Colts (April 22, 2001). ... Released by Colts (August 27, 2001). ... Signed by Oakland Raiders to practice squad (December 5, 2001). ... Assigned by Raiders to Frankfurt Galaxy in 2002 NFL Europe enhancement allocation program (February 12, 2002). ... Released by Raiders (September 1, 2002). ... Re-signed by Raiders to practice squad (September 3, 2002). ... Activated (September 28, 2002).
CHAMPIONSHIP GAME EXPERIENCE: Played in AFC championship game (2002 season).

Year Team	G	GS	RECEIVING			
			No.	Yds.	Avg.	TD
2002—Frankfurt NFLE	...	...	1	2	2.0	1
—Oakland NFL	14	0	0	0	0.0	0
NFL Europe totals (1 year)	...	...	1	2	2.0	1
NFL totals (1 year)	14	0	0	0	0.0	0
Pro totals (2 years)	...	...	1	2	2.0	1

WILLIAMS, MAURICE — OT — JAGUARS

PERSONAL: Born January 26, 1979, in Detroit. ... 6-5/310. ... Full name: Maurice Carlos Williams.
HIGH SCHOOL: Pershing (Detroit).
COLLEGE: Michigan.
TRANSACTIONS/CAREER NOTES: Selected by Jacksonville Jaguars in second round (43rd pick overall) of 2001 NFL draft. ... Signed by Jaguars (July 25, 2001). ... On injured reserve with leg injury (October 14, 2002-remainder of season).
PLAYING EXPERIENCE: Jacksonville NFL, 2001-2002. ... Games/Games started: 2001 (16/16), 2002 (5/5). Total: 21/21.

WILLIAMS, MIKE — OT — BILLS

PERSONAL: Born January 11, 1980, in Dallas. ... 6-6/370. ... Full name: Michael D. Williams.
HIGH SCHOOL: The Colony (Texas).
COLLEGE: Texas.
TRANSACTIONS/CAREER NOTES: Selected by Buffalo Bills in first round (fourth pick overall) of 2002 NFL draft. ... Signed by Bills (July 28, 2002).
PLAYING EXPERIENCE: Buffalo NFL, 2002. ... Games/Games started: 2002 (14/14).
HONORS: Named offensive tackle on THE SPORTING NEWS college All-America second team (2001).

W

WILLIAMS, MOE — RB — VIKINGS

PERSONAL: Born July 26, 1974, in Columbus, Ga. ... 6-1/210. ... Full name: Maurice Jabari Williams.
HIGH SCHOOL: Spencer (Columbus, Ga.).
COLLEGE: Kentucky.
TRANSACTIONS/CAREER NOTES: Selected after junior season by Minnesota Vikings in third round (75th pick overall) of 1996 NFL draft. ... Signed by Vikings (July 22, 1996). ... On injured reserve with foot injury (December 8, 1998-remainder of season). ... Granted free agency (February 12, 1999). ... Re-signed by Vikings (April 30, 1999). ... Granted unconditional free agency (February 11, 2000). ... Re-signed by Vikings (March 20, 2000). ... Released by Vikings (September 2, 2001). ... Signed by Baltimore Ravens (September 4, 2001). ... Granted unconditional free agency (March 1, 2002). ... Signed by Vikings (May 21, 2002). ... Granted unconditional free agency (February 28, 2003). ... Re-signed by Vikings (March 13, 2003).
CHAMPIONSHIP GAME EXPERIENCE: Played in NFC championship game (2000 season).
SINGLE GAME HIGHS (regular season): Attempts—24 (December 2, 2001, vs. Indianapolis); yards—111 (December 2, 2001, vs. Indianapolis); and rushing touchdowns—2 (November 3, 2002, vs. Tampa Bay).
STATISTICAL PLATEAUS: 100-yard rushing games: 2001 (1), 2002 (1). Total: 2.

Year—Team	G	GS	RUSHING				RECEIVING				KICKOFF RETURNS				TOTALS			
			Att.	Yds.	Avg.	TD	No.	Yds.	Avg.	TD	No.	Yds.	Avg.	TD	TD	2pt.	Pts.	Fum.
1996—Minnesota NFL	9	0	0	0	0.0	0	0	0	0.0	0	0	0	0.0	0	0	0	0	0
1997—Minnesota NFL	14	0	22	59	2.7	1	4	14	3.5	0	16	388	24.3	0	1	0	6	0
1998—Minnesota NFL	12	1	0	0	0.0	0	1	64	64.0	0	2	19	9.5	0	0	0	0	1
1999—Minnesota NFL	14	0	24	69	2.9	1	1	12	12.0	0	10	240	24.0	1	2	0	12	0
2000—Minnesota NFL	16	0	23	67	2.9	0	4	31	7.8	0	10	214	21.4	0	0	1	2	0
2001—Baltimore NFL	15	2	65	291	4.5	0	23	210	9.1	0	0	0	0.0	0	0	0	0	1
2002—Baltimore NFL	16	0	84	414	4.9	11	27	251	9.3	0	24	516	21.5	0	11	0	66	1
Pro totals (7 years)	96	3	218	900	4.1	13	60	582	9.7	0	62	1377	22.2	1	14	1	86	3

WILLIAMS, PAT — DT — BILLS

PERSONAL: Born October 24, 1972, in Monroe, La. ... 6-3/315. ... Full name: Patrick Williams.
HIGH SCHOOL: Wossman (Monroe, La.).
JUNIOR COLLEGE: Navarro College (Texas).
COLLEGE: Northeast Oklahoma, then Texas A&M.
TRANSACTIONS/CAREER NOTES: Signed as non-drafted free agent by Buffalo Bills (April 25, 1997). ... Granted free agency (February 11, 2000). ... Re-signed by Bills (March 23, 2000).

Year—Team	G	GS	TOTALS		
			Tk.	Ast.	Sks.
1997—Buffalo NFL	1	0	0	0	0.0
1998—Buffalo NFL	13	0	11	1	3.5
1999—Buffalo NFL	16	0	25	7	2.5
2000—Buffalo NFL	16	4	37	18	2.5
2001—Buffalo NFL	13	13	41	18	1.5
2002—Buffalo NFL	16	16	53	31	0.5
Pro totals (6 years)	75	33	167	75	10.5

WILLIAMS, RANDAL — WR — COWBOYS

PERSONAL: Born May 21, 1978, in Deerfield, Maine. ... 6-3/220. ... Full name: Randal Ellison Williams.
HIGH SCHOOL: Deerfield Academy (Maine).
COLLEGE: New Hampshire.
TRANSACTIONS/CAREER NOTES: Signed as non-drafted free agent by Jacksonville Jaguars (April 27, 2001). ... Claimed on waivers by Dallas Cowboys (October 29, 2001).

Year—Team	G	GS	RECEIVING			
			No.	Yds.	Avg.	TD
2001—Dallas NFL	7	0	0	0	0.0	0
2002—Dallas NFL	11	0	0	0	0.0	0
Pro totals (2 years)	18	0	0	0	0.0	0

WILLIAMS, RICKY — RB — DOLPHINS

PERSONAL: Born May 21, 1977, in San Diego. ... 5-10/228. ... Full name: Errick Lynne Williams.
HIGH SCHOOL: Patrick Henry (San Diego).
COLLEGE: Texas.
TRANSACTIONS/CAREER NOTES: Selected by New Orleans Saints in first round (fifth pick overall) of 1999 NFL draft. ... Signed by Saints (May 14, 1999). ... Traded by Saints with fourth-round pick (TE Randy McMichael) in 2002 draft to Miami Dolphins for first-(DE Charles Grant) and fourth-round (DB Keyon Craver) picks in 2002 draft and third-round pick in 2003 draft (March 8, 2002).
HONORS: Named running back on THE SPORTING NEWS college All-America first team (1997 and 1998). ... Doak Walker Award winner (1997 and 1998). ... Heisman Trophy winner (1998). ... Walter Camp Award winner (1998). ... Maxwell Award winner (1998). ... Named College Football Player of the Year by THE SPORTING NEWS (1998). ... Played in Pro Bowl (2002 season). ... Named Outstanding Player of Pro Bowl (2002). ... Named running back on THE SPORTING NEWS NFL All-Pro team (2002).
RECORDS: Shares NFL record for most consecutive games with 200 or more yards rushing—2 (December 1-9, 2002).
SINGLE GAME HIGHS (regular season): Attempts—40 (October 31, 1999, vs. Cleveland); yards—228 (December 1, 2002, vs. Buffalo); and rushing touchdowns—3 (October 22, 2000, vs. Atlanta).
STATISTICAL PLATEAUS: 100-yard rushing games: 1999 (2), 2000 (5), 2001 (5), 2002 (10). Total: 22.

Year—Team	G	GS	RUSHING				RECEIVING				TOTALS			
			Att.	Yds.	Avg.	TD	No.	Yds.	Avg.	TD	TD	2pt.	Pts.	Fum.
1999—New Orleans NFL	12	12	253	884	3.5	2	28	172	6.1	0	2	0	12	6
2000—New Orleans NFL	10	10	248	1000	4.0	8	44	409	9.3	1	9	0	54	6
2001—New Orleans NFL	16	16	313	1245	4.0	6	60	511	8.5	1	7	0	42	8
2002—Miami NFL	16	16	*383	*1853	4.8	16	47	363	7.7	1	17	0	102	7
Pro totals (4 years)	54	54	1197	4982	4.2	32	179	1455	8.1	3	35	0	210	27

WILLIAMS, RICKY — RB — COLTS

PERSONAL: Born August 29, 1978, in Dallas. ... 5-7/195. ... Full name: Ricky Antwan Williams.
HIGH SCHOOL: Duncanville (Texas).
COLLEGE: Texas Tech.
TRANSACTIONS/CAREER NOTES: Signed as non-drafted free agent by New Orleans Saints (April 23, 2002). ... Traded by Saints to Indianapolis Colts for conditional pick (traded to New England) in 2003 draft (September 1, 2002).
SINGLE GAME HIGHS (regular season): Attempts—5 (December 1, 2002, vs. Houston); yards—21 (October 27, 2002, vs. Washington); and rushing touchdowns—0.

Year—Team	G	GS	RUSHING				RECEIVING				KICKOFF RETURNS				TOTALS			
			Att.	Yds.	Avg.	TD	No.	Yds.	Avg.	TD	No.	Yds.	Avg.	TD	TD	2pt.	Pts.	Fum.
2002—Indianapolis NFL	10	0	11	35	3.2	0	1	20	20.0	1	2	35	17.5	0	1	0	6	0

W

WILLIAMS, ROLAND   TE   RAIDERS

PERSONAL: Born April 27, 1975, in Rochester, N.Y. ... 6-5/265. ... Full name: Roland Lamar Williams.
HIGH SCHOOL: East (Rochester, N.Y.).
COLLEGE: Syracuse (degree in speech communications, 1997).
TRANSACTIONS/CAREER NOTES: Selected by St. Louis Rams in fourth round (98th pick overall) of 1998 NFL draft. ... Signed by Rams (July 13, 1998). ... Granted free agency (March 2, 2001). ... Re-signed by Rams (April 20, 2001). ... Traded by Rams to Oakland Raiders for fourth-round pick (traded to Arizona) in 2001 draft (April 21, 2001). ... On injured reserve with knee and toe injuries (January 18, 2003-remainder of season).
CHAMPIONSHIP GAME EXPERIENCE: Played in NFC championship game (1999 season). ... Member of Super Bowl championship team (1999 season).
SINGLE GAME HIGHS (regular season): Receptions—7 (September 15, 2002, vs. Pittsburgh); yards—55 (September 15, 2002, vs. Pittsburgh); and touchdown receptions—2 (October 24, 1999, vs. Cleveland).

				RECEIVING				TOTALS		
Year Team	G	GS	No.	Yds.	Avg.	TD	TD	2pt.	Pts.	Fum.
1998—St. Louis NFL	13	9	15	144	9.6	1	1	0	6	0
1999—St. Louis NFL	16	15	25	226	9.0	6	6	0	36	0
2000—St. Louis NFL	16	11	11	102	9.3	3	3	1	20	0
2001—Oakland NFL	16	15	33	298	9.0	3	3	0	18	0
2002—Oakland NFL	16	12	27	213	7.9	0	0	0	0	1
Pro totals (5 years)	77	62	111	983	8.9	13	13	1	80	1

WILLIAMS, ROOSEVELT   CB   BEARS

PERSONAL: Born September 10, 1978, in Jacksonville, Fla. ... 5-11/200.
HIGH SCHOOL: Terry Parker (Jacksonville, Fla.).
COLLEGE: Tuskegee.
TRANSACTIONS/CAREER NOTES: Selected by Chicago Bears in third round (72nd pick overall) of 2002 NFL draft. ... Signed by Bears (June 28, 2002).

			TOTALS			INTERCEPTIONS				KICKOFF RETURNS				TOTALS			
Year Team	G	GS	Tk.	Ast.	Sks.	No.	Yds.	Avg.	TD	No.	Yds.	Avg.	TD	TD	2pt.	Pts.	Fum.
2002—Chicago NFL	13	2	9	1	0.0	0	0	0.0	0	0	0	0.0	0	0	0	0	0

WILLIAMS, ROY   S   COWBOYS

PERSONAL: Born August 14, 1980, in Redwood City, Calif. ... 6-0/235.
HIGH SCHOOL: James Logan (Union City, Calif.).
COLLEGE: Oklahoma.
TRANSACTIONS/CAREER NOTES: Selected after junior season by Dallas Cowboys in first round (ninth pick overall) of 2002 NFL draft. ... Signed by Cowboys (July 26, 2002).
HONORS: Named strong safety on THE SPORTING NEWS college All-America first team (2001). ... Jim Thorpe Award winner (2001). ... Bronko Nagurski Award winner (2001).

			TOTALS			INTERCEPTIONS				PUNT RETURNS				TOTALS			
Year Team	G	GS	Tk.	Ast.	Sks.	No.	Yds.	Avg.	TD	No.	Yds.	Avg.	TD	TD	2pt.	Pts.	Fum.
2002—Dallas NFL	16	16	81	11	2.0	5	90	18.0	2	0	0	0.0	0	2	0	12	0

WILLIAMS, SAMMY   OL

PERSONAL: Born December 14, 1974, in Magnolia, Miss. ... 6-5/310.
HIGH SCHOOL: Thornton Township (Harvey, Ill.).
JUNIOR COLLEGE: Coffeyville (Kan.) Community College..
COLLEGE: Oklahoma.
TRANSACTIONS/CAREER NOTES: Selected by Baltimore Ravens in sixth round (164th pick overall) of 1998 NFL draft. ... Signed by Ravens (July 21, 1998). ... On injured reserve with knee and ankle injuries (August 30, 1998-entire season). ... Released by Ravens (September 4, 1999). ... Claimed on waivers by Kansas City Chiefs (September 6, 1999). ... Claimed on waivers by Ravens (November 10, 1999). ... Assigned by Ravens to Berlin Thunder in 2001 NFL Europe enhancement allocation program (February 19, 2001). ... Granted unconditional free agency (March 1, 2002). ... Signed by San Diego Chargers (June 21, 2002). ... Granted unconditional free agency (February 28, 2003).
PLAYING EXPERIENCE: Kansas City NFL, 1999 and 2000; Berlin NFLE, 2001; Baltimore NFL, 2001; San Diego NFL, 2002. ... Games/Games started: 1999 (1/0), 2000 (2/0), NFLE 2001 (games played unavailable), NFL 2001 (15/7), 2002 (12/7). Total: 30/14.
CHAMPIONSHIP GAME EXPERIENCE: Member of Ravens for AFC Championship game (2000 season); inactive. ... Member of Super Bowl championship team (2000 season); inactive.

WILLIAMS, SHAUN   S   GIANTS

PERSONAL: Born October 10, 1976, in Los Angeles. ... 6-2/217. ... Full name: Shaun LeJon Williams.
HIGH SCHOOL: Crespi (Encino, Calif.).
COLLEGE: UCLA.
TRANSACTIONS/CAREER NOTES: Selected by New York Giants in first round (24th pick overall) of 1998 NFL draft. ... Signed by Giants (July 24, 1998). ... Granted unconditional free agency (March 1, 2002). ... Re-signed by Giants (March 29, 2002).
CHAMPIONSHIP GAME EXPERIENCE: Played in NFC championship game (2000 season). ... Played in Super Bowl XXXV (2000 season).
HONORS: Named free safety on THE SPORTING NEWS college All-America second team (1997).

Year	Team	G	GS	TOTALS Tk.	Ast.	Sks.	INTERCEPTIONS No.	Yds.	Avg.	TD
1998—New York Giants NFL		13	0	19	5	0.0	2	6	3.0	0
1999—New York Giants NFL		11	0	13	3	0.0	0	0	0.0	0
2000—New York Giants NFL		16	16	68	17	0.0	3	52	17.3	0
2001—New York Giants NFL		16	16	77	19	1.0	3	25	8.3	0
2002—New York Giants NFL		16	16	64	26	2.0	2	-2	-1.0	0
Pro totals (5 years)		72	48	241	70	3.0	10	81	8.1	0

WILLIAMS, TANK　　　　　S　　　　　TITANS

PERSONAL: Born June 30, 1980, in Bay St. Louis, Miss. ... 6-3/223. ... Full name: Clevan Williams.
HIGH SCHOOL: Bay (Bay St. Louis, Miss.).
COLLEGE: Stanford.
TRANSACTIONS/CAREER NOTES: Selected by Tennesse Titans in second round (45th pick overall) of 2002 NFL draft. ... Signed by Titans (July 22, 2002).
CHAMPIONSHIP GAME EXPERIENCE: Played in AFC championship game (2002 season).

Year	Team	G	GS	TOTALS Tk.	Ast.	Sks.	INTERCEPTIONS No.	Yds.	Avg.	TD
2002—Tennessee NFL		16	16	46	15	2.0	1	0	0.0	0

WILLIAMS, TONY　　　　　DT　　　　　BENGALS

PERSONAL: Born July 9, 1975, in Germantown, Tenn. ... 6-1/294. ... Full name: Anthony Demetric Williams.
HIGH SCHOOL: Oakhaven (Memphis, Tenn.), then Germantown (Tenn.).
COLLEGE: Memphis.
TRANSACTIONS/CAREER NOTES: Selected by Minnesota Vikings in fifth round (151st pick overall) of 1997 NFL draft. ... Signed by Vikings (June 17, 1997). ... Granted free agency (February 11, 2000). ... Re-signed by Vikings (May 18, 2000). ... Granted unconditional free agency (March 2, 2001). ... Signed by Cincinnati Bengals (March 6, 2001).
CHAMPIONSHIP GAME EXPERIENCE: Played in NFC championship game (1998 and 2000 season).

Year	Team	G	GS	TOTALS Tk.	Ast.	Sks.
1997—Minnesota NFL		6	2	9	3	0.0
1998—Minnesota NFL		14	9	26	10	1.0
1999—Minnesota NFL		16	12	30	15	5.0
2000—Minnesota NFL		14	12	27	6	4.0
2001—Cincinnati NFL		13	13	15	23	5.0
2002—Cincinnati NFL		16	16	30	12	5.0
Pro totals (6 years)		79	64	137	69	20.0

WILLIAMS, TYRONE　　　　　CB　　　　　FALCONS

PERSONAL: Born May 31, 1973, in Bradenton, Fla. ... 5-11/193. ... Full name: Upton Tyrone Williams.
HIGH SCHOOL: Manatee (Bradenton, Fla.).
COLLEGE: Nebraska.
TRANSACTIONS/CAREER NOTES: Selected by Green Bay Packers in third round (93rd pick overall) of 1996 NFL draft. ... Signed by Packers (May 15, 1996). ... Granted free agency (February 12, 1999). ... Re-signed by Packers (May 17, 1999). ... Granted unconditional free agency (February 28, 2003). ... Signed by Atlanta Falcons (March 16, 2003).
CHAMPIONSHIP GAME EXPERIENCE: Played in NFC championship game (1996 and 1997 seasons). ... Member of Super Bowl championship team (1996 season). ... Played in Super Bowl XXXII (1997 season).

Year	Team	G	GS	TOTALS Tk.	Ast.	Sks.	INTERCEPTIONS No.	Yds.	Avg.	TD
1996—Green Bay NFL		16	0	22	3	0.0	0	0	0.0	0
1997—Green Bay NFL		16	15	49	17	0.0	1	0	0.0	0
1998—Green Bay NFL		16	16	61	8	0.0	5	40	8.0	0
1999—Green Bay NFL		16	16	53	12	0.0	4	12	3.0	0
2000—Green Bay NFL		16	16	50	8	0.0	4	105	26.3	1
2001—Green Bay NFL		16	16	77	12	0.0	4	117	29.3	1
2002—Green Bay NFL		15	15	60	9	1.0	1	0	0.0	0
Pro totals (7 years)		111	94	372	69	1.0	19	274	14.4	2

W

WILLIAMS, WALLY　　　　　G/OC

PERSONAL: Born February 20, 1971, in Tallahassee, Fla. ... 6-2/321. ... Full name: Wally James Williams Jr.
HIGH SCHOOL: James S. Rickards (Tallahassee, Fla.).
COLLEGE: Florida A&M.
TRANSACTIONS/CAREER NOTES: Signed as non-drafted free agent by Cleveland Browns (April 27, 1993). ... Browns franchise moved to Baltimore and renamed Ravens for 1996 season (March 11, 1996). ... Designated by Ravens as franchise player (February 13, 1998). ... Re-signed by Ravens (August 18, 1998). ... Granted unconditional free agency (February 12, 1999). ... Signed by New Orleans Saints (February 15, 1999). ... On injured reserve with neck injury (November 19, 1999-remainder of season). ... On suspended list for violating league substance abuse policy (November 9-December 7, 2002). ... Released by Saints (April 30, 2003).
PLAYING EXPERIENCE: Cleveland NFL, 1993-1995; Baltimore NFL, 1996-1998; New Orleans NFL, 1999-2002. ... Games/Games started: 1993 (2/0), 1994 (11/7), 1995 (16/16), 1996 (15/13), 1997 (10/10), 1998 (13/13), 1999 (6/6), 2000 (16/16), 2001 (15/15), 2002 (4/0). Total: 108/96.

WILLIAMS, WILLIE   CB   SEAHAWKS

PERSONAL: Born December 26, 1970, in Columbia, S.C. ... 5-9/182. ... Full name: Willie James Williams Jr.
HIGH SCHOOL: Spring Valley (Columbia, S.C.).
COLLEGE: Western Carolina.
TRANSACTIONS/CAREER NOTES: Selected by Pittsburgh Steelers in sixth round (162nd pick overall) of 1993 NFL draft. ... Signed by Steelers (July 9, 1993). ... Granted free agency (February 16, 1996). ... Re-signed by Steelers (June 12, 1996). ... Granted unconditional free agency (February 14, 1997). ... Signed by Seattle Seahawks (February 18, 1997). ... Granted unconditional free agency (March 2, 2001). ... Re-signed by Seahawks (May 3, 2001). ... Granted unconditional free agency (February 28, 2003). ... Re-signed by Seahawks (May 5, 2003).
CHAMPIONSHIP GAME EXPERIENCE: Played in AFC championship game (1994 and 1995 seasons). ... Played in Super Bowl XXX (1995 season).

			TOTALS			INTERCEPTIONS			
Year—Team	G	GS	Tk.	Ast.	Sks.	No.	Yds.	Avg.	TD
1993—Pittsburgh NFL	16	0	7	2	0.0	0	0	0.0	0
1994—Pittsburgh NFL	16	1	3	0	0.0	0	0	0.0	0
1995—Pittsburgh NFL	16	15	69	8	0.0	§7	122	17.4	▲1
1996—Pittsburgh NFL	15	14	66	10	1.0	1	1	1.0	0
1997—Seattle NFL	16	16	58	9	0.0	1	0	0.0	0
1998—Seattle NFL	14	14	53	13	0.0	2	36	18.0	1
1999—Seattle NFL	15	14	66	6	0.0	5	43	8.6	1
2000—Seattle NFL	16	15	51	9	1.0	4	74	18.5	1
2001—Seattle NFL	14	14	60	12	0.0	4	24	6.0	0
2002—Seattle NFL	15	1	21	4	1.0	1	2	2.0	0
Pro totals (10 years)	153	104	454	73	3.0	25	302	12.1	4

WILLIG, MATT   OT

PERSONAL: Born January 21, 1969, in Santa Fe Springs, Calif. ... 6-8/315. ... Full name: Matthew Joseph Willig.
HIGH SCHOOL: St. Paul (Santa Fe Springs, Calif.).
COLLEGE: Southern California.
TRANSACTIONS/CAREER NOTES: Signed as non-drafted free agent by New York Jets (May 5, 1992). ... Released by Jets (August 24, 1992). ... Re-signed by Jets to practice squad (September 2, 1992). ... Activated (December 24, 1992). ... Active for one game (1992); did not play. ... Signed by Jets (February 14, 1995). ... Released by Jets (April 23, 1996). ... Signed by Atlanta Falcons (May 2, 1996). ... Granted unconditional free agency (February 13, 1998). ... Signed by Green Bay Packers (May 5, 1998). ... Released by Packers (February 23, 1999). ... Signed by Cleveland Browns (August 17, 1999). ... Released by Browns (September 5, 1999). ... Signed by St. Louis Rams (November 30, 1999). ... Granted unconditional free agency (February 11, 2000). ... Signed by San Francisco 49ers (June 7, 2000). ... Granted unconditional free agency (March 1, 2002). ... Re-signed by 49ers (March 7, 2002). ... Granted unconditional free agency (February 28, 2003).
PLAYING EXPERIENCE: New York Jets NFL, 1993-1995; Atlanta NFL, 1996 and 1997; Green Bay NFL, 1998; San Francisco NFL, 2000-2002. ... Games/Games started: 1993 (3/0), 1994 (16/3), 1995 (15/12), 1996 (12/0), 1997 (16/13), 1998 (16/0), 2000 (16/3), 2001 (15/0), 2002 (11/3). Total: 120/34.
CHAMPIONSHIP GAME EXPERIENCE: Member of Rams for NFC championship game (1999 season); inactive. ... Member of Super Bowl championship team (1999 season); inactive.

WILLIS, DONALD   G   CHIEFS

PERSONAL: Born July 15, 1973, in Goleta, Calif. ... 6-3/325. ... Full name: Donald Kirk Willis.
HIGH SCHOOL: Cabrillo (Lompoc, Calif.).
COLLEGE: Washington, then North Carolina A&T.
TRANSACTIONS/CAREER NOTES: Signed as non-drafted free agent by Seattle Seahawks (April 27, 1995). ... Claimed on waivers by New Orleans Saints (December 1, 1995). ... Inactive for 16 games (1995). ... Released by Saints (September 8, 1997). ... Signed by Tampa Bay Buccaneers (December 30, 1997). ... Released by Buccaneers (August 30, 1998). ... Signed by Kansas City Chiefs (March 12, 1999). ... Released by Chiefs (September 6, 1999). ... Re-signed by Chiefs (March 6, 2000). ... Granted unconditional free agency (March 1, 2002). ... Re-signed by Chiefs (April 4, 2002).
PLAYING EXPERIENCE: New Orleans NFL, 1996; Kansas City NFL, 2000-2002. ... Games/Games started: 1996 (4/0), 2000 (16/2), 2001 (14/4), 2002 (13/0). Total: 47/6.

WILSON, ADRIAN   DB   CARDINALS

W

PERSONAL: Born October 12, 1979, in High Point, N.C. ... 6-3/217.
HIGH SCHOOL: T.W. Andrews (High Point, N.C.).
COLLEGE: North Carolina State.
TRANSACTIONS/CAREER NOTES: Selected after junior season by Arizona Cardinals in third round (64th pick overall) of 2001 NFL draft. ... Signed by Cardinals (July 24, 2001).

			TOTALS			INTERCEPTIONS			
Year—Team	G	GS	Tk.	Ast.	Sks.	No.	Yds.	Avg.	TD
2001—Arizona NFL	16	0	15	7	0.5	2	97	48.5	1
2002—Arizona NFL	14	14	66	27	1.5	4	35	8.8	0
Pro totals (2 years)	30	14	81	34	2.0	6	132	22.0	1

WILSON, AL   LB   BRONCOS

PERSONAL: Born June 21, 1977, in Jackson, Tenn. ... 6-0/240. ... Full name: Aldra Kauwa Wilson.
HIGH SCHOOL: Central Merry (Jackson, Tenn.).
COLLEGE: Tennessee.

TRANSACTIONS/CAREER NOTES: Selected by Denver Broncos in first round (31st pick overall) of NFL draft. ... Signed by Broncos (July 21, 1999).

HONORS: Named inside linebacker on The Sporting News college All-America second team (1998). ... Played in Pro Bowl (2001 season). ... Named to play in Pro Bowl (2002 season); replaced by Kendrell Bell due to injury.

			TOTALS			INTERCEPTIONS			
Year Team	G	GS	Tk.	Ast.	Sks.	No.	Yds.	Avg.	TD
1999—Denver NFL	16	12	58	16	1.0	0	0	0.0	0
2000—Denver NFL	15	14	47	13	5.0	3	21	7.0	0
2001—Denver NFL	16	16	72	13	3.0	0	0	0.0	0
2002—Denver NFL	16	15	100	32	5.0	0	0	0.0	0
Pro totals (4 years)	63	57	277	74	14.0	3	21	7.0	0

WILSON, ANTONIO LB TEXANS

PERSONAL: Born December 29, 1977, in Seagoville, Texas. ... 6-2/247.
HIGH SCHOOL: Skyline (Dallas).
COLLEGE: Texas A&M-Commerce.
TRANSACTIONS/CAREER NOTES: Selected by Minnesota Vikings in fourth round (106th pick overall) of 2000 NFL draft. ... Signed by Vikings (July 21, 2000). ... Assigned by Vikings to Barcelona Dragons in 2001 NFL Europe enhancement allocation program (February 19, 2001). ... Released by Vikings (September 2, 2001). ... Re-signed by Vikings to practice squad (September 4, 2001). ... Activated (October 9, 2001). ... Released by Vikings (October 25, 2001). ... Re-signed by Vikings (October 30, 2001). ... Released by Vikings (September 17, 2002). ... Re-signed by Vikings (September 24, 2002). ... Granted free agency (February 28, 2003). ... Re-signed by Texans (March 20, 2003).
CHAMPIONSHIP GAME EXPERIENCE: Member of Vikings for NFC championship game (2000 season); inactive.

			TOTALS			INTERCEPTIONS			
Year Team	G	GS	Tk.	Ast.	Sks.	No.	Yds.	Avg.	TD
2000—Minnesota NFL	1	0	0	0	0.0	0	0	0.0	0
2001—Barcelona NFLE	...	...	...	...	2.0	1	6	6.0	0
—Minnesota NFL	10	0	4	3	0.0	0	0	0.0	0
2002—Minnesota NFL	5	1	3	2	0.0	0	0	0.0	0
NFL Europe totals (1 year)	...	...	...	...	2.0	1	6	6.0	0
NFL totals (3 years)	16	1	7	5	0.0	0	0	0.0	0
Pro totals (4 years)	...	...	...	...	2.0	1	6	6.0	0

WILSON, CEDRICK WR/KR 49ERS

PERSONAL: Born December 17, 1978, in Memphis, Tenn. ... 5-10/183.
HIGH SCHOOL: Melrose (Memphis, Tenn.).
COLLEGE: Tennessee.
TRANSACTIONS/CAREER NOTES: Selected by San Francisco 49ers in sixth round (169th pick overall) of 2001 NFL draft. ... Signed by 49ers (July 24, 2001).
SINGLE GAME HIGHS (regular season): Receptions—4 (December 21, 2002, vs. Arizona); yards—56 (December 21, 2002, vs. Arizona); and touchdown receptions—1 (November 3, 2002, vs. Oakland).

			RECEIVING				PUNT RETURNS				KICKOFF RETURNS				TOTALS			
Year Team	G	GS	No.	Yds.	Avg.	TD	No.	Yds.	Avg.	TD	No.	Yds.	Avg.	TD	TD	2pt.	Pts.	Fum.
2001—San Francisco NFL	6	0	0	0	0.0	0	2	4	2.0	0	6	127	21.2	0	0	0	0	0
2002—San Francisco NFL	16	0	15	166	11.1	1	8	59	7.4	0	10	195	19.5	0	1	0	6	0
Pro totals (2 years)	22	0	15	166	11.1	1	10	63	6.3	0	16	322	20.1	0	1	0	6	0

WILSON, JERRY CB CHARGERS

PERSONAL: Born July 17, 1973, in Alexandria, La. ... 5-10/190. ... Full name: Jerry Lee Wilson Jr.
HIGH SCHOOL: La Grange (Lake Charles, La.).
COLLEGE: Southern (degree in rehabilitation counseling).
TRANSACTIONS/CAREER NOTES: Selected by Tampa Bay Buccaneers in fourth round (105th pick overall) of 1995 NFL draft. ... Signed by Buccaneers (May 9, 1995). ... On injured reserve with knee injury (August 31, 1995-entire season). ... Released by Buccaneers (August 20, 1996). ... Signed by Miami Dolphins to practice squad (October 29, 1996). ... Activated (November 5, 1996). ... Granted unconditional free agency (March 2, 2001). ... Signed by New Orleans Saints (January 2, 2002). ... Granted unconditional free agency (March 1, 2002). ... Re-signed by Saints (May 2, 2002). ... Released by Saints (September 1, 2002). ... Re-signed by Saints (September 10, 2002). ... Released by Saints (November 12, 2002). ... Signed by San Diego Chargers (November 19, 2002). ... Granted unconditional free agency (February 28, 2003). ... Re-signed by Chargers (March 17, 2003).

W

			TOTALS			INTERCEPTIONS			
Year Team	G	GS	Tk.	Ast.	Sks.	No.	Yds.	Avg.	TD
1996—Miami NFL	2	0	0	0	0.0	0	0	0.0	0
1997—Miami NFL	16	0	9	1	2.0	0	0	0.0	0
1998—Miami NFL	16	0	13	2	0.0	1	0	0.0	0
1999—Miami NFL	16	1	14	1	3.0	1	13	13.0	0
2000—Miami NFL	16	0	30	9	0.5	1	19	19.0	0
2001—New Orleans NFL	1	0	0	0	0.0	0	0	0.0	0
2002—New Orleans NFL	7	0	4	0	0.0	0	0	0.0	0
—San Diego NFL	5	0	3	0	0.0	0	0	0.0	0
Pro totals (7 years)	79	1	73	13	5.5	3	32	10.7	0

WILSON, REINARD — DE — BENGALS

PERSONAL: Born December 17, 1973, in Lake City, Fla. ... 6-2/270. ... Cousin of Brian Allen, linebacker, Houston Texans. ... Name pronounced ruh-NARD.
HIGH SCHOOL: Columbia (Lake City, Fla.).
COLLEGE: Florida State.
TRANSACTIONS/CAREER NOTES: Selected by Cincinnati Bengals in first round (14th pick overall) of 1997 NFL draft. ... Signed by Bengals (July 18, 1997). ... Granted unconditional free agency (March 1, 2002). ... Re-signed by Bengals (March 28, 2002).
HONORS: Named defensive end on THE SPORTING NEWS college All-America second team (1996).

				TOTALS	
Year Team	G	GS	Tk.	Ast.	Sks.
1997—Cincinnati NFL	16	3	22	2	3.0
1998—Cincinnati NFL	16	15	47	17	6.0
1999—Cincinnati NFL	15	0	14	7	3.0
2000—Cincinnati NFL	14	0	9	6	3.0
2001—Cincinnati NFL	16	5	27	9	9.0
2002—Cincinnati NFL	16	0	11	2	0.0
Pro totals (6 years)	93	23	130	43	24.0

WINBORN, JAMIE — LB — 49ERS

PERSONAL: Born May 14, 1979, in Wetumpka, Ala. ... 5-11/242.
HIGH SCHOOL: Wetumpka (Ala.).
COLLEGE: Vanderbilt.
TRANSACTIONS/CAREER NOTES: Selected after junior season by San Francisco 49ers in second round (47th pick overall) of 2001 NFL draft. ... Signed by 49ers (July 25, 2001). ... On injured reserve with knee injury (January 2, 2003-remainder of season).

			TOTALS			INTERCEPTIONS			
Year Team	G	GS	Tk.	Ast.	Sks.	No.	Yds.	Avg.	TD
2001—San Francisco NFL	14	4	34	11	0.5	2	40	20.0	0
2002—San Francisco NFL	3	3	18	6	1.0	0	0	0.0	0
Pro totals (2 years)	17	7	52	17	1.5	2	40	20.0	0

WINFIELD, ANTOINE — CB — BILLS

PERSONAL: Born June 24, 1977, in Akron, Ohio. ... 5-9/180. ... Full name: Antoine D. Winfield.
HIGH SCHOOL: Garfield (Ohio).
COLLEGE: Ohio State.
TRANSACTIONS/CAREER NOTES: Selected by Buffalo Bills in first round (23rd pick overall) of 1999 NFL draft. ... Signed by Bills (July 30, 1999). ... On injured reserve list with shoulder injury (November 22, 2000-remainder of season).
HONORS: Named cornerback on THE SPORTING NEWS college All-America second team (1997). ... Jim Thorpe Award winner (1998). ... Named cornerback on THE SPORTING NEWS college All-America first team (1998).

			TOTALS			INTERCEPTIONS			
Year Team	G	GS	Tk.	Ast.	Sks.	No.	Yds.	Avg.	TD
1999—Buffalo NFL	16	2	38	1	0.0	2	13	6.5	0
2000—Buffalo NFL	11	11	34	8	0.0	1	8	8.0	0
2001—Buffalo NFL	16	16	69	12	0.0	2	0	0.0	0
2002—Buffalo NFL	13	13	51	5	0.0	0	0	0.0	0
Pro totals (4 years)	56	42	192	26	0.0	5	21	4.2	0

WINTERS, FRANK — C — PACKERS

PERSONAL: Born January 23, 1964, in Hoboken, N.J. ... 6-3/305. ... Full name: Frank Mitchell Winters.
HIGH SCHOOL: Emerson (Union City, N.J.).
JUNIOR COLLEGE: College of Eastern Utah.
COLLEGE: Western Illinois (degree in political science administration, 1987).
TRANSACTIONS/CAREER NOTES: Selected by Cleveland Browns in 10th round (276th pick overall) of 1987 NFL draft. ... Signed by Browns (July 25, 1987). ... Granted unconditional free agency (February 1, 1989). ... Signed by New York Giants (March 17, 1989). ... Granted unconditional free agency (February 1, 1990). ... Signed by Kansas City Chiefs (March 26, 1990). ... Granted unconditional free agency (February 1, 1992). ... Signed by Green Bay Packers (March 17, 1992). ... Granted unconditional free agency (February 17, 1994). ... Re-signed by Packers (April 1, 1994). ... Granted unconditional free agency (February 14, 1997). ... Re-signed by Packers (March 26, 1997). ... On injured reserve with leg injury (December 16, 1998-remainder of season). ... Granted unconditional free agency (February 11, 2000). ... Re-signed by Packers (April 4, 2000). ... Re-signed by Packers (May 1, 2003).
PLAYING EXPERIENCE: Cleveland NFL, 1987 and 1988; New York Giants NFL, 1989; Kansas City NFL, 1990 and 1991; Green Bay NFL, 1992-2002. ... Games/Games started: 1987 (12/0), 1988 (16/0), 1989 (15/0), 1990 (16/6), 1991 (16/0), 1992 (16/11), 1993 (16/16), 1994 (16/16), 1995 (16/16), 1996 (16/15), 1997 (13/13), 1998 (13/13), 1999 (16/16), 2000 (14/14), 2001 (4/0), 2002 (16/10). Total: 233/146.
CHAMPIONSHIP GAME EXPERIENCE: Played in AFC championship game (1987 season). ... Played in NFC championship game (1995-97 seasons). ... Member of Super Bowl championship team (1996 season). ... Played in Super Bowl XXXII (1997 season).
HONORS: Played in Pro Bowl (1996 season).

WIRE, COY — S — BILLS

PERSONAL: Born November 7, 1978, in Camp Hill, Pa. ... 6-0/209.
COLLEGE: Stanford.
TRANSACTIONS/CAREER NOTES: Selected by Buffalo Bills in third round (97th pick overall) of 2002 NFL draft. ... Signed by Bills (July 3, 2002).

W

Year	Team	G	GS	Tk.	Ast.	Sks.	No.	Yds.	Avg.	TD	No.	Yds.	Avg.	TD	TD	2pt.	Pts.	Fum.
				TOTALS			**INTERCEPTIONS**				**KICKOFF RETURNS**				**TOTALS**			
2002—Buffalo NFL		16	15	67	25	3.0	0	0	0.0	0	0	0	0.0	0	0	0	0	0

WISNE, JERRY OT PACKERS

PERSONAL: Born July 28, 1976, in Rochester, Minn. ... 6-6/315. ... Full name: Gerald Edward Wisne. ... Name pronounced WHIZ-knee.
HIGH SCHOOL: Jenks (Tulsa, Okla.).
COLLEGE: Notre Dame.
TRANSACTIONS/CAREER NOTES: Selected by Chicago Bears in fifth round (143rd pick overall) of 1999 NFL draft. ... Signed by Bears (May 26, 1999). ... Released by Bears (September 1, 2001). ... Signed by Minnesota Vikings (September 4, 2001). ... Released by Vikings (September 11, 2001). ... Signed by Houston Texans (December 29, 2001). ... Released by Texans (August 25, 2002). ... Signed by St. Louis Rams (November 27, 2002). ... Claimed on waivers by Green Bay Packers (December 9, 2002).
PLAYING EXPERIENCE: Chicago NFL, 1999; Green Bay NFL, 2002. ... Games/Games started: 1999 (7/1), 2002 (2/0). Total: 9/1.

WISTROM, GRANT DE RAMS

PERSONAL: Born July 3, 1976, in Webb City, Mo. ... 6-4/272. ... Full name: Grant Alden Wistrom.
HIGH SCHOOL: Webb City (Mo.).
COLLEGE: Nebraska.
TRANSACTIONS/CAREER NOTES: Selected by St. Louis Rams in first round (sixth pick overall) of 1998 NFL draft. ... Signed by Rams (July 18, 1998).
CHAMPIONSHIP GAME EXPERIENCE: Played in NFC championship game (1999 and 2001 seasons). ... Member of Super Bowl championship team (1999 season). ... Played in Super Bowl XXXVI (2001 season).
HONORS: Named defensive end on THE SPORTING NEWS college All-America first team (1996 and 1997).

Year	Team	G	GS	Tk.	Ast.	Sks.	No.	Yds.	Avg.	TD
				TOTALS			**INTERCEPTIONS**			
1998—St. Louis NFL		13	0	14	6	3.0	0	0	0.0	0
1999—St. Louis NFL		16	16	33	6	6.5	2	131	65.5	†2
2000—St. Louis NFL		16	16	51	12	11.0	0	0	0.0	0
2001—St. Louis NFL		15	15	47	9	9.0	2	-4	-2.0	0
2002—St. Louis NFL		15	14	45	2	4.5	1	2	2.0	0
Pro totals (5 years)		75	61	190	35	34.0	5	129	25.8	2

WITHERSPOON, WILL LB PANTHERS

PERSONAL: Born August 19, 1980, in Panama City, Fla. ... 6-1/234. ... Full name: William Cordell Witherspoon.
HIGH SCHOOL: Rutherford (Panama City, Fla.).
COLLEGE: Georgia.
TRANSACTIONS/CAREER NOTES: Selected by Carolina Panthers in third round (73rd pick overall) of 2002 NFL draft. ... Signed by Panthers (June 20, 2002).

Year	Team	G	GS	Tk.	Ast.	Sks.	No.	Yds.	Avg.	TD
				TOTALS			**INTERCEPTIONS**			
2002—Carolina NFL		15	8	49	14	1.5	0	0	0.0	0

WITHROW, CORY C VIKINGS

PERSONAL: Born April 5, 1975, in Spokane, Wash. ... 6-2/281.
HIGH SCHOOL: Mead (Spokane, Wash.).
COLLEGE: Washington State.
TRANSACTIONS/CAREER NOTES: Signed as non-drafted free agent by Minnesota Vikings (April 23, 1998). ... Released by Vikings (August 30, 1998). ... Signed by Cincinnati Bengals to practice squad (December 18, 1998). ... Released by Bengals (April 15, 1999). ... Signed by Vikings (April 30, 1999). ... Released by Vikings (September 5, 1999). ... Re-signed by Vikings to practice squad (September 6, 1999). ... Activated (October 26, 1999); did not play. ... Released by Vikings (November 30, 1999). ... Re-signed by Vikings to practice squad (December 1, 1999). ... Granted free agency (February 28, 2003). ... Re-signed by Vikings (April 9, 2003).
PLAYING EXPERIENCE: Minnesota NFL, 2000-2002. ... Games/Games started: 2000 (12/0), 2001 (16/1), 2002 (16/0). Total: 44/1.
CHAMPIONSHIP GAME EXPERIENCE: Played in NFC championship game (2000 season).

WOFFORD, JAMES RB VIKINGS

PERSONAL: Born June 6, 1978, in Bakersfield, Calif. ... 6-0/186.
HIGH SCHOOL: Bakersfield (Calif.).
COLLEGE: UNLV.
TRANSACTIONS/CAREER NOTES: Signed as non-drafted free agent by Minnesota Vikings (April 30, 2001). ... Released by Vikings (September 2, 2001). ... Re-signed by Vikings (January 16, 2002).

Year	Team	G	GS	Att.	Yds.	Avg.	TD	No.	Yds.	Avg.	TD	TD	2pt.	Pts.	Fum.
				RUSHING				**KICKOFF RETURNS**				**TOTALS**			
2002—Minnesota NFL		9	0	0	0	0.0	0	3	62	20.7	0	0	0	0	0

W

WOHLABAUGH, DAVE   C   RAMS

PERSONAL: Born April 13, 1972, in Hamburg, N.Y. ... 6-3/296. ... Full name: David Vincent Wohlabaugh. ... Name pronounced WOOL-uh-buh.
HIGH SCHOOL: Frontier (Hamburg, N.Y.).
COLLEGE: Syracuse.
TRANSACTIONS/CAREER NOTES: Selected by New England Patriots in fourth round (112th pick overall) of 1995 NFL draft. ... Signed by Patriots (June 26, 1995). ... Granted free agency (February 13, 1998). ... Re-signed by Patriots (May 28, 1998). ... Granted unconditional free agency (February 12, 1999). ... Signed by Cleveland Browns (February 16, 1999). ... Released by Browns (February 26, 2003). ... Signed by St. Louis Rams (February 28, 2003).
PLAYING EXPERIENCE: New England NFL, 1995-1998; Cleveland NFL, 1999-2002. ... Games/Games started: 1995 (11/11), 1996 (16/16), 1997 (14/14), 1998 (16/16), 1999 (15/15), 2000 (12/12), 2001 (16/16), 2002 (12/12). Total: 112/112.
CHAMPIONSHIP GAME EXPERIENCE: Played in AFC championship game (1996 season). ... Played in Super Bowl XXXI (1996 season).

WOMACK, FLOYD   OT   SEAHAWKS

PERSONAL: Born November 15, 1978, in Cleveland, Miss. ... 6-4/333. ... Full name: Floyd Seneca Womack.
HIGH SCHOOL: East Side (Cleveland, Miss.).
COLLEGE: Mississippi State.
TRANSACTIONS/CAREER NOTES: Selected by Seattle Seahawks in fourth round (128th pick overall) of 2001 NFL draft. ... Signed by Seahawks (June 22, 2001).
PLAYING EXPERIENCE: Seattle NFL, 2001-2002. ... Games/Games started: 2001 (6/0), 2002 (11/10). Total: 17/10.

WONG, KAILEE   LB   TEXANS

PERSONAL: Born May 23, 1976, in Eugene, Ore. ... 6-2/250.
HIGH SCHOOL: North Eugene (Ore.).
COLLEGE: Stanford.
TRANSACTIONS/CAREER NOTES: Selected by Minnesota Vikings in second round (51st pick overall) of 1998 NFL draft. ... Signed by Vikings (July 25, 1998). ... On injured reserve with leg injury (December 31, 1998-remainder of season). ... Granted free agency (March 2, 2001). ... Re-signed by Vikings (April 16, 2001). ... Granted unconditional free agency (March 1, 2002). ... Signed by Houston Texans (March 7, 2002).
CHAMPIONSHIP GAME EXPERIENCE: Played in NFC championship game (2000 season).

Year Team	G	GS	TOTALS			INTERCEPTIONS			
			Tk.	Ast.	Sks.	No.	Yds.	Avg.	TD
1998—Minnesota NFL	15	0	12	2	1.5	0	0	0.0	0
1999—Minnesota NFL	13	8	34	12	0.0	0	0	0.0	0
2000—Minnesota NFL	16	16	83	28	2.0	2	28	14.0	0
2001—Minnesota NFL	16	16	83	16	3.0	1	27	27.0	1
2002—Houston NFL	16	16	34	10	5.5	0	0	0.0	0
Pro totals (5 years)	76	56	246	68	12.0	3	55	18.3	1

WOODARD, CEDRIC   DT   SEAHAWKS

PERSONAL: Born September 5, 1977, in Bay City, Texas. ... 6-2/320. ... Full name: Cedric Darnell Woodard. ... Cousin of Tracy Simien, linebacker with Pittsburgh Steelers (1989), Kansas City Chiefs (1991-97) and San Diego Chargers (1999); and cousin of Elmo Wright, wide receiver with Kansas City Chiefs (1971-74), Houston Oilers (1975) and New England Patriots (1975).
HIGH SCHOOL: Sweeny (Texas).
COLLEGE: Texas.
TRANSACTIONS/CAREER NOTES: Selected by Baltimore Ravens in sixth round (191st pick overall) of 2000 NFL draft. ... Signed by Ravens (June 15, 2000). ... Claimed on waivers by Seattle Seahawks (September 6, 2000). ... Granted free agency (February 28, 2003). ... Re-signed by Seahawks (April 9, 2003).

Year Team	G	GS	TOTALS		
			Tk.	Ast.	Sks.
2001—Seattle NFL	16	0	3	1	0.0
2002—Seattle NFL	12	0	0	1	0.0
Pro totals (2 years)	28	0	3	2	0.0

WOODBURY, TORY   WR   JETS

PERSONAL: Born July 12, 1978, in Winston-Salem, N.C. ... 6-2/208.
HIGH SCHOOL: Glenn (Winston-Salem, N.C.).
COLLEGE: Winston-Salem State.
TRANSACTIONS/CAREER NOTES: Signed as non-drafted free agent by New York Jets (April 26, 2001).
SINGLE GAME HIGHS (regular season): Receptions—1 (September 29, 2002, vs. Jacksonville); yards—13 (September 29, 2002, vs. Jacksonville); and touchdown receptions—0.

Year Team	G	GS	RECEIVING			
			No.	Yds.	Avg.	TD
2001—New York Jets NFL	10	0	0	0	0.0	0
2002—New York Jets NFL	2	0	1	13	13.0	0
Pro totals (2 years)	12	0	1	13	13.0	0

W

WOODEN, SHAWN   S   DOLPHINS

PERSONAL: Born October 23, 1973, in Philadelphia. ... 5-11/205. ... Full name: Shawn Anthony Wooden.
HIGH SCHOOL: Abington (Pa.).
COLLEGE: Notre Dame (degree in computer science).
TRANSACTIONS/CAREER NOTES: Selected by Miami Dolphins in sixth round (189th pick overall) of 1996 NFL draft. ... Signed by Dolphins (July 10, 1996). ... On injured reserve with knee injury (September 15, 1998-remainder of season). ... Granted free agency (February 12, 1999). ... Re-signed by Dolphins (April 23, 1999). ... Granted unconditional free agency (February 11, 2000). ... Signed by Chicago Bears (March 6, 2000). ... Released by Bears (June 26, 2001). ... Signed by Dolphins (June 29, 2001). ... Released by Dolphins (March 11, 2003). ... Re-signed by Dolphins (April 24, 2003).

			TOTALS			INTERCEPTIONS			
Year Team	G	GS	Tk.	Ast.	Sks.	No.	Yds.	Avg.	TD
1996—Miami NFL	16	11	54	13	0.0	2	15	7.5	0
1997—Miami NFL	16	15	56	27	0.0	2	10	5.0	0
1998—Miami NFL	2	1	10	0	0.0	0	0	0.0	0
1999—Miami NFL	15	6	36	15	0.0	0	0	0.0	0
2000—Chicago NFL	11	0	8	3	0.0	0	0	0.0	0
2001—Miami NFL	13	0	2	0	0.0	0	0	0.0	0
2002—Miami NFL	16	1	12	6	0.0	1	0	0.0	0
Pro totals (7 years)	89	34	178	64	0.0	5	25	5.0	0

WOODS, JEROME   S   CHIEFS

PERSONAL: Born March 17, 1973, in Memphis, Tenn. ... 6-2/207.
HIGH SCHOOL: Melrose (Memphis, Tenn.).
JUNIOR COLLEGE: Northeast Mississippi Community College.
COLLEGE: Memphis.
TRANSACTIONS/CAREER NOTES: Selected by Kansas City Chiefs in first round (28th pick overall) of 1996 NFL draft. ... Signed by Chiefs (August 12, 1996). ... Granted unconditional free agency (February 11, 2000). ... Re-signed by Chiefs (February 11, 2000). ... On injured reserve with broken leg (August 26, 2002-entire season).

			TOTALS			INTERCEPTIONS			
Year Team	G	GS	Tk.	Ast.	Sks.	No.	Yds.	Avg.	TD
1996—Kansas City NFL	16	0	5	1	0.0	0	0	0.0	0
1997—Kansas City NFL	16	16	67	19	1.0	4	57	14.3	0
1998—Kansas City NFL	16	16	56	25	0.0	2	47	23.5	0
1999—Kansas City NFL	15	15	70	9	0.0	1	5	5.0	0
2000—Kansas City NFL	16	16	74	8	2.0	2	0	0.0	0
2001—Kansas City NFL	16	16	74	13	1.0	3	48	16.0	0
2002—Kansas City NFL				Did not play.					
Pro totals (6 years)	95	79	346	75	4.0	12	157	13.1	0

WOODS, LEVAR   LB   CARDINALS

PERSONAL: Born March 15, 1978, in Larchwood, Iowa. ... 6-2/245.
HIGH SCHOOL: West Lyon (Inwood, Iowa).
COLLEGE: Iowa.
TRANSACTIONS/CAREER NOTES: Signed as non-drafted free agent by Arizona Cardinals (April 23, 2001). ... Re-signed by Cardinals (March 16, 2003).

			TOTALS			INTERCEPTIONS			
Year Team	G	GS	Tk.	Ast.	Sks.	No.	Yds.	Avg.	TD
2001—Arizona NFL	15	0	8	0	0.0	0	0	0.0	0
2002—Arizona NFL	15	2	22	7	0.5	0	0	0.0	0
Pro totals (2 years)	30	2	30	7	0.5	0	0	0.0	0

WOODSON, CHARLES   CB   RAIDERS

PERSONAL: Born October 7, 1976, in Fremont, Ohio. ... 6-1/200.
HIGH SCHOOL: Ross (Fremont, Ohio).
COLLEGE: Michigan.
TRANSACTIONS/CAREER NOTES: Selected after junior season by Oakland Raiders in first round (fourth pick overall) of 1998 NFL draft. ... Signed by Raiders (July 20, 1998).
CHAMPIONSHIP GAME EXPERIENCE: Played in AFC championship game (2000 and 2002 seasons). ... Played in Super Bowl XXXVII (2002 season).
HONORS: Named cornerback on THE SPORTING NEWS college All-America second team (1996). ... Heisman Trophy winner (1997). ... Jim Thorpe Award winner (1997). ... Maxwell Award winner (1997). ... Bronko Nagurski Award winner (1997). ... Named College Football Player of the Year by THE SPORTING NEWS (1997). ... Named cornerback on THE SPORTING NEWS college All-America first team (1997). ... Played in Pro Bowl (1998-2000 seasons). ... Named cornerback on THE SPORTING NEWS NFL All-Pro team (2001). ... Named to played in Pro Bowl (2001 season); replaced by Ty Law due to injury.

			TOTALS			INTERCEPTIONS				PUNT RETURNS				TOTALS		
Year Team	G	GS	Tk.	Ast.	Sks.	No.	Yds.	Avg.	TD	No.	Yds.	Avg.	TD	TD	2pt.	Pts.	Fum.
1998—Oakland NFL	16	16	61	3	0.0	5	118	23.6	1	0	0	0.0	0	1	0	6	0
1999—Oakland NFL	16	16	52	9	0.0	1	15	15.0	1	0	0	0.0	0	1	0	6	0
2000—Oakland NFL	16	16	66	13	0.0	4	36	9.0	0	0	0	0.0	0	0	0	0	0
2001—Oakland NFL	16	15	40	13	2.0	1	64	64.0	0	4	47	11.8	0	0	0	0	0
2002—Oakland NFL	8	7	35	2	0.0	1	3	3.0	0	4	6	1.5	0	0	0	0	0
Pro totals (5 years)	72	70	254	40	2.0	12	236	19.7	2	8	53	6.6	0	2	0	12	0

W

PERSONAL: Born April 25, 1969, in Phoenix. ... 6-1/219. ... Full name: Darren Ray Woodson.

HIGH SCHOOL: Maryvale (Phoenix).

COLLEGE: Arizona State (degree in criminal justice).

TRANSACTIONS/CAREER NOTES: Selected by Dallas Cowboys in second round (37th pick overall) of 1992 NFL draft. ... Signed by Cowboys (April 26, 1992). ... On injured reserve with broken forearm (December 14, 2000-remainder of season). ... Granted unconditional free agency (March 1, 2002). ... Re-signed by Cowboys (March 1, 2002). ... On injured reserve with abdominal injury (November 27, 2002-remainder of season).

CHAMPIONSHIP GAME EXPERIENCE: Played in NFC championship game (1992-1995 seasons). ... Member of Super Bowl championship team (1992, 1993 and 1995 seasons).

HONORS: Named strong safety on THE SPORTING NEWS NFL All-Pro team (1994-1996 and 1998). ... Played in Pro Bowl (1994-1996 and 1998 seasons). ... Named to play in Pro Bowl (1997 season); replaced by John Lynch due to injury.

Year Team	G	GS	TOTALS			INTERCEPTIONS			
			Tk.	Ast.	Sks.	No.	Yds.	Avg.	TD
1992—Dallas NFL	16	2	28	5	1.0	0	0	0.0	0
1993—Dallas NFL	16	15	89	66	0.0	0	0	0.0	0
1994—Dallas NFL	16	16	58	19	0.0	5	140	28.0	1
1995—Dallas NFL	16	16	84	11	0.0	2	46	23.0	1
1996—Dallas NFL	16	16	62	16	3.0	5	43	8.6	0
1997—Dallas NFL	14	14	53	20	2.0	1	14	14.0	0
1998—Dallas NFL	16	15	66	12	3.0	1	1	1.0	0
1999—Dallas NFL	15	15	59	10	1.0	2	5	2.5	0
2000—Dallas NFL	11	11	62	10	0.0	2	12	6.0	0
2001—Dallas NFL	16	16	70	11	0.0	3	11	3.7	0
2002—Dallas NFL	10	10	41	9	0.0	1	1	1.0	0
Pro totals (11 years)	162	146	672	189	10.0	22	273	12.4	2

PERSONAL: Born March 10, 1965, in Fort Wayne, Ind. ... 6-0/205. ... Full name: Roderick Kevin Woodson.

HIGH SCHOOL: R. Nelson Snider (Fort Wayne, Ind.).

COLLEGE: Purdue.

TRANSACTIONS/CAREER NOTES: Selected by Pittsburgh Steelers in first round (10th pick overall) of 1987 NFL draft. ... On reserve/unsigned list (August 31-October 27, 1987). ... Signed by Steelers (October 28, 1987). ... Granted roster exemption (October 28-November 7, 1987). ... Granted free agency (February 1, 1991). ... Re-signed by Steelers (August 22, 1991). ... Granted unconditional free agency (February 14, 1997). ... Signed by San Francisco 49ers (July 17, 1997). ... Released by 49ers (February 9, 1998). ... Signed by Baltimore Ravens (February 20, 1998). ... Granted unconditional free agency (March 2, 2001). ... Re-signed by Ravens (May 7, 2001). ... Released by Ravens (February 27, 2002). ... Signed by Oakland Raiders (April 30, 2002).

CHAMPIONSHIP GAME EXPERIENCE: Played in AFC championship game (1994, 2000 and 2002 seasons). ... Member of Steelers for AFC championship game (1995 season); inactive. ... Played in Super Bowl XXX (1995 season). ... Played in NFC championship game (1997 season). ... Member of Super Bowl championship team (2000 season). ... Played in Super Bowl XXXVII (2002 season).

HONORS: Named defensive back on THE SPORTING NEWS college All-America second team (1985). ... Named kick returner on THE SPORTING NEWS college All-America first team (1986). ... Named kick returner on THE SPORTING NEWS NFL All-Pro team (1989). ... Played in Pro Bowl (1989-1994, 1996, 1999-2002 seasons). ... Named cornerback on THE SPORTING NEWS NFL All-Pro team (1990 and 1992-1994).

RECORDS: Holds NFL career records for most yards on interceptions—1,465; and most touchdowns by interception return—12.

MISCELLANEOUS: Active AFC leader for career interceptions (66). ... Shares Baltimore Ravens all-time record for most interceptions (20).

Year Team	G	GS	TOTALS			INTERCEPTIONS				PUNT RETURNS				KICKOFF RETURNS				TOTALS			
			Tk.	Ast.	Sks.	No.	Yds.	Avg.	TD	No.	Yds.	Avg.	TD	No.	Yds.	Avg.	TD	TD	2pt.	Pts.	Fum.
1987—Pittsburgh NFL	8	0	15	5	0.0	1	45	45.0	1	16	135	8.4	0	13	290	22.3	0	1	0	6	3
1988—Pittsburgh NFL	16	16	78	10	0.5	4	98	24.5	0	33	281	8.5	0	37	850	23.0	†1	1	0	6	3
1989—Pittsburgh NFL	15	14	67	13	0.0	3	39	13.0	0	29	207	7.1	0	§36	§982	*27.3	†1	1	0	6	3
1990—Pittsburgh NFL	16	16	54	12	0.0	5	67	13.4	0	§38	§398	10.5	†1	35	764	21.8	0	1	0	6	3
1991—Pittsburgh NFL	15	15	60	11	1.0	3	72	24.0	0	28	320	§11.4	0	*44	§880	20.0	0	0	0	0	3
1992—Pittsburgh NFL	16	16	85	15	6.0	4	90	22.5	0	32	364	§11.4	1	25	469	18.8	0	1	0	6	2
1993—Pittsburgh NFL	16	16	79	16	2.0	8	§138	17.3	▲1	42	338	8.0	0	15	294	19.6	0	1	0	6	2
1994—Pittsburgh NFL	15	15	67	16	3.0	4	109	27.3	2	39	319	8.2	0	15	365	24.3	0	2	0	12	2
1995—Pittsburgh NFL	1	1	0	1	0.0	0	0	0.0	0	0	0	0.0	0	0	0	0.0	0	0	0	0	0
1996—Pittsburgh NFL	16	16	57	10	1.0	6	121	20.2	1	0	0	0.0	0	0	0	0.0	0	2	0	12	1
1997—San Francisco NFL	14	14	43	5	0.0	3	81	27.0	0	1	0	0.0	0	0	0	0.0	0	0	0	0	0
1998—Baltimore NFL	16	16	76	12	0.0	6	108	18.0	▲2	0	0	0.0	0	0	0	0.0	0	2	0	12	0
1999—Baltimore NFL	16	16	54	12	0.0	†7	195	27.9	†2	2	0	0.0	0	0	0	0.0	0	2	0	12	1
2000—Baltimore NFL	16	16	67	10	0.0	4	20	5.0	0	0	0	0.0	0	0	0	0.0	0	0	0	0	0
2001—Baltimore NFL	16	16	56	20	0.0	3	57	19.0	1	0	0	0.0	0	0	0	0.0	0	1	0	6	0
2002—Oakland NFL	16	16	70	12	0.0	†8	§225	28.1	▲2	0	0	0.0	0	0	0	0.0	0	2	0	12	0
Pro totals (16 years)	228	219	928	180	13.5	69	1465	21.2	12	260	2362	9.1	2	220	4894	22.2	2	17	0	102	23

PERSONAL: Born November 3, 1977, in Beaverdam, Va. ... 6-3/320. ... Full name: Damien Michael Woody.

HIGH SCHOOL: Patrick Henry (Beaverdam, Va.).

COLLEGE: Boston College.

W

TRANSACTIONS/CAREER NOTES: Selected after junior season by New England Patriots in first round (17th pick overall) of 1999 NFL draft. ... Signed by Patriots (July 30, 1999).
PLAYING EXPERIENCE: New England NFL, 1999-2002. ... Games/Games started: 1999 (16/16), 2000 (16/16), 2001 (16/15), 2002 (16/15). Total: 64/62.
CHAMPIONSHIP GAME EXPERIENCE: Played in AFC championship game (2001 season). ... Member of Super Bowl championship team (2001 season).
HONORS: Played in Pro Bowl (2002 season).

WORD, MARK   DE   BROWNS

PERSONAL: Born November 23, 1975, in Miami. ... 6-5/275. ... Full name: Mark Bernard Word.
HIGH SCHOOL: Southridge (Miami).
JUNIOR COLLEGE: Hinds Community College (Miss.).
COLLEGE: Jacksonville State.
TRANSACTIONS/CAREER NOTES: Signed as non-drafted free agent by Kansas City Chiefs (April 20, 1999). ... Released by Chiefs (August 27, 2000). ... Signed by Hamilton Tiger-Cats of CFL (September 3, 2000). ... Signed by St. Louis Rams (January 12, 2001). ... Assigned by Rams to Rhein Fire in 2001 NFL Europe enhancement allocation program (February 19, 2001). ... Released by Rams (July 2, 2001). ... Signed by Cleveland Browns (July 20, 2001). ... Released by Browns (August 22, 2001). ... Signed by Hamilton Tiger-Cats of CFL (August 22, 2001). ... Re-signed by Browns (August 31, 2001). ... On injured reserve with shoulder injury (September 1, 2001-entire season).

			TOTALS		
Year Team	G	GS	Tk.	Ast.	Sks.
1999—Kansas City NFL	6	0	0	0	0.0
2001—Rhein NFLE	...	...	...	...	5.0
2002—Cleveland NFL	16	2	18	3	8.0
NFL Europe totals (1 year)	...	...	...	...	5.0
NFL totals (2 years)	22	2	18	3	8.0
Pro totals (3 years)	...	...	...	...	13.0

WRAGGE, TONY   G   CARDINALS

PERSONAL: Born August 14, 1979, in Creighton, Neb. ... 6-4/311. ... Full name: Tony James Wragge.
HIGH SCHOOL: Bloomfield Community (Creighton, Neb.).
COLLEGE: New Mexico State.
TRANSACTIONS/CAREER NOTES: Signed as non-drafted free agent by Arizona Cardinals (April 22, 2002). ... Released by Cardinals (August 26, 2002). ... Re-signed by Cardinals to practice squad (October 30, 2002). ... Activated (November 23, 2002). ... Re-signed by Cardinals (April 2, 2003).
PLAYING EXPERIENCE: Arizona NFL, 2002. ... Games/Games started: 2002 (2/1).

WRIGHT, KENNY   CB   TEXANS

PERSONAL: Born September 14, 1977, in Ruston, La. ... 6-1/205. ... Full name: Kenneth D. Wright.
HIGH SCHOOL: Ruston (La.).
COLLEGE: Arkansas, then Northwestern (La.) State.
TRANSACTIONS/CAREER NOTES: Selected after junior season by Minnesota Vikings in fourth round (120th pick overall) of 1999 NFL draft. ... Signed by Vikings (July 21, 1999). ... Granted free agency (March 1, 2002). ... Re-signed by Vikings (April 16, 2002). ... Claimed on waivers by Houston Texans (August 1, 2002). ... Re-signed by Texans (April 2, 2003).
CHAMPIONSHIP GAME EXPERIENCE: Member of Vikings for NFC championship game (2000 season); inactive.

			TOTALS			INTERCEPTIONS			
Year Team	G	GS	Tk.	Ast.	Sks.	No.	Yds.	Avg.	TD
1999—Minnesota NFL	16	12	64	10	0.0	1	11	11.0	0
2000—Minnesota NFL	16	7	34	6	0.0	0	0	0.0	0
2001—Minnesota NFL	15	8	34	5	0.0	0	0	0.0	0
2002—Houston NFL	16	0	24	5	1.0	0	0	0.0	0
Pro totals (4 years)	63	27	156	26	1.0	1	11	11.0	0

WUERFFEL, DANNY   QB

W

PERSONAL: Born May 27, 1974, in Pensacola, Fla. ... 6-1/212. ... Full name: Daniel Carl Wuerffel. ... Name pronounced WER-ful.
HIGH SCHOOL: Fort Walton Beach (Fla.).
COLLEGE: Florida.
TRANSACTIONS/CAREER NOTES: Selected by New Orleans Saints in fourth round (99th pick overall) of 1997 NFL draft. ... Signed by Saints (July 17, 1997). ... Released by Saints (February 11, 2000). ... Signed by Green Bay Packers (July 5, 2000). ... Granted unconditional free agency (March 2, 2001). ... Signed by Chicago Bears (July 10, 2001). ... Selected by Houston Texans from Bears in NFL expansion draft (February 18, 2002). ... Traded by Texans to Washington Redskins for DT Jerry DeLoach (March 4, 2002). ... Granted unconditional free agency (February 28, 2003).
HONORS: Davey O'Brien Award winner (1995 and 1996). ... Heisman Trophy winner (1996). ... Named College Player of the Year by THE SPORTING NEWS (1996). ... Named quarterback on THE SPORTING NEWS college All-America first team (1996).
SINGLE GAME HIGHS (regular season): Attempts—47 (October 4, 1998, vs. New England); completions—25 (October 4, 1998, vs. New England); yards—278 (October 4, 1998, vs. New England); and touchdown passes—3 (November 28, 2002, vs. Dallas).
MISCELLANEOUS: Regular-season record as starting NFL quarterback: 4-6 (.400).

Year Team	G	GS	Att.	Cmp.	Pct.	Yds.	TD	Int.	Avg.	Skd.	Rat.	Att.	Yds.	Avg.	TD	TD	2pt.	Pts.
					PASSING								RUSHING				TOTALS	
1997—New Orleans NFL	7	2	91	42	46.2	518	4	8	5.69	18	42.3	6	26	4.3	0	0	0	0
1998—New Orleans NFL	5	4	119	62	52.1	695	5	5	5.84	23	66.3	11	60	5.5	0	0	0	0
1999—New Orleans NFL	4	0	48	22	45.8	191	0	3	3.98	5	30.8	2	29	14.5	1	1	0	6
2000—Rhein NFLE	...	...	260	161	61.9	2042	25	7	7.85	0	107.2	24	80	3.3	2	0	0	0
—Green Bay NFL...............	1	0	0	0	0.0	0	0	0	0.0	0	...	2	-2	-1.0	0	0	0	0
2001—Chicago NFL..............	1	0	0	0	0.0	0	0	0	0.0	0	...	0	0	0.0	0	0	0	0
2002—Washington NFL	7	4	92	58	63.0	719	3	6	7.82	11	70.9	10	76	7.6	0	0	0	0
NFL Europe totals (1 year)	...	...	260	161	61.9	2042	25	7	7.85	0	107.2	24	80	3.3	2	0	0	0
NFL totals (6 years)	25	10	350	184	52.6	2123	12	22	6.07	57	56.4	31	189	6.1	1	1	0	6
Pro totals (7 years)	...	...	610	345	56.6	4165	37	29	6.83	57	78.1	55	269	4.9	3	1	0	6

WUNSCH, JERRY   OT   SEAHAWKS

PERSONAL: Born January 21, 1974, in Eau Claire, Wis. ... 6-6/339. ... Full name: Gerald Wunsch. ... Name pronounced WUNCH.
HIGH SCHOOL: West (Wausau, Wis.).
COLLEGE: Wisconsin (degree in history).
TRANSACTIONS/CAREER NOTES: Selected by Tampa Bay Buccaneers in second round (37th pick overall) of 1997 NFL draft. ... Signed by Buccaneers (July 18, 1997). ... Granted unconditional free agency (March 2, 2001). ... Re-signed by Buccaneers (April 10, 2001). ... Released by Buccaneers (August 25, 2002). ... Signed by Seattle Seahawks (August 27, 2002). ... Granted unconditional free agency (February 28, 2003). ... Re-signed by Seahawks (March 18, 2003).
PLAYING EXPERIENCE: Tampa Bay NFL, 1997-2001; Seattle NFL, 2002. ... Games/Games started: 1997 (16/0), 1998 (16/1), 1999 (16/13), 2000 (16/16), 2001 (16/16), 2002 (15/5). Total: 95/51.
CHAMPIONSHIP GAME EXPERIENCE: Played in NFC championship game (1999 season).

WYCHECK, FRANK   TE   TITANS

PERSONAL: Born October 14, 1971, in Philadelphia. ... 6-3/253. ... Name pronounced WHY-check.
HIGH SCHOOL: Archbishop Ryan (Philadelphia).
COLLEGE: Maryland.
TRANSACTIONS/CAREER NOTES: Selected after junior season by Washington Redskins in sixth round (160th pick overall) of 1993 NFL draft. ... Signed by Redskins (July 15, 1993). ... On suspended list for anabolic steroid use (November 29, 1994-remainder of season). ... Released by Redskins (August 17, 1995). ... Signed by Houston Oilers (August 18, 1995). ... Granted free agency (February 16, 1996). ... Re-signed by Oilers (June 28, 1996). ... Oilers franchise moved to Tennessee for 1997 season. ... Oilers franchise renamed Tennessee Titans for 1999 season (December 26, 1998).
CHAMPIONSHIP GAME EXPERIENCE: Played in AFC championship game (1999 and 2002 seasons). ... Played in Super Bowl XXXIV (1999 season).
HONORS: Played in Pro Bowl (1998-2000 seasons).
SINGLE GAME HIGHS (regular season): Receptions—10 (December 5, 1999, vs. Baltimore); yards—100 (October 21, 2001, vs. Detroit); and touchdown receptions—2 (October 1, 2000, vs. New York Giants).
STATISTICAL PLATEAUS: 100-yard receiving games: 2001 (1).

Year Team	G	GS	No.	Yds.	Avg.	TD	No.	Yds.	Avg.	TD	TD	2pt.	Pts.	Fum.
			RECEIVING				KICKOFF RETURNS				TOTALS			
1993—Washington NFL	9	7	16	113	7.1	0	0	0	0.0	0	0	0	0	1
1994—Washington NFL	9	1	7	55	7.9	1	4	84	21.0	0	1	0	6	0
1995—Houston NFL.......................................	16	10	40	471	11.8	1	0	0	0.0	0	2	0	12	0
1996—Houston NFL.......................................	16	16	53	511	9.6	6	2	5	2.5	0	6	0	36	2
1997—Tennessee NFL....................................	16	16	63	748	11.9	4	1	3	3.0	0	4	1	26	0
1998—Tennessee NFL....................................	16	16	70	768	11.0	2	1	10	10.0	0	2	0	12	2
1999—Tennessee NFL....................................	16	16	69	641	9.3	2	0	0	0.0	0	2	0	12	2
2000—Tennessee NFL....................................	16	16	70	636	9.1	4	0	0	0.0	0	4	0	24	2
2001—Tennessee NFL....................................	16	16	60	672	11.2	4	0	0	0.0	0	4	0	24	0
2002—Tennessee NFL....................................	15	15	40	346	8.7	2	0	0	0.0	0	2	0	12	1
Pro totals (10 years)....................	145	129	488	4961	10.2	26	8	102	12.8	0	27	1	164	8

WYMS, ELLIS   DE   BUCCANEERS

PERSONAL: Born April 12, 1979, in Indianola, Miss. ... 6-3/279. ... Full name: Ellis Rashad Wyms.
HIGH SCHOOL: Gentry (Indianola, Miss.).
COLLEGE: Mississippi State.
TRANSACTIONS/CAREER NOTES: Selected by Tampa Bay Buccaneers in sixth round (183rd pick overall) of 2001 NFL draft. ... Signed by Buccaneers (July 16, 2001).
CHAMPIONSHIP GAME EXPERIENCE: Played in NFC championship game (2002 season). ... Member of Super Bowl championship team (2002 season).

Year Team	G	GS	Tk.	Ast.	Sks.
			TOTALS		
2001—Tampa Bay NFL..	4	0	3	0	0.0
2002—Tampa Bay NFL..	14	0	27	8	5.5
Pro totals (2 years)...	18	0	30	8	5.5

WYNN, MILTON   WR   RAVENS

PERSONAL: Born September 21, 1978, in Mission Hills, Calif. ... 6-2/207. ... Full name: Milton Thomas Wynn.
HIGH SCHOOL: Antelope Valley (Calif.).
JUNIOR COLLEGE: Bakersfield (Calif.), then Los Angeles Valley.
COLLEGE: Washington State.

W

				RECEIVING				TOTALS		
Year Team	G	GS	No.	Yds.	Avg.	TD	TD	2pt.	Pts.	Fum.
2001—Tampa Bay NFL	1	0	4	69	17.3	0	0	0	0	0
2002—Baltimore NFL	3	0	0	0	0.0	0	0	0	0	0
Pro totals (2 years)	4	0	4	69	17.3	0	0	0	0	0

WYNN, RENALDO   DE   REDSKINS

PERSONAL: Born September 3, 1974, in Chicago. ... 6-3/290. ... Full name: Renaldo Levalle Wynn.
HIGH SCHOOL: De La Salle Institute (Chicago).
COLLEGE: Notre Dame (degree in sociology, 1996).
TRANSACTIONS/CAREER NOTES: Selected by Jacksonville Jaguars in first round (21st pick overall) of 1997 NFL draft. ... Signed by Jaguars (July 21, 1997). ... On injured reserve with groin injury (December 25, 1998-remainder of season). ... Granted unconditional free agency (March 1, 2002). ... Signed by Washington Redskins (March 28, 2002).
CHAMPIONSHIP GAME EXPERIENCE: Played in AFC championship game (1999 season).

			TOTALS		
Year Team	G	GS	Tk.	Ast.	Sks.
1997—Jacksonville NFL	16	8	23	5	2.5
1998—Jacksonville NFL	15	15	23	11	1.0
1999—Jacksonville NFL	12	10	10	7	1.5
2000—Jacksonville NFL	14	14	31	5	3.5
2001—Jacksonville NFL	16	16	29	11	5.0
2002—Washington NFL	16	16	30	11	2.5
Pro totals (6 years)	89	79	146	50	16.0

WYRICK, JIMMY   CB   LIONS

PERSONAL: Born December 31, 1976, in DeSoto, Texas. ... 5-9/176.
HIGH SCHOOL: DeSoto (Texas).
COLLEGE: Minnesota.
TRANSACTIONS/CAREER NOTES: Signed as non-drafted free agent by Detroit Lions (April 28, 2000). ... On injured reserve with ankle injury (October 16, 2000-remainder of season). ... Granted free agency (February 28, 2003). ... Re-signed by Lions (February 28, 2003).

			TOTALS			INTERCEPTIONS			
Year Team	G	GS	Tk.	Ast.	Sks.	No.	Yds.	Avg.	TD
2000—Detroit NFL	6	0	1	3	0.0	0	0	0.0	0
2001—Detroit NFL	16	0	13	2	0.0	0	0	0.0	0
2002—Detroit NFL	15	1	8	0	0.0	0	0	0.0	0
Pro totals (3 years)	37	1	22	5	0.0	0	0	0.0	0

YODER, TODD   TE   BUCCANEERS

PERSONAL: Born March 18, 1978, in New Palestine, Ind. ... 6-4/250.
HIGH SCHOOL: New Palestine (Ind.).
COLLEGE: Vanderbilt.
TRANSACTIONS/CAREER NOTES: Signed as non-drafted free agent by Tampa Bay Buccaneers (April 17, 2000). ... Granted free agency (February 28, 2003). ... Re-signed by Buccaneers (April 4, 2003).
CHAMPIONSHIP GAME EXPERIENCE: Played in NFC championship game (2002 season). ... Member of Super Bowl championship team (2002 season).
SINGLE GAME HIGHS (regular season): Receptions—2 (January 6, 2002, vs. Philadelphia); yards—24 (December 9, 2001, vs. Detroit); and touchdown receptions—0.

			RECEIVING			
Year Team	G	GS	No.	Yds.	Avg.	TD
2000—Tampa Bay NFL	9	0	1	1	1.0	0
2001—Tampa Bay NFL	16	1	4	48	12.0	0
2002—Tampa Bay NFL	16	0	2	26	13.0	0
Pro totals (3 years)	41	1	7	75	10.7	0

YOUNG, BRIAN   DT   RAMS

PERSONAL: Born July 8, 1977, in Lawton, Okla. ... 6-2/290. ... Full name: James Brian Young.
HIGH SCHOOL: Andress (El Paso, Texas).
COLLEGE: Texas-El Paso.
TRANSACTIONS/CAREER NOTES: Selected by St. Louis Rams in fifth round (139th pick overall) of 2000 NFL draft. ... Signed by Rams (July 7, 2000). ... Granted free agency (February 28, 2003). ... Re-signed by Rams (April 25, 2003).
CHAMPIONSHIP GAME EXPERIENCE: Played in NFC championship game (2001 season). ... Played in Super Bowl XXXVI (2001 season).

			TOTALS			INTERCEPTIONS			
Year Team	G	GS	Tk.	Ast.	Sks.	No.	Yds.	Avg.	TD
2000—St. Louis NFL	11	0	4	2	0.0	0	0	0.0	0
2001—St. Louis NFL	16	16	33	7	6.5	1	25	25.0	0
2002—St. Louis NFL	16	3	25	9	2.0	0	0	0.0	0
Pro totals (3 years)	43	19	62	18	8.5	1	25	25.0	0

W
Y

YOUNG, BRYANT — DT — 49ERS

PERSONAL: Born January 27, 1972, in Chicago Heights, Ill. ... 6-3/291. ... Full name: Bryant Colby Young.
HIGH SCHOOL: Bloom (Chicago Heights, Ill.).
COLLEGE: Notre Dame.
TRANSACTIONS/CAREER NOTES: Selected by San Francisco 49ers in first round (seventh pick overall) of 1994 NFL draft. ... Signed by 49ers (July 26, 1994). ... On injured reserve with broken leg (December 2, 1998-remainder of season). ... On physically unable to perform list with leg injury (July 30-August 10, 1999).
CHAMPIONSHIP GAME EXPERIENCE: Played in NFC championship game (1994 and 1997 seasons). ... Member of Super Bowl championship team (1994 season).
HONORS: Named defensive tackle on THE SPORTING NEWS NFL All-Pro team (1996 and 1998). ... Played in Pro Bowl (1996, 1999, 2001 and 2002 seasons).

| | | | TOTALS | | |
Year Team	G	GS	Tk.	Ast.	Sks.
1994—San Francisco NFL	16	16	45	4	6.0
1995—San Francisco NFL	12	12	25	3	6.0
1996—San Francisco NFL	16	16	61	15	11.5
1997—San Francisco NFL	12	12	39	6	4.0
1998—San Francisco NFL	12	12	43	11	9.5
1999—San Francisco NFL	16	16	36	5	11.0
2000—San Francisco NFL	15	15	33	12	9.5
2001—San Francisco NFL	16	16	33	6	3.5
2002—San Francisco NFL	16	16	28	8	2.0
Pro totals (9 years)	131	131	343	70	63.0

YOUNG, MICHAEL — LB — CARDINALS

PERSONAL: Born June 1, 1978, in St. Louis. ... 6-2/247. ... Full name: Mike Young.
HIGH SCHOOL: Hazelwood East (Hazelwood, Mo.).
COLLEGE: Illinois.
TRANSACTIONS/CAREER NOTES: Signed as non-drafted free agent by Arizona Cardinals (April 23, 2001). ... Released by Cardinals (August 27, 2001). ... Re-signed by Cardinals to practice squad (September 3, 2001).

| | | | TOTALS | | | INTERCEPTIONS | | | |
Year Team	G	GS	Tk.	Ast.	Sks.	No.	Yds.	Avg.	TD
2002—Arizona NFL	16	2	13	4	0.0	0	0	0.0	0

YOUNG, RYAN — OT — COWBOYS

PERSONAL: Born June 28, 1976, in St. Louis. ... 6-5/320.
HIGH SCHOOL: Parkway Central (Chesterfield, Mo.).
COLLEGE: Kansas State.
TRANSACTIONS/CAREER NOTES: Selected by New York Jets in seventh round (223rd pick overall) of 1999 NFL draft. ... Signed by Jets (June 25, 1999). ... Selected by Houston Texans from Jets in NFL expansion draft (February 18, 2002). ... Granted free agency (March 1, 2002). ... Drafted by Texans in expansion draft (February 18, 2002). ... Granted unconditional free agency (February 28, 2003). ... Signed by Dallas Cowboys (March 5, 2003).
PLAYING EXPERIENCE: New York Jets NFL, 1999-2001; Houston NFL, 2002. ... Games/Games started: 1999 (15/7), 2000 (16/16), 2001 (16/16), 2002 (9/8). Total: 56/47.

ZASTUDIL, DAVE — P — RAVENS

PERSONAL: Born October 26, 1978, in Bay Village, Ohio. ... 6-3/225.
HIGH SCHOOL: Bay Village (Ohio).
COLLEGE: Ohio.
TRANSACTIONS/CAREER NOTES: Selected by Baltimore Ravens in fourth round (112th pick overall) of 2002 NFL draft. ... Signed by Ravens (July 26, 2002).
HONORS: Named punter on THE SPORTING NEWS college All-America third team (2001).

| | | PUNTING | | | | |
Year Team	G	No.	Yds.	Avg.	Net avg.	In. 20	Blk.
2002—Baltimore NFL	16	81	3368	41.6	33.7	31	2

ZEIGLER, DUSTY — C

PERSONAL: Born September 27, 1973, in Savannah, Ga. ... 6-5/305. ... Full name: Curtis Dustin Zeigler. ... Name pronounced ZIG-ler.
HIGH SCHOOL: Effingham County (Springfield, Ga.).
COLLEGE: Notre Dame.
TRANSACTIONS/CAREER NOTES: Selected by Buffalo Bills in sixth round (202nd pick overall) of 1996 NFL draft. ... Signed by Bills (June 25, 1996). ... Granted free agency (February 12, 1999). ... Re-signed by Bills (April 15, 1999). ... Granted unconditional free agency (February 11, 2000). ... Signed by New York Giants (March 6, 2000). ... On injured reserve with knee injury (November 12, 2002-remainder of season). ... Released by Giants (June 1, 2003).
PLAYING EXPERIENCE: Buffalo NFL, 1996-1999; New York Giants NFL, 2000-2002. ... Games/Games started: 1996 (2/0), 1997 (13/13), 1998 (16/16), 1999 (15/15), 2000 (16/16), 2001 (16/16), 2002 (2/2). Total: 80/78.
CHAMPIONSHIP GAME EXPERIENCE: Played in NFC championship game (2000 season). ... Played in Super Bowl XXXV (2000 season).

ZELENKA, JOE   TE

PERSONAL: Born March 9, 1976, in Cleveland. ... 6-3/261. ... Full name: Joseph John Zelenka.
HIGH SCHOOL: Benedictine (Cleveland).
COLLEGE: Wake Forest.
TRANSACTIONS/CAREER NOTES: Signed as non-drafted free agent by San Francisco 49ers (April 23, 1999). ... Traded by 49ers to Washington Redskins for seventh-round pick (TE Eric Johnson) in 2001 draft (April 17, 2000). ... Released by Redskins (March 9, 2001). ... Signed by Jacksonville Jaguars (August 13, 2001). ... Granted unconditional free agency (February 28, 2003).

				RECEIVING		
Year Team	G	GS	No.	Yds.	Avg.	TD
1999—San Francisco NFL	13	0	0	0	0.0	0
2000—Washington NFL	16	0	0	0	0.0	0
2001—Jacksonville NFL	16	0	0	0	0.0	0
2002—Jacksonville NFL	16	0	0	0	0.0	0
Pro totals (4 years)	61	0	0	0	0.0	0

ZELLNER, PEPPI   DE   REDSKINS

PERSONAL: Born March 14, 1975, in Forsythe, Ga. ... 6-5/286. ... Full name: Hunndens Guiseppi Zellner.
HIGH SCHOOL: Mary Persons (Forsythe, Ga.).
JUNIOR COLLEGE: Georgia Military College.
COLLEGE: Fort Valley (Ga.) State.
TRANSACTIONS/CAREER NOTES: Selected by Dallas Cowboys in fourth round (132nd pick overall) of 1999 NFL draft. ... Signed by Cowboys (July 27, 1999). ... On injured reserve with knee injury (December 12, 2000-remainder of season). ... On physically unable to perform list with knee injury (July 22-August 14, 2001). ... Granted unconditional free agency (February 28, 2003). ... Signed by Washington Redskins (May 13, 2003).

			TOTALS		
Year Team	G	GS	Tk.	Ast.	Sks.
1999—Dallas NFL	13	0	9	0	1.0
2000—Dallas NFL	12	0	7	3	2.0
2001—Dallas NFL	16	15	36	10	3.0
2002—Dallas NFL	16	2	22	7	0.0
Pro totals (4 years)	57	17	74	20	6.0

ZEREOUE, AMOS   RB   STEELERS

PERSONAL: Born October 8, 1976, in Ivory Coast. ... 5-8/207. ... Name pronounced zer-O-way.
HIGH SCHOOL: W.C. Mepham (Hempstead, N.Y.).
COLLEGE: West Virginia.
TRANSACTIONS/CAREER NOTES: Selected after junior season by Pittsburgh Steelers in third round (95th pick overall) of 1999 NFL draft. ... Signed by Steelers (July 30, 1999). ... Granted free agency (March 1, 2002). ... Re-signed by Steelers (June 13, 2002).
CHAMPIONSHIP GAME EXPERIENCE: Played in AFC championship game (2001 season).
HONORS: Named running back on THE SPORTING NEWS college All-America third team (1997).
SINGLE GAME HIGHS (regular season): Attempts—37 (November 10, 2002, vs. Atlanta); yards—123 (November 10, 2002, vs. Atlanta); and rushing touchdowns—2 (December 29, 2002, vs. Baltimore).
STATISTICAL PLATEAUS: 100-yard rushing games: 2002 (3).

			RUSHING				RECEIVING				KICKOFF RETURNS				TOTALS		
Year Team	G	GS	Att.	Yds.	Avg.	TD	No.	Yds.	Avg.	TD	No.	Yds.	Avg.	TD	TD	2pt.	Pts. Fum.
1999—Pittsburgh NFL	8	0	18	48	2.7	0	2	17	8.5	0	7	169	24.1	0	0	0	0 0
2000—Pittsburgh NFL	12	0	6	14	2.3	0	0	0	0.0	0	0	0	0.0	0	0	0	0 0
2001—Pittsburgh NFL	14	0	85	441	5.2	1	13	154	11.8	1	0	0	0.0	0	2	0	12 3
2002—Pittsburgh NFL	16	5	193	762	3.9	4	42	341	8.1	0	0	0	0.0	0	4	0	24 2
Pro totals (4 years)	50	5	302	1265	4.2	5	57	512	9.0	1	7	169	24.1	0	6	0	36 5

ZGONINA, JEFF   DT   DOLPHINS

PERSONAL: Born May 24, 1970, in Chicago. ... 6-2/305. ... Full name: Jeffrey Marc Zgonina. ... Name pronounced ska-KNEE-na.
HIGH SCHOOL: Mount Carmel (Chicago).
COLLEGE: Purdue (degree in community health promotion, 1992).
TRANSACTIONS/CAREER NOTES: Selected by Pittsburgh Steelers in seventh round (185th pick overall) of 1993 NFL draft. ... Signed by Steelers (July 16, 1993). ... Claimed on waivers by Carolina Panthers (August 28, 1995). ... Granted free agency (February 16, 1996). ... Re-signed by Panthers (April 11, 1996). ... Released by Panthers (August 19, 1996). ... Signed by Atlanta Falcons (October 8, 1996). ... Granted unconditional free agency (February 14, 1997). ... Signed by St. Louis Rams (March 17, 1997). ... Released by Rams (August 30, 1998). ... Signed by Oakland Raiders (October 13, 1998). ... Released by Raiders (October 18, 1998). ... Signed by Indianapolis Colts (November 25, 1998). ... Granted unconditional free agency (February 12, 1999). ... Signed by Rams (April 5, 1999). ... Released by Rams (April 1, 2002). ... Re-signed by Rams (April 2, 2002). ... Granted unconditional free agency (February 28, 2003). ... Signed by Miami Dolphins (March 31, 2003).
CHAMPIONSHIP GAME EXPERIENCE: Played in AFC championship game (1994 season). ... Played in NFC championship game (1999 and 2001 seasons). ... Member of Super Bowl championship team (1999 season). ... Played in Super Bowl XXXVI (2001 season).

			TOTALS		
Year Team	G	GS	Tk.	Ast.	Sks.
1993—Pittsburgh NFL	5	0	11	5	0.0
1994—Pittsburgh NFL	16	0	6	5	0.0
1995—Carolina NFL	2	0	2	0	0.0
1996—Atlanta NFL	8	0	7	5	1.0
1997—St. Louis NFL	15	0	19	2	2.0

Year	Team	G	GS	Tk.	Ast.	Sks.
				TOTALS		
1998—Indianapolis NFL		2	0	0	0	0.0
1999—St. Louis NFL		16	0	26	5	4.5
2000—St. Louis NFL		16	11	30	7	2.0
2001—St. Louis NFL		13	13	32	6	0.0
2002—St. Louis NFL		16	16	29	9	4.0
Pro totals (10 years)		109	40	162	44	13.5

ZUKAUSKAS, PAUL — G — BROWNS

PERSONAL: Born July 12, 1979, in Weymouth, Mass. ... 6-5/306. ... Full name: Paul Malcolm Zukauskas.
HIGH SCHOOL: Boston College (Ma.).
COLLEGE: Boston College.
TRANSACTIONS/CAREER NOTES: Selected by Cleveland Browns in seventh round (203rd pick overall) of 2001 NFL draft. ... Signed by Browns (July 20, 2001). ... Released by Browns (September 1, 2001). ... Re-signed by Browns to practice squad (September 3, 2001). ... Activated (November 21, 2001).
PLAYING EXPERIENCE: Cleveland NFL, 2001-2002. ... Games/Games started: 2001 (1/0), 2002 (16/3). Total: 17/3.
HONORS: Named guard on THE SPORTING NEWS college All-America second team (2000).

ABDULLAH, KHALID   LB   BENGALS

PERSONAL: Born March 6, 1979, in Jacksonville, Fla. ... 6-2/227. ... Brother of Rahim Abdullah, linebacker with Cleveland Browns (1999-2000).
HIGH SCHOOL: Fletcher (Jacksonville, Fla.).
COLLEGE: Mars Hill.
TRANSACTIONS/CAREER NOTES: Selected by Cincinnati Bengals in fifth round (136th pick overall) of 2003 NFL draft.

			INTERCEPTIONS			
Year Team	G	Sks.	No.	Yds.	Avg.	TD
1999—Mars Hill	11	15.0	1	33	33.0	0
2000—Mars Hill	10	2.0	2	125	62.5	2
2001—Mars Hill	11	6.0	1	100	100.0	1
2002—Mars Hill	11	5.0	1	30	30.0	0
College totals (4 years)	43	28.0	5	288	57.6	3

ADAMS, ANTHONY   DT   49ERS

PERSONAL: Born August 18, 1980, in Detroit. ... 6-0/299. ... Full name: Anthony Adams Jr.
HIGH SCHOOL: Martin Luther King (Detroit).
COLLEGE: Penn State.
TRANSACTIONS/CAREER NOTES: Selected by San Francisco 49ers in second round (57th pick overall) of 2003 NFL draft.

Year Team	G	SACKS
1998—Penn State	Redshirted.	
1999—Penn State	12	0.0
2000—Penn State	12	1.0
2001—Penn State	11	3.5
2002—Penn State	13	2.0
College totals (4 years)	48	6.5

ADAMS, BLUE   CB   LIONS

PERSONAL: Born October 15, 1979, in Miami. ... 5-9/182. ... Full name: Daniel L. Adams.
HIGH SCHOOL: Miami Senior (Fla.).
COLLEGE: Cincinnati.
TRANSACTIONS/CAREER NOTES: Selected by Detroit Lions in seventh round (220th pick overall) of 2003 NFL draft.

		INTERCEPTIONS			
Year Team	G	No.	Yds.	Avg.	TD
1998—Cincinnati	7	4	57	14.3	0
1999—Cincinnati		Redshirted.			
2000—Cincinnati	11	0	0	0.0	0
2001—Cincinnati	11	2	16	8.0	0
2002—Cincinnati	14	6	104	17.3	2
College totals (4 years)	43	12	177	14.8	2

AIKEN, SAM   WR   BILLS

PERSONAL: Born December 14, 1980, in Clinton, N.C. ... 6-2/209. ... Full name: Samuel Aiken.
HIGH SCHOOL: James Kenan (Warsaw, N.C.).
COLLEGE: North Carolina.
COLLEGE NOTES: Rushed five times (2000); two times (2001).

		RECEIVING				PUNT RETURNS				KICKOFF RETURNS				TOTALS	
Year Team	G	No.	Yds.	Avg.	TD	No.	Yds.	Avg.	TD	No.	Yds.	Avg.	TD	TD	Pts.
1999—North Carolina	11	3	16	5.3	0	12	23	1.9	0	13	275	21.2	0	0	0
2000—North Carolina	11	29	410	14.1	3	2	20	10.0	0	18	365	20.3	0	3	18
2001—North Carolina	12	46	789	17.2	8	9	79	8.8	0	5	105	21.0	0	8	48
2002—North Carolina	12	68	990	14.6	4	2	5	2.5	0	1	18	18.0	0	4	24
College totals (4 years)	46	146	2205	15.1	15	25	127	5.1	0	37	763	20.6	0	15	90

ANDERSON, BRYAN   G   BEARS

PERSONAL: Born March 30, 1980, in Philadelphia. ... 6-4/321. ... Full name: Bryan Michael Anderson.
HIGH SCHOOL: John Bartram (Philadelphia).
COLLEGE: Pittsburgh.
TRANSACTIONS/CAREER NOTES: Selected by Chicago Bears in seventh round (261st pick overall) of 2003 NFL draft.
COLLEGE PLAYING EXPERIENCE: Pittsburgh, 1998-2002. ... Games played: 1998 (redshirted), 1999 (11), 2000 (11), 2001 (11), 2002 (13). Total: 46.

ANGLIN, TRAVIS   WR   LIONS

PERSONAL: Born April 17, 1980, in Columbus, Ga. ... 6-4/192.
HIGH SCHOOL: John Shaw (Columbus, Ga.).
COLLEGE: Memphis.
TRANSACTIONS/CAREER NOTES: Selected by Detroit Lions in seventh round (260th pick overall) of 2003 NFL draft.

			PASSING							RUSHING				RECEIVING				TOTALS	
Year Team	G	Att.	Cmp.	Pct.	Yds.	TD	Int.	Avg.	Rat.	Att.	Yds.	Avg.	TD	No.	Yds.	Avg.	TD	TD	Pts.
1998—Memphis									Redshirted.										
1999—Memphis	10	125	68	54.4	856	5	10	6.85	109.1	57	123	2.2	3	0	0	0.0	0	3	20
2000—Memphis	4	60	26	43.3	200	1	2	3.33	70.2	29	98	3.4	2	0	0	0.0	0	2	12
2001—Memphis	11	65	43	66.2	403	4	0	6.20	138.5	66	227	3.4	2	4	98	24.5	1	3	18
2002—Memphis	12	0	0	0.0	0	0	0	0.0	0.0	10	52	5.2	0	55	740	13.5	5	5	30
College totals (4 years)	37	250	137	54.8	1459	10	12	5.84	107.4	162	500	3.1	7	59	838	14.2	6	13	80

ANGULO, RICHARD — TE — RAMS

PERSONAL: Born August 13, 1980, in Albuquerque, N.M. ... 6-8/263.
HIGH SCHOOL: Sandia (Albuquerque, N.M.).
COLLEGE: Western New Mexico.
TRANSACTIONS/CAREER NOTES: Selected by St. Louis Rams in seventh round (254th pick overall) of 2003 NFL draft.
COLLEGE NOTES: Returned two kickoffs (2001).

		RECEIVING			
Year Team	G	No.	Yds.	Avg.	TD
2001—Western New Mexico	8	24	362	15.1	5
2002—Western New Mexico	9	28	582	20.8	7
College totals (2 years)	17	52	944	18.2	12

ASKEW, B.J. — FB — JETS

PERSONAL: Born August 19, 1980, in Colerain, Ohio. ... 6-2/241. ... Full name: Bobby DeAngelo Askew Jr.
HIGH SCHOOL: Colerain (Cincinnati).
COLLEGE: Michigan.
TRANSACTIONS/CAREER NOTES: Selected by New York Jets in third round (85th pick overall) of 2003 NFL draft.

		RUSHING				RECEIVING				TOTALS	
Year Team	G	Att.	Yds.	Avg.	TD	No.	Yds.	Avg.	TD	TD	Pts.
1999—Michigan	12	23	70	3.0	1	3	4	1.3	0	1	6
2000—Michigan	11	11	40	3.6	0	15	231	15.4	2	2	12
2001—Michigan	11	190	831	4.4	10	24	213	8.9	1	11	66
2002—Michigan	13	110	568	5.2	6	36	280	7.8	1	7	42
College totals (4 years)	47	334	1509	4.5	17	78	728	9.3	4	21	126

ASOMUGHA, NNAMDI — CB — RAIDERS

PERSONAL: Born July 6, 1981, in Lafayette, La. ... 6-2/213. ... Cousin of Iheanyi Uwaezuoke, wide receiver with four NFL teams (1996-2000).
HIGH SCHOOL: Narbonne (Los Angeles).
COLLEGE: California.
TRANSACTIONS/CAREER NOTES: Selected by Oakland Raiders in first round (31st pick overall) of 2003 NFL draft.

			INTERCEPTIONS			
Year Team	G	Sks.	No.	Yds.	Avg.	TD
1999—California	7	0.0	0	0	0.0	0
2000—California	11	3.0	1	31	31.0	1
2001—California	10	0.0	3	11	3.7	1
2002—California	12	0.0	3	85	28.3	1
College totals (4 years)	40	3.0	7	127	18.1	3

BABERS, RODERICK — CB — GIANTS

PERSONAL: Born October 6, 1980, in Houston. ... 5-9/192. ... Full name: Roderick Henri Babers.
HIGH SCHOOL: Lamar (Houston).
COLLEGE: Texas.
TRANSACTIONS/CAREER NOTES: Selected by New York Giants in fourth round (123rd pick overall) of 2003 NFL draft.
COLLEGE NOTES: Returned one punt (2001).

			INTERCEPTIONS			
Year Team	G	Sks.	No.	Yds.	Avg.	TD
1999—Texas	11	3.0	0	0	0.0	0
2000—Texas	11	0.0	2	39	19.5	1
2001—Texas	11	0.0	1	54	54.0	1
2002—Texas	13	1.0	2	83	41.5	1
College totals (4 years)	46	4.0	5	176	35.2	3

BACON, WAINE — S — FALCONS

PERSONAL: Born April 11, 1979, in Fort Washington, Md. ... 5-10/191.
HIGH SCHOOL: Bishop McNamara (Fort Washington, Md.).
COLLEGE: Alabama.
TRANSACTIONS/CAREER NOTES: Selected by Atlanta Falcons in sixth round (202nd pick overall) of 2003 NFL draft.

			INTERCEPTIONS			
Year Team	G	No.	Yds.	Avg.	TD
1998—Alabama			Redshirted.			
1999—Alabama			Did not play.			
2000—Alabama			Did not play.			
2001—Alabama	11	1	4	4.0	0
2002—Alabama	13	4	32	8.0	0
College totals (2 years)	24	5	36	7.2	0

BAILEY, BOSS   LB   LIONS

PERSONAL: Born October 14, 1979, in Folkston, Ga. ... 6-3/233. ... Brother of Champ Bailey, cornerback, Washington Redskins.
HIGH SCHOOL: Charlton County (Ga.).
COLLEGE: Georgia.
TRANSACTIONS/CAREER NOTES: Selected by Detroit Lions in second round (34th pick overall) of 2003 NFL draft.

| | | | INTERCEPTIONS | | | |
Year Team	G	Sks.	No.	Yds.	Avg.	TD
1998—Georgia	11	0.0	0	0	0.0	0
1999—Georgia	11	0.5	0	0	0.0	0
2000—Georgia			Redshirted.			
2001—Georgia	11	1.0	1	0	0.0	0
2002—Georgia	14	6.0	0	0	0.0	0
College totals (4 years)	47	7.5	1	0	0.0	0

BANTA-CAIN, TULLY   DE   PATRIOTS

PERSONAL: Born August 28, 1980, in Mountain View, Calif. ... 6-2/254. ... Cousin of Jeffrey Leonard, outfielder with five major league teams (1977-90); and cousin of Rodney Rogers, forward, New Jersey Nets.
HIGH SCHOOL: Fremont (Mountain View, Calif.).
COLLEGE: California.
TRANSACTIONS/CAREER NOTES: Selected by New England Patriots in seventh round (239th pick overall) of 2003 NFL draft.

Year Team	G	SACKS
1998—California		Redshirted.
1999—California	5	0.0
2000—California	11	5.5
2001—California	11	8.0
2002—California	12	13.0
College totals (4 years)	39	26.5

BARNETT, NICK   LB   PACKERS

PERSONAL: Born May 27, 1981, in Fontana, Calif. ... 6-2/236. ... Full name: Nicholas Alexander Barnett.
HIGH SCHOOL: A.B. Miller (Fontana, Calif.).
COLLEGE: Oregon State.
TRANSACTIONS/CAREER NOTES: Selected by Green Bay Packers in first round (29th pick overall) of 2003 NFL draft.
COLLEGE NOTES: Intercepted one pass (2001).

Year Team	G	SACKS
1999—Oregon State	11	0.0
2000—Oregon State	11	0.0
2001—Oregon State	11	2.0
2002—Oregon State	13	6.0
College totals (4 years)	46	8.0

BATES, JUSTIN   G/OT   COWBOYS

PERSONAL: Born September 20, 1979, in Lansing, Mich. ... 6-4/300.
HIGH SCHOOL: Pomona (Arvada, Colo.).
COLLEGE: Colorado.
TRANSACTIONS/CAREER NOTES: Selected by Dallas Cowboys in seventh round (219th pick overall) of 2003 NFL draft.
COLLEGE PLAYING EXPERIENCE: Colorado, 1998-2002. ... Games played: 1998 (redshirted), 1999 (9), 2000 (10), 2001 (12), 2002 (14). Total: 45.

BATES, SOLOMON   LB   SEAHAWKS

PERSONAL: Born April 18, 1982, in Carver City, Calif. ... 6-1/243. ... Full name: Solomon Augustus Bates.
HIGH SCHOOL: Canyon Springs (Moreno Valley, Calif.).
COLLEGE: Arizona State.
TRANSACTIONS/CAREER NOTES: Selected by Seattle Seahawks in fourth round (135th pick overall) of 2003 NFL draft.

| | | | INTERCEPTIONS | | | |
Year Team	G	Sks.	No.	Yds.	Avg.	TD
1999—Arizona State	8	0.0	0	0	0.0	0
2000—Arizona State	12	3.0	2	45	22.5	0
2001—Arizona State	11	1.0	0	0	0.0	0
2002—Arizona State	12	1.0	1	22	22.0	0
College totals (4 years)	43	5.0	3	67	22.3	0

BATTLE, ARNAZ   WR   49ERS

PERSONAL: Born February 22, 1980, in Dallas. ... 6-1/217. ... Full name: Arnaz Jerome Battle. ... Cousin of Kevin Ollie, guard, Seattle SuperSonics.
HIGH SCHOOL: C.E. Byrd (Shreveport, La.).
COLLEGE: Notre Dame.
TRANSACTIONS/CAREER NOTES: Selected by San Francisco 49ers in sixth round (197th pick overall) of 2003 NFL draft.
COLLEGE NOTES: Returned 16 kickoffs (2002), two punts (2002).

Year Team	G	PASSING								RUSHING				RECEIVING				TOTALS	
		Att.	Cmp.	Pct.	Yds.	TD	Int.	Avg.	Rat.	Att.	Yds.	Avg.	TD	No.	Yds.	Avg.	TD	TD	Pts.
1998—Notre Dame........	4	20	8	40.0	134	0	2	6.70	76.3	13	53	4.1	0	0	0	0.0	0	0	0
1999—Notre Dame........	7	15	7	46.7	84	0	1	5.60	80.4	19	100	5.3	1	0	0	0.0	0	1	6
2000—Notre Dame........	2	31	13	41.9	173	2	1	5.58	103.7	26	157	6.0	0	0	0	0.0	0	0	0
2001—Notre Dame........	7	1	1	100.0	17	0	0	17.00	242.8	3	8	2.7	0	5	40	8.0	0	0	0
2002—Notre Dame........	13	2	1	50.0	30	0	1	15.00	76.0	3	2	0.7	0	58	786	13.6	5	5	32
College totals (5 years).	33	69	30	43.5	438	2	5	6.35	91.9	64	320	5.0	1	63	826	13.1	5	6	38

BATTLE, JULIAN — CB/SS — CHIEFS

PERSONAL: Born July 11, 1981, in Royal Palm Beach, Fla. ... 6-2/205.
HIGH SCHOOL: Wellington (West Palm Beach, Fla.).
JUNIOR COLLEGE: Los Angeles Valley College.
COLLEGE: Tennessee.
TRANSACTIONS/CAREER NOTES: Selected by Kansas City Chiefs in third round (92nd pick overall) of 2003 NFL draft. ... Signed by Chiefs (May 12, 2003).
COLLEGE NOTES: Returned one punt (2002).

Year Team	G	Sks.	INTERCEPTIONS			
			No.	Yds.	Avg.	TD
2001—Tennessee	11	0.0	2	6	3.0	0
2002—Tennessee	13	2.0	1	0	0.0	0
College totals (2 years)	24	2.0	3	6	2.0	0

BELL, YEREMIAH — CB — DOLPHINS

PERSONAL: Born March 3, 1978, in Winchester, Ky. ... 6-1/193.
HIGH SCHOOL: George Rogers Clark (Winchester, Ky.).
COLLEGE: Eastern Kentucky.
TRANSACTIONS/CAREER NOTES: Selected by Miami Dolphins in sixth round (213th pick overall) of 2003 NFL draft.
COLLEGE NOTES: Returned one punt (1999), one punt (2001).

Year Team	G	Sks.	INTERCEPTIONS			
			No.	Yds.	Avg.	TD
1998—Eastern Kentucky	Redshirted.					
1999—Eastern Kentucky	10	0.0	1	0	0.0	0
2000—Eastern Kentucky	11	0.5	2	68	34.0	1
2001—Eastern Kentucky	10	1.0	6	46	7.7	0
2002—Eastern Kentucky	Did not play.					
College totals (3 years)	31	1.5	9	114	12.7	1

BLACK, JORDAN — OT/OG — CHIEFS

PERSONAL: Born January 28, 1980, in Garland, Texas. ... 6-6/314. ... Full name: Brian Jordan Black.
HIGH SCHOOL: Dallas Christian (Mesquite, Texas).
COLLEGE: Notre Dame.
TRANSACTIONS/CAREER NOTES: Selected by Kansas City Chiefs in fifth round (153rd pick overall) of 2003 NFL draft.
COLLEGE NOTES: Caught one pass (2000).
COLLEGE PLAYING EXPERIENCE: Notre Dame, 1998-2002. ... Games played: 1998 (redshirted), 1999 (9), 2000 (11), 2001 (11), 2002 (12). Total: 43.

BOLDIN, ANQUAN — WR — CARDINALS

PERSONAL: Born October 3, 1980, in Pahokee, Fla. ... 6-1/216.
HIGH SCHOOL: Pahokee (Fla.).
COLLEGE: Florida State.
TRANSACTIONS/CAREER NOTES: Selected after junior season by Arizona Cardinals in second round (54th pick overall) of 2003 NFL draft.
COLLEGE NOTES: Completed 7 of 16 passes, 111 yards and had a quarterback rating of 122.7 (2002).

Year Team	G	RUSHING				RECEIVING				PUNT RETURNS				KICKOFF RETURNS				TOTALS	
		Att.	Yds.	Avg.	TD	No.	Yds.	Avg.	TD	No.	Yds.	Avg.	TD	No.	Yds.	Avg.	TD	TD	Pts.
1999—Florida State...........	7	4	33	8.3	1	12	115	9.6	2	0	0	0.0	0	3	55	18.3	0	3	18
2000—Florida State...........	12	1	8	8.0	0	41	664	16.2	6	10	65	6.5	0	1	15	15.0	0	6	36
2001—Florida State...........	Did not play.																		
2002—Florida State...........	13	21	86	4.1	0	65	1011	15.6	13	0	0	0.0	0	0	0	0.0	0	13	78
College totals (3 years)	32	26	127	4.9	1	118	1790	15.2	21	10	65	6.5	0	4	70	17.5	0	22	132

BOLLER, KYLE — QB — RAVENS

PERSONAL: Born June 17, 1981, in Burbank, Calif. ... 6-3/234.
HIGH SCHOOL: Hart (Newhall, Calif.).
COLLEGE: California.
TRANSACTIONS/CAREER NOTES: Selected by Baltimore Ravens in first round (19th pick overall) of 2003 NFL draft.
COLLEGE NOTES: Caught two passes (2001), two passes (2002).

Year Team	G	PASSING								RUSHING				TOTALS	
		Att.	Cmp.	Pct.	Yds.	TD	Int.	Avg.	Rat.	Att.	Yds.	Avg.	TD	TD	Pts.
1999—California	10	259	100	38.6	1303	9	15	5.03	80.8	60	-105	-1.8	0	0	0
2000—California	11	349	163	46.7	2121	15	13	6.08	104.5	65	-44	-0.7	2	2	12
2001—California	9	272	134	49.3	1741	12	10	6.40	110.2	77	63	0.8	1	1	6
2002—California	12	421	225	53.4	2815	28	10	6.69	126.8	72	-83	-1.2	3	4	24
College totals (4 years)............................	42	1301	622	47.8	7980	64	48	6.13	108.2	274	-169	-0.6	6	7	42

BOLLINGER, BROOKS — QB — JETS

PERSONAL: Born November 15, 1979, in Grand Forks, N.D. ... 6-1/203.
HIGH SCHOOL: Central (Grand Forks, N.D.).
COLLEGE: Wisconsin.
TRANSACTIONS/CAREER NOTES: Selected by New York Jets in sixth round (200th pick overall) of 2003 NFL draft.
COLLEGE NOTES: Caught one pass (2000), one pass (2001), one pass (2002).

Year Team	G	Att.	Cmp.	Pct.	Yds.	TD	Int.	Avg.	Rat.	Att.	Yds.	Avg.	TD	TD	Pts.
					PASSING						RUSHING			TOTALS	
1998—Wisconsin							Redshirted.								
1999—Wisconsin	11	126	75	59.5	1028	8	2	8.16	145.8	96	427	4.4	5	5	30
2000—Wisconsin	11	192	101	52.6	1363	8	7	7.10	118.7	141	404	2.9	6	6	36
2001—Wisconsin	9	177	91	51.4	1257	6	4	7.10	117.7	92	388	4.2	6	6	36
2002—Wisconsin	13	245	131	53.5	1758	14	4	7.18	129.3	160	466	2.9	8	8	48
College totals (4 years)	44	740	398	53.8	5406	36	17	7.31	126.6	489	1685	3.4	25	25	150

BRANCH, COLIN — S — PANTHERS

PERSONAL: Born March 2, 1980, in Carlsbad, Calif. ... 6-0/203. ... Brother of Calvin Branch, safety with Oakland Raiders (1997-2000).
HIGH SCHOOL: Carlsbad (Calif.).
COLLEGE: Stanford.
TRANSACTIONS/CAREER NOTES: Selected by Carolina Panthers in fourth round (119th pick overall) of 2003 NFL draft.

Year Team	G	No.	Yds.	Avg.	TD	No.	Yds.	Avg.	TD	TD	Pts.
		INTERCEPTIONS				PUNT RETURNS				TOTALS	
1998—Stanford					Redshirted.						
1999—Stanford	10	0	0	0.0	0	1	0	0.0	0	0	0
2000—Stanford	10	0	0	0.0	0	1	38	38.0	0	1	6
2001—Stanford	11	1	23	23.0	0	0	0	0.0	0	0	0
2002—Stanford	11	2	0	0.0	0	0	0	0.0	0	0	0
College totals (4 years)	42	3	23	7.7	0	2	38	19.0	0	1	6

BRAYTON, TYLER — DE — RAIDERS

PERSONAL: Born November 20, 1979, in Richland, Wash. ... 6-6/277.
HIGH SCHOOL: Pasco (Wash.).
COLLEGE: Colorado.
TRANSACTIONS/CAREER NOTES: Selected by Oakland Raiders in first round (32nd pick overall) of 2003 NFL draft.

Year Team	G	SACKS
1998—Colorado		Redshirted.
1999—Colorado	11	0.0
2000—Colorado	10	1.0
2001—Colorado	12	4.5
2002—Colorado	14	7.0
College totals (4 years)	47	12.5

BRIDGES, JEREMY — G/OT — EAGLES

PERSONAL: Born April 19, 1980, in McComb, Miss. ... 6-4/301.
HIGH SCHOOL: South Pike (McComb, Miss.).
COLLEGE: Southern Mississippi.
TRANSACTIONS/CAREER NOTES: Selected by Philadelphia Eagles in sixth round (185th pick overall) of 2003 NFL draft.
COLLEGE PLAYING EXPERIENCE: Southern Mississippi, 1998-2002. ... Games played: 1998 (redshirted), 1999 (11), 2000 (11), 2001 (11), 2002 (12). Total: 45.

BRIGGS, LANCE — LB — BEARS

PERSONAL: Born November 12, 1980, in Sacramento. ... 6-1/242. ... Full name: Lance Marell Briggs.
HIGH SCHOOL: Elk Grove (Sacramento).
COLLEGE: Arizona.
TRANSACTIONS/CAREER NOTES: Selected by Chicago Bears in third round (68th pick overall) of 2003 NFL draft.
COLLEGE NOTES: Rushed 25 times for 163 yards and two touchdowns, caught one pass for 12 yards, returned one kickoff (1999).

Year Team	G	Sks.	No.	Yds.	Avg.	TD
			INTERCEPTIONS			
1999—Arizona	10	0.0	0	0	0.0	0
2000—Arizona	11	1.0	2	23	11.5	0
2001—Arizona	11	7.0	0	0	0.0	0
2002—Arizona	11	3.0	1	0	0.0	0
College totals (4 years)	43	11.0	3	23	7.7	0

BROWN, CHRIS — RB — TITANS

PERSONAL: Born April 17, 1981, in Winfield, Ill. ... 6-3/220.
HIGH SCHOOL: Naperville (Ill.).
JUNIOR COLLEGE: Fort Scott (Kan.) Junior College.
COLLEGE: Northwestern, then Colorado.
TRANSACTIONS/CAREER NOTES: Selected after junior season by Tennessee Titans in third round (93rd pick overall) of 2003 NFL draft.

Year Team	G	RUSHING				RECEIVING				TOTALS	
		Att.	Yds.	Avg.	TD	No.	Yds.	Avg.	TD	TD	Pts.
1999—Northwestern		Redshirted.									
2001—Colorado	12	190	946	5.0	16	6	36	6.0	0	16	96
2002—Colorado	12	303	1841	6.1	19	5	40	8.0	0	19	114
College totals (2 years)	24	493	2787	5.7	35	11	76	6.9	0	35	210

BROWN, JOSH — K — SEAHAWKS

PERSONAL: Born April 29, 1979, in Foyil, Okla. ... 6-1/202. ... Full name: Joshua Brown.
HIGH SCHOOL: Foyil (Okla.).
COLLEGE: Nebraska.
TRANSACTIONS/CAREER NOTES: Selected by Seattle Seahawks in seventh round (222nd pick overall) of 2003 NFL draft.

Year Team	G	KICKING						
		50+	Tot.	Pct.	Lg.	XPM	XPA	Pts.
1998—Nebraska		Redshirted.						
1999—Nebraska	12	0-0	14-20	70.0	42	46	47	88
2000—Nebraska	11	0-0	5-10	50.0	40	60	60	75
2001—Nebraska	10	0-1	10-14	71.4	43	34	37	64
2002—Nebraska	13	0-0	14-18	77.8	48	46	46	88
College totals (4 years)	46	0-1	43-62	69.4	48	186	190	315

BURLESON, NATE — WR — VIKINGS

PERSONAL: Born August 19, 1981, in Seattle. ... 6-0/197.
HIGH SCHOOL: O'Dea (Seattle).
COLLEGE: Nevada-Reno.
TRANSACTIONS/CAREER NOTES: Selected by Minnesota Vikings in third round (71st pick overall) of 2003 NFL draft.
COLLEGE NOTES: Rushed two times (2000), three times (2001), 22 times (2002).

Year Team	G	RECEIVING				PUNT RETURNS				KICKOFF RETURNS				TOTALS	
		No.	Yds.	Avg.	TD	No.	Yds.	Avg.	TD	No.	Yds.	Avg.	TD	TD	Pts.
1999—Nevada		Did not play.													
2000—Nevada	12	57	921	16.2	8	14	55	3.9	0	11	177	16.1	0	8	50
2001—Nevada	9	53	737	13.9	2	0	0	0.0	0	3	90	30.0	0	2	14
2002—Nevada	12	138	1629	11.8	12	4	24	6.0	0	3	67	22.3	0	13	78
College totals (3 years)	33	248	3287	13.3	22	18	79	4.4	0	17	334	19.6	0	23	142

BURNS, CURRY — S — TEXANS

PERSONAL: Born February 12, 1981, in Miami. ... 6-0/216.
HIGH SCHOOL: Jackson (Miami).
COLLEGE: Louisville.
TRANSACTIONS/CAREER NOTES: Selected by Houston Texans in seventh round (217th pick overall) of 2003 NFL draft.
COLLEGE NOTES: Returned one punt (2002).

Year Team	G	INTERCEPTIONS			
		No.	Yds.	Avg.	TD
1999—Louisville	11	0	0	0.0	0
2000—Louisville	11	2	33	16.5	0
2001—Louisville	12	4	30	7.5	0
2002—Louisville	13	2	25	12.5	0
College totals (4 years)	47	8	88	11.0	0

CALICO, TYRONE — WR — TITANS

PERSONAL: Born November 9, 1980, in Millington, Tenn. ... 6-4/223.
HIGH SCHOOL: Millington (Tenn.).
COLLEGE: Middle Tennessee State.
TRANSACTIONS/CAREER NOTES: Selected by Tennessee Titans in second round (60th pick overall) of 2003 NFL draft.

Year Team	G	RUSHING				RECEIVING				TOTALS	
		Att.	Yds.	Avg.	TD	No.	Yds.	Avg.	TD	TD	Pts.
1998—Middle Tennessee State		Redshirted.									
1999—Middle Tennessee State	11	3	3	1.0	0	65	695	10.7	5	5	30
2000—Middle Tennessee State	11	0	0	0.0	0	47	752	16.0	3	3	18
2001—Middle Tennessee State	11	1	38	38.0	1	37	583	15.8	5	6	36
2002—Middle Tennessee State	12	10	14	1.4	0	45	606	13.5	4	4	24
College totals (4 years)	45	14	55	3.9	1	194	2636	13.6	17	18	108

CLARK, DALLAS — TE — COLTS

PERSONAL: Born June 12, 1979, in Livermore, Iowa. ... 6-3/257.
HIGH SCHOOL: Twin River Valley (Livermore, Iowa).
COLLEGE: Iowa.
TRANSACTIONS/CAREER NOTES: Selected after junior season by Indianapolis Colts in first round (24th pick overall) of 2003 NFL draft.
COLLEGE NOTES: Returned one kickoff (2000).

Year Team	G	RECEIVING			
		No.	Yds.	Avg.	TD
1998—Iowa		Redshirted.			
1999—Iowa		Did not play.			
2000—Iowa	12	0	0	0.0	0
2001—Iowa	11	34	509	15.0	4
2002—Iowa	13	43	742	17.3	4
College totals (3 years)	36	77	1251	16.2	8

CLAXTON, BEN   C   BRONCOS

PERSONAL: Born July 30, 1980, in Dublin, Ga. ... 6-3/301. ... Full name: Benjamin Claxton.
HIGH SCHOOL: Dublin (Ga.).
COLLEGE: Mississippi.
TRANSACTIONS/CAREER NOTES: Selected by Denver Broncos in fifth round (157th pick overall) of 2003 NFL draft.
COLLEGE PLAYING EXPERIENCE: Mississippi, 1998-2002. ... Games played: 1998 (redshirted), 1999 (12), 2000 (8), 2001 (11), 2002 (13). Total: 44.

COX, TORRIE   CB   BUCCANEERS

PERSONAL: Born October 29, 1980, in Miami. ... 5-9/181. ... Full name: Torrie Tywan Cox.
HIGH SCHOOL: Northwestern (Miami).
COLLEGE: Pittsburgh.
TRANSACTIONS/CAREER NOTES: Selected by Tampa Bay Buccaneers in sixth round (205th pick overall) of 2003 NFL draft.
COLLEGE NOTES: Rushed 26 times for 62 yards and one touchdown (1999), three times (2000).

Year Team	G	INTERCEPTIONS No.	Yds.	Avg.	TD	PUNT RETURNS No.	Yds.	Avg.	TD	KICKOFF RETURNS No.	Yds.	Avg.	TD	TOTALS TD	Pts.
1999—Pittsburgh	7	0	0	0.0	0	0	0	0.0	0	6	128	21.3	0	1	6
2000—Pittsburgh	11	0	0	0.0	0	0	0	0.0	0	5	176	35.2	1	1	6
2001—Pittsburgh	11	1	0	0.0	0	4	21	5.3	0	24	576	24.0	0	0	0
2002—Pittsburgh	13	2	41	20.5	0	0	0	0.0	0	30	690	23.0	0	0	0
College totals (4 years)	42	3	41	13.7	0	4	21	5.3	0	65	1570	24.2	1	2	12

CROCKER, CHRIS   S   BROWNS

PERSONAL: Born March 9, 1980, in Chesapeake, Va. ... 6-0/194. ... Full name: Christopher Alan Crocker.
HIGH SCHOOL: Deep Creek (Chesapeake, Va.).
COLLEGE: Marshall.
TRANSACTIONS/CAREER NOTES: Selected by Cleveland Browns in third round (84th pick overall) of 2003 NFL draft.
COLLEGE NOTES: Returned one punt (2000).

Year Team	G	Sks.	INTERCEPTIONS No.	Yds.	Avg.	TD
1998—Marshall			Redshirted.			
1999—Marshall	12	0.0	0	0	0.0	0
2000—Marshall	12	0.0	3	14	4.7	0
2001—Marshall	12	1.5	1	18	18.0	0
2002—Marshall	13	2.0	0	0	0.0	0
College totals (4 years)	49	3.5	4	32	8.0	0

CROWELL, ANGELO   LB   BILLS

PERSONAL: Born August 16, 1981, in Forsyth County, N.C. ... 6-0/236. ... Full name: Angelo Delvonne Crowell. ... Brother of Germane Crowell, wide receiver with Detroit Lions (1998-2002).
HIGH SCHOOL: North Forsyth (N.C.).
COLLEGE: Virginia.
TRANSACTIONS/CAREER NOTES: Selected by Buffalo Bills in third round (94th pick overall) of 2003 NFL draft.

Year Team	G	Sks.	INTERCEPTIONS No.	Yds.	Avg.	TD
1999—Virginia	11	0.0	0	0	0.0	0
2000—Virginia	11	0.0	0	0	0.0	0
2001—Virginia	11	4.0	2	30	15.0	0
2002—Virginia	14	3.0	0	0	0.0	0
College totals (4 years)	47	7.0	2	30	15.0	0

CURLEY, DAN   TE   RAMS

PERSONAL: Born April 25, 1978, in Tacoma, Wash. ... 6-4/254.
HIGH SCHOOL: Anacortes (Wash.).
COLLEGE: Eastern Washington.
TRANSACTIONS/CAREER NOTES: Selected by St. Louis Rams in fifth round (148th pick overall) of 2003 NFL draft.

Year Team	G	RECEIVING No.	Yds.	Avg.	TD
1998—Eastern Washington	7	14	220	15.7	1
1999—Eastern Washington	11	16	244	15.3	2
2000—Eastern Washington			Redshirted.		
2001—Eastern Washington	1	1	8	8.0	0
2002—Eastern Washington	8	27	249	9.2	4
College totals (4 years)	27	58	721	12.4	7

CURTIN, BRENNAN   OT   PACKERS

PERSONAL: Born June 30, 1980, in Daytona Beach, Fla. ... 6-9/318. ... Full name: John Brennan Curtin.
HIGH SCHOOL: The Benjamin School (Palm Beach, Fla.).
COLLEGE: Notre Dame.
TRANSACTIONS/CAREER NOTES: Selected after junior season by Green Bay Packers in sixth round (212th pick overall) of 2003 NFL draft.
COLLEGE PLAYING EXPERIENCE: Notre Dame, 1999-2002. ... Games played: 1999 (redshirted), 2000 (4), 2001 (11), 2002 (12). Total: 27.

CURTIS, KEVIN — WR — RAMS

PERSONAL: Born July 17, 1978, in Murray, Utah. ... 5-11/186.
HIGH SCHOOL: Bingham (South Jordan, Utah).
JUNIOR COLLEGE: Snow College (Utah).
COLLEGE: Utah State.
TRANSACTIONS/CAREER NOTES: Selected by St. Louis Rams in third round (74th pick overall) of 2003 NFL draft.
COLLEGE NOTES: Attempted three passes (2001), three passes (2002).

		RUSHING				RECEIVING				PUNT RETURNS				TOTALS	
Year Team	G	Att.	Yds.	Avg.	TD	No.	Yds.	Avg.	TD	No.	Yds.	Avg.	TD	TD	Pts.
2000—Utah State						Redshirted.									
2001—Utah State	11	3	25	8.3	0	100	1531	15.3	10	0	0	0.0	0	10	60
2002—Utah State	11	6	21	3.5	1	74	1258	17.0	9	2	12	6.0	0	10	60
College totals (2 years)	22	9	46	5.1	1	174	2789	16.0	19	2	12	6.0	0	20	120

DAVIS, CHRIS — FB — SEAHAWKS

PERSONAL: Born November 8, 1979, in Tampa. ... 5-11/235. ... Full name: Christopher Michael Davis.
HIGH SCHOOL: Hillsborough (Tampa).
COLLEGE: Syracuse.
TRANSACTIONS/CAREER NOTES: Selected by Seattle Seahawks in fifth round (165th pick overall) of 2003 NFL draft.
COLLEGE NOTES: Returned one kickoff (2001).

		RUSHING				RECEIVING				TOTALS	
Year Team	G	Att.	Yds.	Avg.	TD	No.	Yds.	Avg.	TD	TD	Pts
1998—Syracuse						Redshirted.					
1999—Syracuse	2	4	31	7.8	0	0	0	0.0	0	0	0
2000—Syracuse	11	26	86	3.3	3	3	21	7.0	0	3	18
2001—Syracuse	12	12	28	2.3	3	1	-3	-3.0	0	3	18
2002—Syracuse	12	31	85	2.7	1	5	35	7.0	0	1	6
College totals (4 years)	37	73	230	3.2	7	9	53	5.9	0	7	42

DAVIS, DOMANICK — RB — TEXANS

PERSONAL: Born October 1, 1980, in Lafayette, La. ... 5-9/213.
HIGH SCHOOL: Breaux Bridge (La.).
COLLEGE: Louisiana State.
TRANSACTIONS/CAREER NOTES: Selected by Houston Texans in fourth round (101st pick overall) of 2003 NFL draft.

		RUSHING				RECEIVING				PUNT RETURNS				KICKOFF RETURNS				TOTALS	
Year Team	G	Att.	Yds.	Avg.	TD	No.	Yds.	Avg.	TD	No.	Yds.	Avg.	TD	No.	Yds.	Avg.	TD	TD	Pts.
1999—Louisiana State	11	64	274	4.3	3	13	94	7.2	0	12	66	5.5	0	25	618	24.7	0	3	18
2000—Louisiana State	11	123	445	3.6	5	9	120	13.3	0	27	298	11.0	0	24	572	23.8	0	5	30
2001—Louisiana State	11	75	406	5.4	5	3	49	16.3	1	19	263	13.8	1	22	418	19.0	0	7	42
2002—Louisiana State	13	193	931	4.8	7	16	130	8.1	0	36	499	13.9	1	24	560	23.3	0	8	48
College totals (4 years)	46	455	2056	4.5	20	41	393	9.6	1	94	1126	12.0	2	95	2168	22.8	0	23	138

DAVIS, JAMES — LB/SS — LIONS

PERSONAL: Born April 26, 1979, in Stuart, Fla. ... 6-1/221.
HIGH SCHOOL: Martin County (Stuart, Fla.).
COLLEGE: West Virginia.
TRANSACTIONS/CAREER NOTES: Selected by Detroit Lions in fifth round (144th pick overall) of 2003 NFL draft.

Year Team	G	SACKS
1998—West Virginia		Redshirted.
1999—West Virginia	10	0.0
2000—West Virginia	11	6.0
2001—West Virginia	11	8.0
2002—West Virginia	13	4.0
College totals (4 years)	45	18.0

DAVIS, SAMMY — CB — CHARGERS

PERSONAL: Born April 8, 1980, in Humble, Texas. ... 6-0/186. ... Full name: Samuel J. Davis Jr.
HIGH SCHOOL: Humble (Texas).
COLLEGE: Texas A&M.
TRANSACTIONS/CAREER NOTES: Selected by San Diego Chargers in first round (30th pick overall) of 2003 NFL draft.

			INTERCEPTIONS				KICKOFF RETURNS				TOTALS	
Year Team	G	Sks.	No.	Yds.	Avg.	TD	No.	Yds.	Avg.	TD	TD	Pts.
1999—Texas A&M	10	0.0	0	0	0.0	0	0	0	0.0	0	0	0
2000—Texas A&M	11	0.0	4	25	6.3	0	0	0	0.0	0	0	0
2001—Texas A&M	11	0.0	5	52	10.4	0	9	162	18.0	0	0	0
2002—Texas A&M	12	2.0	2	35	17.5	0	0	0	0.0	0	0	0
College totals (4 years)	44	2.0	11	112	10.2	0	9	162	18.0	0	0	0

DIEHL, DAVID　　　　　　　　G　　　　　　　　GIANTS

PERSONAL: Born September 15, 1980, in Chicago. ... 6-6/310. ... Full name: David Michael Diehl.
HIGH SCHOOL: Brother Rice (Oak Lawn, Ill.).
COLLEGE: Illinois (degree in speech communications).
TRANSACTIONS/CAREER NOTES: Selected by New York Giants in fifth round (160th pick overall) of 2003 NFL draft.
COLLEGE PLAYING EXPERIENCE: Illinois, 1998-2002. ... Games played: 1998 (redshirted), 1999 (6), 2000 (11), 2001 (11), 2002 (11). Total: 39.

DOCKERY, DERRICK　　　　　G/OT　　　　　REDSKINS

PERSONAL: Born September 7, 1980, in Garland, Texas. ... 6-6/347.
HIGH SCHOOL: Lakeview Centennial (Lakeview, Texas).
COLLEGE: Texas.
TRANSACTIONS/CAREER NOTES: Selected by Washington Redskins in third round (81st pick overall) of 2003 NFL draft.
COLLEGE PLAYING EXPERIENCE: Texas, 1999-2002. ... Games played: 1999 (13), 2000 (11), 2001 (12), 2002 (13). Total: 49.

DORSEY, KEN　　　　　　　　QB　　　　　　　　49ERS

PERSONAL: Born April 22, 1981, in Orinda, Calif. ... 6-5/208. ... Full name: Kenneth Simon Dorsey.
HIGH SCHOOL: Miramonte (Orinda, Calif.).
COLLEGE: Miami (Fla.).
TRANSACTIONS/CAREER NOTES: Selected by San Francisco 49ers in seventh round (241st pick overall) of 2003 NFL draft.

		PASSING								RUSHING				TOTALS	
Year　Team	G	Att.	Cmp.	Pct.	Yds.	TD	Int.	Avg.	Rat.	Att.	Yds.	Avg.	TD	TD	Pts.
1999—Miami (Fla.)	6	120	74	61.7	807	10	2	6.73	142.3	8	-20	-2.5	1	1	6
2000—Miami (Fla.)	11	322	188	58.4	2737	25	5	8.50	152.3	16	-23	-1.4	1	1	8
2001—Miami (Fla.)	11	318	184	57.9	2652	23	9	8.34	146.1	12	3	0.3	0	0	0
2002—Miami (Fla.)	13	393	222	56.5	3369	28	12	8.57	145.9	23	-39	-1.7	0	0	0
College totals (4 years)	41	1153	668	57.9	9565	86	28	8.30	147.4	59	-79	-1.3	2	2	14

DOSS, MIKE　　　　　　　　S　　　　　　　　COLTS

PERSONAL: Born March 24, 1981, in Canton, Ohio. ... 5-10/207.
HIGH SCHOOL: McKinley (Canton, Ohio).
COLLEGE: Ohio State.
TRANSACTIONS/CAREER NOTES: Selected by Indianapolis Colts in second round (58th pick overall) of 2003 NFL draft.

			INTERCEPTIONS				PUNT RETURNS				KICKOFF RETURNS				TOTALS	
Year　Team	G	Sks.	No.	Yds.	Avg.	TD	No.	Yds.	Avg.	TD	No.	Yds.	Avg.	TD	TD	Pts.
1999—Ohio State	11	0.0	0	0	0.0	0	0	0	0.0	0	0	0	0.0	0	0	0
2000—Ohio State	11	3.0	3	33	11.0	0	0	0	0.0	0	1	15	15.0	0	2	12
2001—Ohio State	11	3.0	3	71	23.7	0	2	25	12.5	0	0	0	0.0	0	1	6
2002—Ohio State	14	0.0	2	80	40.0	1	4	25	6.3	0	2	37	18.5	0	1	6
College totals (4 years)	47	6.0	8	184	23.0	1	6	50	8.3	0	3	52	17.3	0	4	24

DRAKE, CHARLES　　　　　　S　　　　　　GIANTS

PERSONAL: Born September 25, 1981, in Los Angeles. ... 6-1/205. ... Full name: Charles Edward Drake.
HIGH SCHOOL: Westchester (Los Angeles).
COLLEGE: Michigan.
TRANSACTIONS/CAREER NOTES: Selected by New York Giants in seventh round (240th pick overall) of 2003 NFL draft.
COLLEGE NOTES: Rushed 12 times, caught one pass, returned two kickoffs (1999); returned one kickoff (2001).

			INTERCEPTIONS			
Year　Team	G	Sks.	No.	Yds.	Avg.	TD
1999—Michigan	9	0.0	0	0	0.0	0
2000—Michigan	11	0.0	0	0	0.0	0
2001—Michigan	11	2.0	0	0	0.0	0
2002—Michigan	13	3.0	1	46	46.0	0
College totals (4 years)	44	5.0	1	46	46.0	0

DRUMM, BRANDON　　　　　FB　　　　　LIONS

PERSONAL: Born July 5, 1979, in Olympia, Wash. ... 6-1/233.
HIGH SCHOOL: Service (Anchorage, Alaska).
COLLEGE: Colorado.
TRANSACTIONS/CAREER NOTES: Selected by Detroit Lions in seventh round (236th pick overall) of 2003 NFL draft.

		RUSHING				RECEIVING				KICKOFF RETURNS				TOTALS	
Year　Team	G	Att.	Yds.	Avg.	TD	No.	Yds.	Avg.	TD	No.	Yds.	Avg.	TD	TD	Pts.
1998—Colorado							Redshirted.									
1999—Colorado	9	2	8	4.0	0	4	42	10.5	0	1	1	1.0	0	0	0
2000—Colorado	11	3	6	2.0	0	1	13	13.0	0	1	18	18.0	0	0	0
2001—Colorado	12	7	19	2.7	0	14	102	7.3	0	0	0	0.0	0	0	0
2002—Colorado	14	11	128	11.6	4	20	161	8.1	0	0	0	0.0	0	4	24
College totals (4 years)	46	23	161	7.0	4	39	318	8.2	0	2	19	9.5	0	4	24

DUNBAR, LATARENCE   WR   FALCONS

PERSONAL: Born August 15, 1980, in Dallas. ... 5-11/196. ... Full name: LaTarence Eugene Dunbar.
HIGH SCHOOL: South Oak Cliff (Dallas).
COLLEGE: Texas Christian.
TRANSACTIONS/CAREER NOTES: Selected by Atlanta Falcons in sixth round (196th pick overall) of 2003 NFL draft.

		RUSHING				RECEIVING				KICKOFF RETURNS				TOTALS	
Year Team	G	Att.	Yds.	Avg.	TD	No.	Yds.	Avg.	TD	No.	Yds.	Avg.	TD	TD	Pts.
1998—Texas Christian							Redshirted.								
1999—Texas Christian	11	9	57	6.3	0	20	315	15.8	2	3	50	16.7	0	3	20
2000—Texas Christian	11	1	8	8.0	0	17	251	14.8	4	15	506	33.7	2	6	36
2001—Texas Christian	11	13	49	3.8	2	41	529	12.9	3	25	456	18.2	0	5	30
2002—Texas Christian	11	18	120	6.7	1	31	444	14.3	4	18	499	27.7	1	6	36
College totals (4 years)	44	41	234	5.7	3	109	1539	14.1	13	61	1511	24.8	3	20	122

EASON, NICK   DT   BRONCOS

PERSONAL: Born May 29, 1980, in Lyons, Ga. ... 6-3/301. ... Full name: Nicholas Eason.
HIGH SCHOOL: Toombs County (Lyons, Ga.).
COLLEGE: Clemson (degree in sociology).
TRANSACTIONS/CAREER NOTES: Selected by Denver Broncos in fourth round (114th pick overall) of 2003 NFL draft.

Year Team	G	SACKS
1998—Clemson		Redshirted.
1999—Clemson	11	1.0
2000—Clemson	11	7.0
2001—Clemson	11	1.0
2002—Clemson	13	7.0
College totals (4 years)	46	16.0

FAINE, JEFF   C   BROWNS

PERSONAL: Born April 6, 1981, in Milwaukee, Ore. ... 6-3/303. ... Full name: Jeffrey Kalei Faine.
HIGH SCHOOL: Seminole (Sanford, Fla.).
COLLEGE: Notre Dame.
TRANSACTIONS/CAREER NOTES: Selected after junior season by Cleveland Browns in first round (21st pick overall) of 2003 NFL draft.
COLLEGE PLAYING EXPERIENCE: Notre Dame, 1999-2002. ... Games played: 1999 (redshirted), 2000 (11), 2001 (11), 2002 (13). Total: 35.

FARGAS, JUSTIN   RB   RAIDERS

PERSONAL: Born January 25, 1980, in Encino, Calif. ... 6-1/219.
HIGH SCHOOL: Notre Dame (Sherman Oaks, Calif.).
COLLEGE: Michigan, then Southern California.
TRANSACTIONS/CAREER NOTES: Selected by Oakland Raiders in third round (96th pick overall) of 2003 NFL draft.

		RUSHING				RECEIVING				KICKOFF RETURNS				TOTALS	
Year Team	G	Att.	Yds.	Avg.	TD	No.	Yds.	Avg.	TD	No.	Yds.	Avg.	TD	TD	Pts.
1998—Michigan	10	77	277	3.6	1	1	5	5.0	0	16	311	19.4	0	1	6
1999—Michigan							Redshirted.								
2000—Michigan	10	18	85	4.7	0	0	0	0.0	0	7	124	17.7	0	0	0
2001—Southern California							Did not play.								
2002—Southern California	12	161	715	4.4	7	8	101	12.6	0	7	132	18.9	0	7	42
College totals (3 years)	32	256	1077	4.2	8	9	106	11.8	0	30	567	18.9	0	8	48

FLORENCE, DRAYTON   CB   CHARGERS

PERSONAL: Born December 19, 1980, in Waycross, Ga. ... 6-0/198. ... Full name: Drayton Florence Jr.
HIGH SCHOOL: Richland Northeast (Columbia, S.C.), then Vanguard (Ocala, Fla.).
COLLEGE: Tennessee-Chattanooga, then Tuskegee.
TRANSACTIONS/CAREER NOTES: Selected by San Diego Chargers in second round (46th pick overall) of 2003 NFL draft.

			INTERCEPTIONS				KICKOFF RETURNS				TOTALS	
Year Team	G	Sks.	No.	Yds.	Avg.	TD	No.	Yds.	Avg.	TD	TD	Pts.
1999—Tennessee-Chattanooga	11	0.0	0	0	0.0	0	1	27	27.0	0	0	0
2000—Tennessee-Chattanooga	11	0.0	4	7	1.8	0	0	0	0.0	0	0	0
2001—Tuskegee	11	1.0	4	74	18.5	1	1	8	8.0	0	1	6
2002—Tuskegee	11	0.0	5	177	35.4	1	0	0	0.0	0	1	6
College totals (4 years)	44	1.0	13	258	19.8	2	2	35	17.5	0	2	12

FORD, CARL   WR   PACKERS

PERSONAL: Born October 8, 1980, in Monroe, Mich. ... 6-0/174. ... Full name: Carl Ford III.
HIGH SCHOOL: Monroe (Mich.).
COLLEGE: Toledo.
TRANSACTIONS/CAREER NOTES: Selected by Green Bay Packers in seventh round (256th pick overall) of 2003 NFL draft.
COLLEGE NOTES: Caught one pass (2002).

Year	Team	G	RECEIVING				KICKOFF RETURNS				TOTALS	
			No.	Yds.	Avg.	TD	No.	Yds.	Avg.	TD	TD	Pts.
1999—Toledo		11	15	172	11.5	2	13	260	20.0	0	2	12
2000—Toledo		10	9	86	9.6	0	6	97	16.2	0	0	0
2001—Toledo		11	46	646	14.0	6	0	0	0.0	0	6	36
2002—Toledo		14	79	1062	13.4	9	5	98	19.6	0	9	54
College totals (4 years)		46	149	1966	13.2	17	24	455	19.0	0	17	102

FORSEY, BROCK — RB — BEARS

PERSONAL: Born February 11, 1980, in Meridian, Idaho. ... 5-11/198.
HIGH SCHOOL: Centennial (Meridian, Idaho).
COLLEGE: Boise State.
TRANSACTIONS/CAREER NOTES: Selected by Chicago Bears in sixth round (206th pick overall) of 2003 NFL draft.
COLLEGE NOTES: Attempted one pass, passed for one touchdown (2001), attempted two passes (2002).

Year	Team	G	RUSHING				RECEIVING				KICKOFF RETURNS				TOTALS	
			Att.	Yds.	Avg.	TD	No.	Yds.	Avg.	TD	No.	Yds.	Avg.	TD	TD	Pts.
1998—Boise State									Redshirted.							
1999—Boise State		12	75	313	4.2	2	7	125	17.9	2	13	337	25.9	0	4	24
2000—Boise State		10	197	914	4.6	9	23	399	17.3	7	24	517	21.5	0	16	96
2001—Boise State		12	245	1199	4.9	12	35	369	10.5	3	17	362	21.3	0	15	90
2002—Boise State		13	295	1611	5.5	26	36	282	7.8	6	9	234	26.0	0	32	192
College totals (4 years)		47	812	4037	5.0	49	101	1175	11.6	18	63	1450	23.0	0	67	402

FOSTER, GEORGE — OT — BRONCOS

PERSONAL: Born June 9, 1980, in Macon, Ga. ... 6-5/338.
HIGH SCHOOL: Southeast (Macon, Ga.).
COLLEGE: Georgia.
TRANSACTIONS/CAREER NOTES: Selected by Denver Broncos in first round (20th pick overall) of 2003 NFL draft.
COLLEGE PLAYING EXPERIENCE: Georgia, 1998-2002. ... Games played: 1998 (redshirted), 1999 (11), 2000 (11), 2001 (11), 2002 (5). Total: 38.

FRANKLIN, AUBRAYO — DT — RAVENS

PERSONAL: Born August 27, 1980, in Johnson City, Tenn. ... 6-1/307. ... Full name: Aubrayo Razyo Franklin.
HIGH SCHOOL: Science Hill (Johnson City, Tenn.).
JUNIOR COLLEGE: Itawamba Community College (Miss.).
COLLEGE: Tennessee.
TRANSACTIONS/CAREER NOTES: Selected by Baltimore Ravens in fifth round (146th pick overall) of 2003 NFL draft.

Year	Team	G	SACKS
2001—Tennessee		11	0.0
2002—Tennessee		13	2.0
College totals (2 years)		24	2.0

FREITAS, MAKOA — OT — COLTS

PERSONAL: Born November 23, 1979, in Honolulu, Hawaii. ... 6-4/307. ... Full name: Rockne Makoa Freitas. ... Son of Rocky Freitas, offensive tackle with Detroit Lions (1968-77) and Tampa Bay Buccaneers (1978).
HIGH SCHOOL: Kamehameha (Honolulu, Hawaii).
COLLEGE: Arizona.
TRANSACTIONS/CAREER NOTES: Selected by Indianapolis Colts in sixth round (208th pick overall) of 2003 NFL draft.
COLLEGE PLAYING EXPERIENCE: Arizona, 1998-2002. ... Games played: 1998 (13), 1999 (11), 2000 (3), 2001 (11), 2002 (11). Total: 49.

GABRIEL, DOUG — WR — RAIDERS

PERSONAL: Born August 27, 1980, in Miami. ... 6-2/213. ... Full name: Douglas Gabriel.
HIGH SCHOOL: Dr. Phillips (Orlando).
JUNIOR COLLEGE: Mississippi Gulf Coast Junior College.
COLLEGE: Central Florida.
TRANSACTIONS/CAREER NOTES: Selected by Oakland Raiders in fifth round (167th pick overall) of 2003 NFL draft.

Year	Team	G	RUSHING				RECEIVING				KICKOFF RETURNS				TOTALS	
			Att.	Yds.	Avg.	TD	No.	Yds.	Avg.	TD	No.	Yds.	Avg.	TD	TD	Pts.
2001—Central Florida		10	0	0	0.0	0	22	632	28.7	9	6	163	27.2	0	9	54
2002—Central Florida		12	7	52	7.4	1	75	1237	16.5	11	31	632	20.4	0	12	72
College totals (2 years)		22	7	52	7.4	1	97	1869	19.3	20	37	795	21.5	0	21	126

GAGE, JUSTIN — WR — BEARS

PERSONAL: Born January 25, 1981, in Jefferson City, Mo. ... 6-4/203.
HIGH SCHOOL: Jefferson City (Mo.).
COLLEGE: Missouri.
TRANSACTIONS/CAREER NOTES: Selected by Chicago Bears in fifth round (143rd pick overall) of 2003 NFL draft.
COLLEGE NOTES: Returned one kickoff, one punt (2000).

Year Team	G	PASSING								RUSHING				RECEIVING				TOTALS	
		Att.	Cmp.	Pct.	Yds.	TD	Int.	Avg.	Rat.	Att.	Yds.	Avg.	TD	No.	Yds.	Avg.	TD	TD	Pts.
1999—Missouri............	3	41	14	34.1	138	2	3	3.37	63.9	19	3	0.2	0	0	0	0.0	0	0	0
2000—Missouri............	11	5	2	40.0	105	0	0	21.00	216.4	6	-14	-2.3	0	44	709	16.1	4	4	24
2001—Missouri............	11	2	1	50.0	9	1	0	4.50	252.8	1	8	8.0	0	74	920	12.4	5	6	38
2002—Missouri............	12	1	1	100.0	6	1	0	6.00	480.4	2	9	4.5	0	82	1075	13.1	9	9	54
College totals (4 years) .	37	49	18	36.7	258	4	3	5.27	95.7	28	6	0.2	0	200	2704	13.5	18	19	116

GALLOWAY, AHMAAD — RB — BRONCOS

PERSONAL: Born March 10, 1980, in Millington, Tenn. ... 6-0/223.
HIGH SCHOOL: Millington (Tenn.).
COLLEGE: Alabama.
TRANSACTIONS/CAREER NOTES: Selected by Denver Broncos in seventh round (235th pick overall) of 2003 NFL draft.

Year Team	G	RUSHING				RECEIVING				TOTALS	
		Att.	Yds.	Avg.	TD	No.	Yds.	Avg.	TD	TD	Pts.
1998—Alabama					Redshirted.						
1999—Alabama	12	7	33	4.7	0	0	0	0.0	0	0	0
2000—Alabama	11	137	659	4.8	7	4	48	12.0	0	7	42
2001—Alabama	11	174	881	5.1	6	3	20	6.7	0	6	36
2002—Alabama	4	58	257	4.4	4	1	5	5.0	0	4	24
College totals (4 years)	38	376	1830	4.9	17	8	73	9.1	0	17	102

GARAY, ANTONIO — DE — BROWNS

PERSONAL: Born November 30, 1979, in Rahway, N.J. ... 6-3/295.
HIGH SCHOOL: Rahway (N.J.).
COLLEGE: Boston College.
TRANSACTIONS/CAREER NOTES: Selected by Cleveland Browns in sixth round (195th pick overall) of 2003 NFL draft.

Year Team	G	Sks.	INTERCEPTIONS			
			No.	Yds.	Avg.	TD
1998—Boston College................................	7	0.0	0	0	0.0	0
1999—Boston College................................	11	2.0	0	0	0.0	0
2000—Boston College................................	1	0.0	0	0	0.0	0
2001—Boston College................................	8	5.0	1	49	49.0	0
2002—Boston College................................	6	5.0	0	0	0.0	0
College totals (5 years)	33	12.0	1	49	49.0	0

GARDNER, TALMAN — WR — SAINTS

PERSONAL: Born March 10, 1980, in New Orleans. ... 6-1/205.
HIGH SCHOOL: McDonough (New Orleans).
COLLEGE: Florida State.
TRANSACTIONS/CAREER NOTES: Selected by New Orleans Saints in seventh round (231st pick overall) of 2003 NFL draft.

Year Team	G	RUSHING				RECEIVING				KICKOFF RETURNS				TOTALS	
		Att.	Yds.	Avg.	TD	No.	Yds.	Avg.	TD	No.	Yds.	Avg.	TD	TD	Pts.
1998—Florida State..................................								Redshirted.							
1999—Florida State..................................	11	2	23	11.5	0	7	123	17.6	0	8	172	21.5	0	0	0
2000—Florida State..................................	11	2	24	12.0	0	12	198	16.5	0	8	175	21.9	0	0	0
2001—Florida State..................................	10	2	-8	-4.0	0	33	649	19.7	11	0	0	0.0	0	11	66
2002—Florida State..................................	14	1	0	0.0	0	38	625	16.4	8	12	261	21.8	0	8	48
College totals (4 years)	46	7	39	5.6	0	90	1595	17.7	19	28	608	21.7	0	19	114

GARRETT, KEVIN — CB — RAMS

PERSONAL: Born July 29, 1980, in San Benito, Texas. ... 5-9/194. ... Cousin of Quentin Jammer, cornerback, San Diego Chargers.
HIGH SCHOOL: Sweeney (Brazoria, Texas).
COLLEGE: Southern Methodist.
TRANSACTIONS/CAREER NOTES: Selected by St. Louis Rams in fifth round (172nd pick overall) of 2003 NFL draft.
COLLEGE NOTES: Returned one punt (1999).

Year Team	G	INTERCEPTIONS			
		No.	Yds.	Avg.	TD
1998—SMU..			Redshirted.		
1999—SMU..	10	1	-6	-6.0	0
2000—SMU..	12	1	11	11.0	0
2001—SMU..	11	3	88	29.3	1
2002—SMU..	10	2	5	2.5	0
College totals (4 years)	43	7	98	14.0	1

GILBERT, TONY — LB — CARDINALS

PERSONAL: Born October 16, 1979, in Macon, Ga. ... 6-0/251. ... Full name: Antonio C. Gilbert.
HIGH SCHOOL: Central (Macon, Ga.).
COLLEGE: Georgia.
TRANSACTIONS/CAREER NOTES: Selected by Arizona Cardinals in sixth round (210th pick overall) of 2003 NFL draft.

Year	Team	G	Sks.	INTERCEPTIONS No.	Yds.	Avg.	TD
1998—Georgia				Redshirted.			
1999—Georgia		10	0.0	0	0	0.0	0
2000—Georgia		10	0.0	0	0	0.0	0
2001—Georgia		11	1.5	1	5	5.0	0
2002—Georgia		14	2.5	0	0	0.0	0
College totals (4 years)		45	4.0	1	5	5.0	0

GRANT, CIE — LB — SAINTS

PERSONAL: Born November 27, 1979, in New Philadelphia, Ohio. ... 6-0/228. ... Full name: Willie Grant.
HIGH SCHOOL: New Philadelphia (Ohio).
COLLEGE: Ohio State.
TRANSACTIONS/CAREER NOTES: Selected by New Orleans Saints in third round (86th pick overall) of 2003 NFL draft.

Year	Team	G	Sks.	INTERCEPTIONS No.	Yds.	Avg.	TD
1998—Ohio State				Redshirted.			
1999—Ohio State		11	0.0	0	0	0.0	0
2000—Ohio State		10	0.0	0	0	0.0	0
2001—Ohio State		11	0.0	3	21	7.0	0
2002—Ohio State		13	4.0	1	23	23.0	0
College totals (4 years)		45	4.0	4	44	11.0	0

GREEN, BRANDON — DE — JAGUARS

PERSONAL: Born September 5, 1980, in Victoria, Texas. ... 6-2/267. ... Full name: James Brandon Green.
HIGH SCHOOL: Industrial (Vanderbilt, Texas).
COLLEGE: Rice.
TRANSACTIONS/CAREER NOTES: Selected by Jacksonville Jaguars in sixth round (176th pick overall) of 2003 NFL draft.

Year	Team	G	Sks.	INTERCEPTIONS No.	Yds.	Avg.	TD
1999—Rice		11	1.0	0	0	0.0	0
2000—Rice		10	4.0	0	0	0.0	0
2001—Rice		12	12.0	1	27	27.0	0
2002—Rice		11	8.0	1	13	13.0	1
College totals (4 years)		44	25.0	2	40	20.0	1

GREEN, JAMAAL — DE — EAGLES

PERSONAL: Born June 5, 1980, in Camden, N.J. ... 6-2/272. ... Full name: Jamaal Hakeem Green.
HIGH SCHOOL: Woodrow Wilson (Camden, N.J.).
COLLEGE: Miami (Fla.).
TRANSACTIONS/CAREER NOTES: Selected by Philadelphia Eagles in fourth round (131st pick overall) of 2003 NFL draft.

Year	Team	G	SACKS
1998—Miami (Fla.)			Redshirted.
1999—Miami (Fla.)		12	4.0
2000—Miami (Fla.)		9	4.0
2001—Miami (Fla.)		11	6.0
2002—Miami (Fla.)		13	10.0
College totals (4 years)		45	24.0

GRIFFIN, QUENTIN — RB — BRONCOS

PERSONAL: Born January 12, 1981, in Houston. ... 5-7/195.
HIGH SCHOOL: Aldine-Nimitz (Aldine, Texas).
COLLEGE: Oklahoma.
TRANSACTIONS/CAREER NOTES: Selected by Denver Broncos in fourth round (108th pick overall) of 2003 NFL draft.

Year	Team	G	RUSHING Att.	Yds.	Avg.	TD	RECEIVING No.	Yds.	Avg.	TD	TOTALS TD	Pts.
1999—Oklahoma		4	44	285	6.5	3	11	107	9.7	1	4	24
2000—Oklahoma		12	189	783	4.1	16	45	406	9.0	0	16	96
2001—Oklahoma		12	182	804	4.4	9	55	440	8.0	2	11	66
2002—Oklahoma		14	287	1884	6.6	15	35	264	7.5	3	18	108
College totals (4 years)		42	702	3756	5.4	43	146	1217	8.3	6	49	294

GRIFFITH, JUSTIN — FB — FALCONS

PERSONAL: Born July 21, 1980, in Magee, Miss. ... 5-11/232. ... Full name: Justin Montrel Griffith.
HIGH SCHOOL: Magee (Sanatorium, Miss.).
COLLEGE: Mississippi State.
TRANSACTIONS/CAREER NOTES: Selected by Atlanta Falcons in fourth round (121st pick overall) of 2003 NFL draft.

Year	Team	G	RUSHING Att.	Yds.	Avg.	TD	RECEIVING No.	Yds.	Avg.	TD	TOTALS TD	Pts.
1998—Mississippi State		1	3	9	3.0	1	0	0	0.0	0	1	6
1999—Mississippi State		11	62	196	3.2	5	37	380	10.3	2	7	42
2000—Mississippi State		11	44	136	3.1	2	19	240	12.6	2	4	24
2001—Mississippi State		5	13	40	3.1	0	10	118	11.8	0	0	0
2002—Mississippi State		11	91	471	5.2	2	19	199	10.5	0	2	12
College totals (5 years)		39	213	852	4.0	10	85	937	11.0	4	14	84

GROCE, DEJUAN   CB   RAMS

PERSONAL: Born February 17, 1980, in Garfield Heights, Ohio. ... 5-10/192.
HIGH SCHOOL: St. Edward (Garfield Heights, Ohio).
COLLEGE: Nebraska.
TRANSACTIONS/CAREER NOTES: Selected by St. Louis Rams in fourth round (107th pick overall) of 2003 NFL draft.

Year Team	G	INTERCEPTIONS				PUNT RETURNS				TOTALS	
		No.	Yds.	Avg.	TD	No.	Yds.	Avg.	TD	TD	Pts.
1998—Nebraska						Redshirted.					
1999—Nebraska	12	0	0	0.0	0	2	17	8.5	0	0	0
2000—Nebraska	11	1	0	0.0	0	0	0	0.0	0	0	0
2001—Nebraska	11	3	49	16.3	0	33	469	14.2	1	1	6
2002—Nebraska	14	4	26	6.5	0	43	732	17.0	4	4	24
College totals (4 years)	48	8	75	9.4	0	78	1218	15.6	5	5	30

GROSS, JORDAN   OT   PANTHERS

PERSONAL: Born July 20, 1980, in Fruitland, Idaho. ... 6-4/300.
HIGH SCHOOL: Fruitland (Idaho).
COLLEGE: Utah (degree in communications).
TRANSACTIONS/CAREER NOTES: Selected by Carolina Panthers in first round (eighth pick overall) of 2003 NFL draft.
COLLEGE NOTES: Caught one pass (2001), one pass (2002).
COLLEGE PLAYING EXPERIENCE: Utah, 1998-2002. ... Games played: 1998 (redshirted), 1999 (8), 2000 (11), 2001 (11), 2002 (11). Total: 41.

GROSSMAN, REX   QB   BEARS

PERSONAL: Born August 23, 1980, in Bloomington, Ind. ... 6-1/217.
HIGH SCHOOL: Bloomington South (Bloomington, Ind.).
COLLEGE: Florida.
TRANSACTIONS/CAREER NOTES: Selected after junior season by Chicago Bears in first round (22nd pick overall) of 2003 NFL draft.
COLLEGE NOTES: Caught one pass (2000), one pass (2002).

Year Team	G	PASSING								RUSHING				TOTALS	
		Att.	Cmp.	Pct.	Yds.	TD	Int.	Avg.	Rat.	Att.	Yds.	Avg.	TD	TD	Pts.
1999—Florida						Redshirted.									
2000—Florida	11	212	131	61.8	1866	21	7	8.80	161.8	27	-76	-2.8	0	0	0
2001—Florida	11	395	259	65.6	3896	34	12	9.86	170.8	34	8	0.2	5	5	30
2002—Florida	13	503	287	57.1	3402	22	17	6.76	121.5	58	-65	-1.1	1	1	8
College totals (3 years)	35	1110	677	61.0	9164	77	36	8.26	146.7	119	-133	-1.1	6	6	38

HAGGAN, MARIO   LB   BILLS

PERSONAL: Born March 3, 1980, in Clarksdale, Miss. ... 6-3/252. ... Full name: Mario Marcell Haggan.
HIGH SCHOOL: Clarksdale (Miss.).
COLLEGE: Mississippi State.
TRANSACTIONS/CAREER NOTES: Selected by Buffalo Bills in seventh round (228th pick overall) of 2003 NFL draft.

Year Team	G	Sks.	INTERCEPTIONS			
			No.	Yds.	Avg.	TD
1998—Mississippi State				Redshirted.		
1999—Mississippi State	8	1.0	0	0	0.0	0
2000—Mississippi State	11	5.0	1	7	7.0	0
2001—Mississippi State	10	2.5	0	0	0.0	0
2002—Mississippi State	11	0.0	0	0	0.0	0
College totals (4 years)	40	8.5	1	7	7.0	0

HAMDAN, GIBRAN   QB   REDSKINS

PERSONAL: Born February 8, 1981, in San Diego. ... 6-5/239.
HIGH SCHOOL: Bishop O'Connell (North Potomac, Md.).
COLLEGE: Indiana.
TRANSACTIONS/CAREER NOTES: Selected by Washington Redskins in seventh round (232nd pick overall) of 2003 NFL draft.

Year Team	G	PASSING								RUSHING				TOTALS	
		Att.	Cmp.	Pct.	Yds.	TD	Int.	Avg.	Rat.	Att.	Yds.	Avg.	TD	TD	Pts.
1998—Indiana						Redshirted.									
1999—Indiana	11	0	0	0.0	0	0	0	0.0	0.0	0	0	0.0	0	0	0
2000—Indiana	11	5	2	40.0	60	1	0	12.00	206.8	0	0	0.0	0	0	0
2001—Indiana	11	1	1	100.0	-3	0	0	-3.00	74.8	2	9	4.5	0	0	0
2002—Indiana	12	293	152	51.9	2115	9	14	7.22	113.1	55	-52	-0.9	1	1	6
College totals (4 years)	45	299	155	51.8	2172	10	14	7.26	114.5	57	-43	-0.8	1	1	6

HAMLIN, KEN   S   SEAHAWKS

PERSONAL: Born January 20, 1981, in Memphis, Tenn. ... 6-2/209.
HIGH SCHOOL: Fraysar (Memphis, Tenn.).
COLLEGE: Arkansas.
TRANSACTIONS/CAREER NOTES: Selected after junior season by Seattle Seahawks in second round (42nd pick overall) of 2003 NFL draft.
COLLEGE NOTES: Returned one punt (2000).

Year Team	G	Sks.	No.	Yds.	Avg.	TD
				INTERCEPTIONS		
1999—Arkansas			Redshirted.			
2000—Arkansas	11	0.0	2	0	0.0	0
2001—Arkansas	11	0.5	3	33	11.0	0
2002—Arkansas	14	0.0	4	33	8.3	0
College totals (3 years)	36	0.5	9	66	7.3	0

HARRIS, KWAME   OT   49ERS

PERSONAL: Born March 2, 1980, in Jamaica. ... 6-7/310.
HIGH SCHOOL: Newark (Del.).
COLLEGE: Stanford.
TRANSACTIONS/CAREER NOTES: Selected after junior season by San Francisco 49ers in first round (26th pick overall) of 2003 NFL draft.

HAYES, GERALD   LB   CARDINALS

PERSONAL: Born October 10, 1980, in Paterson, N.J. ... 6-1/238.
HIGH SCHOOL: Passaic County Technical Institute (Passaic, N.J.).
COLLEGE: Pittsburgh.
TRANSACTIONS/CAREER NOTES: Selected by Arizona Cardinals in third round (70th pick overall) of 2003 NFL draft.

Year Team	G	Sks.	No.	Yds.	Avg.	TD
				INTERCEPTIONS		
1999—Pittsburgh	10	2.0	0	0	0.0	0
2000—Pittsburgh	10	3.0	0	0	0.0	0
2001—Pittsburgh	11	6.5	0	0	0.0	0
2002—Pittsburgh	13	2.0	2	-5	-2.5	0
College totals (4 years)	44	13.5	2	-5	-2.5	0

HAYNES, MICHAEL   DE   BEARS

PERSONAL: Born September 13, 1980, in Brooklyn, N.Y. ... 6-4/281. ... Full name: Michael Washington Augustis Haynes Jr.
HIGH SCHOOL: Balboa (Panama City, Fla.).
COLLEGE: Penn State.
TRANSACTIONS/CAREER NOTES: Selected by Chicago Bears in first round (14th pick overall) of 2003 NFL draft.

Year Team	G	SACKS
1998—Penn State		Redshirted.
1999—Penn State	9	0.5
2000—Penn State	12	6.0
2001—Penn State	11	4.0
2002—Penn State	13	15.0
College totals (4 years)	45	25.5

HENDERSON, E.J.   LB   VIKINGS

PERSONAL: Born August 3, 1980, in Aberdeen, Md. ... 6-1/245. ... Full name: Eric N. Henderson.
HIGH SCHOOL: Aberdeen (Md.).
COLLEGE: Maryland (degree in criminology and criminal justice).
TRANSACTIONS/CAREER NOTES: Selected by Minnesota Vikings in second round (40th pick overall) of 2003 NFL draft.
COLLEGE NOTES: Returned one kickoff (1999), one kickoff (2000), returned one punt (2002).

Year Team	G	Sks.	No.	Yds.	Avg.	TD
				INTERCEPTIONS		
1998—Maryland			Redshirted.			
1999—Maryland	11	0.5	0	0	0.0	0
2000—Maryland	10	2.0	0	0	0.0	0
2001—Maryland	11	6.0	1	5	5.0	0
2002—Maryland	14	8.5	2	20	10.0	0
College totals (4 years)	46	17.0	3	25	8.3	0

HENSON, DREW   QB   TEXANS

PERSONAL: Born February 13, 1980, in San Diego. ... 6-4/223. ... Full name: Drew Daniel Henson.
HIGH SCHOOL: Brighton (Mich.).
COLLEGE: Michigan.
TRANSACTIONS/CAREER NOTES: Selected by Houston Texans in sixth round (192nd pick overall) of 2003 NFL draft.
COLLEGE NOTES: Caught one pass (1999).
MISCELLANEOUS: Selected by New York Yankees organization in third round of free-agent draft (June 2, 1998).

Year Team	G	PASSING								RUSHING				TOTALS	
		Att.	Cmp.	Pct.	Yds.	TD	Int.	Avg.	Rat.	Att.	Yds.	Avg.	TD	TD	Pts.
1998—Michigan	7	45	19	42.2	233	3	1	5.18	103.3	7	66	9.4	1	1	6
1999—Michigan	9	89	46	51.7	546	3	2	6.13	109.8	26	-22	-0.8	1	1	6
2000—Michigan	8	217	131	60.4	1852	16	4	8.53	152.7	27	30	1.1	2	2	12
College totals (3 years)	24	351	196	55.8	2631	22	7	7.50	135.5	60	74	1.2	4	4	24

HILLENMEYER, HUNTER — LB — PACKERS

PERSONAL: Born October 28, 1980, in Nashville. ... 6-4/241.
HIGH SCHOOL: Montgomery Bell (Nashville).
COLLEGE: Vanderbilt (degree in human and organizational development and economics).
TRANSACTIONS/CAREER NOTES: Selected by Green Bay Packers in fifth round (166th pick overall) of 2003 NFL draft.
COLLEGE NOTES: Caught one pass (1999).

Year Team	G	SACKS
1999—Vanderbilt	11	0.0
2000—Vanderbilt	11	0.0
2001—Vanderbilt	11	2.0
2002—Vanderbilt	12	4.0
College totals (4 years)	45	6.0

HOAG, RYAN — WR — RAIDERS

PERSONAL: Born November 23, 1979, in Minneapolis, Minn. ... 6-2/200.
HIGH SCHOOL: Washburn (Minneapolis, Minn.).
COLLEGE: Wake Forest, then Gustavus Adolphus.
TRANSACTIONS/CAREER NOTES: Selected by Oakland Raiders in seventh round (262nd pick overall) of 2003 NFL draft.
COLLEGE NOTES: Attempted one pass (2002).

		RUSHING				RECEIVING				PUNT RETURNS				KICKOFF RETURNS				TOTALS	
Year Team	G	Att.	Yds.	Avg.	TD	No.	Yds.	Avg.	TD	No.	Yds.	Avg.	TD	No.	Yds.	Avg.	TD	TD	Pts.
1998—Wake Forest							Did not play.												
1999—Gustavus Adolphus.							Did not play.												
2000—Gustavus Adolphus.	10	2	18	9.0	1	34	548	16.1	5	0	0	0.0	0	0	0	0.0	0	6	36
2001—Gustavus Adolphus.	10	4	13	3.3	0	54	876	16.2	14	0	0	0.0	0	0	0	0.0	0	14	84
2002—Gustavus Adolphus.	10	6	61	10.2	0	56	808	14.4	10	4	31	7.8	0	13	397	30.5	0	10	60
College totals (3 years)	30	12	92	7.7	1	144	2232	15.5	29	4	31	7.8	0	13	397	30.5	0	30	180

HOBSON, VICTOR — LB — JETS

PERSONAL: Born February 3, 1980, in Mount Laurel, N.J. ... 6-0/252.
HIGH SCHOOL: St. Joseph's Prep (Philadelphia).
COLLEGE: Michigan.
TRANSACTIONS/CAREER NOTES: Selected by New York Jets in second round (53rd pick overall) of 2003 NFL draft.

			INTERCEPTIONS			
Year Team	G	Sks.	No.	Yds.	Avg.	TD
1998—Michigan			Redshirted.			
1999—Michigan	12	1.0	0	0	0.0	0
2000—Michigan	12	3.0	0	0	0.0	0
2001—Michigan	11	5.0	0	0	0.0	0
2002—Michigan	13	6.0	2	42	21.0	0
College totals (4 years)	48	15.0	2	42	21.0	0

HOLLAND, MONTRAE — G — SAINTS

PERSONAL: Born May 21, 1980, in Ore City, Texas. ... 6-1/333.
HIGH SCHOOL: Jefferson (Ore City, Texas).
COLLEGE: Florida State.
TRANSACTIONS/CAREER NOTES: Selected by New Orleans Saints in fourth round (102nd pick overall) of 2003 NFL draft.
COLLEGE PLAYING EXPERIENCE: Florida State, 1998-2002. ... Games played: 1998 (redshirted), 1999 (9), 2000 (12), 2001 (11), 2002 (11). Total: 43.

HOLT, TERRENCE — S — LIONS

PERSONAL: Born March 5, 1980, in Greensboro, N.C. ... 6-2/208. ... Brother of Torry Holt, wide receiver, St. Louis Rams.
HIGH SCHOOL: Eastern Guilford (Gibsonville, N.C.).
COLLEGE: North Carolina State.
TRANSACTIONS/CAREER NOTES: Selected by Detroit Lions in fifth round (137th pick overall) of 2003 NFL draft.

			INTERCEPTIONS				KICKOFF RETURNS				TOTALS	
Year Team	G	Sks.	No.	Yds.	Avg.	TD	No.	Yds.	Avg.	TD	TD	Pts.
1998—North Carolina State					Redshirted.							
1999—North Carolina State	12	0.5	0	0	0.0	0	0	0	0.0	0	0	0
2000—North Carolina State	11	0.0	1	34	34.0	0	0	0	0.0	0	0	0
2001—North Carolina State	11	0.0	1	22	22.0	0	0	0	0.0	0	0	0
2002—North Carolina State	14	1.0	3	12	4.0	0	0	0	0.0	0	1	6
College totals (4 years)	48	1.5	5	68	13.6	0	0	0	0.0	0	1	6

HOWRY, KEENAN — WR — VIKINGS

PERSONAL: Born June 17, 1981, in Los Angeles. ... 5-10/178. ... Full name: Keenan Rashaun Howry.
HIGH SCHOOL: Los Alamitos (Calif.).
COLLEGE: Oregon.
TRANSACTIONS/CAREER NOTES: Selected by Minnesota Vikings in seventh round (221st pick overall) of 2003 NFL draft.
COLLEGE NOTES: Attempted two passes (1999), two passes (2000), one pass (2001), two passes (2002).

		RUSHING				RECEIVING				PUNT RETURNS				KICKOFF RETURNS				TOTALS	
Year Team	G	Att.	Yds.	Avg.	TD	No.	Yds.	Avg.	TD	No.	Yds.	Avg.	TD	No.	Yds.	Avg.	TD	TD	Pts.
1999—Oregon	11	1	20	20.0	0	26	398	15.3	4	1	12	12.0	0	0	0	0.0	0	4	24
2000—Oregon	11	0	0	0.0	0	47	721	15.3	5	35	281	8.0	0	2	45	22.5	0	5	32
2001—Oregon	11	4	51	12.8	1	49	649	13.2	8	32	465	14.5	2	0	0	0.0	0	11	66
2002—Oregon	13	8	79	9.9	0	40	784	19.6	5	30	401	13.4	2	0	0	0.0	0	7	42
College totals (4 years)	46	13	150	11.5	1	162	2552	15.8	22	98	1159	11.8	4	2	45	22.5	0	27	164

HUNT, AARON — DE — BRONCOS

PERSONAL: Born June 19, 1980, in Denison, Texas. ... 6-3/267. ... Cousin of Fred Washington, defensive tackle with Chicago Bears (1990).
HIGH SCHOOL: Denison (Texas).
COLLEGE: Texas Tech (degree in communications).
TRANSACTIONS/CAREER NOTES: Selected by Denver Broncos in sixth round (194th pick overall) of 2003 NFL draft.
COLLEGE NOTES: Rushed one time (2002).

Year Team	G	SACKS
1998—Texas Tech	Redshirted.	
1999—Texas Tech	10	5.0
2000—Texas Tech	12	8.0
2001—Texas Tech	11	12.0
2002—Texas Tech	14	9.0
College totals (4 years)	47	34.0

HUNTER, WAYNE — OT — SEAHAWKS

PERSONAL: Born July 2, 1981, in Honolulu, Hawaii. ... 6-6/303.
HIGH SCHOOL: Radford (Honolulu, Hawaii).
COLLEGE: California, then Hawaii.
TRANSACTIONS/CAREER NOTES: Selected after junior season by Seattle Seahawks in third round (73rd pick overall) of 2003 NFL draft.
COLLEGE NOTES: Recorded 1.5 sacks (1999).
COLLEGE PLAYING EXPERIENCE: California, 1999; Hawaii, 2001-2002. ... Games played: 1999 (10), 2001 (11), 2002 (13). Total: 34.

JACKSON, ALONZO — DE — STEELERS

PERSONAL: Born September 15, 1980, in Americus, Ga. ... 6-4/266.
HIGH SCHOOL: Americus (Ga.).
COLLEGE: Florida State.
TRANSACTIONS/CAREER NOTES: Selected by Pittsburgh Steelers in second round (59th pick overall) of 2003 NFL draft.

			INTERCEPTIONS			
Year Team	G	Sks.	No.	Yds.	Avg.	TD
1999—Florida State	11	0.0	0	0	0.0	0
2000—Florida State	11	5.0	0	0	0.0	0
2001—Florida State	9	5.0	0	0	0.0	0
2002—Florida State	14	13.0	1	48	48.0	1
College totals (4 years)	45	23.0	1	48	48.0	1

JACOBS, TAYLOR — WR — REDSKINS

PERSONAL: Born May 30, 1981, in Tallahassee, Fla. ... 6-0/205. ... Full name: Taylor Houser Jacobs.
HIGH SCHOOL: Florida A&M (Tallahassee, Fla.).
COLLEGE: Florida.
TRANSACTIONS/CAREER NOTES: Selected by Washington Redskins in second round (44th pick overall) of 2003 NFL draft.

		RUSHING				RECEIVING				TOTALS	
Year Team	G	Att.	Yds.	Avg.	TD	No.	Yds.	Avg.	TD	TD	Pts.
1999—Florida	10	0	0	0.0	0	7	99	14.1	0	0	0
2000—Florida	12	3	11	3.7	1	17	198	11.6	1	2	12
2001—Florida	11	4	27	6.8	0	38	712	18.7	7	7	42
2002—Florida	11	3	43	14.3	0	71	1088	15.3	8	8	50
College totals (4 years)	44	10	81	8.1	1	133	2097	15.8	16	17	104

JAMES, BRADIE — LB — COWBOYS

PERSONAL: Born January 17, 1981, in Monroe, La. ... 6-2/242. ... Full name: Bradie Gene James.
HIGH SCHOOL: West Monroe (Monroe, La.).
COLLEGE: Louisiana State.
TRANSACTIONS/CAREER NOTES: Selected by Dallas Cowboys in fourth round (103rd pick overall) of 2003 NFL draft.
COLLEGE NOTES: Rushed two times (2002).

			INTERCEPTIONS			
Year Team	G	Sks.	No.	Yds.	Avg.	TD
1999—Louisiana State	10	3.0	1	0	0.0	0
2000—Louisiana State	11	5.0	0	0	0.0	0
2001—Louisiana State	12	3.0	0	0	0.0	0
2002—Louisiana State	13	3.0	1	0	0.0	0
College totals (4 years)	46	14.0	2	0	0.0	0

JENKINS, COREY — S — DOLPHINS

PERSONAL: Born August 25, 1976, in Columbia, S.C. ... 6-0/220.
HIGH SCHOOL: Dreher (Columbia, S.C.).
JUNIOR COLLEGE: Garden City (Kan.) Community College.
COLLEGE: South Carolina.
TRANSACTIONS/CAREER NOTES: Selected by Miami Dolphins in sixth round (181st pick overall) of 2003 NFL draft.
MISCELLANEOUS: Selected by Boston Red Sox organization in first round (24th pick overall) of free-agent draft (June 1, 1995).

					PASSING						RUSHING			TOTALS	
Year Team	G	Att.	Cmp.	Pct.	Yds.	TD	Int.	Avg.	Rat.	Att.	Yds.	Avg.	TD	TD	Pts.
2001—South Carolina	11	24	11	45.8	194	0	1	8.08	105.4	58	301	5.2	3	3	18
2002—South Carolina	12	180	100	55.6	1334	7	10	7.41	119.5	160	655	4.1	4	4	24
College totals (2 years)	23	204	111	54.4	1528	7	11	7.49	117.9	218	956	4.4	7	7	42

JOHNSON, AL — C — COWBOYS

PERSONAL: Born January 27, 1979, in Brussels, Wis. ... 6-3/305. ... Cousin of Ben Johnson, offensive tackle, Detroit Lions.
HIGH SCHOOL: Southern Door (Brussels, Wis.).
COLLEGE: Wisconsin.
TRANSACTIONS/CAREER NOTES: Selected by Dallas Cowboys in second round (38th pick overall) of 2003 NFL draft.
COLLEGE PLAYING EXPERIENCE: Wisconsin, 1998-2002. ... Games played: 1998 (redshirted), 1999 (7), 2000 (11), 2001 (12), 2002 (14). Total: 44.

JOHNSON, ANDRE — WR — TEXANS

PERSONAL: Born July 11, 1981, in Miami. ... 6-2/230. ... Full name: Andre Lamont Johnson.
HIGH SCHOOL: Senior (Miami).
COLLEGE: Miami (Fla.).
TRANSACTIONS/CAREER NOTES: Selected after junior season by Houston Texans in first round (third pick overall) of 2003 NFL draft.

		RECEIVING				KICKOFF RETURNS				TOTALS	
Year Team	G	No.	Yds.	Avg.	TD	No.	Yds.	Avg.	TD	TD	Pts.
1999—Miami (Fla.)				Redshirted.							
2000—Miami (Fla.)	11	3	57	19.0	1	12	249	20.8	0	1	6
2001—Miami (Fla.)	11	37	682	18.4	10	13	254	19.5	0	10	60
2002—Miami (Fla.)	12	52	1092	21.0	9	3	91	30.3	0	9	54
College totals (3 years)	34	92	1831	19.9	20	28	594	21.2	0	20	120

JOHNSON, BEN — OT — LIONS

PERSONAL: Born April 7, 1980, in Brussels, Wis. ... 6-6/329. ... Cousin of Al Johnson, offensive center, Dallas Cowboys.
HIGH SCHOOL: South Door (Brussels, Wis.).
COLLEGE: Wisconsin.
TRANSACTIONS/CAREER NOTES: Selected by Detroit Lions in seventh round (216th pick overall) of 2003 NFL draft.
COLLEGE PLAYING EXPERIENCE: Wisconsin, 1998-2002. ... Games played: 1998 (redshirted), 1999 (4), 2000 (10), 2001 (12), 2002 (14). Total: 40.

JOHNSON, BETHEL — WR — PATRIOTS

PERSONAL: Born February 11, 1979, in Corsicana, Texas. ... 5-11/201.
HIGH SCHOOL: Corsicana (Texas).
COLLEGE: Texas A&M.
TRANSACTIONS/CAREER NOTES: Selected by New England Patriots in second round (45th pick overall) of 2003 NFL draft.

		RUSHING				RECEIVING				PUNT RETURNS				KICKOFF RETURNS				TOTALS	
Year Team	G	Att.	Yds.	Avg.	TD	No.	Yds.	Avg.	TD	No.	Yds.	Avg.	TD	No.	Yds.	Avg.	TD	TD	Pts.
1998—Texas A&M								Did not play.											
1999—Texas A&M	10	1	-3	-3.0	0	27	514	19.0	0	2	27	13.5	0	9	174	19.3	0	3	18
2000—Texas A&M	11	2	21	10.5	1	42	440	10.5	0	1	29	29.0	0	1	14	14.0	0	1	6
2001—Texas A&M	2	0	0	0.0	0	8	68	8.5	0	0	0	0.0	0	0	0	0.0	0	0	2
2002—Texas A&M	12	5	37	7.4	0	40	718	18.0	8	12	139	11.6	0	12	252	21.0	0	8	48
College totals (4 years)	35	8	55	6.9	1	117	1740	14.9	11	15	195	13.0	0	22	440	20.0	0	12	74

JOHNSON, BRYANT — WR — CARDINALS

PERSONAL: Born March 7, 1981, in Baltimore. ... 6-2/214. ... Full name: Bryant Andrew Johnson.
HIGH SCHOOL: Baltimore City College (Baltimore).
COLLEGE: Penn State.
TRANSACTIONS/CAREER NOTES: Selected by Arizona Cardinals in first round (17th pick overall) of 2003 NFL draft.
COLLEGE NOTES: Rushed four times (2001).

		RECEIVING				PUNT RETURNS				TOTALS	
Year Team	G	No.	Yds.	Avg.	TD	No.	Yds.	Avg.	TD	TD	Pts.
1999—Penn State	12	7	140	20.0	2	0	0	0.0	0	2	12
2000—Penn State	11	4	85	21.3	1	0	0	0.0	0	1	6
2001—Penn State	11	51	866	17.0	3	0	0	0.0	0	3	18
2002—Penn State	13	48	917	19.1	4	41	528	12.9	1	5	32
College totals (4 years)	47	110	2008	18.3	10	41	528	12.9	1	11	68

JOHNSON, CHRIS   CB   PACKERS

PERSONAL: Born September 25, 1979, in Longview, Texas. ... 6-0/184.
HIGH SCHOOL: Pinetree (Longvew, Texas).
JUNIOR COLLEGE: Blinn College (Texas).
COLLEGE: Louisville.
TRANSACTIONS/CAREER NOTES: Selected by Green Bay Packers in seventh round (245th pick overall) of 2003 NFL draft.

JOHNSON, EDDIE   P   VIKINGS

PERSONAL: Born March 2, 1981, in Costa Mesa, Calif. ... 6-3/232.
HIGH SCHOOL: Newport Harbor (Newport Beach, Calif.).
JUNIOR COLLEGE: Orange Coast College (Calif.).
COLLEGE: Idaho State.
TRANSACTIONS/CAREER NOTES: Selected by Minnesota Vikings in sixth round (180th pick overall) of 2003 NFL draft.

			PUNTING				
Year Team	G	No.	Yds.	Avg.	Net avg.	In. 20	Blk.
2001—Idaho State	11	49	2270	46.3	0	10	0
2002—Idaho State	11	51	2357	46.2	0	15	1
College totals (2 years)	22	100	4627	46.3	0.0	25	1

JOHNSON, JARRET   DE   RAVENS

PERSONAL: Born August 14, 1981, in Chiefland, Fla. ... 6-3/284.
HIGH SCHOOL: Chiefland (Fla.).
COLLEGE: Alabama.
TRANSACTIONS/CAREER NOTES: Selected by Baltimore Ravens in fourth round (109th pick overall) of 2003 NFL draft.

Year Team	G	SACKS
1999—Alabama	12	2.0
2000—Alabama	11	7.0
2001—Alabama	11	10.0
2002—Alabama	13	5.0
College totals (4 years)	47	24.0

JOHNSON, JEREMI   FB   BENGALS

PERSONAL: Born September 4, 1980, in Louisville, Ky. ... 5-11/260.
HIGH SCHOOL: Ballard (Louisville, Ky.).
COLLEGE: Indiana, then Western Kentucky.
TRANSACTIONS/CAREER NOTES: Selected by Cincinnati Bengals in fourth round (118th pick overall) of 2003 NFL draft.

		RUSHING				RECEIVING				KICKOFF RETURNS				TOTALS	
Year Team	G	Att.	Yds.	Avg.	TD	No.	Yds.	Avg.	TD	No.	Yds.	Avg.	TD	TD	Pts.
1999—Indiana	11	69	282	4.1	2	10	90	9.0	1	2	14	7.0	0	3	18
2000—Indiana	11	20	103	5.2	2	11	83	7.5	0	1	10	10.0	0	2	12
2001—Indiana	11	95	546	5.7	7	16	213	13.3	1	0	0	0.0	0	8	48
2002—Western Kentucky	15	102	637	6.2	2	23	310	13.5	2	0	0	0.0	0	4	24
College totals (4 years)	48	286	1568	5.5	13	60	696	11.6	4	3	24	8.0	0	17	102

JOHNSON, LARRY   RB   CHIEFS

PERSONAL: Born November 19, 1979, in State College, Pa. ... 6-1/228. ... Full name: Larry Alphonso Johnson.
HIGH SCHOOL: State College (Pa.).
COLLEGE: Penn State (degree in integrative arts).
TRANSACTIONS/CAREER NOTES: Selected by Kansas City Chiefs in first round (27th pick overall) of 2003 NFL draft.

		RUSHING				RECEIVING				PUNT RETURNS				KICKOFF RETURNS				TOTALS	
Year Team	G	Att.	Yds.	Avg.	TD	No.	Yds.	Avg.	TD	No.	Yds.	Avg.	TD	No.	Yds.	Avg.	TD	TD	Pts.
1999—Penn State	12	43	171	4.0	1	4	74	18.5	1	0	0	0.0	0	13	230	17.7	0	2	12
2000—Penn State	12	75	358	4.8	3	9	122	13.6	1	1	9	9.0	0	18	444	24.7	0	4	24
2001—Penn State	11	71	337	4.7	2	11	136	12.4	2	1	55	55.0	0	17	454	26.7	1	7	42
2002—Penn State	13	271	2087	7.7	20	41	349	8.5	3	0	0	0.0	0	11	219	19.9	0	23	140
College totals (4 years)	48	460	2953	6.4	26	65	681	10.5	7	2	64	32.0	0	59	1347	22.8	1	36	218

JOHNSON, TEYO   WR/TE   RAIDERS

PERSONAL: Born November 29, 1981, in San Diego. ... 6-5/247. ... Brother of Riall Johnson, linebacker, Cincinnati Bengals.
HIGH SCHOOL: Mira Mesa (San Diego).
COLLEGE: Stanford.
TRANSACTIONS/CAREER NOTES: Selected after sophomore season by Oakland Raiders in second round (63rd pick overall) of 2003 NFL draft.
COLLEGE NOTES: Attempted one pass, rushed one time (2002).

		RECEIVING			
Year Team	G	No.	Yds.	Avg.	TD
2000—Stanford			Redshirted.		
2001—Stanford	11	38	565	14.9	7
2002—Stanford	11	41	467	11.4	8
College totals (2 years)	22	79	1032	13.1	15

JOHNSON, TODD   S   BEARS

PERSONAL: Born December 18, 1978, in Sarasota, Fla. ... 6-1/206. ... Full name: Todd Edward Johnson.
HIGH SCHOOL: Riverview (Sarasota, Fla.).
COLLEGE: Florida.
TRANSACTIONS/CAREER NOTES: Selected by Chicago Bears in fourth round (100th pick overall) of 2003 NFL draft.
COLLEGE NOTES: Returned one punt (1999), one punt (2002).

		INTERCEPTIONS			
Year Team	G	No.	Yds.	Avg.	TD
1998—Florida		Redshirted.			
1999—Florida	12	0	0	0.0	0
2000—Florida	12	5	139	27.8	0
2001—Florida	11	2	25	12.5	0
2002—Florida	12	2	0	0.0	0
College totals (4 years)	47	9	164	18.2	0

JOPPRU, BEN   TE   TEXANS

PERSONAL: Born January 5, 1980, in Wayzata, Minn. ... 6-4/272. ... Full name: Benjamin Paul Joppru.
HIGH SCHOOL: Minnetonka (Wayzata, Minn.).
COLLEGE: Michigan.
TRANSACTIONS/CAREER NOTES: Selected by Houston Texans in second round (41st pick overall) of 2003 NFL draft.

		RECEIVING			
Year Team	G	No.	Yds.	Avg.	TD
1998—Michigan		Redshirted.			
1999—Michigan	8	3	27	9.0	2
2000—Michigan	11	11	52	4.7	0
2001—Michigan	11	12	73	6.1	1
2002—Michigan	13	53	579	10.9	5
College totals (4 years)	43	79	731	9.3	8

JOSEPH, WILLIAM   DT   GIANTS

PERSONAL: Born September 3, 1979, in Miami. ... 6-5/308.
HIGH SCHOOL: Edison (Miami).
COLLEGE: Miami (Fla.) (degree in liberal arts).
TRANSACTIONS/CAREER NOTES: Selected by New York Giants in first round (25th pick overall) of 2003 NFL draft.
COLLEGE NOTES: Intercepted one pass (2001).

Year Team	G	SACKS
1998—Miami (Fla.)		Redshirted.
1999—Miami (Fla.)	12	1.5
2000—Miami (Fla.)	11	3.0
2001—Miami (Fla.)	11	10.0
2002—Miami (Fla.)	13	5.0
College totals (4 years)	47	19.5

JOSUE, STEVE   LB   PACKERS

PERSONAL: Born April 5, 1980, in Miami. ... 6-2/233.
HIGH SCHOOL: North Miami (Fla.).
COLLEGE: Carson-Newman.
TRANSACTIONS/CAREER NOTES: Selected by Green Bay Packers in seventh round (257th pick overall) of 2003 NFL draft.

			INTERCEPTIONS			
Year Team	G	Sks.	No.	Yds.	Avg.	TD
1998—Carson-Newman			Redshirted.			
1999—Carson-Newman	9	10.0	0	0	0.0	0
2000—Carson-Newman	10	7.0	0	0	0.0	0
2001—Carson-Newman	7	5.0	1	63	63.0	1
2002—Carson-Newman	13	7.0	0	0	0.0	0
College totals (4 years)	39	29.0	1	63	63.0	1

JUNE, CATO   S   COLTS

PERSONAL: Born November 18, 1979, in Washington, D.C. ... 6-0/218.
HIGH SCHOOL: Anacostia (Washington, D.C.).
COLLEGE: Michigan.
TRANSACTIONS/CAREER NOTES: Selected by Indianapolis Colts in sixth round (198th pick overall) of 2003 NFL draft.

			INTERCEPTIONS				PUNT RETURNS				KICKOFF RETURNS				TOTALS	
Year Team	G	Sks.	No.	Yds.	Avg.	TD	No.	Yds.	Avg.	TD	No.	Yds.	Avg.	TD	TD	Pts.
1998—Michigan					Redshirted.											
1999—Michigan	12	1.0	1	29	29.0	0	1	15	15.0	0	4	59	14.8	0	0	0
2000—Michigan								Did not play.								
2001—Michigan	11	3.0	2	38	19.0	0	0	0	0.0	0	0	0	0.0	0	0	0
2002—Michigan	12	2.0	0	0	0.0	0	0	0	0.0	0	0	0	0.0	0	0	0
College totals (3 years)	35	6.0	3	67	22.3	0	1	15	15.0	0	4	59	14.8	0	0	0

KELLEY, ETHAN   DT   PATRIOTS

PERSONAL: Born February 12, 1980, in Sugar Land, Texas. ... 6-1/301. ... Full name: Ethan Jeffery Arthur Kelley.
HIGH SCHOOL: Kempner (Sugar Land, Texas).
COLLEGE: Baylor.
TRANSACTIONS/CAREER NOTES: Selected by New England Patriots in seventh round (243rd pick overall) of 2003 NFL draft.

Year Team	G	SACKS
1998—Baylor	Redshirted.	
1999—Baylor	11	0.0
2000—Baylor	11	0.0
2001—Baylor	11	2.0
2002—Baylor	12	2.0
College totals (4 years)	45	4.0

KELLY, KAREEM   WR   SAINTS

PERSONAL: Born April 1, 1981, in Long Beach, Calif. ... 6-0/186. ... Cousin of Rashard Cook, safety with Philadelphia Eagles (1999-2002).
HIGH SCHOOL: Polytechnic (Long Beach, Calif.).
COLLEGE: Southern California.
TRANSACTIONS/CAREER NOTES: Selected by New Orleans Saints in sixth round (203rd pick overall) of 2003 NFL draft.

		RUSHING				RECEIVING				PUNT RETURNS				TOTALS	
Year Team	G	Att.	Yds.	Avg.	TD	No.	Yds.	Avg.	TD	No.	Yds.	Avg.	TD	TD	Pts.
1999—Southern California	12	2	17	8.5	0	54	902	16.7	4	5	14	2.8	0	4	24
2000—Southern California	11	5	8	1.6	0	55	796	14.5	4	6	22	3.7	0	4	24
2001—Southern California	11	6	38	6.3	0	46	768	16.7	3	8	51	6.4	0	3	18
2002—Southern California	13	1	1	1.0	0	46	605	13.2	4	11	76	6.9	0	4	24
College totals (4 years)	47	14	64	4.6	0	201	3071	15.3	15	30	163	5.4	0	15	90

KELSAY, CHRIS   DE   BILLS

PERSONAL: Born October 31, 1979, in Auburn, Neb. ... 6-4/273.
HIGH SCHOOL: Auburn (Neb.).
COLLEGE: Nebraska (degree in finance).
TRANSACTIONS/CAREER NOTES: Selected by Buffalo Bills in second round (48th pick overall) of 2003 NFL draft.

Year Team	G	SACKS
1999—Nebraska	11	0.5
2000—Nebraska	11	0.5
2001—Nebraska	12	5.0
2002—Nebraska	9	7.0
College totals (4 years)	43	13.0

KENNEDY, JIMMY   DT   RAMS

PERSONAL: Born November 15, 1979, in Yonkers, N.Y. ... 6-4/320. ... Full name: Jimmy Wayne Kennedy.
HIGH SCHOOL: Roosevelt (Yonkers, N.Y.).
COLLEGE: Penn State (degree in rehabilitation services education).
TRANSACTIONS/CAREER NOTES: Selected by St. Louis Rams in first round (12th pick overall) of 2003 NFL draft.
COLLEGE NOTES: Intercepted one pass (2000).

Year Team	G	SACKS
1998—Penn State	Redshirted.	
1999—Penn State	12	1.0
2000—Penn State	12	6.0
2001—Penn State	11	1.5
2002—Penn State	13	5.5
College totals (4 years)	48	14.0

KIEL, TERRENCE   S   CHARGERS

PERSONAL: Born November 24, 1980, in Lufkin, Texas. ... 5-11/204. ... Full name: Terrence Dewayne Kiel. ... Cousin of Rodney Thomas, running back with Houston/Tennessee Oilers (1995-97), Tennessee Titans (1998-2000) and Atlanta Falcons (2001).
HIGH SCHOOL: Lufkin (Texas).
COLLEGE: Texas A&M.
TRANSACTIONS/CAREER NOTES: Selected by San Diego Chargers in second round (62nd pick overall) of 2003 NFL draft.

			INTERCEPTIONS			
Year Team	G	Sks.	No.	Yds.	Avg.	TD
1999—Texas A&M	11	0.0	0	0	0.0	0
2000—Texas A&M	11	0.0	4	0	0.0	0
2001—Texas A&M	11	1.0	1	0	0.0	0
2002—Texas A&M	12	1.5	3	19	6.3	0
College totals (4 years)	45	2.5	8	19	2.4	0

KING, AUSTIN   C   BUCCANEERS

PERSONAL: Born April 11, 1981, in Cincinnati. ... 6-4/299. ... Full name: Austin Patrick King.
HIGH SCHOOL: Purcell Marian (Cincinnati).
COLLEGE: Northwestern.
TRANSACTIONS/CAREER NOTES: Selected by Tampa Bay Buccaneers in fourth round (133rd pick overall) of 2003 NFL draft.
COLLEGE PLAYING EXPERIENCE: Northwestern, 1999-2002. ... Games played: 1999 (11), 2000 (11), 2001 (11), 2002 (12). Total: 45.

KING, KENNY   DE   CARDINALS

PERSONAL: Born April 23, 1981, in Daphne, Ala. ... 6-3/281.
HIGH SCHOOL: Daphne (Ala.).
COLLEGE: Alabama.
TRANSACTIONS/CAREER NOTES: Selected by Arizona Cardinals in fifth round (141st pick overall) of 2003 NFL draft.
COLLEGE NOTES: Intercepted one pass (2001).

Year Team	G	SACKS
1999—Alabama	12	5.5
2000—Alabama	8	1.5
2001—Alabama	11	2.0
2002—Alabama	12	3.0
College totals (4 years)	43	12.0

KINGSBURY, KLIFF   QB   PATRIOTS

PERSONAL: Born August 9, 1979, in San Antonio. ... 6-4/231.
HIGH SCHOOL: New Braunfels (Texas).
COLLEGE: Texas Tech (degree in management).
TRANSACTIONS/CAREER NOTES: Selected by New England Patriots in sixth round (201st pick overall) of 2003 NFL draft.
COLLEGE NOTES: Caught one pass (2002).

Year Team	G	Att.	Cmp.	Pct.	Yds.	TD	Int.	Avg.	Rat.	Att.	Yds.	Avg.	TD	TD	Pts.
				PASSING							RUSHING			TOTALS	
1998—Texas Tech							Redshirted.								
1999—Texas Tech	6	57	25	43.9	492	4	1	8.63	136.0	27	-23	-0.9	1	1	6
2000—Texas Tech	12	585	362	61.9	3418	21	17	5.84	117.0	78	19	0.2	2	2	12
2001—Texas Tech	11	529	365	69.0	3502	25	9	6.62	136.8	66	-48	-0.7	0	0	0
2002—Texas Tech	14	712	479	67.3	5017	45	13	7.05	143.7	102	-114	-1.1	2	2	12
College totals (4 years)	43	1883	1231	65.4	12429	95	40	6.60	133.2	273	-166	-0.6	5	5	30

KIRCUS, DAVID   WR   LIONS

PERSONAL: Born February 19, 1980, in Imlay City, Mich. ... 6-1/186.
HIGH SCHOOL: Imlay City (Mich.).
COLLEGE: Grand Valley State (Mich.).
TRANSACTIONS/CAREER NOTES: Selected by Detroit Lions in sixth round (175th pick overall) of 2003 NFL draft.

Year Team	G	No.	Yds.	Avg.	TD	No.	Yds.	Avg.	TD	No.	Yds.	Avg.	TD	TD	Pts.
			RECEIVING				PUNT RETURNS				KICKOFF RETURNS			TOTALS	
1998—Grand Valley State								Redshirted.							
1999—Grand Valley State	8	27	533	19.7	5	14	131	9.4	0	0	0	0.0	0	5	30
2000—Grand Valley State	13	56	967	17.3	8	18	219	12.2	0	0	0	0.0	0	8	48
2001—Grand Valley State	14	81	1682	20.8	32	31	359	11.6	0	3	35	11.7	0	32	192
2002—Grand Valley State	14	77	1341	17.4	35	9	76	8.4	0	0	0	0.0	0	35	212
College totals (4 years)	49	241	4523	18.8	80	72	785	10.9	0	3	35	11.7	0	80	482

KLECKO, DAN   DE/DT   PATRIOTS

PERSONAL: Born January 12, 1981, in Colts Neck, N.J. ... 5-11/283. ... Son of Joe Klecko, defensive tackle with New York Jets (1977-87) and Indianapolis Colts (1988).
HIGH SCHOOL: Marlboro (N.J.).
COLLEGE: Temple.
TRANSACTIONS/CAREER NOTES: Selected by New England Patriots in fourth round (117th pick overall) of 2003 NFL draft.

Year Team	G	SACKS
1999—Temple	10	8.0
2000—Temple	8	1.5
2001—Temple	11	6.5
2002—Temple	11	10.0
College totals (4 years)	40	26.0

KOOISTRA, SCOTT   OT   BENGALS

PERSONAL: Born October 14, 1980, in Cary, N.C. ... 6-1/316. ... Full name: Daniel Scott Kooistra.
HIGH SCHOOL: Cary (N.C.).
COLLEGE: North Carolina State.
TRANSACTIONS/CAREER NOTES: Selected by Cincinnati Bengals in seventh round (215th pick overall) of 2003 NFL draft.
COLLEGE PLAYING EXPERIENCE: North Carolina State, 1999-2002. ... Games played: 1999 (5), 2000 (4), 2001 (11), 2002 (13). Total: 33.

KOPPEN, DAN   C   PATRIOTS

PERSONAL: Born August 12, 1978, in Dubuque, Iowa. ... 6-3/297. ... Full name: Daniel Koppen.
HIGH SCHOOL: Whitehall (Pa.).
COLLEGE: Boston College.
TRANSACTIONS/CAREER NOTES: Selected by New England Patriots in fifth round (164th pick overall) of 2003 NFL draft.
COLLEGE PLAYING EXPERIENCE: Boston College, 1999-2002. ... Games played: 1999 (redshirted), 2000 (11), 2001 (11), 2002 (13). Total: 35.

LAFAVOR, TRON — DT — BEARS

PERSONAL: Born November 27, 1979, in Fort Lauderdale, Fla. ... 6-1/290.
HIGH SCHOOL: Dillard (Fort Lauderdale, Fla.).
COLLEGE: Florida.
TRANSACTIONS/CAREER NOTES: Selected by Chicago Bears in fifth round (171st pick overall) of 2003 NFL draft.
COLLEGE NOTES: Intercepted one pass (2000).

Year Team	G	SACKS
1999—Florida	9	0.0
2000—Florida	12	0.0
2001—Florida	11	1.0
2002—Florida	13	2.0
College totals (4 years)	45	3.0

LEE, DONALD — TE — DOLPHINS

PERSONAL: Born August 31, 1980, in Maben, Miss. ... 6-3/249. ... Full name: Donald Tywon Lee.
HIGH SCHOOL: Maben (Miss.).
COLLEGE: Mississippi State.
TRANSACTIONS/CAREER NOTES: Selected by Miami Dolphins in fifth round (156th pick overall) of 2003 NFL draft.
COLLEGE NOTES: Rushed one time (2001).

Year Team	G	No.	Yds.	Avg.	TD
		RECEIVING			
1999—Mississippi State	11	4	49	12.3	1
2000—Mississippi State	11	19	204	10.7	1
2001—Mississippi State	11	16	197	12.3	0
2002—Mississippi State	11	22	161	7.3	1
College totals (4 years)	44	61	611	10.0	3

LEE, JAMES — DT — PACKERS

PERSONAL: Born March 12, 1980, in Salem, Ore. ... 6-4/327. ... Full name: James Franklin Lee.
HIGH SCHOOL: McKay (Salem, Ore.).
JUNIOR COLLEGE: College of the Redwoods (Calif.).
COLLEGE: Oregon State.
TRANSACTIONS/CAREER NOTES: Selected by Green Bay Packers in fifth round (147th pick overall) of 2003 NFL draft.

Year Team	G	SACKS
2001—Oregon State	10	0.0
2002—Oregon State	13	0.0
College totals (2 years)	23	0.0

LEFTWICH, BYRON — QB — JAGUARS

PERSONAL: Born January 14, 1980, in Washington, D.C. ... 6-5/231. ... Full name: Byron A. Leftwich.
HIGH SCHOOL: H.D. Woodson (Washington, D.C.).
COLLEGE: Marshall.
TRANSACTIONS/CAREER NOTES: Selected by Jacksonville Jaguars in first round (seventh pick overall) of 2003 NFL draft.
COLLEGE NOTES: Caught one pass (1999), one pass (2001).

Year Team	G	PASSING								RUSHING				TOTALS	
		Att.	Cmp.	Pct.	Yds.	TD	Int.	Avg.	Rat.	Att.	Yds.	Avg.	TD	TD	Pts.
1998—Marshall	7	13	7	53.8	85	0	2	6.54	78.0	2	-19	-9.5	0	0	0
1999—Marshall	3	11	7	63.6	60	0	0	5.45	109.5	5	26	5.2	0	0	0
2000—Marshall	12	457	279	61.1	3358	21	9	7.35	134.0	82	83	1.0	1	1	6
2001—Marshall	12	470	315	67.0	4132	38	7	8.79	164.6	64	92	1.4	2	3	18
2002—Marshall	12	491	331	67.4	4268	30	10	8.69	156.5	37	-1	0.0	3	3	18
College totals (5 years)	46	1442	939	65.1	11903	89	28	8.25	150.9	190	181	1.0	6	7	42

LEHAN, MICHAEL — CB — BROWNS

PERSONAL: Born November 25, 1979, in Hopkins, Minn. ... 6-0/196.
HIGH SCHOOL: Hopkins (Minn.).
COLLEGE: Minnesota.
TRANSACTIONS/CAREER NOTES: Selected by Cleveland Browns in fifth round (152nd pick overall) of 2003 NFL draft.

Year Team	G	INTERCEPTIONS				PUNT RETURNS				KICKOFF RETURNS				TOTALS	
		No.	Yds.	Avg.	TD	No.	Yds.	Avg.	TD	No.	Yds.	Avg.	TD	TD	Pts.
1998—Minnesota							Redshirted.								
1999—Minnesota	11	1	45	45.0	0	0	0	0.0	0	1	0	0.0	0	0	0
2000—Minnesota	11	0	0	0.0	0	0	0	0.0	0	0	0	0.0	0	0	0
2001—Minnesota	11	2	55	27.5	0	1	11	11.0	0	2	54	27.0	0	0	0
2002—Minnesota	10	2	28	14.0	0	0	0	0.0	0	0	0	0.0	0	0	0
College totals (4 years)	43	5	128	25.6	0	1	11	11.0	0	3	54	18.0	0	0	0

LEJEUNE, NORMAN   S   EAGLES

PERSONAL: Born May 10, 1980, in Brusly, La. ... 6-0/200.
HIGH SCHOOL: Brusly (La.).
COLLEGE: Louisiana State.
TRANSACTIONS/CAREER NOTES: Selected by Philadelphia Eagles in seventh round (244th pick overall) of 2003 NFL draft.

			INTERCEPTIONS			
Year Team	G	Sks.	No.	Yds.	Avg.	TD
1999—Louisiana State	11	0.0	2	37	18.5	0
2000—Louisiana State	11	0.0	0	0	0.0	0
2001—Louisiana State	9	0.0	0	0	0.0	0
2002—Louisiana State	13	5.0	0	0	0.0	0
College totals (4 years)	44	5.0	2	37	18.5	0

LLOYD, BRANDON   WR   49ERS

PERSONAL: Born July 5, 1981, in Kansas City, Mo. ... 6-0/184. ... Full name: Brandon Matthew Lloyd.
HIGH SCHOOL: Blue Springs (Mo.).
COLLEGE: Illinois.
TRANSACTIONS/CAREER NOTES: Selected after junior season by San Francisco 49ers in fourth round (124th pick overall) of 2003 NFL draft.

		RUSHING				RECEIVING				PUNT RETURNS				KICKOFF RETURNS				TOTALS	
Year Team	G	Att.	Yds.	Avg.	TD	No.	Yds.	Avg.	TD	No.	Yds.	Avg.	TD	No.	Yds.	Avg.	TD	TD	Pts.
1999—Illinois	12	2	35	17.5	0	27	454	16.8	2	3	54	18.0	0	10	171	17.1	0	2	12
2000—Illinois								Redshirted.											
2001—Illinois	11	5	5	1.0	0	60	1006	16.8	8	1	17	17.0	0	3	52	17.3	0	8	48
2002—Illinois	12	5	15	3.0	0	65	1010	15.5	9	0	0	0.0	0	1	23	23.0	0	9	54
College totals (3 years)	35	12	55	4.6	0	152	2470	16.3	19	4	71	17.8	0	14	246	17.6	0	19	114

LONG, RIEN   DT   TITANS

PERSONAL: Born August 7, 1981, in Los Angeles. ... 6-6/302. ... Full name: Rien M. Long.
HIGH SCHOOL: Anacortes (Wash.).
COLLEGE: Washington State.
TRANSACTIONS/CAREER NOTES: Selected after junior season by Tennessee Titans in fourth round (126th pick overall) of 2003 NFL draft.

Year Team	G	SACKS
1999—Washington State		Redshirted.
2000—Washington State	10	1.0
2001—Washington State	12	3.0
2002—Washington State	12	13.0
College totals (3 years)	34	17.0

LUCIER, WAYNE   C/OG   GIANTS

PERSONAL: Born December 5, 1979, in Amesbury, Mass. ... 6-4/301. ... Name pronounced loo-SEAR.
HIGH SCHOOL: St. John's (Salem, N.H.).
COLLEGE: Northwestern, then Colorado.
TRANSACTIONS/CAREER NOTES: Selected by New York Giants in seventh round (249th pick overall) of 2003 NFL draft.
COLLEGE NOTES: Caught one pass (1998).
COLLEGE PLAYING EXPERIENCE: Northwestern, 1998-1999; Colorado, 2000-2002. ... Games played: 1998 (7), 1999 (11). (Northwestern Total: 18). 2000 (did not play), 2001 (12), 2002 (14). (Colorado Total: 26). Total: 44.

MABRY, MIKE   C   RAVENS

PERSONAL: Born April 26, 1980, in Houston. ... 6-1/295.
HIGH SCHOOL: Dayton (Texas).
JUNIOR COLLEGE: Southwest Mississippi Junior College.
COLLEGE: Central Florida.
TRANSACTIONS/CAREER NOTES: Selected by Baltimore Ravens in seventh round (250th pick overall) of 2003 NFL draft.
COLLEGE PLAYING EXPERIENCE: Central Florida, 2001-2002. ... Games played: 2001 (11), 2002 (12). Total: 23.

MACKENZIE, MALAEFOU   RB   JAGUARS

PERSONAL: Born July 24, 1979, in Apia, Western Samoa. ... 5-10/233.
HIGH SCHOOL: Capistrano Valley (Mission Viejo, Calif.).
COLLEGE: Southern California.
TRANSACTIONS/CAREER NOTES: Selected by Jacksonville Jaguars in seventh round (218th pick overall) of 2003 NFL draft.

		RUSHING				RECEIVING				KICKOFF RETURNS				TOTALS	
Year Team	G	Att.	Yds.	Avg.	TD	No.	Yds.	Avg.	TD	No.	Yds.	Avg.	TD	TD	Pts.
1997—Southern California	9	96	332	3.5	3	5	22	4.4	0	1	7	7.0	0	3	18
1998—Southern California	1	7	28	4.0	0	0	0	0.0	0	0	0	0.0	0	0	0
1999—Southern California	8	25	121	4.8	3	5	40	8.0	0	0	0	0.0	0	3	18
2000—Southern California	12	41	284	6.9	0	27	249	9.2	0	4	91	22.8	0	0	0
2001—Southern California								Did not play.							
2002—Southern California	13	47	174	3.7	2	39	365	9.4	7	0	0	0.0	0	9	54
College totals (5 years)	43	216	939	4.3	8	76	676	8.9	7	5	98	19.6	0	15	90

MADISE, ADRIAN   WR   BRONCOS

PERSONAL: Born March 23, 1980, in Lancaster, Texas. ... 5-11/215. ... Full name: Adrian James Madise.
HIGH SCHOOL: Lancaster (Texas).
JUNIOR COLLEGE: Middle Georgia Junior College.
COLLEGE: Texas Christian.
TRANSACTIONS/CAREER NOTES: Selected by Denver Broncos in fifth round (158th pick overall) of 2003 NFL draft.

		RECEIVING			
Year Team	G	No.	Yds.	Avg.	TD
2001—Texas Christian	11	50	819	16.4	5
2002—Texas Christian	11	32	523	16.3	2
College totals (2 years)	22	82	1342	16.4	7

MAHAN, SEAN   G   BUCCANEERS

PERSONAL: Born May 28, 1980, in Tulsa, Okla. ... 6-3/301. ... Full name: Sean Christopher Mahan.
HIGH SCHOOL: Jenks (Okla.).
COLLEGE: Notre Dame.
TRANSACTIONS/CAREER NOTES: Selected by Tampa Bay Buccaneers in fifth round (168th pick overall) of 2003 NFL draft.
COLLEGE PLAYING EXPERIENCE: Notre Dame, 1998-2002. ... Games played: 1998 (redshirted), 1999 (6), 2000 (11), 2001 (11), 2002 (13). Total: 41.

MANNING, RICKY   CB   PANTHERS

PERSONAL: Born November 18, 1980, in Fresno, Calif. ... 5-9/185. ... Full name: Ricky Manning Jr.
HIGH SCHOOL: Edison (Fresno, Calif.).
COLLEGE: UCLA.
TRANSACTIONS/CAREER NOTES: Selected by Carolina Panthers in third round (82nd pick overall) of 2003 NFL draft.
MISCELLANEOUS: Selected by Minnesota Twins organization in 22nd round of free-agent draft (1999).

			INTERCEPTIONS				PUNT RETURNS				KICKOFF RETURNS				TOTALS	
Year Team	G	Sks.	No.	Yds.	Avg.	TD	No.	Yds.	Avg.	TD	No.	Yds.	Avg.	TD	TD	Pts.
1999—UCLA	11	2.0	2	83	41.5	0	9	95	10.6	0	1	20	20.0	0	0	0
2000—UCLA	10	2.0	4	64	16.0	0	18	120	6.7	0	0	0	0.0	0	0	0
2001—UCLA	11	0.0	3	51	17.0	0	16	53	3.3	0	2	15	7.5	0	0	0
2002—UCLA	13	0.0	4	47	11.8	1	0	0	0.0	0	2	29	14.5	0	1	6
College totals (4 years)	45	4.0	13	245	18.8	1	43	268	6.2	0	5	64	12.8	0	1	6

MANUWAI, VINCENT   G   JAGUARS

PERSONAL: Born July 12, 1980, in Honolulu, Hawaii. ... 6-2/304.
HIGH SCHOOL: Farrington (Honolulu, Hawaii).
COLLEGE: Hawaii.
TRANSACTIONS/CAREER NOTES: Selected by Jacksonville Jaguars in third round (72nd pick overall) of 2003 NFL draft.
COLLEGE PLAYING EXPERIENCE: Hawaii, 1999-2002. ... Games played: 1999 (12), 2000 (11), 2001 (12), 2002 (14). Total: 49.

MATHIS, RASHEAN   S   JAGUARS

PERSONAL: Born August 27, 1980, in Jacksonville, Fla. ... 6-1/202.
HIGH SCHOOL: Englewood (Jacksonville, Fla.).
COLLEGE: Bethune-Cookman.
TRANSACTIONS/CAREER NOTES: Selected by Jacksonville Jaguars in second round (39th pick overall) of 2003 NFL draft.
COLLEGE NOTES: Caught three passes, scored two touchdowns (2002).

		INTERCEPTIONS				PUNT RETURNS				KICKOFF RETURNS				TOTALS	
Year Team	G	No.	Yds.	Avg.	TD	No.	Yds.	Avg.	TD	No.	Yds.	Avg.	TD	TD	Pts.
1999—Bethune-Cookman	10	2	5	2.5	0	10	120	12.0	1	0	0	0.0	0	1	6
2000—Bethune-Cookman	11	11	157	14.3	0	11	212	19.3	0	0	0	0.0	0	1	6
2001—Bethune-Cookman	10	4	65	16.3	0	21	321	15.3	2	2	18	9.0	0	2	12
2002—Bethune-Cookman	13	14	455	32.5	3	22	145	6.6	0	2	39	19.5	0	6	36
College totals (4 years)	44	31	682	22.0	3	64	798	12.5	3	4	57	14.3	0	10	60

MATHIS, ROBERT   DE   COLTS

PERSONAL: Born February 26, 1981, in Atlanta. ... 6-0/231.
HIGH SCHOOL: McNair (Atlanta).
COLLEGE: Alabama A&M.
TRANSACTIONS/CAREER NOTES: Selected by Indianapolis Colts in fifth round (138th pick overall) of 2003 NFL draft.

Year Team	G	SACKS
1999—Alabama A&M	9	1.0
2000—Alabama A&M	11	14.0
2001—Alabama A&M	11	8.0
2002—Alabama A&M	12	20.0
College totals (4 years)	43	43.0

McDONALD, SHAUN — WR — RAMS

PERSONAL: Born June 30, 1981, in Phoenix. ... 5-8/169. ... Full name: Shaun Terrance McDonald.
HIGH SCHOOL: Shadow Mountain (Phoenix).
COLLEGE: Arizona State.
TRANSACTIONS/CAREER NOTES: Selected after junior season by St. Louis Rams in fourth round (106th pick overall) of 2003 NFL draft.

Year Team	G	RUSHING Att.	Yds.	Avg.	TD	RECEIVING No.	Yds.	Avg.	TD	PUNT RETURNS No.	Yds.	Avg.	TD	KICKOFF RETURNS No.	Yds.	Avg.	TD	TOTALS TD	Pts.
1999—Arizona State										Redshirted.									
2000—Arizona State	11	4	21	5.3	0	18	297	16.5	1	24	265	11.0	1	3	42	14.0	0	2	12
2001—Arizona State	11	4	8	2.0	1	47	1104	23.5	10	3	1	0.3	0	3	52	17.3	0	11	68
2002—Arizona State	14	5	25	5.0	0	87	1405	16.1	13	2	29	14.5	0	0	0	0.0	0	13	80
College totals (3 years)	36	13	54	4.2	1	152	2806	18.5	24	29	295	10.2	1	6	94	15.7	0	26	160

McDOUGLE, JEROME — DE — EAGLES

PERSONAL: Born December 15, 1978, in Pompano Beach, Fla. ... 6-2/264. ... Full name: Jerome McDougle Jr. ... Brother of Stockar McDougle, offensive tackle, Detroit Lions.
HIGH SCHOOL: Ely (Pompano Beach, Fla.).
JUNIOR COLLEGE: Hinds Community College (Miss.).
COLLEGE: Pittsburg State (Kan.), then Miami (Fla.).
TRANSACTIONS/CAREER NOTES: Selected by Philadelphia Eagles in first round (15th pick overall) of 2003 NFL draft.

Year Team	G	Sks.	INTERCEPTIONS No.	Yds.	Avg.	TD
1998—Pittsburg State			Did not play.			
2000—Miami (Fla.)			Redshirted.			
2001—Miami (Fla.)	11	6.0	1	14	14.0	1
2002—Miami (Fla.)	12	7.0	0	0	0.0	0
College totals (2 years)	23	13.0	1	14	14.0	1

McGAHEE, WILLIS — RB — BILLS

PERSONAL: Born October 20, 1981, in Miami. ... 6-0/223. ... Full name: Willis Andrew McGahee.
HIGH SCHOOL: Central (Miami).
COLLEGE: Miami (Fla.).
TRANSACTIONS/CAREER NOTES: Selected after sophomore season by Buffalo Bills in first round (23rd pick overall) of 2003 NFL draft.
COLLEGE NOTES: Returned one kickoff (2001).

Year Team	G	RUSHING Att.	Yds.	Avg.	TD	RECEIVING No.	Yds.	Avg.	TD	TOTALS TD	Pts.
2000—Miami (Fla.)						Redshirted.					
2001—Miami (Fla.)	8	67	314	4.7	3	1	-7	-7.0	0	3	18
2002—Miami (Fla.)	13	282	1753	6.2	28	27	355	13.1	0	28	168
College totals (2 years)	21	349	2067	5.9	31	28	348	12.4	0	31	186

McGEE, TERRENCE — CB — BILLS

PERSONAL: Born October 14, 1980, in Athens, Texas. ... 5-9/201.
HIGH SCHOOL: Athens (Texas).
COLLEGE: Northwestern State.
TRANSACTIONS/CAREER NOTES: Selected by Buffalo Bills in fourth round (111th pick overall) of 2003 NFL draft.
COLLEGE NOTES: Rushed one time (2001), rushed two times, caught one pass (2002).

Year Team	G	INTERCEPTIONS No.	Yds.	Avg.	TD	PUNT RETURNS No.	Yds.	Avg.	TD	KICKOFF RETURNS No.	Yds.	Avg.	TD	TOTALS TD	Pts.
1999—Northwestern State	10	4	61	15.3	1	0	0	0.0	0	1	2	2.0	0	1	6
2000—Northwestern State	11	3	78	26.0	1	18	427	23.7	3	0	0	0.0	0	4	24
2001—Northwestern State	11	1	0	0.0	0	24	391	16.3	0	14	309	22.1	0	0	0
2002—Northwestern State	11	3	27	9.0	0	18	208	11.6	0	0	0	0.0	0	0	0
College totals (4 years)	43	11	166	15.1	2	60	1026	17.1	3	15	311	20.7	0	5	30

McMULLEN, BILLY — WR — EAGLES

PERSONAL: Born March 8, 1980, in Richmond, Va. ... 6-4/210. ... Full name: Wilbur Anthony McMullen Jr.
HIGH SCHOOL: Henrico (Richmond, Va.).
COLLEGE: Virginia.
TRANSACTIONS/CAREER NOTES: Selected by Philadelphia Eagles in third round (95th pick overall) of 2003 NFL draft.
COLLEGE NOTES: Attempted two pass (2001), one pass (2002).

Year Team	G	RUSHING Att.	Yds.	Avg.	TD	RECEIVING No.	Yds.	Avg.	TD	TOTALS TD	Pts.
1999—Virginia	11	0	0	0.0	0	28	483	17.3	6	6	36
2000—Virginia	11	0	0	0.0	0	30	541	18.0	3	3	18
2001—Virginia	12	0	0	0.0	0	83	1060	12.8	12	12	72
2002—Virginia	14	7	37	5.3	1	69	894	13.0	3	4	28
College totals (4 years)	48	7	37	5.3	1	210	2978	14.2	24	25	154

McNEAL, BRYANT   DE   BRONCOS

PERSONAL: Born July 13, 1979, in Swansea, N.C. ... 6-4/248. ... Full name: Bryant A. McNeal.
HIGH SCHOOL: Swansea (S.C.).
COLLEGE: Clemson.
TRANSACTIONS/CAREER NOTES: Selected by Denver Broncos in fourth round (128th pick overall) of 2003 NFL draft.

Year Team	G	SACKS
1998—Clemson	Redshirted.	
1999—Clemson	11	3.0
2000—Clemson	11	2.0
2001—Clemson	11	6.5
2002—Clemson	13	9.0
College totals (4 years)	46	20.5

MILLIGAN, HANIK   S   CHARGERS

PERSONAL: Born November 3, 1979, in U.S. Virgin Islands. ... 6-2/201.
HIGH SCHOOL: Coconut Creek (North Fort Lauderdale, Fla.).
JUNIOR COLLEGE: Iowa Central Community College.
COLLEGE: Houston.
TRANSACTIONS/CAREER NOTES: Selected by San Diego Chargers in sixth round (188th pick overall) of 2003 NFL draft.

Year Team	G	No.	Yds.	Avg.	TD
			INTERCEPTIONS		
2000—Houston	11	5	77	15.4	0
2001—Houston	11	1	18	18.0	0
2002—Houston	12	1	19	19.0	0
College totals (3 years)	34	7	114	16.3	0

MITCHELL, CLINT   DE   BRONCOS

PERSONAL: Born September 21, 1980, in Austin, Texas. ... 6-7/257. ... Full name: Clint Edward Mitchell. ... Brother of Jeff Mitchell, offensive center, Carolina Panthers.
HIGH SCHOOL: Coiuntryside (Clearwater, Fla.).
COLLEGE: Florida.
TRANSACTIONS/CAREER NOTES: Selected by Denver Broncos in seventh round (227th pick overall) of 2003 NFL draft.

Year Team	G	SACKS
1999—Florida	Redshirted.	
2000—Florida	12	3.5
2001—Florida	2	0.0
2002—Florida	12	2.3
College totals (3 years)	26	5.8

MITCHELL, KAWIKA   LB   CHIEFS

PERSONAL: Born October 10, 1979, in Winter Springs, Fla. ... 6-2/255.
HIGH SCHOOL: Lake Howell (Casselberry, Fla.).
COLLEGE: Georgia, then South Florida.
TRANSACTIONS/CAREER NOTES: Selected by Kansas City Chiefs in second round (47th pick overall) of 2003 NFL draft.

Year Team	G	Sks.	No.	Yds.	Avg.	TD
				INTERCEPTIONS		
1998—Georgia	Redshirted.					
1999—South Florida	11	1.5	1	22	22.0	0
2000—South Florida	11	1.0	0	0	0.0	0
2001—South Florida	10	1.5	0	0	0.0	0
2002—South Florida	11	4.0	1	39	39.0	0
College totals (4 years)	43	8.0	2	61	30.5	0

MOORE, CASEY   FB   PANTHERS

PERSONAL: Born July 26, 1980, in Largo, Fla. ... 6-2/240.
HIGH SCHOOL: St. Petersburg Catholic (St. Petersburg, Fla.).
COLLEGE: Stanford.
TRANSACTIONS/CAREER NOTES: Selected by Carolina Panthers in seventh round (247th pick overall) of 2003 NFL draft.

Year Team	G	RUSHING				RECEIVING				TOTALS	
		Att.	Yds.	Avg.	TD	No.	Yds.	Avg.	TD	TD	Pts.
1998—Stanford					Redshirted.						
1999—Stanford	11	23	190	8.3	4	11	109	9.9	1	5	30
2000—Stanford	11	50	224	4.5	3	8	115	14.4	2	5	30
2001—Stanford	11	31	199	6.4	3	15	146	9.7	0	3	18
2002—Stanford	11	54	348	6.4	1	16	143	8.9	2	3	18
College totals (4 years)	44	158	961	6.1	11	50	513	10.3	5	16	96

MOORE, EDDIE   LB   DOLPHINS

PERSONAL: Born July 5, 1980, in South Pittsburg, Tenn. ... 6-0/237. ... Full name: Eddie Deon Moore.
HIGH SCHOOL: Pittsburg (Tenn.).
COLLEGE: Tennessee.
TRANSACTIONS/CAREER NOTES: Selected by Miami Dolphins in second round (49th pick overall) of 2003 NFL draft.
COLLEGE NOTES: Intercepted one pass (2001).

Year Team	G	SACKS
1999—Tennessee	11	0.0
2000—Tennessee	11	1.0
2001—Tennessee	11	2.0
2002—Tennessee	12	3.0
College totals (4 years)	45	6.0

MOORE, LANGSTON   DT   BENGALS

PERSONAL: Born July 17, 1981, in Charleston, S.C. ... 6-1/303.
HIGH SCHOOL: James Island (Charleston, S.C.).
COLLEGE: South Carolina.
TRANSACTIONS/CAREER NOTES: Selected by Cincinnati Bengals in sixth round (174th pick overall) of 2003 NFL draft.
COLLEGE NOTES: Intercepted one pass (2002).

Year Team	G	SACKS
1999—South Carolina	11	0.0
2000—South Carolina	10	2.0
2001—South Carolina	11	1.0
2002—South Carolina	12	3.0
College totals (4 years)	44	6.0

MOORE, RASHAD   DT   SEAHAWKS

PERSONAL: Born March 16, 1979, in Huntsville, Ala. ... 6-3/324. ... Full name: Glenn Rashad Moore.
HIGH SCHOOL: Johnson (Huntsville, Ala.).
COLLEGE: Tennessee.
TRANSACTIONS/CAREER NOTES: Selected by Seattle Seahawks in sixth round (183rd pick overall) of 2003 NFL draft.
COLLEGE NOTES: Intercepted one pass (2001).

Year Team	G	SACKS
1998—Tennessee	Redshirted.	
1999—Tennessee	7	0.0
2000—Tennessee	7	1.5
2001—Tennessee	11	0.0
2002—Tennessee	12	2.0
College totals (4 years)	37	3.5

MOOREHEAD, KINDAL   DE   PANTHERS

PERSONAL: Born October 14, 1978, in Memphis, Tenn. ... 6-2/285.
HIGH SCHOOL: Melrose (Memphis, Tenn.).
COLLEGE: Alabama (degree in general health studies).
TRANSACTIONS/CAREER NOTES: Selected by Carolina Panthers in fifth round (145th pick overall) of 2003 NFL draft.
COLLEGE NOTES: Intercepted one pass (2001).

Year Team	G	SACKS
1998—Alabama	11	5.0
1999—Alabama	12	5.5
2000—Alabama	Redshirted.	
2001—Alabama	10	6.0
2002—Alabama	13	9.0
College totals (4 years)	46	25.5

MUGHELLI, OVIE   FB   RAVENS

PERSONAL: Born June 10, 1980, in Boston. ... 6-1/255.
HIGH SCHOOL: Porter-Gaud (Charleston, S.C.).
COLLEGE: Wake Forest.
TRANSACTIONS/CAREER NOTES: Selected by Baltimore Ravens in fourth round (134th pick overall) of 2003 NFL draft.

Year Team	G	RUSHING				RECEIVING				TOTALS	
		Att.	Yds.	Avg.	TD	No.	Yds.	Avg.	TD	TD	Pts.
1998—Wake Forest			Redshirted.								
1999—Wake Forest	9	16	80	5.0	0	0	0	0.0	0	0	0
2000—Wake Forest	11	40	128	3.2	1	1	0	0.0	0	1	6
2001—Wake Forest	11	0	0	0.0	0	7	53	7.6	0	0	0
2002—Wake Forest	13	81	322	4.0	12	10	111	11.1	0	12	72
College totals (4 years)	44	137	530	3.9	13	18	164	9.1	0	13	78

NATTIEL, MICHAEL   LB   VIKINGS

PERSONAL: Born November 8, 1980, in Gainesville, Fla. ... 6-0/228. ... Full name: Michael Dondrill Nattiel. ... Nephew of Ricky Nattiel, wide receiver with Denver Broncos (1987-92).
HIGH SCHOOL: Newberry (Archer, Fla.).
COLLEGE: Florida.
TRANSACTIONS/CAREER NOTES: Selected by Minnesota Vikings in sixth round (190th pick overall) of 2003 NFL draft.

			INTERCEPTIONS			
Year Team	G	Sks.	No.	Yds.	Avg.	TD
1999—Florida	12	0.0	0	0	0.0	0
2000—Florida	12	0.0	2	28	14.0	0
2001—Florida	11	1.0	1	25	25.0	0
2002—Florida	13	2.0	0	0	0.0	0
College totals (4 years)	48	3.0	3	53	17.7	0

NEAD, SPENCER   TE   PATRIOTS

PERSONAL: Born November 3, 1977, in Tacoma, Wash. ... 6-4/259.
HIGH SCHOOL: Teton (Tetonia, Idaho).
JUNIOR COLLEGE: Ricks College (Idaho).
COLLEGE: Brigham Young.
TRANSACTIONS/CAREER NOTES: Selected by New England Patriots in seventh round (234th pick overall) of 2003 NFL draft.

		RECEIVING				KICKOFF RETURNS				TOTALS	
Year Team	G	No.	Yds.	Avg.	TD	No.	Yds.	Avg.	TD	TD	Pts.
2001—Brigham Young	13	22	266	12.1	5	2	20	10.0	0	5	30
2002—Brigham Young	12	40	449	11.2	1	0	0	0.0	0	1	6
College totals (2 years)	25	62	715	11.5	6	2	20	10.0	0	6	36

NELSON, BRUCE   C   PANTHERS

PERSONAL: Born May 12, 1979, in Emmetsburg, Iowa. ... 6-5/301.
HIGH SCHOOL: Emmetsburg (Iowa).
COLLEGE: Iowa.
TRANSACTIONS/CAREER NOTES: Selected by Carolina Panthers in second round (50th pick overall) of 2003 NFL draft.
COLLEGE PLAYING EXPERIENCE: Iowa, 1998-2002. ... Games played: 1998 (redshirted), 1999 (11), 2000 (11), 2001 (12), 2002 (13). Total: 47.

NEWMAN, TERENCE   CB   COWBOYS

PERSONAL: Born September 4, 1978, in Salina, Kan. ... 5-10/189.
HIGH SCHOOL: Central (Salina, Kan.).
COLLEGE: Kansas State.
TRANSACTIONS/CAREER NOTES: Selected by Dallas Cowboys in first round (fifth pick overall) of 2003 NFL draft.
COLLEGE NOTES: Rushed two times, caught four passes for 98 yards and one touchdown (2002).

		INTERCEPTIONS				PUNT RETURNS				KICKOFF RETURNS				TOTALS	
Year Team	G	No.	Yds.	Avg.	TD	No.	Yds.	Avg.	TD	No.	Yds.	Avg.	TD	TD	Pts.
1998—Kansas State								Redshirted.							
1999—Kansas State	11	1	8	8.0	0	0	0	0.0	0	8	211	26.4	0	0	0
2000—Kansas State	13	1	4	4.0	0	0	16	0.0	0	3	44	14.7	0	1	6
2001—Kansas State	11	3	0	0.0	0	1	13	13.0	0	9	211	23.4	0	0	0
2002—Kansas State	13	5	21	4.2	0	26	388	14.9	2	13	370	28.5	1	4	24
College totals (4 years)	48	10	33	3.3	0	27	417	15.4	2	33	836	25.3	1	5	30

NICKEY, DONNIE   S   TITANS

PERSONAL: Born April 25, 1980, in Plain City, Ohio. ... 6-2/220.
HIGH SCHOOL: Jonathan Alder (Plain City, Ohio).
COLLEGE: Ohio State.
TRANSACTIONS/CAREER NOTES: Selected by Tennessee Titans in fifth round (154th pick overall) of 2003 NFL draft.

			INTERCEPTIONS			
Year Team	G	Sks.	No.	Yds.	Avg.	TD
1998—Ohio State				Redshirted.		
1999—Ohio State	11	0.0	1	0	0.0	0
2000—Ohio State	11	1.0	2	11	5.5	0
2001—Ohio State	11	1.0	2	79	39.5	0
2002—Ohio State	14	0.0	0	0	0.0	0
College totals (4 years)	47	2.0	5	90	18.0	0

NIMMO, LANCE   OT   BUCCANEERS

PERSONAL: Born September 13, 1979, in New Castle, Pa. ... 6-5/303.
HIGH SCHOOL: Laurel (New Castle, Pa.).
COLLEGE: West Virginia.
TRANSACTIONS/CAREER NOTES: Selected by Tampa Bay Buccaneers in fourth round (130th pick overall) of 2003 NFL draft.
COLLEGE PLAYING EXPERIENCE: West Virginia, 1998-2002. ... Games played: 1998 (redshirted), 1999 (8), 2000 (11), 2001 (11), 2002 (13). Total: 43.

ODOM, JOE — LB — BEARS

PERSONAL: Born December 14, 1979, in Bethalto, Ill. ... 6-1/241. ... Full name: Joe Edward Odom.
HIGH SCHOOL: Civic Memorial (Bethalto, Ill.).
COLLEGE: Purdue.
TRANSACTIONS/CAREER NOTES: Selected by Chicago Bears in sixth round (191st pick overall) of 2003 NFL draft.
COLLEGE NOTES: Returned one kickoff (1999), rushed one time (2001), returned one kickoff (2002).

Year Team	G	Sks.	INTERCEPTIONS No.	Yds.	Avg.	TD
1998—Purdue			Redshirted.			
1999—Purdue	12	2.0	0	0	0.0	0
2000—Purdue	9	2.0	1	12	12.0	0
2001—Purdue	11	2.0	3	35	11.7	0
2002—Purdue	13	1.0	0	0	0.0	0
College totals (4 years)	45	7.0	4	47	11.8	0

OGDEN, MARQUES — OT — JAGUARS

PERSONAL: Born November 15, 1980, in Washington, D.C. ... 6-4/317. ... Brother of Jonathan Ogden, offensive tackle, Baltimore Ravens.
HIGH SCHOOL: St. John's (Washington, D.C.).
COLLEGE: Howard.
TRANSACTIONS/CAREER NOTES: Selected by Jacksonville Jaguars in sixth round (193rd pick overall) of 2003 NFL draft.
COLLEGE PLAYING EXPERIENCE: Howard, 1998-2002. ... Games played: 1998 (redshirted), 1999 (11), 2000 (11), 2001 (9), 2002 (11). Total: 42.

OLINGER, JON — WR — FALCONS

PERSONAL: Born August 24, 1980, in Hazard, Ky. ... 6-3/223.
HIGH SCHOOL: Hazard (Ky.).
COLLEGE: Cincinnati.
TRANSACTIONS/CAREER NOTES: Selected by Atlanta Falcons in fifth round (159th pick overall) of 2003 NFL draft.

Year Team	G	RECEIVING No.	Yds.	Avg.	TD
1998—Cincinnati		Redshirted.			
1999—Cincinnati	7	5	63	12.6	0
2000—Cincinnati	7	3	23	7.7	0
2001—Cincinnati	11	27	469	17.4	7
2002—Cincinnati	14	54	1114	20.6	7
College totals (4 years)	39	89	1669	18.8	14

PACE, CALVIN — DE — CARDINALS

PERSONAL: Born October 28, 1980, in Detroit. ... 6-4/269.
HIGH SCHOOL: Lithia Springs (Douglasville, Ga.).
COLLEGE: Wake Forest.
TRANSACTIONS/CAREER NOTES: Selected by Arizona Cardinals in first round (18th pick overall) of 2003 NFL draft.

Year Team	G	SACKS
1998—Wake Forest		Redshirted.
1999—Wake Forest	7	2.0
2000—Wake Forest	11	9.0
2001—Wake Forest	11	10.0
2002—Wake Forest	12	0.0
College totals (4 years)	41	21.0

PAGEL, DEREK — S — JETS

PERSONAL: Born October 24, 1979, in Plainfield, Iowa. ... 6-1/208.
HIGH SCHOOL: Nashua-Plainfield (Plainfield, Iowa).
COLLEGE: Iowa.
TRANSACTIONS/CAREER NOTES: Selected by New York Jets in fifth round (140th pick overall) of 2003 NFL draft.

Year Team	G	Sks.	INTERCEPTIONS No.	Yds.	Avg.	TD
1998—Iowa			Redshirted.			
1999—Iowa	11	0.0	0	0	0.0	0
2000—Iowa	10	1.0	0	0	0.0	0
2001—Iowa	11	0.0	1	1	1.0	0
2002—Iowa	13	0.0	4	89	22.3	1
College totals (4 years)	45	1.0	5	90	18.0	1

PALMER, CARSON — QB — BENGALS

PERSONAL: Born December 27, 1979, in Laguna Niguel, Calif. ... 6-5/232.
HIGH SCHOOL: Santa Margarita (Rancho Santa Margarita, Calif.).
COLLEGE: Southern California.
TRANSACTIONS/CAREER NOTES: Selected by Cincinnati Bengals in first round (first pick overall) of 2003 NFL draft. ... Signed by Bengals (April 25, 2003).

HONORS: Heisman Trophy winner (2002). ... Named College Football Player of the Year by THE SPORTING NEWS (2002). ... Named quarterback on THE SPORTING NEWS college All-America first team (2002).
COLLEGE NOTES: Granted medical redshirt (1999).

Year Team	G	PASSING								RUSHING				TOTALS	
		Att.	Cmp.	Pct.	Yds.	TD	Int.	Avg.	Rat.	Att.	Yds.	Avg.	TD	TD	Pts.
1998—Southern California	13	235	130	55.3	1755	7	6	7.47	118.2	47	-116	-2.5	0	1	6
1999—Southern California	3	53	39	73.6	490	3	3	9.25	158.6	7	2	0.3	0	1	6
2000—Southern California	12	415	228	54.9	2914	16	18	7.02	118.0	63	5	0.1	2	2	12
2001—Southern California	12	377	221	58.6	2717	13	12	7.21	125.5	88	34	0.4	1	1	6
2002—Southern California	13	489	309	63.2	3942	33	10	8.06	149.1	50	-122	-2.4	4	4	24
College totals (5 years)	53	1569	927	59.1	11818	72	49	7.53	131.2	255	-197	-0.8	7	9	54

PASHOS, TONY — OT — RAVENS

PERSONAL: Born August 3, 1980, in Palos Heights, Ill. ... 6-6/337. ... Full name: Anthony George Pashos.
HIGH SCHOOL: Locksport Township (Ill.).
COLLEGE: Illinois.
TRANSACTIONS/CAREER NOTES: Selected by Baltimore Ravens in fifth round (173th pick overall) of 2003 NFL draft.
COLLEGE PLAYING EXPERIENCE: Illinois, 1998-2002. ... Games played: 1998 (redshirted), 1999 (11), 2000 (11), 2001 (11), 2002 (12). Total: 45.

PATTERSON, ELTON — DE — BENGALS

PERSONAL: Born June 13, 1981, in Tallahassee, Fla. ... 6-2/271.
HIGH SCHOOL: Rickards (Tallahassee, Fla.).
COLLEGE: Central Florida.
TRANSACTIONS/CAREER NOTES: Selected by Cincinnati Bengals in seventh round (259th pick overall) of 2003 NFL draft.

Year Team	G	SACKS
1999—Central Florida	11	2.0
2000—Central Florida	11	10.0
2001—Central Florida	11	9.0
2002—Central Florida	12	10.0
College totals (4 years)	45	31.0

PEARCE, CHANCE — C — TEXANS

PERSONAL: Born May 11, 1980, in Brownwood, Texas. ... 6-1/246. ... Full name: Chance Douglas Pearce.
HIGH SCHOOL: Brownwood (Texas).
COLLEGE: Texas A&M.
TRANSACTIONS/CAREER NOTES: Selected by Houston Texans in seventh round (233rd pick overall) of 2003 NFL draft.
COLLEGE PLAYING EXPERIENCE: Texas A&M, 1999-2002. ... Games played: 1999 (11), 2000 (11), 2001 (11), 2002 (11). Total: 44.

PEEK, ANTWAN — LB — TEXANS

PERSONAL: Born October 29, 1979, in Cincinnati. ... 6-3/246.
HIGH SCHOOL: Woodward (Cincinnati).
COLLEGE: Cincinnati.
TRANSACTIONS/CAREER NOTES: Selected by Houston Texans in third round (67th pick overall) of 2003 NFL draft.
COLLEGE NOTES: Returned one punt (2001).

Year Team	G	Sks.	INTERCEPTIONS			
			No.	Yds.	Avg.	TD
1998—Cincinnati	8	0.0	0	0	0.0	0
1999—Cincinnati	1	0.0	0	0	0.0	0
2000—Cincinnati	11	8.5	1	21	21.0	0
2001—Cincinnati	10	11.5	0	0	0.0	0
2002—Cincinnati	14	6.5	0	0	0.0	0
College totals (5 years)	44	26.5	1	21	21.0	0

PETERSON, KENNY — DE — PACKERS

PERSONAL: Born November 21, 1978, in Canton, Ohio. ... 6-3/298.
HIGH SCHOOL: McKinley (Canton, Ohio).
COLLEGE: Ohio State.
TRANSACTIONS/CAREER NOTES: Selected by Green Bay Packers in third round (79th pick overall) of 2003 NFL draft.
COLLEGE NOTES: Intercepted one pass (1999).

Year Team	G	SACKS
1998—Ohio State	Redshirted.	
1999—Ohio State	8	0.0
2000—Ohio State	11	3.0
2001—Ohio State	11	3.0
2002—Ohio State	14	6.0
College totals (4 years)	44	12.0

PIERCE, TERRY — LB — BRONCOS

PERSONAL: Born June 21, 1981, in Fort Worth, Texas. ... 6-1/251.
HIGH SCHOOL: Western Hills (Fort Worth, Texas).
COLLEGE: Kansas State.
TRANSACTIONS/CAREER NOTES: Selected after junior season by Denver Broncos in second round (51st pick overall) of 2003 NFL draft.
COLLEGE NOTES: Returned one kickoff (2001), one kickoff (2002).

Year Team	G	Sks.	INTERCEPTIONS			
			No.	Yds.	Avg.	TD
1999—Kansas State			Redshirted.			
2000—Kansas State	11	0.0	1	0	0.0	0
2001—Kansas State	11	2.0	0	0	0.0	0
2002—Kansas State	13	5.0	0	0	0.0	0
College totals (3 years)	35	7.0	1	0	0.0	0

PIERSON, SHURRON — DE — RAIDERS

PERSONAL: Born May 31, 1982, in Inverness, Fla. ... 6-2/243. ... Full name: Shurron Torian Pierson.
HIGH SCHOOL: Wildwood (Fla.).
COLLEGE: South Florida.
TRANSACTIONS/CAREER NOTES: Selected after junior season by Oakland Raiders in fourth round (129th pick overall) of 2003 NFL draft.
COLLEGE NOTES: Returned one punt (2001), returned one punt, intercepted one pass (2002).

Year Team	G	SACKS
2000—South Florida		Did not play.
2001—South Florida	11	10.0
2002—South Florida	11	8.0
College totals (2 years)	22	18.0

PILE, WILLIE — S — CHIEFS

PERSONAL: Born May 25, 1980, in New York City. ... 6-2/206. ... Full name: Willie Marquis Pile.
HIGH SCHOOL: West Potomac (Alexandria, Va.).
JUNIOR COLLEGE: degree in management.
COLLEGE: Virginia Tech.
TRANSACTIONS/CAREER NOTES: Selected by Kansas City Chiefs in seventh round (252nd pick overall) of 2003 NFL draft. ... Signed by Chiefs (May 12, 2003).

Year Team	G	Sks.	INTERCEPTIONS			
			No.	Yds.	Avg.	TD
1998—Virginia Tech			Redshirted.			
1999—Virginia Tech	3	1.0	0	0	0.0	0
2000—Virginia Tech	11	0.0	6	22	3.7	1
2001—Virginia Tech	11	4.0	4	77	19.3	1
2002—Virginia Tech	14	0.0	4	171	42.8	1
College totals (4 years)	39	5.0	14	270	19.3	2

PINNER, ARTOSE — RB — LIONS

PERSONAL: Born January 5, 1978, in Hopkinsville, Ky. ... 5-10/229. ... Full name: Artose Deonce Pinner.
HIGH SCHOOL: Hopkinsville (Ky.).
COLLEGE: Kentucky.
TRANSACTIONS/CAREER NOTES: Selected by Detroit Lions in fourth round (99th pick overall) of 2003 NFL draft.

Year Team	G	RUSHING				RECEIVING				TOTALS	
		Att.	Yds.	Avg.	TD	No.	Yds.	Avg.	TD	TD	Pts.
1999—Kentucky	4	16	62	3.9	0	0	0	0.0	0	0	0
2000—Kentucky	7	39	188	4.8	0	9	28	3.1	0	0	0
2001—Kentucky	11	100	441	4.4	4	12	115	9.6	0	4	24
2002—Kentucky	12	283	1414	5.0	13	37	264	7.1	2	15	90
College totals (4 years)	34	438	2105	4.8	17	58	407	7.0	2	19	114

PINNOCK, ANDREW — FB — CHARGERS

PERSONAL: Born March 12, 1980, in Bloomfield, Conn. ... 5-10/265.
HIGH SCHOOL: Bloomfield (Conn.).
COLLEGE: South Carolina.
TRANSACTIONS/CAREER NOTES: Selected by San Diego Chargers in seventh round (229th pick overall) of 2003 NFL draft.
COLLEGE NOTES: Returned one kickoff (2000).

Year Team	G	RUSHING				RECEIVING				TOTALS	
		Att.	Yds.	Avg.	TD	No.	Yds.	Avg.	TD	TD	Pts.
1999—South Carolina	7	73	261	3.6	3	2	2	1.0	0	3	18
2000—South Carolina	11	99	373	3.8	7	5	37	7.4	0	7	42
2001—South Carolina	11	103	573	5.6	10	3	30	10.0	0	10	60
2002—South Carolina	12	124	563	4.5	5	16	106	6.6	0	5	32
College totals (4 years)	41	399	1770	4.4	25	26	175	6.7	0	25	152

POLAMALU, TROY   S   STEELERS

PERSONAL: Born April 19, 1981, in Garden Grove, Calif. ... 5-10/206. ... Full name: Troy Polamalu Aumua. ... Cousin of Nicky Sualua, running back with Dallas Cowboys (1997-98).
HIGH SCHOOL: Douglas (Winston, Ore.).
COLLEGE: Southern California.
TRANSACTIONS/CAREER NOTES: Selected by Pittsburgh Steelers in first round (16th pick overall) of 2003 NFL draft.

			INTERCEPTIONS				KICKOFF RETURNS				TOTALS	
Year Team	G	Sks.	No.	Yds.	Avg.	TD	No.	Yds.	Avg.	TD	TD	Pts.
1999—Southern California	8	2.0	0	0	0.0	0	0	0	0.0	0	0	0
2000—Southern California	12	1.0	2	43	21.5	1	0	0	0.0	0	1	6
2001—Southern California	11	1.0	3	116	38.7	2	3	27	9.0	0	2	12
2002—Southern California	12	3.0	1	33	33.0	0	0	0	0.0	0	0	0
College totals (4 years)	43	7.0	6	192	32.0	3	3	27	9.0	'0	3	18

PONDER, WILLIE   WR   GIANTS

PERSONAL: Born February 14, 1980, in Tulsa, Okla. ... 6-0/205. ... Full name: Willie Columbus Ponder Jr.
HIGH SCHOOL: Central (Tulsa, Okla.).
JUNIOR COLLEGE: Coffeyville (Kan.).
COLLEGE: Tulsa, then Southeast Missouri State.
TRANSACTIONS/CAREER NOTES: Selected by New York Giants in sixth round (199th pick overall) of 2003 NFL draft.
COLLEGE NOTES: Rushed one time (2001), intercepted one pass (2002).

		RECEIVING				PUNT RETURNS				KICKOFF RETURNS				TOTALS	
Year Team	G	No.	Yds.	Avg.	TD	No.	Yds.	Avg.	TD	No.	Yds.	Avg.	TD	TD	Pts.
1998—Tulsa	2	8	71	8.9	0	0	0	0.0	0	0	0	0.0	0	0	0
1999—Tulsa								Did not play.							
2001—Southeast Missouri State	11	70	1090	15.6	11	5	2	0.4	0	13	283	21.8	0	11	66
2002—Southeast Missouri State	12	87	1453	16.7	15	2	25	12.5	0	12	257	21.4	0	16	98
College totals (3 years)	25	165	2614	15.8	26	7	27	3.9	0	25	540	21.6	0	27	164

PONTBRIAND, RYAN   C   BROWNS

PERSONAL: Born October 1, 1979, in Houston. ... 6-2/250. ... Full name: Ryan David Pontbriand. ... Name pronounced pownt-bree-AWND.
HIGH SCHOOL: W.P. Clements (Sugar Land, Texas).
COLLEGE: Rice.
TRANSACTIONS/CAREER NOTES: Selected by Cleveland Browns in fifth round (142nd pick overall) of 2003 NFL draft.
COLLEGE PLAYING EXPERIENCE: Rice, 1998-2002. ... Games played: 1998 (redshirted), 1999 (11), 2000 (11), 2001 (12), 2002 (11). Total: 45.

PROVOST, TIM   OT   DOLPHINS

PERSONAL: Born August 24, 1980, in Downey, Calif. ... 6-5/301.
HIGH SCHOOL: Perris (Calif.).
COLLEGE: San Jose State.
TRANSACTIONS/CAREER NOTES: Selected by Miami Dolphins in sixth round (209th pick overall) of 2003 NFL draft.
COLLEGE PLAYING EXPERIENCE: San Jose State, 1998-2002. ... Games played: 1998 (redshirted), 1999 (11), 2000 (12), 2001 (12), 2002 (13). Total: 48.

RAGONE, DAVE   QB   TEXANS

PERSONAL: Born October 3, 1979, in Middleburg Heights, Ohio. ... 6-4/249.
HIGH SCHOOL: St. Igantius (Middleburg Heights, Ohio).
COLLEGE: Louisville.
TRANSACTIONS/CAREER NOTES: Selected by Houston Texans in third round (88th pick overall) of 2003 NFL draft.
COLLEGE NOTES: Caught one pass (2000).

		PASSING								RUSHING				TOTALS	
Year Team	G	Att.	Cmp.	Pct.	Yds.	TD	Int.	Avg.	Rat.	Att.	Yds.	Avg.	TD	TD	Pts.
1998—Louisville						Redshirted.									
1999—Louisville	4	2	1	50.0	7	0	0	3.50	79.4	2	31	15.5	0	0	0
2000—Louisville	11	354	216	61.0	2621	27	11	7.40	142.2	101	252	2.5	6	6	36
2001—Louisville	12	383	231	60.3	3056	23	7	7.98	143.5	92	66	0.7	3	3	20
2002—Louisville	13	441	237	53.7	2880	24	11	6.53	121.6	131	248	1.9	0	0	0
College totals (4 years)	40	1180	685	58.1	8564	74	29	7.26	134.8	326	597	1.8	9	9	56

REDDING, CORY   DE   LIONS

PERSONAL: Born November 15, 1980, in Houston. ... 6-4/279. ... Full name: Cory B. Redding.
HIGH SCHOOL: North Shore (Houston).
COLLEGE: Texas.
TRANSACTIONS/CAREER NOTES: Selected by Detroit Lions in third round (66th pick overall) of 2003 NFL draft.

2003 DRAFT PICKS

Year Team	G	Sks.	INTERCEPTIONS			
			No.	Yds.	Avg.	TD
1999—Texas	13	2.0	0	0	0.0	0
2000—Texas	11	6.5	0	0	0.0	0
2001—Texas	12	4.5	1	22	22.0	0
2002—Texas	13	8.5	0	0	0.0	0
College totals (4 years)	49	21.5	1	22	22.0	1

ROBERTSON, DEWAYNE — DT — JETS

PERSONAL: Born October 16, 1981, in Memphis, Tenn. ... 6-1/317.
HIGH SCHOOL: Melrose (Memphis, Tenn.).
COLLEGE: Kentucky.
TRANSACTIONS/CAREER NOTES: Selected after junior season by New York Jets in first round (fourth pick overall) of 2003 NFL draft.
COLLEGE NOTES: Intercepted one pass (2000).

Year Team	G	SACKS
2000—Kentucky	11	3.0
2001—Kentucky	9	1.0
2002—Kentucky	11	5.0
College totals (3 years)	31	9.0

ROGERS, CHARLES — WR — LIONS

PERSONAL: Born May 23, 1981, in Saginaw, Mich. ... 6-2/202.
HIGH SCHOOL: Saginaw (Mich.).
COLLEGE: Michigan State.
TRANSACTIONS/CAREER NOTES: Selected after junior season by Detroit Lions in first round (second pick overall) of 2003 NFL draft.

Year Team	G	RUSHING				RECEIVING				PUNT RETURNS				TOTALS	
		Att.	Yds.	Avg.	TD	No.	Yds.	Avg.	TD	No.	Yds.	Avg.	TD	TD	Pts.
2000—Michigan State						Did not play.									
2001—Michigan State	11	4	36	9.0	1	57	1200	21.1	12	18	158	8.8	1	14	84
2002—Michigan State	12	6	74	12.3	0	68	1351	19.9	13	3	19	6.3	0	13	78
College totals (2 years)	23	10	110	11.0	1	125	2551	20.4	25	21	177	8.4	1	27	162

RUBIN, DEANDREW — WR — PACKERS

PERSONAL: Born October 8, 1978, in St. Petersburg, Fla. ... 5-11/190.
HIGH SCHOOL: Dixie Hollins (St. Petersburg, Fla.).
COLLEGE: South Florida.
TRANSACTIONS/CAREER NOTES: Selected by Green Bay Packers in seventh round (253rd pick overall) of 2003 NFL draft.
COLLEGE NOTES: Rushed one time (1999).

Year Team	G	RECEIVING				PUNT RETURNS				KICKOFF RETURNS				TOTALS	
		No.	Yds.	Avg.	TD	No.	Yds.	Avg.	TD	No.	Yds.	Avg.	TD	TD	Pts.
1998—South Florida	Redshirted.														
1999—South Florida	11	22	228	10.4	5	0	0	0.0	0	23	578	25.1	0	5	30
2000—South Florida	10	17	189	11.1	2	9	211	23.4	1	14	389	27.8	0	3	18
2001—South Florida	11	34	532	15.6	4	26	406	15.6	1	8	165	20.6	0	5	30
2002—South Florida	10	18	357	19.8	3	29	432	14.9	2	15	402	26.8	1	6	36
College totals (4 years)	42	91	1306	14.4	14	64	1049	16.4	4	60	1534	25.6	1	19	114

RYKERT, DUSTIN — OT — RAIDERS

PERSONAL: Born April 18, 1980, in Carmichael, Calif. ... 6-6/327.
HIGH SCHOOL: Oakmont (Calif.).
COLLEGE: Brigham Young.
TRANSACTIONS/CAREER NOTES: Selected by Oakland Raiders in sixth round (204th pick overall) of 2003 NFL draft.
COLLEGE PLAYING EXPERIENCE: Brigham Young, 1998-2002. ... Games played: 1998 (redshirted), 1999 (8), 2000 (11), 2001 (13), 2002 (12). Total: 44.

SAMUEL, ASANTE — CB — PATRIOTS

PERSONAL: Born January 6, 1981, in Fort Lauderdale, Fla. ... 5-11/185.
HIGH SCHOOL: Boyd Anderson (Lauderdale Lake, Fla.).
COLLEGE: Central Florida.
TRANSACTIONS/CAREER NOTES: Selected by New England Patriots in fourth round (120th pick overall) of 2003 NFL draft.

Year Team	G	INTERCEPTIONS				PUNT RETURNS				KICKOFF RETURNS				TOTALS	
		No.	Yds.	Avg.	TD	No.	Yds.	Avg.	TD	No.	Yds.	Avg.	TD	TD	Pts.
1999—Central Florida	10	0	0	0.0	0	0	0	0.0	0	0	0	0.0	0	0	0
2000—Central Florida	11	2	27	13.5	0	25	275	11.0	0	10	168	16.8	0	0	0
2001—Central Florida	11	2	18	9.0	0	19	165	8.7	0	0	0	0.0	0	0	0
2002—Central Florida	12	4	26	6.5	0	19	233	12.3	0	0	0	0.0	0	0	0
College totals (4 years)	44	8	71	8.9	0	63	673	10.7	0	10	168	16.8	0	0	0

SANDERS, ANTWOINE — S — RAVENS

PERSONAL: Born September 22, 1977, in Fayetteville, N.C. ... 6-2/202.
HIGH SCHOOL: Terry Sanford (Fayetteville, N.C.).
JUNIOR COLLEGE: Arizona Western College.
COLLEGE: Utah.
TRANSACTIONS/CAREER NOTES: Selected by Baltimore Ravens in seventh round (258th pick overall) of 2003 NFL draft.

		INTERCEPTIONS			
Year Team	G	No.	Yds.	Avg.	TD
2001—Utah	11	4	69	17.3	0
2002—Utah	11	2	30	15.0	0
College totals (2 years)	22	6	99	16.5	0

SAPE, LAUVALE — DT — BILLS

PERSONAL: Born August 29, 1980, in American Samoa. ... 6-2/297.
HIGH SCHOOL: Leilehua (Hawaii).
COLLEGE: Utah.
TRANSACTIONS/CAREER NOTES: Selected by Buffalo Bills in sixth round (187th pick overall) of 2003 NFL draft.

Year Team	G	SACKS
1998—Utah	Did not play.	
1999—Utah	2	0.0
2000—Utah	11	0.0
2001—Utah	11	4.5
2002—Utah	11	0.5
College totals (4 years)	35	5.0

SAPP, GEROME — S — RAVENS

PERSONAL: Born February 8, 1981, in Houston. ... 6-0/216. ... Full name: Gerome Daren Sapp.
HIGH SCHOOL: Lamar (Houston).
COLLEGE: Notre Dame.
TRANSACTIONS/CAREER NOTES: Selected by Baltimore Ravens in sixth round (182nd pick overall) of 2003 NFL draft.

		INTERCEPTIONS			
Year Team	G	No.	Yds.	Avg.	TD
1999—Notre Dame	12	1	0	0.0	0
2000—Notre Dame	10	0	0	0.0	0
2001—Notre Dame	9	0	0	0.0	0
2002—Notre Dame	11	4	17	4.3	0
College totals (4 years)	42	5	17	3.4	0

SCIFRES, MIKE — P — CHARGERS

PERSONAL: Born October 8, 1980, in Norco, La. ... 6-2/236. ... Full name: Michael Scifres.
HIGH SCHOOL: Destrehan (Norco, La.).
COLLEGE: Western Illinois.
TRANSACTIONS/CAREER NOTES: Selected by San Diego Chargers in fifth round (149th pick overall) of 2003 NFL draft.
COLLEGE NOTES: Attempted three passes (2000), two passes (2001), one pass, rushed two times(2002).

		PUNTING						KICKING						
Year Team	G	No.	Yds.	Avg.	Net avg.	In. 20	Blk.	50+	Tot.	Pct.	Lg.	XPM	XPA	Pts.
1998—Western Illinois								Redshirted.						
1999—Western Illinois	11	53	2171	41.0	0	8	0	0-0	0-0	0.0	0	0	0	0
2000—Western Illinois	12	58	2485	42.8	0	10	0	1-1	1-1	100.0	56	3	4	6
2001—Western Illinois	10	44	1867	42.4	0	13	1	0-1	2-5	40.0	46	0	0	6
2002—Western Illinois	13	53	2545	48.0	0	16	0	0-1	0-1	0.0	0	0	0	0
College totals (4 years)	46	208	9068	43.6	0.0	47	1	1-3	3-7	42.9	56	3	4	12

SCIULLO, STEVE — OT — COLTS

PERSONAL: Born August 27, 1980, in Pittsburgh. ... 6-5/330. ... Full name: Steven William Sciullo.
HIGH SCHOOL: Shaler Area (Pittsburgh).
COLLEGE: Marshall.
TRANSACTIONS/CAREER NOTES: Selected by Indianapolis Colts in fourth round (122nd pick overall) of 2003 NFL draft.
COLLEGE NOTES: Caught one pass (2001).
COLLEGE PLAYING EXPERIENCE: Marshall, 1998-2002. ... Games played: 1998 (redshirted), 1999 (12), 2000 (12), 2001 (11), 2002 (12). Total: 47.

SCOTT, BRYAN — CB/SS — FALCONS

PERSONAL: Born April 13, 1981, in Washington, D.C. ... 6-1/219. ... Full name: Bryan Anderson Scott. ... Cousin of Ryan Stewart, safety with Detroit Lions (1996-2000).
HIGH SCHOOL: Central Bucks (Pa.).
COLLEGE: Penn State.
TRANSACTIONS/CAREER NOTES: Selected by Atlanta Falcons in second round (55th pick overall) of 2003 NFL draft.

Year Team	G	Sks.	No.	Yds.	Avg.	TD
			INTERCEPTIONS			
1999—Penn State	11	0.0	1	0	0.0	0
2000—Penn State	11	0.0	1	14	14.0	0
2001—Penn State	11	1.0	0	0	0.0	0
2002—Penn State	13	0.0	4	47	11.8	0
College totals (4 years)	46	1.0	6	61	10.2	0

SCOTT, IAN — DT — BEARS

PERSONAL: Born November 8, 1981, in Greenville, S.C. ... 6-2/312. ... Full name: Josef Ian Scott.
HIGH SCHOOL: Gainesville (Fla.).
COLLEGE: Florida.
TRANSACTIONS/CAREER NOTES: Selected after junior season by Chicago Bears in fourth round (116th pick overall) of 2003 NFL draft.

Year Team	G	SACKS
2000—Florida	8	0.0
2001—Florida	11	2.5
2002—Florida	12	1.0
College totals (3 years)	31	3.5

SEIDMAN, MIKE — TE — PANTHERS

PERSONAL: Born February 11, 1981, in Westlake, Calif. ... 6-4/261. ... Full name: Michael H. Seidman.
HIGH SCHOOL: Westlake (Calif.).
COLLEGE: UCLA.
TRANSACTIONS/CAREER NOTES: Selected by Carolina Panthers in third round (76th pick overall) of 2003 NFL draft.

Year Team	G	RECEIVING				KICKOFF RETURNS				TOTALS	
		No.	Yds.	Avg.	TD	No.	Yds.	Avg.	TD	TD	Pts.
1999—UCLA	10	2	28	14.0	0	0	0	0.0	0	0	0
2000—UCLA	11	4	47	11.8	1	1	9	9.0	0	1	6
2001—UCLA	11	12	250	20.8	1	2	17	8.5	0	1	6
2002—UCLA	13	41	631	15.4	5	0	0	0.0	0	5	30
College totals (4 years)	45	59	956	16.2	7	3	26	8.7	0	7	42

SHABAZZ, SIDDEEQ — S — RAIDERS

PERSONAL: Born February 5, 1981, in Frankfurt, Germany. ... 5-11/202. ... Full name: Siddeeq Muneer Shabazz.
HIGH SCHOOL: Gadsden (Anthony, N.M.).
COLLEGE: New Mexico State.
TRANSACTIONS/CAREER NOTES: Selected by Oakland Raiders in seventh round (246th pick overall) of 2003 NFL draft.

Year Team	G	Sks.	No.	Yds.	Avg.	TD
			INTERCEPTIONS			
1998—New Mexico State			Redshirted.			
1999—New Mexico State	11	0.0	0	0	0.0	0
2000—New Mexico State	11	0.0	0	0	0.0	0
2001—New Mexico State	12	0.0	2	0	0.0	0
2002—New Mexico State	12	1.0	2	53	26.5	0
College totals (4 years)	46	1.0	4	53	13.3	0

SHANLE, SCOTT — LB — RAMS

PERSONAL: Born November 23, 1979, in St. Edward, Neb. ... 6-2/245.
HIGH SCHOOL: St. Edward (Neb.).
COLLEGE: Nebraska (degree in family and consumer science).
TRANSACTIONS/CAREER NOTES: Selected by St. Louis Rams in seventh round (251st pick overall) of 2003 NFL draft.

Year Team	G	Sks.	No.	Yds.	Avg.	TD
			INTERCEPTIONS			
1998—Nebraska			Redshirted.			
1999—Nebraska	12	0.0	0	0	0.0	0
2000—Nebraska	11	1.0	1	18	18.0	0
2001—Nebraska	12	3.0	0	0	0.0	0
2002—Nebraska	13	2.0	0	0	0.0	0
College totals (4 years)	48	6.0	1	18	18.0	0

SHARPE, MONTIQUE — DT — CHIEFS

PERSONAL: Born March 10, 1980, in Washington, D.C. ... 6-2/296.
HIGH SCHOOL: Dunbar (Washington, D.C.).
COLLEGE: Wake Forest.
TRANSACTIONS/CAREER NOTES: Selected by Kansas City Chiefs in seventh round (230th pick overall) of 2003 NFL draft.
COLLEGE NOTES: Intercepted one pass (2002).

Year Team	G	SACKS
1998—Wake Forest		Redshirted.
1999—Wake Forest	7	0.0
2000—Wake Forest	11	0.0
2001—Wake Forest	11	5.0
2002—Wake Forest	13	0.0
College totals (4 years)	42	5.0

SHIANCOE, VISHANTE   TE   GIANTS

PERSONAL: Born June 18, 1980, in Laurel, Md. ... 6-4/251.
HIGH SCHOOL: Blair (Laurel, Md.).
COLLEGE: Morgan State.
TRANSACTIONS/CAREER NOTES: Selected by New York Giants in third round (91st pick overall) of 2003 NFL draft.

		RECEIVING			
Year Team	G	No.	Yds.	Avg.	TD
1998—Morgan State		Redshirted.			
1999—Morgan State	1	2	55	27.5	0
2000—Morgan State	1	1	23	23.0	1
2001—Morgan State	10	22	350	15.9	5
2002—Morgan State	10	26	502	19.3	5
College totals (4 years)	22	51	930	18.2	11

SIMMS, CHRIS   QB   BUCCANEERS

PERSONAL: Born August 29, 1980, in Franklin Lakes, N.J. ... 6-4/220. ... Full name: Christopher David Simms. ... Son of Phil Simms, quarterback with New York Giants (1979-93).
HIGH SCHOOL: Ramapo (N.J.).
COLLEGE: Texas.
TRANSACTIONS/CAREER NOTES: Selected by Tampa Bay Buccaneers in third round (97th pick overall) of 2003 NFL draft.

		PASSING								RUSHING				TOTALS	
Year Team	G	Att.	Cmp.	Pct.	Yds.	TD	Int.	Avg.	Rat.	Att.	Yds.	Avg.	TD	TD	Pts.
1999—Texas	6	36	19	52.8	223	2	1	6.19	117.6	11	22	2.0	0	0	0
2000—Texas	10	117	67	57.3	1064	8	7	9.09	144.3	26	-25	-1.0	0	0	0
2001—Texas	12	362	214	59.1	2603	22	11	7.19	133.5	52	-10	-0.2	6	6	36
2002—Texas	13	396	235	59.3	3207	26	12	8.10	143.0	70	-124	-1.8	4	4	24
College totals (4 years)	41	911	535	58.7	7097	58	31	7.79	138.4	159	-137	-0.9	10	10	60

SMITH, L.J.   TE   EAGLES

PERSONAL: Born May 13, 1980, in Highland Park, N.J. ... 6-3/258. ... Full name: John Smith.
HIGH SCHOOL: Highland Park (N.J.).
COLLEGE: Rutgers.
TRANSACTIONS/CAREER NOTES: Selected by Philadelphia Eagles in second round (61st pick overall) of 2003 NFL draft.
COLLEGE NOTES: Rushed 16 times (2001), one time (2002).

		RECEIVING			
Year Team	G	No.	Yds.	Avg.	TD
1998—Rutgers		Redshirted.			
1999—Rutgers	11	26	418	16.1	3
2000—Rutgers	11	34	374	11.0	1
2001—Rutgers	11	30	282	9.4	3
2002—Rutgers	11	32	384	12.0	3
College totals (4 years)	44	122	1458	12.0	10

SMITH, MUSA   RB   RAVENS

PERSONAL: Born May 31, 1982, in Elliottsburg, Pa. ... 6-1/232.
HIGH SCHOOL: West Perry (Pa.).
COLLEGE: Georgia.
TRANSACTIONS/CAREER NOTES: Selected after junior season by Baltimore Ravens in third round (77th pick overall) of 2003 NFL draft.

		RUSHING				RECEIVING				KICKOFF RETURNS				TOTALS	
Year Team	G	Att.	Yds.	Avg.	TD	No.	Yds.	Avg.	TD	No.	Yds.	Avg.	TD	TD	Pts.
2000—Georgia	9	75	330	4.4	5	2	-7	-3.5	0	4	93	23.3	0	5	30
2001—Georgia	9	119	548	4.6	6	10	87	8.7	0	0	0	0.0	0	6	36
2002—Georgia	13	260	1324	5.1	8	15	107	7.1	0	0	0	0.0	0	8	48
College totals (3 years)	31	454	2202	4.9	19	27	187	6.9	0	4	93	23.3	0	19	114

SMITH, ONTERRIO   RB   VIKINGS

PERSONAL: Born December 8, 1980, in Sacramento. ... 5-10/220. ... Full name: Onterrio Raymond Smith.
HIGH SCHOOL: Grant (Sacramento).
COLLEGE: Tennessee, then Oregon.
TRANSACTIONS/CAREER NOTES: Selected after junior season by Minnesota Vikings in fourth round (105th pick overall) of 2003 NFL draft.
COLLEGE NOTES: Attempted two passes, threw for one touchdown (2001).

		RUSHING				RECEIVING				KICKOFF RETURNS				TOTALS	
Year Team	G	Att.	Yds.	Avg.	TD	No.	Yds.	Avg.	TD	No.	Yds.	Avg.	TD	TD	Pts.
1999—Tennessee	8	31	189	6.1	4	2	25	12.5	1	1	23	23.0	0	5	30
2000—Oregon		Did not play.													
2001—Oregon	11	161	1007	6.3	7	8	63	7.9	1	12	338	28.2	1	9	54
2002—Oregon	10	244	1141	4.7	12	13	78	6.0	0	7	175	25.0	0	12	72
College totals (3 years)	29	436	2337	5.4	23	23	166	7.2	2	20	536	26.8	1	26	156

SMITH, TRENT — TE — RAVENS

PERSONAL: Born September 15, 1979, in Norman, Okla. ... 6-5/243.
HIGH SCHOOL: Clinton (Okla.).
COLLEGE: Oklahoma.
TRANSACTIONS/CAREER NOTES: Selected by Baltimore Ravens in seventh round (223rd pick overall) of 2003 NFL draft.

			RECEIVING		
Year Team	G	No.	Yds.	Avg.	TD
1999—Oklahoma	11	15	142	9.5	2
2000—Oklahoma	12	29	310	10.7	3
2001—Oklahoma	12	61	564	9.2	6
2002—Oklahoma	14	46	396	8.6	5
College totals (4 years)	49	151	1412	9.4	16

SMITH, WADE — OT — DOLPHINS

PERSONAL: Born April 26, 1981, in Dallas. ... 6-4/296.
HIGH SCHOOL: Lake Highlands (Dallas).
COLLEGE: Memphis.
TRANSACTIONS/CAREER NOTES: Selected by Miami Dolphins in third round (78th pick overall) of 2003 NFL draft.
COLLEGE NOTES: Caught one pass, recorded one sack (1999), caught five passes, returned one kickoff (2000).

SMITH, ZURIEL — WR — COWBOYS

PERSONAL: Born January 15, 1980, in Mechanicsville, Va. ... 5-11/168.
HIGH SCHOOL: Altee (Mechanicsville, Va.).
COLLEGE: Hampton.
TRANSACTIONS/CAREER NOTES: Selected by Dallas Cowboys in sixth round (186th pick overall) of 2003 NFL draft.
COLLEGE NOTES: Attempted two passes (1999), rushed two times (2000).

		RECEIVING				PUNT RETURNS				KICKOFF RETURNS				TOTALS	
Year Team	G	No.	Yds.	Avg.	TD	No.	Yds.	Avg.	TD	No.	Yds.	Avg.	TD	TD	Pts.
1998—Hampton								Redshirted.							
1999—Hampton	9	31	429	13.8	4	7	91	13.0	0	0	0	0.0	0	4	24
2000—Hampton	11	47	816	17.4	5	5	40	8.0	0	0	0	0.0	0	5	30
2001—Hampton	11	58	732	12.6	6	29	514	17.7	4	0	0	0.0	0	10	62
2002—Hampton	11	53	773	14.6	6	27	500	18.5	1	1	57	57.0	0	7	42
College totals (4 years)	42	189	2750	14.6	21	68	1145	16.8	5	1	57	57.0	0	26	158

SOBIESKI, BEN — G/OT — BILLS

PERSONAL: Born May 3, 1979, in Mahtomedi, Minn. ... 6-5/307.
HIGH SCHOOL: Mahtomedi (Minn.).
COLLEGE: Iowa.
TRANSACTIONS/CAREER NOTES: Selected by Buffalo Bills in fifth round (151st pick overall) of 2003 NFL draft.
COLLEGE PLAYING EXPERIENCE: Iowa, 1997-2002. ... Games played: 1997 (11), 1998 (11), 1999 (redshirted), 2000 (redshirted), 2001 (4), 2002 (13). Total: 39.

ST. PIERRE, BRIAN — QB — STEELERS

PERSONAL: Born November 28, 1979, in Danvers, Mass. ... 6-3/218.
HIGH SCHOOL: St. John's Prep (Danvers, Mass.).
COLLEGE: Boston College.
TRANSACTIONS/CAREER NOTES: Selected by Pittsburgh Steelers in fifth round (163rd pick overall) of 2003 NFL draft.

		PASSING								RUSHING				TOTALS	
Year Team	G	Att.	Cmp.	Pct.	Yds.	TD	Int.	Avg.	Rat.	Att.	Yds.	Avg.	TD	TD	Pts.
1998—Boston College							Redshirted.								
1999—Boston College	9	40	24	60.0	295	1	2	7.38	120.2	24	105	4.4	0	0	0
2000—Boston College	11	77	47	61.0	543	4	3	7.05	129.6	13	-29	-2.2	1	1	6
2001—Boston College	11	279	149	53.4	2016	25	10	7.23	136.5	67	217	3.2	0	0	0
2002—Boston College	13	407	237	58.2	2983	18	17	7.33	126.0	68	126	1.9	1	1	6
College totals (4 years)	44	803	457	56.9	5837	48	32	7.27	129.7	172	419	2.4	2	2	12

STEINBACH, ERIC — G — BENGALS

PERSONAL: Born April 4, 1980, in New Lenox, Ill. ... 6-6/297.
HIGH SCHOOL: Providence Catholic (New Lenox, Ill.).
COLLEGE: Iowa.
TRANSACTIONS/CAREER NOTES: Selected by Cincinnati Bengals in second round (33rd pick overall) of 2003 NFL draft.
COLLEGE PLAYING EXPERIENCE: Iowa, 1998-2002. ... Games played: 1998 (redshirted), 1999 (11), 2000 (5), 2001 (11), 2002 (13). Total: 40.

STINCHCOMB, JON   OT   SAINTS

PERSONAL: Born August 27, 1979, in Lilburn, Ga. ... 6-5/302. ... Full name: Jonathan Stinchcomb. ... Brother of Matt Stinchcomb, offensive tackle, Oakland Raiders.
HIGH SCHOOL: Parkview (Lilburn, Ga.).
COLLEGE: Georgia.
TRANSACTIONS/CAREER NOTES: Selected by New Orleans Saints in second round (37th pick overall) of 2003 NFL draft.
COLLEGE PLAYING EXPERIENCE: Georgia, 1998-2002. ... Games played: 1998 (redshirted), 1999 (11), 2000 (11), 2001 (10), 2002 (13). Total: 45.

STRICKLAND, DONALD   CB   COLTS

PERSONAL: Born November 24, 1980, in Redwood, Calif. ... 5-10/187.
HIGH SCHOOL: Archbishop Riordan (San Francisco).
COLLEGE: Colorado.
TRANSACTIONS/CAREER NOTES: Selected by Indianapolis Colts in third round (90th pick overall) of 2003 NFL draft.
COLLEGE NOTES: Returned one kickoff (2000), returned one punt (2002).

			INTERCEPTIONS		
Year Team	G	Sks.	No.	Yds.	Avg.	TD
1998—Colorado			Redshirted.			
1999—Colorado	7	0.0	0	0	0.0	0
2000—Colorado	9	2.0	0	0	0.0	0
2001—Colorado	12	0.0	2	34	17.0	2
2002—Colorado	14	1.0	2	186	93.0	2
College totals (4 years)	42	3.0	4	220	55.0	4

SUGGS, LEE   RB   BROWNS

PERSONAL: Born August 11, 1980, in Roanoke, Va. ... 6-0/202. ... Full name: Lee Ernest Suggs Jr.
HIGH SCHOOL: William Fleming (Roanoke, Va.).
COLLEGE: Virginia Tech.
TRANSACTIONS/CAREER NOTES: Selected by Cleveland Browns in fourth round (115th pick overall) of 2003 NFL draft.
COLLEGE NOTES: Returned one punt (2000).

		RUSHING				RECEIVING				KICKOFF RETURNS				TOTALS	
Year Team	G	Att.	Yds.	Avg.	TD	No.	Yds.	Avg.	TD	No.	Yds.	Avg.	TD	TD	Pts.
1998—Virginia Tech							Redshirted.								
1999—Virginia Tech	9	44	136	3.1	2	1	1	1.0	0	0	0	0.0	0	2	12
2000—Virginia Tech	11	222	1207	5.4	27	3	44	14.7	1	3	45	15.0	0	28	168
2001—Virginia Tech	1	12	99	8.3	2	0	0	0.0	0	0	0	0.0	0	2	12
2002—Virginia Tech	14	257	1325	5.2	22	11	126	11.5	2	5	132	26.4	0	24	144
College totals (4 years)	35	535	2767	5.2	53	15	171	11.4	3	8	177	22.1	0	56	336

SUGGS, TERRELL   DE   RAVENS

PERSONAL: Born October 11, 1982, in Minneapolis. ... 6-3/262. ... Full name: Terrell Raynonn Suggs.
HIGH SCHOOL: Hamilton (Chandler, Ariz.).
COLLEGE: Arizona State.
TRANSACTIONS/CAREER NOTES: Selected after junior season by Baltimore Ravens in first round (10th pick overall) of 2003 NFL draft.

			INTERCEPTIONS		
Year Team	G	Sks.	No.	Yds.	Avg.	TD
2000—Arizona State	11	10.0	1	48	48.0	1
2001—Arizona State	11	10.0	0	0	0.0	0
2002—Arizona State	14	24.0	1	22	22.0	0
College totals (3 years)	36	44.0	2	70	35.0	1

SULLIVAN, JOHNATHAN   DT   SAINTS

PERSONAL: Born January 21, 1981, in Griffin, Ga. ... 6-3/313.
HIGH SCHOOL: Griffin (Ga.).
COLLEGE: Georgia.
TRANSACTIONS/CAREER NOTES: Selected after junior season by New Orleans Saints in first round (sixth pick overall) of 2003 NFL draft.

Year Team	G	SACKS
2000—Georgia	10	1.0
2001—Georgia	11	4.0
2002—Georgia	14	4.0
College totals (3 years)	35	9.0

TAYLOR, IVAN   CB   STEELERS

PERSONAL: Born May 5, 1980, in New Orleans. ... 6-0/202.
HIGH SCHOOL: Abramson (Gretna, La.).
COLLEGE: Louisiana-Lafayette.
TRANSACTIONS/CAREER NOTES: Selected by Pittsburgh Steelers in fourth round (125th pick overall) of 2003 NFL draft.
COLLEGE NOTES: Played running back (2001).

Year Team	G	RUSHING				RECEIVING				KICKOFF RETURNS				TOTALS	
		Att.	Yds.	Avg.	TD	No.	Yds.	Avg.	TD	No.	Yds.	Avg.	TD	TD	Pts.
1999—Louisiana-Lafayette								Did not play.							
2000—Louisiana-Lafayette								Did not play.							
2001—Louisiana-Lafayette	11	70	323	4.6	3	18	125	6.9	0	18	280	15.6	0	3	18
2002—Louisiana-Lafayette	12	0	0	0.0	0	0	0	0.0	0	9	210	23.3	0	0	0
College totals (2 years)	23	70	323	4.6	3	18	125	6.9	0	27	490	18.1	0	3	18

TERCERO, SCOTT — G — RAMS

PERSONAL: Born October 28, 1981, in Whittier, Calif. ... 6-4/303.
HIGH SCHOOL: Loyola (Pico Rivera, Calif.).
COLLEGE: California.
TRANSACTIONS/CAREER NOTES: Selected by St. Louis Rams in sixth round (184th pick overall) of 2003 NFL draft.
COLLEGE PLAYING EXPERIENCE: California, 1999-2002. ... Games played: 1999 (9), 2000 (10), 2001 (11), 2002 (12). Total: 42.

THOMPSON, CHAUN — LB — BROWNS

PERSONAL: Born May 22, 1980, in Mount Pleasant, Texas. ... 6-2/240.
HIGH SCHOOL: Mount Pleasant (Texas).
COLLEGE: West Texas A&M.
TRANSACTIONS/CAREER NOTES: Selected by Cleveland Browns in second round (52nd pick overall) of 2003 NFL draft.

Year Team	G	Sks.	INTERCEPTIONS			
			No.	Yds.	Avg.	TD
1998—West Texas A&M	8	1.0	0	0	0.0	0
1999—West Texas A&M	11	3.0	1	0	0.0	0
2000—West Texas A&M			Redshirted.			
2001—West Texas A&M	11	3.0	0	0	0.0	0
2002—West Texas A&M	11	1.0	2	33	16.5	0
College totals (4 years)	41	8.0	3	33	11.0	0

TILLMAN, CHARLES — CB — BEARS

PERSONAL: Born February 23, 1981, in Copperas Cove, Texas. ... 6-1/207.
HIGH SCHOOL: Copperas Cove (Texas).
COLLEGE: Louisiana-Lafayette.
TRANSACTIONS/CAREER NOTES: Selected by Chicago Bears in second round (35th pick overall) of 2003 NFL draft.
COLLEGE NOTES: Rushed one time (2001).

Year Team	G	Sks.	INTERCEPTIONS				KICKOFF RETURNS				TOTALS	
			No.	Yds.	Avg.	TD	No.	Yds.	Avg.	TD	TD	Pts.
1999—Louisiana-Lafayette	11	0.0	0	0	0.0	0	0	0	0.0	0	0	0
2000—Louisiana-Lafayette	11	2.0	6	15	2.5	0	0	0	0.0	0	0	0
2001—Louisiana-Lafayette	11	0.0	4	13	3.3	0	0	0	0.0	0	0	0
2002—Louisiana-Lafayette	12	0.0	2	8	4.0	0	3	57	19.0	0	0	0
College totals (4 years)	45	2.0	12	36	3.0	0	3	57	19.0	0	0	0

TINOISAMOA, PISA — LB — RAMS

PERSONAL: Born July 15, 1981, in San Diego. ... 6-0/231.
HIGH SCHOOL: Vista (Calif.).
COLLEGE: Hawaii.
TRANSACTIONS/CAREER NOTES: Selected by St. Louis Rams in second round (43rd pick overall) of 2003 NFL draft.

Year Team	G	Sks.	INTERCEPTIONS			
			No.	Yds.	Avg.	TD
2000—Hawaii	10	4.0	0	0	0.0	0
2001—Hawaii	9	5.0	0	0	0.0	0
2002—Hawaii	14	6.5	2	23	11.5	0
College totals (3 years)	33	15.5	2	23	11.5	0

TOEFIELD, LABRANDON — RB — JAGUARS

PERSONAL: Born September 24, 1980, in Independence, La. ... 5-11/233. ... Full name: LaBrandon Cordell Toefield.
HIGH SCHOOL: Independence (La.).
COLLEGE: Louisiana State.
TRANSACTIONS/CAREER NOTES: Selected after junior season by Jacksonville Jaguars in fourth round (132nd pick overall) of 2003 NFL draft.
COLLEGE NOTES: Attempted one pass (2001).

Year Team	G	RUSHING				RECEIVING				TOTALS	
		Att.	Yds.	Avg.	TD	No.	Yds.	Avg.	TD	TD	Pts.
1999—Louisiana State				Redshirted.							
2000—Louisiana State	10	165	682	4.1	5	7	44	6.3	0	5	30
2001—Louisiana State	12	230	992	4.3	19	13	148	11.4	0	19	114
2002—Louisiana State	9	116	475	4.1	2	5	41	8.2	1	3	18
College totals (3 years)	31	511	2149	4.2	26	25	233	9.3	1	27	162

TOLVER, J.R. — WR — DOLPHINS

PERSONAL: Born January 13, 1980, in Long Beach, Calif. ... 6-1/202. ... Full name: Gregory D. Tolver Jr.
HIGH SCHOOL: Mira Mesa (San Diego).

COLLEGE: San Diego State (degree in information decision making).
TRANSACTIONS/CAREER NOTES: Selected by Miami Dolphins in fifth round (169th pick overall) of 2003 NFL draft.
COLLEGE NOTES: Attempted three passes (2002).

Year Team	G	RUSHING Att.	Yds.	Avg.	TD	RECEIVING No.	Yds.	Avg.	TD	PUNT RETURNS No.	Yds.	Avg.	TD	KICKOFF RETURNS No.	Yds.	Avg.	TD	TOTALS TD	Pts.
1998—San Diego State										Redshirted.									
1999—San Diego State	7	0	0	0.0	0	9	101	11.2	2	0	0	0.0	0	0	0	0.0	0	2	12
2000—San Diego State	11	0	0	0.0	0	62	808	13.0	1	0	0	0.0	0	2	33	16.5	0	1	6
2001—San Diego State	11	2	-6	-3.0	0	63	878	13.9	2	0	0	0.0	0	1	33	33.0	0	2	12
2002—San Diego State	13	6	40	6.7	1	128	1785	13.9	13	2	5	2.5	0	0	0	0.0	0	14	86
College totals (4 years)	42	8	34	4.3	1	262	3572	13.6	18	2	5	2.5	0	3	66	22.0	0	19	116

TRUFANT, MARCUS   CB   SEAHAWKS

PERSONAL: Born December 25, 1980, in Tacoma, Wash. ... 5-11/199. ... Full name: Marcus Lavon Trufant.
HIGH SCHOOL: Wilson (Tacoma, Wash.).
COLLEGE: Washington State.
TRANSACTIONS/CAREER NOTES: Selected by Seattle Seahawks in first round (11th pick overall) of 2003 NFL draft.

Year Team	G	INTERCEPTIONS No.	Yds.	Avg.	TD	PUNT RETURNS No.	Yds.	Avg.	TD	TOTALS TD	Pts.
1999—Washington State	11	2	48	24.0	0	0	0	0.0	0	0	0
2000—Washington State	11	3	7	2.3	0	0	0	0.0	0	0	0
2001—Washington State	7	3	51	17.0	0	7	47	6.7	0	0	0
2002—Washington State	13	3	33	11.0	0	38	402	10.6	0	0	0
College totals (4 years)	42	11	139	12.6	0	45	449	10.0	0	0	0

TUCKER, B.J.   CB   COWBOYS

PERSONAL: Born October 12, 1980, in Sierra Leone, West Africa. ... 5-10/188.
HIGH SCHOOL: Nicolet (Bayside, Wis.).
COLLEGE: Wisconsin.
TRANSACTIONS/CAREER NOTES: Selected by Dallas Cowboys in sixth round (178th pick overall) of 2003 NFL draft.

Year Team	G	INTERCEPTIONS No.	Yds.	Avg.	TD
1999—Wisconsin	5	0	0	0.0	0
2000—Wisconsin	9	0	0	0.0	0
2001—Wisconsin	9	0	0	0.0	0
2002—Wisconsin	14	5	67	13.4	1
College totals (4 years)	37	5	67	13.4	1

TYREE, DAVID   WR   GIANTS

PERSONAL: Born January 3, 1980, in Livingston, N.J. ... 6-1/197. ... Full name: David Mikel Tyree.
HIGH SCHOOL: Montclair (N.J.).
COLLEGE: Syracuse.
TRANSACTIONS/CAREER NOTES: Selected by New York Giants in sixth round (211th pick overall) of 2003 NFL draft.
COLLEGE NOTES: Rushed four times (2002).

Year Team	G	RECEIVING No.	Yds.	Avg.	TD	PUNT RETURNS No.	Yds.	Avg.	TD	TOTALS TD	Pts.
1998—Syracuse					Redshirted.						
1999—Syracuse	11	7	89	12.7	0	0	0	0.0	0	0	0
2000—Syracuse	11	14	333	23.8	3	2	33	16.5	1	4	26
2001—Syracuse	12	18	233	12.9	0	1	12	12.0	0	0	0
2002—Syracuse	12	36	559	15.5	3	1	25	25.0	0	3	20
College totals (4 years)	46	75	1214	16.2	6	4	70	17.5	1	7	46

UMENYIORA, OSI   DE   GIANTS

PERSONAL: Born November 16, 1980, in London, England. ... 6-3/278.
HIGH SCHOOL: Auburn (Ala.).
COLLEGE: Troy State.
TRANSACTIONS/CAREER NOTES: Selected by New York Giants in second round (56th pick overall) of 2003 NFL draft.

Year Team	G	SACKS
1998—Troy State		Redshirted.
1999—Troy State	11	2.0
2000—Troy State	12	0.0
2001—Troy State	11	6.0
2002—Troy State	12	16.0
College totals (4 years)	46	24.0

VAN BUREN, COURTNEY   OT   CHARGERS

PERSONAL: Born February 22, 1980, in St. Louis. ... 6-6/353.
HIGH SCHOOL: Ladue Horton Watkins (St. Louis).
COLLEGE: Arkansas-Pine Bluff.
TRANSACTIONS/CAREER NOTES: Selected by San Diego Chargers in third round (80th pick overall) of 2003 NFL draft.
COLLEGE PLAYING EXPERIENCE: Arkansas-Pine Bluff, 1998-2002. ... Games played: 1998 (redshirted), 1999 (6), 2000 (10), 2001 (10), 2002 (11). Total: 37.

VEAL, DEMETRIN — DE — FALCONS

PERSONAL: Born August 11, 1981, in Paramount, Calif. ... 6-2/288. ... Full name: Demetrin Leeotis Veal.
HIGH SCHOOL: Paramount (Calif.).
JUNIOR COLLEGE: Cerritos Junior College (Calif.).
COLLEGE: Tennessee.
TRANSACTIONS/CAREER NOTES: Selected by Atlanta Falcons in seventh round (238th pick overall) of 2003 NFL draft.

Year Team	G	SACKS
2001—Tennessee	11	4.0
2002—Tennessee	12	3.0
College totals (2 years)	23	7.0

WADE, BOBBY — WR — BEARS

PERSONAL: Born February 25, 1981, in Phoenix. ... 5-10/193. ... Full name: Robert Louis Wade Jr.
HIGH SCHOOL: Desert Vista (Phoenix).
COLLEGE: Arizona.
TRANSACTIONS/CAREER NOTES: Selected by Chicago Bears in fifth round (139th pick overall) of 2003 NFL draft.

Year Team	G	RUSHING				RECEIVING				PUNT RETURNS				KICKOFF RETURNS				TOTALS	
		Att.	Yds.	Avg.	TD	No.	Yds.	Avg.	TD	No.	Yds.	Avg.	TD	No.	Yds.	Avg.	TD	TD	Pts.
1999—Arizona	12	0	0	0.0	0	30	454	15.1	4	0	0	0.0	0	10	191	19.1	0	4	24
2000—Arizona	10	8	27	3.4	0	45	626	13.9	3	26	262	10.1	1	3	66	22.0	0	4	24
2001—Arizona	11	3	22	7.3	0	62	882	14.2	8	23	239	10.4	0	3	67	22.3	0	8	48
2002—Arizona	12	1	4	4.0	0	93	1389	14.9	8	16	224	14.0	0	17	332	19.5	0	8	48
College totals (4 years)	45	12	53	4.4	0	230	3351	14.6	23	65	725	11.2	1	33	656	19.9	0	24	144

WALKER, AARON — TE — 49ERS

PERSONAL: Born March 14, 1980, in Titusville, Fla. ... 6-6/252. ... Full name: Aaron Scott Walker.
HIGH SCHOOL: Astronaut (Mims, Fla.).
COLLEGE: Florida.
TRANSACTIONS/CAREER NOTES: Selected by San Francisco 49ers in fifth round (161st pick overall) of 2003 NFL draft.

Year Team	G	RECEIVING			
		No.	Yds.	Avg.	TD
1998—Florida			Redshirted.		
1999—Florida	10	1	13	13.0	0
2000—Florida	12	11	130	11.8	3
2001—Florida	11	16	179	11.2	2
2002—Florida	13	27	376	13.9	4
College totals (4 years)	46	55	698	12.7	9

WALKER, FRANK — CB — GIANTS

PERSONAL: Born August 6, 1980, in Tuskegee, Ala. ... 5-11/202. ... Full name: Frank Bernard Walker Jr.
HIGH SCHOOL: Booker T. Washington (Tuskegee, Ala.).
COLLEGE: Tuskegee.
TRANSACTIONS/CAREER NOTES: Selected by New York Giants in sixth round (207th pick overall) of 2003 NFL draft.

Year Team	G	Sks.	INTERCEPTIONS				KICKOFF RETURNS				TOTALS	
			No.	Yds.	Avg.	TD	No.	Yds.	Avg.	TD	TD	Pts.
1999—Tuskegee	9	0.0	0	0	0.0	0	4	59	14.8	0	0	0
2000—Tuskegee	12	0.0	0	0	0.0	0	1	15	15.0	0	0	0
2001—Tuskegee	9	0.0	0	0	0.0	0	0	0	0.0	0	0	0
2002—Tuskegee	11	1.0	3	0	0.0	0	0	0	0.0	0	0	0
College totals (4 years)	41	1.0	3	0	0.0	0	5	74	14.8	0	0	0

WALL, J.T. — FB — STEELERS

PERSONAL: Born September 12, 1979, in Milledgeville, Ga.) ... 5-11/261. ... Full name: John Thomas Wall.
HIGH SCHOOL: John Milledge (Milledgeville, Ga.).
COLLEGE: Southwest Baptist, then Georgia.
TRANSACTIONS/CAREER NOTES: Selected by Pittsburgh Steelers in seventh round (242nd pick overall) of 2003 NFL draft.

Year Team	G	RUSHING				RECEIVING				KICKOFF RETURNS				TOTALS	
		Att.	Yds.	Avg.	TD	No.	Yds.	Avg.	TD	No.	Yds.	Avg.	TD	TD	Pts.
1998—Southwest Baptist University	11	129	465	3.6	3	8	75	9.4	0	0	0	0.0	0	0	0
1999—Southwest Baptist University	11	118	450	3.8	3	0	0	0.0	0	0	0	0.0	0	0	0
2000—Georgia				Did not play.											
2001—Georgia	11	15	58	3.9	0	2	21	10.5	0	2	9	4.5	0	0	0
2002—Georgia	14	30	149	5.0	3	9	84	9.3	2	0	0	0.0	0	5	30
College totals (4 years)	47	292	1122	3.8	9	19	180	9.5	2	2	9	4.5	0	5	30

WALLACE, SENECA   QB   SEAHAWKS

PERSONAL: Born August 6, 1980, in Sacramento. ... 5-11/196.
HIGH SCHOOL: Rancho Cordova (Sacramento).
JUNIOR COLLEGE: Sacramento City Junior College.
COLLEGE: Iowa State.
TRANSACTIONS/CAREER NOTES: Selected by Seattle Seahawks in fourth round (110th pick overall) of 2003 NFL draft.
COLLEGE NOTES: Caught one pass, returned one kickoff (2002).

Year Team	G	PASSING								RUSHING				TOTALS	
		Att.	Cmp.	Pct.	Yds.	TD	Int.	Avg.	Rat.	Att.	Yds.	Avg.	TD	TD	Pts.
2001—Iowa State	11	269	167	62.1	2044	11	9	7.60	132.7	114	475	4.2	7	7	42
2002—Iowa State	14	443	244	55.1	3245	15	18	7.33	119.7	123	437	3.6	8	8	50
College totals (2 years)	25	712	411	57.7	5289	26	27	7.43	124.6	237	912	3.8	15	15	92

WALLACE, TACO   WR   SEAHAWKS

PERSONAL: Born April 14, 1981, in Harbor City, Calif. ... 6-0/196.
HIGH SCHOOL: Taft (Woodlands Hills, Calif.).
JUNIOR COLLEGE: Mount San Antonio College (Calif.).
COLLEGE: Kansas State.
TRANSACTIONS/CAREER NOTES: Selected by Seattle Seahawks in seventh round (224th pick overall) of 2003 NFL draft.
COLLEGE NOTES: Rushed two times (2002).

Year Team	G	RECEIVING			
		No.	Yds.	Avg.	TD
2001—Kansas State	1	2	17	8.5	0
2002—Kansas State	12	39	704	18.1	5
College totals (2 years)	13	41	721	17.6	5

WALTER, KEVIN   WR   GIANTS

PERSONAL: Born August 4, 1981, in Libertyville, Ill. ... 6-3/221. ... Full name: Kevin Patrick Walter.
HIGH SCHOOL: Libertyville (Ill.).
COLLEGE: Eastern Michigan.
TRANSACTIONS/CAREER NOTES: Selected by New York Giants in seventh round (255th pick overall) of 2003 NFL draft.
COLLEGE NOTES: Attempted one pass (2001).

Year Team	G	RECEIVING			
		No.	Yds.	Avg.	TD
1999—Eastern Michigan	10	1	1	1.0	0
2000—Eastern Michigan	11	55	721	13.1	5
2001—Eastern Michigan	11	62	748	12.1	6
2002—Eastern Michigan	12	93	1368	14.7	9
College totals (4 years)	44	211	2838	13.5	20

WALTERS, MATT   DT   JETS

PERSONAL: Born August 22, 1979, in Melbourne, Fla. ... 6-4/272. ... Full name: Matthew Jeremy Walters.
HIGH SCHOOL: Eau Galle (Melbourne, Fla.).
COLLEGE: Miami (Fla.).
TRANSACTIONS/CAREER NOTES: Selected by New York Jets in fifth round (150th pick overall) of 2003 NFL draft.
COLLEGE NOTES: Intercepted one pass (2001).

Year Team	G	SACKS
1998—Miami (Fla.)	Redshirted.	
1999—Miami (Fla.)	12	2.0
2000—Miami (Fla.)	11	3.0
2001—Miami (Fla.)	11	4.0
2002—Miami (Fla.)	13	5.0
College totals (4 years)	47	14.0

WALTON, SHANE   CB   RAMS

PERSONAL: Born October 9, 1979, in San Diego. ... 5-11/184. ... Full name: Shane Scott Walton.
HIGH SCHOOL: The Bishop's School (San Diego).
COLLEGE: Notre Dame.
TRANSACTIONS/CAREER NOTES: Selected by St. Louis Rams in fifth round (170th pick overall) of 2003 NFL draft.

Year Team	G	Sks.	INTERCEPTIONS				KICKOFF RETURNS				TOTALS	
			No.	Yds.	Avg.	TD	No.	Yds.	Avg.	TD	TD	Pts.
1998—Notre Dame					Redshirted.							
1999—Notre Dame	9	0.0	0	0	0.0	0	0	0	0.0	0	0	0
2000—Notre Dame	10	0.0	2	60	30.0	1	0	0	0.0	0	1	6
2001—Notre Dame	11	1.0	2	37	18.5	0	1	10	10.0	0	0	0
2002—Notre Dame	13	0.0	7	84	12.0	2	9	85	9.4	0	2	12
College totals (4 years)	43	1.0	11	181	16.5	3	10	95	9.5	0	3	18

WAND, SETH OT TEXANS

PERSONAL: Born August 6, 1979, in Springfield, Mo. ... 6-7/321.
HIGH SCHOOL: Springfield Catholic (Springfield, Mo.).
COLLEGE: Northwest Missouri State.
TRANSACTIONS/CAREER NOTES: Selected by Houston Texans in third round (75th pick overall) of 2003 NFL draft.

WARREN, TY DT PATRIOTS

PERSONAL: Born February 6, 1981, in Bryan, Texas. ... 6-5/307. ... Full name: Ty'ron Markeith Warren. ... Nephew of Curtis Dickey, running back with Baltimore/Indianapolis Colts (1980-85) and Cleveland Browns (1985-86).
HIGH SCHOOL: Bryan (Texas).
COLLEGE: Texas A&M.
TRANSACTIONS/CAREER NOTES: Selected by New England Patriots in first round (13th pick overall) of 2003 NFL draft.

Year Team	G	SACKS
1999—Texas A&M	9	0.0
2000—Texas A&M	11	5.0
2001—Texas A&M	10	4.0
2002—Texas A&M	10	4.5
College totals (4 years)	40	13.5

WASHINGTON, KELLEY WR BENGALS

PERSONAL: Born August 21, 1979, in Stephens City, Va. ... 6-2/223. ... Full name: James Kelley Washington.
HIGH SCHOOL: Sherando (Stephens City, Va.).
COLLEGE: Tennessee.
TRANSACTIONS/CAREER NOTES: Selected after junior season by Cincinnati Bengals in third round (65th pick overall) of 2003 NFL draft.
COLLEGE NOTES: Rushed one time (2002).
MISCELLANEOUS: Selected by Florida Marlins organization in 10th round of free-agent draft (June 2, 1997).

Year Team	G	RECEIVING			
		No.	Yds.	Avg.	TD
2001—Tennessee	12	64	1010	15.8	5
2002—Tennessee	4	23	443	19.3	1
College totals (2 years)	16	87	1453	16.7	6

WEATHERSBY, DENNIS CB BENGALS

PERSONAL: Born June 16, 1980, in Glendora, Calif. ... 6-1/204.
HIGH SCHOOL: Duarte (Calif.).
COLLEGE: Oregon State.
TRANSACTIONS/CAREER NOTES: Selected by Cincinnati Bengals in fourth round (98th pick overall) of 2003 NFL draft.

Year Team	G	Sks.	INTERCEPTIONS			
			No.	Yds.	Avg.	TD
1998—Oregon State			Redshirted.			
1999—Oregon State	11	0.0	0	0	0.0	0
2000—Oregon State	11	0.0	2	0	0.0	0
2001—Oregon State	11	0.0	2	76	38.0	0
2002—Oregon State	13	1.0	1	0	0.0	0
College totals (4 years)	46	1.0	5	76	15.2	0

WELLS, REGGIE OT CARDINALS

PERSONAL: Born November 3, 1980, in Liberty, Pa. ... 6-3/300.
HIGH SCHOOL: South Park (Liberty, Pa.).
COLLEGE: Clarion.
TRANSACTIONS/CAREER NOTES: Selected by Arizona Cardinals in sixth round (177th pick overall) of 2003 NFL draft.

WHITE, DEWAYNE DE BUCCANEERS

PERSONAL: Born October 19, 1979, in Marbury, Ala. ... 6-2/273.
HIGH SCHOOL: Marbury (Ala.).
COLLEGE: Louisville.
TRANSACTIONS/CAREER NOTES: Selected after junior season by Tampa Bay Buccaneers in second round (64th pick overall) of 2003 NFL draft.

Year Team	G	Sks.	INTERCEPTIONS			
			No.	Yds.	Avg.	TD
1999—Louisville			Redshirted.			
2000—Louisville	11	12.0	1	35	35.0	1
2001—Louisville	12	15.0	0	0	0.0	0
2002—Louisville	13	10.5	1	55	55.0	1
College totals (3 years)	36	37.5	2	90	45.0	2

WHITESIDE, KEYON   LB   COLTS

PERSONAL: Born January 31, 1980, in Forest City, N.C. ... 6-0/229. ... Full name: Keyon Shontel Whiteside.
HIGH SCHOOL: Chase (Forest City, N.C.).
COLLEGE: Tennessee.
TRANSACTIONS/CAREER NOTES: Selected by Indianapolis Colts in fifth round (162nd pick overall) of 2003 NFL draft.

| | | | | INTERCEPTIONS | | |
Year Team	G	Sks.	No.	Yds.	Avg.	TD
1998—Tennessee			Redshirted.			
1999—Tennessee	10	0.0	0	0	0.0	0
2000—Tennessee	7	0.0	0	0	0.0	0
2001—Tennessee	11	2.0	0	0	0.0	0
2002—Tennessee	13	5.0	2	26	13.0	0
College totals (4 years)	41	7.0	2	26	13.0	0

WHITLEY, TAYLOR   G   DOLPHINS

PERSONAL: Born February 21, 1980, in Baytown, Texas. ... 6-4/321.
HIGH SCHOOL: Sudan (Texas).
COLLEGE: Texas A&M.
TRANSACTIONS/CAREER NOTES: Selected by Miami Dolphins in third round (87th pick overall) of 2003 NFL draft.
COLLEGE PLAYING EXPERIENCE: Texas A&M, 1998-2002. ... Games played: 1998 (redshirted), 1999 (11), 2000 (11), 2001 (11), 2002 (11). Total: 44.

WILHELM, MATT   LB   CHARGERS

PERSONAL: Born February 2, 1981, in Lorain, Ohio. ... 6-4/245.
HIGH SCHOOL: Elryia Catholic (Lorain, Ohio).
COLLEGE: Ohio State.
TRANSACTIONS/CAREER NOTES: Selected by San Diego Chargers in fourth round (112th pick overall) of 2003 NFL draft.

| | | | | INTERCEPTIONS | | |
Year Team	G	Sks.	No.	Yds.	Avg.	TD
1999—Ohio State	10	1.0	0	0	0.0	0
2000—Ohio State	11	3.0	1	25	25.0	1
2001—Ohio State	10	1.0	0	0	0.0	0
2002—Ohio State	14	3.0	2	0	0.0	0
College totals (4 years)	45	8.0	3	25	8.3	1

WILKERSON, JIMMY   DE   CHIEFS

PERSONAL: Born January 4, 1981, in Omaha, Texas. ... 6-3/271.
HIGH SCHOOL: Paul H. Pewitt (Omaha, Texas).
COLLEGE: Oklahoma.
TRANSACTIONS/CAREER NOTES: Selected after junior season by Kansas City Chiefs in sixth round (189th pick overall) of 2003 NFL draft.

Year Team	G	SACKS
2000—Oklahoma	11	1.0
2001—Oklahoma	12	5.0
2002—Oklahoma	14	0.0
College totals (3 years)	37	6.0

WILLIAMS, ANDREW   DE   49ERS

PERSONAL: Born April 18, 1979, in Tampa. ... 6-2/263. ... Full name: Andrew B. Williams.
HIGH SCHOOL: Hillsborough (Tampa, Fla.).
JUNIOR COLLEGE: Hinds Community College (Miss.).
COLLEGE: Miami (Fla.).
TRANSACTIONS/CAREER NOTES: Selected by San Francisco 49ers in third round (89th pick overall) of 2003 NFL draft.

Year Team	G	SACKS
2001—Miami (Fla.)	8	4.0
2002—Miami (Fla.)	13	4.0
College totals (2 years)	21	8.0

WILLIAMS, BRETT   OT   CHIEFS

PERSONAL: Born May 2, 1980, in Kissimmee, Fla. ... 6-5/321.
HIGH SCHOOL: Osceola (Kissimmee, Fla.).
COLLEGE: Florida State.
TRANSACTIONS/CAREER NOTES: Selected by Kansas City Chiefs in fourth round (113th pick overall) of 2003 NFL draft.
COLLEGE PLAYING EXPERIENCE: Florida State, 1999-2002. ... Games played: 1999 (11), 2000 (12), 2001 (10), 2002 (14). Total: 47.

WILLIAMS, DAVERN — DT — DOLPHINS

PERSONAL: Born February 13, 1980, in Brewton, Ala. ... 6-3/300. ... Nephew of Bob Meeks, offensive center with Denver Broncos (1993).
HIGH SCHOOL: Jefferson Davis (Montgomery, Ala.).
COLLEGE: Auburn, then Troy State.
TRANSACTIONS/CAREER NOTES: Selected by Miami Dolphins in seventh round (248th pick overall) of 2003 NFL draft.
COLLEGE NOTES: Intercepted one pass (2001).

Year Team	G	SACKS
1998—Auburn	2	0.0
1999—Troy State	Did not play.	
2000—Troy State	12	3.0
2001—Troy State	11	1.0
2002—Troy State	11	2.0
College totals (4 years)	36	6.0

WILLIAMS, KEVIN — DT — VIKINGS

PERSONAL: Born August 16, 1980, in Arkdelphia, Ark. ... 6-5/304.
HIGH SCHOOL: Fordyce (Ark.).
COLLEGE: Oklahoma State.
TRANSACTIONS/CAREER NOTES: Selected by Minnesota Vikings in first round (ninth pick overall) of 2003 NFL draft.

Year Team	G	SACKS
1998—Oklahoma State	Redshirted.	
1999—Oklahoma State	11	2.0
2000—Oklahoma State	11	4.0
2001—Oklahoma State	11	5.5
2002—Oklahoma State	13	7.0
College totals (4 years)	46	18.5

WILLIAMS, MELVIN — DE — SAINTS

PERSONAL: Born February 2, 1979, in St. Louis, Mo. ... 6-2/269.
HIGH SCHOOL: Mehlville (St. Louis, Mo.).
COLLEGE: Kansas State.
TRANSACTIONS/CAREER NOTES: Selected by New Orleans Saints in fifth round (155th pick overall) of 2003 NFL draft.

Year Team	G	SACKS
1998—Kansas State	Redshirted.	
1999—Kansas State	6	2.0
2000—Kansas State	12	4.5
2001—Kansas State	7	1.0
2002—Kansas State	13	5.0
College totals (4 years)	38	12.5

WILLIAMS, SAM — LB — RAIDERS

PERSONAL: Born July 28, 1980, in Clayton, Calif. ... 6-4/244.
HIGH SCHOOL: Clayton Valley (Clayton, Calif.).
COLLEGE: Fresno State.
TRANSACTIONS/CAREER NOTES: Selected by Oakland Raiders in third round (83rd pick overall) of 2003 NFL draft.

Year Team	G	Sks.	No.	Yds.	Avg.	TD
			INTERCEPTIONS			
1998—Michigan State	Redshirted.					
1999—Michigan State	12	5.0	0	0	0.0	0
2000—Michigan State	11	1.0	2	0	0.0	0
2001—Michigan State	11	1.0	2	13	6.5	0
2002—Michigan State	12	1.5	4	91	22.8	1
College totals (4 years)	46	8.5	8	104	13.0	1

WILLIAMS, TODD — G/OT — TITANS

PERSONAL: Born April 9, 1978, in Bradenton, Fla. ... 6-5/360.
HIGH SCHOOL: Southeast (Bradenton, Fla.).
COLLEGE: Florida State.
TRANSACTIONS/CAREER NOTES: Selected by Tennessee Titans in seventh round (225th pick overall) of 2003 NFL draft.
COLLEGE PLAYING EXPERIENCE: Florida State, 1998-2002. ... Games played: 1998 (redshirted), 1999 (6), 2000 (12), 2001 (11), 2002 (14). Total: 43.

WILSON, EUGENE — CB — PATRIOTS

PERSONAL: Born August 17, 1980, in Merrillville, Ind. ... 5-10/192. ... Full name: Eugene W. Wilson II.
HIGH SCHOOL: Merrillville (Ind.).
COLLEGE: Illinois.
TRANSACTIONS/CAREER NOTES: Selected by New England Patriots in second round (36th pick overall) of 2003 NFL draft.

Year	Team	G	Sks.	INTERCEPTIONS				PUNT RETURNS				KICKOFF RETURNS				TOTALS	
				No.	Yds.	Avg.	TD	No.	Yds.	Avg.	TD	No.	Yds.	Avg.	TD	TD	Pts.
1999—Illinois		10	0.0	0	0	0.0	0	29	297	10.2	1	0	0	0.0	0	1	6
2000—Illinois		10	0.0	4	22	5.5	0	14	72	5.1	0	2	30	15.0	0	0	0
2001—Illinois		11	1.0	6	29	4.8	0	24	241	10.0	0	9	177	19.7	0	0	0
2002—Illinois		12	1.0	1	0	0.0	0	23	270	11.7	1	4	73	18.3	0	1	6
College totals (4 years)		43	2.0	11	51	4.6	0	90	880	9.8	2	15	280	18.7	0	2	12

WITTEN, JASON — TE — COWBOYS

PERSONAL: Born May 6, 1982, in Elizabethon, Tenn. ... 6-6/264. ... Full name: Christopher Jason Witten.
HIGH SCHOOL: Elizabethon (Tenn.).
COLLEGE: Tennessee.
TRANSACTIONS/CAREER NOTES: Selected after junior season by Dallas Cowboys in third round (69th pick overall) of 2003 NFL draft.
COLLEGE NOTES: Returned one kickoff (2001).

Year	Team	G	RECEIVING			
			No.	Yds.	Avg.	TD
2000—Tennessee		11	1	11	11.0	0
2001—Tennessee		12	28	293	10.5	2
2002—Tennessee		13	39	493	12.6	5
College totals (3 years)		36	68	797	11.7	7

WOOLFOLK, ANDRE — CB — TITANS

PERSONAL: Born January 26, 1980, in Denver. ... 6-1/197. ... Cousin of Butch Woolfolk, running back with New York Giants (1982-84), Houston Oilers (1985-86) and Detroit Lions (1987-88).
HIGH SCHOOL: Thomas Jefferson (Denver).
COLLEGE: Oklahoma.
TRANSACTIONS/CAREER NOTES: Selected by Tennessee Titans in first round (28th pick overall) of 2003 NFL draft.
COLLEGE NOTES: Rushed one time (2000).

Year	Team	G	INTERCEPTIONS				RECEIVING				KICKOFF RETURNS				TOTALS	
			No.	Yds.	Avg.	TD	No.	Yds.	Avg.	TD	No.	Yds.	Avg.	TD	TD	Pts.
1998—Oklahoma									Redshirted.							
1999—Oklahoma		8	0	0	0.0	0	11	129	11.7	1	0	0	0.0	0	1	6
2000—Oklahoma		12	0	0	0.0	0	39	573	14.7	5	1	3	3.0	0	5	30
2001—Oklahoma		9	1	39	39.0	0	6	134	22.3	0	0	0	0.0	0	0	0
2002—Oklahoma		12	2	0	0.0	0	0	0	0.0	0	0	0	0.0	0	0	0
College totals (4 years)		41	3	39	13.0	0	56	836	14.9	6	1	3	3.0	0	6	36

WRIGHSTER, GEORGE — TE — JAGUARS

PERSONAL: Born April 1, 1981, in Memphis, Tenn. ... 6-2/249. ... Full name: George Fredrick Wrighster III.
HIGH SCHOOL: Sylmar (Calif.).
COLLEGE: Oregon.
TRANSACTIONS/CAREER NOTES: Selected after junior season by Jacksonville Jaguars in fourth round (104th pick overall) of 2003 NFL draft.
COLLEGE NOTES: Rushed one time, scored one touchdown (2002).

Year	Team	G	RECEIVING			
			No.	Yds.	Avg.	TD
1999—Oregon				Redshirted.		
2000—Oregon		11	0	0	0.0	0
2001—Oregon		11	11	123	11.2	1
2002—Oregon		13	41	568	13.9	6
College totals (3 years)		35	52	691	13.3	7

WRIGHT, KEITH — DT — TEXANS

PERSONAL: Born June 8, 1980, in Sacramento, Calif. ... 6-1/275.
HIGH SCHOOL: Arizona Boys Ranch.
JUNIOR COLLEGE: Sacramento City Junior College.
COLLEGE: Missouri.
TRANSACTIONS/CAREER NOTES: Selected by Houston Texans in sixth round (214th pick overall) of 2003 NFL draft.
COLLEGE NOTES: Intercepted one pass (2000).

Year	Team	G	SACKS
2000—Missouri			Redshirted.
2001—Missouri		11	2.0
2002—Missouri		12	6.0
College totals (2 years)		23	8.0

YOUNG, DAVID — S — JAGUARS

PERSONAL: Born May 17, 1979, in Columbia, S.C. ... 6-1/211. ... Full name: David F. Young.
HIGH SCHOOL: Keenan (Columbia, S.C.).
COLLEGE: Georgia Southern.
TRANSACTIONS/CAREER NOTES: Selected by Jacksonville Jaguars in sixth round (179th pick overall) of 2003 NFL draft.
COLLEGE NOTES: Returned one kickoff (2001).

Year Team	G	INTERCEPTIONS				PUNT RETURNS				TOTALS	
		No.	Yds.	Avg.	TD	No.	Yds.	Avg.	TD	TD	Pts.
1998—Georgia Southern						Redshirted.					
1999—Georgia Southern	15	3	91	30.3	1	1	32	32.0	0	2	12
2000—Georgia Southern	14	3	17	5.7	0	0	0	0.0	0	0	0
2001—Georgia Southern	11	2	32	16.0	0	1	7	7.0	0	0	0
2002—Georgia Southern	14	2	27	13.5	0	2	26	13.0	0	1	6
College totals (4 years)	54	10	167	16.7	1	4	65	16.3	0	3	18

YOUNG, WALTER — WR — PANTHERS

PERSONAL: Born December 7, 1979, in Chicago Heights, Ill. ... 6-5/214. ... Full name: Walter Young Jr.
HIGH SCHOOL: Rich East (Park Forest, Ill.).
COLLEGE: Illinois.
TRANSACTIONS/CAREER NOTES: Selected by Carolina Panthers in seventh round (226th pick overall) of 2003 NFL draft.
COLLEGE NOTES: Attempted one pass and rushed twice (1999), returned one kickoff (2002).

Year Team	G	RECEIVING			
		No.	Yds.	Avg.	TD
1998—Illinois			Redshirted.		
1999—Illinois	9	13	236	18.2	1
2000—Illinois	11	27	403	14.9	0
2001—Illinois	11	44	712	16.2	6
2002—Illinois	12	56	822	14.7	6
College totals (4 years)	43	140	2173	15.5	13

YOVANOVITS, DAVE — OT — JETS

PERSONAL: Born March 6, 1981, in Hopatcong, N.J. ... 6-3/294.
HIGH SCHOOL: Hopatcong (N.J.).
COLLEGE: Temple.
TRANSACTIONS/CAREER NOTES: Selected by New York Jets in seventh round (237th pick overall) of 2003 NFL draft.
COLLEGE PLAYING EXPERIENCE: Temple, 1999-2002. ... Games played: 1999 (11), 2000 (11), 2001 (11), 2002 (12). Total: 45.

HEAD COACHES

BELICHICK, BILL — PATRIOTS

PERSONAL: Born April 16, 1952, in Nashville. ... Full name: William Stephen Belichick. ... Son of Steve Belichick, fullback with Detroit Lions (1941); head coach at Hiram (Ohio) College (1946-49); assistant coach, Vanderbilt (1949-53); assistant coach, North Carolina (1953-56); assistant coach, Navy (1956-83); and administrative assistant, Navy (1983-89).
HIGH SCHOOL: Annapolis (Md.) and Phillips Academy (Andover, Mass.).
COLLEGE: Wesleyan University (degree in economics, 1975).

HEAD COACHING RECORD

BACKGROUND: Assistant special teams coach, Baltimore Colts NFL (1975). ... Assistant special teams coach, Detroit Lions NFL (1976 and 1977). ... Assistant special teams coach/assistant to defensive coordinator, Denver Broncos NFL (1978). ... Special teams coach, New York Giants NFL (1979 and 1980). ... Special teams/linebackers coach, Giants (1981 and 1982). ... Linebackers coach, Giants (1983 and 1984). ... Defensive coordinator/linebackers coach, Giants (1985-1988). ... Defensive coordinator/secondary coach, Giants (1989 and 1990). ... Assistant head coach/secondary coach, New England Patriots NFL (1996). ... Assistant head coach/secondary coach, New York Jets NFL (1997-1999).

	W	L	T	Pct.	Finish	W	L
					REGULAR SEASON	**POST-SEASON**	
1991—Cleveland NFL	6	10	0	.375	3rd/AFC Central Division	0	0
1992—Cleveland NFL	7	9	0	.438	3rd/AFC Central Division	0	0
1993—Cleveland NFL	7	9	0	.438	3rd/AFC Central Division	0	0
1994—Cleveland NFL	11	5	0	.688	2nd/AFC Central Division	1	1
1995—Cleveland NFL	5	11	0	.313	4th/AFC Central Division	0	0
2000—New England NFL	5	11	0	.313	5th/AFC Eastern Division	0	0
2001—New England NFL	11	5	0	.688	1st/AFC Eastern Division	3	0
2002—New England NFL	9	7	0	.563	2nd/AFC East Division	0	0
Pro totals (8 years)	61	67	0	.477	**Pro totals (2 years)**	4	1

NOTES:
1994—Defeated New England, 20-13, in first-round playoff game; lost to Pittsburgh, 29-9, in conference playoff game.
2001—Defeated Oakland, 16-13 (OT), in conference playoff game; defeated Pittsburgh, 24-17, in AFC championship game; defeated St. Louis, 20-17, in Super Bowl XXXVI.

BILLICK, BRIAN — RAVENS

PERSONAL: Born February 28, 1954, in Fairborn, Ohio. ... Full name: Brian Harold Billick. ... Played tight end.
HIGH SCHOOL: Redlands (Calif.).
COLLEGE: Air Force, then Brigham Young.
TRANSACTIONS/CAREER NOTES: Selected by San Francisco 49ers in 11th round of 1977 NFL draft. ... Signed by 49ers for 1977 season. ... Released by 49ers (August 30, 1977). ... Signed by Dallas Cowboys (May 1978). ... Released by Cowboys before 1978 season.

HEAD COACHING RECORD

BACKGROUND: Assistant coach, University of Redlands (1977). ... Graduate assistant, Brigham Young (1978). ... Assistant public relations director, San Francisco 49ers NFL (1979 and 1980). ... Assistant coach and recruiting coordinator, San Diego State (1981-1985). ... Offensive coordinator, Utah State (1986-1988). ... Assistant coach, Stanford (1989-1991). ... Tight ends coach, Minnesota Vikings (1992). ... Offensive coordinator, Minnesota Vikings (1993-1998).

	W	L	T	Pct.	Finish	W	L
					REGULAR SEASON	**POST-SEASON**	
1999—Baltimore NFL	8	8	0	.500	3rd/AFC Central Division	0	0
2000—Baltimore NFL	12	4	0	.750	2nd/AFC Central Division	4	0
2001—Baltimore NFL	10	6	0	.625	2nd/AFC Central Division	1	1
2002—Baltimore NFL	7	9	0	.438	3rd/AFC North Division	0	0
Pro totals (4 years)	37	27	0	.578	**Pro totals (2 years)**	5	1

NOTES:
2000—Defeated Denver, 21-3, in first-round playoff game; defeated Tennessee, 24-10, in conference playoff game; defeated Oakland, 16-3, in AFC championship game; defeated New York Giants, 34-7, in Super Bowl XXXV.
2001—Defeated Miami, 20-3, in first-round playoff game; lost to Pittsburgh, 27-10, in conference playoff game.

CALLAHAN, BILL — RAIDERS

PERSONAL: Born July 31, 1956, in Chicago.
HIGH SCHOOL: Mendel (Chicago).
COLLEGE: Illinois Benedictine.

HEAD COACHING RECORD

BACKGROUND: Head coach, Oak Lawn (Ill.) High School (1978). ... Head coach, De La Salle Institute, Chicago (1979). ... Graduate assistant, University of Illinois (1980). ... Tight ends coach/offensive line coach/quarterbacks coach/special teams coach, University of Illinois (1981-1986). ... Offensive line coach, Northern Arizona (1987 and 1988). ... Offensive coordinator, Southern Illinois University (1989). ... Offensive line coach, University of Wisconsin (1990-1994). ... Offensive line coach, Philadelphia Eagles NFL (1995-1997). ... Offensive coordinator/tight ends coach, Oakland Raiders NFL (1998). ... Offensive coordinator/offensive line coach, Raiders (1999-2001).

	W	L	T	Pct.	Finish	W	L
					REGULAR SEASON	**POST-SEASON**	
2002—Oakland NFL	11	5	0	.688	1st/AFC West Division	2	1

NOTES:
2002—Defeated New York Jets, 30-10, in conference playoff game; defeated Tennessee, 41-24, in AFC championship game; lost to Tampa Bay, 48-21, in Super Bowl XXXVII.

CAPERS, DOM — TEXANS

PERSONAL: Born August 7, 1950, in Cambridge, Ohio. ... Full name: Dominic Capers.
HIGH SCHOOL: Meadowbrook (Byesville, Ohio).
COLLEGE: Mount Union, Ohio (bachelor's degree in psychology and physical education), then Kent (master's degree in administration).

HEAD COACHING RECORD

BACKGROUND: Graduate assistant, Kent State (1972-1974). ... Graduate assistant, Washington (1975). ... Defensive backs coach, Hawaii (1976). ... Defensive backs coach, San Jose State (1977). ... Defensive backs coach, California (1978 and 1979). ... Defensive backs coach, Tennessee (1980 and 1981). ... Defensive backs coach, Ohio State (1982 and 1983). ... Defensive backs coach, Philadelphia Stars USFL (1984). ... Defensive backs coach, Baltimore Stars USFL (1985). ... Defensive backs coach, New Orleans Saints NFL (1986-1991). ... Defensive coordinator, Pittsburgh Steelers NFL (1992-1994). ... Defensive coordinator, Jacksonville Jaguars NFL (1999 and 2000).
HONORS: Named NFL Coach of the Year by THE SPORTING NEWS (1996).

	REGULAR SEASON					POST-SEASON	
	W	L	T	Pct.	Finish	W	L
1995—Carolina NFL	7	9	0	.438	4th/NFC Western Division	0	0
1996—Carolina NFL	12	4	0	.750	1st/NFC Western Division	1	1
1997—Carolina NFL	7	9	0	.438	2nd/NFC Western Division	0	0
1998—Carolina NFL	4	12	0	.250	4th/NFC Western Division	0	0
2002—Houston NFL	4	12	0	.250	4th/AFC South Division	0	0
Pro totals (5 years)	34	46	0	.425	**Pro totals (1 year)**	1	1

NOTES:
1996—Defeated Dallas, 26-17, in conference playoff game; lost to Green Bay, 30-13, in NFC championship game.

COWHER, BILL — STEELERS

PERSONAL: Born May 8, 1957, in Pittsburgh. ... Full name: William Laird Cowher. ... Played linebacker.
HIGH SCHOOL: Carlynton (Carnegie, Pa.).
COLLEGE: North Carolina State (bachelor of science degree in education, 1979).
TRANSACTIONS/CAREER NOTES: Signed as non-drafted free agent by Philadelphia Eagles (May 8, 1979). ... Released by Eagles (August 14, 1979). ... Signed by Cleveland Browns (February 27, 1980). ... On injured reserve with knee injury (August 20, 1981-entire season). ... Traded by Browns to Eagles for ninth-round pick (WR Don Jones) in 1984 draft (August 21, 1983). ... On injured reserve with knee injury (September 25, 1984-remainder of season).
PLAYING EXPERIENCE: Cleveland NFL, 1980 and 1982; Philadelphia NFL, 1983 and 1984. ... Games: 1980 (16), 1982 (9), 1983 (16), 1984 (4). Total: 45.
PRO STATISTICS: 1983—Recovered one fumble.

HEAD COACHING RECORD

BACKGROUND: Special teams coach, Cleveland Browns NFL (1985 and 1986). ... Defensive backs coach, Browns (1987 and 1988). ... Defensive coordinator, Kansas City Chiefs NFL (1989-1991).
HONORS: Named NFL Coach of the Year by THE SPORTING NEWS (1992).

	REGULAR SEASON					POST-SEASON	
	W	L	T	Pct.	Finish	W	L
1992—Pittsburgh NFL	11	5	0	.688	1st/AFC Central Division	0	1
1993—Pittsburgh NFL	9	7	0	.563	2nd/AFC Central Division	0	1
1994—Pittsburgh NFL	12	4	0	.750	1st/AFC Central Division	1	1
1995—Pittsburgh NFL	11	5	0	.688	1st/AFC Central Division	2	1
1996—Pittsburgh NFL	10	6	0	.625	1st/AFC Central Division	1	1
1997—Pittsburgh NFL	11	5	0	.688	1st/AFC Central Division	1	1
1998—Pittsburgh NFL	7	9	0	.438	3rd/AFC Central Division	0	0
1999—Pittsburgh NFL	6	10	0	.375	4th/AFC Central Division	0	0
2000—Pittsburgh NFL	9	7	0	.563	3rd/AFC Central Division	0	0
2001—Pittsburgh NFL	13	3	0	.813	1st/AFC Central Division	1	1
2002—Pittsburgh NFL	10	5	1	.656	1st/AFC North Division	1	1
Pro totals (11 years)	109	66	1	.622	**Pro totals (8 years)**	7	8

NOTES:
1992—Lost to Buffalo, 24-3, in conference playoff game.
1993—Lost to Kansas City, 27-24 (OT), in first-round playoff game.
1994—Defeated Cleveland, 29-9, in conference playoff game; lost to San Diego, 17-13, in AFC championship game.
1995—Defeated Buffalo, 40-21, in conference playoff game; defeated Indianapolis, 20-16, in AFC championship game; lost to Dallas, 27-17, in Super Bowl XXX.
1996—Defeated Indianapolis, 42-14, in first-round playoff game; lost to New England, 28-3, in conference playoff game.
1997—Defeated New England, 7-6, in conference playoff game; lost to Denver, 24-21, in AFC championship game.
2001—Defeated Baltimore, 27-10, in conference playoff game; lost to New England, 24-17, in AFC championship game.
2002—Defeated Cleveland, 36-33, in first-round playoff game; lost to Tennessee, 34-31 (OT), in conference playoff game.

DAVIS, BUTCH — BROWNS

PERSONAL: Born November 17, 1951, in Tahlequah, Okla. ... Full name: Paul Hilton Davis.
HIGH SCHOOL: Bixby (Okla.).
COLLEGE: Arkansas (degree in biology and life science).

BACKGROUND: Assistant coach, Fayetteville (Ark.) High School (1973). ... Assistant coach, Pawhuska (Okla.) High School (1974 and 1975). ... Assistant coach, Sand Springs (Okla.) High School (1976 and 1977). ... Head coach, Rogers High School, Tulsa, Okla. (1978). ... Assistant coach, Oklahoma State (1979-1983). ... Assistant coach, University of Miami (1984-1988). ... Assistant coach, Dallas Cowboys NFL (1989-1992). ... Defensive coordinator, Cowboys (1993 and 1994).

	W	L	T	Pct.	Finish	W	L
					REGULAR SEASON	**POST-SEASON**	
1995—Miami (Fla.)	8	3	0	.727	T1st/Big East Conference	0	0
1996—Miami (Fla.)	9	3	0	.750	T1st/Big East Conference	1	0
1997—Miami (Fla.)	5	6	0	.455	T5th/Big East Conference	0	0
1998—Miami (Fla.)	9	3	0	.750	T2nd/Big East Conference	1	0
1999—Miami (Fla.)	9	4	0	.692	2nd/Big East Conference	1	0
2000—Miami (Fla.)	11	1	0	.917	1st/Big East Conference	1	0
2001—Cleveland NFL	7	9	0	.438	3rd/AFC Central Division	0	0
2002—Cleveland NFL	9	7	0	.563	2nd/AFC North Division	0	1
College totals (6 years)	**51**	**20**	**0**	**.718**	**College totals (4 years)**	**4**	**0**
Pro totals (2 years)	**16**	**16**	**0**	**.500**	**Pro totals (1 year)**	**0**	**1**

NOTES:
1996—Defeated Virginia, 31-21, in CarQuest Bowl.
1998—Defeated North Carolina State, 46-23, in Micron PC Bowl.
1999—Defeated Georgia Tech, 28-13, in Gator Bowl.
2000—Defeated Florida, 37-20, in Sugar Bowl.
2002—Lost to Pittsburgh, 36-33, in first-round playoff game.

DEL RIO, JACK   JAGUARS

PERSONAL: Born April 4, 1963, in Castro Valley, Calif. ... Full name: Jack Del Rio Jr.
HIGH SCHOOL: Hayward (Calif.).
COLLEGE: Southern California.
TRANSACTIONS/CAREER NOTES: Selected by Los Angeles Express in 1985 USFL territorial draft. ... Selected by New Orleans Saints in third round (68th pick overall) of 1985 NFL draft. ... Signed by Saints (July 31, 1985). ... Traded by Saints to Kansas City Chiefs for fifth-round pick (TE Greg Scales) in 1988 draft (August 17, 1987). ... On injured reserve with knee injury (December 13, 1988-remainder of season). ... Claimed on waivers by Dallas Cowboys (August 31, 1989). ... Granted free agency (February 1, 1991). ... Re-signed by Cowboys (July 25, 1991). ... Granted unconditional free agency (February 1, 1992). ... Signed by Minnesota Vikings (March 3, 1992). ... Released by Vikings (February 13, 1996). ... Signed by Miami Dolphins (June 2, 1996). ... Released by Dolphins (August 5, 1996).
HONORS: Played in Pro Bowl (1994 season).
PRO STATISTICS: 1985—Recovered five fumbles for 22 yards and one touchdown. 1986—Rushed once for 16 yards. 1988—Recovered one fumble. 1989—Returned two fumbles for 57 yards and one touchdown. 1991—Recovered one fumble. 1992—Recovered two fumbles. 1993—Returned one kickoff for four yards. 1994—Recovered two fumbles. 1995—Recovered one fumble.
MISCELLANEOUS: Selected by Toronto Blue Jays organization in 22nd round of free-agent baseball draft (June 8, 1981); did not sign.

			INTERCEPTIONS				SACKS
Year Team	G	GS	No.	Yds.	Avg.	TD	No.
1985—New Orleans NFL	16	9	2	13	6.5	0	0.0
1986—New Orleans NFL	16	1	0	0	0.0	0	0.0
1987—Kansas City NFL	10	7	0	0	0.0	0	3.0
1988—Kansas City NFL	15	10	1	0	0.0	0	1.0
1989—Dallas NFL	14	12	0	0	0.0	0	0.0
1990—Dallas NFL	16	16	0	0	0.0	0	1.5
1991—Dallas NFL	16	16	0	0	0.0	0	0.0
1992—Minnesota NFL	16	16	2	92	46.0	1	2.0
1993—Minnesota NFL	16	16	4	3	0.8	0	0.5
1994—Minnesota NFL	16	16	3	5	1.7	0	2.0
1995—Minnesota NFL	9	9	1	15	15.0	0	3.0
Pro totals (11 years)	**160**	**128**	**13**	**128**	**9.8**	**1**	**13.0**

HEAD COACHING RECORD
BACKGROUND: Linebackers coach/assistant strength coach, New Orleans Saints NFL (1997 and 1998). ... Linebackers coach, Baltimore Ravens NFL (1999-2001). ... Defensive coordinator, Carolina Panthers NFL (2002).

DUNGY, TONY   COLTS

PERSONAL: Born October 6, 1955, in Jackson, Mich. ... Full name: Anthony Kevin Dungy. ... Played defensive back and quarterback. ... Name pronounced DUN-gee.
HIGH SCHOOL: Parkside (Jackson, Mich.).
COLLEGE: Minnesota (degree in business administration, 1978).
TRANSACTIONS/CAREER NOTES: Signed as non-drafted free agent by Pittsburgh Steelers (May 1977). ... Traded by Steelers to San Francisco 49ers for 10th-round pick in 1980 draft (August 21, 1979). ... Traded by 49ers with RB Mike Hogan to New York Giants for WR Jimmy Robinson and CB Ray Rhodes (March 27, 1980).
CHAMPIONSHIP GAME EXPERIENCE: Played in AFC championship game (1978 season). ... Played in Super Bowl XIII (1978 season).
PRO STATISTICS: 1977—Attempted eight passes with three completions for 43 yards and two interceptions, rushed three times for eight yards and fumbled once. 1978—Recovered two fumbles for eight yards. 1979—Returned eight punts for 52 yards and recovered two fumbles.

Year Team				INTERCEPTIONS		
	G	No.	Yds.	Avg.	TD
1977—Pittsburgh NFL	14	3	37	12.3	0
1978—Pittsburgh NFL	16	6	95	15.8	0
1979—San Francisco NFL	15	0	0	0.0	0
Pro totals (3 years)	45	9	132	14.7	0

HEAD COACHING RECORD

BACKGROUND: Defensive backs coach, University of Minnesota (1980). ... Defensive assistant, Pittsburgh Steelers NFL (1981). ... Defensive backs coach, Steelers (1982 and 1983). ... Defensive coordinator, Steelers (1984-1988). ... Defensive backs coach, Kansas City Chiefs NFL (1989-1991). ... Defensive coordinator, Minnesota Vikings NFL (1992-1995).

	REGULAR SEASON					POST-SEASON	
	W	L	T	Pct.	Finish	W	L
1996—Tampa Bay NFL	6	10	0	.375	4th/NFC Central Division	0	0
1997—Tampa Bay NFL	10	6	0	.625	2nd/NFC Central Division	1	1
1998—Tampa Bay NFL	8	8	0	.500	3rd/NFC Central Division	0	0
1999—Tampa Bay NFL	11	5	0	.688	1st/NFC Central Division	1	1
2000—Tampa Bay NFL	10	6	0	.625	2nd/NFC Central Division	0	1
2001—Tampa Bay NFL	9	7	0	.563	3rd/NFC Central Division	0	1
2002—Indianapolis NFL	10	6	0	.625	2nd/AFC South Division	0	1
Pro totals (7 years)	64	48	0	.571	Pro totals (5 years)	2	5

NOTES:
1997—Defeated Detroit, 20-10, in first-round playoff game; lost to Green Bay, 21-7, in conference playoff game.
1999—Defeated Washington, 14-13, in conference playoff game; lost to St. Louis, 11-6, in NFC championship game.
2000—Lost to Philadelphia, 21-3, in first-round playoff game.
2001—Lost to Philadelphia, 31-9, in first-round playoff game.
2002—Lost to New York Jets, 41-0, in first-round playoff game.

EDWARDS, HERMAN — JETS

PERSONAL: Born April 27, 1954, in Fort Monmouth, N.J. ... Full name: Herman Lee Edwards. ... Played cornerback.
HIGH SCHOOL: Monterey (Calif.).
JUNIOR COLLEGE: Monterey (Calif.) Peninsula College.
COLLEGE: California, then San Diego State (degree in criminal justice).
TRANSACTIONS/CAREER NOTES: Signed as non-drafted free agent by Philadelphia Eagles (May 1977). ... Released by Eagles (September 8, 1986). ... Signed by Los Angeles Rams (September 15, 1986). ... Released by Rams (October 20, 1986). ... Signed by Atlanta Falcons (November 3, 1986). ... Announced retirement (November 11, 1986).
CHAMPIONSHIP GAME EXPERIENCE: Played in NFC championship game (1980 season). ... Played in Super Bowl XV (1980 season).
PRO STATISTICS: 1977—Recovered two fumbles and fumbled once. 1978—Recovered one fumble for 26 yards and a touchdown and fumbled once. 1979—Recovered one fumble. 1981—Recovered one fumble for four yards. 1985—Recovered one fumble for four yards.

Year Team				INTERCEPTIONS		
	G	No.	Yds.	Avg.	TD
1977—Philadelphia NFL	14	6	9	1.5	0
1978—Philadelphia NFL	16	7	59	8.4	0
1979—Philadelphia NFL	16	3	6	2.0	0
1980—Philadelphia NFL	16	3	12	4.0	0
1981—Philadelphia NFL	16	3	1	0.3	0
1982—Philadelphia NFL	9	5	3	0.6	0
1983—Philadelphia NFL	16	1	0	0.0	0
1984—Philadelphia NFL	16	2	0	0.0	0
1985—Philadelphia NFL	16	3	8	2.7	1
1986—Los Angeles Rams NFL	4	0	0	0.0	0
—Atlanta NFL	3	0	0	0.0	0
Pro totals (10 years)	142	33	98	3.0	1

HEAD COACHING RECORD

BACKGROUND: Defensive backs coach, San Jose State (1987-1989). ... Scout, Kansas City Chiefs NFL (1990, 1991 and 1995). ... Defensive backs coach, Chiefs (1992-1994). ... Assistant head coach/defensive backs coach, Tampa Bay Buccaneers NFL (1996-2000).

	REGULAR SEASON					POST-SEASON	
	W	L	T	Pct.	Finish	W	L
2001—New York Jets NFL	10	6	0	.625	3rd/AFC Eastern Division	0	1
2002—New York Jets NFL	9	7	0	.563	1st/AFC East Division	1	1
Pro totals (2 years)	19	13	0	.594	Pro totals (2 years)	1	2

NOTES:
2001—Lost to Oakland, 38-24, in first-round playoff game.
2002—Defeated Indianapolis, 41-0, in first-round playoff game; lost to Oakland, 30-10, in conference playoff game.

ERICKSON, DENNIS — 49ERS

PERSONAL: Born March 24, 1947, in Everett, Wash.
HIGH SCHOOL: Everett (Wash.).
COLLEGE: Montana State (degree in physical education, 1969).

HEAD COACHING RECORD

BACKGROUND: Graduate assistant, Montana State (1969). ... Graduate assistant, Washington State (spring 1970). ... Head coach, Billings (Mont.) Central High (1970; record: 7-2). ... Offensive backs coach, Montana State (1971-73). ... Offensive coordinator, Idaho (1974 and 1975). ... Offensive coordinator, Fresno State (1976-78). ... Offensive coordinator, San Jose State (1979-81)
HONORS: Named College Football Coach of the Year by THE SPORTING NEWS (1992 and 2000).

	W	L	T	Pct.	Finish	W	L
1982—Idaho	8	3	0	.727	T2nd/Big Sky Conference	1	1
1983—Idaho	8	3	0	.727	T3rd/Big Sky Conference	0	0
1984—Idaho	6	5	0	.545	T3rd/Big Sky Conference	0	0
1985—Idaho	9	2	0	.818	1st/Big Sky Conference	0	1
1986—Wyoming	6	6	0	.500	T4th/Western Athletic Conference	0	0
1987—Washington State	3	7	1	.318	9th/Pacific-10 Conference	0	0
1988—Washington State	8	3	0	.727	T3rd/Pacific-10 Conference	1	0
1989—Miami (Fla.)	10	1	0	.909	Independent	1	0
1990—Miami (Fla.)	9	2	0	.818	Independent	1	0
1991—Miami (Fla.)	11	0	0	1.000	Independent	1	0
1992—Miami (Fla.)	11	0	0	1.000	1st/Big East Conference	0	1
1993—Miami (Fla.)	9	2	0	.818	2nd/Big East Conference	0	1
1994—Miami (Fla.)	10	1	0	.909	1st/Big East Conference	0	1
1995—Seattle NFL	8	8	0	.500	3rd/AFC Western Division	0	0
1996—Seattle NFL	7	9	0	.438	5th/AFC Western Division	0	0
1997—Seattle NFL	8	8	0	.500	3rd/AFC Western Division	0	0
1998—Seattle NFL	8	8	0	.500	3rd/AFC Western Division	0	0
1999—Oregon State	7	5	0	.583	5th/Pacific 10 Conference	0	1
2000—Oregon State	11	1	0	.917	1st/Pacific 10 Conference	1	0
2001—Oregon State	5	6	0	.455	7th/Pacific 10 Conference	0	0
2002—Oregon State	8	4	0	.615	4th/Pacific 10 Conference	0	1
College totals (17 years)	139	51	1	.730	**College totals (12 years)**	6	7
Pro totals (4 years)	31	33	0	.484			

NOTES:
1982—Defeated Montana, 21-7, in first round of NCAA Division I-AA playoffs; lost to Eastern Kentucky, 38-30, in second round of NCAA Division I-AA play-offs.
1985—Lost to Eastern Washington, 42-38, in first round of NCAA Division I-AA playoffs.
1988—Defeated Houston, 24-22, in Aloha Bowl.
1989—Defeated Alabama, 33-25, in Sugar Bowl.
1990—Defeated Texas, 46-3, in Cotton Bowl.
1991—Defeated Nebraska, 22-0, in Orange Bowl.
1992—Lost to Alabama, 34-13, in Sugar Bowl.
1993—Lost to Arizona, 29-0, in Fiesta Bowl.
1994—Lost to Nebraska, 24-17, in Orange Bowl.
1999—Lost to Hawaii, 23-17, in O'ahu Bowl.
2000—Defeated Notre Dame, 41-9, in Fiesta Bowl.
2002—Lost to Pittsburgh, 38-13, in Insight.com Bowl.

FASSEL, JIM   GIANTS

PERSONAL: Born August 31, 1949, in Anaheim. ... Full name: James Fassel. ... Played quarterback.
HIGH SCHOOL: Anaheim (Calif.) High.
JUNIOR COLLEGE: Fullerton (Calif.) College.
COLLEGE: Southern California, then Long Beach State (degree in physical education, 1972).
TRANSACTIONS/CAREER NOTES: Selected by Chicago Bears in seventh round of 1972 NFL draft.

HEAD COACHING RECORD
BACKGROUND: Quarterbacks coach, Fullerton College (1973). ... Player/coach, Hawaii Hawaiians WFL (1974). ... Quarterbacks/receivers coach, Utah (1976). ... Offensive coordinator, Weber State (1977 and 1978). ... Offensive coordinator, Stanford (1979-1983). ... Offensive coordinator, New Orleans Breakers USFL (1984). ... Quarterbacks coach, New York Giants NFL (1991). ... Offensive coordinator, Giants (1992). ... Assistant head coach/offensive coordinator, Denver Broncos NFL (1993 and 1994). ... Quarterbacks coach, Oakland Raiders NFL (1995). ... Offensive coordinator/quarterbacks coach, Arizona Cardinals NFL (1996).
HONORS: Named NFL Coach of the Year by THE SPORTING NEWS (1997).

	W	L	T	Pct.	Finish	W	L
1985—Utah	8	4	0	.667	3rd/Western Athletic Conference	0	0
1986—Utah	2	9	0	.182	9th/Western Athletic Conference	0	0
1987—Utah	5	7	0	.417	7th/Western Athletic Conference	0	0
1988—Utah	6	5	0	.545	5th/Western Athletic Conference	0	0
1989—Utah	4	8	0	.333	7th/Western Athletic Conference	0	0
1997—New York Giants NFL	10	5	1	.656	1st/NFC Eastern Division	0	1
1998—New York Giants NFL	8	8	0	.500	3rd/NFC Eastern Division	0	0
1999—New York Giants NFL	7	9	0	.438	3rd/NFC Eastern Division	0	0
2000—New York Giants NFL	12	4	0	.750	1st/NFC Eastern Division	2	1
2001—New York Giants NFL	7	9	0	.438	3rd/NFC Eastern Division	0	0
2002—New York Giants NFL	10	6	0	.625	2nd/NFC East Division	0	1
College totals (5 years)	25	33	0	.431			
Pro totals (6 years)	54	41	1	.568	**Pro totals (3 years)**	2	3

NOTES:
1997—Lost to Minnesota, 23-22, in first-round playoff game.
2000—Defeated Philadelphia, 20-10, in conference playoff game; defeated Minnesota, 41-0, in NFC championship game; lost to Balitmore, 34-7, in Super Bowl XXXV.
2002—Lost to San Francisco, 39-38, in first-round playoff game.

FISHER, JEFF   TITANS

PERSONAL: Born February 25, 1958, in Culver City, Calif. ... Full name: Jeffrey Michael Fisher. ... Played safety.
HIGH SCHOOL: Taft (Woodland Hills, Calif.).
COLLEGE: Southern California (degree in public administration, 1981).
TRANSACTIONS/CAREER NOTES: Selected by Chicago Bears in seventh round (177th pick overall) of 1981 NFL draft. ... On injured reserve with broken leg (October 24, 1983-remainder of season). ... On injured reserve with ankle injury entire 1985 season.
CHAMPIONSHIP GAME EXPERIENCE: Played in NFC championship game (1984 season).
PRO STATISTICS: 1981—Recovered one fumble. 1984—Recovered one fumble.

		INTERCEPTIONS			PUNT RETURNS				KICKOFF RETURNS				TOTALS			
Year Team	G	No.	Yds.	Avg.	TD	No.	Yds.	Avg.	TD	No.	Yds.	Avg.	TD	TD	2pt.	Pts. Fum.
1981—Chicago NFL	16	2	3	1.5	0	43	509	11.8	1	7	102	14.6	0	1	0	6	3
1982—Chicago NFL	9	3	19	6.3	0	7	53	7.6	0	7	102	14.6	0	0	0	0	2
1983—Chicago NFL	8	0	0	0.0	0	13	71	5.5	0	0	0	0.0	0	0	0	0	0
1984—Chicago NFL	16	0	0	0.0	0	57	492	8.6	0	0	0	0.0	0	0	0	0	4
1985—Chicago NFL								Did not play.									
Pro totals (4 years)	49	5	22	4.4	0	120	1125	9.4	1	14	204	14.6	0	1	0	6	9

HEAD COACHING RECORD

BACKGROUND: Defensive backs coach, Philadelphia Eagles NFL (1986-1988). ... Defensive coordinator, Eagles (1989 and 1990). ... Defensive coordinator, Los Angeles Rams NFL (1991). ... Defensive backs coach, San Francisco 49ers NFL (1992 and 1993). ... Defensive coordinator, Houston Oilers NFL (February 9-November 14, 1994). ... Oilers franchise moved to Tennessee for 1997 season.

		REGULAR SEASON					POST-SEASON	
	W	L	T	Pct.	Finish		W	L
1994—Houston NFL	1	5	0	.167	4th/AFC Central Division		0	0
1995—Houston NFL	7	9	0	.438	3rd/AFC Central Division		0	0
1996—Houston NFL	8	8	0	.500	4th/AFC Central Division		0	0
1997—Tennessee NFL	8	8	0	.500	3rd/AFC Central Division		0	0
1998—Tennessee NFL	8	8	0	.500	2nd/AFC Central Division		0	0
1999—Tennessee NFL	13	3	0	.813	2nd/AFC Central Division		3	1
2000—Tennessee NFL	13	3	0	.813	1st/AFC Central Division		0	1
2001—Tennessee NFL	7	9	0	.438	4th/AFC Central Division		0	0
2002—Tennessee NFL	11	5	0	.688	1st/AFC South Division		1	1
Pro totals (9 years)	76	58	0	.567	Pro totals (3 years)		4	3

NOTES:
1994—Replaced Jack Pardee as head coach (November 14) with 1-9 record and club in fourth place.
1999—Defeated Buffalo, 22-16, in first-round playoff game; defeated Indianapolis, 19-16, in conference playoff game; defeated Jacksonville, 33-14 in AFC championship game; lost to St. Louis, 23-16, in Super Bowl XXXIV.
2000—Lost to Baltimore, 24-10, in conference playoff game.
2002—Defeated Pittsburgh, 34-31 (OT), in conference playoff game; lost to Oakland, 41-24, in AFC championship game.

FOX, JOHN   PANTHERS

PERSONAL: Born February 8, 1955, in Virginia Beach, Va.
HIGH SCHOOL: Castle Park (Chula Vista, Calif.).
JUNIOR COLLEGE: Southwestern Junior College (Calif.).
COLLEGE: San Diego State (degree in physical education).

HEAD COACHING RECORD

BACKGROUND: Graduate assistant, San Diego State (1978). ... Assistant coach, U.S. International University, Calif. (1979). ... Secondary coach, Boise State (1980). ... Secondary coach, Long Beach State (1981). ... Secondary coach, University of Utah (1982). ... Secondary coach, University of Kansas (1983). ... Secondary coach, Iowa State (1984). ... Secondary coach, Los Angeles Express USFL (1985). ... Defensive coordinator/secondary coach, University of Pittsburgh (1986-1988). ... Secondary coach, Pittsburgh Steelers NFL (1989-1991). ... Secondary coach, San Diego Chargers NFL (1992-1993). ... Defensive coordinator, Los Angeles Raiders NFL (1994). ... Defensive coordinator, Oakland Raiders NFL (1995). ... Consultant, St. Louis Rams NFL (1996). ... Defensive coordinator, New York Giants NFL (1997-2001).

		REGULAR SEASON					POST-SEASON	
	W	L	T	Pct.	Finish		W	L
2002—Carolina NFL	7	9	0	.438	4th/NFC South Division		0	0

GRUDEN, JON   BUCCANEERS

PERSONAL: Born August 17, 1963, in Sandusky, Ohio. ... Son of Jim Gruden, scout, San Francisco 49ers; and brother of Jay Gruden, quarterback with Tampa Bay Storm of Arena League (1991-96) and current head coach, Orlando Predators of Arena League.
HIGH SCHOOL: Clay (South Bend, Ind.).
COLLEGE: Dayton, then Tennessee (degree in communications, 1985).

HEAD COACHING RECORD

BACKGROUND: Graduate assistant, Tennessee (1986 and 1987). ... Passing game coordinator, Southeast Missouri State (1988). ... Wide receivers coach, Pacific (1989). ... Assistant coach, San Francisco 49ers NFL (1990) ... Wide receivers coach, University of Pittsburgh (1991). ... Offensive/quality control coach, Green Bay Packers NFL (1992). ... Wide receivers coach, Packers (1993 and 1994). ... Offensive coordinator, Philadelphia Eagles NFL (1995-1997).

	W	L	T	Pct.	REGULAR SEASON Finish	POST-SEASON W	L
1998—Oakland NFL	8	8	0	.500	2nd/AFC Western Division	0	0
1999—Oakland NFL	8	8	0	.500	4th/AFC Western Division	0	0
2000—Oakland NFL	12	4	0	.750	1st/AFC Western Division	1	1
2001—Oakland NFL	10	6	0	.625	1st/AFC Western Division	1	1
2002—Tampa Bay NFL	12	4	0	.750	1st/NFC South Division	3	0
Pro totals (5 years)	50	30	0	.625	**Pro totals (3 years)**	5	2

NOTES:

2000—Defeated Miami, 27-0, in conference playoff game; lost to Baltimore, 16-3, in AFC championship game.
2001—Defeated New York Jets, 38-24, in first-round playoff game; lost to New England, 16-13 (OT), in conference playoff game.
2002—Defeated San Francisco, 31-6, in conference playoff game; defeated Philadelphia, 27-10, in NFC championship game; defeated Oakland, 48-21, in Super Bowl XXXVII.

HASLETT, JIM   SAINTS

PERSONAL: Born December 9, 1957, in Pittsburgh. ... Full name: James Donald Haslett. ... Cousin of Hal Stringert, defensive back with San Diego Chargers (1974-80). ... Played linebacker.
HIGH SCHOOL: Avalon (Pittsburgh).
COLLEGE: Indiana University, Pa. (degree in elementary education).
TRANSACTIONS/CAREER NOTES: Selected by Buffalo Bills in second round (51st pick overall) of 1979 NFL draft. ... On injured reserve with back injury (September 13-November 17, 1983). ... On injured reserve with broken leg (September 1, 1986-entire season). ... Released by Bills (September 7, 1987). ... Signed by New York Jets as replacement player (September 30, 1987). ... On injured reserve with back injury (October 20, 1987-remainder of season).
HONORS: Played in Pro Bowl (1980 and 1981 seasons).
PRO STATISTICS: 1979—Recovered two fumbles. 1980—Recovered one fumble. 1982—Recovered one fumble and caught one pass for four yards. 1984—Recovered three fumbles for ten yards. 1985—Recovered three fumbles and fumbled once. 1987—Recovered one fumble.

			INTERCEPTIONS			
Year Team	G	No.	Yds.	Avg.	TD	
1979—Buffalo NFL	16	2	15	7.5	0	
1980—Buffalo NFL	16	2	30	15.0	0	
1981—Buffalo NFL	16	0	0	0.0	0	
1982—Buffalo NFL	6	0	0	0.0	0	
1983—Buffalo NFL	5	0	0	0.0	0	
1984—Buffalo NFL	15	0	0	0.0	0	
1985—Buffalo NFL	16	1	40	40.0	0	
1986—Buffalo NFL			Did not play.			
1987—New York Jets NFL	3	1	9	9.0	0	
Pro totals (8 years)	93	6	94	15.7	0	

HEAD COACHING RECORD

BACKGROUND: Linebackers coach, University of Buffalo (1988). ... Defensive coordinator, University of Buffalo (1989 and 1990). ... Defensive coordinator, Sacramento Surge W.L. (1991 and 1992). ... Linebackers coach, Los Angeles Raiders NFL (1993 and 1994). ... Linebackers coach, New Orleans Saints NFL (1995). ... Defensive coordinator, Saints (1996). ... Defensive coordinator, Pittsburgh Steelers NFL (1997-1999).

	W	L	T	Pct.	REGULAR SEASON Finish	POST-SEASON W	L
2000—New Orleans NFL	10	6	0	.625	1st/NFC Western Division	1	1
2001—New Orleans NFL	7	9	0	.438	3rd/NFC Western Division	0	0
2002—New Orleans NFL	9	7	0	.563	3rd/NFC South Division	0	0
Pro totals (3 years)	26	22	0	.542	**Pro totals (1 year)**	1	1

NOTES:

2000—Defeated St. Louis, 31-28, in first-round playoff game; lost to Minnesota, 34-16, in conference playoff game.

HOLMGREN, MIKE   SEAHAWKS

PERSONAL: Born June 15, 1948, in San Francisco. ... Full name: Michael George Holmgren. ... Played quarterback.
HIGH SCHOOL: Lincoln (San Francisco).
COLLEGE: Southern California (degree in business finance, 1970).
TRANSACTIONS/CAREER NOTES: Selected by St. Louis Cardinals in eighth round of 1970 NFL draft. ... Released by Cardinals (1970).

HEAD COACHING RECORD

BACKGROUND: Coach, Lincoln High, San Francisco (1971). ... Assistant coach, Sacred Heart Cathedral Prep School, San Francisco (1972 and 1973). ... Assistant coach, Oak Grove High School, San Jose, Calif. (1975-1980). ... Offensive coordinator/quarterbacks coach, San Francisco State (1981). ... Quarterbacks coach, Brigham Young (1982-1985). ... Quarterbacks coach, San Francisco 49ers NFL (1986-1988). ... Offensive coordinator, 49ers (1989-1991).

	W	L	T	Pct.	REGULAR SEASON Finish	POST-SEASON W	L
1992—Green Bay NFL	9	7	0	.563	2nd/NFC Central Division	0	0
1993—Green Bay NFL	9	7	0	.563	3rd/NFC Central Division	1	1
1994—Green Bay NFL	9	7	0	.563	2nd/NFC Central Division	1	1
1995—Green Bay NFL	11	5	0	.688	1st/NFC Central Division	2	1
1996—Green Bay NFL	13	3	0	.813	1st/NFC Central Division	3	0

	W	L	T	Pct.	REGULAR SEASON Finish	POST-SEASON W	L
1997—Green Bay NFL	13	3	0	.813	1st/NFC Central Division	2	1
1998—Green Bay NFL	11	5	0	.688	2nd/NFC/Central Division	0	1
1999—Seattle NFL	9	7	0	.563	1st/AFC Western Division	0	1
2000—Seattle NFL	6	10	0	.375	4th/AFC Western Division	0	0
2001—Seattle NFL	9	7	0	.563	2nd/AFC Western Division	0	0
2002—Seattle NFL	7	9	0	.438	3rd/NFC West Division	0	0
Pro totals (11 years)	106	70	0	.602	**Pro totals (7 years)**	9	6

NOTES:
1993—Defeated Detroit, 28-24, in first-round playoff game; lost to Dallas 27-17, in conference playoff game.
1994—Defeated Detroit, 16-12, in first-round playoff game; lost to Dallas, 35-9, in conference playoff game.
1995—Defeated Atlanta, 37-20, in first-round playoff game; defeated San Francisco, 27-17, in conference playoff game; lost to Dallas, 38-27, in NFC championship game.
1996—Defeated San Francisco, 35-14, in conference playoff game; defeated Carolina, 30-13, in NFC championship game; defeated New England, 35-21, in Super Bowl XXXI.
1997—Defeated Tampa Bay, 21-7, in first-round playoff game; defeated San Francisco, 23-10, in NFC championship game; lost to Denver, 31-24, in Super Bowl XXXII.
1998—Lost to San Francisco, 30-27, in first-round playoff game.
1999—Lost to Miami, 20-17, in first-round playoff game.

JAURON, DICK   BEARS

PERSONAL: Born October 7, 1950, in Peoria, Ill. ... Full name: Richard Manual Jauron. ... Played defensive back.
HIGH SCHOOL: Swampscott (Mass.).
COLLEGE: Yale (degree in history).
TRANSACTIONS/CAREER NOTES: Selected by Detroit Lions in fourth round of 1973 NFL draft. ... Released by Lions (August 23, 1978). ... Signed by Cincinnati Bengals (August 29, 1978). ... On injured reserve with knee injury (November 12, 1980-remainder of season).
HONORS: Played in Pro Bowl (1974 season).

		INTERCEPTIONS				PUNT RETURNS				KICKOFF RETURNS				TOTALS			
Year Team	G	No.	Yds.	Avg.	TD	No.	Yds.	Avg.	TD	No.	Yds.	Avg.	TD	TD	2pt.	Pts.	Fum.
1973—Detroit NFL	14	4	208	52.0	1	6	49	8.2	0	17	405	23.8	0	1	0	6	2
1974—Detroit NFL	14	1	26	26.0	0	17	286	16.8	0	2	21	10.5	0	0	0	0	0
1975—Detroit NFL	10	4	39	9.8	0	6	29	4.8	0	0	0	0.0	0	0	0	0	0
1976—Detroit NFL	6	2	0	0.0	0	0	0	0.0	0	0	0	0.0	0	0	0	0	0
1977—Detroit NFL	14	3	55	18.3	0	11	41	3.7	0	0	0	0.0	0	0	0	0	0
1978—Cincinnati NFL	16	4	52	13.0	1	3	32	10.7	0	0	0	0.0	0	1	0	6	0
1979—Cincinnati NFL	16	6	41	6.8	0	1	10	10.0	0	0	0	0.0	0	0	0	0	0
1980—Cincinnati NFL	10	1	11	11.0	0	0	0	0.0	0	0	0	0.0	0	0	0	0	0
Pro totals (8 years)	100	25	432	17.3	2	44	447	10.2	0	19	426	22.4	0	2	0	12	2

HEAD COACHING RECORD
BACKGROUND: Secondary coach, Buffalo Bills NFL (1985). ... Defensive backs coach, Green Bay Packers NFL (1986-94). ... Defensive coordinator, Jacksonville Jaguars NFL (1995-1998).
HONORS: Named NFL Coach of the Year by The Sporting News (2001).

	W	L	T	Pct.	REGULAR SEASON Finish	POST-SEASON W	L
1999—Chicago NFL	6	10	0	.375	5th/NFC Central Division	0	0
2000—Chicago NFL	5	11	0	.313	5th/NFC Central Division	0	0
2001—Chicago NFL	13	3	0	.813	1st/NFC Central Division	0	1
2002—Chicago NFL	4	12	0	.250	3rd/NFC North Division	0	0
Pro totals (4 years)	28	36	0	.438	**Pro totals (1 year)**	0	1

NOTES:
2001—Lost to Philadelphia, 33-19, in conference playoff game.

LEWIS, MARVIN   BENGALS

PERSONAL: Born September 23, 1958, in McDonald, Pa.
HIGH SCHOOL: Fort Cherry (McDonald, Pa.).
COLLEGE: Idaho State (degree in physical education, 1981; master's in athletic administration, 1982).

HEAD COACHING RECORD
BACKGROUND: Linebackers coach, Idaho State (1981-1984). ... Linebackers coach, Long Beach State (1985 and 1986). ... Linebackers coach, University of New Mexico (1987-1989). ... Outside linebackers coach, University of Pittsburgh (1990 and 1991). ... Linebackers coach, Pittsburgh Steelers NFL (1992-1995). ... Defensive coordinator, Baltimore Ravens NFL (1996-2001). ... Defensive coordinator/assistant head coach, Washington Redskins NFL (2002).

MARIUCCI, STEVE   LIONS

PERSONAL: Born November 4, 1955, in Iron Mountain, Mich. ... Full name: Steven Mariucci. ... Played quarterback.
HIGH SCHOOL: Iron Mountain (Mich.).
COLLEGE: Northern Michigan.
TRANSACTIONS/CAREER NOTES: Signed with Hamilton Tiger-Cats of CFL for 1978 season.

HEAD COACHING RECORD

BACKGROUND: Quarterbacks/running backs coach, Northern Michigan (1978 and 1979). ... Quarterbacks/special teams coordinator, Cal State Fullerton (1980-1982). ... Assistant head coach, Louisville (1983 and 1984). ... Receivers coach, Orlando Renegades USFL (1985). ... Quality control coach, Los Angeles Rams NFL (fall 1985). ... Wide receivers/special teams coach, University of California (1987-1989). ... Offensive coordinator/quarterbacks coach, University of California (1990 and 1991). ... Quarterbacks coach, Green Bay Packers NFL (1992-1995).

	W	L	T	Pct.	REGULAR SEASON Finish	POST-SEASON W	L
1996—California	6	6	0	.500	T5th/Pacific-10 Conference	0	1
1997—San Francisco NFL	13	3	0	.813	1st/NFC Western Division	1	1
1998—San Francisco NFL	12	4	0	.750	2nd/NFC Western Division	1	1
1999—San Francisco NFL	4	12	0	.250	4th/NFC Western Division	0	0
2000—San Francisco NFL	6	10	0	.375	4th/NFC Western Division	0	0
2001—San Francisco NFL	12	4	0	.750	2nd/NFC Western Division	0	1
2002—San Francisco NFL	10	6	0	.625	1st/NFC West Division	1	1
College totals (1 year)	6	6	0	.500	**College totals (1 year)**	0	1
Pro totals (6 years)	57	39	0	.594	**Pro totals (4 years)**	3	4

NOTES:
1996—Lost to Navy, 42-38, in Aloha Bowl.
1997—Defeated Minnesota, 38-22, in conference playoff game; lost to Green Bay, 23-10, in NFC championship game.
1998—Defeated Green Bay, 30-27, in first-round playoff game; lost to Atlanta, 20-18, in conference playoff game.
2001—Lost to Green Bay, 25-15, in first-round playoff game.
2002—Defeated New York Giants, 39-38, in first-round playoff game; lost to Tampa Bay, 31-6, in conference playoff game.

MARTZ, MIKE   RAMS

PERSONAL: Born May 13, 1951, in Sioux Falls, S.D.
HIGH SCHOOL: Madison (San Diego).
JUNIOR COLLEGE: San Diego Mesa Community College.
COLLEGE: UC Santa Barbara, then Fresno State.

HEAD COACHING RECORD

BACKGROUND: Assistant coach, Bullard High School, Fresno, Calif. (1973). ... Assistant coach, San Diego Mesa Community College (1974, 1976 and 1977). ... Assistant coach, San Jose State (1975). ... Assistant coach, Santa Ana College (1978). ... Coach, Fresno State (1979). ... Assistant coach, Pacific University (1980 and 1981). ... Running backs coach, University of Minnesota (1982). ... Quarterbacks/receivers coach, Arizona State (1983, 1986 and 1987). ... Offensive coordinator, Arizona State (1984 and 1988-1991). ... Offensive assistant, Los Angeles Rams NFL (1992 and 1993). ... Quarterbacks coach, Rams (1994). ... Wide receivers coach, St. Louis Rams NFL (1995 and 1996). ... Quarterbacks coach, Washington Redskins NFL (1997 and 1998). ... Offensive coordinator, Rams (1999).

	W	L	T	Pct.	REGULAR SEASON Finish	POST-SEASON W	L
2000—St. Louis NFL	10	6	0	.625	2nd/NFC Western Division	0	1
2001—St. Louis NFL	14	2	0	.875	1st/NFC Western Division	2	1
2002—St. Louis NFL	7	9	0	.438	2nd/NFC West Division	0	0
Pro totals (3 years)	31	17	0	.646	**Pro totals (2 years)**	2	2

NOTES:
2000—Lost to New Orleans, 31-28, in first-round playoff game.
2001—Defeated Green Bay, 45-17, in conference playoff game; defeated Philadelphia, 29-24, in NFC championship game; lost to New England, 20-17, in Super Bowl XXXVI.

McGINNIS, DAVE   CARDINALS

PERSONAL: Born August 7, 1951, in Independence, Kan.
HIGH SCHOOL: Snyder (Texas).
COLLEGE: Texas Christian (degree in business administration).

HEAD COACHING RECORD

BACKGROUND: Freshman coach, Texas Christian (1973 and 1974). ... Linebackers/secondary coach, University of Missouri (1975-1977). ... Secondary coach, Indiana State (1978-1981). ... Defensive backfield coach, Texas Christian (1982). ... Defensive ends/linebackers coach, Kansas State (1983-1985). ... Linebackers coach, Chicago Bears NFL (1986-1995). ... Defensive coordinator, Arizona Cardinals (1996-October 23, 2000).

	W	L	T	Pct.	REGULAR SEASON Finish	POST-SEASON W	L
2000—Arizona NFL	1	8	0	.111	5th/NFC Eastern Division	0	0
2001—Arizona NFL	7	9	0	.438	4th/NFC Eastern Division	0	0
2002—Arizona NFL	5	11	0	.313	4th/NFC West Division	0	0
Pro totals (3 years)	13	28	0	.317			

NOTES:
2000—Replaced Vince Tobin as head coach (October 23), with 2-5 record and club in fifth place.

PARCELLS, BILL — COWBOYS

PERSONAL: Born August 22, 1941, in Englewood, N.J. ... Full name: Duane Charles Parcells.
HIGH SCHOOL: River Dell (Oradell, N.J.).
COLLEGE: Colgate, then Wichita State (degree in education, 1964).

HEAD COACHING RECORD

BACKGROUND: Defensive assistant coach, Hastings (Neb.) College (1964). ... Defensive line coach, Wichita State (1965). ... Linebackers coach, Army (1966-1969). ... Linebackers coach, Florida State (1970-1972). ... Defensive coordinator, Vanderbilt (1973 and 1974). ... Defensive coordinator, Texas Tech (1975-1977). ... Assistant coach, New York Giants NFL (1979). ... Linebackers coach, New England NFL (1980). ... Defensive coordinator/linebackers coach, New York Giants NFL (1981 and 1982). ... NFL Analyst, NBC Sports (1991 and 1992).
HONORS: Named NFL Coach of the Year (1986).

		REGULAR SEASON				POST-SEASON	
	W	L	T	Pct.	Finish	W	L
1978—Air Force	3	8	0	.273	Independent	0	0
1983—New York Giants NFL	3	12	1	.219	5th/NFC Eastern Division	0	0
1984—New York Giants NFL	9	7	0	.563	2nd/NFC Eastern Division	1	1
1985—New York Giants NFL	10	6	0	.625	2nd/NFC Eastern Division	1	1
1986—New York Giants NFL	14	2	0	.875	1st/NFC Eastern Division	3	0
1987—New York Giants NFL	6	9	0	.400	5th/NFC Eastern Division	0	0
1988—New York Giants NFL	10	6	0	.625	2nd/NFC Eastern Division	0	0
1989—New York Giants NFL	12	4	0	.750	1st/NFC Eastern Division	0	1
1990—New York Giants NFL	13	3	0	.813	1st/NFC Eastern Division	3	0
1993—New England NFL	5	11	0	.313	4th/AFC Eastern Division	0	0
1994—New England NFL	10	6	0	.625	2nd/AFC Eastern Division	0	1
1995—New England NFL	6	10	0	.375	4th/AFC Eastern Division	0	0
1996—New England NFL	11	5	0	.688	1st/AFC Eastern Division	2	1
1997—New York Jets NFL	9	7	0	.563	3rd/AFC Eastern Division	0	0
1998—New York Jets NFL	12	4	0	.750	1st/AFC Eastern Division	1	1
1999—New York Jets NFL	8	8	0	.500	4th/AFC Eastern Division	0	0
College totals (1 year)	3	8	0	.273			
Pro totals (15 years)	138	100	1	.579	**Pro totals (8 years)**	11	6

NOTES:
1984—Defeated Los Angeles Rams, 16-13, in wild-card playoff game; lost to San Francisco, 21-10, in conference playoff game.
1985—Defeated San Francisco, 17-3, in wild-card playoff game; lost to Chicago, 21-0, in conference playoff game.
1986—Defeated San Francisco, 49-3, in conference playoff game; defeated Washington, 17-0, in NFC championship game; defeated Denver, 39-20, in Super Bowl XXI.
1989—Lost to Los Angeles Rams, 19-13 (OT), in conference playoff game.
1990—Defeated Chicago, 31-3, in conference playoff game; defeated San Francisco, 15-13, in NFC championship game; defeated Buffalo, 20-19, in Super Bowl XXV.
1994—Lost to Cleveland, 20-13, in first-round playoff game.
1996—Defeated Pittsburgh, 28-3, in conference playoff game; defeated Jacksonville, 20-6, in AFC championship game; lost to Green Bay, 35-21, in Super Bowl XXXI.
1998—Defeated Jacksonville, 34-24, in conference playoff game; lost to Denver, 23-10, in AFC championship game.

REEVES, DAN — FALCONS

PERSONAL: Born January 19, 1944, in Rome, Ga. ... Full name: Daniel Edward Reeves. ... Played running back.
HIGH SCHOOL: Americus (Ga.).
COLLEGE: South Carolina.
TRANSACTIONS/CAREER NOTES: Signed as non-drafted free agent by Dallas Cowboys for 1965 season.
CHAMPIONSHIP GAME EXPERIENCE: Played in NFL championship game (1966 and 1967 seasons). ... Played in NFC championship game (1970 and 1971 seasons). ... Played in Super Bowl V (1970 season). ... Member of Super Bowl championship team (1971 season).
HONORS: Named halfback on The Sporting News NFL Eastern Conference All-Star team (1966).
PRO STATISTICS: 1965—Returned two kickoffs for 45 yards. 1966—Returned two punts for minus one yard, returned three kickoffs for 56 yards and fumbled six times. 1967—Fumbled seven times. 1969—Fumbled twice. 1970—Fumbled four times. 1971—Fumbled once.

		PASSING						RUSHING				RECEIVING				TOTALS		
Year Team	G	Att.	Cmp.	Pct.	Yds.	TD	Int.	Avg.	Att.	Yds.	Avg.	TD	No.	Yds.	Avg.	TD	TD	2pt.	Pts.
1965—Dallas NFL	13	2	1	50.0	11	0	0	5.50	33	102	3.1	2	9	210	23.3	1	3	0	18
1966—Dallas NFL	14	6	3	50.0	48	0	0	8.00	175	757	4.3	8	41	557	13.6	8	16	0	96
1967—Dallas NFL	14	7	4	57.1	195	2	1	27.86	173	603	3.5	5	39	490	12.6	6	11	0	66
1968—Dallas NFL	4	4	2	50.0	43	0	0	10.75	40	178	4.5	4	7	84	12.0	1	5	0	30
1969—Dallas NFL	13	3	1	33.3	35	0	1	11.67	59	173	2.9	4	18	187	10.4	1	5	0	30
1970—Dallas NFL	14	3	1	33.3	14	0	1	4.67	35	84	2.4	2	12	140	11.7	0	2	0	12
1971—Dallas NFL	14	5	2	40.0	24	0	1	4.80	17	79	4.6	0	3	25	8.3	0	0	0	0
1972—Dallas NFL	14	2	0	0.0	0	0	0	0.0	3	14	4.7	0	0	0	0.0	0	0	0	0
Pro totals (8 years)	100	32	14	43.8	370	2	4	11.56	535	1990	3.7	25	129	1693	13.1	17	42	0	252

HEAD COACHING RECORD

BACKGROUND: Player/coach, Dallas Cowboys NFL (1970 and 1971). ... Offensive backs coach, Cowboys (1972 and 1974-1976). ... Offensive coordinator, Cowboys (1977-1980).
HONORS: Named NFL Coach of the Year by The Sporting News (1993 and 1998).

	REGULAR SEASON					POST-SEASON	
	W	L	T	Pct.	Finish	W	L
1981—Denver NFL	10	6	0	.625	2nd/AFC Western Division	0	0
1982—Denver NFL	2	7	0	.222	12th/AFC	0	0
1983—Denver NFL	9	7	0	.563	3rd/AFC Western Division	0	1
1984—Denver NFL	13	3	0	.813	1st/AFC Western Division	0	1
1985—Denver NFL	11	5	0	.688	2nd/AFC Western Division	0	0
1986—Denver NFL	11	5	0	.688	1st/AFC Western Division	2	1
1987—Denver NFL	10	4	1	.700	1st/AFC Western Division	2	1
1988—Denver NFL	8	8	0	.500	2nd/AFC Western Division	0	0
1989—Denver NFL	11	5	0	.688	1st/AFC Western Division	2	1
1990—Denver NFL	5	11	0	.313	5th/AFC Western Division	0	0
1991—Denver NFL	12	4	0	.750	1st/AFC Western Division	1	1
1992—Denver NFL	8	8	0	.500	3rd/AFC Western Division	0	0
1993—New York Giants NFL	11	5	0	.688	2nd/NFC Eastern Division	1	1
1994—New York Giants NFL	9	7	0	.563	2nd/NFC Eastern Division	0	0
1995—New York Giants NFL	5	11	0	.313	4th/NFC Eastern Division	0	0
1996—New York Giants NFL	6	10	0	.375	5th/NFC Eastern Division	0	0
1997—Atlanta NFL	7	9	0	.438	3rd/NFC Western Division	0	0
1998—Atlanta NFL	14	2	0	.875	1st/NFC Western Division	2	1
1999—Atlanta NFL	5	11	0	.313	3rd/NFC Western Division	0	0
2000—Atlanta NFL	4	12	0	.250	5th/NFC Western Division	0	0
2001—Atlanta NFL	7	9	0	.438	4th/NFC Western Division	0	0
2002—Atlanta NFL	9	6	1	.594	2nd/NFC South Division	1	1
Pro totals (22 years)	**187**	**155**	**2**	**.547**	**Pro totals (9 years)**	**11**	**9**

NOTES:

1983—Lost to Seattle, 31-7, in wild-card playoff game.

1984—Lost to Pittsburgh, 24-17, in conference playoff game.

1986—Defeated New England, 22-17, in conference playoff game; defeated Cleveland, 23-20 (OT), in AFC championship game; lost to New York Giants, 39-20, in Super Bowl XXI.

1987—Defeated Houston, 34-10, in conference playoff game; defeated Cleveland, 38-33, in AFC championship game; lost to Washington, 42-10, in Super Bowl XXII.

1989—Defeated Pittsburgh, 24-23, in conference playoff game; defeated Cleveland, 37-21, in AFC championship game; lost to San Francisco, 55-10, in Super Bowl XXIV.

1991—Defeated Houston, 26-24, in conference playoff game; lost to Buffalo, 10-7, in AFC championship game.

1993—Defeated Minnesota, 17-10, in first-round playoff game; lost to San Francisco, 44-3, in conference playoff game.

1998—Defeated San Francisco, 20-18, in conference playoff game; defeated Minnesota, 30-27 (OT), in NFC championship game; lost to Denver, 34-19, in Super Bowl XXXIII.

2002—Defeated Green Bay, 27-7, in first-round playoff game; lost to Philadelphia, 20-6, in conference playoff game.

REID, ANDY   EAGLES

PERSONAL: Born March 19, 1958, in Los Angeles. ... Full name: Andrew Walter Reid.

HIGH SCHOOL: John Marshall (Los Angeles).

JUNIOR COLLEGE: Glendale (Calif.).

COLLEGE: Brigham Young (bachelor's degree in physical education; master's degree in professional leadership, physical education and athletics).

HEAD COACHING RECORD

BACKGROUND: Graduate assistant, Brigham Young University (1982). ... Offensive coordinator, San Francisco State (1983-1985). ... Offensive line coach, Northern Arizona University (1986). ... Offensive line coach, University of Texas-El Paso (1987 and 1988). ... Offensive line coach, University of Missouri (1989-1991). ... Tight ends coach, Green Bay Packers NFL (1992-1996). ... Quarterbacks coach, Packers (1997 and 1998).

HONORS: Named NFL Coach of the Year by THE SPORTING NEWS (2000 and 2002).

	REGULAR SEASON					POST-SEASON	
	W	L	T	Pct.	Finish	W	L
1999—Philadelphia NFL	5	11	0	.313	5th/NFC Eastern Division	0	0
2000—Philadelphia NFL	11	5	0	.688	2nd/NFC Eastern Division	1	1
2001—Philadelphia NFL	11	5	0	.688	1st/NFC Eastern Division	2	1
2002—Philadelphia NFL	12	4	0	.750	1st/NFC East Division	1	1
Pro totals (4 years)	**39**	**25**	**0**	**.609**	**Pro totals (3 years)**	**4**	**3**

NOTES:

2000—Defeated Tampa Bay, 21-3, in first-round playoff game; lost to New York Giants, 20-10, in conference playoff game.

2001—Defeated Tampa Bay, 31-9, in first-round playoff game; defeated Chicago, 33-19, in conference playoff game; lost to St. Louis, 29-24, in NFC championship game.

2002—Defeated Atlanta, 20-6, in conference playoff game; lost to Tampa Bay, 27-10, in NFC championship game.

SCHOTTENHEIMER, MARTY   CHARGERS

PERSONAL: Born September 23, 1943, in Canonsburg, Pa. ... Full name: Martin Edward Schottenheimer. ... Played linebacker. ... Brother of Kurt Schottenheimer, defensive coordinator, Detroit Lions; father of Brian Schottenheimer, quarterbacks coach, San Diego Chargers.

HIGH SCHOOL: Fort Cherry (McDonald, Pa.).

COLLEGE: Pittsburgh (degree in English, 1964).

TRANSACTIONS/CAREER NOTES: Selected by Buffalo Bills in seventh round of 1965 AFL draft. ... Released by Bills (1969). ... Signed by Boston Patriots (1969). ... Patriots franchise renamed New England Patriots for 1971 season. ... Traded by New England Patriots to Pittsburgh Steelers for OT Mike Haggerty and a draft choice (July 10, 1971). ... Released by Steelers (1971).

CHAMPIONSHIP GAME EXPERIENCE: Member of AFL championship team (1965 season). ... Played in AFL championship game (1966 season).

HONORS: Played in AFL All-Star Game (1965 season).

PRO STATISTICS: 1969—Returned one kickoff for 13 yards. 1970—Returned one kickoff for eight yards.

			INTERCEPTIONS			
Year Team		G	No.	Yds.	Avg.	TD
1965—Buffalo AFL		14	0	0	0.0	0
1966—Buffalo AFL		14	1	20	20.0	0
1967—Buffalo AFL		14	3	88	29.3	1
1968—Buffalo AFL		14	1	22	22.0	0
1969—Boston AFL		11	1	3	3.0	0
1970—Boston NFL		12	0	0	0.0	0
AFL totals (5 years)		67	6	133	22.2	1
NFL totals (1 year)		12	0	0	0.0	0
Pro totals (6 years)		79	6	133	22.2	1

HEAD COACHING RECORD

BACKGROUND: Linebackers coach, Portland Storm WFL (1974). ... Linebackers coach, New York Giants NFL (1975 and 1976). ... Defensive coordinator, Giants (1977). ... Linebackers coach, Detroit Lions NFL (1978 and 1979). ... Defensive coordinator, Cleveland Browns NFL (1980-October 22, 1984).

	REGULAR SEASON					POST-SEASON	
	W	L	T	Pct.	Finish	W	L
1984—Cleveland NFL	4	4	0	.500	3rd/AFC Central Division	0	0
1985—Cleveland NFL	8	8	0	.500	1st/AFC Central Division	0	1
1986—Cleveland NFL	12	4	0	.750	1st/AFC Central Division	1	1
1987—Cleveland NFL	10	5	0	.667	1st/AFC Central Division	1	1
1988—Cleveland NFL	10	6	0	.625	2nd/AFC Central Division	0	1
1989—Kansas City NFL	8	7	1	.531	2nd/AFC Western Division	0	0
1990—Kansas City NFL	11	5	0	.688	2nd/AFC Western Division	0	1
1991—Kansas City NFL	10	6	0	.625	2nd/AFC Western Division	1	1
1992—Kansas City NFL	10	6	0	.625	2nd/AFC Western Division	0	1
1993—Kansas City NFL	11	5	0	.688	1st/AFC Western Division	2	1
1994—Kansas City NFL	9	7	0	.563	2nd/AFC Western Division	0	1
1995—Kansas City NFL	13	3	0	.813	1st/AFC Western Division	0	1
1996—Kansas City NFL	9	7	0	.563	2nd/AFC Western Division	0	0
1997—Kansas City NFL	13	3	0	.813	1st/AFC Western Division	0	1
1998—Kansas City NFL	7	9	0	.438	4th/AFC Western Division	0	0
2001—Washington NFL	8	8	0	.500	2nd/NFC Eastern Division	0	0
2002—San Diego NFL	8	8	0	.500	3rd/AFC West Division	0	0
Pro totals (17 years)	161	101	1	.614	Pro totals (11 years)	5	11

NOTES:

1984—Replaced Sam Rutigliano as coach of Cleveland (October 22), with 1-7 record and in third place.

1985—Lost to Miami, 24-21, in conference playoff game.

1986—Defeated New York Jets, 23-20 (2 OT), in conference playoff game; lost to Denver, 23-20 (OT), in AFC championship game.

1987—Defeated Indianapolis, 38-21, in conference playoff game; lost to Denver, 38-33, in AFC championship game.

1988—Lost to Houston, 24-23, in wild-card playoff game.

1990—Lost to Miami, 17-16, in first-round playoff game.

1991—Defeated Los Angeles Raiders, 10-6, in first-round playoff game; lost to Buffalo, 37-14, in conference playoff game.

1992—Lost to San Diego, 17-0, in first-round playoff game.

1993—Defeated Pittsburgh, 27-24 (OT), in first-round playoff game; defeated Houston, 28-20, in conference playoff game; lost to Buffalo, 30-13, in AFC championship game.

1994—Lost to Miami, 27-17, in first-round playoff game.

1995—Lost to Indianapolis, 10-7, in conference playoff game.

1997—Lost to Denver, 14-10, in conference playoff game.

SHANAHAN, MIKE — BRONCOS

PERSONAL: Born August 24, 1952, in Oak Park, Ill. ... Full name: Michael Edward Shanahan.

HIGH SCHOOL: East Leyden (Franklin Park, Ill.).

COLLEGE: Eastern Illinois (bachelor's degree in physical education, 1974; master's degree in education, 1975).

HEAD COACHING RECORD

BACKGROUND: Graduate assistant, Eastern Illinois (1973 and 1974). ... Running backs/wide receivers coach, Oklahoma (1975 and 1976). ... Backfield coach, Northern Arizona (1977). ... Offensive coordinator, Eastern Illinois (1978). ... Offensive coordinator, University of Minnesota (1979). ... Offensive coordinator, University of Florida (1980-1983). ... Receivers coach, Denver Broncos NFL (1984). ... Offensive coordinator, Broncos (1985-1987 and 1991). ... Quarterbacks coach, Broncos NFL (1989 and 1990). ... Offensive coordinator, San Francisco 49ers NFL (1992-1994).

	REGULAR SEASON					POST-SEASON	
	W	L	T	Pct.	Finish	W	L
1988—Los Angeles Raiders NFL	7	9	0	.438	3rd/AFC Western Division	0	0
1989—Los Angeles Raiders NFL	1	3	0	.250	3rd/AFC Western Division	0	0
1995—Denver NFL	8	8	0	.500	4th/AFC Western Division	0	0
1996—Denver NFL	13	3	0	.813	1st/AFC Western Division	0	1
1997—Denver NFL	12	4	0	.750	2nd/AFC Western Conference	4	0
1998—Denver NFL	14	2	0	.875	1st/AFC Western Division	3	0
1999—Denver NFL	6	10	0	.375	5th/AFC Western Division	0	0
2000—Denver NFL	11	5	0	.688	2nd/AFC Western Division	0	1
2001—Denver NFL	8	8	0	.500	3rd/AFC Western Division	0	0
2002—Denver NFL	9	7	0	.563	2nd/AFC West Division	0	0
Pro totals (10 years)	**89**	**59**	**0**	**.601**	**Pro totals (4 years)**	**7**	**2**

NOTES:
1989—Replaced as Raiders coach by Art Shell (October 3) with club tied for fourth place.
1996—Lost to Jacksonville, 30-27, in conference playoff game.
1997—Defeated Jacksonville, 42-17, in first-round game; defeated Kansas City, 14-10, in conference playoff game; defeated Pittsburgh, 24-21, in AFC championship game; defeated Green Bay, 31-24, in Super Bowl XXXII.
1998—Defeated Miami, 38-3, in conference playoff game; defeated New York Jets, 23-10, in AFC championship game; defeated Atlanta, 34-19, in Super Bowl XXXIII.
2000—Lost to Baltimore, 21-3, in first-round playoff game.

SHERMAN, MIKE   PACKERS

PERSONAL: Born December 19, 1954, in Norwood, Mass. ... Full name: Michael Francis Sherman.
COLLEGE: Central Connecticut State (degree in English).

HEAD COACHING RECORD
BACKGROUND: Head coach, Stamford High School, Stamford, Conn. (1978). ... Head coach, Worcester (Mass.) Academy (1979 and 1980). ... Graduate assistant, University of Pittsburgh (1981 and 1982). ... Offensive line coach, Tulane (1983 and 1984). ... Offensive line coach, Holy Cross (1985-1987). ... Offensive coordinator, Holy Cross (1988). ... Offensive line coach, Texas A&M (1989-1993). ... Offensive line coach, UCLA (1994). ... Offensive line coach, Texas A&M (1995-1996). ... Tight ends coach, Green Bay Packers NFL (1997-1998). ... Offensive coordinator/tight ends coach, Seattle Seahawks NFL (1999).

	REGULAR SEASON					POST-SEASON	
	W	L	T	Pct.	Finish	W	L
2000—Green Bay NFL	9	7	0	.563	3rd/NFC Central Division	0	0
2001—Green Bay NFL	12	4	0	.750	2nd/NFC Central Division	1	1
2002—Green Bay NFL	12	4	0	.750	1st/NFC North Division	0	1
Pro totals (3 years)	**33**	**15**	**0**	**.688**	**Pro totals (2 years)**	**1**	**2**

NOTES:
2001—Defeated San Francisco, 25-15, in first-round playoff game; lost to St. Louis, 45-17, in conference playoff game.
2002—Lost to Atlanta, 27-7, in first-round playoff game.

SPURRIER, STEVE   REDSKINS

PERSONAL: Born April 20, 1945, in Miami Beach. ... Full name: Stephen Orr Spurrier Sr.
HIGH SCHOOL: Science Hill (Johnson City, Tenn.).
COLLEGE: Florida.
TRANSACTIONS/CAREER NOTES: Selected by San Francisco 49ers in first round (third pick overall) of 1967 AFL-NFL draft. ... Traded by 49ers to Tampa Bay Buccaneers for WR Willie McGee, LB Bruce Elia and second-round pick (April 2, 1976).
HONORS: Heisman Trophy winner (1966). ... Named College Football Player of the Year by THE SPORTING NEWS (1966). ... Named quarterback on THE SPORTING NEWS college All-America team (1966).
PRO STATISTICS: 1967—Punted 73 times for 2,745 yards. 1968—Punted 68 times for 2,651 yards. 1969—Punted 12 times for 468 yards. 1970—Punted 75 times for 2,877 yards. 1971—Punted twice for 77 yards. 1972—Recovered two fumbles. 1973—Recovered one fumble.
MISCELLANEOUS: Played quarterback and punter.

		PASSING								RUSHING				TOTALS		
Year Team	G	Att.	Cmp.	Pct.	Yds.	TD	Int.	Avg.	Rat.	Att.	Yds.	Avg.	TD	TD	2pt.	Pts.
1967—San Francisco NFL	14	50	23	46.0	211	0	7	4.22	18.4	5	18	3.6	0	0	0	0
1968—San Francisco NFL	14	0	0	0.0	0	0	0	0.0	...	1	-15	-15.0	0	0	0	0
1969—San Francisco NFL	6	146	81	55.5	926	5	11	6.34	54.8	5	49	9.8	0	0	0	0
1970—San Francisco NFL	14	4	3	75.0	49	1	0	12.25	155.2	2	-18	-9.0	0	0	0	0
1971—San Francisco NFL	6	4	1	25.0	46	0	0	11.50	75.0	1	2	2.0	0	0	0	0
1972—San Francisco NFL	13	269	147	54.6	1983	18	16	7.37	75.9	11	51	4.6	0	0	0	0
1973—San Francisco NFL	11	157	83	52.9	882	4	7	5.62	59.5	9	32	3.6	2	2	0	12
1974—San Francisco NFL	3	3	1	33.3	2	0	0	0.67	42.4	0	0	0.0	0	0	0	0
1975—San Francisco NFL	11	207	102	49.3	1151	5	7	5.56	60.3	15	91	6.1	0	0	0	0
1976—Tampa Bay NFL	14	311	156	50.2	1628	7	12	5.23	57.1	12	48	4.0	0	0	0	0
Pro totals (10 years)	**106**	**1151**	**597**	**51.9**	**6878**	**40**	**60**	**5.98**	**60.1**	**61**	**258**	**4.2**	**2**	**2**	**0**	**12**

HEAD COACHING RECORD
BACKGROUND: Quarterbacks coach, Florida (1978). ... Offensive coordinator/quarterbacks coach, Georgia Tech (1979). ... Offensive coordinator and quarterbacks coach, Duke (1980-1982).

		REGULAR SEASON				POST-SEASON	
	W	**L**	**T**	**Pct.**	**Finish**	**W**	**L**
1983—Tampa Bay USFL	11	7	0	.611	3rd/Central Division	0	1
1984—Tampa Bay USFL	14	4	0	.778	2nd/Southern Division	0	1
1985—Tampa Bay USFL	10	8	0	.556	5th/Eastern Division	0	0
1987—Duke	5	6	0	.455	7th/Atlantic Coast Conference	0	0
1988—Duke	7	3	1	.682	6th/Atlantic Coast Conference	0	0
1989—Duke	8	4	0	.667	1st/Atlantic Coast Conference	0	1
1990—Florida	9	2	0	.818	1st/Southeastern Conference	0	0
1991—Florida	10	1	0	.833	1st/Southeastern Conference	0	1
1992—Florida	8	4	0	.692	1st/Southeastern Conference East Division	1	0
1993—Florida	10	2	0	.846	1st/Southeastern Conference East Division	1	0
1994—Florida	10	1	1	.808	1st/Southeastern Conference East Division	0	1
1995—Florida	12	0	0	.923	1st/Southeastern Conference East Division	0	1
1996—Florida	11	1	0	.923	1st/Southeastern Conference East Division	1	0
1997—Florida	9	2	0	.833	T2nd/Southeastern Conference East Division	1	0
1998—Florida	9	2	0	.833	2nd/Southeastern Conference East Division	1	0
1999—Florida	9	3	0	.692	2nd/Southeastern Conference East Division	0	1
2000—Florida	10	2	0	.769	1st/Southeastern Conference East Division	0	1
2001—Florida	9	2	0	.833	2nd/Southeastern Conference East Division	1	0
2002—Washington NFL	7	9	0	.438	3rd/NFC Eastern Division	0	0
College totals (15 years)	136	35	2	.795	**College totals (12 years)**	6	6
USFL totals (3 years)	35	19	0	.648	**USFL totals (2 years)**	0	2
NFL totals (1 year)	7	9	0	.438			
Pro totals (4 years)	42	28	0	.600	**Pro totals (2 years)**	0	2

NOTES:
1984—Lost to Birmingham, 36-17, in conference playoff.
1985—Lost to Oakland, 48-27, in conference playoff game.
1989—Lost to Texas Tech, 49-21, in All America Bowl.
1991—Lost to Notre Dame, 39-28, in Sugar Bowl.
1992—Defeated North Carolina State, 27-10, in Gator Bowl.
1993—Defeated West Virginia, 41-7, in Sugar Bowl.
1994—Lost to Florida State, 23-17, in Sugar Bowl.
1995—Lost to Nebraska, 62-24, in Fiesta Bowl.
1996—Defeated Florida State, 52-20, in Sugar Bowl.
1997—Defeated Penn State, 21-6, in Citrus Bowl.
1998—Defeated Syracuse, 31-10, in Orange Bowl.
1999—Lost to Michigan State, 37-34, in Citrus Bowl.
2000—Lost to Miami, 37-20, in Sugar Bowl.
2001—Defeated Maryland, 56-23, in Orange Bowl.

TICE, MIKE   VIKINGS

PERSONAL: Born February 2, 1959, in Bayshore, N.Y. ... Full name: Michael Peter Tice. ... Brother of John Tice, tight end, New Orleans Saints (1983-1992).
HIGH SCHOOL: Central Islip (N.Y.).
COLLEGE: Maryland.
TRANSACTIONS/CAREER NOTES: Signed as non-drafted free agent by Seattle Seahawks (April 30, 1981). ... On injured reserve with fractured ankle (October 15-December 7, 1985). ... Granted unconditional free agency (February 1, 1989). ... Signed by Washington Redskins (February 20, 1989). ... Released by Redskins (September 4, 1990). ... Signed by Seahawks (November 28, 1990). ... Granted unconditional free agency (February 1-April 1, 1991). ... Re-signed by Seahawks (July 19, 1991). ... Granted unconditional free agency (February 1, 1992). ... Signed by Minnesota Vikings (March 18, 1992). ... On injured reserve with back injury (September 25-October 21, 1992). ... Granted unconditional free agency (March 1, 1993). ... Re-signed by Vikings (May 4, 1993). ... Released by Vikings (August 30, 1993). ... Re-signed by Vikings (August 31, 1993). ... Granted unconditional free agency (February 17, 1994). ... Re-signed by Vikings (December 7, 1995). ... Granted unconditional free agency (February 16, 1996).
CHAMPIONSHIP GAME EXPERIENCE: Played in AFC championship game (1983 season).
PRO STATISTICS: 1982—Recovered one fumble. 1983—Recovered one fumble. 1986—Recovered one fumble. 1991—Recovered one fumble. 1992—Recovered one fumble for four yards.

			RECEIVING			KICKOFF RETURNS				TOTALS			
Year Team	G	GS	No.	Yds.	Avg.	TD	No.	Yds.	Avg.	TD	TD	2pt.	Pts.	Fum.
1981—Seattle NFL	16	3	5	47	9.4	0	0	0	0.0	0	0	0	0	0
1982—Seattle NFL	9	9	9	46	5.1	0	0	0	0.0	0	0	0	0	0
1983—Seattle NFL	15	1	0	0	0.0	0	2	28	14.0	0	0	0	0	0
1984—Seattle NFL	16	8	8	90	11.3	3	0	0	0.0	0	3	0	18	0
1985—Seattle NFL	9	2	2	13	6.5	0	1	17	17.0	0	0	0	0	0
1986—Seattle NFL	16	15	15	150	10.0	0	1	17	17.0	0	0	0	0	0
1987—Seattle NFL	12	12	14	106	7.6	2	0	0	0.0	0	2	0	12	0
1988—Seattle NFL	16	16	29	244	8.4	0	1	17	17.0	0	0	0	0	1
1989—Washington NFL	16	5	1	2	2.0	0	0	0	0.0	0	0	0	0	0
1990—Seattle NFL	5	2	0	0	0.0	0	0	0	0.0	0	0	0	0	0
1991—Seattle NFL	16	15	10	70	7.0	4	3	46	15.3	0	4	0	24	0
1992—Minnesota NFL	12	9	5	65	13.0	1	0	0	0.0	0	1	0	6	0
1993—Minnesota NFL	16	12	6	39	6.5	1	0	0	0.0	0	1	0	6	1
1995—Minnesota NFL	3	1	3	22	7.3	0	0	0	0.0	0	0	0	0	0
Pro totals (14 years)	177	110	107	894	8.4	11	8	125	15.6	0	11	0	66	2

HEAD COACHING RECORD

BACKGROUND: Tight ends coach, Minnesota Vikings NFL (1996). ... Offensive line coach, Vikings (1997-2000). ... Assistant head coach/offensive line coach, Vikings (2001).

				REGULAR SEASON		POST-SEASON	
	W	L	T	Pct.	Finish	W	L
2001—Minnesota NFL	0	1	0	.000	4th/NFC Central Division	0	0
2002—Minnesota NFL	6	10	0	.375	2nd/NFC North Division	0	0
Pro totals (2 years)	6	11	0	.353			

NOTES:
2001—Replaced Dennis Green as head coach (January 4) with 5-10 record and club in fourth place.

VERMEIL, DICK   CHIEFS

PERSONAL: Born October 30, 1936, in Calistoga, Calif. ... Full name: Richard Albert Vermeil. ... Brother of Al Vermeil, conditioning coach with San Francisco 49ers (1979-82) and brother-in-law of Louie Giammona, running back with Philadelphia Eagles (1978-82).
HIGH SCHOOL: Calistoga (Calif.).
JUNIOR COLLEGE: Napa College.
COLLEGE: San Jose State (master's degree in physical education, 1959).

HEAD COACHING RECORD

BACKGROUND: Assistant coach, Del Mar High School, San Jose, Calif. (1959). ... Head coach, Hillsdale High School, San Mateo, Calif. (1960-1962; record: 17-9-1). ... Assistant coach, College of San Mateo (1963). ... Assistant coach, Stanford (1965-1968). ... Assistant coach, Los Angeles Rams NFL (1969 and 1971-1973). ... Offensive coordinator, UCLA (1970).
HONORS: Named NFL Coach of the Year by THE SPORTING NEWS (1979 and 1999).

				REGULAR SEASON		POST-SEASON	
	W	L	T	Pct.	Finish	W	L
1964—Napa Junior College	8	1	0	.889	2nd/Golden Valley Conference	0	0
1974—UCLA	6	3	2	.636	T3rd/Pacific-8 Conference	0	0
1975—UCLA	8	2	1	.773	T1st/Pacific-8 Conference	1	0
1976—Philadelphia NFL	4	10	0	.286	4th/NFC Eastern Division	0	0
1977—Philadelphia NFL	5	9	0	.357	4th/NFC Eastern Division	0	0
1978—Philadelphia NFL	9	7	0	.563	2nd/NFC Eastern Division	0	1
1979—Philadelphia NFL	11	5	0	.688	2nd/NFC Eastern Division	1	1
1980—Philadelphia NFL	12	4	0	.750	1st/NFC Eastern Division	2	1
1981—Philadelphia NFL	10	6	0	.625	2nd/NFC Eastern Division	0	1
1982—Philadelphia NFL	3	6	0	.333	5th/NFC Eastern Division	0	0
1997—St. Louis NFL	5	11	0	.313	5th/NFC Western Division	0	0
1998—St. Louis NFL	4	12	0	.250	5th/NFC Western Division	0	0
1999—St. Louis NFL	13	3	0	.813	1st/NFC Western Division	3	0
2001—Kansas City NFL	6	10	0	.375	4th/AFC Western Division	0	0
2002—Kansas City NFL	8	8	0	.500	4th/AFC West Division	0	0
College totals (3 years)	22	6	3	.758	**College totals (1 year)**	1	0
Pro totals (12 years)	90	91	0	.497	**Pro totals (5 years)**	6	4

NOTES:
1975—Defeated Ohio State, 23-10, in Rose Bowl.
1978—Lost to Atlanta, 14-13, in conference playoff game.
1979—Defeated Chicago, 27-17, in first-round playoff game; lost to Tampa Bay, 24-17, in conference playoff game.
1980—Defeated Minnesota, 31-16, in conference playoff game; defeated Dallas, 20-7, in NFC championship game; lost to Oakland, 27-10, in Super Bowl XV.
1981—Lost to New York Giants, 27-21, in conference playoff game.
1982—Only nine of 16 games were played due to the cancellation of games because of a players strike.
1999—Defeated Minnesota, 49-37, in conference playoff game; defeated Tampa Bay, 11-6, in NFC championship game; defeated Tennessee, 23-16, in Super Bowl XXXIV.

WANNSTEDT, DAVE   DOLPHINS

PERSONAL: Born May 21, 1952, in Pittsburgh. ... Full name: David Raymond Wannstedt.
HIGH SCHOOL: Baldwin (Pittsburgh).
COLLEGE: Pittsburgh (bachelor of science degree in physical education, 1974; master's degree in education, 1975).
TRANSACTIONS/CAREER NOTES: Selected by Green Bay Packers in 15th round (376th pick overall) of 1974 NFL draft. ... On injured reserve with neck injury for entire 1974 season.

HEAD COACHING RECORD

BACKGROUND: Graduate assistant, University of Pittsburgh (1975). ... Assistant coach, University of Pittsburgh (1976-1978). ... Defensive line coach, Oklahoma State (1979 and 1980). ... Defensive coordinator, Oklahoma State (1981 and 1982). ... Defensive line coach, Southern California (1983-1985). ... Defensive coordinator, Miami, Fla. (1986-1988). ... Defensive coordinator, Dallas Cowboys NFL (1989-1992). ... Assistant head coach, Miami Dolphins NFL (1999).

HEAD COACHES

	W	L	T	Pct.	REGULAR SEASON Finish	POST-SEASON W	L
1993—Chicago NFL	7	9	0	.438	4th/NFC Central Division	0	0
1994—Chicago NFL	9	7	0	.563	4th/NFC Central Division	1	1
1995—Chicago NFL	9	7	0	.563	3rd/NFC Central Division	0	0
1996—Chicago NFL	7	9	0	.438	3rd/NFC Central Division	0	0
1997—Chicago NFL	4	12	0	.250	5th/NFC Central Division	0	0
1998—Chicago NFL	4	12	0	.250	5th/NFC Central Division	0	0
2000—Miami NFL	11	5	0	.688	1st/AFC Eastern Division	1	1
2001—Miami NFL	11	5	0	.688	2nd/AFC Eastern Division	0	1
2002—Miami NFL	9	7	0	.563	3rd/AFC East Division	0	0
Pro totals (9 years)	71	73	0	.493	Pro totals (3 years)	2	3

NOTES:
1994—Defeated Minnesota, 35-18, in first-round playoff game; lost to San Francisco, 44-15, in conference playoff game.
2000—Defeated Indianapolis, 23-17 (OT), in first-round playoff game; lost to Oakland, 27-0, in conference playoff game.
2001—Lost to Baltimore, 20-3, in first-round playoff game.

WILLIAMS, GREGG — BILLS

PERSONAL: Born July 15, 1958, in Excelsior Springs, Mo.
COLLEGE: Northeast Missouri, then Central Missouri (master's degree in education).

HEAD COACHING RECORD
BACKGROUND: Assistant coach, Excelsior Springs (Mo.) High School (1980-1983). ... Head coach, Belton (Mo.) High School (1984-1987). ... Graduate Assistant, University of Houston (1988 and 1989). ... Quality control coach, Houston Oilers NFL (1990-1992). ... Special teams coach, Oilers (1993). ... Linebackers coach, Oilers (1994-1996). ... Defensive coordinator, Tennessee Oilers NFL (1997 and 1998). ... Defensive coordinator, Tennessee Titans NFL (1999 and 2000).

	W	L	T	Pct.	REGULAR SEASON Finish	POST-SEASON W	L
2001—Buffalo NFL	3	13	0	.188	5th/AFC Eastern Division	0	0
2002—Buffalo NFL	8	8	0	.500	4th/AFC East Division	0	0
Pro totals (2 years)	11	21	0	.344			

Get Inside The Game

☑ YES!

Send me 30 issues of
Sporting News Magazine
for just 99¢ each.
I SAVE 75% OFF
the newsstand price.
For new subscribers only.

ONLY 99¢ AN ISSUE!

NAME (Please Print)

_____

ADDRESS

_____

CITY   STATE   ZIP

☐ Payment enclosed ☐ Bill me later   5GCE6

Canada add $20.80 for subscription postage (U.S. funds only). Other international
rates available on request. Sporting News Magazine is published weekly, with
special double issues. **www.sportingnews.com**

MAIL THIS CARD OR CALL TOLL-FREE:
1-800-238-0452

Get Inside The Game

☑ YES!

Send me 30 issues of
Sporting News Magazine
for just 99¢ each.
I SAVE 75% OFF
the newsstand price.
For new subscribers only.

ONLY 99¢ AN ISSUE!

NAME (Please Print)

_____

ADDRESS

_____

CITY   STATE   ZIP

☐ Payment enclosed ☐ Bill me later   5GCE6

Canada add $20.80 for subscription postage (U.S. funds only). Other international
rates available on request. Sporting News Magazine is published weekly, with
special double issues. **www.sportingnews.com**

MAIL THIS CARD OR CALL TOLL-FREE:
1-800-238-0452

BUSINESS REPLY MAIL

FIRST-CLASS MAIL   PERMIT NO 1397   BOULDER CO

POSTAGE WILL BE PAID BY ADDRESSEE

PO BOX 51576
BOULDER CO 80323-1576

NO POSTAGE
NECESSARY
IF MAILED
IN THE
UNITED STATES

BUSINESS REPLY MAIL

FIRST-CLASS MAIL   PERMIT NO 1397   BOULDER CO

POSTAGE WILL BE PAID BY ADDRESSEE

PO BOX 51576
BOULDER CO 80323-1576